MARKETING PLANNING AND STRATEGY

Second Edition

Subhash C. Jain

School of Business Administration
University of Connecticut

Published by

S13 **SOUTH-WESTERN PUBLISHING CO.**

CINCINNATI   WEST CHICAGO, IL   DALLAS   PELHAM MANOR, NY   PALO ALTO, CA

ISBN: 0-538-19130-9

Library of Congress Catalog Card Number: 84-71039

1 2 3 4 5 6 7 8 9 D 3 2 1 0 9 8 7 6 5

Printed in the United States of America

With love to
my wife, Sadhna

PREFACE

A significant change in the field of management in the 1970s was the emergence of strategic planning as an important area of endeavor. Initially, as strategic planning began to make inroads in business circles, marketing assumed a secondary role. With growing experience, however, it became obvious that strategic planning cannot be effective without the inputs that marketing provides, especially in an environment characterized by far-reaching economic, social, and technological changes. Developing a winning marketing strategy in such a climate is, indeed, the new priority, as reported in the business press (e.g., *Business Week, Fortune*), stressed in executive speeches, and explored in academia.

Marketing Planning and Strategy, Second Edition, is designed to help students understand the development of the sophisticated marketing strategies necessary for businesses to survive in today's highly competitive marketplace. The book offers new ideas, new insights, and a reliable perspective on marketing strategy formulation. Readers will become informed about such matters as:

- How to determine what marketing strategy can realistically accomplish for a business.
- How to determine that a business ought to reformulate its marketing strategy.
- How marketing strategy differs from marketing management.
- What underlying factors must be considered in determining marketing strategy.
- How to analyze corporate perspective and measure strengths and weaknesses.
- How basic changes in America's social and industrial environments have led to the new emphasis on marketing strategy.
- What a mission statement can do to advance marketing efforts.
- How to set realistic marketing objectives.
- How to determine respective roles for different products of a business unit.
- How portfolio techniques may be usefully employed in strategy determination and resource allocation.
- How to organize for successful strategy implementation.
- What the latest techniques are for gathering information, undertaking strategic analysis, and formulating strategies.

In recent years, to clearly delineate the role of marketing in strategy development, a new term, strategic marketing, has been coined. Marketing may be viewed in three ways: as marketing management; as marketing strategy or strategic marketing; and as corporate marketing. Marketing management deals with strategy implementation, usually at the product/market or brand level. Strategic marketing focuses on strategy formulation, while corporate marketing provides inputs for corporate-wide strategy.

Strategy is commonly considered at the business unit level. At the heart of the business unit strategy is marketing strategy, which becomes the basis of strategy in other functional areas. Integration of all functional strategies represents the business unit strategy. *Marketing Planning and Strategy* focuses on marketing strategy from the viewpoint of the business unit.

Hallmarks of the Second Edition

This second edition presents a much more comprehensive treatment of the subject than the first edition. Developments in the field as evidenced by numerous journal articles, reports, and books on strategic marketing, and extension of my own thinking on the subject have enabled me to provide state-of-the-art coverage of the discipline.

Preparation of the second edition was guided by the following objectives:

1. To provide a clear perspective on strategic marketing.
2. To develop a conceptual framework for formulating marketing strategy.
3. To bring in the customer focus in developing marketing strategy.
4. To strengthen the material on competition, portfolio analysis, and strategy implementation.
5. To include cases reflecting a variety of strategic marketing situations.
6. To update concepts, illustrations, and statistics to 1984.

Accomplishment of these objectives led to the following distinguishing features of the second edition:

- A new chapter on competitive analysis.
- A new chapter on the customer, focusing on marketing's boundary role.
- Clear-cut distinction between strategic marketing and marketing management.
- A comprehensive model for marketing strategy formulation.
- New and expanded material on defining strategic corporate direction and business mission.
- Complete revision of the chapters on corporate appraisal, environmental scanning, and measuring strengths and weaknesses.
- A thorough examination and critique of various portfolio techniques.

- Discussion of problems and their solution for successful marketing strategy implementation.
- Substantial revision of the chapters on market, product, pricing, distribution, and promotion strategies, with inclusion of an outline in an appendix at the end of each of these five chapters to provide a quick review of the points covered.
- Updating of references to provide the most current perspectives on the subject.
- Inclusion of a case at the end of each chapter—seventeen cases in all, twelve more than in the first edition. Five of the cases represent service industries, the new and growing segment in the economy. Several of the cases pertain to situations in such well-known companies as AT&T, Anheuser-Busch, Apple Computer, and Chesebrough Pond's.
- A completely rewritten instructor's manual with a variety of new pedagogical aids: answers to the end-of-chapter discussion questions in the book; true/false, multiple-choice, and fill-in exam questions; solutions to cases; suggestions for further reading; and a listing of additional cases.

Assumptions about the audience significantly affect the style and content of a book. Primarily, this book is intended for advanced undergraduates and graduate students. Thus, the material has been developed from a classroom-tested conceptual framework. Many of the conceptual schemes included in the book have been presented at both academic and professional conferences and have been reshaped and modified, based on the feedback provided by many distinguished marketers. Where appropriate, the book incorporates ideas generated by such esteemed strategy development consultants as the Boston Consulting Group, McKinsey & Company, and Arthur D. Little, Inc. The experiences of a large number of companies have been drawn upon and are cited throughout the book as illustrations.

This book concentrates on areas of strategic importance only, especially those having significant implications and particular relevance for the making of policy decisions in competitive situations. Discussion of routine, day-to-day decisions is intentionally avoided to keep the focus intact. The overall approach of this book is analytic rather than normative. This is necessary because strategy development is, currently at least, more an art than a science. In addition, strategy formulation is a highly complex process for which neat models and econometric equations, no matter how diligently worked out, will not suffice.

Acknowledgments

A project of this nature cannot be completed without active support from different sources. I have been lucky in this respect to have received advice and assistance from many directions.

My colleagues at the University of Connecticut have contributed to the task of preparing this second edition in a variety of ways for which I am indebted to them. I acknowledge the valuable feedback provided by students at the University of Connecticut who read early drafts of the text as a part of their assignments during 1983–84.

A special mention of appreciation must go to my graduate assistants Jack Herbert and Navin Suri, for gathering information and performing other chores, and to the departmental secretary, Mrs. Ruth Pfeifer, and student-helpers Ami Khachoyan and Carol Frechette for typing portions of the manuscript. I am indebted to many writers and publishers for granting me permission to include excerpts from their works. I wish to express gratitude to the following individuals for their permission to include cases written by them or under their supervision: Derek Abell, IMEDE, Switzerland; Sexton Adams, North Texas State University; Adelaide Griffin, Texas Woman's University; Peter J. LaPlaca, University of Connecticut; Edwin A. Murray, Jr., Boston University; and Stuart U. Rich, University of Oregon. I appreciate the case-writing help received from my graduate students: Sharon Huxley, Elizabeth R. Igleheart, Janet Lenore, and Colette M. Nakhoul.

While it is not feasible to list them all, I must single out the following individuals for helping me to gain additional insights into strategy formulation: Theodore Gordon, President, The Futures Group; Charles Lillis, General Electric Company (now Dean, University of Colorado); Donald C. Powell, Champion International Corporation (now Dean, University of Toledo); Robert W. Pratt, Jr., Group Vice-President, Avon Products, Inc.; and William F. Souders, Executive Vice-President, Xerox Corporation.

I owe a special word of gratitude to my former teacher, Professor Stuart U. Rich of the University of Oregon, who taught me what I know about marketing strategy. Dean Ronald J. Patten of the University of Connecticut encouraged me to undertake this project and inspired me to complete it. I owe these individuals my greatest debt of appreciation.

Finally, my gratitude must go to my wife and our children for their support and inspiration in seeing this book to completion. The book belongs more to them than to me.

Storrs, CT   S.C.J.
September, 1984

CONTENTS

PART SIX - Strategy Implementation and Control

PART SEVEN - Marketing Strategies

13   Product Strategies   637

14   Pricing Strategies   711

PART ONE
Introduction

CHAPTER 1 - Marketing and the Concept of Planning and
Strategy

CHAPTER 2 - Strategic Marketing

CHAPTER 1
Marketing and the Concept of Planning and Strategy

We must plan for the future, because people who stay in the present will remain in the past.

Abraham Lincoln

Over the years marketers have been presented with a series of philosophical approaches to marketing decision making. One widely touted approach is the marketing concept approach, which directs the marketer to develop the product offering, and indeed the entire marketing program, to meet the needs of the customer base. A key element in this approach is the need for information flow from the market to the decision maker. Another approach is the systems approach, which instructs the marketer to view the product not as an individual entity but as just one aspect of the customers' total need-satisfaction system. A third approach, the environmental approach, portrays the marketing decision maker as the focal point of numerous environments within which the firm operates and which affect the success of the firm's marketing program. These environments frequently bear such labels as legal-political, economic, competitive, consumer, market structure, social, technological, and international.

Indeed, these and other approaches to marketing decision making are merely descriptive frameworks which stress certain aspects of the firm's role vis-à-vis the strategic planning process. No matter what approach a firm follows, it needs a reference point for its decisions which is provided by the strategy and the planning process involved in designing the strategy. Thus the strategic planning process is the guiding force behind decision making, whichever framework one adopts for it. This relationship between the strategic planning process and approaches to marketing decision making is depicted in Exhibit 1-1.

Planning perspectives develop in response to needs that arise internally or impinge on the organization from outside. During the 1950s and 1960s, growth was the dominant fact of the economic environment, and the planning processes developed during that time were typically geared to the discovery and exploitation of entrepreneurial opportunities. Decentralized planning was the order of the day. Top management focused on reviewing major investment proposals and approving annual operating budgets. Long-range corporate plans were occasionally put together, but

EXHIBIT 1-1   Relationship Between the Strategic Planning Process and Approaches to Marketing Decision Making

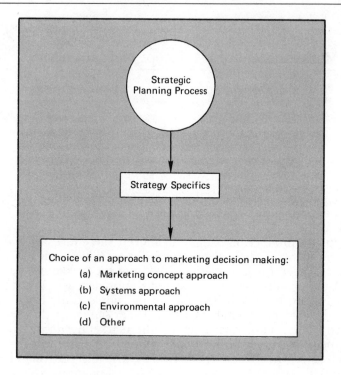

they were primarily extrapolations and were rarely used for strategic decision making.

This changed in the 1970s. With the quadrupling of energy costs and the emergence of competition from new quarters, followed by a recession and reports of an impending capital crisis, companies found themselves surrounded by new needs. Reflecting these new management needs and concerns, a process aimed at more centralized control over resources soon pervaded planning efforts. Strategically, sorting out winners and losers, setting priorities, and conserving capital became the name of the game. A new era of strategic planning dawned over corporate America.

Today, the value of effective strategic planning is virtually unchallenged in the business world. A majority of the *Fortune* 1000 firms in the United States, for instance, now have senior executives responsible for developing strategic plans.[1]

Strategic planning requires that company assets (i.e., resources) be

---

[1]Walter Kiechel III, "Corporate Strategists Under Fire," *Fortune*, December 27, 1982, p. 36.

managed to maximize the financial return through the selection of a viable business in accordance with the changing environment. One very important component of strategic planning is the establishment of the product/market scope of a business. It is within this scope that strategic planning becomes relevant for marketers. Thus as companies adopted and made progress in their strategic planning capabilities, a new strategic role for marketing emerged. In this role, marketing concentrates on the markets to serve, the competition to be tackled, and the timing of market entry/ exit.

CONCEPT OF PLANNING

Throughout human history, people have been engaged in achieving specific purposes, and in this effort some sort of planning has always found a place. In modern times the Soviet Union was the first nation to come up with an economic plan for growth and development. After World War II national economic planning became a popular activity, particularly among the developing countries, with the goal of systematic and organized action designed to achieve stated objectives within a given period. Among the market economies France has gone furthest in planning its economic affairs. In the business world, Henri Fayol, the French industrialist, is credited with the first successful attempts at formal planning.

Accomplishments attributed to planning have been summarized as follows:

1. It leads to a better position or standing for the organization.
2. It helps the organization progress in the ways that its management considers most suitable.
3. It helps every manager think, decide, and act more effectively for progress in the desired direction.
4. It helps keep the organization flexible.
5. It stimulates a cooperative, integrated, enthusiastic approach to organizational problems.
6. It indicates to management how to evaluate and check up on progress toward the planned objectives.
7. It leads to socially and economically useful results.[2]

In modern times, planning among business corporations emerged as an important activity in the 1960s. Several studies during that time showed that companies attached significant importance to planning. A Conference Board survey, for example, revealed that 85 percent among 420 separate companies had formalized corporate planning activity.[3] As Steiner claimed in 1969:

---

[2]David W. Ewing, *The Practice of Planning* (New York: Harper & Row, 1968), pp. 9–14.
[3]James Brown, Saul S. Sands, and G. Clark Thompson, "The Status of Long Range Planning," *The Conference Board Record*, September, 1966, p. 11.

No self-respecting company today can afford to be without planning capability. It is not surprising that the majority of security analysts and institutional investors passing through companies insist on spending time with the planner and often emphasize his capabilities in their evaluation reports.[4]

Currently, most companies are insisting on some sort of planning exercise to meet the rapidly changing environment. For many, however, the exercise is cathartic rather than creative.

In the United States growth is an accepted expectation of a firm; however, it does not happen by itself. Growth must be carefully planned: questions such as how much, when, in which areas, and where to grow, and who will be responsible for different tasks, must be answered. Unplanned growth will be haphazard and may fail to provide the desired levels of profit. Therefore, in order for a company to realize orderly growth, to maintain a high level of operating efficiency, and to achieve its goals fully, it must plan for the future in a systematic manner. Products, markets, facilities, personnel, and financial resources must be evaluated and selected wisely.

Today's business is more complex than ever. In addition to the keen competition that firms face from both domestic and overseas companies, a variety of other concerns such as environmental protection, employees' welfare, consumerism, and antitrust action impinge on business moves. Thus, it is desirable for a firm to be cautious in undertaking risks. This again calls for a planned effort.

Many firms pursue growth internally through the R&D effort. This route to growth not only is time-consuming but also requires a heavy commitment of resources with a high degree of risk. In such a context, planning is needed to choose the right type of risks.

Since World War II, technology has had a major impact on markets and marketers. Presumably, the trend of technological changes will continue to rise in the future. The impact of technological innovations may be felt in any industry or in any firm. Therefore, such changes need to be anticipated as far in advance as possible in order for a firm to take advantage of new opportunities and to avoid the harmful consequences of major new developments. Here again planning achieves significance.

Finally, planning is required in making a choice among the many equally attractive alternative investment opportunities a firm may have. No firm can afford to invest in each and every "good" opportunity. Thus, planning becomes essential in making the selection.

Planning done for future action has been called by many different names, such as long-range planning, corporate planning, comprehensive planning, and formal planning. Whatever the name used for it, the reference is obviously to the future.

---

[4]George Steiner, *Top Management Planning* (New York: Macmillan Co., 1969), p. 14.

Definition of Planning

Warren defines planning as:

> . . . essentially a process directed toward making today's decisions with tomorrow in mind and a means of preparing for future decisions so that they may be made rapidly, economically, and with as little disruption to the business as possible.[5]

Though there are as many definitions of planning as there are writers on the subject, Warren's emphasis on the future is the common thread underlying all planning theory. In practice, however, different meanings are attached to planning. Often a distinction is made between a budget—a yearly program of operations—and a long-range plan. Some people consider planning as something done by staff specialists, while budgeting falls within the purview of line managers.

It is necessary for a company to be clear about the nature and scope of planning that it intends to adopt. A definition of planning should then be based on what planning is supposed to be in an organization. It is not necessary for every company to engage in comprehensive planning of the same style. The basis of all planning should be to design courses of action to be pursued for achieving stated objectives in the future such that opportunities are marshalled and threats are guarded against, but the exact planning posture must be custom-made, based on the decision-making needs of the organization.

Operational management, which emphasizes the current programs of an organization, and planning, which essentially deals with the future, are two intimately related activities. Operational management or budgeted programs should emerge as the result of planning. In the outline of a five-year plan, for example, years two through five may be described in general terms, but the activities of the first year should be budgeted and accompanied by detailed operational programs.

A distinction should also be made between planning and forecasting. Forecasting considers future changes in areas of importance to a company and tries to assess the impact of these changes on company operations. Planning takes over from there to set objectives and goals and develop strategy.

Significance of Planning

No business, however small or poorly managed, can do without planning. While planning per se may be nothing new for an organization, the current emphasis on it is indeed different. No longer considered to

---

[5]Kirby E. Warren, *Long Range Planning: The Executive Viewpoint* (Englewood Cliffs, NJ: Prentice-Hall, 1966), p. 5.

be just one of several important functions of the organization, in its new role planning demands linkage of various parts of an organization into an integrated system. The emphasis has shifted from planning as an aspect of the organization to planning as a basis of all its efforts and decisions, building the entire organization toward the achievement of designated objectives. As a matter of fact, it can be considered as a new business orientation. Whereas the 1960s required each firm to have a marketing orientation as a condition for growth and survival, the firm of the 1970s reached a point where only long-term direction could underwrite success. Future years will demand even greater emphasis on planning.

A variety of reasons can be ascribed to the recent increase in the emphasis placed on planning. Dynamic technological developments, new dimensions of sociological changes in the environment, increasing involvement of all levels of government, and fierce competition at home and abroad have introduced far-reaching complexities into today's business. To survive in these environments, a firm must look sufficiently far ahead to provide against the uncertainties of a dynamic world. The economic slowdown during the early 1970s led many people to wonder whether they should do something right away to ensure growth in the future or merely accept growth as something built into the system. In the past, corporations were able to adjust themselves to changes in technology, competition, and markets through intuitive leadership. But seat-of-the-pants methods are not adequate to deal with the complexities of today's constantly changing environment. Further, when a firm becomes large and the new generation of managers emerges, its environment changes substantially. Under these circumstances it becomes essential to use a systematic approach to change. This calls for a planned posture.

There is little doubt about the importance of planning, but to be useful, planning should be done properly. Planning just for the sake of it can be injurious; half-hearted planning can cause more problems than it solves. In practice, however, many business executives simply pay lip service to planning, partly because they find it difficult to incorporate planning into their decision process and partly because they are uncertain how to adopt it.

Requisites for Successful Planning

If planning is to succeed, proper arrangements must be made to put it into operation. The Boston Consulting Group suggests the following concerns for effective planning:

> There is the matter of outlook, which can affect the degree to which functional and professional viewpoints, versus corporate needs, will dominate the work of planning.
> There is the question of the extent of involvement for members of the management. Who should participate and to what extent?

There is the problem of determining what part of the work of planning should be accomplished through joint effort, and of how to achieve effective collaboration among the participants in the planning process.

There is the matter of incentives of making planning an appropriately emphasized and rewarded kind of managerial work.

There is the question of how to provide staff coordination for planning, and this raises the issues of how a planning unit should be used in the organization.

And there is the role of the chief executive in the planning process . . . What should it be?[6]

Though planning is conceptually rather simple, implementing it is far from easy. Successful planning requires a blend of many forces in different areas, not the least of which are behavioral, intellectual, structural, philosophical, and managerial. Achieving the proper blend of these forces requires making difficult decisions, as indicated in the above quotation. While planning is complex indeed, successful planning systems do have common fundamental characteristics despite differing operational details. First, it is essential that the chief executive officer be completely supportive. Second, planning must be kept simple, in agreement with the managerial style, unencumbered by detailed numbers and fancy equations. Third, planning is a shared responsibility, and it would be wrong to assume that the president or vice-president of planning, staff specialists, or line managers could do it single-handedly. Fourth, the managerial incentive system should give due recognition to the fact that decisions made with long-term implications may not appear good in the short run. Fifth, the goals of planning should be achievable without excessive frustrations and workload and with a widespread understanding and acceptance of the process. Sixth, overall flexibility should be encouraged in order to accommodate changing conditions.

Initiating Planning Activities

There is no one best time for initiating planning activities in an organization; however, before developing a formal planning system, the organization should be prepared to establish a strong planning foundation. The chief executive should stand behind it wholeheartedly and be willing to perform the necessary functions of the job. A planning framework should be developed to match the company's perspective and should be generally accepted by the executives. A planning manual giving the work flow, information links, format of various documents, and time schedule for completing various activities must be prepared by the plan-

---

[6]*Perspectives on Corporate Planning* (Boston: The Boston Consulting Group, 1968), p. 48.

ner. Once these foundations are completed, the company can initiate the planning process anytime.

Planning should not be put off until bad times prevail; it is not a cure for poor performance. While planning is probably the best way to avoid bad times, planning efforts which are begun when operational performance is at an ebb (e.g., low or no profitability) will only make things worse, since planning efforts tend initially to create an upheaval by challenging the traditional patterns of decision making. The company facing the question of survival should concentrate on alleviating the current crisis.

Planning should evolve gradually over a period of time. It is wishful thinking to expect full-scale planning to be instituted in a few weeks or months. Initial planning may be formalized in one or more functional areas. Then, as experience is gained, a company-wide planning system may be designed. IBM, a pioneer in formalized planning, followed this pattern. First, financial planning and product planning were attempted in the post–World War II period. Gradual changes toward increased formality were made over the years. Since 1966, "increased attention has been given to planning contents, and a compatible network of planning data systems was initiated."[7]

Philosophies of Planning

In an analysis of three different philosophies of planning, Ackoff establishes the labels *satisfying, optimizing,* and *adaptivizing.*[8] Planning on the basis of the *satisfying* philosophy aims at easily achievable goals and molds the planning efforts accordingly. This type of planning requires setting objectives and goals that are "high enough" and not as "high as possible." Therefore, the satisfying planner devises only one feasible and acceptable way of achieving these goals, which may not necessarily be the best possible way. Under a satisfying philosophy, confrontations that might be caused by conflicts in programs are avoided through politicking, underplaying change, and accepting a fall in performance as unavoidable.

The philosophy of *optimizing* planning has its foundation in operations research. The optimizing planner seeks to model various aspects of the organization and define them as objective functions. Then efforts are directed so that an objective function is maximized (or minimized), subject to the constraints imposed by the management or forced by the environment. For example, an objective may be to obtain the highest feasible market share; planning will then amount to making a search for different

[7]Harold W. Henry, "Formal Long Range Planning and Corporate Performance," in Subhash C. Jain and Surendra Singhvi, *Essentials of Corporate Planning* (Oxford, OH: Planning Executives Institute, 1973), pp. 22–23.
[8]Russell L. Ackoff, *A Concept of Corporate Planning* (New York: John Wiley & Sons, 1970), p. 13.

variables that affect market share, such as price elasticity, plant capacity, competitive behavior, the product's stage in the life cycle, and so on. The effect of each variable will be reduced to constraints on the market share. Then an analysis will be undertaken to find out the optimum market share to shoot for.

Unlike the satisfying planner, the optimizer endeavors with the use of mathematical models to find the best available course to realize the objectives and goals. The success of an optimizing planner will depend on how completely and accurately the model framework depicts the underlying situation and how well the planner can figure out solutions from the model once it has been built.

Ackoff considers the philosophy of *adaptivizing* planning as an innovative approach, not yet popular in practice. To understand the nature of this type of planning, let us compare it to optimizing planning. In optimization the significant variables and their effects are taken for granted. Given these, an effort is made to achieve the optimal result. With an adaptivizing approach, on the other hand, planning may be undertaken to produce changes in the underlying relationships themselves to create a desired future. The underlying relationships refer to an organization's internal and external environment and the dynamics of the values of the actors in the environments—i.e., how values relate to needs and their satisfaction, how changes in needs produce changes in values, and what produces changes in needs.

CONCEPT OF STRATEGY

Strategy in a firm is concerned with

the basic goals and objectives of the business, the product-market matches chosen on which to compete, the major patterns of resource allocations, and the major operating policies used to relate the firm to its environment.[9]

Any organization needs strategy (a) when resources are finite; (b) when there is uncertainty about competitive strengths and behavior; (c) when commitment of resources is irreversible; (d) when decisions must be coordinated between far-flung places and over time; and (e) when there is uncertainty about control of the initiative.[10]

---

[9]Arnold C. Cooper and Dan Schendel, "Strategy Determination in Manufacturing Firms: Concepts and Research Findings," *Proceedings* of the Fall Conference (Chicago: American Marketing Association, 1971).

[10]Bruce D. Henderson, "The Concept of Strategy," in *A Special Commentary* (Boston: The Boston Consulting Group, 1981), p. 3. See also Frederick W. Gluck, Stephen P. Kaufman, and A. Steven Walleck, "Strategic Management for Competitive Advantage," *Harvard Business Review*, July–August, 1980, pp. 154–161; and "Texas Instruments Cleans Up Its Act," *Business Week*, September 19, 1983, pp. 56–64.

An explicit statement of strategy is the key to success in a changing business environment. Strategy provides a unified sense of direction to which all members of the organization can relate. Where there is no clear concept of strategy, decisions rest on either subjective or intuitive assessment and are made without regard to other decisions. Such decisions become increasingly unreliable as the pace of change accelerates or decelerates rapidly. Without a strategy, an organization is like a ship without a rudder, going around in circles.

Strategy is concerned with the deployment of potential for results and the development of a reaction capability to adapt to environmental changes. Quite naturally, we find that there are hierarchies of strategies: corporate strategy and business strategy. At the corporate level, strategy is mainly concerned with defining the set of businesses that should form the company's overall profile. Corporate strategy seeks to unify all the business lines of a company and point them toward an overall goal. At the business level, strategy focuses on defining the manner of competition in a given industry or product/market segment. A business strategy usually covers a plan for a single product or a group of related products. Today most of the action is at the business unit level, where sophisticated tools and techniques permit analysis of a business, forecasting of such variables as market growth, pricing, and the impact of government regulation, and establishment of a plan that can sidestep threats from competitors, economic cycles, and social, political, and consumer changes in an erratic environment. As a General Electric Company executive illustrates:

> The key feature of our decentralized planning is the development of business strategies at the level of the Strategic Business Unit (SBU),* each a complete business, responsible for formulating its own business strategy. . . . However, we have also found that it is essential, at the corporate level, to develop a strategic planning framework that emphasizes overall goals and permits a more rational allocation of resources. The four tasks that our experience shows should be performed at the corporate level are:
>
> • shaping the corporate business scope and diversification thrust;
> • setting objectives and priorities for the corporation as a whole and for each SBU;
> • estimating and allocating corporate resources;
> • designing corporate management systems.[11]

Each functional area (e.g., marketing) makes its own unique contribution to strategy formulation at different levels. In a great many firms, the marketing function represents the greatest degree of contact with the external environment, the environment least controllable by the firm. In such firms, marketing plays a pivotal role in strategy development.

---

*Discussed later in the chapter.

[11]Ian H. Wilson, William R. George, and Paul J. Solomon, "Strategic Planning for Marketers," *Business Horizons,* December, 1978, pp. 68–69.

In its strategic role, marketing consists of establishing a match between the firm and its environment to seek solutions to problems of deciding (a) what business the firm is in and what kinds of business it may enter in the future, and (b) how the chosen field(s) of endeavor may be successfully run in a competitive environment by pursuing product, price, promotion, and distribution perspectives to serve target markets. In the context of strategy formulation, marketing has two dimensions: present and future. The present dimension deals with the existing relationships of the firm to its environments. The future dimension encompasses intended future relationships—in the form of a set of objectives—and the action programs necessary to reach those objectives. The following example illustrates the point.

McDonald's, the hamburger chain, has among its corporate objectives the goal of increasing the productivity of its operating units. Given the high proportion of costs in fixed facilities, it was decided to increase facility utilization during off-peak hours, particularly during the morning hours. The program developed to accomplish these goals was the Egg McMuffin, followed by a breakfast menu consistent with the limited product-line strategy of McDonald's regular fare. In this example, the corporate goal of increased productivity led to the marketing perspective of the breakfast fare (intended relationship) and favorable customer attitudes toward the chain (an existing relationship).

Generally, organizations have identifiable existing strategic perspectives; however, not many organizations have explicit strategy for the intended future. This is frequently the result of a lack of the top management involvement and commitment required for the development of proper perspectives of the future within the scope of current corporate activities.

Marketing provides the core element for future relationships between the firm and its environment. It specifies inputs for defining objectives and helps in formulating plans to achieve them.

CONCEPT OF STRATEGIC PLANNING

Strategy specifies the direction. Its intent is to influence the behavior of competitors and the evolution of the market to the advantage of the strategist. It seeks to change the competitive environment. Thus, a strategy statement includes a description of the new competitive equilibrium to be created, the cause-and-effect relationships that will bring it about, and the logic to support the course of action.

Planning articulates the means of implementing strategy. A strategic plan specifies the sequence and timing of steps that will alter competitive relationships.

The strategy and the strategic plan are quite different things. The strategy may be brilliant in content and logic but the sequence and timing of the plan inadequate. The plan may be the laudable implementation of a worthless strategy. Put together, strategic planning concerns the rela-

EXHIBIT 1-2   A Strategic Planning Scorecard

- Is our planning really strategic?
  —Do we try to anticipate change or only project from the past?
- Do our plans leave room to explore strategic alternatives?
  —or do they confine us to conventional thinking?
- Do we have time and incentive to investigate truly important things?
  —or do we spend excessive planning time on trivia?
- Have we ever seriously evaluated a new approach to an old market?
  —or are we locked into the status quo?
- Do our plans critically document and examine strategic assumptions?
  —or do we not really understand the implications of the plans we review?
- Do we consistently make an attempt to examine consumer, competitor and distributor responses to our programs?
  —or do we assume that changes will not affect the relationships we have seen in the past?

Source: Thomas P. Hustad and Ted J. Mitchell, "Creative Market Planning in a Partisan Environment," *Business Horizons*, March–April, 1982, p. 64. Copyright, 1982, by the Foundation for the School of Business at Indiana University. Reprinted by permission.

tionship of an organization to its environment. Conceptually, the organization monitors its environment, incorporates the effects of environmental changes into the corporate decision making, and formulates new strategies. Exhibit 1-2 provides a scorecard to evaluate the viability of a company's strategic planning effort.

Companies that do well in strategic planning define their goals clearly and develop rational plans to implement them. In addition, they take the following steps to make their strategic planning most effective:

- Shaping the company into logical business units that can identify markets, customers, competitors, and the external threats to their business. These are managed semiautonomously by executives who operate under corporate financial guidelines and with an understanding of the unit's assigned role in the corporate plan.
- Demonstrating a willingness at the corporate level to compensate line managers on long-term achievements, not just the yearly bottom line; to fund research programs that could give the unit a long-term competitive edge; and to offer the unit the type of planning support that provides data on key issues and encourages and teaches sophisticated planning techniques.
- Developing at the corporate level the capacity to evaluate and balance competing requests from business units for corporate funds, based on the degree of risk and reward.
- Matching shorter-term business unit goals to a long-term concept of the company's evolution over the next 15 to 20 years. This is exclu-

sively the chief executive's function—and his effectiveness here may be tested by the board.[12]

Strategic Planning—An Example

The importance of strategic planning for a company may be illustrated by the example of the Mead Corporation. The Mead Corporation is basically in the forest products business. More than 75 percent of its earnings are derived from trees—from the manufacture of pulp and paper to the conversion of paperboard to beverage carriers and the distribution of paper supplies to schools. It also has an array of businesses outside the forest products industry and is developing new technologies and businesses for its future, primarily in storing, retrieving, and reproducing data electronically. In short, Mead was, and is, a company growing in the industries in which it started, as well as expanding into areas which fit the capabilities and style of its management.

Although Mead was founded in 1846, it did not begin to grow rapidly until around 1955, reaching the $1-billion mark in sales in the late '60s. Unfortunately, its competitive position did not keep pace. In 1972, the company ranked twelfth among fifteen forest products companies. Clearly, if Mead was to become a leading company, its philosophy, its management style and focus, and its sense of urgency—its whole corporate culture—had to change. The vehicle for that change was the company's strategic planning process.

When the top managers began to discuss ways to improve Mead, they quickly arrived at the key question: "What kind of performing company should Mead be?" They decided that Mead should be in the top quartile of those companies with which it normally compared. Articulation of such a clear and simple objective provided all levels of management with a sense of direction and with a frame of reference within which to make and test their own decisions. This objective was translated into specific long-term financial goals.

In 1972, a rigorous assessment of Mead's businesses was made. The results were not comforting—several small units were in very weak competitive positions. They were substantial users of cash, which was needed elsewhere in businesses where Mead had opportunities for significant growth. Mead's board decided that by 1977, the company should get out of certain businesses, even though some of those high cash users were profitable.

Setting goals and assessing the mix of businesses were only the first steps. Strategic planning had to become a way of life if the corporate culture was going to be changed. Five major changes were instituted.

---

[12]"The New Planning," *Business Week*, December 18, 1982, pp. 62–63.

First, the corporate goals were articulated throughout the company—over and over and over again.

Second, the management system was restructured. This was much easier said than done. In Mead's pulp and paper businesses, the culture expected top management to be heavily involved in the day-to-day operation of major facilities and intimately involved in major construction projects. That style had served the company well when it was simply a producer of paper. By the early '70s, however, Mead was simply too large and too diverse for such a hands-on approach. The non–pulp and paper businesses, which were managed with a variety of styles, needed to be integrated into a more balanced management system.

Therefore, it was essential for top management to stay out of day-to-day operations. This allowed division managers to become stronger and to develop a greater sense of personal responsibility for their operations. By staying away from major construction projects, top managers allowed on-site managers to complete under budget and ahead of schedule the largest and most complex programs in the company's history.

Third, simultaneously with the restructuring, seminars were used to teach strategic planning concepts and techniques. These seminars were sometimes week-long sessions, held off the premises, with groups of 5 to 20 people at a time. Eventually, the top 300 managers in the company became graduates of Mead's approach to strategic planning.

Fourth, specific and distinctly different goals were developed and agreed upon for each of Mead's two dozen or so business units. Whereas the earlier Mead culture had charged each operation to grow in any way it could, each business unit now had to achieve a leadership position in its markets or, if a leadership position was not practical, to generate cash.

Finally, the board began to fund agreed-upon strategies, instead of approving capital projects piecemeal or yielding to emotional pleas from favorite managers.

The first phase was the easiest. Between 1973 and 1976, Mead disposed of 11 units that offered neither growth nor significant cash flow. Over $100 million was obtained from the divestitures, and that money was promptly reinvested in Mead's stronger businesses. As a result, Mead's mix of businesses showed substantial improvement by 1977. In fact, Mead achieved its portfolio goals one year ahead of schedule.

For the remaining businesses, developing better strategies and obtaining better operating performance were much harder. After all, on a relative basis, the company was performing well. With the exception of 1975, 1973 through 1979 were all-time record years. The evolution of Mead's strategic planning system and the role it played in helping the good businesses of the company improve their relative performance are public knowledge. The financial results speak for themselves. In spite of the divestitures of businesses with sales over $200 million, Mead's sales grew at a compound rate of 13 percent from 1972 to reach $2.6 billion in 1979. In addition, by the end of 1979, Mead's return on total capital

(ROTC) reached 13.3 percent. More important, among the 15 forest product companies with which Mead is normally compared, it had moved from twelfth place in 1972 to second place in 1983. These were the results of using a strategic planning system as the vehicle for improving a company's financial performance.

By 1979, Mead managers were proud of their strategic planning process. Information was more accurate, manager's considerations of alternatives were more thorough and more thoughtful, and, with these changes, their judgments were more sound. Consequently, Mead became much more cohesive and developed the confidence to take calculated risks. Today, Mead is still a well-managed, highly focused, aggressive company. It is expected to be exceptionally successful in the rest of the '80s and '90s.

But it is important to remember that it took seven years to change Mead's corporate culture. Seven years is a long time. Changing or creating a corporate culture is no task for the impatient.

STRATEGIC BUSINESS UNIT

Frequent reference has been made in this chapter to the "business unit." This refers to a unit comprised of one or more products having a common market base whose manager has complete responsibility for integrating all functions into a strategy against an identifiable competitor. Usually referred to as a strategic business unit (SBU), it has also been called a strategy center, strategic planning unit, or independent business unit. The philosophy behind the SBU concept has been described this way:

> The diversified firm should be managed as a "portfolio" of businesses, with each business unit serving a clearly defined product-market segment with a clearly defined strategy.
> Each business unit in the portfolio should develop a strategy tailored to its capabilities and competitive needs, but consistent with the overall corporate capabilities and needs.
> The total portfolio of businesses should be managed by allocating capital and managerial resources to serve the interests of the firm as a whole—to achieve balanced growth in sales, earnings, and asset mix at an acceptable and controlled level of risk. In essence, the portfolio should be designed and managed to achieve an overall corporate strategy.[13]

---

[13]William K. Hall, "SBU: Hot New Topic in the Management of Diversification," *Business Horizons*, February, 1978, p. 17.

Identification of Strategic Business Units (SBUs)

Since formal strategic planning began to make inroads in corporations in the 1970s, a variety of new concepts have been developed for identifying the opportunities of a corporation and speeding up the process of strategy development. These newer concepts create problems of internal organization. In a dynamic economy all functions of a corporation (i.e., R&D, finance, and marketing) are interrelated. Optimizing certain functions instead of the company as a whole is far from adequate for achieving superior corporate performance. Such an organizational perspective leaves only the chief executive officer in a position to think in terms of the corporation as a whole. Large corporations have tried many different structural designs to broaden the scope of the chief executive in dealing with complexities. One such design is the profit center concept. Unfortunately, the profit center concept emphasizes short-term consequences; also, its emphasis is on optimizing the profit center instead of the corporation as a whole.

The strategic business unit concept has been developed to overcome the difficulties posed by the profit center type of organization. Thus, the first step in integrating the product/market strategies is to identify the SBUs or "strategy centers." This amounts to identifying natural businesses in which the corporation is involved. SBUs are not necessarily synonymous with existing divisions or profit centers. An SBU is composed of a product or product lines having identifiable independence from other products or product lines in terms of competition, prices, substitutability of product, style/quality, and impact of product withdrawal. It is around this configuration of products that a business strategy should be designed. In today's organizations this strategy may encompass products found in more than one division. By the same token, some managers may find themselves managing two or more natural businesses. This does not necessarily mean that divisional boundaries need to be redefined; often a strategic business unit can overlap divisions, and a division can include more than one unit.

Strategic business units may be created by applying a set of criteria consisting of price, competitors, customer groups, and shared experience. To the extent that price changes in a product entail a review of the pricing policy of other products, these products may have a natural alliance. If various products/markets of a company share the same group of competitors, they may be amalgamated into an SBU for the purpose of strategic planning. Likewise, products/markets sharing a common set of customers belong together. Finally, products/markets in different parts of the company having common R&D, manufacturing, and marketing components may be included in the same SBU. For purposes of illustration, consider the case of a large, diversified company, one division of which manufactures car radios. The following possibilities exist: the car radio division, as it stands, may represent a viable SBU; alternatively, luxury car radios with automatic tuning may constitute a different SBU from the SBU for standard models; or it may be that other areas of the company, such as the TV division, are combined with all or parts of the car radio division for the creation of an SBU.[14]

Overall, an SBU should be established at a level where it can rather freely address: (a) all key segments of the customer group having similar objectives; (b) all key functions of the corporation, so that it can deploy whatever functional expertise is needed to establish positive differentiation from the competition in the eyes of the customer; and (c) all key aspects of the competition, so that the corporation can seize the advantage when opportunity offers—and, conversely, so that competitors will not be able to catch the corporation off balance by exploiting unsuspected sources of strength.

A conceptual question becomes relevant in identifying SBUs: How much aggregation is desirable? Higher levels of aggregation give a relatively smaller and more manageable number of SBUs. Besides, the existing management information system may not have to be modified, since a higher level of aggregation yields SBUs of the size and scope of present divisions or product groups. However, higher levels of aggregation permit at the SBU level only general notions of strategy, which may lack relevance for promoting action at the operating level.

For example, an SBU for medical care would be too broad. It could embrace equipment, service, hospitals, education, self-discipline, even social welfare. On the other hand, lower levels of aggregation make SBUs identical to product/market segments which may lack "strategic autonomy."[15] An SBU for farm tractor engines would be ineffective because it is at too low a level in the organization to (a) consider product applications and customer groups other than farmers; and /or (b) cope with new competitors who might enter the farm tractor market at almost any time with a totally different product set of "boundary conditions." Further, at that low an organizational level, one SBU may compete with another, thereby shifting to higher levels of management the strategic issue of which SBU should formulate what strategy. The optimum level of aggregation, one that is neither too broad nor too narrow, can be determined by applying the criteria discussed above, then further refining it by using managerial judgment. Exhibit 1-3 points out factors which may be considered in the process.

Definition of the strategic business unit always contains gray areas which may lead to dispute. It is helpful, therefore, to review the creation of the SBU, halfway into the strategy development process, by raising the following questions:

---

[14]Peter Patel and Michael Younger, "A Frame of Reference for Strategy Development," *Long Range Planning*, April, 1978, pp. 37–38.
[15]*Ibid.*

—Are customers' wants well defined and understood by the industry, and is the market segmented so that differences in these wants are treated differently?

—Is the business unit equipped to respond functionally to the basic wants and needs of customers in the defined segments?

—Do competitors have different sets of operating conditions that could give them an unfair advantage over the business unit in question?[16]

If the answers give reason to doubt the SBU's ability to compete in the market, it is better to redefine the SBU, with a view to increasing its degrees of strategic freedom in meeting customer needs and competitive threats.

EXHIBIT 1-3   Factors to Consider When Identifying/Creating SBUs

1. All SBUs must have:
   a. A distinct mission
   b. Identifiable external competitors
   c. Control over all functional activities
2. Overall, one should consider:
   a. The total number of SBUs that will be created.
   b. The size of each individual SBU
   c. The degree to which it is meaningfully possible to separate or combine markets, distribution systems, production technologies, and R&D technologies.
   d. The degree of SBU overlap
   e. Competitor SBU selection
3. Remember:
   The choice of how an organization will be broken down into SBUs is really the choice of the number, the level, and the nature of the points at which competitive resource allocation decisions will occur in the organization.

Source: Charles W. Hofer, "Conceptual Constructs for Formulating Corporate and Business Strategies," p. 5. Available from *Stanford Business Cases 1977* or The Case Publishing Company (#BP-0041), Dover, MA 02030. Copyright © 1977 by Charles W. Hofer. Reprinted by permission.

SUMMARY

This chapter focuses on the concept of planning and strategy. Planning is the ongoing management process of choosing the objectives to be achieved during a certain period, setting up a plan of action, and maintaining continuous surveillance of results so as to make regular evaluations and, if necessary, to modify the objectives and plan of action. Also described are requisites for successful planning and a time frame for initi-

---

[16]Kenichi Ohmae, "The 'Strategic Triangle' and Business Unit Strategy," *The McKinsey Quarterly*, Winter, 1983, p. 13.

ating planning activities and philosophies of planning (i.e., satisfying, optimizing, and adaptivizing). Strategy is the course of action selected from alternatives as the optimum way to attain objectives, consistent with current policies and in the light of anticipated competitive actions.

The concept of strategic planning has been examined. Most large companies have made significant progress in the last 10 or 15 years in improving their strategic planning capabilities. There are two levels of strategic planning: corporate and business unit level. Corporate strategic planning is concerned with the management of a firm's portfolio of businesses and with issues of firmwide impact, such as resource allocation, cash flow management, government regulation, and capital market access. Business strategy focuses more narrowly on the strategic business unit level and involves the design of plans of action and objectives based on analysis of both internal and external factors affecting each business unit's performance. A strategic business unit is defined as a stand-alone business within a corporation facing (an) identifiable competitor(s) in a given market.

DISCUSSION QUESTIONS

1. *Why is planning significant?*
2. *Is the concept of strategic planning relevant only to profit-making organizations? Can nonprofit organizations or the national government also embrace planning?*
3. *Traditionally, planning has always been considered an important function of management. How is strategic planning different from traditional planning?*
4. *What is a strategic business unit? How is it different from a division or a group?*
5. *What are the requisites for successful strategic planning?*
6. *Differentiate between satisfying, optimizing, and adaptivizing philosophies of planning.*

The A&S Company, a button manufacturer, had an operating loss of $470,567 in 1979, continuing a downward trend of recent years (Exhibit 1-4). Unfavorable conditions in the apparel and automotive markets were the cause and were felt to confirm the need for the diversification program begun six months earlier. John Green, new president of A&S Company, summed up the future perspectives of the company in the 1979 Annual Report in the following words:

> Major attention during 1979 was given to three factors vitally important in moving a business from losses to profits, ensuring competent people in key positions, clearly defining business objectives with supporting budgets and action plans, and instituting strong operating controls. . . .
>
> During 1979 we prepared a three-year strategic business plan with objectives and action plans to achieve them. Our priority objective for 1980–81 is to eliminate the serious losses due to low production volume at our C location.
>
> Two actions are underway to achieve this. First, a major contract manufacturing program is being initiated. . . . Second, we are seeking to acquire a company which can be moved into our C plant or to provide volume for it. About fifty companies have been screened, and we are in discussion with several. . . .
>
> Management's priority objective is an early return to profitability at C, but diversification of our business is also a very important goal. During 1980 we will identify and evaluate markets which can provide profitable growth and diversification for our company through acquisition, product development, and contract manufacturing. We plan to maintain a profitable position in our established automotive and garment markets without further major investment, and steadily reduce our dependence on them.
>
> The single overriding goal for 1980 is to achieve operating trends and results that clearly indicate we are accomplishing the business turnaround and are on the way to profitable growth.

COMPANY BACKGROUND

The A&S Company was established in 1850 as the C Manufacturing Company. Its product was metal shoe buttons. In time, the company en-

This case was prepared by Sharon Huxley, graduate student at the University of Connecticut, under the supervision of the author.

EXHIBIT 1-4   A&S Company: Operating Results, 1969–1979

| YEAR | NET SALES | NET INCOME | | |
		AMOUNT	PER SHARE	% SALES
1969	$3,991,738	$495,226	$8.25	12.4%
1970	4,309,223	443,293	7.39	10.3
1971	4,817,280	589,268	9.82	12.2
1972	4,052,886	316,854	5.28	7.8
1973	3,900,691	261,348	4.36	6.7
1974	3,858,145	234,241	3.91	6.1
1975	4,304,418	345,024	5.71	8.0
1976	4,282,930	194,366	3.25	4.5
1977	3,804,950	87,795	1.47	2.3
1978	3,129,264	(124,713)	(2.08)	(4.0)
1979	3,096,048	(470,567)	(7.87)	(15.2)

Source: Company financial reports.

tered several markets with its metal buttons: the garment market, the automotive seat button market, and the upholstery button market.

In time, the button product line was expanded to include covered metal buttons and novelty items such as jingle bells. Primarily, however, A&S was a metal stamping business engaged in manufacturing buttons for the garment and automotive industries. The business was subject to sales fluctuations resulting from fashion and styling decisions over which the company had no control. The major markets the company served were competitively price intensive, with demands for excellence in customer service and quality. They could not be characterized as growth markets, but there was modest potential for increased market share.

The company was capable of contract manufacturing in metal stamping, eyelet work, metal finishing, and assembly. However, the company had not successfully sought this type of business for many years. Actually, the company had shown no real growth (except as a result of inflation and after the company's much earlier entry into the automotive market) in 130 years of business, with the current trend seriously downward. Exhibit 1-4 shows the operating results for the last ten years. Certain other selected financial statistics are given in Exhibit 1-5.

After the economic downturn of the early seventies and its effect on the garment and automotive industries and therefore on A&S, the company contacted a consulting firm, Technical Marketing Associates, Inc., which in 1976 submitted a lengthy report recommending a new business planning program for the A&S Company. The objectives of the planning program were as follows:

1. To find satisfactory means to participate in new businesses which

EXHIBIT 1-5   A&S Company: Selected Statistics—10-Year Summary

Year	Interest and Dividend Income	Declared Dividends per Share	Expenditures for Plant and Equipment	Number of Employees
1969	$156,413	$4.00	$350,153	180
1970	148,065	4.50	186,686	179
1971	141,334	5.10	321,092	180
1972	144,417	5.25	187,072	170
1973	152,698	5.25	252,642	163
1974	148,356	4.75	99,913	141
1975	148,259	5.00	75,600	133
1976	169,223	5.00	138,910	138
1977	179,539	3.50	35,467	131
1978	190,381	3.00	15,985	108
1979	220,145	2.75	614,332	160

Source: Company financial reports and management interviews.

could be expected to contribute $2 to $3 million of additional sales volume by 1981.

2. To select new businesses in such a way as:
    a. to take maximum advantage of the company's present reputation, marketing contacts, manufacturing skills and facilities, and financial strength.
    b. to diminish the company's dependence upon buttons and related products for the garment, automotive, and furniture industries.
3. To enter new businesses in such a way as:
    a. to complement and strengthen the management of A&S Company, rather than spreading it thinner.
    b. to offer a reasonable prospect that the profitability of the company (at that time averaging 11 percent on sales and $12\frac{1}{2}$ percent on net worth) would not be adversely affected.

A summary of the findings and recommendations of the study is contained in Case Appendix A. The consultant identified five promising new business opportunities and at least seven likely candidates for acquisition. The seven companies were from four of the five possible business areas, and were engaged in the manufacture of luggage hardware, furniture hardware, furniture casters, and a process called "fineblanking." The consulting firm made additional recommendations concerning the "best" fit of the luggage hardware business, with a proposed management and marketing strategy if A&S did enter that business, and also offered its services to pursue negotiations with the candidates.

The recommendations of the study were not implemented, however, and A&S saw further market erosion and decline in earnings. During 1978, the A&S Company hired its first marketing vice-president, Anne Lewis, who came to A&S from a much larger international firm with similar technologies. In another significant management change, toward the end of 1978, President Don Allen retired. His background had been financial, and A&S now needed someone with strong marketing skills to lead them. John Green joined the company as president early in 1979, and the 1979 Annual Report announced his coming on board:

> He spent 15 years with Comer & Keunyon Corporation, progressing from salesman to president of a division. He then went to Saunders Georgia, a subsidiary of Saunders and Peterson Company, for 11 years, serving as president for the last three years. After a three-year period as president of the Sheerwood Division of Fantom-Sartax, and a short period as a consultant to a small venture firm, we welcome him to A&S Company. His business experience has been primarily in management, with heavy emphasis on business planning, new products, acquisitions, and "turnaround" situations, areas which are vital to the long-range success of our company.

Late in 1979, A&S acquired the assets of a plastic button manufacturer. The New Jersey plant of the manufacturer was closed, and A&S began to market plastic buttons with its own name. In addition, the plastics technology was adapted to the production of plastic game pieces, such as checkers, markers, and blanks for dominos. A&S has had some success in this market.

Metal and plastic buttons were sold to the garment industry through trim distributors. The company had a New York sales office staffed by a vice-president–sales and three salespeople, who called directly on approximately 200 trim distributors active in the market. There was considered to be little brand awareness on the part of the garment manufacturers or loyalty to any particular button supplier. However, cost and service were very important in their decision process, as well as the availability of the desired styles and colors. The distributors handled buttons and other trim items, and typically added 50 to 60 percent to the cost of the items. A manufacturer who tried to sell directly to a garment manufacturer was dropped by the trim distributors and had difficulty gaining access to potential customers. It was considered suicidal to try to deal directly with the garment manufacturers.

Automotive buttons often consisted of three parts and were covered with the fabric used for the rest of the interior upholstery. Sales to the automotive business for A&S were handled by a four-person manufacturer's representative organization in Detroit. This was typical of sales to the automotive industry. The representatives dealt directly with the engineers and car designers. In addition, the representatives dealt with purchasing people of the automotive manufacturers, negotiating contracts for an entire model year far in advance of production for the expected total volume.

A&S was considered an important "source" supplier for automotive buttons. Service, quality, and price were the primary considerations in the automotive market along with some loyalty to suppliers. Upholstery buttons were sold through an 11-person manufacturer's representative organization that called upon manufacturers of furniture, recreational vehicles (vans and campers), and boats. There was considerable loyalty to suppliers here, and service, quality, and price were all important in choosing the supplier. These buttons also were sold in Canada through jobbers.

A minor product line consisting of stamped metal jingle bells and "Liberty" bells was sold to toy manufacturers and novelty and "home and hobby" centers.

OVERVIEW OF EXISTING BUTTON MARKETS

Neither the button industry nor major button users had a trade association or other medium for collecting and disseminating button sales data or trend information. Therefore, the company had estimated market size, market share, and trends based on its own operations and on discussions with industry contacts. Its current major market positions were summarized as follows:

1. Automotive Market
   a. *Size*: A&S estimated the total market for its type of seat buttons to be $3–$4 million. This was based on probable usage by the automobile companies, A&S supplier position with each customer, knowledge about competitors, and discussions with industry contacts. A&S sales to the recreational vehicles market were not included in automotive market considerations.
   b. *Market Share*: Based on knowledge of its five competitors and their relative position, A&S Company estimated its share of the total market to be around 25 to 30 percent. A&S had served this market for 16 years. Annual sales for 1964–69 averaged $413,254, and little growth had occurred. Sales for the ten-year period 1970–79 are shown below:

1979 (est.)	$1,050,000	1974	$1,308,264
1978	1,638,739	1973	1,274,179
1977	1,867,231	1972	856,550
1976	1,815,711	1971	689,197
1975	1,432,570	1970	365,992

   Since 1977, sales had declined primarily because of styling changes and increased competitive activity. In 1979, sales to the Fisher Body Division of General Motors Corporation were about $400,000 lower than in 1978 because of styling changes and Fisher's decision to assemble buttons in-house.

Although its pricing was competitive, A&S had not increased its market share of unassembled button components, partly because automotive companies used multiple suppliers for such products.

c. *Profitability*: There had been a declining pretax profit on sales as shown below:

1978–79	Loss	1975	10.1%
1977	3.7%	1974	12.0%
1976	8.7%	1973	12.1%

A combination of factors had caused the decline in profits: pricing pressures; underabsorption of costs in both automotive and garment buttons because of declining volume; and failure to cover increased material costs. In addition, during 1979 a series of major tooling and manufacturing problems added to losses in the line.

d. *Trends*: Some new, negative trends had been identified. The most important was Fisher Body's experimentation with injection-molded plastic buttons (metal back and stud) for weight and cost control. The company's best estimate was that plastic buttons would begin to encroach on the vinyl-covered metal button in the 1982–83 model years. In addition to the development of injection-molded buttons, a method of "tufting" of automobile upholstery which gave the gathered effect of a button was being used more widely. On the positive side, however, there was the possibility that the move to smaller cars might create competition among the automobile companies to use more decorative trim to suggest more luxury.

e. *Current Major Problems*:
   (1) Depressed sales of automobiles.
   (2) Major efforts by the automotive manufacturers to reduce weight and costs (either switch to plastic buttons or eliminate the use of buttons entirely).
   (3) Continuing heavy pressure on suppliers to *reduce* prices; some competitors were willing to respond.

2. Garment Market
   a. *Size*: A&S estimated that in 1980 the total domestic garment button market would be somewhat over $50 million in metal buttons, $30–35 million in plastic buttons from U.S. manufacturers, $6–$8 million in imported plastic buttons, and $2–$3 million in other types of buttons (pewter, glass, wood, etc.).

   The market had two segments: garment manufacturers and companies which sold carded buttons to retail stores. A&S sold to both, but data were not available on the size of the segments. A majority of A&S plastic button sales were to jobbers selling to garment manufacturers.

b. *Market Share*: On the basis of estimated market size, A&S's share of the metal button market was probably 20 to 25 percent. Eliminating the precious-metal and uniform-button segments of the market (monopolized by a single competitor with sales of $3–$4 million), the A&S market share was estimated to be about 35 percent. A&S total unit button sales to the garment industry amounted to 530,000 in 1979, down from 604,097 in 1978. Sales in 1973 were 1,740,343 units.

A&S used to be dominant in the metal button market, but in the past two years it had been losing some of its share of the declining market as price competition had become more intense and A&S had tried to maintain its position at the higher end of the price scale. In addition, there was some evidence that A&S had lost touch with some major metal button customers because it had failed to offer new designs as its competition was doing. Of the total domestic plastic button market of about $35 million, A&S estimated that 65 percent was high-volume "shirt-type" buttons. A&S did not sell to this segment, and estimated its share of the remaining or "fashion" and "custom-type" plastic button market was about 8 to 10 percent.

According to the records of the recently acquired New Jersey company, plastic button sales increased by 24 percent from 1973 through 1975 but then declined 37 percent for the three years through 1978. In 1979 sales were expected to be about 15 percent below 1978, attributed to a general weakening in the plastic button market.

c. *Profitability*: Profitability of metal buttons dropped from 18.7 percent of sales in 1975 to 10 percent in 1976, 2 percent in 1977, and with losses in 1978 and 1979. Cost of sales increased from 70 percent in 1975 to 86.2 percent in 1978. Currently, material costs were relatively stable; direct labor increased from 10 percent in 1975 to 14.5 percent in 1978–79. Factory overhead increased from 32.9 percent in 1975 to 49 percent in 1978 and 54 percent in 1979, reflecting the underabsorption of costs resulting from the sales drop in both metal button markets. The rapid decline in sales volume along with delays in adjusting to it caused some of the profit problems with metal buttons. Because the plastic button company was privately owned, comparative cost data were not available. The company's auditors reported profits in 1972–78 with the exception of a modest loss in 1977 due to an accounting practice change.

Exhibit 1-6 summarizes market size and market share positions.

EXHIBIT 1-6   The Button Market (est.)

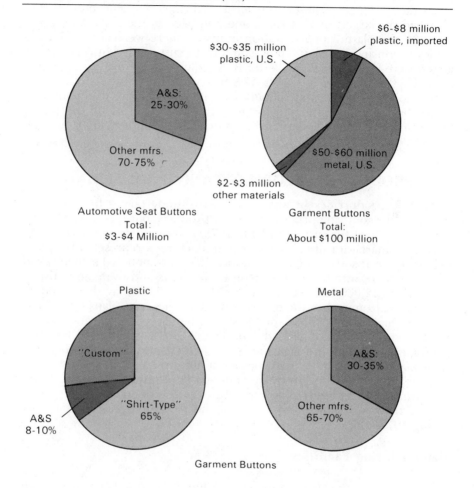

Automotive Seat Buttons
Total:
$3-$4 Million

$30-$35 million plastic, U.S.

A&S:
25-30%

Other mfrs.
70-75%

$6-$8 million plastic, imported

$50-$60 million metal, U.S.

$2-$3 million other materials

Garment Buttons
Total:
About $100 million

Plastic

"Custom"

"Shirt-Type"
65%

A&S
8-10%

Metal

A&S:
30-35%

Other mfrs.
65-70%

Garment Buttons

COMPETITION

A&S Company identified three major competitors in the automotive button market. Two of the firms, C&C Metals (NJ) and Royal Button (NY), were of approximately the same size as the A&S Company, with probably slightly less market share. Much larger was Neider & Company (KY), which did other contract stamping in addition to producing buttons.

In the metal apparel button market, there were three competitors at the higher end of the market. Waterbury Button, Talley, and Phoenix all dealt in buttons of precious metals and special construction. Of these, Waterbury Button was considered far and away the market leader. In the market for standard metal buttons for the garment trade, C&C Metals,

Jaffee & Jaffee of New York, and Emco, also of New York, were the major competitors of A&S. These firms all dealt in quality metal buttons, but A&S had the largest market share and had been in the market longer.

In the plastic apparel button industry, there were about 15 companies producing "fashion," fancy buttons to custom designs. The three largest were U.S. Plastics, Rochester Button (also a trim distributor; Rochester filled in its metal line with A&S buttons), and Emsig, another trim distributor carrying A&S metal buttons. The plastic button company now owned by A&S was estimated to be in the lower half of all the plastic button manufacturers. Exhibit 1-7 summarizes the information on competition.

PRODUCT DEVELOPMENT AND ENGINEERING

New product design was not an active undertaking for A&S. Occasionally the company produced custom products, but this was generally at the initiative of the customer. Until 1978, marketing activities were confined to contact with distributors or manufacturer's representatives, and to attendance at some trade shows. Since 1978, promotional activities had been increased, with the emphasis on trade shows and trade advertising. A&S spent $12,000 to develop a trade show booth display that could be changed to accommodate the different product lines, and plans were made to attend major trade shows for OEM suppliers to garment, automotive, and furniture manufacturers. Additionally, $30,000 was budgeted for 1979 for trade advertising in magazines such as *Playthings* (bells and buttons, game markers), *Apparel Industry*, (garment buttons), and *Sales Agent* (manufacturer's reps). A sales brochure outlining the company's contract manufacturing and metal stamping capability was also developed.

Exhibit 1-8 shows the change in the company's product-sale mix during 1977–1979.

Manufacturing Facilities

A&S's manufacturing capability included the C location plant with 70,000 square feet, with facilities for metal stamping, polishing, and some assembly, and the M location plant with 40,000 square feet, with facilities for rod and sheet casting of small plastic products. Both plants were operating at less than 50 percent of capacity. A new computerized production control system had been installed in the C plant which was expected to help with cost information and cost control in the future.

PLANNING

The new management team at A&S Company had put together the first "long-range" plan in the company's history. The time frame of the plan was necessarily short because the situation was critical, with too many

EXHIBIT 1-7 Major Competitors of A&S Company

INDUSTRY	COMPETITOR	LOCATION	REL. SIZE	CHANNEL
Automotive	C&C Metals	NJ	Same size	Mfr. representative
	Royal Button Co.	NY	Same size	Mfr. representative
	Neider & Company[a]	KY	Much larger	Mfr. representative
Metal Apparel	C&C Metals	NJ	Same size	Trim distributor
	Jaffee & Jaffee	NY	Smaller	Trim distributor
	Emco	NY	Smaller	Trim distributor
	Waterbury Button[b]	CT	Larger	Trim distributor
Plastic Apparel	U.S. Plastics	VA	Much larger	Trim distributor
	Rochester Button[c]	NY	Much larger	Trim distributor
	Emsig[c]	NY	Much larger	Trim distributor

[a]Also does contract stamping. [b]High-end precious-metal products. [c]These two companies are themselves trim distributors and carry A&S metal buttons to fill in their line.

EXHIBIT 1-8   A&S Company: Change in Product/Sales Mix

	1977	1978	1979	(After 6 Months) 1980 Projected	1980 Budgeted
Location C					
Metal buttons	1,821	1,235	1,217	1,500	1,350
Automotive	1,881	1,682	1,123	900	1,154
Jingle bells	49	73	108	150	87
Miscellaneous	30	22	24	50	50
Contract mfg.	—	—	—	200	150*
Upholstery	24	117*	216*	350	254*
Subtotal	3,805	3,129	2,688	3,150	3,045
Location M					
Polyester buttons	—	—	380*	900	1,011*
Game pieces	—	—	28*	750	300*
Subtotal			408	1,650	1,311
Total	3,805	3,129	3,096	4,800	4,356

*New business, 39%; traditional businesses, 61%.

unknowns for effective planning beyond a survival time frame. The planning process, a cooperative effort of the top management team, involved the following major steps:

1. Assessing the present situation
   a. Company strengths
   b. Company weaknesses
   c. Major current problems
   d. Overview of current markets
2. Determining what business the company wants to be in—its "mission"
   a. Short range (1981)
   b. Longer range (1982)
3. Planning to achieve short- and longer-range goals
   a. Strategy statement
   b. Planning assumptions
   c. Operating projections
   d. Operational plans to achieve goals
   e. Resource requirements
4. Providing for review and modification of plans

Case Appendix B contains an abstract of the plan.

The new management team was committed to the concept of planning as a continual process, and saw it as necessary for survival. Twice before, the company had paid consultants to develop strategic alternatives (1960 and 1976), but the commitment to follow through was not there. At this time, the strategic plan was being used as a working document, reviewed at intermediary dates for progress, and some targets and target dates were being revised. Because the company was in a very fluid situation, this kind of adaptability in both management and plan was seen as mandatory. Most of the performance objectives and one diversification objective had been met or exceeded to date.

President John Green summarized the goals of the strategic planning effort as follows:

> We need to change the character of our business to achieve our goals. Maintenance of our existing products and markets alone will result in a continuing downward trend in sales, probable operating losses, and unsatisfactory return on investment. . . .
>
> Our strategic actions and their timing are naturally influenced by the fact that our turnaround cannot be achieved with our existing business segments. Turnaround and diversification must be accomplished almost simultaneously. This requires emphasis on the acquisition route.
>
> Some important actions were taken in 1979 to begin a business turnaround, but 1980 will be the target year for achieving a visible reversal of the 4-year downward trend and establishment of the stronger business base needed for longer-range profit growth and satisfactory return on investment. The broad goals of our strategic planning are to increase profit return, stimulate business growth, bring more stability to operations and ensure long-term survival of the company.

CASE APPENDIX A: SUMMARY FINDINGS OF STUDY CONDUCTED FOR A&S BY TECHNICAL MARKETING ASSOCIATES, INC. (TMA)

A. Overall Summary and Conclusions
   1. Not surprisingly, more intensive investigation of the industries selected for deeper study reveals both positive and negative characteristics in each. Although, at this point, one industry appears more suitable for A&S than the others, this preference could be outweighed by features discovered later in individual companies.
   2. In TMA's judgment, negative characteristics loom largest in the leadframe and furniture hardware industries.
      a. Leadframes appear too risky for A&S: the business is both capital-intensive and cyclical. Furthermore, A&S cannot buy a producer large enough to be diversified and hence gain a measure of stability.
      b. Furniture hardware proves to be a doubtful match for A&S. Makers of decorative hardware are primarily die casters, and are all too large to be acquirable. Makers of functional hardware, for the most part, are little more than job-shop stamping houses.

Hardware Specialties, Inc., however, seems to be an exception which warrants further investigation.

3. While the fineblanking business is an interesting one, with unusual growth and profit potential, it must be regarded as a "long shot" for A&S. Successful participation appears to require:

    a. Acquisition of the facilities and manufacturing staff of American Feintool. Both are rumored to be available and are believed to be of excellent quality, but the company seems seriously deficient in marketing.

    b. To fill the marketing gap at American, A&S must also acquire a key sales manager from one of American's competitors, such as Connecticut Fineblanking or International Fineblanking.

    c. Acquisition of Connecticut Fineblanking or International Fineblanking.

    While prospects of executing such a program are uncertain at best, appropriate inquiries would appear worthwhile.

4. The luggage hardware industry, while it lacks the glamor of fineblanking or integrated circuit components, would appear to be the most attractive choice for A&S because:

    a. Though not growing rapidly, the industry is large enough to provide adequate opportunity for expansion for A&S.

    b. The industry has many characteristics in common with metal buttons, so that A&S management could expect to play an effective role in the business with little need for adjustment.

    c. There are at least three healthy companies in the industry which might be considered as acquisition candidates.

    d. While it appears that companies in this industry can be viable at a $2-million sales level, without unusual downside risks, the injection of sharper marketing, more innovative design, and stronger financial backing could yield substantial gains in growth and profits.

5. Little is known as yet about the availability of management talent among the small companies in these industries. The chances of securing good management appear best in the furniture and luggage hardware industries, however, because specialized technical skill is not an important consideration there, and because the pool of experienced talent on which A&S could draw is very large.

B. Principal Recommendations

1. The diversification opportunities identified in this study warrant continuation of active interest on the part of A&S.

2. Specifically, TMA recommends that the following companies be sounded out as possibilities for acquisition or merger: Excelsior Hardware Company (Stamford, CT); Long Manufacturing, Inc. (Petersburg, VA); Worcester Tool and Stamping Company (Rockdale, MA); American Feintool Inc. (White Plains, NY); Connecticut Fineblanking (Bridgeport, CT); International Fineblanking (Dayton, OH); Hardware Designers, Inc. (Mt. Kisco, NY). If requested,

TMA will be glad to make preliminary contact with these companies.

3. Should the fineblanking facility of American Feintool be found available for acquisition, A&S should immediately investigate the availability of experienced sales management from Connecticut Fineblanking or International Fineblanking.

4. Should it be found possible to enter the hardware business, the need for stronger management will depend on A&S's assessment of the management of candidate companies. Should A&S have reservations about available personnel, a search firm should be used to look for alternatives.

5. If A&S enters the luggage hardware industry, its management strategy should stress:
    a. An aggressive marketing program designed to increase market share.
    b. Design of proprietary products on which higher-than-average margins can be realized.
    c. Willingness to make relatively large investments in tooling so as to broaden the company's product base.

6. It also should be noted that participation in the luggage hardware business will almost automatically bring with it opportunities for further diversification into related types of hardware. In fact, such diversification is the rule rather than the exception among luggage hardware manufacturers. The challenge will be to find additional products in which skills in distinctive design and superior appearance can be reflected in satisfactory margins.

CASE APPENDIX B: ABSTRACT FROM A&S COMPANY'S STRATEGIC PLAN

I. Assessment of Company Strengths and Weaknesses
    A. Strengths
        1. General
            a. Long business history provides a good company image for entering new fields.
            b. Satisfactory physical location of C plant in relation to our markets and to attract key employees.
            c. Management with strong profit and growth motivation.
        2. Marketing
            a. A good reputation in the garment and automotive industries.
            b. More financial resources than most competitors in the markets we serve.
            c. The only button company with both metal and plastic button manufacturing capabilities.

3. Manufacturing
   a. Know-how in stamping, finishing, and assembling small metal parts.
   b. Good production equipment and extensive tooling available for metal buttons.
   c. Available plant capacity (metal and plastic) for a substantial increase in volume of garment and automotive products without significant capital investment.
   d. Knowledge of rod and sheet casting of small plastic products.
   e. Non-union plants; reasonably competitive wage structures.
4. Financial
   a. Internally available funds to finance early growth, with the ability to borrow if necessary.
   b. A start on computerized management control systems.

B. Weaknesses
   1. General
      a. The management team is still in the development stage.
      b. Assimilation of plastic button operations is creating time demands on several key people.
      c. Plastic plant is located 300 miles from company headquarters.
      d. Inadequate purchasing function.
   2. Marketing
      a. The garment and automotive markets will not satisfy our longer-range profit goals.
      b. Dependence on jobbers and sales representatives; little or no influence with ultimate users of our products.
      c. Highly price-intensive competition in garment and automotive markets, plus competition from lower-priced plastic button imports.
      d. Increasing imports of garments (with buttons) from the Far East.
      e. Limited product development capability. Much copying of competitors' button styles.
      f. No brand identification of our products.
      g. Growth potential in the furniture/upholstery market restricted by our limited product line.
      h. Little knowledge of markets served: size, trends, and growth rates.
      i. Decreasing demand for metal automobile buttons of the type we manufacture.
      j. Most competitors are family-owned companies with very "informal" approaches to profitability.
   3. Manufacturing
      a. Metal-stamping capabilities are restricted to a relatively small size range.
      b. Little attention has been given to plant layout for improved

production flow, availability of more cost-effective equipment, opportunities for improving manufacturing methods, and supervisory training.

c. Weak production scheduling, process and quality controls.

d. Insufficient industrial engineering capability for setting manufacturing standards and conducting special projects to increase efficiency.

4. Personnel

a. Weak technical/engineering support at metal and plastic plants.

5. Financial

a. Serious underabsorption at C location plant.

b. Four years of rapidly declining earnings, with one or two years of profit rebuilding required.

c. Inadequate departmental budgeting, cost systems, variance reporting, and control of materials.

d. Very low inventory turnover.

e. Incomplete accounting system for M location plant.

II. Short and Long-Range Goals

A. Short-Range (1981)

By the end of 1981 we plan to be at least a $7–$9 million business with a pretax profit of 7–8 percent of sales. Actual operating results and return on investment will depend on the size and profitability of our acquisition(s).

We'll still be selling buttons to the garment and automotive industries, but will have contract work and new products for growing markets where we have more direct control over our destiny and are not subject to fashion and styling factors that have had a continuing negative effect on our company for so many years.

Our sales increase for 1980 will be primarily from new manufacturing work in our C location plant and development of our non-button plastic product sales at the M plant. By the end of 1981, at least 50 percent of our sales volume and about 60 percent of our profits will come from products and markets that are not a part of our 1979 business. During 1981 we will make a significant acquisition for diversification and growth.

We will have a competent organization, sound budgeting and strategic planning, and effective management control systems.

The amount of sales and profit growth we achieve by the end of 1981 will depend upon these major factors:

1. Our ability to develop the necessary key employee organization.

2. The type of acquisition and contract manufacturing arrangements we make.

3. Fashion trends in the garment and automotive markets.

4. The length of the current economic downturn and the speed of the recovery after it.

B. Longer-Range (1982)

By the end of 1982 we plan to be at least a $9–$11 million business with percentage profit returns somewhat higher than those targeted for the end of 1981.

No more than 40 percent of our business will be in the automotive and garment industries. The balance will be in markets offering profitable growth, stability, and proprietary product positions.

A major acquisition during 1981 for diversification and growth (not necessarily related to volume for the C plant) will be a key factor in 1982 sales and profit growth.

Our organization will be further strengthened, particularly with backup support for key people, and we will have cost-effective manufacturing facilities and productive channels of distribution to the markets we serve. Our technical support functions will be well developed and we will have internal new product development capabilities.

III. Strategy Statement

The focus of this Business Plan is on earliest possible elimination of operating losses. Actions to begin moving the company toward our longer-range goals will be taken when they will not delay our short-term return to profitability.

Satisfactory short-term profit improvement will come from acquisitions, contract manufacturing, and non-button plastic products. The prime objective is work for the C location plant.

We will take actions to improve the profitability of our established businesses in the garment and automotive industries as we diversify into new fields.

It will be very difficult to achieve satisfactory profit growth if C plant losses or low profits dilute the profits generated by new business ventures. Therefore, it is imperative that we resolve the C plant problem.

During the next three years we plan to combine acquisitions, contract manufacturing, and internal new product development to achieve profit growth and diversification. Whenever practical, we will try to maintain some relationship between our existing skills and our new endeavors.

In summary, our major strategic routes to profitable growth will be as follows:

1. Develop a strong results-oriented management and supervisory organization.
2. Bring new business volume into the C plant.
3. Develop and market non-button plastic products.
4. Broaden and diversify the scope of our business by acquisitions and contract manufacturing.
5. Maintain a profitable business in buttons to support growth in new areas.

IV. Planning Assumptions

Our business goals and plans are based on the following assumptions. Any significant change in one or more of them may require adjustments in our plan.

1. By the end of 1982, net profits from our business segments will be as follows:

    business existing in 1979, 4 percent
    contract manufacturing, 5 percent
    acquisitions, 5 percent

2. By June, 1980, we will have the key people functioning as necessary to support our growth plans.

3. The U.S. economy will be moving out of the current recession by the 4th quarter of 1980.

4. Our unit sales of metal and plastic garment buttons will not drop below 1979 levels during the next two years.

5. Our 1980 selling-price increases for buttons will offset the major portion of increased material and labor costs.

6. Management's objective on behalf of the stockholders will continue to be the building of a larger and more profitable diversified company.

V. Operational Plans to Achieve Goals

This portion of our Business Plan includes those action plans necessary to reduce our weaknesses and move the company toward its goals. The management group will meet monthly to review progress with each action and agree on new ones as necessary.

Because of time pressures related to resolving the underabsorption problem at the C plant, we have already instituted the following strategic actions:

1. An *acquisition program* with focus on a metal stamping company in the Northeast which can be moved into the C plant or provide significant work for it promptly. Several such acquisitions are now in early evaluation stages.

2. Preparation of a *contract manufacturing* program. This will involve preparation of a C facilities brochure, appointment of qualified metal stamping sales representatives in selected industrial areas, and a planned promotional program. When the C plant is again busy and profitable, contract manufacturing decisions will be more selective and based on higher margins and the potential for longer-term proprietary positions.

    The contract manufacturing program is scheduled for introduction in March, 1980.

The following actions in each functional area of our business are necessary to achieve our operating goals:

A. Management

1. Develop the management group into a cooperative working team, meeting monthly to monitor major operating problems, budget variances, and strategic planning progress. Beginning in January, 1980.

2. Make one acquisition to help relieve the C plant underutilization problem. By 3/31/80.
3. Ensure effective development and initiation of the contract manufacturing program. By 3/31/80.
4. Evaluate four new markets and identify acquisition opportunities in them: game industry; lamp hardware; furniture hardware; luggage hardware. By 3/31/80.

B. Marketing
  1. Automotive market
    a. Find another product niche (not just subcontract). By 12/31/80.
    b. Explore combination plastic-metal product possibilities. By 3/31/80.
    c. Expand product line by adding new button and trim products using epoxy-on-metal designs. By 3/31/80.
    d. Regular management review of all automotive product quotations to maximize profitability. Continuing action.
  2. Apparel market
    a. Design and implement new button sampling techniques. By 1/1/80.
    b. Add new styles to our plastic button product line. Continuing action.
    c. Add a junior commissioned salesman in New York to spend full time making calls on a specific list of approximately 100 button jobbers. By 1/15/80.
    d. Ensure pricing strategies to maximize profitability. Continuing action.
    e. Test sale of buttons direct to one garment manufacturer. By 3/31/80.
    f. Decision on development of precious-metal button line. By 2/29/80.
  3. Make decision regarding two new products for upholstery market. By 3/31/80.
  4. Identify and justify product development projects, especially in plastics and plastic-metal products. Continuing action.
  5. Evaluate desirability of modest promotional program for jingle bells. By 4/30/80.

C. Manufacturing
  1. Strengthen tool engineering support for new products and contract manufacturing program. By 2/29/80.
  2. Recruit an industrial engineer for standard cost system and other cost reduction projects. By 1/31/80.
  3. Develop a materials management function. By 6/30/80.
  4. Work with accounting and marketing to reduce inventory levels. Continuing action.

D. Financial
  1. Initiate development of standards for cost systems at both plants. By 3/31/80.

2. Maximize the return on invested capital. Continuing action.

3. Increase inventory turnover to three times. By 12/31/80.

VI. Financial Resource Requirements

    A. *Operating Expenses.* The 1980 budget will include organizational and other operating expenses related to achieving our planned goals.

    B. *Capital.* The 1980 capital budget will make specific reference to investments necessary to achieving our strategic goals.

    As indicated in the plan, an evaluation is being made of the manufacturing equipment at the C plant with the objective of selectively disposing of certain old and excess machines to help fund capital requirements for the turnaround.

    C. *Acquisition(s).* The most significant capital requirements will be for acquisitions. Each will be presented with its own investment justification.

*Marketing is merely a civilized form of warfare in which most
battles are won with words, ideas, and disciplined thinking.*

Albert W. Emery

In its strategic role, marketing focuses on a business's intentions in
a market and the means and timing of realizing those intentions. This is
quite different from marketing management, which deals with developing, implementing, and directing programs to achieve designated intentions. To clearly differentiate between marketing management and marketing in its new role, a new term—strategic marketing—has been coined
to represent the latter. The chapter discusses different aspects of strategic
marketing and examines how it differs from marketing management.

Also noted are the trends pointing to the continued growth of strategic marketing in the future. The chapter ends with a plan for the rest
of the book.

CONCEPT OF STRATEGIC MARKETING

Exhibit 2-1 shows the role that the marketing function plays at different levels in the organization. At the corporate level, marketing inputs
(e.g., competitive analysis, market dynamics, environmental shifts) are essential to formulate a corporate strategic plan. Marketing represents the
boundary between the marketplace and the company, and knowledge of
current and emerging happenings in the marketplace is extremely important in any strategic planning exercise. At the other end of the scale,
marketing management deals with formulation and implementation of
marketing programs to support the marketing strategy. Marketing strategy is developed at the business unit level.

Essentially, within a given environment, marketing strategy deals
with the interplay of three forces, known as "the strategic 3 C's": the customer, the competition, and the corporation. Marketing strategies should
devise ways in which the corporation can differentiate itself effectively from
its competitors, capitalizing on its distinctive strengths to deliver better
value to its customers. A good marketing strategy should be characterized
by: (a) a clear market definition; (b) a good match between corporate
strengths and the needs of the market; and (c) superior performance, relative to the competition, in the key success factors of the business.

EXHIBIT 2-1   Marketing's Role in the Organization

ORGANIZATIONAL LEVEL	ROLE OF MARKETING*	FORMAL NAME
Corporate	Provide customer and competitive perspective for corporate strategic planning	Corporate Marketing
Business Unit	Assist in the development of strategic perspective of the business unit to direct its future course	Strategic Marketing
Product/Market	Formulate and implement marketing programs	Marketing Management

*Like marketing, other functions, i.e., finance, research and development, production, accounting, and personnel, play their own unique role at each organizational level. The business unit strategy emerges from the interaction of marketing with other disciplines.

Put together, the strategic 3 C's form the marketing strategy triangle (see Exhibit 2-2). All three are dynamic, living creatures with their own objectives to pursue. If what the customer wants does not match the needs of the corporation, the latter's long-term viability may be at stake. Positive matching of the needs and objectives of the two parties involved is required for a lasting good relationship. But such matching is relative, and if the competition is able to offer a better match, the corporation will be at a disadvantage over time. In other words, the matching of needs between the customer and the corporation must be not only positive, but better or stronger than that between the customer and the competitor. When the corporation's approach to the customer is identical to that of the competition, the customer cannot differentiate between them and the result could be a price war, which may satisfy the customer's needs but not the corporation's. Marketing strategy must then be defined in terms of these three key constitutents as *an endeavor by a corporation to differentiate itself positively from its competitors, using its relative corporate strengths to better satisfy customer needs, in a given environmental setting.*[1]

Based on the interplay of the strategic 3 C's, formation of marketing strategy requires the following three decisions:

    a. *Where to compete*—i.e., definition of the market. For example, entire market versus one or more segments.

---

[1]See Kenichi Ohmae, *The Mind of the Strategist* (New York: McGraw-Hill Book Co., 1982).

EXHIBIT 2-2 Key Elements of Marketing Strategy Formulation

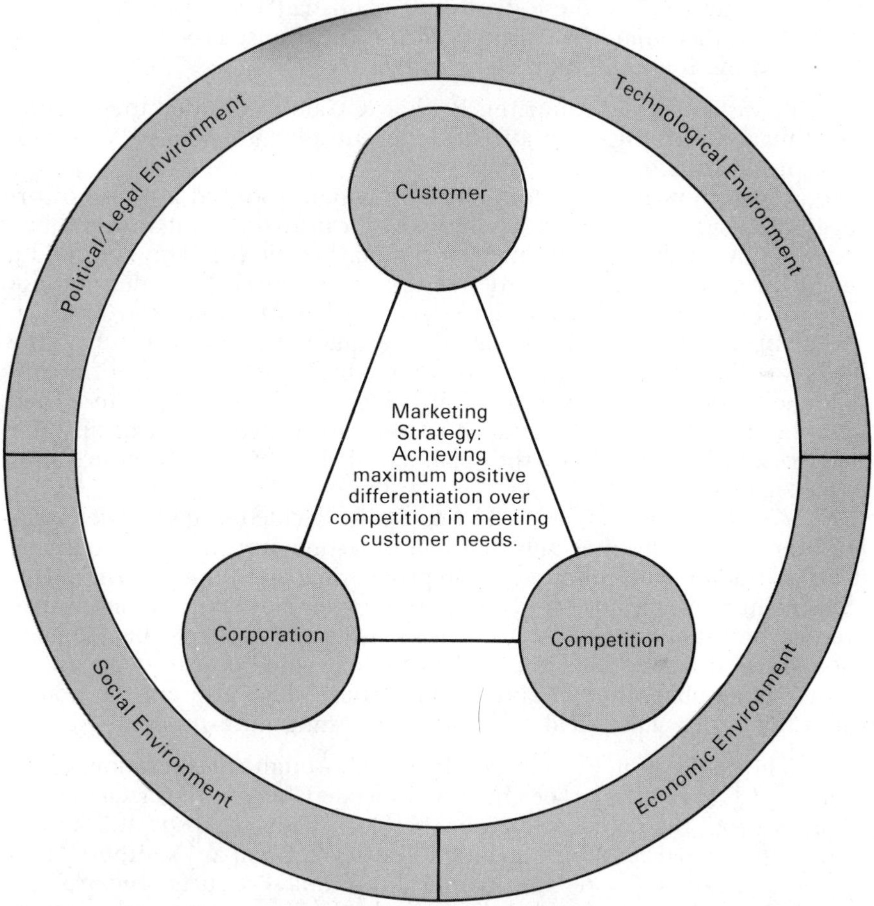

b. *How to compete*—i.e., means for competing. For example, introducing a new product to meet customer need; establishing a new image for an existing product, etc.

c. *When to compete*—i.e., timing of market entry. For example, be first in the market or wait until primary demand is established.

The concept of strategic marketing may be illustrated with reference to Procter & Gamble Company's entry into the orange juice market.[2] In 1982, faced with flagging growth in its core markets, Procter & Gamble

---

[2]"P&G Dives into Orange Juice with a Big Splash," *Business Week*, October 31, 1983, p. 50.

looked around for new opportunities. The orange juice field looked attractive. Orange juice ranked behind only soft drinks and coffee in beverage sales, and unlike these drinks, demand had been growing as consumers were becoming increasingly health-conscious. Procter & Gamble delineated the following marketing strategy:

Market (where to compete): Procter & Gamble decided to enter the broad market, offering both a frozen concentrate and a chilled, ready-to-serve product nationally.

Means (how to compete): The company introduced a brand of orange juice, Citrus Hill, which was not significantly different from others. Interestingly, at the time of entering the market the company did hold a patent for a process that yielded a better-tasting juice. But it decided not to use it initially but rather to enter the market with a me-too product. The company budgeted $400 million to promote the product during the first year, the most money ever for a new brand. The rollout of a conventional, me-too product, instead of bringing out its best product first, was seen as a P&G ploy to draw out rivals' ad strategies and drain their resources, to be followed by the relaunch of the improved product after a year or two.

Time (when to compete): The company decided to introduce Citrus Hill brand nationally after only one year of testing, unusual for a company that has traditionally followed a foolproof, time-consuming formula for introducing new brands: study the competition, develop an innovative product, and cautiously test-market it—sometimes for years—before making a move. It is said that Procter & Gamble decided on early entry to be ahead of Campbell, Lipton, and General Mills, which also saw the potential in the orange juice field and had been testing juice products.

The above strategy emerged from a thorough consideration of the strategic 3 C's. First, market entry was dictated by growing *customer* demand. Second, the decision to enter the market was based on full knowledge of the *competition,* which included Coca-Cola Company's Minute Maid label and Beatrice Foods Company's Tropicana Products, Inc. As expected, both these companies dramatically increased their advertising, consumer promotion, and trade deals for retailers. Third, the *corporation's* strength as an aggressive, successful marketer of packaged goods adequately equipped it to seek entry into new fields. Finally, the environment (in this case, increasing health consciousness) substantiated the continued opportunity in the field.

ASPECTS OF STRATEGIC MARKETING

Strategic marketing represents a new perspective in the area of marketing. Examined in this section are the importance, characteristics, origin, and future of strategic marketing.

Importance of Strategic Marketing

Strategic planning deals with the relationship of the organization to its environment and thus relates to all areas of a business. Among all the areas of a business, however, marketing is the most susceptible to outside influences. Thus marketing concerns become pivotal in strategic planning. For example, a key question that must be raised in formulating strategic plans is "What business are we in?" This question is directly related to the product/market perspective of a company. Thus the strategic perspective of the marketing side of business assumes significance in defining a company's purpose.

The experience of companies well versed in strategic planning indicates that failure on the marketing front can block the way to the goals established by strategic planning. A prime example is provided by Texas Instruments, a pioneer in developing the system of strategic planning called the OST system (see Chapter 11). Yet marketing negligence forced it to withdraw from the digital watch business. When the external environment is stable, a company can successfully ride on its technological leads, manufacturing efficiency, and financial acumen. As shifts in the environment take place, however, lack of marketing perspective makes the best-planned strategies treacherous. With the intensification of competition in the watch business and the loss of uniqueness of the digital watch, Texas Instruments began to lose ground. Its experience has been summarized as follows:

> The lack of marketing skills certainly was a major factor in the . . . demise of its watch business. T.I. did not try to understand the consumer, nor would it listen to the marketplace. They had the engineer's attitude.[3]

Characteristics of Strategic Marketing

Strategic marketing holds different perspectives from those of marketing management. Its salient features are as follows.

Emphasis on Long-Term Implications. Strategic marketing decisions usually have far-reaching implications. In the words of a marketing strategist, strategic marketing is a *commitment,* not an *act.* For example, a strategic marketing decision would not be simply a matter of providing an immediate delivery to a favorite customer but of offering 24-hour delivery service to all customers alike.

In 1980, the Goodyear Tire Company made a strategic decision to

---

[3]"When Marketing Failed at Texas Instruments," *Business Week,* June 22, 1981, p. 91. See also Bro Uttal, "Texas Instruments Regroups," *Fortune,* August 9, 1982, p. 40.

continue its focus on the tire business. At a time when other members of the industry were de-emphasizing tires, Goodyear opted for the opposite route.[4] This decision will have far-reaching implications for the company over the years. If its calculations were correct, with its new entries it should come to dominate the tire business not only in North America but to an extent in Western Europe as well, the home base of the Michelin tire, currently a strong challenger worldwide. On the other hand, if things turn sour, Goodyear may end up paying a high price for choosing greater involvement in tires than such competitors as Uniroyal and Firestone, which are now diversifying into other fields.

The long-term orientation of strategic marketing requires greater concern for the environment. Environmental changes are more probable in the long run than in the short run. In other words, in the short run, one may assume that the environment will remain stable, but that is not at all likely in the long run.

Proper monitoring of the environment requires strategic intelligence inputs. Strategic intelligence differs from traditional marketing research in requiring much deeper probing. For example, simply knowing that a competitor has a cost advantage is not enough. Strategically, one ought to find out how much flexibility the competitor has in further reducing the price.

Corporate Inputs. Strategic marketing decisions require inputs from three corporate aspects, i.e., corporate culture, corporate publics, and corporate resources. Corporate culture refers to the style, whims, fancies, traits, taboos, customs, rituals, etc., of the top management which over time have come to be accepted as intrinsic to the corporation. Corporate publics are the various stakeholders with an interest in the organization. Typically customers, employees, vendors, governments, and society constitute the stakeholders. Corporate resources include the human, financial, physical, and technological assets/experience of the company. The corporate perspectives set the degree of freedom a marketing strategist has in deciding which market to enter, which business to divest, which business to invest in, etc. The use of corporate-wide inputs in formulating marketing strategy also helps to maximize overall benefits for the organization.

Varying Roles for Different Products/Markets. Traditionally it had been held that all products exert effort to maximize profitability. Strategic marketing starts from the premise that different businesses have varying roles for the company.[5] For example, some may be in the growth stage

---

[4]*Business Week*, September 25, 1978, p. 126.

[5]Derek F. Abell, "Metamorphosis in Marketing Planning," in Subhash C. Jain (ed.), *Research Frontiers in Marketing: Dialogues and Directions* (Chicago: American Marketing Association, 1978), pp. 257–259.

of the product life cycle, some in the maturity stage, others in the introduction stage. Each position in the life cycle requires a different strategy
and affords different expectations. Products in the growth stage need extra investment while those in the maturity stage should generate a cash
surplus. While conceptually this was understood for many years, it has
been articulated for real-world application only in recent years—different
products serve different purposes. The lead in this regard was provided
by the Boston Consulting Group (BCG) in the form of a portfolio matrix,
in which products are positioned on a two-dimensional matrix of market
share and growth rate, both measured on a continuous scale from high
to low.[6]

The matrix is based on the assumption that the firm with the highest market share relative to its competitors should be able to produce at
the lowest cost. Conversely, firms with a low market share relative to competition will be high-cost producers. An important characteristic of the
framework is that it isolates businesses into four categories, reflecting their
cash use and cash generation capabilities. The BCG matrix essentially has
two properties: (a) it ranks diverse businesses according to uniform criteria; (b) it provides a tool to balance a company's cash flow by showing
which businesses are likely to be cash providers and which cash users.[7]

The practice of strategic marketing seeks first to examine each
product/market before determining its appropriate role. Further, different products/markets are synergistically related to maximize total marketing effort. Finally, each product/market is paired with a manager who
has the proper background and experience to manage it.

Organizational Level. Strategic marketing is conducted primarily at
the business unit level in the organization. At General Electric Company,
for example, major appliances are organized into a separate business unit
for which strategy is separately formulated. At Heublein Corporation,
strategy for white spirits is developed at the white spirits business unit
level.

Relationship to Finance. Strategic marketing decision making is closely
related to the finance function. The importance of maintaining a close
relationship between marketing and finance, and for that matter with other
functional areas of a business, is nothing new. But in recent years, frameworks have been developed that make it convenient to simultaneously relate marketing to finance in making strategic decisions.[8]

---

[6]See Yoram Wind and Vijay Mahajan, "Designing Product and Business Portfolios," *Harvard Business Review,* January–February, 1981, pp. 155–165.
[7]For further discussion of the portfolio matrix see Chapter 10.
[8]See Chapter 16.

Origin of Strategic Marketing

Strategic marketing did not originate in a systematic fashion. As already noted, the difficult environment of the early 1970s forced management to develop strategic plans for more centralized control of resources. It happened that these pioneering efforts at strategic planning had a finance focus. Certainly it was recognized that marketing inputs were required, but they were gathered as needed or were simply assumed. For example, most strategic planning approaches emphasized cash flow and return on investment, which of course must be examined in relation to market share. Perspectives on such marketing matters as market share, however, were either obtained on an ad hoc basis or assumed as constant. Marketing inputs such as market share became the result instead of the cause; a typical conclusion was that market share *must* be increased to meet cash flow target. The financial bias of strategic planning systems demoted marketing to a necessary but not important role in the long-term perspective of the corporation.

In a few years' time, as strategic planning was becoming firmly established, corporations began to realize that there was a missing link in the planning process. Without properly relating the strategic planning effort to marketing, the whole process tended to become static. Business exists in a dynamic setting and, by and large, it is only through marketing inputs that perspectives of changing social, economic, political, and technological environments can be brought into the strategic planning process.

In brief, while initially marketing got lost in the emphasis on strategic planning, lately the role of marketing is better understood and is re-emerging in the form of strategic marketing.

Future of Strategic Marketing

A variety of factors point to an increasingly important role for strategic marketing in future years. First, the battle for market share is intensifying in many industries as a result of declining growth rates. Faced with insignificant growth, companies have no choice but to grasp for new weapons to increase their share, and strategic marketing could provide extra leverage in share battles. Second, deregulation in many industries is mandating a move to strategic marketing. Take, for example, the case of the airline, trucking, banking, and telecommunications industries. In the past, with territories protected and prices regulated, the need for strategic marketing was limited. With deregulation, it is an entirely different story. Emphasis on strategic marketing is no longer a matter of choice if these companies are to perform well. Third, many packaged-goods companies are acquiring companies in hitherto nonmarketing-oriented industries and are attempting to gain market share through strategic marketing. For example, apparel makers traditionally have depended on production excellence to gain competitive advantage. But when marketing-oriented consumer products companies purchased apparel companies, the picture changed. General Mills, through marketing strategy, has turned Izod (the alligator shirt) into a highly successful business. Chesebrough-Pond's has done much the same with Health-Tex, making it the leading marketer of children's apparel.[9] Since acquiring Columbia Pictures in 1982, the Coca-Cola Company has been successfully testing the proposition that it can sell movies like soft drinks. Coke installed its No. 2 marketing manager as an executive vice-president at Columbia and has been applying its methodical techniques to a business famous for a more seat-of-the-pants style.[10]

Fourth, competition from overseas companies both in the United States and abroad is intensifying. More and more countries around the world are developing the capacity to compete aggressively in world markets. Businessmen in both developed and developing countries are aware of world market trends and are confident that they can reach new markets. Eager to improve their economic conditions and their living standards, they are willing to learn, adapt, and innovate. Thirty years ago, most American companies were confident that they could beat foreign competitors with relative ease. After all, they reasoned, we have the best technology, the best management skills, and the famous American "can do" attitude. Today competition from Europe, Japan, and elsewhere is becoming insurmountable. To cope with worldwide competition, renewed emphasis on marketing strategy achieves significance.

Finally, the demographic shift in the American society has created a new customer environment which makes strategic marketing an imperative.

In years past, the typical American family consisted of a working dad, a homemaker mom, and two kids. But the 1980 census revealed that only 7 percent of the 82 million households then surveyed fit that description. Of those families reporting children under the age of 17, 54 percent of the mothers worked full or part time outside their homes. Smaller households now predominate: more than 50 percent of all households comprise only one or two persons (see Exhibit 2-3). Even more startling, and frequently overlooked, is the fact that 24 percent of all households are now headed by singles. This fastest-growing segment of all—up some 80 percent over the previous decade—expanded mainly because of an increase in the number of men living alone. Some 20 percent of households now include persons 65 or older, a group that will grow rapidly. Already, almost one out of six Americans is over age 55. These statistics have strategic significance. The mass market has splintered, and companies can't sell their products the way they used to. The largest number of households may fall into the two-wage-earner grouping, but that includes

---

[9]Edward G. Michaels, "Marketing Muscle: Who Needs It?," *The McKinsey Quarterly*, Summer, 1982, pp. 37–55.

[10]Myron Magnet, "Coke Tries Selling Movies Like Soda Pop," *Fortune*, December 26, 1983, p. 119.

EXHIBIT 2-3   Demographic Profile of the U.S. Market

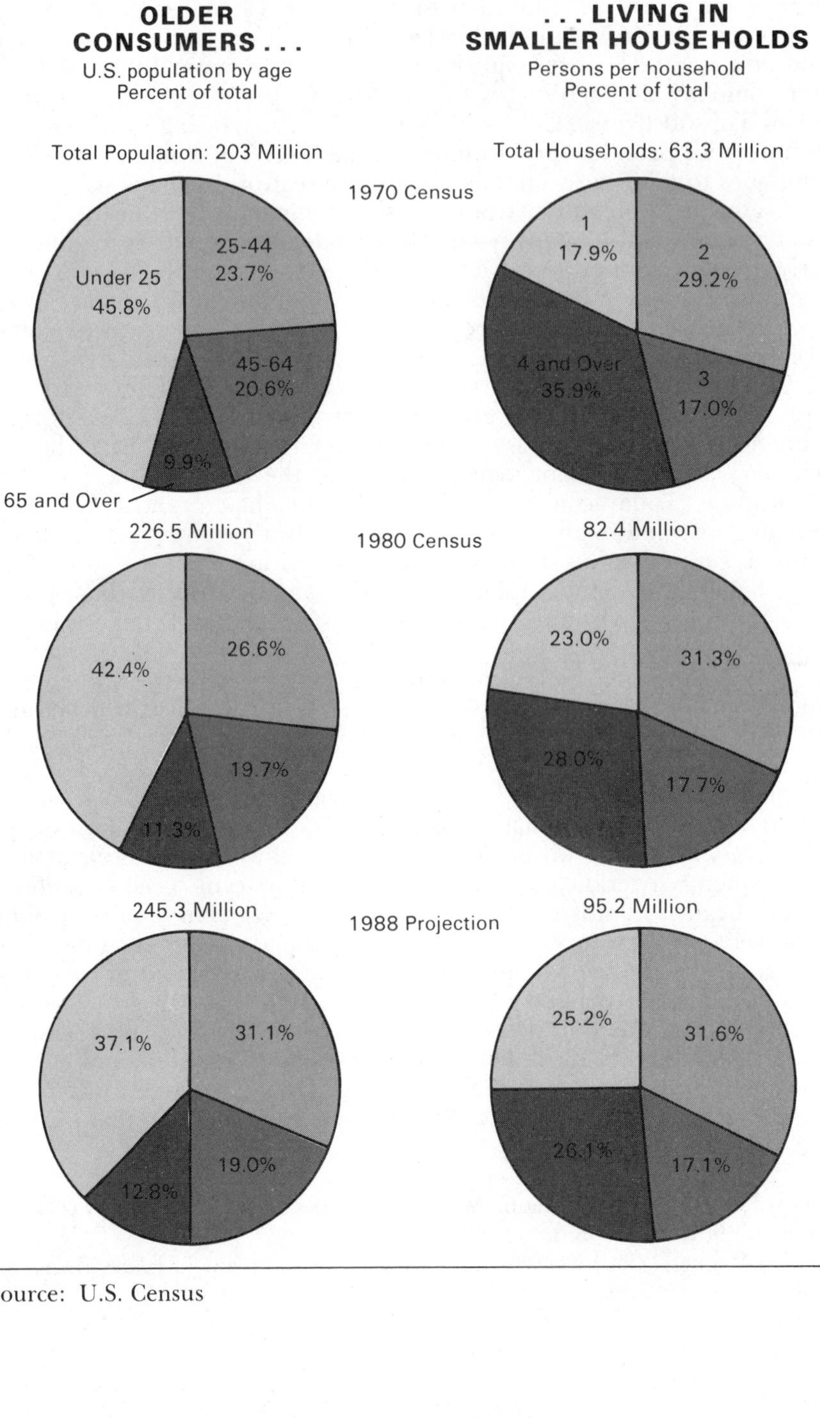

OLDER CONSUMERS . . .
U.S. population by age
Percent of total

. . . LIVING IN SMALLER HOUSEHOLDS
Persons per household
Percent of total

Total Population: 203 Million   Total Households: 63.3 Million

1970 Census

Under 25
45.8%

25-44
23.7%

45-64
20.6%

9.9%

65 and Over

1
17.9%

2
29.2%

4 and Over
35.9%

3
17.0%

226.5 Million   1980 Census   82.4 Million

42.4%

26.6%

19.7%

11.3%

23.0%

31.3%

28.0%

17.7%

245.3 Million   1988 Projection   95.2 Million

37.1%

31.1%

19.0%

12.8%

25.2%

31.6%

26.1%

17.1%

Source: U.S. Census

everyone from a manicurist to a Wall Street broker—too diverse in life-style and income to qualify as a mass market. We may foresee every market breaking into smaller and smaller units, with unique products aimed at defined segments.[11]

To sum up, the emergence of this fragmented consumer population, together with an array of economic factors—intense international competition, the impact of rapid technological change, the maturing or stagnation of certain markets, and deregulation—has altered the shape of competition, signalling the importance of strategic marketing.

STRATEGIC MARKETING AND MARKETING MANAGEMENT

Strategic marketing focuses on choosing the right products for the right growth markets at the right time. It may be argued that these decisions are no different from those emphasized in marketing management. However, the two disciplines approach these decisions from a different angle. For example, in marketing management, market segments are defined by grouping customers according to marketing-mix variables. In the strategic marketing approach, market segments are formed to identify the group(s) that would provide the company with a sustainable economic advantage over competition. To clarify the matter, Henderson labels the latter grouping a strategic sector. Henderson notes:

> A strategic sector is one in which you can obtain a competitive advantage and exploit it. . . . Strategic sectors are the key to strategy because each sector's frame of reference is competition. The largest competitor in an industry can be unprofitable in that the individual strategic sectors are dominated by smaller competitors.[12]

A further difference is that in marketing management the resources and objectives of the firm, however defined, are viewed as an uncontrollable variable in developing a marketing mix. In strategic marketing, objectives are systematically defined at different levels after a thorough examination of necessary inputs. Resources are allocated to maximize overall corporate performance. Finally, the resulting strategies are formulated with a more inclusive view. As has been said:

> A strategic market plan *is not* the same . . . as a marketing plan; it is a plan of *all* aspects of an organization's strategy in the market place. A marketing plan, in contrast, deals primarily with the delineation of target segments and the product, communication, channel, and pric-

---

[11]"Marketing: The New Priority," *Business Week*, November 21, 1983, p. 96.

[12]Bruce D. Henderson, *Henderson on Corporate Strategy* (Cambridge, MA: Abt Books, 1981), p. 38.

ing policies for reaching and servicing those segments—the so-called marketing mix.[13]

Marketing management deals with developing a marketing mix to serve designated markets. The development of a marketing mix should be preceded by a definition of the market. Traditionally, however, market has been loosely defined. In an environment of expansion, even marginal operations could exist profitably. Therefore, there was no reason to be precise, especially since the task of defining the market is at best difficult. Besides, corporate culture emphasized short-term orientation, which by implication stressed a winning marketing mix rather than an accurate definition of the market.

To illustrate how problematic it may be to define a market, consider the laundry product Wisk. The market for Wisk can be defined in many different ways: for example, laundry detergent market, liquid laundry detergent market, and prewash-treatment detergent market. In each market, the product would have a different market share and would be challenged by a different set of competitors. Which definition of the market would be most viable for a long-term healthy performance is a question that strategic marketing would address. As has been said:

> A market can be viewed in many different ways, and a product can be used in many different ways. Each time the product-market pairing is varied, the relative competitive strength is varied, too. Many businessmen do not recognize that a key element in strategy is choosing the competitor whom you wish to challenge, as well as choosing the marketing segment and product characteristics with which you will compete.[14]

Exhibit 2-4 summarizes the differences between strategic marketing and marketing management. Strategic marketing differs from marketing management in many respects: orientation, philosophy, approach, relationship with the environment and other parts of the organization, and the management style required. For example, strategic marketing requires a manager to forgo short-term performance in the interest of long-term results. Strategic marketing deals with the business to be in, while marketing management stresses running a delineated business.

In marketing management the question is: Given the array of environmental forces affecting my business, the past and the projected performance of the industry and/or market, and my current position in it, which kind of investments am I justified in making in this business? In strategic marketing, on the other hand, the question is rather: What are

---

[13]Derek F. Abell and John S. Hammond, *Strategic Market Planning* (Englewood Cliffs, NJ: Prentice-Hall, 1979), p. 9.

[14]*Ibid.*, p. 4. See also Paul F. Anderson, "Marketing, Strategic Planning and the Theory of the Firm," *Journal of Marketing*, Spring, 1982, pp. 15–26.

EXHIBIT 2-4   Major Differences Between Strategic Marketing and Marketing Management

POINT OF DIFFERENCE	STRATEGIC MARKETING	MARKETING MANAGEMENT
Timeframe	Long-range; i.e., decisions have long-term implications	Day-to-day; i.e., decisions have relevance in a given financial year
Orientation	Inductive and intuitive	Deductive and analytical
Decision process	Primarily bottom-up	Mainly top-down
Relationship with environment	Environment considered ever-changing and dynamic	Environment considered constant with occasional disturbances
Opportunity sensitivity	Ongoing to seek new opportunities	Ad hoc search for a new opportunity
Organizational behavior	Achieve synergy between different components of the organization, both horizontally and vertically	Pursue interests of the decentralized unit
Nature of job	Requires high degree of creativity and originality	Requires maturity, experience, and control orientation
Leadership style	Requires proactive perspective	Requires reactive perspective
Mission	Deals with what business to emphasize	Deals with running a delineated business

my options for upsetting the equilibrium of the marketplace and re-establishing it in my favor? Marketing management takes market projections and competitive position as a given, and seeks to optimize within those constraints. Strategic marketing, by contrast, seeks to throw off those constraints wherever possible. Marketing management is deterministic. Strategic marketing is opportunistic. Marketing management is deductive and analytical, while strategic marketing is inductive and intuitive.

PROCESS OF STRATEGIC MARKETING—AN EXAMPLE

The process of strategic marketing planning charted in Exhibit 2-5 may be illustrated with reference to the Gums and Other Specialty Foods strategic business unit of the Terris International Company.* Headquartered in New Haven, Connecticut, Terris is a worldwide manufacturer and marketer of ethical and nonprescription health care and consumer products, including gums and other specialty foods. The company conducts its business in more than 140 countries, employs approximately 56,000 people, operates more than 140 manufacturing facilities, and maintains three major research centers. In 1982 the company's worldwide sales amounted to $4.3 billion.

Corporate Strategy. In 1982, the company's strategic plan established the following goals:

- To strengthen significantly the company's existing basic businesses in pharmaceuticals and consumer products.
- To identify and pursue emerging high-technology health care markets.
- To remove Terris International from those businesses that were not meeting the company's criteria for profitability and growth, thus providing additional resources to achieve other objectives.
- To make an 18 percent return on total capital invested.
- To a great extent, to depend on retained earnings for financing growth.

The above strategy rested on the five factors shown in Exhibit 2-5 as feeding into corporate strategy:

Value system—always to be in a strong financial position, achieving growth through self-funding whenever possible;

Corporate publics—the willingness of Terris's stockholders to forgo short-term profits and dividends in the interest of long-term growth and profitability;

Corporate resources—strong financial position, high brand recognition;

Business unit's performance—chewing gum sales, for example, were higher worldwide despite recessionary conditions;

External environment—increased health consciousness among consumers.

Business Unit Mission. The mission for one of Terris International's 14 business units, Gums and Other Specialty Foods, emerged from a simultaneous review of corporate strategy, competitive conditions, cus-

---

*Disguised name.

EXHIBIT 2-5   Process of Strategic Marketing

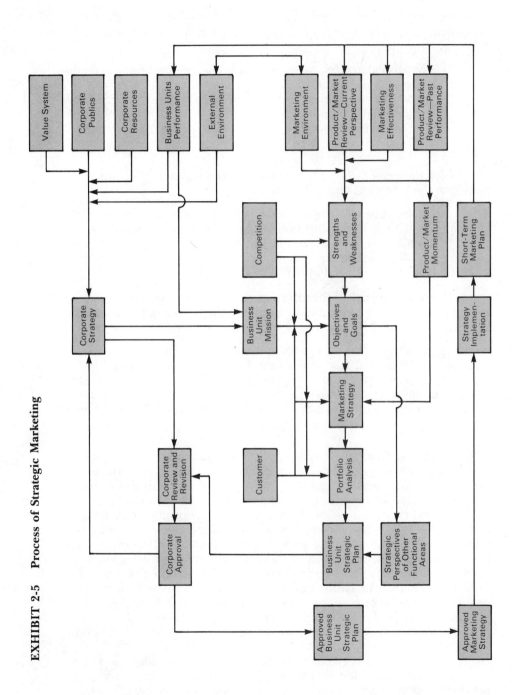

tomers' perspectives, past performance of the business unit, and marketing environment, as charted in Exhibit 2-5. The business unit mission was delineated as follows:

- To consolidate U.S. operations of gums, breath mints, and confections.
- To accelerate business in Latin America and Asia, regarded as areas of high potential growth.
- To expand baked goods operations to cover the entire continental United States.

Objectives and Goals. The mission for the business unit was translated into the following objectives and goals:

- To invest heavily to grow to achieve $1.5 billion in sales by 1986.
- To achieve leadership position in Latin America and Asia.
- To maintain position in the United States.
- To adopt marketing innovations to grow and become number one or two in the industry.

Marketing objectives for different products/markets emerged from overall business unit objectives. For example, the marketing objectives for baked goods in the Midwest and South were identified as follows:

- To achieve at least 5 percent annual growth in the United States to be counted among the first three producers of baked goods.
- To accelerate the process of new product development to offer a full range of baked goods.
- To work out new methods of distribution to become number three in baked goods.

Marketing Strategy. Marketing objectives, customer and competitive perspectives, and product/market momentum (i.e., extrapolation of past performance into the future) formed the basis of marketing strategy. In the case of Terris International, the major emphasis of marketing strategy for gums and mints was on advertising and on new product development and positioning. Thus the company decided to increase advertising support throughout the planning period and to broaden R&D efforts. Expansion was sought in Japan and other Pacific area countries via heavy promotion, and plans were made to invade the Canadian market with new product categories. In Latin America, expansion was based on intensive distribution. In the case of baked goods, an adequate delivery system was planned by establishing regional bakeries. Further new and innovative products were to be developed and introduced to stay ahead of competition.

The overall strategy of the Gums and Other Specialty Foods business unit was determined by the industry maturity and the unit's competitive position. The industry was established to be *growing*, while the competitive position was held as *strong*. These inputs, along with the business unit's goals, led to the following business unit strategy: to attempt to improve position; to push for share.

Portfolio Analysis. The marketing strategy for each product/market was reviewed using the portfolio technique. Positioning different products/markets on a portfolio matrix (high/low industry growth, and high/low market share), strategy for each product/market was examined and approved from the viewpoint of meeting the business unit mission and goals.

Following the portfolio analysis, the approved marketing strategy became a part of the business unit's strategic plan, which, when approved by top management, was ready to be implemented. As a part of implementation, an annual marketing plan was formulated which became the basis for operating managers to pursue their objectives.

Implementation of the Strategic Plan. A few highlights of the activities of the Gums and Other Specialty Foods business unit since 1982 will demonstrate how the strategic plan was implemented.

Steps were taken to reinforce and improve Terris International's position in the important sugarless sector of the gum market. In the United States, distribution of a new formulation of liquid-center sugarless gum was completed in the third quarter of 1982. In extensive preference tests, consumers consistently rated reformulated gum the best-tasting among sugarless gums.

A current brand of sugarless gum is now being distributed in an improved package that greatly prolongs product freshness. This new "fin-seal" package, employed successfully by companies in Japan and other international markets, is expected to enhance consumer acceptance and satisfaction in the United States.

The sugar-based stick gum first introduced in 1980 has been reformulated and relaunched into U.S. test markets. The new gum contains a milder flavor formulation aimed at a broader market. Sales of soft bubble gum increased substantially in 1982. In the United States, Terris International achieved a larger share of the continually expanding soft bubble gum market. Overseas, the product has been introduced successfully in 18 countries.

Terris took steps during the year to realign gum manufacturing capacity for greater efficiencies. As a result of a rationalization study of facilities within European Common Market countries, an inefficient chewing gum plant in France was closed. Consumer products for these countries are being produced by an existing facility in the United Kingdom.

Also in 1982, the company established a joint venture with a state-owned company in Egypt for the production and marketing of chewing gums and confections. Majority-owned by the parent, the Egyptian plant has been manufacturing its products in a new $5-million plant near Alexandria. The venture takes advantage of the company's technology for large-scale production of gum.

The company has been considering creating a new vitality in the mints business by introducing three products in the sugarless mint category, which now accounts for nearly 30 percent of all mint sales. A tablet mint with unique breath-protection properties has been launched. Two other sugarless mints have been introduced in U.S. test markets.

The specialty baked goods business was extremely successful in 1982. Expansion into the Midwest and other regions continued, while an extensive program of new product introductions was being implemented. Annual sales of baked products increased to nearly $280 million in 1982 from $168 million at the time of acquisition in late 1978, a 67 percent improvement. This growth is consistent with earlier projections of a $500-million sales level by the late 1980s.

During 1982, distribution of baked products was expanded to Cleveland, Ohio; Pittsburgh, Pennsylvania; and St. Louis, Missouri. The Detroit, Michigan, market was added in the first quarter of 1982. Expansion into additional Midwest metropolitan areas was planned for 1983.

In other parts of the country, baked goods were expanded into the Atlanta, Georgia, area with product distribution from the Miami plant. Albany, New York, was reached during the year from the Long Island plant. At year-end, these products were available to more than 30 percent of the nation's population, compared with 19 percent at the time of its acquisition. Response to the company's baked products within all new regions has been very favorable.

Growth of the baked line also has been stimulated by new baked goods and diversification into nonbaked products. A high-quality fudge was introduced in the Northeast in 1982 and expanded into the South and Midwest early in 1983, thus creating an entirely new market category for baked goods. New product introduction included doughnut holes and cream-filled cupcakes to form the basis of an aisle display of snacks and treats, a new marketing concept aimed at impulse purchases of baked goods. The innovation was tried first in the Northeast.

PLAN OF THE BOOK

Today's business and marketing managers are faced with a continuous stream of decisions, each with its own degree of risk, uncertainty, and payoff. Broadly, these decisions may be categorized into two classes: operating and strategic. With reference to marketing, operating decisions are the domain of marketing management. Strategic decisions constitute the field of strategic marketing.

Operating decisions are those dealing with the current operations of the business. The typical objective of these decisions in a business firm is profit maximization. During times of business stagnation or recession as experienced in the past several years, these efforts at increasing efficiency have typically encompassed a cost minimization perspective. Under these conditions managers are pressured into shorter and shorter time horizons. All too frequently decisions are made regarding pricing, discounts, promotional expenditures, collection of marketing research information, inventory levels, delivery schedules, and a host of other areas with far too little regard for the long-term impact of the decision. As would be expected, the decision which may be optimal for one time period is not so in the long run.

The second category of decision making deals with the determination of strategy: the selection of the proper markets and the products that best suit the needs of those markets. While strategic decisions may represent a very small fraction of the multitude of management decisions, they are truly the most important as they provide the definition of the business and the general relationship between the firm and its environment. Despite their importance, the need to make strategic decisions is not always as apparent as is the need (sometimes urgency) for successfully completing operating decisions.

Strategic decisions are characterized by the following distinctions:

1. They are likely to effect a *significant departure from the established product-market mix.* (This might involve branching out technologically or innovating in other ways.)
2. They are likely to hold provisions for undertaking programs with an unusually *high degree of risk relative to previous experience* (e.g., using untried resources or entering uncertain markets and competitive situations where predictability of success is noticeably limited).
3. They are likely to *include a wide range of available alternatives* to cope with a major competitive problem, the scope of these alternatives providing for significant differences in both the results and resources required.
4. They are likely *to involve important timing options,* both for starting development work and for deciding when to make the actual market commitment.
5. They are likely *to call for major changes in the competitive "equilibrium,"* creating a new operating and customer acceptance pattern.
6. They are likely *to resolve the choice of either leading or following certain market or competitive advances,* based on a trade-off between the costs and risks of innovating and the timing vulnerability of letting others pioneer (in the expectation of catching up and moving ahead at a later date on the strength of a superior marketing force).[15]

This book deals with strategic decisions in the area of marketing. Chapter 1 deals with planning and strategy concepts. Chapter 2 examines various aspects of strategic marketing. Chapters 3 through 6 deal with analysis of strategic information relative to company (e.g., corporate appraisal), competition, customer, and external environment. Chapter 7 fo-

---

[15]J. Thomas Cannon, *Business Strategy and Policy* (New York: Harcourt, Brace & World, 1968), p. 20.

cuses on the measurement of strategic capabilities, while Chapter 8 concentrates on strategic direction via goals and objectives.

Chapters 9 and 10 are devoted to strategy formulation. Organization for strategy implementation and control is examined in Chapter 11. The next five chapters, Chapters 12 through 16, review major market, product, price, distribution, and promotion strategies. The final chapter, Chapter 17, discusses strategic techniques and models.

SUMMARY

This chapter introduces the concept of strategic marketing and differentiates it from marketing management. Strategic marketing focuses on marketing strategy, i.e., direction of business. This is achieved by identifying markets to serve, competition to be tackled, and the timing of market entry/exit. Marketing management deals with developing a marketing mix to serve a designated market.

The complex process of marketing strategy formulation is described. Marketing strategy is developed at the strategic business unit level. Essentially, it emerges from the interplay of three forces—customer, competition, and corporation—in a given environment.

A variety of internal and external information is needed to formulate marketing strategy. Internal information flows both down from top management (e.g., corporate objectives and goals), and up from operations management (e.g., past performance of products/markets). External information pertains to social, economic, political, and technological trends and products/markets environment. The effectiveness of marketing perspectives of the company is another input in strategy formulation. The above information is analyzed to identify the strategic business unit's strengths and weaknesses, which together with competition and customer are considered to define strategic business unit objectives. The strategic business unit objectives lead to marketing objectives and strategy formulation. The process of marketing strategy development is illustrated with reference to an example.

Finally, the plan to be followed in this book is articulated. Of the two types of business decisions, operating and strategic, this book concentrates on strategic decision making with reference to marketing.

DISCUSSION QUESTIONS

1. *Define strategic marketing. Differentiate it from marketing management.*
2. *What are the distinguishing characteristics of strategic marketing?*
3. *What emerging trends support the continuation of strategic marketing as an important area of business endeavor?*

4. *Differentiate between operating and strategic decisions. Suggest three examples of each type of decision from the viewpoint of a food processor.*
5. *How might the finance function have an impact on marketing strategy? Explain.*
6. *Adapt to a small business the process of marketing strategy formulation presented in Exhibit 2-5.*
7. *Specify the corporate inputs needed to formulate marketing strategy.*

CASE 2
Wilmington Corporation

In June, 1975, executives in the Consumer Products Division of the Wilmington Corporation were considering the introduction of a range of cook and bakeware products made from a glass-ceramic material. The sole existing producer of pressed glass-ceramic cookware, Corning Glass Works, held a patent on the product which was due to expire in January, 1977. Corning's product range, marketed under the trade name of CORNING WARE®[1] cookware, was considered to be well established and held a strong position in the marketplace. While Wilmington did not have detailed figures on CORNING WARE® sales or profits, it was felt that this line provided a sizable proportion of the sales and profits of Corning's Consumer Products Division. The expiration of Corning's patent in 1977 would remove a major barrier to entry into the glass-ceramic market. In anticipation of this event, Wilmington had already developed the technology to produce a product comparable in quality and performance to CORNING WARE® cookware.

The investigation of Wilmington's possible entry into the glass-ceramic market was the responsibility of a three-man task force appointed in March, 1975, by Thomas Alstone, marketing vice-president for the Consumer Products Division. The task force included as its members F. Henderson Bruit, product manager for Wilmington's Country Squire line; John P. Middle, a market analyst from the Market Research Department; and Allen S. Stern, an engineer from the manufacturing staff. In his initial discussions with the task force, Mr. Alstone had indicated that their final report should include:

1. a detailed study of the glass-ceramic market;
2. a recommendation as to whether or not Wilmington should enter the market; and
3. if yes, detailed plans for entry.

Mr. Alstone felt that fairly heavy capital expenditure would be required for the glass-ceramic project and he knew that the plans would have to be placed before the New Products Review Committee and the

Capital Expenditure Review Committee before any final decisions could be made. Preliminary estimates had shown that a twelve-month period would be required to develop the facility to produce glass-ceramic products. Some existing facilities at Wilmington's Marygold, New York, plant were being phased out and could be converted to production of glass-ceramic products at a lower capital cost than would be required to construct a completely new manufacturing plant. Mr. Alstone felt that a decision about whether or not to enter the glass-ceramic business had to be made as soon as possible, and if the company were to go ahead, further decisions about plant size and capital expenditure should follow fairly quickly.

In his preliminary discussions with the engineering staff, Mr. Alstone had been assured that Wilmington was capable of producing a product at least as good as CORNING WARE® cookware. He had been shown some laboratory samples which were very similar to CORNING WARE® in material and weight, though their shape and appearance were somewhat different.

COMPANY BACKGROUND

Wilmington Corporation was a large, diversified manufacturer of glass and glass-related products. The company was started in 1901 to manufacture glass tumblers, and had grown in sales to $510 million per year by 1974. (See Exhibit 2-6 for a ten-year statistical history of the company.) The major share of this growth had come from expansion of company operations in the glass industry. Currently, the company had twenty-one plants in operation: seventeen in the United States, two in Canada, and one each in Germany and Brazil. Although the company marketed its products in seventy-five countries, 76 percent of its sales came from the United States and Canada. Wilmington divided its business into four major areas—consumer products, packaging, commercial products, and technical. Exhibit 2-7 shows the net sales and income before taxes of the company's major lines of business.

While the Consumer Products Division had always been an important part of the company's business, the Packaging Division had provided the major share of the growth and earnings in the 1960s. During the late sixties, however, the glass packaging industry's growth was slowed by growth in the use of plastic materials. As a result, both sales and earnings from packaging declined. The company did try to enter the plastic packaging business by acquiring two plastic packaging companies in the United States and one in Canada. The Canadian plant was moderately successful, but both the United States plastics operations had failed to make money.

The Consumer Products Division

The company manufactured over 2,000 different items in its Consumer Products Division. These were sold both as individual pieces, which

EXHIBIT 2-6   Wilmington Corporation: Ten-Year Financial Summary, 1965–1974

	1974	1973	1972	1971	1970
Operations					
Net sales	$509,975,200	$455,493,300	$422,242,800	$387,705,500	$363,824,800
Costs and expenses:					
Cost of products sold	423,283,900	366,793,000	331,191,000	303,253,900	281,590,700
Selling and administrative	48,993,500	44,296,800	40,311,100	36,604,600	34,547,200
	472,277,400	411,089,800	371,502,100	339,858,500	316,138,000
Income from operations	37,697,800	44,403,500	50,740,700	47,846,900	47,686,900
Other income	1,984,200	1,713,600	1,338,900	959,200	1,625,500
Interest expenses	(2,418,500)	(1,755,800)	(1,511,400)	(1,428,200)	(1,531,200)
Income before income tax	37,263,500	44,361,300	50,568,200	47,377,900	47,781,200
Net income	17,032,300	21,124,700	24,832,400	23,613,900	24,246,700
Financial Position Data					
Working capital	97,556,400	95,969,300	93,209,600	85,098,000	73,385,400
Property, plant and equipment	288,970,200	270,854,700	249,155,500	232,867,700	223,824,200
Accumulated depreciation	127,883,400	116,048,000	103,783,100	97,696,600	92,596,600
Long-term debt	22,009,400	24,468,800	23,919,100	24,837,400	26,255,700
Common stockholders' equity	223,614,500	214,913,500	203,887,100	185,718,200	170,181,200
Statistics					
Property, plant and equipment expenditures	24,679,800	24,661,200	24,025,800	17,538,500	22,845,800
Depreciation expense	15,673,500	14,863,200	13,273,600	12,964,700	12,119,600
Weighted average no. of common shares	8,489,195	8,705,625	8,701,510	8,666,405	8,652,421
No. of common stockholders	10,253	10,114	9,139	8,522	8,140
No. of employees	18,489	19,109	18,116	17,868	18,240

	1969	1968	1967	1966	1965
Operations					
Net sales	$344,655,800	$290,852,600	$265,016,400	$249,283,300	$212,013,600
Costs and expenses:					
Cost of products sold	256,711,200	219,946,500	210,975,000	195,869,800	172,495,400
Selling and administrative	32,230,500	29,758,700	26,055,900	24,638,800	19,746,100
	288,941,700	249,705,200	237,030,900	220,508,600	192,241,500
Income from operations	55,714,100	41,147,400	27,985,500	28,774,700	19,772,100
Other income	1,801,800	2,089,600	1,301,700	1,340,100	596,900
Interest expenses	(1,503,900)	(1,377,400)	(1,341,400)	(959,200)	—
Income before income tax	56,011,900	41,859,700	27,945,800	29,155,600	20,369,000
Net income	29,206,700	21,693,000	13,127,200	13,499,500	9,374,800
Financial Position Data					
Working capital	68,383,400	68,599,300	62,911,200	59,439,700	39,951,200
Property, plant and equipment	206,581,000	176,704,500	158,342,000	144,768,000	117,945,300
Accumulated depreciation	85,791,700	77,918,300	69,986,600	65,072,800	57,724,300
Long-term debt	26,961,800	26,289,200	26,286,700	24,817,500	—
Common stockholders' equity	155,210,000	133,627,400	118,527,200	108,682,100	93,215,800
Statistics					
Property, plant and equipment expenditures	33,584,300	20,558,800	16,951,600	24,193,400	14,902,900
Depreciation expense	11,082,300	9,598,200	8,117,800	6,630,000	5,304,700
Weighted average no. of common shares	8,595,710	8,502,468	8,476,516	8,440,523	7,376,960
No. of common stockholders	7,614	7,350	7,921	7,954	8,337
No. of employees	18,240	17,496	16,875	16,441	15,262

EXHIBIT 2-7   Wilmington Corporation: Sales and Income Before Taxes

| | PERCENTAGE | | | | |
	1970	1971	1972	1973	1974
Net Sales:					
Consumer Products	25%	27%	29%	30%	30%
Packaging	57	56	55	54	54
Commercial	12	11	10	10	10
Technical	6	6	6	6	6
Total net sales	100%	100%	100%	100%	100%
Income Before Taxes:					
Consumer Products	37%	44%	44%	51%	51%
Packaging	44	40	40	34	34
Commercial	12	8	7	7	7
Technical	7	8	9	8	8
Total income before taxes	100%	100%	100%	100%	100%

were shipped to retailers in bulk, as well as in sets. The sets were mostly sold in gift packs, though company research showed that a number of the so-called gift sets were used by the purchasers in their own home or given to a person in the same house.

The product range had initially started with drinking glasses, but had been expanded over the years to include dinnerware, decorative items, giftware, ovenware, and a great variety of miscellaneous glass pieces. A description of the product range is presented in Exhibit 2-8. Traditionally the company had concentrated in the low-price, high-volume end of the market, and competed by offering "good value for the money." The product range was subsequently broadened, however, to include a number of middle-price-range pieces as well.

The company used a great variety of styles and designs in its glassware, but the bulk of them tended to be either traditional or "popular." Some of its lines were promoted as being "modern," but these lines represented only a small proportion of total sales and did not fare well in competition with imported glassware. Generally speaking, each product was offered in three or four colors or designs. Wilmington executives believed that few consumers recognized the name Wilmington or associated it with any of the products in their line.

Though not highly innovative in the application of technology to consumer glassware manufacture, the company did monitor consumer tastes and preferences quite closely. Product development activities were guided by analysis of this research data, as well as through preference testing of new products at both the regional and national levels. Before products were put into distribution, they were generally test marketed; after the test market, the company often conducted post-test follow-up research with consumers to find out how well the product performed in actual use and whether consumers were satisfied with it.

EXHIBIT 2-8   Wilmington Corporation Consumer Products Division: Product Range, 1974

	No. of designs/ decorations/colors	No. of sizes/items	Total no. of pieces
1. Mugs and bowls	9	3	27
2. Decorated mugs	9	3	27
3. Ovenware	10	11	31
4. Ovenware gift sets	5	12	20
5. Mixing bowls	4	3	11
6. Mixing bowl gift sets	8	12	40
7. Kitchen aids	4	10	10
8. Dinnerware gift sets	7	12	184
9. Serving dish gift sets	4	6	31
10. Table server gift sets	2	8	16
11. Salad gift sets	4	3	12
12. Salt and pepper shakers	4	2	8
13. Salt and pepper gift sets	4	2	8
14. Punch gift sets	5	5	25
15. Chip'n dip gift sets	7	3	21
16. Decorated novelty gift	35	97	435
17. Decorated cocktail ware	24	6	78
18. Glass/refreshment	13	14	122
19. Decorated glasses	2	14	38
20. Cocktail glasses	5	11	60
21. Miscellaneous drinking	19	12	201
22. Decorative glasses	5	7	42
23. Cut glass	6	12	72
24. Beer glasses and mugs	16	3	49
25. Brandy snifters	1	12	12
26. Whiskey glasses	1	12	12
27. Wine and decanter sets	7	6	54
28. Beverage gift sets	9	4	42
29. Refreshment gift sets	5	4	31
30. Decorated gift sets	26	81	312
31. Decorated cocktail gift sets	3	18	31
32. Decorated juice gift sets	2	5	12
33. Dinnerware	7	12	184
34. Accessories for dinnerware	4	27	208
35. Serving dishes	4	11	31
36. Punch cups	5	2	7
37. Fountainware	7	12	12
38. Terrarium	3	3	3
39. Imaginarium gift sets	3	3	3
40. Vases and planters	6	36	42
41. Ash trays	38	54	54
42. Storage jar gift sets	4	5	20
43. Storage jars	21	32	38
44. Fish bowls	5	14	14
45. Miscellaneous ornaments	12	12	12
46. Candleholders	5	14	14
47. Ashtray gift sets	8	13	13
48. Snack and buffet gift sets	4	2	8
49. Lazy susan gift sets	2	3	66
50. Miscellaneous gift sets	12	12	12

Note: There was considerable overlap between pieces offered individually and in sets. The total number of different pieces manufactured by Wilmington was a little over 2,000.

Distribution

The Consumer Products Division distributed its products direct to retailers in major market areas through 15 field offices in 43 states. Each field office consisted of a district sales manager with a staff of three to five salespersons, two or three sales promotion assistants, and clerical staff. In addition, the national account sales manager and a staff of ten salespersons handled sales to large multiple-unit retailers, mail order houses, premium companies, and government. The sales force called regularly on the retail trade to book orders, arrange sales promotion and displays in stores, and handle routine customer problems. The Consumer Products Division operated fifteen distribution centers, six at plants where the products were produced, and the other nine at key distribution locations.

The company serviced about 13,000 retail outlets through its direct distribution network, plus 175 national accounts which accounted for about 9,000 locations. In addition, the company had a network of 87 wholesalers to service those areas which were uneconomical to call on directly. It was estimated that these wholesalers serviced about 10,000 additional outlets, though they accounted for only 11 percent of sales. The breakdown of sales by type of outlet is shown in Exhibit 2-9.

Wilmington's suggested list prices provided the retailer with average margins of approximately 42 percent. However, because of differences among suggested trade margins for various items in the Wilmington line, as well as regular discounting from list on certain more standard products, substantial variation existed in the actual margins received.

Typically, Wilmington spent between 1 percent and 2 percent of sales on advertising and sales promotion activities. The bulk of these funds

EXHIBIT 2-9   Wilmington Corporation Consumer Products Division: Estimated Breakdown of Sales by Type of Outlet, 1974

	NO. OF OUTLETS	%	$ MILLION	%
Department Stores	3840	12	32.1	21
Supermarkets	9280	29	18.4	12
Discount Stores	5420	17	36.5	24
Hardware Stores	6440	20	16.8	11
Chain Stores	2540	8	12.2	8
Premium	660	2	10.7	7
Institutional	1600	5	6.1	4
Government	1290	4	12.3	8
Mail Order	300	1	6.2	4
Others	630	2	1.7	1
Total	32,000	100%	153.0	100%

Source: Company records.

went to support in-store display and merchandising activities. Advertising expenditures were confined to the few branded products within the Wilmington line.

Country Squire Product Line

The first line of heat-resistant glass cook and bakeware was launched by Corning in 1915. The product, branded PYREX® ware,[2] was protected by strong patents which were ultimately extended until 1957. When the patent for PYREX® ware expired, Wilmington considered the introduction of a range of heat-resistant glass bakeware similar to PYREX® ware. However, the management of the company was reluctant to make the investment in the new technology for a product which was somewhat different from the rest of its range. The company had a large range of glass products at the time, but none of them were suitable for cooking or baking. While the company hesitated, American Glass introduced its Blue Flame range of heat-resistant glass bakeware at 20–25 percent below PYREX® ware prices. This was followed by Ajay Corporation with a similar range. By this time, Wilmington was convinced that there was a good opportunity for it to add a line of heat-resistant glass ovenware to its line. It developed the Country Squire line of opal ovenware which was made available in four colors and two decorations. Later, the company added a range of clear glass items to the Country Squire line.

Wilmington experienced some difficulty in obtaining distribution for the Country Squire line. By the time the product was ready for distribution, both American Glass and Ajay Corporation had achieved substantial distribution. Most stores were already carrying one or two lines and were reluctant to add a third. Exhibit 2-10 shows the market penetration of Country Squire.

EXHIBIT 2-10   Market Shares, Heat-Resistant Glass Bakeware

	1957	1958	1959	1960	1961	1965	1974
PYREX® ware	98%	90%	83%	71%	60%	61%	58%
American Glass	2	8	12	18	19	18	18
Ajay Corporation	—	2	4	7	11	12	13
Country Squire	—	—	1	4	9	8	8
Others	—	—	—	—	1	1	3
	100%	100%	100%	100%	100%	100%	100%

[2]PYREX® ware is a registered trademark of Corning Glass Works.

THE HOUSEWARES INDUSTRY

The housewares industry was reported to have retail sales on the order of $14 billion per year in 1973. A fairly common breakdown of the industry is shown in Exhibit 2-11.

The industry was highly fragmented. More than 1,500 firms produced houseware products, and over 60 percent of these firms had sales of less than $5 million per year. However, several of the largest U.S. corporations had a stake in the housewares business, including General Electric's Consumer Products Division, the Hardware Division of American Home Products Corporation, National Presto Industries, Inc., and General Housewares, Inc.

The growth of the industry is illustrated in the figures on total industry shipments shown in Exhibit 2-12.

It was generally believed that the sale of housewares was related to

EXHIBIT 2-11   Breakdown of the Housewares Industry, 1973

	MANUFACTURER'S SHIPMENTS (in $ MILLIONS)
Small electrics	$3,033
Serving/buffet	1,127
Cook and bakeware	1,040
Outdoor	433
Bath and closet	260
Kitchen tools and gadgets	173
Others	2,601
Total	$8,667

Source: National Housewares Manufacturers Association, Seventh Annual Survey of Housewares Manufacturers, 1973.

EXHIBIT 2-12   Manufacturers' Shipments of Housewares, 1966–1973

1966	$4,035 million
1967	4,535
1968	5,700
1969	5,475
1970	5,400
1971	6,135
1972	7,061
1973	8,667

Source: National Housewares Manufacturers Association, various reports and publications.

the rate of family formation. This had been running at approximately two million households per year since 1970, and was expected to continue at about this level into the early 1980s. One observer of the industry commented:

> Young housewives tend to stock up on pots and pans and other kitchen paraphernalia even before they get married, and housewares were traditionally regarded as good gifts for weddings and showers.

Industry growth was attributed in part to the rapid introduction of new products. New products seldom tended to originate from fundamental technological breakthroughs, however. Rather, the industry appeared to concentrate on the use of innovative materials, design, and color to introduce newness into its products. Corning's original breakthrough in heat-resistant glass, and later pressed glass-ceramic, were included with DuPont's nonstick Teflon among the few fundamental technological changes in the industry.

There appeared to be definite fashion trends in color and design, analogous in many ways to fashion trends in the clothing industry. Observers attributed these partly to trends in the development of consciousness about kitchen decor and color coordination. Housewives were encouraged to plan the appearance of their kitchens because this was a room where they and the rest of the family spent a great deal of time. This had introduced a fashion element into the cook and bakeware market. The color and decor of kitchen utensils had thus become an important purchase consideration. The cook and bakeware industry expended a considerable amount of effort in tracking and predicting these trends. The trade literature devoted considerable space to identifying the latest "in color," as indicated by the following two extracts:

> Color is still a tricky point. While avocado continues to be the number one seller, red and harvest are still vying for the number two spot. It looks like red will come out ahead of harvest, but harvest may prove somewhat harder to knock out of the running than earlier anticipated. Blue is still being talked about as a potentially strong seller, and spring selling may make or break the talk about blue.[3]

> One noticeable product trend was heavy emphasis on color. Floral designs were splashed on everything from cookware and toilet-seat covers to pastry servers. "Our market research tells us the fashion concept is extremely important," noted Corning's Stemski.[4]

The industry was to some extent less affected by general business conditions than most other industries, as indicated by the following abstract from *Barron's:*[5]

---

[3]*Merchandising Week,* December 14, 1970, p. 23.
[4]*Business Week,* January 22, 1972, p. 14.
[5]*Barron's,* November 30, 1970, p. 12.

While many a business is suffering recession pains, the housewares trade is booming. Reason: sales are benefiting from more leisure time, higher discretionary income, and the willingness of customers to continue buying reasonably priced products, while holding back on such big ticket items as refrigerators and stoves.

The Cook and Bakeware Industry

In general, cookware is used for range-top cooking and bakeware products are used only for baking in the oven. Exact sales figures for the total cook and bakeware industry were not available and only rough estimates could be made. In 1973, the National Housewares Manufacturers Association estimated that the annual sales of the cook and bakeware industry were about $1,040 million and were growing at the rate of 5.3 percent per year. In 1972, the Metal Cookware Manufacturers Association estimated that shipments of metal cookware had reached an estimated $431 million and were growing at the rate of 4 percent per year. From these and other sources, Wilmington produced the estimated breakdown of industry sales by type of material shown in Exhibit 2-13.

It was generally acknowledged in the industry that a considerable proportion of sales were purchased by the customer as gifts, but Wilmington executives did not have figures on the proportion of gifts within each product or material category. They felt that gift purchasing was more common for the higher-priced products, while the lower-priced products were typically bought for the consumer's own use.

EXHIBIT 2-13   Estimates of Manufacturers' Shipments of Cook and Bakeware, 1974

	COOKWARE	BAKEWARE
	(PERCENT OF TOTAL SALES)	
Stainless steel	23%	6%
Glass/heat-resistant glass	17	25
Aluminum	13	14
Cast iron	8	15
Porcelain clad metal	15	24
Stoneware*	9	6
Copper	5	—
Others	10	10
Total	100%	100%

*Recently several manufacturers had begun to sell "stoneware dinnerware" in supermarkets. Some sets contained casseroles in addition to place settings. These casseroles were promoted in supermarket-sponsored advertising as "freezer-to-oven-to-table" items. In Mr. Alstone's judgment their quality was inferior to heat-resistant glass products of the Country Squire type.

Data were also collected to provide an estimate of cookware and bakeware sales by major product type. These are shown in Exhibit 2-14.

Wilmington executives felt that the breakdown for CORNING WARE® cookware was different from the figures in Exhibit 2-14, but they did not have accurate figures to back this up.

General Environmental Trends

Home cooking habits in the United States were being influenced by several trends in the general environment. On the one hand, the popularity of convenience foods had reduced the amount of time that the average housewife spent on meal preparation, particularly when combined with the impact of kitchen gadgets and appliances in the cooking process. On the other hand, there had been a surge of interest in ethnic, specialty, and gourmet foods, evidenced by the popularity of cookbooks on these subjects. The popularity of these foods had created demand for more, and often specialized, cooking utensils. *Barron's* reported:

> The latest trend to catch the imagination of housewives—and the marketing managers of the industry—is so-called gourmet cooking. Popular television shows like Julia Child's workmanlike French Chef and the good-natured Galloping Gourmet, Graham Kerr, have spurred interest in the "joy of cooking." Best-selling cookbooks are doing like-

EXHIBIT 2-14 Estimated Breakdown of Cook and Bakeware Market by Product Type, 1974

		PERCENT OF TOTAL SALES
Cookware		
Casseroles (1½ qt. or larger)	19%	
Frying pans	15	
Saucepots (below 1½ qts.)	8	
Subtotal		42%
Bakeware		
Pans	11%	
Baking dishes	13	
Baking trays	4	
Special items	2	
Subtotal		30%
Measuring and Mixing		
Bowls	11	
Cups	4	
Subtotal		15%
Miscellaneous	13	13%
Total		100%

wise. To cash in on the trend, West Bend is offering French-style skillets. Others are rushing out with fondue sets in every shade of the rainbow. Many new entries allow food to be cooked and served from the same utensils at the table—sort of a rich man's TV dinner.

To the Tube

Just as television is whetting the appetites of would-be Cordon Bleu chefs, it also is becoming more popular as a medium for selling housewares. APL, for example, has gone on the air to promote its line of "Superseal" air-tight, food storage containers. The firm already advertises in selected TV markets and will go national next year.[6]

Merchandise Week reported:

The metal cookware industry . . . has accepted the challenge of homemakers who prepare more than 45 million custom-prepared meals daily, to provide glamorous cooking utensils of top quality with color, no-stick, easy-to-clean pans, with a purpose.

For the first time, stores can offer fashion colors and a choice of styles to customers who prefer stainless steel. But some buyers have doubts, believing consumers will, in the words of one buyer, choose "Farberware to cook in and Copco to serve in"—or, in other words, prefer the decorative look of enameled cast iron to enameled stainless steel.[7]

Further, more and more meals were being eaten outside the home. A recent *Business Week* article reported that by 1980 two out of every three meals would be eaten out. The impact this would have on cookware purchase decisions was uncertain.

Finally, cooking technology also appeared to be undergoing some changes. This had been marked by the introduction of flat-top stoves and microwave ovens.[8] Microwave oven sales exceeded 900,000 units in 1975 and amounted to approximately $360 million. This represented a growth of 25 percent and 63 percent over 1974 and 1973, respectively. Since metal cookware was not suitable for use with these new ovens, some observers foresaw the possibility of a substantial change in cook and bakeware purchases in the future.

CORNING GLASS WORKS

Corning Glass Works ranked 190th in the *Fortune* 500 1974 listing of the largest manufacturing companies in the United States. Its 1974 sales exceeded $1,051 million, of which some 68 percent were in the United

---

[6]*Barron's*, November 30, 1970, p. 12.

[7]*Merchandise Week*, November 9, 1970, p. 21.

[8]A flat-top stove is a cooking range with a flat sheet over the top of individual burners.

States. Consumer products accounted for 25 percent of the company's sales, electrical and electronic products for 44 percent, and "technical" and other products for the remaining 31 percent. The company depended heavily on sales to industrial customers. Among the most important were manufacturers of television tubes who bought glass blanks from Corning.

The Consumer Products Division

The Consumer Products Division handled the manufacture and marketing of the PYREX® ware and CORNING WARE® ranges of cook and bakeware, the CORELLE® Livingware[9] range of tableware, the Electromatics range of small electrical appliances, a range of domestic major appliances such as stoves, and some miscellaneous products including decorative glassware. The world-renowned Steuben range of crystal glassware was handled by another division. The marketing staff of the Consumer Products Division was divided into two sections. One handled PYREX® ware, CORNING WARE®, and CORELLE® and generally distributed its products through a chain of wholesale distributors who in turn sold to the retail stores. The other section handled all the other products and sold through a variety of distribution methods, as appropriate.

The PYREX® ware line of heat-resistant glass cook and bakeware had been launched by Corning in 1915. It was promoted on the basis of a combination bake and serve utensil—strong and heat resistant enough to bake products in an oven and yet good-looking enough to serve on the table. PYREX® ovenware was not recommended, however, for range-top cooking and could not be heated directly on a flame. PYREX® ware was protected by patents and until the expiration of its patents in 1957 enjoyed an unchallenged position in the market for glass cookware. Wilmington executives estimated that by 1975 PYREX® ware still accounted for between 10 percent and 15 percent of the Consumer Products Division's sales.

CORNING WARE®

CORNING WARE® cookware was introduced to the United States market with nationwide distribution in 1959. Manufactured from pressed glass-ceramic, trademarked PYROCERAM®,[10] it not only had a superior appearance to PYREX® ware but also was suitable for range-top cooking. There was some research evidence, however, that some consumers did not recognize this functional distinction between the two products and thought of CORNING WARE® cookware as merely being a superior type of oven-to-table ceramic-glass product.

---

[9]CORELLE® Livingware is a registered trademark of Corning Glass Works.
[10]PYROCERAM® is a registered trademark of Corning Glass Works.

Only rough estimates were available of CORNING WARE® sales, since the company did not publish these figures. The 1974 Annual Report of the company indicated that sales of consumer products was $235 million for that year. Industry sources estimated that about half of these sales were of housewares products, and about half of the houseware sales were CORNING WARE®. However, since some of the CORNING WARE® brand products were part of the Electromatic range of small electrical houseware products, the sales of cook and bakeware under the CORNING WARE® label were somewhat less than total CORNING WARE® sales. One trade source estimated that the Electromatics represented 12 percent of the sales of housewares for Corning. Based on overall industry trends and their own perception of CORNING WARE® products' market acceptance, Wilmington executives estimated that CORNING WARE® had probably doubled its unit sales over the previous seven years.

Product Line

The CORNING WARE® product line consisted of twenty-four individual pieces, ranging from the one-quart covered saucepan to the four-quart saucepot (see Exhibit 2-15). In addition, items were combined into sets; Corning currently offered ten such sets. The company also made available several accessories, such as handles, as well as spare parts and replacement of broken items.

The product line was fairly narrow by industry standards (see Exhibit 2-16); only one basic color and two types of decoration were available (see Exhibit 2-17). The available decorations were the traditional Cornflower Emblem, which was closely associated with the CORNING WARE® name, and the Spice O' Life®, which was available in all the sets and in a limited number of individual pieces. Up to 1970, only the Cornflower Emblem was available. In that year, the company introduced the Floral Bouquet design. According to industry reports, CORNING WARE® sales grew 24 percent over the previous year and the new design accounted for 14 percent of total CORNING WARE® sales.

Spice O' Life was introduced in the second half of 1972, and demand for this decoration grew so fast that the company discontinued the Floral Bouquet in June, 1974. This decision was apparently taken in order to be able to produce the Spice O' Life® design in sufficient quantities. Reports indicated that CORNING WARE® sales had grown 27 percent over the previous year, with Spice O' Life® attaining 46 percent of the total. There were trade rumors that the company was planning to introduce a third decoration in the middle of 1975.

Wilmington estimated that over 60 percent of CORNING WARE® was sold in sets, and the remainder was sold as single pieces. The company felt that the majority of the sets were bought for gifts and that gift purchasing accounted for a large part of the sales of single pieces as well. Some sales were for accessories and replacement of broken parts.

Pricing

Retail prices of CORNING WARE® products were near the top end of cook and bakeware products though they were lower than those of the top-quality stainless steel and enamel ware. The prices of PYREX® ware were much lower than CORNING WARE®, as shown in Exhibit 2-18.

The Wilmington task force studied the history of CORNING WARE® prices and concluded that Corning had kept prices relatively stable with only four major increases between 1958 and 1974. CORNING WARE® prices had kept up with inflation, and gained ground somewhat in the last few years. A summary history of CORNING WARE® prices is presented in Exhibit 2-19.

Distribution

Corning used a two-level distribution system for its PYREX® ware, CORNING WARE®, and CORELLE® product lines: the company sold directly to a network of 350 independent distributors who, in turn, sold to retailers. The Corning sales force sold to and serviced the distributors and in addition, assisted at the retail level, mainly by doing in-store displays, promotion, and merchandising. Over the years, the company had managed to build up a strong network of loyal, competent distributors in most marketing areas. The typical Corning distributor was financially sound and a major force in the housewares trade in the area in which he operated. This strong distribution network was considered a major factor in Corning's competitive position.

Although Wilmington executives knew that CORNING WARE® products were broadly distributed in many different types of stores, they had little idea of the exact extent of this coverage or its effectiveness. As a result, a group of MBA students were commissioned to do a trade survey of both PYREX® ware and CORNING WARE® distribution. This involved a retail store audit as well as interviews with store buyers. An extract from the student report is presented in Case Appendix A. Wilmington executives did know, however, that Corning had developed particularly strong relationships with Sears, as well as other large chains such as Montgomery Ward and J. C. Penney Co. It had been rumored in the trade that Corning was about to embark on the production of a special pattern to be distributed by Sears through all of its outlets in North America. Sears was known to be a major outlet for CORNING WARE® as well as PYREX® and CORELLE® products.

According to industry sources, Corning was reputed to have a reputation in the trade of "selling itself"; it had a strong brand name, a high reputation for quality, and was manufactured by a well-known company.

Up to 1974, trade margins were guaranteed by Corning's fair trading rules. The company set the retail prices for all its CORNING WARE®, PYREX®, and CORELLE® products and generally speaking managed to

EXHIBIT 2-15   Extract From Corning's Suggested Retail Price List, 1975

Catalog Number	Description	Price Each	Pieces Per Pack	Packs Per Shipper	Weight Per Shipper	Price Per Shipper
A-1	1-Qt. Covered Saucepan—Cornflower Emblem	$ 7.95	1	3	9 lbs.	$23.85
A-1-8	1-Qt. Covered Saucepan—Spice O'Life™ design	8.95	1	3	9 lbs.	26.85
A-1½	1½-Qt. Covered Saucepan—Cornflower Emblem	8.95	1	3	10 lbs.	26.85
A-1½-8	1½-Qt. Covered Saucepan—Spice O'Life	9.95	1	3	10 lbs.	29.85
A-2	2-Qt. Covered Saucepan—Cornflower Emblem	9.95	1	3	13 lbs.	29.85
A-2-8	2-Qt. Covered Saucepan—Spice O'Life	10.95	1	3	13 lbs.	32.85
A-3	3-Qt. Covered Saucepan—Cornflower Emblem	11.95	1	3	17 lbs.	35.85
A-3-8	3-Qt. Covered Saucepan—Spice O'Life	12.95	1	3	17 lbs.	38.85
A-5	5-Qt. Covered Saucepot—Cornflower Emblem	16.95	1	3	25 lbs.	50.85
A-5-8	5-Qt. Covered Saucepot—Spice O'Life	17.95	1	3	25 lbs.	53.85
A-8	1½-Qt. Covered 8″ Skillet—Cornflower Emblem	9.95	1	3	12 lbs.	29.85
A-8-8	1½-Qt. Covered 8″ Skillet—Spice O'Life	10.95	1	3	12 lbs.	32.85
A-10	2½-Qt. Covered 10″ Skillet—Cornflower Emblem	11.95	1	3	20 lbs.	35.85
A-10-8	2½-Qt. Covered 10″ Skillet—Spice O'Life	12.95	1	3	20 lbs.	38.85
A-84	4-Qt. Covered Saucepot—Cornflower Emblem	14.95	1	3	23 lbs.	44.85
A-84-8	4-Qt. Covered Saucepot—Spice O'Life	15.95	1	3	23 lbs.	47.85
A-115-S	Dollar Days Special complete with covered 1-Qt. saucepan and 10″ skillet—Cornflower Emblem	12.95	1 set	2 sets	20 lbs.	25.90
A-115-8-S	Dollar Days Special complete with covered 1-Qt. saucepan and 10″ skillet—Spice O'Life	13.95	1 set	2 sets	20 lbs.	27.90

A-300	Kitchen Starter Set complete with 1½-Qt. and 2-Qt. covered saucepans and 10" covered skillet—Cornflower Emblem	22.88	1 set	1 set	15 lbs.	22.88
A-300-8	Kitchen Starter Set complete with 1½-Qt. and 2-Qt. covered saucepans and 10" skillet—Spice O'Life	25.88	1 set	1 set	15 lbs.	25.88
A-300-P	Kitchen Starter Set with Bonus Value complete with 1½-Qt. and 2-Qt. covered saucepans, 10" covered skillet, and a 9" pie plate—Cornflower Emblem	22.88	1 set	1 set	17 lbs.	22.88
A-300-8-P	Kitchen Starter Set with Bonus Value complete with 1½-Qt. and 2-Qt. covered saucepans, 10" covered skillet, and an undecorated 9" pie plate—Spice O'Life	25.88	1 set	1 set	17 lbs.	25.88
A-500	Chef Master Set complete with 1-Qt. and 2-Qt. covered saucepans, 4-Qt. saucepot, 8" and 10" skillets—Cornflower Emblem	39.88	1 set	1 set	27 lbs.	39.88
A-500-8	Chef Master Set complete with 1-Qt. and 2-Qt. covered saucepans, 4-Qt. saucepot, 8" and 10" skillets—Spice O'Life	44.88	1 set	1 set	27 lbs.	44.88
A-700	Great Cook's Set complete with 1-Qt. saucepan bowl with plastic storage cover, 1½-Qt. and 3-Qt. covered saucepans, 8" and 10" covered skillets, 6-Cup teapot, and two 1¾-Cup petite pans with two plastic storage covers—Cornflower Emblem	44.88	1 set	1 set	26 lbs.	44.88
A-700-8	Great Cook's Set—Spice O'Life	49.88	1 set	1 set	26 lbs.	49.88
P-4	1½-Qt. Covered Baking Dish (7" × 5½" × 3")—Cornflower Emblem	7.95	1	3	10 lbs.	23.85
P-4-8	1½-Qt. Covered Baking Dish (7" × 5½" × 3")—Spice O'Life	8.95	1	3	10 lbs.	26.85

EXHIBIT 2-15   continued

Catalog Number	Description	Price Each	Pieces Per Pack	Packs Per Shipper	Weight Per Shipper	Price Per Shipper
P-19	13" Serving Platter with spatter shield—Cornflower Emblem	$11.95	1	3	11 lbs.	$35.85
P-20	1³/₄-Qt. Party Buffet cover and candlewarmer—Cornflower Emblem	12.95	1	3	13 lbs.	38.85
P-21 P-21-8	13" Roaster with rack—Cornflower Emblem 13" Roaster with rack—Spice O'Life™ design	12.95 13.95	1 1	3 3	13 lbs. 13 lbs.	38.85 41.85
P-34	5-Qt. Dutch Oven with cover and rack—Cornflower Emblem	15.95	1	3	20 lbs.	47.85
P-40	2¹/₂-Qt. Royal Buffet with cover and candlewarmer—Cornflower Emblem	14.95	1	3	18 lbs.	44.85
P-42	1³/₄-Cup Petite Pan Set (set of 4 pans and 4 plastic covers)—Cornflower Emblem	10.95	1 set	3 sets	10 lbs.	32.85
P-42-8	1³/₄-Cup Petite Pan Set (set of 2 pans and 2 plastic covers)—Spice O'Life	12.95	1 set	3 sets	10 lbs.	38.85
P-43	2³/₄-Cup Petite Pan Set (set of 2 pans and 2 plastic covers)—Cornflower Emblem	6.95	1 set	3 sets	7 lbs.	20.85
P-43-8	2³/₄-Cup Petite Pan Set (set of 2 pans and 2 plastic covers)—Spice O'Life	8.95	1 set	3 sets	7 lbs.	26.85
P-46	1³/₄-Cup Petite Pan—Cornflower Emblem	2.95	6	3	14 lbs.	53.10
P-64	1-Qt. Covered Saucemaker—Cornflower Emblem	6.95	1	3	9 lbs.	20.85

Item	Description	Price			Weight	
P-76	15½" Open Roaster with 2-section wire rack—Cornflower Emblem	16.95	1	3	16 lbs.	50.85
P-100	Menu-ette Set complete with 1 and 1½-Pt. covered saucepans and 6½" covered skillet—Cornflower Emblem	12.88	1 set	3 sets	18 lbs.	38.64
P-100-8	Menu-ette Set—Spice O'Life	15.88	1 set	3 sets	18 lbs.	47.64
P-104	6-Cup Teapot—Cornflower Emblem	9.95	1	3	5 lbs.	29.85
P-104-8	6-Cup Teapot—Spice O'Life	10.95	1	3	5 lbs.	32.85
P-146	6-Cup Percolator—Cornflower Emblem	12.95	1	3	10 lbs.	38.85
P-146-8	6-Cup Percolator—Spice O'Life	13.95	1	3	10 lbs.	41.85
P-149	10-Cup Percolator—Cornflower Emblem	14.95	1	3	11 lbs.	44.85
P-149-8	10-Cup Percolator—Spice O'Life	15.95	1	3	11 lbs.	47.85
7186-FP	Filter Paper for P-186-N, pk of 100	2.95	1 pk	6	6 lbs.	17.70
P-250	Baker's Helper Set complete with 9" Pie Plate, 2-Qt. Loaf Dish, Square Cake Dish and 1½-Qt. Covered Baking Dish—Cornflower Emblem	18.88	1 set	1 set	11 lbs.	18.88
P-250-8	Baker's Helper Set complete with 9" undecorated Pie Plate, 2-Qt. Loaf Dish, Square Cake Dish and 1½-Qt. Covered Baking Dish—Spice O'Life	21.88	1 set	1 set	11 lbs.	21.88
P-309	9" Pie Plate—Cornflower Emblem	3.95	1	4	8 lbs.	15.80
P-315	9" × 5" × 3", 2-Qt. Loaf Dish—Cornflower Emblem	5.95	1	3	8 lbs.	17.85
P-315-8	9" × 5" × 3", 2-Qt. Loaf Dish—Spice O'Life	6.95	1	3	8 lbs.	20.85
P-322	8" × 8" × 2", Square Cake Dish—Cornflower Emblem	7.95	1	3	11 lbs.	23.85
P-322-8	8" × 8" × 2", Square Cake Dish—Spice O'Life design	8.95	1	3	11 lbs.	26.85

EXHIBIT 2-15   continued

Catalog Number	Description	Price Each	Pieces Per Pack	Packs Per Shipper	Weight Per Shipper	Price Per Shipper
P-332	12" × 7½" × 2", 2¾-Qt. Oblong Baking Dish—Cornflower Emblem	$ 9.95	1	3	12 lbs.	$29.85
P-332-8	12" × 7½" × 2", 2¾-Qt. Oblong Baking Dish—Spice O'Life™	10.95	1	3	12 lbs.	32.85
P-423	Petite Fours 2 ea. 1¾-Cup and 2¾-Cup Petite Pans with 2 plastic covers and 2 glass covers—Cornflower Emblem	8.88	1 set	1 set	5 lbs.	8.88
P-423-8	Petite Fours 2 ea. 1¾-Cup and 2¾-Cup Petite Pans with 2 plastic covers and 2 glass covers—Spice O'Life	11.88	1 set	1 set	5 lbs.	11.88
P-81	1-Pt. Menu-ette Saucepan with Cover—Cornflower Emblem	4.50	1	3	6 lbs.	13.50
P-81-8	1-Pt. Menu-ette Saucepan with Cover—Spice O'Life	5.50	1	3	6 lbs.	16.50
P-82	1½-Pt. Menu-ette Saucepan with Cover—Cornflower Emblem	5.50	1	3	7 lbs.	16.50
P-82-8	1½-Pt. Menu-ette Saucepan with Cover—Spice O'Life	6.50	1	3	7 lbs.	19.50
P-83	6½" Menu-ette Skillet with Cover—Cornflower Emblem	5.50	1	3	7 lbs.	16.50
P-83-8	6½" Menu-ette Skillet with Cover—Spice O'Life	6.50	1	3	7 lbs.	19.50

EXHIBIT 2-16   Range of Products Sold—Cook and Bakeware, 1975

Company/Brand	Number of Individual Pieces	Number of Sets	Number of Colors	Number of Decorations
CORNING WARE®	24	10	1	2
PYREX® ware	56	20	5	4
Wilmington's Country Squire	31	13	7	2
American Glass (heat-resistant glass line)	15	5	5	3
Ajay Corporation (heat-resistant glass line)	20	—	2	6

Source: Catalogues of the companies concerned, 1975.

get the retail trade to maintain these prices. It sold the products to its wholesale distributors at $52\frac{1}{2}$ percent discounts from retail price and expected the wholesaler to sell to the retailer at 40 percent discount from retail price.

In January, 1974, Corning discontinued its practice of fair trading at the wholesale level and permitted each wholesaler to set its own price to the retailer. While this move apparently caused some concern among distributors and large department store buyers, there was very little change in the market situation as a result of this move.

In April, 1975, Corning discontinued its retail fair trade policy and allowed each retailer to set its own price for CORNING WARE®, PYREX® and CORELLE® products. This move was followed by substantial discounting by some retailers. *Business Week* reported that, in Massachusetts, Corning products began selling at discounts of 20 percent to 40 percent.[11] It was, however, too early for Wilmington to assess the full impact of this move.

Advertising and Promotion

Although no exact figures were available, Wilmington executives estimated that Corning typically spent between 2 percent and 3 percent of sales on advertising and promotional expenses. These percentages appeared to apply to both the PYREX® and CORNING WARE® lines with the split between advertising and promotion being approximately 50/50.

---

[11]*Business Week.* April 21, 1975, p. 38.

EXHIBIT 2-17   CORNING WARE® Patterns

Cornflower

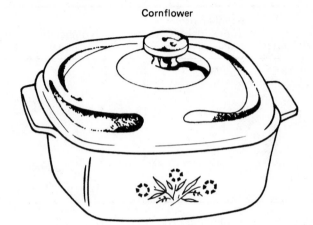

Spice O' Life

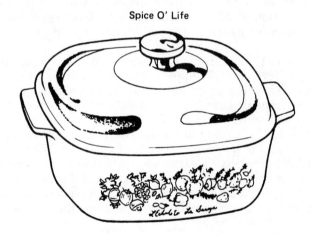

Advertising was primarily national in scope, with women's service magazines and TV being used. The bulk of the sales promotion for CORNING WARE® was tied in with the company's cooperative program for retailers. This consisted of special displays, company designed promotions operated through stores, and advertising assistance. The company introduced these programs to the trade at the housewares shows organized by the National Housewares Manufacturers Association in Chicago in January and July of each year. The company made elaborate ar-

EXHIBIT 2-18   Comparison of PYREX® and CORNING WARE® Retail Prices—Selected Items, 1975

	Unit	PYREX®	CORNING WARE® Cornflower	CORNING WARE® Spice O'Life®
1 qt. covered casserole	ea.	$2.29	$ 7.95	$ 8.95
1½ qt. covered casserole	ea.	2.59	8.95	9.95
2 qt. covered casserole	ea.	2.99	9.95	10.95
3 qt. covered casserole	ea.	3.99	11.95	12.95
Baking dish	ea.	1.89	9.95	10.95
3 pc. bake set	set	8.95	22.88	25.88
4 qt. saucepot	ea.	9.95	14.95	15.95

EXHIBIT 2-19   Inflation Adjusted Pricing for CORNING WARE® 1½-Qt. Saucepan at Retail

YEAR	PRICE	CONSUMER PRICE INDEX	INFLATION ADJUSTED PRICE LEVEL
1958	$4.50	$ 86.6	$5.20
1959	4.50	87.3	5.15
1960	4.50	88.7	5.07
1961	4.50	89.6	5.02
1962	4.50	90.6	4.97
1963	4.50	91.7	4.91
1964	4.50	92.9	4.84
1965	4.50	94.5	4.76
1966	4.95	97.2	5.09
1967	4.95	100.0	4.95
1968	4.95	104.2	4.75
1969	5.95	109.8	5.42
1970	5.95	116.3	5.12
1971	5.95	121.3	4.91
1972	6.50	125.3	5.19
1973	6.50	133.1	4.88
1974	7.95	147.7	5.38

rangements for participation in these shows. The plans for CORNING WARE® for the first half of 1975 are presented in Exhibit 2-20.

THE WILMINGTON TASK FORCE

The task force began its assignment by collecting information from a variety of sources. Production and capital costs estimates were easy to gather because a great deal of the engineering data was already available

EXHIBIT 2-20   Extract from Wilmington Corporation Report on Plans for Sales Promotion and Advertising of CORNING WARE® for the First Half of 1975

This report was prepared on the basis of a visit to the Corning stand at the Chicago Housewares Show in January 1975. It covers plans for the first half of fiscal year 1975 for CORNING WARE®:

1. Gift Promotion—which consisted of the following:
   a. A full color two-page advertisement in the Sunday supplements of April 25, 1975, that would reach about 80% of the U.S. households.
   b. Local advertising aids that helped retailers tie in with local newspaper advertisements, radio spots and store announcements.
   c. A four-page full color enclosure provided free by Corning for retailers to insert into their direct mail advertisements or with bills, etc.
   The entire promotion was built around the theme, "Corning—Gifts That Make Life Easier," and featured PYREX® Ware and CORELLE® Livingware in addition to CORNING WARE®. It helped to position CORNING WARE® in the high quality, gifting end of the cook and bakeware market where its slightly higher prices made sense.
2. In-store displays—Corning salesmen would assist and encourage stores to set up shelves with special CORNING WARE® displays. Retailers were to be provided with full color brochures with suggestions for shelf displays running from eight feet to twenty-four feet as well as six foot end cap displays. They were also to be provided with special printed set organizers for displaying the individual sets. Eight such set organizers were available.
3. Dollar Day Special—This was a set containing a ten-inch covered skillet and a one quart covered saucepan which sold for $1.00 more than the regular price of the skillet. The consumer paid $13.95 for a set which would cost $21.95 if purchased separately, a saving of $8.00. The sets were specially packed and labelled and Corning would supply stores with ads to insert in local newspapers at the store's expense.
4. Kitchen Starter Set—A similar promotion in which the consumer got a free nine-inch pie plate and a savings of $7.97 to make a total savings of $11.92. Supported with full color ad in the April/May issue of *Reader's Digest*.
5. Cookware Set—Corning would provide stores with ads to promote cookware sets—at the store's expense.
6. New Spice O'Life® ads to promote new items in the Spice O'Life® range—at the store's expense.

in the company. These figures were confirmed by discussion with equipment and raw material suppliers, trade association data, and technical literature.

Capital and Cost Estimates

Estimates of the cost of converting existing facilities, new capital equipment, start-up, and front-end costs indicated that a capital investment of $10 million would be necessary to set up a production facility with a capacity of about 75 percent of Corning's current production. This was considered the minimum economic plant size. A completely new production facility was estimated to cost $15 million. Preliminary estimates also indicated that total manufacturing overheads for either plant would amount to $2 million per year (exclusive of depreciation). The variable costs of production for the two-quart casserole, a typical item of the proposed product line, were estimated to be as shown in Exhibit 2-21. It was believed that these variable cost levels could be attained within six months of start-up provided the plant was running at more than 30 percent capacity. Wilmington executives guessed that equivalent costs for Corning might be lower than these because of their greater experience, but they had no way of knowing exactly how low they might be.

Product Line

Several decisions had to be made about the proposed product line. Four possibilities were considered by the task force:

Alternative A: "Me too" line. Similar to existing CORNING WARE®, i.e., "square" shape, white color, decorations similar to the Cornflower Emblem and Spice O' Life®.

Alternative B: Similar shape to above, but in solid "fashion" colors, some dark and some pastel.

Alternative C: Round shapes, solid colors, some dark and some pastel.

Alternative D: Round shapes with all-over floral and/or geometric patterns.

Samples of these four types were made up in the company's development laboratories and were reviewed by the task force and other marketing and sales personnel. Since opinion on these alternatives was divided, the task force decided to conduct consumer research to evaluate the alternatives. This research, consisting of focus group interviews with panels of housewives, was conducted in February, 1975. An extract from the findings of this study is contained in Case Appendix B.

In evaluating the impact of design on sales, the task force reported:

EXHIBIT 2-21   Variable Cost for a Two-Quart Saucepan with Decal Decoration

Raw material	$ .23
Direct labor	.73
Packing and cover	.70
Freight	.62
Other	.48
Total variable cost	$2.76

There is considerable evidence that varying the traditional CORN-ING WARE® design could expand sales volume. Specifically by changing the shape from rectangular to round the market could be expanded by increasing the number of ways in which the consumer would want to use glass-ceramic products. When consumers at our focus group interviews discussed CORNING WARE®, some considered the product oven and table ware. When exposed to a round version they indicated they would also use it as a saucepan for range-top cooking.

Proposed Prices

The task force was considering three alternative price ranges for the new product line:

  A. About the same as CORNING WARE® products
  B. 5–10% lower—i.e., shallow price cuts
  C. 20–25% lower—i.e., deep price cuts

The first alternative was rejected as impractical. The task force felt that since Wilmington would be facing an established competitor who had had patent protection for 18 years in a fairly mature market, it would have to offer the consumer a better deal before a switch could be expected.

The choice then boiled down to whether the task force should recommend a shallow or deep price cut. The shallow cut was obviously attractive in that it would permit the product line to deliver a better contribution. This contribution would fall substantially if the firm chose a deep price cut; on the other hand, it was recognized that a shallow price cut might not give the consumer sufficient incentive to switch, and the resultant sales volume would be too small to justify entry. In its analysis of the price factor, the task force reported:

> That price is an important factor is evident from the consumer research. Fifty-nine percent of consumers expected cookware to be inexpensive, yet our research shows that CORNING WARE® cookware is considered to be expensive. Twenty-eight percent of the nonowners say that they do not, in fact, own it because it is too expensive. Industry research shows that 26 percent of all consumers purchase bakeware on price alone. Lowering the price may also have an indirect effect on the potential uses of the product. In our focus group interviews it became apparent that most consumers considered CORNING WARE® to be a serving vessel, while when it was presented at a lower price consumers saw it as a saucepan. Thus, lowering the price allowed the product to compete in an entirely different market.

Proposed Distribution

CORNING WARE® cookware was sold mainly in department stores, national chains, discount stores, hardware stores, and specialty stores. It was generally not sold in supermarkets, although PYREX® ware and other heat-resistant glass products were available in a number of supermarkets. Wilmington estimated that its present direct distribution system had managed to put its Country Squire range into 35 percent of the supermarkets and 75 percent of the stores where Corning products were available.

Wilmington was debating whether to use its own direct distribution system for the new product or to set up a chain of wholesalers similar to Corning's two-tiered distribution system. Most management personnel were in favor of using the company's direct distribution, even though several felt that the quality of service to the retail trade provided by independent wholesalers was superior to the company's system. In support of this position they noted that Corning had a high degree of loyalty with key wholesalers, and Wilmington might have to content itself with marginal distributors.

Further, Wilmington had to decide whether to extend distribution to supermarkets; it was unclear how much sales would result from supermarket distribution. On the other hand, the absence of CORNING WARE® from the supermarket shelves was looked upon as an opportunity for Wilmington.

The national sales manager was asked to prepare estimates of how well the Wilmington sales force would be able to achieve distribution for the new product. His report indicated that at least 25 percent of the retail outlets served by Wilmington might be persuaded to carry the product at the time of the product launch because of the good relations that Wilmington enjoyed with the retail trade. This could perhaps be increased to about 40 percent in three months after launch. After that, he indicated that "progress would depend on how the consumer accepts our product."

Sales Promotion and Advertising

It was believed that the new line would require heavy sales promotion and advertising in order to compete with the well-established and highly regarded CORNING WARE® brand name and image. A somewhat arbitrary figure of $700,000 was agreed upon as the recommended budget for advertising and promotion, partly because the task force felt that Wilmington management would not be willing to spend a larger amount on a new product line.

The task force then addressed itself to the problem of finding the optimal method of spending this money. This boiled down to three alternatives:

   A. Spend most of the money on a media advertising campaign, with a small back-up budget for sales promotion.
   B. Spend about equal amounts on advertising and sales promotion.
   C. Develop a heavy sales promotion campaign, particularly at launch, and spend a smaller amount of money on media advertising.

In addition, the task force intended to develop a cooperative advertising campaign in which Wilmington would provide designs and advertising materials and the trade would pay for media space costs. It was expected, however, that trade support for such a program would be only marginal, since the trade was usually reluctant to invest its own funds in promoting a new product or brand. Therefore, the coop program did not figure heavily in the preliminary plans.

Other Factors

F. Henderson Bruit conducted a brief study of what he believed to be analogous situations in the housewares industry to find out what happened when a patent expired or competitors entered a market which had been dominated by one producer. A summary of his findings is presented in Case Appendix C.

The task force was grappling with two additional sets of unknown factors. First, there was a question as to whether other firms would attempt to bring out glass-ceramic lines after the expiration of the patent. The task force felt that it would have to take into account the potential impact of these entries on Wilmington's entry. A crucial element in this problem was the question of timing. It was felt that the timing and success or failure of the first entrant would have a bearing on both the strategy and success of other entrants. If the first entrant was highly successful or a conspicuous failure, this might cause other firms to change their plans.

The task force could not gather any substantial information about the plans of other potential competitors. It believed that Ajay Corporation was studying the possibility, but it had no information about the direction of their efforts. Ajay had a reputation in the industry as a manufacturer of high-quality glassware and tableware and distributed its products broadly through department stores, discount stores, variety stores, and home furnishings specialty outlets. Although it was felt unlikely, the task force believed that there was also some possibility of either a Japanese or European entry into the glass-ceramic cook and bakeware market if the market potential proved to be substantial.

The other set of unknowns that the task force had to consider was the possible moves by Corning to protect its market for CORNING WARE® cookware. These moves could be made either before, during, or after the expiration of Corning's patent. The task force felt that the most likely move by Corning would be a lowering of price. It was felt that a factory price cut of 5 percent would do little harm to the profitability of the line for Corning. Accompanied by the drop in trade margins due to the abandonment of fair trading this could result in a substantial drop in consumer prices. On the other hand, a deep price cut of around 20 percent would probably have a large impact on the profitability of the line for Corning, and was therefore deemed to be unlikely.

Further, if Corning chose not to drop prices, Wilmington executives were concerned that they might impede and perhaps destroy a potential competitor by heavy sales promotion and advertising at the time of a competitor's launch.

Finally, there was the possibility that Corning would consider its position so secure that it would choose to do nothing before or during the launch of the competitor and would react only if it found that the competitor was making substantial inroads into its market.

CASE APPENDIX A: EXTRACT FROM STUDENT TRADE SURVEY CONDUCTED ON CORNING WARE® AND PYREX® WARE IN ONE MAJOR METROPOLITAN AREA

Introduction

This study was conducted through retail store audits and telephone interviews with buyers in a sample of twenty-one stores in the Boston metropolitan area. The sample consisted of five department stores, four discount stores, six variety stores, four hardware stores, and two supermarkets. About one-third were located in downtown areas, one-third in nearby suburban shopping centers, and the rest in small adjacent towns.

The survey attempts to evaluate retailer merchandising of CORNING WARE® and PYREX® ware with respect to stock conditions, display, promotion, and pricing. Attention was focused on the five most popular CORNING WARE® items and six most popular PYREX® ware items. Stores that carried four or five items (5–6 PYREX® ware items) were considered well stocked; two or three moderately stocked (3–4 PYREX® ware items); and one or two, poorly stocked. The final determination of the stock condition took into consideration the amount of stock in other items in the product line.

The display ratings reflected our opinion of shelf condition (neatness or otherwise), shelf location, and general appearance. The promotion category indicates the presence of either point-of-purchase displays or sales promotions.

Finally, the selling prices column compares retailer prices with list prices or, in the case of PYREX® ware, comparison between the mean prices of the items in the twenty-one stores and the particular store in question.

The overall results of the retail store audit are tabulated in Exhibits 2-22 and 2-23.

Store Buyer Attitudes

Houseware buyers were contacted to determine their attitudes toward CORNING WARE® cookware and the distribution process that places CORNING WARE® on their shelves. A summary of the attitudes of buyers from Jordan Marsh, Kresge, Zayre, Bradlees, Tags, and Lechmere is contained below.

EXHIBIT 2-22   CORNING WARE®

Company	Stock Conditions			Display		Promo		Price		
	Well	Mod	Poor	Good	Poor	Yes	No	List	Above	Below
Department										
Jordan Marsh (Bos)	X			X		X		X		
Jordan Marsh (Burl)		X		X		X		X		
Sears (Camb)	X			X		X		X		
Sears (Burl)	X			X		X		X		
Coop	X			X		X		X	X	
Discount										
Lechmere (Camb)	X			X			X			X
Zayre (128)			X	X		X				X
Bradlees (Wob)		X		X			X			X
Turnstyle (Walt)		X			X		X	X		
Variety										
Woolworth (Bos)		X			X		X	X		
Woolworth (Camb)		X			X		X	X		
Woolworth (Harv)		X			X		X			X
Kresge (Bos)					X		X	X		
Kresge (Camb)		NONE								
WT Grant (Bos)					X		X	X		
Grocery										
Stop and Shop (Walt)		NONE								
Broadway Super		NONE								
Hardware										
Almys (Camb)	X			X				X	X	
Tags (Camb)		X		X		X		X	X	
Dickson Bros (Camb)		X			X			X	X	
Pharmacy Super (Camb)			X	X			X	X		

Product Characteristics

The buyers placed special emphasis on the brand image of CORN-ING WARE® products, stating that it would be virtually impossible to compete with the product's design and quality. CORNING WARE® products' competitive strength, tenure in the market, and its well-scheduled promotion and advertising campaign have created a formidable brand name and image. The buyers' universal faith in the strength of CORNING WARE® has been reinforced by PYREX® ware successes, and the realization that consumer awareness pulls the product through the distribution channels.

EXHIBIT 2-23   PYREX® Ware and Competition

Company	Stock Conditions			Display		Promo		Price*		
	Well	Mod	Poor	Good	Poor	Yes	No	Medium	Above	Below
Department										
Jordan Marsh (Bos)	X			X		X		X		
Jordan Marsh (Burl)	X			X		X		X		
Sears (Camb)			X	X		X		X		
Sears (Burl)	X			X		X				X
Coop	X				X		X	X		
Discount										
Lechmere (Camb)		X		X			X			X
Zayre (128)		X			X	X		X		
Bradlees (Wob)		X		X			X	X		
Turnstyle (Walt)		X		X			X		X	
Variety										
Woolworth (Bos)		X			X		X		X	
Woolworth (Cent)	X				X		X	X		
Woolworth (Harv)			X		X		X	X		
Kresge (Bos)	X				X		X	X		
Kresge (Camb)	no Pyrex				X		X			X
WT Grant (Bos)		X								
Grocery										
Stop and Shop (Walt)			X	X	X					X
Broadway Super		X			X		X		X	
Hardware										
Almys (Camb)		X		X	X					X
Tags (Camb)	X			X	X					X
Dickson Bros (Camb)	X			X			X			X
Pharmacy Super (Camb)			X	X			X			

*In stores which carried both Pyrex and competitive products, the latter were invariably priced lower than Pyrex.

The buyers feel that no company could provide the same quality and brand name product. Confronted with the question of carrying a CORNING WARE® type product at a reduced price, the majority of the buyers indicated a willingness to carry such a line only if the price reduction was substantial (15%–20%), and most importantly, if the product's quality was acceptable.

All buyers predicted that CORNING WARE® cookware would

maintain market share if a new product was introduced, yet none, with the exception of the local hardware retailer, would rule out the possibility of taking on such a brand.

Distribution

All buyers were enthusiastic about the service they had been receiving from the two-tiered distribution system. All were especially content not to carry excess inventory in recessionary times. The buyers of a large, national chain agreed that the local wholesalers provided a much quicker response to their needs than the bureaucracy of a central office. Orders were being filled quite adequately for PYREX® ware and CORNING WARE®, but the buyers were a little disgruntled with the lack of CORELLE® Livingware. Finally, the services provided by the local distributors (order taking and shelf service) were excellent; the buyers did not want to sacrifice this amenity.

The only buyers who expressed any interest in a direct system predicated their remarks on the state of the economy; that is, only with a booming economy where products were "jumping off those shelves" would they prefer to switch systems.

Although the decision to carry a brand to compete with CORNING WARE® cookware would be made at a central headquarters level, the buyers (who are an important input in the decision making process) say that CORNING WARE® is very strong. No company could compete on image, brand, or quality. Only a price reduction would provide incentive for the stores to consider carrying the product.

CASE APPENDIX B: EXTRACT FROM REPORT ON FOCUS GROUP INTERVIEWS

Focus Group Interviews were conducted with six different panels, each one consisting of approximately ten housewives. Participants were selected on the following basis:

Group Number	Social Group	Ownership of CORN-ING WARE®
1	white collar	no
2	white collar	yes
3	blue collar	no
4	blue collar	yes
5	working women	no
6	working women	yes

The moderator was instructed to first lead the group into a general discussion of cook and bakeware and then focus the discussion on oven-to-table and stove-to-table products. The groups were then shown four sets of samples, as follows:

Set 1: Similar to existing CORNING WARE® cookware, i.e., square shape, blue decoration

Set 2: Similar to CORNING WARE® in shape, but in solid colors, some dark and some pastel

Set 3: Round shape, in solid colors, both dark as well as pastel

Set 4: Round shape, in white with all-over floral designs and geometric patterns.

The order in which the sets were shown to each group was rotated systematically to eliminate the end-bias effect. In addition, two price levels were exhibited, one about the same as Corning's current prices and the other 25 percent lower. Prices were attached to the bottom of each piece and the interviewees were allowed to handle the items before discussing them.

Attitudes Toward CORNING WARE® Cookware

A majority of CORNING WARE® owners (73%) had received the product as a gift, and did not add to the sets once they received them. When asked why, most respondents said that they preferred to buy less costly products, such as PYREX® ware and other brands for their own use. The respondents did not think of CORNING WARE® cookware as being a different class of product from heat-resistant glass products, but rather thought of it as more expensive and of higher quality. Many respondents were not aware that CORNING WARE® could be used on top of the range.

Most purchases of CORNING WARE® cookware were for gifts; only 19 percent of the respondents reported buying CORNING WARE® for their own use. The most commonly reported reasons for buying CORNING WARE® as a gift were its high quality, brand name and reputation, colors and design, and warranty. Purchases of CORNING WARE® were usually planned in advance (87% vs. 13%).

Reaction to Set 1—CORNING WARE® Imitation. The groups generally characterized this set as being "like CORNING WARE®." The general reaction was that if they were to purchase this type of product, they would prefer to buy CORNING WARE® because of its brand name, reputation, and warranty. Most of the respondents said that they would prefer CORNING WARE® if the price was the same; a few indicated that they might buy the new set at the 25 percent lower price, provided it carried a guarantee like CORNING WARE® and was made by a well-known company. However, most respondents said that the brand name was more important than the price differential, particularly if they were buying a gift. Several respondents said that the cheaper price version might be

PYREX® ware, and a few of these said that they would buy it for themselves, but not as a gift.

Reaction to Set 2—Solid Color, Corning Shape. Most respondents
thought that this set was PYREX® ware. The general reaction was that
this set looked "cheap" and "gaudy." They thought that it was definitely
inferior to CORNING WARE® and would only buy it at a lower price.
Among those who indicated that they would buy, the most commonly stated
reason was that it "suited the color scheme" of their kitchen. There was
a slightly greater preference for the dark colors among the blue-collar and
professional families, while the white-collar and working women appeared
to prefer the pastel colors. Most respondents who said that they might
buy the product said that they would buy it for their own use, but would
prefer CORNING WARE® for gifts. Owners of CORNING WARE® were
less inclined to buy this product than nonowners.

Reaction to Set 3—Solid Colors, Round Shape. The reaction to this
set was similar to Set 2, except that a number of respondents who thought
they might buy the product said that these products could be used on top
of the stove because they were shaped like a pot. A number of respondents said that this set looked very similar to PYREX® mixing bowls. When
asked whether they would use this product for baking, most respondents
said that it was not suitable because of the round shape and the colors.
The proportion of respondents who said they might buy the product was
highest among the blue-collar workers.

Reaction to Set 4—Decorated, Round Shape. The reaction to this set
was mixed—some liked the patterns and said they would buy it, while
others did not like the patterns for a variety of reasons. Most of the respondents who said they would buy it also said they would use it themselves for everyday use. There was some resistance to price at the CORN-
ING WARE® level: most respondents said they would buy it only if the
price was cheaper. On the whole, more respondents appeared to like this
set than dislike it. The floral pattern was preferred to the geometric designs which were said to look "too much like metal utensils." However,
for gifts, most people said they would prefer CORNING WARE® products.

CASE APPENDIX C: SUMMARY OF TASK FORCE
INVESTIGATION OF OTHER HOUSEWARES MARKETS

In attempting to assess the share of market that Corning might be
expected to lose to an aggressive competitor, we investigated the market
structure of a number of rather mature markets within the general housewares industry. In these markets a strong nationally advertised brand

commands a premium price despite the existence of lower priced substitutes. A summary description of these "two-tiered" markets follows:

1. Plastic Housewares (exclusive of Tupperware type storage containers)

	SOM	Price	Distribution
Rubbermaid	.65	1.00	2-step intensive
Festival	.15	.70	direct
Sterilite	.08	.66	direct to national chains, manufacturer's reps.
Eagle	.06	.66	direct to discounters, chains
Loma	.06	.66	direct, manufacturer's reps.

Source: Wilmington estimates.

Price promotions in this category are extremely effective. Often, different products are grouped in sets, and sold at prices nearer to 50 percent of Rubbermaids. These sets are designed for retailers' purchase, *not* for ultimate consumer purchase.

2. Tupperware

	SOM	Price	Distribution
Tupperware	.70	1.00	home party selling
Rubbermaid	.12	.75	85% distribution, 15% party
Eagle	.10	.75	direct, mainly supermarkets
Republic Molding	.08	.75	direct, mainly supermarkets

Source: Wilmington estimates.

The price differential may be substantially greater than the indicated 75 percent in some cases. What is particularly significant is that Tupperware, in response to several entrants in the late sixties, *did not* lower prices. Their basic response has been to add new products, further differentiating through design. Apparently, the new entrants in this market did "cherry pick," typically coming in with the most popular fifteen or so items in the product line.

3. Ekco (gadgets only)

Many competitors abound in the gadget segment of Ekco's market. The overall market structure looks approximately as follows:

	SOM	*Price*	*Distribution*
Ekco	.40	1.00	direct
Kenberry	.15	.80	through distributors
Tasco	.15	.80	through distributors
Elpo	.10	.80	through distributors
Foley	.10	.80	through distributors
Others	.10	.80	through distributors

Source: Wilmington estimates.

It appears that Ekco's competitors try to fill in the gaps that Ekco leaves for them, rather than competing directly. Indeed in a few audits, directly competitive products could be found for only 20–25 percent of the Ekco line.

PART TWO
Strategic Analysis

CHAPTER 3
Corporate Appraisal

We that acquaint ourselves with every zone
And pass both tropics and behold the poles
When we come home are to ourselves unknown
And unacquainted still with our souls.

John Davies

One important reason for formulating marketing strategy is to prepare the company to interact with the changing environment in which it operates. Implicit in this is the significance of predicting what shape the environment is likely to take in the future. Then with a perspective of the company's present position the task ahead can be determined. Study of the environment is reserved for a later chapter. This chapter is devoted to self-appraisal.

An analogy to corporate self-appraisal is provided by a career counselor's job. Just as it is relatively easy to make a list of the jobs available to a young person, it is simple to produce a superficial list of investment opportunities open to a company. With the career counselor the real skill comes in taking stock of each applicant, examining the applicant's qualifications, personality, and temperament, defining the areas in which some sort of further development may be required, such as training, and matching these characteristics and the applicant's aspirations against the various options which are open. Well-established techniques exist that can be used to find out most of the necessary information about an individual. Digging deep into the psyche of a company is a more complex operation, but no less important. Failure by the company in the area of self-appraisal can be as stunting to future development in the corporate sense as can the misplacement of a young graduate in the personal sense.

How should the strategist approach the task of appraising corporate perspectives? What needs to be discovered? These and other similar questions are explored in this chapter.

MEANING OF CORPORATE APPRAISAL

Broadly, corporate appraisal refers to an examination of the entire organization from different angles. It is a measurement of the readiness of the internal culture of the corporation to interact with the external environment. Marketing strategists are concerned with those aspects of the corporation which have a direct bearing on corporate-wide strategy because it must be referred to in defining the business unit mission. As shown in Exhibit 3-1, corporate publics, the value system of top management, corporate resources, past performance of business units, and the external environment are all variables that affect the development of corporate strategy. Of these, the first four variables are discussed in this chapter.

Two important characteristics of strategic marketing planning are its concern with issues having far-reaching effects on the entire organization and change as an essential ingredient in its implementation. These two characteristics make the entire process of marketing strategy formulation a difficult job and demand creativity and adaptability on the part of the organization. Creativity, however, is not everybody's forte. By the same token, adaptation to changing conditions may come to be considered as a threat to existing style, norms of behavior, and relationships. As has been said:

> Success in the past always becomes enshrined in the present by the over-valuation of the policies and attitudes which accompanied that success. . . . with time these attitudes become embedded in a system of beliefs, traditions, taboos, habits, customs, and inhibitions which constitute the distinctive culture of that firm. Such cultures are as dis-

EXHIBIT 3-1   Scope of Corporate Appraisal

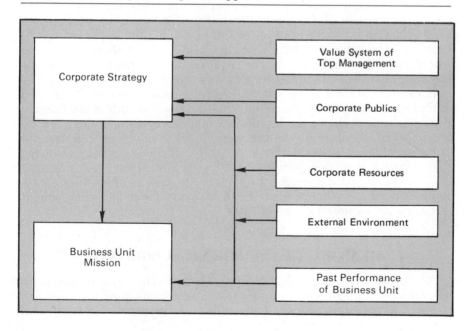

tinctive as the cultural differences between nationalities or the personality differences between individuals. They do not adapt to change very easily.[1]

Human history is full of instances where communities and cultures were wiped out over time, the apparent reason for downfall being a failure to change to keep up with the times. In the context of business, why is it that organizations like Xerox, R. J. Reynolds, Litton, and IBM, comparative newcomers among the large organizations, are considered blue-chip companies? Why should United States Rubber and American Tobacco lag behind? Why are General Motors, DuPont, and 3M continually ranked as the "successful" companies? The outstanding common denominator found in the successful companies is the element of change. When the perspective of an organization undergoes a change as demanded by time, success is the outcome.

Obviously, the marketing strategist must take a close look at the perspectives of the organization before formulating future strategy. Strategies must bear a close relationship to the internal culture of the corporation if they are to be successfully implemented.

FACTORS IN APPRAISAL: CORPORATE PUBLICS

Business exists for people. Thus, the first consideration in the strategic process is to recognize the individuals and groups who have an interest in the fate of the corporation and the extent and nature of their expectations.

Meaning of Corporate Publics

The following groups generally constitute the interest-holders in business organizations:

1. Owners
2. Employees
3. Customers
4. Suppliers
5. Banking community and other lenders
6. Government
7. Community in which the company does business
8. Society at large

For the healthy growth of the organization, all eight groups must be served adequately. The traditional organization paid little attention to the community in which it operated; today, however, the importance of

---

[1]*Perspectives on Corporate Strategy* (Boston, MA: The Boston Consulting Group, 1968), p. 93.

service to community and society is widely acknowledged. The community may force a company to refrain from activities which are detrimental to the environment. For example, the Boise Cascade Company was denounced in 1971 as harsh, stingy, socially insensitive, and considerably short of the highest ethical standards because of its unplanned land development. Ultimately, the community interest prevailed, forcing the company either to give up its land development activities or make proper arrangements for sewage, etc., to keep the environment clean.[2] Similarly, social concern may prevent a company from becoming involved in certain types of business. A publishing company responsive to community standards may refuse to publish pornographic material. Student demonstrations against Dow Chemical in the early 1970s for manufacturing napalm provide another example of how societal constraints bear heavily on the operations of a business corporation. Likewise, Gulf Oil's involvement in Angola was resented by various social groups. In brief, the requirements and expectations of today's society must serve as basic ingredients in the development of strategy. As the Committee for Economic Development in its statement on the subject has mentioned:

> The great growth of corporations in size, market power, and impact on society has naturally brought with it a commensurate growth in responsibilities; in a democratic society, power sooner or later begets equivalent responsibility.[3]

It was social concern that led Control Data Corporation to locate four new plants in depressed inner cities, a far from easy move. For example, to counter absenteeism at one of the plants, the Northside plant in Minneapolis, the company had to send a lawyer with a book of bail bonds to the city jail every Monday morning. But with time things worked out. As Control Data's chairman William C. Norris puts it: "By whatever criteria are used to measure these plants—tenure, absenteeism, profitability—they are equal to or better than the company's conventional operations."[4]

Limits of Corporate Response to Different Publics

Historically, a business organization considered its sole purpose to be economic gain, concerning itself with other spheres of society only when required to by law or motivated by philanthropy, charity, etc. The latter was merely a celebration of a corporation's good fortunes which it desired

---

[2]"Boise Cascade Shifts Toward Tighter Control," *Business Week,* May 15, 1971, p. 90.

[3]*Social Responsibilities of Business Corporations: A Statement on National Policy* (New York: Committee for Economic Development, 1971), p. 21.

[4]Thornton Bradshaw and David Vogel (eds.), *Corporations and Their Critics* (New York: McGraw-Hill Book Co., 1981), p. 106.

to share with the "outsiders" or a display of pity for the unfortunate. In-directly, of course, even this meant a good name for the company and thus served the public relations function of the corporation. In slack times, the company reduced its activities in all areas, which meant both inside cost-cutting measures and lowering of commitments to all publics other than stockholders. This system worked well until recently. With economic prosperity almost assured, different stakeholders began to demand a more equitable deal from the corporation. For example, during the 1960s, con-cern over environmental pollution by corporations became a major issue in both the public and the private sector. Similarly, customers expected products to be wholesome; employees wanted opportunities for advance-ment and self-improvement; the community hoped that the local corpo-ration would assume some of its concerns, such as unemployment among blacks. Society now expects business corporations to help in resolving so-cial problems. In brief, the role of the business corporation has shifted from that of an economic institution solely responsible to stockholders to that of a multifaceted force owing its existence to different stakeholders to whom it must be responsible.

As the most progressive institution in the society, the business cor-poration is expected to provide balanced prosperity in all fields. This new outlook extends the mission of the business beyond the primary obligation to owners.

Much has been said and written on the desirability and feasibility of enlarging the role of the corporation. *Business Week* states:

> Two generations ago, the idea that business is party to a contract with the society in which it operates would have provoked an indignant snort from most businessmen. Even 10 years ago it was more likely to be material for a corporate president's speech to the stockholders than a basis for policy. It is a measure of how much the middle-of-the-road group of businessmen can set it up as the basic assumption for their statement on the social responsibilities of the business.[5]

In today's environment, corporate strategy must be developed not simply to enhance financial performance, but to maximize performance across the board, delivering highest gains to all the stakeholders or cor-porate publics.

One company that systematically and continuously examines the in-terests of its stakeholders is General Electric. It identified 14 groups among its publics and derived a list of 97 of their demands, which included fed-eral chartering of corporations; more stringent effluents/emissions stan-dards; provision of day-care centers for working mothers; representation of interests other than those of the stockholders on the board of directors; disclosure of more information about products; and an end to tax defer-

---

[5]"The New 'Social Contract,' " *Business Week,* July 3, 1971, p. 72.

rals for offshore profits.[6] The company ranked these demands in terms of their convergence with major domestic trends perceived over the next decade. Among the trends considered were increasing affluence, rising level of education, proliferating technology, increasing emphasis on individualism, and growing emphasis on quality of life. A second score was computed from a subjective evaluation of how much pressure each of the 14 groups of stakeholders might exert for each demand. On this basis the leading potential demands on General Electric Company over the next decade were identified.[7] The above analysis resulted in six areas of challenge (in descending order) to General Electric which became an input to the corporate-level strategic planning process:

1. Constraints on corporate growth—a spectrum of issues ranging from national growth policy through economic controls and environmental protection to questions of antitrust policy and industrial structure.
2. Corporate governance—including matters of accountability, personal liability of managers and directors, board representation, and disclosure of information.
3. Managing the "new work force"—dealing with the growing demands for job enlargement, more flexible scheduling, more equality of opportunity, greater participation, and individualization.
4. External constraints on employee relations—the new pressures from government (employment opportunities, health and safety, "federalization" of benefits), unions (coalition bargaining), and other groups (class action suits, "whistle-blowing").
5. Problems and opportunities of business-government partnership—including a redefinition of the role of the private sector in public problem solving.
6. "Politicizing" of economic decision making—the growing government involvement in corporate decisions through consumerism, environmentalism, industrial reorganization, inflation control, etc.[8]

Corporate Publics—Analysis of Expectations

While the expectations of different groups vary, in our society growth and improvement are the common expectations of any institution. But this broad definition does not take into account the stakes of different groups

---

[6]For a complete list of these demands see George A. Steiner, *Business and Society,* 2d Ed. (New York: Random House, 1975), pp. 95–97.

[7]Ian Wilson, "What One Company Is Doing About Today's Demands on Business," in George A. Steiner (ed.), *Changing Business-Society Interrelationships* (Los Angeles: Graduate School of Management, UCLA, 1975).

[8]Robert E. Estes, in George A. Steiner (ed.), *Selected Major Issues in Business's Role in Modern Society* (Los Angeles: Graduate School of Management, UCLA, 1973), p. 30.

within the business. For planning purposes, a clearer definition of each group's anticipations is needed.

Exhibit 3-2 summarizes the factors against which the expectations of different groups can be measured. The broad categories shown here should be broken down into subcategories as far as possible. For example, in a community where juvenile delinquency is rampant, youth programs become an important area of corporate concern. One must be careful, however, not to make unrealistic or typical assumptions about the expectations of different groups. Take owners, for example. Typically, 50 percent of earnings after taxes must be invested to sustain the normal growth of a business. But the payout desired by the owners may render it difficult to finance growth. Thus, a balance must be struck between payment of dividends and plowing back of earnings. A vice-president of finance for a chemical company with yearly sales over $100 million said in a conversation with the author:

> While we do recognize the significance of retaining more money, we must consider the desires of our stockholders. They happen to be people who actually live on dividend payments. Thus, a part of long-term growth must be given up in order to maintain their short-term needs of regular dividend payments.

Apparently, this company would not be correct in assuming that growth alone is the objective of stockholders. Thus it behooves the marketing strategists to gain clear insights into the demands of different corporate publics.

Who in the company should undertake the study of stakeholders' expectations? This task constitutes a project in itself and should be assigned either to someone inside the company (such as a corporate planner, an assistant to the president, a director of public affairs and/or a marketing researcher) or to a consultant who may be hired for this purpose. The first time around it will be fairly difficult to specify stakeholders, designate their areas of concern, and make their expectations explicit. Later on, updating from year to year should become fairly routine.

The groups which constitute the stakeholders of a business organization are usually the same from one business to another. Mainly, they are the owners, employees, customers, suppliers, the banking community and other lenders, government, community, and society. The areas of concern of each group and their expectations, however, require surveying. As with any other survey project, this amounts to seeking information from an appropriate sample within each group. A structured questionnaire is preferable for obtaining objective answers. Before surveying the sample, however, it is desirable to give in-depth interviews to a few members of each group. The information provided by these interviews is helpful in developing the questionnaire. While overall areas of concern may not vary from one time period to another, expectations certainly do. For example, during a recession stockholders may desire higher payout in dividends than at other times. Besides, in a given time period, the public may

EXHIBIT 3-2   Corporate Publics and Their Concerns

PUBLICS	AREA OF CONCERN
Owners	Payout Equity Stock prices Nonmonetary desires
Customers	Business reliability Product reliability Product improvement Product price Product service Continuity Marketing efficiency
Employees of all ranks	Monetary reward Reward of recognition Reward of pride Environment Challenge Continuity Advancement
Suppliers	Price Stability Continuity Growth
Banking community and other lenders	Sound risk Interest payment Repayment of principal
Government (federal, state, and local)	Taxes Security and law enforcement Management expertise Democratic government Capitalistic system Implementation of programs
Immediate community	Economic growth and efficiency Education Employment and training
Society at large	Civil rights and equal opportunities Urban renewal and development Pollution abatement Conservation and recreation Culture and arts Medical care

not articulate expectations in all of its areas of concern. During inflationary periods, for example, customers may only emphasize stable prices, while product improvement and marketing efficiency may figure prominently in times of prosperity.

Corporate Publics and Corporate Strategy

The expectations of different publics provide the corporation with a focus for working out its objectives and goals. However, a company may not be able to satisfy the expectations of all stakeholders for two reasons: limited resources and conflicting expectations among stakeholders. For example, customers may want low prices and simultaneously ask for product improvements. Likewise, to meet exactly the expectations of the community the company may be obliged to reduce dividends paid out to the stockholders. Thus, a balance must be struck between the expectations of different stakeholders and the company's ability to honor them.

The corporate response to stakeholders' expectations emerges in the form of its objectives and goals, which in turn determine corporate strategy. While objectives and goals are discussed in detail in Chapter 8, a sample of corporate objectives with reference to customers is given below.

Assume the following customers' expectations for a food processing company:

1. The company should provide wholesome products.
2. The company should clearly state the ingredients of different products in words which are easily comprehensible to an ordinary consumer.
3. The company should make all efforts to keep the prices down.

The company, based on the aforementioned expectations, may set the following goals:

Wholesome Products

1. Create a new position—vice-president, product quality—effective January 1, 19—. No new products will be introduced into the market until they are approved for wholesomeness by this vice-president. The vice-president's decision will be upheld no matter how bright a picture of consumer acceptance of a product is painted by marketing research and marketing planning.
2. Create a panel of nutrient testers to analyze and judge different products for their wholesomeness.
3. Communicate with the consumers about the wholesomeness of the company's products, suggesting that they deal directly with the vice-president of product quality should there be any questions. (Incidentally, a position similar to vice-president of product quality was created at Gillette a few years ago. This exec-

utive's decisions overruled the market introduction of products despite numerous other reasons for early introduction.)

Information on Ingredients

1. Create a new position: director, consumer information. The person in this position will decide what information about product ingredients, nutritive value, etc., should be included on each package.
2. Seek feedback every other year from a sample of consumers concerning the effectiveness and clarity of the information provided.
3. Encourage customers through various forms of promotions to communicate with the director of consumer information on a toll-free phone number to clarify any part of the information that may be unclear.
4. Revise information contents based on numbers 2 and 3.

Keeping Prices Low

1. Communicate with customers on what leads the company to raise different prices (i.e., cost of labor is up, cost of ingredients is up, etc.).
2. Design various ways to reduce the price pressure on consumers. For example, develop family packs.
3. Let customers know how much they can save by buying family packs. Assure them that quality of the product will remain intact for a specified period.
4. Work on new ways to reduce costs. For example, a substitute may be found for a product ingredient whose cost has gone up tremendously.

By using the illustration given above, the expectations of each group of stakeholders can be translated into specific goals.

FACTORS IN APPRAISAL: VALUE ORIENTATION OF TOP MANAGEMENT

The ideologies and philosophies of the top management as a team and the chief executive as the leader of the team have a profound effect on the managerial policy and the strategic development process. As Steiner has said:

> [The chief executive's] aspirations about his personal life, the life of his company as an institution, and the lives of those involved in his business are major determinants of choice of strategy. His mores, habits, and ways of doing things determine how he behaves and decides.

His sense of obligation to his company will decide his devotion and choice of subject matter to think about.[9]

For example, Rene McPherson, former chief executive officer of Dana Corporation, incessantly emphasized cost reduction and productivity improvement, and the company doubled its productivity in seven years. Similarly, IBM chairmen have always preached the importance of calling on customers—even stressing the proper dress for the call, which has over time become an accepted norm of behavior in the entire corporation. Texas Instruments' ex-chairman Patrick Haggerty made it a point to drop in at a development laboratory on his way home each night when he was in Dallas to emphasize his view of the importance of new products for the company. Such single-minded focus on a value becomes a culture for the company. As the employees who are steeped in the corporate culture move up the ladder, they become role models for newcomers, and the process continues.[10]

How companies in essentially the same business may move in different strategic directions because of different top management values is illustrated by the example of American Can Company and Continental Group, Inc. Throughout the 1970s, both Robert S. Hatfield, then Continental's chairman, and William F. May, his counterpart at American Can, made deep changes in their companies' product portfolios. Both closed numerous aged canmaking plants. Both divested themselves of tangential businesses they deemed to have lackluster growth prospects. And both sought either to hire or promote executives who would steer the companies in profitable directions.

But similar as their overall strategies might seem, their concepts of their companies diverged markedly. May envisioned American Can as a corporate think tank, serving as both a trend-spotter and a trend-setter. He put his trust in the advice of financial experts who, although lean on operating experience, were adept in the perspectives of business theory. They took American Can into such diverse fields as aluminum recycling, record distribution, and mail-order consumer products. By contrast, Hatfield sought executives with proven records in spotting new potential in old areas. The company acquired Richmond Corporation, an insurance holding company, and Florida Gas Company.[11]

---

[9]George A. Steiner, *Top Management Planning* (New York: Macmillan Co., 1969), p. 241.

[10]Thomas J. Peters, "Putting Excellence into Management," *The McKinsey Quarterly,* Autumn, 1980, p. 37.

[11]"Where Different Styles Have Led Two Canmakers," *Business Week,* July 27, 1981, pp. 81–82. See also Alexander Stuart, "What Makes Mobil Run," *Fortune,* December 14, 1981, pp. 93–97.

Importance of Value Orientation in the Corporate Environment

It would be wrong to assume that every firm wants to grow. There are companies which probably could grow faster than their current rate indicates. But where top management is averse to expansion, sluggishness prevails throughout the organization, inhibiting growth. A large number of companies started small, with the family managing the organization. Some entrepreneurs at the helm of affairs in such companies are quite satisfied with what they have been able to achieve. They would rather not grow than give up their complete control of the organization. Obviously if managerial values promote stability rather than growth, the strategy will be formed accordingly. Of course, if the owners find that their expectations are in conflict with the value system of the top management, they may seek to replace them with a more philosophically compatible team. As an example, a flamboyant CEO may emphasize growth and introduce changes in the organization to the extent of creating suspicion among owners, board members, and colleagues. This may lead to the CEO's exit from the organization. An unconventionally high debt-equity ratio exhibited in the balance sheet can be sufficient cause for a chief executive to be dismissed. Similarly, a CEO's style of management may create upheavals in the organization. As Jennings narrates:

> Under the leadership of William C. Stolk, American Can acquired Marathon Paper Company, and its president, Roy J. Sund, was made head of the parent company. Sund was plainly ticketed to become the chief executive officer when Stolk reached the mandatory retirement age of sixty-five. Now Sund believed in a highly decentralized structure in opposition to the highly centralized organization that Stolk was building. Roy Sund resigned because he did not want to take over a company that did not have his style. Sund went over to Champion Paper and took George Walker with him.[12]

In brief, the value systems of the individual members of the top management serve as important inputs in strategy development. If people at the top hold conflicting values, the chosen strategy will lack the willing cooperation and commitment of all the executives. Generally, differing values are reflected in conflicts over policies, objectives, strategies, and structure.

Top Management Values and Corporate Culture

Over time, top management values come to characterize the culture of the entire organization. The corporate culture gives people a sense of direction, a sense of how to behave and what they ought to be doing.

---

[12]Eugene E. Jennings, *Routes to the Executive Suite* (New York: Alfred A. Knopf, 1971), p. 219.

Employees who fail to live up to the cultural norms of the organization find the going tough. The point may be illustrated with reference to PepsiCo, Inc., and J. C. Penney Company. At PepsiCo, beating the competition is the surest path to success. In its soft-drink operation, Pepsi takes on Coke directly, asking consumers to compare the taste of the two colas. That direct confrontation is reflected inside the company as well. Managers are pitted against each other to grab more market shares, to work harder, and to wring more profits out of their businesses. Because winning is the key value at Pepsi, losing has its penalties. Consistent runners-up find their jobs gone. Employees know they must win merely to stay in place—and must devastate the competition to get ahead.[13]

But the aggressive manager who succeeds at Pepsi would be sorely out of place at J. C. Penney Company, where a quick victory is far less important than building long-term loyalty. As has been said:

> Indeed, a Penney store manager once was severely rebuked by the company's president for making too much profit. That was considered unfair to customers, whose trust Penney seeks to win. The business style set by the company's founder—which one competitor describes as avoiding "taking unfair advantage of anyone the company did business with"—still prevails today. Customers know they can return merchandise with no questions asked; suppliers know that Penney will not haggle over terms; and employees are comfortable in their jobs, knowing that Penney will avoid layoffs at all costs and will find easier jobs for those who cannot handle more demanding ones. Not surprisingly, Penney's average executive tenure is 33 years while Pepsi's is ten.[14]

These vastly different methods of doing business are just two examples of corporate culture. People who work at Pepsi and Penney sense that the corporate values are the yardstick by which they will be measured. Just as tribal cultures have totems and taboos that dictate how each member will act toward fellow members and outsiders, so does a corporation's culture influence employees' actions toward customers, competitors, suppliers, and one another. Sometimes the rules are written out. More often they are tacit. Most often, they are laid down by a strong founder and hardened by success into custom.

Measurement of Values

In emphasizing the significance of the value system in strategic planning, several questions become pertinent. Should the corporation attempt to formally establish values for important members of the manage-

---

[13]"Corporate Culture," *Business Week*, October, 27, 1980, p. 148. See also Geoffrey Colvin, "The De-Geneening of ITT," *Fortune*, January 11, 1982, p. 34.

[14]*Ibid.* See also Bro Uttal, "The Corporate Culture Vultures," *Fortune*, October 17, 1983, pp. 66–73.

ment? If so, who should do it? What measures or techniques should be used? If values of the senior executives are in conflict, what should be done? Can values be changed?

It is generally agreed that the values of top management in a company should be measured. If nothing else, such measurement will familiarize the CEO with the orientation of the top executives and will help the CEO to better appreciate their viewpoints. Opinions differ, however, on who should do the measuring. While a good case can be made for giving the assignment to a staff person—for example, a strategic planner or a human resources planner, hiring an outside consultant is probably the most effective way to gain an objective perspective on management values. If a consultant's findings appear to create conflict in the organization, they can be scrapped. Once the initial effort is made with help from the consultant, the human resources planner in the company, working closely with the strategic planner, can design a system for measurement of values.

There are various ways in which values can be measured. A popular technique is the self-evaluating scale developed by Allport et al.[15] This scale divides values into six classes: religious, political, theoretical, economic, aesthetic, and social. A manual is available that lists the average scores of different groups. Executives can complete the test in about 30 minutes and determine the structure of their values individually. Difficulties with using this scale lie in relating the executives' values to their jobs and in figuring out the impact of these values on corporate strategy.

A more specific way is to pinpoint those aspects of human values which are likely to affect strategy development and measure one's score on these values on a simple five- or seven-point scale. For example, we can measure executives' orientation on factors such as leadership image, performance standards and evaluation, decision-making techniques, use of authority, attitude on change, and nature of involvement. Exhibit 3-3 shows a sample scale for measuring values.

As a matter of fact, a formal value-orientation profile of executives may not be entirely necessary. By raising questions like the following about each top executive, one can gather insights into value orientations:[16]

> Does the executive:
>   seem efficiency-minded?
>   like repetition?
>   like to be first in a new field instead of second?
>   revel in detail work?
>   seem willing to pay the price of keeping in personal touch with
>   the customer, etc.?

---

[15]Gordon W. Allport, Philip E. Vernon, and Gardner Lindzey, *Study of Values and the Manual of Study of Values* (Boston: Houghton Mifflin Co., 1960).
[16]See Charles Margerison, *How to Assess Your Managerial Style* (New York: AMACOM, 1979).

EXHIBIT 3-3   Measuring Value Orientation

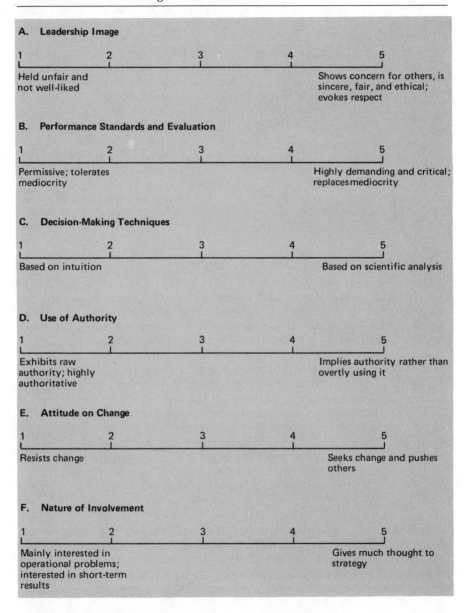

A.   Leadership Image

| 1 | 2 | 3 | 4 | 5 |

Held unfair and
not well-liked

Shows concern for others, is
sincere, fair, and ethical;
evokes respect

B.   Performance Standards and Evaluation

| 1 | 2 | 3 | 4 | 5 |

Permissive; tolerates
mediocrity

Highly demanding and critical;
replaces mediocrity

C.   Decision-Making Techniques

| 1 | 2 | 3 | 4 | 5 |

Based on intuition

Based on scientific analysis

D.   Use of Authority

| 1 | 2 | 3 | 4 | 5 |

Exhibits raw
authority; highly
authoritative

Implies authority rather than
overtly using it

E.   Attitude on Change

| 1 | 2 | 3 | 4 | 5 |

Resists change

Seeks change and pushes
others

F.   Nature of Involvement

| 1 | 2 | 3 | 4 | 5 |

Mainly interested in
operational problems;
interested in short-term
results

Gives much thought to
strategy

Can the value system of an individual be changed? Traditionally, it has been held that a person's behavior is determined mainly by the inner self reacting within a given environment. In line with this thinking, major shifts in values should be difficult to achieve. In recent years a new school of behaviorists has begun to emerge who assign a more significant role to the environment. They challenge the concept of "self" as the underlying force in determining behavior.[17] If this "environmental" thesis is accepted, it should be possible to bring about a change in individual values so that the senior executives become more unified. However, the science of human behavior has yet to provide tools that can be used to change values. Thus it would be appropriate to say that minor changes in personal values can be produced through manipulation of the environment. But where the values of an individual executive differ significantly from those of the executive's colleagues, an attempt to alter the former would be difficult.

Differing values caused a key executive, John W. Hanley, to leave the top management of Procter & Gamble for the chief executive officer position at Monsanto. Other members of the P&G management team found him too aggressive, too eager to experiment and change practices, and too quick to challenge his superior. Since he could not be brought around to the conservative style of the other executives, he was passed over for the presidency and eventually left the company.[18]

Value Orientation and Corporate Strategy

The influence of the value orientation of top management on the perspectives of their business has already been emphasized. This section examines how a particular type of value orientation may lead to certain objectives and strategy perspectives. Two examples are presented in Exhibit 3-4. In the first example the president is rated high on social and aesthetic values, which seems to indicate a greater emphasis on the quality of a single product than on growth per se. In the second example, again, the theoretical and social orientations of the top management appear to stress "truth and honesty" rather than strictly growth. If the strategic plans of these two companies were to emphasize growth as the major goal, they would undoubtedly fail. Planned perspectives may not be implemented if they are constrained by the top management's value system.

Further evidence on the subject is provided by a study undertaken to find out which approaches, among those that chief executive officers use in their jobs, contribute most to superior performance of companies over time. The study is based on a survey in which 211 CEOs of the *Fortune* 1000 corporations participated. The highlights of the findings are presented in Exhibit 3-5. Participants were classified according to "role patterns" (activist, aloof strategist, etc.) and rated according to their degree of involvement in various activities of the firm. Note, for example, that an activist exhibits very high involvement in organization and moti-

---

[17]B. F. Skinner, *Beyond Freedom and Dignity* (New York: Alfred A. Knopf, 1971).

[18]Aimee L. Horner, "Jack Hanley Got There by Selling Harder," *Fortune*, November, 1976, p. 162.

EXHIBIT 3-4   **Influence of Personal Values on Objectives and Strategies**

Example A

Values
The president of a small manufacturer of office duplicating equipment ranked relatively high on social values, giving particular attention to the security, welfare, and happiness of the employees. Second in order of importance to the president were aesthetic values.

Objectives and Strategies
1. Slow-to-moderate company growth
2. Emphasis on a single product
3. An independent-agent form of sales organization
4. Very high-quality products with aesthetic appeal
5. Refusal to compete on a price basis

Example B

Values
The top-management team members of a high-fidelity loudspeaker systems manufacturer placed greater emphasis on theoretical and social values than on other values.

Objectives and Strategies
1. Scientific truth and integrity in advertising
2. Lower margins to dealers than competitors were paying
3. Maintenance of "truth and honesty" in relationships with suppliers, dealers, and employees

Source: Reprinted by permission of the *Harvard Business Review*. Excerpt from "Personal Values and Corporate Strategies" by William D. Guth and Renato Tagiuri (September–October, 1965), pp. 137–138. Copyright © 1965 by the President and Fellows of Harvard College; all rights reserved.

vation of personnel but low involvement in strategic planning for growth, and very low involvement in anything related to acquisitions. On the other hand, an aloof strategist shows only medium involvement in organization and motivation of personnel but high involvement in strategic planning for growth and in acquisitions. Here again, the message is clear. Strategy formulation should be based on the orientation of the top management. If it is not, top management will give inadequate support to the activities outlined by the strategic plans, and the strategy will become meaningless. For example, an executive with activist orientation will not be very keen on strategic planning. Thus, the strategic planning effort in a company with an activist CEO should be rather simple.

EXHIBIT 3-5   Expressed Degree of Personal Involvement in Important Activities for Different Role Patterns

	CEO Role Pattern							
Nature of Involvement	Activist	Growth Entre- preneur	Remote Con- troller	Product Manager	Aloof Strat- egist	Acquirer	R&D Planner	Growth Director
New-product development								
Growth source								
Sales, existing products	H	VH	L	H	M	H	M	H
Product modifications	M	M	L	H	L	M	L	H
New products in present markets	H	H	L	H	M	M	M	M
New products in new markets	L	H	VL	M	M	M	M	L
Activities								
Strategic planning for growth	L	M	L	H	H	M	H	M
Direction of growth activities	H	H	L	H	L	M	L	L
Specifying areas for development	H	VH	M	VH	H	L	H	H
Creation of new-product ideas	H	H	VL	M	L	VL	L	L
Specifying development budget	H	VH	M	H	H	L	VH	H
Allocating budget among activities	M	VH	VL	L	M	VL	H	M
Selection of personnel	H	VH	L	M	M	L	M	H

Activity						
"Go–no go" decisions on products	H	VH	L	H	M	M
Organization and motivation of personnel	VH	H	L	M	M	M
Review of progress versus plans	M	M	M	L	VH	L
Acquisitions						
Growth source						
Acquisitions in present markets	VL	M	VL	L	H	H
Acquisitions in new markets	VL	M	M	L	VH	M
Activities						
Strategic planning	VL	M	M	VL	H	H
Identification of candidates and negotiation	VL	H	H	M	VH	VH
Analysis of candidates	VL	H	M	L	L	L
Integration and organization of acquired companies	VL	L	L	L	H	M

Key: VH = Very high involvement H = High involvement M = Medium involvement L = Low involvement VL = Very low involvement

Source: Reprinted by permission of the *Harvard Business Review.* Exhibit from "CEO's Role in Corporate Growth" by Joseph O. Eastlack, Jr., and Philip R. McDonald (May–June, 1970), p. 156. Copyright © 1970 by the President and Fellows of Harvard College; all rights reserved.

A corporation's culture can be its major strength when it is consistent with its strategies. This is demonstrated by the following examples:

—International Business Machines Corporation, where marketing drives a service philosophy that is almost unparalleled. The company keeps a hot line open 24 hours a day, seven days a week, to service IBM products.

—International Telephone and Telegraph Corporation, where financial discipline demands total dedication. To beat out the competition in a merger, an executive once called former chairman Harold S. Geneen at 3 A.M. to get his approval.

—Digital Equipment Corporation, where an emphasis on innovation creates freedom with responsibility. Employees can set their own hours and working style, but they are expected to articulate and support their activities with evidence of progress.

—Delta Air Lines Inc., where a focus on customer service produces a high degree of teamwork. Employees will substitute in other jobs to keep planes flying and baggage moving.

—Atlantic Richfield Company, where an emphasis on entrepreneurship encourages action. Operating men have the autonomy to bid on promising fields without hierarchical approval.[19]

In summary, an organization in the process of strategy formulation must study the values of its important executives. While exact measurement of values may not be possible, some awareness of the values held by top management is helpful to planners. Care should be taken not to threaten or alienate the executives by challenging their beliefs, traits, outlooks, etc. The strategy should be duly formulated considering the value package of the management team even if it means making a compromise on growth and profitability. Where no such compromise is feasible, it is better to transfer or change the assignment of the dissenting executive.

The experience of William Hartman, chairman of Interpace Corporation, is relevant here. After moving from International Telephone and Telegraph Corporation (ITT) in 1974, he drew on his ITT background to manage Interpace, a miniconglomerate with interests in such diverse products as teacups and concrete pipes. He used a formula that had worked well for ITT that consisted of viewing assets primarily as financial pawns to be shifted around at the chief executive's will, of compelling managers to abide by financial dicta and of focusing on financial results. The approach seemed reasonable. But its implementation at Interpace has been fraught with problems. ITT's management style did not fit with the Interpace culture despite the fact that Hartman had replaced 35 members of a 51-man team.[20] Culture that prevents a company from meeting competitive threats or from adapting to changing economic or social environments can lead to the company's stagnation and ultimate demise unless it makes a conscious effort to change.

---

[19]"Corporate Culture," *op. cit.*
[20]"How a Winning Formula Can Fail," *Business Week*, May 25, 1981, pp. 119–120.

FACTORS IN APPRAISAL: RESOURCES OF THE FIRM

The resources of a firm are its distinctive capabilities and strengths. The resources are relative in nature and must always be measured with reference to competition. The resources can be categorized as financial strength, human resources, raw material reserve, engineering and production, overall management, and marketing strength. The marketing strategist needs to consider not only marketing resources, but also resources of the company across the board. For example, price setting is a part of marketing strategy, yet it must be considered in the context of the financial strength of the company if the firm is to grow as rapidly as it should. It is obvious that profit margins on sales, combined with dividend policy, determine the amount of funds a firm can generate internally. It is less well understood, but equally true, that if a firm uses more debt than its competitors or pays lower dividends, it can generate more funds for growth by decreasing profit margins. Thus it is important in strategy development that all of the firm's resources are fully utilized in a truly integrated way. The firm that will not use its resources fully is a target for the firm that will—even if the latter has fewer resources. Full and skillful utilization of resources can give a distinct competitive edge to a firm.

Resources and Marketing Strategy

Consider the following resources of a company:

1. Has ample cash on hand (financial strength).
2. Average age of key management personnel is 42 years (human resources).
3. Has a superior raw material ingredient in reserve (raw material reserve).
4. Manufactures parts and components that go into the final product using the company's own facilities (plant and equipment).
5. The products of the company, if properly installed and serviced regularly, never stop while being used (technical competence).
6. Has a knowledge of, close relationship with, and expertise in doing business with the grocery chains (marketing strength).

How do these resources affect marketing strategy? The cash-rich company, unlike the cash-tight company, will be in a position to provide liberal credit accommodation to customers. General Electric Company, for example, established the General Electric Credit Corporation to help its dealers and ultimate customers to obtain credit. In the case of a manufacturer of durable products, which are usually bought on credit, availability of easy credit accommodation to the customers can itself make a difference between success and failure for the company.

If a company has a new raw material reserve, it will not have to depend on outside suppliers when shortages occur. From 1972 to 1974 there was a shortage of high-grade paper. A magazine publisher with its own forests and paper manufacturing facilities did not have to depend on paper companies to acquire paper. Thus, even when there was a shortage which forced the competitors to reduce the sizes of their magazines, the company not dependent on outsiders was still able to provide the same product to the customers.

In the initial stages of the development of color television, RCA was the only company that manufactured color picture tubes. In addition to using these tubes in its own television sets, RCA also sold them to other manufacturers/competitors such as General Electric. When the market for color television began to grow, RCA was in a strong position to obtain a larger share of the growth partly because of its easy access to picture tubes. General Electric, on the other hand, was weaker in this respect.[21]

IBM's technical capabilities, among other things, helped it to be an innovator in developing data processing equipment and introducing it to the market. IBM's excellent after-sale service facilities in themselves serve as a promotion for the company's products. The servicing provides a promotional tool in the hands of salespeople to promote the company's products.

Procter & Gamble is noted for its superior strength in dealing with grocery channels. The fact that this strength has served Procter & Gamble well hardly needs to be mentioned. More than anything else, marketing strength has helped Procter & Gamble to compete successfully with established companies like Kimberly Clark and Scott Paper Company in the paper product market.[22]

In brief, the resources of a company help it to establish and maintain itself in the marketplace. It is, of course, necessary for resources to be appraised objectively.

Measurement of Resources

A firm is a conglomerate of different entities, each having a number of variables that affect performance. How far should a strategist probe into these variables to designate the resources of the firm? Exhibit 3-6 is a listing of 85 possible strategic factors in different areas of a business. Not all of these factors will be important for every business; attention should be focused on those that could play a critical role in the success or failure of the particular firm. Therefore, the first step in designating resources

---

[21]"General Electric Radio and Television Division," a case copyrighted by the President and Fellows of Harvard College, 1967.

[22]"Marketing Classic: How Firms Put the Big Squeeze on Scott Paper Co.; Latter Napped, Diversified, While P&G and Mr. Whipple Invaded Its Paper Business," *The Wall Street Journal*, October 20, 1971, p. 1.

is to have executives in different areas of the business go through the listing shown in Exhibit 3-6 and choose those variables which they deem strategic. Then each strategic factor may be evaluated either qualitatively or quantitatively. One way of conducting the evaluation is to frame relevant question(s) around each strategic factor, which may be rated on either a dichotomous or a continued scale. As an example, the following questions were found relevant by a men's sportswear manufacturer in different areas of its concern.

Top Management. Which executives form the top management? Which one of them can be held responsible for the firm's performance during the past few years? Is each one of them capable of undertaking future challenges as well as in the past? Is something needed to boost the morale of top management? What are the distinguishing characteristics of each top executive? Are there any conflicts, such as personality conflicts, among them? If so, between whom, and for what reasons? What has been done and is being done for organizational development? What are the reasons for the company's performance during the past few years? Are the old ways of managing obsolete? What more can be done to enhance the company's capabilities?

Marketing. What are the major products/services of the company? Determine the basic facts about each product—e.g., market share, profitability, position in the life cycle, major competitors and their strengths and weaknesses, etc. In which field can the firm be considered a leader? Why? What can be said about the firm's pricing policies (i.e., price compared with value and with prices of competitors)? What is the nature of new product development efforts of the company, such as coordination with R&D and manufacturing? How does the market look in the future for the planning period? What steps are being taken or proposed to meet future challenges? What can be said about the company's channel arrangements, physical distribution, and promotional efforts? What is the behavior of marketing costs? What new products are expected to be launched, when, and with what expectations? What has been done towards consumer satisfaction?

Production. Are people capable of working on new machines, new processes, designs, etc., that may be developed in the future? What new plant, equipment, and facilities are needed? Determine the basic facts about each product—e.g., cost structure, quality control, work stoppages, etc. What is the nature of labor relations? Are any problems anticipated? What steps have been proposed and/or taken to avert strikes, work stoppages, etc.? Does production perform its part effectively in the process of manufacturing new products? How flexible are the operations? Can they be made suitable for future competition and new products well on the way to being produced and marketed commercially? What steps have been

EXHIBIT 3-6   Strategic Factors in Business

A. General Managerial
  1. Ability to attract and maintain high-quality top management
  2. Developing future managers for overseas operations
  3. Developing future managers for domestic operations
  4. Developing a better organizational structure
  5. Developing a better long-range planning program
  6. Achieving better overall control of company operations
  7. Using more new quantitative tools and techniques in decision making at:
     a. Top management levels
     b. Lower management levels
  8. Assuring better judgment, creativity and imagination in decision making at:
     a. Top management levels
     b. Lower management levels
  9. Ability to use computers for problem solving and planning
 10. Ability to use computers for information handling and financial control
 11. Ability to divest nonprofitable enterprises
 12. Ability to perceive new needs and opportunities for products
 13. Ability to motivate sufficient managerial drive for profits

B. Financial
  1. Ability to raise long-term capital at low cost:
     a. Debt
     b. Equity
  2. Ability to raise short-term capital
  3. Ability to maximize value of stockholder investment
  4. Ability to provide a competitive return to stockholders
  5. Willingness to take risks with commensurate returns in what appear to be excellent new business opportunities in order to achieve growth objectives
  6. Ability to apply ROI criteria to R&D investments
  7. Ability to finance diversification by means of:
     a. Acquisitions
     b. In-house research and development

C. Marketing
  1. Ability to accumulate better knowledge about markets
  2. Establishing a wide customer base
  3. Establishing a selective consumer base
  4. Establishing an efficient product distribution system
  5. Ability to get good business contracts (government and others)
  6. Assuring imaginative advertising and sales promotion campaigns
  7. Using pricing more effectively (including discounts, customer credit, product service, guarantees, delivery, etc.)
  8. Better relationships between marketing and new product engineering and production
  9. Producing vigor in sales organization

D. Engineering and Production
  1. Developing effective machinery and equipment replacement policies
  2. Providing more efficient plant layout
  3. Developing sufficient capacity for expansion
  4. Developing better materials and inventory control
  5. Improving product quality control
  6. Improving in-house product engineering
  7. Improving in-house basic product research capabilities
  8. Developing more effective profit improvement (cost-reduction) programs
  9. Developing better ability to mass-produce at low per-unit cost
  10. Relocating present production facilities
  11. Automating production facilities
  12. Better management of, and better results from, research and development expenditures
  13. Establishing foreign production facilities
  14. Developing more flexibility in using facilities for different products
  15. Being in the forefront of technology and being extremely scientifically creative

E. Products
  1. Improving present products
  2. Developing more efficient and effective product-line selection
  3. Developing new products to replace old ones
  4. Developing new products in new markets
  5. Developing sales for present products in new markets
  6. Diversifying products by acquisition
  7. More subcontracting
  8. Getting bigger share of product market

F. Personnel
  1. Attracting scientists and highly technically qualified employees
  2. Establishing better relationships with employees
  3. Ability to get along with labor unions
  4. Better utilizing the skills of employees
  5. Motivating more employees to remain abreast of developments in their fields
  6. Ability to level peaks and valleys of employment requirements
  7. Ability to stimulate creativity in employees
  8. Ability to optimize employee turnover (not too much and not too little)

G. Materials
  1. Getting geographically closer to raw material sources
  2. Assuring continuity of raw material supplies
  3. Finding new sources of raw materials
  4. Owning and controlling sources of raw materials
  5. Bringing "in-house" presently purchased materials and components
  6. Reducing raw material costs

Source: George Steiner, *Strategic Factors in Business Success* (New York: Financial Executives Research Foundation, 1969), pp. 4–5. Reprinted by permission.

proposed and/or taken to cut down pollution? What are the important raw materials being used or likely to be used? What are the important sources for each raw material? How reliable are these sources?

Finance. What is the financial standing of the company as a whole and of its different products/divisions in terms of earnings, sales, tangible net worth, working capital, earnings per share, liquidity, inventory, cash flow position, capital structure, etc.? What is the cost of capital? Can money be used in a more productive fashion? What is the reputation of the company in the financial community? How does our performance compare with that of competitors and other corporations of our size? What steps have been proposed and/or taken to line up new sources of capital, to increase return on investment through more productive use of resources, to lower break-even points, etc.? Has the company managed tax matters aggressively? What contingency steps are proposed to avert threats of capital shortage, takeover, etc.?

R&D. What is the R&D reputation of the company? What percentage of sales and profits in the past can be directly attributed to R&D efforts? Are there any conflicts or personality clashes in the department? If so, what has been proposed and what is being done? What is the status of current major projects? When are they expected to be completed? In what way will they help the company's performance? What kind of relationships do the R&D people have with those in marketing and manufacturing? What steps have been proposed and are being taken to cut down overhead and improve quality? Are all scientists/researchers adequately used? If not, why not? Can we expect any breakthroughs from R&D? Are there any resentments? If so, what are they, and for what reason?

Miscellaneous. What has been proposed and/or done to serve minorities, the community, the cause of education, etc.? What is the nature of productivity gains for the company as a whole and for each part of the company? How do we stand in comparison to industry trend and national goal? How well do we compete in the world market? Which countries/companies constitute tough competitors? What are their strengths and weaknesses? What is the nature and scope of our public relations function? Is it adequate? How does it compare with that of competitors and other companies of our size and character? Which government agencies—federal, state, or local—do we deal with most often? Are our relationships with them satisfactory? Who are our stockholders? Do a few individuals/institutions hold majority stock? What are their corporate expectations? Do they prefer capital gains or dividend income?

The ratings on the above questions may be added up to compute the total resource score in each area. It must be understood that not all questions can be evaluated using the same scale. In many cases quantitative measurement may be difficult and subjective evaluation will have to be accepted. Further, measurement of resources should be done for current effectiveness and for future perspectives. Exhibit 3-7 shows two nine-point scales: one for current effectiveness and one for future perspectives. These scales can be simplified and/or altered to meet specific needs.

The strategic factors for success lie in different functional areas, distribution channels, and so on, and they vary by industry. As shown in Exhibit 3-8, the success factors for different industries fall at different points along the continuum of functional activities that begins with raw materials sourcing and ends with servicing. In the uranium industry, raw material sourcing is the key to success since low-quality ore requires much more complicated and costly processing. Inasmuch as the uranium price does not vary among producers, the choice of the source of uranium supply is the crucial determinant of profitability. In contrast, the critical factor in the soda industry is production technology.[23] Since the mercury process is more than twice as efficient as the semipermeable membrane method of obtaining soda of similar quality, a company using the latter process will be at a disadvantage no matter what else it might do to reduce the extra cost. In other words, use of mercury technology would become a strategic resource for a soda company to count on if the competitors have chosen not to go to the expense and difficulty of a changeover from the semipermeable membrane method.

PAST PERFORMANCE OF BUSINESS UNITS

The past performance of business units serves as an important input in formulating corporate-wide strategy. It helps in the assessment of

EXHIBIT 3-7   Scales for Measuring Resources

Current Effectiveness	*Future Perspectives*
(9) Completely effective	(9) Completely sound
(8) Almost completely effective	(8) Almost completely sound
(7) Quite effective	(7) Quite sound
(6) Moderately effective	(6) Moderately sound
(5) As effective as ineffective	(5) As sound as unsound
(4) Moderately ineffective	(4) Moderately unsound
(3) Quite ineffective	(3) Quite unsound
(2) Almost completely ineffective	(2) Almost completely unsound
(1) Completely ineffective	(1) Completely unsound

Source: Adapted from Robert R. Blake and Jane Srygley Mouton, *How to Assess the Strengths and Weaknesses of Corporate Leadership* (Austin, TX: Scientific Methods, 1972). Reprinted by permission.

---

[23]Kenichi Ohmae, *The Mind of the Strategist* (New York: McGraw-Hill Book Co., 1982), pp. 46–47.

EXHIBIT 3-8   How Success Factors Vary by Industry

KEY FACTOR OR FUNCTION	SPECIMEN INDUSTRIES	
	TO INCREASE PROFIT	TO GAIN SHARE
Raw materials sourcing	Uranium	Petroleum
Production facilities (economies of scale)	Shipbuilding, steelmaking	Shipbuilding, steelmaking
Design	Aircraft	Aircraft, hi-fi
Production technology	Soda, semiconductors	Semiconductors
Product range/variety	Department stores	Components
Application engineering/engineers	Minicomputers	LSI, microprocessors
Sales force (quality × quantity)	ECR	Automobiles
Distribution network	Beer	Films, home appliances
Servicing	Elevators	Commercial vehicles—e.g., taxis

Source: Kenichi Ohmae, *The Mind of the Strategist* (New York: McGraw-Hill Book
Co., 1982), p. 47. Reprinted by permission.

the current situation and possible developments in the future. For example, if the profitability of a strategic business unit (SBU) has been declining over the past five years, an appraisal of current performance as
being satisfactory cannot be justified assuming the trend continues. In addition, any projected rise in profitability must be thoroughly justified in
the light of this trend. The perspectives of different SBUs over time, vis-
à-vis other factors (i.e., top management values, concerns of stakeholders,
corporate resources, and the socioeconomic-political-technological environment), would show which ones have the potential for profitable growth.
     SBU performance is based on such measures as *financial* (sales—dol-
lar and/or volume, operating profit before taxes, cash flow, depreciation,
sales per employee, profits per employee, investment per employee, return on investment/sales/assets, asset turnover); *human resources* (use of
employee skills, productivity, turnover, and ethnic and racial composition); *facilities* (rated capacity, capacity utilization, modernization); *inven-*

tories (raw materials, finished products, and obsolete inventory); *marketing* (research and development expenditures, new products to be introduced, number of salespersons, sales per salesperson, independent distributors, exclusive distributors, promotion expenditures); *international business* (growth rate, geographic coverage); and *managerial performance* (leadership capabilities, planning, development of personnel, and delegation).

Usually, the volume of data that the above information would generate is much greater than required. It is desirable, therefore, for management to specify what measures it considers important in appraising the performance of the SBUs. To ensure consistency in information received from different SBUs, it is worthwhile to develop a *pro forma* sheet listing the categories of information that corporate management desires. The general profile produced from the evaluation of information obtained through the *pro forma* sheets provides a quick picture of how well things are going.

SUMMARY

Corporate appraisal constitutes an important ingredient in the strategy development process since it lays the foundation for the company to interact with the future environment. Corporate publics, value orientation of top management, and corporate resources are the three principal factors in appraisal which are discussed in this chapter. Appraisal of the past performance of business units, which also affects formulation of corporate strategy for the future, is covered briefly.

Corporate publics are all those groups having a stake in the organization, i.e., owners, employees, customers, suppliers, the banking community and other lenders, government, the community in which the company does business, and the society at large. Expectations of all stakeholders should be considered in formulating corporate strategy. Corporate strategy is also deeply influenced by the value orientation of the corporation's top management. Thus, values of top management should be studied and duly figured in setting objectives. Finally, the company's resources in different areas should be carefully evaluated. They serve as a major criterion for the company to accept certain future perspectives.

DISCUSSION QUESTIONS

1. *How often should a company undertake self-appraisal? What are the arguments for and against yearly self-appraisal?*
2. *Discuss the pros and cons of having a consultant conduct the appraisal.*
3. *Identify five companies which in your opinion have failed to change with time and have either pulled out or continue as laggards. Justify your selection of companies.*
4. *Identify five companies which in your opinion have kept pace with time as evidenced by their performance.*

5. What expectations does a community have of (a) a bank, (b) a medical group, and (c) a manufacturer of cyclical goods?
6. What type of top-management values are most likely to lead to growth orientation?
7. Is growth orientation necessarily good? Discuss.
8. In your opinion what marketing resources are the most critical for success in the cosmetics industry?
9. How should a company go about identifying the critical factors for success in its business?

The Eugene Star

The Eugene Star is a daily newspaper serving Wayne County in a relatively isolated area of New England. The newspaper was independently owned by the Lyon family until 1978, when it was purchased by the Southern Newspaper Group following the death of Richard Lyon, its long-time publisher. Founded in 1848 as a weekly, it was converted to a five-day daily in 1872. It acquired its chief competitor, *The Eugene Tribune,* after a lengthy newspaper war which culminated in 1940. Physical facilities were consolidated at the *Star* headquarters, and 78 percent of the combined personnel were retained. The remainder were given generous severance arrangements, reflecting the benevolent management practices which guided the Lyon family and which had generated high regard in the community. This regard, coupled with the virtual monopoly position in print media that the *Star* enjoyed, resulted in the paper's prosperity. Saturday and Sunday editions were added in 1946 and 1948, respectively. Although technological changes such as photocomposition and front-end systems were adopted only after the majority of newspapers had embraced such innovations, a relatively inexpensive labor force had partially compensated for the additional costs incurred because of lack of mechanization.

Since the *Star's* acquisition by Southern, there had been a notable shift in all aspects of the operation. Aside from the obvious financial changes, there had been heavy staff turnover, including three publishers. Growing hostility to the newspaper by both its staff and the community had fostered a serious morale problem, in addition to jeopardizing its status in its community. Resentment precipitated by Southern's suspension of the Saturday edition continued to fester. By April of 1983, the situation had further worsened. The management of the *Star* now has to consider what strategic changes should be made to straighten things out.

ORGANIZATIONAL STRUCTURE

The Eugene Star is composed of five functional departments, each with a department manager reporting directly to the publisher (see Exhibit 3-9). The publisher reports to the Eastern Division Manager of the Southern Newspaper Group. Although Southern espouses the theory that complete autonomy be retained by all its publications, their actual authority is somewhat limited, focusing primarily on the editorial rather than the financial area.

The *Star* employs approximately 46 full-time employees, with 15 to

EXHIBIT 3-9   The Eugene Star: Organizational Structure

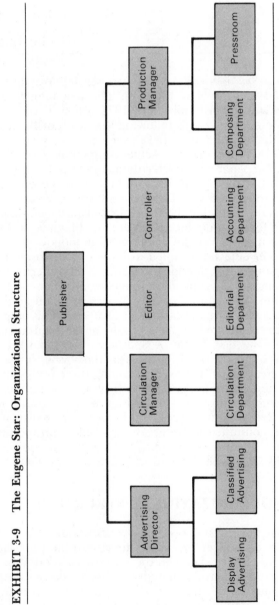

Source: Company records.

25 additional part-time employees utilized mostly to distribute the paper. Home delivery is accomplished by youth carriers operating as independent contractors.

DISTRIBUTION PATTERN

As of March 31, 1983, the *Star* had a paid circulation averaging 9,340 Monday through Friday and 10,160 on Sunday. An audit by the Audit Bureau of Circulations (ABC), an independent newspaper audit firm, indicated that over the previous four-year period circulation had declined by nearly 15 percent (see Exhibit 3-10).

The paper is approximately 85 percent home delivered, with the balance sold in stores and vending racks. The most recent ABC report estimated primary market households (Wayne County) at 13,160, an increase of 840 over the 1980 Census Bureau figures. Households had been increasing at the rate of 2 to 3 percent each year, stemming in large part from the demographic change to fewer persons per household. In the spring of 1983 the circulation of the *Star* in its primary market was 8,570 daily and 9,660 on Sunday. This gave the newspaper 65 percent penetration of its primary market on a daily basis and 73 percent penetration on Sunday. This statistic, critical to the newspaper's advertisers, had been declining for the past four years from the combined effect of a drop in paid circulation and an increase in the number of primary market households (see Exhibit 3-11).

CIRCULATION PRICING AND REVENUE

In 1983 the retail price of the *Star* was $1.80 per week for home delivery. Single copies were available at store and vending-rack locations for 30¢ daily and 75¢ on Sunday. Audit Bureau of Circulations reports

EXHIBIT 3-10   The Eugene Star: Paid Circulation History

SIX-MONTH AVERAGES, PERIOD ENDING*	DAILY	SUNDAY
3/31/79	10,680	11,490
3/31/80	10,230	11,080
3/31/81	10,010	10,740
3/31/82	9,760	10,480
3/31/83	9,340	10,160
*Based on ABC (Audit Bureau of Circulations) figures.		

Source: Company records.

EXHIBIT 3-11   The Eugene Star: Primary Market Penetration

Date	Primary Market Households	Primary Market Daily Circulation	Percentage Penetration
3/31/79	12,040	9,860	82%
3/31/80	12,370	9,390	76%
3/31/81	12,715	9,210	72%
3/31/82	12,975	8,955	69%
3/31/83	13,160	8,570	65%
		Primary Market Sunday Circulation	**Percentage Penetration**
3/31/79	12,040	10,915	91%
3/31/80	12,370	10,505	85%
3/31/81	12,715	10,200	80%
3/31/82	12,975	9,955	77%
3/31/83	13,160	9,660	73%

Source: Company records.

EXHIBIT 3-12   The Eugene Star: Pricing and Revenue Data

(a) PRICES

Date	Retail			Wholesale		
	Daily	Sunday	Weekly	Carrier	Store Daily	Sunday
3/31/79	.20	.40	1.25	.94	.15	.30
3/31/80	.25	.50	1.50	1.12	.19	.375
3/31/81	.25	.55	1.60	1.20	.19	.41
3/31/82	.25	.65	1.70	1.28	.19	.49
3/31/83	.30	.75	1.80	1.35	.225	.56

(b) CIRCULATION REVENUE HISTORY

Year Ended	Daily Circulation	Wholesale Price	Revenue	Sunday Revenue	Total Revenue
3/31/79	10,680	.94	$522,038	$12,636	$534,674
3/31/80	10,230	1.12	595,795	16,575	612,370
3/31/81	10,010	1.20	624,624	15,564	640,188
3/31/82	9,760	1.28	649,626	18,346	667,972
3/31/83	9,340	1.35	655,668	23,878	679,546

EXHIBIT 3-12   continued

(c) ADVERTISING LINAGE & REVENUE (Year ended 3/31/83)

Advertising Category	Linage	Average Line Rate	Advertising Revenue
Display	2,876,000	.22	$632,720
National	124,000	.35	43,400
Classified	964,000	.24	231,360
Legal	46,000	.30	13,800
Total	4,010,000	.2297	$921,280

(d) ADVERTISING LINAGE, RATE AND REVENUE HISTORY

Year Ended	Total Linage	Average Line Rate	Advertising Revenue
3/31/79	6,035,000	.1751	$1,056,729
3/31/80	5,944,000	.1874	1,113,906
3/31/81	5,387,000	.2005	1,080,009
3/31/82	5,125,000	.2146	1,099,825
3/31/83	4,010,000	.2297	921,280

(e) ADVERTISING INSERT REVENUE

Year Ended	Number of Inserts	Average Price Per Insert	Insert Revenue
3/31/79	135	$391	$ 52,785
3/31/80	135	391	52,785
3/31/81	364	391	142,324
3/31/82	364	391	142,324
3/31/83	156	340	53,040

(f) TOTAL REVENUE HISTORY

Year Ended	Circulation Revenue	Advertising Revenue	Insert Revenue	Total Revenue
3/31/79	$534,674	$1,056,729	$ 52,785	$1,644,188
3/31/80	612,370	1,113,906	52,785	1,726,276
3/31/81	640,188	1,080,009	142,324	1,862,521
3/31/82	667,972	1,099,825	142,324	1,910,121
3/31/83	679,546	921,280	53,040	1,653,866

Source: Company records.

indicated that the price of the paper had increased four times since 1979, which had undoubtedly added to the decline in paid circulation (see Exhibit 3-12a).

Newspaper carriers were earning approximately 25 percent of the retail home-delivery price as compensation for their services. The same margin applied to retail outlets.

Despite the decline in circulation, the circulation revenues had increased substantially over the last four years because of price increases. Estimated net circulation revenues for the year ended 3/31/83 were $679,546 (see Exhibit 3-12b).

ADVERTISING LINAGE AND REVENUE

Advertising linage at the *Star* is sold on the basis of agate lines. A full eight-column page contains 2,408 agate lines.

The newspaper's 1983 advertising rates, which varied with the customer's earned rate, ranged from 18¢ to 25¢ per agate line for display, 20¢ to 28¢ per agate line for classified, 35¢ per agate line for national, and 30¢ per agate line for legal advertising. These were the published rates on the advertising rate card effective 9/30/82.

Monthly and year-to-date advertising linage figures published by the New England Newspaper Association indicated that for the year ended 3/31/83 total advertising linage in the *Star* was 4,010,000 lines, broken down as 2,876,000 lines of display, 964,000 lines of classified, 124,000 lines of national, and 46,000 lines of legal advertising. The estimated advertising revenue for the year ended 3/31/83 was $921,280, based on applying an average rate per line to each category of advertising (see Exhibit 3-12c).

Information on advertising revenues in the *Star* for the prior years was available only in totals. The decline in advertising revenues shown in Exhibit 3-12(d) can be attributed, in part, to competition from a rival advertising medium, *The Bargain Hunter,* which began publication in November, 1981. Another factor influencing the decline had been the *Star*'s increase in advertising rates, which had averaged 7 percent annually since the *Star*'s acquisition by Southern. Estimated advertising rates and ad dollars indicated a decline in advertising revenue dollars of 16 percent from prior years despite higher ad rates. This was a consequence of the 22 percent drop in ad linage. Advertising revenue had declined by 13 percent since 1979, a serious situation when compounded by the effects of inflation. The cumulative increase of 31 percent in advertising rates since 1979 needed to be examined since it appeared to be a short-term solution and a long-term irritant.

The *Star* also ran advertising supplements which were inserted in the newspaper after being preprinted by the advertiser. In the year ended 3/31/83, the *Star* ran approximately 156 advertising inserts for which it received an average of $340 each, or $53,040 for the year. Approximately one year earlier, four grocery store advertising supplements which had formerly been placed in the *Star* were abruptly withdrawn from the newspaper and began appearing in *Bargain Hunter.* Advertising inserts during the two prior years had numbered about 364 (see Exhibit 3-12e). Pricing was about 15 percent higher. Earlier years' advertising inserts numbered

approximately 135 per year, since in those years grocers and other retailers used "Run of Paper" (ROP) advertising as their primary focus.

Total advertising revenue for the *Star* was lower in the most recent
year than four years earlier because of competition from *Bargain Hunter*
beginning in November, 1981. Total revenues of the newspaper were slightly
higher than four years ago because of a 27 percent increase in circulation
revenue realized from higher pricing on lower circulation. Since the new
competitor entered the business, however, total revenue had declined by
13 percent (see Exhibit 3-12f).

EXPENSE AND PROFIT STRUCTURE

In the year ended 3/31/83 the *Star* made an estimated pretax profit
of $163,898, or 9.9 percent of revenue. This estimate was based on av-
erages obtained from daily newspapers in this revenue size category as
reported by the Cost and Revenue Study of the Inland Daily Press Association, Inc., covering the year 1981. This annual survey was the result
of participation of almost 300 newspapers in the United States and Canada (see Exhibit 3-13a).

Since many of the expenses of producing a newspaper are of a fixed
nature, profit for the prior year was approximated at $409,554, or 21.4
percent of the $1,910,121 total revenue (see Exhibit 3-13b). The slippage
in revenue of 13 percent and in profit of 60 percent from one year to
the next signaled a disturbing trend for *The Eugene Star*. The competing
paper had gained market share to the extent of endangering the *Star*'s
viability. The high profit component of incremental revenue is indicated
by analyzing the comparative financial statements in Exhibit 3-13.

THE COMPETITION

Since its inception in November, 1981, the weekly *Bargain Hunter*
had steadily gained advertising revenue and market share. It was started
by the former advertising director of *The Eugene Star* soon after she was
dismissed from her job by the Southern management. She then hired the
two top *Star* ad salespersons to assist her.

The Bargain Hunter was distributed on Mondays to 13,000 households in the primary market. Distribution was accomplished through a
force of adult carriers. An additional 3,000 copies of the shopper were
distributed through retail store drops on a free basis. Since there is no
charge for the paper, it must derive its entire revenue from advertising.

According to the advertising rate card of *The Bargain Hunter*, the
average rate is 20¢ per line of advertising. This rate combined with *The
Bargain Hunter*'s classified rate averaged about 13 percent less than the
Star's average rate (see Exhibit 3-14). *The Bargain Hunter*'s selling advantage lay in both this rate advantage and its total circulation of 16,000,
versus 9,340 daily and 10,160 Sunday circulation for the *Star*. Since *The*

**EXHIBIT 3-13   The Eugene Star: Estimated Expenses and Profit,
                 1982 and 1983**

(a) Year ended 3/31/83		
Newspaper Revenue	$1,653,866	Percentage
Expenses*		of Revenue
Editorial	208,364	12.6%
Advertising	145,524	8.8%
Circulation	203,403	12.3%
Newsprint	229,862	13.9%
Production	224,901	13.6%
Administrative & Accounting	477,914	28.9%
Total Expense	$1,489,968	90.9%
Newspaper Net Profit	$163,898	9.9%
(b) Year ended 3/31/82		
Newspaper Revenue	$1,910,121	Percentage
Expenses*		of Revenue
Editorial	198,442	10.4%
Advertising	152,800	8.0%
Circulation	193,717	10.1%
Newsprint	265,507	13.9%
Production	234,945	12.3%
Administrative & Accounting	455,156	23.8%
Total Expense	$1,500,567	78.6%
Newspaper Net Profit	$409,554	21.4%

*Estimated utilizing the Inland Daily Press Association, Inc., Cost and Revenue
Study covering 1981.

Bargain Hunter was delivered to every household in the primary market,
it boasted total market coverage as its prime selling point.

Advertising space in *The Bargain Hunter* was averaging 24 tabloid
pages per week or about $293,500 per year, based on $2.80 per inch (20¢
per agate line). Since about 20 percent of the linage was made up of $1.00

EXHIBIT 3-14   Advertising Rate Comparison

	Bargain Hunter	Eugene Star
Local rate per line	$ .20	$ .22
Classified rate per line	.20	.24
Want ad cost	1.00	4.50 minimum
Insert price per thousand	25.00	34.00
Total distribution	16,000	9,340
Primary market penetration	100%	65%

want ads and the *Star* personnel claimed that many of the large advertisers received special discounts (a practice disdainfully referred to as selling off the rate card), a more realistic estimate of *The Bargain Hunter*'s revenues, according to the *Star* executives, should be 70 percent of the original total, or $205,471.

The Bargain Hunter also carried four advertising insert supplements each week which were formerly delivered in the *Star*. Based on 16,000 inserts at $25 per thousand, or $400 per week, insert revenue for *The Bargain Hunter* amounted to $83,200. Together, the total advertising revenue of *The Bargain Hunter* appeared to be $288,671 (see Exhibit 3-15).

FUTURE PROSPECTS

Although the immediate financial picture is not grave, if the present trend of deterioration of market share remains unchecked, the long-term consequences for the *Star* appear decidedly negative. Despite the fact that little is known about actual expenses, distinct variances in revenue-generating mechanisms are apparent from the 1981 Inland Cost and Revenue Study summarizing industry averages (see Exhibit 3-16). Since daily newspapers in relatively small, isolated markets are generally economically sound, the *Star* management feels that the potential exists to recreate a healthy paper that will continue to meet the needs of its community. They are concerned about what strategic path they should develop to secure long-term viability of the paper. The Case Appendix provides the perspectives of the newspaper industry.

CASE APPENDIX: PERSPECTIVES OF THE NEWSPAPER INDUSTRY

Newspapers have a place in our society and our daily lives which helps guarantee our freedom and our way of life. Recent publicity surrounding the demise of metropolitan papers has colored industry prospects negatively. When newspaper publishing is examined in its entirety, however, the complexion is quite different. Each day more than 100,000,000 people across America rely on daily newspapers for information, entertainment, and advertising. Newspapers remain strong today, despite challenges posed by changing technologies and shifting social habits.

EXHIBIT 3-15   Market Share Comparison

	Bargain Hunter	Eugene Star
Year ended 3/31/80	0	$1,166,691 (100%)
Year ended 3/31/83	$288,671 (23%)	$974,320 (77%)

EXHIBIT 3-16   The Eugene Star: Cost and Revenue Study, 1981

Regression # Subject	Predicted Value	Actual Position	Variance/ Predicted[a]
1 Local advertising revenue	$800,000	$632,720	−21%
2 National advertising revenue	$50,000	$43,400	−13%
3 Classified advertising revenue	$190,000	$245,160	+29%
4 Total advertising revenue	$1,100,000	$921,280	−16%
5 Advertising as a % of total space	43%	NA	—
6 Homeprint pages per issue	22 pages	NA	—
7 Total inches of advertising	450,000″	286,429″	−36%
8 Inches of local advertising	330,000″	205,429″	−38%
9 Local ad revenue per inch	$2.30	$3.08[b]	+34%
10 Inches of national advertising	20,000″	8,857″	−56%
11 National ad revenue per inch	$2.70	$4.90	+81%
12 Inches of classified advertising	85,000″	72,143″	−15%
13 Classified ad revenue per inch	$2.25	$3.40	+51%
14 Preprint revenue	$100,000	$53,040	−47%
15 Total revenue	$1,500,000	$1,653,866	+10%
16 Total expense	$1,300,000	NA	—
17 News-editorial expense	$200,000	NA	—
18 Advertising department expense	$135,000	NA	—
19 Circulation & distribution expense	$150,000	NA	—
20 Newsprint, ink & handling expense	$200,000	NA	—
21 General and administrative expense	$440,000	NA	—
22 Composing room expense	$130,000	NA	—
23 Composing room hours per page	2.4 hours	NA	—
24 Other mechanical expense	$85,000	NA	—
25 Other mechanical hours per page	1.2 hours	NA	—
26 Total mechanical expense	$220,000	NA	—
27 Total mechanical hours per page	3.6 hours	NA	—
28 Advertising expense/total ad inches	$80,000	NA	—
29 Circulation revenue	$350,000	$679,546	+94%
30 Total payroll	$650,000	NA	—
31 News-editorial pages/n.-e. expense	NA	NA	—
32 News-editorial payroll	$140,000	NA	—
33 Advertising payroll	$120,000	NA	—
34 Circulation & distribution payroll	$70,000	NA	—
35 Total mechanical payroll	$150,000	NA	—
36 General & administrative payroll	$120,000	NA	—
37 Total depreciation expense	$65,000	NA	—
38 Business office expense	$70,000	NA	—
39 Administrative & all other expense	$250,000	NA	—

[a]The accuracy of the variance is affected by an inflation factor resulting from differences in the study of predicted values (calendar year 1981) and the actual values (fiscal year ending 3/31/83).
[b]Based on ROP (Run of Paper) linage and dollars only; does not include any insert revenue.

Source: Inland Daily Press Association, Inc., Cost and Revenue Study Covering 1981.

American newspapers continue to be among the largest national employers. Department of Labor statistics show an increase in newspaper employment from 421,900 in 1981 to 424,800 in 1982, continuing a long-established trend.

Circulation

Newspaper circulation increased in 1982 by 1,000,000 to record levels of 62,438,074 daily and 56,152,405 on Sunday. There were 1,710 daily newspapers in 1982: 433 morning papers, 1,311 evening papers, 34 "all day" papers, and 768 Sunday papers. A shift from evening to morning distribution is evident, along with an increase in the number of Sunday papers. An analysis of the industry reveals that in 1946, before the advent of commercial television, there were 1,763 daily papers and 497 Sunday papers circulating 50,927,505 daily and 43,665,364 on Sunday.

Nearly three out of every four daily newspapers now cost 25¢ a copy and the predominant price for Sunday papers is 50¢. Increasing circulation prices are functioning to counterbalance recent stagnation in the growth of circulation.

Advertising

Daily newspapers remained the number one advertising medium in 1982, capturing 27.3 percent of all advertising dollars spent. Although this was a gain of 5.4 percent in total revenues over 1981, higher ad rates accounted for the vast majority of these gains, reflecting a flattening of linage increases. Actual advertising in newspapers totaled $18,355,000,000. This amount outdistanced television by $4,000,000,000, radio by $13,700,000,000, magazines by $14,600,000,000, and direct mail by $8,000,000,000 (see Exhibit 3-17).

Since advertising revenues represent approximately 80 percent of the newspaper industry's total revenues, negative trends should be carefully noted. Market share has slipped from its all-time high of 33 percent of all advertising dollars in the 1950s. This was caused largely by additional advertising dollars being spent on television and direct mail. Classified advertising, consisting primarily of automotive, real estate, and help wanted ads, has been detrimentally affected by adverse economic conditions. It also responds favorably to prospects of recovery such as lowering of interest rates and renewed consumer confidence.

Recent years have seen a trend of large advertisers shifting away from "Run of Paper" (ROP) advertising toward the use of preprinted advertising supplements inserted in newspapers as "stuffers." Use of these inserts has made many advertisers susceptible to a newer and more ominous trend, that of "marriage mail." In 1979, the United States Post Office enacted legislation granting a favorable "shared mail" postage rate, resulting in the formation of independent companies known as "baggies" or "breadwrappers." These firms group preprint inserts together and di-

EXHIBIT 3-17   Perspectives of Newspaper Advertising

(a) Newspapers' Share of Advertising Revenue (1981 and 1982 Sales and Percentages)

		1981 (millions)	% of Total	1982[1] (millions)	% of Total	% of Change
Daily Newspapers	Total	$17,420	28.3	$18,355	27.3	+ 5.4
	National	2,729	4.4	2,975	4.4	+ 9.0
	Local	14,691	23.9	15,380	22.8	+ 4.7
Magazines		3,533	5.7	3,745	5.6	+ 6.0
Television	Total	12,650	20.6	14,280	21.2	+12.9
	Network	5,575	9.1	6,275	9.3	+12.6
	Spot	3,730	6.1	4,290	6.4	+15.0
	Local	3,345	5.4	3,715	5.5	+11.1
Radio	Total	4,230	6.9	4,625	6.9	+ 9.3
	Network	230	0.4	254	0.4	+10.4
	Spot	879	1.4	931	1.4	+ 5.9
	Local	3,121	5.1	3,440	5.1	+10.2
Farm Publications		146	0.2	146	0.2	0.0
Direct Mail		8,918	14.5	10,345	15.4	+16.0
Business Publications		1,841	3.0	1,860	2.8	+ 1.0
Outdoor	Total	650	1.1	720	1.1	+10.8
	National	419	0.7	465	0.7	+11.0
	Local	231	0.4	255	0.4	+10.4
Miscellaneous	Total	12,122	19.7	13,254	19.7	+ 9.3
	National	6,440	10.5	7,199	10.7	+11.8
	Local	5,682	9.2	6,055	9.0	+ 6.6
Grand Total National		34,440	56.0	38,485	57.2	+11.7
Grand Total Local		27,070	44.0	28,845	42.8	+ 6.6
TOTAL—ALL MEDIA		$61,510	100.0	$67,330	100.0	+ 9.5

[1]Preliminary figures

Source: McCann-Erickson Inc.

(b) Advertising Content: Ratio of Advertising to Total Content of U.S. Daily and Sunday Newspapers, 1946–1982

Year	Morning	Evening	Sunday	Total
1946	52.9%	55.9%	53.1%	54.5%
1950	57.5	60.4	54.6	58.3
1955	60.9	61.8	58.2	60.7
1960	60.2	60.3	56.4	59.4
1965	60.9	61.0	59.1	60.5
1970	61.6	61.4	61.5	61.5
1975	63.2	63.0	65.7	63.7
1980	62.1	59.9	66.8	62.6
1981	61.2	59.7	67.3	62.3
1982		(Not Available)		

Source: *Media Records.*

EXHIBIT 3-17   continued

(c) Daily Newspaper Advertising Volume: Growth of Daily Newspaper Advertising and the U.S. Economy, 1946–1982

Year	National Advertising (millions)	Local Advertising (millions)	Total Newspaper Advertising (millions)	Index	Gross National Product[1] (billions)	Index
1946	$ 238	$ 917	$ 1,155	100.0	$ 208.5	100.0
1950	518	1,552	2,070	179.2	284.8	136.6
1955	712	2,365	3,077	266.4	398.0	190.9
1960	778	2,903	3,681	318.7	503.7	241.6
1965	784	3,642	4,426	383.2	684.9	328.5
1970	891	4,813	5,704	493.9	977.1	468.6
1975	1,221	7,221	8,442	730.9	1,516.3	727.2
1980	2,353	13,188	15,541	1,345.5	2,626.1	1,259.5
1981[1]	2,729	14,691	17,420	1,508.2	2,937.7	1,408.9
1982[2]	2,975	15,380	18,355	1,589.2	3,057.6	1,466.5

[1]Revised figures
[2]Preliminary figures

Source: U.S. Department of Commerce, McCann-Erickson Inc.

rect-mail them to all households. In areas of high population densities, they may even be hand delivered. Weekly newspapers and the advertising papers called "shoppers" have also been the beneficiaries of this trend toward preprints, by offering blanket coverage of an area without the high rates necessitated by a daily newspaper's large overhead.

Many newspapers are retaliating with their own mail supplement programs to reach nonsubscribers. These supplements, called TMCs (Total Market Coverage), can be programmed to target selected markets by zoning them, thus ensuring 100 percent penetration of demographically attractive areas at relatively low additional cost. Other tactics being employed to strengthen their competitive position include package sales of advertising space in groups of newspapers under both diverse and common ownership. Encouraging progress is being made in establishing SAUs, or Standard Advertising Units. It is hoped that the advent of SAUs will facilitate easier placement of national advertising, thus elevating this area from its plateau. Ultimate goals of SAUs incorporate their use in conjunction with direct broadcasting by satellite of national ads. At such time, the vast potential of increasing newspapers' market share of national advertising from 7.7 percent to more closely approximate the 53.3 percent market share of local advertising that newspapers now enjoy can be explored.

Expense Reduction

Labor and newsprint are the two most significant cost items in the newspaper industry, together making up roughly 70 percent of a newspaper's total expense. The newspaper industry has made dramatic improvements in productivity in recent years. Capital expenditures of around $1,000,000,000 in 1982 were double the 1977 level. The areas of composition and page make-up have received the most attention, with front-end computer systems replacing typewriters in the newsroom and eliminating the need for re-keyboarding in the composing room. Video display terminals make it possible to set full-page-width type at speeds of 1,500 lines (1/2 page) per minute. Years ago typesetting was accomplished on a linotype machine by an individual operator at about six lines per minute. Composing rooms at medium-size newspapers which had 100 workers are now staffed by eight to ten workers. Electronic reproduction of photographs and advertising art should eliminate the composing room altogether. Whole newspaper pages can now be produced by simply keying the information into a terminal. Future plans anticipate parlaying this capability with direct transmission to ink jet presses, thus streamlining all prepress operations. As this obstacle is surmounted, plant investment will be transferred to improved material handling, sorting, and delivery.

Newsprint prices have skyrocketed over the past twelve years, necessitating a reduction in newsprint consumption. This is being effected by various measures including the reduction of page widths, use of lighter-weight newsprint, tightening of space between lines, compression of typefaces, and reduction in the amount of space available for news stories. These measures, coupled with the recession in 1982, cut demand and caused the first retrenchment of newsprint pricing in recent history. United States consumption in 1982 by all newspapers was 10,200,000 metric tons, with daily newspapers consuming 7,700,000 metric tons and paying an average of $469 a ton. Some large newspaper publishers are attempting to integrate backwards into newsprint mills to assure themselves access to the lifeblood of the industry.

At least 1,400 U.S. newspapers are now printed by offset presses as opposed to letterpresses. Better reproduction is obtained this way, yet since a new offset press for a typical 25,000 circulation daily costs over $1,000,000, many papers are reconciling themselves to the conversion of their existing letterpresses to allow compatibility with inexpensive page negatives produced by photocomposition.

Future Projections

New forms of competition are challenging newspapers. Cable television has achieved 30 percent penetration and is beginning to attract the interest of local advertisers. In 1982 cable systems won $38,000,000 of local advertising. This is only 1 percent of newspaper local ad revenue, but the future of cable is promising. Newspaper marketing people argue

EXHIBIT 3-18   Results of Survey of Newspaper Readers and Publishers

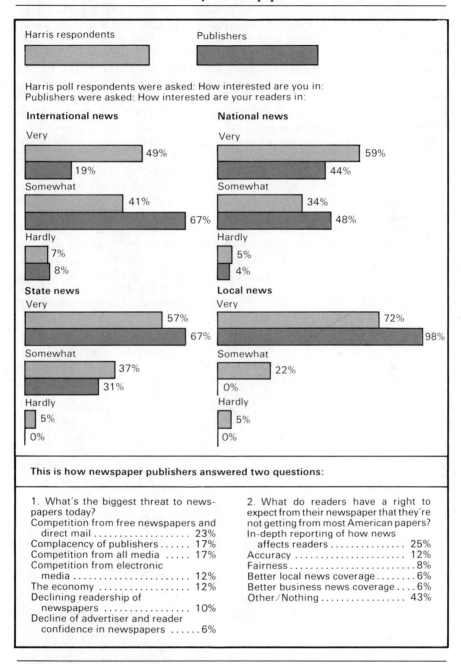

Harris respondents   Publishers

Harris poll respondents were asked: How interested are you in:
Publishers were asked: How interested are your readers in:

International news

Very
49%
19%

Somewhat
41%
67%

Hardly
7%
8%

State news

Very
57%
67%

Somewhat
37%
31%

Hardly
5%
0%

National news

Very
59%
44%

Somewhat
34%
48%

Hardly
5%
4%

Local news

Very
72%
98%

Somewhat
22%
0%

Hardly
5%
0%

This is how newspaper publishers answered two questions:

1. What's the biggest threat to newspapers today?
Competition from free newspapers and
   direct mail 23%
Complacency of publishers 17%
Competition from all media 17%
Competition from electronic
   media 12%
The economy 12%
Declining readership of
   newspapers 10%
Decline of advertiser and reader
   confidence in newspapers 6%

2. What do readers have a right to
expect from their newspaper that they're
not getting from most American papers?
In-depth reporting of how news
   affects readers 25%
Accuracy 12%
Fairness 8%
Better local news coverage 6%
Better business news coverage 6%
Other/Nothing 43%

Source: *USA TODAY.*

that cable advertising is a novelty and, with cable systems carrying an increasing number of channels, the viewing audience will become fragmented. Nevertheless, many newspaper companies are acquiring cable companies or at least leasing cable channels not only to protect themselves from incursions, but also to augment their delivery of the news. They are in the preliminary stages of recognizing that they are in the wider market of communications, rather than the restricted area of simply delivering newspapers. Along this line, they are actively pursuing other forms of the dissemination of information, including direct delivery of news and advertising into the home by way of computers. Utilizing their existing data bases, they are conducting experiments with both videotex, a two-way interactive system, and teletext, a less sophisticated but cheaper system which provides information retrieval but lacks customer-response capability. A key factor in these trials will be the effectiveness with which newspapers assess and satisfy the ever-changing demands of their potential market (see Exhibit 3-18).

Future profit margins are expected to continue to grow. This will result from increased advertising volume in conjunction with stable circulation at higher prices. Together they are expected to outpace expenses, which will be reduced through higher productivity generated by innovative technology. Newspapers are expected to remain the number one advertising medium through the 1980s, with a continued melding of print and electronic formats as the decade unfolds.

CHAPTER 4
Understanding Competition

*The most complete and happy victory is this: to compel one's enemy
to give up his purpose, while suffering no harm oneself.*

Belisarius

In a free market economy, each company tries to exceed its competitors in performance. A competitor is like an enemy. To outperform its competitors, a company must know how it stands against each one of them with regard to "arms and ammunition"—skill in maneuvering opportunities, preparedness in reacting to threats, and so on. To get adequate knowledge about the competition it faces, the company needs an excellent intelligence network.

Typically, whenever one talks in terms of competition, emphasis is placed on price, quality of product, delivery time, and other marketing variables. For the purposes of strategy development, however, one needs to go far beyond these marketing tactics employed by a competitor. Simply knowing that a competitor has been lowering prices, for example, is not sufficient. Over and above that, we must know how much flexibility the competitor has in further reducing the price. Implicit here is the need for information about the competitor's cost structure.

This chapter begins by examining the meaning of competition. The theory of competition is reviewed and a scheme for classifying competitors is advanced. Various sources of competitive intelligence are mentioned, and models for understanding competitive behavior are discussed. Finally, the impact of competition in formulating marketing strategy is analyzed.

MEANING OF COMPETITION

The term competition defies true definition because the view of competition held by different groups (e.g., lawyers, economists, government officials, and businesspeople) varies. Most firms define competition in crude, simplistic, and unrealistic terms. Some firms fail to identify the true sources of competition, while others underestimate the capabilities and reactions of their competitors. When the business climate was stable, this shallow outlook on competition used to work, but in the current environment, business strategies must be competitively oriented.

Natural and Strategic Competition

Perhaps the best way to define competition is to differentiate between natural and strategic competition. Natural competition refers to the survival of the fittest in a given environment. It is an evolutionary process that weeds out the weaker of the two rivals. Applied to the business world, it means that no two firms doing business across the board the same way in the same market can coexist forever. To survive, each firm must define how it is uniquely superior to other competitors.

Natural competition is the extension of the biological phenomenon to the business world, the Darwinian natural selection. Characteristically, this type of competition—evolution by adaptation—occurs by trial and error; is wildly opportunistic, day to day; pursues growth for its own sake; and is very conservative, because growth from successful trial by chance must prevail over death (e.g., bankruptcy) by random mistake.

Strategic competition, on the other hand, tries to leave nothing to chance. In Bruce Henderson's definition, strategic competition is the "studied deployment of resources based on a high degree of insight into the systematic cause and effect in the business ecological system."[1] Strategic competition is a new phenomenon in the business world which may well have the same impact upon business productivity that the industrial revolution had upon individual productivity. Strategic competition requires (a) an adequate amount of information surrounding the situation; (b) development of a framework to understand the dynamic interactive system; (c) postponement of current consumption to provide investment capital; (d) commitment to invest major resources to an irreversible outcome; and (e) ability to predict the output consequences, even with incomplete knowledge of inputs. Henderson identifies the basic elements of strategic competition as follows:

> —The ability to understand competitive interaction as a complete dynamic system that includes the interaction of competitors, customers, money, people, and resources.
> —The ability to use this understanding to predict the consequences of a given intervention in that system and how that intervention will result in new patterns of stable dynamic equilibrium.
> —The availability of uncommitted resources that can be dedicated to different uses and purposes in the present even though the dedication is permanent and the benefits will be deferred.
> —The ability to predict the risk and return with sufficient accuracy and confidence to justify the commitment of such resources.
> —The willingness to deliberately act to make the commitment.[2]

---

[1]Bruce D. Henderson, "New Strategies for the Global Competition," *A Special Commentary* (Boston: The Boston Consulting Group, 1981), p. 6.
[2]Bruce D. Henderson, "Understanding the Forces of Strategic and Natural Competition," *Journal of Business Strategy*, Winter, 1981, p. 11.

Japan's emergence as a major industrial power over a short span of time illustrates the practical application of strategic competition:

> The differences between Japan and the U.S. deserve some comparative analysis. There are lessons to be learned. These two leading industrial powers came from different directions, developed by different methods and followed different strategies.
>
> Japan is a small group of islands whose total land area is smaller than a number of our 50 states. The U.S. by comparison is a vast land.
>
> Japan is mountainous with very little arable land. The U.S. is the world's largest and most fertile agricultural area in a single country.
>
> Japan has virtually no energy or natural resources. The U.S. is richly endowed with energy, minerals and other vital resources.
>
> Japan has one of the oldest, most homogenous, most stable cultures. For 2,000 years or more, there was virtually no immigration, no dilution of culture or any foreign invasion. The U.S. has been a melting pot of immigrants from many cultures and many languages over one-tenth the time span. For most of our history, the U.S. has been an agrarian society and a frontier society.
>
> The Japanese developed a high order of skill in living together in cooperation over many centuries. We Americans developed a frontier mentality of self-reliance and every man for himself.
>
> The evolution of the U.S. into a vast industrial society was a classic example of natural competition in a rich environment with no constraints or artificial barriers.
>
> This option was not open to Japan. It had been in self-imposed isolation from the rest of the world for several hundred years until Commodore Perry sailed into Tokyo harbor and forced the signing of a navigation and trade treaty. Japan had been unaware of the industrial revolution already well underway in the West. It decided to compete in that world. But it had no resources.
>
> To rise above a medieval economy, Japan had to obtain foreign materials. To obtain foreign materials, it had to buy them. To buy abroad required foreign exchange. To obtain foreign exchange exports were required. Exports became Japan's lifeline. But effective exports meant the maximum value added, first with minimum material and then with minimum direct labor. Eventually this led Japan from labor intensive to capital intensive and then to technology intensive businesses. Japan was forced to develop strategic business competition as part of national policy.[3]

THEORY OF COMPETITION

Competition is basic to the free enterprise system. It is involved in all observable phenomena of the market—the prices at which products

---

[3]Bruce D. Henderson, "New Strategies for the Global Competition," *A Special Commentary* (Boston: The Boston Consulting Group, 1981), pp. 5–6. Reprinted by permission.

are exchanged, the kinds and qualities of products produced, the quantities exchanged, the methods of distribution employed, and the emphasis placed on promotion. Economists have contributed over many decades to the theory of competition. There has emerged a well-recognized body of theoretical knowledge which can be grouped, broadly, into two categories: (a) economic theory and (b) industrial organization perspective. These and certain hypotheses on competition from the viewpoint of businesspeople will be introduced.

Economic Theory of Competition

Economists have worked with many different models of competition. Still central to much of their work is the model of perfect competition, based on the premise that there are a large number of buyers and sellers in the market dealing in homogeneous products; that there is complete freedom to enter or exit the market; and that everyone possesses complete and accurate knowledge about each other.

Industrial Organization Perspective

Essentially, the study of industrial organization (IO) focuses on three variables: market structure, market conduct, and market performance. The essence of the IO framework is that a firm's performance in the marketplace depends critically on the characteristics of the industry environment in which it competes.[4] The industry environment comprises structure, conduct, and performance. Market or industry *structure* refers to the economic and technical perspectives of the industry in the context of which competition occurs. Structure includes: (a) concentration in the industry (i.e., the number and size distribution of firms); (b) barriers to entry in the industry; and (c) product differentiation among the offerings of different firms comprising the industry. *Conduct*, which is essentially strategy, refers to firms' behavior decisions in such matters as pricing, advertising, and distribution. *Performance* includes social performance, measured in terms of allocative efficiency (profitability), technical efficiency (cost minimization), and innovativeness.

Following the IO thesis, the structure of each industry vis-à-vis concentration, product differentiation, and entry barriers varies. Structure plays an important role in the competitive behavior of different firms in the market.[5] As has been said:

---

[4]See Michael E. Porter, "The Contributions of Industrial Organization to Strategic Management," *Academy of Management Review*, No. 4, 1981, pp. 609–620.

[5]Richard E. Caver, "Industrial Organization, Corporate Strategy and Structure," *Journal of Economic Literature*, March, 1980, pp. 64–92.

Businessmen must be continually aware of the structure of the markets they are presently in or of those they seek to enter. Their appraisal of their present and future competitive posture will be influenced substantially by the size and concentration of existing firms as well as by the extent of product differentiation and the presence or absence of significant barriers to entry.

If a manager has already introduced his firm's products into a market, the existence of certain structural features may provide him with a degree of insulation from the intrusion of firms not presently in that market. The absence, or relative unimportance, of one or more entry barriers, for example, supplies the manager with insights into the direction from which potential competition might come. Conversely, the presence or absence of entry barriers indicates the relative degree of effort required and the success that might be enjoyed if he attempted to enter a specific market. In short, a fundamental purpose of marketing strategy involves the building of entry barriers to protect present markets and the overcoming of existing entry barriers around markets that have an attractive potential.[6]

Business Viewpoint

From the businessperson's perspective, competition refers to rivalry among firms operating in a market to fill the same customer's need. The businessperson's major interest is to keep the market to himself/herself by adopting appropriate strategies. How and why competition occurs, its intensity, and what escape routes are feasible through adopting what strategies has not been conceptualized.[7] In other words, there has been no formulation of a theory of competition by businesspeople.

In recent years, however, Bruce Henderson has developed the theory of strategic competition discussed above. The hypotheses on which this theory rests, shown in the appendix at the end of this chapter, are derived from military warfare. This is an interesting new way of looking at the marketplace, as a battleground where opposing forces (competitors) devise ways (strategies) to outperform each other.[8] According to Henderson, some of his hypotheses can be readily observed, tested, and validated and could lead to a general theory of business competition. However, many interlocking hypotheses must still be revised and tested. In this process, the science of sociobiology would play a big role. Henderson observes:

---

[6]Louis W. Stern and John R. Grabner, Jr., *Competition in the Marketplace* (Glenview, IL: Scott, Foresman and Company, 1970), p. 29.

[7]See E. T. Grether, *Marketing and Public Policy* (Englewood Cliffs, NJ: Prentice-Hall, 1960), p. 25; and George Fisk, *Marketing Systems: An Introductory Analysis* (New York: Harper & Row, 1967), p. 622.

[8]Philip Kotler and Ravi Singh, "Marketing Warfare in the 1980's," *Journal of Business Strategy*, Winter, 1981, pp. 30–41. See also Hans Widmer, "Business Lessons from Military Strategy," *The McKinsey Quarterly*, Spring, 1980, pp. 59–67.

To understand competition and its homeostasis, we must be able to integrate its entire system. The quantification of sociobiology has demonstrated the power of analysis when competition is viewed as a dynamic, ever-changing system.

If competition is fully understood as a system, the benefits in rationalization of public policy with respect to antitrust regulation and international trade can be far-reaching.

I believe that insight into strategic competition has the promise of quantum increase in our productivity and our ability to both control and expand the potential of our own future.[9]

CLASSIFYING COMPETITORS

A business may face competition from various sources either within or outside the industry. Competition may come from essentially similar products or from substitutes. The competitor may be a small firm or a large, multinational corporation. To gain an adequate perspective on competition, a firm needs to identify all current and potential sources of competition.

Competition is triggered when different industries try to serve the customer's needs and demands. For example, the customer's entertainment needs may be filled by such industries as television, sports, publishing, and travel. New industries may enter the arena to satisfy these needs. In the early 1980s, for example, the computer industry entered the entertainment field via video games. Different industries position themselves to serve different customer demands—existing, latent, and incipient. *Existing demand* occurs when a product is bought to satisfy a recognized need. *Latent demand* refers to a situation where a particular need has been recognized, but no products have yet been offered to satisfy the need. *Incipient demand* occurs when certain trends project the emergence of a need that the customer is not yet aware of.

Often an industry competes by offering different product lines. General Foods Corporation, for example, offers ground, regular instant, freeze-dried, decaffeinated, and "international" coffee to compete in the coffee industry. The competitor may be an existing firm or a new entrant. The new entrant may come in via a product developed through research and development, or through acquisition. For example, Texas Instruments entered the educational toys business through R&D, which led to development of their Speak and Spell product. Philip Morris entered the beer market by acquiring Miller Brewery Company.

The product lines offered can be grouped into three categories: a me-too product, an improved product, or a breakthrough product. A me-too product is similar to current offerings. One of many brands currently

---

[9]Bruce D. Henderson, "Understanding the Forces of Strategic and Natural Competition," *op. cit.*, p. 15.

available in the market, it offers no special advantage over the competing products. An improved product is one which, while not unique, is generally superior to many existing brands. A breakthrough product is an innovation, usually technical in nature, such as a digital watch or a color television set.

In the watch business, companies have traditionally competed by offering me-too products. Occasionally, a competitor came out with an improved product, as in the early 1960s when Bulova introduced the Caravelle line of watches, which were a little fancier and supposedly more accurate. Texas Instruments, however, entered the watch business via a breakthrough product, i.e., the digital watch.

Finally, the scope of a competing firm's activities may be limited or extensive. For example, PepsiCo may not worry if a regional chain of pizza parlors is established to compete against its Pizza Hut subsidiary. However, if Procter & Gamble were to enter the pizza restaurant business, PepsiCo would be concerned at the entry of such a strong and seasoned competitor.

Exhibit 4-1 illustrates various sources of competition with reference to liquid requirements of the human body. Let us analyze the competition here for the Procter & Gamble Company, assuming the company maintains interest in this field. Currently, the thrust of the market is to satisfy existing demand. An example of a product to satisfy latent demand would be a liquid that promotes weight loss; a liquid to prevent aging would be an example of a product to satisfy incipient demand.

The industries that currently offer products to quench customer thirst are the liquor, beer, wine, soft-drink, milk, coffee, tea, drinking water, and fruit-juice industries. A potential entrant, however, is mineral water. Looking just at the soft-drink industry, assuming that this is the field that interests Procter & Gamble the most, the majority of competitors offer me-too products (e.g., regular cola, diet cola, lemonade, and other fruit-based drinks). Recently, however, caffeine-free cola has been introduced by two major competitors, Coca-Cola Company and PepsiCo. A breakthrough in the form of a low-calorie, caffeine-free drink with a day's nutritional requirement is feasible.

The companies that currently compete in the regular cola market are Coca-Cola, Pepsi-Cola, Seven-Up, Dr. Pepper, and a few others. Among these, however, the first two have a major share of the cola market. Among the new entrants in the business, General Foods Corporation and Nestlé Company are the likely candidates (an assumption). The two principal competitors, Coca-Cola Company and PepsiCo, are large, multinational, multibusiness companies. This is the competitive arena where Procter & Gamble will have to fight if it enters the soft-drink business.

INTENSITY OF COMPETITION

The degree of competition in a market depends on the moves and countermoves of the various firms that are active in the market. Usually

EXHIBIT 4-1   Sources of Competition

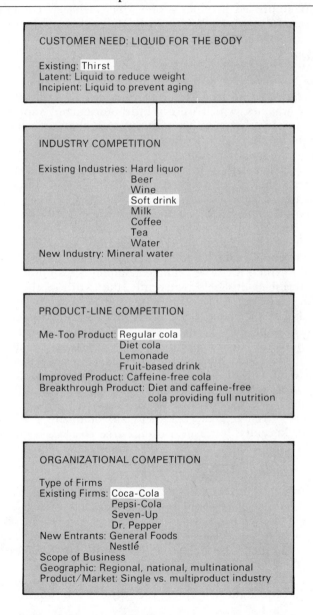

CUSTOMER NEED: LIQUID FOR THE BODY

Existing: Thirst
Latent: Liquid to reduce weight
Incipient: Liquid to prevent aging

INDUSTRY COMPETITION

Existing Industries: Hard liquor
                     Beer
                     Wine
                     Soft drink
                     Milk
                     Coffee
                     Tea
                     Water
New Industry: Mineral water

PRODUCT-LINE COMPETITION

Me-Too Product: Regular cola
                Diet cola
                Lemonade
                Fruit-based drink
Improved Product: Caffeine-free cola
Breakthrough Product: Diet and caffeine-free
                      cola providing full nutrition

ORGANIZATIONAL COMPETITION

Type of Firms
Existing Firms: Coca-Cola
               Pepsi-Cola
               Seven-Up
               Dr. Pepper
New Entrants: General Foods
              Nestlé
Scope of Business
Geographic: Regional, national, multinational
Product/Market: Single vs. multiproduct industry

it starts with one firm trying to achieve a favorable position by pursuing appropriate strategies. Since what is good for one firm may be harmful to the rival firms, however, the latter then respond with counterstrategies to protect their own interests.

Intense competitive activity may or may not be injurious to the industry. For example, while a price war may result in lower profit for all members of the industry, an advertising battle may increase demand, which would be mutually beneficial. Exhibit 4-2 lists the factors that affect the intensity of competition in the marketplace. In a given situation, a combination of factors determines the degree of competition.

Opportunity Potential. A promising market is likely to attract more firms to capitalize on the opportunity. As the number of firms interested in sharing the pie goes up, rivalry increases. An interesting example is the household computer market in early 1980s. Everyone from the mighty IBM to such unknowns in the field as Timex Watch Company wanted to participate. As firms started jockeying for position, the intensity of competition increased manifold. Texas Instruments, for example, drastically reduced the price of its 99 4/A home computer, leaving such firms as Apple Computer Company and Atari no choice but to slash their own prices.[10]

Ease of Entry. Where entry into an industry is relatively easy, many firms, including some marginal ones, are attracted to it. The long-standing, committed members of the industry, however, do not want the "outsiders" to break into their territory. Therefore these firms discourage potential entrants by adopting strategies that enhance competition.

Nature of Product. Where the products offered by different competitors are perceived by customers to be more or less similar, the firms are forced into price and, to a lesser degree, service competition. In such a situation the competition can be really severe.

EXHIBIT 4-2   Factors Contributing to Competitive Rivalry

Opportunity Potential
Ease of Entry
Nature of Product
Exit Barriers
Homogeneity of the Market
Industry Structure or Competitive Position of Firms
Commitment to the Industry
Feasibility of Technological Innovations
Scale Economies
Economic Climate
Diversity of Firms

---

[10]Bro Uttal, "Sudden Shake-Up in Home Computers," *Fortune*, July 11, 1983, p. 105.

Exit Barriers. For a variety of reasons, it may be difficult for a firm to get out of a business. Such reasons include the interrelationship of the business to other businesses of the firm; high investment in assets of the business for which there may not be an advantageous alternative use; high cost of discharging the commitments—for example, fixed labor contract, futures purchasing agreements—made on behalf of the business; top management's emotional attachment to that business; and government regulations prohibiting exit—as, for example, the requirement that a utility must serve all customers.

Homogeneity of the Market. When the entire market represents one large, homogeneous unit, the intensity of competition is much greater than when the market can be segmented. Even if the product sold is a commodity type, segmentation of the market is possible—for example, frequent buyers of the product as one segment, occasional buyers as another. But if the market is not suited to segmentation, firms must compete to serve it in a homogeneous manner, intensifying competition.

Industry Structure. When the number of firms active in a market is large, there is a good chance that one of the firms may aggressively seek an advantageous position. This would lead to intense competitive activity as the others retaliate. On the other hand, if there are only a few firms in the industry, usually there is little doubt about industry leadership. In this situation, care is taken not to irritate the leader since a resulting fight could be very costly.

Commitment to the Industry. When a firm has wholeheartedly committed itself to a business, it will do everything to hang on, even becoming the maverick who fearlessly makes moves without worrying about the impact either on the industry or on its own resources. Polaroid Corporation, for example, with its strong commitment to instant photography, must maintain its position in the field at any cost.

Feasibility of Technological Innovations. In industries where technological innovations are frequent, each firm likes to do its best to cash in while the technology lasts. This triggers greater competitive activity.

Scale Economies. Where economies realizable through large-scale operations are substantial, a firm will do all it can to achieve scale economies. This may lead the firm to aggressively compete for the market share, escalating pressures on other firms. A similar situation occurs when the business's fixed costs are high and the firm must spread them over a large volume. If capacity can only be added in large increments, the resulting excess capacity will also intensify competition.

Economic Climate. During depressed economic conditions and otherwise slow growth, competition is much more volatile as each firm tries to make the best of the situation.

Diversity of Firms. Firms active in a field over a long period come to acquire a kind of industry standard of behavior. But when an industry is invaded by new participants, they do not necessarily like to play the old game. The newcomers may have different strategic perspectives to pursue and may be willing to go to any lengths to achieve their goals without worrying about industry patterns. The Miller Brewery Company's unconventional marketing practices are a case in point. Miller, nurtured and guided by its parent, Philip Morris, segmented the market by introducing light beer in an industry that had hitherto considered beer to be a commodity-type product. When different cultures meet in the marketplace, competition can be fierce.

COMPETITIVE INTELLIGENCE

Competitive intelligence is the publicly available information on competitors, current and potential, which serves as an important input in formulating marketing strategy. No general orders an army to march without first fully knowing about the enemy's position and intentions. Likewise, before deciding on the competitive moves to make, a firm must be aware of the perspectives of its competitors. Competitive intelligence includes information beyond industry statistics and trade gossip. It involves close observation of competitors to learn what they do best and why, or where they goofed and why. No self-respecting business will admit to not doing an adequate job of scanning the competitive environment. What sets the outstanding companies apart, however, is that they watch their competition in such depth and with such dedication that, as a marketing executive once remarked, "The information on competitive moves reaches them before even the management of the competing company learns about them."

Three types of competitive intelligence may be distinguished: defensive, passive, and offensive intelligence.[11] Defensive intelligence, as the name suggests, is conducted to avoid being caught off balance. A deliberate attempt is made to gather information on the competition in a structured fashion and to keep track of moves that are relevant to the firm's business. Passive intelligence is ad hoc information gathered for a specific decision. A company may, for example, seek information on a competitor's sales compensation plan to devise its own compensation plan. Finally,

---

[11]David Montgomery and Charles Weinberg, "Toward Strategic Intelligence Systems," *Journal of Marketing*, Fall, 1979, pp. 41–52.

offensive intelligence is undertaken to identify new opportunities to capitalize upon. From a strategic perspective, offensive intelligence is the most relevant.

Strategic Usefulness of Competitive Intelligence

Such information as how competitors make, test, distribute, price, and promote their products can go a long way in developing a viable marketing strategy. The Ford Motor Company, for example, has an ongoing program for tearing down competitors' products to learn about their cost structure. Exhibit 4-3 summarizes the process followed at Ford. This competitive knowledge has helped Ford in its strategic moves in Europe. For example, from regularly tearing down the Leyland Mini (a small truck), the company concluded that (a) Leyland was not making money on the Mini at its current price, and (b) Ford should not enter the Mini market at the current price level. Based on these conclusions, Ford was able to arrive at a firm strategic decision not to assemble the Mini.

The following example compares two companies that sought the

**EXHIBIT 4-3   Ford Motor Company's Competitive Product Tear-Down
Process**

---

1. **Purchase the product.** The high cost of product tear-down, particularly for a carmaker, gives some indication of the value successful competitors place on the knowledge they gain.
2. **Tear the product down—literally.** First, every removable component is unscrewed or unbolted; then rivets are undone; finally, individual spot welds are broken.
3. **Reverse-engineer the product.** While the competitor's car is being dismantled, detailed drawings of parts are made and parts lists are assembled, together with analyses of the production processes that were evidently involved.
4. **Build up costs.** Parts are costed out in terms of make-or-buy, the variety of parts used in a single product and the extent of common assemblies across model ranges. Among the most important facts to be established in a product tear-down, obviously, are the number and variety of components and the number of assembly operations. The costs of the processes are then built up from both direct labour requirements and overheads (often vital to an understanding of competitor cost structures).
5. **Establish economies of scale.** Once the individual cost elements are known, they can be put together with the volume of cars produced by the competitor, and with the total numbers of people he employs, to develop some fairly reliable guides to his economies of scale. Having done this, Ford can calculate model-run lengths and volumes needed to achieve, first, break-even and then profit.

Source: Robin Leaf, "How to Pick Up Tips from Your Competitors," *Director*, February, 1978, p. 60.

opportunity to enter the automatic dishwasher market at about the same time. One of the companies did a superior job of learning from the competition and came out on top; the other ignored the competition, floundered, and eventually abandoned the field.

When the chief executive of the first company, a British company, learnt from his marketing department about the market growth potential and current competitors' shares, he lost no time setting up an R&D project to develop a suitable machine.

Finding little useful information available on dishwasher design, the R&D director decided to begin by investigating the basic mechanics of the dishwashing process. Accordingly, he set up a series of pilot projects to evaluate the cleaning performance of different jet configurations, the merits of alternative washing-arm designs, and the varying results obtained with different types and quantities of detergent on different washing loads. At the end of a year he had amassed a great deal of useful knowledge. He also had a pilot machine running that cleansed dishes well, and a design concept for a production version. But considerable development work was still needed before the prototype could be declared a satisfactory basis for manufacture.

To complicate matters, management had neglected to establish effective linkages among the company's three main functions—marketing, technology and production. So it was not until the technologists had produced the prototype and design concepts that marketing and production began asking for revisions and suggesting new ideas—further delaying the development of a marketable product.

So much for the first company, with its fairly typical traditional response to market opportunities. The second company, which happened to be Japanese, started with the same marketing intelligence but responded in very different fashion.

First, it bought three units of every available competitive dishwasher. Next, management formed four special teams: (1) a product test group of marketing and technical staff; (2) a design team of technologists and production people; (3) a distribution team of marketing and production staff; and (4) a field team of production staff.

The product test group was given one of each competitive model and asked to evaluate their performance: dishwashing effectiveness, ease of use, and reliability (frequency and cause of breakdown).

The remaining two units of each competitive model were given to the design team of technologists and production people, who stripped down one of each pair to determine the number and variety of parts, the cost of each part and the ease of assembly. The remaining units were stripped down to "life-test" each component, to identify design improvements and potential sources of supply; and to develop a comprehensive picture of the competitors' technology. Meanwhile, the distribution team was evaluating each competitor's sales and distribution system (numbers of outlets, product availability and service offered), and the field team was investigating the competitors' factories and evaluating their production facilities in terms of cost of labour, cost of supplies, and plant productivity.

All this took a little less than a year. At the end of that time, the

Japanese still knew a lot less than their UK rivals about the physics and chemistry of dishwashing, but the knowledge developed by their business teams had put them far ahead. In two more months they had designed a product that out-performed the best of the competition, yet would cost 30 per cent less to build, based on a preproduction prototype and production process design. They also had a marketing plan for introducing the new dishwasher on the Japanese domestic market before taking it overseas. This plan positioned the product relative to competition and defined the distribution system requirements in terms of stocking and service levels needed to meet the expected production rate. Finally, the Japanese had prepared detailed plans for building a new factory, establishing supply contracts and training the labour force.

The denouement of this story is what one might expect: the competitive Japanese manufacturer brought its new product to market two years ahead of the more traditionally-minded British manufacturer, and achieved its planned market share ten weeks later. The traditional company steadily lost money and eventually dropped out of the market.[12]

Knowing the Competition

Knowledge about the competition may be gained by raising the following questions. The answer to each question requires systematic probing and data gathering on different aspects of competition:

—Who is the competition—now? Five years from now?
—What are the strategies, objectives, and goals of major competitors?
—How important is a specific market to each competitor and what is the level of its commitment?
—What are the competitors' relative strengths and limitations?
—What weaknesses make the competitor vulnerable?
—What changes are competitors likely to make in their future strategies?
—So what? What will be the effects on the industry, the market and our strategy of all the competitors' strategies?[13]

The following procedure may be adopted to review competition:

1. Recognize key competitors in market segments in which the company is active. Presumably, a product will be positioned to serve one or more market segments. In each segment there may be different competitors to reckon with; an attempt should be made to recognize all important competitors in each seg-

---

[12]Robin Leaf, "How to Pick Up Tips from Your Competitors," *Director*, February, 1980, pp. 61–62.

[13]Michael G. Allen, "Strategic Planning with a Competitive Focus," *The McKinsey Quarterly*, Autumn, 1978, p. 6.

ment. If the number of competitors is excessive, it is sufficient to limit the consideration to the first three competitors. Each competitor may be briefly profiled to indicate total corporate proportion.

2. Analyze the track record of each competitor in terms of sales, profits, growth, and share. Performance of a competitor can be measured with reference to a number of criteria. As far as marketing is concerned, sales growth, market share, and profitability are the important measures of success. Thus, a review of each competitor's sales growth, market share, and profitability for the past several years will be desirable. In addition, any ad hoc reasons which bear upon a competitor's performance should be noted. For example, a competitor may have lined up some business, in the nature of a windfall from Saudi Arabia, without making any strategic moves to secure the business. Such events should be duly pointed out. Occasionally a competitor may intentionally pad up the result to reflect good performance at year end. Such tactics should be noted too. Rothschild advises the following:

> To make it really useful, you must probe how each participant keeps its books and records its profits. Some companies stress earnings; others report their condition in such a way as to delay the payment of taxes; still others bookkeep to increase cash availability.
>
> These measurements are important because they may affect the company's ability to procure financing and attract people as well as influence stockholders' and investors' satisfaction with current management.[14]

3. Study how satisfied each competitor appears to be with its performance. To study this question, reference will have to be made to the objective(s) each competitor has for the product. If the results are in concert with the expectations of the firm's management and stakeholders, the competitor will be satisfied. A satisfied competitor is most likely to follow the current successful strategy. On the other hand, if the results as exhibited by the track record are at odds with management expectations, the competitor is most likely to come out with a new strategy.

4. Probe each competitor's marketing strategy. The strategy of each competitor can be inferred from the game plans (i.e., different moves in the area of product, price, promotion, and distribution) which are pursued to achieve the objective. Information on the game plans will be available partly from published stories on the competitor and partly from the company salespeo-

---

[14]William E. Rothschild, *Putting It All Together* (New York: AMACOM, 1976), p. 85.

ple in contact with the competitor's customers and salespeople.

To clarify the point, consider a competitor in the small appliances business who spends heavily for consumer advertising and sells products mainly through discount stores. From this brief description it will be safe to conclude that as a matter of strategy, the competitor desires to establish the brand in the mass market through the discounters. In other words, the competitor is trying to reach customers who would like to buy a reputable brand at discount prices and hopes to make money by creating a large sales base.

5. Analyze the current and future resources and competencies of each competitor. In order to study a competitor's resources and competencies, the first step is to designate the broad areas of concern: facilities and equipment, personnel skills, organizational capabilities, and management capabilities are the categories established in the checklist in Exhibit 4-4. Each area may then be examined generally with reference to different functional areas (i.e., general management and finance, research and development, operations, and especially marketing). In the area of finance, availability of a large credit line would be a strength under "management capabilities." Owning a warehouse and refrigerated trucks is a marketing strength under "facilities and equipment." With the use of the checklist, an attempt should be made to specifically pinpoint those strengths which one's competitor can use to pursue goals against one's firm and other firms in the market. Simultaneously, areas in which the competitor looks particularly vulnerable should also be noted. The purpose here is not to get involved in a ritualistic, detailed account of each competitor, but to demarcate those aspects which may account for substantial difference in performance.

6. Predict the future marketing strategy of each competitor. The above competitive analysis provides enough information to make predictions concerning the future strategic directions which each competitor may pursue. The prediction, however, must be made qualitatively, using management consensus. The use of management consensus as the basic means for developing forecasts is based on the presumption that, by virtue of their experience in gauging market trends, executives should be able to make some credible predictions about each competitor's behavior in the future. A senior member of the marketing research staff may be assigned the task of soliciting executive opinions and consolidating the information into specific predictions on the moves competitors are likely to make in the future. Management consensus may, however, be systematized to a certain extent by using the delphi technique, described in Chapter 17. To summarize the method briefly, the executive in charge of

the product develops perspectives on the future strategy of each competitor. Then the marketing researcher presents these predictions to a panel of marketing executives who presumably are familiar with the industry-wide marketing of the product. Their opinions are then used to refine the predictions made by the product executive.

7. Assess the impact of competitive strategy on the company's product/market. The delphi technique discussed above can also be used to specify the impact of competitive strategy. Here again, the product executive must first analyze the impact using as a basis competitive information and his or her experiences on the job. Thereafter, the consensus of a larger group of executives can be obtained on the impact analysis performed by the product executive.

Needless to say, an analysis of impact using the delphi technique will be expensive and time-consuming. The amount of money and time that can be devoted to analyze such matters will depend on the strategic importance of the product.

Sources of Competitive Information

Essentially, three sources of competitive information may be distinguished: (a) what competitors say about themselves; (b) what others say about them; and (c) what the employees of the firm engaged in competitive analysis have observed and learned about competitors. Information from the first two sources, as shown in Exhibit 4-5, becomes available through public documents, trade associations, government, and investors. Take, for example, the information from government sources. Under the Freedom of Information Act, a great amount of information can be obtained at low cost.

As far as information from its own sources is concerned, the company should develop a structured program to gather competitive information. First, a tear-down program like Ford's (Exhibit 4-3) may be undertaken. Second, salespeople may be trained to carefully gather and provide information on competition, using such sources as customers, distributors, dealers, and competitors' former salespeople.[15] Third, senior marketing people should be encouraged to call on customers and speak to them in depth. Such contacts should provide valuable information on competitors' products and services. Fourth, other people in the company who happen to have some knowledge of competitors should be encouraged to channel that information to an appropriate office.

---

[15]Robert Hershey, "Commercial Intelligence on a Shoestring," *Harvard Business Review*, September–October, 1980, p. 22.

EXHIBIT 4-4   Checklist for Competitive Strengths and Competencies

	FACILITIES AND EQUIPMENT	PERSONNEL SKILLS	ORGANIZATIONAL CAPABILITIES	MANAGEMENT CAPABILITIES
General Management & Finance				
R&D				
Operations				
Marketing	Warehousing Retail outlets Sales offices Service offices Transportation equipment Training facilities for sales staff	Door-to-door selling Retail selling Wholesale selling Direct industry selling Department of Defense selling Cross-industry	Direct sales Distributor chain Retail chain Consumer service organization Industrial service organization Department of Defense	Industrial marketing Consumer merchandising Department of Defense marketing State and municipality marketing Well-informed and receptive management

Data processing equipment	selling	product support	Large customer base
	Applications engineering	Inventory distribution and control	Decentralized control
	Advertising	Ability to make quick response to customer requirements	Favorable public image
	Sales promotion	Ability to adapt to socio-political upheavals in the marketplace	Future orientation
	Servicing	Loyal set of customers	Ethical standards
	Contract administration	Cordial relations with media and channels	
	Sales analysis	Flexibility in all phases of corporate life	
	Data analysis	Consumer financing	
	Forecasting	Discount policy	
	Computer modeling	Teamwork	
	Product planning	Product quality	
	Background of people		
	Corporate culture		

Source: Adapted, by permission of the publisher, from H. Igor Ansoff, *Corporate Strategy* (New York: McGraw-Hill Book Co., 1965), pp. 98–99.

EXHIBIT 4-5   Sources of Competitive Information

	PUBLIC	TRADE PROFES-SIONALS	GOVERN-MENT	INVESTORS
What competitors say about themselves	• Advertising • Promotional materials • Press releases • Speeches • Books • Articles • Personnel changes • Want ads	• Manuals • Technical papers • Licenses • Patents • Courses • Seminars	• SEC reports • FIC • Testimony • Lawsuits • Antitrust	• Annual meetings • Annual reports • Prospectuses • Stock/bond issues
What others say about them	• Books • Articles • Case studies • Consultants • Newspaper reporters • Environmental groups • Consumer groups • Unions • "Who's Who" • Recruiting firms	• Suppliers/vendors • Trade press • Industry study • Customers • Subcontractors	• Lawsuits • Antitrust • State/federal agencies • National plans • Government programs	• Security analyst reports • Industry studies • Credit reports

Source: Adapted, by permission of the publisher, from "Competitor Analysis: The Missing Link in Strategy," by William E. Rothschild, *Management Review*, July, 1979, p. 27. © AMACOM, a division of American Management Associations, New York. All rights reserved.

Organization for Competitive Intelligence

Competitive activities can be monitored in-house or assigned to an outside firm. Usually, companies combine the two sources, depending partly on their own people to scan the competitive environment and partly on external help.

Within the organization, competitive information should be acquired both at the corporate level and at the SBU level. At the corporate level competitive intelligence is concerned with competitors' investment strengths and priorities. At the SBU level, the major interest is in marketing strategy, i.e., the pricing, product, distribution, and promotion strategies that a competitor is likely to pursue. The true payoff of competitive intelligence comes from the SBU review.

Organizationally, the competitive intelligence task can be assigned to an SBU strategic planner; a marketing person within the SBU, who may be a marketing research or a product/market manager; or to a staff person. Whoever is given the task of gathering competitive intelligence should be allowed adequate time and money to do a thorough job.

As far as outside help is concerned, there are three main types of organizations that may be hired to gather competitive information. First, many marketing research firms (e.g., A. C. Nielsen, Frost and Sullivan, SRI International, Predicasts) provide different types of competitive information, some on a regular basis and others on an ad hoc arrangement. Second, clipping services scan newspapers, financial journals, trade journals, and business publications for articles concerning designated competitors and make copies of relevant clippings for their clients. Third, different brokerage firms specialize in gathering information on various industries. Arrangements may be made with the brokerage firms to have regular access to their information on a particular industry.

SEEKING COMPETITIVE ADVANTAGE

To outperform competitors and to grow despite them, a company must understand why competition prevails, why firms attack, and how firms respond. Insights into competitors' perspectives can be gained by undertaking two types of analysis: industry and competitive. Industry analysis assesses the attractiveness of a market based on its economic structure. Competitive analysis indicates how every firm in a particular market is likely to perform given the structure of the industry.

Industry Analysis

Every industry has a few peculiar characteristics of its own. These characteristics are bound by time and thus are subject to change. We may call them the dynamics of the industry. No matter how hard a company tries, if it fails to fit into the dynamics of the industry, ultimate success may be difficult to achieve.

An example of how the perspectives of an entire industry may change over time is provided by the cosmetics industry. The cosmetics business has traditionally been run according to a seat-of-the-pants method with ultimate dependence on the marketing genius of the inventors. In the 1970s a variety of pressures began to engulf the industry. The regulatory climate became tougher. Consumers became more demanding and unpredictable. Inflationary economic conditions and rising costs made profits smaller. Many leading companies were acquired by large corporations. For example, Eli Lilly bought Elizabeth Arden, Squibb acquired Lanvin-Charles of the Ritz, Pfizer got Coty, Norton Simon added Max Factor, Colgate-Palmolive bought Helena Rubinstein, and British-American Tobacco scooped up Germaine Monteil. These changes have made competition in the industry fierce. Capital investment in the industry is small, but inventory and distribution costs are extremely high, partly because of the number of shades and textures in each product line. For example, nail polish and lipstick have to be available in over 50 different shades.

The cosmetics industry has gone through a tremendous change since the 1950s and 1960s. In those days, success in the industry depended on having a glamorous product. As has been observed, Revlon was manufacturing lipstick in its factories, but what it was selling was beautiful lips. In the 1970s, however, success rested on such nuts-and-bolts matters as securing distribution to achieve specific objectives in sales, profit, and market share. Basic inventory and financial controls, budgeting, and planning are now utilized to the fullest extent to cut costs and waste. This type of shift in direction and style in the industry may have important ramifications for marketing strategy.[16]

Exhibit 4-6 provides a checklist of items which may be examined to get an understanding of the dynamics of industry. Basically considered here are:

1. Scope of competitors' business (i.e., location and number of industries)
2. New entrants in the industry
3. Other current and potential offerings which appear to serve similar functions or satisfy the same need
4. Industry's ability to raise capital, attract people, avoid government probing, and compete effectively for the consumers' dollars
5. Industry's current practices (i.e., price setting, warranties, distribution structure, after-sales service, etc.)
6. Trends in volume, costs, prices, and return on investment, compared with other industries
7. Industry profit economics: key factors determining profits, such as volume, materials, labor, capital investment, market penetration, and dealer strength
8. Ease of entry into the industry, including capital investment
9. Relationship between current and future demand and manufacturing capacity, and its probable effects on prices and profits
10. Effect of integration, both forward and backward
11. Effect of cyclical swings in the relationship between supply and demand

---

[16]"Management Realists in the Glamour World of Cosmetics," *Business Week*, November 29, 1976, p. 42.

EXHIBIT 4-6   Industry Dynamics Checklist

Classification of Competitors

1. List all of your current major competitors and then classify them in terms of the following categories: United States, foreign, international, multinational; single industry or multi-industry.
2. Anticipate changes which you think may take place over the next five to ten years.
3. What are the positive (opportunities) and negative (threats) implications of these changes?

New Entries

Draw a diagram depicting:

1. Competitors in other geographic regions or other segments who do not currently, but may decide to, compete in your markets or segments.
2. Customers served by your industry. Note those who may want to move backwards, and consider the reasons why such a move may make sense.
3. Suppliers to your industry; note movement and reasons.
4. Companies on the periphery—those who serve the same customers with different but related products. This might include other pieces of equipment related to yours or equipment that would be included in a broader definition of the market. It is impossible to list all related items, but those of closest proximity should be included.
5. Any other companies that might be enticed to serve your customers or markets. This should include conglomerates or diversified companies that might be attracted by the growth, size, or profitability of your markets. Choose the most likely new entries and quiz yourself about what you know about them and their strategies.

Substitutions and Innovations

1. List other products or services that provide the same or a similar function. Record the percentage of total market sales for each substitute product.
2. Anticipate product innovations which can replace or reduce the sales of your products. When do you think these products will be commercially feasible? (Note: Information about potentially competitive products can be found by searching the U.S. Patent Office or foreign patent offices.)

Other Forms of Competition

1. Think about your industry's and product's ability to compete effectively for the consumers' dollar and how this may be modified in the future.
2. Identify the type of financial resources required, and evaluate the ability of the industry to obtain capital and at what cost.
3. Record the image your industry has and how this can impact on its ability to attract the quantity and quality of people it requires now and in the planning period. There is also a cost dimension to this aspect of competition, since people can be bought.

Source: William E. Rothschild, *Putting It All Together* (New York: AMACOM, 1976), pp. 80–81.

To formulate marketing strategy, a company should determine the relevance of each of the above factors in its industry and the position it occupies with respect to competitors. An attempt should be made to highlight the dynamics of the company in the industry environment. It should be said here that the study of dynamics does not mean making projections of industry growth rates and assessing the likelihood that the company will match the industry's growth pattern, since the fortunes of a particular company may not necessarily be related to the overall growth of its industry. An alternative way to analyze an industry is to apply the Porter model described below.

Porter's Model of Industry Structure Analysis

Porter's five-factor model for industry analysis is shown in Exhibit 4-7.[17] The model identifies five key structural features that determine the strength of the competitive forces within an industry and hence industry profitability.

As shown in this model, the *degree of rivalry* among different firms is a function of the number of competitors, industry growth, assets intensity, product differentiation, and exit barriers. Among these variables, the number of competitors and industry growth are the most influential. Further, industries with high fixed costs tend to be more competitive since the competing firms are forced to cut price to enable them to operate at capacity. Differentiation, both real and perceived, among the competing offerings, however, lessens rivalry. Finally, difficulty of exit from an industry intensifies competition.

Threat of entry into the industry by new firms is likely to enhance competition. There are, however, several barriers that make it difficult to seek entry into an industry. There are two cost-related entry barriers: economies of scale and absolute cost advantage. Economies of scale require potential entrants either to establish high levels of production or to accept a cost disadvantage. Absolute cost advantage is enjoyed by firms with proprietary technology or favorable access to raw materials and by firms with production experience. In addition, high capital requirements, high switching costs (i.e., the cost to a buyer of changing suppliers), limited access to distribution channels, and government policy can act as entry barriers.

Substitute products that serve essentially the same function as the industry products are another source of competition. Since substitute products place a ceiling on the prices that firms can charge, they affect the industry potential. The threat posed by a substitute also depends on its long-term price/performance trend relative to the industry's product.

---

[17]See Michael E. Porter, *Competitive Strategy* (New York: The Free Press, 1980), and "How Competitive Forces Shape Strategy," *Harvard Business Review*, March–April, 1979, pp. 137–145.

EXHIBIT 4-7 Porter's Model of Industry Competition

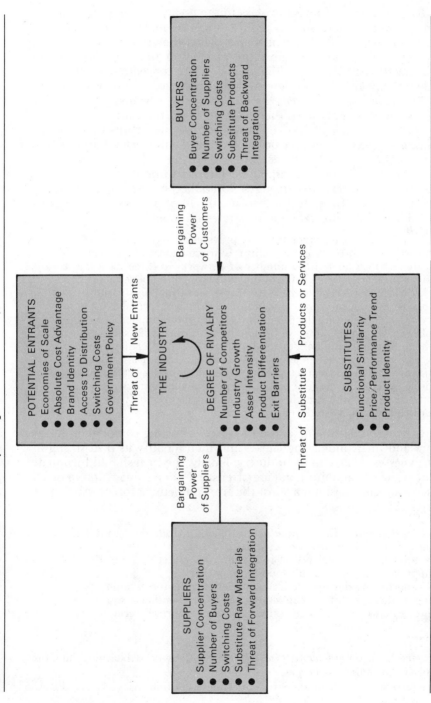

Source: Adapted with permission of The Free Press, a Division of Macmillan, Inc., from *Competitive Strategy* by Michael E. Porter, p. 4. Copyright © 1980 by The Free Press.

Bargaining power of buyers refers to the ability of the industry's customers to force the industry to reduce prices or increase features, thus bidding away profits. Buyers gain power when they have choices—when their needs can be met by a substitute product or the same product offered by another supplier. In addition, high buyer concentration, the threat of backward integration, and low switching costs add to buyer power.

Bargaining power of suppliers is the degree to which suppliers of the industry's raw materials have the ability to force the industry to accept higher prices or reduced service, thus affecting the profits. The factors influencing supplier power are the same as those influencing buyer power. In this case, however, industry members act as buyers.

These five forces of competition interact to determine the attractiveness of an industry. The strongest forces become dominant in determining industry profitability and become the focal points of strategy formulation. The following example illustrates the point:

> The network television industry provides an excellent example of the way these forces affect an industry's profitability. Government regulations which limited the number of networks to three have had a great influence on the profile of the industry. This impenetrable entry barrier created weak buyers (advertisers), weak suppliers (writers, actors, etc.) and a very profitable industry. However, several exogenous events are influencing the power of the buyers and suppliers. The suppliers have gained power with the advent of cable television because the number of customers to whom the artists can offer their services has increased rapidly. In addition, as cable television firms reduce the size of the network market, the advertisers may find substitute advertising media more cost effective. In sum, while the industry is still very attractive and profitable, the changes in its structure imply that future profitability may be reduced.[18]

A firm should first diagnose the forces affecting competition in the industry and their underlying causes and then identify its own strengths and weaknesses relative to the industry. Finally, the firm should formulate its strategy, which amounts to taking offensive or defensive action in order to achieve a secure position against the five competitive forces. According to Porter this involves:

> —Positioning the firm so that its capabilities provide the best defense against the existing array of competitive forces;
> —Influencing the balance of forces through strategic moves, thereby improving the firm's relative position; or
> —Anticipating shifts in the factors underlying the forces and responding to them, hopefully exploiting change by choosing a strategy appropriate to the new competitive balance before rivals recognize it.[19]

---

[18]*Understanding the Competition: A Practical Guide to Competitive Analysis* (Arlington, VA: Michael M. Kaiser Associates, Inc., no date), p. 96.

[19]Michael E. Porter, "Note on the Structural Analysis of Industries," Harvard Business School Case Service, 1975, p. 22.

Take, for example, the U.S. blue jeans industry.[20] In the 1970s most firms except for Levi Strauss and Blue Bell, maker of Wrangler Jeans, took low profits. The situation can be explained with reference to industry structure. The extremely low entry barriers allowed almost 100 small jeans manufacturers to join the competitive ranks; all that was needed was some equipment, an empty warehouse, and some relatively low-skilled labor. All such firms competed on price.

Further, these small firms had little control over raw materials pricing. The production of denim is in the hands of about four major textile companies, so no one small manufacturer was important to them—jeans makers had to take their price or leave it. Thus suppliers (of denim) had a strong bargaining power. Store buyers also were in a strong bargaining position. Most of the jeans sold in the United States are handled by relatively few buyers in major store chains. As a result, a small manufacturer basically must sell for the price the buyers want to pay, or they will easily find someone else who will.

But then, along came Jordache, creating designer jeans with heavy up-front advertising. It designed a new way to compete that changed the industry forces. First, it significantly lowered the bargaining power of its customers (i.e., store buyers) by creating strong consumer preference. The buyer had to meet Jordache's price rather than the other way around. Second, emphasis on the designer's name created significant entry barriers.

In summary, Jordache formulated a strategy that neutralized many of the structural forces surrounding the industry and gave itself a competitive advantage.

Competitive Analysis

Competitive analysis examines the comparative advantage of competitors within a given market. Two types of comparative advantage may be distinguished: structural and response.[21] *Structural* advantages are those built into the business. For example, a manufacturing plant in South Korea may, because of low labor costs, have a built-in advantage over another firm. *Responsive* advantages refer to positions of comparative advantage built over time as a result of certain decisions. This type of advantage is based on leveraging the strategic phenomena which are at work in the business.

Every business is a unique mixture of strategic phenomena. For example, in the soft-drink industry a unit of investment in advertising may lead to a unit of market share. In contrast, the highest-volume producer in the electronics industry is usually the lowest-cost producer. In industrial

---

[20]Ennlus E. Bergsma, "In Strategic Phase, Line Management Needs 'Business' Research, Not Market Research," *Marketing News*, January 21, 1983, pp. 21–22.
[21]Peter R. Sawers, "How to Apply Competitive Analysis to Strategic Planning," *Marketing News*, March 18, 1983, p. 11.

product businesses, up to a point, sales and distribution costs tend to decline as the density of sales coverage (the number of salespeople in the field) increases. Beyond this optimum point, costs tend to rise dramatically. Cost is only one way of achieving a competitive advantage. In the business system, there are different things a firm may do to score over competition. For example, a company may find distribution through dealers giving it a competitive leverage. Another company may find seeking product differentiation strategically more desirable.

In order to survive, any company, regardless of size, must be different in one of two dimensions. It must have lower costs than its direct head-to-head competitors, or it must have unique values for which its particular customers will pay more. Competitive distinctiveness is essential to survival. Competitive distinctiveness can be achieved in different ways: (a) by concentrating on particular market segments; (b) by offering products which differ from, rather than mirror, the competing products; (c) by using alternative distribution channels and manufacturing processes; and (d) by employing selective pricing and fundamentally different cost structures. Presented below are three analytical tools that may be used by a company seeking a position of competitive advantage/distinction: (a) the business-system framework; (b) the experience curve; and (c) the customer value/utility curve.

Business-System Framework. Examination of the business system operating in an industry is useful in analyzing competitors and searching out innovative options for gaining a sustainable competitive advantage. It enables a firm to discover the sources of greatest economic leverage, i.e., stages in the system where it may build cost or investment barriers against competitors. The business-system framework may also be used to analyze a competitor's costs and to gain insights into the sources of a competitor's current advantage in either cost or economic value to the customer.

Exhibit 4-8 depicts the business system of a manufacturing company. At each stage of the system, i.e., technology, product design, manufacturing, and so on, a company may have several options. These options are often interdependent. For example, product design will partially constrain the choice of raw materials. Likewise, the perspectives of physical distribution will affect manufacturing capacity and location, and vice versa. At each stage a variety of questions may be raised the answers to which provide insights into strategic alternatives a company may consider. Such questions are: How are we doing this now? How are our competitors doing it? What is better about their way? About ours? How else might it be done? How would these options affect our competitive position? If we change what we are doing at this stage, how would the other stages be affected? Answers to these questions reveal the sources of leverage to gain competitive advantage (see Exhibit 4-9).

The use of the business-system framework may be illustrated with reference to Savin Business Machines Corporation. In 1975, this company with $63 million in revenues was a minor factor in the U.S. office-copier

EXHIBIT 4-8 Business System of a Manufacturing Company

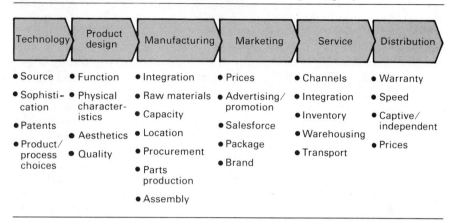

Technology	Product design	Manufacturing	Marketing	Service	Distribution
• Source	• Function	• Integration	• Prices	• Channels	• Warranty
• Sophistication	• Physical characteristics	• Raw materials	• Advertising/promotion	• Integration	• Speed
• Patents	• Aesthetics	• Capacity	• Salesforce	• Inventory	• Captive/independent
• Product/process choices	• Quality	• Location	• Package	• Warehousing	• Prices
		• Procurement	• Brand	• Transport	
		• Parts production			
		• Assembly			

Source: Roberto Buaron, "New-Game Strategies," *The McKinsey Quarterly*, Spring, 1981, p. 34. Reprinted by permission of the publisher.

market. The market was obviously dominated by Xerox, with domestic copier revenues approaching $2 billion. Xerox at that time accounted for almost 80 percent of the plain-paper copiers in the United States. In November, 1975, Savin introduced a plain-paper copier to serve customers who wanted low- and medium-speed machines (i.e., those producing fewer than 40 copies per minute). Two years later Savin's revenues crossed $200 million annually; the company had captured 40 percent of all new units installed in the low-end plain-paper copier market in the United States. Savin managed to earn a 64 percent return on equity while maintaining a conservative 27 percent debt ratio. Meanwhile Xerox, which in 1974 had

EXHIBIT 4-9 Sources of Economic Leverage in the Business System

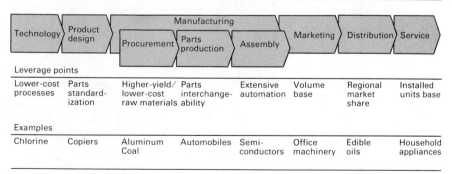

		Manufacturing					
Technology	Product design	Procurement	Parts production	Assembly	Marketing	Distribution	Service

Leverage points

Lower-cost processes	Parts standardization	Higher-yield/lower-cost raw materials	Parts interchangeability	Extensive automation	Volume base	Regional market share	Installed units base

Examples

Chlorine	Copiers	Aluminum Coal	Automobiles	Semiconductors	Office machinery	Edible oils	Household appliances

Source: Roberto Buaron, "New-Game Strategies," *The McKinsey Quarterly*, Spring, 1981, p. 35. Reprinted by permission of the publisher.

accounted for more than half of the low-end market, saw its share shrink
to 10 percent in 1978. What reasons may be ascribed to Savin's success
against the mighty Xerox? Through careful analysis of the plain-paper
copier business system, Savin combined the various options feasible at different stages of the system to develop a competitive advantage to successfully confront Xerox. As shown in Exhibit 4-10, by combining a different technology with different manufacturing, distribution, and service
approaches, it had been able to offer business customers, at some sacrifice
in copy quality, a much cheaper machine than the competitive machines.
The option of installing several cheaper machines in key office locations
in lieu of a single large, costly, centrally located unit proved attractive to
many large customers.

At virtually every stage of the business system, Savin took a radically
different approach. First, it used a low-cost technology which had been
avoided by the industry because it produced a lower-quality copy. Next,
its product design was based on low-cost standardized parts that were
available in volume from Japanese suppliers. Further, the company opted
for low-cost assembly in Japan. These business-system innovations per-

EXHIBIT 4-10   Plain-Paper Copier Strategy: Xerox vs. Savin

		Technology	Product design	Manu-facturing	Distribution channel	Terms/pricing	Service
XEROX	Choices	• Dry xerography	• Feature rich • High speed	• United States • Custom parts • Backward integrated	• Own sales force	• Lease emphasis	• Own technical service force
	Attributes	• High copy quality	• Complex • Relatively high failure rate	• Higher costs/prices	• Limited outreach to small accounts	• High fixed expense at low volume	• Good service but thin coverage?
SAVIN	Choices	• Liquid toner	• Modular • Low speed • Human factors engineer-ing	• Japan • Standard parts • Subcon-tractors	• Office supplies dealers	• Sales emphasis	• Dealers
	Attributes	• Medium quality • Reliability	• Reli-ability • Fool-proof	• Lower costs/prices	• Good coverage of small accounts	• One time capital cost—low expenses	• Better service response time for small accounts?

Source: Peter R. Sawers, "How to Apply Competitive Analysis to Strategic Planning," *Marketing News*, March 18, 1983, p. 11. Reprinted by permission
of the American Marketing Association.

mitted Savin to offer a copier of comparable reliability and acceptable quality for half the price of Xerox's equivalent model.[22]

The Experience Curve. Competitor cost is one of the most fundamental, yet elusive, information needs of the producer attempting to develop a product strategy. Experience curve analysis provides a sound basis for estimating the cost positions of competitors. The experience curve, developed by the Boston Consulting Group, empirically demonstrates the relationship between an industry's cost and market experience. As shown in Exhibit 4-11, the curve plots experience, i.e., units of total accumulated volume, against cost or price per unit on a log-log scale. The curve for most industries depicts a linear relationship between the total *real* cost per unit and the total volume. The slope of the curve represents the percentage reduction in real costs with every doubling of cumulative experience. For example, if a doubling of cumulative experience causes total real costs per unit to drop from $100 to $90, then for the next doubling of cumulative experience the cost per unit will again be reduced by 10 percent, to $81. Chapter 17 discusses the experience curve and its construction procedure at length. Examined here is how experience curve analysis can be used to estimate the competitor's cost advantage/disadvantage.

Suppose, for illustrative purposes, that company A has constructed its own experience curve. The company is interested in estimating the cur-

EXHIBIT 4-11   The Experience Curve

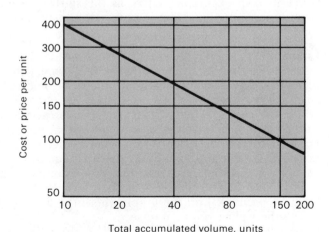

Total accumulated volume, units

---

[22]Roberto Buaron, "New-Game Strategies," *The McKinsey Quarterly*, Spring, 1981, pp. 24–40.

rent unit cost of a competitor, company B. If it is reasonable to assume that (a) A and B are equally cost-effective, i.e., they have the same cost-reduction rate or intensity with experience, and (b) they began producing the product at approximately the same time, then B's experience curve should be nearly identical to A's. Therefore, if A can assess B's current experience level, it can estimate B's current unit cost directly from its own experience curve.

If A and B have maintained their current market shares for some length of time, the ratio of their current experience levels will approximate the ratio of their market shares. If information on market share is available, B's current experience level can be estimated from the following formula:

$$\frac{\text{Market Share of B}}{\text{Market Share of A}} \quad * \quad \text{Experience of A}$$

This formula requires only the ratio of the market shares of the two producers. Consequently, if absolute shares are unknown but the relative shares of A and B can be assessed, the formula is equally applicable.

There may be reason for A to believe that B's cost reduction rate or intensity is significantly less than its own. This difference might be attributed to any number of factors: less-efficient management, failure to implement an industry technological advance, less-skilled labor force, lack of a captive raw material source, etc. In experience curve terms, B's slope would be less steep than A's.

If A can estimate (a) the time that B began to lose relative cost effectiveness, and (b) the extent of the difference in cost-reduction rates, A can again use its own experience curve as the starting point in estimating B's current unit cost. The following procedure may be utilized (see Exhibit 4-12):

1. Estimate B's experience level (E_1) at the time B became less cost-effective than A. If necessary, use the formula above, which relates B's experience level at that time to A's and to their relative market shares.
2. Locate the corresponding point (X_1) on A's experience curve and, from that, B's estimated unit cost at that time (C_1).
3. Locate E_2 on the experience axis, where E_2 equals E_1 times 2. Locate C_2 on the unit-cost axis, where C_2 equals C_1 times the quantity ($1 - $ B's intensity fraction). (For example, if E_1 is 500, C_1 is 10, and B's intensity is 10%, then E_2 is 1000 and C_2 is 9.) Find the point (X_2) on the graph where the lines up from E_2 and to the right from C_2 intersect.
4. Draw a line through X_1 and X_2. This is the estimated experience curve for B.
5. Estimate B's current experience level (E_3); locate the corresponding point on B's experience curve; and, from that, B's estimated current unit cost in *constant* dollars (C_3).

EXHIBIT 4-12

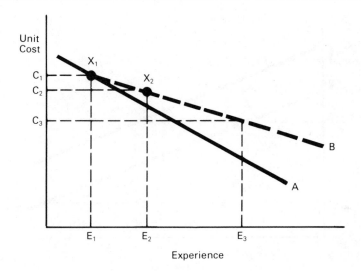

6. To transform the estimate to real dollars, multiply it by the projected deflator for the year.

The above procedure would also apply if B's intensity were assumed to be greater than A's.

The procedures presented thus far have assumed that A and B began business with the product at approximately the same time. With a further assumption that the producers' intensities are equal, it follows that their experience curves would be nearly identical.

However, if producer B had been a late starter in the industry, it is unlikely that its initial costs, *in constant dollars*, would have been as high as A's. Normally, some part of the effect on costs of the industry's past experience would have been immediately available to B.

The forces behind the experience effect might be broadly categorized into (a) technological advances, many of which would have been accessible to B, and (b) "learning" and "scale" factors, which have little transferability. Therefore, the magnitude of the reduction in initial cost would have been closely related to the relative importance of technology to the industry.

If A has been cost-effective, that is, has availed itself of the new technology, and has realized the full cost-reduction potential of its experience through "learning" and "scale," then its unit cost at the time B entered the market must have been lower than B's initial cost.

These concepts can be used by A to estimate B's current unit cost, following the procedure discussed below (see Exhibit 4-13):

EXHIBIT 4-13

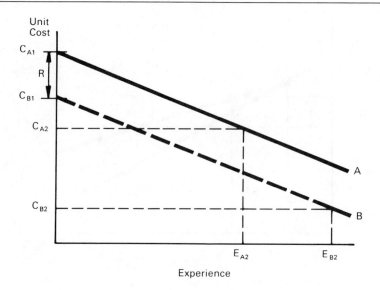

1. Estimate A's experience level (E_{A2}) at the time B entered the market. Locate E_{A2} on the experience axis and, from A's experience curve, determine B's corresponding unit cost at that time (C_{A2}).
2. Estimate the relative (percentage) importance of technology to cost reduction for the industry. Multiply this percentage by the quantity ($C_{A1} - C_{A2}$), where C_{A1} is A's initial unit cost. The result (R) is the estimated reduction in initial unit cost realized by B.
3. Subtract R from C_{A1} to obtain B's estimated initial constant-dollar unit cost (C_{B1}) on the unit-cost axis.
4. Draw a line through C_{B1} *parallel* to A's experience curve. This is the estimated experience curve for B.
5. Estimate B's current experience level (E_{B2}); locate the corresponding point on B's experience curve; and, from that, B's estimated current unit cost in constant dollars (C_{B2}).
6. To transform the estimate to real dollars, multiply it by the projected deflator for the year.

The Customer Value/Utility Curve. The customer value/utility curve is developed to compare the maximum number of different product features various customer segments are willing to pay for. The curve may be used to examine the perspectives of product/service offerings of different firms in the market. A firm may gain competitive advantage by aligning its product offered as close to the actual customer utility curve as is feasible. The point may be illustrated with reference to gasoline retailers. In 1960, the integrated oil companies believed that the customer would be willing to pay a price premium for gasoline if their service stations offered additional features including credit cards, windshield washes, oil checks, etc. The independent gasoline retailers, on the other hand, felt that the majority of the customers wanted inexpensive gasoline. As it turned out, the latter group had more accurately positioned the customer utility curve than had the integrated firms (see Exhibit 4-14). This forced the former to cut their prices to meet the challenge of the smaller gasoline vendors.

A utility curve may be generated by plotting the total number of product features against the cost/value of all features. The manufacturer's total cost rises linearly with each additional feature; the marginal cost of each feature is assumed to remain constant. However, the marginal value to the customer of each additional feature does not remain constant. Conceptually, the value of the first few features added to the basic product may be high, but thereafter the value of each additional feature begins to diminish, eventually reaching a point at which it costs the producer more to add a feature than it is worth to the customer. The intersection

EXHIBIT 4-14   Customer Value/Utility Curve

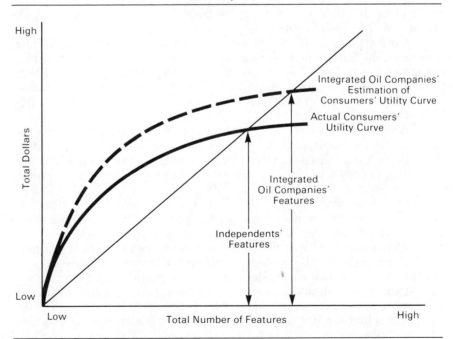

Source: *Understanding the Competition: A Practical Guide to Competitive Analysis* (Arlington, VA: Michael M. Kaiser Associates, Inc., no date), p. 85. Reprinted by permission.

of the two curves defines the point at which the producer should cease adding features. A competitor's deviation from the optimum point provides an opportunity for a firm to capitalize upon.

SUSTAINING COMPETITIVE ADVANTAGE[23]

A good strategist seeks not only to "win the hill, but hold on to it." In other words, a business should not only seek competitive advantage but also sustain it over the long haul. Sustaining competitive advantage requires erecting barriers against the competition. Barriers are based on competitive cost differentials and/or price or service differentials. In all cases a successful barrier allows higher margins than the competition. Further, a successful barrier must be sustainable and, in a practical sense, unbreachable by the competition; that is, it must cost the competition more to surmount than it costs the protected competitor to defend.

The nature of the barrier depends on the competitive economics of the business. A heavily advertised consumer product with a leading market share enjoys a significant cost barrier, and perhaps a price-realization barrier, against its competition. If a consumer product has, for example, twice the market share of its competition, it need spend only one-half the advertising dollar per unit to produce the same impact in the marketplace. It will always cost the competition more, per unit, to attack than it costs the leader to defend.

On the other hand, barriers cost money to erect and defend. The expense of the barrier may become an umbrella under which new forms of competition can grow. For example, while advertising is a barrier that protects a leading consumer brand from its other branded competitors, the cost of maintaining the barrier is an umbrella under which a private-label product may hide and grow.

A wide product line, large sales and service forces, and systems capabilities are all examples of major barriers. Each of these has a cost to erect and maintain. Each is effective against smaller competitors who are attempting to copy the leader but have less volume over which to amortize the barrier costs.

Each barrier, however, holds a protective umbrella over focused competitors. The competitor with a narrow product line faces fewer costs than the wide-line leader. The mail order house may live under the umbrella of costs associated with the large sales and service force of the leader. The "cherry picker" may produce components compatible with the systems of the leader without bearing the systems engineering costs.

Exhibit 4-15 shows the relationship between the barrier and umbrella strategies in sustaining competitive advantage. The best position in the system is high-barrier and low-umbrella. This is a product or business

---

[23]This section relies heavily on Sandra O. Moose, "Barriers and Umbrellas," in *Perspectives* (Boston: The Boston Consulting Group, 1980).

EXHIBIT 4-15   Strategies for Sustaining Competitive Advantage

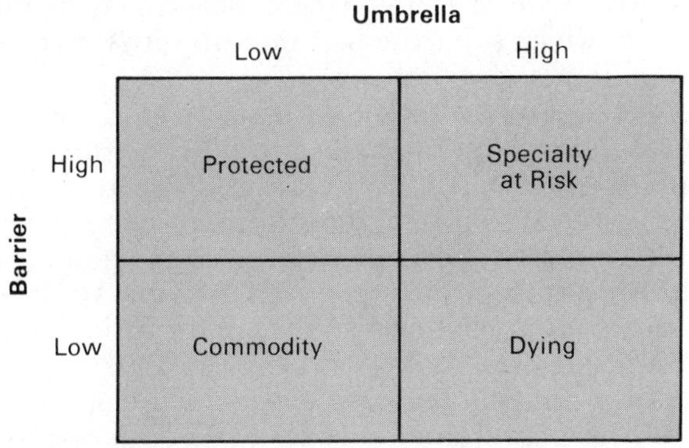

Umbrella

	Low	High
High	Protected	Specialty at Risk
Low	Commodity	Dying

(vertical axis label: **Barrier**)

Source: Sandra O. Moose, "Barriers and Umbrellas," *Perspectives* (Boston: The Boston Consulting Group, 1980). Reprinted by permission.

with a position strong enough so that the costs of maintaining the barrier are, on a per unit basis, insignificant. The low-barrier, low-umbrella quadrant is, by definition, a commodity without high profitability.

Most interesting is the high-barrier, high-umbrella quadrant. The business is protected by the existence of the barrier. At the same time, it is at risk because the cost of supporting the barrier is high. Profitability may be high, but the risk of competitive erosion, too, may be substantial. The marketplace issue is the tradeoff in consumer preferences for more service, quality, choice, or "image" versus lower prices from more narrowly focused competitors.

These businesses face profound decisions. Making no change in direction means continual threats from focused competition. Yet any change in spending to lower the umbrella means changing the nature of the competitive protection—that is, eroding the barrier.

Successful marketing strategy requires being aware of the size of the umbrella and continually testing whether to maintain investment to preserve or heighten the barrier or to withdraw investment to "cash out" as the barrier erodes.

SUMMARY

Competition is one of the strategic factors that affect marketing strategy formulation. Traditionally, marketers have considered competition as one of the uncontrollable variables to be reckoned with in developing the marketing mix. It is only in the last few years that the focus of business strategy has shifted to competition. It is becoming more and more evident that the chosen marketing strategy should be based on a competitive advantage to achieve sustained business success. To implement such a perspective, resources should be concentrated in those areas of competitive activity which offer the best opportunity for continuing profitability and sound investment returns.

There are two very different forms of competition: natural and strategic. Natural competition implies survival of the fittest in a given environment. In business terms, it means firms compete from very similar strategic positions, relying on operating differences to separate the successful from the unsuccessful. With strategic competition, on the other hand, the underlying strategy differences vis-à-vis market segments, product offerings, distribution channels, and manufacturing process become the paramount consideration.

Conceptually, competition may be examined from the viewpoint of economists, industrial organization theorists, and businesspeople. The major thrust of economic theories has centered on the model of perfect competition. Industrial organization emphasizes the industry environment (i.e., industry structure, conduct, and performance) as the key determinant of a firm's performance. There hardly exists a theoretical framework of competition from the viewpoint of businesspeople, other than the pioneering efforts of Bruce Henderson, whose hypotheses on competition are reproduced in the appendix at the end of this chapter.

Firms compete to satisfy customer needs which may be classified as existing, latent, or incipient. A firm may face competition from different sources, categorized as (a) industry competition, (b) product-line competition, and (c) organizational competition. The intensity of competition is determined by a combination of factors.

A firm needs a competitive intelligence system to keep track of various facets of its rivals' businesses. The system should include proper data gathering and analysis of each major competitor's current and future perspectives. Various sources of competitive information are identified, including what competitors say about themselves, what others say about them, and what a firm's own people have observed. To gain competitive advantage, i.e., to choose those product/market positions where victories are clearly attainable, two forms of analysis may be undertaken: industry analysis and competitive analysis. Porter's five-factor model is useful in industry analysis. Tools useful in competitive analysis are the business-system framework, the experience curve, and the customer value/utility curve.

DISCUSSION QUESTIONS

1. *Differentiate between natural and strategic competition. Give examples.*
2. *What are the basic elements of strategic competition? Are there any prerequisites to pursue strategic competition?*
3. *How do economists approach competition? Does this approach suffice for businesspeople?*

4. *What is the industrial organization viewpoint of competition?*
5. *What is the underlying thesis supporting Henderson's hypotheses on competition?*
6. *Identify, with examples, different sources of competition.*
7. *How does industry structure affect intensity of competition?*
8. *What are the major sources of competitive intelligence?*
9. *Briefly explain Porter's five-factor model of industry structure analysis.*

APPENDIX: HENDERSON'S HYPOTHESES ON COMPETITION

- All competitors who persist and survive have a unique advantage over all others. If they did not, then others would crowd them out. In biology this is known as Gause's Principle of Mutual Exclusion.
- The more similar competitors are to each other, the more severe their competition. This observation was made by Darwin in "The Origin of Species."
- If competitors are different and coexist, then each must have a distinct advantage over the other. Such an advantage can only exist if differences in the competitor's characteristics match differences in the environment that give those characteristics their relative value.
- Competitors that coexist must be in equilibrium. Such equilibrium can exist only if any change produces forces that tend to restore the conditions prior to the disturbance.
- If competitors must each have an advantage and each must match different environmental factors, then there must be a point or series of points where the advantage shifts from one competitor to the other. These points of no relative advantage define the "competitive segment" boundary.
- There must be as many significant variables or combinations of variables in the competitive environment as there are competitive survivors. If this were not true, then it would be impossible for some competitor to find a combination of factors that would outweigh the advantages of others in any part or segment of the environment and, therefore, permit survival for that competitor.
- If multiple competitors coexist, then any given pair of competitors must differ from any other possible pair by a different combination of characteristics or factors. Otherwise two or more of the competitors would be nearly identical and as a consequence, be conditionally unstable.
- Since each and every pair of competitors acts as a constraint on each other, then the equilibrium point between them constitutes a segment boundary. However, characteristically there are multiple simultaneous competitors.
- If a given competitor has multiple coexisting competitors, then each such competitor defines a sector of the "competitive segment" boundary. Wherever one such sector ends and another begins, all three are equal

and have no advantage over each other. However, any two of the three always constitute a constraint on the third.

- Any given competitor may have a large number of competitors, each of which defines a sector of the "competitive segment" and acts as a constraint. However, each sector of the "competitive segment" is defined by only one competitor.

- Failure to maintain a competitive segment and monopolize the advantage within that "competitive segment" is failure to have an advantage over any competitor. The eventual consequence must be extinction.

- Any change in the environment changes the factor weighting of environment characteristics and, therefore, shifts the boundaries of competitive equilibrium and "competitive segments." Competitors who can adapt best or fastest gain an advantage from environmental change.

- For virtually all competitors their critical environment constraint is their interface with other competitors. Therefore any change in the environment that affects any competitor will have consequences that require some degree of adaptation. This requires continual change and adaptation by all competitors merely to maintain relative position. This is the "Red Queen Syndrome" of Van Valen.

- Only in the harshest and most severe environment, where only a very limited number of factors and characteristics outweigh all others, can there be a limited number of interfacing competitors. The richer and more varied the environment, then the greater the number of potential competitors and the smaller the potential advantage for any one of them relative to others. The competition will be correspondingly more severe between them because the relative advantage they can individually obtain compared to their total competition will become correspondingly diminished.

- The total competitive environment, therefore, consists of a fabric or web of interfacing competitors, all of whom are uniquely advantaged, all of whom are constrained by their competition and all of whom are in dynamic equilibrium with those with whom they interface.

- The competition within the web is for resources. These can be of many kinds, but the basic starting point for all of these are the natural resources of energy and materials. These are fundamental to everything else. Such resources are converted to more complex and specialized uses by successive trophic levels. In nature there are rarely as many as six trophic levels. In business there can be more. The ecological food chain is the biological parallel to vertical integration in business.

- Each level of a trophic resource chain is dependent upon those links below it and is limited by the continuity, stability and abundance of each link below. No one preys on the top predator but its supply line is the most fragile. The most severe and critical competition is between adjacent elements of parallel vertical resource chains that can also use the resources of a parallel chain. This horizontal competition produces the interaction that creates the competitive fabric or web. Any significant disturbance of any part of this web will affect to some degree all elements of the array of competition.

- Such a complex interactive web of mutual dependence has an inherent and prerequisite range of characteristics and variety. Specialization of function is a prerequisite for effectiveness. Differentiation is a requirement for survival. Interdependence is unavoidable. As a result the leverage, value and weighting of any characteristic will be a variable whose distribution will follow a log normal or Pareto pattern. The consequence is a characteristic pattern of major ecological roles that are constantly repeated in form but never in detail. This is as true of the business community as it is of the biological community.

- The control of the relationships within the competitive web and its elements is based on the Darwinian Fitness Factor, defined as the ratio of the numbers of a species of one generation compared to the numbers of the preceding generation. If that ratio is 1.00, then there is no growth or shrinkage from one generation to another. If the Darwinian Fitness Factor is other than 1.00, then the population will be defined by $(DFF)^n$ where n is the number of generations. Any DFF over 1.00 will grow to infinity if compounded indefinitely. Conversely any DFF less than 1.00 will lead to extinction.

- The corollary of the above is that all significant populations of any species have had an extensive period of successive generations in which the DFF was in excess of 1.00. However, all species must inevitably at some point in time have a decrease in DFF to no more than 1.00. Failure of that to happen would cause all resources on earth to be diverted to a single survivor. However, history gives many examples of extremely long periods during which populations were static on trend. The understanding of the system dynamics that controls the DFF is the fundamental prerequisite for a basic theory of competition.

- For these purposes a species, an industry or a combination of businesses that share common evolution must all also share a common gene pool in which natural selection within that pool affects the characteristics of each subsequent generation of that pool. Specialization of function which results in mutually exclusive selection of characteristics to the point that the gene pool is not shared by the alternative specialization is effectively the emergence of two separate species with independent DFFs.

Source: Bruce D. Henderson, "The Anatomy of Competition," *Journal of Marketing*, Spring, 1983, pp. 8–9. Reprinted by permission of the American Marketing Association.

CASE 4
AT&T

On January 1, 1984, AT&T divested itself of its 22 local telephone companies, and what was known as the Bell System was over. With the increased competition in the long-distance market, would the new AT&T entity be able to maintain and possibly increase its share of this market?

COMPANY HISTORY

On February 14, 1876, Alexander Graham Bell submitted a patent application in Boston for an invention ("a telephone"). On March 10, 1876, the first telephone was working and made possible the construction of the American telephone network. From 1878 to 1887, Theodore N. Vail, president of the company at that time, put together the pieces of the Bell System. He created the engineering department (future Bell Labs) and a manufacturing department (future Western Electric) to develop new technology and manufacture telephone equipment. On January 30, 1894, the last patent ran out and American Bell Telephone Company (its name at that time) had to fight for its survival. It did survive, and by the early 1900s the company had become a nationwide corporation. On December 19, 1913, the company became a regulated monopoly, privately controlled and financed.

AT&T's quasi-monopoly status, however, was always an uncomfortable arrangement. The company wanted to get into unregulated fields like computer technology while other firms were eager to enter the telephone business, and the government was worried by the size and the power of the telephone company. In 1968, the FCC allowed a telephone company to sell a device, called a cataphone, that connected mobile radios to AT&T's lines. At the end of the '60s, certain forms of long-distance communications were approved by the FCC. In 1971, MCI Communications Corporation filed a suit against AT&T, which had denied it the right to connect its long-distance operations to Bell local companies. The lawsuit was still being debated in court in 1984 and could end in damages that AT&T would have to pay to MCI. On November 20, 1974, the Justice Department filed a suit to break off Western Electric from the rest of AT&T. This antitrust lawsuit dragged on endlessly in court. It was finally settled on August 4, 1982, when Federal Judge Harold Greene approved the modified final judgment accepted by the Department of Justice and AT&T. For details on the different phases of the lawsuit and a chronology of events since this agreement, see Exhibit 4-16.

EXHIBIT 4-16   Chronology of the Lawsuit

January 24, 1956: The Bell System agrees to a consent decree to end a seven-year-old Justice Department antitrust case against the company. The decree limits the Bell System to providing communication services, with charges subject to regulation. The company may also manufacture equipment needed to furnish those services.

November 20, 1974: The Justice Department files another antitrust suit against the Bell System, charging it with anticompetitive behavior in providing intercity services and procuring terminal equipment. AT&T denies the charges, claiming the company's structure is essential for efficient communications, and that it is already subject to state and federal regulations. Massive discovery proceedings and negotiations begin shortly after.

January 5, 1981: Ten days before the scheduled start of the trial, the Department of Justice and AT&T receive a postponement to pursue settlement talks.

March 4, 1981: The trial starts after AT&T and the Justice Department are unable to reach an agreement.

July 1, 1981: The prosecution rests its case. AT&T files for dismissal.

July 29, 1981: The Justice Department asks Judge Greene to delay the trial. Greene refuses, but the Justice Department indicates it will ask Congress for legislation while pursuing the case.

January 8, 1982: AT&T and the Justice Department announce an agreement that would modify the 1956 consent decree. AT&T agrees to divest itself of its 22 local telephone companies. In return, certain restrictions imposed by the 1956 decree would be abolished and the 1974 antitrust case dropped.

May 25, 1982: Hearings start in Washington, DC.

August 11, 1982: Greene asks for major changes in the decree before approving it.

August 19, 1982: AT&T accepts the modifications suggested by Greene.

August 24, 1982: Judge Greene approves the modified final judgment.

October 4, 1982: AT&T files maps showing 161 calling areas nationwide, with definition of calls handled by the local telephone companies and those handled by long-distance carriers.

December 16, 1982: AT&T files detailed divestiture plan with Judge Greene.

December 17, 1982: Pacific Telephone & Telegraph tells Greene it needs more financial help from AT&T under the divestiture plan.

February 28, 1983: Supreme Court affirms Judge Greene's handling of divestiture agreement.

April 7, 1983: AT&T agrees to provide Pacific Telephone with added financial help in breakup.

April 20, 1983: Greene approves boundaries for most of AT&T's proposed 161 calling areas nationwide.

July 8, 1983: Greene outlines changes in AT&T's divestiture, including giving local companies almost exclusive use of the Bell name.

August 3, 1983: AT&T agrees to the loss of the Bell name. Greene approves divestiture plan, clearing way for the breakup.

Source: Newspaper reports. See *The Wall Street Journal,* August 26, 1982, and November 17, 1983.

MAIN POINTS OF THE AGREEMENT

The 22 local Bell operating companies (BOCs) represented about two-thirds of AT&T's assets and 50 percent of its profits. After divestiture the 22 companies were grouped into seven regional companies, each independent of the others and of AT&T (see Exhibit 4-17). The following are the highlights of the breakup:

1. The BOCs will be divided into seven companies.
2. The Bell name and logo will belong to the BOCs only.
3. The BOCs will be allowed to sell but not manufacture telephone equipment.
4. The BOCs will keep the Yellow Pages business and be permitted to offer mobile phone services.
5. AT&T is allowed to enter the data-processing and computer business.
6. AT&T is barred for seven years from offering any electronic publishing services, such as those providing news or financial reports on home computer screens through telephone line connections, over any of its own telephone lines.
7. The boundaries of the divested companies' new local service areas will be based on communities of interest. Called Local Access and Transport Areas (LATA), these service areas will each cover local telephone exchanges. Calls within these areas will be handled by the BOCs. Calls between them, commonly referred to as "interexchange or long distance," will be handled by AT&T and other long-distance carriers.
8. The BOCs are required to provide all long-distance carriers, AT&T and the others, with access to their facilities that is equal in type, quality, and price.

CONSEQUENCES OF THE DIVESTITURE

Structural Changes

Exhibit 4-18 shows the AT&T structure before and after the divestiture. After the divestiture AT&T was left with the following businesses:

—Bell Laboratories: in charge of research and development.
—Western Electric: in charge of manufacturing and supplying equipment.
—AT&T Communications (interexchange organization): in charge of providing nationwide long-distance service.
—AT&T Information Systems: in charge of providing enhanced communications and information services and equipment for businesses, government, and residential customers.

EXHIBIT 4-17   Reorganization of the Bell Operating Companies

Pacific Telesis

Far West

● Pacific Telephone
● Nevada Bell

U.S. West

Mountains and Great Plains

● Northwestern Bell
● Mountain Bell
● Pacific Northwest Bell

Ameritech

Midwest

● Illinois Bell
● Indiana Bell
● Michigan Bell
● Ohio Bell
● Wisconsin Telephone

Southwestern Bell Corporation

Southwest

● Southwestern Bell

Bell South

Southeast

● South Central Bell
● Southern Bell

Bell Atlantic

Mid-Atlantic

● Bell of Pennsylvania
● Diamond State Telephone Company
● Chesapeake and Potomac Companies (4)
● New Jersey Bell

NYNEX

Northeast

● New England Telephone
● New York Telephone

—AT&T International: in charge of marketing products and services overseas (switching and transmission equipment).

In the post-divestiture era AT&T will have to mobilize all its power and strength to enter and compete in new markets, such as data processing, and also to keep its share of the long-distance communications market.

EXHIBIT 4-18 AT&T Structure Before and After Divestiture

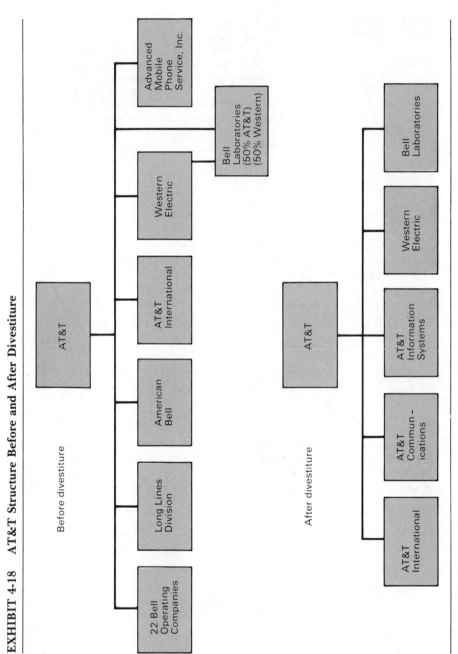

Before divestiture

After divestiture

Source: AT&T.

Long-Distance Services

In 1984, AT&T Communications had 118,000 employees and $15 to $20 billion in assets. This division offered the following services:

1. Long-distance telephone communications (nationwide and overseas).
2. WATS (Wide Area Telecommunications Service) and 800-number services.
3. Special services for government and businesses such as large private networks, video and audio teleconferencing, high-speed data links, satellite transmissions, etc.

Regular AT&T Long-Distance Services

Through an extensive nationwide network, AT&T connects its telephone subscribers to every location in the United States as well as to overseas telephone networks. In 1983, AT&T had 70 million subscribers to its long-distance services. Together with regular long-distance services, AT&T also offered special cheaper long-distance communications—WATS lines—to residential and business customers having a high volume of telephone communications (see Exhibit 4-19 for an example of WATS service and prices). In 1984, AT&T basic long-distance services remained regulated.

Prices Charged by AT&T

Under the Bell System, a single nationwide network handled local and long-distance communications. AT&T had been sharing long-distance

EXHIBIT 4-19   AT&T's WATS Line Price for the State of Connecticut

NUMBER OF HOURS	INWARD LINE (800-NUMBERS), MONTHLY CHARGES	OUTWARD LINE, MONTHLY CHARGES
First 10 hours	$185	$180
Each additional hour, up to 35 hours	$9.75	$9.50
Each additional hour, after the first 35 hours	$6.25	$6.00
Labor charges for installation of the service	$30 for the first 15 minutes + $10.00 per additional minute	

Source: New England Telephone.

EXHIBIT 4-20   MCI's Long-Distance Prices Compared with AT&T's Prices

LONG DISTANCE CALLS	MINS.	BELL	MCI	SAVINGS
St. Louis to Belleville	1	$ .32	$ .15	53.1%
New York City to Erie	1	.59	.36	39.0
Washington, D.C., to Atlanta	2	1.05	.75	28.6
San Francisco to Denver	3	1.52	1.15	24.3
Dallas to Milwaukee	5	2.34	1.87	20.1
Memphis to Fresno	9	4.16	3.46	16.8
Baltimore to Boston	4	1.85	1.45	21.6
Los Angeles to Chicago	7	3.28	2.69	18.0
Richmond to Baltimore	13	5.26	4.45	15.4
Cincinnati to Louisville	8	3.16	2.62	17.1
Cheyenne to Ft. Wayne	10	4.60	3.84	16.5
Houston to Phoenix	3	1.52	1.15	24.3
Atlanta to Cincinnati	6	2.69	2.18	19.0
Boston to Providence	1	.48	.27	43.8
Chicago to Cleveland	11	4.79	4.00	16.5
Knoxville to St. Louis	4	1.85	1.45	21.6

Source: MCI's ad in newspapers.

revenues with the local telephone companies. As a result of this sharing and the nationwide coverage, AT&T long-distance services had been priced higher than their actual cost. Telephone communications offered by MCI, GTE, and other competitors, in the heavy traffic areas they connected, were usually cheaper than those offered by AT&T. (For an example, see Exhibit 4-20.)

After the divestiture, depending on FCC decisions on access charges, AT&T planned to decrease its long-distance rates by 10 percent annually. For more details about the access charges controversy and future possible AT&T long-distance rates, refer to Exhibits 4-21 and 4-22.

After the divestiture, MCI, GTE Sprint, and AT&T's other competitors did not need FCC approval for rate changes, but AT&T had to get FCC permission in advance and submit cost data to justify a request for a rate change.

EXHIBIT 4-21   Access Charges Controversy

Telephone access charges have become one of the biggest issues in the restructuring of the telephone system.

Access charges are the fee that the Federal Communications Commission wants people, businesses and long-distance companies to pay for access between local phone systems and long-distance lines. The fee has been approved by the FCC and is supposed to take effect April 3 [1984]. But it has bewildered politicians, investors and telephone users, and the reaction has been heated.

Bills have been introduced in Congress to limit the fee. . . . Consumer advocates and competitors of American Telephone & Telegraph Co. have vigorously opposed the fee. AT&T, which is being split up Jan. 1, has lobbied for it just as vigorously. . . .

Customers have paid access charges for many years. They just didn't know it because the fee was part of long-distance rates. Then in the mid-1970s other companies started offering long-distance service, ending AT&T's monopoly. That meant the FCC had to untangle the old system of using revenue from AT&T's long-distance rates to pay part of the cost of local telephone service. (The subsidy was used to hold down the cost of local service, keeping it affordable for almost everyone.)

In December 1982, the FCC decided to unscramble the system by shifting more of the cost of local telephone service to those who use the service—people, businesses and AT&T's long-distance competitors, such as MCI Communications Corp. The access charge was the way chosen to shift the cost. . . .

Perhaps it's best to think of the nation's phone system as a system of highways and city streets. Long-distance telephone lines are like the highways. Local phone lines are like the web of city streets. Under the access-charge plan, consumers would pay a special flat-rate fee to the local phone companies to get onto the long-distance network. The long-distance carriers would pay a fee to the local companies for the privilege of getting traffic off the highway and onto the local roads—that is, hooking into the local phone network.

And, in effect, the additional charges to consumers would replace some of the subsidies that have been collected through AT&T's long-distance rates. . . .

Under the FCC plan, people who use the telephone at home or at work will pay the "subscriber" access charge. It will start at $2 a month per line for residential customers and as much as $6 a month per line for business customers. By the end of the decade, those charges would be about $5 a month for each home or business line, or $60 a year.

Long-distance companies would pay a "carrier" access charge based on the number of calls they put through the local network. AT&T, which will still have the long-distance business after the breakup, estimates that it would pay $16.3 billion in 1984 if access charges were started on Jan. 1. MCI, GTE Corp.'s Sprint service and other long-distance carriers would pay less because they funnel fewer calls into the local system and because they would pay a lower rate than AT&T.

AT&T is the strongest supporter. That's because with access charges, the hidden subsidy would be removed from AT&T's long-distance rates, letting AT&T charge less for long-distance calls. AT&T has proposed a $1.75 billion reduction next year

EXHIBIT 4-21   continued

---

in basic long-distance rates. Presumably, that would stimulate calling and increase AT&T's long-distance profit to the limits set by the FCC. Access charges would also benefit local Bell companies and other local phone companies, since the fee is being paid to them.

Heavy users of long-distance service also generally support access charges. These include the hotel industry and many large companies such as Mobil Corp. and Merrill Lynch & Co.

Source: Excerpted from *The Wall Street Journal,* November 9, 1983.

THE MARKET

The long-distance market represented $40 billion in 1983 and had been growing at an annual rate of 10 percent. In 1983, AT&T's market share was 93 percent versus 3 percent for MCI and 1 percent for GTE, its main competitors. (See Case Appendixes A and B for background on these companies.) Since 1978, AT&T's market share had dropped from 99 percent to 93 percent. This decrease may be explained by (1) increasing competition from new, smaller companies which had entered the market; (2) the failure of AT&T's marketing department to promote its long-distance services as aggressively as its competitors; and (3) AT&T's prices, which were higher than those charged by its competitors. Also, recently, some large companies and agencies had legally bypassed the public telephone companies and built up their own telecommunication systems, by building microwave dish antennas and aiming them at communication satellites.

AT&T's Marketing Moves

In the past, protected by its monopoly, AT&T had not aggressively marketed its long-distance services. In the middle of 1983, however, because the long-distance market is a profitable one that generates a good deal of income for the company, AT&T launched a nationwide advertising campaign to try to maintain and increase its market share after divestiture. Ads were placed in magazines and newspapers such as *Fortune, Business Week,* and *The Wall Street Journal,* as well as on television. The objectives of these ads were to associate AT&T with its new logo, to maintain its image as a company whose primary goal was to serve public needs, and to offer high-quality long-distance service everywhere in the United States and overseas. AT&T's WATS lines were now advertised in telephone directories with a toll-free number to get information.

To prepare itself for the divestiture, AT&T strengthened its marketing capabilities by hiring a large number of people for marketing and sales positions, and by developing its certification and training programs.

EXHIBIT 4-22   Future Long-Distance Rates

American Telephone & Telegraph Co. is touting its proposed long-distance rates as the biggest price cut in its history. But for many businesses, the proposal could mean bigger phone bills.

AT&T wants to cut basic long-distance rates by $1.75 billion annually beginning next year, after the breakup of the company. But only some of its rates are being cut, and the ones that are rising could hit businesses hard, especially some of the biggest and most sophisticated phone users.

Large companies that have put together their own networks, often using private lines for which they pay a flat fee for unlimited calls, would pay an average of 15.3% more for the lines and as much as 100% more in some cases, under rates proposed by AT&T. Like consumers, businesses would have to pay the proposed 75-cent charge for long-distance directory assistance and may have to pay local phone companies a charge for access to long-distance lines.

All this is creating a lot of anxiety and confusion. And Congress or the Federal Communications Commission may change the proposed rate structure, making it even more difficult to estimate costs. Some companies are so concerned that they are considering ways to bypass AT&T and its new rates.

. . . Many companies are trying to make estimates, and they aren't pleased with the results. American Airlines figures that the $60 million it spends for phone service a year may have to be increased by $11 million to $27 million a year. Security Pacific Corp., a bank holding company, says its $30 million annual bill could increase 15% to 25%. And Westinghouse Electric Co. says its $35 million annual bill would rise about 15%.

How a company is affected by the rate changes depends on how it uses phones. Businesses that mostly use regular long-distance service or WATS lines—a service that gives volume callers a lower rate—will, on average, pay lower rates. And businesses that use 800 numbers, which let people call in for free, should pay about the same amount as they are now. . . .

But businesses that depend on private lines will be hit hard, because the rates for private lines are increasing. Kemper Group, a financial-services company that is a heavy user of private lines, expects its private-line charges to rise as much as 20%. . . .

Businesses are concocting several ways to avoid the increases. Companies that don't already have them may install computerized switches that are programmed to find the cheapest line for each call. The computer could route the call over lines belonging to AT&T or to an independent phone system such as MCI Communications Corp. or GTE Corp.'s Sprint service. . . .

Other companies are considering heavier use of satellites or microwave transmission—ways of avoiding AT&T entirely. Security Pacific, which spends more than $30 million a year on telecommunications, is talking with a microwave company about installing its own microwave-transmission system. . . .

Source: Excerpted from *The Wall Street Journal*, October 25, 1983.

The company also set up large marketing centers where salespersons sell business services by phone and talk with people calling in response to media or direct-mail solicitations.

Competitors

More than 200 companies entered the long-distance market over the past few years and now share 6 or 7 percent of the market. Most of these companies use microwave transmission networks and cover heavy traffic areas, where the big profits are. They have more flexibility than AT&T because they are smaller. Because their costs are lower, they can offer service at lower rates than AT&T can.

Their current weaknesses are the difficulties in using their services: in some cases the customer needs a touch-phone to have access to the service and may have to dial up to 23 numbers to be connected. These problems are expected to disappear in the near future. However, because of their small size, these AT&T rivals are limited in their capacity to expand their services. Further, they compete with one another, which weakens them in relation to AT&T.

CASE APPENDIX A: MCI CORPORATION

MCI grew up from a company called Microwave Communications, Inc., 15 years ago. In 1969, the FCC permitted MCI to provide long-distance services, such as telephone calls transmitted by microwaves instead of cable, to challenge AT&T's monopoly. In 1973, AT&T denied MCI the right to connect its long-distance operations to Bell's local networks. MCI filed a suit. Depending on the decision of the court, AT&T might have to pay MCI $1.8 billion for antitrust violations.

Today, MCI provides mobile radio and paging services and international communication services as well as its long-distance services. With 3 percent of the long-distance market, MCI is AT&T's main competitor.

MCI customers originally needed push-button phones and had to press 12 digits before the number they were calling. Starting on September, 1984, about one-third of MCI's customers could simply dial 1 before the number, just as they would in making any other long-distance call. And they could use rotary-dial as well as push buttons. Over the following two years, MCI will be phasing in these services to the rest of its customers.

With the AT&T divestiture and equal access in the future to local networks, MCI expects a boom in its long-distance services. In order to prepare for this, MCI spent $1 billion in 1983 and planned to spend $2 billion in 1984 to expand its technical capacity (increased use of optical fiber cable, microwave transmitters, satellite and switching capacities).

MCI's rates were expected to rise as a result of convenient services offered and the access charges. However, MCI would try to keep its rates below AT&T's, because it had built its market by pricing below AT&T. Even if its discounts were likely to shrink, it planned to keep some price advantage by making sure its costs were lower than its rival's. After AT&T announced it planned to reduce its long-distance rates by 10 percent annually, MCI announced plans to reduce its rates by an average of 5 percent yearly.

To compete aggressively against AT&T and the other companies MCI recently took several actions:

1. It set up a telemarketing center in Rye Brook, New Jersey. There, 200 salespersons, strongly assisted by computers, call up potential customers and answer questions about long-distance services from people responding to ads or direct-mail solicitations.

2. MCI surveyed 2,000 people who had terminated its service without moving to a city not served by the company. The main reasons given were (a) that the company did not serve the whole United States; and (b) that some customers did not make enough calls to justify the $5 or $10 monthly subscription fee. After this survey, MCI created Omnicall Corporation, which leases AT&T's WATS lines to complete interstate off-network calls. About 70 percent of the 300 metropolitan areas served by MCI now use Omnicall. MCI also decided that customers who were not making enough calls would pay a one-time $10 fee instead. Each call would cost more than under the monthly-fee system but less than with Bell's rates.

3. MCI reached an agreement with American Express and Sears. Now these two companies offer long-distance services to their credit card customers through MCI.

4. To attract more business and build its image as a full-service company, MCI announced that it planned to lift restrictions on when customers could place calls, letting all subscribers make daytime calls, as only some of its subscribers were permitted to do in the past. It also hoped to make its credit card service easier to use and eventually to offer operator and toll-free 800 numbers.

5. MCI launched an advertising campaign in newspapers and TV stations offering, during sporting events and in shopping malls, a three-minute free long-distance call to potential customers. With this method, MCI collected the names and addresses of the persons calling as well as those of the persons called. Such a list should help the company to target its marketing effort more closely in the future.

Source: Newspaper reports.

CASE APPENDIX B: GTE CORPORATION

GTE is a worldwide leader in developing, manufacturing, and marketing telecommunications, electrical and electronic products, and network services and systems. The company is also engaged in advanced research and development work in such high-technology areas as fiberoptic communications, satellite communications, packet switching, etc.

One of the five principal groups of GTE is GTE Sprint Communications Corporation, acquired from the Southern Pacific Satellite Company in 1983. This group has 1 percent of the American long-distance market. With revenues of $393 million in 1982, it employed over 3,000 people and served more than 600,000 business and residential customers. GTE Sprint's microwave network connects about 300 cities and surrounding communities in 46 states and the District of Columbia.

GTE is not aggressively marketing its long-distance services to increase its market share, because it is concerned about the consequences of a possible increase in access charges, to connect its network to local phone lines.

The following table compares GTE services with those of its competitors:

Year Ending December 31, 1982

	INDEPEN-DENTS*	BELL SYSTEM**	GTE (DOMESTIC ONLY)	GRAND TOTAL*
Access Lines	21,700,000	86,920,600	9,702,000[a]	108,620,600
Operating Companies	1,432	25	16	1,457
Number of Exchanges	11,074	6,874	2,251	17,948
Gross Investment in Plant	$41.9 billion	$160.2 billion	$19.3 billion	$202.1 billion
Gross Plant Addition in 1982	$4.7 billion	$17.1 billion	$2.3 billion	$21.8 billion
Operating Revenues	$14 billion	$66 billion	$6.6 billion[b]	$80 billion
Operating Revenues per Access Line	$648	$760	$681	
Number of Employees	192,100	840,675	97,200	1,032,775
Investment per Access Line	$1,933	$1,843	$1,993	
Percent Direct Distance Dialing	Nearly 100%	Nearly 100%	Nearly 100%	

*Includes GTE.
**Includes Southern New England Telephone Co. and Cincinnati Bell Inc.
[a]Represents nearly 9 percent of total U.S. access lines and 45 percent of total independent access lines.
[b]Represents 8 percent of total U.S. revenues and 47 percent of total independent revenues.

Source: Newspaper reports and GTE.

CHAPTER 5
Focusing on the Customer

Consumption is the sole end and purpose of production; and the interest of the producer ought to be attended to only so far as it may be necessary for promoting that of the consumer.

Adam Smith

Businesses compete to serve customer needs. Not only are there different types of customers, but their needs vary too. Thus the market is not a homogeneous place. Further, the markets that are homogeneous today may not remain so in the future. In brief, the market represents a dynamic phenomenon that, influenced by customer needs, evolves over time.

In a free economy, each customer group tends to want a slightly different service or product. But a business unit cannot reach out to all customers with equal effectiveness; it must distinguish the easily accessible customer groups from the hard-to-reach ones. Moreover, a business unit faces competitors whose ability to respond to customer needs and cover customer groups differs from its own. To establish a strategic edge over its competition with a viable marketing strategy, it is important for the business unit to clearly define the market it intends to serve. It must segment the market, identifying one or more subsets of customers within the total market and concentrating its efforts on meeting their needs. Fine differentiation of the structure within the total customer group offers the opportunity to establish a competitive leverage.

This chapter introduces a framework for identifying markets to serve. Various underlying concepts of market definition are examined. The chapter ends with a discussion of alternative ways of segmenting the market.

IDENTIFYING MARKETS

Contemporary approaches to strategic planning require proper definition of the market. However, there is question about what the proper definition is. Depending on which definition is used, two companies and their two products can reverse their relative market share positions, as shown below:

BRANDS

	Segment 1				Segment 2		
	S	T	U	V	X	Y	Z
MARKET							
Mass	32	24	16	8	12	6	2
Segmented	40	30	20	10	60	30	10

Though brand X has a low share in the mass market, it has a much higher share within its own segment of the mass market than does brand S. Which of the two shares shown above is the correct one for the business: the total mass market for the product category or some segmented portion of that market? The arguments go both ways, some pointing out the merits of having a larger share of industry volume and others noting the favorable profit consequences of holding a larger share within one of the smaller market niches. Does Sanka compete in a mass market with Maxwell House and Folgers or in a decaffeinated market segment against Brim and Nescafe?[1]

Considering the importance of adequately defining the market, it is desirable to develop a systematic approach for the purpose in the form of a conceptual framework. Exhibit 5-1 presents such a framework. The

EXHIBIT 5-1   Identifying Markets to Serve

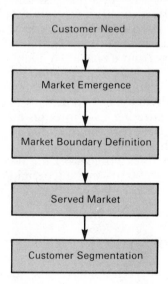

---

[1]William T. Moran, "Market Share and Market Boundaries," unpublished paper (Greenwich, CT: Moran & Tucker, Inc., no date).

first logical step in defining the market is to determine customer need. Based on the need, the market emerges. Since this provides a broad perspective of the market, it is desirable to establish market boundaries. Traditionally, market boundaries have been defined in terms of product/market scope, but recent work on the subject suggests that markets be defined multidimensionally.

The market boundary delineates the total limits of the market. An individual business must select and serve those parts of the total market in which it is best equipped to compete over the long run. Further, at a given point in time, a business may choose to concentrate on only a part of the total market that it intends to cover over time.

CUSTOMER NEED

Satisfaction of customer need is the ultimate test of a business unit's success. Thus an effective marketing strategy should aim at serving customer needs and wants better than the competitors do. Focus on customers is the essence of marketing strategy. As Robertson and Wind have said:

> Marketing performs a boundary role function between the company and its markets. It guides the allocation of resources to product and service offerings designed to satisfy market needs while achieving corporate objectives. This boundary role function of marketing is critical to strategy development. Before marshalling a company's resources to acquire a new business, or to introduce a new product, or to reposition an existing product, management must use marketing research to cross the company-consumer boundary and to assess the likely market response.
>
> The logic and value of consumer needs assessment is generally beyond dispute, yet frequently ignored. It is estimated, for example, that a majority of new products fail. Yet, there is most often nothing wrong with the product itself; that is, it works. The problem is simply that consumers do not want the product.
>
> ATT's Picture Phone is a classic example of a technology-driven product which works; but people do not want to see each other on a telephone. It transforms a comfortable, low involvement communication transaction into a demanding, high involvement one. The benefit is not obvious to consumers. Of course, the benefit could become obvious if transportation costs continue to outpace communication costs, and if consumers could be "taught" the benefits of using a Picture Phone.
>
> Marketing's boundary role function is similarly important in maintaining a viable competitive positioning in the marketplace. The passing of Korvette from the American retail scene, for example, can be attributed to consumer confusion as to what Korvette represented— how it was positioned relative to competition. Korvette's strength was as a discount chain—high turnover and low margin. This basic mission of the business was violated, however, as Korvette traded-up in soft

goods and fashion items and even opened a store on Manhattan's Fifth Avenue. The result was that Korvette became neither a discount store nor a department store and lost its previous customer base. Sears has encountered a similar phenomenon as it opted for higher margins in the 1970s and lost its reputation for "value" in the marketplace. The penalty has been declining sales and profitability for its retail store operation, which it is now trying valiantly to arrest by reestablishing its "middle America" value orientation. Nevertheless, consumer research could have indicated the beginning of the problem long before the crisis in sales and profits occurred.[2]

Concept of Need

Traditionally, needs have been classified according to Maslow's hierarchy of human needs listed below:

—physiological
—safety
—belongingness
—self-esteem
—self-actualization

Needs at each level of the hierarchy can be satisfied only after needs at the levels below it have been satisfied. A need unsatisfied becomes a source of frustration. When the frustration is sufficiently intense, it motivates a relief action—for example, the purchase of a product. Once a need is satisfied, it is forgotten, creating space for awareness of other needs. In a marketing context, this suggests that customers need periodic reminders of their association with a product, *particularly when satisfied.*

Business strategy can be based on the certainty that needs exist. As needs are satisfied at lower levels, room is created for higher-level needs. As we move up the hierarchy, needs become less and less obvious. The challenge in marketing is to expose non-obvious needs to fill needs at all levels of the hierarchy.

Maslow's first two levels can be called the survival levels. Most businesses operate at level 2 (safety) with occasional spikes into higher levels. Satisfying need here is what a business must do to have a viable operation. The customer must feel both physically and economically safe in buying the product. The next higher levels—belongingness and self-esteem—are customer reward levels, where benefits accrue to the customer personally, enhancing his or her sense of worth as an individual. At the highest level, self-actualization, the customer feels a close identification with the prod-

---

[2]Thomas S. Robertson and Yoram Wind, "Marketing Strategy," in *Handbook of Business Strategy* (New York: McGraw-Hill Book Co., 1982). Reprinted by permission. See also Yoram Wind and Thomas S. Robertson, "Marketing Strategy: New Directions for Theory and Research," *Journal of Marketing,* Spring, 1983, pp. 12–25.

uct. Of course, not all needs of customers can be filled, nor would it be economically feasible to attempt to do so. But a business can move further toward satisfaction of customer needs by utilizing the insights of the Maslow hierarchy.

MARKET EMERGENCE

Customer need gives rise to a market opportunity, and a market emerges. To judge the worth of this market an estimate of market potential becomes important. If the market appears attractive, the strategist would take the next step of delineating the market boundary. This section examines the potential of the market.

Market Potential

Simply stated, market potential is the total demand for a product in a given environment. While theoretically this definition appears adequate, its meaning in practice creates problems. This is because the two aspects of the definition—demand and environment—are dynamic concepts, and their meaning varies from one situation to another.[3] Realizing this difficulty, Kotler defines market potential as "the limit approached by demand as marketing effort goes to infinity."[4] But such an abstract definition still leaves the meaning of market potential open to interpretation. As has been said:

> Herein lies the first discrepancy, for philosophers and mathematicians have long debated the concept and measurement of infinity with little resolution, so marketing researchers are unlikely to be very interested or successful in pursuing such an abstruse matter. Thus, the term potential is often used as being synonymous with demand and forecast, in that it is related to a finite, rather than an infinite level of marketing effort.[5]

It is clear that market potential defies precise definition. We know, however, that it can be approached through the estimation of maximum reasonable limits of a saturation point in a given environment for a given product at a given time. Within these constraints, market potential for any product or service can be extrapolated using various methods discussed below.

---

[3]See Morgan McDonald, *Appraising the Market for New Industrial Products* (New York: The Conference Board, 1967).

[4]Philip Kotler, *Marketing Management,* 5th Ed. (Englewood Cliffs, NJ: Prentice-Hall, 1984), p. 230.

[5]Francis E. Hummel, *Market and Sales Potential* (New York: Ronald Press, 1961), p. 18.

Measuring Market Potential

There are various ways to measure market potential. Different methods are required for new versus established products.

Methods for estimating market potentials for established products may be classified into two groups based on their contrasting approaches. Breakdown methods begin with aggregate industry or market data and then break down the data into segments of interest to the firm. Build-up methods start with individual accounts (customer and prospects) and aggregate the data to the industry or market level.

Breakdown methods. The Total Market Measure method is characterized by the use of available total industry or market data to estimate market and sale potentials. The Statistical Series Method is based on the determination of observed statistical relationships between industry and market data, and socioeconomic variables descriptive of industry and market.

Build-up methods. The Census Method involves making a separate appraisal of every user or prospective user in a market. The market potential is derived from a summation of the individual potentials. The Market Survey Method is very often used when goods and services have relatively unconcentrated markets. It involves the collection of data on past purchases, together with classification data on the principal products/services produced, number of employees, and other relevant statistical series. The Secondary Data Method relies on internal sales data rather than survey data on product purchases.

Estimating market and sales potential for new rather than established products tends to be more subjective and speculative. The research is heavily dependent on four factors: the availability of secondary data, degree of precision required or obtainable, market structure and situation, and degree of product newness.

Some authors have suggested that test marketing is the best approach to determine potentials for new products, but estimates of potentials are usually required long before products/services are developed to the point that they are ready for test marketing. Therefore, in order to obtain timely, relevant, and reliable estimates of market and sales potentials, relatively objective measures of possible demand for products or services are needed.[6] Three methods meet this requirement. The Usage Factor Method, a multi-step process, estimates market potential for each segment by multiplying a developed usage factor ratio by the economic activity of the segments. The Possible Use Method is based on a market survey of prospective users to determine whether a given business can use a specific product, or component part, and if so, to what extent. The Analogy/Substitution Method is the weakest of the three. It is based on the

---

[6]See Robert Patty, *Managing Sales People*, 2d Ed. (Reston, VA: Reston Publishing Co., 1982).

hypothesis (1) that past diffusion processes for similar or related products are analogous to and a useful guide to the market growth process for new products and services, or (2) that virtually all new products and services are basically substitutes for existing products and services; therefore, estimation of potential is merely a process of determining the substitution rate of the new product for the old product.

Measurement of market potential is undertaken to gain insights into five elements: market size, market growth, profitability, type of buying decision, and customer market structure. These elements may be defined as follows:

> The first element, market size, is best expressed in both units and dollars. Dollar expression in isolation is inadequate because of distortion by inflation and international currency fluctuations. Also, because of inflationary distortion, the screening criteria for new product concepts and product line extensions should separately specify both units and dollars. Market size can be expressed as total market sales potential or company market share, although most companies through custom utilize market share figures.

> The second element, market growth, is meant to reflect the secular trend of the industry. Again, the screening criteria should be specified for new product concepts and product line extensions. The criteria and projections should be based on percentage growth in units. Projections in industrial settings often are heavily dependent on retrofit possibilities, and plans for equipment replacement.

> The third element in this evaluation of strategic potential is profitability. It usually is expressed in terms of contribution margin, or in one of the family of return calculations. Most U.S. companies view profitability in terms of return on investment (ROI), return on sales (ROS), or return on net assets (RONA). Return on capital employed (ROCE) is often calculated in multinational companies. For measuring market potential, no one of these calculations appears to function better than another.

> The fourth element is the type of buying decision. The basis for a buying decision must be predicated on whether the decision is straight rebuy, modified rebuy, or new task.

> The fifth and final element is the structure of the customer market. Based on the same criteria as competitive structure, the market can be classified as monopsony, oligopsony, differentiated competition (monopsonistic competition) or pure competition.[7]

Exhibit 5-2 summarizes the above elements and shows a *pro forma* scheme for measuring market potential.

---

[7]Terry C. Wilson, "An Opportunity Screening Model," in *1983 AMA Educators' Proceedings* (Chicago: American Marketing Association, 1983), pp. 324–325. Reprinted by permission of the American Marketing Association.

EXHIBIT 5-2   Measurement of Market Potential

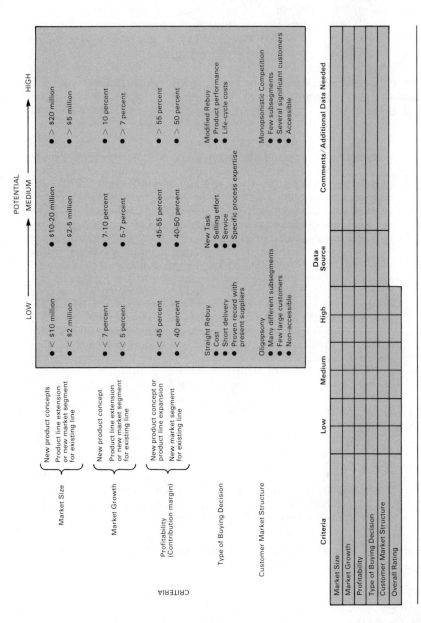

Source: Reprinted by permission of Dr. Terry C. Wilson, West Virginia University.

DEFINING MARKET BOUNDARIES[8]

The crux of any strategy formulation effort is market definition. As has been said:

> The problem of identifying competitive product-market boundaries pervades all levels of marketing decisions. Such strategic issues as the basic definition of a business, the assessment of opportunities presented by gaps in the market, the reaction to threats posed by competitive actions, and the decisions on major resource allocations are strongly influenced by the breadth or narrowness of the definition of competitive boundaries. The importance of share of market for evaluating performance and for guiding territorial advertising, sales force, and other budget allocations and the growing number of antitrust prosecutions also call for defensible definitions of product-market boundaries.[9]

Defining the market is a difficult task, however, since market can be defined in many ways.

Consider the cooking appliance business.[10] Overall in 1983, about 10 million gas and electric ranges and microwave ovens were sold for household use. All these appliances serve the basic function of cooking, but their similarity ends there. They differ in many ways: (a) with reference to fuels, primarily gas vs. electricity; (b) in cooking method, heat vs. radiation; (c) with reference to type of cooking function served: e.g., surface heating, baking, roasting, charcoal broilings, etc.; (d) in design: free-standing ranges, built-in countertop ranges and wall ovens, countertop microwave ovens, and combinations of microwave units with conventional ranges; and (e) in price and product features.

The above differences raise an important question: Should all household cooking appliances be considered as constituting a single market? Or do they represent several distinct markets? If they are several distinct markets, how should these markets be defined? There are different possibilities for defining the market: (a) with reference to product characteristics; (b) in terms of private brand sales vs. manufacturers' brand sales; (c) with reference to sales in specific regions; (d) in terms of sales target, e.g., sales to building contractors for installation in new houses vs. replacement sales for existing homes.

Depending on the criterion adopted to define the market, the size of the market will vary considerably. The strategic question of how the

---

[8]This section relies heavily on Robert D. Buzzell, "Note on Market Definition and Segmentation," a Harvard Business School Note, 1978, distributed by HBS Case Services.

[9]George S. Day and Allan D. Shocker, *Identifying Competitive Product-Market Boundaries: Strategic and Analytical Issues* (Cambridge, MA: Marketing Science Institute, 1976), p. 1.

[10]Robert D. Buzzell, *op. cit.*

marketer of home cooking appliances should define the market is explored below.

Dimensions of Market Boundary

Traditionally, market boundaries have been defined in terms of product/market space.[11] For example, consider the following definitions:

> A market is sometimes defined as a group of firms producing identical or closely related products. . . . A preferable approach is to define the markets in terms of products. . . . [What is meant by] a close relationship among products? Goods and services may be closely related in the sense that they are regarded as substitutes by consumers, or they may be close in that the factors of production used in each are similar.[12]

> A market usually is identified with a generic class of products. One hears of the beer market, the cake-mix market or the cigarette market. These are *product markets,* referring to individuals who in the past have purchased a given class of products.[13]

These two definitions view the market as either who the buyers are or what the products are. In the first definition, the buyers are implicitly assumed to be homogeneous in their behavior. The second definition propounds that the products and brands within the category are easily identified and interchangeable, and that the problem is to search for market segments.

In recent years it has been considered inadequate to perceive market definitions as simply a choice of products for chosen markets. Instead, it is suggested that the product be considered as a physical manifestation of the application of a particular *technology* to the provision of a particular *customer function* for a particular *customer segment.* Market boundaries should then be determined by the choices along these three dimensions.[14]

Technology. A particular customer function can be performed by different technologies. In other words, alternative technologies can be ap-

---

[11]See George S. Day, Allan D. Shocker, and Rajendra K. Srivastava, "Customer-oriented Approaches to Identifying Product Markets," *Journal of Marketing,* Fall, 1979, pp. 8–19. See also Rajendra K. Srivastava, Robert P. Leone, and Allan D. Shocker, "Market Structure Analysis: Hierarchical Clustering of Products Based on Substitution-in-Use," *Journal of Marketing,* Summer, 1981, pp. 38–48.

[12]Peter Asch, *Economic Theory and the Antitrust Dilemma* (New York: John Wiley & Sons, 1970), p. 168.

[13]Jack Z. Sissors, "What Is a Market?," *Journal of Marketing,* July, 1968, p. 17.

[14]Derek F. Abell, *Defining the Business: The Starting Point of Strategic Planning* (Englewood Cliffs, NJ: Prentice-Hall, 1980).

plied to satisfy a particular customer need. To illustrate the point, consider home cooking appliances. In terms of fuel, traditionally the alternative technologies have been gas and electric. In recent years, a new form of technology, microwave radiation, has also been used. In another industry the alternative technologies may be based on the use of different materials. For example, containers may be made from metal or glass or plastic. In defining the market boundary, a decision must be made whether the products of all relevant technologies or only a particular technology are to be included.

Customer Function. Products can be considered in terms of the functions they serve or the ways they are used. To take the cooking appliance example again, some bake and roast, others fry and boil. Some perform all these functions and perhaps more. Different functions provide varying customer benefits. In establishing marketing boundary the customer benefits to be served should be spelled out.

Customer Segment. A segment refers to a homogeneous set of customers with similar needs and characteristics. The market for cooking appliances, for example, can be split into different segments: building contractors, individual households buying through retail stores, etc. The retail stores segment can be further broken down into traditional appliance specialty stores, mass merchandisers, and so on. The decision on market boundary should indicate which types of customers are to be served.

In addition to the above three dimensions for determining market boundary, Buzzell recommends adding a fourth—*level of production/distribution.*[15] A business has the option of operating at one or more levels of the production/distribution process. For example, producers of raw materials (e.g., aluminum) or component products (e.g., semiconductors, motors, compressors) may limit their business to selling only to other producers or they may produce finished products themselves, or both. The decision on production/distribution level has a direct impact on the market boundary definition. The point may be illustrated with reference to Texas Instruments:

> The impact that a business unit's vertical integration strategy can have on competition in a market is dramatically illustrated by Texas Instruments' decision, in 1972, to enter the calculator business. At the time, it was a principal supplier of calculator components (integrated circuits) to the earlier entrants into the market, including the initial market leader, Bowmar Instruments. As most readers undoubtedly know, TI quickly took over a leadership position in calculators through a combination of "pricing down the experience curve" and aggressive promotion. For purposes of this discussion, the important point is one of a finished product. Some other component suppliers also entered

---

[15]Robert D. Buzzell, *op. cit.*

the calculator business, while others continued to supply OEMs. In light of these varying strategies, is there a "calculator component market" *and* a "calculator market," or do these constitute a single market?[16]

Exhibit 5-3 shows the dimensions of market boundary definition from the viewpoint of the packaging industry. The market boundary is defined in terms of customer groups, customer functions, and technologies. The fourth dimension, i.e., level of production/distribution, is not included because it is not feasible to incorporate four dimensions in a single chart. The exhibit shows a matrix developed around customer groups on the vertical axis, customer functions on the northeast-southwest axis, and technologies on the northwest-southeast axis. Any three-dimensional

EXHIBIT 5-3   Dimensions of Market Definition

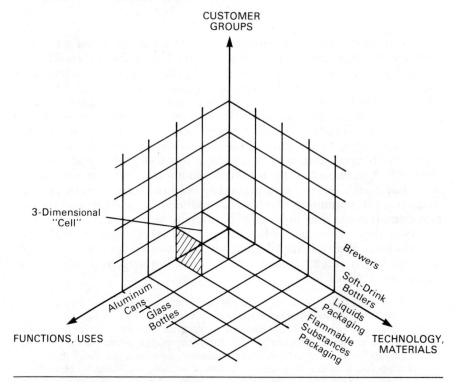

Source: Robert D. Buzzell, Note on Market Definition and Segmentation, p. 7. Harvard Business School Note 9-579-083. Copyright © 1978 by the President and Fellows of Harvard College. Reprinted by permission.

---

[16]*Ibid.*, p. 6.

cell in the matrix constitutes an elementary "building block" of market definition: Aluminum cans for liquid packaging by soft-drink bottlers is an example of such a cell. To sum up, the task of market boundary definition amounts to grouping together a set of market cells, each defined in terms of three dimensions: customer groups, customer functions, and technologies.[17]

Market Boundary Redefinition

As markets evolve, the boundary definition may need to be restated. George Day and Allan Shocker point to five sets of "environmental influences" affecting product/market boundaries. These influences are technological change (displacement by a new technology); market-oriented product development (for example, combining the features of several products into one multipurpose offering); price changes and supply constraints (which influence the perceived set of substitutes); social, legal, or government trends (which influence patterns of competition); and international trade competition (which changes geographic boundaries).[18] For example, when management introduces a new product, markets an existing product to new customers, diversifies the business through acquisition, or liquidates a part of the business through sale, the market undergoes a process of evolution. Redefinition of market boundary may be based on any one or more of the three basic dimensions. The market may be extended by the penetration of new customer groups, the addition of products serving related customer functions, or the development of products based on new technologies. As shown in Exhibit 5-4, these changes are caused by three fundamentally different phenomena: "The *adoption and diffusion* process underlies the penetration of new customer groups, a process of *systemization* results in the operation of products to serve combinations of functions, and the *technology substitution* process underlies change on a technology dimension."[19]

SERVED MARKET

Earlier in this chapter, it was concluded that the task of market boundary definition amounts to grouping together a set of market cells (see Exhibit 5-3), each defined in terms of three dimensions: customer groups, customer functions, and technologies. In other words, a *market* may comprise any combination of these cells. At this time an additional question must be answered. Should a business unit serve the entire market or limit itself to serving just a part of it? While it is conceivable that a

---

[17]*Ibid.*
[18]George S. Day and Allan D. Shocker, *op. cit.*
[19]Derek F. Abell, *op. cit.,* p. 207.

EXHIBIT 5-4   Market Evolution in Three Dimensions

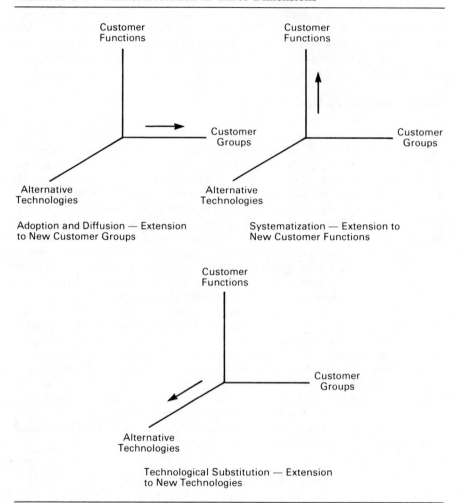

Adoption and Diffusion — Extension to New Customer Groups

Systematization — Extension to New Customer Functions

Technological Substitution — Extension to New Technologies

Source: Derek F. Abell, DEFINING THE BUSINESS: The Starting Point of Strategic Planning, © 1980, p. 207. Reprinted by permission of Prentice-Hall, Inc., Englewood Cliffs, NJ.

business unit may decide to serve the total market, usually the served market is considerably narrower in scope and smaller in size than the total market. The decision on what market to serve is based on such factors as the following:

   (a) perceptions of which product function and technology groupings
       can best be protected and dominated,

(b) internal resource limitations which force a narrow focus,
(c) cumulative trial-and-error experience in reacting to threats and opportunities, and
(d) unusual competencies stemming from access to scarce resources or protected markets.[20]

In practice, the choice of served market is not based on conscious, deliberate effort. Rather, circumstances and perceptions surrounding the business unit dictate the decision making. For some businesses lack of adequate resources limits the range of possibilities. Apple Computer, for example, would be naive to consider competing against IBM across the board. Further, as a business unit gains experience through trial and error, it may extend the scope of its served market. For example, the U.S. Post Office entered the *overnight* package delivery market to participate in the opportunity established by the Federal Express Company.[21]

The task of delineating the served market, however, is full of complications. As has been said:

> In practice, the task of grouping market cells to define a market is complicated. First, there is usually no one defensible criterion for grouping cells. There may be many ways to achieve the same function. Thus, boxed chocolates compete to some degree with flowers, records, and books as semicasual gifts. Do all of these products belong in the total market? To confound this problem, the available statistical and accounting data are often aggregated to a level where important distinctions between cells are completely obscured. Second, there are many products which evolve by adding new combinations of functions and technologies. Thus, radios are multifunctional products which include clocks, alarms, and appearance options. To what extent do these variants dictate new market cells? Third, different competitors may choose different combinations of market cells to serve or to include in their total market definitions. In these situations there will be few direct competitors; instead, businesses will encounter each other in different but overlapping markets, and, as a result, may employ different strategies.[22]

Strategically, the choice of a business unit's served market may be based on the following approaches:[23]

I. Breadth of Product Line
    A. Specialized in terms of technology, broad range of product uses

---

[20]George S. Day, "Strategic Market Analysis and Definition: An Integrated Approach," *Strategic Management Journal*, Vol. 2, 1981, p. 284.
[21]See Kenichi Ohmae, *The Mind of the Strategist* (New York: McGraw-Hill Book Co., 1982), pp. 242–268.
[22]George S. Day, *op. cit.*
[23]Robert D. Buzzell, *op. cit.*, p. 16.

  B. Specialized in terms of product uses, multiple technologies
  C. Specialized in a single technology and a narrow range of product uses
  D. Broad range of (related) technologies *and* uses
  E. Broad vs. narrow range of quality/price levels
 II. Types of Customers
  A. Single customer segment
  B. Multiple customer segments
   1. Undifferentiated treatment
   2. Differentiated treatment
 III. Geographic Scope
  A. Local or regional
  B. National
  C. Multinational
 IV. Level of Production/Distribution
  A. Raw or semi-finished materials or components
  B. Finished products
  C. Wholesale or retail distribution

An Example[24]

The choice of served market may be illustrated with reference to one company's entry into the snowmobile business. The management of this company found snowmobiles an attractive market in terms of sales potential. The boundaries of this market are extensive. For example, in terms of technology, a snowmobile may be powered by gas, diesel fuel, or electricity. A snowmobile may fulfill such customer functions as delivery, recreation, and emergency transportation. Customer groups include household consumers, industrial buyers, and the military.

Since the company could not cover the total market, it had to define the market it would serve. To accomplish this task, the company developed a product/market matrix (see Exhibit 5-5a). The company could manufacture and market any one of three product types: gasoline, diesel, or electric. Further, it could design a snowmobile for any one of three customer groups: consumer, industrial, or military. The matrix in Exhibit 5-5(a) furnished nine possibilities for the company. Considering market potential and its competencies to compete, the part of the market that looked best was the diesel-driven snowmobile for the industrial market segment, the shaded area in Exhibit 5-5(a).

But further narrowing of the market to be served was necessary. A second matrix (see Exhibit 5-5b) laid out the dimensions of customer use (function) and customer size. Thus, as shown in Exhibit 5-5(b), snow-

---

[24]See Philip Kotler, "Strategic Planning and the Marketing Process," *Business*, May–June, 1980, pp. 2–9.

EXHIBIT 5-5   Defining Served Market

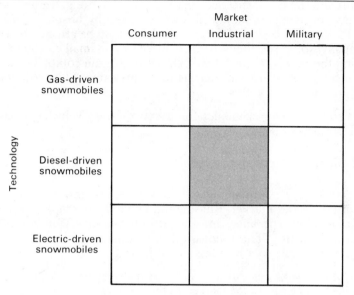

(a) Technology/Market Matrix

(b) Customer Use/Customer Size Matrix

Source: Philip Kotler, "Strategic Planning and the Marketing Process," *Business,* May–June, 1980, pp. 6–7. Reprinted by permission of the author.

mobiles could be designed for use as delivery vehicles (e.g., used by business firms and the post office), as recreation vehicles (e.g., rented at resort hotel sites), or as emergency vehicles (e.g., used by hospitals and police forces). Further, the design of the snowmobile would be affected by whether the company would sell them to large, medium, or small customers. After evaluating the nine alternatives in Exhibit 5-5(b), the company found the "large customer, delivery use" market to be attractive. Thus, this company defined its served market as:

> Diesel-driven snowmobiles for use as delivery vehicles by large industrial customers.

Served Market Alternatives

In the above example, the company settled on a rather narrow definition of the served market. But it could expand the scope of the served market as it gains experience and the opportunities elsewhere in the market appear attractive. The following is a summary of the served market alternatives available to a business like this one:

1. *Product/market concentration* consists of the company's niching itself in only one part of the market. In the above example, making only diesel-driven snowmobiles for industrial buyers.
2. *Product specialization* consists of the company's deciding to produce only diesel-driven snowmobiles for all customer groups.
3. *Market specialization* consists of the company's deciding to make a variety of snowmobiles that serve the varied needs of a particular customer group, such as industrial buyers.
4. *Selective specialization* consists of the company's entering several product markets that have no relation to each other except that each provides an individually attractive opportunity.
5. *Full coverage* consists of the company's making a full range of snowmobiles to serve all the market segments.[25]

CUSTOMER SEGMENTATION

In the example discussed above, the served market consisted of one segment. But conceivably, the served market could be much broader in scope. For example, the company could decide to serve all industrial customers (large, medium, small) by offering diesel-driven snowmobiles for delivery use. The "broader" served market, however, must be segmented; because the market is not homogeneous, it cannot be served by one type of product/service offering.

The United States represents the largest market in the world for most products. But it is not a homogeneous market. Not all customers

---

[25]*Ibid.*, p. 7.

want the same thing. Particularly in well-supplied markets, customers generally prefer products or services that are tailored to their needs. The difference can be expressed in terms of product or service features, service levels, quality levels, or something else.

In other words, the large market has a variety of submarkets or segments which vary substantially. One of the crucial elements of marketing strategy is to choose the segment or segments that are to be served. This, however, is not always easy. There can be different methods for dissecting the market. Deciding which method to use may pose a problem.

Virtually all strategists segment their markets. Typically, they use SIC code, annual purchase volume, age, and income as differentiating variables. Categories based on these variables, however, may not suffice as far as the development of strategy is concerned.

RCA, for example, initially classified potential customers for color television sets according to age, income, and social class. The company soon realized that these segments were not crucial ones for continued growth since buyers were not confined to those groups. Later analysis discovered that there were "innovators" and "followers" in each of the above groups. This finding led the company to tailor its marketing strategy to various segments according to their "innovativeness." Mass acceptance of color television might have been delayed substantially if RCA had followed a more traditional approach.[26]

An American food processor achieved rapid success in the French market after discovering that "modern" French women like processed foods while "traditional" French housewives look upon them as a threat. A leading industrial manufacturer discovered that its critical variable was the amount of annual usage per item, not per order or per any other conventional variable. This proved to be critical since heavy users can be expected to be more sensitive to price and may be more aware of and responsive to promotional perspective.

Segmentation is aimed at increasing the scope of business by closely aligning a product or brand with an identifiable customer group. Take, for example, cigarettes. Thirty years ago, most cigarette smokers chose from among three brands: Camel, Chesterfield, and Lucky Strike. Today more than 160 brands adorn retail shelves. In order to sell more cigarettes, tobacco companies have been dividing the smoking public into relatively tiny sociological groups and then aiming one or more brands at each group. Vantage and Merit, for example, are aimed at young women, and Camel and Winston are aimed mostly at rural smokers.[27] Cigarette marketing success hinges on how effectively a company can design a brand

---

[26]"Strategy and Market Segment Research," an informal statement issued by the Boston Consulting Group, 1968.

[27]John Koten, "Tobacco Marketer's Success Formula: Make Cigarettes in Smoker's Own Image," *The Wall Street Journal*, February 29, 1980, p. 22. See also "Banking Squeeze: The Search for Special Niches," *Business Week*, April 12, 1982, p. 70.

to appeal to a particular type of smoker, and then how well it can reach that smoker with sharply focused packaging, product design, and advertising.

What is true of cigarettes applies to many, many products; it applies even to services. Banks, for example, have recently been vying with one another for important customers by offering innovative services that will set each bank apart from its competition.

The above illustrations underscore not only the significance of segmenting the market, but also the importance of carefully choosing the segmentation criteria.

Segmentation Criteria

Segmentation criteria will vary depending on the nature of the market. In consumer goods marketing, one may use simple demographic and socioeconomic variables, personality and lifestyle variables, or situation-specific events (such as use intensity, brand loyalty, attitudes, etc.) as the bases of segmentation. In industrial marketing, segmentation is achieved by forming end-use segments, product segments, geographic segments, common buying factor segments, and customer-size segments. Exhibit 5-6 provides an inventory of different bases for segmentation. Most of these bases are self-explanatory. For a detailed account, however, reference may be made to an advanced book on the subject.[28]

In addition to the above criteria, creative analysts may well identify others. For example, a shipbuilding company dissects its tanker market into large, medium, and small markets; similarly, its cargo ship market is classified into high-, medium-, and low-grade markets. A forklift truck manufacturer divides its market on the basis of product-performance requirements. Many consumer goods companies, General Foods, Procter & Gamble, and Heublein among them, base their segments on lifestyle analysis.

Data for forming customer segments may be analyzed with the use of simple statistical techniques (e.g., averages) or multivariate methods. Caution is necessary to avoid the impression that a good job in forming segments necessarily calls for the use of multivariate techniques or other high-level statistical analysis. As has been said;

> Clearly, all this exotic segmentation research—multivariate, life-style, benefits, nonparametric, factor analytic—is an expensive toy for hypothesis generation. It is an over-intellectualized exercise of powerful statistical methods which, unfortunately, too often are hooked up to

---

[28]See Ronald E. Frank, William F. Massy, and Yoram Wind, *Market Segmentation* (Englewood Cliffs, NJ: Prentice-Hall, 1972). See also B. P. Shapiro and T. V. Bonoma, "How to Segment Industrial Markets," *Harvard Business Review*, May–June, 1984, pp. 104–110.

EXHIBIT 5-6   **Bases for Customer Segmentation**

A. Consumer Markets
1. Demographic Factors (age, income, sex, etc.)
2. Socioeconomic Factors (social class, stage in the family life cycle)
3. Geographic Factors
4. Psychological Factors (lifestyle, personality traits)
5. Consumption Patterns (heavy, moderate, and light users)
6. Perceptual Factors (benefit segmentation, perceptual mapping)
7. Brand-Loyalty Patterns

B. Industrial Markets
1. End Use Segments (identified by SIC code)
2. Product Segments (based on technological differences or production economics)
3. Geographic Segments (defined by boundaries between countries or by regional differences within them)
4. Common Buying Factor Segments (cut across product/market and geographic segments)
5. Customer Size Segments

inadequate marketing theory. If hypothesis generation is the goal, there are other ways (and talking to your spouse is a respectable substitute for all that statistical manipulation).[29]

Conceptually, the following procedure may be adopted to choose a criterion for segmentation:

1. Identify potential customers and the nature of their needs.
2. Segment all customers into groups having:
   a. Common requirements
   b. The same value system with respect to the importance of these requirements.
3. Determine the theoretically most efficient means of serving each market segment, making sure that the distribution system selected will differentiate each segment from all others with respect to cost and price.
4. Adjust this ideal system to the constraints of the real world: existing commitments, legal restrictions, practicality, and so forth.

A market can also be segmented by level of customer service, stage of production, price-performance characteristics, credit arrangements with

[29]William T. Moran, "Segments Are Made, Not Born," in Earl L. Bailey (ed.), *Marketing Strategies* (New York: The Conference Board, 1974), pp. 15–16.

customers, location of plants, characteristics of manufacturing equipment, channels of distribution, and financial policies.[30]

The key is to choose a variable or variables which so divide the market that customers in a segment have similar responsiveness to some aspect of the marketer's strategy. The variable should be measurable, i.e., it should represent an objective value such as income, rate of consumption, frequency of buying, etc., not simply a qualitative viewpoint such as the degree of customer happiness. Also, the variable should create segments which may be accessible through promotion. Even if it is feasible to measure happiness, segments based on the happiness variable cannot be reached by a specific promotional medium.

Once segments have been formed, the next strategic issue is deciding which segment should be selected. The selected segment should comply with the following conditions:

1. It should be one in which the maximum differential in competitive strategy can be developed.
2. It must be capable of being isolated so that the competitive advantage can be preserved.
3. It must be valid, even though imitated.

The success of Volkswagen in the United States in 1960 can be attributed to its fit into a market segment which had two unique characteristics. First, the segment served by VW could not be adequately served by a modification of conventional U.S. cars. Second, manufacturing economies of scale could not be brought to bear by U.S. manufacturers to the disadvantage of VW. In contrast, American Motors was equally successful in identifying a special segment to serve with its compact car, i.e., the Rambler. The critical difference was that American Motors could not protect that segment from the superior scale of manufacturing volume of the other three U.S. automobile manufacturers.

The choice of strategically critical segments is not a straightforward task. It requires a careful evaluation of business strengths as compared with the competition. It also requires analytical marketing research to uncover market segments in which these competitive strengths can be significant.

Rarely do market segments conveniently coincide with obvious categories such as religion, age, profession, or family income in consumer markets or industrial sector and size of company where industrial customers are concerned. For this reason, market segmentation is emphatically not a job for statisticians. Rather, it is a task that can be mastered only by the creative strategist.

---

[30]See Robert A. Garda, "A Strategic Approach to Market Segmentation," *The McKinsey Quarterly*, Autumn, 1981, pp. 16–29.

SUMMARY

This chapter examines the role of the third "strategic C"—i.e., the customer—in formulating marketing strategy. One strategic consideration in determining marketing strategy is the definition of the market. A conceptual framework for defining the market is outlined.

The underlying factor in the formation of a market is customer need. The concept of need is discussed with reference to Maslow's hierarchy of needs. Once a market emerges, its worth must be determined through examining its potential. Different methods may be employed to study market potential.

Based on its potential, if the market appears worth tapping, its boundaries must be identified. Traditionally, market boundaries have been defined on the basis of product/market scope. Recent work on the subject recommends that market boundaries be established around the following dimensions: *technology, customer function,* and *customer group.* In addition, *level of production/distribution* is suggested as the fourth dimension. The task of market boundary definition amounts to grouping together a set of market cells, each defined in terms of the above dimensions.

The market boundaries set the limits of the market. Should a business unit serve this total market or choose a part of it? While it is conceivable to serve the entire market, usually the served market is considerably narrower in scope and smaller in size than the total market. Factors that influence the choice of served market are examined.

The served market may be too broad to be served by a single marketing program. If so, then the served market must be segmented. The rationale for segmentation is given, and a procedure for segmenting the market is outlined.

DISCUSSION QUESTIONS

1. *Elaborate on marketing's boundary role function. How is it related to customer needs?*
2. *What methods may be employed to measure market potential?*
3. *Identify the elements determined by market potential.*
4. *What dimensions may be used to define market boundaries?*
5. *Illustrate the use of these dimensions with a practical example.*
6. *What is served market? What factors determine the served market?*
7. *How may a business unit choose the criteria for segmenting the market?*

Anheuser-Busch, Inc.

In 1982, Anheuser-Busch (A-B) controlled 32 percent of the United States beer market and had clearly established itself as the ruler in the industry. The self-proclaimed "King of Beers" had successfully fought off a challenge by Miller, the second-largest brewer in the industry, to take over the throne. Several of the other top ten companies in the industry were in trouble and seeking merger partners. Therefore, they offered no threat to the firmly placed crown of A-B, which was seeking to capitalize on its competitors' turmoil.

August Busch III, chairman of A-B, felt very smug about his company's strong leadership position within the industry. He was confident that the company could "continue to dominate its rivals simply by redoubling its efforts—building huge and efficient breweries, spending heavily on advertising and promotion, maintaining price leadership where it holds commanding share, and cutting prices where needed to gain business." According to Dennis Long, president of A-B's Beer Division, "If you segment this country geographically, demographically, and by competitors, it gives you great confidence that there is still considerable room for us to grow."

A-B intended to increase its market share to 40 percent by 1990. It was seeking to increase its capacity 27 percent by means of a five-year capital expansion plan. This involved an investment of approximately $2 billion. A previous five-year expansion program costing $1.8 billion had increased the capacity of A-B by 50 percent. The major question facing A-B and its chairman was whether A-B would be able to achieve its objectives of increased market share and capacity, in light of the decrease in beer consumption growth from 5 percent annually in the 1970s to less than 3 percent in 1982. This decrease was a direct result of the increased popularity of other beverages and a decrease in the number of 18- to 34-year-olds.

INDUSTRY BACKGROUND

Small-scale brewing in the United States began in 1633 when the first commercial brewery was founded in the Dutch colonial town of New

---

This case was prepared by Elizabeth R. Igleheart and Colette M. Nakhoul, graduate students at the University of Connecticut, under the supervision of the author.

Amsterdam, now New York City. It was not until the 1840s that large-scale brewing began to take place as a result of the introduction of a different type of yeast from Germany. The 1870s saw the continued evolution of the beer industry when Louis Pasteur developed the process for controlling fermentation. This made the bottling of beer commercially feasible. During the 1900s, two events had a serious impact upon the industry. These events were the results of regulatory and technological changes. The first, Prohibition, occurred in 1920, at a time when the industry consisted almost exclusively of local and regional brewers, numbering approximately 1,500 brewers. When Prohibition was repealed in 1933, fewer than 800 of these brewers had survived. The second event, the introduction of commercial television, occurred in 1946. National advertising began to play an important role in determining market leadership. Television had given a definite edge to those brewers who could afford to advertise by placing their brand first in the consumer's mind.

Consolidation of the Industry

Over the past decade, the $10.5-billion beer industry had undergone considerable change. Consolidation had occurred as a result of the absorption by large brewers of many regional brewers. There were 92 breweries in 1970, and in 1982 that number had decreased to 43. In 1982, 95 percent of all the beer sold came from only 10 of these brewers, and 56 percent was accounted for by A-B and Miller. Exhibit 5-7 shows who were the 10 largest brewers in 1977 and 1981.

EXHIBIT 5-7   Market Shares in Beer Industry

COMPANY	SHARE IN 1977	SHARE IN 1981
Anheuser-Busch	23.0%	30.3%
Miller	15.2	22.4
Schlitz	13.9	7.9
Pabst	10.1	7.5[a]
Heileman	3.9	7.8
Coors	8.0	7.4
Olympia	4.3	3.2
Stroh	3.8	5.0[b]
Schaefer	2.9	—
Carling National	2.6	—
Genesee	—	2.0
C. Schmidt	—	1.8
Other	12.3	4.7
Total	100.0%	100.0%

[a]Includes acquisition of Carling National.
[b]Includes acquisition of Schaefer.

This market dominance by A-B and Miller had drastically altered the industry. A-B and Miller paid their unionized employees more than the average wage in the industry, took advantage of economies of scale, and spent more than their competitors for advertising. They gained considerable control over the market as a result of their marketing expertise, an avalanche of money, and a great deal of animosity toward each other. The remaining brewers provided little challenge for the two leaders. The smaller brewers were suffering from such nightmares as ineffective production and pricing decisions, poor marketing, and continuous management turnover. As a result of their weak position, the smaller brewers had banded together. It had been necessary for several of them to merge in order to survive. In 1982, Stroh acquired Schlitz, and Pabst acquired Olympia Brewing. The long-run outlook for the industry was even greater consolidation.

It appeared that the beer industry was headed toward a controlled oligopoly, similar to that of the tobacco industry. Companies were dissuaded from entering the industry because of high entry costs and low-growth prospects. The high entry costs involved two separate considerations: first, the expense required to build marketing and production groups able to compete with A-B and Miller; and second, the expense and difficulty involved in competing, based on product differentiation. Product differentiation was necessary since price competition alone was not sufficient. However, small brewers were resorting to price cutting in an effort to simply maintain current market shares. This made the low-growth prospects of the industry very apparent. The only small brewer that could possibly compete with A-B and Miller was G. Heileman because of its low-cost production facilities.

Along with reduction in the number of brewers over the long run, it was expected that the number of brands would also decrease. However, this could be offset by new types of beer being offered to new market segments. If greater industry consolidation and stronger competition were to occur in the future, A-B and Miller could potentially benefit from it. A more stable industry would result in an end to the vicious price cutting of the past, and profits would be more easily achieved for the few firms remaining in the industry.

Market Shifts

The existing brewers sold different types of beer in all segments of the market. In order to continue expansion, new types of beer were continually being produced. The most recent opportunity for growth had come from the light segment. In the 1970s, only 3 percent of the total market was attributed to light beer. By 1982, light beer accounted for 15 percent of the total market with only 20 percent penetration. Three factors had contributed to the growth in this segment. First, 25- to 34-year-olds drank the greatest amount of diet soft drinks, and their health-conscious attitude had had an effect on their beer-drinking habits. While the total population was growing at a rate of 1 percent annually, this age segment was forecast to grow at a 2 percent annual rate over the next five years. The second factor involved the increased importance of women in the light beer market. As a group, women appeared to prefer light beer. The third factor contributing to the growth of the light beer segment was advertising. In 1982, Miller held 60 percent of the light beer market; it had achieved its market leadership by appealing to the more-weight-conscious drinker, such as the older male beer drinker.

Imports were another area in which the possibility for growth existed. In 1982, imported beer represented only 2.9 percent of total beer consumption. This market segment was expected to almost double in size by 1990. Competition in this area is a matter of taste and image. The leading imports were marketed by companies that were not involved with domestic beer products, but most of the larger domestic brewers sold at least one import. Major brewers obviously considered it important to be represented in all segments and regions of the beer market (see Exhibit 5-8).

Market Segmentation

To be successful in the national market, three types of strengths were required: marketing skill, product mix, and distribution. The current leaders in the national beer market, A-B and Miller, were strong in all three areas (see Exhibit 5-9). They possessed marketing expertise, powerful wholesaler networks, and broad product lines. The strength of their product lines was their focus on the high-margin and high-growth light, premium, and super-premium beer segments. In 1982, A-B and Miller held 56 percent of the market, and it was projected that by the end of the decade they would hold 70 percent. Consolidation had accelerated because many small competitors were unable to execute effective marketing programs. It was obvious from this that marketing prowess was necessary for success. Product mix was important because the value of the product mix must be greater than the summed values of the individual products, otherwise referred to as synergy. If this is not the case, it would be cost-prohibitive to introduce a brand. Effective distribution was also a necessary ingredient to success. There was a tendency among consumers to purchase the brand sold in their neighborhood tavern. In order to capture these on-premise sales, effective distribution was essential. While distribution strength varied from segment to segment, A-B was strongest in distribution overall.

As mentioned above, imported beer represented a mere 2.9 percent of the market in 1982. This market segment had grown slowly over the preceding five years but was expected to grow to 5 percent by 1990. Importers continued to expand their markets by introducing new types of beers to appeal to different segments of the drinking-age population (e.g., Amstel Light). Heineken controlled 39 percent of the imported beer market and Molson controlled 20 percent, but recently these brewers had

EXHIBIT 5-8 Principal Brands of Major Brewers

COMPANY	PREMIUM	SUPER	LIGHT	IMPORTED
Anheuser-Busch	Budweiser	Michelob	Budweiser Light	Wurzburger Hofbrau
Miller	Miller High Life	Lowenbrau	Lite	Munich Oktoberfest
Schlitz	Schlitz	Erlanger	Schlitz Lite	
			Old Milwaukee Lite	
Pabst	Pabst Blue Ribbon	Andeker	Pabst Extra Lite	Fuerstenberg
Coors	Coors	Herman Joseph's 1868	Coors Light	Stella Arto
Heileman	Old Style Rainier	Special Export	[several entries]	Beck's

EXHIBIT 5-9   Strengths of Major Competitors in the Beer Industry in Three Key Areas

COMPANY	DISTRIBUTION	MARKETING STRENGTH	PRODUCT MIX
Anheuser-Busch	Strongest in the industry.	Superior—after the expenditure of considerable money, time, and effort.	The best in the industry. Something for everyone, but unit volume predominantly in the most profitable segment.
	Excellent unit-volume increases.	Benefits to both unit volume and productivity.	A plus for productivity.
Miller (Philip Morris)	Far superior to the industry average.	Deepest pockets in the industry. Proven skill.	Limited, but concentrated in the most profitable segment.
	Promotes good unit volume growth.	Benefits to both unit volume and productivity.	A plus for productivity.
Heileman	Very strong in some areas and weak in most others.	Limited financial strength but very efficient with the dollars it spends.	Limited in the most profitable. Very strong in the least profitable.
	Unit growth at industry average or slightly better.	Makes it a viable competitor in the industry.	No impact on productivity.
Coors	Deteriorating in traditional markets, weak in new markets.	Thus far, underwhelming.	Limited, but concentrated in the most profitable segments.
	Continuing declines in unit volumes.	Both unit volume and productivity declining.	A potential but unrealizable plus for productivity.
Pabst	Weak and getting weaker.	Ineffective and low budget.	Concentrated in the least profitable segments.
	Continuing declines in unit volume.	Effecting declines in both unit volume and productivity.	No impact on productivity.

Source: Prudential-Bache's *Brewery Industry Outlook*, March 10, 1983.

been losing part of their market share to Beck, Moosehead, and Labatt. The major U.S. producers had only recently begun to market one or more types of imported beers. Imported beers had a distinctive taste and were marketed to appeal to consumers who were inner-directed, upscale, and urban. The imported segment was the sole segment of the total beer market that could experience a sales slowdown when the economy decelerated.

The smaller brewers also marketed beer that had a distinctive taste. These brewers tended to sell on a regional basis, staying in well-defined areas close to home. They specialized in lower-priced beers and controlled 10 percent of the total beer market in 1982. The number of small, local, family-owned breweries had decreased, and it was expected that this trend would continue. Between 1970 and 1980 this market declined substantially in size. As a result of increased fixed costs, many of these brewers had been unable to afford to continue in business on their own. With those that were able to survive, one of the key factors had been community pride and interest in the local brewery.

Competition

There are three areas in which brewers compete with one another: packaging, advertising, and price. Packaging provides brewers with a method of segmentation. Packaging choices include the traditional 12-oz. six-pack in bottles or cans; 20-oz. cans; 40-oz. bottles; 7-oz. eight-pack in bottles or cans; 12-oz. twelve-pack in bottles or cans; and various keg sizes. During 1981, 59 percent of the total beer consumed was from cans, 9 percent was from returnable bottles, and 32 percent was from nonreturnable bottles. The use of returnable bottles had increased significantly since 1981 as a result of the passage of deposit laws in 19 states.

Over the past decade, advertising had become the major marketing tool. Since 1977, the advertising expenditures of the major brewers had been growing by more than 12 percent annually. Effective advertising had increased brand loyalties. There was an understanding among the brewers to advertise in a legal and morally responsible manner. In order to promote the image of being socially responsible, brewers sponsored many public service commercials involving the subjects of teenage pregnancy and drunk driving. They did not show minors, intoxicated people, or the actual consumption of beer in their advertising. There were several market segments that were important targets of advertising campaigns. These included college students, sports fans, and ethnic groups. The brewers attempted to instill brand loyalty in college students by sending representatives to the campuses (Schlitz) or sponsoring activities with promotional samples (Budweiser). The Hispanic market was large and important. To appeal to this market segment, Coors used actors of Hispanic background in its advertising, and A-B used a Spanish advertising agency to promote Michelob.

As new products were introduced they were being targeted directly toward certain market segments. This was achieved mainly through advertising campaigns. Miller Lite was targeted toward older men while Michelob 7-oz. bottles were targeted toward 24- to 35-year-old women. In all the advertisements focus was placed on identification with males, females, or couples. Beer is an extremely image-oriented product, and advertising campaigns were using a new emphasis. Instead of promoting beer just as a beverage that goes with a simple, relaxed lifestyle, the focus was on beer as a reward for a job well done. In these commercials, beer was the reward after a hard day's work or for winning at a sport. Humor was often injected into the commercials. Advertising played an important role in the beer industry, and it gave those brewers who could afford it a definite competitive advantage.

Price was no longer the important marketing tool it once was. It had lost its competitive importance. The emphasis had shifted to media. Pricing policies now depended upon product positioning. Brewers sold a number of brands that were price-sensitive, including super-premium, premium, popular-priced, light, and generic beer. It was expected that the premium, super-premium, and light-beer brands would seek annual price increases of 6–7 percent compared with the smaller increases of 3–5 percent sought by the popular-priced brands.

Environmental Factors Affecting the Beer Industry

There were certain economic and demographic factors that affected the beer industry. Two of these factors were the unpredictability of changes in consumer tastes and preferences, and the effect of extended recessionary forces. If the demand for beer were to weaken substantially, this could result in an overcapacity in the industry. Other factors were increased beer consumption by women, and the health-conscious attitude regarding lightness and moderation. The potential impact of these factors would be a favoring of beer over distilled spirits that would provide opportunity for enlargement and further segmentation of the beer market. A final factor encompassed all future movements in consumer economics and demographics. One of these forecasted trends was an increase of 20 percent in the 25-to-44 age group by 1987. This age group had a greater amount of discretionary income, tended to eat out more frequently, and was more likely to entertain at home. Another forecasted trend involved the primary beer drinking age segment. The 18-to-24 age group was expected to decrease in size. These projected trends would not be beneficial to the beer industry.

There were also regulatory factors that affected the beer industry. These included stricter litter-control requirements, additional legislation requiring bottle deposits, the raising of the drinking age, and increases in the excise tax. If brewers were required to make alterations in their packaging and methods of distribution, the possible result would be increased costs and, therefore, lower profit margins. This also might result if additional legislation were passed requiring bottle deposits. Raising the drinking age would result in a shrinking of the number of 18- to 24-year-olds who could legally drink, which would also negatively affect brewers' profits. If there were a flat increase in the excise tax, this could lead to a redistribution of profits. The hardest hit by the increase, on a percentage basis, would be the popular-priced and generic beers. This could lead consumers to believe that the price differential among the brands was narrowing and, therefore, cause them to change to the more expensive beers. This might prove devastating to the small, regional brewers who specialized in lower-priced beers. The granting of permission for territorial agreements between wholesalers would also affect the beer industry. The provision of exclusive regional rights would widen the gap between the strong and the weak wholesalers.

Industry Financial and Operating Performance

In the past, the financial success of brewers had paralleled their performance in marketing, distribution, and product mix. The brewers who had displayed strength in these three areas had gained increasing control over the beer market, while the weaker performers had been losing market share.

Even though the gap between the strong and weak brewers had been widening, most brewers' profit margins had been hurt by the price wars of the past. This had limited somewhat the flexibility in pricing. As a result, several other components of profitability had become important. These were productivity, unit volume, and gross margin. Productivity could be increased through changes to more favorable product mixes. There had been a shift to brands which had growth opportunities and/or appealing gross profit margins. The gross profit margin of each beer segment and its 3- to 5-year growth within each segment is shown in Exhibit 5-10.

Both A-B and Miller had focused their product lines on the fast-

EXHIBIT 5-10   Financial Perspectives of Different Types of Beer

BEER SEGMENT	GROSS PROFIT MARGIN	3–5 YEAR GROWTH	CURRENT SHARE
Popular-Priced	13%	(6)%	30%
Premium-Priced	20	4	37
Light Beers	24	11	15
Super Premiums	33	8	7
Imports	NA	10	6
Specialty	25	10	5
Total			100%

Source: Prudential-Bache's *Brewery Industry Outlook*, March 10, 1983.

growing and high-margin light, premium, and super-premium market segments. Light beer was a good brand to market since it was usually less costly to produce, sold at a premium, had a high profit margin, and was, therefore, more profitable than other brands. In 1982, another factor of productivity, operating rate, did not look good for most of the producers in the industry. The average operating rate for the industry was 75 percent of capacity, far below the optimum rate of 90 to 95 percent. A-B was the only brewer with strength in this area; its plants were operating at approximately 98 percent of capacity.

The second important component of profitability was unit volume, total barrelage; the higher the unit volume the greater the profitability. Since a flattening of beer consumption trends was forecast, the ability of individual brewers to increase their unit volume would depend upon several factors. These included their capacity to finance strong marketing programs and the presence of strong distribution systems.

The third component of profitability was gross margin, which is equal to sales minus cost of goods sold. This figure represented the maximum amount that could be spent on marketing and administrative expenditures without incurring an operating loss. Past and projected industry gross profit are shown in Exhibit 5-11. The industry gross profit per barrel, excluding A-B and Miller, equaled only two-thirds that of A-B. It was not within the financial means of most brewers to reach a com-

EXHIBIT 5-11   Past and Estimated Future Changes in Industry Gross Profit

	(PROFIT AND BARRELAGE IN MILLIONS)			
	1972	1977	1982	1987
Industry				
Total Barrelage	131.8	156.9	180.0	209.0
Total Gross Profit	$1,479.5	$1,915.5	$2,454.5	$3,224.2
Gross Profit/Barrel	$11.23	$12.21	$13.64	$15.43
Anheuser-Busch				
Total Barrelage	26.5	36.6	59.1	86.6
Total Gross Profit	$392.6	$571.1	$976.1	$1,555.7
Gross Profit/Barrel	$14.82	$15.60	$16.52	$17.96
Miller				
Total Barrelage	5.3	24.2	39.3	54.5
Total Gross Profit	$71.6	$368.2	$580.7	$865.7
Gross Profit/Barrel	$13.51	$15.21	$14.78	$15.88
Industry—Less Bud & Miller				
Total Barrelage	100.0	96.1	81.6	67.9
Total Gross Profit	$1,015.3	$976.2	$897.7	$802.8
Gross Profit/Barrel	$10.15	$10.96	$11.00	$11.82

Source: Prudential-Bache's *Brewery Industry Outlook*, March 10, 1983.

petitive level of marketing, since this would necessitate a substantial increase in spending. There was apparently a dichotomy in the industry which could be expressed as "The rich get richer and the not-so-rich are lucky to keep running in place." In summation, higher gross margins represented more available funds for marketing expenditures. This in turn led to increased market share and sales, the results of which were greater volume and productivity, and, therefore, increased profitability.

The factors which would affect the future performance of the industry were a slow growth environment, recession, and the cost outlook. The first factor, a slow growth environment, would necessitate that even more emphasis be placed on increasing productivity and unit volume. Recession, the second factor, would have an impact upon certain brands of beer, the brands marketed to the people most affected by a recession. A good example of this is Miller High Life, which is strongly marketed towards blue-collar workers. Lastly, the outlook for costs was that the costs of raw materials and packaging would increase at a rate lower than that of inflation, and that advertising would not exceed an annual growth rate of 12 percent. Such a favorable cost outlook would enable brewers to keep operating margins within a 3 to 5 percent increase. Exhibit 5-12 presents a breakdown of the costs of the major brewers.

ANHEUSER-BUSCH PERSPECTIVES

Company Background

Anheuser-Busch was founded in 1852. Its corporate headquarters are in St. Louis, Missouri. The present chairman is August Busch III, a fourth-generation brewer. In 1957, A-B took the industry leadership away from Schlitz and has held this leadership position ever since. During that period A-B has had to fend off challenges from both Schlitz and Miller. By the 1970s, A-B had grown so contented that even a challenge by Schlitz did not elicit any response. The brewer was running out of beer every summer and saw no need to market aggressively. The challenge by Schlitz

EXHIBIT 5-12   Estimated Cost Breakdown for Major Brewers

Packaging	50%
Raw Materials	14
Labor	12
Marketing	8
All Other	16
Total	100%

Source: Prudential-Bache's *Brewery Industry Outlook*, March 10, 1983.

failed only as a result of several marketing blunders which lost Schlitz many loyal customers. It was a challenge by Miller, acquired in 1969–70 by Philip Morris, Inc., that posed a definite threat to the leadership position of A-B and prompted it to act. A-B was in the middle of an awkward transition of management when Miller attacked, but what made matters considerably worse was a strike during the summer season of 1976 that kept its beer off the shelves. In retaliation, A-B made an all-out effort to defeat Miller and successfully retained its leadership position. The war between A-B and Miller badly crippled the rest of the brewers in the industry, who were constantly struggling to survive.

Since 1976, A-B has increased its number of brands from 3 to 8 to target all market segments. Busch and Natural Light are marketed as popular-priced brands, Budweiser and Budweiser Light as premium brands, and Michelob, Michelob Light, Michelob Dark, and an import, Wurzberger, as super-premium brands. All of its brands are backed by heavy advertising and promotion expenditures. The amount spent by A-B on media rose 170 percent, to $145 million, between 1977 and 1982. A-B was outspending all other brewers in the sponsoring of sporting events. In 1982, it sponsored 98 professional and 310 college sports events and successfully bid $10 million for beer sponsorship of the 1984 Summer Olympics.

Brewers have used "image" advertising to position their products ever since advertising was first employed, but its use has been on the rise in the past few years. The original targeted beer segment of Budweiser had a strong, rugged image and, therefore, from the beginning, Budweiser had been associated with the Clydesdale horses. A team of these horses pulled the original Budweiser wagon, but their use had become primarily ceremonial. The type of people now drinking Budweiser were higher-income, middle-aged individuals, more likely to be men and less likely to be minorities. In order to attract a broader market, including women, minorities, and older and younger people, A-B had established a new campaign to promote Budweiser based on the slogan "This Bud's for you." The overall consumption of Budweiser tended to be evenly distributed geographically. As a result, it did not face the same problem as Miller High Life brands, which tended to be skewed geographically toward the economically depressed areas of the country. Exhibit 5-13 presents the estimated media costs of Budweiser, Miller High Life, and Schlitz in 1973, 1977, and 1981.

A-B marketed three light beers, Budweiser Light, Michelob Light, and Natural Light. These three brands were marketed toward the premium, super-premium, and mid-price market segments, respectively. When Budweiser Light was introduced in 1982, it met with unexpected success. This brand emphasized sports and was marketed with a sport-oriented theme, "Bring out your best . . ." Budweiser Light was targeted toward the heavy beer drinker who was athletic and active, whereas Miller Lite was targeted toward the older male beer drinker who was weight-conscious.

EXHIBIT 5-13   Estimated Media Costs per Barrel of Different Brands of Beer

(MEDIA AND BARRELAGE IN MILLIONS)			5-YEAR GROWTH	
1973	1977	1981	73–77	77–81
Budweiser				
Total Media	$7.2	$22.7	$42.6	33.3%	17.0%
Total Barrelage	22.5	25.7	37.6	3.4	10.0
Media/Barrel	$0.32	$0.88	$1.13	28.8	6.5
Miller High Life				
Total Media	$8.2	$14.6	$37.6	15.5	26.7
Total Barrelage	6.4	16.7	24.0	27.1	9.5
Media/Barrel	$1.28	$0.87	$1.57	(9.2)	15.9
Schlitz				
Total Media	$10.3	$19.0	$17.6	16.5	(1.9)
Total Barrelage	17.5	16.2	8.0	(1.9)	(16.1)
Media/Barrel	$0.59	$1.17	$2.20	18.7	17.1

Busch, a popular-priced beer, was targeted toward the free-spirited man. Promotional campaigns for this brand were geared toward the hard-working blue-collar employee who headed to the mountains for relaxation. The super-premium market segment was dominated by Michelob, an A-B brand, and close behind was Lowenbrau, a Miller brand. There had been a slowing in the growth of this market segment. The new promotional campaign for Michelob Light targeted white-collar men and women who entertained, belonged to country clubs, and could afford to spend a little more for a special-occasion beer. This campaign centered on heritage, tradition, quality, and distinctiveness. A-B, with its many expenditures on advertising, closely followed by Miller, was the leader of the industry.

Wholesalers have high fixed expenses as a result of the large capital outlays required to purchase trucks, etc. Therefore, a wholesaler depends on volume sales for profit and concentrated effort upon the brands that offer the greatest volume. It can be seen in Exhibit 5-14 that A-B and Miller had greater volume than competing brewers. A-B achieved product distribution through a network of 950 wholesalers and was reputed to have the most effective network of wholesalers in the industry. A-B had provided considerable support to its wholesalers, including the establishment of in-depth training seminars on financial management and warehousing. Wholesaler performance was evaluated on the basis of the frequency with which calls were made upon accounts, the weekly and monthly sales of all beers, and several other factors. It was normal for an A-B wholesaler to hold from 12 to more than 20 days' inventory, depending upon the season. With a high inventory turnover rate, a wholesaler was able to generate profits much more quickly. The effective wholesaler system of A-B proved invaluable since it was forecast that, in the future, the fight between the brewers would be focused at the wholesaler level.

Company Financial and Operating Performance

A-B's many interests include baking operations, snack foods, transportation services, a baseball franchise, and real estate development. Despite these other interests, A-B's beer operations dominate its revenue base. The beer operations accounted for approximately 85 percent of revenue in 1982. As of June, 1982, A-B controlled 31.4 percent of the United States beer market. It controlled 29.8 percent in 1981, 28.2 percent in 1980, and 23 percent in 1977 (see Exhibit 5-15). This was an increase in market share of 37 percent over a five-year period. The volume of beer sold by A-B also increased significantly over these five years. Between 1977 and 1982, beer volume rose from $36 million to $59.1 million, an increase of 64 percent. In 1981, A-B had total sales of $3.8 billion, and its profit for the year was $217.4 million. Exhibit 5-16 presents the financial and operating performance of A-B over a five-year period.

Over this five-year period A-B had experienced an increase in sales and profits of 111 percent and 136 percent, respectively. It had a unit profitability of approximately $3.59 per barrel of beer sold, greater than that of the rest of the industry. While it was forecast that total market earnings would increase by 15 to 20 percent in 1983, it was projected that A-B earnings would increase by 30 to 40 percent. As a result of its profit leadership in the industry, A-B had price elasticity.

A-B had experienced operating and financial success as a result of both productivity gains and unit volume increases. It had spent more than $2 billion over the past five years on a program to increase capacity. This had both expanded and upgraded the cost effectiveness of the A-B plants.

EXHIBIT 5-14   Average Case Volume per Brand per Distributor for Different Brewers

Anheuser-Busch	859,000
Miller	637,000
Heileman	108,000
Coors	438,000
Stroh/Schlitz	280,000
Pabst	154,000
Industry Average	541,000
Industry Average Less A-B	405,000

Source: Prudential-Bache's *Brewery Industry Outlook*, March 10, 1983.

EXHIBIT 5-15 Top Brewers' Volume Share of Market 1965–85 (in Millions of 31-Gallon Barrels)

(% Market Shares)	1965	1975	1978	1979	1980	1981	1982E	1985E
Anheuser-Busch	11.7%	23.4%	25.1%	26.8%	28.2%	29.8%	32.0%	34.5%
Miller	3.7	8.6	18.9	20.7	21.0	22.0	22.0	23.6
Heileman	1.0	3.0	4.3	6.5	7.5	7.7	7.8	8.8
Schlitz	8.5	15.5	11.8	9.7	8.4	7.8	7.5	6.9
Stroh-Schaefer	—	7.3	6.2	5.6	5.5	5.0	4.8	5.2
Pabst*	8.1	10.4	9.3	8.7	8.5	7.4	6.6	5.5
Coors*	3.6	7.9	7.6	7.5	7.8	7.3	6.8	6.8
Olympia	—	4.4	4.0	3.5	3.4	3.1	2.9	2.5
All Others	63.4	19.4	12.8	10.9	9.7	9.9	9.7	6.2
A-B and Miller	15.4	32.0	44.0	47.5	49.2	51.9	54.0	58.1
% Point change in annual market share(s)								
Anheuser-Busch	—	+1.2	+0.6	+1.7	+1.4	+1.6	+2.2	+0.8
Miller	—	+0.5	+3.4	+1.8	+0.3	+1.0	0.0	+0.5
Heileman	—	+0.2	+0.4	+2.2	+1.0	+0.2	+0.1	+0.3
Schlitz	—	+0.7	-1.2	-2.1	-1.3	-0.6	-0.4	-0.1
Stroh-Schaefer	—	—	-0.3	-0.6	-0.1	-0.5	-0.1	+0.1
Pabst*	—	+0.2	-0.4	+0.6	-0.2	-1.1	-0.8	-0.4

Coors*	—	+0.4	-0.1	-0.1	+0.3	-0.5	+0.4	0.0
Olympia	—	—	-0.1	-0.5	-0.1	-0.3	-0.2	-0.?
All Others	—	-3.2	-2.2	-1.9	-1.1	+0.2	-0.2	-1.2
A-B and Miller	—	+1.7	+4.0	+3.5	+1.7	+2.6	+2.1	+1.4
Industry Volume	100.8	150.3	165.8	172.6	177.9	182.8	185.0	207.5
Anheuser-Busch	11.8	35.2	41.6	46.2	50.2	54.5	59.3	71.5
Miller	3.7	12.9	31.3	35.8	37.3	40.3	40.7	49.0
Heileman	1.0	4.5	7.1	11.2	13.3	14.0	14.5	18.3
Schlitz	8.6	23.3	19.6	16.8	15.0	14.3	13.8	14.5
Stroh-Schaefer	—	11.0	10.2	9.6	9.7	9.1	8.8	10.8
Pabst*	8.2	15.7	15.4	15.1	15.1	13.5	12.3	11.0
Coors*	3.6	11.9	12.6	12.9	13.8	13.3	12.5	14.1
Olympia	—	6.6	6.7	6.0	6.1	5.7	5.3	5.2
Total Top Six	36.9	103.5	127.6	138.0	144.7	149.9	153.1	178.4
% Market Share of Top Six	36.6%	68.9%	77.0%	80.0%	81.3%	82.0%	82.8%	86.0%
% Share of A-B and Miller	15.4%	32.0%	44.0%	47.5%	49.2%	51.9%	54.1%	58.1%

E—Estimated

Source: *Advertising Age*, December 24, 1983

EXHIBIT 5-16 Anheuser-Busch, Inc.: Five-Year Composite Summary of Financial Performance (in Millions of Dollars)

	1978	1979	1980	1981	1982	Industry Comparison (1982)
Volume (7.2% growth)	41.6	46.2	50.2	54.5	59.1	1–2% Growth
Sales	$2259.6	$2775.9	$3295.4	$3847.2	$4576.6	$7297.9
Profit Margin	4.9%	5.2%	5.2%	5.7%	6.3%	5.1%
Capital Expenditures	228.7	432.3	590.0	421.3	350.0E	NA
Capitalization	36.1%	35.8%	43.2%	42.4%	33.9%*	NA
Interest Coverage	8.1x	6.5x	4.0x	3.9x	4.0x	NA

*6 months ended June 30, 1982.

Source: Information provided by Anheuser-Busch, Inc.

Over the next five years, A-B intended to invest another $2 billion in order to increase capacity from 62 million barrels to over 75 million. A significant portion of these funds was likely to be internally generated. A-B recently acquired the second-largest domestic baker, Campbell-Taggert, which should result in an increase in the amount of funds generated internally.

A-B had successfully positioned its products in the high-margin and fast-growing beer segments. It had also employed an aggressive marketing strategy. As a result, A-B had achieved increases in unit volume that were greater than the growth in industry sales. Over the next five years, it was projected that annual unit growth for A-B would be 8 to 10 percent. This is shown in Exhibit 5-17. The exhibit also shows projected annual unit growth for five other companies and breaks down each of their market shares among the brands they offer. In order to obtain operating flexibility, A-B had also employed vertical integration. Many of the processes involved in the manufacturing of beer were carried on in-house at the A-B facilities. These included barley malting, metalized paper printing, and can manufacturing. While A-B was putting considerable effort into expansion, other brewers were attempting to increase their return on investment by restricting capacity.

Expansion

In the 1970s, A-B was unsuccessful in its efforts to market root beer and a low-alcohol lemon-lime drink. As a result of these past failures, the company was moving into new areas more cautiously. Also, A-B had teamed up with partners for certain ventures. It had recently moved into the rapidly expanding "wine on tap" business with a partner, LaMont Winery Inc. In this business, A-B was marketing larger kegs which distributed, under the Master Cellars brand name, white, red, and rosé wines. A-B had most recently expanded through diversification into the snack food business. Its Eagle Snacks were being distributed nationwide through bars and convenience stores. The company's latest offering in the beer market was Budweiser Light. It was hoped that this brand would succeed, where Michelob Light and Natural Light had failed, in denting Miller's 60 percent share of the light beer market. The Budweiser Light brand was backed by substantial financial support, $40–$50 million.

In planning the future expansion of A-B, August Busch III had several strategic alternatives to consider. These could be divided into two categories, those involving beer operations and those involving non-beer operations. Within the beer operations category there were several possible alternatives for expansion, including the light beer segment, acquisitions, European markets, divestitures, the "Eastern" bloc, and the 3.2-beer segment. There was definitely opportunity for expansion through the light beer segment since it was estimated that the potential for market penetration was at least 35 percent and currently penetration was only 20

EXHIBIT 5-17   Growth Potential of Different Brewers (3–5 Years Out)

	Projected Annual Unit Growth	Estimated Current Market Share	Projected Net Price Increase Realized by Company
Anheuser-Busch	8%–10%	32%	6%–7%
Budweiser		22	
Budweiser Light		1	
Michelob		5	
Michelob Light		2	
Busch		1	
Natural Light		1	
Miller	6%–8%	22%	6%–7%
Miller		11	
Lite		9	
Lowenbrau		2	
Stroh/Schlitz	3%–5%	12%	4%–6%
(privately held)			
Stroh		5	
Old Milwaukee		4	
Schlitz		3	
Heileman	3%–5%	8%	4%–6%
Major Brand			
Old Style &			
numerous other			
brands including			
Blatz, Carling,			
Black Label, and			
Tuborg			
Coors	declines	7%	6%–7%
Coors		5	
Coors Light		2	
Herman Joseph's		NF	
George Killian		NF	
Pabst	declines	7%	4%
Pabst			
Pabst Light			
Andeker		NF	
Henry Weinhard			
NF = Not forecastable			

Source: Prudential-Bache's *Brewery Industry Outlook,* March 10, 1983.

percent. It would also be possible for A-B to expand through the acquisition of smaller brewers. The disadvantage to A-B of acquiring smaller brewers would be that most of these brewers tended to concentrate upon unique market segments which would be too small or uneconomical for A-B to serve. Therefore, these acquisitions might offer few advantages. However, it might prove necessary to acquire some of the smaller brewers in order to stop them from banding together and establishing a third power in the industry.

Another way in which A-B could promote expansion was through the European markets. It would be beneficial for A-B to explore and evaluate untapped European markets. The question mark in this alternative was whether A-B brands would be able to compete successfully against the heavier, fuller European brands. It could also prove beneficial to A-B to divest its Natural Light brand of beer, which had proved to be unsuccessful. In 1982, this brand was lowered in price when selling to supermarket accounts, since this was where consumers were extremely price-sensitive. It appeared that the consumer was not attracted to A-B's idea of a "natural" beer as A-B had expected. There was potential for further expansion if A-B divested its Natural Light brand and used these brewing facilities for the production of its Budweiser Light brand.

Another possible alternative for A-B was to put a vigorous effort into pursuing the "Eastern" markets. It appeared that the Japanese were extremely attracted to products which project the "Western" culture. The Japanese company which marketed Suntory whiskey was promoting the product in California to encourage its projection of a "Western" image so that it would be accepted in Japan. An aggressive marketing effort in this area of the world should promote the expansion of A-B. Expansion could also be promoted through pursuit of the 3.2-beer market segment. This variety of beer has half the alcohol, and thus half the calories, of regular beer. The only problem with pursuing this market segment was that it could affect the sales of light beer, which also has fewer calories than regular beer.

The other category of alternatives through which expansion could be achieved involved non-beer operations. The major questions concerning Eagle Snacks and their potential for expansion involved the growth of the "junk food" market, how the product could be differentiated, and whether or not the product could obtain a significant part of the retail business, considering Frito-Lay's market domination. A-B could potentially expand through growth in the snack food business.

The other area through which A-B could expand was wine and spirits. Exhibit 5-18 compares the 1982 consumption of various liquids such as beer, wine, spirits, etc. A-B had already moved into the "wine on tap" business with a partner. There were a number of other possibilities in this area it could explore. One of these possibilities involved determining the feasibility of acquiring a winery and taking advantage of A-B's strengths in distribution and marketing. Another possibility involved exploring the potential for developing a product to compete with "Club

EXHIBIT 5-18   1982 Liquid Consumption in the U.S. (Gallons per Capita)

Soft Drinks	40.1	Juices	6.6
Coffee	26.1	Spirits	1.9
Beer	24.4	Wines	2.3
Milk	20.5	Bottled Water	2.2
Tea	6.3	Water	46.1
Powdered Drinks	NA		
	TOTAL		176.5

Source: *Beverage Industry,* May 23, 1983.

Cocktails," currently being marketed by Heublein, Inc. A-B has great potential for further expansion since its strengths allow it to diversify. It has
many possibilities to consider for future expansion.

To sum up, the future outlook for A-B is good. Its facilities were
operating at 98 percent of capacity, and the brewer was confident that it
could maintain its dominance in the industry. August Busch III was not
fazed by the slowing of beer-consumption growth and was confident that
A-B could achieve its objectives of increased market share and capacity.
If the company continued its aggressive marketing strategy and capitalized upon its ability to diversify and expand in other areas, there appeared
to be no reason why it would not achieve its objectives.

CHAPTER 6
Scanning the Environment

I hold that man is in the right who is most in league with the future.

Henrik Ibsen

An organization is a creature of its environment. Its very survival and all of its perspectives/resources, problems, and opportunities are generated and conditioned by the environment. Thus, it is important for an organization to monitor the relevant changes taking place in the environment surrounding the organization and formulate strategies to adapt to these changes.

In other words, in order for an organization to survive and prosper in the future, the strategist must master the challenges of the profoundly changing political, economic, technological, and social environment. In order to achieve this broad perspective, the strategist needs to develop and implement a systematic approach to environmental scanning. As the rate and magnitude of change increase, this scanning activity must be intensified and directed by explicit definitions of purpose, scope, and focus. The efforts of businesses to cope with these problems is contributing to the development of systems for exploring alternatives with greater sensitivity to long-run implications. This emerging science has the promise of providing a better framework for maximizing opportunities and allocating resources in anticipation of environmental changes.

This chapter reviews the state of the environmental scanning art and suggests a general approach for environmental scanning which may be used by a marketing strategist. Specifically, the chapter discusses the criteria to determine the scope and focus of scanning, the procedure for examining the relevance of environmental trends, the techniques to evaluate the impact of an environmental trend on a particular product/market, and the linkage of environmental trends and other "early warning signals" to strategic planning processes.

IMPORTANCE OF ENVIRONMENTAL SCANNING

Without taking into account the relevant environmental influences, a company cannot expect to develop its strategy. It is the environmental influences emerging out of the energy crisis which are responsible for the high popularity of smaller, more-fuel-efficient automobiles and which brought about the demise of the less-efficient rotary engines. Similar influences resulting from the severe winter of 1976–77 and uncertainty about fossil fuels have renewed and expanded the interest in solar energy and wind energy and in more-energy-conservative homes and buildings. It was the environmental influence of a coffee bean shortage and geometric price increases that spawned the "coffee-saver" modification for Mr. Coffee automatic drip coffee makers, hastened the development of a ground tea for automatic coffee machines, and even produced a coffee substitute, Bravo, made of a common weed. Shopper and merchant complaints of an earlier era contributed to the virtual elimination of deposit bottles; recent pressures from environmental groups have forced their return and have prompted Monsanto to develop a low-cost recyclable plastic bottle, the Easy Goer, for the Coca-Cola Company.

The sad tales of companies that seemingly did everything right and yet lost competitive leadership as a result of technological change abound. DuPont was beaten by Celanese when bias-ply tire cords changed from nylon to polyester. B. F. Goodrich was beaten by Michelin when the radial overtook the bias-ply tire. NCR wrote off $139 million in electromechanical inventory, and the equipment to make it, when solid-state point-of-sale terminals entered the market. Indeed, none of the leading vacuum tube manufacturers in 1957 remained as a competitive force by 1977. These companies lost even though they were low-cost producers. They lost even though they were close to their customers. They lost even though they were market leaders. They lost because they failed to make an effective transition from old to new technology.[1]

In brief, business derives its existence from the environment. Thus, it should monitor its environment constructively. To do so the business should scan the environment and incorporate the impact of environmental trends on the organization by reviewing the corporate strategy on a continual basis. Glover said the following:

> Perceiving in the environment needs and opportunities for adaptation—even before they actually materialize—and designing and seeing through a continuous procession of actions to carry out adaptive innovation, these are the essence of business *strategy*. More—these are the distinguishing functions of the top management. It is the job of corporate top management to direct and to manage the *transformation* of every aspect of the corporation in response to developments of the dynamic environment. A corporation gets left behind whose management lacks these capacities—The environment represents an ever-changing sum total of the "facts of life" with which the corporation has to come to terms. Willy-nilly the environment is the unyielding,

---

[1]Richard N. Foster, "To Exploit New Technology, Know When to Junk the Old," *The Wall Street Journal*, May 2, 1983, p. 30. See also John Diebold, "Where We Are Heading in the Age of Automation," *Management Review*, March, 1983, pp. 9–15.

unforgiving frame of reference for everything top management does as it guides the corporation.[2]

John Naisbitt has identified ten megatrends that would deeply affect individuals and businesses for the rest of the 1980s (see Exhibit 6-1). We are indeed living in a rapidly changing world. Many things that we take for granted today could not be even perceived in the 1960s. Before the end of this century many more "wonders" will come to exist.

To survive and prosper in the midst of such a changing environment companies must stay at the forefront of changes affecting their industries. First, it must be recognized that all products and processes have performance limits and that the closer one comes to these limits the more expensive it becomes to squeeze out the next generation of performance improvements. Second, one must take all competition seriously. Normally competitor analyses seem to implicitly assume that the most serious competitors will be the ones with the largest resources. But in the context of taking advantage of environmental shifts this is frequently not the case. Texas Instruments was a $5 million to $10 million company in 1955 when it took on the mighty vacuum tube manufacturers—RCA, General Electric, Sylvania, and Westinghouse—and beat all of them with its semiconductor technology. Boeing was nearly bankrupt when it successfully introduced the commercial jet plane, vanquishing the larger and more financially secure Lockheed, McDonnell, and Douglas Corporations. Third, if the environmental change promises potential advantage, one has to attack to win or even play in the game. Attack means gaining access to the new technology, training people in its use, investing in capacity to use it, devising strategies to protect the position, and holding off on investments in mature lines. Fourth, the attack has to begin early. The substitution of one product or process for another proceeds at a slow pace and then explodes—rarely in a predictable fashion. One cannot wait for the explosion to occur to react. There is simply not enough time. B. F. Goodrich lost 60 percentage points of market share to Michelin in four years. Texas Instruments passed RCA in sales of active electronic devices in five to six years. Fifth, a close tie is needed between the chief executive officer and the operating managers facing the change to incorporate the environmental shifts in the strategy.[3]

What Scanning Can Accomplish

Scanning improves an organization's abilities to deal with a rapidly changing environment in a number of ways:

---

[2]J. D. Glover, "Rise and Fall of Corporations: Challenge and Response," unpublished note prepared at Harvard Business School, No. 9-367-017, 1967, p. 4.
[3]Yezdi M. Godiwalla, Wayne A. Meinhart, and William D. Warde, "Environmental Scanning—Does It Help the Chief Executive?," *Long Range Planning*, October, 1980, pp. 87–99.

1. It helps an organization capitalize on early opportunities, rather than lose these to competitors.
2. It provides an early signal of impending problems, which can be defused if recognized well in advance.
3. It sensitizes an organization to the changing needs and wishes of its customers.
4. It provides a base of objective qualitative information about the environment that strategists can utilize.
5. It provides intellectual stimulation to strategists in their decision making.
6. It improves the image of the organization with its publics by showing that it is sensitive to its environment and responsive to it.
7. It is a means of continuing, broad-based education for executives, especially the strategy developers.

EXHIBIT 6-1   Naisbitt's Megatrends

1. The United States is today an information society. Nearly 20 million new jobs were created in the 1970s, 90 percent of them in the information/knowledge/service sector. While the current transition to an information society is painful, adjustments will be made throughout the decade, and unemployment will return to acceptable levels. Retraining will be necessary, and economists will have to learn to regroup data—deemphasizing the link between goods and services—to give the United States a clearer view of its economic situation.
2. We are no longer a national economy but instead part of a new, truly global economy. The "global village" concept has become a reality, with nations sharing information and technology. As developing nations increasingly play a role in the world economy, developed countries—especially the United States—must deemphasize investment in declining industries. Rather, we should look to the new technological adventures: electronics, biotechnology, alternative energy sources, financial services, leisure/travel, mining the seabeds. Ironically, as the new global economy materializes, nations will reassert their various languages and cultures to maintain individuality.
3. During the past decade and a half we have profoundly shifted from a centralized society to a decentralized society. President Reagan rode the crest of decentralization by returning powers (and financial responsibilities) to states and localities. Congressional legislation is becoming less important than legislation at the local level. Decentralization is also apparent in the divestiture of AT&T, the specialization of mass-market publications, and cable TV's multitude of specialized networks.
4. A decade-long shift from institutional help to self-help has brought about a reemergence of the traditional American value of self-reliance. Americans' newfound urge to help themselves is implicit in the health craze, the rise of the entrepreneur, and the fledgling education-at-home industry.
5. The restructuring of America from North to South is irreversible in our lifetime.

EXHIBIT 6-1 continued

Exodus to the South—really, from the Northeast to the Southwest—will grow stronger. This means that most new industries will be concentrated in the South-Southwest. The ten "cities of great opportunity" are Albuquerque, Austin, Denver, Phoenix, Salt Lake City, San Antonio, San Diego, San Jose, Tampa, and Tucson.

6. There are no either/ors anymore; in today's Baskin-Robbins world, everything comes in at least 31 flavors. Diversity in consumer product choices has mushroomed in the 1980s and will continue to do so, heralding the "market-segmented, market-decentralized society." Diversity will also increase in work choices (flexible schedules, work-at-home options, part- or full-time work), the arts, religion, and foods. In the multiple-option society, there will be a market and a market niche for just about everything.

7. American is moving in the dual directions of high tech/high touch, where the introduction of every new technology must be accompanied by a compensatory human response or the new technology is rejected. The "high tech/high touch" philosophy holds that Americans will only welcome those new technologies that, somewhat ironically, permit them greater access to each other as human beings. Every new technology will be evaluated in terms of quality of life. Factory-floor robots will increase in number, but so will quality circles. Compensation practices, abetted by computer technology, will focus increasingly on the individual worker.

Source: Excerpted from different sources.

THE CONCEPT OF ENVIRONMENT

Philosophically, the environment of a corporation includes all those realities whose existence may affect the corporation directly or indirectly in any perceptible way. These realities may be sorted out in the following four categories:

(1) The *"community"* that is made up of all the human beings that inhabit it and all their social organizations of all kinds; (2) the *"culture"* that is made up of all the constructs of the human mind that affect the behavior of all these individuals and organizations; (3) the *"habitat"* that includes all the physical features of this environment; and (4) the *"product"* that includes all things made and services rendered by man.[4]

Applying the prevailing *culture* and using and consuming natural features of the *habitat* and the *product* of past periods, the entities of the *community* have an existence and generate goods and services.

---

[4]J. D. Glover, "Environment: Community, Culture, Habitat, and Product," unpublished note prepared at Harvard Business School, No. 9-367-018, 1966, p. 1.

Operationally, however, five different types of environments may be identified: technological, political, economic, regulatory, and social. The environment may be scanned at three different levels in the organization—corporate, SBU, and product/market level. Perspectives of environmental scanning vary from level to level (see Exhibit 6-2). Corporate scanning examines happenings in different environments broadly, focusing on trends with corporate-wide implications. For example, IBM, at the corporate level, may review the impact of AT&T divestiture on the availability and rates of long-distance telephone lines to its customers. Emphasis at the SBU level is given to those changes in the environment that may influence the future direction of the business. At IBM the SBU concerned with personal computers may study such environmental perspectives as diffusion rate of personal computers, new developments in integrated circuit technology, and political debate in progress on registration (similar to that for automobiles) of personal computers. At the product/market level, the scanning is limited to day-to-day aspects. For example, an IBM personal computer marketing manager may review the significance of giving a rebate to buyers as has been popularly practiced by competitors.

The emphasis in this chapter is on environmental scanning from the viewpoint of the strategic business unit. The primary purpose is to gain a comprehensive view of the future business world as a foundation on which to base major strategic decisions.

EXHIBIT 6-2   Constituents of Environment

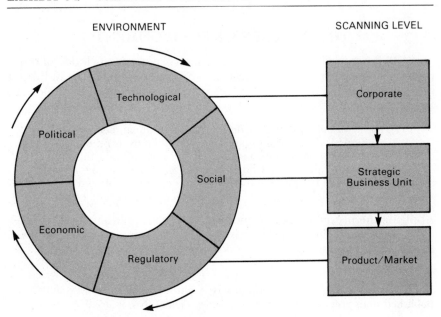

STATE-OF-THE-ART

Scanning serves as an early warning system for the environmental forces that may impact a company's products and markets in the future. Environmental scanning is a comparatively new development. Traditionally corporations evaluated themselves mainly on the basis of financial performance. Generally the environment was studied only for the purpose of making economic forecasts. Other factors of the environment were brought in haphazardly, if at all, and in an intuitive fashion. In recent years, however, most large corporations have started doing systematic work in this area.[5]

The slow progress made in relating the environment to one's business can be explained by the difficulty involved in undertaking such an analysis. It is only during the past decade that management science has concerned itself with environmental analysis. The work done at or sponsored by institutions like the Hudson Institute, the Rand Corporation, SRI International, the Club of Rome,* and the World Future Society has made it easier for business corporations to undertake scientific analysis of the environment.

A pioneering study on environmental scanning has been done by Francis Aguilar. In his investigation of selected chemical companies in the United States and Europe, he found a lack of a systematic approach to environmental scanning. Aguilar's sixteen types of information (see Exhibit 6-3) about the environment that the companies found interesting has been consolidated into five groupings: market tidings, acquisition leads, technical tidings, broad issues, and other tidings. Among those, market tidings was found to be the dominant category and was of most interest to managers across the board. Aguilar identified four patterns for viewing information: *undirected viewing* (exposure without a specific purpose), *conditioned viewing* (directed exposure but without undertaking an active search), *informal search* (collection of purpose-oriented information in an informal manner), and *formal search* (a structured process for collection of specific information for a designated purpose). Both internal and external sources were used in seeking the above information. The external was comprised of both personal sources (i.e., customers, suppliers, bankers, consultants, and other knowledgeable individuals) and impersonal sources (various publications, conferences, trade shows, exhibitions, and so on). The in-

---

[5]See Philip S. Thomas, "Environmental Scanning—The State of the Art," *Long Range Planning*, February, 1980, pp. 20–28. See also Liam Fahey, William R. King, and Vadake K. Narayanan, "Environmental Scanning and Forecasting in Strategic Planning—The State of the Art," *Long Range Planning*, February, 1981, pp. 32–39.

*Supported by the Volkswagen Foundation in Germany, the Club of Rome was formed in 1969 by a small group of people from Europe and the United States to analyze global problems in the context of changing environment.

EXHIBIT 6-3   What External Information Do Managers Obtain?

CATEGORY	GENERAL CONCEPT
Market Tidings	
Market potential	Supply and demand consideration for market areas of current or potential interest: e.g., capacity, consumption, imports, exports.
Structural change	Mergers, acquisitions, and joint ventures involving competitors, new entries into the industry.
Competitors and industry	General information about a competitor, industry policy, concerted actions in the industry, and so forth.
Pricing	Effective and proposed prices for products of current and potential interest.
Sales negotiations	Information relating to a specific current or potential sale or contract for the firm.
Customers	General information about current or near-potential customers, their markets, their problems.
Acquisition Leads	
Leads for mergers, joint ventures, or acquisitions	Information concerning possibilities for the manager's own company.
Technical Tidings	
New products, processes, and technology	Technical information relatively new and unknown to the company.
Product problems	Problems involving existing products.
Costs	Costs for processing, operations, and so forth for current and potential competitors, suppliers, and customers, and for proposed company activities.
Licensing and patents	Products and processes.
Broad Issues	
General conditions	Events of a general nature: political, demographic, national, and so forth.
Government actions and policies	Governmental decisions affecting the industry.
Other Tidings	
Suppliers and raw materials	Purchasing considerations for products of current or potential interest.
Resources available	Persons, land, and other resources possibly available for the company.
Miscellaneous	Items not elsewhere classified.

Source: Francis Joseph Aguilar, *Scanning the Business Environment* (New York: Macmillan Co., 1967), p. 40. Copyright © 1967 by the Trustees of Columbia University in the City of New York. Reprinted by permission.

ternal personal sources included peers, superiors, and subordinates. The internal impersonal sources included regular and general reports and scheduled meetings. Aguilar's study concluded that while the process is not simple, a company can systematize its environmental scanning activity for strategy development.[6]

Aguilar's framework may be illustrated with reference to the Coca-Cola Company. The company looks at its environment through a series of analyses. At the corporate level considerable information is gathered on economic, social, and political factors affecting the business and on competition both in the United States and overseas. The corporate office also becomes involved in special studies when it feels that some aspect of the environment requires special attention. For example, to address itself to a top-management concern about the possible market saturation of soft drinks, the company undertook a study to understand what was going on in the minds of their consumers and what they were looking for. How was the consumption of Coca-Cola related to their lifestyle, to their set of values, to their needs? Back in the early 1970s the corporate office also made a study of the impact of antipollution trends in the government on regulations on packaging. It was noted that at the corporate level environment was scanned rather broadly. Mostly, *market tidings, technical tidings,* and *broad issues* were dealt with. Whenever necessary, in-depth studies were done on a particular area of concern. The corporate information was made available to different divisions of the company.

In addition, at the division level (e.g., Coca-Cola, USA) considerable attention is given to the market situation, acquisition leads, and new business ventures. The division also studies general economic conditions (trends in GNP, consumption, income); government regulation (especially antitrust actions); social factors; and even the political situation. Part of this scanning duplicates the efforts of the corporate office. Such redundancy resulted because the divisional planning staff felt that it was in a position to do a better job for its own purpose than could the corporate office, which had to serve the needs of the other divisions as well. The division also undertakes special studies. For example, a few years ago they wondered whether a caffeine-free drink should be introduced, and if so, when.

The information received from the corporate office and that which the division had collected itself was analyzed to study events and happenings that could affect the company's current and potential business. Analysis was done mostly through meetings and discussions rather than through the use of any statistical model. It has been said that "the environmental analysis activity is a sort of forum. In the Coca-Cola Company, there is relatively little cohesion among managers. The meetings, therefore, respond to a need for exchange of information between people."[7]

---

[6]Francis Joseph Aguilar, *Scanning the Business Environment* (New York: Macmillan Co., 1967), p. 40.

[7]"The Coca-Cola Company (E), A Case Study," copyrighted by the President and the Fellows of Harvard College, 1970.

A recent study of environmental scanning[8] identifies four evolutionary phases of activity, from primitive to proactive (see Exhibit 6-4). The scanning activities in most business corporations can be characterized by one of the four labels.

In Phase 1, the primitive phase, the environment is taken as something inevitable and random for which nothing can be done other than to accept each impact as it occurs. Management is exposed to information, both strategic and nonstrategic, without making any effort to distinguish the difference. No discrimination is used to discern strategic information, and the information is rarely related to strategic decision making. As a matter of fact, scanning takes place without management devoting any effort to it.

Phase 2, the ad hoc phase, makes improvements over Phase 1 in that management identifies a few areas which need to be watched carefully. However, no formal system exists for scanning and no initiative is taken to scan the environment. Additionally, the fact that management is sensitive to information on specific areas does not imply that this information is subsequently related to strategy formulation. This phase is characterized by statements such as this one: "From all reliable sources we learned that rates of interest would not decline substantially in the late 1980s but our management never sat down to seriously consider what we might do or not do as a company to meet this challenge in the pursuit of our goals." Typically, this phase characterizes companies that have traditionally done well and where the management, which is intimately tied to day-to-day operations, recently happened to hire a young MBA to do strategic planning.

In Phase 3, the reactive phase, environmental scanning begins to be viewed as important, and efforts are made to monitor the environment to seek information in different areas. In other words, the management fully recognizes the significance of environment and dabbles in scanning but in an unplanned, unstructured fashion. Everything in the environment appears to be important, and the company is swamped with information. Some of the scanned information may never be looked into; some is analyzed, understood, and stored. As soon as the leading firm in the industry makes a strategic move in a particular matter, presumably in response to an environmental shift, the company in Phase 3 is quick to react, following the footsteps of the leader. For example, if the use of glass bottles for soft drinks appears uncertain, the Phase 3 company will understand the problem on the horizon but hesitate to take a strategic lead. If the leading firm decides to experiment with plastic bottles, the Phase 3 firm will make a similar response fast. In other words, the Phase 3 firm understands the problems and opportunities which the future holds, but its management is unwilling to be the first to take steps to avoid the prob-

---

[8]Subhash C. Jain, "Environmental Scanning—How the Best Companies Do It," *Long Range Planning*, April, 1984, pp. 117–128.

EXHIBIT 6-4   Four Phases in the Evolution of Environmental Scanning

Phase 1	Phase 2	Phase 3	Phase 4
Primitive	Ad hoc	Reactive	Proactive
Face the environment as it appears	*Watch out for a likely impact of the environment*	*Deal with the environment to protect the future*	*Predict the environment for a desired future*
• Exposure to information without purpose and effort	• No active search • Be sensitive to information on specific issues	• Unstructured and random effort • Less specific information collection	• Structured and deliberate effort • Specific information collection • Pre-established methodology
Scanning without an impetus	Scanning to enhance understanding of a specific event	Scanning to make an appropriate response to markets and competition	Strategic scanning to be on the lookout for competitive advantage

lems or capitalize on the opportunities. Such a company waits for a leading competitor to pave the way.

The firm in Phase 4, the proactive phase, practices environmental scanning with vigor and zeal, employing a structured effort. Careful screening focuses the scanning effort on specified areas considered crucial. Time is taken to establish a proper methodology to scan the environment, disseminate the scanned information, and incorporate it into the strategy. A hallmark of scanning in Phase 4 is the distinction between macro and micro scanning. The former refers to scanning of interest to the entire corporation and is undertaken at the corporate level. Micro scanning is often practiced at the product/market or strategic business unit level. A corporate-wide scanning system is created to ensure that macro and micro scanning activity complement each other. The system is designed to provide open communication between different micro scanners to avoid duplication of effort and information.

TYPES OF ENVIRONMENT

Corporations today, more than ever before, are profoundly sensitive to technological, political, economic, social, and regulatory changes. While such environmental changes may be felt throughout the organization, the impact most affects strategic perspectives. To cope with a changing and shifting environment, the marketing strategist must find new ways to forecast the shape of things to come and to analyze strategic alternatives, at the same time developing greater sensitivity to long-term implications. Various techniques which are especially relevant for projecting long-range trends are discussed in the appendix at the end of this chapter. Suffice it to say here that environmental scanning necessarily implies a forecasting perspective.

Technological Environment

Technological developments come out of the research effort. Two types of research can be distinguished: basic and applied. A company may engage in applied research only or may undertake both basic and applied research. In either case, a start will have to be made at the basic level, and from there the specific effect on a company's product or process will have to be derived. A company may choose not to undertake any research on its own, accepting a secondary role as an imitator. The research efforts of such a company will be limited mainly to the adaptation of a particular technological change to its business.

Exhibit 6-5 shows three different aspects of technology: types, process, and impetus. Five general areas of technology are recognized: energy, materials, transportation, communications and information, and genetic. The original impetus for technological breakthroughs can come from any or all of three sources: meeting defense needs, seeking the welfare of

EXHIBIT 6-5   A Framework for Assessing Technological Conditions at the National Level

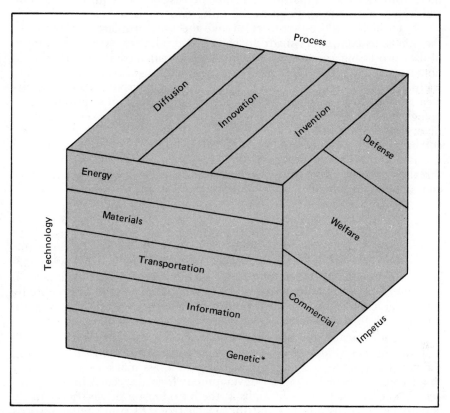

*Includes agronomic and biomedical developments.

Source: Philip S. Thomas, "Environmental Analysis for Corporate Planning," *Business Horizons,* Vol. XVII (October, 1974), p. 36. Copyright, 1974, by the Foundation for the School of Business at Indiana University. Reprinted by permission.

the masses, and making a mark commercially. The three stages in the process of technological development are invention (the creation of a new product or process); innovation (the introduction of that product or process into use); and diffusion (the spread of the product or process beyond first use).

The area of technology which a company prefers is of course dictated by the company's interests. The impetus will point to the market for technological development, and the process of development will show the state of technological development and whether the company is in a position to interface with the technology in any stage. For example, the invention and innovation stages may call for basic research which is beyond the resources of a company. Diffusion, however, will require adaptation which may not be as difficult as the other two stages.

To illustrate the point, let us take the area of microcomputers. In the 1960s, as computers made inroads in the business world, a number of data processing bureaus were born to service small companies that could not afford a computer. Over the years these bureaus have rendered a very useful service by processing such information as payroll, accounts receivable, and accounts payable. Developments in the field of computer technology made it feasible in the late 1970s to build and market small computers at a price within the reach of small businesses. While a typical computer in the 1960s sold for over $100,000, in 1984 one could get a small computer for as little as $1,000. The small computer has become a threat to the data processing bureaus because the small business can now choose between buying a small computer and using the services of a bureau.

Let us also consider technology's impact on the consumer goods industry. Before the 1980s are out, technology will enable a music fan to pull out a small sheet of plastic about as big as a slice of toast and put this "record" containing millions of bits of computer data on a playing machine that reads the computer code with a low-power laser beam. Such computerized or digital records will be capable of playing uninterruptedly for two and a half hours, long enough to encompass a full-length opera on one side alone.

Prototypes of this futuristic gear already exist, and more than 20 manufacturers in Japan, the United States, and Europe are racing to bring the new technology to a stage suitable for the mass market by the end of the decade. This technological development for the record industry has been likened to such breakthroughs as the introduction of electrically made commercial records in 1925 and the switch from 78 rpm shellac records to vinyl LP disks in the 1950s. Needless to say, this new technological leap will pose a great threat to the $3.4-billion-a-year record and tape industry. Many members of the industry may join the race to embrace the new development and themselves offer computerized records. Others may be obliged to leave the industry. A changeover to the new technology cannot be done overnight. A newcomer to the industry, Minnesota Mining & Manufacturing Company, has been working on a variety of digital recording projects since 1971. Thus, those record companies which have scanned their technological environment and followed the trend will be able to make a positive response. Those who have not kept up with the changing technology will have a hard time coping with the technological breakthrough.[9]

Startling things have been happening to the television set in the last

---

[9]Berhard Wysocki, Jr., "Computerized System May Free Recordings of Distortion Problems," *The Wall Street Journal*, February 27, 1979, p. 1.

few years.[10] For example, Panasonic now offers a color-projection system with a 60-inch screen. Even traditional 19-inch sets aren't just for looking at anymore; they are basic equipment to attach gadgets to—to play video games, to learn how to spell, or to practice math. Videodisc players produce TV images from discs; videocassette recorders tape TV shows and play prerecorded videotapes. With two-way TV the viewer can respond to questions flashed on the screen. Teleprint enables the conversion of TV sets into video-display tubes so that viewers can scan the contents of newspapers, magazines, catalogs, or whatever and call up any sections of interest. Finally, cable TV permits the viewer to call on the system's library for a game, movie, or even a French lesson.

The rest of the '80s and '90s are almost certain to be a period of technological change and true innovation. One of the impacts is going to be in communications. Until now, electronic communication has largely adapted itself to the traditional definition of voice (telephone), pictures (television), and graphics (computer) as distinct and separate kinds of communications. From now on, electronics will increasingly produce total communications. In 1980, the Business Communications Satellite, a joint venture of IBM, Xerox, and COMSAT, came into operation in this country, making simultaneous and instantaneous electronic transmission of voice, pictures, and graphics possible. People scattered over the face of the globe can now talk to each other directly, see each other, and if need be, share the same reports, documents, and graphs simultaneously without leaving their own offices or homes. Consider the impact of the above innovation on the airline industry. Business travel should diminish in importance—though its place may well be taken by travel for vacation and learning.

Technological innovation is not limited to electronics and computers alone. In other fields as well a variety of developments are providing new opportunities and threatening existing businesses. The point may be illustrated with reference to the packaging industry.[11] Packages have been developed which permit liquids (e.g., milk, juice) to be stored unrefrigerated for months without being spoiled. Such a package is already popular in Europe and Japan and is slowly making its way into the U.S. market. Innovated by Tetra Pak Company of Sweden, the new container is likely to have a deep effect on U.S. shopping habits. Many companies are experimenting with the new package. Ocean Spray, the New England cooperative, is using the new pack for all its single-serving cranberry concoctions and other juices. Similarly, Coca-Cola Company is successfully marketing its Hi-C beverage in Tetra Pak boxes.[12]

To analyze technological changes and capitalize on them, market-

---

[10]See Robert F. Hartley and Thomas A. Moore, "New Video Technology Poses Perils for Some Advertisers," *Harvard Business Review*, September–October, 1981, p. 24.

[11]"Paper 'Bottles' Are Coming On Strong," *Business Week*, January 16, 1984, p. 56.

[12]Robert Ball, "Revolution in the Packaging Industry," *Fortune*, August 9, 1982, pp. 79–82.

ing strategists may utilize the technology management matrix shown in Exhibit 6-6. It should aid in choosing appropriate strategic options based on a business's technological position. The matrix has two dimensions: technology and product. The technology dimension describes technologies in terms of their relationships to one another, while the product dimension establishes competitive position. The interaction of these two dimensions suggests desirable strategic action. For example, if a business's technology is superior to anything else on the market, the company should enhance its leadership by identifying and introducing new applications for the technology. On the other hand, if a business's technology lags behind the competition, it should either make a technological leap to the competitive process, abandon the market, or identify and pursue those elements which are laggards in terms of adopting new technologies.

EXHIBIT 6-6   Technology Management Matrix

PRODUCT POSITION	TECHNOLOGY POSITION		
	SAME TECHNOLOGY	DIFFERENT TECHNOLOGY	
		OLDER TECHNOLOGY	NEWER TECHNOLOGY
Behind competitors	• Take traditional strategic actions —Assess marketing strategy and target markets —Enhance product features —Improve operational efficiency	• Evaluate viability of your technology —Implement newer technology —Divest products based on older technology	• Evaluate availability of resources to sustain technology development and full market acceptance —Continue to define new applications and product enhancements —Scale back operations
Ahead of competitors	• Define new applications for the technology and enhance products accordingly	• Take advantage of all possible profit	• Define new applications for the technology and enhance products accordingly

Source: Susan J. Levine, "Marketers Need to Adopt a Technological Focus to Safeguard Against Obsolescence," *Marketing News,* October 28, 1983, p. 16. Reprinted by permission of the American Marketing Association.

Political Environment

In stable governments the political trends may not be as important as in countries where governments are weak. Yet even in stable countries political trends may have a significant impact on business. For example, in the United States one can expect greater emphasis on social programs and an increase in government spending when Democrats are in power in the White House. Therefore, companies in the business of providing social services may expect greater opportunities during such a period.

More important, however, are the political trends overseas because the U.S. economy is intimately connected with the global economy. And, therefore, what goes on in the political spheres of other countries (both free-world and state-controlled economies) may be significant for U.S. corporations, particularly the multinational corporations.

The following are examples of political trends and events affecting business planning and strategy:

1. The increase of geopolitical federations
   a. Economic interests: resource countries vs. consumer countries
   b. Political interests: third world vs. the rest
2. Rising nationalism vs. world federalism
   a. Failure of the United Nations
   b. Trend toward world government or world law system
3. Limited wars: Middle East, Russia-China; China-India-international conflict
4. Increase in political terrorism; revolutions
5. Third-party gains in the United States; rise of socialism
6. U.S. parliamentary government; cabinet becoming ad hoc leaders
7. Decline of the major powers; rise of emerging nations (e.g., Brazil)
8. Minority (woman) president
9. Rise in senior-citizen power in developed nations
10. Political turmoil in Saudi Arabia, threatening world oil supplies and peace in the Middle East
11. Revolutionary change in Indonesia, jeopardizing Japanese oil supplies
12. Revolutionary change in South Africa, limiting Western access to important minerals and threatening huge capital losses to the economies of Great Britain, the United States, and West Germany
13. Instability in other places where the economic consequences could be important, including Mexico, Turkey, Zaire, Nigeria, South Korea, Brazil, Chile, and the People's Republic of China. While the chances of any particular crisis occurring may be small, the odds that at least one or two shocks will occur may be pretty high.

Already in the past decade we have seen the overwhelming impact that political shocks can have on the world economy. Inflation is the perfect illustration: it is not just the product of an arbitrary monetary policy that is temporarily out of control, but a rational response to problems that are fundamentally political. In the 1980s, the problem of adjusting to the new terms of trade created by the oil embargo of 1973 and, more recently, the Iranian revolution, and the problem of trading off the costs of higher unemployment in the short run against the longer-run benefits of lower inflation continue to be a concern.

The marketing strategist needs to study both domestic and foreign political happenings, reviewing selected published information to keep in touch with political trends and interpret the information as it relates to the particular company. Exhibit 6-7 shows the types of information a multinational corporation may find useful to gather and review with reference to the political environment.

Economic Environment

Examples of economic trends and events affecting businesses include the following possibilities:

—Depression; worldwide economic collapse
—Increasing foreign ownership of U.S. economy
—Increasing regulation and management of national economies
—Several developing nations become superpowers (e.g., Brazil, China)
—World food production: Famine relief vs. holistic management
—Decline in real world growth; or stable growth
—Collapse of world monetary system
—Continuing high inflation
—Significant employee-union ownership of U.S. businesses
—Worldwide free trade

It is not unrealistic to say that all companies, small or large, engaged in strategic planning examine the economic environment. Relevant published information is usually gathered, analyzed, and interpreted for use in planning. In some corporations the entire process of dealing with economic information may be manual and intuitive. The large ones, however, not only buy specific and detailed economic information from private sources, over and above what may be available from government sources, but they analyze the information for meaningful conclusions by constructing econometric models. For example, one large corporation with 9 divisions has developed 26 econometric models of its different businesses. The data used for these models are stored in a data bank and regularly updated. The information is available on-line to all the divisions for further analysis at any time. Some other companies may occasionally buy information from outside and selectively undertake modeling.

EXHIBIT 6-7   Political Risk: A Conceptual Framework

SOURCES OF POLITICAL RISK	GROUPS THROUGH WHICH POLITICAL RISK CAN BE GENERATED	EFFECTS ON INTERNATIONAL BUSINESS OPERATIONS
Competing political philosophies (nationalism, socialism, communism)	Government in power and its operating agencies	Confiscation: loss of assets without compensation
Social unrest and disorder	Parliamentary opposition groups	Expropriation with compensation: loss of freedom to operate
Vested interests of local business groups	Nonparliamentary opposition groups (Algerian "FLN," guerrilla movements working within or outside country)	Operational restrictions: market shares, product characteristics, employment policies, locally shared ownership, and so on
Recent and impending political independence	Nonorganized common interest groups: students, workers, peasants, minorities, and so on	Loss of transfer freedom: financial (dividends, interest payments, goods, personnel, or ownership rights, for example)
Armed conflicts and internal rebellions for political power	Foreign governments or intergovernmental agencies such as the EEC	Breaches or unilateral revisions in contracts and agreements
New international alliances	Foreign governments willing to enter into armed conflict or to support internal rebellion	Discrimination such as taxes or compulsory subcontractings
		Damage to property or personnel from riots, insurrections, revolutions, and wars

Source: Stefan H. Robock, "Political Risk: Identification and Assessment," *Columbia Journal of World Business* July–August, 1971, p. 7. Reprinted by permission.

Usually, the economic environment is analyzed with reference to the following key economic indicators: employment, consumer price index, housing starts, auto sales, weekly unemployment claims, real gross national product, industrial production, personal income, savings rate, capacity utilization, productivity, money supply (weekly M1: currency and checking accounts), retail sales, inventories, and durable goods orders. Information on these indicators is available from government sources.

The above indicators are adequate for short-run analysis and decision making, because by and large they track developments over the business cycle reasonably well. However, companies that try to base strategic plans on these indicators can run into serious trouble. The deficiencies in the data will prove most dangerous if the government moves to take a more interventionist role in the economy. Further, rapid changes in the structure of the economy, coming at a time when the ability of the statistical agencies to respond has been hampered by unprecedented budget stringency, are causing a gradual deterioration in the quality of many of the figures the government puts out.

The problem begins with a recondite document called the Standard Industrial Classification (SIC) Manual, which divides all economic activity into 12 "divisions" and 84 "major groups" of industries. The SIC dictates the organization of and the amount of available data about production, income, employment, and other vital economic indicators. Each major group has a two-digit numerical code. The economy is then subdivided into hundreds of secondary groups, each with a three-digit code, and then further subdivided into thousands of industries, with four-digit codes. But detail in most government statistical series is available only at the major-group level; data at the three-digit level are scarce and at the four-digit level almost nonexistent. Hopefully, review of future information needs of the society may lead the government to examine and change its data collection procedures.

To illustrate the effect of economic climate on strategy consider the following trends:

> In the more elderly capitalist countries, it is expected that old markets will become saturated much faster than new markets will take their place. Staple consumer goods such as cars, radios and television sets already outnumber households in North America and much of Western Europe, and other products are fast approaching the same fate. The slow growth of populations in most of these countries means that the number of households is likely to grow at only about 2 percent per year in the 1980s and demand for consumer goods is unlikely to grow any faster.
>
> Furthermore, while demand in these markets decreases, supply will increase, leading to intensified price competition and pressure on profit margins. Already the market concentration in many consumer sectors has fallen significantly, mainly because of increased foreign competition. And the expansion of production capacity in primary industries like metals and chemicals, especially in developing countries,

threatens to bring some kind of increased competition to producer goods.

Many observers also believe the rate of technical progress in capitalist countries may be slowing down. The number of new patents granted each year to large firms in many different industries—at least in the United States—has fallen during the 1970s. Also, the share of GNP committed to R&D by public and private sources in OECD countries has leveled off since the late 1960s—or, in the case of the United States, actually dropped. And the rate of private investment in many countries has been rather slow to recover from the last recession, so that the speed with which innovations get translated into new processes and products may also have fallen.

Finally, many Western countries have experienced lower rates of productivity growth in the 1970s relative to past trends. While there are many factors besides the rate of innovation that might contribute to this, it is consistent with the other information. Another factor is the national economic policies. It is well known that these policies have had great trouble achieving stable economic growth in the past decade, not only in high-income countries, but also in the poorest developing countries with per-capita incomes below $200 per year. The expectation is that economic policy will do even worse in the 1980s, with perhaps as many as three worldwide recessions in the next decade and serious famines appearing as soon as 1988 in the poorer LDCs.[13]

Social Environment

The ultimate test of a business is its social relevance. This is particularly true in a society where survival needs are already met. It therefore behooves the strategic planner to be familiar with emerging social trends and concerns. The relevance of the social environment to a particular business will of course vary depending on the nature of the business. For a technologically oriented business, the scanning of the social environment will be limited to aspects of pollution control and environmental safety. For a consumer products company, however, the impact of the social environment will go much further.

An important aspect of the business environment is the values people hold. In recent years changes in these values have stimulated massive regulations, deep criticisms, new demands, and challenges of the very foundation on which business rests. For example, a substantial percentage of people in the United States are less and less willing to accept the impartial operation of the market mechanism as the best way to allocate resources. They expect government to intervene in their behalf. Another interesting value shift is what Daniel Bell calls the Revolution of Rising

---

[13]Carter F. Bales, Donald J. Gogel, and James S. Henry, "The Environment for Business in the 1980s," *The McKinsey Quarterly*, Winter, 1980, pp. 3, 4.

Entitlements, challenging the traditional concept of egalitarianism.[14] Equality had meant that conditions should permit individuals, whatever their origins, to make a life on the basis of ability and character. It was believed that everyone should have an equal place at "the starting line." More recently the emphasis has shifted to the finish line, a guarantee of an equal outcome for all. A central tenet of the new egalitarianism argues that because people are born with different natural abilities and are raised under different circumstances, not everyone approaches the starting line equally. In this light, it is argued, fairness and justice necessitate equalization of results.

Observers have noted many other value shifts that directly or indirectly influence business.[15] For example, people today seek self-gratification now rather than later. They want the good things of life immediately. They want to lead lives that are continuously improving in quality. There is a growing attitude of cynicism toward authority. There seems to be an erosion of that part of the Protestant ethic that motivates people to high standards of work performance. People seem to want a more comfortable and less risky life. People are no longer willing to accept traditional rights of property ownership but want to influence how property is used. Profit is no longer universally accepted as the end purpose of business. Society is coming more and more to expect that societal interests be considered, as well as business self-interest, in pursuing profit objectives. Some observers see in such trends a serious erosion of the fundamental institutional values of the classical free enterprise system.[16]

Information on social trends may be derived from published sources. The impact of social trends on a particular business can be studied in-house or with the help of outside consultants. A number of consulting firms specialize in making this kind of study. Exhibit 6-8 shows 31 social trends which, according to the firm of Yankelovich, Skelley and White, Inc., will have a tremendous effect on business in the coming years. One of these, female careerism (#30 in Exhibit 6-8), is of particular interest to the retail industry. It has been predicted, for example, that by the end of the 1980s 70 percent of women as opposed to 80 percent of men will be working. This structural social change leads retailers to ask such questions as: Where does the working wife like to do most of her shopping? What type of store does she prefer? How fashion-conscious is she? What sources of information does she use before she makes a purchase? What kinds of services does she expect retailers to provide?

---

[14]Daniel Bell, "The Revolution of Rising Entitlements," *Fortune*, April, 1975, pp. 98–185.

[15]John Cobbs, "Egalitarianism: Threat to a Free Market," *Business Week*, December 1, 1975, pp. 62–65.

[16]See Gerald F. Cavanaugh, *American Business Values in Transition* (Englewood Cliffs, NJ: Prentice-Hall, 1976).

EXHIBIT 6-8 Social Trends Having Marketing Significance

PSYCHOLOGY OF AFFLUENCE TRENDS, reflecting the increasing assumption that the essentials of economic survival are assured, leading to a focus on having more or doing more to improve the quality of living.

Trend 1 Personalization
       2 Physical Self-Enhancement
       3 Physical Fitness and Well-Being
       4 Social/Cultural Self-Expression
       5 Personal Creativity
       6 Anti-Materialism
       7 Meaningful Work

ANTI-FUNCTIONALISM TRENDS, reflecting reaction to the emphasis on the functional and "scientific," seen as leading to drabness and boredom in everyday life.

Trend 8 Mysticism
       9 Sensuousness
      10 New Romanticism
      11 Introspection
      12 Novelty and Change
      13 Beauty in the Home

REACTION AGAINST COMPLEXITY TRENDS, reflecting the belief that life has become excessively complicated, that the individual has lost control of his destiny, and that there is much to be gained by returning to a more natural and more simple style of life.

Trend 14 Return to Nature
      15 Simplification
      16 Anti-Bigness
      17 Scientism and Technology
      18 Ethnic Orientation
      19 Local Community Involvement

TRENDS RELATED TO THE WEAKENING OF THE "PROTESTANT ETHIC," reflecting questioning of a value system, termed the "Protestant Ethic" by sociologists, which, put very simply, is based on the belief that ambition, striving, hard work, self-sufficiency, self-denial, and other familiar virtues will lead to a successful life.

Trend 20 Living for Today
      21 Hedonism
      22 Away from Self-Improvement
      23 Noninstitutional Religion
      24 Liberal Sex Attitudes
      25 Blurring of the Sexes
      26 Acceptance of Drugs

EXHIBIT 6-8   continued

TRENDS REFLECTING PERMISSIVENESS IN CHILD REARING, deriving from the
psychological guidelines which have been widely used in the upbringing of our current youth population. These guidelines were based largely on concern about the
negative aftereffects of a rigid, demanding, punishment-oriented childhood.

Trend   27   Anti-Hypocrisy
        28   Rejection of Authority
        29   Tolerance for Chaos and Disorder
        30   Female Careerism
        31   Familism

Source: These trends have been extracted from *Marketing News*, Mid-March, 1971,
         p. 8; First-of-April, 1971, p. 8; Mid-April, 1971, pp. 7–8; First-of-May,
         1971, p. 8; Mid-May, 1971, p. 7; and First-of-June, 1971, p. 8. Reprinted
         by permission of the American Marketing Association.

A proprietary study on the subject (conducted for a major department store) with which the author was associated brought out interesting
findings. It was found that in general, working wives are better educated,
are more experienced metropolitans, and have more sophisticated tastes
than wives who do not work outside the home. Their shopping behavior
is considerably different from that of the traditional woman shopper. The
working-wife market cannot be served by a store that is "all things to all
customers." It is predicted that a new kind of store is on the horizon which
may emerge either within a department store or as a separate institution
to cater to this market. The working wife was found to prefer suburban
stores to downtown stores even though she may be working downtown.
She is likely to be interested in the latest fashions and looks for clothing
that is stylish but practical on the job. The above findings bear heavily on
retailers' strategies in such areas as merchandising, the role of the suburban store, store positioning, fashion orientation, promotion, and store
services.

Let us take two additional trends—physical fitness and well-being
(trend #3 in Exhibit 6-8) and meaningful work (#7)—and examine their
impact on marketing strategy.

Physical Fitness and Well-Being. Salads and fish are replacing the
traditional American dinner of meat and potatoes. Increasing varieties of
decaffeinated coffee and tea and substitutes for sugar and salt are crowd-
ing supermarket shelves. Shoppers are reading the small print to check
for artificial ingredients in foods and beverages they once bought without
a thought. Smoking is finally declining. Manufacturers and retailers of
natural foods are building a healthy "health industry" in the midst of a
slow economy.

The nation's dramatic new awareness of health is prompting these
changes. The desire to feel better, look younger, and live longer exerts a

powerful influence on what people put into their bodies, and this strong force is now moving against a well-entrenched habit that affects millions and dates back to Biblical times—the consumption of too much alcohol.

Health substitutes for alcoholic beverages, labeled "dealcoholized," are now being offered to American consumers. For some time, gourmet food shops have stocked champagne-like bottles of carbonated grape juice and cans containing a not-fully-brewed mixture of water, malt, corn, yeast, and hops. But except for the packaging, these alcohol-free imitations failed to resemble wine and beer, especially in the crucial area of taste.

The new dealcoholized beverages, however, are fully fermented or brewed before their alcohol is separated out—either by pressure or heat—to below an unnoticeable 0.5 percent, which is the federal maximum before classifying a drink as alcoholic. The taste and body of the beverages match that of their former alcoholized selves.

This 0.5 percent level is so low that a drinker would need to consume 24 glasses of dealcoholized wine or 8 cans of dealcoholized beer to obtain the same amount of alcohol as in one 4-ounce glass of regular wine or one 12-ounce can of regular beer. Thus the drinker avoids not only intoxication but also worthless calories, since a regular glass of wine or beer has about 150 calories, while their dealcoholized copies contain about 40 to 60 calories respectively. And their prices are the same.[17]

Introduced in Europe about two years ago, dealcoholized wines are just now entering the United States.

Meaningful Work. The following changes are producing a new challenge at work. First, people want good jobs, not make-work. Second, workers want their individual rights to be respected. Third, the concept of the professional appears to be under siege. It is increasingly difficult for professionals to maintain their special status in a society that is becoming more and more knowledge-oriented, more and more bureaucratic, and more and more participatory. The growth of the two-income family is also blurring status distinctions, since it has brought a new degree of affluence to the so-called working class. For example, a secretary and her laborer husband can have a family income of $30,000 a year, while a family headed by a sole-earner college professor or attorney can have an income well under that. Fourth, the oncoming generation has doubts about the ideals of efficiency. They are unwilling to pay the crushing price of loss of pride, mind-killing monotony, dehumanization, and stress diseases in return for the highest wages in history. Fifth, today a woman's place can be wherever she wants it to be, and so a greater number of women are expected to find their place in the labor market. As mentioned above, 70 percent of working age females will participate in the labor force by 1990.

---

[17]Allan Luks, "Dealcoholized Beverages: Changing the Way Americans Drink," *The Futurist*, October, 1982, pp. 44–49.

Stated below are the strategic implications of the above changes from the viewpoint of the insurance industry:

1. Workers don't stay at one job as long as they used to and there are projections that typical employees may change jobs—or occupations—as many as seven times during a career. Continuation of some employee benefits during non-working time is one answer to the coverage gap problem, although it is an answer that may lead to reduced incentive to purchase individual policies. Life and health insurance companies may have to provide more group insurance portability in their services to fit new needs.

2. Even though the rush of women into paid employment will slow down, women in greater numbers will be entering the labor market. The full implications of these developments will not be felt for some time. The most serious long-term impact on the life insurance business could be decisions by working couples to limit the size of their families.

3. The women's market for life insurance may parallel men's as more women begin to have the same type of life cycle as men . . . full work-lives along with spouse/children. Marketing plans and criteria should be examined carefully to take advantage of the underinsured female segment of our working population.

4. Greater federal pressure for equal employment opportunities, including affirmative action, could from a company's point of view lead to increasing strictures on employment practices to the point where hiring and promotions are guided more by regulation than by merit. What can life insurance companies do to deal with a situation when a sense of job "security" among corporate workers diminishes the individual employee's incentive to provide for the future through life insurance?

5. As employees obtain more power in the governance of organizations, they will bring a different perspective to the consideration of fringe benefits. Group coverage will almost certainly be affected by employee decision making. For example, will employees be more concerned about health insurance first or dollar coverage? Would they be willing to share high premiums? Would young single or two-income family employees prefer options like increased leisure time to an emphasis on group life insurance coverage?[18]

Regulatory Environment

Even in a capitalistic society like the United States, government influence on business appears to be increasing. It is estimated that businesses spend, on the average, twice as much time fulfilling government requirements today as they did ten years ago. As has been said:

---

[18]"The Changing Nature of Work," *Trend Analysis Report #17* (Washington, DC: American Council of Life Insurance, no date).

Few businesses, large or small, can operate without considering a myriad of government restrictions and regulations. Costs and profits can be affected as much by a regulation written by a government official as by their own management decision or their customers' changing preferences. The types of management decisions which increasingly are subject to governmental influence, review, or control are fundamental to the business system:

—What lines of business to go into?
—What products can be produced?
—Which investments can be financed?
—Under what conditions can products be produced?
—Where can they be made?
—How can they be marketed?
—What prices can be charged?
—What profit can be kept?

Virtually every major department of the typical corporation in the United States has one or more counterparts in a federal agency that controls, or strongly influences, its internal decision making.[19]

Interestingly, government in recent years has changed its emphasis from regulating specific industries to focusing on problem areas of national interest, including environmental cleanup, elimination of job discrimination, establishment of safe working conditions, and reduction of product hazards. A number of steps have been taken toward deregulation since 1968. For example:

1968: The Supreme Court's Carterfone decision permitted non-AT&T equipment to be connected to the AT&T system.
1969: The FCC gave MCI the right to hook its long-distance network into local phone systems.
1970: The Federal Reserve Board freed interest rates on bank deposits over $100,000 with maturities of less than six months.
1974: The Justice Department filed antitrust suit against AT&T.
1975: The SEC ordered brokers to cease fixing commission on stock sales.
1977: Merrill Lynch offered the Cash Management Account, competing more closely with commercial banks.
1978: Congress deregulated the airlines.
1979: The FCC allowed AT&T to sell non-regulated services, such as data processing.
1980: The Fed allowed banks to pay interest on checking accounts.
1981: Sears Roebuck became the first one-stop financial supermarket, offering insurance, banking, brokerage services.

---

[19]Murray L. Weidenbaum, "The Future of Business/Government Relations in the United States," in Max Ways (ed.), *The Future of Business* (New York: Pergamon Press, 1978), p. 50. See also Robert Reich, "The Fourth Wave of Regulation," *Across the Board*, May, 1982.

1982: Congress deregulated intercity bus services.
1984: AT&T divested itself of its local phone companies.[20]

The above shift in focus deeply affects the internal operations of business. Consider the major developments in the area of products liability (Exhibit 6-9). During the past 150 years product liability law has undergone a radical change. Caveat emptor is now caveat venditor. The doctrine of privity of contract, the code that governs most businesspeople's thinking, has been eroded. The result has not been a uniform system of

EXHIBIT 6-9   Major Developments in Products Liability

Winterbottom v. Wright, 1842

Doctrine of "privity of contract" upheld.
Circumscribes the parties who have legal rights and duties under a contract.

Thomas v. Winchester, 1852

Exception to "privity of contract." Customer may sue manufacturer when manufacturer's business is inherently dangerous.

MacPherson v. Buick Motor Co., 1916

Further exceptions to "privity of contract." Artificiality of "manufacturer-dealer-consumer" relationship. Manufacturer may not be shielded from direct suit.

Escola v. Coca-Cola Bottling of Fresno, 1944

Ideas of "liability in tort" and "liability in contract" explicitly brought together. Harm done apart from contractual relations and development of liability for defective goods.

Greenman v. Yuba Power Products, 1969

Doctrine of manufacturer's strict liability for damage caused by its products, even though:

• The seller has exercised all possible care in the preparation and sale of his product.
• The consumer has not bought the product from nor has entered into any contractual arrangement with the seller.

Source: Ram Charan and R. Edward Freeman, "Planning for the Business Environment of the 1980s," *Journal of Business Strategy,* p. 15. Reprinted by permission.

---

[20]"Deregulating America," *Business Week,* November 28, 1983, p. 80. See also Bro Uttal, "How to Deregulate AT&T," *Fortune,* November 30, 1981, p. 70.

products liability law but a confused collection of precedents, at times too favorable to consumers, at times simply confused in application.

To study the impact of the regulatory environment, i.e., of laws already on the books and pending legislation, legal assistance is required. Small firms may seek legal assistance on an ad hoc basis. Large firms may maintain offices in Washington staffed by people with legal backgrounds and well versed in company business. They know the important government agencies from the point of view of their companies and maintain a close liaison with them. They pass on the relevant information to planners in different departments of the companies. For example, a company that did a substantial amount of business in less-developed countries had a person in Washington who closely followed the developments in the Agency for International Development (AID). As soon as foreign aid to a country was approved, this legal expert signalled the company headquarters, which in turn alerted its office in that country to begin seeking business.[21]

ENVIRONMENTAL SCANNING AND MARKETING STRATEGY

The impact of environmental scanning on marketing strategy can be illustrated with reference to videotex technology.[22] Videotex technology—the merging of computer and communications technology—delivers information directly to the consumer. For the first time, the consumer may instantly retrieve desired textual and visual information from on-line data bases to television screens or other video receivers. She/he need only push the appropriate buttons or type in the proper commands.

Possibilities for business and personal use are as endless as the imagination. Consumers are already utilizing videotex information for shopping, travel, personal protection, financial transactions, and entertainment, in greater privacy and autonomy than ever before.

With videotex as the mechanism for getting things done most efficiently and cost-effectively, marketing strategists have begun to explore the implications on marketing decisions. Videotex will alter the demand for certain kinds of goods and services and the ways in which consumers interact with marketing activities. For the first time, the average consumer, not just the affluent, can interact directly with the production process, dictating final product specifications as the product is manufactured. Especially as small-batch production becomes more cost-effective, this will become more common.

---

[21]Carol J. Loomis, "The Fight for Financial Turf," *Fortune*, December 28, 1981, p. 54.

[22]The following discussion is adapted from W. Wayne Talarzyk and Robert E. Widing II, "Introduction to and Issues with Videotex: Implications for Marketing," *Working Paper Series*, #WPS82-16 (Columbus, OH: College of Administrative Science, The Ohio State University, 1982).

Product selection might also be enhanced by videotex, as sellers stock at fewer, more central locations with a more complete inventory, rather than having to deal with many retail outlets. Since packages will no longer serve as the communications vehicle for selling the product, less money will need to be spent on packaging. Product changes can also be kept up to date. Information on videotex will be current, synthesized, and comprehensive. The user will have the power to access only desired information at the time it is desired. Advertising messages and articles will be available in index form.

Direct consumer interaction with manufacturers will eliminate distribution channels. Reduced or zero-based inventory will reduce obsolescence and turnover costs. Central warehouses and new delivery routes will become increasingly cost-effective. The remaining retail stores will be transformed into showrooms with direct-order possibilities via viewdata-like terminals.

Promotional material will become more educational and information based, including the provision of product specifications and independent product evaluations. Interactive video channels will provide advertisers and interested shoppers with prepackaged commercials and live shopping programs.

With more accurate price and product information, more perfect competition will result. Price discrepancies will be reduced. Consumers will engage in more pre-shopping planning, price-comparison shopping, and in-home shopping.

The market segment concept will be more important than ever before. The individualizing possibilities of videotex will enable the seller to measure and reach segments with unparalleled accuracy and will also enable consumers to effectively self-segment. Advertisers and consumers will benefit from 24-hour, 7-day-a-week salespeople, at their service, with everyone better prepared through videotex information to satisfy the customers.

ENVIRONMENTAL SCANNING PROCEDURE

Like any other new program, the scanning activity in a corporation evolves over time. There is no way to introduce a foolproof system from the beginning. If conditions are favorable—i.e., if there is an established system of strategic planning in place and the CEO is interested in a structured effort at scanning—the evolutionary period shortens, of course, but the state-of-the-art may not permit the introduction of a fully developed system at the outset. Besides, behavioral and organizational constraints require that things be done over a period of time.

The level and type of scanning activity that a corporation undertakes should be custom-designed. And a customized system takes time to emerge into a viable system.

Exhibit 6-10 shows the process by which environmental scanning is linked to marketing strategy. Listed below are the procedural steps which explain this relationship.

EXHIBIT 6-10 Linking Environmental Scanning to Corporate Strategy

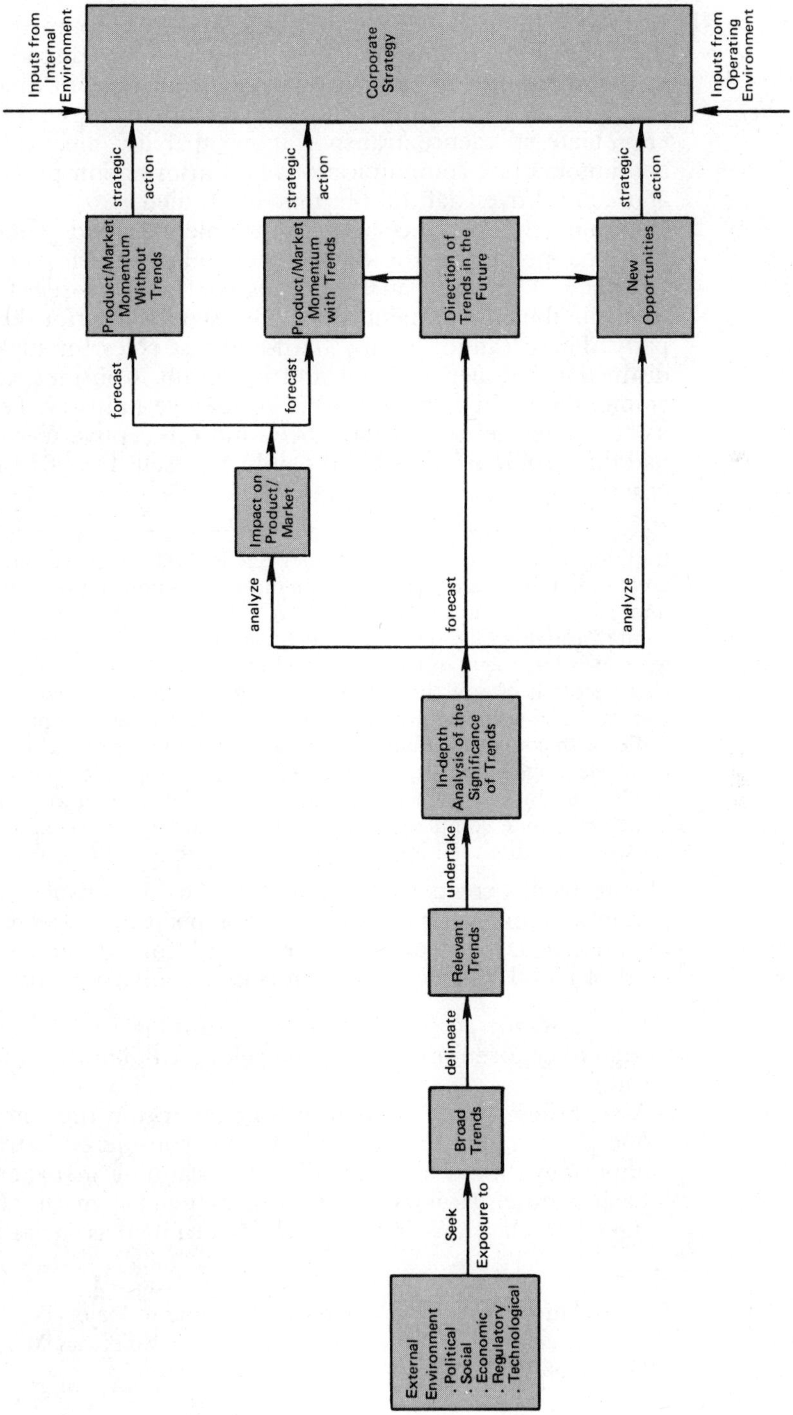

1. Keep a tab on broad trends appearing in the environment. Once the scope of environmental scanning is determined, broad trends in the chosen areas may be reviewed from time to time. For example, in the area of technology, trends in mastery of energy, material science, transportation capability, mechanization and automation, communications and information processing, and control over natural life may be studied.
2. Determine the relevance of an environmental trend. Not everything happening in the environment may be relevant for a company. Therefore attempts must be made to select those trends in the environment which have significance for the company. There cannot be any hard-and-fast rules for making a distinction between relevant and irrelevant. Consider, for example, the demise of the steam locomotive industry. Perhaps its constituencies would have been more receptive to changes had these come from within the industry itself. In 1967 Cooper observed:

> I would hypothesize that if the new threat is very similar to a firm's traditional way of meeting consumer needs, such as the turbine-powered automobile being similar to the internal combustion-powered automobile, then management often would perceive the new development threatening. However, if it meets consumer needs in very different ways, it is less likely to be recognized at an early point. For instance, I suspect that one of the major threats to the future growth of commercial airlines is originating not with transportation companies, but rather with communication firms. I'm thinking in particular of American Telephone and Telegraph's development of the "television phone." As that product is perfected and as the costs of using it are lowered, it may eliminate completely the need for many business flights, with consequent substantial impact upon the future growth of airlines.[23]

Management's creativity and farsightedness would play an important role in a company's ability to pinpoint the relevant areas of concern. Described below is one way (for a large corporation) of identifying relevant trends in the environment:

—Place a senior person in charge of scanning.
—Identify a core list of about 100 relevant publications worldwide.
—Assign these publications to volunteers within the company, one per person. Selected publications considered extremely important should be scanned by the scanning manager.
—Each scanner reviews stories/articles/news items in the assigned publication that meet predetermined criteria, based

---

[23]Arnold C. Cooper, "Identifying, Appraising, and Reacting to Major Technological Change," in *Proceedings*, Winter Conference (Chicago: American Marketing Association, 1967), p. 56.

on the company's aims. Scanners might also review books, conference proceedings, lectures, and presentations.

—The scanned information is given a predetermined code. For example, a worldwide consumer goods company used the following codes: subject (e.g., politics); geography (e.g., Middle East); function (e.g., marketing); application (e.g., promotion, distribution); and "uniterm" or keyword for organizing the information. An abstract is prepared on the story, etc., in a few lines.

—The abstract along with the codes is submitted to a scanning committee consisting of several managers, to determine the relevance in terms of effect on corporate/SBU/product-market strategy. An additional relevance code is added at this time.

—The codes and the abstract are computerized.

—A newsletter is prepared to disseminate the information company-wide. Managers whose areas are directly affected by the information are encouraged to contact the scanning department for further analysis.

3. Study the impact of an environmental trend on a product/market. An environmental trend can pose either a threat or an opportunity for a company's product/market; which one it will turn out to be must be studied. The task of determining the impact of a change is the responsibility of the SBU manager. Alternatively, it may be assigned to another executive who is supposedly familiar with the product/market. If the whole subject appears controversial, it may be safer to have an ad hoc committee look into it, or even consultants, either internal or external, may be approached. There is a good chance that a manager who has been involved with a product or service for a good many years would look at any change as a threat. He or she may, therefore, avoid the issue by declaring the impact to be irrelevant at the outset. If such sabotage is feared, perhaps it would be better to rely on the committee or a consultant.

4. Forecast the direction of an environmental trend into the future. If an environmental trend does appear to have significance for a product/market, it is desirable to determine the course that the trend is likely to adopt in the future. In other words, attempts must be made at environmental forecasting.

5. Analyze the momentum of the product/market business in the face of the environmental trend. Assuming the company takes no action, what will be the shape of the product/market performance in the midst of the environmental trend and its direction into the future? The impact of an environmental trend is usually gradual. While it is helpful to be "first" to recognize

and take action when perceiving an environmental trend, all is not lost even if a company waits to see which way the trend proceeds. But how long one can wait depends on the diffusion process of the adoption of change necessitated by the trend. People did not jump to replace their black-and-white television sets overnight. Such examples abound. There are a variety of reasons which would prohibit an overnight shift in markets due to an environmental trend which may deliver a new product or process. High prices, religious taboos, legal restrictions, and unfamiliarity with the product or service would restrict change-over. In brief, the diffusion process should be predicted before arriving at a conclusion.

6. Study the new opportunities that an environmental trend appears to provide. An environmental trend may not be relevant for a company's current product/market. But it may indicate promising new business opportunities for a company. For example, the energy crisis provided an easy entry point for Honda cars in the United States. Such opportunities should be duly pinpointed and analyzed for action.

7. Relate the outcome of an environmental trend to corporate strategy. Based on environmental trends and their impacts, the company needs to review its strategy on two counts: changes which may be introduced in the current products/markets, and feasible opportunities which the company may embrace for action. Even if an environmental trend poses a threat for a company's product/market, it is not necessary for the company to come out with a new product to replace the existing one. Neither is it necessary for every competitor to embrace the "change." Even without developing a new product, a company may find a niche in the market which it could cater to despite introduction of a new product by the competitor. The electric razor did not make the use of safety razor blades obsolete. Use of automatic transmission in automobiles did not throw the standard shift out of vogue. New markets and new uses can be found which give the existing product an advantage despite the overall popularity of the new product.

While there are procedural steps listed above for scanning the environment, scanning is nevertheless an art in which creativity plays an important role. Thus, to adequately study the changing environment and relate it to corporate strategy, companies should inculcate a habit of creative thinking on the part of the managers. The following steps adopted by the Coca-Cola Company in this regard are noteworthy:

> Managers concerned with products and new business would ultimately be withdrawn from the line organization and would serve as staff people at the corporate level. There they would be granted considerable

freedom of action. A serious effort would have to be undertaken to "open up" line managers to new ideas and to encourage innovation in their plans.[24]

CONDUCTING ENVIRONMENTAL SCANNING—AN EXAMPLE

Following the steps in Exhibit 6-11, an attempt is made here to illustrate how specific trends in the environment may be systematically scanned.

A *literature search* in the area of politics shows that the following federal laws were considered during the late '70s:

1. Eliminating inside directors
2. Requiring companies to meet the cost of "unfriendly" proxy contests
3. Barring nominee ownership of stock
4. Reducing a company's right to fire workers at will
5. Guarding worker privacy
6. Mandating due-process procedures for grievances
7. Disclosing lobbying efforts in detail

EXHIBIT 6-11   Systematic Approach to Environmental Scanning

1. Pick up events in different environments (via literature search).
2. Delineate events of interest to the SBU in one or more of the following areas: production, labor, markets (household, business, government, foreign), finance, R&D. This could be achieved via trend-impact analysis of the events.
3. Undertake cross-impact analysis of the events of interest.
4. Relate the trends of the noted events to current SBU strategies in different areas.
5. Select the trends which appear either to provide new opportunities or to pose threats.
6. Undertake trends' forecasts
   —wild card prediction
   —most probable occurrence
   —conservative estimate
7. Develop three scenarios for each trend based on three types of forecasts.
8. Pass on the information to strategists.
9. Strategists may repeat steps 4 to 7 and develop more specific scenarios vis-à-vis different products/markets. These scenarios will then be incorporated in SBU strategy.

---

[24]"The Coca-Cola Company (E), A Case Study," copyrighted by the President and Fellows of Harvard College, 1970, p. 15.

8. Requiring that all ad claims be substantiated
9. Publishing corporate actions that endanger workers or the environment[25]

The marketing strategist of a consumer goods company may want to determine if these trends have any relevance for the company. To do so the marketing strategist will undertake *trend-impact analysis*. This will require the formation of a delphi panel (see Chapter 17) to determine the desirability (0-1), technical feasibility (0-1), probability of occurrence (0-1), and probable time of occurrence (1990, 1995, 2000, beyond 2000) of each event listed above. The panel may also be asked to suggest the area(s) which may be affected by each event; i.e., production, labor, markets (household, business, government, foreign), finance, or R&D.

The above information about an event may be studied by managers in areas which, according to the delphi panel, are likely to be affected by the event. If their consensus is that the event is indeed important, the scanning may continue (see Exhibit 6-12).

Next, *cross-impact analysis* may be undertaken. This type of analysis is planned to study the impact of an event on other events. Where events are mutually exclusive, such analysis may not be necessary. But where an event seems to reinforce or inhibit other events, the cross-impact analysis is highly desirable for uncovering the true strength of an event.

The cross-impact analysis amounts to studying the impact of an event (given its probability of occurrence) upon other events. The impact may be delineated either in qualitative terms (such as critical, major, significant, slight, or none) or in quantitative terms in the form of probabilities.

Exhibit 6-13 shows how cross-impact analysis may be undertaken. The cross-impact ratings or probabilities can best be determined with the help of another delphi panel. To further sharpen the analysis, it may also be determined whether the impact of an event on other events will be felt immediately or after a certain number of years.

The cross-impact analysis provides the "time" probability of occurrence of an event and indicates other key events which may be monitored to keep track of the first event. Cross-impact analysis is more useful for project-level scanning than for general scanning.

To relate the environmental trends to strategy, consider the following assumed environmental trends and strategies of a cigarette manufacturer.

Trends:

T_1: Requiring that all ad claims be substantiated
T_2: Publishing corporate actions that endanger workers or the environment
T_3: Disclosing lobbying efforts in detail

---

[25]*Business Week*, November 21, 1977, p. 64.

EXHIBIT 6-12   Trend-Impact Analysis: An Example

EVENT	REQUIRING THAT ALL AD CLAIMS BE SUBSTANTIATED	REDUCING A COMPANY'S RIGHT TO FIRE WORKERS AT WILL
Desirability	.8	.5
Feasibility	.6	.3
Probability of occurrence	.5	.1
Probable time of occurrence	1990	Beyond 2000
Area(s) impacted	Household markets Business markets Government markets Finance R&D Production	Labor Finance
Decision	Carry on scanning	Drop from further consideration

Note: Two to three rounds of delphi would be needed to arrive at the above probabilities.

T_4: Reducing a company's right to fire workers at will
T_5: Eliminating inside directors

Strategies:

S_1: Heavy emphasis on advertising, using emotional appeals
S_2: Seasonal adjustments in labor force for agricultural operations of the company
S_3: Regular lobbying effort in Washington against further legislation imposing restrictions on the cigarette industry
S_4: Minimum number of outside directors on the board[26]

The analysis in Exhibit 6-14 shows that strategy S_1, heavy emphasis on advertising, is most susceptible and requires immediate management action. Among the trends, trend T_5, eliminating inside directors, will have the most positive overall impact. Trends T_1 and T_2, requiring that all ad

[26]F. Friedrich Neubauer and Norman B. Solomon, "A Managerial Approach to Environmental Assessment," *Long Range Planning*, April, 1977, pp. 13–20.

EXHIBIT 6-13   Cross-Impact Analysis: An Example

EVENT	PROBABILITY OF OCCURRENCE	IMPACT								
		a	b	c	d	e	f	g	h	i
a. Eliminating inside directors	.6		.3*							
b. Requiring companies to meet the cost of "un-friendly" proxy contests	.3									
c. Barring nominee owner-ship of stock	.5									
d. Reducing a company's right to fire workers at will	.1									
e. Guarding worker privacy	.4									
f. Mandating due-process procedures for grievances	.3									
g. Disclosing lobbying ef-forts in detail	.4									
h. Requiring that all ad claims be substantiated	.5									
i. Publishing corporate ac-tions that endanger work-ers or the environment	.4								.7**	

*This means that elimination of inside directors has no effect on the probability of event b.
**This means that if publishing corporate actions that endanger workers or the environment occurs (probability .4), the probability of requiring that all ad claims be substantiated increases from .5 to .7.

EXHIBIT 6-14   Use of Matrix to Determine the Impact of Selected Trends on Different Corporate Strategies

Trends	Strategies				Impact (I_1)	
	S_1	S_2	S_3	S_4	+	–
T_1	–8	0	+2	–2		8
T_2	–4	–2	–6	0		12
T_3	0	+4	–4	+2	2	
T_4	0	–4	0	+6	2	
T_5	–2	+6	+4	+2	10	
Impact (I_2) +	–	4	–	8		
–	14	–	4	–		

Scale

+8	Enhance the implementation of strategy	Critical
+6		Major
+4		Significant
+2		Slight
0		No effect
–2	Inhibit the implementation of strategy	Slight
–4		Significant
–6		Major
–8		Critical

claims be substantiated and publishing corporate actions that endanger workers or the environment, will have a devastating impact. This type of analysis indicates where management concern and action should be directed.

Thus, it will be desirable to undertake forecasts of trends T_1 and T_2. The forecasts may predict when the legislation will be passed, what will be the major provisions of the legislation, etc. Three different forecasts may be obtained:

1. Extremely unfavorable legislation
2. Most probable legislation
3. Most favorable legislation

Three different scenarios (using three types of forecasts) may be developed indicating the impact of each trend. This information may then be passed on to product/market managers for action. Product/market managers may repeat steps 4 through 7 (see Exhibit 6-11) to study the selected trend(s) in depth.

ORGANIZATIONAL ARRANGEMENTS AND PROBLEMS

Structuring Responsibility for Scanning

There are three different ways in which corporations organize scanning activity: (1) line managers undertake environmental scanning in addition to their other work; (2) scanning is made a part of the strategic planner's job; (3) scanning responsibility is instituted in a new office of environmental scanning. Most companies use a combination of the first two types of arrangements. The strategic planner may scan the corporate-wide environment while line managers concentrate on product/market environment. In some companies, notably General Electric Company, a new office of environmental scanning has been established with a responsibility for all types of scanning. GE's environmental scanning office undertakes scanning both regularly and on an ad hoc basis (i.e., on a request from one of the groups of the company). Information which is scanned on a regular basis is passed on to all those in the organization for whom it may have relevance. For example, GE is organized into sectors, groups, and strategic business units (SBUs).[27] The SBU is the level at which product/market planning takes place. Thus, the scanned information is channeled to those SBUs, groups, and sectors for which it has relevance. The ad hoc scanning may be undertaken at the request of one or more SBUs. These SBUs then share the cost of scanning and are the principal recipients of the information.

---

[27]"GE's New Billion-Dollar Small Businesses," *Business Week*, December 19, 1977, pp. 78–79.

The environmental scanner serves to split the work of the planner. If the planner already has many responsibilities and if the environment of a corporation is complex, it is desirable to have a person specifically responsible for scanning. Further, it is desirable that both planners (and/or scanners) and line managers undertake scanning. This is because managers usually limit their scanning perceptions to their own industry; i.e., they may limit their scanning to the environment with which they are most familiar. At the corporate level, scanning should go beyond the industry. Morrison H. Beach, chairman of the board and chief executive officer, Travelers Insurance Companies, advises:

> Traditional planning seeks to identify the environment in which we will be operating and then lays out the alternative strategies for accomplishing our objectives within that environment. It generally assumes that a vast number of organizational regulatory and economic factors are beyond our control. I encourage you to challenge such traditional assumptions. In fact, some of these factors may be at least partially within our ability to control, and modifying our environment may be part of the answer to accomplishing our objectives.[28]

Whoever is assigned to scan the environment should undertake the following six tasks:

1. Trend Monitoring – systematically and continuously monitoring trends in the external environments of the company and studying their impact upon the firm and its various constituencies.
2. Forecast Preparation – periodically developing alternative scenarios, forecasts, and other analyses that serve as inputs to various types of planning and issue management functions in the organization.
3. Internal Consulting – providing a consulting resource on long-term environmental matters and conducting special futures research studies as needed to support decision-making and planning activities.
4. Information Center – providing a center to which intelligence and forecasts about the external environment can be sent from all over the organization for interpretation, analysis, and storage in a basic library on long-range environmental matters.
5. Communications – communicating information on the external environment to interested decision makers through a variety of media including newsletters, special reports, internal lectures, and periodic analyses of the environment.
6. Process Improvement – continually improving the process of environmental analysis by developing new tools and techniques, designing forecasting systems, applying methodologies developed elsewhere, and engaging in a continuing process of self-evaluation and self-correction.[29]

---

[28]Morrison H. Beach, "Corporate Planning," remarks at Regional Invitational Meeting, American Management Association, November 19, 1976.
[29]Burt Nanus, "The Corporate Futurist," *World Future Society Bulletin*, March/April, 1981, p. 13.

Successful implementation of the above tasks should provide increased awareness and understanding of long-term environments which should improve the strategic planning capabilities of the firm. More specifically, the environmental inputs are helpful in product design, formulation of marketing strategies, determination of marketing mix, and research and development strategies.

In addition, the scanner should train and motivate line managers to become sensitive to environmental trends, encouraging them to identify strategic versus tactical information and to understand the strategic problems of the firm as opposed to short-term sales policy and tactics.

Time Horizon of Scanning

Scanning may be for a short term or a long term. Short-term scanning is useful for programming various operations and the term may last up to two years. Long-term scanning is needed for strategic planning, and the term may vary from three years to 25 years. Rarely does the term of scanning go beyond 25 years. The actual time horizon would be determined by the nature of the product. Forest products, for example, may require a longer time horizon since the company must make a decision almost 25 years ahead on tree planting for lumber. The fashion designer, however, may not extend scanning beyond four years. As a rule of thumb, the appropriate time horizon for environmental scanning for a company would be twice as long as the duration of its strategic plan. For example, if a company's strategic plan is extended eight years into the future, the environmental scanning time horizon for this company should be 16 years. Likewise, a company with a five-year planning horizon should scan the environment for ten years into the future. Presumably, then, a multiproduct, multimarket company should have different time horizons for environmental scanning. Working on the above rule of thumb, a company can be sure not only of discovering relevant trends and their impact on its products/markets, but also of implementing necessary changes in its strategy to marshal opportunities provided by the environment or to avert environmental threats.

Problems Faced

Discussed below are the major problems which companies face in the context of environmental scanning. Many of these problems are, in fact, dilemmas which may be attributed to lack of theoretical frameworks on the subject.

1. The environment per se is too broad to be tracked by an organization. Thus, it is necessary to separate the relevant from the irrelevant environment. But this may not be easy since in terms of perceptible realities, the environment of all large cor-

porations is as broad as the world itself. For example, the steam locomotive industry, presumably, would have been more receptive to changes had they emerged within the industry itself rather than outside (via General Motors). Therefore, a company needs to determine what criteria to develop to select information on a practical basis.

2. Another problem is concerned with determining the impact of an environmental trend, i.e., its meaning for business. For example, what does the feminist movement mean for a company's sales and new business opportunities?

3. Even if the relevance of a trend and its impact are determined, making forecasts of the trend poses another problem. For example, how many women will be in managerial positions ten years from now?

4. A variety of organizational problems hinder environmental scanning. Presumably managers are the company's ears and eyes and therefore could be a good source to perceive, study, and channel pertinent information within the organization. But managers are usually so tied up mentally and physically within their little world of specific roles that they simply ignore happenings in the environment. The structuring of organizations by specialized functions can be blamed for this problem to a certain extent. In addition, organizations lack a formal system for receiving, analyzing, and finally disseminating environmental information to the decision points.

5. Environmental scanning requires "blue sky" thinking and "ivory tower" working patterns to encourage creativity. But such work perspectives are often not justifiable in the midst of corporate culture.

6. Frequently the top management, because of their own values, consider dabbling in the future to be a waste of resources; therefore, they adopt an unkindly attitude towards such projects.

7. Many companies as a matter of corporate strategy like to wait and see; therefore, they let the industry leaders act on their behalf, the ones who want to be first in the field.

8. Lack of normative approaches on environmental scanning is another problem.

9. Often the change is too out of the way. It may be perceived, but its relationship to the company is not conceivable.

10. It is also problematic to decide what department of the organization should be responsible for environmental scanning. Should marketing research undertake environmental scanning? How about the strategic planning office? Who else should participate? Is it possible to divide the work? For example, the SBUs may concentrate on their products, product lines, markets, and industry. The corporate level may deal with the rest of the information.

11. Often information is gathered which is overlapping, leading to a waste of resources. Frequently there are informational gaps which require duplication of effort.

SUMMARY

Environment is ever-changing and complex. Thus firms must constantly scan and monitor the environment. Environmental scanning may be undertaken at three levels in the organization: corporate level, strategic business unit (SBU) level, and product/market level. This chapter approaches scanning primarily from the SBU viewpoint. The various environments discussed are technological, political, economic, social, and regulatory.

Environmental scanning evolves over a long haul. It is sufficient, therefore, to make a humble beginning rather than designing a fully structured system.

The impact of different environments on marketing strategy is illustrated by numerous examples. A step-by-step procedure for scanning the environment is outlined. A systematic approach to environmental scanning using such techniques as trend-impact analysis, cross-impact analysis, and the delphi technique is illustrated. Feasible organizational arrangements for environmental scanning are examined, and problems that companies face in their scanning endeavors are discussed.

DISCUSSION QUESTIONS

1. *Explain the meaning of environmental scanning. Which constituents of the environment, from the viewpoint of a business corporation, require scanning?*
2. *Why did the state of the scanning art not keep pace with the popularity of strategic planning?*
3. *Illustrate with the help of examples the relevance of technological, political, economic, social, and regulatory environments in the context of marketing strategy.*
4. *Who in the organization should be responsible for scanning the environment? What role may consultants play to help corporations in their environmental scanning activity?*
5. *Explain the use of trend-impact analysis and cross-impact analysis with reference to environmental scanning.*
6. *How may the delphi technique be useful in the context of environmental scanning? Give an example.*
7. *What type of responsibilities should be assigned to the person in charge of environmental scanning?*
8. *How may the managers be involved in environmental scanning?*

APPENDIX: SCANNING TECHNIQUES

Environmental scanning has been implemented mainly with the use of conventional methodologies such as marketing research, economic indicators, demand forecasting, and industry studies. But the use of such conventional techniques for environmental scanning has not been without pitfalls, for two major reasons. One, these techniques have failed to provide reliable insights into the future. As Ewing has said, "the most careful and sophisticated forecasts of market demand have gone awry, and there is no technical improvement in sight that promises to change matters."[30] Two, these techniques, in any event, provide a narrow view of the environment:

> Direct competition . . . is only one of the basic dimensions of the company's total strategic environment—The competitive audit must be augmented by assessment of the broader governmental, social, economic, ideological and other forces which all influence the company's character, purpose and strategies over the longer term.[31]

Discussed below are a variety of techniques which have been adapted for use in environmental scanning.

Extrapolation Procedures

These procedures require the use of information from the past to explore the future. Obviously their use assumes that the future is some function of the past. There are a variety of extrapolation procedures which range from a simple estimate of the future (based on past information) to regression analysis.

Historical Analogy

Where past data cannot be used to scan an environmental phenomenon, the phenomenon may be studied by establishing historical parallels with other phenomena. Assumed here is the availability of sufficient information on the other phenomena. The turning points in the progression of these phenomena become the guideposts for predicting the behavior of the phenomenon under study.

---

[30]David Ewing, "Corporate Planning at Crossroads," *Harvard Business Review*, Vol. 45, July–August, 1967, p. 84.

[31]J. Thomas Cannon, "Auditing the Competitive Environment," in John W. Bonge and Bruce P. Coleman (eds.), *Concepts of Corporate Strategy* (New York: Macmillan Co., 1972), pp. 263–264.

Intuitive Reasoning

This technique bases the future on the "rational feel" of the scanner. Intuitive reasoning requires free thinking unconstrained by past experience and personal biases. This technique, therefore, may provide better results when used by free-lance think tanks than when used by managers on the job.

Scenario Building

This technique calls for developing a time-ordered sequence of events bearing a logical cause-effect relationship to one another. The ultimate forecast is based on multiple contingencies each with its respective probability of occurrence.

Cross-Impact Matrices

When two different trends in the environment point toward conflicting futures, this technique may be used to study these trends simultaneously for their effect. As the name implies, this technique uses a two-dimensional matrix, arraying one trend along the rows and the other along the columns.

Some of the features of cross-impact analyses that make them attractive for strategic planning are: (1) they can accommodate all types of eventualities (social or technological, quantitative or qualitative, and binary events or continuous functions); (2) they rapidly discriminate important from unimportant sequences of developments; and (3) the underlying rationale is fully retraceable from the analysis.

Morphological Analysis

This technique requires identification of all possible ways to achieve an objective. For example, the technique can be employed to anticipate innovations and to develop the optimum configurations for a particular mission or task.

Network Methods

There are two types of network methods: contingency trees and relevance trees. A contingency tree is simply a graphical display of logical relationships among environmental trends that focuses on branch-points where several alternative outcomes are possible. A relevance tree is a logical network similar to a contingency tree, but drawn in a way that assigns degrees of importance to various environmental trends with reference to an outcome.

Missing-Link Approach

The missing-link approach combines morphological analysis and the network method. Many developments and innovations that appear promising and marketable may be held back because something is missing. Under such circumstances this technique may be used to scan new trends to see if they provide answers to the missing links.

Model Building

This technique emphasizes construction of models following deductive or inductive procedures. Two types of models may be constructed: phenomenological models and analytic models. Phenomenological models identify trends as a basis for prediction but make no attempt to explain the underlying causes. Analytic models seek to identify the underlying causes of change so that future developments may be forecast on the basis of a knowledge of their causes.

Delphi Technique

The delphi technique is the systematic solicitation of expert opinion. Based on reiteration and feedback, this technique gathers opinions of a panel of experts on happenings in the environment.

Laskin Ski Company

Laskin Ski Company is a wholly owned subsidiary of the Laskin Corporation, engaged in the development, manufacture, and worldwide distribution of high-quality alpine skis. The company objective has been to establish Laskin skis as the number one premium brand in all major world markets.

In 1980, in light of the then current demographic, economic, and legal developments, the company was concerned with its ability to hold on to the number one position in high-end ski sales in the United States. Laskin's product philosophy has been the belief that skiers are a demanding group of purchasers who will respond favorably to a high-quality product which is honestly and factually presented. This philosophy combined with good distribution has been the key to Laskin's present success.

The job of maintaining this success falls on the company's Recreation Products Strategic Business Unit (SBU). Because of changeable environmental forces, this department has to follow skiing trends and develop an appropriate marketing strategy.

One such force in the ski industry is the weather. Obviously, if it does not snow, people cannot ski. Additionally, the industry is vulnerable to energy shortages. If people cannot get fuel, they cannot get to the ski areas. The industry also faces a threat from the environmental movement, which has halted the development of new skiing facilities in the United States. As the sport grows and the area growth remains static, the quality of the skiing declines because of overcrowding of existing areas. These areas also face a legal threat from a liability standpoint. Recent court cases have raised insurance premiums, forcing some areas to close and others to respond by increasing the price of lift tickets. Faced with these current industry trends, in the fall of 1980 the Recreation Products SBU general manager, Paul Angelico, was concerned about what strategies to employ over the next several years to maintain Laskin's current market position.

The focus of Mr. Angelico's concern was a recent survey conducted by *Ski Business Magazine* which highlighted certain trends developing within the ski industry. The survey showed that consumers were spending considerably less for skis than they had planned, a trend which could be detrimental to both manufacturer and retailer. The average price skiers were expecting to spend was $173, but they ended up spending $139 (see Exhibit 6-15a). Mr. Angelico felt that if such a trend persisted, it could have a long-term effect on Laskin's market position and he would have to formulate a new strategy that considered its overall implications. Alterna-

EXHIBIT 6-15   Aspects of the Ski Market

(a) Ski Business Magazine Equipment Survey: Planned Spending vs. Actual

PLANNED			ACTUAL		
$ 0-100	6%		$ 0-100	22%	
101-125	10%		101-125	17%	
126-150	18%		126-150	19%	
151-175	19%	⎤	151-175	13%	⎤
176-200	29%	⎬ 66%	176-200	16%	⎬ 38%
200+	18%	⎦	200+	9%	⎦
No answer	2%		No answer	5%	
	102%			101%	

Average: $173.00   Average: $139.00

Note: Because of rounding of individual figures,
total percentages exceed 100%.

(b) Comparison of Percentage Change: Total Equipment,
High-Priced Equipment, and Skier Population

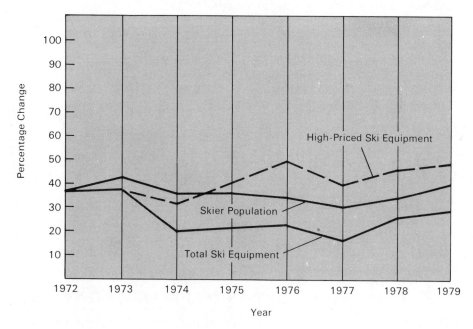

tively, there was a feeling within the SBU that the company was strong enough to reverse this trend by following the existing strategy. Exhibits 6-15(b), 6-15(c), and 6-15(d) provide additional insights into the ski market and Laskin's position.

(c) Population of Serious U.S. Skiers

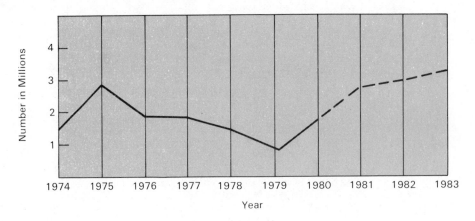

(d) Laskin's Share of Market for High-End Skis ($150 and up)

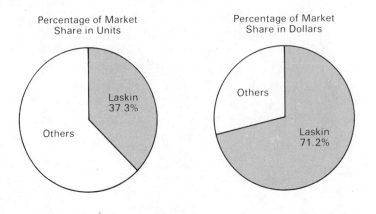

Source: Company files.

COMPANY HISTORY AND SKI DEVELOPMENT

Headquarters for all Laskin Ski manufacturing and domestic marketing operations is a newly expanded 100,000-square-foot plant in Springfield, Massachusetts. This modern facility, built in 1970, handles Laskin Ski's worldwide production requirements. Throughout its history, Laskin Ski has been successful in introducing innovations in ski design and in spotting new trends in market demand. By putting itself in front of competition from the start, the company has been able to keep itself in that position.

The company's history dates back to 1968 when Laskin Corporation, a major diversified company, decided to expand its efforts in the outdoor recreational field. In 1969, the Laskin Ski Company was incorporated as an independent subsidiary. Laboratory and field testing programs were carried out during the winter of 1968–69 to evaluate the construction of leading brands of skis. Specifications on the first Laskin prototypes were completed in June, 1969; then extensive field testing was conducted.

By early 1970 an outstanding recreational ski, the "Mark I," had evolved. The company also had developed a patent on a unique cracked-edge configuration. Company engineers used this "variable cracked edge" to introduce their "Mark II" model. Later that year, the "Mark II V.C.E." was introduced. The ski proved to be ideal for experts and racers. Using this model, the Laskin Ski professional racing team compiled the most successful team record on the ISRA (International Ski Racers Association) circuit.

In 1971, the new trend in skiing was a move toward shorter ski length. The company began to develop a ski for recreational skiers who prefer shorter lengths. The Mark I "D Series" was introduced in June of 1971. This marked the beginning of a new era that saw short skis become popular with skiers of all abilities.

In 1972, many expert skiers began switching to shorter-length skis for increased mobility. In response to this trend, Laskin Ski began development of a short, high-performance model. In August, an exceptional freestyle ballet and fast mogul ski, the "Mark IV," was introduced. This ski was greeted with immediate success and has been the number one selling ski in the $150-and-above price range for the past four seasons.

The "Mark V" was developed in the spring of 1974 as the newest model in the company's line of top-quality, high-performance skis. This year also saw the development of another unique company patent. Engineers successfully used the first "constrained visoelastic layer" in ski construction. This material controls vibration and reduces the level of ski decay.

Since 1974, the company has used these innovations to expand its product line to the present number of seven. In 1980 the company was continuing to improve these models. Engineers concluded that the absence of a bottom groove would improve the swiveling characteristics of certain skis without any loss in stability or turning ease. This led to removal of the groove in all 1980 high-performance models.

These individual achievements have helped Laskin to reach its present leadership position. The principles of a quality product, advertised and promoted honestly, remain the fundamental elements of the company's strategy.

PRODUCT LINE

Since skiers vary widely in their abilities and tastes, Laskin has designed each model with a specific type of skier and a specific kind of skiing in mind. To help match a particular model to a certain skier, the Laskin line has been divided into four categories: recreational models, advanced/expert models, high-performance models, and special-purpose/junior models.

Recreational Models. Weekend recreational skiers comprise the largest segment of the skier population. These skiers need easy-turning, forgiving skis that will handle a variety of snow conditions. They also require a dependable, durable ski. The company makes two such skis, the Laskin Mark I "K Series" and the Laskin Mark I "M Series," designed for those novice-through-intermediate skiers who are looking for a fun, easy ski. Advertisements claimed: "At Laskin Ski, quality and dependability are just as important in our recreational models as they are in our high-performance and racing skis."

Advanced/Expert Models. A large number of skiers belong in the advanced-through-expert category. They are good, strong recreational skiers who enjoy moderate to high speeds of skiing over a wide variety of terrains. Laskin offers these skiers two models, the "Mark III" and the "Mark IV."

The Laskin "Mark III" is a mid-length ski designed for the good skier looking for a quick-turning, stable ski that will give good performance without demanding it. The Laskin "Mark IV" is a high-performance short ski designed for the aggressive recreational skier who prefers the shorter length for maneuverability. The ski's soft rolling tip, cracked edges, and turned-up tail make it ideally suited for the aggressive mogul skier.

High Performance Models. Skiers in this group are generally experts, very demanding in their performance requirements. To satisfy different performances in this group, the company offers three models.

The Laskin Mark III "S Series" is a full-length ski for the expert who does not want to be limited to any single area of the mountain. It is an extremely quick, soft-flex ski that provides stability even at high speeds.

The "Mark IV Competition" is a new model that delivers high performance in mid-length sizes. It is ideal for the expert who wants a high-performance, maneuverable ski.

The "Mark VI" remains the company's top-performance, full-length ski. It is designed for the skier who prefers a responsive, quiet ski that is ideal for use on hard snow and icy surface conditions.

Special Purpose/Junior Models. The Laskin "Ballet" is a top ski for serious ballet skiers. Its turned-up tail and convex base, without a bottom groove, make it ideal for ballet maneuvers on smooth, packed surfaces.

The "Mark IV Junior" is a short ski for the more advanced junior. Like the adult version, it is ideally suited for skiing the bumps. The "Mark VI Junior," a junior version of the Mark VI, is designed to provide a high-performance ski for top juniors.

MANUFACTURING

Step one in manufacturing is designing and testing the desired ski. The next step is building it. When manufacturing Laskin skis, consistency is the key. From the time the materials arrive until the finished skis are ready for shipping, even the slightest flaw anywhere along the line warrants an inspector's rejection. Materials either fall within a 5/1000 level of tolerance or are sent back. Once accepted, they undergo a variety of preparatory steps. All metal parts are sandblasted to remove any oil. From this point on, no metal piece is ever touched without the use of plastic gloves, because even a slight smudge could cause a weak bond.

The core provides the basic control of the skis' flex properties. At Laskin, an electronically programmed machine—the first of its kind—shapes the core to an exact tolerance of 1/10 of a millimeter. Another unique assurance of consistency is the temperature/humidity-controlled bonding room, which ensures stability of the materials during final assembly. At each step in the production process, materials are subjected to rigid inspections. Provided the materials pass inspection, they are brought to the bonding room for assembly. Here workers in teams of two build one pair of skis at a time, carefully laying up the epoxied parts in precision molds. The molds are placed in a press where the skis are shaped under controlled heat and 40,000 pounds of pressure.

The finished steps are carried out with the same care, some by machine and some by hand. The ski has to pass thirty-one final checks before it is finally shipped. These methodical steps in manufacturing assure the consistency of quality needed to make each Laskin ski as good as the next.

Organizational Structure

Exhibit 6-16 shows Laskin's organization. Laskin Ski is unique in its structure because of its status as a subsidiary. Since the company's external financing is taken care of by the parent company, it concentrates its efforts in product development, marketing, and sales. Thus, the company is in a position to concentrate on those areas needed to produce and sell a superior product. Operations at Laskin are centered around four main departments:

(a) Marketing and Sales determine customer needs, follow skiing trends, analyze performance requirements in the market, and develop programs in sales, advertising, and promotion.
(b) Engineering and Product Development is responsible for designing skis that will meet customers' varying performance requirements.

EXHIBIT 6-16   Laskin Ski Company: Organizational Structure

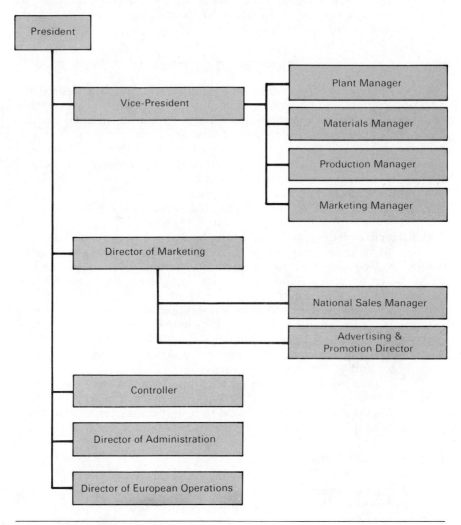

Source: Company records.

(c) Finance makes sure that the business is running smoothly; orders are processed quickly and bills reported accurately. The objective here is to keep the company as financially sound as possible.

(d) Manufacturing takes the skis from raw materials to finished product, making sure all skis are built to the highest standards of excellence. Its goal is to make the best skis possible.

In addition to these departments, the company is staffed with employees assigned to answer questions from dealers. A dealer placing an order or checking on shipments calls the representative for his or her sales territory.

SALES FORCE

The company employs 11 highly trained full-time regional sales representatives. They are located across the country (see Exhibit 6-17) and do nothing else but call on Laskin dealers on a year-round basis. These salespeople are ski specialists whose only product is Laskin skis.

The salespeople are responsible for approximately 90 dealers each. They stay in contact with them throughout the season either by phone or by personal visits. During the busiest portion of the selling season, the salespeople provide efficient service by maintaining a reorder telephone campaign with each of their dealers. They also supply dealers with weekly inventory summary forms so they can determine exactly what they have in stock and what they need before it becomes a problem.

Finally, these salespeople provide in-store clinics to give dealers and their staff a better understanding of the company and the product line.

EXHIBIT 6-17   Laskin Ski Company: Geographic Sales and Distribution Setup

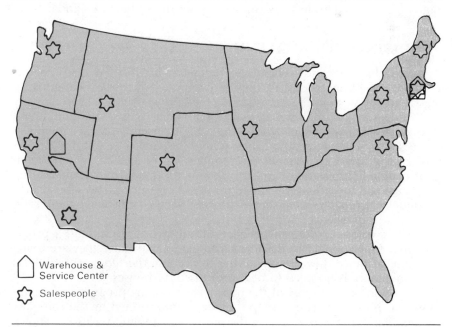

Source: Company records.

EXHIBIT 6-18   Laskin Ski Company: Channel Structure

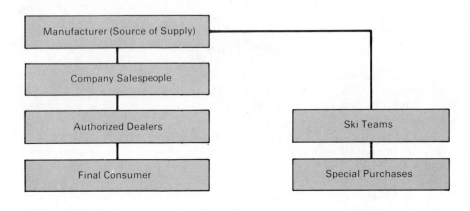

Source: Company records.

Their most recent clinic format includes an audiovisual presentation highlighting the product line and covering the basic skills of retail sales. These clinics offered by Laskin have continually set the industry's standards.

DISTRIBUTION CHANNEL—DEALER SELECTION

Exhibit 6-18 shows Laskin's channel structure. To distribute its product to the final consumer, the company uses one direct channel, selling its line of skis only to high-quality specialty ski shops. The company believes this is the only way to assure the skiing public the quality and service they demand when purchasing a high-priced consumer good.

The company is not in the position of having to search for dealers to sell its product. Its number one position in the market and frequent participation in trade shows are sufficient to attract more than the desired number of dealers willing to distribute its line. The company is, in fact, continually turning away dealers who they feel do not meet their rigid standards of excellence.

The company does not engage in any private branding, a procedure they believe would be detrimental to the quality image they are trying to maintain. Since they are not trying to become the most profitable ski company, there is no need to deal with discount houses.

Laskin provides one of the best dealer-support programs in the industry, as is evident from a recent survey commissioned by the company (see Exhibit 6-19). Prices, dealer discounts, and pricing terms are shown in Exhibit 6-20.

EXHIBIT 6-19   Laskin Ski Company: Retailer Evaluation of Sales Representatives and Service

CRITERIA	LASKIN	MAJOR COMPETITORS K-2	ROSSIGNOL
Product availability	1	7	5
Product delivery	1	7	2
Price	5	10	2
Quality	1	6	8
Profitability	10	6	9
Sales personnel	2	6	5
Point-of-purchase aids	1	2	5
Promotional assistance	1	1	4
Vendor representation	1	11	3
Vendor warranty	1	6	10
Return policy	3	3	7
1-EXCELLENT 13-POOR			

Source: Company records.

ADVERTISING AND PROMOTION

To generate maximum exposure and demand for Laskin skis, the company has developed one of the most extensive support programs in the industry. They recognize the important role advertising and promotion play in successful marketing of ski products. The combination of programs which follow was selected for its benefits in affecting consumer attitudes in a positive way:

1. A major national advertising campaign was run in *Ski, Skiing,* and *Powder* magazines to reach approximately 20 million skiers.

EXHIBIT 6-20   Laskin Ski Company: Pricing Structure

LINE	RECREATION	ADVANCED/ EXPERT	HIGH- PERFORMANCE
At plant	$ 50	$ 55	$ 60
To retailer (dealer)	$120 $109	$114 $126	$126 $129
40% retail markup	$150 $160	$190 $190	$210 $215

Source: Company records.

2. Freestyle skiers on both the professional and amateur level have made Laskin skis a top choice of competitors all over the world. The Laskin Professional Freestyle Team contributed to this by capturing the Manufacturer Team Award twice in the last three seasons.
3. Laskin sponsors a professional racing team which has been extremely competitive for the past three seasons.
4. The company provides point-of-purchase material and a variety of in-shop selling aids to authorized company dealers.
5. Dealer clinics are conducted to provide shop salespeople with the materials and information necessary to improve their selling efficiency.
6. Influential skiers are selected at key resorts as part of the company's ambassador program. These individuals represent the company, making demonstrations to the public and providing product information.
7. In-store promotions using company personnel help to increase store traffic and familiarity with products.
8. The company sponsors an on-hill program where they make Laskin skis available for people to try for the day. The program brings the Laskin name directly to skiers by giving them an opportunity to actually use the company's product.
9. The company sponsors radio coverage for pro ski races carried on the Winter Sports Network.
10. The company uses a cooperative advertising program to help share the cost of radio and newspaper advertising with dealers. This helps consumers associate Laskin with the authorized dealer in the area.
11. The company has created a new information center that is unique to the industry. This electronic unit serves as a silent salesperson conveying the advantages of purchasing a quality product. It sets Laskin dealers apart from the rest, since it is available only to those authorized to sell the Laskin line.

These are some of the elements that have taken Laskin from a start-up company in 1969 to an industry leader in 1980. The company continues its commitment to manufacture the best possible product and to give dealers the best possible service and support in selling its skis.

LOOKING TO THE FUTURE

Reviewing Laskin's past status, Mr. Angelico and the entire staff could be nothing less than extremely pleased with their performance. Will this success continue into the future? This is the problem currently facing the company's planning board.

Many members feel that this current success will indeed continue. Their argument is as follows:

Skiers have always been an affluent segment of the consumer market, and they will become even more so in the future. More women will be working, which will add to the family's discretionary income, and they are having fewer children, which increases the family's mobility. Shorter work weeks will also increase participation in the sport.

The healthiest portion of the U.S. economy continues to be the quality, prestige spending for cars, boats, real estate, and recreation. Industry statistics reveal that the number of skiers who are willing to pay for top-line, prestigious products is strong and growing.

The overall ski market is not expected to grow much more than 5 percent per year. Therefore, a specialty shop must look for its continued growth from the profitable high-end market segment. The market for high-end skis represents the major portion of the average shop's total dollar volume in skis.

Although these shops sell only 37.3 percent of their units in the high end, this segment contributes more than 70 percent to the shop's total ski-dollar volume.

Much of Laskin's management expressed the view that these favorable trends in demographics, combined with past market performance, indicate an optimistic outlook for the company in the high-priced segment.

Mr. Angelico, on the other hand, was hesitant to be so optimistic. He continued to cite the growing environmental and legal threats facing the industry:

> Can we continue to expect people to pay $250 for a pair of skis, when it costs them $30 to ski for the day and another $30 to fill up their car in order to get to the area? On top of this, once they do get to the area, can we expect them to enjoy the sport when they are faced with a 45-minute wait in a lift line?

These factors deeply concerned Mr. Angelico and several other members of his staff.

The planning board seemed to be sitting in limbo. To break the stalemate, Mr. Angelico suggested the development of a new growth strategy. He felt both sides would be able to incorporate their argument into the company's future strategic considerations if the problem was approached with both long-term and short-term goals in mind.

PART THREE
Strategic Capabilities

CHAPTER 7 - Measuring Strengths and Weaknesses

CHAPTER 7
Measuring Strengths and Weaknesses

To measure is the first step to improve.

Sir William Petty

A business does not perform well by accident. Good performances occur because the people directing its affairs interact well with the environment, capitalizing on strengths and eliminating underlying weaknesses. In other words, to operate successfully in a changing environment, the business should plan its future objectives around its strengths and downplay moves which bear on its weaknesses. Thus, assessment of strengths and weaknesses becomes an essential task in the strategic process.

In this chapter a framework will be presented for identifying and describing a business's strengths and weaknesses. This framework provides a systematic scheme for an objective appraisal of the performance and strategic moves of the marketing side of business. It can also be used for identifying those perspectives which can be considered as strengths, and those which constitute weaknesses, for meeting the future.

Traditionally the appraisal of the marketing function has been pursued in the form of a marketing audit which stresses the review of current problems. From the strategic point of view, the review should go further to include the future as well. The importance of the measurement of strengths and weaknesses in the context of marketing strategy is well described by Alderson:

> The marketing executive may be visualized as operating on the basis of a sort of map. There are boundaries or limits marking off the class of customers he is trying to reach or the trade channels through which he is willing to sell. There are routes over which he can move in attaining his objectives which experience or investigation has indicated are better than other routes. This map may have to be brought up to date by a validation or a revision of operating assumptions.[1]

---

[1] Wroe Alderson, *Marketing Behavior and Executive Action* (Homewood, IL: Richard D. Irwin, 1957), p. 419. See also Philip Kotler, William Gregor, and William Rogers, "The Marketing Audit Comes of Age," *Sloan Management Review*, Winter, 1977, pp. 25–44.

Strengths and weaknesses in the context of marketing are a relative phenomenon. Strengths today may become weaknesses tomorrow and vice versa. This is why a penetrating look at the different aspects of a business's marketing program is essential. This chapter is directed toward this end—searching for opportunities and the means for exploiting them, as well as identifying weaknesses and the ways in which they may be eliminated.

MEANING OF STRENGTHS AND WEAKNESSES

Strengths refer to the competitive advantages and other distinctive competencies which the company can exert in the marketplace. Andrews notes:

> The distinctive competence of an organization is more than what it can do; it is what it can do particularly well. Thus, the hapless manufacturer of chocolate candy who finally lost his chain of candy stores was not really a surpassingly efficient retailer of candy. He just thought he was. His real skill lay in production, in his ability to design special machinery to perform quality production at low cost. The proper application of his real strengths would probably have confined him to manufacturing for wholesalers and supermarket chains.[2]

Weaknesses are constraints which hinder movements in certain directions. For example, a business short of cash cannot afford to undertake a large-scale promotional offensive. In developing marketing strategy, the business should, among other things, dig deeply into its skills and competencies and chart its future in accordance with these competencies.

As an example, in many businesses, service—speed, efficiency, personal attention—makes a crucial difference in gaining leverage in the marketplace. Companies that score high on service over their rivals have a real competitive strength. McDonald's may not be everyone's idea of the best place in town to dine, but at its level, McDonald's provides a quality of service that is the envy of the industry. Whether at a McDonald's in a rural area or in the downtown area of a large city, the customer gets exactly the same service. Every McDonald's employee is supposed to strictly follow the rules. Cooks must turn, never flip, hamburgers one, never two, at a time. If they haven't been purchased, Big Macs must be discarded ten minutes after being cooked and french fries after seven minutes. Cashiers must make eye contact with and smile at every customer.

Similarly, visitors to Disney World come home impressed with its cleanliness and the courtesy and competence of the staff. The Disney World management works hard to make sure the 14,200 employees are, as described in a *Fortune* article, "people who fulfill an expectation of wholesomeness, always smiling, always warm, forever positive in their approach." The article goes on:

---

[2]Kenneth R. Andrews, *The Concept of Corporate Strategy* (Homewood, IL: Dow Jones-Irwin, 1971), pp. 97–98.

Even for dishwashers, employment at Disney World begins with three days of training and indoctrination in an on-site center known as Disney University. Disney doesn't "hire" people for a "job" but "casts" them in a "role" to look after the "guests" (never "customers"). If employees are to work in costume in the Magic Kingdom, they are told not to hesitate to go underground to the vast wardrobe for a fresh costume if the one they're wearing gets soiled during the shift.

They learn that everyone pitches in to make Disney World work. When the crowds get too big to handle—a record 93,000 visitors turned up last New Year's Day—even the top managers and their secretaries leave their offices to work behind counters or in ticket booths. New employees begin to pick up the pride that goes with working for a first-class organization.[3]

STUDYING STRENGTHS AND WEAKNESSES:
STATE-OF-THE-ART

A systematic scheme for analyzing strengths and weaknesses is still in embryonic form. One hardly finds any scholarly work on the subject of strengths and weaknesses. The only formal study with which the author is familiar was done by Stevenson, who studied six companies. He was interested in the process of defining strengths and weaknesses in the context of strategic planning. He was concerned with the company attributes examined, the organizational scope of the strengths and weaknesses identified, the measurement employed in the process of definition, the criteria used for distinguishing a strength from a weakness, and the sources of information utilized. Exhibit 7-1 illustrates the process in detail.

Companies should make targeted efforts to identify their competitive strengths and weaknesses. This is far from easy, however. Many companies have only the vaguest notion of the nature and degree of whatever competencies they may possess, especially the large ones. The sheer multiplicity of production stages and the overlapping among product lines hinder clear-cut assessment of the competitive strength of a single product line. Despite such problems, development of competitive strategy depends on having a complete perspective on strengths and weaknesses. Success requires putting the best foot forward.

The unique strengths may lie in different areas of the business and may impact the entire company. Stevenson found a general lack of agreement on suitable definitions, criteria, and information used to measure strengths and weaknesses. In addition to the procedural difficulties, he noted a variety of situational factors contributing to difficulties faced by managers in their attempts to measure strengths and weaknesses. These factors included the need for situational analysis, the need for self-pro-

---

[3]Jeremy Main, "Toward Service Without a Snare," *Fortune*, March 23, 1981, pp. 64–66.

EXHIBIT 7-1   Steps in the Process of Assessing Strengths and Weaknesses

Which attributes can be examined?	What organizational entity is the manager concerned with?	What types of measurements can the manager make?	What criteria are applicable to judge a strength or a weakness?	How can the manager get the information to make these assessments?
Organizational structure	The corporation	Measure the existence of an attribute	Historical experience of the company	Personal observation
Major policies				Customer contacts
Top manager's skills	Groups	Measure an attribute's efficiency	Intracompany competition	Experience
				Control system documents
Top manager's experience	Divisions			
Information system				Meetings
Operation procedures	Departments	Measure an attribute's effectiveness	Direct competitors	Planning system documents
Planning system				
Employee attitudes	Individual employees		Other companies	Employees
Manager's attitudes				Subordinate managers
Union agreements			Consultants' opinions	Superordinate managers
Technical skills			Normative judgments	Peers

Research skills New product ideas Production facilities Demographic characteristics of personnel Distribution network Sales force's skill Breadth of product line Quality control procedures Stock market reputation Knowledge of customer's needs Market domination	based on management's understanding of literature Personal opinions Specific targets of accomplishment such as budgets, etc.	Published documents Competitive intelligence Board members Consultants Journals Books Magazines Professional meetings Government economic indicators

Source: Reprinted from "Defining Corporate Strengths and Weaknesses," by Howard H. Stevenson, *Sloan Management Review*, Vol. 17, No. 3 (Spring, 1976), p. 54, by permission of the publisher. Copyright © 1976 by the Sloan Management Review Association. All rights reserved.

tection, the desire to preserve the status quo, and the problems of definition and computational capacity.[4] Stevenson makes the following suggestions for improvement of the process of defining strengths and
weaknesses. The manager should:

—Recognize that the process of defining strengths and weaknesses is
primarily an aid to the individual manager in the accomplishment
of his task.
—Develop lists of critical areas for examination which are tailored to
the responsibility and authority of each individual manager.
—Make the measures and the criteria to be used in evaluation of
strengths and weaknesses explicit so that managers can make their
evaluations against a common framework.
—Recognize the important strategic role of defining attributes as opposed to efficiency or effectiveness.
—Understand the difference in the use of identified strengths and
identified weaknesses.[5]

Despite the primitive state-of-the-art, however, many more companies in the process of developing strategic plans review their strengths
and weaknesses today than did ten years ago. The strengths and weaknesses may be found in the functional areas of the business, or they may
result from some unusual interaction of functions.

The following example illustrates how a study of strengths and
weaknesses may uncover opportunities which otherwise might not have
even been conceived of. A national distiller and marketer of whiskeys may
possess such strengths as

. . . sophistication in natural commodity trading associated with its grain
purchasing procedures; knowledge of complex warehousing procedures and inventory control; ability and connections associated with
dealing in state political structures—i.e., state liquor stores, licensing
agencies, and so on; marketing experience associated with diverse
wholesale and retail outlets; advertising experience in creating brand
images.[6]

If these strengths are properly analyzed with a view to seeking diversification opportunities, it will appear that the distiller has unique abilities for
successfully entering the business of selling building products, e.g., wood
flooring or siding, composition board, and the like. This is because experience in commodity trading can be transferred to trading in lumber;
experience in dealing with political groups can be used to gain building

---

[4]Howard H. Stevenson, "Defining Corporate Strengths and Weaknesses: An Ex-
ploratory Study," unpublished doctoral dissertation, Harvard Business School, 1969.
[5]Howard H. Stevenson, "Defining Corporate Strengths and Weaknesses," *Sloan
Management Review*, Spring, 1976, p. 66.
[6]Gordon R. Conrad, "Unexplored Assets for Diversification," *Harvard Business Review*, September–October, 1963, p. 71.

code acceptances; and experience in marketing can apply to wholesalers (e.g., hardware stores and do-it-yourself centers) of building products.

The case of Apeco Corporation illustrates how a company can get into trouble if it does not carefully consider its strengths and weaknesses. Apeco is a Des Plaines, Illinois, company with a penchant for diversifying into businesses that are in vogue in the stock market. It has been, or still is, in the following businesses: office copying machines, mobile homes, recreational vehicles, speedboats and cabin cruisers, computers, video recording systems, and small buses. Despite entry into some glamorous fields, Apeco did not share the growth and profits that other companies in some of these fields achieved. This is because Apeco entered new and diverse businesses without relating its moves to its basic skills and competencies. For example, despite the fact that it was the first company to develop a photocopy process, even before Xerox, its total market share for all types of copier machines and supplies is now well under 5 percent. Apeco could not keep pace with the technological improvements and service on installed machines, essential in the copier business. In addition, it overextended itself so much that managerial controls were rendered inadequate.[7]

SYSTEMATIC MEASUREMENT OF STRENGTHS AND WEAKNESSES

The strengths and weaknesses of a business can be measured at different levels in the organization: corporate, strategic business unit, and product/market level. The thrust of this chapter is on the measurement of strengths and weaknesses at the strategic business unit level. Inasmuch as the strengths and weaknesses of the strategic business unit are a composite of the strengths and weaknesses of different products/markets, the major portion of the discussion will be devoted to the measurement of the marketing strengths and weaknesses of a product/market.

Exhibit 7-2 illustrates the factors which require examination in order to delineate the strengths and weaknesses of a product/market. These factors, along with competitive perspectives, describe the strengths and weaknesses of the product.

Current Strategic Posture

Current strategic posture constitutes a very important variable in developing future strategy. While it is difficult and painful to try to understand current strategy if formal planning has not been done in the past, it is worth the effort for a good beginning in strategic planning.

---

[7]"Apeco Puts Its Money on Small Bus," *Business Week*, February 2, 1974, pp. 40–41.

EXHIBIT 7-2   Measurement of Product Strengths and Weaknesses

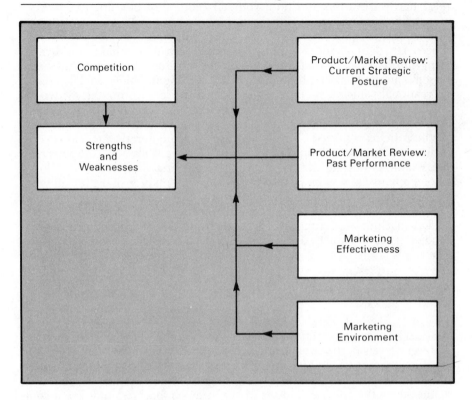

The emphasis here is on the study of the current strategy of a product/market. Before undertaking such a study, however, it is desirable to gain company-wide perspectives by raising such questions as:

1. What underlies our company's success, given competitor's patterns of doing business?
2. Are there any characteristics and traits which have been followed regularly?
3. To what strategic posture do these characteristics and traits lead?
4. What are the critical factors which could make a difference in the success of the strategy?
5. To what extent are critical factors likely to undergo a change? What may be the direction of change?[8]

These questions cannot be answered entirely objectively; they call

---

[8]*Perspectives on Corporate Strategy* (Boston: The Boston Consulting Group, 1968), p. 42.

for creative responses. Often managers will disagree on various issues. For example, the vice-president of marketing of a company which had recently made a heavy investment in sales training considered this investment to be a critical factor in success. He thought a well-trained sales staff was crucial in developing new business. On the other hand, the vice-president of finance saw only that the investment in training had increased overheads. Though disagreements of this sort are inevitable, a review of current strategy is very important. The following operational scheme for studying current strategy from the point of view of the entire corporation has been found useful:

1. Begin with an identification of the actual current scope of the company's activities. The delineation of customer/product/market emphasis and concentration will give an indication of what kind of a company it is currently.
2. This analysis should be followed by identification of the pattern of actual past and existing resource deployments. This description will show which functions and activities have received the greatest management emphasis and where the greatest sources of strength currently lie.
3. Given the identification of scope and deployment patterns, an attempt should be made to deduce the actual basis on which the company has been competing. Such competitive advantages or distinctive competences represent the central core of present performance and future opportunities.
4. Next, on the basis of observation of key management personnel, the actual performance criteria (specifications), emphasis, and priorities which have governed strategic choices in the past should be determined.[9]

Current Strategy of a Product/Market. As far as marketing is concerned, the strategy for a product is formulated around one or more marketing-mix variables. In examining present strategy the purpose is to pinpoint those perspectives of the marketing mix which currently dominate strategy. The current strategy of a product may be examined by seeking answers to the following two questions:

1. What markets do we have?
2. How is each market served?

What Markets Do We Have? Answering this question involves consideration of several aspects of the market:

1. Recognize different market segments in which the product is sold.

---

[9]Robert L. Katz, *Cases and Concepts in Corporate Strategy* (Englewood Cliffs, NJ: Prentice-Hall, 1970), p. 210.

2. Build a demographic profile of each segment.
3. Identify important customers in each segment.
4. Identify also those customers who, while important, also do business with competitors.
5. Identify reasons each important customer may have in buying the product from us. These reasons may be economic (i.e., lower prices); functional (e.g., product features not available in competing products); and psychological (e.g., "this perfume matches my individual chemistry").
6. Examine the strategic perspective of each important customer as it concerns the purchase of our product. This aspect will be relevant primarily for business customers. For example, an aluminum company should attempt to study the strategy a can manufacturer may have as far as its aluminum can business is concerned. Suppose prices of aluminum are consistently rising, and more and more can manufacturers are replacing aluminum cans with cans of a new alloy of plastic and paper. Such strategic perspectives of an important customer should be examined.
7. Consider changes in each customer's perspectives which may occur in the next few years. These changes may become necessary because of shifts in the customer's environment (both internal and external), abilities, and resources.

The above information should, if properly analyzed, provide a good knowledge of customers: why they buy our products, and their likelihood of doing business with us in the future. For example, a paper manufacturer discovered that most customers did business with him because, in their opinion, his delivery schedules were more flexible than those of other suppliers. The quality of paper might have been superior too, but this was not strategically important for the customers.

How Is Each Market Served? The means which the company employs to serve its different customers may be studied by analyzing the information contained in Exhibit 7-3.

A careful examination of this information will reveal the current strategy which the company utilizes to serve its main markets. For example, analysis of the information in Exhibit 7-3 may reveal the following facts pertaining to a breakfast cereal:

Of the seven different segments in the market, the product is extremely popular in two segments. Customers buy the product mainly for health reasons or because of a desire for "natural" foods. This desire is strong enough for them to pay a premium price for the product. Further, customers are willing to make a trip to another store (other than their regular grocery store) to buy this product. Different promotional devices keep the customers conscious of the "natural" ingredients of the product.

EXHIBIT 7-3   Information for Recognizing Present Marketing Strategy

1. Basis for segmenting the market
2. Definition of the markets for the product
3. Profile of customers in each segment: age, income level, occupation, geographical location, etc.
4. Scope and dimensions of each market: size, profitability, etc.
5. Expected rate of growth of each segment
6. Requirements for success in each market
7. Market standing with established customers in each segment: market share, pattern of repeat business, expansion of customer's product use
8. Benefits which customers in different segments derive from the product: economics, better performance, displaceable cost, etc.
9. Reasons for buying the product in different segments: product features, awareness, price, advertising, promotion, packaging, display, sales assistance, other
10. Customer attitudes in different segments: brand awareness, brand image (mapping), etc.
11. Overall reputation of the product in each segment
12. Purchase or use habits which contribute to these attitudes
13. Reasons which reinforce customer's faith in the company and product
14. Reasons which force customers to turn elsewhere for help in using the product
15. Life-cycle status of the product
16. Story of the product line: quality development, delivery, service
17. Product research and improvements planned
18. Market share—overall and in different segments
19. Deficiencies in servicing or assisting customers in using the product
20. Possibility of reducing services in areas where customers are becoming more self-sufficient
21. Resource base: nature of emerging and developing resources—technical, marketing, financial—which could expand or open new markets for the product
22. Geographic coverage of the product market
23. Identification of principal channels (dealer or class of trade)
24. Buying habits and attitudes of these channels
25. Sales history through each type of channel
26. Industry sales by type of outlet (i.e., retail, wholesale, institutional, and further by major types of outlets within each area—department store, chain store, specialty store, etc.)
27. Overall price structure for the product
28. Trade discount policy
29. Variations in price in different segments
30. Frequency of price changes
31. Promotional deals offered for the product
32. Emphasis on different advertising media
33. Major thrust of advertising copy
34. Sales tips or promotional devices used by salespeople

This may point toward the following strategy for the product:

1. Concentrate on limited segments.
2. Emphasize the naturalness of the product as its unique attribute.
3. Keep the prices high.
4. Pull the product through with heavy doses of consumer advertising.

Where strategy in the past has not been systematically formulated, recognition of current strategy will be more difficult. In such situations, strategy must be inferred from the perspectives of different marketing decisions.

The discussion above on present strategy of a product has been approached from two angles: which strategic aspects of the product are indeed valued by the customer, and what constitutes marketing strategy in the eyes of the company.

Past Performance

Evaluation of past performance is invaluable in measuring strengths and weaknesses since it provides historical insights into a company's marketing strategy and its success. Historical examination should not be limited to simply noting the directions the company adopted and the results it achieved, but should also include a search for reasons for these results. Exhibit 7-4 shows the type of information which is helpful in measuring past performance. Our discussion in this section will not deal with all the different types of information listed therein; however, this exhibit summarizes the type of past information which a company uses in its marketing planning efforts.

Strategically, the following three types of analysis should be undertaken to measure past performance: product performance profile, market performance profile, and financial performance profile.

Information utilized for developing a product performance profile is shown in Exhibit 7-5. A product may contribute to company performance in six different ways: through profitability, image of product leadership, furnishing a base for further technological growth, support of total product line, utilization of company resources (e.g., utilization of excess plant capacity), and provision of customer benefits (vis-à-vis the price paid).[10] An example of this last type of contribution would be a product which is a small but indispensable part of another product or process with low cost relative to the value of the whole finished product. Tektronics, Inc., a manufacturer of oscilloscopes, is an example. When a computer is in-

---

[10]See Stuart U. Rich, "Planning the Future Strategy of Your Business," *Oregon Business Review*, April, 1964, p. 3.

**EXHIBIT 7-4   General Foods: Post Division
Historical and Supporting Data for Marketing Plans**

A. The Consumer
Identify if possible the current "light," "moderate," and "heavy" user of the product in terms of:
1. Recent trends in % of brand's volume accounted for by each group.
2. The characteristics of each group as to sex, age, income, occupation, income group, geographical location.
3. Attitudes towards the product and category and copy appeals most persuasive to each group.

B. The Product
Identify the current consumer preference of the brand versus primary competition (and secondary competition if available), according to:
1. Light, moderate, heavy usage (if available).
2. The characteristics of each group as to sex, age, income, occupation, income group, geographical location, size of family, etc.

C. Shipment History
Identify the recent shipment trends on the brand by total units and units/M population (brand development) according to districts, regions, and nationally.

D. Spending History
Identify the recent spending trends on the brand by total dollars, dollar/M population, per unit sold for advertising, for promotion, and for total A & P by districts, regions, and nationally.

E. Profitability History
Identify the recent trends of list price, average retail price (by sales areas), gross profit margins, and PBT *in addition* to trends in:
1. Gross profit as % of net sales.
2. Total marketing as % of gross profit and per unit sold.
3. PBT as % of net sales and per unit sold.
4. ROFE (Return of Funds Employed) for each recent fiscal year.

F. Share of Market History
Identify recent trends of:
1. The brands of share-of-market nationally, regionally, district-wide.
2. Consumption by total units and % gain/loss versus year ago nationally, regionally, district-wide.
3. Distribution by pack size nationally, regionally, district-wide.

Where applicable, trends in all of the above data should also be identified by store classification, chain versus independent (large, medium and small).

EXHIBIT 7-4   continued

G. Total Market History
   Identify recent trends of the total market in terms of units and % gain/loss versus year ago nationally, regionally, district-wide, per M population, store type, county size, type of user (exclusive versus partial user), retail price trends, by user characteristics (age, income, etc.).

H. Competitive History (major brands), where available
   Identify significant competitive trends in share, consumption levels by sales areas, store types; media and promotion expenditures; types of media, promotion; retail price differentials, etc.

Source: E. Raymond Corey and Steven H. Star, *Organization Strategy: A Marketing Approach* (Boston: Division of Research, Harvard Business School, 1971), p. 224. Reprinted by permission.

stalled, an oscilloscope is sold along with it and is used to help set up the computer to test it, and to monitor its performance. The cost of the oscilloscope is small when one considers the essential role it plays in the use of the much more expensive computer.

A market performance profile is illustated in Exhibit 7-6. In analyzing how well a company is doing in the segments it serves, a good place to begin is the marginal profit contribution of each customer or customer group. Other measures used are market share, growth end-user markets, size of customer base, distribution strength, and degree of customer loyalty.[11] Of all these, only distribution strength requires some explanation. Distribution and dealer networks can greatly influence a company's per-

EXHIBIT 7-5   Product Performance Profile
Contribution to Company Performance

Product Line	Profit-ability	Product Leader-ship	Techno-logical Growth	Support of Total Product Line	Utiliza-tion of Company Resources	Provision of Customer Benefits
_____						
_____						
_____						
_____						

Source: Stuart U. Rich, University of Oregon. Reprinted by permission.

---

[11]*Ibid.*, p. 4.

EXHIBIT 7-6 Market Performance Profile
Contribution to Company Performance

Market Segments	Profit-ability	Market Share	Growth End-user Markets	Size of Customer Base	Distribu-tion Strength	Degree of Customer Loyalty
_____						
_____						
_____						
_____						

Source: Stuart U. Rich, University of Oregon. Reprinted by permission.

formance. This is because it takes an enormous effort to cultivate dealers' loyalty and get repeated business from them. Distribution strength, therefore, can make a significant difference in overall performance.

The real value of a strategy must be reflected in financial gains and market achievements. To measure financial performance, four standards may be employed for comparison: (1) the company's performance, (2) competitors' performance, (3) management expectations, and (4) performance in terms of resources committed. With these standards, for the purposes of marketing strategy, financial performance can be measured with respect to the following variables:

1. Growth rate (percentage)
2. Profitability (percentage), i.e., rate of return on investment
3. Market share (percentage as compared with that of principal competitors)
4. Cash flow

It is desirable to analyze financial performance for a number of years to determine the historical trend of performance. To show how financial performance analysis may figure in formulating marketing strategy, the following excerpt from a recent study on the subject may be used:

A maker of confectionery that offers more than one hundred brands, flavors and packagings, prunes its lines—regularly and routinely—of those items having the lowest profit contribution, sales volume, and vitality for future growth.

Since the early 1970s each individual product has been ranked on these three factors, and an "index of gross profitability" has been prepared for each in conjunction with annual marketing plans. These plans take into account longer-term objectives for the business, trends in consumer wants and expectations, competitive factors in the marketplace and, lastly, a deliberately ordered "prioritization" of the company's resources. Sales and profit performance are then checked against projected targets at regular intervals through the year, and the indexes of gross profitability are adjusted when necessary.

The firm's chief executive emphasizes that even individual items whose indexes of profitability are ranked at the very bottom are none-theless profitable and paying their way by any customary standard of return on sales and investment. But the very lowest-ranking items are regularly reviewed; and, on a judgmental basis, some are marked for pruning at the next convenient opportunity. This opportunity is most likely to arrive when stocks of special ingredients and packaging labels for the items have been exhausted.

In a recent year, the company dropped 16 items that were judged to be too low on its index of gross profitability. Calculated and selective pruning is regarded within the company as a healthy means of work-ing toward the best possible mix of products at all times. It has the reported advantages of increasing efficiencies in manufacturing as a result of cutting the "down time" between small runs, reducing inven-tories, and freeing resources for the expansion of the most promising items—or the development of new ones—without having to expand productive capacity. Another important benefit is that the sales force concentrates on a smaller line containing only the most profitable products with the largest volumes. On the negative side, however, it is acknowledged that pruning, as the company practices it, may result in near-term loss of sales for a line until growth of the rest of the items can compensate.[12]

Appraising Marketing Effectiveness

Marketing is concerned with the activities required to facilitate the exchange process toward managing demand. The perspectives of these activities are founded on marketing strategy. To develop the strategy a company needs a philosophical orientation. Four different types of ori-entation may be considered: manufacturing, sales, technology, and mar-keting. Manufacturing orientation emphasizes a physical product or a ser-vice and assumes that the customer will be pleased with it if it has been well conceived and developed. Sales orientation focuses on promoting the product to make the customer want it. The thrust of technology orien-tation is on reaching the customer through new and varied products made feasible through technological innovations. Under marketing orientation, first the customer group that the firm wishes to serve should be desig-nated. Then, the requirements of the target group should be carefully examined. These requirements should become the basis of product or ser-vice conception and development, its pricing, promotion, and distribution. Exhibit 7-7 contrasts marketing-oriented companies with manufacturing-, sales- and technology-oriented firms.

---

[12]David S. Hopkins, *Business Strategies for Problem Products* (New York: The Con-ference Board, 1977), p. 29.

EXHIBIT 7-7   Comparison of Four Kinds of Companies

	Orientation			
	Manufac-turing	Sales	Technology	Marketing
Typical strategy	Lower cost	Increase volume	Push research	Build share profitability
Normal structure	Functional	Functional or profit centers	Profit centers	Market or product or brand; decentralized profit responsibility
Key systems	Plant P&L's Budgets	Sales forecasts Results vs. plan	Performance tests R&D plans	Marketing plans
Traditional skills	Engineering	Sales	Science and engineering	Analysis
Normal focus	Internal efficiencies	Distribution channels; short-term sales results	Product performance	Consumers Market share
Typical response to competitive pressure	Cut costs	Cut price Sell harder	Improve product	Consumer research, planning, testing, refining
Overall mental set	"What we need to do in this company is get our costs down and our quality up."	"Where can I sell what we make?"	"The best product wins the day."	"What will the consumer buy that we can profitably make?"

Source: Edward G. Michaels, "Marketing Muscle: Who Needs It?," *Business Horizons*, May–June, 1982, p. 72. Copyright, 1982, by the Foundation for the School of Business at Indiana University. Reprinted by permission.

An examination of Exhibit 7-7 shows that good marketers should think like general managers. Their approach should be unconstrained by functional boundaries. Without neglecting either near- or medium-term profitability, they concentrate on building a position for tomorrow.

Despite the lip service that has been paid to marketing for over 30 years, it remains one of the most misunderstood functions of a business. According to Kotler only a few corporations, such as Procter & Gamble, Eastman Kodak, Avon, McDonald's, IBM, Xerox, General Electric, and Caterpillar, really understand and practice true marketing. Inasmuch as marketing orientation is a prerequisite to developing successful marketing strategy, it behooves a company to thoroughly examine its marketing orientation.[13] The following checklist of ten questions provides a quick self-test for a company that wants a rough measure of its marketing capability:[14]

—Has your company carefully segmented the various segments of the consumer market that it serves?

—Do you routinely measure the profitability of your key products or services in each of these consumer market segments?

—Do you use market research to keep abreast of the needs, preferences, and buying habits of consumers in each segment?

—Have you identified the key buying factors in each segment, and do you know how your company compares with its competitors on these factors?

—Is the impact of environmental trends (demographic, competitive, lifestyle, governmental) on your business carefully gauged?

—Does your company prepare and use an annual marketing plan?

—Is the concept of "marketing investment" understood—and practiced—in your company?

—Is profit responsibility for a product line pushed below the senior management level?

—Does your organization "talk" marketing?

—Did one of the top five executives in your company come up through marketing?

The number of "yes" answers to the above questions would determine the marketing orientation of a company. For example, a score of 9 or 10 "yes" answers would mean that the company has a strong marketing capability; 6 to 8 would indicate that the firm is on the way, and fewer than 6 "yes" answers would stress that the firm is vulnerable to marketing-minded competitors. Essentially, truly marketing-oriented firms are consumer-oriented, take an integrated approach to planning, look further ahead, and have highly developed marketing systems. In such firms marketing dominates the corporate culture.

The marketing orientation perspective of a firm should reflect its

---

[13]Philip Kotler, "From Sales Obsession to Marketing Effectiveness," *Harvard Business Review*, November–December, 1977, p. 68.

[14]Edward G. Michaels, "Marketing Muscle: Who Needs It?," *Business Horizons*, May–June, 1982.

marketing effectiveness. A more detailed procedure for measuring marketing effectiveness is given in the appendix at the end of this chapter. It consists of a questionnaire which uses the following five measures of effectiveness: customer philosophy, integrated marketing organization, adequate marketing information, strategic orientation, and operational efficiency. If the questionnaire is thoughtfully completed, it will reveal the overall marketing effectiveness of the company and highlight the areas that are weak and require management action. The management may take appropriate action, such as management training, reorganization, or installation of measures designed to seek improvements with or without the help of consultants. If the weaknesses cannot be addressed, the company must live with them, and the marketing strategist should take note of them in the process of outlining the company's future direction.

Marketing Environment

Chapter 6 was devoted to scanning the environment at the macro level. This section looks at the environment from the product/market perspective. Environmental scanning at the macro level is the job of a staff person who may be positioned at the corporate, division, group, or business unit level. The person concerned may go by any of these titles: corporate planner, environmental analyst, environmental scanner, strategy planner, or marketing researcher.

Monitoring of the environment from the viewpoint of products/ markets is a line function which should be carried out by those who are involved in making marketing decisions. This is so since the product/market managers, being in close touch with various marketing aspects of the product/market, are in a better position to read between the lines and make more meaningful interpretations of the environment than are the staff people. The constituents of the product/market environment are: social and cultural effects, political influences, ethical considerations, legal requirements, competition, economic climate, technological changes, institutional evolution, consumerism, population, location of consumers, income, expenditure patterns, and education. Not all aspects of the environment will be relevant for every product/market. The scanner, therefore, should first choose which parts of the environment influence the product/ market before attempting to monitor them.

The strategic significance of product/market environment is well illustrated by the experience of Nabisco Brands, Inc., an established leader in the cookie industry. Review of the environment in the early 1980s showed that because the U.S. population was not growing much, overall food consumption was not growing much either. Also, increasing health consciousness among consumers was changing eating habits. Interestingly, however, while consumption of supermarket cookies was not growing, sales of chewy, fresh-baked cookies from specialty shops were—even though comparatively little money was being spent to advertise or promote them.

Equipped with this analysis of the environment, new entrants in the cookie business (Frito-Lay, a division of PepsiCo; and Procter & Gamble) figured that if they could offer a grocery store cookie that was chewy instead of dry and hard, advertise it heavily, then sell it for less than the fresh-baked kind, they could scoop up sales from Nabisco, British-owned Keebler Co., and American Brands' Sunshine Biscuits, the top three cookie makers. As a matter of fact, they anticipated that such a product might get people to eat more cookies generally.[15]

In May, 1982, Frito-Lay introduced its Grandma's Cookies in seven varieties, ranging from sandwich to chocolate chip. Initially distributed west of the Mississippi, Grandma's Cookies went national by 1984. About nine months later, Procter & Gamble's Duncan Hines Chocolate Chip Cookies followed with the promise that they were crispy outside and chewy inside, just like a good homemade cookie. After successful test marketing in Kansas City, Procter & Gamble also went national in 1984. The company even applied for a patent for its cookies, something unusual in the cookie business. (The detailed 45-page patent application even included a diagram of a cookie with soft dough sandwiched inside stiff dough.) Shelf life of this more perishable type of cookie might have been a problem, but the successful introduction of aseptic packaging (a technological breakthrough) in the United States provided the answer.[16]

Failure to respond soon enough to the changing cookie market environment posed a threat to Nabisco, which for decades had enjoyed a leading position in the market. As a quick reaction, Nabisco rushed to add more chocolate chips to its Chips Ahoy! cookies, but this did not help much. Apparently Nabisco needs a new strategic thrust to hold/advance its position in the cookie market. Environmental perspectives would serve as an input in defining objectives and formulating strategy.

ANALYZING STRENGTHS AND WEAKNESSES

The study of competition, current strategic perspectives, past performance, marketing effectiveness, and marketing environment provides insights into information necessary for designating strengths and weaknesses. Exhibit 7-8 provides a rundown of areas of strength as far as marketing is concerned. Where feasible, strengths should be stated in objective terms. Exhibit 7-8 does not provide an all-inclusive listing, but it is indicative of the kind of strength which a company may have over its competitors. It will be noted that most areas of strength are related to the excellence of personnel or are resource-based. Not all factors will have the same significance for every product/market. Therefore, it will be desir-

---

[15]Janet Guyon, "Nabisco's New Cookie Line Marks the Beginning of a Fierce Sales War," *The Wall Street Journal*, October 17, 1983, p. 33.
[16]See Robert Ball, "The Packaging Industry," *Fortune*, August 9, 1982, p. 79.

EXHIBIT 7-8   Areas of Strength

1. Excellence in product design and/or performance (engineering ingenuity)
2. Low-cost, high-efficiency operating skill in manufacturing and/or in distribution
3. Leadership in product innovation
4. Efficiency in customer service
5. Personal relationships with customers
6. Efficiency in transportation and logistics
7. Effectiveness in sales promotion
8. Merchandising efficiency—high turnover of inventories and/or of capital
9. Skillful trading in volatile price movement commodities
10. Ability to influence legislation
11. Highly efficient, low-cost facilities
12. Ownership or control of low-cost or scarce raw materials
13. Control of intermediate distribution or processing units
14. Massive availability of capital
15. Widespread customer acceptance of company brand name (reputation)
16. Product availability, convenience
17. Customer loyalty
18. Dominant market share position
19. Effectiveness of advertising
20. Quality sales force

Source: Points 1 through 16 are taken from Robert L. Katz, *Cases and Concepts in Corporate Strategy,* © 1970, p. 215. Reprinted by permission of Prentice-Hall, Englewood Cliffs, NJ.

able to first recognize the critical factors which could directly or indirectly bear on a product's performance. For example, the development of an improved product may be strategic for drug companies. On the other hand, in the case of cosmetic products, where image building is usually important, advertising may be a critical factor. After-sales service may have significance for products such as copying machines, computers, and elevators. The critical factors may be chosen with reference to Exhibit 3-6 (p. 126). From among the critical factors, an attempt should be made to sort out strengths. It will be desirable to rate different strengths for a more objective analysis.

The strengths should be further examined to undertake what may be called opportunity analysis (i.e., matching strengths or competencies to opportunity). The opportunity analysis will serve as an input in establishing a company's economic mission. The opportunity analysis is useful in developing both an individual product's objectives and the corporate-wide mission. In Exhibit 7-9 the objectives for a food product are shown as they emerged from a study of its strengths. These objectives are a premium product, an unscored segment, and a new channel outlet. In other words, at the level of a product the opportunity analysis seeks to answer such questions as: What opportunity does the company have to capitalize on a

EXHIBIT 7-9   Matching Strengths with Opportunities

STRENGTH	LIKELY IMPACT	OPPORTUNITY (FURNISHED BY THE ENVIRONMENT)	OBJECTIVES AND GOALS
Customer loyalty	Incremental product volume increases Price increases for premium quality/service New product introductions	A trend of changing taste An identified geographic shift of part of the market A market segment neglected by the industry	Develop a premium product Introduce the existing product in the segment hitherto not served Develop a new channel outlet for the product, etc.
Cordial relationships with channels	New product introductions Point-of-purchase advertising Reduction of delivered costs through distribution innovations Tied-in products Merchandising differentiation	A product-related subconscious need not solicited by competition A product weakness of competition A distribution weakness of competition Technical feasibility for improving existing package design A discovered new use for the product or container	

competitor's weaknesses? Modify or improve the product line or add new products? Serve the needs of more customers in existing markets, or develop new markets? Improve the efficiency of current marketing operations?

The opportunities emerge from the changing environment. Thus, the environmental analysis provides an important input in pinpointing opportunities. Exhibit 7-10 suggests a simple format for analyzing the impact of the environment.

As far as the corporate-wide mission is concerned, consider the case of a ballpoint pen manufacturer. One of the strengths of a successful manufacturer is the ability to handle extensive advertising and massive distribution. This strength is transferable and could be used for running a suc-

EXHIBIT 7-10   Impact of Environmental Trends

Trends	Impact	Timing of Impact	Response Time	Urgency	Threats	Opportunities

cessful razor-blade business as well. This is what has happened, of course, at BIC Pen Corporation. In other words, the opportunity analysis can direct a company toward the course it should pursue.

An interesting observation with regard to opportunity analysis, made by Andrews, is relevant here:

> The match is designed to minimize organizational weakness and to maximize strength. In any case, risk attends it. And when opportunity seems to outrun present distinctive competence, the willingness to gamble that the latter can be built up to the required level is almost indispensible to a strategy that challenges the organization and the people in it. It appears to be true, in any case, that the potential capability of a company tends to be underestimated. Organizations, like individuals, rise to occasions, particularly when the latter provide attractive reward for the effort required.[17]

In the process of analyzing strengths, certain weaknesses will also be noted. Exhibit 7-11 is a list of typical marketing weaknesses. Basically,

EXHIBIT 7-11   Typical Marketing Weaknesses

1. Inadequate definition of customer for product/market development
2. Ambiguous service policies
3. Too many levels of reporting in the organizational setup
4. Overlapping channels
5. Lack of top-management involvement in new product development
6. Lack of quantitative goals

---

[17]Kenneth R. Andrews, *The Concept of Corporate Strategy* (Homewood, IL: Dow Jones-Irwin, 1971), p. 100.

appropriate action must be taken to correct the weaknesses. However, some weaknesses may have corporate-wide bearing, while others may be weaknesses of a specific product. The corporate-wide weaknesses must be examined, and necessary corrective action must be incorporated into the overall marketing strategy. For example, weaknesses #3, 5, and 6 in Exhibit 7-11 could have corporate-wide ramifications. These must be addressed by the chief marketing strategist. The remaining three weaknesses can be corrected by the person in charge of the product/market with which these weaknesses are associated.

Measurement of strengths and weaknesses may be illustrated with reference to the personal computer business. In 1982, Apple Computer, Atari (Warner Bros.), Commodore International, Digital Equipment, Fortune Systems, International Business Machines, Japanese firms, Radio Shack (Tandy Company), and Texas Instruments were active in the field. Of these, Tandy, IBM, Apple, and Commodore were the leading competitors. Exhibit 7-12 lists the relative strengths of the different firms.

At that time, success in the personal computer business depended on mastery of three critical areas, summarized as follows in a *Business Week* article:

EXHIBIT 7-12   Relative Strengths of Personal Computer Firms

COMPANIES	Applications software	Brand image	Depth of management	Financial muscle	Low-cost production	National sales force	Retail distribution	Service and support
Apple Computer	•	•					•	
Atari (Warner)	•	•	•				•	
Commodore International					•		•	
Digital Equipment			•	•	•	•		•
Fortune Systems	•							
International Business Machines	•	•	•	•	•	•	•	•
Japan Inc.*			•	•	•			
Radio Shack (Tandy)	•	•		•			•	•
Texas Instruments			•	•	•		•	•

*At least one Japanese company is expected to succeed,
 but it is too early to pick which one.

Low-cost Production. As personal computer hardware becomes increasingly standardized, the ability to provide the most value for the dollar will greatly influence sales. The most vertically integrated companies will have the edge.

Distribution. Retailers have shelf space for just four or five brands; only those makers that keep their products in the customer's line of sight will survive.

Software. Computer sales will suffer unless a wide choice of software packages is offered to increase the number of applications.[18]

Without all the above three strengths in place, a company could not make it in the personal computer business. Thus, Texas Instruments withdrew from the field in 1983 for lack of applications software. Both Apple Computer and Atari appeared to be in trouble in 1984, at the time of this writing, since they were high-cost manufacturers. To overcome its weaknesses, Apple has been working to come out with a computer for which users will need no training. The company believes that pursuing this goal will differentiate Apple computers from those of competitors, thus compensating for its high costs. This is one more illustration of the importance of analyzing strengths and weaknesses to define objectives and strategies for the future.

CONCEPT OF SYNERGY

Before concluding the discussion of strengths and weaknesses, it will be desirable to briefly introduce the concept of synergy. Synergy, simply stated, is the concept that the combined effect of certain parts is greater than the sum of their individual effects. Let us say, for example, that Product 1 contributes X and Product 2 contributes Y. If they are produced together, they may contribute X + Y + Z. Then, Z is the synergistic effect of X and Y being brought together, and Z represents positive synergy. There can be negative synergy as well. Study of synergy helps in analyzing new growth opportunities. A new product, for instance, may have such a high synergistic effect on a company's existing product(s) that it may be an extremely desirable addition.

Quantitative analysis of synergy is far from easy. Ansoff, however, has provided a framework for evaluation of synergy which will be discussed here with reference to a new product/market entry (see Exhibit 7-13). A new product/market entry contribution could take place at three levels: contribution to the parent company (from the entry), contribution to the new entry (from the parent), and joint opportunities (i.e., benefits which will accrue to both as a result of consolidation). As far as it is feasible, entries in Exhibit 7-13 should be assigned a numerical value, such

---

[18]"The Coming Shakeout in Personal Computers," *Business Week*, November 22, 1982, p. 73.

EXHIBIT 7-13   Measurement of Synergy of a New Product/Market Entry

Synergistic Contribution to:	Synergy Measures						
	Startup Economies			Operating Economies		New Product and Market Areas	Overall Synergy
	Investment	Operating	Timing	Investment	Operating	Expansion of Present Sales	
Parent							
New entry							
Joint opportunities							

Source: Adapted from H. Igor Ansoff, *Corporate Strategy* (New York: McGraw-Hill Book Co., 1965), p. 189. Reprinted by permission of the publisher.

as increase in unit sales by 20 percent, time saving by two months, reduction in investment requirements by 10 percent, and so on. Finally, various numerical values may be given a common value in the form of return on investment or cash flow.[19]

SUMMARY

This chapter has provided a scheme for an objective measurement of strengths and weaknesses of a product/market. Strengths and weaknesses are tangible and intangible resources which may be utilized for seeking growth for the product. Factors which need to be studied in order to designate strengths and weaknesses are: competition, current strategic perspectives, past performance, marketing effectiveness, and marketing environment. Present strategy may be examined with reference to the markets being served and the means utilized to serve these markets. Past performance is considered in the form of financial analysis ranging from simple measurements such as market share and profitability to developing product and market performance profiles.

Marketing effectiveness is related to marketing orientation, which may be determined with reference to the questions raised in the chapter. Finally, various aspects of product/market marketing environment should be analyzed.

The above five factors are brought together to delineate strengths and weaknesses. An operational scheme is introduced to conduct opportunity analysis. Also discussed is the concept of synergy. The analysis of strengths and weaknesses sets the stage for developing marketing objectives and goals, to be discussed in the next chapter.

DISCUSSION QUESTIONS

1. *Why is it necessary to measure strengths and weaknesses?*
2. *Since it is natural for managers and other employees to want to justify their actions and decisions, is it possible for a company to make a truly objective appraisal of its strengths and weaknesses?*
3. *Evaluate the current strategy of IBM related to personal computers and compare it with the strategy pursued by Apple Computer and Commodore International.*
4. *Develop a conceptual scheme to evaluate the current strategy of a bank and a department store.*
5. *Evaluate the past performance of Chrysler Corporation in the light of its comeback in 1983.*

---

[19]H. Igor Ansoff, *Corporate Strategy* (New York: McGraw-Hill Book Co., 1965), pp. 88–90.

6. *Is it necessary for a firm to be marketing-oriented to succeed? What may a firm do to overcome its lack of marketing orientation?*
7. *Making necessary assumptions, perform an opportunity analysis for a fast-food firm and a packaged-goods manufacturer.*
8. *Explain the meaning of synergy. Examine what sort of synergy Procter & Gamble achieved by going into the frozen orange juice business.*

APPENDIX: RATING MARKETING EFFECTIVENESS

	Customer Philosophy
	A. Does management recognize the importance of designing the company to serve the needs and wants of chosen markets?
Score	
0 ☐	Management primarily thinks in terms of selling current and new products to whoever will buy them.
1 ☐	Management thinks in terms of serving a wide range of markets and needs with equal effectiveness.
2 ☐	Management thinks in terms of serving the needs and wants of well-defined markets chosen for their long-run growth and profit potential for the company.
	B. Does management develop different offerings and marketing plans for different segments of the market?
0 ☐	No.
1 ☐	Somewhat.
2 ☐	To a good extent.
	C. Does management take a whole marketing system view (suppliers, channels, competitors, customers, environment) in planning its business?
0 ☐	No. Management concentrates on selling and servicing its immediate customers.
1 ☐	Somewhat. Management takes a long view of its channels although the bulk of its effort goes to selling and servicing the immediate customers.
2 ☐	Yes. Management takes a whole marketing systems view recognizing the threats and opportunities created for the company by changes in any part of the system.

		Integrated Marketing Organization
		D. Is there high-level marketing integration and control of the major marketing functions?
0	☐	No. Sales and other marketing functions are not integrated at the top and there is some unproductive conflict.
1	☐	Somewhat. There is formal integration and control of the major marketing functions but less than satisfactory coordination and cooperation.
2	☐	Yes. The major marketing functions are effectively integrated.
		E. Does marketing management work well with management in research, manufacturing, purchasing, physical distribution, and finance?
0	☐	No. There are complaints that marketing is unreasonable in the demands and costs it places on other departments.
1	☐	Somewhat. The relations are amicable although each department pretty much acts to serve its own power interests.
2	☐	Yes. The departments cooperate effectively and resolve issues in the best interest of the company as a whole.
		F. How well-organized is the new product development process?
0	☐	The system is ill-defined and poorly handled.
1	☐	The system formally exists but lacks sophistication.
2	☐	The system is well-structured and professionally staffed.
		Adequate Marketing Information
		G. When were the latest marketing research studies of customers, buying influences, channels, and competitors conducted?
0	☐	Several years ago.
1	☐	A few years ago.
2	☐	Recently.
		H. How well does management know the sales potential and profitability of different market segments, customers, territories, products, channels, and order sizes?

0	☐	Not at all.
1	☐	Somewhat.
2	☐	Very well.

I. What effort is expended to measure the cost-effectiveness of different marketing expenditures?

0	☐	Little or no effort.
1	☐	Some effort.
2	☐	Substantial effort.

Strategic Orientation

J. What is the extent of formal marketing planning?

0	☐	Management does little or no formal marketing planning.
1	☐	Management develops an annual marketing plan.
2	☐	Management develops a detailed annual marketing plan and a careful long-range plan that is updated annually.

K. What is the quality of the current marketing strategy?

0	☐	The current strategy is not clear.
1	☐	The current strategy is clear and represents a continuation of traditional strategy.
2	☐	The current strategy is clear, innovative, data-based, and well-reasoned.

L. What is the extent of contingency thinking and planning?

0	☐	Management does little or no contingency thinking.
1	☐	Management does some contingency thinking although little formal contingency planning.
2	☐	Management formally identifies the most important contingencies and develops contingency plans.

Operational Efficiency

M. How well is the marketing thinking at the top communicated and implemented down the line?

0	☐	Poorly.
1	☐	Fairly well.
2	☐	Successfully.

N. Is management doing an effective job with the marketing resources?

0	☐	No. The marketing resources are inadequate for the job to be done.
1	☐	Somewhat. The marketing resources are adequate but they are not employed optimally.
2	☐	Yes. The marketing resources are adequate and are deployed efficiently.

O. Does management show a good capacity to react quickly and effectively to on-the-spot developments?

0	☐	No. Sales and market information is not very current and management reaction time is slow.
1	☐	Somewhat. Management receives fairly up-to-date sales and market information; management reaction time varies.
2	☐	Yes. Management has installed systems yielding highly current information and fast reaction time.

Total Score

Rating Marketing Effectiveness

The auditing outline can be used in this way. The auditor collects information as it bears on the 15 questions. The appropriate answer is checked for each question. The scores are added—the total will be somewhere between 0 and 30. The following scale shows the equivalent in marketing effectiveness:

0–5	None
6–10	Poor
11–15	Fair
16–20	Good
21–25	Very good
26–30	Superior

To illustrate, 15 senior managers in a large building materials company were recently invited to rate their company using the auditing instrument in this exhibit. The resulting overall marketing effectiveness scores ranged from a low of 6 to a high of 15. The median score was 11, with three fourths of the scores between 9 and 13. Therefore, most of the managers thought their company was at best "fair" at marketing.

Several divisions were also rated. Their median scores ranged from a low of 3 to a high of 19. The higher scoring divisions tended to have higher profitability. However, some of the lower scoring divisions were also profitable. An examination of the latter showed that these divisions were in industries where their competition also operated at a low level of marketing effectiveness. The managers feared that these divisions would be vulnerable as soon as competition began to learn to market more successfully.

An interesting question to speculate on is the distribution of median marketing effectiveness scores for *Fortune* "500" companies. My suspicion is that very few companies in that roster would score above 20 ("very good" or "superior") in marketing effectiveness. Although marketing theory and practice have received their fullest expression in the United States, the great majority of U.S. companies probably fail to meet the highest standards.

Intertel, Inc.

Intertel develops, manufactures, and markets data communication products and services. The company is a leader in the emerging field of network control systems, which are used to maintain and trouble-shoot large, distributed processing computer systems such as airline reservation systems and branch-bank ATMs.

The company also has a product line of modems, black boxes used to interface computer equipment to communication lines. This was the company's original product line. In the fall of 1981, Dr. Jerry Holsinger, inventor of the first commercially available, high-speed (9600 bps) modem and president of Intertel, Inc., was interested in launching a strategic planning effort to ensure long-term prosperity for the company. He was especially concerned with developing a viable marketing strategy to continue to hold the leadership position in the field.

COMPANY BACKGROUND

Intertel was founded in 1969 by Dr. Holsinger and two associates to design and manufacture state-of-the-art modems in the emerging independent modem market. A modem is a device which accepts data from a computer and makes it suitable for transmission over an existing communications facility, such as leased telephone lines. Back in the 1960s, AT&T was the only supplier of commercially available modems. This was due to protective tariffs which prohibited the connection of non-AT&T devices to the Bell System network. This restriction was removed in 1969 after a decision made by the Supreme Court in the Carterfone case which opened up the data communications equipment market to independent companies, such as Intertel.

Intertel started making custom, high-speed modems for the OEM market and developed a reputation for technical expertise and competitive pricing. Intertel's OEM modems are regularly incorporated into products made by TRW, Bunker Ramo, and Data General, among others.

By 1972, Intertel had entered the end-user modem market, specializing in high performance modems for large, on-line systems. At that time, the company recognized an unmet need for an integrated tool to perform diagnostic and restoral functions on the communications network from a central location. These functions were then being performed in an ad hoc manner, using an inefficient system of oscilloscopes, signal generators, and hit-or-miss testing. Intertel began a development effort to build a product that combined the communication function with this diagnostic capability.

In 1973 Intertel introduced the "Network Control System," which it described as enabling a person to test an entire on-line data system's communication network from the central site. It would allow a technician to locate and by-pass modem failures or bad telephone lines anywhere in the system in a very short time.

In 1976, a second-generation system, the NCS 4000, was introduced. This system was specifically designed for on-line, distributed intelligence systems, such as an airline reservation system.

In 1978, the EMS-1, a third-generation network control system, was introduced. This system allowed network communications system control at a much higher level of automation than had previously been available.

In 1980, the 90/10 system was introduced. This system continued the trend toward automating the testing and restoral function as well as providing a data base on the system's communication network status.

This history shows the company's commitment to the network communications field.

CORPORATE STRATEGY

The data communication products field has been described as a marketing-driven business, supported by continual product innovation. This requires the appropriate marketing expertise, including a sufficient sales force with the information, tools, and training needed to do a good job. Also, product development is needed to ensure an ongoing supply of innovative products.

In order to meet its long-range goals, which included market position in an increasingly competitive marketplace, Intertel had recently increased spending in the areas of marketing and engineering by more than 60 percent.

Intertel's commitment to long-term goals was strong despite the depressed state of the data communications business and lower profit margins due to increased competition, both of which had put pressure on Intertel's earnings. Exhibit 7-14 outlines the company's purpose as defined by Dr. Holsinger.

PRESENT POSITION

Intertel had recently moved into a new facility, enabling all departments to be housed under one roof. The company had previously been spread out in a few smaller buildings.

The company's financial position in 1981 was good. After a few lean years in the beginning, typical for a company that depended on the proprietary technology it had developed, the company had shown strong growth paced by sales which have averaged a 35 percent increase each

EXHIBIT 7-14   Intertel, Inc.: Corporate Statement of Purpose

---

What is our business?

Intertel develops, manufactures, and markets data communication products and services.

Who are our customers?

Intertel customers use interactive, real-time, on-line systems to access data bases and computing power. These systems operate over a complex network of leased telephone lines to interconnect geographically distributed remote terminals with centralized computers and data bases. There is typically no technical expertise at remote sites.

What are their needs?

Intertel customers use these systems in a manner integral to the operating of their business and thus present unusually demanding requirements for network availability (e.g., airlines and banks).

What do we do to fulfill these needs?

Intertel products and services function as an integrated set of tools to help its customer achieve high network availability in a controlled, cost-effective manner from a central location.

How do we service our customers?

Intertel products and services are sold and serviced directly to the customer.

---

year. Earnings as a percentage of sales had risen from zero in 1974 to a high of 16.6 percent in 1979. A recent drop was due in part to decreased profit margins resulting from increased competition and higher interest rates. The company had no long-term debt, and had an unused $1-million line of credit. The company's quick ratio had declined slightly, from a high of 4 to 1. This was due to an increased effort to get the fixed assets necessary to support growth in all functional areas, such as a corporate data base, automatic test equipment, etc. These types of expenditures had not been made in the past, so the company was currently playing a catch-up game.

The number of employees at Intertel had increased from 50 in 1970 to 100 in 1974 and currently stood at 375.

Organization

Organizationally the company was divided into four operating units:

1. *Finance and Administration.* This included top management, accounting, personnel, and human development.

2. *Manufacturing.* This included production and quality control. The manufacturing facility in Andover, Massachusetts, provided enough space for growth through 1988. In addition, the company operated a manufacturing facility in Puerto Rico to take advantage of the tax write-offs available. Puerto Rico was also a very good pool of production labor. The company built all its own products from the component level up, with the exception of the minicomputers and printers used in the network control systems for data base management. The manufacturing group had recently purchased new, semiautomated production and ATE equipment, which had significantly improved productivity in these areas.

3. *Engineering.* This department was responsible for all product development as well as manufacturing quality assurance. Because of the high priority placed on product innovation, this group had a relatively high percentage (20%) of the company's total employees. In the past, Intertel had had problems finding engineering professionals because of the large demand, but at present the department was staffed to planned levels.

4. *Marketing.* The marketing function at Intertel had not been given the support that it should have had in the past. There were two main reasons for this. The company's focus on developing its unique products had required much of top management attention. Besides, for a number of years, the company had had a virtual monopoly in the area of network control systems and felt little need for marketing.

The company now realized, however, that changes in the industry had made it much more market-driven and that, in order to achieve its goals, it must now make a strong commitment to marketing.

Because the two basic products of the company, network control systems and modems, were part of a system, the marketing department was organized in the following way:

Product marketing group. This group functioned as a link to the engineering group. It forecast future product developments to ensure successful product introduction, including the development of training programs and instruction manuals.

Industry marketing group. This group was formed in response to increased competition in the network control field and to increased end-user sophistication. The group's purpose was to maintain a group of specialists in areas such as airline reservation systems, bank systems, etc. Because these specialists could talk the same language as the end-user's computer systems people, they did a better job of meeting their needs. This group was also responsible for salesperson training and support.

Sales. A large part of Intertel's strategy to strengthen its market position was an increased commitment to the sales force. Intertel did all its selling through its own sales offices (15 in 1980) and had increased the sales force from 40 to 70 in the last two years, making the necessary increases in training programs and promotional effort as well.

International sales. The company had a division, Intertel International, which was responsible for international sales of the company's products. This group had been functioning for two years and had not been successful. While other companies had made progress in overseas markets, Intertel felt it had not for two reasons. First, the diversity of regulations covering communications equipment and the number of different engineering standards in the foreign markets made the development costs for products very high. Second, management felt that the growth and competition in the United States had prevented them from making a strong enough effort overseas.

Service. Because many end-users depended on their systems to be operating continuously, service was a critical part of the product package. Intertel maintained a 24-hour-service clearinghouse from the company headquarters. Service was provided from sales offices around the United States. Intertel had set up these offices near concentrations of central sites for distributed processing systems, such as Boston, New York, Chicago, Dallas, and Los Angeles. This allowed for fast response time, which was currently at a 4-hour industry average.

Where direct servicing was not feasible, Intertel used a third party, such as Western Union or AT&T. This had proved to be a cost-effective way to handle many outlying branch sites.

Service people were also used for on-site installation of systems. Exhibits 7-15 and 7-16 provide financial information on the company.

Product/Markets—Network Control Systems

Intertel was the first company to recognize a need and develop a product for the control of data communication systems used by distributed, on-line computer systems. Use of these systems had been increasing because of Intertel's strength in the service sector and its understanding of the benefits of distributed-intelligence information management systems.

The same forces in the industry that were making it cheaper and more efficient to have computer networks were making it easier to build an automated control system for the communication systems. This increased system "up-time" and replaced the need for a skilled service technician at every location.

Intertel was the first to develop this product. The perceived advantage of the idea was so great that Intertel sold ten systems while the first one was still on the drawing board.

Succeeding generations of the product increased the capability of the system and the automation of the testing procedures. Current capabilities allow monitoring and testing of over 9,000 remote sites of any different configuration or speed. Testing and restoral are done continually and so automatically that the system operator usually learns about it after

EXHIBIT 7-15   Intertel, Inc.: Comparative Financial Data, 1978–1980

	1976	1977	1978	1979	1980
Revenues and Net Earnings					
Revenues ($000)	5,730	8,450	12,210	14,840	19,730
Net earnings ($000)	465	975	1,885	2,370	2,409
Net earnings (%)	8.2	11.6	15.4	16.0	12.2
Earnings per share					
fully diluted ($)	0.23	0.43	0.80	0.94	0.95
Backlog at year-end ($000)	2,000	5,000	5,500	6,500	7,000
Balance Sheet Items					
Working capital ($000)	1,430	2,420	5,470	5,895	6,365
Net investment sales-type					
leases	—	—	1,030	3,850	4,720
Recourse borrowings ($000)	330	150	150	-0-	-0-
Net worth ($000)	1,350	2,235	4,710	7,330	9,870

Source: Company records.

the fact. System status data bases are developed and printed in report format to give facility managers historical reports on system status and maintenance actions.

Technology. The technical capabilities of these control systems have reached a limit; any increase in the number of drops serviced, restoral time, etc., would not be useful.

There is a trend toward providing redundancy at the remote site in the modem. This is possible because of declining hardware costs. An additional circuit board costs less than $750, and can be made for easy removal so that it can be mailed back to the factory in the event of a failure.

The technological barriers to entry in this product area are minimal; anyone with an established data communication hardware and software capability can enter.

Market environment. Intertel had had a monopoly on the network control system market for three to four years. During this time the company did not have to try hard to convince end-users of the product's advantages. Once convinced, end-users had only one source for such a product.

Intertel's main competitors in the mature modem market, such as Paradyne, Milgo and Codex, took three to four years to respond with the development of their own network control products.

By 1981, the needs of computer system users had grown more complex and consequently more diverse. For example, a hotel chain's reservation system had requirements different from those of a bank's branch office network. Also, end-users had increased the sophistication of their own in-house computer staff. This had made the end-users much more

EXHIBIT 7-16   Intertel, Inc., and Subsidiaries: Consolidated Statement of Income

	Year ended October 31, 1980	1979
Revenues:		
Sales	$10,824,566	$ 8,420,509
Leases treated as sales	5,221,734	3,773,943
Field service revenues and operating lease revenues	3,684,357	2,646,396
Total revenues	$19,730,657	$14,840,848
Cost of revenues	8,964,098	5,647,363
Gross profit	$10,766,559	$ 9,193,485
Engineering and development costs	$ 1,822,878	$ 1,165,658
Selling expenses	4,098,627	2,472,184
General and administrative expenses	1,467,134	1,315,249
Total expenses	$ 7,388,639	$ 4,953,091
Income from operations	$ 3,377,920	$ 4,240,394
Other income (expense):		
Interest income	841,519	377,204
Interest expense	(45,729)	(12,644)
Income before income taxes	$ 4,173,710	$ 4,604,954
Provision for income taxes:		
Federal—		
Current	$ 838,000	$ 1,002,000
Deferred	637,000	798,000
State—		
Current	160,000	257,000
Deferred	130,000	178,000
	$ 1,765,000	$ 2,235,000
Net income	$ 2,408,710	$ 2,369,954
Earnings per common and common equivalent share, primary	$ .95	$ .99
Earnings per common and common equivalent share, assuming full dilution	$ .95	$ .94
Weighted average number of shares, primary	2,525,673	2,399,565
Weighted average number of shares, assuming full dilution	2,541,653	2,540,455

Source: Company records.

knowledgeable and selective in their choice of data products.

While the growth in the service sector and decline in hardware costs had caused growth in the number of computer networks, the profit margins on network control systems had attracted very aggressive competition. This competition, however, had not grown to include computer manufacturers like IBM, etc.

Marketing strategy. Intertel was aware of the focus in the marketplace and in spite of the pressure on earnings had remained committed to investing in the company to maintain a strong position.

Part of its effort had been to focus its marketing effort on those specific segments which seemed to show the most promise, such as branch banking. Also, the company had increased both the size and capability of its sales force in response to competitive pressures.

Product thrusts had been aimed at delivering more benefits to the user, such as data base formation and report writing. Also, declining hardware costs had been used to build redundancy at remote sites, reducing the need for expensive service calls.

Both of these product developments were designed to provide the end-user with less costly, more effective "up-time," which was the principal benefit derived from the product.

PART FOUR
Strategic Direction

CHAPTER 8 - Developing Marketing Objectives and Goals

CHAPTER 8
Developing Marketing Objectives and Goals

*"Would you tell me, please, which way I ought to go from here?"
said Alice. "That depends a good deal on where you want to get
to," said the Cheshire Cat.*

Lewis Carroll
Alice in Wonderland

An organization must have an objective to guide its destiny. While the objective does not in itself guarantee the success of a business, its presence will certainly mean more efficient and financially less wasteful management of operations.

Objectives form a specific expression of purpose, thus helping to remove any uncertainty about the company's policy or about the intended purpose of any effort. To be effective, objectives must provide a startling challenge to jolt managers away from traditional in-a-rut thinking. If properly designed, objectives permit measurement of progress. Without some form of progress measurement, it may not be possible to know whether adequate resources are being applied or whether these resources are being managed effectively. Finally, objectives facilitate the relationships between units, especially in a diversified corporation where the separate goals of different units may not be consistent with some higher corporate purpose.

Despite their overriding importance, defining objectives is far from easy: "There is no mechanical or expert instant answer method. Rather, defining goals as the future becomes the present is a long, time-consuming, and continuous process."[1] In practice, many businesses are run either without any commonly accepted objectives and goals or with conflicting objectives and goals. In some cases objectives may be understood in different ways by different executives. At times the objectives may be defined in such general terms that their significance for the job is not understood. For example, one product manager of a large company said, "Our objective is to satisfy the customer and increase sales." After cross-checking with the vice-president of sales, however, it was found that the company had a goal of making a minimum of 6 percent after-tax profit even if it meant

---

[1] Myles L. Mace, "The President and Corporate Planning," *Harvard Business Review*, January–February, 1965, p. 56.

losing market share. "Our objective, or whatever you choose to call it, is to grow," the vice-president of sales said. "This is a profit-oriented company, and thus, we must earn a minimum profit of 10 percent on everything we do. You may call this our objective." These are examples of how different departments in a company define their objectives. In brief, setting a company's direction is a difficult task. It is the task of the chief executive to set the company's objectives and goals and obtain for them the support of his or her senior colleagues, thus paving the way for other parts of the organization to do the same.

The purpose of this chapter is to provide a framework for goal setting in a large, complex organization. Usually a first step in planning is to state your objectives so that, knowing where you are trying to go, you can figure out how to get there. However, objectives cannot be stated in isolation without the perspectives of the company's current business, past performance, resources, and environment. Thus, the subject matter discussed in the previous chapters becomes the background material for defining objectives and goals.

FRAMEWORK FOR DEFINING OBJECTIVES

This chapter deals with defining objectives and goals at the strategic business unit (SBU) level. Because the SBU objectives should bear a close relationship to corporate strategic direction, the chapter will start with a discussion of corporate direction and then examine the SBU objectives and goals. Product/market objectives will also be discussed, since they are usually defined at the SBU level and derived from the SBU objectives.

The above scheme assumes the perspectives of a large corporation. In a small company which manufactures a limited line of related products, corporate and SBU objectives may be identical. Likewise, in a company with a few unrelated products, an SBU's objectives may be no different from those of the product/market.

It will be desirable to define a few terms which one often confronts in the context of goal setting. These are mission, policy, objective, goal, and strategic direction. A mission (also referred to as corporate concept, vision, or aim) is the chief executive officer's conception of the organization's raison d'être, or what it should work toward, in the light of long-range opportunity. A policy is a written definition of general intent or company position designed to guide and regulate certain actions and decisions, especially those of major significance or of a recurring nature. An objective is a long-range purpose which is not quantified or limited to a time period, such as increasing the return on the stockholders' equity. A goal is a measurable objective of the business, judged by management to be attainable at some specific future date through planned actions. An example of a goal would be to achieve 10 percent growth in sales within the next two years. Strategic direction is an all-inclusive term referring to the network of mission, objectives, and goals. Although we recognize the distinction between an objective and a goal, we will consider these terms simultaneously in order to give the discussion more depth.

The following are the frequently cited types of frustrations, disappointments, or troubling uncertainties which should be avoided when dealing with objectives:

1. Lack of credibility, motivation, and/or practicality
2. Poor information inputs
3. Defining objectives without considering different options
4. Lack of consensus regarding corporate values
5. Disappointing committee effort to define objectives
6. Sterility (lack of uniqueness and competitive advantage).[2]

Briefly, if objectives and goals are to serve their purpose well, they should represent a careful weighing of the balance between the performance desired and the probability of its being accomplished:

> Strategic objectives which are too ambitious result in the dissipation of assets and the destruction of morale, and create the risk of losing past gains as well as future opportunities. Strategic objectives which are not ambitious enough represent lost opportunity and open the door to complacency.[3]

CORPORATE STRATEGIC DIRECTION

Corporate strategic direction is defined in different ways. In some corporations it takes the form of a corporate creed, or code of conduct, which defines the perspectives from the viewpoint of different stakeholders. At other corporations policy statements are made which provide guidelines for implementing strategy. In still others, corporate direction is outlined in terms of objective statements. However expressed, corporate direction consists of broad statements which represent a company's position on various matters and serve as an input in defining objectives and formulating strategy at lower echelons in the organization.

A company can reasonably expect to achieve a leadership position or superior financial results only when it has purposefully laid out its strategic direction. Every outstanding corporate success is based on a direction that differentiates the firm's approach from that of others.[4] Specifically, strategic direction helps in:

---

[2]Robert F. Stewart, "Setting Corporate Aims," a report of the Long Range Planning Service of the Stanford Research Institute, 1971, p. 5.

[3]*Perspectives on Corporate Strategy* (Boston: The Boston Consulting Group, 1970), p. 44.

[4]Milton Lauenstein, "The Need for Strategic Concept," *Journal of Business Strategy*, Spring, 1981, pp. 66–68.

(a) Identifying what "fits" and what *needs* the company is well suited to meet.
(b) Analyzing potential synergies.
(c) Undertaking risks that simply cannot be justified on a project basis. For example, willingness to pay for what might appear, on a purely financial basis, to be a premium for acquisition.
(d) Providing the ability to act fast. . . . Presence of strategic direction not only helps in adequately and quickly scanning opportunities in the environment but capitalizing on them without waiting.
(e) Focussing the search for opportunities and options more clearly.[5]

Corporate Strategic Direction: An Example

To illustrate the point, consider the *corporate direction* of Dow Chemical Company, which has persisted for over 50 years.[6] Herbert Dow founded and built Dow Chemical on one fundamental and energizing idea: start with a cheap and basic raw material; then develop the soundest, lowest-cost process possible. This idea or direction defined certain imperatives which Dow has pursued consistently over time:

(a) First, don't copy or license anyone else's process. In other words, as Dow himself put it: "Don't make a product unless you can find a better way to do it."
(b) Second, build large, vertically integrated complexes to achieve the maximum economies of scale—i.e., cut out obsolete plant and equipment and maintain cost leadership by building the most technologically advanced facilities in the industry.
(c) Third, locate near and tie up abundant sources of cheap raw materials.
(d) Fourth, build in bad times as well as good. In other words, become the large-volume supplier for the long pull and preempt competitors from coming in. Be there, in place, when the demand develops.
(e) Fifth, maintain a high cash flow so the corporation can pursue its vision.

Over the years, Dow has consistently acted in concert with this direction or vision. They have built enormous, vertically integrated complexes at Midland, Michigan; Freeport, Texas; Rotterdam, Holland; and the Louisiana Gulf Coast. And they have pursued with almost fanatical consistency the obtaining of secure, low-cost sources of raw materials.

In 1947 the company formed its wholly owned Brazos Oil and Gas

---

[5]Frederick W. Gluck, "Vision and Leadership in Corporate Strategy," *The McKinsey Quarterly*, Winter, 1981, pp. 22–23.
[6]The discussion on Dow Chemical Company draws heavily on information provided by the company.

subsidiary, which was engaged in oil and gas exploration in Texas. In 1952, Dow paid what were then considered high prices to secure very long-term commitments for benzene supplies from the new oil industry plants; benzene was at that time the only basic raw material Dow did not make itself. In 1954, Dow acquired an 86 percent interest in Columbia Oil Shale & Refining Company, owner of large shale oil reserves in Colorado. In 1956, it bought Bay Refining Corporation and Bay Pipeline Corporation, refiners and distributors of petroleum products. In 1972, it bought an interest in the Oasis Gas Pipeline, and in 1973 it acquired 600 million tons of lignite reserves, a 35- to 40-year supply. Finally, the company recently built a 200,000-barrel-per-day petroleum refinery in Louisiana with adjacent facilities for cracking naphtha into ethylene.

Dow likes to say that it has always regarded money as just another raw material, and indeed it has been as aggressive about securing adequate supplies of money as it has been about securing other key raw materials. The company has long been recognized for its aggressive, progressive financial policies. Its financial policies go back to the very early days of the company's founding, when Earl Bennett was named one of Herbert Dow's top executives—first his bookkeeper and later his chief financial officer. Bennett had an abiding belief in the persistence of inflation, and he recognized that borrowing heavily made a great deal of sense during inflationary periods, since repayment could always be made in cheaper dollars. Bennett believed in high leverage and used Dow's leverage to build aggressively for the future. Bennett's fundamental business principle may have been quoted even more often than Herbert Dow's: "We build in boom times to keep up with demand; we build in slump times for the future; so we never stop building."

As a result, Dow has the highest ratio of depreciation to sales in the industry; it uses double-declining balance depreciation for tax and book purposes and it leverages financial resources through heavy long-term borrowing and joint ventures—some 16 joint venture companies worldwide.

Strategic Direction and Organizational Perspectives. Pursuing the above direction has, in turn, mandated certain human and organizational characteristics of the company and its leadership. For example, Dow has been characterized as a company whose management shows "exceptional willingness to take sweeping but carefully thought out gambles."[7] The company has had to make leaps of faith about the pace and direction of future market and technological developments. Sometimes, as in the case of shale oil, these have taken a very long time to materialize. Other times these leaps of faith have resulted in failure. But as Ben Branch, a top Dow executive for many years, was fond of saying: "Dow encourages well-intentioned failure."

---

[7]"Dow's Rising Star," *Forbes*, July 15, 1974, p. 37.

To balance this willingness to take large risks, the company has had to maintain an extraordinary degree of organizational flexibility to give it the ability to respond quickly to unexpected changes. For example, "Dow places little emphasis on, and does not publish, organization charts, preferring to define areas of broad responsibility without rigid compartments. Its informal style has given the company the flexibility to react quickly to change."[8]

Dow has also used product/market diversification combined with functional excellence to counterbalance its aggressive capital and financial risk taking. It is very widely diversified by product, producing basic, intermediate, and end-use products as well as organic and inorganic chemicals, pharmaceuticals, and metals. Yet in all these product areas, Dow has been "single-minded about doing what they do best." In all, Dow produces more than 2,300 products and services, with no single one accounting for more than 4 percent of consolidated sales. Its markets are also highly diversified, covering virtually every basic human need, including food, apparel, transportation, health, and housing. It is highly diversified geographically, with approximately 47 percent of sales and 38 percent of plant investment outside the United States at the end of 1983. It has 28 foreign production facilities in North America, South America, Europe, and the Pacific.

Dow maintains a ratio of 45 to 50 percent debt to total capitalization. Moreover, it keeps in reserve substantial unused lines of credit to meet unanticipated short-term needs. It also has a long-practiced policy of cash balancing across both its country and its product portfolios.

Changing the Strategic Direction. Over the years, Dow's direction has had to expand to accommodate a changing world, its own growth, and expanding horizons of opportunity. The expansion of its direction or vision has included, for example:

(a) Recognition of the opportunities and need to diversify downstream into higher-value-added, technologically more sophisticated intermediate and end-use products, with the concomitant requirement for greater technical selling capability after World War II.

(b) The opportunity, and imperative, to expand abroad. In fact, Herbert Dow's core vision may have retarded expansion abroad initially, since raw material availability was not as good in Europe or Japan and it was harder to get economies of scale comparable to those achievable in the United States.

(c) The need to reorganize and decentralize foreign operations,

---

[8]Lee Smith, "Dow vs. DuPont: Rival Formulas for Leadership," *Fortune*, September 10, 1979, p. 74.

setting them up on a semiautonomous basis in the mid-1960s to give them room for growth and flexibility.

But throughout its history, Dow's leadership has consistently held to a guiding concept which perhaps has been articulated as: "In this business, it's who's there with the vision, the money, and the guts to seize an opportunity."

Corporate Strategic Direction and Strategy Development. What can be concluded from this brief history of Dow Chemical's corporate direction? First, it seems clear that, for over 50 years, all of Dow's major strategic and operating decisions have been amazingly consistent. They have been consistent because they have been firmly grounded in some basic beliefs about where and how to compete. The direction has evidently made it easier to make the always difficult and risky long-term/short-term decisions, such as investing in research for the long haul, or aggressively tying up sources of raw materials.

This direction or vision has also driven Dow to be aggressive in generating the cash required to make these risky investments possible. Most important, top management seems never to have eschewed its leadership role to become merely stewards of a highly successful enterprise. They have been constantly aware of the need to question and reshape their direction, while maintaining those elements that have been instrumental in achieving their long-term competitive success. Dow's example illustrates that corporate direction gives coherence to a wide range of apparently unrelated decisions, serving as the crucial link among them.

Another Example

Harry Gray of United Technologies came from Litton Industries in 1971 to what was then the United Aircraft Company. As a newcomer to United, brought in essentially to create a new direction for the company, his task was substantially different from that of a long line of Dow top management. He spent his first few years fixing problems and building financial strength. In 1973, he announced the areas in which the company would compete—electronics, communications, transportation, energy, and environmental systems. He communicated his notions of what United's competitive leadership would be based on: market dominance; excellence in technology management and transfer; willingness to invest to become the technology leader; and the determination to share corporate UTC capabilities in electronics, services, and R&D.[9]

In the years since then, Gray has persistently and consistently pur-

---

[9]A. F. Ehrbar, "United Technologies Master Plan," *Fortune,* September 22, 1980, p. 46.

sued this vision, culminating with his most recent acquisition of Mostek, which he regards as his strategic linchpin. In accomplishing his goals, Gray has exerted strong leadership not only in shaping and communicating United's direction, but also in some other areas where leadership is frequently required if the link between strategy and operational decision making is to be made firm. For example, he has aggressively redeployed United's assets in pursuit of decreased dependence on government spending and to establish positions in his target market areas. He has shaped the capability of the organization through major management changes and has published a booklet entitled *Bottom-Line Technology* describing United's management approach. Finally, he has communicated extensively to the investment community and through institutional advertising his determination to be an innovative leader in each area in which he competes. There can be no doubt of either Harry Gray's clarity of direction or the commitment of United Technologies to that direction.

Corporate Strategic Direction and Marketing Strategy

The corporate direction of all successful companies, without exception, is based not only on a clear notion of the markets in which they will compete but also on specific concepts of how they will sustain an economically attractive position in those markets. Their direction is grounded in deep understanding of industry and competitive dynamics, and company capabilities and potential. Corporate direction should focus in general on continually strengthening the company's economic or market position, or both, in some substantial way. For example, Dow and United Technologies were not immobilized by existing industry relationships, such as current market shares or their past shortcomings. They sought—and found—new ways to influence industry dynamics in their favor. Corporate direction should foster creative thinking about realistic and achievable options. In other words, in addition to having thought through the questions of where and how to compete, top management should also make realistic judgments on: (a) the capital and human resources that would be required to compete and where they would come from; (b) the changes in the corporation's functional and cultural biases that would have to be accomplished; (c) the unique contributions that would be required of the corporation (top management and staff) to support pursuit of the new direction by the strategic business units; and (d) a guiding notion of the timing or pace of change within which the corporation could realistically move toward the new vision.

In summary, strategic direction is not an abstruse construct based on the inspiration of a solitary genius. It is a hard-nosed, practical concept based on thorough understanding of the dynamics of industries, markets, and competition, and of the potential of the corporation for influencing and exploiting these dynamics. It is only rarely the result of a flash of insight; much more often it is the product of deep and disciplined analysis.

Formulating Corporate Strategic Direction

Strategic direction frequently starts out fuzzy and is refined through a messy process of trial and error. It generally emerges in its full clarity only when it is well on its way to being realized. Likewise, changes in corporate direction occur by a long process and in stages.

Changing an established direction is much more difficult than starting from scratch, since one must overcome inherited biases and set norms of behavior. Usually, the change is effected through a sequence of steps.[10] First, a *need for change* is recognized. Second, *awareness* of the need for change is built throughout the organization by commissioning study groups, staff, or consultants to examine problems, options, contingencies, or opportunities posed by the sensed need. Third, *broad support* for the change is sought through unstructured discussions, probing of positions, definition of differences of opinion, etc., among executives. Fourth, *pockets of commitment* are created by building necessary skills or technologies within the organization, testing options, and taking opportunities to make decisions to build support. Fifth, a *clear focus* is established either by creating an ad hoc committee to formulate a position or by expressing in written form the specific direction that the chief executive officer desires. Sixth, a *definite commitment* to change is obtained by designating someone to champion the goal and be accountable for its accomplishment. Finally, after the organization arrives at the new direction, efforts are made to be sensitive to the need for further change in direction, if necessary.

Specific Statements on Corporate Strategic Direction

Many companies make specific statements of objectives to designate their direction. Some of these companies make only brief statements of objectives while others elaborate on each objective in detail. Hewlett-Packard's list, shown in Exhibit 8-1, defines its objectives through brief statements on profit, customers, field of interest, growth, people, management, and citizenship. Green Giant has defined its objectives, which it calls policies, separately for each functional area in a long report. The Barnes group, a Connecticut-based industrial company, defined its objectives five years into the future with detailed statements under the following headings: corporate concept, internal growth, external growth, sales goal, financial, planning for growth and performance, management and personnel, corporate citizenship, and stockholders and financial community.[11]

Exhibit 8-2 illustrates how corporate objectives and goals may be organized. Objectives and goals are split into three categories: measure-

---

[10]James Brian Quinn, "Strategic Goals: Process and Politics," *Sloan Management Review*, Fall, 1977, pp. 34–36.
[11]*Corporate Objectives: 1980–85* (Bristol, CT: The Barnes Group, 1980).

EXHIBIT 8-1   Hewlett-Packard's Corporate Objectives

Profit. To achieve sufficient profit to finance our company growth and to provide the resources we need to achieve our other corporate objectives.

Customers. To provide products and services of the greatest possible value to our customers, thereby gaining and holding their respect and loyalty.

Field of interest. To enter new fields only when the ideas we have, together with our technical, manufacturing and marketing skills, assure that we can make a needed and profitable contribution to the field.

Growth. To let our growth be limited only by our profits and our ability to develop and produce technical products that satisfy real customer needs.

People. To help our own people share in the company's success, which they make possible: to provide job security based on their performance, to recognize their individual achievements, and to help them gain a sense of satisfaction and accomplishment from their work.

Management. To foster initiative and creativity by allowing the individual great freedom of action in attaining well-defined objectives.

Citizenship. To honor our obligations to society by being an economic, intellectual and social asset to each nation and each community in which we operate.

Source: Y. K. Shetty, "New Look at Corporate Goals." © 1979 by the Regents of the University of California. Reprinted from *California Management Review*, Vol. 22, No. 2 (Winter, 1979), p. 72, by permission of the Regents.

ment, growth/survival, and constraint. Measurement objectives are usually financial in nature. Growth/survival objectives have a reference to the marketing side of the business. Constraint objectives indicate certain external and internal limitations and impositions which must be adhered to. For example, the objective of giving a square deal to all people may prohibit a company from seeking a course which would hurt the interest of a special group. Also, the objective of equal opportunity has led many corporations to encourage employment of women executives.

STRATEGIC BUSINESS UNIT OBJECTIVES

A strategic business unit (SBU) was defined in Chapter 1 as a unit comprising one or more products having a common market base whose manager has complete responsibility for integrating all functions into a strategy against an identifiable external competitor. We will examine the development and meaning of strategic business units again in this chapter to make it clear why objectives must be defined at this level. Abell's explanation is as follows:

EXHIBIT 8-2   Classifying Corporate Objectives and Goals

MEASUREMENT		GROWTH/SURVIVAL		CONSTRAINT	
OBJECTIVES	GOALS	OBJECTIVES	GOALS	OBJECTIVES	GOALS
1. Make satisfactory profit.	a. 10 percent return on investment. b. $2 per share earnings.	1. Become leader in the industry.	Achieve 55 percent market share in the traditional business.	1. Do not dilute stockholder equity.	Growth should be achieved without equity financing. A small amount of dilution of shareholders' equity will be tolerated as a result of present stock option and incentive compensation plans.
2. Control water pollution in the area.	Reduce the fluoride concentration in the waste discharge of a plant from 3.8 milligrams per liter to the government-prescribed limit of 1.0 mg.	2. Be among *Fortune*'s first 500 corporations.	Add another $100 million to sales by 1983–1984.		
3. Fight back acquisition efforts by other corporations.	a. Seek recapitalization by borrowing to repurchase 10 percent common shares. b. Trim marketable current assets to raise enough funds to double dividend payouts.	3. Achieve a stronger position in the Eastern European markets.	a. Undertake a study of market potential, country by country. b. Choose a country for initial entry and for opening an office.	2. Do not do business with countries that pursue apartheid policy.	Attempts to develop business with South Africa may be called off.
				3. Depend less on government business.	Government business should not constitute more than 50 percent of sales.
				4. New venture must provide satisfactory return on investment.	Aim at 12 to 15 percent return on investment.

The development of marketing planning has paralleled the growing complexity of business organizations themselves. The first change to take place was the shift from functionally organized companies with relatively narrow product lines and served-market focus to large diversified firms serving multiple markets with multiple product lines. Such firms are usually divided into product or market divisions, divisions may be divided into departments, and these in turn are often further divided into product lines or market segments. As this change gradually took place over the last two decades, "sales planning" was gradually replaced by "marketing planning" in most of these organizations. Each product manager or market manager drew up a marketing plan for his product line or market segment. These were aggregated together into an overall divisional "marketing plan." Divisional plans in turn were aggregated into the overall corporate plan.

But a further important change is now taking place. There has been over the last decade a growing acceptance of the fact that individual units or subunits within a corporation, e.g., divisions, product departments, or even product lines or market segments, may play different *roles* in achieving overall corporate objectives. Not all units and subunits need to produce the same level of profitability; not all units and subunits have to contribute equally to cash flow objectives.

This concept of the organization as a "portfolio" of units and subunits having different objectives is at the very root of contemporary approaches to strategic marketing planning. It is commonplace today to hear businesses defined as "cash cows," "stars," "question marks," "dogs," etc.* It is in sharp contrast to practice in the 1960s and earlier which emphasized primarily sales and earnings (or return on investment) as a major measure of performance. Although different divisions or departments were intuitively believed to have different capabilities to meet sales and earning goals, these differences were seldom made explicit. Instead, each unit was expected to "pull its weight" in the overall quest for growth and profits.

With the recognition that organizational entities may differ in their objectives and roles, a new organizational concept has also emerged. This is the concept of a "business unit." A business unit may be a division, a product department, or even a product line or major market, depending on the circumstances. It is, however, usually regarded by corporate management as a reasonably autonomous profit center. Usually it has its own "general manager" (even though he may not have that title, he has general managerial responsibilities). Often it has its own manufacturing, sales, research and development, and procurement functions although in some cases some of these may be shared with other businesses (e.g., pooled sales). A business unit usually has a clear market focus. In particular it usually has an identifiable strategy and an identifiable set of competitors. In some organizations (the General Electric Company, for example), business units are clearly identified and defined. In other organizations, divisions or product departments are treated as relatively autonomous business units although they are not explicitly defined as such.

---

*These terms are defined in Chapter 10.

A business unit will usually comprise several "program" units. These may be product lines, geographic market segments, end-user industries to which the company sells, or units defined on the basis of any other relevant segmentation dimension. Program units may also sometimes differ in their objectives. In such cases, the concept of a portfolio exists both in terms of business units within a corporate structure (or substructure, such as a group) or in terms of programs within a business unit. Usually, however, the business unit is a major focus of strategic attention, and strategic market plans are of prime importance at this level.[12]

As Abell notes, a large, complex organization may have a number of SBUs, each playing its unique role in the organization. Obviously, then, at the corporate level, objectives can be defined only in generalities. It is only at each SBU level that more specific statements of objectives can be made. Actually it is the SBU mission and its objectives and goals that product/market managers will need to consider in their strategic plans.

BUSINESS MISSION

Chapter 5 discussed the topic of market boundary. Definition of business mission has an intimate, chicken-and-egg relationship to market boundary definition. On the one hand, business mission must be defined, at least in part, in terms of market scope. On the other hand, the market scope should emerge from the business mission. To resolve the problem, Abell suggests:

One useful distinction is between "served market" and "total market." When describing the way an individual business is defined, the market referred to in the term "product/market scope" is the served market— that portion of the total market which the firm specifically selects to serve. When describing the market arena in which the business competes, the term "market" usually means the total market.[13]

To continue the discussion, it is necessary to make a working assumption here that market boundary definition determines the individual business definition. Such a view is commonly accepted by marketing scholars. George Day and Allan Shocker state, for example: "Such issues as the basic definition of the business . . . are strongly influenced by the breadth or narrowness of the definition of competitive boundaries."[14] The above

---

[12]Derek F. Abell, "Metamorphosis in Marketing Planning," in Subhash C. Jain (ed.), *Research Frontiers in Marketing: Dialogues and Directions* (Chicago: American Marketing Association, 1978), p. 257.

[13]Derek F. Abell, *Defining the Business—The Starting Point of Strategic Planning* (Englewood Cliffs, NJ: Prentice-Hall, 1980), p. 23.

[14]George S. Day and Allan D. Shocker, *Identifying Competitive Product-Market Boundaries: Strategic and Analytical Issues* (Cambridge, MA: Marketing Science Institute, 1976), p. 1.

assumption helps to bring in the customer perspective in defining the business.

Defining Business Mission—The Traditional Viewpoint

Mission is a broad term that refers to the total perspectives or purpose of a business. Traditionally the mission of a business corporation was framed around its product line and expressed in mottoes such as: "Our business is textiles," "We manufacture cameras," and so on. With the advent of marketing orientation and technological innovations, this method of defining the business mission has been decried. It has been held that building the perspectives of a business around its product limits the scope of management to enter new fields and thus make use of growth opportunities. Levitt observed in a key article published in 1960:

> The railroads did not stop growing because the need for passengers and freight transportation declined. That grew. The railroads are in trouble today not because the need was filled by others (cars, trucks, airplanes, even telephones), but because it was not filled by the railroads themselves. They let others take customers away from them because they assumed themselves to be in the railroad business rather than in the transportation business. The reason they defined their industry wrong was because they were railroad-oriented instead of transportation-oriented; they were product-oriented instead of customer-oriented.[15]

According to Levitt's thesis, the mission of a business should be defined broadly: an airline might consider itself in the vacation business, a publisher in the education industry, an appliance manufacturer in the business of preparing nourishment, and so on. Recently Levitt's proposition has been criticized and the question asked whether simply extending the scope of a business leads far enough. The Boston Consulting Group, for example, has pointed out that the railroads could not have protected themselves by defining their business as transportation:

> Unfortunately, there is a prevalent notion that if one merely defines one's business in increasingly general terms—such as transportation rather than railroading—the road to successful competitive strategy will be clear. Actually, that is hardly ever the case. More often, the opposite is true. For example, in the case of the railroads, passengers and freight represent very different problems, and short haul vs. longer haul are completely different strategic issues. Indeed, as the unit train demonstrates, just coal handling is a meaningful strategic issue.[16]

---

[15]Theodore Levitt, "Marketing Myopia," *Harvard Business Review*, July–August, 1960, p. 46.

[16]*Perspectives on Corporate Strategy* (Boston: The Boston Consulting Group, 1970), p. 42.

The problem with Levitt's thesis is that it is too broad and does not provide what those involved in finance call a *common thread:* a relationship between a firm's past and future which indicates where the firm is headed and helps management to institute directional perspectives. The common thread may be found in the area of marketing, production technology, finance, or management. ITT took advantage of its managerial abilities when it ventured into such diverse businesses as hotels and bakeries. Armco Inc. found a common thread via finance in entering the airplane leasing business. BIC Pen Company used its marketing strength to involve itself in the razor blade business. The Singer Company considered common technology as the basis for entering the business machines industry. Thus, the mission cannot be defined by making abstract statements which one hopes will pave the way for entry into new fields.

It would appear that the mission of a business is neither a statement of current business nor a random extension of current involvements. It signifies the scope and nature of business, not as it is today, but as it could be in the future. The mission plays an important role in designating opportunities for diversification either through R&D or acquisitions. To be meaningful, the mission should be based on a comprehensive analysis of the business's technology and customer mission. Examples of companies with technology-based definitions are computer companies and aerospace companies. Customer mission refers to the fulfillment of a particular type of customer need, such as the need for basic nutrition, household maintenance, or entertainment.

Whether the company has a written business mission statement or not is immaterial. What is important, however, is that due consideration has been given to technological and marketing factors (as related to particular segments and their needs) in defining the mission. Ideally, business definitions should be based on a combination of technology and market mission variables, but some companies venture into new fields on the basis of one variable only. For example, Texas Instruments entered the digital watch market on the basis of its lead in integrated circuits technology. Procter & Gamble added Folger's coffee to its business out of its experience in fulfilling the ordinary daily needs of customers.

To sum up, the mission deals with the questions: What type of business do we want to be in at some future time? What do we want to become? At any given point in time, most of the resources of a business are frozen or locked into their current uses, and the outputs in services and/or products are for the most part defined by current operations. Over an interval of a few years, however, environmental changes place demands on the business for new types of resources. Further, because of personnel attrition and depreciation of capital resources, management has the option of choosing the environment in which the company will operate and acquiring commensurate new resources rather than replacing the old ones in kind. This explains the importance of defining the business's mission. The mission should be so defined that it has a bearing on the business's strengths and weaknesses.

Defining Business Mission: A New Approach

In his pioneering work on the subject Abell has argued against defining a business as simply a choice of products, or markets.[17] He proposes that a business be defined in terms of three measures: (a) scope; (b) differentiation of the company's offerings, one from another, across segments; and (c) differentiation of the company's offerings from those of competitors. The scope pertains to the breadth of a business. For example, do life insurance companies consider themselves to be in the business of only underwriting insurance or do they provide complete family financial planning services? Likewise, should a manufacturer of toothpaste define the scope of his business as preventing tooth decay or providing complete oral hygiene? There are two separate contexts in which differentiation can occur: differentiation across segments and across competitors. Differentiation across segments measures the degree to which business segments are treated differently. An example is personal computers marketed to young children as educational aids, and to older people as financial planning aids. Differentiation across competitors measures the degree to which competitors' offerings differ.

The above three measures, according to Abell, should be viewed in *three dimensions:* (a) customer groups served; (b) customer functions served; (c) technologies utilized.

These three dimensions, (and a fourth one, level of production/distribution) were examined at length in Chapter 5 in the context of defining market boundaries and will not be elaborated further here. An example will illustrate how a business may be defined using the Abell thesis.

Customer groups describe *who* is being satisfied, customer functions describe *what* needs are being satisfied, and technologies describe *how* the needs are being satisfied. Consider a thermometer manufacturer. Depending on which measure is used, the business can be defined as follows:

Customer groups	Customer functions	Technologies utilized
Households	Body temperature	Mercury-base
Restaurants	Cooking temperature	Alcohol-base
Health care facilities	Atmospheric temperature	Electronic-digital

The manufacturer can confine the business to just health care facilities or broaden the scope to include restaurants and households. Thermometers can be provided only for measurement of body temperature or the line can be extended to offer cooking and/or atmospheric thermometers. The manufacturer could decide to produce only mercury-base thermometers or could also produce alcohol-base and/or electronic-digital

---

[17]This section relies heavily on Derek F. Abell, *Defining the Business—The Starting Point of Strategic Planning* (Englewood Cliffs, NJ: Prentice-Hall, 1980).

EXHIBIT 8-3   Defining Business Mission – Narrow Scope

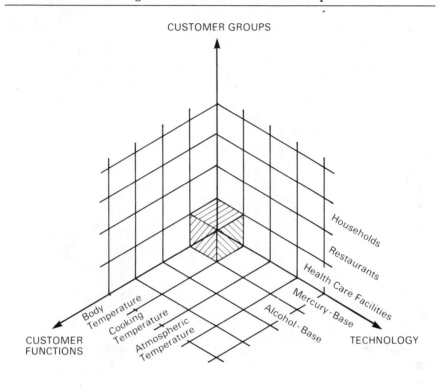

thermometers. The decisions that the manufacturer makes regarding customer groups, customer functions, and technologies would ultimately affect the definition of the business, in terms of both scope and differentiation. Exhibits 8-3 and 8-4 graphically show how business can be defined narrowly or broadly around the above three dimensions. In Exhibit 8-3, the manufacturer limits the business to service only health care facilities, offering just mercury-base thermometers for measuring body temperatures. In Exhibit 8-4, however, the definition has been broadened to serve three customer segments: households, restaurants, and health care facilities; two types of thermometers: mercury-base and alcohol-base; and three customer functions. The manufacturer could further expand the definition of the business in all three directions. Physicians could be added as a customer group. A line of electronic-digital thermometers could be offered. Finally, thermometers could be produced to measure industrial-process temperatures.

An adequate business definition requires proper consideration of the strategic 3 C's: customer (e.g., buying behavior); competition (e.g., competitve definitions of the business); and company (e.g., cost behavior such as efficiencies via economies of scale, resources/skills such as finan-

EXHIBIT 8-4   Defining Business Mission – Broader Scope

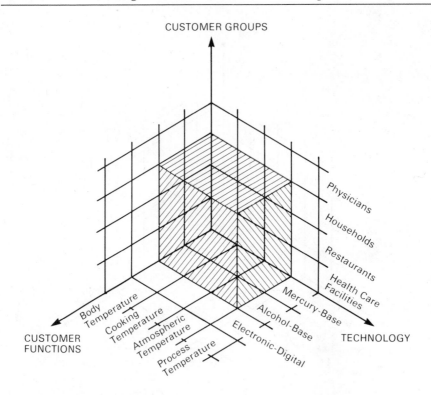

cial strength, managerial talent, engineering/manufacturing capability, physical distribution system, etc., and differences in marketing, manufacturing, R&D requirements, and so on, resulting from market segmentation).

Typology of Business Definitions

Abell proposed defining business in terms of three measures: scope, differentiation across segments, and differentiation across competitors. According to Abell, scope and both kinds of differentiation are related to one another in complex ways. One way to conceptualize these interrelationships is in terms of typology of business definitions. Three alternative strategies for defining a business are recommended: (a) a focused strategy, (b) a differentiated strategy, and (c) an undifferentiated strategy:

> *Focused strategy.* A business may choose to focus on a particular customer group, customer function, or technology segment. Focus implies a certain basis for segmentation along one or more of these dimensions, narrow scope involving only one or a few chosen segments,

and differentiation from competitors through careful tailoring of the offering to the specific need of the segment(s) targeted.

Differentiated strategy. When a business combines broad scope with differentiation across any or all of the three dimensions, it may be said to follow a differentiated strategy. Differentiation across segments may also be related to competitive differentiation. By tailoring the offering to the specific needs of each segment, a company automatically increases the chance for competitive superiority. Whether or not competitive differentiation also results is purely a function of the extent to which competitors have also tailored their offerings to the same specific segments. If they have, segment differentiation may be substantial, yet competitive differentiation may be small.

Undifferentiated strategy. When a company combines broad scope across any or all of the three dimensions with an undifferentiated approach to customer group, customer function, or technology segments, it is said to follow an undifferentiated strategy.[18]

Each of the above strategies can be applied to the three dimensions (customer groups, customer functions, and technologies) separately. In other words, there is a possibility of 27 different combinations: (a) focused, differentiated, or undifferentiated across customer groups; (b) focused, differentiated, or undifferentiated across customer functions, and (c) focused, differentiated, or undifferentiated across technologies.

A focused strategy serves a specific customer group, customer function, or technology segment. It has a narrow scope. Docutel Corporation's strategy in the late 1960s exemplifies a focused strategy relative to customer function. When Docutel first pioneered the development of the automated teller machine (ATM), they defined customer function very narrowly, concentrating on one function only—cash dispensing.

A differentiated strategy combines broad scope with differentiation across one or more of the three dimensions. A differentiated strategy would serve several customer groups, functions, or technologies while tailoring the product offered to each segment's specific needs. An example of a differentiated strategy applied to customer groups is athletic footwear. Athletic footwear serves a broad range of customer groups and is differentiated across those groups. Tennis shoes are tailored to meet the needs of one specific customer group; basketball shoes another.

An undifferentiated strategy combines a broad scope across one or more of the three dimensions and an undifferentiated approach to the three dimensions. This strategy would be applied to customer groups in a business that serves a wide range of customer groups but does not differentiate its offerings among those groups. Docutel's strategy was focused with respect to customer function but not with respect to customer groups: they offered exactly the same product to commercial banks, savings and loans, mutual savings banks, and credit unions. To sum up, the strategy

---

[18]*Ibid.*, pp. 174–175.

that a business chooses to follow, based on the amount of scope and differentiation applied to the three dimensions, determines the definition of the business.

SBU OBJECTIVES AND GOALS

The objectives and goals of the SBU may be stated in terms of activities (manufacturing a specific product, selling in a particular market); financial indicators (achieving targeted return on investment); desired positions (market share, quality leadership); and combinations of these factors.[19] Generally an SBU has a series of objectives to cater to the interests of different stakeholders. One way of organizing objectives is to split them into the following classes: measurement objectives, growth/survival objectives, and constraint objectives. It must be emphasized that objectives and goals should not be based just on facts, but also on values and feelings. What facts should one look at? How should they be weighed and related to one another? It is in seeking answers to such questions that value judgments become crucial.

The perspectives of an SBU will determine how far an objective can be broken down into minute details. If the objective applies to a number of products, only broad statements of objectives specifying the role of each product/market from the vantage point of the SBU will be feasible. On the other hand, when an SBU has been created around one or two products, objectives may be stated in detail.

Exhibit 8-5 illustrates how SBU objectives and goals can be identified and split into three groups: measurement, growth/survival, and constraint. Measurement objectives and goals define an SBU's aims from the point of view of the stockholders. Traditionally the word *profit* was used instead of measurement. But, as is widely recognized today, a modern corporation has several corporate publics besides the stockholders. Therefore it is erroneous to use the word *profit*. On the other hand, the company's very existence and ability to serve different stakeholders depend on financial viability. Thus, profit constitutes an important measurement objective. To emphasize the real significance of profit, it is more appropriate to label it as a measurement tool.

It will be useful here to draw a distinction between corporate objectives and measurement objectives and goals at the level of an SBU. Corporate objectives define the company's outlook for various stakeholders as a general concept. But the SBU's objectives and goals are specific statements. For example, keeping the environment clean may be one of the

---

[19]See Y. K. Shetty, "New Look at Corporate Goals," *California Management Review*, Winter, 1979, pp. 71–79. See also Charles P. Edmonds III and John H. Hand, "What Are the Real Long-Run Objectives of Business?," *Business Horizons*, December, 1976, pp. 75–81.

EXHIBIT 8-5   Illustration of an SBU's Objectives

I. SBU
   Cooking Appliances

II. Mission
   To market to *individual homes* cooking appliances that perform such *functions* as baking, boiling, and roasting, using electric fuel *technology*.

III. Objectives (general statements in the following areas):
   A. Measurement
      1. Profitability
      2. Cash flow
   B. Growth/Survival
      1. Market standing
      2. Productivity
      3. Innovation
   C. Constraint
      1. Capitalize on our research in certain technologies
      2. Avoid style businesses with seasonal obsolescence
      3. Avoid antitrust problems
      4. Assume responsibility to public

IV. Goals
   Specific targets and time frame for achivement of each objective listed above.

corporate objectives. Using this as a basis, in a particular time frame an SBU may define prevention of water pollution as one of its objectives. In other words, it is not necessary to repeat the company's obligation to various stakeholders in defining an SBU's objectives since this is already covered in the corporate objectives. Objectives and goals should underline the areas that need to be covered during the time horizon of planning.

Growth objectives and goals have a reference to getting ahead, accepted as a normal goal in a capitalistic society. Thus, companies often aim at growth. While measurements are usually stated in financial terms, growth is described with reference to the market. Constraint objectives and goals depend on the internal environment of the company and how it wishes to interact with the outside world.

An orderly description of objectives may not always work out. Overlapping may occur among the three types of objectives and goals. It is important, however, that the final draft of objectives be based on investigation, analysis, and contemplation. The SBU's objectives and goals as outlined in Exhibit 8-5 comprise all functional areas of a business; the objectives mainly concerned with marketing are the growth/survival objectives. However, as far as strategy development is concerned, at the SBU level, the functional breakdown of a business is outdated.

PRODUCT/MARKET OBJECTIVES

Product/market objectives may be defined in terms of profitability, market share, and growth. Most businesses state their product/market purpose through a combination of these terms. Some companies, especially the very small ones, may use just one of these terms to communicate their product/market objectives. Usually product/market objectives are stated at the SBU level.

Profitability

Profits in one form or another constitute a desirable goal for a product/market venture to pursue. As objectives they may be expressed either in absolute monetary terms or as a percentage of capital employed or total assets.

At the corporate level emphasis on profit in a statement of objectives is sometimes avoided since it seems to convey a limited perspective of the corporate purpose. But at the product/market level an objective in terms of profitability provides a measurable criterion with which the management can evaluate performance. Since product/market objectives are an internal matter, the corporation is not constrained by any ethical questions in its emphasis on profits. Of course, attainment of objectives should always be subject to good across-the-board conduct and be within the ethical standards laid down by the corporate management.

Burroughs Corporation, a computer manufacturer, is an ardent user of the profitability objective. The company aims at achieving a pretax margin of 20 percent and increasing pretax return on invested capital to 20 percent. Burroughs' emphasis on profits is unusual in the computer industry. The orthodox view has been that before the computer business could be expected to pay off, many years of unprofitable investment were required. But Burroughs' chief executive officers over time have insisted on the profit goal, and the outcome has been very satisfactory. Burroughs' overall performance has been twice as good as that of any other competitor in the industry except IBM.[20]

How can the profitability goal be realized in practice? First, the corporate management determines the desired profitability, i.e., rate of return on investment. There may be a single goal set for the entire corporation, or it may vary for different businesses. Using the given rate of return, the SBU may compute the percentage of markup on cost for its product(s). To do so, the normal rate of production, averaged over the business cycle, is computed. The total cost of the normal production then becomes the standard cost. Next, the ratio of invested capital (in the SBU)

---

[20]Bro Uttal, "How Ray Macdonald's Growth Theory Created IBM's Toughest Competitor," *Fortune*, January, 1977, p. 94. See also "Mike Blumenthal's Battle to Make Burroughs No. 2," *Business Week*, December 19, 1983, p. 73.

to a year's standard cost (i.e., capital turnover) is computed. The capital turnover multiplied by the rate of return gives the markup percentage to be applied to standard cost. This markup is an average figure which may be adjusted both among products and through time.

Market Share

In many industries, the cigarette industry for example, gain of a few percentage points in market share has a positive effect on profits. Thus, market share has traditionally been considered a desirable goal to pursue. In recent years extensive research on the subject has uncovered new evidence on the positive impact of market share on profitability.

While market share was traditionally considered in absolute terms, current thinking on it requires that it be defined in relative terms (i.e., in relation to the share of the leader). It is held that absolute share is meaningful only to the extent that it is an indicator of market stability and competitive maturity.

The importance of market share is explainable by the fact that it is related to cost. Cost is a function of scale or experience. Thus the market leader has a lower cost than the competitors because superior market share permits the accumulation of more experience. Prices, however, are determined by the cost structure of the least effective competitor. The high-cost competitor must generate enough cash to hold the market share and meet expenses. If this is not accomplished, the high-cost competitor drops out and is replaced by a more effective, lower-cost competitor. The profitability of the market leader is ascertained by the same price level that determines the profit of even the least effective competitor. Thus, higher market share gives a competitive edge to a firm. As a matter of fact, effect of market share goes much further. Henderson states:

> Ability to have a basic cost differential in a market sector provides the opportunity to gain a differential growth rate and a differential market share in that sector. This leads to an even greater differential advantage in cost. This advantage can be compounded until it becomes an advantage of such proportions that quite adequate profits can be earned even though competitors can barely finance the maintenance of their own shares.[21]

One strong proponent of market share goal is Texas Instruments. The company takes a long-term view and commits itself to obtaining a big share of the growth market. It keeps building new plants even though its first plant for a product has yet to run at full capacity. It does so hoping large-scale operations will provide a cost advantage which it can utilize in

---

[21]Bruce D. Henderson, "Market Share," an informal statement by the Boston Consulting Group, 1978.

the form of lower prices to customers. The latter in turn lead to a higher market share.[22]

While market share is a viable goal to pursue, tremendous foresight and effort are needed to achieve and maintain the market share position. A company aspiring to aim at a large share of the market should carefully consider two aspects: (1) its ability to finance the market share, and (2) its ability to effectively defend itself against the antitrust action which may be instigated by large increases in market share.[23] For example, both GE and RCA found that to meet their corporate profitability objectives they needed to achieve specific market share positions in the computer business. To realize the targeted market share positions required huge investment. The question, then, was whether they should gamble in an industry which was dominated by one large competitor (IBM) or invest their monies in other fields where there was the probability of earning a return equal to or higher than that in the computer field. Both GE and RCA decided to get out of the computer field.[24] Fear of antitrust suits also prohibits the seeking of higher market shares. A number of corporations—Kodak, Gillette, Xerox, and IBM, for example—have been the target of such action.

The above reasons have led Bloom and Kotler to suggest that while market share should be pursued as a desirable goal, companies should opt not for share maximization, but for an optimal market share. They suggest the following procedure for figuring out the optimal point:

1. Estimate the relationship between market share and profitability.
2. Estimate the amount of risk associated with each share level.
3. Determine the point at which an increase in market share can no longer be expected to bring enough profit to compensate for the added risks to which the company would expose itself.[25]

The advantages of higher market share do not mean that a company with a lower share may not have a chance in the industry. There are companies which earn a respectable return on their equity despite low market shares. Examples of such corporations are Burroughs, Crown Cork & Seal, Union Camp, and Inland Steel. The following characteristics explain the success of low-share companies: They compete only in those market segments where their strengths have the greatest impact, they make

---

[22]"The Strategy That Took T.I. to the Top," *Business Week*, September 18, 1978, p. 67.

[23]William E. Fraham, Jr., "Pyrrhic Victories in Fights for Market Share," *Harvard Business Review*, September–October, 1972, p. 100.

[24]Allan T. Demaree, "G.E.'s Costly Ventures into Future," *Fortune*, October, 1970, p. 158.

[25]Paul N. Bloom and Philip Kotler, "Strategies for High Market Share Companies," *Harvard Business Review*, November–December, 1975, p. 63.

efficient use of their modest R&D budgets, they shun growth for growth's sake, and they have innovative leaders.[26]

In brief, market share goal should not be taken lightly. Rather, a firm should aim at a market share after careful examination.

The following example illustrates the importance of market share. Exhibit 8-6 shows the experience of the industry leader in an industrial product. With an initially high share of a growing and competitive market, the management shifted its emphasis from market share to high earnings. A manager with proven skills was put in charge of the business. Earnings increased for six years at the expense of some slow erosion in market share. In the seventh year, however, market share fell so rapidly that, although efforts to hold profits were redoubled, they dropped sharply. Share was never regained. The manager had been highly praised and richly rewarded for his profit results up to 1975. These results, however, were

EXHIBIT 8-6   Relationship Between Market Share and After-Tax Profit

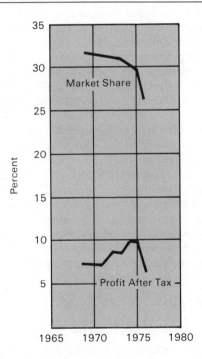

[26]R. G. Hamermesh, M. J. Anderson, Jr., and J. E. Harris, "Strategies for Low Market Share Businesses," *Harvard Business Review*, May–June, 1978, p. 95. See also Carolyn Y. Woo and Arnold C. Cooper, "The Surprising Case for Low Market Share," *Harvard Business Review*, November–December, 1982, pp. 106–113.

achieved in exchange for a certain *unreported* damage to the firm's long-term competitiveness. Only by knowing both, and by weighing the gain in current income against the degree of market share liquidation entailed, can the true value of performance be judged. In other words, reported earnings do not tell the true story unless market share is constant. Loss of market share is liquidation of an unbooked asset upon which the value of all other assets depends. Gain in market share is like an addition to cost potential, just as real an asset as credit rating, brand image, organization resources, or technology. In brief, market share guarantees the long-term survival of the business. Liquidation of market share to realize short-term earnings should be avoided. High earnings make sense only when market share is stable.

Growth

Growth is an accepted phenomenon of American life. All institutions should progress and grow. Those which do not grow invite extinction. Static corporations are often subject to a proxy fight.

There are a variety of reasons which make growth a viable objective to pursue. These are growth expectations of the stockholders, growth orientation of top management, employees' enthusiasm, growth opportunities furnished by the environment, corporate need to compete effectively in the marketplace, and corporate strengths and competencies which make it easy to grow. Exhibit 8-7 elaborates these under customer reasons; competitive reasons; company reasons; and distributor, dealer, and agent reasons.

An example of growth encouraged by corporate strength is provided by Time Inc. Around 1978 the company was in an extremely strong cash position. This helped it to acquire Book-of-the-Month Club, Inc., American Television & Communications Corporation, and the *Washington Star*. H. S. Geneen's passion for growth led ITT into different industries (bakeries, car-rental agencies, hotels, insurance firms, parking lots) in addition to its traditional communications business. Any field that promised growth was acceptable to him. Thus, the chief executive officer's growth orientation is the most valuable prerequisite for growth.

Growth ambitions led Procter & Gamble to venture into the orange juice and cookie businesses. The company even has an eye on the soft-drink business.[27]

Other Objectives

In addition to the commonly held objectives of profitability, market share, and growth, discussed above, a company may sometimes pursue a

---

[27]"Is P&G Thirsty for Some of Coke's Knowhow?," *Business Week*, May 30, 1983, p. 62.

EXHIBIT 8-7   Reasons for Growth

Customer Reasons

The product line or sizes too limited for customer convenience.
Related products needed to serve a specific market.
Purchasing economies: one source, one order, one bill.
Service economies: one receiving and processing, one source of parts, service, other assistance.
Ability to give more and better services.
Production capacity not enough to fill needs of important customers who may themselves be growing.

Competitive Reasons

To maintain or better industry position, growth is necessary in any but a declining industry.
To counter or better chief competitors on new offerings.
To maintain or better position in specific product or market areas where competition is making strong moves.
To permit more competitive pricing ability by greater volume.
To possess greater survival strength in price wars, product competition and economic slumps by greater size.

Company Reasons

To fulfill the growth expectations of stockholders, directors, executives and employees.
To utilize available management, selling, distribution, research or production capacity.
To supplement existing products and services that are not growth markets or are on downgrade of the profit cycle.
To stabilize seasonal or cyclical fluctuations.
To add flexibility by broadening the market and product base of opportunities.
To attain greater borrowing and financial influence with size.
To be able to attract and pay for better management personnel.
To attain the stability of size and move to management-by-planning.

Distributor, Dealer and Agent Reasons

To add products, sizes, and ranges necessary to attract interest of better distributors, dealers and agents.
To make additions necessary to obtain needed attention and selling effort from existing distributors, dealers and agents.

Source: John M. Brion, *Corporate Marketing Planning*, copyright © 1967 by John Wiley & Sons, Inc., pp. 70–71. Reprinted by permission of John Wiley & Sons, Inc.

unique objective. Such an objective might be technological leadership, social contribution, strengthening of national security, or international economic development.[28]

Technological Leadership. A company may consider technological leadership a worthwhile goal to achieve. In order to accomplish this, it may develop new products or processes or adopt innovations ahead of the competition, even when economics may not justify doing so. The underlying purpose in seeking this objective is to keep the name of the company in the forefront as a technological leader among security analysts, customers, distributors, and other stakeholders. Pan Am, for example, was the first airline to fly a Boeing 747 jumbo jet. This conveyed the image of a modern airline which uses up-to-date equipment.

Social Contribution. A company may pursue as an objective something which will make a social contribution. Ultimately that something may lead to higher profitability, but initially it is intended to provide a solution to a social problem. A beverage company, for example, may attack the problem of litter by not offering its product in throwaway bottles. Another company may decide to hire minority youths during the summer to keep the streets calm.

Strengthening of National Security. In the interest of strengthening national defense, a company may undertake activities not otherwise justifiable. For example, concern for national security may lead a company to deploy resources to develop a new fighter plane. The company may do so despite little encouragement from the air force, if only because the company sincerely feels that the country will need the plane in the coming years to match the Russian stockpile.

International Economic Development. Improvement of human welfare, the economic progress of less-developed countries, promotion of a worldwide free enterprise system, etc., may also serve as objectives. For example, a company may undertake the development of a foolproof method of birth control which can be easily afforded and conveniently used by poor and illiterate masses in the less-developed countries of the world.

PROCESS OF SETTING OBJECTIVES

At the very beginning of the process of setting objectives, an SBU should attempt to take an inventory of objectives as they are currently

---

[28]J. Thomas Cannon, *Business Strategy and Policy* (New York: Harcourt, Brace & World, 1968), pp. 41–42.

understood. For example, the SBU's head and senior executives may state what the current objectives of the SBU are and what type of SBU they want it to be in the future. Various executives will perceive current objectives differently; of course they will have varying ambitions for the SBU's future. It will take several top-level meetings and a good deal of effort on the part of the head to settle on the final objectives.

Each executive may be asked to make a presentation on the objectives and goals he or she would like the SBU to adopt for accomplishment in the future. The executives should be asked to justify the significance of each objective in terms of measuring performance, satisfying environmental conditions, and achieving growth. Foreseeably, the executives will have different objectives, or may express the same objectives in terms that make them appear different, but there should emerge, on analysis, a desire for a common destiny for the SBU. Sometimes inharmony of objectives may be based on diverse perceptions of a business's resource potential and corporate strategy. Thus, before embarking on setting objectives, it is helpful if information on the resource potential and corporate strategy is circulated among the executives.

Before finalizing the objectives, it is necessary that the executive team show a consensus; i.e., each one of them should believe in the viability of the set objectives and willingly agree to work toward their achievement. A way must be found to persuade a dissenting executive to cooperate. For example, if a very ambitious executive works with stability-oriented people, in the absence of an opportunity to be creative the executive may fail to perform adequately even on routine matters, thus becoming a liability to the organization. In such a situation, it may be better to encourage the executive to look around for another job. This is useful for the organization as well as for the dissenting executive. This type of situation occurs when most of the executives have risen through the ranks and an "outsider" joins them. The dynamism of the latter is perceived as a threat, which may result in conflict. The author is familiar with a $100-million company where the vice-president of finance, an "outsider," in his insistence on long-range planning came to be perceived as such a danger by the old-timers that they made it necessary for him to quit.

To sum up, objectives should be set through a series of executive meetings. The organizational head plays the role of mediator in the process of screening varying viewpoints and perceptions and developing consensus from them.

Once broad objectives have been worked out, they should be translated into specific goals. This is an equally challenging task. Should the goals be set so high that only an outstanding manager can achieve them, or should they be set so that they are attainable by the average manager? At what level does frustration inhibit a manager's best efforts? Does an attainable budget lead to complacency? Presumably a company should start with three levels of goals: (1) easily attainable, (2) most desirable, and (3) optimistic. Thereafter, the company may choose a position somewhere between the most desirable goals and the optimistic goals, depending on the organization's resources and the value orientation of the management. In no case, however, should the performance fall below the easily attainable level, even if everything goes wrong. Attempts should be made to make the goals realistic and achievable. Overly elusive goals can cause discouragement and affect motivation.

There are no universally accepted standards, procedures, or measures for defining objectives. Each organization must work out its own definitions of objectives and goals—what constitutes growth, what measures to adopt for their evaluation, etc. For example, consider the concept of return on investment. For decades this has been considered to be a good measure of corporate performance. A large number of corporations consider a specified return on investment as the most sacrosanct of goals to achieve. But ponder over its limitations. In a large, complex organization, ROI tends to optimize divisional performance at the cost of total corporate performance. Further, its orientation is a short-term one. Investment refers to assets. Different projects require a varying amount of assets before beginning to yield results, and the return may be slow or fast, depending on the nature of the project. Thus the value of assets may lose significance as an element in performance measurement. As the president of a large company remarked, "Profits are often the result of expenses incurred several years previously." The president suggested that the current amount of net cash flow in dollars serves as a better measure of performance than the potential amount of net cash flow: "The net cash contribution budget is a precise measure of expectations with given resources."

Authors have suggested different procedures for developing objectives and goals. According to Boyd and Levy, the following six sources may be used to generate objectives and goals:

1. Focus on material resources (e.g., oil, minerals, forest).
2. Concern with fabricated objects (e.g., paper, nylon).
3. Major interest in events and activities requiring certain products or services, such as golfing and handling emergencies (Emery Air Freight).
4. Emphasis on the kind of person whose needs are to be met: "Babies Are Our Business" (Gerber).
5. Catering to specific parts of the body; i.e., eyes (Maybelline), teeth (Dr. West), feet (Florsheim), skin (Noxzema), hair (Clairol), beard (Gillette), and legs (Hanes).
6. Examination of wants and needs and seeking to adapt to them; i.e., generic use to be satisfied (nutrition, comfort, energy, self-expression, development, conformity, etc.) and consumption systems (for satisfying nutritional needs, for example).[29]

---

[29]Harper W. Boyd, Jr., and Sidney J. Levy, "What Kind of Corporate Objectives," *Journal of Marketing*, October, 1966, pp. 53–58.

The above categories are especially useful for defining growth/survival objectives, particularly at the SBU or product/market level.

A different scheme for defining objectives has been proposed by SRI International. As shown in Exhibit 8-8, three approaches for working out objectives are the "rational" approach, the "experimental" approach, and the "creative" approach. Each approach follows a different cause, means, and outcome sequence to arrive at objectives.[30] The SRI scheme appears to be better suited to defining corporate objectives than SBU and product/market objectives.

Whichever approach is utilized for finally coming out with a set of objectives and goals, the following serve as basic inputs in the process. At the corporate level objectives are influenced by corporate publics, the value system of top management, corporate resources, performance of business units, and external environment. The SBU objectives are based on the strategic 3C's of customer, competition, and corporation. The product/ market objectives are dictated by the product/market strengths and weaknesses, and by momentum. Strengths and weaknesses are determined on the basis of current strategy, past performance, marketing effectiveness, and marketing environment. Momentum refers to future trends—extrapolation of past performance with the assumption that no major changes will occur either in the product/market environment or in its marketing mix.

EXHIBIT 8-8   Approaches to Objective Selling

	Cause	Means	Outcome
"Rational" Approach	Recognize Need	Formulate Options	Rate and Choose
"Experimental" Approach	Determine Priority	Explore Options	Evaluate Merit
"Creative" Approach	Determine Priority	Test Feasibility	Conceptualize Outputs

Source: Robert F. Stewart, *Setting Corporate Aims* (Menlo Park, CA: SRI International, 1971), p. 5. Reprinted by permission.

---

[30]Robert F. Stewart, "Setting Corporate Aims," a report of the Long Range Planning Service of SRI International, 1971, p. 8.

Identified above are the conceptual frameworks and underlying information useful in defining objectives at different levels. Unfortunately there is no computer model which would neatly relate all the available information to give a set of acceptable objectives. Thus, whichever conceptual scheme is followed and no matter how much information is available, in the final analysis objective setting remains a creative exercise. A creativity test which SRI International recommends to executives for determining their creativity vis-à-vis objective setting is shown in Exhibit 8-9.

Internal and external forces may require a business to redefine its objectives, shifting emphasis from one aspect to another. To give an example, Control Data Corporation has traditionally been concerned more with building volume than with bolstering profit margins. This was necessary for survival. Unlike other computer firms, CDC had no established business-machines sales to lean on, so year after year it had to be satisfied with slim profits. But in early 1980s, CDC's core businesses (i.e., large computer systems, data processing services, and peripheral equipment) matured, making it feasible for the company to stress profits over volume. This change to a bottom-line orientation is attributed in part to the new president of the company.[31]

Once an objective has been set, it may be tested for validity using the following criteria:

1. Is it, generally speaking, a guide to action? Does it facilitate decision making by helping management select the most desirable alternative courses of action?
2. Is it explicit enough to suggest certain types of action? In this sense, "to make profits" does not represent a particularly meaningful guide to action, but "to carry on a profitable business in electrical goods" does.
3. Is it suggestive of tools to measure and control effectiveness? "To be a leader in the insurance business" and "to be an innovator in child-care services" are suggestive of measuring tools in a helpful way; but statements of desires merely to participate in the insurance field or child-care field are not.
4. Is it ambitious enough to be challenging? The action called for should in most cases be something in addition to resting on one's laurels. Unless the enterprise sets objectives which involve reaching, there is the threat that the end of the road may be at hand. It might be perfectly appropriate for some enterprises which have accomplished their objectives to quietly disband. However, for an undertaking to have continuity, it needs the vitality of challenging objectives.
5. Does it suggest cognizance of external and internal constraints? Most enterprises operate within a framework of external constraints (e.g., legal and competitive restrictions) and internal constraints (e.g., lim-

---

[31]"Control Data Beats the Industry," *Business Week*, November 30, 1981, p. 88.

EXHIBIT 8-9   Creativity Test

A group whose members would like to test how far out in the spectrum of creative methodology it can go can do so by a rather simple experiment. To illustrate:

Question: What are the end products of our business?

Conventional answer: We make light, off-the-road vehicles and ancillary mowing, raking, and baling equipment.

Generic answer: We are in the motorized agricultural equipment business.

Analog answer: Our products are to sickle and rake as seining nets are to the fishing pole.

Metaphor answer: We are obstetricians to Mother Earth.

Let us assume that Mr. A offered the analog that mentioned the fishing pole. Mr. B asks derisively, "What the hell have fish got to do with making tractors?" Mr. C interrupts before A can answer with, "Say! Speaking of fish—have we ever looked into either the threats or opportunities of hydroponics?" Mr. D: "I thought of worms. Has anybody ever tried mechanically stocking a field with fertile earthworm eggs like they stock streams with trout?" The power of unconventional ways of looking at familiar things is illustrated without Mr. A's having to rationalize his analogy.

Or, let us also assume that the group agrees that the metaphoric allusion to obstetricians is interesting but too abstract to be useful. The fact that the group acknowledges interest—especially if accompanied by any evidence of humor or elation—may be the kind of signal that W. J. J. Gordon refers to in his research at Synetics. If the moderator deems it to be such, a short exercise called "force fit" may be tried. This consists of asking the group to imagine some line of thought by which the metaphor and the existing business might be connected. For example, one individual trying to force the Mother Earth metaphor and power mowers might muse: "It seems to me that obstetricians, like ourselves, only get into the life stream on 'labor day' when the sweat and tears and pressure are greatest." (Grins break out around the table.) "All right, you guys are ahead of me. What should our role be at planting time?"

If the above experiment indicates that the planning committee finds the latter two levels of abstraction more stimulating than frustrating, it is probably worthwhile to take advantage of this stimulation by seeking professional counsel in group creativity.

Source: Robert F. Stewart, *Setting Corporate Aims* (Menlo Park, CA: SRI International, 1971), p. 5. Reprinted by permission.

itations in financial resources). For instance, if objectives are to be a guide to action, it appears that American Motors, because of its particular set of constraints, should have somewhat different objectives than General Motors.

6. Can it be related to both the broader and the more specific objectives at higher and lower levels in the organization? For example,

are the SBU's objectives relatable to the corporate objectives, and in turn do they also relate to the objectives of one of its products/markets?[32]

SUMMARY

The thrust of this chapter is on defining objectives and goals at the strategic business unit level. Objectives may be defined as general statements on the long-term purpose that the business wants to pursue. Goals are specific targets that the corporation would like to achieve within a given time frame. Because SBU objectives should bear a close relationship to overall corporate direction, the chapter first examines the networks of mission, objectives, and goals through which corporate direction is implemented. The example of the Dow Chemical Company is given.

The discussion of SBU objectives begins with business mission, which defines the total perspectives or purpose of a business. In addition to presenting the traditional viewpoint on business mission, a new framework for defining the business is introduced. The SBU objectives and goals are defined in terms of either financial indicators or desired positions, or combinations of these factors. Also considered are product/market objectives. Usually set at the SBU level, product/market objectives are defined in terms of profitability, market share, growth, and several other aspects. Finally, the process of setting objectives is outlined.

DISCUSSION QUESTIONS

1. *Define the terms policy, objective, and goal.*
2. *What is meant by corporate direction? Why is it necessary to set corporate direction?*
3. *Does corporate direction undergo change? Discuss.*
4. *How does the traditional view of business mission differ from the new approach?*
5. *Examine the perspectives of the new approach to defining business mission.*
6. *Using the new approach, how may an airline define its business mission?*
7. *In what way is the market share objective viable?*
8. *Give two examples of product/market objectives in terms of technological leadership, social contribution, and strengthening of national security.*

---

[32]Reprinted by permission of the *Harvard Business Review*. Excerpt from "The Hierarchy of Objectives" by Charles H. Granger, May–June, 1964, p. 65. Copyright © 1964 by the President and Fellows of Harvard College; all rights reserved.

Bloomington Bank and Trust Company

Bloomington Bank and Trust (BBT hereafter) is a state-chartered commercial bank located in an affluent eastern state. The bank's assets currently stand at approximately $35 million, a figure which ranks the bank as medium-sized in comparison with the other commercial banking institutions of the state. At the close of 1975 BBT found itself in better shape than ever, at least in pure numbers. Demand deposits had increased 14.6 percent during 1975 (55 percent since 1970); time deposits had grown 10 percent in the past year and 75.4 percent in the recent five-year period. Also, total assets had risen 62.3 percent, and total capital had grown 43.5 percent since 1970.

The bank's market had also grown geographically in recent years as branches had been opened in three area towns, and plans were being formulated for the creation of two more. Formerly bank management had been hesitant about expanding into new towns, fearing that the bank would lose its close identification with Bloomington residents. However, at the same time, larger commercial banks were not hesitating to install branches of their own in Bloomington, and as a result, BBT had gradually been losing market share. BBT's first branch opening was experimental in nature, but its success encouraged bank officers to plan for more in the future.

Now that BBT had established itself as a highly successful bank not only in its base town but in the state's most competitive banking region as well, its president, Jim McGowan, felt it an opportune time to retire. He announced his plans in June of 1975, and a search for his successor, who would take office at the start of 1976, was immediately initiated.

On January 2, 1976, McGowan's successor, Brian McQuade, began his stewardship as president of BBT. McQuade had been a vice-president of the state's largest commercial bank before accepting his new post and possessed an exceptional financial background, developed from previous executive positions at banking institutions throughout the East. The bank's board of directors was extremely satisfied with its selection, and McQuade felt confident that he would continue where Jim McGowan left off.

The new president's first task involved an investigation of BBT's past and present strategies. He studied all memos left to him by the bank's former president and analyzed the programs employed by the institution,

This case is printed here with the permission of Professor Peter J. LaPlaca of the University of Connecticut.

but still, after weeks of painstaking research, McQuade felt his efforts were wasted. Upon accepting his executive role, McQuade had pledged to the board of directors that he would continue to lead BBT toward highly successful operation, that he would continue to strive for goals toward which the bank had progressed under the leadership of Jim McGowan. Unfortunately McQuade could not determine what these goals were. Nowhere had the former president explicitly stated any formal goals or objectives by or toward which the bank would operate. In fact, the only material that McQuade could proceed on was a list, compiled by himself, of various strategies BBT had undertaken in the last 15 years. This list, however, was an inadequate basis from which to plan future programs.

Next, McQuade conferred with four of the bank's top executives in hope that they might clarify the problem. He found that all were top-flight and knowledgeable concerning strategies they were responsible for, and information gathered from these meetings was helpful to McQuade in determining the commercial and consumer markets toward which BBT concentrated activity. Nevertheless, McQuade still could not uncover a list of specific goals or objectives around which past strategies were planned or toward which future strategies might be geared.

Finally, the new president decided to meet with Jim McGowan himself. The meeting lasted approximately three hours, and McQuade left the McGowan home with a clearer picture of the past administration's planning process; however, planning for the future was as vague a concept as ever. In his conference with BBT's former chief executive, McQuade confirmed what he had suspected; that is, all programs had been initiated *instinctively* by McGowan. Whenever McGowan had felt that a new program was "right" for the bank, he had ordered it implemented. Perhaps McGowan had acted toward some type of long-term goals subconsciously, but they were not formal or written objectives. Moreover, McGowan himself could not articulate these subconscious goals for McQuade.

Now McQuade knew that the greater part of his first year as BBT's president would have to be spent formulating goals and objectives. He felt that BBT, especially now that it was expanding significantly each year, could no longer be operated according to an executive's intuition. What the bank needed now was a written operating plan. If such a plan could be drawn up, he felt, new strategies could be implemented as part of the plan. Also, any proposed strategy would be considered by management only if that strategy was consistent with the goals set forth in the plan. Conceptually, the idea seemed perfect, but McQuade knew that it could fail in actual practice. In fact, McQuade's former bank had attempted to utilize an operating plan. In theory that plan was still in existence; in practicality it was all but useless. Still, McQuade felt that the situation was different at Bloomington. BBT was much smaller than the other bank, with 1/60 the assets, and its interests were not as diverse and uncontrollable as those in the larger bank. McQuade knew that an operating plan could work at BBT if it were wisely and efficiently conceived.

McQuade also knew that he wouldn't be able to draw up the plan

EXHIBIT 8-10   Bloomington Bank and Trust Company: Planning Milestones

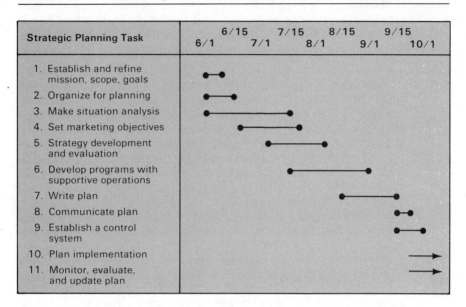

Strategic Planning Task	6/1 6/15 7/1 7/15 8/1 8/15 9/1 9/15 10/1
1. Establish and refine mission, scope, goals	
2. Organize for planning	
3. Make situation analysis	
4. Set marketing objectives	
5. Strategy development and evaluation	
6. Develop programs with supportive operations	
7. Write plan	
8. Communicate plan	
9. Establish a control system	
10. Plan implementation	
11. Monitor, evaluate, and update plan	

himself. Consequently, he informed his four top aides of his plans and asked them to think about the bank's operations: where they presently stood and where they should head in the future. McQuade also realized his limitations as a professional planner; therefore, he called an outside consultant, Dr. Richard Baker, whom he knew to be an expert in business planning.

On May 4, 1976, McQuade and Baker met in McQuade's office. The bank president explained the situation to Baker, stressing the need for an operating plan that would be specific enough to establish direction toward predetermined goals yet flexible enough to encompass innovative strategies. Baker responded favorably to the idea and felt confident that a written operating plan was a viable system for management of BBT. He immediately suggested that a schedule be drawn up for the completion of the various stages involved in creating the plan and that every effort be made to follow the timetable. The two men spent the remainder of the evening developing the schedule (Exhibit 8-10). As the meeting ended, Baker suggested to McQuade that work begin on accomplishing Task #1 as soon as possible.

The suggestion was actually unnecessary, as Brian McQuade had already planned to confer with his department heads the very next morning. McQuade was now firmly committed to the planning idea, and made this known to his officers when he arrived at the bank on May 5. A meeting was arranged for May 18 at which Baker and McQuade would meet with McQuade's four top aides: Jim Carlson (Commercial and Mortgage Lending, Marketing), Bob Delaney (Operations, Personnel), John Erickson (Trust, Portfolio Investments), and Ted Fredericks (Consumer Lending, Credit and Debit Cards). That meeting opened as McQuade introduced Baker to the executives and explained the nature of the meeting:

McQUADE: Gentlemen, today we're to lay the groundwork for an operating plan which I hope will serve as a management guide for all of us. By November, it is hoped that a strategic operating plan for the year 1977 will have been developed. But the development of a short-term plan necessitates reference to longer-term strategic goals. Therefore, today, through a brainstorming session of sorts, we will attempt to devise BBT's mission and its goals. Later, we'll attempt to build strategies that can be used to attain those goals. Before we begin, are there any questions that you would care to ask either Dr. Baker or myself?

DELANEY: I'm a little confused. Many concepts that are considered to be goals are but means towards achieving more generally defined goals. Are we distinguishing between the two?

BAKER: That's very true, Bob, but today we're just trying to assemble a list of any objectives for the operation of BBT. After we've compiled the list we might separate the goals into separate groups; for instance, *ends* goals and *means* goals. But again, the separation can be done some other time. Today we want to get all of the objectives down on paper.

McQUADE: OK; I guess we're all set now. Let fly with any concepts which you feel best describe what we're trying to achieve here at BBT. I'll be taking the minutes of the meeting.

ERICKSON: Well, for starters, I feel that one of our main objectives is to provide a full range of banking services to the markets in which we're located.

McQUADE: Good! In fact, that may even be our mission here.

CARLSON: Another goal might be to increase profits substantially.

BAKER: Can we make it more specific than that? To be effective, the goal should contain a fairly exact range to strive towards.

CARLSON: I see. Well, how does 8 to 10 percent sound? Increasing profits after taxes 8 to 10 percent compounded annually.

McQUADE: Much better. Some more ideas . . . ?

The meeting continued for three hours as goals of the institution were established and a division of responsibility in the planning process was discussed. As the men became more involved, possible strategies to be used in 1977 were discussed, but it soon became apparent that an exhaustive inventory of possible strategies could not be accomplished in just one evening. Therefore, McQuade cut short the session and suggested that all concerned deliberate for a few weeks upon further proposals. On June 1 he issued the following memo, a recapitulation of the thoughts that were expressed on May 18.

<u>MEMO</u>

TO: James Carlson   June 1, 1976
       Robert Delaney
       John Erickson
       Ted Fredericks

FROM: Brian J. McQuade

SUBJECT: PLANNING

   Here is a first stab at outlining the goals, objectives, and strategies we have been
discussing. During the next several months, we will be working to develop a marketing plan for late 1976 and 1977, a 1977 budget, and the foundation for a longer-
term strategic plan. Your suggestions and comments are essential.

1. <u>BBT Goals</u>
    A. Provide full range of banking services to market in which located.
    B. Increase profits after taxes 8–10%, compounded annually.
    C. Build and retain capital to maintain capital to deposit ratio of 1:12–15.
    D. Increase stock value steadily over time.
    E. Provide a "stimulating" and financially rewarding work atmosphere for em-
       ployees.
    F. Maintain and build an image of BBT as a quality, imaginative, service-ori-
       ented, and "professional" institution.
    G. Maintain size and profitability advantage over other banks in town.
    H. Build towards a profit goal of 1%+ of assets (reduced by check deposit
       float).
    I. Specifically develop the capacity of BBT to meet the operational, investment,
       and lending needs of commercial and professional customers and pros-
       pects in our marketing area.
    J. Increase demand deposits 8–12%± annually.
    K. Increase time deposits 10–15%± annually.
    L. Build from the present 50%+ loan to deposit ratio to one of 65–70% by
       1980.

2. <u>Planning</u>
    A. The overall bank planning shall be directly the responsibility of the president.
    B. Primary assistance will come from four department heads:

James Carlson	—	Branch Administration Commercial and Mortgage Lending Marketing
Bob Delaney	—	Operations Personnel
John Erickson	—	Trust Portfolio Investments
Ted Fredericks	—	Consumer Lending Credit and Debit Cards

C. All officers and key supervisory personnel will be encouraged to participate in the planning function through submission of ideas and reaction to ideas and periodic meetings.

3. Strategies
    A. Intensify BBT commercial/professional exposure.
        a. Direct call program
        b. Direct mail program
        c. Educational forums/seminars
    B. Activate statement saving d/d–d/w.
    C. Issue debit card to DDA and savings account customers.
    D. Telephone transfers including non-BBT/DDA a/cs.
    E. Alter NOW charges—perhaps full analysis basis (?)
    F. Offer personal reconciliations via serialized checks onto statement.
    G. Make Master Charge Picture Card optional.
    H. Install a personal/commercial revolving credit service.
    I. Install equipment for competitive check-clearing service.
    J. Institute "Working Trust" service.
    K. Extend drive-in hours for commercial activity.
    L. Institute accounts receivable financing service.
    M. Branch into more commercially developed areas such as East Harrington, Jackson, Westfield, etc.
    N. Open Cookston Branch on Sunday.
    O. Eliminate 78 method on installment loans—go to simple interest.
    P. Intensify bill-paying services.
    Q. Offer account reconciliation services.
    R. Provide lock box service.
    S. Intensify and formalize government securities facilities including perhaps repurchase agreement handling.

We have a Planning Meeting scheduled for 2 P.M. on Thursday, June 3. Please be prepared to comment on the items in this memo and to add your own suggestions. Particularly as relates to your area of responsibility, let's get all ideas "out on the table" regardless of what you feel might be their final disposition after more thorough study.

(Signed)
Brian J. McQuade

On June 3 all six men met again in order to complete the file of possible projects to be implemented in 1977. Once again, the president of BBT displayed his commitment to the operating plan by recording the minutes of the meeting.

McQUADE: Gentlemen, today we're going to go through another brainstorming session. Our meeting of May 18 was highly successful; still, it was only a beginning. Today I want to hear your ideas concerning possible programs that might contribute to our objectives. We won't be discussing the viability of the various programs today; therefore, I want to hear of any ideas that come to mind. Assessment of their significance or workability can wait until later. To keep some semblance of order, Dr. Baker has suggested that we divide our ideas among four categories: loan service oriented programs, deposit/operations service oriented programs, public relations oriented programs, and other or multiple service oriented programs. I think that we can start with those projects that are loan-oriented. Of course, Jim and Ted, since these are your areas of responsibility, we may be looking to you for many suggestions. However, we're looking for recommendations from the entire group; therefore, I hope, Bob and John, that you won't hesitate to contribute whenever an idea comes to mind. OK, I guess we're ready now. Please feel free to start.

DELANEY: How about if we develop contractor and dealer business in the home improvement and construction areas?

McQUADE: Got it. Anybody else?

FREDERICKS: I think that our commercial customers would benefit if we provided financial analysis programs for them. We might be able to do this through time-sharing facilities.

McQUADE: Definitely something to investigate. Some more ideas . . . ?

The session went on for five hours, and when the six men broke up that night, they had compiled no fewer than 113 possible programs. The president took the list home with him that night and reviewed it with mixed emotions. He was extremely pleased with the production of the meeting. Nevertheless, he now faced a fresh problem; that is, deciding upon the priority of the various programs. Certainly, it was impossible to implement each of the suggestions, but choosing the more viable alternatives was not an easy task. The next morning he called Dr. Baker and informed him of his dilemma. The consultant didn't appear surprised by the problem and suggested that some type of collaborative rating system be used. He recommended that the president and his department heads rank each of the programs on a scale in terms of meeting the goals of the institution. McQuade accepted the advice and drafted the following memo. The complete list of programs was attached and appears as Exhibit 8-11.

<u>MEMO</u>

TO: Department Heads   June 15, 1976
FROM: Brian J. McQuade
SUBJECT: Planning

Based on our 6/3 meeting and my 6/1 memo, we broadly defined BBT goals as meeting specifics to do with:

1. Increased profits
2. Improved employee effectiveness
3. Meeting of growth objectives
4. Meeting of market share objectives
5. Meeting of service objectives

We came up with one hundred thirteen possible ideas that might contribute to these objectives. Please review the attached list* and rate each idea on a scale of 1 (low) to 10 (high) in terms of meeting the broad goals outlined above. Obviously, your rating will be based on less than full understanding of each idea but give it a try.

I would appreciate your giving your copy to Jean by 9 A.M. Wednesday. You should be able to complete this in thirty to sixty minutes.

(Signed)
Brian J. McQuade

On June 17, McQuade sent the final compilation of the ratings to his department heads and to Dr. Baker. On that same day a meeting between the six men was scheduled for the purpose of making preliminary decisions concerning projects to be undertaken. The memo is followed by Exhibit 8-11, the rating results of the various proposals.

MEMO

TO: Department Heads   June 17, 1976
FROM: Brian J. McQuadé
SUBJECT: Planning

Attached is a resume of the responses to my memo of June 15 on ranking the ideas generated on June 3. The highest-rated twenty-five items have been so annotated to the right of the total weight column. Also attached is a sheet showing the distribution of responses for the entire one hundred thirteen ideas submitted.

We will be discussing this further at our session this afternoon. The results of this survey should be viewed simply as advisory and one of a number of inputs that will go into a specific action plan.

(Signed)
Brian J. McQuade

On June 28 another meeting was held at which 62 of the 113 proposals were designated as workable for the year 1977. Each of the officers was assigned responsibilities for the implementation of programs covered by his department. The projects to be effected and the names of those responsible for the systematic planning of their implementation were presented to all officers. Items were designated as the sole responsibility of one officer, the joint responsibility of two or more officers, or delegated to other employees. Also several programs needed review by Bob Delaney prior to receiving a go-ahead. All officers were expected to have completed all planning reports by August 9, when another meeting was scheduled.

---

*List is shown in Exhibit 8-11 after the four department heads had ranked each item. The highest possible score is 40. The top 25 items are so indicated in the right column.

EXHIBIT 8-11   Loan Service Oriented

	Points Received	Rank
A. Program		
1. Make Master Charge Picture Card optional	38	24
2. Install a personal/commercial revolving credit service	40	12
3. Institute an accounts receivable financing service	24	
4. Eliminate 78 method on installment loans—go to simple interest computations	23	
5. Develop contractors/dealer business in home improvement and construction areas	38	25
6. Provide financial analysis programs for commercial customers—perhaps via time sharing facilities	30	
7. Install a lease financing program	21	
8. Utilize Master Charge for under-$500 loans	36	
9. Computerize commercial loan function	37	
10. Institute short-term line of credit facility for both individuals and businesses	38	
11. Intensify sales effort for large dollar direct installment loans	44	1
12. Develop a second mortgage loan program	41	11
13. Develop a formalized house-to-house loan program	35	
14. Develop a MGIC and other low down payment mortgage program	26	
15. Expand dealer financing on selective basis	32	
16. Develop a mortgage product with ascending amount payments	26	
17. Formalize a skip payment installment loan program	33	
18. Install a variable rate mortgage program	33	
19. Extend new car installment loans to forty-eight months	36	
20. Institute a balloon payment installment loan program	22	
21. Give rate breaks on Master Charge finance charges to employees and preferred customers	27	
22. Provide coupon books for mortgage payments	33	
23. Activate automatic installment loan and mortgage payments	29	
24. Institute a private label credit card program using Master Charge facilities	32	
25. Add BancAmericard to present Master Charge program	28	
26. Install American Express Gold Card program	28	
B. Deposit/Operations Service Oriented		
27. Activate statement savings d/d–d/w	40	13
28. Issue debit card to DDA and savings customers	42	6
29. Install telephone transfer service including facilities for non-BBT, DDA customers	38	
30. Alter NOW charges—perhaps to full analysis basis	31	

EXHIBIT 8-11   continued

	Points Received	Rank
B. Deposit/Operations Service Oriented		
31. Offer personal reconciliations via serialized checks on the statement	32	
32. Install equipment for competitive check clearing service	40	14
33. Extend drive-in hours for commercial activity	38	
34. Intensify bill paying services	33	
35. Offer account reconciliation services for commercial DDA customers	32	
36. Provide a lock box service	29	
37. Institute a "goal" savings account program	28	
38. Make available for sale, packages of foreign currency	20	
39. Institute a courier deposit pick-up service for commercial businesses	40	15
40. Intensify bank by mail program	26	
41. Institute an emergency 24-hour, wide area money transfer facility using outside sources	24	
42. Institute an automatic savings program for BBT customers with and without our checking accounts	32	
43. Institute GIRO bill payments product	27	
44. Expand automated tellers to other offices	19	
45. Install complete in-house computer facilities	32	
46. Install lobby depositories and/or automated tellers	27	
47. Install mini-max checking account	30	
48. Provide facsimile transmission among our offices	21	
49. Institute a pre-paid interest program using dollars or premiums	27	
50. Expand branch courier service	28	
51. Install out-going WATS	20	
52. Institute service charges for checking accounts	30	
C. Other or Multiple Service Oriented		
53. Intensify commercial/professional direct call program	44	2
54. Intensify commercial/professional direct mail program	40	16
55. Institute "Working Trust" service	26	
56. Branch into more commercially developed areas such as East Harrington, Jackson, Westfield, etc.	42	7
57. Open Cookston Branch on Sunday	22	
58. Intensify/formalize government securities service	30	
59. Provide a commercial service information kit	38	
60. Provide a more formalized municipal finance assistance program		
61. Create and staff a new marketing department	28	
62. Expand East Harrington Branch with safe deposit facilities, etc.	31	
63. Provide more service "breaks" for senior citizens	23	

EXHIBIT 8-11   continued

	Points Received	Rank
C. Other or Multiple Service Oriented		
64. Simplify paperwork on a bank-wide basis	26	
65. Develop a more formalized advertising program	44	3
66. Create a consumer advisory service	30	
67. Create and staff a new business development sales force	43	4
68. Expand through acquisition of other banks	32	
69. Develop a physical facilities plan	36	
70. Institute a 24-hour telephone transfer service	31	
71. Improve customer forms bank-wide	36	
72. Provide MICR encoded coupons for all customer transactions possible	31	
73. Increase use of premiums	27	
74. Install free incoming WATS line	22	
75. Install closed circuit TV facilities between offices	16	
76. Purchase Texas Instruments high-powered calculator	40	17
77. Expand Cookston parking facilities through property acquisition	31	
D. Public Relations Oriented		
78. Intensify commercial/professional educational forums/ seminars	40	18
79. Play music on telephone holds	21	
80. Acquire jai alai passes for and with customers	20	
81. Provide service starter kits for individuals	37	
82. Intensify local school education program	28	
83. Institute merchants relationship program	35	
84. Institute new apartment dwellers call program	29	
85. Institute a home consulting program	27	
86. Institute a business consulting program	37	
87. Institute a consumer information program	34	
88. Run a photo contest for a BBT calendar	42	8
89. Make available a BBT "24-hour" tee-shirt	25	
90. Install coffee bars in branches for customers	18	
91. Renovate main office stairway	25	
92. Redecorate East Harrington Branch	32	
93. Construct a children's waiting facility at main office	32	
94. Procure benches and/or fountains, bird baths, etc. for main office outside	21	
95. Improve outside lighting for main office	30	
96. Provide customer service area in Operations Department	32	
97. Utilize more "exhibits" in main office	34	
98. Acquire season tickets for pro hockey games for and with customers	40	19
99. Acquire Pro Am slot at Greater Columbia Open	26	

EXHIBIT 8-11   continued

E. Employee Effectiveness Oriented	Points Received	Rank
100. Provide customer contact employees with uniforms	20	
101. Enlarge employee lunchroom	40	20
102. Constitute an employees' club for discounts, joint activities, etc.	36	
103. Improve employee job descriptions, salary ranges, etc.	43	5
104. Eliminate cash pay day for employees	36	
105. Provide payroll deduction facilities for employees	39	22
106. Institute an employees' sales incentive program	42	9
107. Activate a formalized employee training and education program	40	21
108. Conduct thorough staffing evaluation survey throughout the bank	42	10
109. Institute a profit center accounting system	35	
110. Institute an officer bonus/incentive program	39	23
111. Eliminate employee Christmas bonus with base pay increases	34	
112. Conduct off-premises and non-work day educational program for employees	30	
113. Conduct off-premises and non-work day educational program for Board of Directors	35	

On August 9, BBT's officers met in order to submit final planning reports concerning strategies from their respective departments. Each of these department heads had spent a considerable amount of time constructing schedules and plans for the projects' implementations, and their resultant work was top-rate. Excerpts from two of the officers' final reports appear below:

Selected Portions of Planning Report of John Erickson, Vice-President
and Trust Officer

PROJECT #36—"THE WORKING TRUST"
     Brian McQuade has proposed the establishment of a new service which he has labeled "The Working Trust." He is recommending that we consider the establishment of this service to provide investment advice to the relatively small investor who either does not have the time, is not interested, or does not have the expertise needed to make economical and intelligent decisions regarding the investment of liquid funds. There are many items to be considered in regard to this matter such as:

     a. other alternatives available to the customer
     b. charges to be assessed
     c. demand use of BBT savings

d. bookkeeping reports required and costs thereof
e. computer capability of handling
f. estimated demand for the service
g. proper pricing
h. legality of pooling funds
i. possible use of money market funds
j. profitability to bank

These items, in addition to many others, must be thoroughly addressed before "The Working Trust" may be proposed to the Board of Directors. I will take the responsibility for investigating this project during 1977, with the intention of presenting a recommendation to Brian McQuade and the Board of Directors no later than March 30, 1977, regarding the possible inception of a new service entitled "The Working Trust."

Selected Portions of Planning Report of Ted Fredericks, Assistant Vice-President (Consumer Lending, Credit and Debit Cards)

I. Issue debit card to DDA and savings account customers.
A. *Goals:* to increase customer awareness and usage of automated teller service, thereby reducing transacting costs.
Control: (a) increase cardholder base by 400% (to 8000 cardholders) by June, 1977; (b) increase total usage/week as % to base to 8–10% by June, 1977.
B. *Steps*
1. Determine eligibility criteria—usage per day, availability of credit line, and geographical considerations (Aug. 1976).
2. Design appropriate artwork for card. Determine promotional and distribution strategies. Use ad agency (Sept. 1976).
3. Order plastics from manufacturer—8–10 weeks lead time—in house by Oct. 1976.
4. Emboss and encode cards—distribute to customers. If credit line offered cards cannot be mass mailed. (Time?)
5. Institute promotional campaign to stimulate usage—establish personal demonstration program. (Timing—ad agency to decide)
C. *Resources/costs/regulatory problems*
1. Approximate cost per thousand cards issued will be $250 (includes embossing).
2. As transactions increase more work time required to process paper—need feasibility study on on-line vs. off-line.
3. Have experience in operating debit card program.
Related project: Install lobby depositories and automated tellers.
A. *Goal:* to reduce lobby congestion; to offer unlimited banking hours; to expedite customer transaction time; to enhance innovative image.
B. *Steps*
1. Determine feasibility of lobby depositories and need for automated teller services at branch locations. For lobby depository, simple queuing theory formulas can be utilized.

2. If feasible lobby depositories would have to be procured and promoted. In the case of the ATM's (automated teller machine) a decision would have to be made with regard to manufacturer.
3. ATM installation schedule would be prepared.
4. ATM promotion at branch location would have to be planned and coordinated with debit card promotion.
5. Balancing and credit procedures would have to be established.

C. *Resources*
1. State U. MBA student doing queuing theory study at East Harrington Branch.
2. ATM scheduled to be installed at Westfield Office.
3. Plans to expand debit card base in process.

For the next month, McQuade reviewed the minutes of the meetings of the past four months and gradually completed a preliminary draft of a 1977 Operating Plan. To do so, he, along with Dr. Baker, first re-examined the list of goals which had been prepared at their May 18 meeting. A further subdivision was made: approximately one-half of the objectives were categorized as general goals while the remainder, "means goals," were included as a plan to meet the more general goals. The two men also reviewed the reports that had been submitted by the department heads and incorporated ideas under appropriate headings. The preliminary plan was submitted to each of the department heads on September 6 to make certain that their findings had not been distorted in any manner, and finally, after minor revisions, the finalized plan was submitted to BBT's board of directors for final approval on September 22 (see Exhibit 8-12). Budgets for each of the programs were prepared, and the plan began operation in November, 1976, two months ahead of schedule.

After six months of painstaking work by all involved, Bloomington Bank and Trust was operating according to a formal written plan for the first time in its history, and its president, Brian J. McQuade, felt confident his bank was headed toward even greater success.

EXHIBIT 8-12   Final Operating Plan

MEMORANDUM

TO: Board of Directors and Officers
FROM: Brian J. McQuade
SUBJECT: 1977 Operating Plan   September 22, 1976

This plan has been developed over the last several months through input, discussion, and suggestions from customers, employees and directors. To plan for one year necessitates reference to longer term strategic goals. We have just begun to formalize a strategic plan and have done enough to construct the shorter term operating plan. This plan is intended as a guide, a summary, and a reference point. It should be studied in detail by all officers.

EXHIBIT 8-12   continued

Mission of BBT: To provide to our market a full range of conveniently delivered banking services of high quality at competitive prices. At the same time, to develop a record of growth and profitability which will be financially rewarding to our stockholders.

A. *Goals:*
   1. Increase profits after taxes 10–15% compounded annually.
   2. Build towards a profit goal of 1% return on assets (less check-float-created due from balances).
   3. Build towards realizing a return on invested capital of 10–12%.
   4. Build and retain capital to maintain capital to deposit rates of 1:12–15.
   5. Increase stock value steadily.
   6. Maintain and build BBT as an imaginative, service oriented and professionally operated institution.
   7. Provide a stimulating and financially rewarding work environment for employees.

B. *General Plan to Meet Goals:*
   1. Increase demand deposits 8–12% annually.
   2. Increase savings and time deposits 10–15% annually.
   3. Build from the present 50%+ loan to deposit ratio, to one of 65–70% by 1980.
   4. Adopt a posture of more aggressive sales through a combination of more rapid product enhancement and development, improved and intensified advertising, improved development and communications, intensified calling on the business community, and a progressive branching program.
   5. Specifically develop the capacity of BBT to meet the operational, investment and lending needs of professional and commercial customers in our marketing area.
   6. Increase market penetration in towns having branches with particular emphasis on Bloomington. Intensify efforts to penetrate more fully towns contiguous to those in which branches are located.
   7. Intensify efforts to improve the profitability of that part of the investment portfolio which prudently need not be considered primary reserves.

C. *Prime 1977 Programs*
   Some of the '77 programs may be implemented during the remainder of 1976 but are included here to solidify this initial written operating plan. Quantitative details will be developed during a budgeting process to be conducted in the fourth quarter.
   1. *Organizational Structure*
      a. President—will be responsible for overall results and management including planning. His role will include a major public relations effort, sales initiatives, with selected prominent prospective customers, and contact with current major customers. He will be assisted by three department heads, each reporting directly to him.
      b. Department Heads
         1. James Carlson
            (a) banking services including commercial lending

EXHIBIT 8-12   continued

    (b) branch administration
    (c) marketing
 2. Bob Delaney
    (a) operations
    (b) financial reporting
    (c) personnel administration
 3. John Erickson
    (a) trust marketing and operations
    (b) investment services
    (c) investment portfolio management
2. *Intensify lending activities*
   a. Install a personal/commercial revolving credit service (in addition to Master Charge).
   b. Institute a short term line of credit facility for both individuals and businesses.
   c. Intensify installment lending activity
      1. formalize a deferred/tailored installment loan program.
      2. develop contractor/dealer business in home improvement areas.
      3. intensify efforts to develop a more competitive pricing posture consistent with BBT goals.
      4. develop a second mortgage loan program.
   d. Implement a formalized house-to-house loan program.
   e. Computerize the commercial loan function.
   f. Make Master Charge Picture Card optional.
3. *Intensify overall marketing effort on a wide basis*
   a. Hire an advertising agency.
   b. Institute a formal officer call program.
   c. Initiate a program of business/professional seminars/forums.
   d. Intensify social program for selected major customers and prospects.
   e. Add to staff a business development officer to concentrate on non-customers in Bloomington and selected parts of E. Harrington in 1977.
4. *Improve and intensify non-lending product lines and sales effort*
   a. Institute d/d–d/w statement savings.
   b. Institute serialized check service.
   c. Issue a debit (noncredit) card for automated teller activation.
   d. Institute a telephone transfer service.
   e. Investigate and implement if feasible a deposit pick-up service for businesses.
   f. Investigate and implement if feasible a mini-max checking account service.
   g. Revise NOW account service charges to present more competitive product.
   h. Implement a formalized government security service.
   i. Investigate and implement if feasible "The Working Trust" service.

EXHIBIT 8-12   continued

    j. Develop operational service "starter kits" for individuals and businesses.

    k. Review service pricing schedules and revise to increase revenues where possible.

    l. Build customer service conference area outside Bookkeeping Department.

5. Open Westfield Branch in early 1977.

6. Open Four Corners and/or Buckingham Branches in late 1977, early 1978.

7. *Improve internal operations*

    a. Accounting

        1. Install remote entry data processing equipment

        2. Place all loan accounting functions in one centralized "back-office" operation.

    b. Financial Reporting

        1. Automatic investment portfolio accounting.

        2. Eliminate cash basis accounting and install a full accrual system (while retaining cash basis tax reporting while advisable).

        3. Progress towards a profit center accounting system.

    c. Formalize a facilities plan and ongoing facilities plan procedure for action to be taken in 1978 and beyond.

    d. Develop formalized job descriptions (and possibly salary ranges).

    e. Develop a more formalized officer evaluation program.

    f. Evaluate and implement better performance oriented compensation programs for officers.

    g. Intensify communications between Board of Directors and Cookston Advisory Board and bank management.

8. Investigate and where possible implement changes in trust services and charges consistent with overall BBT goals.

9. Complete Main Office banking floor renovations.

D. *Five Year Financial Scenario*

Tables 1–9 attached describe a possible course that could develop based on tentative longer range goals and the continuation of the overall philosophy of business being developed in this plan. From our current vantage point, the 1976 and 1977 net income projections may be difficult to achieve. Hopefully near term deficiencies may be overcome during the period 1978–1981.

E. *Conclusion*

The planning process is a continuing one involving all personnel in management positions. I believe that the meetings, memos, studies, discussions and surveys that have gone into this initial plan have already proven beneficial to the individuals involved and the bank. Bloomington Bank is a solid and respected institution—it has performed well in its marketplace and for its stockholders. We have the opportunity to create an even more interesting and exciting institution—one that can serve its present and an expanded marketplace better than it has. We have the opportunity to create a more dynamic work environment for all employees and to obtain better financial results for stockholders and employees. The task is not an easy one. The business of banking shares with other businesses the pressures of regulation, increasing costs, and the resultant squeeze on profits and increasing competition.

I suggest that we view our challenge as opportunities to grow personally and as an institution. Better management in its broadest sense, and including all levels, is the greatest need in banking today—I believe we can learn together to manage better.

1977 will be an exciting and interesting year for Bloomington Bank. Much of what we have planned is basic and simply positions us better vis-a-vis our competition. In the planning process we have deferred for 1977 some of the more creative steps that we may have wished to take. Experience confirms the wisdom of learning to walk before running. We have chosen to walk more quickly—we may or may not ultimately decide to run.

I seek both your support and cooperation and in turn offer you mine.

(Signed)
Brian J. McQuade

Approved by Board of Directors on
September 22, 1976

TABLE 1   Demand Deposits

Deposits	Historical Demand	% Increase
1970	7,185,000	
1971	7,937,000	8.0
1972	8,901,000	12.1
1973	8,893,000	(.1%)
1974	9,713,000	9.2
1975	11,136,000	14.6
(5 Year: 55%)		

	Projection 8% Growth Projection	12% Growth Projection
1976	10,500,000*	10,500,000*
1977	11,340,000	11,760,000
1978	12,247,200	13,171,200
1979	13,226,976	14,751,744
1980	14,285,134	16,521,953
1981	15,427,944	18,504,587

*'76 estimate down from '75

TABLE 2   Time/Savings Deposits

	Historical Time/Savings Deposits	% Increase
1970	10,620,000	
1971	11,985,000	12.8
1972	13,181,000	10.0
1973	14,413,000	9.3
1974	16,933,000	17.5
1975	18,631,000	10.0
(5 Year: 75.4%)		
	Projection 10% Growth Projection	15% Growth Projection
1976	20,460,000	21,390,000
1977	22,506,000	24,598,500
1978	24,756,600	28,288,275
1979	27,232,260	32,531,516
1980	29,955,468	37,411,243
1981	32,951,014	43,022,929

TABLE 3   Total Deposits

	Historical Total Deposits	% Increase
1970	17,805,000	
1971	19,923,000	11.9
1972	22,082,000	10.8
1973	23,304,000	5.5
1974	26,646,000	14.3
1975	27,818,000	4.4
(5 Year: 56.2%)		
	Projection Low Growth Projection	High Growth Projection
1976	30,960,000	31,890,000
1977	33,846,000	36,358,500
1978	37,003,800	41,459,475
1979	40,459,236	47,283,260
1980	44,240,602	53,933,196
1981	48,378,958	61,527,516

TABLE 4   Total Loans

	Historical Total Loans		Deposit to Loan Ratios
			1:—
1970	8,708,000		.489
1971	10,073,000		.506
1972	11,927,000		.540
1973	13,271,000		.569
1974	14,372,000		.529
1975	15,118,000		.507
	(5 Year: 73.6%)		
	Projection		Projected Deposit to Loan Ratio
	Low Growth Projection	High Growth Projection	
1976	16,718,400	17,220,600	.54
1977	19,292,220	20,724,345	.57
1978	22,202,280	24,875,685	.60
1979	25,489,318	29,788,453	.63
1980	29,198,797	35,595,909	.66
1981	33,865,270	43,069,261	.70

TABLE 5   Net Income

	Historical Net Income	% Increase
1970	160,000	
1971	174,500	9.1
1972	135,100	(22.6)
1973	216,200	60.0
1974	245,000	13.3
1975	230,000	(6.1)
	Projection 10% Growth Projection	15% Growth Projection
1976	236,500	247,250
1977	260,150	284,337
1978	286,165	326,988
1979	314,781	376,036
1980	346,259	432,411
1981	380,885	497,308

TABLE 6   **Dividends**

		Historical Dividend*	% Increase
1970	70,000	.70	
1971	70,000	.70	-0-
1972	72,500	.725	3.5
1973	75,000	.75	3.4
1974	80,000	.80	6.6
1975	85,000	.85	6.2

*Adjusted for 5/20/74 100% stock dividend

	Projection Low	High
1976	85,000	85,000
1977	94,600	98,900
1978	104,060	113,735
1979	114,466	150,415
1980	138,504	172,977
1981	152,354	198,923

40% of earnings used for all projections 1977–1981

TABLE 7   **Capital**

	Historical Capital	% Increase
1970	1,761,000	
1971	1,874,000	6.4
1972	1,951,000	4.1
1973	2,163,000	10.9
1974	2,381,000	10.1
1975	2,527,000	6.1

(5 Year: 43.5%)

	Projection Low	High
1976	2,641,900	2,662,250
1977	2,797,990	2,847,687
1978	2,969,689	3,060,940
1979	3,170,004	3,286,562
1980	3,377,760	3,546,027
1981	3,606,291	3,844,412

TABLE 8   Ratio of Deposits to Capital

	Historical		
	Total Capital	Deposits	1:—
1970	1761.1	17805.2	10.1
1971	1874.1	19923.1	10.6
1972	1951.5	22082.5	11.3
1973	2163.1	23304.1	10.8
1974	2382.6	26646.6	11.2
1975	2527.6	29818.1	11.8
	Projection		
	Low		High
1976	11.7		12.0
1977	12.1		12.8
1978	12.5		13.5
1979	12.8		14.4
1980	13.1		15.2
1981	13.4		16.0

TABLE 9   Percentage Return on Capital

	Historical	
	%	
	1970	9.1
	1971	9.3
	1972	6.9
	1973	10.0
	1974	10.3
	1975	9.1
	Projection	
	Low %	High %
1976	8.95	9.29
1977	9.30	9.98
1978	9.64	10.68
1979	9.93	11.44
1980	10.25	12.20
1981	10.56	12.94

PART FIVE
Strategy Formulation and Approval

CHAPTER 9
Strategy Selection

*All men can see the tactics whereby I conquer, but what none can
see is the strategy out of which victory is achieved.*

Sun-tzu

Two things were achieved in the earlier chapters. First, the internal and external information required for formulating marketing strategy was identified, and the methods for analyzing such information were examined. Second, using the available information, the formulation of objectives was covered. This chapter takes us to the next step toward strategy formulation by establishing a framework for it.

Our principal concern in this chapter is with business unit strategy. Among several inputs required to formulate the business unit strategy, a basic input is the strategic perspective of different products/markets that comprise the business unit. Therefore, as a first step toward formulating the business unit strategy, a framework for developing product/market strategies is introduced.

Bringing product/market strategies within the framework for business unit strategy formulation emphasizes the importance of inputs from both top down and bottom up in strategy formulation. As a matter of fact, it can be said that strategic decisions in a diversified company are best made at three different levels: by product/market managers and the SBU manager jointly when questions of implementation are involved, by the chief executive officer and the SBU manager jointly when formulation of strategy is the concern, and by the chief executive officer when the mission of the business is at issue.

CONCEPTUAL SCHEME

Exhibit 9-1 depicts the framework for developing marketing strategy. As delineated earlier, marketing strategy is based on three key factors: corporation, customer, and competition. The interaction between these three factors is rather complex. For example, the *corporation* factor impacts marketing strategy formulation through (a) the business unit mission and its goals and objectives, (b) perspectives of strengths and weaknesses in different functional areas of the business at different levels, and (c) perspectives of the different products/markets that constitute the business

409

EXHIBIT 9-1   Framework for Formulating Marketing Strategy

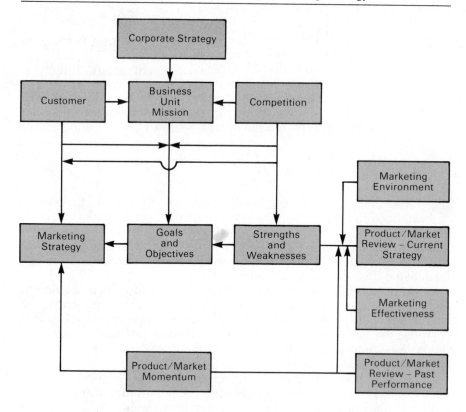

unit. *Competition* affects the business unit mission as well as the measurement of strengths and weaknesses. The *customer* factor is omnipresent, affecting the formation of goals and objectives to support the business unit mission and affecting marketing strategy directly.

PRODUCT/MARKET STRATEGY

The following is the step-by-step procedure for formulating product/market strategy:

1. Start with the present business. Predict what the momentum of the business will be over the planning period if no significant changes in the policies or methods of operation are made. The prediction will be based on historical performance.
2. Forecast what will happen to the environment over the planning period. This will include overall marketing environment and product/market environment.

3. Modify the prediction in step 1 in the light of forecasted shifts in the environment in step 2.
4. Stop if the predicted performance is fully satisfactory vis-à-vis objectives. Continue if the prediction is not fully satisfying.
5. Appraise the significant strengths and weaknesses of the business in comparison with those of important competitors. This appraisal should include any factors which may become important both in marketing (market, product, price, promotion, and distribution) and in other functional areas (finance, R&D, costs, organization, morale, reputation, management depth, etc.).
6. Evaluate the differences between your marketing strategies and those of your major competitors.
7. Undertake an analysis to discover some variation in marketing strategy which would produce a more favorable relationship in your competitive posture in the future.
8. Evaluate the proposed alternate strategy in terms of possible risks, competitive response, and potential payout.
9. Stop if the alternate strategy appears satisfactory in terms of objectives.
10. Broaden the definition of the present business and repeat steps 7, 8, and 9 if there is still a gap between the objective and the alternative strategy. Here, redefining the business means looking at other products that can be supplied to a market which is known and understood. Sometimes this means supplying existing products to a different market. It may also mean applying technical or financial abilities to new products and new markets simultaneously.
11. The process of broadening the definition of the business to provide a wider horizon can be continued until one of the following occurs:
    a. The knowledge of the new area becomes so thin that a choice of the sector to be studied is determined by intuition or obviously inadequate judgment.
    b. The cost of studying the new area becomes prohibitively expensive because of lack of related experience.
    c. It becomes clear that the prospects of finding a competitive opportunity are remote.
12. Lower the objectives if the existing business is not satisfactory and if broadening of the business offers unsatisfactory prospects.

There are three tasks involved in the strategy procedure described above: information analysis, strategy formulation, and implementation. At the product/market level these tasks are performed by either the product/market manager or an SBU executive. In practice, analysis and implementation are usually handled entirely by the product/market manager, while strategy formulation is done jointly by the product/market manager and the SBU executive.

Essentially, all firms have some kind of strategy and plans to carry on their operations. In the past, both the plans and the strategy were made intuitively. However, the increasing pace of change is forcing businesses to make their strategies explicit and often to change them. Strategy per se is getting more and more attention.

Any approach to strategy formulation leads to a conflict between objectives and capabilities. Attempting the impossible is not a good strategy; it is just a waste of resources. On the other hand, setting inadequate objectives is obviously self-defeating. Setting the proper objectives depends upon prejudgment of the potential success of the strategy; however, you cannot determine the strategy until you know the objectives. Strategy development is a reiterative process requiring art as well as science. The above dilemma may explain why many strategies are intuitively made rather than logically and tightly reasoned. But there are concepts which can be usefully applied in approximating the opportunities and speeding up the process of strategy development. Take market segmentation, for example. A market can be viewed in many different ways; a product can be used in many different ways. Each time the product/market pairing is varied, the relative competitive strength is varied, too. Thus, a key element in strategy is choosing the competitor whom you wish to challenge, as well as choosing the market segment and product characteristics with which you will compete. The above procedure is designed not only to systematically analyze information, but also to formulate or change strategy in an explicit fashion and implement it.

Measuring the Momentum

Planning is undertaken to achieve a desired future which, while the probability is low, may come about without any changes in strategy being made. The first phase in developing product/market plans is to determine the state of affairs in the future, assuming that the environment and the strategy remain the same. This future state of affairs is what we call momentum. If the momentum projects a desirable future, little planning is needed. More often, however, the future implied by the momentum may not be the desired future.

The momentum may be measured using modeling, forecasting, and simulation techniques. Let us describe how these techniques were applied to a bank. This bank grew by opening two to three new branches per year in the trading area defined by state law. The measurement of momentum consisted of projecting income statement and balance sheet figures for new branches and merging them with the projected income statement and balance sheet of the original bank. A model was constructed to project the bank's future performance. The first step in construction of the model was the prediction of B_{ijt}, i.e., balances for an account of type i in area j and in time period t. Account types included checking, savings, and certificates of deposit, and areas were chosen to coincide with counties in the state. County areas were desirable since most state data were available by county and the current branching areas were defined by counties. Balances were projected using multiple linear regression. County per capita income and rate of population growth were found to be important variables for predicting total checking account balances, and these variables, along with the last period's savings balance, were shown to be important in describing savings account balances.

The next step was to predict M_{jt} (i.e., the market share of the bank being considered in area j and time period t). This was done using a combination of data of past performances and managerial judgment. The total expected deposit level for the branch being considered, D_{it}, was then calculated as:

$$D_{it} = \sum_{jb} (B_{ijt} M_{jt})$$

For the existing operations of the bank, the past data were utilized to produce a ten-year set of deposit balances. These deposit projections were added to those of new branches. Turning to other figures, certain line items on the income statement could be attributed directly to checking accounts, others to savings accounts. The remaining figures were related to the total of account balances.

For this model, ratios of income and expense items to appropriate deposit balances were predicted by a least-squares regression on historical data. This was not considered the most satisfactory method since some changing patterns of incurring income and expenses were not taken into account. However, more sophisticated forecasting techniques, such as exponential smoothing and Box-Jenkins, were rejected because of the potential amounts of management misunderstanding they could generate. As Ackoff points out, managers will rarely use results of a model they do not understand.[1]

Once the ratio matrix was developed, the income statements could be generated by simply multiplying the ratios by the proper account balance projection to arrive at the ten-year projection for the income statement line items. These income statements, in conjunction with the bank's policy on dividends and capitalization, were then used to generate a ten-year balance-sheet projection. The net results were presented to the bank's senior executive committee to be reviewed and modified. After incorporating executive judgment, final ten-year income statements and balance sheets were obtained, indicating the bank's momentum into the future.[2]

---

[1]Russell L. Ackoff, *A Concept of Corporate Strategy* (New York: John Wiley & Sons, 1970).

[2]Robert J. Graham, "Some Useful Techniques for Implementing a Planning Process," in Justin D. Stolen and James J. Conway (eds.), *Ninth Annual Conference Proceedings* (Atlanta: American Institute for Decision Sciences, 1977), pp. 525–527.

Gap Analysis

In the preceding example, momentum was extrapolated from the historical data. Little attention was given to either internal or external environmental considerations in developing the momentum. However, for a realistic projection of future outcomes, careful analysis of the overall marketing environment as well as the product/market environment is necessary.

As a part of gap analysis, therefore, the momentum should be examined and adjusted with reference to environmental assumptions. Analysis of the industry, the market, and the competitive environment should be performed to identify important threats and opportunities. This should be combined with a careful evaluation of the product/market competitive strengths and weaknesses. On the basis of this, the momentum should be evaluated and refined.

In the midst of continued inflation toward the end of 1981, the chairman of the Federal Reserve System, Paul Volcker, decided to restrict the money supply. Consequently, the prime and short-term rates of interest increased quite a bit. For example, the rate of interest on a 30-month certificate of deposit went up to 15.8 percent annually. This led many depositors to withdraw their money (even at the cost of substantial penalty for early withdrawal) from the six-year certificates of deposit, which earned 7.75 percent annual interest. In the illustration discussed in the previous section, the impact of such an increase in interest rate was not considered in arriving at the momentum (i.e., in making forecasts of deposit balances). But as a part of gap analysis, this shift in the environment should be duly taken into account by making adequate adjustments in the momentum.

The "new" momentum should then be measured against the objectives to see if there will be a gap between expectation and potential realization. More often than not, there will be a gap between what objectives are desired and what momentum, as revised with reference to environmental assumptions, can deliver. How this gap may be filled will be discussed in the next section.

Filling the Gap

The gap must be filled in order to bring the planned results as close to objectives as possible. Essentially, gap filling amounts to reformulating the product/market strategy. Exhibit 9-2 describes a six-step procedure which may be used for examining the current strategy and coming up with a new one which can fill the gap.

While basically using a procedure similar to the one depicted in Exhibit 9-2, the discussion here is planned under the following headings: *issue assessment, identification of key variables,* and *strategy selection.* The experience of companies with which the author is familiar suggests that the gap-filling exercise should be assigned to a multifunctional team. Non-

EXHIBIT 9-2   Procedure for Filling the Gap

1. Record current strategy:
   a. What is the current strategy?
   b. What kind of business does management want to operate (considering such management values as desired return on investment, growth rate, share of market, stability, flexibility, character of the business, and climate)?
   c. What kind of business does management feel it ought to operate (considering management's concepts of social responsibility and obligations to stockholders, employees, community, competitors, customers, suppliers, government, and the like)?
2. Identify problems with the current strategy:
   a. Are trends discernible in the environment that may become threats and/or missed opportunities if the current strategy is continued?
   b. Is the company having difficulty implementing the current strategy?
   c. Is the attempt to carry out the current strategy disclosing significant weaknesses and/or unutilized strengths in the company?
   d. Are there other concerns with respect to the validity of the current strategy?
   e. Is the current strategy no longer valid?
3. Discover the core of the strategy problem:
   a. Does the current strategy require greater competence and/or resources than the company possesses?
   b. Does it fail to exploit adequately the company's distinctive competence?
   c. Does it lack sufficient competitive advantage?
   d. Will it fail to exploit opportunities and/or meet threats in the environment, now or in the future?
   e. Are the various elements of the strategy internally inconsistent?
   f. Are there other considerations with respect to the core of the strategy problem?
   g. What, then, is the real core of the strategy problem?
4. Formulate alternative new strategies:
   a. What possible alternatives exist for solving the strategy problem?
   b. To what extent do the company's competence and resources limit the number of alternatives that should be considered?
   c. To what extent do management's preferences limit the alternatives?
   d. To what extent does management's sense of social responsibility limit the alternatives?
   e. What strategic alternatives are acceptable?
5. Evaluate alternative new strategies:
   a. Which alternative best solves the strategy problem?
   b. Which alternative offers the best match with the company's competence and resources?
   c. Which alternative offers the greatest competitive advantage?
   d. Which alternative best satisfies management's preferences?
   e. Which alternative best meets management's sense of social responsibility?
   f. Which alternative minimizes the creation of new problems?
6. Choose a new strategy:
   a. What is the relative significance of each of the preceding considerations?
   b. What should the new strategy be?

marketing people often provide fresh inputs; their objectivity and healthy skepticism are generally of great help in sharpening the focus and in maintaining business-wide perspectives. The process the team follows should be carefully structured and the analytical work punctuated with regular review meetings to synthesize findings, check progress, and refocus work when such is considered desirable. The SBU staff should be deeply involved in the evaluation and approval of the strategies.

Issue Assessment. The primary purpose of this step is to raise issues about the status quo to evaluate the business's competitive standing in view of present and expected market conditions. Typically, a beginning should be made by working through a series of questions in order to identify those few issues that will most crucially affect the future of the business. The following questions might be included: How mature is the product/ market segment under review? What new avenues of market growth are conceivable? Is the industry becoming more cyclical? Are competitive factors changing (for example, is product-line elaboration declining and cost control gaining in importance)? Is our industry as a whole likely to be hurt by continuing inflation? Are new regulatory restrictions pending?

As the company moves toward evaluation of its own competitive position, the following questions may be raised: How mature is our product line? How do our products perform compared with those of leading competitors? How does our marketing capability compare? What about our cost position? What are our customers' most common criticisms? Where are we most vulnerable to competitors? How strong are we in our distribution channels? How productive is our technology? How good is our record in new-product introduction?

Some critical issues are immediately apparent in many companies. For example, a company in a highly concentrated industry might find it difficult to hold on to its market share if a stronger, larger competitor were to launch a new low-priced product with intensive promotional support. Also, in a capital-intensive industry the cyclical pattern and possible pressures on pricing are usually critical. If a product's transport costs are high, preemptive investments in regional manufacturing facilities may be desirable. Other important issues may be concerned with threats of backward integration by customers or forward integration by suppliers, technological upset, new regulatory action, or the entry of foreign competition into the home market. Most strategy teams supplement this brainstorming exercise with certain basic analyses that often lead to fresh insights and a more-focused list of critical business issues. Three such issues which may be mentioned here are profit economics analysis, market segmentation analysis, and competitor profiling.

Profit economics analysis will indicate how product costs are physically generated and where the economic leverage lies. The contribution of the product to fixed costs and profits may be calculated by classifying the elements of cost as fixed, variable, or semivariable and by subtracting variable cost from product price to yield contribution per item sold. It is then possible to test the sensitivity of profits to possible variations in volume, price, and cost elements. Similar computations may be made for manufacturing facilities, distribution channels, and customers.

Segmenting the market will show alternate methods of segmentation and whether there are any segments not being properly cultivated. Once the appropriate segment is determined, efforts should be made to project the determinants of demand (including cyclical factors and any constraints on market size or growth rate) and to explain pricing patterns, relative market shares, and other determinants of profitability.

Profiling competitors may involve examining their sales literature, talking with experts or representatives of industry associations, and interviewing shared customers and any known former employees of competitors. If more information is needed, the team may acquire and analyze competing products and perhaps even arrange to have competitors interviewed by a third party. With these data competitors may be compared in terms of product features and performance, pricing, likely product costs and profitability, marketing and service efforts, manufacturing facilities and efficiency, and technology and product development capabilities. Finally, each competitor's basic strategy may be inferred from these comparisons.

Identification of Key Variables. The above information on issues should be analyzed to isolate the critical factors on which success in the industry depends. In any business there are usually about five to ten factors which have a decisive effect on performance. As a matter of fact, in some industries one single factor may be the key to success. For example, in the airline industry, with its high fixed costs, a high load factor is critical to success. In the automobile industry, a strong dealer network is a key success factor, since the manufacturer's sales crucially depend on the dealer's ability to finance a wide range of model choices and offer competitive prices to the customer. In a commodity component market such as switches, timers, and relays, both market share and profitability are heavily influenced by product range. An engineer who is designing circuitry normally reaches for the thickest catalog with the richest product selection. In this industry, therefore, the manufacturer with a wide selection can collect more share points with only a meager sales force.

The key factors may vary from industry to industry. Even within a single company they may vary according to shifts in industry position, product superiority, distribution methods, economic conditions, availability of raw materials, and the like. Therefore, suggested here is a set of questions which may be raised to identify the key success factors in any given situation:

1. What things have to be done exceptionally well to win in this industry? In particular, what must we do well today to lead the industry in profit results and competitive vitality in the years ahead?
2. What factors have caused or could cause companies in this industry to fail?

3. What are the unique strengths of our principal competitors?
4. What are the risks of product or process obsolescence? How likely are they to occur and how critical could they be?
5. What things have to be done to increase sales volume? How does a company in this industry go about increasing its share of the market? How could each of these ways of growing affect profits?
6. What are our major elements of cost? In what ways might each of them be reduced?
7. What are the big profit leverage points in this industry—i.e., what would be the comparative impact on profits of equal management efforts expended on each of a whole series of possible improvement opportunities?
8. What key recurring decisions have to be made in each major functional segment of the business? What impact on profits could a good or bad decision in each of these categories have?
9. How, if at all, could the performance of this function give the company a competitive advantage?[3]

Once these key factors have been identified, they should be examined with reference to the current status of the product/market to define alternative strategies which may be pursued to gain competitive advantage over the long term. Each alternative strategy should be evaluated for profit payoff, investment costs, feasibility, and risk.

It is important that strategy alternatives be described as specifically as possible. Simply stating "maintain product quality," "provide high-quality service," and "expand market overseas" is not enough. Precise and concrete descriptions, such as "extend the warranty period from one year to two years," "enter English, French, and German markets by appointing agents in these countries," and "provide a $25 cash rebate to every buyer to be handed over by the company directly," are essential before alternatives can be adequately evaluated.

Initially the strategy group may generate a long list of alternatives, but informal discussion with management can soon pare these down to a handful. Each surviving alternative should be weighed in terms of projected financial consequences (sales, fixed and variable costs, profitability, investment, and cash flow) and relevant nonfinancial measures (market shares, product quality and reliability indices, channel efficiency, and so on) over the planning period.

At this time due attention should be paid to examining any contingencies and making appropriate responses to them. For example, if market share increases by only half of what was planned, what pricing and promotional actions might be undertaken? If customer demand instantly shoots up, how can orders be filled? What ought to be done if the Consumer Product Safety Commission should promulgate new product usage controls? Additionally, if the business is in a cyclical industry, each alter-

---

[3]Richard F. Nenschel, "Improving Management Information Systems," *The McKinsey Quarterly*, Winter, 1976, pp. 51–52.

native should also be tested against several market-size scenarios, simultaneously incorporating varying assumptions about competitive-pricing pressures. In industries dominated by a few competitors, an evaluation should be made of the ability of the business to adapt each strategy to competitive actions such as pricing moves, shifts in advertising strategy, or attempts to dominate a distribution channel.

Strategy Selection. After information on trade-offs between alternative strategies has been gathered, as discussed above, a preferred strategy will be chosen for recommendation to management. Usually the chosen strategy will have a focus on one of the areas of the marketing mix (i.e., product, price, promotion, or distribution). For example, the preferred strategy may be to "reduce prices to maintain market share." Here the emphasis of the strategy is on pricing. Thus, pricing may be labeled as the *core strategy,* i.e., area of primary concern. However, in order to make an integrated marketing decision, appropriate changes may have to be made in product, promotion, and distribution areas. The strategic perspectives in these areas may be called *supporting strategies.* Thus, once strategy selection has been undertaken, the core and supporting strategy areas should be delineated.

Occasionally more than one decision area may constitute core strategy. For example, in holding prices and introducing a new, improved version of the product, both product and price are core strategies, while promotion and distribution are supporting ones. Exhibit 9-3 shows core and supporting strategies for an industrial product and a consumer product. Note that in the case of the microcomputer, product constitutes the only core strategy. For the movie camera, however, both price and promotion are core strategies.

Let us examine the concept of core and supporting strategies with reference to a furniture store in New Jersey. For a long time this store stocked furniture of the Early American style. With the change in consumers' tastes, the Early American style was going out of fashion, and the future of the business looked bleak. The store, therefore, needed a new strategy. On analysis, it was found that the store catered primarily to 20- to 35-year-old professionals struggling to establish careers and households. To continue to serve this segment adequately, the store decided that the product and price areas would constitute the core strategy while promotion and distribution strategies would be supporting ones. To implement the core strategy, the store needed a line of furniture which would be appropriate for those with "a high level of taste and a not-so-high level of income." It finally decided on contemporary furniture to be sold unassembled and packed in cartons. This type of furniture, known in the trade as K.D. (for "knocked down"), was developed in Europe over 30 years ago for sale in the United States. European K.D. had a low profile in this country until recently. Either high-price retailers imported the furniture in K.D. form and assembled it in their workrooms, or cheap K.D. shelving made of plastic or pressboard was sold at budget houseware prices.

EXHIBIT 9-3   Core and Supporting Strategies

PRODUCT/MARKET	CORE STRATEGY	SUPPORTING STRATEGY
1. Microcomputer for small business people	*Product*: Develop new stand-alone product within 3 years for companies with annual sales of less than $5 million.	*Price*: Keep the price low to compete aggressively. *Promotion*: Hire and train a new sales force to call on the customers; provide excellent after-sales service. *Distribution*: Seek intensive distribution through office equipment wholesalers.
2. Movie camera for upper-middle-class families	*Promotion*: Promote heavily by mail among families with annual income over $25,000. Follow through with telephone calls. *Price*: Keep prices down. Make up for reduced prices by selling a package deal for film and processing.	*Product*: Develop instructions in a very lucid fashion (i.e., a step-by-step procedure in easy-to-comprehend language). Develop appropriate packaging for mail delivery. *Distribution*: Arrange with a mail delivery organization such as UPS for fast and dependable delivery.

Now retailers are finding a growing demand for K.D., since it satisfies the desire for contemporary furniture at moderate prices. The following supporting strategies were required: (1) promoting the new line in appropriate media; (2) emphasizing K.D. as tasteful furniture at a reasonable price which required only that the customer assemble it; and (3) stocking the right mix of furniture so that the product was available without delay.[4]

Exhibit 9-4 describes the major elements of marketing strategy, which obviously revolve around the product, price, promotion, and distribution decisions. For each of these four marketing decisions, the exhibit lists the "effort" and "activities" involved. The marketing strategy is formulated around the "effort"; the implementation of the strategy is achieved through the "activities." In other words, when a change in marketing strategy is called for, look under "effort" to develop strategy alternatives in each area.

Once strategy alternatives in each of the four areas have been generated and before an alternative is selected, a decision must be made on core strategy. What this is, is a very difficult question to answer. Conceptually, all major facets of marketing strategy are essential. But which particular area is the most critical is something that depends on a variety of factors. While this question has not been examined deeply in the literature, an original study on the relative importance of the elements of marketing strategy was reported by Udell in the 1960s.[5] A team of professors updated this study in the 1970s and found that sales effort remained the most important facet of marketing strategy, followed by product effort, pricing effort, and distribution effort. While the emphasis on different areas as such did not vary in the two studies, the activities comprising these areas did reveal changes, especially when respondents were classified according to the type of product produced:

> Mid-1970 industrial goods manufacturers assigned less importance to presale service, technical research and development, warehousing and inventory control, pricing at the competitive level, and pricing according to government rules and regulations. Conversely, these manufacturers gave less weight to style research and development, branding and promotional packaging, cost-plus pricing, and pricing according to what the market will bear.
>
> Mid-1970 consumer durable goods manufacturers de-emphasized the importance of presale service, technical research and development, selection of establishments in the channel, assisting channel members, and pricing at the competitive level. Upgraded in importance were style research and development, marketing research, transportation, determination of channels used, and cost-plus pricing.
>
> Finally, mid-1970 producers of consumer nondurable goods placed less emphasis on presale service, postsale service, technical research

---

[4]"The Upswing in Knock-down Furniture," *Business Week*, September 18, 1978, p. 61.

[5]Jon G. Udell, "The Perceived Importance of the Elements of Strategy," *Journal of Marketing*, January, 1968, pp. 34–40.

EXHIBIT 9-4   Major Elements of Marketing Strategy and Component Activities

A. **Product Effort.** Includes product planning, product research and development, product testing, and the service accompanying the product. Activities:
1. Market research relating to product planning, development, and product testing.
2. Technical research, development, and laboratory testing of new products and improvements of existing products.
3. Product research relating to the development of product styling and fashions.
4. Presale service such as product application engineering.
5. Postsale service such as product installation, maintenance, and guarantee service.

B. **Sales Effort.** Includes such areas as sales management, personal selling, advertising, promotional programs, and all other forms of marketing communications.
Activities:
1. Product branding and promotional packaging.
2. Printed media advertising in newspapers, magazines, and brochures.
3. Broadcast media advertising on radio and television.
4. Sales management and personal selling including all sales management activities (e.g., training supervision) and the sales efforts of company management personnel.
5. Special promotional activities such as promotional warranties, trade shows, dealer aids, and product displays.

C. **Distribution.** Includes the selection, coordination, and evaluation of channels, transportation, warehousing, and inventory control.
Activities:
1. Transportation.
2. Warehousing and inventory control.
3. Determination of the basic channels of distribution to be utilized.
4. Selection of individual establishments within the basic channels.
5. Manufacturer's efforts to develop and assist the channel of distribution.

D. **Pricing Effort.** Includes price determination, pricing policies, and specific pricing strategies over which some degree of control is exercised.
Activities:
1. Cost plus desired profit or standard cost pricing.
2. Pricing according to competitive levels, pricing at the prevailing competitive price.
3. Pricing at a certain percent above or below competitors' prices.
4. Pricing according to what the market will bear based on estimated value of the product to the consumer.
5. Pricing based on governmental rules and regulations.

Source: Clyde E. Harris, Jr., Richard R. Still, and Melvin R. Crask, "Stability or Change in Marketing Methods?," *Business Horizons,* October, 1978, p. 33. Copyright, 1978, by the Foundation for the School of Business at Indiana University. Reprinted by permission.

and development, print advertising, assistance to channel members, and pricing according to a percentage above or below competition. The producers gave more weight to style research and development, and branding and promotional packaging.[6]

While the above findings are helpful, the fact remains that determination of core strategy will vary from case to case. What may be said, however, is that the core strategy is formulated around the critical variable(s) which, for the same product, may differ from one segment to another. This is well supported by the following quote taken from a case study of the petroloids business, which deals with manufactured substances based on the synthesis of organic hydrocarbons into a family of such unique materials as oils, petro-rubbers, foams, adhesives, and sealants:

> Major producers competed with one another on a variety of dimensions. Among the most important were price, technical assistance, advertising and promotion, and product availability. Price was used as a competitive weapon primarily in those segments of the market where products and applications had become standardized. However, where products had been developed for highly specialized purposes and represented only a small fraction of a customer's total material cost, the market was often less price sensitive. Here customers were chiefly concerned with the physical properties of the product and operating performance.
>
> Technical assistance was an important means of obtaining business. A sizeable percentage of total petroloid sales were accounted for by products developed to meet the unique needs of particular customers. Products for the aerospace industry were a primary example. Research engineers of petroloid producers were expected to work closely with customers to define performance requirements and to insure the development of acceptable products.
>
> Advertising and promotional activities were important marketing tools in those segments which utilized distribution channels and/or which reached end users as opposed to OEM's. This was particularly true of foams, adhesives and sealants which were sold both to industrial and consumer markets. A variety of packaged consumer products were sold to hardware, supermarkets, and "do-it-yourself" outlets by our company as well as other competitors. Advertising increased awareness and stimulated interest among the general public while promotional activities improved the effectiveness of distribution networks. Since specialty petroloid products accounted for only a small percentage of a distributor's total sales, product promotion insured that specific products received adequate attention.
>
> Product availability was a fourth dimension on which producers competed. With manufacturing cycles from 2–16 weeks in length and thousands of different products, no supplier could afford to keep all

---

[6]Clyde E. Harris, Jr., Richard R. Still, and Melvin R. Crask, "Stability or Change in Marketing Methods," *Business Horizons*, October, 1978, p. 40.

his items in stock. In periods of heavy demand, many products were often in short supply. Those competitors with adequate supplies and quick deliveries could readily attract new business.[7]

Apparently, strategy development is difficult because different emphases may be needed in different product/market situations. The emphasis is built around the critical variables, which may be difficult to identify. Luck plays a part in making the right move; occasionally sheer intuition suffices. Despite all this, a careful review of past performance, current perspectives, and environmental changes should go a long way in choosing the right areas to concentrate on. Appendix A at the end of this chapter gives a framework of business strategy concepts and provides an interesting review for strategic direction. This framework is not meant to introduce a new scheme for strategy development. Rather, it provides an opportunity to reflect on business strategy formulation as an aid in articulating a system for one's own use.

Reformulation of current strategy may range from making slight modifications in the existing perspectives to coming out with an entirely different strategy. For example, in the area of pricing, one alternative for an automobile manufacturer may be to keep the prices from year to year stable (i.e., no yearly price increases). A different alternative may be to lease cars, instead of selling them, directly to consumers. The decision on the first alternative may be made by the strategic business unit executive. But the second alternative, being far-reaching in nature, may require the review and approval of top management. In other words, how much examination and review a product/market strategy will require depends on the nature of the strategy (in terms of the change it seeks from existing perspectives) and the resource commitment required.

One final point about developing core strategy is that the emphasis should always be placed on searching for new ways to compete. The marketing strategist should develop the strategy around those key factors in which the business has more freedom than its competitors have. A food manufacturer, for example, had been losing strength in inverse relation to the growing power of the grocery chains. A strategic response to this threat might take one of three forms. The food manufacturing firm could intensify its efforts by introducing better products or more competing brands, extending its product lines, creating new segments for specialty customer groups, or battling on retail price. It could respond by strengthening trade marketing, i.e., strengthening the key-account management function, offering better trade discounts and deals, or agreeing to provide more and more in-store services at its own expense. Or it could compete on cost advantage—a very different strategy indeed, implying much greater

---

[7]"Tex-Fiber Industries—Petroloid Products Division (A)," a case developed by John Craig under the supervision of Derek F. Abell, copyrighted by the President and Fellows of Harvard College, 1970, p. 7.

concentration on operations management and less on marketing. Exhibit 9-5 illustrates these three degrees of freedom available to the food manufacturer. The company decided to focus its strategy on strengthened distribution and rationalized product lines, areas ignored by the competition.

DETERMINING STRATEGIC BUSINESS UNIT STRATEGY

To repeat a basic principle, marketing strategy at the strategic business unit level is determined by the three C's, i.e., customer, competition, and company (including both top management and product/market perspectives). The experience of different companies shows that for strategy formulation, the strategic three C's can be articulated by placing SBUs on a two-by-two matrix with industry maturity or attractiveness as one dimension and strategic competitive position as the other.

EXHIBIT 9-5   Degrees of Competitive Freedom for a Food Manufacturer

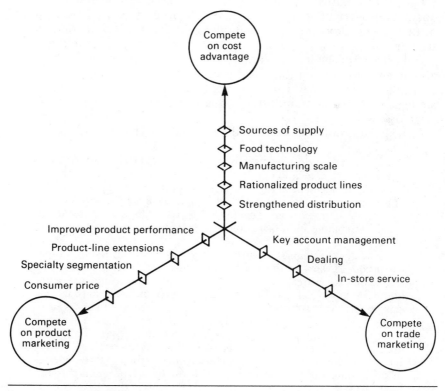

Source: J. Roger Morrison and James G. Lee, "The Anatomy of Strategic Thinking," *The McKinsey Quarterly*, Autumn, 1979, p. 8. Reprinted by permission.

Industry attractiveness may be studied with reference to the life-cycle stage of the industry (i.e., embryonic, growth, mature, or aging). Such factors as growth rate, industry potential, breadth of product line, number of competitors, market share perspectives, purchasing patterns of customers, ease of entry, and technology development determine the maturity status of the industry. As illustrated in Exhibit 9-6, the above factors behave in different ways according to the stage of industry maturity. For example, in the embryonic stage the product line is generally narrow, and frequent changes to tailor the line to customer needs are common. In the growth stage, product lines undergo rapid proliferation. In the mature stage, attempts are made to orient products to specific segments. During the aging stage, the product line begins to shrink.

Going through the four stages of the industry life cycle can take decades or a few years. The different stages are generally of unequal duration. To cite a few examples, home computers and solar energy devices are in the embryonic category. Home smoke alarms and sporting goods in general fall into the growth category. Golf equipment and steel represent mature industries. Men's hats and rail cars are in the aging category. It is important to remember that industries can experience reversals in their aging processes. For example, roller skates have experienced a tremendous resurgence (i.e., moving from the aging stage back to the growth stage) because of the introduction of polyurethane skate wheels. It should also be emphasized that there is no "good" or "bad" life-cycle position. A particular stage of maturity becomes "bad" only if the expectations or strategies adopted by an industry participant are inappropriate for a given stage of maturity.

The four different stages in the life cycle are characterized as follows:

Embryonic industries usually experience rapid sales growth, frequent changes in technology, and fragmented, shifting market shares. The cash deployment to these businesses is often high relative to sales as investment is made in market development, facilities, and technology. These businesses are generally not profitable, but investment is usually warranted in anticipation of gaining position in a developing market.

The growth stage of maturity is generally characterized by a rapid expansion of sales as the market develops. Customers, shares, and technology are better known than in the embryonic stage, and entry into the industry can be more difficult. Growth businesses are usually capital borrowers from the corporation, producing low to good earnings.

In mature industries the competitors, technology, and customers are all known and there is little volatility in market shares. The growth rate of these industries is usually about equal to the GNP. Businesses in these industries tend to provide cash for the corporation through high earnings.

The aging stage of maturity is characterized by:

1. Falling demand for the product and limited growth potential.

2. A shrinking number of competitors. Survivors gain market share through attrition.
3. Little product line variety.
4. Little, if any, investment in research and development or plant and equipment even though the business generates extremely high earnings.[8]

The competitive position of an SBU should depend not only on market share, but also on such factors as capacity utilization, current profitability, degree of integration (forward or backward), distinctive product advantages (such as patent protection), and management strength (such as willingness to take risks). The above factors may be studied for classifying a given SBU in one of the following competitive positions: dominant, strong, favorable, tenable, or weak.

Exhibit 9-7 summarizes the typical characteristics of firms in different competitive positions. An example of a *dominant* firm is IBM in the computer field; its competitors pattern their behavior and strategies on what IBM does. In the beer industry Anheuser-Busch exemplifies a *strong* firm, able to make an independent move without being punished by the major competition.

Determining strategic competitive position is one of the most complex elements of business analysis and one of the least researched. With little state-of-the-art guidance available, often there is a temptation to fall back on the single criterion of market share, but experience of successful companies makes it clear that determining competitive position is a multifaceted problem embracing, for example, technology, breadth of product line, market share, share movement, and special market relationships. Such factors change in relative importance as industry maturity changes.

Choice of Strategy

Once the position of an SBU is located on the industry maturity/competitive position matrix, the guide shown in Exhibit 9-8 may be used to determine what strategy the SBU should pursue. Actually the strategies shown in the exhibit are guides to strategic thrust rather than strategies per se. They show the normal strategic path a business unit may adopt, given its industry maturity and competitive position. Appendix B at the end of this chapter further examines the strategic thrusts identified in Exhibit 9-8. Each strategic thrust is defined, and its objective, requirements, and expected results are noted.

To bridge the gap between broad guidelines and specific strategies for implementation, further analysis is required. A three-stage process is

---

[8]*A Management System for the 1980s* (Cambridge, MA: Arthur D. Little, Inc., no date), pp. 18–20. See also Robert V. L. Wright, *A System for Managing Diversity* (Cambridge, MA: Arthur D. Little, Inc., no date).

Exhibit 9-6   Industry Maturity Guide

| DESCRIPTORS | STAGES OF INDUSTRY MATURITY | | | |
	EMBRYONIC	GROWTH	MATURE	AGING
Growth Rate	Accelerating. Meaningful rate cannot be calculated because base is too small.	Substantially faster than GNP. Industry sales expanding significantly.	Growing at rate equal to or slower than GNP. More subject to cyclicality.	Industry volume declining.
Industry Potential	Usually difficult to determine.	Demand exceeds current industry volume, but is subject to unforeseen developments.	Well known. Primary markets approach saturation.	Saturation is reached. Supply capability exceeds long-term demand.
Product Line	Line generally narrow. Frequent changes tailored to customer needs.	Product lines undergo rapid proliferation. Some evidence of products oriented toward multiple industry segments.	Product line turnover but little or no change in breadth. Products frequently oriented toward narrow industry segments.	Product line shrinking, but tailored to major customer needs.
Number of Competitors	Few competing at first, but number increasing rapidly.	Number and types are unstable. Increase to peak, followed by shake-out and consolidation.	Generally stable or declining slightly.	Declines, or industry may break up into many small regional suppliers.

Market Share Stability	Volatile. Share difficult to measure. Share frequently concentrated.	Rankings can change. A few firms have major shares.	Little share volatility. Firms with major shares are entrenched. Significant niche competition. Firms with minor shares are unlikely to gain major shares.	Some change as marginal firms drop out. As market volume declines, market share generally becomes more concentrated.
Purchasing Patterns	Varies. Some customers have strong loyalties; others have none.	Some customer loyalty. Buyers are aggressive, but evidence of repeat or add-on purchases. Some price sensitivity.	Suppliers are well known. Buying patterns are established. Customers generally loyal to limited number of acceptable suppliers. Increasing price sensitivity.	Strong customer loyalty as number of alternatives decreases. Customers and suppliers may be tied to each other.
Ease of Entry (Exclusive of capital considerations)	Usually easy. Opportunity may not be apparent.	Usually easy. Presence of competitors is offset by vigorous growth.	Difficult. Competitors are entrenched. Growth is slowing.	Little incentive.
Technology	Important to match performance to market needs. Industries started on technological breakthrough or application. Multiple competing technologies.	Fewer competing technologies. Significant product line refinements or extensions likely. Performance enhancement is important.	Process and materials refinement. Technologies developed outside this industry are used in seeking efficiencies.	Minimal role in ongoing products. New technology may be sought to renew growth.

Source: Arthur D. Little, Inc. Reprinted by permission.

EXHIBIT 9-7   Classification of Competitive Strategic Positions

Dominant	• Controls behavior and/or strategies of other competitors • Can choose from widest range of strategic options, independent of competitors' actions
Strong	• Can take independent stance or action without endangering long-term position • Can generally maintain long-term position in the face of competitors' actions
Favorable	• Has strengths which are exploitable with certain strategies if industry conditions are favorable • Has more than average ability to improve position • If in a niche, holds a commanding position relatively secure from attack
Tenable	• Has sufficient potential and/or strengths to warrant continuation in business • May maintain position with tacit consent of dominant company or the industry in general, but is unlikely to significantly improve position • Tends to be only marginally profitable • If in a niche, is profitable, but clearly vulnerable to competitors' actions
Weak	• Has currently unsatisfactory performance, but has strengths which may lead to improvement • Has many characteristics of a better position, but suffers from past mistakes or current weaknesses • Inherently short-term position; must change (up or out)
Nonviable	• Has currently unsatisfactory performance and few, if any, strengths which may lead to improvement (may take years to die)

Source: Arthur D. Little, Inc. Reprinted by permission.

EXHIBIT 9-8   Guide to Strategic Thrust Options

COMPETITIVE POSITION	STAGES OF INDUSTRY MATURITY			
	EMBRYONIC	GROWTH	MATURE	AGING
Dominant	Fast grow Start-up	Fast grow Attain cost leadership Renew Defend position	Defend position Attain cost leadership Renew Fast grow	Defend position Focus Renew Grow with industry
Strong	Start-up Differentiate Fast grow	Fast grow Catch-up Attain cost leadership Differentiate	Attain cost leadership Renew, focus Differentiate Grow with industry	Find niche Hold niche Hang-in Grow with industry Harvest
Favorable	Start-up Differentiate Focus Fast grow	Differentiate, focus Catch-up Grow with industry	Harvest, hang-in Find niche, hold niche Renew, turnaround Differentiate, focus Grow with industry	Retrench Turnaround
Tenable	Start-up Grow with industry Focus	Harvest, catch-up Hold niche, hang-in Find niche Turnaround Focus Grow with industry	Harvest Turnaround Find niche Retrench	Divest Retrench
Weak	Find niche Catch-up Grow with industry	Turnaround Retrench	Withdraw Divest	Withdraw

Source: Arthur D. Little, Inc. Reprinted by permission.

suggested here. First, using the broad guidelines, the SBU management may be asked to state the strategies pursued during the previous years. Second, these strategies may be reviewed by using selected performance ratios to analyze the extent to which the strategies were successfully implemented. Similarly, current strategies may be identified and their link to past strategies established. Third, having identified and analyzed past and current strategy with the help of strategic guidelines, the management, using the same guidelines, selects the strategy it proposes to pursue in the future. The future perspective may call for the continuation of current strategies and/or the development of new ones. Before accepting the future strategic course, however, it is desirable to measure its *cash consequences* or *internal deployment* (i.e., percentage of funds generated which are reinvested). Exhibit 9-9 illustrates an SBU earning 22 percent on assets with an internal deployment of 80 percent. Such an SBU would normally be considered to be in the mature stage. However, if the previous analysis

EXHIBIT 9-9   Profitability and Cash Position of a Business

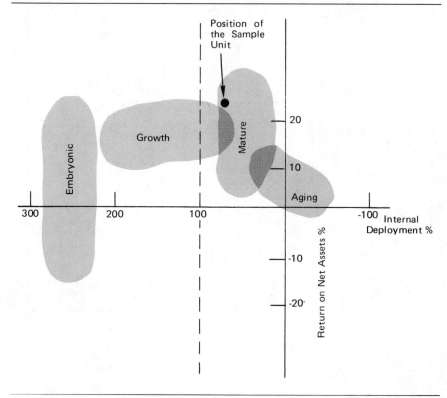

Source: Peter Patel and Michael Younger, "A Frame of Reference for Strategy Development," *Long Range Planning*, April, 1978, p. 78. Reprinted by permission.

showed that the SBU was in fact operating in a growth industry, the corporation would need to rethink its investment policy for this SBU. All quantitative information pertaining to an SBU may be summarized on one form, as shown in Exhibit 9-10.

Different product/market plans are reviewed at the SBU level. The purpose of this review is twofold: (a) to consider product/market strategies in finalizing the SBU strategies, and (b) to approve the product/market strategies. The underlying criterion for evaluation is a balanced achievement of SBU goals, which may be specified in terms of profitability and cash consequences. If there is a conflict of interest between two product/market groups in the way the strategy is either articulated or implemented, the conflict should be resolved so that SBU goals are maximized. Assume that both product/market groups seek additional investments during the next two years. Of these, the first product/market will start delivering positive cash flow in the third year. The second one, however, is not likely to generate positive cash flow until the fourth year, but it will provide a higher overall return on capital. If the SBU's need for cash is urgent and if it desires additional cash for its goals during the third year, the first product/market group will appear more attractive. Thus, despite higher profit expectations from product/market group two, the SBU may approve investment in product/market group one with a view to maximizing the realization of its own goals.

At times the SBU may require a product/market group to make additional changes in its strategic perspective before giving its final approval. On the other hand, a product/market plan may be totally rejected and the group instructed to pursue its current perspective.

The industry maturity and competitive position analysis may also be used in further refining the SBU itself. In other words, after an SBU has been created and it is analyzed for industry maturity and competitive position, it may be found that it has not been properly constituted. This would require redefining the SBU and undertaking the analysis again. Drawing an example from the car radio industry, considerable differences with reference to industry maturity may become apparent between car radios with built-in cassette players and traditional car radios. Differences in industry maturity and/or competitive position may also exist with regard to regional markets, consumer groups, and distribution channels. For example, the market for cheap car radios sold by discount stores to end users doing their own installation may be growing faster than the market served by specialty retail stores providing installation services. Such revelations may require further refinement in formulating SBUs. This may continue until the SBUs represent the highest possible level of aggregation consistent with the need for clear-cut analyses of industry maturity and competitive position.[9]

---

[9]Peter Patel and Michael Younger, "A Frame of Reference for Strategy Development," *Long Range Planning*, April, 1978, p. 8.

EXHIBIT 9-10   Financial Record of an SBU

PERFORMANCE

	INDICES OF:					RETURN					
						INVESTMENT (PER $ SALES)					
Year	Industry Capacity	Business Unit's Product Capacity	Business Unit's Sales	Profits After Taxes	Net Assets	Receivables	Inventories	Net Current Liabilities	Working Capital	Other Assets	Total Net Assets
	(A)	(B)	(C)	(D)	(E)	(F)	(G)	(H)	(I)	(J)	(K)

INVESTMENT

RETURN (continued)

	COST AND EARNINGS (PER $ SALES)						RONA		FUNDS GENERATION AND DEPLOYMENT			
									(PER $ SALES)			(%)
Year	Cost of Goods Sold	Research and Development	Sales and Marketing	General and Administrative	Other Income and Expenses	Profit Before Taxes	Profit After Taxes	Return on Net Assets	Operating Funds Flow	Change in Assets	Net Cash Flow to Corporation	Internal Deployment (U ÷ T)
	(L)	(M)	(N)	(O)	(P)	(Q)	(R)	(S)	(T)	(U)	(V)	(W)

Source: Arthur D. Little, Inc. Reprinted by permission.

STRATEGY EVALUATION

"The time required to develop resources is so extended, and the time-scale of opportunities is so brief and fleeting, that a company which has not carefully delineated and appraised its strategy is adrift in white water." This quotation from an article by Seymour Tilles underlines the importance of strategy evaluation. He suggests the following six criteria for evaluating the adequacy of a strategy:

1. Internal consistency
2. Consistency with the environment
3. Appropriateness in the light of available resources
4. Satisfactory degree of risk
5. Appropriate time horizon
6. Workability[10]

An attempt is made in this section to evaluate product/market strategy using these criteria.

Internal Consistency

The strategy should be in tune with the different policies of the corporation, the SBU, and the product/market area. For example, if the corporation has decided to limit the government business of any unit to 40 percent of total sales, a product/market strategy emphasizing greater than 40 percent reliance on the government market will be internally inconsistent.

Consistency with the Environment

The strategy should be consistent with the external product/market environment. After the fall of the Shah of Iran in 1979, gas prices shot up, and a nationwide gas shortage for the coming years became imminent. In such an environment as this, an automobile company which introduces to its middle-of-the-line car new features which will substantially increase gas consumption may not be doing the right thing. At a time when more and more women are seeking jobs, a strategy assuming traditional roles for women (i.e., raising children and staying home) is inconsistent with the environment.

Appropriateness in the Light of Available Resources

Money, competence, and physical facilities are the critical resources which a manager should be aware of in finalizing strategy. A resource may

---

[10]Seymour Tilles, "How to Evaluate Corporate Strategy," *Harvard Business Review*, July–August, 1963, pp. 111–121. See also Milton Lauenstein, "Keeping Your Corporate Strategy on Track," *Journal of Business Strategy*, Summer, 1981, pp. 61–64.

be examined in two different ways: (1) as a constraint limiting the achievement of goals, and (2) as an opportunity to be exploited as the basis for strategy. It is desirable for a strategist to make correct estimates of the resources available without being excessively optimistic about them. This implies that even if the resources are available in the corporation, a particular product/market group may not be able to lay claim to them. Alternatively, the resources currently available to a product/market group may be transferred to another group if the SBU strategy deems it necessary.

Satisfactory Degree of Risk

The degree of risk may be determined on the basis of the perspectives of the strategy and the available resources. A pertinent question here is: Will the resources be available as planned in appropriate quantities and for as long as it is necessary to implement the strategy? The overall proportion of resources committed to a venture becomes a factor to be reckoned with here: the greater these quantities, the greater the degree of risk.

Appropriate Time Horizon

A viable strategy will have a time frame for its realization. The time horizon of the strategy should be set up to allow its implementation without either creating havoc in the organization or missing market availability. For example, in introducing a new product to the market, enough time should be allotted for market testing, salespeople's training, etc. But the time should not be so long that a competitor can enter the market first and skim the cream off the top.

Workability

The workability of a strategy should be realistically evaluated with reference to quantitative data. Sometimes, however, it may be difficult to undertake such objective analysis. In such a case, other indications may be used to assess the contributions of a strategy. One such indication could be the degree of consensus among key executives about the viability of the strategy. Identifying ahead of time alternate strategies for achieving the goal is another indication of the workability of the strategy. Finally, establishing resource requirements in advance, which eliminates the need to institute crash programs of cost reduction or seek reduction in planned programs, also substantiates the workability of the strategy.

In addition to reviewing the strategy with reference to the above criteria, a quick evaluation of the viability of specific strategies (i.e., product, price, promotion, and distribution strategies) can be made by referring to a compendium of strategies like the one shown in Exhibit 9-11. It

EXHIBIT 9-11   Impact of Multibusiness Strategic Planning on Marketing

MARKETING DECISION AREA	STRATEGY ADOPTED FOR DIVISION OR PRODUCT LINE		
	INVEST FOR FUTURE GROWTH	MANAGE FOR EARNINGS	MANAGE FOR IMMEDIATE CASH
Market share	Aggressively build across all segments	Target efforts to high-return/high-growth segments Protect current franchises	Forego share development for improved profits
Pricing	Lower to build share	Stabilize for maximum profit contribution	Raise, even at expense of volume
Promotion	Invest heavily to build share	Invest as market dictates	Avoid
Existing product line	Expand volume Add line extensions to fill out product categories	Shift mix to higher-profit product categories	Eliminate low-contribution products/varieties
New products	Expand product line by acquisition, self-manufacture or joint venture	Add products selectively and in controlled stages of commitment	Add only sure winners

Source: Louis V. Gerstner, "Can Strategic Planning Pay Off?," *Business Horizons*, December, 1972, p. 15. Copyright, 1972, by the Foundation for the School of Business at Indiana University. Reprinted by permission.

is desirable that such a compendium be custom developed for a company, either internally or with the help of a consultant.

SUMMARY

This chapter is devoted to strategy formulation for the strategic business unit. A conceptual framework for developing the SBU strategy is outlined. Strategy formulation at the SBU level requires, among different inputs, the perspectives of product/market strategies. For this reason, a procedure for developing product/market strategy is discussed first.

Product/market strategy development requires predicting the momentum of current operations into the future (assuming constant conditions), modifying the momentum in the light of environmental changes, and reviewing the adjusted momentum against goals. If there is no gap between the set goal and the prediction, the present strategy may well be continued. Usually, however, there is a gap between the goal and expectations from current operations. Thus, the gap must be filled.

The following three-step process has been suggested for filling the gap: (1) issue assessment (i.e., raising issues with the status quo vis-à-vis the future); (2) identification of key variables (i.e., isolating the key variables on which success in the industry depends) and development of alternative strategies; and (3) strategy selection (i.e., choosing the preferred strategy). The thrust of the preferred strategy is on one or more of the four variables of the marketing mix—product, price, promotion, and distribution. The major emphasis of marketing strategy, the core strategy, is on this chosen variable. Strategies for the remaining variables are supporting strategies.

The SBU strategy is based on the three C's, i.e., customer, competition, and company (including both top management and product/market perspectives). SBUs are placed on a two-by-two matrix with industry maturity or attractiveness as one dimension and strategic competitive position as the other. Stages of industry maturity are identified: embryonic, growth, mature, and aging. Competitive position can be classified as dominant, strong, favorable, tenable, or weak. Classification by industry maturity and competitive position generates 20 different quadrants in the matrix. In each quadrant an SBU requires a different strategic perspective. A compendium of strategies is provided to figure out the appropriate strategy in a particular case.

The chapter concludes with a procedure for evaluating the selected strategy. This consists of examining the following aspects of the strategy: internal consistency, consistency with the environment, appropriateness in the light of available resources, satisfactory degree of risk, appropriateness of time horizon, and workability.

DISCUSSION QUESTIONS

1. *Describe how a manufacturer of television sets may measure the momentum of his or her business for the next five years.*

2. *Discuss how the increasing impact of Japanese competition may be taken into account by the television manufacturer to adjust momentum.*
3. *List five issues which Sears may raise to review its large-appliances strategy.*
4. *List five key variables on which success in the home-construction industry depends.*
5. *In what industry stage would you position (a) light beer and (b) color television?*
6. *Based on your knowledge of the company, what would you consider to be Miller's competitive position in the light beer business, and GE's position in the color television business?*
7. *Referring to the guide to strategic thrust options (Exhibit 9-8), examine the soundness of strategies pursued by Miller and GE in the light beer and color television business respectively.*
8. *Discuss how the strategy evaluation criteria may be employed to review the strategy of an industrial goods manufacturer (assume a particular type of company).*
9. *Apply the marketing strategy framework outlined in this chapter to a service business such as a bank, an airline, etc.*

APPENDIX A: BUSINESS STRATEGY CONCEPTS

Spectacular business successes are usually new ways of doing business in familiar markets with familiar products. These are the true strategic victories, won by using corporate resources to substantially outperform a competitor with superior strength.

The concept of superior performance without superior resources is usually identified with trying harder. Yet most companies seem to work very hard to produce only minor differentials in performance.

The underlying principle of a good strategy is simple: "Concentrate your strength against your competitor's relative weakness." This principle has a major corollary in a dynamic competitive environment—concentration of effort will inevitably produce a counter-concentration by competition; therefore, timing and sequence are critical. A major attack should never be launched against a competent well-entrenched competitor without first eliminating his ability or willingness to respond in kind.

There are many prerequisites to a successful strategy:

1. The characteristics of the competition must be known in detail, including their characteristic attitude and behavior.
2. The environment in which competition will take place must be equally well understood.
3. Your own relative strengths must be accurately and objectively appraised.
4. The strategic concept must not be based on the obvious exercise of known strengths. If it is, you don't need a strategy, just a plan.
5. It must be possible to achieve stability if the strategy succeeds.

6. Your own organization must not be misled by your efforts to outmaneuver competition. Strategic goals must be very explicit.

Once the strategic framework has been designed, the tactics of attack must be selected. Concentration of resources can be achieved in several ways:

1. Choose the most vulnerable market segment.
2. Choose products or markets that require response rates beyond a competitor's ability.
3. Choose products or markets which require capital that a competitor is unwilling to commit.
4. Recognize the commercial potentials of new technology early.
5. Exploit managerial differences in style, method, or system such as overhead rate, distribution channels, market image, or flexibility.

The value of the initiative depends on when and how the competition responds. Therefore, an effective strategy must choose the best initiative and also dissuade competition from responding. This is a fundamental strategic concept that is often neglected. Most strategic success depends upon the competition's decision not to compete. Therefore, strategic success almost always depends upon the ability to influence competitors' decisions. It is necessary to win in the mind of the competition.

Diversion and dissuasion fall into classic categories:

1. Appear to be unworthy of attention. Quickly cut off a part of the market which is too small to justify a major response. Repeat, and repeat, etc.
2. Appear to be unbeatable. Convince competition that if they follow your lead and practices, they will gain nothing since you will equal or better any market actions they take.
3. Avoid attention. Be secretive. Do not let competition know about new products, new policies or capabilities until it is too late to respond effectively.
4. Redirect attention. Focus competitive attention on the major volume areas of company sales, not the high potential areas.
5. Attract attention but discredit significance. Overstate and overpublicize the potentials of new products or policies.
6. Be apparently irrational. Take actions which seem emotional or impulsive but which make competitive investment unattractive.

These and other patterns have exact counterparts in military behavior. In business as in war, the lessons of experience teach the same thing.

. . . We can at least crystallize the lessons into two simple maxims—one negative, the other positive. The first is that, in the face of the overwhelming evidence of history, no general is justified in launching his troops in a direct attack upon an enemy firmly in position. The second, that instead of seeking to upset the enemy's equilibrium by one's attack, it must be upset before a real attack is, or can be, successfully launched.

(Liddell Hart, *Strategy*, Praeger)

Source: Bruce D. Henderson, "Business Strategy Concepts" (Boston: The Boston Consulting Group, Inc., 1969), Perspectives No. 61. Reprinted by permission.

APPENDIX B: PERSPECTIVES OF STRATEGIC THRUSTS

A. Start-Up

Definition: Introduction of new product or service with clear, significant technology breakthrough.

Objective: To develop a totally new industry to create and satisfy new demand where none existed before.

Requirements: Risk taking attitude of management; capital expenditures; expense.

Expected Results: Negative cash flow; low-to-negative returns; a leadership position in new industry.

B. Grow With Industry

Definition: To limit efforts to those necessary to maintain market share.

Objective: To free resources to correct market, product, management or production weaknesses.

Requirements: Management restraint; market intelligence; some capital and expense investments; time-limited strategy.

Expected Results: Stable market share; profit, cash flow and RONA not significantly worse than recent history, and fluctuating only as do industry averages.

C. Fast Grow

Definition: To pursue aggressively larger share and/or stronger position relative to competition.

Objective: To grow volume and share faster than competition and faster than general industry growth rate.

Requirements: Available resources for investment and follow up; risk taking management attitude; an appropriate investment strategy.

Expected Results: Higher market share; short term, perhaps lower returns; above average returns in longer term; competitive retaliation.

D. Attain Cost Leadership

Definition: To achieve lowest delivered costs relative to competition with acceptable quality levels.

Objective: To increase freedom to defend against powerful entries, strong customer blocks, vigorous competitors or potential substitute products.

Requirements: Relatively high market share; disciplined, persistent management efforts; favorable access to raw materials; substantial capital expenditures; aggressive pricing.

Expected Results: In early stages may result in start-up losses to build share; ultimately, high margins; relatively low capital turnover rates.

E. Differentiate

Definition: To achieve the highest degree of product/quality/service difference (as perceived by customers) in the industry with acceptable costs.

Objective: To insulate the company from switching, substitution, price competition, and strong blocks of customers or suppliers.

Requirements: Willingness to sacrifice high market share; careful target marketing; focused technological and market research; strong brand loyalty.

Expected Results: Possibly lowered market share; high margins; above average earnings; highly defensible position.

F. Focus

Definition: To select a particular segment of the market/product line more narrow in scope than competing firms.

Objective: To serve the strategic target area (geographic, product or market) more efficiently, more fully and more profitably than it can be served by broad line competitors.

Requirements: Disciplined management; persistent pursuit of well defined scope and mission; premium pricing; careful target selection.

Expected Results: Above average earnings; may be low-cost producer in its area; may attain high differentiation.

G. Renew

Definition: To restore the competitiveness of a product line in anticipation of future industry sales.

Objective: To overcome weakness in product/market mix in order to improve share, or to prepare for a new generation of demand, competition or substitute products.

Requirements: Strong enough competitive position to generate necessary resources for renewal efforts; capital and expense investments; management capable of taking risk; recognition of potential threats to existing line.

Expected Results: Short-term decline in sales, then sudden or gradual break-out of old volume/profit patterns.

H. Defend Position

Definition: To insure that relative competitive position is stable or improved.

Objective: To create barriers which make it difficult, costly and risky for competitors, suppliers, customer blocks or new entries to erode your firm's market share, profitability and growth.

Requirements: Establishment of one or more of the following: proprietary technology; strong brand; protected sourcing; favorable locations; economies of scale; government protection; exclusive distribution; or customer loyalty.

Expected Results: Stable or increasing market share.

I. Harvest

Definition: To convert market share or competitive position into higher returns.

Objective: To bring returns up to industry averages by trading, leasing or selling technology, distribution rights, patents, brands, production capacity, locations or exclusive sources to competitors. '

Requirements: A better than average market share; rights to entry or mobility barriers that the industry values; alternative investment opportunities.

Expected Results: Sudden surge in profitability and return; a gradual decline of position, perhaps leading to withdrawal strategy.

J. Find Niche

Definition: To opt for retaining a small, defensible portion of the available market rather than withdraw.

Objective: To define the opportunity so narrowly that large competitors with broad lines do not find it attractive enough to dislodge you.

Requirements: "Think Small" management style; alternative uses for excess production capacity; reliable sources for supplies and materials; superior quality and/or service with selected sector.

Expected Results: Pronounced decline in volume and share; improved return in medium to longer term.

K. Hold Niche

Definition: To protect a narrow position in the larger product/market arena from larger competitors.

Objective: To create barriers (real or imagined) which make it unattractive for competitors, suppliers or customer blocks to enter your segment or switch to alternative products.

Requirements: Designing, building and promoting "switching costs" into your product.

Expected Results: Lower than industry average returns, but steady and acceptable.

L. Catch-Up

Definition: To make up for poor or late entry into an industry by aggressive product/market activities.

Objective: To overcome early gains made by first entrants into the market by careful choice of optimum product, production, distribution, promotion and marketing tactics.

Requirements: Management capable of taking risk in flexible environment; resources to make high investments of capital and expense; corporate understanding of short-term low returns; probably necessary to dislodge weak competitors.

Expected Results: Low to negative returns in near term; should result in favorable to strong position by late growth stage of industry.

M. Hang-In

Definition: To prolong existence of the unit in anticipation of some specific favorable change in the environment.

Objective: To continue funding a tenable (or better) unit only long enough to take advantage of unusual opportunity known to be at hand; this might take the form of patent expiration, management change, government action, technology breakthrough, or socioeconomic shift.

Requirements: Clear view of expected environmental shift; a management willing and able to sustain poor performance; opportunity and resources to capitalize on new environment; a time limit.

Expected Results: Poorer than average performance, perhaps losses; later, substantial growth and high returns.

N. Turnaround

Definition: To overcome inherent, severe weaknesses in performance in a limited time.

Objective: To halt further declines in share and/or volume; to bring about at least stability, or preferably a small improvement in position; to protect the line from competitive and substitute products.

Requirements: Fast action to prevent disaster; reductions or redirection to reduce losses; change in morale.

Expected Results: Stable condition and average performance.

O. Retrench

Definition: To cut back investment in the business and reduce level of risk and exposure to losses.

Objective: To stop unacceptable losses or risks; to prepare the business for divestment or withdrawal; to strip away loss operations in hopes of exposing a "little jewel."

Requirements: Highly disciplined management system; good communication with employees to prevent wholesale departures; clear strategic objective and timetable.

Expected Results: Reduced losses or modestly improved performance.

P. Divest

Definition: To strip the business of some or all of its assets through sale of the product line, brands, distribution facilities or production capacity.

Objective: To recover losses sustained through earlier strategic errors; to free up funds for alternative corporate investments; to abandon part or all of a business to competition.

Requirements: Assets desirable to others competing or desiring to compete in the industry; a recognition of the futility of further investments.

Expected Results: Increase in cash flow; reduction of asset base; probable reduction in performance levels and/or losses.

Q. Withdraw

Definition: To remove the business from competition.

Objective: To take back from the business whatever corporate assets or expenses can be recovered through shut-down, sale, auction or scrapping of operations.

Requirements: A decision to abandon; a caretaker management; a phased timetable; a public relations plan.

Expected Results: Losses and write offs.

Source: Arthur D. Little, Inc. Reprinted by permission.

CASE 9
Apple Computer, Inc.

A familiar sight at the headquarters of Apple Computer, Inc., in Cupertino, California, is a boyish-looking fellow sporting a stringy mustache and often wearing jeans, boots, and a cowboy shirt. His name is Steven Jobs, and at age 28 he is chairman of the board of a company that in 1982 had sales of $583 million.

Steve Jobs grew up in California in an area known as Silicon Valley, because tiny semiconductors made with chips of silicon were first manufactured there at the end of the 1960s. During the early 1970s Jobs attended high school in Los Altos, where he developed an interest in technology. He also began a friendship with a fellow named Stephen Wozniak. Pooling their talents, the two Steves built and sold so-called blue boxes, which were illegal electronic attachments for telephones that allowed users to make long-distance calls for free.

Jobs entered college in 1972 in Oregon. His college career lasted for only two years because of financial hardships. After dropping out, he took a position at Atari, designing video games. His close friend, Steve Wozniak, had also dropped out of college (Berkeley) to work at Hewlett-Packard as a designer. On his own time, Wozniak began working on the construction of a small computer, and in 1976 he succeeded with a machine about the size of a portable typewriter.

Steve Wozniak did not fully appreciate the commercial potential of his new creation. To him, it was more of a gadget to impress fellow computer hobbyists. Jobs, on the other hand, felt that the invention had real market potential and urged that they form a company. The two raised $1,300 to open a makeshift production line by selling Jobs's Volkswagen Microbus and Wozniak's Hewlett-Packard scientific calculator. Jobs wanted the new computer to be something personal that one could easily become familiar with. He rejected any technical-sounding names for the new computer as being inconsistent with this goal. Remembering the pleasant times he had had working in the orchards of Oregon, he selected the name Apple.

Silicon Valley, meanwhile, had developed quite a reputation for having an effective start-up support network for new companies. Says Jobs:

This case was prepared by Mark Kever, George Macias, John Sanders, and Ken Schoenherr, under the supervision of Professor Sexton Adams, North Texas State University, and Professor Adelaide Griffin, Texas Woman's University. It is printed here with the permission of Professors Sexton Adams and Adelaide Griffin.

"We didn't know what the hell we were doing, but we were very careful observers and learned quickly." Jobs persuaded a public relations specialist to take on Apple as a client. On the recommendation of his former boss at Atari and the public relations firm, Jobs contacted Don Valentine, a venture capitalist, to seek funds for the new company. When Valentine made a visit to inspect the new computer, he found Jobs dressed in cutoff jeans and sandals, wearing shoulder-length hair and a Ho Chi Minh beard. Valentine later recalled his first impression of Jobs: "a renegade from the human race."

Don Valentine did, however, mention the new company to A. C. (Mike) Markkula, formerly a marketing manager at Intel (a manufacturer of computer chips) and Fairchild Semiconductor. Markkula was so impressed with the new company's potential that he put up $250,000 of his own money and became an equal partner with Jobs and Wozniak. One of Markkula's first acts was to arrange a credit line with the Bank of America. He also persuaded two venture capital firms to invest in Apple.

From the very beginning, things went very well for the new company. The original computer was redesigned and called the Apple II. The company also designed instruction manuals to make the computer much easier to use. Sales were $2.7 million in 1977 and just three years later, in 1980, the young company had sales of $200 million.

The sudden growth, however, had not been without problems. In the words of Markkula, the problem was "to keep the race car on the track." According to Markkula, the 1980 introduction of Apple III, a more powerful version of Apple II, was premature because of enormous market pressures. The Apple III had to be reworked before it met its specifications and was temporarily withdrawn from the market. As a result, 40 employees were fired, and the project manager of Apple III resigned.

Apple is now at a very critical time. A multitude of aggressive competitors have entered the market. Tandy Corporation's Radio Shack, with its 8,400 retail outlets, has a market share equal to that of Apple. Xerox has a computer nicknamed "The Worm" because they claim it can eat an Apple. More important, however, is the fact that IBM, the computer industry giant, has entered the field.

In addition to competitive threats, Apple must deal with maintaining a superior management team. Although Steve Wozniak is a major shareholder, he is not active in company affairs. Mr. Markkula is retiring and is to be succeeded by John Sculley, former president of PepsiCo, Inc. Jobs, who took a company that six years ago didn't exist and built it to $1 billion, must demonstrate that he has the expertise to guide a major corporation.

THE PERSONAL COMPUTER INDUSTRY

Since 1977—when Apple Computer, Inc., first introduced the personal computer—the market for this product has grown dramatically. Worldwide computer shipments of U.S.-based manufacturers, which totaled $29.4 billion in 1981, up 12 percent from a year earlier, are expected to rise some 16 percent annually between 1981 and 1986, according to International Data Corporation, a Waltham, Massachusetts, research firm. The personal computer segment of this industry, which is still in its infancy, is expected to show the most vigorous expansion over the next five years. Personal computers, which currently hold 10 percent of the total computer market, should increase their market share to about 30 percent in 1986, according to IDC. The value of these shipments, which was $3.0 billion in 1981, up nearly 70 percent from $1.8 billion a year earlier, is projected to increase at a compounded annual rate of about 43.5 percent over the next five years.

Growth in the personal computer segment is spurred by improved software, lower hardware costs, and the search by many industries for ways to increase productivity. Which type of software will solve the user's problem is a question constantly asked by potential purchasers of hardware, as buyers have become much more software conscious. *Visi-Calc,* a powerful management software package, was the first major breakthrough in personal computer software and, according to Rosen Research, Inc., has proved to be one of the most effective hardware-selling software products ever.

The largest personal computer market is the business/professional market, which accounted for more than half of the U.S. personal computer units shipped in 1981. Market sources have projected a very healthy growth rate for this segment—some 50 percent through 1986, in dollar-value terms. This high rate can be attributed to the very large number of potential buyers, from one-person businesses to large corporations that need to increase productivity, and the increasing applications and capabilities of the machine. Businesses have discovered that white-collar productivity has been declining and that new information/analysis tools are needed to solve this problem. Some advantages of personal computers are their "user-friendly" feature, the advantage of not adding to the mainframe load, and the ability to link personal computers to form a load network capable of performing several of the functions of an automated office, such as word processing and electronic mail.

The dollar volume of the home/hobby market is expected to grow at a compounded annual rate of about 40 percent through 1986. This rate could be spurred by the continuing decline in hardware costs and increased exposure of people to computers at school and at work. Given the 80 million households in the United States, the potential of home/hobby buyers is very large. Sales of lower-priced ($100–$1000) home computers have been particularly brisk, benefiting from the popularity of video games.

The scientific/engineering market of the personal computer segment is the third largest in terms of units. This market is expected to grow at a compounded annual rate of 15 to 20 percent in dollar terms through 1986.

The educational market, currently the smallest, is expected to grow at a compounded annual rate of 15 percent through 1986. This market is important because exposure to a computer in school may encourage the user—and perhaps the user's parents—to buy a personal computer. This could also lead to increased business sales.

The current trends in the personal computer industry can be summarized as a shrinking in computer size, a decline in hardware costs, and an increase in the number of personal computer vendors. A newer trend is a move to a 16-bit machine versus the old 8-bit. The 16-bit computer allows more computing power, which is especially useful in the business/professional and scientific markets.

Many large computer manufacturers have been experiencing a stagnant mainframe market and have turned to the personal computer market for new growth. IBM, for instance, introduced its version of the personal computer in August, 1981, and is currently shipping over 20,000 units per month. The increasing number of new vendors is not expected to last, and a gradual shakeout is likely to occur over the next few years. John J. McDonald, president of CISIO, Inc. (a Japanese firm), predicts that firms will be unable to maintain profitability with less than 15 percent market share and at least $100 million in revenues. Joel Schwartz, vice-president of DEC, also predicts that the personal computer market will be dominated by the large companies. David Gold, an industry consultant, predicts that only a handful of the new firms will survive. Firms will either be acquired, go out of business, or end up as small companies with unique applications. The next three to five years should witness an era of price-cutting and intense competition.

Another factor to be considered is the entry of Japanese manufacturers. Initial predictions were that the Japanese would obtain 50 percent of the personal computer market by 1985. That forecast has since been reduced to a maximum of 25 percent. The primary reason for this reduction is that domestic Japanese demand has increased so rapidly that local manufacturers are hard pressed to satisfy their domestic market. Industry analysts agree, however, that the Japanese will be a major factor in the personal computer market within the next few years.

Exhibit 9-12 illustrates the trend of the personal computer (sometimes called the desktop computer) segment of the total computer industry.

THE COMPETITION

Competition within the personal computer market is intense as companies scramble for market share and new technological breakthroughs. Currently there are three major competitive threats confronting Apple Computer, Inc., but instabilities within the market could cause a sudden change in the lineup. Now, however, those firms most competitive to Apple are Commodore, Tandy, and IBM.

EXHIBIT 9-12   The Changing Structure of the Computer Market

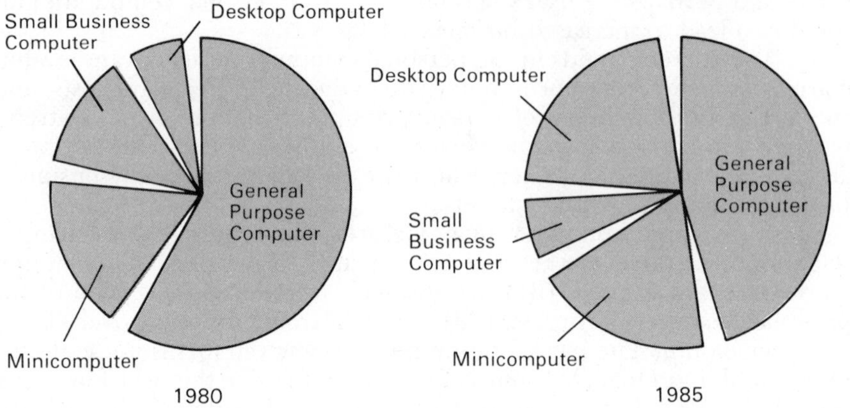

Source: "The Incredible Explosion of Startups," *Business Week,* August 2, 1982,
          p. 63.

Commodore

Commodore International sold $275 million in personal computers
in 1982, ranking it number four in the market. Industry analysts see the
company's strength in its highly functional, low-priced system. Commodore says that it wants to be known as the American Japanese entry. "Our
strategy is to offer more versatility in a single desktop computer with pe-
ripherals built in at a lower price than anyone else," says Michael Tom-
czyk, Commodore product marketing manager. "We are more Japanese
in our thinking than any Western company because we have been doing
business in Japan for a decade."

Commodore recently intensified its efforts in the video game market by stressing that its products could compute as well as play games. In
1983, Commodore intends to stress price and performance. The message
in their ad campaign will emphasize: "Why buy a simple ordinary home
computer when you can buy a more powerful one that can be used both
at home and at work?"

Commodore spends little on research and development. They have
no national sales force and do not plan to create one. Their success in
tapping the home market, however, has encouraged other producers to
make cost-cutting moves and emphasize new product introductions.

Tandy (Radio Shack)

Tandy's TRS-80 Model I was a pioneer product that quickly gained
acceptance and captured a significant market share in the home and small-

business market. Tandy is currently targeting *Fortune* 1000 firms and small businesses. Tandy has an established distribution channel through its Radio Shack stores which has enabled it to be one of the market leaders in the personal computer market. All of the company's 6,460 stores stock the personal computers. Tandy also distributes its more powerful computers through computer centers and its 480 Super Shacks.

Along with good retail marketing, Tandy offers good service and support. Service has been a problem for most companies, but because of its already existing service centers Tandy has provided excellent service to its customers. According to industry experts, Tandy is fortunate to have such a good service network because some of its products suffer from an image of poor quality. Its TRS-80 line was nicknamed the TRASH-80, and that nickname has persisted in industry circles. Poor quality has probably stemmed from one of Tandy's weaknesses—lack of qualified personnel, from the computer divisions management down to the line workers.

IBM

In August, 1981, IBM entered the personal computer market and rapidly captured one-third of the market. IBM sold 200,000 units in 1982 and could double that figure in 1983. Mike Markkula declares that Apple's three biggest rivals are "IBM, IBM, and IBM."

The IBM personal computer offers attractive features and pricing, easy expandability, and most important, the IBM name. IBM is everywhere in corporate America, its image and presence almost intimidating the other manufacturers. Says Charles Johnson of Wang, "IBM sells on their image; we have to sell ourselves first, then the product second."

Software abounds for the IBM personal computer and hundreds of new compatible programs are being created on the assumption that it will eventually be the dominant model. IBM markets only 39 of its own titles; nearly 1,200 are produced by outside programmers. A marketing rule of thumb in the computer business says that the more programs the computer can use, the more attractive it is for the buyer.

IBM has a network of strategically located dealers and company-owned stores in the largest markets. IBM is also attuned to the potential in the farmer-rancher market and displays a presence in small communities as well. It also utilizes 600 retailers to move its product. IBM is industry renowned for the quality of its sales force. Because IBM mainframes are already installed in many companies, the sales force already has a well-established relationship with potential customers for the personal computer.

Exhibit 9-13 presents major product comparisons.

ORGANIZATION OF APPLE COMPUTER, INC.

During Apple's early days, when the company had just a few hundred employees and a single major product on the market, its organizational

EXHIBIT 9-13 Competitor Model Comparison

COMPUTER	RADIO SHACK TRS-80 MODEL III	COMMODORE PET	IBM PERSONAL	APPLE II PLUS	APPLE III
HARDWARE					
RAM Memory	4k to 48k	16k to 32k	16k to 256k	48k to 64k	128k to 256k
ROM Memory	4k or 14k	18k	40k	12k	4k
B/W Display	yes	yes	yes	yes	yes
Color Display	no	no	yes	yes	yes
Graphics	64 char. + dot graphics	128 full-screen char.	line graphic char.	15 colors	15 colors
Keyboard	basic + keypad	basic	83 key, keypad, func. keys	basic	basic + keypad
SOFTWARE					
Languages	basic cobol, pascal, author, pilot, fortran	basic	basic, cobol, pascal, fortran	basic, cobol, pascal	basic, pascal
Documentation	20 books, manuals	about 12 manuals	2 manuals	about 100 manuals	about 100 manuals
CONSUMER INFO					
Support	dealer training	none	dealer train.	none	none
Maintenance	dealer on-site	dealer	dealer	on-site	on-site
Warranty	90 days p + 1	90 days p + 1	90 days	90 days	90 days
APPLICATIONS					
Personal Inv.	yes	yes	yes	yes	yes
Invest. Mgmt.	yes	yes	yes	yes	yes
Personal Fin.	yes	yes	yes	yes	yes
Research	yes	yes	yes	yes	yes
Games	yes	yes	yes	yes	yes
Writing/Editing Text	yes	yes	yes	yes	yes
Base List Price	$699 to $2295	$995 to $1295	$1565	$1530	$3495

Source: "How to Buy a Home Computer," *Forbes*, August 2, 1982, p. 64.

structure was simple: a few managers backed by small staffs performing whatever needed to be done. With unparalleled growth, however, Apple restructured its organization to be certain that activities received the proper attention. Apple's organization is still designed loosely and for maximum freedom and flexibility. The structure is evolving week by week into new areas of specialization and organization form.

Apple's various teams work together and support one another, for Apple is, in fact, a team of teams working together to achieve its goals. The company's flexible, decentralized structure tries to ensure enough freedom for individual creativity. According to Steven Jobs, the management philosophy is "to give people enough rope to hang themselves." Apple hires specialists to instruct the company what to do. Jobs describes his position as being "to help run the company and [plan] the directions we ought to go in."

There are two types of divisions within Apple—product divisions, responsible for developing and manufacturing the various products, and the product support divisions, which handle marketing, distribution, and post-sale support. There are, in addition, a number of administrative departments such as finance, legal, and human resources.

In August of 1980, Apple Computer went through a major restructuring phase. Michael M. Scott was demoted from president to vice-president and lost most of his authority after he fired 40 mid- to upper-level managers. He later resigned. Scott's management style was termed, "decisive, authoritarian and insensitive." Soon after this "shakeout" one Apple executive was quoted as saying: "There seems to be so little control and so much chaos that I can't believe the company isn't flying off into space in a thousand pieces. On the other hand, it does seem to keep pulling off its plans." A veteran manager of the semiconductor industry describes the company as "Camp Run Amok."

Exhibit 9-14 presents a list of officers and directors of Apple Computer, Inc.

Key Management Personnel

Stephen G. Wozniak co-founded Apple Computer in 1977. He served as secretary of the company from 1977 to 1980 and as a director from 1977 to 1978. He also has held the position of vice-president of research and development. Although Wozniak remains a major shareholder, he is no longer active in company affairs. He has returned to Berkeley, where he is pursuing the completion of his college studies. Wozniak received the Grace Murray Hopper Award from the Association for Computing Machinery for his contributions to the computer industry. He has been generous with his recently acquired wealth, giving nearly $3 million in Apple stock to his parents and other family members.

A. C. Markkula was promoted to president and CEO in March, 1981. He previously held the position of chairman of the board and vice-president of marketing. Markkula was formerly with Intel Corporation, where

EXHIBIT 9-14   Apple Computer, Inc.: Officers and Directors

OFFICERS
> A. C. Markkula, Jr.—President and Chief Executive Officer
> Kenneth R. Zerbe—Executive Vice-President, Finance and Administration
> Albert A. Eisenstat—Vice-President, Secretary, and General Counsel
> Joseph A. Graziano—Vice-President and Chief Financial Officer
> Gene P. Carter—Vice-President, Sales
> S. P. Jobs—Chairman and Vice-President
> C. H. Carlson—Executive Vice-President, Operations

DIRECTORS
> P. O. Crisp—a founding and managing partner of Venrock Associates, a limited partnership formed by the Rockefeller family to invest in technology-based firms.
> P. S. Schlein—chairman of the board and chief executive officer of Macy's California.
> Arthur Rock—former general partner of Arthur Rock and Associates, venture capitalists. Currently a limited partner of a San Francisco–based investment banking firm.
> H. E. Singleton—chairman of the board and chief executive officer of Teledyne, Inc., a diversified manufacturing company.
> A. C. Markkula, Jr.
> S. P. Jobs

Source: Apple Computer, Inc., 1982 Annual Report.

he spent four years as marketing manager. Markkula was also a product marketing manager for Fairchild Semiconductor Corporation as well as a former member of the technical staff of the research and development laboratory at Hughes Aircraft Corporation. An electrical engineer, he received his B.S. and M.S. degrees from the University of Southern California. Markkula plans to retire shortly from his position but remain as a director and consultant, doing long-range research and planning for Apple. He describes his new title as "Markkula-at-large."

Stephen P. Jobs co-founded Apple Computer in 1977, and has served as vice-president and director since that time. He has also served as chairman of the board since March, 1981. Previously he held the position of vice-chairman of the board. Prior to 1977, he worked as a design engineer for Atari, Inc., a computer games manufacturer. He attended Reed College in Portland, Oregon, but did not receive a degree. Overseeing Apple's growth has kept Jobs too busy to spend the millions he has earned. His Tudor-style house in Los Altos Hills is essentially empty because he has not decided how to furnish it. As an executive, Jobs has sometimes been petulant and harsh on subordinates. He says, "I've got to learn to keep my feelings private."

The newest addition to the Apple team is John Sculley, former president of PepsiCo, Inc. He replaces Markkula as president and CEO. Sculley is passing up an opportunity at Pepsi to become chairman of the board because he says he has to be totally turned on to what he is doing. He sees the computer business as being where the soft-drink business was ten years ago. Sculley has long had an interest in technology. He applied for a cathode-ray-tube patent at age 14, built projection television sets while a student at Brown University, and designed his house in Greenwich, Connecticut. Sculley has a bachelor's degree in architecture but later attended business school. He joined Pepsi as a trainee but worked his way up to president where he built Pepsi into a strong number two behind Coke. He describes Pepsi as "a Marine boot camp" and believes Apple has a similar work-hard ethic. Apple considered more than 126 executives for the job but selected Sculley because of his broad domestic and international management and marketing experience. Additionally, his experience in motivating franchised Pepsi bottlers to sell Pepsi-Cola will help him build dealer loyalty at Apple. To induce Sculley to leave a very promising career at Pepsi, Apple will pay him a $1-million bonus when he starts, $1 million in salary and bonus the first year and $1 million in severance pay if he leaves. He also gets a package of "wealth creation" benefits, including options on 350,000 shares of Apple stock and financial help in buying a $2-million Tudor-style house with a kidney-shaped pool in Woodside, California.

Product Line

There was nothing really new in the first Apple. It was just a small board fixed up to do simple things for an individual, rather than for a professional data processing department. When it became evident that there was real demand for such a product, the prototype was redesigned and christened Apple II. With a capacity of 48 thousand bits of memory storage and a compatibility with virtually every major software system available, the Apple II quickly became one of the top-selling personal computers.

As the computer industry exploded throughout the 1970s, it became evident that the Apple II would be unable to meet growing business demands. As a result, in 1978, the Apple II Plus was introduced. This revised model upgraded memory to 64K, expanded its software capability, allowed itself to be adapted with more peripheral accessories (printers, disk drives, etc.), and more important, maintained cost compatibility with comparable units already in the marketplace.

In 1979 the company unveiled the Apple III, and from the start things began to go wrong. Production delays and design foul-ups kept the computer from being released earlier. After it was released, reports started coming in regarding safety hazards. Overheating terminals and electrical current surges were common complaints. The Apple III was withdrawn from the market and later reintroduced after improvements had been made.

The Apple III is a more powerful version of the Apple II and as of 1983 its sales are doing very well.

The Apple IIe ("e" standing for enhanced) was introduced in early 1983. Walt Broedner, co-designer, and David Larson, marketing coordinator for the IIe, were given the task of redesigning the Apple II Plus to include the best features of modern machines, make it less expensive to manufacture, make it compatible with the thousands of Apple II software packages, and do it quickly. Working alone and with hardware design manager Peter Quinn, Broedner created two custom computer chips within 22 weeks, and Larson was able to demonstrate a fully operational Apple IIe, complete with an expanded keyboard, 128K memory capacity, lowercase and uppercase typing capability, and a more efficient cooling system.

In 1980 Apple began work on a new machine named LISA (local integrated software architecture) and spent $50 million developing it. Although the LISA was introduced in early 1983, it won't be available to most customers until about June, Apple estimates. This new system is viewed as state-of-the-art in computer technology. Instead of having to learn complex languages to operate the machine, type cumbersome commands, and limit the computer to only a few tasks at a time, LISA enables the user to use the keyboard only for data entry, uses icons (graphics symbols) to replace commands and task descriptions, and employs an electronic pointer called a "mouse." The mouse replaces a cursor and enables the user to select functions and tasks without ever referring to the keyboard. Although LISA is targeted for *Fortune* 1000 companies, price may be a major issue. At $10,000, LISA is in the high end of the market, according to Egil Juliussen of *Future Computing*. In addition to price, Juliussen stresses that LISA's novelty will be an issue and it will be about a year before companies start deciding to make volume purchases. Finally, companies want to be assured that Apple will be able to provide the maintenance and program advice that a company like IBM is famous for.

Work is currently under way on a computer called the "Macintosh" that will utilize elements of LISA technology but will cost less and aim at a different market. The Macintosh will have a video screen, disk drive, and keyboard integrated into one unit which can be transported easily by an individual. The unit will be encased in a soft container and weigh only about 24 pounds. The machine is a 16-bit computer and will have a minimum of 64K random access memory, improved over the old Apple II, which had an 8-bit computer. Additionally, Macintosh will have the "mouse" feature as on the LISA. Enabling the user to obtain operational ability in only four to eight hours is the goal of the Macintosh design team. This compares to approximately twenty hours with the Apple II. The computer is expected to sell for $1,000 when introduced. It was originally decided that production of the Macintosh would take place in the Carrollton, Texas, facility. One building was cleared out specifically to set up work on Macintosh. Project managers were chosen from within the firm and several high-level individuals were hired from Xerox and Texas Instruments to bolster the program. In order to avoid past production problems, an expensive "bench-made" computerized process was to be utilized in production. Just as final production plans were being completed, a memo was received from Steven Jobs instructing the Carrollton facility that the entire production project was being moved to Cupertino, near corporate headquarters.

Marketing, Distribution, and Servicing

Apple does not have the army of direct salespeople that is characteristic of IBM. For this reason it has relied strongly on the ties forged with the over 1,400 retail outlets that sell its computers. Among its other marketing tools are sales and product training, toll-free software hot lines manned by applications specialists, monthly newsletters, and a handsome magazine that focuses on a particular application area in each issue.

There is also the Apple Means Business (AMB) Program, which is designed to help dealers go after targeted markets. AMB provides dealers with a series of objectives and a method of obtaining those objectives. For example, to make dealers more sales productive, Apple designed sales seminars, for 6 to 20 prospects at a time, built around a single application, and created structured presentations the dealers could use, along with a kit of 172 color slides for illustrating the various applications. The dealers are then given tips on seminar organization and post-meeting follow-up.

Apple, in 1983, appointed E. Floyd Kvamme as executive vice-president of marketing and sales with the primary mission of getting Apple into the overseas market and into American offices. Assisting Kvamme in his efforts is the National Accounts Program to service large customers. This program was also implemented in anticipation of forthcoming products. Sculley, the newly designated president, wants Apple to become a bigger factor in the market for small office computers, selling whole systems rather than individual units.

Two areas that IBM excels at, a direct selling force and a highly rated dealer network, have presented problems for Apple. Apple has a very small sales force, but it is expanding. Also, Apple was plagued by a rash of sales by its retail outlets to wholesalers, who then sold the machines at discounts. Apple then refused to service computers not sold through an authorized dealer. The problem really became a question of dealer loyalty. Most retail store outlets, however, usually give shelf preference and advertising support to the model that sells, and currently IBM is selling. "IBM's approach is like the classic Procter & Gamble approach," says the advertising executive that handles Texas Instruments. "If you can sell the consumer, you don't have to sell the grocery store managers in addition."

To meet this challenge, Apple has been making use of TV and magazine advertising. Magazine double gatefolds illustrate the dozens of ways the personal computer can be used from talking to animals to catching a thief, thus using a funny/informational route. Apple also inserted a booklet in *Fortune* and other business publications entitled: "What the average business person doesn't know about personal computers could fill a 12-page ad." Paul Wiefels, manager of product advertising, explains Apple's ad philosophy: "People don't fundamentally understand what computers are all about. While other advertisers are talking about 28K versus 48K, we attempt to educate, to show how the personal computer will make meaningful contributions to their lives." Exhibit 9-15 presents media expenditures by manufacturers.

In the area of service, both Apple and IBM rely on authorized dealers to provide routine repairs. More complicated repairs are provided at regional service centers, of which Apple has six and IBM has fifteen. Additionally, service contracts providing for on-site coverage of Apple hardware are not offered by every authorized Apple dealer. Service contracts are available at all authorized dealers if the customer is willing to carry equipment into Apple-authorized service centers.

Financial Matters

Apple's first four years of operation were financed by private investment and venture capital. The first public offering was in December, 1980, when 96.8 million common shares were sold at $22 a share. Apple's steady record of earnings advances has endeared the firm to Wall Street; the stock traded at $43 a share on March 30, 1983, and moved to $52 by the end of April. According to *Value Line*, there is little reason to expect the earnings trend to be broken.

EXHIBIT 9-15   Personal Computer Media Expenditures (January through September, 1983)

	Total	Magazines	News Supps	TV	Radio
Apple	$3,450.2	$3,110.3		$ 87.1	$232.0
Commodore	650.9	650.9			
Digital	482.8	482.8			
IBM	3,620.4	3,307.0	313.4		
Osborne	1,069.3	954.3		115.0	
Sinclair	1,286.9	1,245.5	19.8	21.6	
Tandy (TRS80)	2,027.8	652.3		1,375.5	
Texas Instruments	3,183.8			3,183.8	
Timex	2,058.9	756.9		1,302.5	
Wang	918.0	720.7		197.3	
Warner (Atari)	7,786.4	1,306.0		6,480.1	
Xerox	274.0	274.0			

Note: Figures are in thousands of dollars.

Source: *Marketing & Media Decisions*, February, 1983, p. 144.

EXHIBIT 9-16   Apple Computer, Inc.: Consolidated Statement of Income

	Year ended September 24,		
(in thousands, except per-share amounts)	1982	1981	1980
Net sales	$583,061	$334,783	$117,126
Cost and expenses:			
Cost of sales	288,001	170,124	66,490
Research and development	37,979	20,956	7,282
Marketing and distribution	119,945	55,369	12,619
General and administrative	34,927	22,191	7,150
	$480,852	$268,640	$ 93,541
Operating income	102,209	66,143	23,585
Interest, net	14,563	10,400	567
Income before taxes on income	$116,772	$ 76,543	$ 24,152
Provision for taxes on income	55,466	37,123	12,454
Net income	$ 61,306	$ 39,420	$ 11,698
Earnings per common and common			
equivalent share	$ 1.06	$ .70	$ .24
Common and common equivalent shares			
used in the calculation of earnings per			
share	57,798	56,161	48,412

Source: Apple Computer, Inc., 1982 Annual Report.

Apple makes use of cash management techniques by encouraging dealers to pay in full within two weeks but usually takes six weeks to pay its own suppliers. Exhibits 9-16 through 9-19 present financial data on Apple Computer, Inc.

Research and Development

Apple maintains a continuing program of research and development. Apple is developing personal computer systems to address new markets and applications, including products for use in the office automation and information-processing segments of the business and office market. Several major products resulting from this effort will be announced in 1983, including enhancements to the present line. Investment in research and development was 6.5 percent of sales in fiscal 1982, a total of $38 million or 81 percent more than in 1981. Exhibit 9-20 illustrates Apple's increasing emphasis on research and development.

Plant and Facilities

Apple's dramatic rise in revenues has been matched by its facility expansion. In a little over six years Apple has grown from a company housed in a two-car garage to a company with over 1.5 million square feet

EXHIBIT 9-17   Apple Computer, Inc.: Consolidated Balance Sheet

(in thousands)	Year ended Sept. 24, 1982	Sept. 25, 1981
Assets		
Current assets:		
Cash and temporary cash investments	$153,056	$ 72,834
Accounts receivable, not of allowance for doubtful accounts of $3,606 ($1,823 in 1981)	71,478	42,330
Inventories	81,229	103,873
Other current assets	11,312	8,067
Total current assets	317,075	227,104
Property, plant and equipment:		
Land and buildings	7,220	4,815
Machinery and equipment	26,136	14,688
Office furniture and equipment	13,423	6,192
Leasehold improvements	10,515	5,129
	57,294	30,824
Accumulated depreciation and amortization	(22,811)	(8,453)
Net property, plant and equipment	34,483	22,371
Other assets	6,229	5,363
	$357,787	$254,838
Liabilities and Shareholders' Equity		
Current liabilities:		
Notes payable to banks	$ 4,185	$ 10,745
Accounts payable	25,125	26,613
Accrued compensation and employee benefits	11,774	7,759
Income taxes payable	15,307	8,621
Accrued advertising	8,815	3,540
Other current liabilities	20,550	13,002
Total current liabilities	85,756	70,280
Non-current obligations under capital leases	2,052	1,909
Deferred taxes on income	12,887	5,262
Shareholders' equity:		
Common stock, no par value, 160,000,000 shares authorized	141,070	123,317
Retained earnings	118,332	57,026
	259,402	180,343
Notes receivable from shareholders	(2,310)	(2,956)
Total shareholders' equity	257,092	177,387
	$357,787	$254,838

Source: Apple Computer, Inc., 1982 Annual Report.

EXHIBIT 9-18   Apple Computer, Inc.: Consolidated Statement of Changes in Financial Position

(in thousands)	Year ended September 24, 1982	1981	1980
Working capital was provided by:			
Operations:			
Net income	$ 61,306	$ 39,420	$ 11,698
Charges to operations not affecting working capital:			
—Depreciation & amortization	16,556	8,590	1,377
—Deferred taxes on income (non-current) ..	7,625	4,311	747
Total working capital provided by operations	$ 85,487	$ 52,321	$ 13,822
Increases in common stock and related tax benefits, net of changes in notes receivable from shareholders ...	18,399	112,019	4,569
Increases in non-current obligations under capital leases	1,172	1,747	752
Total working capital provided	$105,058	$166,087	$ 19,143
Working capital was applied to:			
Purchase of property, plant & equipment, net	$ 26,470	$ 24,529	$ 4,878
Reacquisition of distribution rights	—	—	5,401
Other	4,093	1,060	1,298
Total working capital applied	$ 30,563	$ 25,589	$ 11,577
Increase in working capital	$ 74,495	$140,498	$ 7,566
Increase (decrease) in working capital by component:			
Cash and temporary cash investments	80,222	72,471	(200)
Accounts receivable	29,148	26,516	6,688
Inventories	(22,644)	69,682	24,089
Other current assets	3,245	4,329	3,685
Notes payable to banks	6,560	(2,895)	(7,850)
Accounts payable	1,488	(12,118)	(9,084)
Accrued compensation & employee benefits	(4,015)	(5,206)	(1,727)
Income taxes payable	(6,686)	(486)	(4,205)
Accrued advertising and other current liabilities	(12,823)	(11,795)	(3,830)
Increase in working capital	$ 74,495	$140,498	$ 7,566

Source: Apple Computer, Inc., 1982 Annual Report.

EXHIBIT 9-19   Apple Computer, Inc.: Selected Financial Information

(in thousands, except per-share amounts)	Year ended September 24,				
	1982	1981	1980	1979	1978
Net sales	$583,061	$334,783	$117,126	$47,867	$ 7,856
Net income	61,306	39,420	11,698	5,073	793
Earnings per common and common equivalent share ...	1.06	.70	.24	.12	.03
Common and common equivalent shares used in the calculation of earnings per share	57,798	56,161	48,412	43,620	31,544
Cash and temporary cash investments ..	153,056	72,834	363	563	775
Total assets	357,787	254,838	65,350	21,171	4,341
Non-current obligations under capital leases	$ 2,052	$ 1,909	$ 671	$ 203	$ ——

Source: Apple Computer, Inc., 1982 Annual Report.

of office and manufacturing facilities. Currently, Apple has manufacturing plants in California, Texas, Ireland, and Singapore. Apple's corporate office is located in Cupertino, California. Of the total 1.5 million square feet, over 50 percent is dedicated to manufacturing.

Apple management is very proud of its procedures for new facility implementation. It has a facility crew of five people who oversee the movement into new facilities from the time the request is made until the final person is in place. At one point Apple made five separate facility moves in ten days with zero production slowdown. This was all accomplished through careful planning and, of course, through use of Apple computers. Managers are asked to forecast space and personnel requirements for the next few years.

Apple has increased efficiency and reduced inventories and warehousing, storage, and handling costs by what it calls "just in time" scheduling. This is the procedure of taking daily delivery of inventory material. Raw materials are delivered on an as-needed basis for the manufacture of the finished goods.

Management measures its productivity very meticulously, paying attention to small details. With increased emphasis on automation, Apple hopes to increase productivity with its existing facilities. Greater utilization of its plants is one of the goals of management in 1983. Management expects to double capacity in 1983 within its existing plants.

Litigation and Copycats

Apple Computer is involved in both defending itself and actively seeking relief from injustices in a number of important lawsuits. In December, 1981, six dealers filed suit against Apple seeking to restrain implementation of its prohibition on mail-order and telephone sales. The litigation is now in the discovery stage with respect to the plaintiffs' request for permanent injunctive relief and Apple's counterclaims. On May 12, 1982, Apple brought suit against Franklin Computer Corporation, alleging patent, trademark, and copyright infringement. The Franklin Computer Company's Model Ace 1000 is not only a functional copy of the Apple IIe, but it has also been designed to look like the Apple model. It has almost all the features of the Apple IIe.

Apple Computer is in the process of trying to contain the many "copycats" such as Franklin which have emerged in foreign markets. Per-

EXHIBIT 9-20   Apple Computer, Inc.: Research and Development (in Millions)

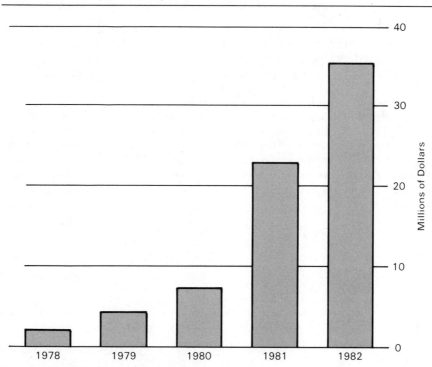

Source: Apple Computer, Inc., 1982 Annual Report.

sonal computers with names such as "The Orange" and "The Lemon" are having a major impact on Apple's international sales, especially in Japan. In Australia, for example, Apple's market share dropped from 80 percent to 20 percent in two years chiefly because of foreign duplication, according to industry expert John R. Lindel, security analyst at Goldman Sachs.

Until recently Apple has had little luck in prosecuting firms overseas, but some positive signs are surfacing. Taiwan's high court ruled that U.S. companies can initiate criminal cases against Taiwan-based companies, permitting Apple to prosecute companies that copy its computers. In Cupertino, California, Apple's general counsel, Albert A. Eisenstat, hailed the ruling as "a spectacular piece of news. If we can stop these actions out of Taiwan, we will have solved 75 percent of our counterfeit problems." Eisenstat added that Hong Kong was also a major breeding ground for problems: "We feel a little bit like the Dutch boy sticking his finger in the dike." After the Taiwan court decision, Dan Wendin, head of Apple's internal legal department, said: "We will continue to go after the counterfeiters, but the fire is under control—maybe even contained."

THE FUTURE

Most astute observers agree that the personal computer is going to revolutionize the home and workplace over the next few years. *Time* magazine selected the personal computer as its 1982 "person" of the year, *Time*'s editorial board having decided that the personal computer had done more to affect mankind than had any single human being during that year. Much has also happened at Apple since it first introduced the personal computer just seven years ago. Over 100 competitors have entered the market, including some of the world's most familiar and respected names. In a recent article, Steven Jobs said that within three years no more than five major computer makers will remain, and he vows that Apple will be among them. As the industry is not short of challenges, Apple must be careful to relate better than anyone else to the customer's needs and markets.

CHAPTER 10
Portfolio Analysis

Induce your competitors not to invest in those products, markets, and services where you expect to invest the most. That is the most fundamental rule of strategy.

Bruce D. Henderson

The previous chapters dealt with strategy development for individual strategic business units. Different SBU strategies must ultimately be judged from the viewpoint of the total organization before being implemented. In today's environment most companies operate with a variety of businesses. Even if a company is primarily involved in a single broad business area, it may actually be operating in multiple product/market segments. From a strategy angle, the different products/markets may constitute different businesses of a company, since they have different roles to play. This chapter is devoted to the analysis of the different businesses of an organization so that each may be assigned the unique role for which it is suited, thus maximizing the long-term growth and earnings of the company.

Years ago Peter Drucker suggested classifying products into six categories which reveal whether the potential for future sales growth is present. These are: tomorrow's breadwinners, today's breadwinners, products capable of becoming net contributors if something drastic is done, yesterday's breadwinners, the "also rans," and the failures. Drucker's classification provides an interesting scheme for determining whether a company is developing enough new products to ensure future growth and profits.

In the past few years the emphasis has shifted from product to business. Usually a company discovers that some of its business units are competitively well placed, while others are not. Since resources, particularly cash resources, are limited, not all SBUs can be treated alike. In this chapter three different frameworks are presented to enable management to select the optimum combination of individual SBU strategies from a spectrum of possible alternatives and opportunities open to the company, still satisfying the resource limitations within which the company must operate. The frameworks may also be used at the SBU level to review the strategic perspective of its different product/market segments.

The first framework to be discussed, product life cycle, is a tool which many marketers have traditionally used to formulate marketing strategies for different products. The second framework was developed

by the Boston Consulting Group and is commonly called the product portfolio approach. The third one, the multifactor portfolio approach, owes
its development to the General Electric Company.

PRODUCT LIFE CYCLE (PLC)

Products tend to go through different stages, each stage being affected by different competitive conditions.[1] These stages require different
marketing strategies at different times if sales and profits are to be efficiently realized. The length of a product's life cycle is in no way a fixed
period of time. It can last from weeks to years, depending on the type of
product. The discussion of PLC in most texts portrays the sales history of
a typical product as following an S-shaped curve. The curve is divided
into four stages known as introduction, growth, maturity, and decline. (Some
authors include a stage called saturation.)

Not all products follow the S-shaped curve. Marketing scholars have
identified varying product life cycle patterns. For example, Tellis and
Crawford[2] identify 17 PLC patterns, while Swan and Rink name ten.[3] Exhibit 10-1 illustrates a typical PLC curve showing the relationship between
profits and corresponding sales throughout the product life cycle.

Introduction is the period during which initial market acceptance is
in doubt; thus, it is a period of slow growth. Profits are almost nonexistent
because of high marketing and other expenses. Setbacks in the product's
development, manufacturing, and market introduction exact a heavy toll.
Marketing strategy during this stage is based on different combinations
of product, price, promotion, and distribution variables. For example, price
and promotion variables may be combined to generate the following strategy alternatives: (a) high price/high promotion; (b) high price/low promotion; (c) low price/heavy promotion; and (d) low price/low promotion.

Survivors of the introduction stage enjoy a period of rapid *growth.*
During this period there is substantial profit improvement. Strategy in this
stage takes the following shape: (a) product improvement: addition of new
features and models; (b) development of new market segments; (c) addition of new channels; (d) selective demand stimulation; and (e) price
reductions to vie for new customers.

---

[1] This section draws heavily on Philip Kotler, *Marketing Management*, 5th Ed. (Englewood Cliffs, NJ: Prentice-Hall, 1984), pp. 362–372. See also David R. Rink and
John E. Swan, "Product Life Cycle Research: A Literature Review," *Journal of Business Research*, September, 1979, pp. 219–242.

[2] Gerald J. Tellis and C. Merle Crawford, "An Evolutionary Approach to Product
Growth Theory," *Journal of Marketing*, Fall, 1981, pp. 125–134.

[3] John E. Swan and David R. Rink, "Fitting Market Strategy to Varying Product
Life Cycles," *Business Horizons*, January–February, 1982, pp. 72–76; and Yoram
J. Wind, *Product Policy: Concepts, Methods, and Strategy* (Reading, MA: Addison-Wes-
ley Publishing Co., 1982).

EXHIBIT 10-1   Product Life Cycle

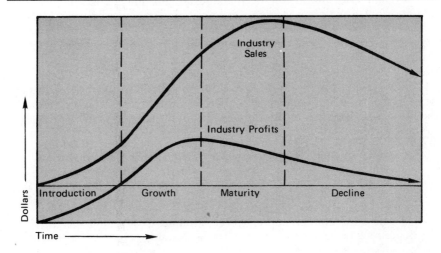

During the next stage, *maturity*, there is intense rivalry for a mature market, which may be limited to efforts to attract a new population. This leads to a proliferation of sizes, colors, attachments, and other product variants. Battling to retain the company's share, each marketer steps up persuasive advertising, opens new channels of distribution, and grants price concessions. Unless new competitors are obstructed by patents or other barriers, entry is easy. Thus, maturity is a period when sales growth slows down and profits peak and then start to decline.

Strategy in the maturity stage comprises the following steps: (a) search for new markets and new and varied uses for the product; (b) improvement of product quality through changes in features and style; and (c) new marketing-mix perspectives. For the leader firm (c) may mean introducing an innovative product, fortifying the market through multibrand strategy, or engaging in a price-promotion war against the weaker members of the industry; the non-leader firm may seek a differential advantage to find a niche in the market through either product or promotional variables.

Finally, there is the *decline* period. Though sales and profits continue their downward trend, the declining product is not necessarily unprofitable. Some of the competition may have been removed by this stage. Customers who remain committed to the product may be willing to use standard models, pay higher prices, and buy at selected outlets. Promotional expenses can also be reduced.

An important consideration in strategy determination in this stage is exit barrier. Even when it appears appropriate to leave the industry, one or more barriers may exist to prevent easy exit. For example, there may be durable and specialized assets which are peculiar to the business and which outside the business would carry little value; the cost of exit may be prohibitive because of labor settlement costs or contingent liabilities for land use; there may be managerial resistance; the business may be important in gaining access to financial markets; quitting the business may have a negative impact on other businesses in the company; or there may be government pressure to continue in the business, a situation which a multinational corporation may face, particularly in developing countries.[4]

Overall, in the decline stage, the following alternative strategies appear appropriate. The choice of a specific alternative would be based on the business's strengths and weaknesses and attractiveness of the industry to the company:

(a) Increasing the firm's investment (to dominate or get a good competitive position).
(b) Holding the firm's investment level until the uncertainties about the industry are resolved.
(c) Decreasing the firm's investment posture selectively, by sloughing off the unpromising customer groups, while simultaneously strengthening the firm's investment posture within the lucrative niches of enduring customer demands.
(d) Harvesting (or milking) the firm's investment to recover cash quickly, regardless of the resulting investment posture.
(e) Divesting the business quickly by disposing of its assets as advantageously as possible.[5]

In summary, in the introduction stage, the choices are primarily with what force to enter the market and whether to target a relatively narrow segment of customers or a broader customer group. In the growth stage, the choices appear to be to fortify and consolidate previously established market positions or to develop new primary demand. In the latter case this may be accomplished by a variety of means, including the development of new applications, geographic extension, trading down to previously untapped consumer groups, or adding related products. In the late growth and early maturity stages, the choices lie among the various alternatives for achieving a larger share of the existing market. This may involve product improvement, product-line extension, finer positioning of the product line, a shift from breadth of offering to in-depth focus, invading the market of a competitor who has invaded one's own market, or cutting out some of the "frills" associated with the product to appeal better to certain classes of customers. In the maturity stage, market positions have become established and the primary emphasis is on nose-to-nose

[4]Kathryn Rudie Harrigan, "The Effect of Exit Barriers upon Strategic Flexibility," *Strategic Management Journal*, Vol. 1, 1980, pp. 165–176; and Kathryn Rudie Harrigan and Michael E. Porter, "End-Game Strategies for Declining Industries," *Harvard Business Review*, July–August, 1983, pp. 111–120.
[5]Kathryn Rudie Harrigan, "Strategies for Declining Industries," *Journal of Business Strategy*, Fall, 1980, p. 27.

competition in the various segments of the market. This may take the
form of price competition, minor feature competition, or promotional
competition. In the decline stage the choices are to continue current prod-
uct/market perspectives as is, to continue selectively, or to divest.

Exhibit 10-2 identifies the characteristics, marketing objectives, and
marketing strategies of each stage of the S-shaped product life cycle. The
characteristics help in locating the product on the curve. The objectives
and strategies indicate what marketing perspective is relevant in each stage.
Actual choice of strategies will rest on the objective set for the product,
the nature of the product, and environmental characteristics operating at
the time. For example, in the introductory stage, if a new product is
launched without any competition and the firm has spent huge amounts
of funds on research and development, the firm may pursue a high price–
low promotion strategy (i.e., skim the cream off the top of the market).
As the product gets established and enters the growth stage, the price may
be cut to bring new segments into the fold. This reflects the type of strategic perspective followed by Texas Instruments for its digital watches.

On the other hand, if the product is introduced into a market where
there is already a well-established brand, the firm may follow a high price–
high promotion strategy. Seiko, for example, introduced its digital watch
with a high price and heavy promotion among well-to-do buyers without
any intention of competing against Texas Instruments head on.

Of the four stages, the maturity stage of the life cycle offers the
greatest opportunity to shape the duration of a product's life cycle. These
critical questions must be answered: Why have sales tapered off? Has the
product approached obsolescence because of a superior substitute or a
fundamental change in consumer needs? Can obsolescence be attributed
to management's failure to identify and reach the right consumer needs,
or has a competitor done a better market job? The answer is crucial if an
appropriate strategy is to be employed to strengthen the product's position. For example, the product may be redirected on a growth path through
repacking, physical modifications, repricing, appeals to new users, the addition of new distribution channels, or the use of some combination of
marketing strategy changes. The choice of a right strategy here can be
extremely beneficial, since a successfully revitalized product offers a higher
return on management time and funds invested than does a new product.

Product Life Cycle Controversy

Product life cycle is a useful concept which may serve as an important aid in marketing planning and strategy. A concept familiar to most
marketers, it is given a prominent place in every marketing textbook. Its
use in practice remains limited, however, partly because of the lack of
normative models available for its application and partly because of the
vast amount of data needed for, and subjectivity involved in, its use. As
a matter of fact, the PLC concept has many times been criticized for its

EXHIBIT 10-2   Perspectives of the Product Life Cycle

	Introduction	Growth	Maturity	Decline
CHARACTERISTICS				
Sales	Low sales	Rapidly rising sales	Peak sales	Declining sales
Costs	High cost per customer	Average cost per customer	Low cost per customer	Low cost per customer
Profits	Negative	Rising profits	High profits	Declining profits
Customers	Innovators	Early adopters	Middle majority	Laggards
Competitors	Few	Growing number	Stable number beginning to decline	Declining number

MARKETING OBJECTIVES				
	Create product awareness and trial	Maximize market share	Maximize profit while defending market share	Reduce expenditure and milk the brand

STRATEGIES				
Product	Offer a basic product	Offer product extensions, service, warranty	Diversify brands and models	Phase out weak items
Price	Use cost-plus	Price to penetrate market	Price to match or beat competitors	Cut price
Distribution	Build selective distribution	Build intensive distribution	Build more intensive distribution	Go selective: phase out unprofitable outlets
Advertising	Build product awareness among early adopters and dealers	Build awareness and interest in the mass market	Stress brand differences and benefits	Reduce to level needed to retain hardcore loyals
Sales Promotion	Use heavy sales promotion to entice trial	Reduce to take advantage of heavy consumer demand	Increase to encourage brand switching	Reduce to minimal level

Source: Philip Kotler, *Marketing Management: Analysis, Planning and Control,* 5th Ed., © 1984, p. 373. Reprinted by permission of Prentice-Hall, Inc., Englewood Cliffs, NJ.

lack of relevance to businesspeople. Years ago Buzzell remarked: "There is very little empirical evidence to show how the life cycles operate and how they are related to competition and marketing strategy."[6] A few years ago, Dhalla and Yuspeh challenged the whole concept of product life cycle. They contend that PLC has led many companies to make costly mistakes and pass up promising opportunities.[7] Such criticism of PLC may be attributed to the lack of a research base on the subject. As Levitt has said:

> Most alert and thoughtful senior marketing excutives are by now familiar with the concept of the product life cycle. Even a handful of uniquely cosmopolitan and up-to-date corporate presidents have familiarized themselves with this tantalizing concept. Yet a recent survey I took of such executives found none who used the concept in any strategic way whatever and pitifully few who used it in any kind of tactical way. It has remained—as have so many fascinating theories in economics, physics, and sex—a remarkably durable but almost totally unemployed and seemingly unemployable piece of professional baggage whose presence in the rhetoric of professional discussions adds a much-coveted but apparently unattainable legitimacy to the idea that marketing management is somehow a profession.
>
> The concept of the product life cycle is today at about the stage that the Copernican view of the universe was 300 years ago: a lot of people know about it, but hardly anybody seems to use it in any effective or productive way.[8]

While Levitt's criticism is very penetrating, many academicians and practitioners feel that even in its present stage of development, PLC has proved to be remarkably durable because it has been valuable to those who know how to use it. Smallwood claims:

> The product life cycle is a useful concept. It is the equivalent of the periodic table of the elements in the physical sciences. The maturation of production technology and product configuration along with marketing programs proceeds in an orderly, somewhat predictable course over time with the merchandising nature and marketing environment noticeably similar between products that are in the same stage of their life cycle. Its use as a concept in forecasting, pricing, advertising, product planning, and other aspects of marketing management can make it a valuable concept, although considerable amounts of judgment must be used in its application.[9]

---

[6]Robert D. Buzzell, "Competitive Behavior and Product Life Cycles," in John S. Wright and Jac L. Goldstrucker (eds.), *New Ideas for Successful Marketing* (Chicago, IL: American Marketing Association, 1966), p. 47.

[7]Nariman K. Dhalla and Sonia Yuspeh, "Forget the Product Life Cycle Concept," *Harvard Business Review*, January–February, 1976, pp. 102–109.

[8]Theodore Levitt, "Exploit the Product Life Cycle," *Harvard Business Review*, November–December, 1965, p. 81.

[9]John E. Smallwood, "The Product Life Cycle: A Key to Strategic Market Planning," *MSU Business Topics*, Winter, 1973. p. 35.

One caution which is in order when using PLC is to keep in mind that not all products follow the typical life cycle pattern. According to Kotler, the same product may be viewed in different ways—for example, as a brand (Tab), a product form (diet cola), and a product class (cola drink). Among these, the PLC concept is most relevant for product forms.[10] Despite criticisms and limitations, it is important not to lose sight of the PLC concept of basing marketing strategies on the position of a product in its life cycle.[11]

Though questions remain on its universal application, the PLC concept is a useful model for a product's progression. In recent years, research on the subject has provided new and interesting insights which should help in its further refinement. For example, Tellis and Crawford suggest that products, influenced by market dynamics, managerial creativity, and government intervention, are in a state of constant evolution in the direction of greater efficiency, greater complexity, and greater diversity. The five stages in this evolutionary process, which the authors call the product evolutionary cycle (PEC), are as follows:

1. *Divergence* . . . is the start of a new product type (e.g., TV). This term is suggested because most often a product is not an entirely new concept but a modification or combination of existing products and technologies. It is a divergence from a line of product evolution. Thus TV may be considered an evolutionary divergence from the radio and the motion picture.
2. *Development* . . . is the pattern where a new product's sales increase rapidly and the product is increasingly adapted to suit consumer needs best. Thus in the 50's, TV sales increased rapidly accompanied by frequent product improvements.
3. *Differentiation* . . . is the pattern that occurs when a highly successful product is differentiated to suit varying consumer interests. More recently TV's are available as black and white, color, portable, and console sets, and variation has extended to CRTs, rear-projection screens, home computers, and videodiscs.
4. *Stabilization* . . . is a pattern characterized by few and minor changes in the product category, but numerous changes in packaging, service deals, product accessories, and stable or fluctuating sales. Black and white television was in stabilization for years prior to differentiation into portable sets and the other uses mentioned above.
5. *Demise* occurs when a product fails to meet consumer expectations or can no longer satisfy changes in consumer demand. Sales decline and the product is ultimately discontinued.[12]

Following the above framework, the growth of a product is to some extent a function of the strategy being pursued. Thus, a product is not

---

[10]Philip Kotler, *op. cit.*, p. 355.
[11]See George S. Day. "The Product Life Cycle: Analysis and Applications Issues," *Journal of Marketing*, Fall, 1981, pp. 60–67.
[12]Gerald J. Tellis and C. Merle Crawford, "An Evolutionary Approach to Product Growth Theory," *Journal of Marketing*, Fall, 1981, pp. 125–134.

necessarily predestined to mature as propounded by the traditional concept of product life cycle, but can be kept profitable by proper adaptation to the evolving market environment.

Locating Products in Their Life Cycles

The easiest way to locate a product in its life cycle is to study its performance, competitive history, and current position and match this information with the characteristics of a particular stage of the life cycle. Analysis of past performance of the product will include examination of the following:

1. Sales-growth progression since introduction
2. Any design problems and technical bugs that need to be sorted out
3. Sales and profit history of allied products (those similar in general character or function as well as those directly competitive)
4. Number of years the product has been on the market
5. Casualty history of similar products in the past

The review of competition will focus on:

1. Profit history
2. Ease with which other firms can get into the business
3. Extent of initial investment needed to enter the business
4. Number of competitors and their strengths
5. Number of competitors that have left the industry
6. Life cycle of the industry
7. Critical factors for success in the business

In addition, current perspectives may be reviewed to gauge whether sales are on the upswing, have leveled out for the last couple of years, or are heading down; whether any competitive products are moving up to replace the product under consideration; whether customers are becoming more demanding vis-à-vis price, service, or special features; whether additional sales efforts are necessary to keep the sales going up; and whether it is becoming harder to sign up dealers and distributors.

The above information on the product may be related to the characteristics of the different stages of the product life cycle as discussed above; the PLC stage with which the product perspectives match will indicate the position of the product in its life cycle. Needless to say, the whole process is highly qualitative in nature, and managerial intuition and judgment will bear heavily on the final placement of the product in its life cycle. As a matter of fact, making appropriate assumptions, the types of information described above can be used to construct a model to predict the industry volumes of a newly introduced product through each stage of the PLC.[13]

---

[13]Stephen G. Harrell and Elmer D. Taylor, "Modeling the Product Life Cycle for Consumer Durables," *Journal of Marketing*, Fall, 1981, pp. 68–75.

A slightly different approach for locating a product in its life cycle has been recommended by Clifford. He suggests the use of past accounting information for the purpose. Listed below are steps Clifford recommends using to position a product in its life cycle:

1. Develop historical trend information for a period of three to five years (longer for some products). Data included will be unit and dollar sales, profit margins, total profit contribution, return on invested capital, market share, and prices.
2. Check recent trends in the number and nature of competitors; number and market-share rankings of competing products, and their quality and performance advantages; shifts in distribution channels; and relative advantages enjoyed by products in each channel.
3. Analyze development in short-term competitive tactics such as competitors' recent announcements of new products or plans for expanding production capacity.
4. Obtain (or update) historical information on the life cycle of similar or related products.
5. Project sales for the product over the next three to five years, based on all the information gathered, and estimate an incremental profit ratio for the product during each of these years (the ratio of total direct costs—manufacturing, advertising, product development, sales, distribution, etc.—to pretax profits). Expressed as a ratio—e.g., 4.8 to 1 or 6.3 to 1—this measures the number of dollars required to generate each additional dollar of profit. The ratio typically improves (becomes lower) as the product enters its growth period; begins to deteriorate (rise) as the product approaches maturity; and climbs more sharply as it reaches obsolescence.
6. Estimate the number of profitable years remaining in the product's life cycle, and—based on all the information at hand—fix the product's position on its life-cycle curve: (1) introduction, (2) early or late growth, (3) early or late maturity, or (4) early or late obsolescence.[14]

Developing a Portfolio

The current positions of different products in the product life cycle may be determined by following the above procedure, and the net results (i.e., the cash flow and profitability) of these positions may be computed. Similar analyses may be performed for a future time period. The difference between the current and future positions will indicate what results management may expect if no strategic changes are made. These results may be compared with corporate expectations to determine the gap. The gap can be filled either by making strategic changes to extend the life cycle of a product, or by bringing in new products through research and de-

---

[14]Donald K. Clifford, Jr., "Managing the Product Life Cycle," *The McKinsey Quarterly*, Spring, 1965, pp. 14–20.

velopment or acquisition. The above procedure may be put into operation by following the steps given below:

1. Determine what percentage of the company's sales and profits fall within each phase of the product life cycle. These percentage figures indicate the present life-cycle (sales) profile and the present profit profile of the company's current line.
2. Calculate changes in the life-cycle and profit profiles over the past five years, and project these profiles over the next five years.
3. Develop a target life-cycle profile for the company and measure the company's present life-cycle profile against it. The target profile, established by marketing management, specifies the desirable share of company sales that should fall within each phase of the product life cycle. It can be determined by industry obsolescence trends, the pace of new-product introduction in the field, the average length of product life cycles in the company's line, and top management's objectives for growth and profitability. As a rule, the target profile for growth-minded companies whose life cycles tend to be short will call for a high proportion of sales in the introductory and growth phases.

    With these steps completed, management can assign priorities to such functions as new-product development, acquisition, and product-line pruning, based on the discrepancies between the company's target profile and its present life-cycle profile. Once corporate effort has been broadly allocated in this way among products at various stages of their life cycles, marketing plans can be detailed for individual product lines.[15]

PORTFOLIO MATRIX

A good planning system must guide the development of strategic alternatives for each of the company's current businesses and new business possibilities. It must also provide for management's review of these strategic alternatives and for the corresponding resource allocation decisions. The result is a set of approved business plans which, taken as a whole, represent the direction of the firm. This process starts with, and its success is largely determined by, the creation of sound strategic alternatives.

The top management of a multibusiness firm cannot generate these strategic alternatives. They must rely on the managers of their business ventures and on their corporate development personnel. However, they can and should establish a conceptual framework within which these plan alternatives can be developed. One such framework is the portfolio matrix associated with the Boston Consulting Group (BCG). Briefly, the portfolio concept is used to establish the best mix of businesses in order to maximize the long-term earnings growth of the firm. The portfolio concept represents a real advance in strategic planning in several ways:

---

[15]*Ibid.*, p. 226.

It encourages top management to evaluate the prospects of each of the company's businesses individually, and to set tailored objectives for each business based on the contribution it can realistically make to corporate goals.

It has stimulated the use of externally focused, empirical data to supplement managerial judgment in evaluating the potential of a particular business.

It explicitly raises the issue of cash flow balancing as management plans for expansion and growth.

It gives managers a potent new tool for analyzing competitors and predicting competitive responses to strategic moves.

It provides not just a financial but a strategic context for evaluating acquisitions and divestitures.[16]

As a consequence of these benefits, the widespread application of the portfolio approach to corporate planning has sounded the death knell for planning by exhortation, the kind of strategic planning that sets uniform financial performance goals across the entire company—such as "15 percent growth in earnings" or "15 percent return on equity"—and then expects each business to meet those goals year in and year out. The portfolio approach has given top management the tools to evaluate each business in the context of both its environment and its unique contribution to the goals of the company as a whole and to weigh the entire array of business opportunities available to the company against the financial resources required to support them.

The portfolio concept addresses the issue of the potential value that a particular business has for the firm. This value has two variables: first, the potential for generating attractive earnings levels now; and second, the potential for growth, or in other words, for significantly increased earnings levels in the future. The portfolio concept holds that these two variables can be quantified. Current earnings potential is measured by comparing the market position of the business to that of its competitors. Empirical studies have shown that profitability is directly determined by relative market share. There are some types of businesses, however, in which the economies do not respond significantly to scale, and other factors are important determinants of return. In such cases the terminology for the earnings-potential yardstick may be changed from "market share" to "market leadership."

Growth potential is measured by the growth rate of the market segment in which the business competes. Clearly, if the segment is in the decline stage of its life cycle, the only way the business can increase its market share is by taking volume away from competitors. While this is sometimes possible and economically desirable, it is usually expensive, it leads to destructive pricing and erosion of profitability for all competitors,

---

[16]See Philippe Haspeslagh, "Portfolio Planning: Uses and Limits," *Harvard Business Review*, January–February, 1982, pp. 60, 73.

and it ultimately results in a market which is ill served. On the other hand, if a market is in its rapid growth stage, the business can gain share by preempting the incremental growth in the market. So if these two dimensions of value are arrayed in matrix form, we have the basis for a business classification scheme. This is essentially what the Boston Consulting Group portfolio matrix is. Each of the four business categories tends to have specific characteristics associated with it. The two quadrants corresponding to high market leadership have current earnings potential, and the two corresponding to high market growth have growth potential.

Exhibit 10-3 shows a matrix with its two sides labeled as "product sales growth rate" and "relative market share." The area of each circle represents dollar sales. The market-share position of each circle is determined by its horizontal position. Each circle's product sales growth rate (corrected for inflation) in the market in which it competes is shown by its vertical position.

With regard to the two axes of the matrix, the relative market share

EXHIBIT 10-3   Product Portfolio Matrix

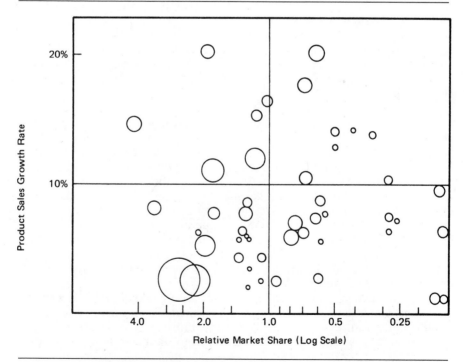

Source: Bruce D. Henderson, "The Experience Curve Reviewed: IV. The Growth Share Matrix or the Product Portfolio" (Boston: The Boston Consulting Group, Inc., 1973), Perspectives No. 135. Reprinted by permission.

is plotted on a logarithmic scale in order to be consistent with the experience curve effect, which implies that profit margin or rate of cash generation differences between two competitors tends to be proportionate to the ratio of their competitive positions. A linear axis is used for growth, for which the most generally useful measure is volume growth of the business concerned; in general, rates of cash use should be directly proportionate to growth.

The lines dividing the matrix into four quadrants are arbitrary. Usually high growth is taken to include all businesses growing in excess of 10 percent annually in volume. The line separating areas of high and low relative competitive position is set at 1.0.

The importance of growth variables for strategy development is based on two factors. First, growth is a major influence in reducing cost because it is easier to gain experience or build market share in a growth market than in a low-growth situation. Second, growth provides opportunity for investment. The relative market share affects the rate at which the business will generate cash. The stronger the relative-market-share position of a product, the higher the margins it will have, because of the experience effect.

Classification of Businesses

Using the two dimensions discussed above, one can classify businesses into four categories (see Exhibit 10-4). Businesses in each category exhibit different financial characteristics and offer different strategic choices.[17]

Stars. High-growth market leaders are called stars. They generate large amounts of cash, but the cash they generate from earnings and depreciation is more than offset by the cash that must be put back into these businesses in the form of capital expenditures and increased working capital. Such heavy reinvestment is necessary to fund the capacity increases and inventory and receivable investment that go along with market share gains. Thus, star products represent probably the best profit opportunity available to a company, and their competitive position must be maintained. If a star's share is allowed to slip because the star has been used to provide large amounts of cash in the short run or because of cutting back on investment and raising prices (creating an umbrella for competitors), the star will ultimately become a dog.

The ultimate value of any product or service is reflected in the stream of cash it generates net of its own reinvestment. For a star, this stream of cash is in the future, sometimes the distant future, and to obtain real value, the stream of cash must be discounted back to the present at a rate equal

---

[17]See Bruce D. Henderson, *Henderson on Corporate Strategy* (Cambridge, MA: Abt Associates, 1979).

EXHIBIT 10-4 Matrix Quadrants

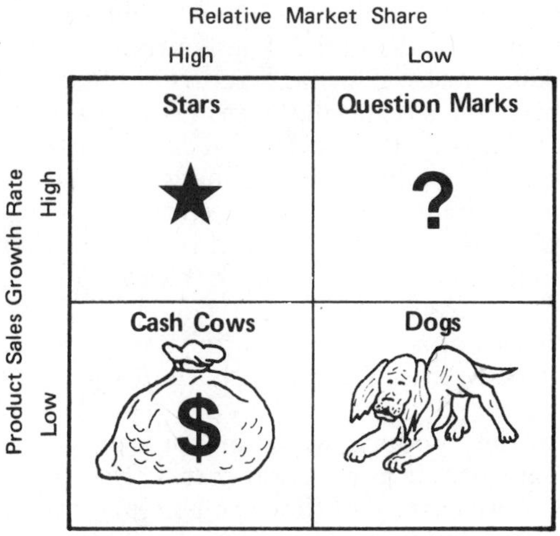

Relative Market Share

Source: The Boston Consulting Group, Inc., 1970. Reprinted by permission.

to the return on alternative opportunities. It is the future payoff of the star that counts, not the present reported profit.

Lone Star Industries, Inc., provides an example of how a company attempts to take care of its star. The company's two main businesses were cement manufacturing operations and building-materials outlets, ranging from wholesale centers that catered to professional homebuilders to retail stores selling mostly to do-it-yourselfers. Both businesses happened to be in the star category, but the company, as a matter of strategy, decided that it could not afford to support both the stars. Therefore, it harvested the latter. In doing so, it parted with 40 percent of the $1.1 billion in sales in 1978. Simultaneously, the company planned a $300-million expansion of the cement business. Lone Star explained it in this manner: "The company could not afford rapid growth campaigns for both businesses. So we are going with cement. It is the business Lone Star managers are most familiar with and where we see the better returns."[18]

Cash Cows. Cash cows are characterized by low growth and high market share. They are net providers of cash. Their high earnings coupled with their depreciation represent high cash inflows, while they need very little in the way of reinvestment. Thus, these products generate large

[18]"Lone Star Industries: Selling the Source of One-Third Its Profits," *Business Week*, May 28, 1979, p. 79.

cash surpluses which help to pay dividends and interest, provide debt capacity, supply funds for R&D, meet overheads, and also make cash available for investment in other products. Thus, cash cows are the foundation on which everything else depends. These products must be protected. Technically speaking, a cash cow has a return on assets which exceeds its growth rate. Only if that is true will the cash cow generate more cash than it uses. For NCR Company, the mechanical cash register business is a cash cow. The company still maintains a dominant share of this business even though growth since the introduction of electronic cash registers has slowed down. The company uses the surplus cash from the mechanical cash registers to develop electronic machines with a view to creating a new star. Likewise, the tire business can be categorized as a cash cow for the Goodyear Tire & Rubber Company. The industry is characterized by slow market growth, and Goodyear has a major share of the market.

Question Marks. Products which are in a growth market but have a low share are categorized as question marks. Because of growth, these products require more cash than they are able to generate on their own. If nothing is done to increase its market share, the question mark will simply absorb large amounts of cash in the short run and later, as the growth slows down, become a dog. Thus, unless something is done to change its perspective, a question mark remains a cash loser throughout its existence and ultimately becomes a "cash trap."

What can be done to make a question mark more viable? One alternative is to gain share increases for it. Since the business is growing, it can be funded to dominance so that it may become a star, and later a cash cow when growth slows down. This strategy is a costly one in the short run. An abundance of cash must be poured into the question mark in order for it to win a major share of the market, but in the long run this is the only way of developing a sound business from the question mark stage. The other strategy is to divest the business. Outright sale is the most desirable alternative. But if this does not work out, a firm decision must be made not to invest further in the business, and the business must be allowed simply to generate whatever cash it can while none is reinvested.

For both General Electric and RCA, the computer business was a question mark. Both giants ultimately decided to quit this business. Although the market was growing rapidly, the major competitor (i.e., IBM) was so well established that to grow at a faster rate than IBM, GE (as well as RCA) would have needed to invest rather heavily in computer operations. An examination of the investment needed and the potential long-term cash expected showed that it was not a good business for them to be in.

Dogs. Products with low market share and positioned in a low-growth situation are called dogs. Their poor competitive position condemns them to poor profits. Because growth is low, there is little potential for gaining sufficient share to achieve a viable cost position. Usually they are net users of cash. Their earnings are low, and the reinvestment required just to keep the business together eats cash inflow. The business, therefore, becomes a "cash trap" which is likely to regularly absorb cash unless further investment in the business is rigorously avoided. An alternative is to convert dogs into cash if there is an opportunity to do so.

In 1981, American Can Company's forest-products business had assets with a book value of $450 million, comprising 588,000 acres of timberland, cutting rights on an additional 1.6 million acres, five pulp mills, seven folding-carton plants, three lumber mills, and a lignin chemical operation. Accounting for a quarter of American Can's total business, forest products in 1980 had sales of $1.1 billion and employed 11,000 people. Despite these impressive statistics, it was in the dog category, with a small percentage of the available market and in a period of slow growth. The company decided to unload the business and invest the proceeds to strengthen its existing stars and acquire a new business in the star category.[19]

Exhibit 10-5 summarizes the investment, earning, and cash-flow characteristics of stars, cash cows, question marks, and dogs. Also shown are viable strategy alternatives for products in each category.

Strategy Implications

In a typical company there are products scattered in all four quadrants of the portfolio matrix. The appropriate strategy for products in each cell is given briefly in Exhibit 10-5. The first goal of a company should be to secure a position with cash cows but to guard against the frequent temptation to reinvest in them excessively. The cash generated from cash cows should first be used to support those stars which are not self-sustaining. The surplus cash may be used to finance selected question marks to dominance. Any question mark which cannot be funded should be divested. A dog may be restored to a position of viability by shrewdly segmenting the market; i.e., rationalizing and specializing the business into a small niche which the product concerned may dominate. If this is not practical, a firm should manage the dog for cash; i.e., cut off all investment in the business and liquidate it when an opportunity develops.

Exhibit 10-6 shows the consequences of an incorrect strategic move. For example, if a star is not appropriately funded, it will become a question mark, and finally a dog (disaster sequence). On the other hand, if a question mark is given adequate support, it may become a star, and ultimately a cash cow (success sequence).

There are two strategic questions that top management needs to answer: (1) How promising is the current set of businesses with respect to long-term return and growth? (2) Which business should be developed?

---

[19]"Why American Can Is Unloading So Much," *Business Week*, April 13, 1981, p. 45.

EXHIBIT 10-5 **Characteristics and Strategy Implications of Products in the Strategy Quadrants**

QUADRANT	INVESTMENT CHARACTERISTICS	EARNING CHARACTERISTICS	CASH-FLOW CHARACTERISTICS	STRATEGY IMPLICATION
Stars	—Continual expenditures for capacity expansion —Pipeline filling with cash	Low to high	Negative cash flow (net cash user)	Continue to increase market share. If necessary, at the expense of short-term earnings.
Cash Cows	—Capacity maintenance expenditures	High	Positive cash flow (net cash contributor)	Maintain share and cost leadership until further investment becomes marginal.
Question Marks	—Heavy initial capacity expenditures —High R&D costs	Negative to low	Negative cash flow (net cash user)	Assess chances of dominating segment. If good, go after share. If bad, redefine business or withdraw.
Dogs	—Gradually deplete capacity	High to low	Positive cash flow (net cash contributor)	Plan an orderly withdrawal so as to maximize cash flow.

EXHIBIT 10-6   Product Portfolio Matrix: Strategic Consequences

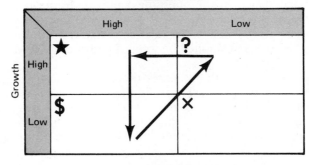

SUCCESS SEQUENCE

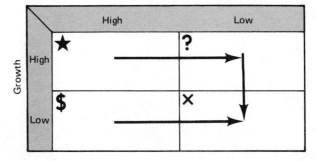

DISASTER SEQUENCE

Source: Bruce D. Henderson, "The Product Portfolio" (Boston: The Boston Consulting Group, Inc., 1970), Perspectives No. 66. Reprinted by permission.

maintained as is? liquidated? Following the portfolio approach discussed above, a company needs a cash-balanced portfolio of businesses, i.e., cash cows and dogs, to throw off sufficient cash to fund stars and question marks. There should be an ample supply of question marks to ensure long-term growth and businesses with return levels appropriate to their matrix position. In response to the second question, the capital budgeting theory requires the lining up of capital project proposals, assessment of incremental cash flows attributable to each project, computation of discounted rate of return of each, and approval of the project with the highest rate of return until available funds are exhausted. But the capital budgeting approach misses the strategic content; i.e., how to validate the assumptions of volume, price, cost, and investment and how to eliminate the natural biases. This problem is solved by the portfolio approach.

Product Portfolio and Product Life Cycle

The product portfolio approach propounded by the Boston Consulting Group may be related to the product life cycle by letting the introduction stage begin in the question mark quadrant; growth starts toward the end of this quadrant and continues well into the star quadrant. Going down from the star to the cash cow quadrant, the maturity stage begins. The decline is positioned between the cash cow and dog quadrants (see Exhibit 10-7).

Ideally a company should enter the product/market segment in its introduction stage, gain market share in the growth stage, attain a position of dominance when the product/market segment enters its maturity stage, maintain this dominant position until the product/market segment enters its decline stage, and then determine the optimum point for liquidation.[20]

EXHIBIT 10-7   Relationship Between Product Portfolio Matrix and Product Life Cycle

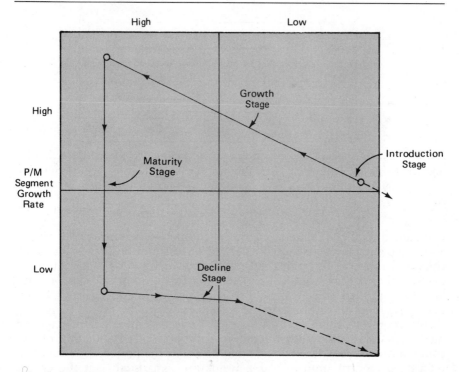

[20]See Hiram C. Barksdale and Clyde E. Harris, Jr., "Portfolio Analysis and the Product Life Cycle," *Long Range Planning*, December, 1982, pp. 74–83.

Balanced and Unbalanced Portfolios

Exhibit 10-8 gives an example of a balanced portfolio. With two (actually three) cash cows, this company is well positioned with stars to provide growth and to yield high cash returns in the future when they mature. The company has four question marks, two of which offer a good opportunity to emerge as stars at an investment which the cash cows should be able to support (based on the area of the circles). The company does have dogs, but they can be managed in order to avoid drain on cash resources.

Unbalanced portfolios may be classified into four types:

1. Too many losers (due to inadequate cash flow, inadequate profits, and inadequate growth)
2. Too many question marks (due to inadequate cash flow and inadequate profits)
3. Too many profit producers (due to inadequate growth and excessive cash flow)

EXHIBIT 10-8   Illustration of a Balanced Portfolio

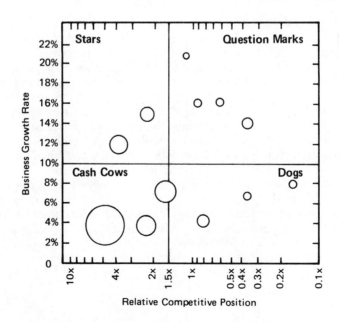

Source: The Boston Consulting Group, Inc., 1973. Reprinted by permission.

4. Too many developing winners (due to excessive cash demands, excessive demands on management, and unstable growth and profits)[21]

Exhibit 10-9 illustrates an unbalanced portfolio. The company has just one cash cow, three question marks, and no stars. Thus, the cash base of the company is actually inadequate to support question marks. The company may allocate the available cash among all question marks in an equal proportion. Dogs may also be given occasional cash nourishment. If the company continues its current strategy, it may find itself in a dangerous position in five years, particularly when the cash cow moves closer to being a dog. To take corrective action, the company must face the fact that it cannot support all the question marks. It must choose one or maybe two of the three question marks and fund them adequately to move them into star positions. Besides, disbursement of cash in dogs should be totally prohibited. In brief, the strategic choice for the company, considered in portfolio terms, is obvious. It cannot fund all question marks and dogs equally. The portfolio matrix focuses on the real fundamentals of the businesses and their relationships to each other within the portfolio. It is not possible to develop effective strategy in a multiproduct, multimarket company without considering the mutual relationships of different businesses.

Conclusion

The portfolio approach provides for the simultaneous comparison of different products. It also underlines the importance of cash flow as a strategic variable. Thus, when continuous long-term growth in earnings is the objective, it is necessary to identify high-growth product/market segments early, develop businesses, and preempt the growth in these segments. If necessary, short-term profitability in these segments may be forgone to ensure achievement of the dominant share. Costs must be managed to meet experience-effect standards. The appropriate point at which to shift from an earnings focus to a cash-flow focus must be determined and a liquidation plan for cash-flow maximization established. A cash-balanced mix of businesses should be maintained.

There are many companies worldwide that have used the portfolio approach in their strategic planning. The first company to use this approach was the Norton Company in the late 1960s. Since then, many large corporations have reported following this approach. Among them are Mead, Borg-Warner, Eaton, and Monsanto.

This approach, however, is not a panacea for strategy development.

---

[21]Charles W. Hofer and Merritt J. Davoust, *Successful Strategic Management* (Chicago, IL: A. T. Kearney, Inc., 1977), p. 52.

EXHIBIT 10-9   Illustration of an Unbalanced Portfolio

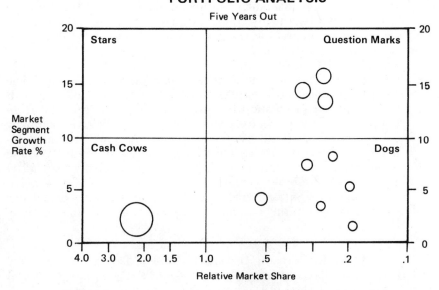

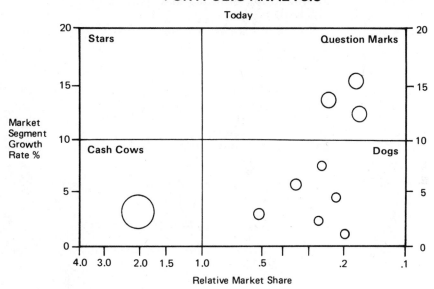

In reality, many difficulties limit the workability of the approach. These difficulties are listed below:

1. Overinvesting in low-growth segments (lack of objectivity and "hard" analysis)
2. Underinvesting in high-growth segments (lack of guts)
3. Misjudging the segment growth rate (poor market research)
4. Not achieving market share (because of improper market strategy, sales capabilities, or promotion)
5. Losing cost effectiveness (lack of operating talent and control system)
6. Not uncovering emerging high-growth segments (lack of corporate development effort)
7. Unbalanced business mix (lack of planning and financial resources)

Thus, the portfolio approach should be used with great care.

MULTIFACTOR PORTFOLIO MATRIX

The two-factor portfolio matrix discussed above provides a useful approach for reviewing the role that different products play in a company. Generally, however, the growth rate–relative market share matrix approach leads to many difficulties. At times, factors other than market share and growth rate may bear heavily on the cash flow, which is the mainstay of this approach. Some managements may consider return on investment a more suitable criterion than cash flow for making investment decisions. Further, this approach does not address itself to major investment decisions between dissimilar businesses. The above difficulties can lead a company into too many traps and errors. For this reason many companies (such as General Electric and the Shell Group) have developed a multifactor portfolio approach.

Exhibit 10-10 illustrates the General Electric matrix. This matrix has two dimensions, "industry attractiveness" and "business strengths." The two dimensions of the matrix have been based on a variety of factors. It is this multifactor characteristic which differentiates this approach from the one discussed in the previous section. The General Electric Company in 1980, for example, used the criteria and measures shown in Exhibit 10-11 to determine industry attractiveness and business strengths.[22] These criteria and measures are only suggestions; another company may adopt a different list. For example, General Electric added cyclicality as a criterion under industry attractiveness later on. The measure of relative profitability, as shown in the exhibit, was used for the first time in 1980.

---

[22]Francis J. Aguilar and Richard Hamermesh, "General Electric: Strategic Position: 1981," p. 25. Harvard Business School Case 9-381-174. Copyright © 1981 by the President and Fellows of Harvard College; reprinted by permission.

EXHIBIT 10-10   Multifactor Portfolio Matrix

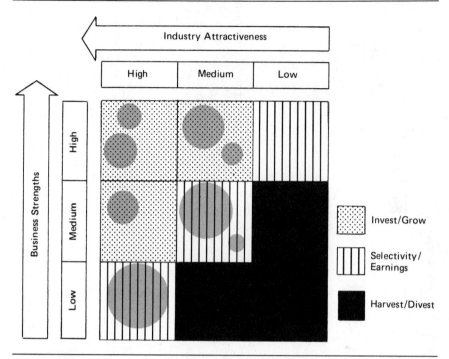

Source: *Maintaining Strategies for the Future Through Current Crises* (Fairfield, CT: General Electric Co., 1975). Reprinted by permission.

Rothschild recommends taking into consideration the following factors in measuring both "industry environment" (industry attractiveness) and "our position" (business strengths): market, competition, financial and economic factors, technological factors, sociopolitical factors, and overall factors. Each factor may be treated equally or assigned a different weight.[23] Exhibits 10-12 and 10-13 illustrate how the factors may be weighed and a final industry attractiveness and business strengths score computed. Management may establish cutoff points for high, medium, and low industry attractiveness and competitive position scores.

It is worthwhile to mention that the development of the multifactor matrix discussed above may not be as easy as it appears. The actual analysis required may take considerable amounts of foresight and experience and many, many days of work. The major difficulties lie in identifying

---

[23]William E. Rothschild, *Putting It All Together* (New York: AMACOM, 1976), pp. 141–162.

EXHIBIT 10-11   Portfolio Criteria and Measures Used by General Electric

INDUSTRY ATTRACTIVENESS		BUSINESS STRENGTHS	
CRITERION	MEASURE	CRITERION	MEASURE
1. Market Size	• 3-year average served industry market dollars	1. Market Position	• 3-year average market share (total market)
2. Market Growth	• 10-year constant dollar average annual market growth rate		• 3-year average international market share
3. Industry Profitability	• 3-year average ROS, SBU, and Big 3 competitors: • Nominal • Inflation adjusted		• 2-year average relative market share (SBU/Big 3 competitors)
4. Cyclicality	• Average annual percent variation of sales from trend	2. Competitive Position	Superior, equal, or inferior to competition in 1980: • Product quality • Technological leadership • Manufacturing/cost leadership • Distribution/marketing leadership
5. Inflation Recovery	• 5-year average ratio of combined selling price and productivity change to change in cost due to inflation	3. Relative Profitability	• 3-year SBU ROS less average ROS, Big 3 competitors: • Nominal • Inflation adjusted
6. Importance of Non-U.S. Markets	• 10-year average ratio of international to total market		

☐ Indicates measure used for first-time in 1980.

Source: General Electric Co. Reprinted by permission.

EXHIBIT 10-12   Assessing Industry Attractiveness

CRITERIA	WEIGHTS*	× RANKINGS** =	WEIGHTED RANK
Size	.15	4	.60
Growth	.12	3	.36
Pricing	.05	3	.15
Customer financials	.10	5	.50
Market diversity	.05	2	.10
Demand cyclicality	.05	2	.10
Expert opportunities	.05	5	.25
Competitive structure	.05	3	.15
Industry profitability	.20	3	.60
Inflation vulnerability	.05	2	.10
Value added	GO	4	—
Capital intensity	GO	4	—
Raw material availability	GO	4	—
Technological role	.05	4	.20
Energy impact	.08	4	.32
Social	GO	4	—
Environmental	GO	4	—
Legal	GO	4	—
Human	GO	4	—
	1.00	1 to 5	3.43

*Some criteria may be of a GO/NO GO type. For example, many *Fortune* 500 firms would probably not invest in industries viewed negatively by society even if it were legal and profitable to do so.
**"1" denotes very unattractive; "5" denotes very attractive.

Source: Charles W. Hofer, "Conceptual Constructs for Formulating Corporate and Business Strategies," p. 6. Available from *Stanford Business Cases 1977* or The Case Publishing Company (#BP-0041), Dover, MA 02030. Copyright © 1977 by Charles W. Hofer. Reprinted by permission.

the relevant factors, relating the factors to industry attractiveness and business strengths, and weighing the factors.[24]

Strategy Development

The overall strategy for a business in a particular position was illustrated in Exhibit 10-10. The area of the circle refers to the business's sales. Investment priority is given to products in the "high" area (upper

---

[24]Derek F. Abell and John S. Hammond, *Strategic Market Planning* (Englewood Cliffs, NJ: Prentice-Hall, 1979), pp. 211–227.

EXHIBIT 10-13   Assessing Business Strengths

CRITERIA	WEIGHTS* ×	RANKINGS** =	WEIGHTED RANK
Market share	.10	5	.50
SBU growth rate	X	3	—
Breadth of product line	.05	4	.20
Sales/distribution effectiveness	.20	4	.80
Proprietary & key account effectiveness	X	3	—
Price competitiveness	X	4	—
Advertising & promotion effectiveness	.05	4	.20
Facilities location & newness	.05	5	.25
Capacity and productivity	X	3	—
Experience curve effects	.15	4	.60
Value added	X	4	—
Investment utilization	.05	5	.25
Raw materials cost	.05	4	.20
Relative product quality	.15	4	.60
R & D advantages/ position	.05	4	.20
Cash throwoff	.10	5	.50
Caliber of personnel	X	4	—
Organizational synergies	X	4	—
General image	X	5	—
	1.00	1 to 5	4.30

*For any particular industry, there will be some factors that, while important in general, will have little or no effect on the relative competitive position of firms within that industry.
**"1" denotes a very weak competitive position; "5" denotes a very strong competitive position.

Source: Charles W. Hofer, "Conceptual Constructs for Formulating Corporate and Business Strategies," p. 6. Available from *Stanford Business Cases 1977* or The Case Publishing Company (#BP-0041), Dover, MA 02030. Copyright © 1977 by Charles W. Hofer. Reprinted by permission.

left), where a stronger position is supported by the attractiveness of an industry. Along the diagonal, selectivity is desired to achieve a balanced earnings performance. The businesses in the "low" area (lower right) are the candidates for harvesting and divestment.

A company may position its products or businesses on the matrix to study their present standing. Forecasts may be made to examine the direction different businesses may go in the future, assuming no changes are made in the strategy. The future perspectives may be compared to the corporate mission to identify gaps between what is desired and what may be expected if no measures are taken now. Filling the gap will require making strategic moves for different businesses. Once strategic alternatives for an individual business have been identified, the final choice of a strategy will be based on the scope of the overall corporation vis-à-vis the matrix. For example, the prospects for a business along the diagonal may appear good, but this business cannot be funded in preference to a business in the "high-high" cell. In devising future strategy a company generally would like to have a few businesses on the left to provide growth and furnish potential for investment and a few on the right to generate cash for investment in the former. The businesses along the diagonal may be selectively supported (based on resources) for relocation on the left. If this is not feasible, they may be slowly harvested or divested. Exhibit 10-14 summarizes desired strategic perspective in different cell positions.

For an individual business there can be four strategy options: investing to maintain, investing to grow, investing to regain, and investing to exit. The choice of a strategy will depend on the current position of the business in the matrix (i.e., toward the high side, along the diagonal,

EXHIBIT 10-14   Prescriptive Strategies for Businesses in Different Cells

		INDUSTRY ATTRACTIVENESS		
		High	Medium	Low
BUSINESS STRENGTHS	High	—Grow —Seek dominance —Maximize investment	—Identify growth segments —Invest strongly —Maintain position elsewhere	—Maintain overall position —Seek cash flow —Invest at maintenance levels
	Medium	—Evaluate potential leadership via segmentation —Identify weaknesses —Build strengths	—Identify growth segments —Specialize —Invest selectively	—Prune lines —Minimize investment —Position to divest
	Low	—Specialize —Seek niches —Consider acquisitions	—Specialize —Seek niches —Consider exit	—Trust leader's statemanship —Sic on competitors' cash generators —Time exit and divest

Source: Charles W. Hofer and Merritt J. Davoust, *Successful Strategic Management* (Chicago: A. T. Kearney, Inc., 1977), p. 82. Copyright © 1977 by Charles W. Hofer and Merritt J. Davoust. Reproduced by permission.

or toward the low side) and its future direction, assuming the current strategic perspective continues to be followed. If the future appears unpromising, a new strategy for the business will be called for.

Analysis of present position on the matrix may not pose any problem. At General Electric, for example, there was little disagreement on the position of the business.[25] The mapping of future direction, however, may not be easy. A rigorous analysis will have to be performed taking into account the environmental shifts, competitors' perspectives, and internal strengths and weaknesses.

The four strategy options are shown in Exhibit 10-15. Strategy to maintain the current position (strategy 1 in the exhibit) may be adopted if, in the absence of a new strategy, erosion is expected in the future. Investment will be sought to hold the position; hence the name *invest-to-maintain strategy.* The second option is the *invest-to-grow strategy.* Here, the product's current position is perceived as less than optimum vis-à-vis industry attractiveness and business strength. In other words, considering the opportunities furnished by the industry and the strength exhibited by the business, the current position is considered inadequate. The growth strategy is adopted with the aim of shifting the product position upward and/or toward the left. Movement in both directions is an expensive option with high risk.

The *invest-to-regain strategy* (strategy 3 in Exhibit 10-15) is an attempt to rebuild the product or business to its previous position. Usually, when environment (i.e., industry) continues to be relatively attractive but the business position has slipped because of some strategic mistake in the past (e.g., premature harvesting), it may be decided to revitalize the business through new investments. The fourth and final option, the *invest-to-exit strategy,* is directed toward leaving the market through harvesting or divesting. Harvesting amounts to making very low investments in the business so that in the short run the business will secure positive cash flow and in a few years die out. (With no new investments, the position will continue to deteriorate.) Alternatively, the whole business may be divested, i.e., sold to another party in a one-time deal. Sometimes small investments may be made to maintain the viability of business if divestment is desired but there is no immediate suitor. In this way the business can eventually be sold at a higher price than would have been possible right away.

Unit of Analysis

The framework discussed above may be applied to either a product/market or a strategic business unit. As a matter of fact, it may be

---

[25]*Organizing and Managing the Planning Function* (Fairfield, CT: General Electric Company, no date).

EXHIBIT 10-15 Strategy Options

1. Invest to Maintain

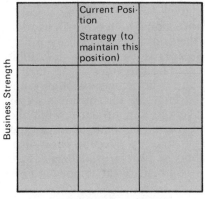

2. Invest to Grow

3. Invest to Regain

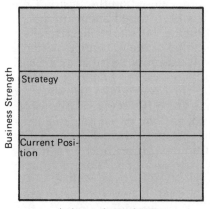

4. Invest to Exit

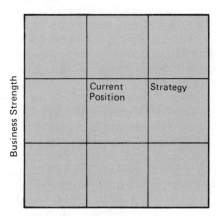

equally applicable to a much higher level of aggregation in the organization, such as a division or a group. Of course, at the group or division level, it may be very difficult to measure industry attractiveness and business strength positions unless the group or division happens to be in one business.

In the scheme followed in this book, the analysis may be performed first at the SBU level to determine the strategic perspective of different products/markets. Finally, all SBUs may be simultaneously positioned on the matrix to determine a corporate-wide portfolio.

Directional Policy Matrix

A slightly different technique, the directional policy matrix, is popularly used in Europe. It was initially worked out at the Shell Group but later on caught the fancy of many businesses across the continent. Exhibit 10-16 illustrates a directional policy matrix. The two sides of the matrix are labeled "business sector prospects" (industry attractiveness) and "company's competitive capabilities" (business strengths). The business sector prospects are categorized as unattractive, average, and attractive, while the company's competitive capabilities are categorized as weak, average, and strong. Shown within each cell is the overall strategy direction for a business depicted by the cell. The consideration of factors used to measure business sector prospects and a company's competitive capabilities follows the same logic and analyses discussed above.

PORTFOLIO MATRIX: CRITICAL ANALYSIS

In recent years, a variety of criticisms have been leveled at the portfolio framework.[26] Most of the criticism has centered on the Boston Consulting Group matrix. First, a question has been raised about the use of market share as the most important influence on marketing strategy.[27] The BCG matrix is derived from an application of the learning experience curve to manufacturing and other costs. It was observed that as a firm's product output (and thus market share) increases, the total cost declines by a fixed percentage. This may be true for commodities. However, in most product/market situations, products are differentiated, new products and brands are continually introduced, and the pace of technological changes keeps increasing. As a result, one may move from learning curve to learning curve, or encounter a discontinuity. More concrete evidence is needed before the validity of market share as a dimension in strategy formulation is established or rejected.

A second issue, closely related to the first, is how product/market boundaries are defined. Market share will vary depending upon the definition of the corresponding product/market. Hence, a product may be

---

[26]See Ravi Singh Achrol and David L. Appel, "New Developments in Corporate Strategic Planning," in *1983 AMA Educators' Proceedings* (Chicago: American Marketing Association, 1983), pp. 305–310. See also Walter Kiechel III, "Oh Where, Oh Where Has My Little Dog Gone? or My Cash Cow? or My Star?," *Fortune*, November 2, 1981, p. 148.

[27]Yoram Wind and Vijay Mahajan, "Designing Product and Business Portfolios," *Harvard Business Review*, January–February, 1981, pp. 155–165.

EXHIBIT 10-16   Directional Policy Matrix

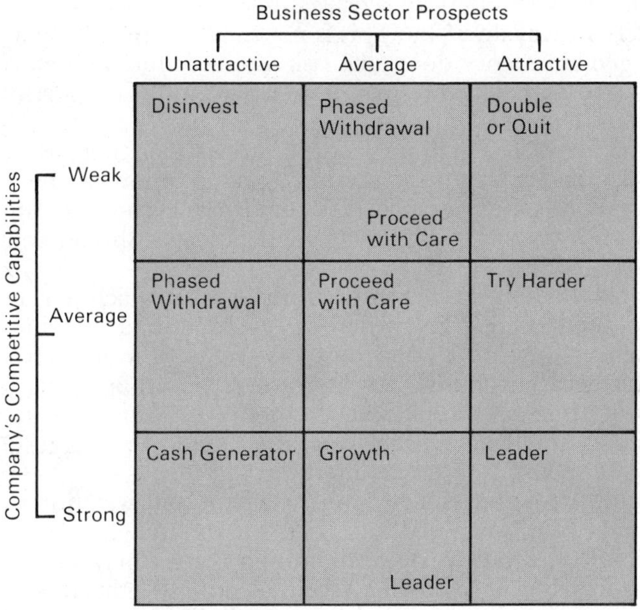

Business Sector Prospects

	Unattractive	Average	Attractive
Weak	Disinvest	Phased Withdrawal	Double or Quit
		Proceed with Care	
Average	Phased Withdrawal	Proceed with Care	Try Harder
Strong	Cash Generator	Growth	Leader
		Leader	

Company's Competitive Capabilities

classified in different cells depending on the market boundaries used.[28]

Third, the stability of product life cycles is implicitly assumed in some of the portfolio models. However, as in the case of the learning curve, it is possible for the product life cycle to change during the life of the product. For example, recycling can extend the life cycle of a product, sparking a second growth stage after the maturity stage.[29] A related subissue concerns the assumption that investment in high-growth markets is more desirable than in low-growth ones. There is insufficient evidence to support this proposition.[30] This overall issue becomes more problematic for international firms because a given product may be in different stages of its life cycle depending upon the country.

Fourth, the BCG portfolio framework was developed for balancing

[28]Rajendra K. Srivastava, Robert P. Leone, and Allan D. Shocker, "Market Structure Analysis: Hierarchical Clustering of Products Based on Substitution-in-Use," *Journal of Marketing*, Summer, 1981, pp. 38–48.

[29]George Day, "Diagnosing the Product Portfolio," *Journal of Marketing*, April, 1977, pp. 29–38.

[30]Robin Wensley, "Strategic Marketing: Betas, Boxes, or Basics," *Journal of Marketing*, Summer, 1981, pp. 173–182.

cash flows. This ignores the existence of capital markets. Cash balancing is not always an important consideration.

Fifth, the portfolio framework assumes that investments in all products/markets are equally risky. This is not the case. In fact, financial portfolio management theory does take risk into account. The more risky an investment, the higher the return expected of it.[31] The portfolio matrix does not consider the risk factor.

Sixth, the BCG portfolio model assumes that there is no interdependency between products/markets. This assumption can be questioned on various grounds. For instance, different products/markets might share technology and/or costs.[32] These interdependencies should be accounted for in a portfolio framework.

Seventh, there is no consensus on the level at which portfolio models are appropriately used.[33] Five levels can be identified: product, product line, market segment, SBU, and business sector. The most frequent application has been at the SBU level. However, it has been suggested that the framework is equally applicable at other levels. Since it is unlikely that any one model could have such wide application, the suggestion that it *does* has cast doubt on the model itself.

Eighth, there are issues of measurement and weighting. Different measures have been proposed and used for the dimensions of portfolio models. However, a product's position on a matrix may vary depending on the measures used.[34] In addition, the dimension weights used for models having composite dimensions may impact the results; the position of a business on the matrix may change with the weighting scheme used.

Ninth, the portfolio models ignore the impact of both the external and internal environments of a company. Since a firm's strategic decisions are made within its environments, their potential impact must be taken into account. Day highlights a few situational factors which might affect a firm's strategic plan—rate of capacity utilization, union pressures, barriers to entry, extent of captive business, and so on, as examples of internal factors; GNP, interest rates, and social, legal, and governmental environment as external factors.[35] No systematic treatment has been accorded to such environmental influences in the portfolio models. Since these influences are always unique to a company, the importance of customizing a portfolio approach becomes clear.

Apart from these problems, the relevance of a particular strategy for a business depends on its correct categorization on the matrix. If a

---

[31]H. Markowitz, "Portfolio Selection," *Journal of Finance*, March, 1952, pp. 77–79.

[32]Michael E. Porter, *Competitive Strategy* (New York: The Free Press, 1981).

[33]Yoram Wind and Vijay Mahajan, *op. cit.*

[34]Yoram Wind, Vijay Mahajan, and Donald J. Swire, "An Empirical Comparison of Standardized Portfolio Models," *Journal of Marketing*, Spring, 1983, pp. 89–99.

[35]George Day, *op. cit.*

mistake is made in locating a business in a particular cell of the matrix, the failure of the prescribed strategy cannot be blamed on the framework.[36] In other words, superficial and uncritical application of the portfolio framework can misdirect a business's strategy. As has been said:

> Portfolio approaches have their limitations, of course. First, it's just not all that easy to define the businesses or product/market units appropriately before you begin to analyze them. Second, some attractive strategic opportunities can be overlooked if management treats its businesses as independent entities when there may be real advantages in their sharing resources at the research or manufacturing or distribution level. And third, like more sophisticated models, when it's used uncritically the portfolio can give its users the illusion that they're being rigorous and scientific when in fact they've fallen prey to the old garbage-in, garbage-out syndrome.[37]

Finally, the portfolio models fail to answer such questions as (a) how a company may determine whether its strategic goals are consistent with its financial objectives; (b) how a company may relate strategic goals to its affordable growth; and (c) how relevant the designated strategies are vis-à-vis competition from overseas companies. In addition, many marketers have raised other questions on the viability of portfolio approaches as a strategy development tool. For example, it has been claimed that the BCG matrix approach is relevant only for positioning existing businesses and fails to prescribe how a problem child may be reared to emerge as a star, how new stars can be located, etc.[38]

In response to the above criticisms, it should be pointed out that the BCG portfolio framework was developed to be an aid in formulating business strategies in complex environments. Its aim was not to *prescribe* strategy, though many executives and academicians misused it in this way. As has been said:

> No simple, monolithic set of rules or strategy imperatives will point automatically to the right course. No planning system guarantees the development of successful strategies. Nor does any technique. The Business Portfolio [the growth/share matrix] made a major contribution to strategic thought. Today it is misused and overexposed. It can be a helpful tool, but it can also be misleading or, worse, a straightjacket.[39]

---

[36]D. E. Hussey, "The Brief Case—A Portfolio of Commentary and Opinion," *Long Range Planning*, February, 1981, pp. 100–103.

[37]Frederick W. Gluck, "Strategic Choice and Resource Allocation," *The McKinsey Quarterly*, Winter, 1980, p. 24.

[38]Yoram Wind and Vijay Mahajan, *op. cit.*

[39]*The Boston Consulting Group Annual Perspective* (Boston, MA: The Boston Consulting Group, 1981).

NEW PRODUCT PORTFOLIO APPROACHES

In spite of its shortcomings, the portfolio approach appears to be an attractive strategy formulation tool. An empirical study estimates that as many as 75 percent of diversified companies widely use portfolio frameworks.[40] This may be explained by the fact that a two-variable approach condenses a considerable amount of information into a simple framework for decision making. The framework also facilitates communication. Examined in this section are three new portfolio approaches: (a) the Boston Consulting Group's new framework, (b) Porter's generic strategies framework, and (c) the commodity/specialty matrix.

Boston Consulting Group's New Approach[41]

According to BCG, the requirements for strategic success vary depending upon the economic environment and competitive dynamics. In the 1970s most successful companies achieved their success by anticipating market evolution and creating unique and defensible advantage over their competitors in the new environment. In the 1980s, the focus of strategy development has shifted to competitive environment and the potential for change in that environment. To articulate this focus, BCG has developed a new portfolio matrix around two factors: (a) size of the advantage that can be created over other competitors, and (b) number of unique ways in which that advantage can be created. The combination of these two factors provides a long-term value for a business and dictates the strategy requirements.

There is a fundamental difference between businesses in which the size of the potential advantage that can be created by a competitor over all other competitors is large and those in which it is small. The reward potential for a successful strategy is only large where the size of the advantage that can be created is also large. There is also a fundamental difference between businesses that offer only one or a few ways to achieve advantage and those that present several ways. When product differentiation is costly and not valued by customers, only low price and relative cost position determine success. When a variety of approaches are possible, however, then so are a variety of strategies. Competitors can succeed by tuning their offering and costs exactly to meet a specific segment's demand. If advantage can be created by doing this, a small competitor can thrive as an industry specialist.

These two factors—the size of the advantage and the number of ways it can be achieved—can be combined into a simple matrix to help

---

[40]Philippe Haspeslagh, *op. cit.*, p. 63.
[41]Discussion of this framework draws heavily on "Strategy in the 1980s," in *Perspectives* (Boston, MA: The Boston Consulting Group, 1981).

guide more creative strategy development (see Exhibit 10-17). The specific requirements for success are different in each quadrant.

Corporate success depends on retaining advantaged positions in volume and specialization businesses. Even high market share or relatively low cost position in stalemated and fragmented industries may not be exceptionally valuable. In fact, the value of success in businesses which best fit on the right side of the matrix is always higher than in those that fit best on the left.

Following this framework, too many companies pursue strategies that are inappropriate to their specific competitive environments. Market share, for example, often lacks value in stalemated and fragmented businesses. In specialization businesses, focus and superior brand image may be more rewarding than mere size.

Over time, the nature of the competitive environment can change. Businesses that start out as fragmented industries can evolve toward specialization and even on to the volume category. McDonald's did this in away-from-home eating. Businesses that start out as volume businesses can migrate toward stalemate. This has happened to much of the world's paper industry. Others that were clearly volume businesses have moved toward specialization, as both the Japanese auto producers and a few European companies have proved to the large U.S. auto companies. Some have remained volume businesses by going toward world-scale economies, as Caterpillar has shown in construction equipment. The challenge for

EXHIBIT 10-17   Boston Consulting Group's New Portfolio Matrix

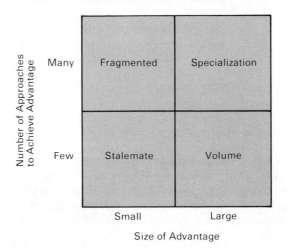

Source: "Strategy in the 1980s," in *Perspectives* (Boston: The Boston Consulting Group, 1981). Reprinted by permission.

companies is to anticipate, or even cause, these major evolutions toward a new basis of competition.

In a diversified company, the challenge is immense. A portfolio of businesses that is disadvantaged in specialization and volume businesses and weighed down by assets tied up in stalemated and fragmented industries will mean failure. The successful companies will be those with advantaged positions in volume and specialization businesses. Extraordinary success will accrue to those few strategists willing and able to create sustainable advantage, but especially to those able to change the basis of competition.

Porter's Generic Strategies Framework[42]

Porter has identified three generic strategies: (a) overall cost leadership (i.e., making units of a fairly standardized product and underpricing everybody else); (b) differentiation (i.e., turning out something customers will perceive as unique, an item whose quality, design, brand name, or reputation for service will command higher-than-average prices); and (c) focus (i.e., concentrating on a particular group of customers, geographic market, channel of distribution, or distinct segment of the product line).

As shown in Exhibit 10-18, the choice of strategy is based on two factors: the strategic target that the business aims at, and the strategic advantage that the business has in aiming at that target. According to Porter, forging successful strategy begins with understanding what is happening in one's industry and deciding which of the competitive niches available one should attempt to dominate. For example, it may be discovered by a firm that the largest competitor is aggressively pursuing cost leadership, while the other members of the industry have been trying the differentiation route; and no one has attempted to focus on some small specialty market. On the basis of this information, the firm might sharpen its efforts to distinguish its product from others, or switch to a focus game plan. As Porter says, the idea is to position the firm "so it won't be slugging it out with everybody else in the industry; if it does it right, it won't be directly toe-to-toe with anyone." The objective is to mark out a defensible competitive position—defensible not just against rival companies but also against the forces driving industry competition (discussed in Chapter 4). What it means is that the give-and-take between firms already in the business represents only one such force. The others are the bargaining power of suppliers, the bargaining power of buyers, the threat of substitute products or services, and the threat of new entrants. In conclusion, Porter's framework emphasizes not only that certain characteristics of the industry

---

[42]Michael Porter, *op. cit.*

EXHIBIT 10-18   Three Generic Strategies

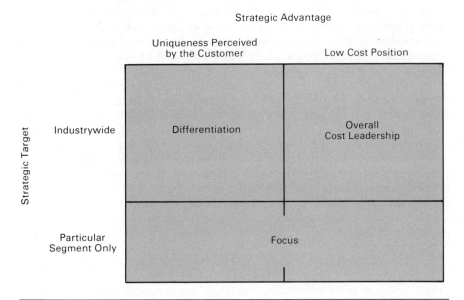

Source: Reprinted with permission of The Free Press, a Division of Macmillan, Inc., from *Competitive Strategy* by Michael E. Porter, p. 39. Copyright © 1980 by The Free Press.

must be considered in choosing a generic strategy, but that in fact they dictate the proper choice.

Commodity/Specialty Matrix[43]

The commodity/specialty matrix uses two concepts—product differentiation and price sensitivity—to categorize an industry and the customer segments served by that industry. The positioning of a product on the matrix requires a qualitative assessment of the level of product differentiation in the industry and the degree of price sensitivity exercised by consumers.

The degree of product differentiation can be determined by analysis of the product quality, the number of features, the functional use, and the impact of advertising. For example, Rolls-Royces, Calvin Klein

---

[43]Discussion of this matrix draws heavily on *Understanding the Competition: A Practical Guide to Competitive Analysis* (Arlington, VA: Michael M. Kaiser Associates, Inc., no date).

jeans, and specialty plastics are all differentiated; sugar, gasoline, and lumber are not. The level of price sensitivity exercised by the buyers depends on several factors. If the cost of the product is high relative to that of other purchases, buyers tend to be more price-sensitive. If the product does not have a great impact on the buyers' budget, they tend to be less price-sensitive. Finally, unprofitable businesses tend to be more price-sensitive than successful businesses.

To illustrate the point, personal computers, from the perspective of home buyers, are a relatively undifferentiated product; they all perform similar functions and are of similar quality. Since business buyers place greater demands on the machines, they are likely to perceive greater differences between the competitors' offerings. The degree of price sensitivity also differs between the two buyer segments. Home buyers are more price-sensitive because the purchase accounts for a large part of their total discretionary expenditures; they are more concerned with cost than quality. For business buyers, on the other hand, the product's cost is small relative to total purchases. As a result this segment is less price-sensitive and more feature-sensitive, since the purchase can have a major impact on their operations.

The commodity/specialty matrix explains the impact of industry evolution on the product (see Exhibit 10-19). When a product is introduced, it tends to be a specialty, unless it is a relatively minor substitute for an existing product. New products are usually expensive. Sales depend upon the goodwill of a limited number of customers who are less price-sensitive and care more about the novelty of the product. For example, super-strong engineered plastics, a potential replacement for other, more expensive raw materials, currently earn high margins for the few firms which manufacture these compounds.

As more firms enter the industry, however, the market becomes more competitive. The buyers begin to understand how the product works and which features are important. As the competitors start to make similar products, the customers get more choice and are able to exercise their natural price sensitivity. Products which still have differentiated characteristics but sell to price-sensitive buyers are termed "transitional." The stock brokerage industry is currently in transition as customers are switching from full-service to discount brokers. Most industries do not remain in the transitional mode. As the industry matures, and the growth slows, the competitors fight harder to increase their sales. Firms that want large market shares are in a race to appeal to the largest segment of customers. Since all firms are receiving the same signals from the customers, the products start to look alike. This lack of differentiation, in combination with the price sensitivity of the buyers, implies a commodity product; it would be difficult to differentiate Exxon's gasoline from the gasoline pumped by Shell Oil.

While most products tend to become commodities, as in the auto industry, there are usually segments which retain the characteristics of specialties. Only a few products fall in the "hybrid" category, i.e., undif-

EXHIBIT 10-19   The Commodity/Specialty Matrix

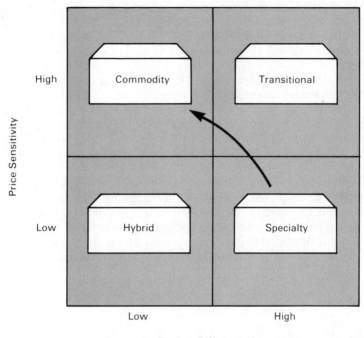

Source: *Understanding the Competition: A Practical Guide to Competitive Analysis* (Arlington, VA: Michael M. Kaiser Associates, Inc., no date). Reprinted by permission.

ferentiated products which sell to non–price-sensitive buyers. An example is the fine abrasives sold to eyeglass manufacturers. These products usually represent a very small percentage of the customer's purchases. The customer has little reason to exercise price sensitivity and remains loyal to its supplier, regardless of the price.

The commodity/specialty framework implies that there are two basic strategies which businesses can employ. A business unit can either attempt to make a product at lower cost than the competition but sell it at a comparable price, or it can attempt to make a product which meets the needs of a particular customer segment and therefore earns a higher price than the competitors' offerings. These basic strategies can be used to serve an entire market, or a particular segment of the market, but the basic functional requirements do not change.

A firm which chooses to serve commodity markets must be the low-cost producer. The cost-effective firm will price low enough to gain sales and still earn a required return. The higher-cost competitors will have to meet the market price. Specialty manufacturers are less concerned with cost; they must isolate the customer segments they wish to serve and develop a superior product at an appropriate price. Businesses that do not pursue either strategy may "fall in the middle"; by not focusing their efforts on either product development or cost reduction they may succeed at neither.

The ability to pursue one of these two strategies successfully depends on the environment and the strengths of the business. An examination of the environment in which the business operates determines whether or not there are external constraints placed on the firm's actions or chances of success. The ability of the firm to develop and market a specialty product or to be a low-cost producer depends on its ability to overcome environmental constraints.

To sum up, following the commodity/specialty matrix approach, in a majority of cases a business has two strategic options depending upon its position on the matrix. In the case of commodity products, the emphasis should be on low cost and large customer segments. Specialty products call for differentiated product focus and small customer segments. The other two matrix positions, hybrid and transitional, are either temporary in nature or only infrequently faced.

Conclusion

Portfolio approaches provide a useful tool for strategists. Granted, these approaches have limitations. But all these limitations can be overcome with a little imagination and foresight. The real concern about the portfolio approach is that its elegant simplicity often tempts managers to believe that it can solve all problems of corporate choices and resource allocation. The truth is that it addresses only half the problem: the back half. The portfolio approach is a powerful tool for helping the strategist select from the menu of opportunities. But it does not put the menu into his or her hands. That is the front half of the problem, the other critical dimension in making strategic choices: the need to generate a rich array of business options from which to choose. No simple tool is available that can provide this option-generating capability. Here only creative thinking about one's environment, one's business, one's customers, and one's competitors can help.

For successful introduction of the portfolio framework, the strategist should heed the following advice:

(a) once introduced, move quickly to establish the legitimacy of portfolio analysis;
(b) educate line managers in its relevance and use;
(c) redefine strategic business units explicitly, since their definition is the "genesis—and nemesis"—of adequately using the portfolio framework;

(d) use the portfolio framework to seek the strategic direction for different businesses, without haggling over the fancy labels by which to call these businesses;

(e) make top management acknowledge SBUs as portfolios to be managed;

(f) seek top management time for reviewing different businesses using the portfolio framework;

(g) rely on a flexible, informal management process to differentiate influence patterns at the SBU level;

(h) tie resource allocation to the business plan;

(i) consider strategic expenses and human resources as explicitly as capital investment;

(j) plan explicitly for new business development; and

(k) make a clear strategic commitment to a few selected technologies and/or markets early.[44]

SUMMARY

A diversified organization needs to examine its widely different businesses at the corporate level to see how they fit within the overall corporate purpose and to come to grips with the resource allocation problem. The portfolio approaches described in this chapter help management determine the role that each business plays in the corporation and allocate resources accordingly.

Three portfolio approaches are introduced: product life cycle, growth rate–relative market share matrix, and multifactor portfolio matrix. The product life cycle approach determines what the life status of different products is and whether the company has enough viable products to provide desired growth in the future. If the company lacks new products with which to generate growth in coming years, investments may be made in new products. If growth is hurt by the early maturity of promising products, the strategic effort may be directed toward extension of their life cycles.

The second approach, the growth rate–relative market share matrix, suggests locating products or businesses on a matrix with relative market share and growth rate as its dimensions. The four cells in the matrix, whose positions are based on whether growth is high or low and whether relative market share is high or low, are labeled stars, cash cows, question marks, and dogs. The strategy for a product or business in each cell, which is primarily based on the business's cashflow implications, is outlined.

The third approach, the multifactor portfolio matrix, again uses two variables (i.e., industry attractiveness and business strengths), but they are based on a variety of factors. Here again, a desired strategy for a product/business in each cell is recommended. The focus of the multifactor

---

[44]Philippe Haspeslagh, *op. cit.*, pp. 70–71.

matrix approach is on the return-on-investment implications of strategy alternatives, rather than on cash flow as in the growth rate–relative market share matrix approach.

Various portfolio approaches are critically examined. The criticism relates mainly to operational definition of dimensions used, weighting of variables, and product/market boundary determination. The chapter concludes with a discussion of three new portfolio approaches—the Boston Consulting Group's new framework, Porter's generic strategies, and the commodity/specialty matrix.

DISCUSSION QUESTIONS

1. *What purpose may a product portfolio serve in the context of marketing strategy?*
2. *How may the position of a product in its life cycle be located?*
3. *What is the strategic significance of products in the maturity stage of the product life cycle?*
4. *What is the meaning of relative market share?*
5. *How does the experience curve concept fit into the growth rate–relative market share portfolio scheme?*
6. *What sequence should products follow for success? What may management do to ensure this sequence?*
7. *What factors may a company consider to measure industry attractiveness and business strengths? Should these factors vary from one business to another in a company?*
8. *Illustrate how industry attractiveness and business strengths may be weighed.*
9. *What is the basic difference between the growth rate–relative market share matrix approach and the multifactor portfolio matrix approach?*
10. *What major problems with portfolio approaches have their critics identified?*
11. *What generic strategies does Porter recommend? Discuss.*

CASE 10
Chesebrough-Pond's, Inc.

In the fall of 1981, Charles J. Chapman, president of the Health and Beauty Products division of Chesebrough-Pond's, was faced with a sudden increase in competition for one of its major products. For the past decade, Chesebrough-Pond's had enjoyed a respectable share (28 percent) of the hand and body lotion market because of the outstanding success of its Vaseline Intensive Care (VIC) lotions and their complement, Pond's Cream and Cocoa Butter lotion. However, within the past eight months, several new products had been introduced in the market by present competitors and new competitors. S. C. Johnson & Son, Inc., had been aggressively advertising a new lotion called Soft Sense, emphasizing that Soft Sense had outperformed the two other leading skin lotions in a major consumer test. The makers of Jergens lotion had also introduced a new hand and body lotion to complement their existing lotion. Noxzema, the maker of Raintree face cream and body lotion, had recently introduced a "new" Raintree hand and body lotion. In addition, there was a new Rosemilk hand and body lotion to complement the old lotion.

Because of Chesebrough-Pond's strength in the market, Mr. Chapman felt that there was no reason to be alarmed by the added competition. However, all precautions had to be taken to assure that these new products would in no way disrupt the company's share of the lotion market. Mr. Chapman evaluated his division's product portfolio to see how the company could counterattack competition either by introducing a new but similar product, by diversifying further into new categories, or by changing the cost structure of the division to make it more profitable.

COMPANY HISTORY

Chesebrough-Pond's was the result of a merger that occurred on June 30, 1955, between Chesebrough Manufacturing Company Consolidated and the Pond's Extract Company. Chesebrough was incorporated on May 11, 1880, in New York. The company's success was due to an oil by-product its founder, Robert Chesebrough, had developed, which he named Vaseline petroleum jelly. In addition to manufacturing its Vaseline brand products, the company also bought, refined, and marketed oil, gas, and other volatile or mineral substances and acquired other companies for that purpose. The company manufactured 25 medicinal products and toiletries and distributed these products exclusively in the United States through the Colgate Palmolive Company.

The Pond's Extract Company manufactured and marketed the famous old Pond's creams. Prior to merging with Chesebrough, the company had acquired the Pond's Extract Company of Canada and the Pond's Extract Company of London. Both companies were actively involved in international sales, and after the merger the new company became one of the largest producers of health products and toiletries.

In the latter half of the 1950s, following the merger, the company adopted a strategy of growth by acquisition, at which time they acquired a number of companies from diverse industries. Seek & Kade Inc., makers of Pertussin cough syrup, was acquired in 1956; Prince Matchabelli, makers of several perfumes and cosmetics, was acquired in 1958; Northan Warren Inc., makers of Cutex nail care products, in 1960; and Q-tips Inc. in 1962. However, the real transformation took place when Ralph E. Ward, the company's present chairman, took command of the company in 1968. The company continued to acquire more companies, but emphasis was placed on new product activities, and heavy investment spending for people, research, and facilities followed. As a result, Chesebrough-Pond's (C-P) was transformed from a highly profitable but mature health and beauty products company into a profitable, diversified consumer-products company. Diversification was for the company the "thing" of the Ward era. Ragu Packing Company, the makers of the famous Ragu spaghetti sauce, was acquired in 1969, followed by Health-Tex infants' and children's apparel in 1973. In the following year, Adolph's meat tenderizer was acquired, and the latest acquisition, completed in July, 1978, was G. H. Bass & Company, a shoe manufacturer.

CORPORATE STRUCTURE

Through its many acquisitions C-P has been able to diversify into many different industries. The company is organized into seven major divisions (Exhibit 10-20). The International division, being the largest, accounted for 30 percent of 1980 sales. This division coordinates the activities of 41 foreign branches and subsidiaries and is responsible for sales in more than 140 foreign markets. The second largest division, Packaged Foods, accounted for 18 percent of sales and includes all the products in the Ragu lines and Adolph's meat tenderizer. The other divisions are the Health and Beauty Products division, the Health-Tex division, the Prince Matchabelli division, the Bass division, and the Hospital Products division. Financial information relative to the different divisions is given in Exhibit 10-21.

Each division is operated as an autonomous and independent unit. Each is headed by a president and has its own manufacturing facility and marketing, sales, finance, and systems departments. Marketing is such an important aspect of each division that it operates independently of the sales department. Marketing research, research and development centers, corporate engineering, legal systems, and creative services are centralized in order to minimize duplication and therefore reduce costs. During an

EXHIBIT 10-20   Chesebrough-Pond's, Inc.:: Corporate Organization

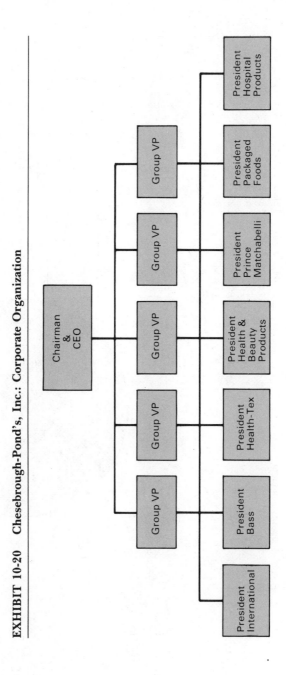

EXHIBIT 10-21   Chesebrough-Pond's, Inc.: Net Sales by Operating Division (in Thousands of Dollars)

Division	1980	1979	1978	1977
Packaged Foods	$ 245,708	$ 221,059	$182,623	$145,824
Health & Beauty Products	238,811	223,415	198,540	179,484
Health-Tex	203,542	174,002	158,805	143,698
Prince Matchabelli	124,179	113,370	96,159	86,213
Bass	112,968	80,284	28,798	—
Hospital Products	39,687	33,614	28,366	26,261
International	412,589	328,560	276,542	226,517
TOTAL	$1,377,484	$1,174,304	$969,833	$807,997

1980 Net Sales by Operating Division

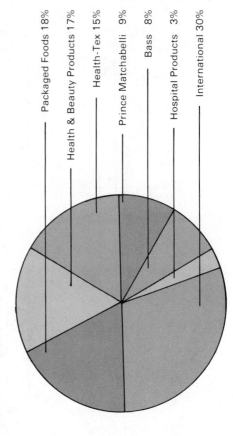

Packaged Foods 18%

Health & Beauty Products 17%

Health-Tex 15%

Prince Matchabelli 9%

Bass 8%

Hospital Products 3%

International 30%

interview, Mr. Ward stated that he is not so much interested in promoting the corporation as he is in making sure that the consumer knows the product name and what the product will do.

All of the company's divisions have been growing rapidly, with sales totaling $1,377,484,000 in 1980, a 17 percent increase over 1979's figure. Net income increased 21 percent in 1980, topping $100 million for the first time. In 1980, for the first time in its history, C-P acquired its first U.S. debt offering for $100 million. The proceeds were to be used to repay the Bass acquisition and to reduce short-term debt.

The Health and Beauty Products Division

The Health and Beauty Products division, the oldest division in C-P's family, can be said to have set the foundation for the company's success. Exhibit 10-22 shows the division's organization. This division has enjoyed the prosperity brought by some of C-P's oldest trademarks, such as Vaseline and Pond's. Vaseline petroleum jelly, the original product, holds a very large percentage of its market, while Pond's cold cream has grown steadily over the years. In addition, with the Pond's and Vaseline trademarks, C-P entered the lotion market a decade ago with Vaseline Intensive Care lotion and more recently with Pond's Cream and Cocoa Butter lotion. In 1980 Vaseline Intensive Care lotion held a stable 28 percent market share. Among the other products developed or held by the division are Cutex nail care products, Pond's Angel Face brand pressed powder, Vaseline lip balm, Q-tips cotton swabs, Vaseline Intensive Care bath beads, and the more recently introduced Rave soft perm and Rave soft hairspray. Among the division's less profitable products are Pond's Naturally Dry body powder, Pertussin cough syrup, Vaseline hair tonic, Vaseline Intensive Care baby products, and Groom and Clean hairdressing. Within the division there is a specific staff in marketing responsible for the development and marketing of each major product line; for example, one group has responsibility only for the Vaseline Intensive Care products.

The Lotion Market

The lotion market has three main segments. Because of varied applications, however, it can be difficult for the marketer to define his/her market or product (see Exhibit 10-23). The largest segment is face lotions/moisturizers with Richardson Merrill's Oil of Olay as the leader, holding a 21.5 percent estimated market share in 1980. Rosemilk from J. B. Williams and Raintree from Noxell are close seconds, each holding about 14 percent market share in 1980.

Another segment is the body lotions/therapeutic skin care market, with the most important product being Lubriderm from Texas Pharmaceutical, holding a 31.7 percent share of the market in 1980. Alpha-Keri from Westwood and Noxzema from Noxell are the other leading brands

EXHIBIT 10-22   Chesebrough-Pond's, Inc.: Health and Beauty Products Division Organization

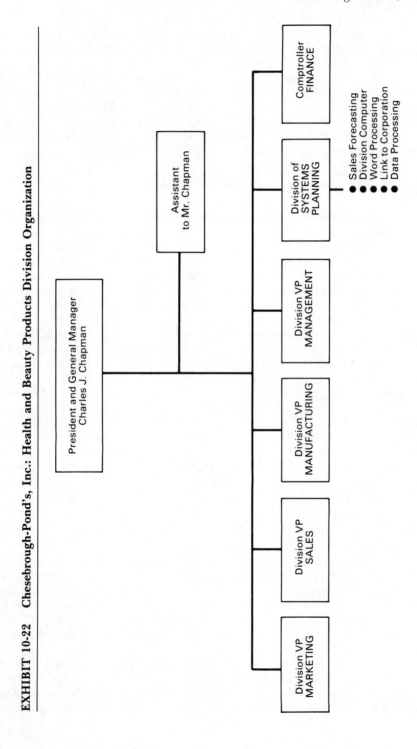

EXHIBIT 10-23 **Sales Position of Different Skin Preparations (in Thousands of Dollars)**

	1979	1978	% CHANGE
SKIN PREPARATIONS	$1,552,360	$1,365,118	+13.7
Acne Products	144,140	130,737	+10.3
OTC	57,951	53,253	+ 8.8
Proprietary	86,189	77,504	+11.2
Suntan Products	107,976	104,885	+ 2.9
Sun Screens/Blocks	52,039	36,143	+44.0
Lip Protectors	34,068	28,365	+20.1
Face Creams/Cleansers	323,320	256,600	+26.0
Face Lotions/Moisturizers	321,050	288,492	+11.3
Body Lotions/Emollients	260,456	216,572	+20.3
OTC	35,743	33,035	+ 8.2
Proprietary	224,713	183,537	+22.4
Wrinkle Removers/Astringents	74,065	42,750	+73.3
Depilatories	19,657	20,577	− 4.5
Talcum Powder	18,620	63,170	NA
Cleansing Pads	59,627	66,147	− 9.9
Hand Creams	63,379	56,708	+11.8
Beauty Masks/Skin Whiteners	73,963	53,972	+37.0

Source: *Product Marketing,* July, 1980.

with estimated market share of 28.1 percent and 21 percent, respectively. In the fall of 1981, C-P entered this $100-million therapeutic skin care market with its new Vaseline Dermatology Formula lotion. One company spokesman projected that C-P's share of this market would reach 25 percent by the fall of 1982.

The third segment is the hand and body lotion market, in which C-P's Vaseline Intensive Care lotion is the leader, holding 28 percent share of the market. C-P has three kinds of VIC lotions in the market: the regular lotion, the lotion for extra-dry skin, and the new extra-strength formula to appeal to individuals with more serious skin problems. The company makes drug claims, promising that the product will help "sore, red, and itching hands." In addition, C-P manufactures Pond's Cream and Cocoa Butter lotion, which is more cosmetic than therapeutic. A company spokesman noted:

> What consumers want in a hand lotion is a nice, soft, silky-smooth feeling immediately after applying the lotion. In addition, they are concerned about consistency. They don't want a runny lotion. Since any product rubbed into the hands will leave them soft and smooth, C-P concentrated on achieving absorption, good consistency, and a nongreasy feeling in its products.

Chesebrough-Pond's puts its primary advertising focus on active women between the ages of 18 to 49 but attempts to attract other groups as well. For example, using as its theme "Working Hands of America," one series of ads pictured farmers, students, and older persons of both sexes.

INDUSTRY AND COMPETITION

Although there are many competitors in the market, C-P's principal competition comes from five major companies: American Brands with Jergens, Revlon with Milk Plus Six, J. B. Williams with Rosemilk, Noxell with Raintree, and Procter & Gamble with Wondra.

Before 1970, American Brands' Jergens lotion had such a substantial share of the market that "Jergens" was almost a synonym for "lotion." At that time the other products on the market included J. B. Williams' Rosemilk, Richardson Merrill's Oil of Olay, and Revlon's Milk Plus Six. Because of the lack of new products, however, the hand and body lotion market had an annual growth rate of only 4 to 5 percent. In 1970, C-P changed the whole concept of hand and body lotions when it introduced its Vaseline Intensive Care lotion. C-P carved out a niche in the market by putting less stress on the effect of aging on the body and more on the therapeutic aspects of its product. Vaseline Intensive Care lotion became the number one hand lotion in the market, demoting Jergens to the number two position. Since then several companies have entered the market, including Miller Morton with Skin Quencher and Noxell with Raintree. In 1977, the giant Procter & Gamble, realizing that the hand and body lotion market was far from reaching full potential, also made an entry with its new Wondra lotion. In 1981 there were many new entries in the market—a new Jergens hand and body lotion, a new Raintree lotion, a new Rosemilk lotion, and S. C. Johnson's new Soft Sense lotion. Adding to the competition, though with small market shares, were numerous store brands such as CVS and Woolworth's.

Procter & Gamble spent years developing its market entry, Wondra lotion. When the product was finally introduced in 1977, many competitors noted that it wasn't very much different from the lotions already on the market. However, others perceived it as being much thicker and, as one noted, "You can almost feel it working." Despite heavy advertising efforts, P&G managed to capture only a 10 percent market share, at the expense of Rosemilk and Jergens.

One may wonder why a big company like P&G entered such a small market after it was saturated with competition. At the time of P&G's entry, *Advertising Age* (October 24, 1977 issue) noted:

> The company chose this relatively small market because it realizes that new categories that fit all its criteria are hard to find. P&G reportedly looks for large categories in which it can produce all the materials needed to market the product. P&G wants to limit its products to those that require distribution in all three major retail outlets—grocery, drug, and mass merchandise stores. P&G also aims for a field where it can attain a leadership position within a reasonable period of time. Since all of these standards are becoming harder to meet, P&G is considering smaller categories than in the past.

Rosemilk hand and body lotion was originally manufactured by Century Creations, which in 1967 began marketing the product through a very unique channel of distribution—the local milkman. The product was packaged in a pink container shaped like a milk bottle and brought into homes with the orders of milk and cream through 450 home-delivery dairies. As home milk delivery began to decline in the early '70s, Rosemilk's distribution strategy became obsolete and ineffective. In 1973, J. B. Williams purchased the company and repositioned the product using the more traditional distribution channels. In addition, actress Julie London endorsed the product, and thus the commercials and the product's image fit neatly into the current marketing swing toward the mature woman. In 1976, J. B. Williams spent $6,000,000 advertising the product in a battle with Jergens for the number two position in the market.

Jergens, on the other hand, had been slacking for years. Since the promotional battle with Rosemilk in 1976 (which it lost), it still hadn't been able to regain any strength. In 1981, Jergens introduced a new lotion on the market to complement its dying formula and to revive the name. In 1980, Jergens and Rosemilk, combined, controlled only 30 percent of the market.

STRENGTHS AND WEAKNESSES

The major competitive strength of Chesebrough-Pond's Health and Beauty Products division is its strong consumer franchise—its trademarks. Words like Vaseline and Pond's have been common household words since the early 1900s. People have relied on Vaseline petroleum jelly for cuts, burns, dry skin, and diaper rash ever since the product was introduced. Housewives trust the products and find many uses for them. Though the original Pond's and Vaseline products have matured and are dying out, C-P has developed new products using the old established names to obtain quick customer acceptance.

Among C-P's other strengths are a strong commitment to advertising and to new product development and a pool of reliable marketing people. When asked about the company's weaknesses, Mark Hedges, a senior marketing executive of the company, stated, "I honestly don't think we have any." He said the only failure he could think of was letting Oil of Olay enter the market and obtain such a large market share. Mr. Hedges stated that C-P should have been able to produce a similar product with the Pond's name to compete in the face moisturizer market; not being able to foresee a competitor's move was a bad mistake.

ADVERTISING AND PROMOTION

C-P invests heavily in advertising the products of the Health and Beauty Products division to help pull the products through the channels of distribution. Mr. Hedges stated, "We spend more money on advertising than any of our competitors. The only time they are able to outspend us is when they are introducing a new product." For example, P&G spent over $15,000,000 to launch its new Wondra lotion. Similarly, when S. C. Johnson introduced its Soft Sense lotion in the fall of 1981, they promoted it heavily, using media advertising, point-of-purchase displays, and sample and coupon distribution to residential homes. During these heavy promotional periods, C-P increased its advertising expenditures, not so much to match the competitors as to get a better exposure in the market and reinforce the message "Remember we're better." The company made heavy use of media advertising, point-of-purchase displays, and coupons. In 1980, the division spent $18,783,000 on advertising, an increase of 9 percent over 1979. Of this total, $5,618,800 was spent on Vaseline Intensive Care products, $1,810,200 on Q-tips swabs, $586,500 on Vaseline petroleum jelly, $6,922,500 on Pond's cold creams and lotions, $1,646,100 on Cutex nail products, and $2,198,600 on Rave home permanent.

In its heavy emphasis on advertising the division's objective is to create such a demand for its products that retailers will really have no choice but to stock them. Mr. Hedges explained:

> We've always concentrated our efforts on advertising, but every now and then, we would slack off on a few products because we have to employ our resources where they are needed the most. However, since Chapman became the president of the division four years ago, we have adopted a new policy of keeping our advertising expenditures high under all circumstances.

The division's goal is to have a more efficient production system, thereby cutting costs, so that the extra revenues can be applied to new product development and advertising. Though C-P had not advertised its Vaseline petroleum jelly in a long time, in 1980 they decided to take a different approach and advertise it again extensively in order to revitalize it. By showing new uses for this maturing and dying product, the company succeeded in increasing its sales tremendously.

C-P's promotional strategy was best exemplified in 1977 when the division was testing its new improved VIC lotion. Just before the company introduced the improved lotion and the new Pond's Cream and Cocoa Butter lotion, P&G started test marketing its new Wondra lotion. In order to stall P&G, the company flooded the market with a 2-for-1 promotion of its 10-ounce bottle of VIC lotion. This succeeded in stalling P&G long enough for the division to begin pushing its two new lotions. Through heavy promotion and new product development, C-P was able to maintain its 28 percent share of the lotion market. P&G managed to capture 10 percent of the market.

Through skillful advertising and promotion, C-P has been able to change the total concept of the markets it has entered. As noted earlier, before 1970 American Brands' Jergens lotion had dominated the market. Its advertising, which portrayed little old ladies rubbing in Jergens faithfully, brought an unfortunate association with aging. When Milk Plus Six and Rosemilk were introduced to the market, the image was still unchanged.

When C-P entered the market, however, with advertising aimed at younger as well as older users and promising "It's good for you," it changed the total concept of lotion. Similarly, before C-P entered the home hair permanent market, it was a slow-growth category. When C-P introduced its Rave home hair permanent as a product that was odorless and would leave the hair feeling soft, the product created such excitement in the market that within the first year, C-P captured the leadership position with a 27 percent market share.

DISTRIBUTION

The division's products are distributed through mass merchandisers, large department stores, drug stores, grocery stores, and most of the mom-and-pop stores. The division's sales department operates through eight sales offices throughout the country, with the major offices in Stamford, Connecticut; Chicago, and Houston. The division's 150 salespersons report to district managers in the sales offices. The majority of the salespeople call on large retailers; some are assigned to call on wholesalers. The division uses wholesalers primarily to distribute to the small mom-and-pop stores and other stores that the sales force cannot reach.

The salespeople sell only the division's major products: Vaseline Intensive Care lotions, VIC bath beads, Rave soft perm and hairsprays, Vaseline petroleum jelly, Q-tips cotton swabs, Pond's cold creams and lotion, and Cutex nail products. The company's maturing products, including the VIC baby products, Vaseline hair tonic, Pond's body powder, Pertussin cough formula, and Groom and Clean hairdressing, are distributed through brokers who know specifically where to locate a market for them.

The division has eight selling periods during the year. Products such as VIC lotions, Rave, and other major products are pushed during all eight periods; other products such as Vaseline petroleum jelly and Q-tips cotton swabs are pushed only during five or six of the selling periods.

C-P engages in very few distributor incentive programs. As Mr. Hedges stated, "We rely basically on a pull strategy. We do some pushing mostly because our competitors are doing it." C-P gives its distributors quantity discounts and allowances and engages in co-op advertising. Occasionally, C-P uses push money to encourage retailers to carry a new line.

The health and beauty products that are sold overseas are the sole responsibility of the International division. They locate the right markets for the products and handle all packaging, distribution, promotion, and other marketing-related activities. The Health and Beauty Products division handles the domestic market exclusively.

C-P'S STRATEGIES

C-P's objective is to grow consistently and profitably. Over the past decades, it has achieved this objective mainly through acquisitions. Profitable companies have become very scarce, however, because "Everyone is after the good ones." Mr. Hedges reported that Ralph Ward, the chairman, looks at hundreds of possible acquisitions each year. Although C-P's executives are constantly on the lookout for attractive acquisitions, they have also chosen to achieve growth internally through new product development, with the objective of introducing a new product every year. For the most part, the products introduced have been extensions of ex-

EXHIBIT 10-24   Chesebrough-Pond's, Inc.: Consolidated Statement of Income

(in thousands except per-share data)	Year ended December 31, 1980	1979
Net sales	$1,377,484	$1,174,274
Royalties	2,912	2,819
Operating revenues	1,380,396	1,177,093
Cost of products sold	662,527	567,205
Selling, advertising, and administrative expenses	524,430	446,336
Operating costs and expenses	1,186,957	1,013,541
Income from operations	193,439	163,552
Other income (expense):		
Interest expense	(22,517)	(17,341)
Interest income	4,809	3,928
Loss on foreign exchange	(383)	(1,253)
Miscellaneous—net	408	(1,050)
	(17,683)	(15,716)
Income before provision for income taxes	175,756	147,836
Provision for income taxes	75,553	65,227
Net income	$ 100,203	$ 82,609
Earnings per share	$3.10	$2.56

isting products rather than major new entries. For instance, when C-P introduced the new VIC lotion in 1978, it wasn't so much its ingredients as its promotion as a therapeutic product that was new. A number of minor improvements have been made over the years in the lotion, but the major breakthrough was the new VIC dermatology formula developed in 1981. The one truly new product was Rave home perm and Rave soft

EXHIBIT 10-25   Chesebrough-Pond's, Inc.: Consolidated Balance Sheet (in Thousands)

| | December 31, | | |
	1980	1979	1978
Assets			
Current assets:			
Cash and short-term investments ...	$ 65,332	$ 24,913	$ 30,429
Accounts receivable	254,214	228,625	194,882
Inventories	296,370	258,891	233,189
Prepaid expenses.................	18,253	16,200	15,279
Total current assets	634,169	528,629	473,779
Property, plant and equipment:			
At cost	315,605	273,137	236,131
Less accumulated depreciation	111,241	94,259	80,946
Net property, plant and equipment	204,364	178,878	155,185
Investments and other assets	25,647	23,865	23,020
Goodwill and trademarks	57,288	57,711	54,271
	$921,468	$789,083	$706,255
Liabilities and Shareholders' Equity			
Current liabilities:			
Notes payable....................	$ 32,428	$ 23,858	$ 40,517
Accounts payable and accrued liabilities......................	145,915	132,250	101,604
Income taxes payable.............	43,033	34,081	21,744
Long-term debt due within one year	36,095	36,265	7,390
Total current liabilities	257,471	226,454	171,255
Long-term debt	130,632	97,701	120,900
Deferred income taxes..............	10,251	9,108	9,038
Other non-current liabilities..........	20,471	17,486	13,930
Shareholders' equity:			
Common stock....................	32,598	32,466	32,466
Additional paid-in capital	49,948	46,417	46,386
Retained earnings	423,050	364,263	316,523
	505,596	443,146	395,375
Less treasury stock, at cost	2,953	4,812	4,243
Total shareholders' equity	502,643	438,334	391,132
	$921,468	$789,083	$706,255

hairspray. The company tried to differentiate the product from those of its competitors by making the perm the first of its kind that was odorless. Exhibits 10-24 and 10-25 show the company's income statement and balance sheet.

CORPORATE PORTFOLIO

Discussing the corporation's portfolio and the Health and Beauty Products division's position in that portfolio, Charles Chapman noted:

> We really don't have a cash cow or a question mark or a dog. All of our divisions are stars. Our newest strategy is to try to minimize production cost in all the divisions by having reliable, cost-efficient machinery, and by having the best personnel. As such, by cutting costs we can invest more in research and development and advertising in all the divisions.

Mr. Chapman added, however, that within the product portfolio of a division, there might be cash cows, question marks, stars, and dogs. For example, in the Health and Beauty Products division, some of the products, such as Pond's Naturally Dry body powder, Vaseline hair tonic, and Groom and Clean hairdressing, could be considered cash cows and perhaps even dogs. Although these products are still on the market, the division has discontinued all investments in these products and is harvesting them. These products are not sold through national distributors but through brokers. The division periodically reevaluates its products in order to eliminate any unprofitable ones. For example, early in 1981, the division conducted an extensive evaluation, and discontinued many products whose

EXHIBIT 10-26   Chesebrough-Pond's, Inc.: Health and Beauty Products Division Product Portfolio

Market Growth	RAVE Q-tips VIC Lotions	
	Pond's Cold Creams	
	Vaseline Petroleum Jelly	Groom & Clean Hairdressing Vaseline Hair Tonic

Market Share

EXHIBIT 10-27 Chesebrough-Pond's, Inc.: Competitive Information

COMPANY	COSMETICS (in thousands of dollars)		
	1980 NET SALES (1979)	1980 COST OF GOODS (1979)	1980 NET INCOME (1979)
Bristol-Myers, Inc.	$3,158,283 ($2,752,777)	$ 959,900 (—)	$270,579 ($231,545)
Avon Products, Inc.	2,569,100 (2,380,000)	1,092,200 (—)	241,253 (250,700)
Gillette Co.	2,315,300 (1,984,722)	— (—)	124,000 (110,618)
Revlon Inc.	2,203,324 (1,717,993)	— (—)	192,407 (152,688)
Chesebrough-Pond's, Inc.	1,377,484 (1,174,274)	— (567,205)	100,203 (82,609)
Faberge Inc.	248,200 (245,307)	133,588 (91,081)	2,100 (7,056)
Alberto-Culver Inc.	232,024 (190,025)	117,250 (—)	10,435 (5,799)
Noxell Corp.	204,160 (179,665)	82,600 (—)	14,699 (13,335)
Carter-Wallace	208,206 (177,972)	81,013 (70,255)	8,065 (6,504)
Mary Kay Cosmetics	166,900 (91,400)	— (27,800)	— (9,600)
MEM Inc.	60,800 (59,430)	— (32,200)	3,600 (3,500)
Minnetonka Inc.	73,210 (25,100)	34,170 (—)	5,530 (1,522)
LaMaur Inc.	50,015 (41,823)	29,496 (24,093)	1,396 (744)
Cosmetic Sciences, Inc.	506 (461)	— (—)	53 (33)

Source: *Drug & Cosmetics*, July, 1981.

markets had declined to an unprofitable level. Exhibit 10-26 provides a brief view of the division's portfolio.

FUTURE OF THE DIVISION

When asked about new competition that the division was facing, Mr. Chapman stated:

> Well, we can't panic everytime someone introduces a new product in the market. However, we have to be concerned. When a new product is introduced, we would first analyze it to see how different it is from the products that are presently on the market. We would also have our chemists test it to determine if it is better. Next, we would evaluate the new competitor's marketing plans, such as when they plan to ship the product, how big their advertising expenditures are, etc. When they advertise extensively, we don't try to match them, but we do add some weight to our present expenditures.

The future looks promising for C-P's Health and Beauty Products division because "they don't have all their eggs in one basket." Despite the threat of increased competition in the lotion market, C-P has several strong trademarks and a strong marketing staff to rely on. In addition, the division is continuously diversifying with new product development (e.g., the Rave line) so that its dependence on any particular product will lessen.

The company as a whole has diversified into several growing markets. Many years back, the company decided not to depend entirely on its traditional lines because of fear that larger competitors would buy them out. In 1981 the company stood as a large, international conglomerate, with increasing sales and earnings in all of its divisions. The company's overall position vis-à-vis its major competitors is summarized in Exhibit 10-27.

PART SIX
Strategy Implementation and Control

CHAPTER 11 - Organizational Structure

CHAPTER 11
Organizational Structure

Whatever action is performed by a great man, common men follow in his footsteps, and whatever standards he sets by exemplary acts, all the world pursues.

Bhagavad Gita

A strategic planning system should provide answers to two basic questions: what to do and how to do it. The first question refers to selection of a strategy, the second to organizational arrangements. An organization must have not only a winning strategy to pursue, but also a matching structure to facilitate its implementation. The emphasis in the preceding chapters has been on strategy formulation. This chapter is devoted to building a viable organizational structure to administer the strategy.

William Durant, the founder of General Motors, had a winning strategy: "a car for every pocket and taste." Despite this superb strategy, General Motors in its early history ran into problems because a matching structure did not accompany the strategy. Alfred Sloan discovered the missing link in General Motors' strategic perspective and restructured the company around the concepts of decentralization and the profit center. How General Motors continued to grow and eventually emerged as the world's largest corporation is history.[1]

Fitting a company's structure and organization to its strategies is a delicate process that requires a finely tuned management sense. Today's changing business environment—an outgrowth of diversification, acquisition and agglomeration, the creation of new industries and the phasing out of old ones—is causing a new wave of strategic reorganization for the future. More often than not, the successful implementation of strategic plans requires structural reorganization. Executives are finding that planning for organizational change is a difficult task. There is no magic for-

---

[1]See Alfred D. Chandler, Jr., *Strategy and Structure: Chapters in the History of the Industrial Enterprise* (Cambridge, MA: M.I.T. Press, 1962); and Alfred P. Sloan, Jr., *My Years with General Motors* (New York: Doubleday & Co., 1964). See also David J. Hall and Maurice A. Saias, "Strategy Follows Structure," *Strategic Management Journal*, Vol. 1, 1980, pp. 149–163.

mula to ensure successful reorganization and, generally, no "perfect" prototype available to follow. This chapter, therefore, provides some real-life examples to help the reader develop a sensitivity to the factors that require consideration in building a customized prototype. The thrust of the chapter is on:

—Evaluating the fit between present corporate structure and long-range corporate plans.
—Identifying and assessing realistic organizational options.
—Drawing up the tactics and determining the pace for corporate change.

The discussion is planned around three dimensions of strategy implementation and control: (a) strategic reorganization (i.e., formal authority-responsibility patterns to simplify and encourage strategy implementation; (b) leadership style (i.e., establishing an interpersonal environment that is conducive to strategy implementation); and (c) measuring strategic performance (i.e., developing a network of control and communication to monitor and evaluate progress in achieving strategic goals). In addition, the impact of strategic planning on marketing organization is studied.

STRATEGIC REORGANIZATION

Traditionally corporations have been organized with a strong emphasis on pursuing and achieving established objectives. Such organizations adapt well to growing internal complexities and provide adequate incentive mechanisms and systems of accountability to support objectives. However, they fail to provide a congenial environment for strategic planning. For example, one of the organizational capabilities needed for strategic planning is that of modifying or redefining the objectives themselves so that the corporation is prepared to meet future competition. The traditional organizational structure resists change, and this is why a new type of structure is needed for strategic planning. Mainer explains this point as follows:

> The crux of the matter is that the behavorial requirements of planning as a management task are often different from, or in conflict with, the processes and content of management work normally prevalent in the organization. Thus, it is quite possible that an organization optimally geared to the pursuit of established objectives may be less than optimally prepared to work on the evaluation and adoption of new objectives or strategies. To a very real extent, planning is a new kind of management activity.[2]

---

[2]Robert Mainer, "The Impact of Strategic Planning on Executive Behavior," a special commentary (Boston: The Boston Consulting Group, 1968), pp. 4–5.

Exhibit 11-1 differentiates the characteristics of operational management (i.e., the traditional organization with emphasis on the achievement of established objectives) and strategic planning. By and large, operational management works in known territory and is concerned with immediate issues. Strategic planning stresses unfamiliar perspectives and is oriented toward the future.

How an organization's process, system, and structure may be modified and changed to accommodate strategic perspectives is illustrated with reference to three large corporations: Texas Instruments, General Electric, and General Motors.

Texas Instruments' OST System[3]

Because of its calculators, Texas Instruments Incorporated (TI) is well known today. The company has grown over the years at an average compound rate of 25 percent annually, reaching $2.5 billion in sales in 1978. Over the same period profits have grown at a rate of 24 percent. Although in the early 1980s the company ran into problems, ascribed to its computer business, by 1984 it was on the way to recovery.

Exhibit 11-2 shows the traditional organizational structure at TI. The company is divided into four groups supported by four staff departments. The groups break down further into divisions, which in turn divide into product/customer centers. There are a total of 77 product/ customer centers (PCCs). The PCCs operate like complete small business organizations, each having its own profit responsibility. Each PCC manager has decentralized responsibility for the creation, manufacturing, and marketing functions of products serving a particular class of customers in a specific product area. The range of a PCC business may be between $1 million and $80 million in sales.

Basically, the PCC environment has a short-term emphasis. Traditionally long-term planning at TI was carried out by top management, with the group and division managers serving as communicators between PCCs and top management. The traditional structure worked well until the early 1960s, when certain developments in the semiconductor field and the loss of some government business led TI to change its strategic perspective. The traditional structure posed some problems for the pursuit of new strategic directions. For example, in many cases one PCC duplicated the staff work of other PCCs. Each PCC operated to maximize its own benefits without any concern for the corporation as a whole—a typical characteristic of a decentralized unit. New ideas were keyed to cur-

---

[3]This section draws heavily on executive speeches available from Texas Instruments. For example, see Charles H. Phipps, "Management of Innovation: The OST System," a presentation made at the *Business Week* Strategic Planning Conference in New York on October 5, 1978.

EXHIBIT 11-1   Organizational Characteristics

OPERATIONAL MANAGEMENT	STRATEGIC PLANNING
1. Concerned with goals derived from established objectives.	1. Concerned with the identification and evaluation of new objectives and strategies.
2. Goals usually have been validated through extensive past experience.	2. New objectives and strategies can be highly debatable; experience within the organization or in other companies may be minimal.
3. Goals are reduced to specific sub-goals for functional units.	3. Objectives usually are evaluated primarily for corporate significance.
4. Managers tend to identify with functions or professions and to be preoccupied with means.	4. Managers need a corporate point of view oriented to the environment.
5. Managers obtain relatively prompt evidence of their performance against goals.	5. Evidence of the merit of new objectives or strategies is often available only after several years.
6. Incentives, formal and social, are tied to operating goals.	6. Incentives are at best only loosely associated with planning.
7. The "rules of the game" become well understood. Experienced individuals feel competent and secure.	7. New fields of endeavor may be considered. Past experience may not provide competence in a "new game."
8. The issues are immediate, concrete, and familiar.	8. Issues are abstract, deferrable (to some extent), and may be unfamiliar.

Source: Robert Mainer, "The Impact of Strategic Planning on Executive Behavior," a special commentary (Boston: The Boston Consulting Group, 1968), pp. 4–5. Reprinted by permission of the publisher.

EXHIBIT 11-2   Texas Instruments Inc.: Traditional Organization (1970)

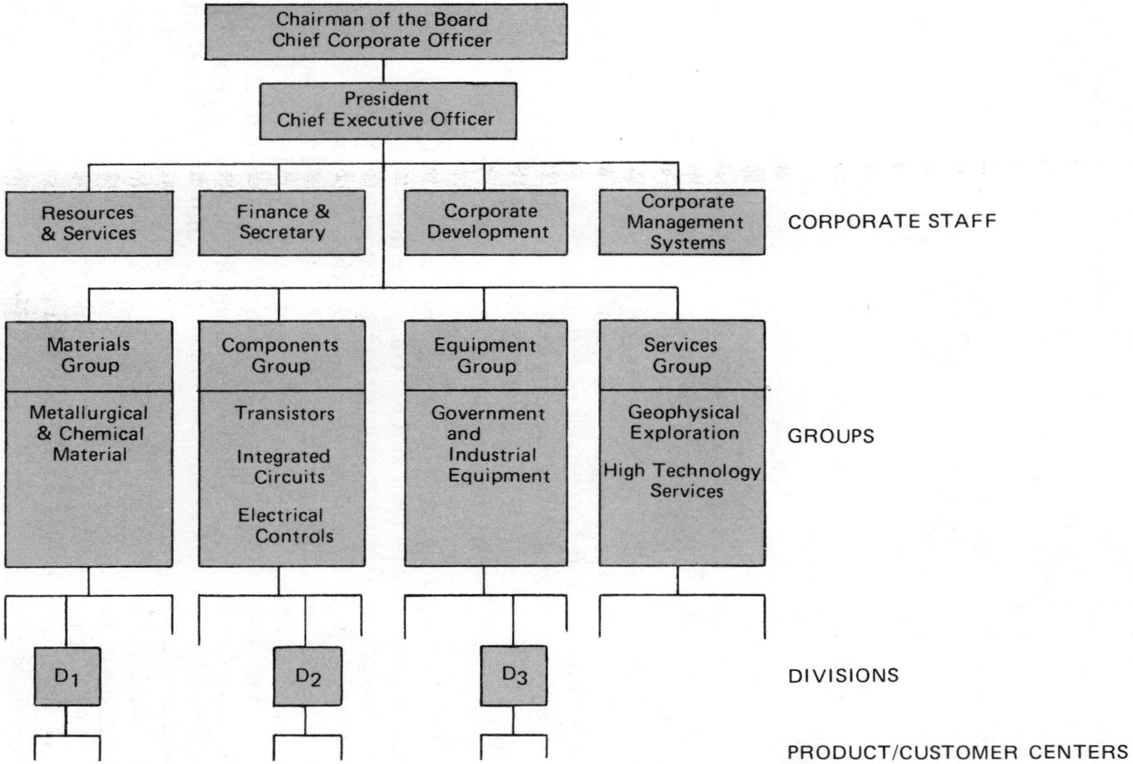

Source: Texas Instruments Incorporated. Reprinted by permission.

rent strengths and were mostly incremental in nature. In short, there was a lack of synergistic effort.

The OST (objectives, strategies, and tactics) system was created to offset the above problems and to provide an aggressive perspective for facing the future. The system was established to supplement, not replace, the traditional organization. Having complete budgetary responsibility, the PCCs continue to be the operating units for implementation of plans. The OST system is designed for strategic planning (including resource allocation).

Exhibit 11-3 presents the OST system. At the top is the corporate objective, which refers to (1) the economic purpose of the company; (2) product, market, and technical goals; (3) responsibilities to employees, shareowners, community, and society; and (4) financial goals. The corporate objective is supported by a set of nine business objectives, each of which is expressed in the following terms:

1. *Scope* (a business charter which establishes the boundaries of the business, appraises the potential opportunities in the business, and studies the technical and market trends and the overall competitive structure of industry serving the business)
2. *Performance measures* (sales, profit, return on assets, and served available market penetration for five and ten years ahead)
3. *Market and product goals* (served available market projections by product and percentage penetration by product)
4. *Technical goals* (technical constraints and innovations required)
5. *Critique* (competitive evaluation, threats and contingencies, and market shifts)

The business objectives for a company using the OST system are stated by the top management and the corporate development committee. Objectives which pertain to an industry (e.g., the auto industry) or a geographic area (e.g., Latin America) often cut across groups and divisions. For each objective an objective manager, who may be a group or division manager, is appointed. In other words, an executive in the traditional organization has an additional responsibility in the OST system. The objective manager for TI's auto industry, for example, may be the components group executive, since most of the sales for this industry come from integrated circuits. When a manager has dual responsibility, about one fourth of the manager's time is spent on strategy-related work and the remaining three fourths of the time on the responsibilities to the product line or on short-run profit performance.

At the next level in the OST system is the strategy statement, which describes in detail the environment of the business opportunity to be pursued in support of the objective. Normally there are several strategies for supporting an objective. For example, in the auto industry the company may have one strategy involving automobile electronics, one involving material applications, and perhaps one for safety systems. The strategy looks

EXHIBIT 11-3 Texas Instruments Inc.: The OST System

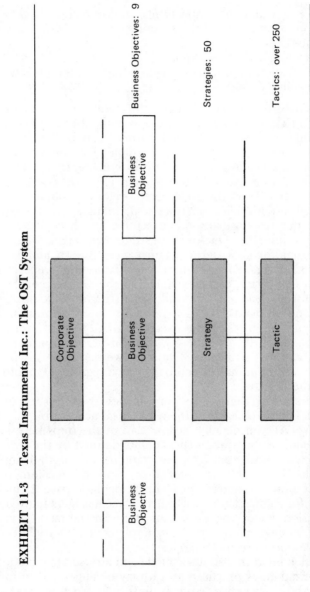

Source: Texas Instruments Incorporated. Reprinted by permission.

ahead a number of years (normally five to ten) and defines intermediate checkpoints along the way so as to provide milestones against which to judge progress. Each strategy is defined by taking the following factors into consideration:

1. Strategy statement (opportunity environment, required innovations, competitive actions, contingencies, and major commitments)
2. Major long-range checkpoints
3. Contribution to and/or possible impact on the objective
4. Probability of success

Texas Instruments has over 60 strategies throughout the company.

There is a strategy manager for each strategy. In the auto industry, the strategy manager for automobile electronics may be a division manager in the components group (see D_2 in Exhibit 11-2); the strategy manager for materials applications may be a division manager in the materials group (D_1). The safety-systems strategy manager may come from the equipment group (D_3). Thus, the group executive of the components group has an additional responsibility for strategic planning as an objective manager. For the latter responsibility this executive has three strategy managers reporting to him/her. One of these strategy managers (i.e., D_2) also reports to him/her for short-term performance. But D_1 and D_3 report only as strategy managers. For short-term performance they report to other group executives. In brief, each manager has the two responsibilities of short-term performance under the traditional structure and strategy-oriented performance under the OST system. For these two responsibilities a manager may report to the same executive or to two different executives. In about one fourth of the cases, there are cross-group and cross-divisional objectives and strategies. The objective manager is expected to identify strategies throughout the company and integrate them into a strategic plan for the objective.

For each strategy there are several tactics (over 250 for the company as a whole), and for each of them a tactical action program (TAP) is developed. A TAP is a detailed action plan of the steps necessary for reaching the major or long-range checkpoints defined by the strategy. A TAP is normally a short-term program ranging in length from six to eighteen months. Each tactic is assigned to a product/customer center manager; the resources required for its implementation are defined, and a time schedule for completion is established. PCC managers may cut across group and division lines. Progress on the status of the tactic is reported monthly. Thus, strategic planning and its implementation are linked since the same people operate in both modes.

The relation between a strategic mode and an operating mode within the same organization, as practiced at TI, may be illustrated in the form of a matrix, as shown in Exhibit 11-4. It must be noted that there are not two separate and distinct organizations; there is a single organization with

EXHIBIT 11-4   Texas Instruments Inc.: Relationship Between Strategic and Operating Modes

(a) Organization Matrix
OST/Operating

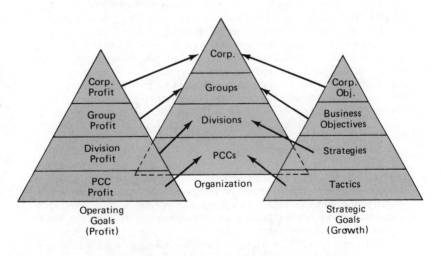

(b) Dual Organizational Roles

Source: Texas Instruments Incorporated. Reprinted by permission.

clearly defined responsibilities for both the strategic and the operating modes.

For example, one of the roles of a strategy manager, as indicated in Exhibit 11-4, is to identify the TAPs required (represented by X's) and to pull them together from across the company into a coordinated strategic plan. Sometimes the strategy manager may also be the manager of a product/customer center, especially if there is one PCC which occupies a dominant position in the strategy. Almost invariably the strategy or tactic manager will also have an operating role to play. Only rarely does the strategy manager or tactic manager serve only in a strategy role. Dove explains the manager's roles at TI as follows:

> To understand how this works, let's look at the differences between what we would call operating investments and strategic investments. Suppose that you were an operating manager and were concerned only about short-term profit and loss goals. The investments you would make would tend to be only those necessary for current operations, those required to meet your current commitments. In other words, you probably would invest about what was necessary to maximize the year-ahead results.
>
> Now, on the other hand, suppose you were a strategy manager concerned mainly with long-term goals. First—let's face it—your investments would be completely discretionary to current operations; that is, we can choose not to undertake them at all. They are always avoidable or postponable, but they are key to our long-term growth.
>
> Now, with these definitions in mind, let us say you are a young manager somewhere within one of the company's product-customer centers. You might be in Research, or Manufacturing, or Marketing, or any area, but let's say you are performing a line function within your center and a large measure of your day-to-day responsibility is the profitability of that center. Suppose that you thought you could see the possibility for a new business entry for TI, or possibly for a major impact on one of the existing strategies. You are excited about the proposal and would like to spend more time digging into the possibilities of its success. The problem is that every minute you give to this idea is a minute you have not given to your product-customer center. In a way, this might be considered wasteful. In many organizations, short-term pressures for operating profits might completely block your efforts. This would be a very frustrating and demotivating experience. You might soon learn to avoid wasting time on such innovative thinking. But in terms of future business growth, these are precisely the kinds of ideas the organization needs to stay alive. This is the activity we are attempting to institutionalize through the OST system. How does this come about?
>
> Through the OST overlay, we have a goal structure for strategic activities as well as operating activities. Not only can we measure profit and loss performance operationally, but we also can allocate resources through the OST structure and measure our progress toward these strategic goals. Now your new idea has a home. It can be given resources for further development and, if the progress warrants, heavier

support later. A number of outcomes are possible. Your idea might develop as a tactic. Or it might be big enough to stimulate an entire strategy. Or it might even be the catalyst which would lead to a new major corporate goal at the objective level. Whatever the case, your idea would be clearly a part of the OST structure and would be recognized and supported by deliberate choice. It won't have to be bootlegged or dropped completely through the crack.[4]

The OST cycle begins in the spring of each year with the strategic planning conference. About 400 managers from TI's worldwide operations attend this meeting along with corporate officers and board members. Each business objective manager presents his/her current assessment of opportunities and redefines the long-range goals. His/her position is supported by presentations from his/her key strategy managers, who define their business directions and goals and the resources required for each of these. By the end of the second quarter, the plans are appraised, goals reviewed, and corrective action defined. In the third quarter the corporate OST expenditure level for the forthcoming year is defined, and the corporate development committee allocates funds to each business objective according to its growth opportunities, competitive status, and progress made in the execution of its plans. The objective and strategy managers define their tactical programs, rank them in order of importance, and, after several iterations, present them to the corporate development committee for approval. During the process of this approval, tactical programs may be reoriented and funds shifted between objectives. Thereafter, during the course of the year, the business objective managers are encouraged to continually appraise the progress of their programs and shift funds as necessary.

For the first five years of OST implementation, although plans were developed and action programs defined, there was no control on the extent of resources being used on a current basis. In order to close this loophole and control the resources actually being applied to the strategic program, the expense budgets were divided into operating and strategic expenses.

A strategic expense is directed toward the attainment of long-term perspectives. It is project oriented (not level-of-effort oriented); that is, it must have a beginning and an end as well as milestones in between. Most of all, it is directed toward optimizing long-term results. An operating expense, on the other hand, is necessary for current operations. It is required to meet operational goals and should optimize year-end results.

The OST system has worked well for TI. The company has developed an appropriate compensation structure which measures both stra-

---

[4]Grant A. Dove, "The OST System of Texas Instruments Incorporated," an address made to the London Graduate School of Business Studies, May 22, 1970, pp. 22–23; copy available from Texas Instruments Inc., Richardson, TX.

tegic and operating performances. Over the years a variety of adjustments have been made to resolve difficulties. Despite that, many problems remain. For example, the drainage of strategic resources to meet short-term problems continues to be a difficulty. Another problem is the uneven quality of longer-range quantitative data available for developing strategies and tactics. Besides this, there are the occasional conflicts which arise because managers have multiple bosses. Also, there are arguments that detailed project planning is an over-regimented approach. Another problem often arises, ironically as a result of the success of the OST system. Often more tactical action programs or good ideas are generated than can be undertaken in a given year. This means that many well-developed proposals fall below the funding-approval line. This is a major disappointment to the individuals who have worked very hard to formulate these proposals.

No organizational structure, however well designed it may be, can work forever. During 1981–82, Texas Instruments was obliged to make drastic changes in its matrix management system. This became necessary to reverse the record of delayed product introductions and missed opportunities, resulting in profit decline for six consecutive quarters and the loss to Motorola of number one position in sales in the key U.S. semiconductor market. The company's problems were directly attributed to a turgid management system that had become increasingly inept at coping with TI's 25 percent compound annual growth rate of the past decade.

As a part of reorganization, the company created several new profit centers and delegated unprecedented responsibility to the managers of these businesses. Further, marketing was accorded a central role so that customer inputs would be sought and adequately considered in strategy development and implementation. Also, the PCC management structure was brought into line with TI's strategic planning organization, so that PCC managers would be responsible for making and marketing their products as well as for developing extensions to their product families.

The most dramatic changes, however, were the complete reorganization of TI's two sickest operating groups, semiconductors and distributed computing. For both, TI redefined its basic profit-and-loss unit, the PCC, to encompass a complete business. Each PCC manager was given full control of the resources—people, capital, and facilities—needed to run the business. Previously, PCC managers in the semiconductor group had had to beg for those resources from huge central support entities, while the PCC structure in computers had been fragmented into a series of individual product lines that were difficult to team together for sale as a system.[5]

---

[5]Based on telephone interview with a company executive. See also "An About-Face in TI's Culture," *Business Week*, July 5, 1982, p. 77.

General Electric Company's Strategic Business Unit Structure[6]

Exhibit 11-5 is a chart of GE's line organization and strategic business unit setup. The company has a chairperson and chief executive officer, three vice-chairpersons, and five business sectors comprising a number of product groups. Each product group is split into divisions and departments. To superimpose a strategic business planning process on the existing structure, GE established basic planning blocks which it refers to as strategic business units (SBUs). The SBUs are at various levels and of various sizes. Some at the group level have sales in excess of $1.5 billion. Each business unit has a strategic plan, and resource allocation among SBUs is at the corporate level.

GE's SBUs are similar to the strategies at TI. Like the OST system, the SBU structure is intended for strategic planning, while the line organization is oriented toward short-term operations and control. In 1984 GE had 43 SBUs, 6 managed by group executives, 18 by division managers, and 19 by department managers. The level of an SBU is determined by whether it is cross-departmental or cross-divisional and by the size of the business. The SBU structure anticipates change and positions itself to meet the challenges posed by the change. The line structure provides real-time response to change.

Further, to deal with compounding complexity, at GE planning is extended from a single level (SBU) to multiple levels (SBU, sector, corporate). The idea is to achieve decentralized management of integrated objectives. Each level is expected to add value through business development within the unique scope of the level. For example, at the SBU level this is accomplished through contiguous product/market extension; at the sector level, through diversification within assigned scope; and at the corporate level, through diversification into an unserved economic sector.

GE also changed its corporate staff from a functional organization to one that emphasizes administration under one senior vice-president. The planning activity was formerly staffed by four senior vice-presidents. Under the new system the administration and coordination of functions was taken off the shoulders of the chief executive officer. The corporate executive staff was strengthened so as to be able to advise the CEO on key decisions. An executive board made up of a vice-chairperson and the senior vice-presidents was organized for each group. The board functions as a mechanism for the continual review of operations and plans within each group.

---

[6]This section draws heavily on executive speeches available from General Electric Company. See also "General Electric: Strategic Position: 1981," a Harvard Business School case by Francis J. Aguilar and Richard Hamermesh, 1981.

EXHIBIT 11-5   General Electric Co.: Line Organization and Strategic Business Units

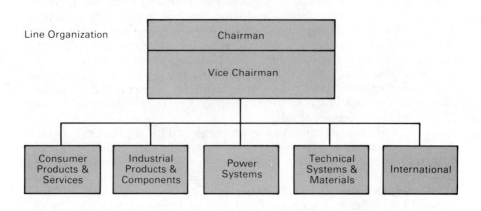

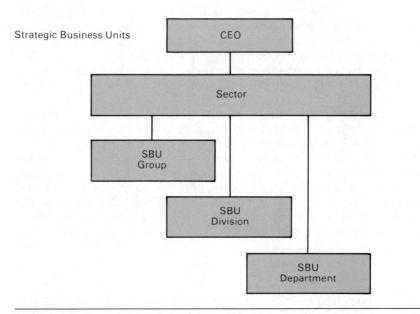

Source: General Electric Company. Reprinted by permission.

EXHIBIT 11-6   General Electric Co.: Corporate Strategic Planning Organization

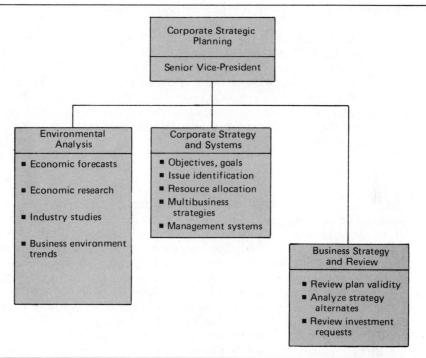

Source: General Electric Company. Reprinted by permission.

As shown in Exhibit 11-6, Corporate Strategic Planning, headed by a senior vice-president, has three sections: Environmental Analysis, Corporate Strategy and Systems, and Business Strategy and Review. Environmental Analysis handles economic forecasts, economic research, and industry studies; it also follows up and advises on business, social, and legal trends that may lead to future legislation. Corporate Strategy and Systems deals with company objectives and goals, issue identification, and resource allocation strategies which may involve a number of businesses and management systems. The particular emphasis here is on the corporate plan. The third component, Business Strategy and Review, reviews the validity of the plans as they are submitted by each of the SBUs. This department analyzes alternate strategies and reviews specific investment requests to make certain they conform to the approved strategy of the business. In 1984 there were 42 professionals in these three departments.

In the SBUs themselves, about 43 lead planners were identified and appointed. Additionally, some 123 staff members were added to the SBUs. The turnover among SBU planners is high. For example, the turnover for ten group-level planners was 100 percent in three years, mostly because of promotions. Fifty percent of the other planners in the company also turned over in that time. This is perceived as evidence that an individual planner's performance is relatively easy to assess in a short period of time.

It must be emphasized that it is the line manager's responsibility to develop a strategy for the business. The staff members are merely assistants. This is true at both the corporate and P&L center levels. GE undertook an extensive operation to train its planners. The top 320 executives attended a four-day orientation session organized internally. More extensive training was given to strategic planners in a two-week strategic planning workshop, and an audiovisual program described the basics to 10,000 people in the company.

Reorganization at General Motors

Organization structures evolve through continuing attention to forces of change. The upheaval in the auto industry in the late 1970s and early 1980s led General Motors to make extensive changes in the structure of its U.S. auto operations in 1984. The company consolidated engineering and centralized product development and manufacturing.

GM will continue to market autos through the same five car divisions—Chevrolet, Pontiac, Oldsmobile, Buick, and Cadillac—it has operated since 1916. But developing new models for the divisions will be done by two new units. Small cars will be engineered and built by the Chevrolet-Pontiac-GM Canada group. Intermediate and large cars will be developed by the Buick-Cadillac-Oldsmobile group. In brief, the five car divisions will continue to exist, but primarily as marketing arms of the two car groups.

The two groups are responsible for engineering, manufacturing, and marketing their own cars. They may be considered as self-contained business units. To give them more control over engineering and costing out their cars, the groups have created their own engineering staffs out of those working at Fisher Body and GM Assembly divisions.

Overall, the reorganization was undertaken to:

—Help GM launch its new models on schedule.
—Provide more cost control.
—Boost quality control so the company can compete more effectively with foreign auto makers.
—Make its divisions build more distinctive models instead of the current look-alikes, which are confusing consumers.[7]

The last point made above is especially significant from the viewpoint of marketing strategy. As GM opted to cut costs in the 1970s by letting more and more car divisions share nearly identical body styles, they lost the marketing advantage of product differentiation—without gaining

---

[7]"Can GM Solve Its Identity Crisis?," *Business Week*, January 23, 1984, p. 32.

the desired cost advantage. The new structure should help solve this problem. It is expected that each car group, with fewer models to worry about, can soon develop more distinctive products.

Integration at the Top

In today's environment the chief executive officer cannot handle alone the various demands that are made on his/her time. To ensure top-level involvement in strategic planning, companies have adopted two types of organizational changes, which are examined here. The first of these is the formation of the office of chief executive officer, and the other is the creation of a sector-executive position.

CEO Office. A large number of companies now have an office of the chief executive officer (CEO office) rather than just one chief executive officer (CEO). The term "office" implies here that more than one executive is assigned to the chief executive office. For example, at Mead Corporation the CEO office includes the chairperson of the board (who is also the chief executive officer), the vice-chairperson, and the president. The vice-chairperson is responsible for strategic planning, while the president looks after the operations. This type of structure permits the chief executive officer to draw a proper balance between operations and strategy while it also frees the CEO for interaction with the outside world.

Conceptually, an activity needs to be integrated at the top when it is spread across the company in many groups and divisions and its coordination is scattered throughout the organization. The number of executives in the CEO office may range from two to five. The responsibilities assigned to individuals depend on their backgrounds and interests. Operational, strategic, international, and government responsibilities are among the duties that may be assigned to executives in the CEO office. People who constitute the CEO office are expected to visualize things from the total corporate viewpoint. Their individual performances and rewards are based on the performance of the entire corporation. Large companies with established planning systems, like Mead, often have an executive in the CEO office who is responsible for strategic planning. In this way top management is able to play the key role required for successful strategic planning.

Sector Organization. In some corporations a new level has been created between the chief executive officer and the group managers. This has been achieved by forming clusters of groups which are interdependent in their work and relatively independent of other groups not in their cluster. For example, GE recently added five sector executives, each of whom is in charge of a sector. One of the sectors is concerned with consumer products and services. Thus, all groups doing business in the consumer sector of the economy, as opposed to those selling to industry or

EXHIBIT 11-7   General Electric Co.: Sector-SBU Structure

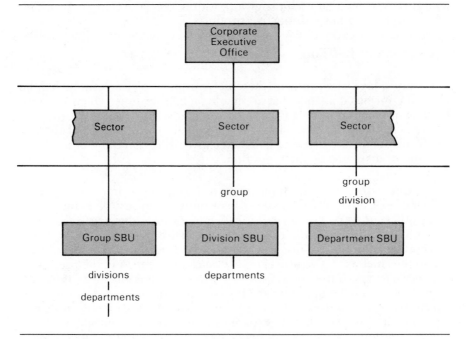

Source: General Electric Company. Reprinted by permission.

the government, report to the executive in charge of the consumer sector.[8] The new level of management at GE was installed just below the corporate executive office. Group heads who formerly reported to the executive office now report to a sector executive, who in turn reports to one of the two vice-chairpersons. GE's 43 strategic-business-unit heads also report to sector executives. Previously strategic plans for each SBU had to be reviewed by the top office. Now the executive office sees only the sector plans, which are summaries of all the SBU plans. Each sector executive at GE absorbed many chief executive functions in the company reorganization (see Exhibit 11-7).

The sector concept has also been adopted by the American Can Company. The company appointed five of its ten senior vice-presidents to the position of sector executive. The five sectors at American Can are (1) Packaging; (2) Consumer Products; (3) Technology and Development (including recovery systems and chemicals); (4) Specialty Wholesaling and

---

[8]"G.E.'s New Billion-Dollar Small Businesses," *Business Week*, December 19, 1977, pp. 78–79 (information updated based on an interview with a company executive).

Retailing, and (5) International Business.[9] Similarly, W. R. Grace & Co. has established four new sector-executive positions.

The sector arrangement is considered a vehicle for cross-fertilization. Corporate-wide trade-offs in capital, technology, and human resources can be dealt with at the sector level without creating any suspicions at the group or division levels. In addition, the sector structure relieves the chief executive officer of strategic planning responsibility, thus permitting the CEO to get involved in external matters. As a matter of fact, the sector executives become the representatives for an industry insofar as the company's participation in the industry is concerned. This is a function people traditionally expected the chief executive officer to perform. Thus, sector organization is a way of developing institutional leadership.

LEADERSHIP STYLE

However strategic plans are arrived at, only one person, the chief executive officer, can ensure that energies and efforts throughout the organization are orchestrated to attain the desired objectives. What the Chinese general and philosopher Sun-tzu said in 514 B.C. is still true today: "Weak leadership can wreck the soundest strategy; forceful execution of even a poor plan can often bring victory."

This section examines the key role that the CEO plays in shaping the organization for strategy implementation. Also discussed is the role of the strategic planner, since his/her activities have a major impact on the organization and its attitude toward strategic change. Finally, the importance of matching strategic planning with executives' skills and of designing the compensation system to reward long-term performance is discussed.

Role of the Chief Executive

The chief executive officer of a company is the chief strategist. He/she communicates the importance of strategic planning to the organization. Personal commitment on the part of the CEO to the significance of planning must not only be highly visible but also be consistent with all the other decisions the CEO makes to influence the work of the organization. To be accepted within the organization, the strategic planning process needs the CEO's support. People accustomed to short-term orientations may resist the strategic planning process, which requires different methods. But the CEO can set an example for them by adhering to the planning process. Essentially, the CEO is responsible for creating a corporate climate

---

[9]"Canco Adds a Rung to Its Executive Ladder," *Business Week*, April 30, 1979, p. 25.

which is conducive to strategic planning. The CEO can also set a future perspective for the organization. One CEO remarked:

> My people cannot plan or work beyond the distance of my own vision. If I focus on next year, I'll force them to become preoccupied with next year. If I can try to look five to ten years ahead, at least I'll make it possible for the rest of the organization to raise their eyes off the ground immediately in front of them.[10]

The CEO should focus attention on the corporate purpose and approve strategic decisions accordingly. To perform these tasks well, the CEO should support the staff work and analysis upon which his or her decisions are based. Along the same lines, the CEO should ensure the establishment of a noise-free communications network in the organization. Communications should flow downward from the CEO with respect to organizational goals, aspirations, and values of top management. Similarly, information about risks, results, plans, concepts, capabilities, competition, and the environment should flow upward. The CEO should avoid seeking false uniformity, trying to eliminate risk, trusting tradition, dominating discussion, and delegating strategy development. A CEO who does these things could inadvertently discourage strategy implementation.[11]

Concern for the future may require a change in organizational perspectives. The CEO should not only perceive the need for a change but also be instrumental in making it happen. Change is not easy, however, since past success provides a strong motive for preserving the status quo. As long as the environment and competitive behavior do not change, the past perspectives are fine. However, as the environment undergoes a shift, changes in policies and attitudes become essential. The CEO must rise to the occasion and not only initiate change but also encourage others to accept it and adapt to it. The timing of the change may be more important than the change itself. The need for change must be realized before the optimum time for it has passed so that competitive advantage and flexibility are not lost.

Zalesink makes a distinction between the CEO who is a manager and the CEO who is a leader. Managers keep things running smoothly, while leaders provide longer-term direction and thrust.[12] Successful strategic planning requires that the CEO be a good leader. In this capacity the CEO should:

1. Gain complete and willing acceptance of his leadership.

---

[10]Robert Mainer, "The Impact of Strategic Planning on Executive Behavior," a special commentary (Boston: The Boston Consulting Group, 1968), p. 24.
[11]Robert D. Paulson, "Making It Happen: The Real Strategic Challenge," *The McKinsey Quarterly*, Winter, 1982, p. 59.
[12]See Abraham Zalezink, "Managers and Leaders: Are They Different?," *Harvard Business Review*, May–June, 1977, pp. 67–68.

2. Determine those business goals, objectives, and standards of behavior which are as ambitious as the potential abilities of the organization will permit.
3. Introduce these objectives and motivate the organization to accept them as their own. The rate of introduction will be the maximum consistent with continued acceptance of leadership. Because of this need for acceptance, the new manager must always go slowly, except in emergencies. In emergencies the boss must not go slowly if he is to maintain leadership.
4. Change the organizational relationships internally as necessary to facilitate both the acceptance and attainment of the new objectives.[13]

A coordinated program of change in pursuit of a sound and relevant strategy, under the active direction of the chief executive and the chief planner, can lead to significant progress. While this may only begin a long-term program, it should yield benefits far beyond the time and effort invested. Although pace and effectiveness of strategic change cannot be judged in quantitative terms, there are useful criteria by which they may be assessed. These are some of the more important hallmarks of progress:

—Strategies are principally developed by line managers, with direct, constructive support by the staff.
—Real strategic alternatives are openly discussed at all levels within the corporation.
—Corporate priorities are relatively clear to senior management, but permit flexible response to new opportunities and threats.
—Corporate resources are allocated based on these priorities, and in view of future potential as well as historical performance.
—The strategic roles of business units are clearly differentiated; so are the performance measures applied to their managers.
—Realistic responses to likely future events are worked out well in advance.
—The corporate staff adds real value to the consideration of strategic issues and receives cooperation from most of the divisions.[14]

Role of the Strategic Planner

A strategic planner is a staff person who assists line executives in their planning efforts. Thus, there may be a corporate strategic planner working closely with the chief executive officer. A strategic planner may also be attached to an SBU. This section examines the role of a strategic planner at the SBU level.

---

[13]Bruce D. Henderson, *Henderson on Corporate Strategy* (Cambridge, MA: Abt Associates, 1979), p. 54. See also Thomas J. Peters, "A Style for All Seasons," *Best of Business*, Spring, 1981, pp. 23–27.
[14]Robert D. Paulson, *op. cit.*, p. 65.

The planner conceptualizes the planning process and helps translate it for line executives who actually do the planning. As part of this function, the planner works out a planning schedule and may develop a planning manual. He or she may also design a variety of forms, charts, tables, etc., which may be used to collect, analyze, and communicate planning-oriented information. The planner may also serve as a trainer in orienting line managers to strategic planning.

The planner generates innovative ways of performing difficult tasks and educates the line management in the new techniques and tools needed for an efficient job of strategic planning. The planner also coordinates the efforts of other specialists (i.e., marketing researchers, systems persons, econometricians, environmental monitors, and management scientists) with those of the line management. In this role the planner exposes managers to the newest and most sophisticated concepts and techniques in planning.

The planner serves as an adviser to the head of the SBU. In matters of concern, the SBU head may ask the planner to undertake a study. For example, the SBU head may seek the advice of the SBU strategic planner in such matters as deciding whether private branding should be accepted so as to increase market share and gain experience, or whether it should be rejected for eroding the quality image of the brand.

Another key role that the planner plays is that of evaluator of strategic plans. For example, strategic plans relative to various products/markets are submitted to the SBU head. The latter may ask his or her planner to develop an evaluation system for the products/markets. In addition, the planner may also be asked to express an opinion on strategic issues.

The planner may be involved in integrating different plans. For example, the planner may integrate different product/market plans into an SBU strategic plan. Similarly, the SBU's plans may be integrated by the corporate strategic planner from the perspectives of the entire corporation. For example, if the company uses the growth rate–relative market share matrix (see Exhibit 10-4) to judge plans submitted by different businesses, the planner may be asked not only to establish the position of these businesses on the matrix but also to furnish a recommendation on such matters as which of two question marks (businesses in the high-growth-rate, low-market-share quadrant of the matrix in Exhibit 10-4) should be selected for additional funding. The planner's recommendation on such strategic issues helps in the crystallization of executive thinking.

Matters of a nonroutine nature may be assigned to the planner for study and recommendation. For example, the planner may head a committee to recommend structural changes in the organization. The committee that recommended sector organization at General Electric was headed by the corporate senior vice-president of strategic planning.

Obviously the job of strategic planner is not an easy one. The strategic planner must:

1. Be well versed in theoretical frameworks relevant to planning, at the same time realizing their limitations as far as practical applications are concerned.

2. Be capable of making a point with conviction and firmness and at the same time be a practical politician who can avoid creating conflict in the organization.
3. Maintain a working alliance with other units in the organization.
4. Command the respect of other executives and managers.
5. Be a salesperson who can help managers accept new and difficult tools and techniques.

In short, a planner needs to be a jack-of-all-trades.

Motivating Managers

Motivating managers to keep a balanced view of short-term problems and future opportunities is an important concern. The critical issue is, "On what basis do managers get promoted or rewarded?" One can have elegant strategic plans, but if managers are rewarded on short-term results alone, then plans for the future will not be considered along with short-term actions.

At General Electric Company, managers receive clear instructions as to their strategic assignments, and the incentive compensation program has been modified to reflect these assignments. As shown in Exhibit 11-8, managers are assigned according to key characteristics. The entrepreneurial managers are aligned with the growth businesses; the more sophisticated, critical managers with businesses where great selectivity is needed; and the more solid, experienced managers with the tough cost-control and investment-reduction tasks in the weaker businesses. Bonuses to these different groups are duly adjusted, with low emphasis on current results in the invest/grow type of business.

Different companies use different criteria to match executive skills with strategic perspectives of the business. For its premium wine business, Heublein looks for people knowledgeable about wine, while those in the standard wine business come out of consumer products and food companies. At Texas Instruments, as a product moves through different phases of its life cycle, managers with different skills and style are given charge to see it through. When the Chase Manhattan Bank's trust manager retired, corporate management decided that the department, whose operations had been essentially stable, should focus on a more aggressive growth strategy. Instead of seeking a veteran banker, Chase hired a man whose main experience had been with IBM and who had a strong marketing orientation.[15]

In brief, businesses should give explicit attention to the personality attributes, behavior traits, and previous experience of managers when a

---

[15]"Wanted: A Manager to Fit Each Strategy," *Business Week*, February 25, 1980, p. 166.

EXHIBIT 11-8   General Electric Co.: Managerial Incentive Compensation

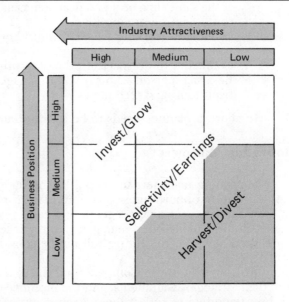

Portfolio Category	Manager's Key Characteristics	Weighting of I.C. Based On	
		Current Results	Future Benefits
Invest/Grow	Entrepreneur	Low	High
Selectivity/ Earnings	Sophisticated/ Critical	←———— Balanced ————→	
Harvest/Divest	Solid/Experienced	High	Low

Source: General Electric Company. Reprinted by permission.

significant change in strategy is being considered. It will be self-defeating to put the best guard into the quarterback's slot.

An additional factor in adequately motivating managers is to link the reward system with the long-term perspectives of the business. General Electric Company has made pioneering efforts in orienting its compensation plans to reward long-term performance. Shown in Exhibit 11-9 are some of the financial measures of current performance that GE uses—income compared with the previous year and income compared with budget. Also used are the performance factors concerned with future benefits: performance in building manpower, in developing facilities, in designing and executing programs for market or product development, and in strengthening the strategy of the business. There are additional criteria to cover unforeseen events or unique contributions.

In the growth businesses only 40 percent of a manager's bonus award

EXHIBIT 11-9   General Electric Co.: Matching Performance Factors to Business Portfolio Position

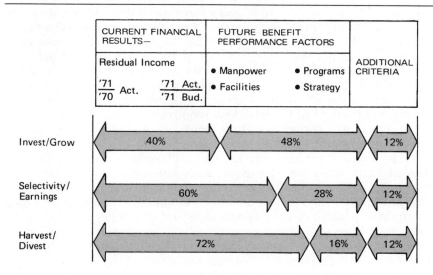

Source: General Electric Company. Reprinted by permission.

depends on current financial results; the predominant portion depends on the manager's performance in building the future of the business. The proportion is reversed when the role of the business is to produce short-term results. In the harvest/divest business, 72 percent of the bonus depends on the manager's short-term financial results. The planning system at General Electric gives each business a firm role in the overall company picture, defining that role and paying for it. The planning system is based on the premise that at the corporate level one cannot know enough about every business to develop its strategy. Nor can a manager set goals effectively alone; the manager needs someone to augment his or her efforts. That is what is done at the corporate level.

What is true at GE is hardly common practice, however. Too many compensation plans still bias executive behavior toward the short term, at the expense of long-term strategic growth. Only a handful of the top *Fortune* 500 companies measure results over a period greater than one year for annual bonus purposes. Tying executive incentives to short-term target growth in reported earnings can have disastrous effects on longer-term strategic vitality. To encourage managers to support business strategies, companies should revamp their reward systems to recognize and pay for achievement of strategic milestones and thus underscore the importance of strategic performance.[16]

---

[16]See Paul J. Stonich, "Using Rewards in Implementing Strategy," *Strategic Management Journal*, Vol. 2, 1981, pp. 345–352.

MEASURING STRATEGIC PERFORMANCE

Tracking strategy, or evaluating progress toward established objectives, is an important task in strategy implementation. There are three basic considerations in putting together a performance measurement system: (a) selecting performance measures; (b) setting performance standards; (c) designing reports. A strategic performance measurement system requires reporting not by profit center or cost center, but by strategic business unit. This may require allocation or restatement of financial results based on the new type of reporting center. Most management reporting is geared to SEC and FASB requirements, and focuses on the bottom line. For many business units, however, profit is not the pertinent measure of that unit's strategic performance.

In selecting performance measures, only those measures that are relevant to the strategies adopted by each strategic business unit should be chosen. Further, when setting performance standards, the targets or expected values should be so established that they are consistent with both the strategic position of the business units and the strategies selected. Finally, the reports should be designed to focus management attention on the key performance measures. Exhibit 11-10 summarizes significant issues in measuring strategic performance.

ACHIEVING STRATEGIC PLANNING EFFECTIVENESS

Most companies have made significant progress in the last 10 to 15 years in improving their strategic planning capabilities. Clear, concise methods have been developed for analyzing and evaluating market segments, business performance, and pricing and cost structures. Creative, even elegant, methods have been devised for displaying the results of these strategic analyses to top management.

Few today would argue the value—in theory at least—of the strategic approach to business planning. Reginald Jones, former chairman of General Electric Company, described that value in the following words:

> More and more, strategic planning is no longer just a buzz phrase or a paperwork exercise. At GE, we entered the 1970s getting 80 percent of our earnings from electrical equipment. By 1979, that was down to 47 percent. If you take this longer-term strategic approach, it will get you more capital investment, increased productivity, and take you out of dying industries and into ones that are growing.[17]

Unfortunately, GE's successful experience appears to be more the exception than the rule. Much more typical are reports of dissatisfaction with the results of strategic planning.

---

[17]Quoted from his speech at the University of Connecticut's Centenary Celebration program, Stamford, CT, September 8, 1981.

EXHIBIT 11-10   Strategic Performance Measurements

(1) To be effective, strategic performance measures must be tailored to the particular strategy of each individual business unit. While there is a basket of generic strategic measurement tools, selection and application is highly dependent on detailed understanding of the particular business' strategy and situation.

(2) Strategic performance measurements have two dimensions:
- **Monitoring key program implementation** to ensure that the necessary elements of strategy are being provided.
- **Monitoring results** to ensure that the programs are having the desired effects.

(3) Strategy performance necessarily involves trade-offs—costs and benefits. Both must be recognized in any useful strategic performance measurement system:
- **Objectives** assessing progress toward primary goals;
- **Constraints** monitoring other dimensions of performance which may be sacrificed, to some degree and for some period, in order to achieve strategic objectives.

(4) Strategic performance measurements do not replace, but rather supplement, short-term financial measurements. They provide management with a view of long-term progress in contrast to short-term performance. They may indicate that fundamental objectives are being met in spite of short-term problems, and that strategic programs should be sustained despite adversity. They may also show that fundamentals are *not* being met although short-term performance is satisfactory, and, therefore, strategy needs to be changed.

(5) Strategic-performance measurement is linked to competitive analysis. Performance measurements should be stated in competitive terms (share, relative profitability, relative growth). While quantitative goals must be established, evaluating performance against them should include an assessment of what competition has been able to attain.

(6) Strategic-performance measurement is linked to environmental monitoring. Reasonable goals cannot always be met by dint of effort if the external world turns against us. Strategic-performance measurement systems must attempt to filter uncontrollable from controllable performance, and provide signals when the measures themselves may be the problem, rather than performance against them.

Source: Rochelle O'Conner, *Tracking the Strategic Plan* (New York: The Conference Board, Inc., 1983), p. 11. Reprinted by permission of the publisher.

Why the "achievement gap" between strategic planning and strategic performance? While the reasons undoubtedly vary from corporation to corporation, certain ones appear to be critical. First, many companies have found that top-down strategic planning produces resistance behavior on the part of their operating managers. Second, strategic planning efforts have failed to encourage innovative ideas, techniques, and products and to create an innovative business strategy to implement them. Third, even in companies known for excellence in strategic planning, lack of adequate emphasis on marketing has led to poor implementation of strategic plans.

Strategy Implementation and Management Behavior

Strategic planning as currently practiced has produced resistance behavior on the part of operating managers. One observer has identified three types of resistance behavior: measurement myopia (i.e., managers behave in ways that show good short-term performance); measurement invalidation (i.e., managers supply top management with distorted or selected biased data); and measurement justification (i.e., managers adopt excessive justification behavior and become excessively cautious on specific factors identified as critical cash flow or ROI determinants).[18]

To solve the problem, it is important to remember that sophisticated management tools and the up-to-the-minute techniques of the business schools may be a help in identifying a desirable strategic course, but implementation of the strategy requires the time-honored simple and straightforward approaches. As a matter of fact, the latter are still vital prerequisites for success. The following are the eight basic attributes that are common to the management of companies generally regarded successful:[19]

(a) *A bias toward action*—i.e., avoid analyzing and questioning products to death and avoid complicated procedures for developing new ideas; rather, perpetuate a *do it, fix it, try it* attitude.

(b) *Simple form and lean staff*—i.e., keep staffs small to avoid bureaucracies.

(c) *Continued contact with customers*—i.e., maintain constant contact with the customer to seek insights that direct the company; in other words, view the customer as an integral element of the business.

(d) *Productivity improvement via people*—i.e., motivate and stimulate employees by giving them autonomy, and use effective means to reward them.

(e) *Operational autonomy to encourage entrepreneurship*—i.e., authorize and encourage managers to act like entrepreneurs.

(f) *Stress on one key business value*—i.e., identify and pursue a key

---

[18]Steven R. Palesy, "Implementing Strategic Planning Systems in Diversified Companies," a note prepared at Harvard Business School, 1979, pp. 5–7.

[19]Thomas J. Peters, "Putting Excellence into Management," *Business Week*, July 21, 1980, p. 196. See also Walter Kiechel III, "Corporate Strategists Under Fire," *Fortune*, December 27, 1982, p. 34.

value with religious zeal; for example, IBM's emphasis on solving the problems of individual customers.

(g) *Emphasis on doing what they know best*—i.e., define and build on strengths, such as product innovation, low-cost manufacturing, etc.

(h) *Simultaneous loose-tight controls*—i.e., control a few variables tightly, but allow flexibility and looseness in others.

The above attributes should help to put excellence into management. As has been said:

> By sticking to these eight basics, the successful companies have achieved better-than-average growth. Their managements are able not only to change but also to change quickly. They keep their sights aimed externally at their customers and competitors, and not on their own financial reports.
>
> Excellence in management takes brute perseverance—time, repetition and simplicity. The tools include plant visits, internal memos and focused systems. Ignoring these rules may mean that the company slowly loses its vitality, its growth flattens and its competitiveness is lost.[20]

Effective Innovative Planning

Effective strategic planning should eliminate organizational restraints, not multiply them; it should contribute to innovation, not inhibit it. In the upcoming years strategic planners face a unique challenge because innovation and new product development must be stimulated within the structure of the large, multinational corporate enterprise. A number of companies have proved that innovation and entrepreneurial drive can be institutionalized and fostered by a responsive organization structure. Celanese and IBM, for example, have established technology review boards to ensure that promising product ideas and new technologies receive adequate start-up support. Adopting another approach, Dow Chemical recently instituted an "innovation department" to streamline technology commercialization.

To encourage perpetuation of new ideas and innovation, management should:[21]

(a) focus management attention on the goals of strategic planning rather than its process—i.e., concentrate on substance, not form;

(b) integrate into business strategy the analysis of emerging technologies and technology management, consumer trends and

---

[20]*Ibid.*, p. 205.

[21]See Shelby H. McIntyre, "Obstacles to Corporate Innovation," *Business Horizons*, January–February, 1982, pp. 23–28. See also Peter F. Drucker, "The Innovative Company," *The Wall Street Journal*, February 26, 1982, p. 36.

demographic shifts, regulatory impact and global economics;
(c) design totally new planning processes, review standards and acceptance criteria for technological advances and new business "thrusts" that may not conform completely to a firm's current corporate base;
(d) adopt a longer planning horizon to ensure that a promising business or technological development won't be cut off prematurely;
(e) ensure that overly stringent financial requirements aren't imposed during the start-up phase of a promising project;
(f) create special organizational "satellites," such as new venture groups whose mission is to pursue new ideas, free from the pressures of day-to-day operations; and
(g) institute financial and career reward systems that encourage bold, innovative development programs.

STRATEGIC PLANNING AND MARKETING ORGANIZATION

Strategic planning deals with the relationship of the organization to its environment and thus relates to all areas of a business. Among all these areas, however, marketing is the most susceptible to outside influences. Thus, marketing concerns become pivotal in strategic planning. Unfortunately, with the advent of strategic planning, the role of marketing in the organization declined. As Kotler noted in 1978:

> . . . strategic planning threatens to demote marketing from a strategic to an operational function. Instead of marketing being in the driver's seat, strategic planning has moved into the driver's seat. Marketing has moved into the passenger seat and in some companies into the back seat.[22]

It has generally been believed that the only marketing decision which has strategic content is the one concerned with product/market perspectives. As far as other marketing decisions are concerned, while they may occasionally have strategic elements, they are mainly operational in nature, i.e., they deal with short-term performance. Product/market decisions, however, being the most far-reaching in nature as far as strategy is concerned, are frequently made by top management; the marketing organization is relegated to making operating decisions. In brief, the inroads of strategic planning tend to lower marketing's status in the organization. Empirical evidence on the role of marketing vis-à-vis strategic plan-

---

[22]Philip Kotler, "The Future Marketing Manager," in Betsy D. Gelb (ed.), *Marketing Expansion in a Shrinking World: 1978 Business Proceedings* (Chicago: American Marketing Association, 1978), p. 3.

ning is provided by Rich. In his study of 20 forest-products companies in 1979, he found that not one had a marketing executive with the title of vice-president at the corporate level:

> The highest level at which most marketing executives were found was just under the head of a strategic business unit be it at the group or at the division level. Those few marketing executives who were found up at the corporate level tended to be one of three types. The first type was a "V.P., Distribution Division" and was found in companies with strong captive distribution systems. His job was overseeing the distribution, usually at the wholesale level, of all or some of the products of the company's mills. Sometimes he drew on outside sources of supply as well. The second type carried a title such as "Manager of Marketing Planning" and reported to a "Director of Strategic Planning" who came under the CEO. The third type, sometimes carrying the title "Marketing Service Manager," reported to the president or executive vice-president, but his duties were confined mainly to handling important national accounts, that is, large customers who bought from many different divisions of the company. Such national account sales managers, however, were more likely to be found down at the group level.[23]

According to Rich, this was not true in the 1960s, when in every company except one a vice-president of marketing reported directly to the president. He further noted that the highest marketing executive was a vice-president or director of marketing who reported to the SBU head. Marketing and sales managers were involved mainly in day-to-day operations and occasionally in the strategic planning of the SBU. With the emergence of strategic planning, the marketing function was gradually relegated to the background.

A recent Conference Board survey on the subject supports Rich's findings:

> Seventy percent of the multibusiness manufacturing companies surveyed do not have a senior executive at the corporate level who is generally regarded as being the chief marketing executive. The other 30 percent of these companies do have a corporate chief marketing executive. This is, without question, a substantially lower proportion than in former times.
>
> On balance, it seems reasonable to conclude that, in the early 1970's, the proportion of those large multibusiness manufacturing companies then having a corporate-level chief marketing executive was on the order of 50 percent, at a minimum. This finding is consistent with earlier Conference Board surveys, reported in 1965 and 1971, which found, respectively, that 52 percent and 53 percent of the divisional-

---

[23]Stuart U. Rich, "Organization Structure and the Marketing Function in Forest Products Companies," a paper presented at the AMA Western Marketing Educators' conference, San Jose, CA, April 20, 1979.

ized manufacturing companies then surveyed had corporate marketing heads. . . . the decline of the chief marketing position has, within
many affected companies, proved to be an event of profound importance for the marketing function as a whole, and for its organizational
structuring in particular.[24]

Many marketers opined that marketing would continue to be important, but mainly for day-to-day operations. For example, Kotler predicted:

1. The marketer's job will be harder than ever in the 1980s because
   of the tough environment.
2. The strategic planner will provide the directive force to the company's growth, not the marketer.
3. The marketer will be relied on to contribute a great deal of data
   and appraisal of corporate purposes, objectives and goals, growth
   decisions, and portfolio decisions.
4. The marketer will assume more of an operational and less of a strategic role in the company.
5. The marketer will still have to champion the customer concept because companies tend to forget it.[25]

Experience has shown, however, that marketing definitely has an
important strategic role to play. How neglect of marketing can affect strategy implementation and performance is illustrated by Atari's problems.
This company has been a pioneer in developing video games. Because of
negligence in the area of marketing, it failed to realize how quickly the
market for video games would mature. Atari based earnings projections
on the assumption that demand would grow at the same rate as in the
past and that the company would hold onto its share of the market. But
its assumption proved to be wrong. The market for video games grew at
a much lower rate than anticipated.

Continuous close contact with the marketplace is an important prerequisite to excellent performance which no firm can ignore. As has been
said:

Stay close to the customer. No company, high tech or low, can afford
to ignore it. Successful companies always ask what the customer needs.
Even if they have strong technology, they do their marketing home-
work.[26]

More and more businesses today than during the establishment years
of strategic planning are making organizational arrangements to bring in

---

[24]David S. Hopkins and Earl L. Bailey, *Organizing Corporate Marketing* (New York:
The Conference Board, Inc., 1984), p. 5.
[25]Philip Kotler, *op. cit.*, p. 5.
[26]Susan Fraker, "High-Speed Management for the High-Tech Age," *Fortune*, March
5, 1984, p. 62.

marketing perspectives. This is understandable since with the emergence of strategic planning, particularly in organizations that have adopted the SBU concept, marketing has become a more pervasive function than it was before. Thus, while marketing positions at the corporate level may have vanished, the marketing function still plays a key strategic role at the SBU level.

Businesses, by and large, have recognized an important missing link in their strategic planning process: inadequate attention to marketing. Without properly relating the strategic planning effort to marketing, the whole process tends to become static. Business exists in a dynamic setting and it is only through marketing inputs that perspectives of changing social, economic, political, and technological environments can be brought into the strategic planning process.

Overall, marketing is once again assuming more prominence. Businesses are finding that marketing is not just an operations function relevant for day-to-day decision making. It has strategic content as well.

As has been mentioned before, strategic planning emerged largely as an outgrowth of the budgeting and financial planning process, which demoted marketing to a secondary role. However, things are different now. In some companies, of course, concern with broad strategy considerations has long forced routine, high-level attention to issues closely related to markets and marketing. There is abundant evidence, however, of renewed emphasis on such issues on the part of senior management—and hence of staff planners—in a growing number of other companies as well. Moreover, both marketers and planners are drawing increasingly from the same growing body of analytical techniques for futurist studies, market forecasts, competitive appraisals, and the like. Such overlapping in orientation, resources, and methods no doubt helps to reinstate the crucial importance of marketing in the strategic planning effort.

Accumulating forces have caused most firms to reassess their marketing perspectives at both the corporate and the SBU level. While initially marketing got lost in the midst of emphasis on strategic planning, now the role of marketing is better understood and is re-emerging in the form of strategic marketing. The 1980s will indeed be considered as the period of *marketing renaissance*. There is no better way to support this thesis than to refer the reader to an extensive quote from the chief executive officer of the General Electric Company, included here as an appendix at the end of this chapter.

SUMMARY

The chapter examines three dimensions of strategy implementation and control: (a) strategic reorganization, (b) leadership style, and (c) measuring strategic performance.

It is not enough for an organization to develop a sound strategy. It must at the same time structure the organization in a manner that will ensure the implementation of the strategy. This chapter examines how the latter task, i.e., the matching of organizational structure to strategy, may be accomplished.

Inasmuch as strategic planning is a recent activity in most corporations, no basic principles have been developed on the subject. As a matter of fact, little academic research has been reported in this area. The structuring of an organization to accommodate strategic planning is illustrated with reference to three pioneering companies in the field. Thus, discussed in this chapter are Texas Instruments' objective, strategy, and tactics (OST) system, General Electric's strategic business unit structure, and strategic reorganization at General Motors.

Also discussed is the integration of strategic planning at the level of the chief executive officer. In this area two recent developments, the CEO office and the position of sector executive, are examined.

Strategy implementation requires establishing an appropriate climate in the organization. The chief executive officer plays a key role in adapting the organization for strategic planning. Also examined is the role of the strategic planner in the context of strategic planning and its implementation. Discussed also are the matters of matching strategic planning requirements to executive skills and developing an adequate compensation system to reward long-term performance.

Many companies have not been satisfied with their strategic planning experiences. Three reasons are given for the gap between strategic planning and strategic performance: (a) resistance behavior on the part of operating managers, (b) lack of emphasis on innovations, and (c) neglect of marketing. Suggestions are made for eliminating dysfunctional behavior among managers and for improving innovation planning.

As far as the strategic role of marketing is concerned, initially, with the advent of strategic planning, marketing appeared to lose ground. Lately, however, marketing is re-emerging as an important force in strategy formulation and implementation.

DISCUSSION QUESTIONS

1. *Why is it that traditional organizational structures may not be suited for strategic planning?*
2. *Discuss the main features of Texas Instruments' OST system. Does it have a matrix form of organization?*
3. *How did General Electric Company create the SBU organization? What are its major characteristics?*
4. *Which is more productive, the OST system or the SBU organization? Why?*
5. *How did General Electric Company adjust its compensation package for its managers of different types of businesses (i.e., invest/grow, selectivity/earnings, and harvest/divest)?*
6. *What is the significance of the CEO office in strategic planning?*

7. *What is a sector organization? What impact does it have on strategic planning?*
8. *What are the conclusions of the Rich study on the impact of strategic planning on marketing organization?*
9. *How far may Rich's conclusions be applied to other industries?*
10. *What are the chances that strategic planning will succeed in a company whose chief executive is not interested in it and delegates the task to staff people?*
11. *How does the role of a strategic planner at the corporate level differ from the role of a planner with the strategic business unit?*

APPENDIX

Where Is Marketing Now That We Really Need It?

"My concern with marketing is not productivity, but purpose; not efficiency, but effectiveness. Marketing's special role, because of its external focus, is for showing us the way, for picking up the reins in American business that, judging by our collective performance, have gotten a bit slack.

"I suggest that the bigger decisions and dislocations in the world outside—the world whose customers we compete for—don't hinge on marketing technique these days, if they ever did. Rather, the world outside is urging us to get on with it: To acquit ourselves well in the marketplace; to get on with our primary purpose of providing quality products and solutions relevant to contemporary tastes and needs; to lead through market innovation; to win.

"Customers want value and are unquestionably willing to pay a premium when it fits their priorities. Employees want vigor—corporate health, a sharp competitive cutting edge. They want to be part of a winning enterprise. The edge has been dulled, and the effects are there: loss of productivity growth; loss of quality; loss of world share; loss of entire markets; and what's worse, loss of jobs.

"There are lots of reasons why we are out of condition. And I can subscribe to all of them as elements of the picture. But that's all they are—piecemeal causes. By themselves, they don't account for the decline of our competitiveness in so many industries.

"Yet I suggest that there is another cause—perhaps even a more comprehensive one—on which I haven't seen much public debate. I believe one could argue that our most significant miss has been in marketing—something that we in America pioneered as a management concept nearly 30 years ago, but of late haven't practiced too well, and something that the imperatives of the 1980's will force us to rediscover.

"I mean marketing in its original, fundamental sense: Creating customers, as opposed to pushing products, making markets with relevant innovation. In using the word, I mean the attitude, not the function; the primacy of marketing as a total company perspective that shapes a company's destiny; and everyone's issue, now more than ever.

"Since my premise is that 'we lost our way,' it is useful to go back to the original signpost. Although selling and marketing of one kind or another have probably always been done, the full significance of marketing as a *management concept* was first recognized in the 1950's. GE, among others, was one of its exponents.

"According to the thinking of the times: 'The major purpose of business is taken from the need to solve some problem in the outer environment—some betterment for the customer—and all subsidiary decisions dealing with allocation of resources within the business should be bent to that objective. Focus on the end-user and base your competitive offering on some superiority of value that matches the needs of a particular group of these users. Try to design an industrial enterprise from the customer backward into the factory, rather than from the production process forward.'

"What it said was less significant than what it meant. It meant: Don't just make your product cheaper, make it better. It meant: Use *all* your company's resources to obsolete old ways of doing things. Its very essence was the new and the different—constant innovation.

"Above all else, it meant: Have a healthy respect for the external world, which means changes in the environment. It grasped the concept of change, and understood risk. It saw the quicksilver of modern markets, the huge risks involved in having large resource commitments dependent on the fickleness of the customer. My shorthand for the meaning of marketing as a management concept would be: *Constant innovation in a world of constant change*. It was something of a new bearing for postwar business.

"That was the theory. What happened in execution? First, in the 1950's: pent-up demand from the war, an economy of scarcity and of emerging appetites and affluence. What we could produce, we could sell. The 1960's brought more growth: a rising tide of demographics and affluence that carried all boats. Enough business for everyone. Still no need to practice marketing, but the ideal role models were there in both decades. The examples of fundamental, as opposed to incremental, innovation—IBM, Xerox, Polaroid—companies which creatively coupled technology with market insight to create entirely new businesses—not just new segments. These were authentic executions of the marketing concept: a real example and direction for business.

"But elsewhere, a lot of the energy of marketing and management in the late 1960's could, with hindsight, be called a diversion. By seeking certainty in numbers, managements tried to take the risk out of marketing. It was a time of marketing technique and short-view tactics, not market innovation and strategy with the long view.

"Then came the 1970's, with all those cost shocks—energy costs, inflation costs, capital costs—hardly conducive to real strategy, real innovation, the long view. We sought 'sure things'—who wouldn't in turbulent times? But sure things go against the grain of the idea of marketing, which, reflecting change and life itself, insists on constant innovation.

"The desire for sure things, and the long-view vacuum left by marketing, brought on strategic planning. At financial planning, at resource allocation—the internalities—strategic planning did well. But not too well at marketing, 'the crucial externality'. Comfortable with quantification, strategic planning mapped the external world—market size and share—beautifully. It made huge contributions to resource allocation, but strategic planning didn't, or couldn't, chart a market course. It didn't navigate. It didn't lead. And, unfortunately, too often it was seen to replace marketing.

"This numbers thing is a balancing challenge for us in business, especially big business. I like a statement by New York's Senator Patrick Moynihan, who said that 'governments seldom do anything about a problem until they have learned to count it.' Most of us in business are a bit that way with numbers—the trap being that by the time you've got the security that the numbers afford, the world may have passed you by. You may have missed the market niche.

"There's another trap in numbers that the 1970's demonstrated in spades—an even bigger miss for marketing. It's hard to quantify quality, and the world was moving to quality. Americans graduated from wanting more to wanting better. How could so many U.S. companies have missed this simple truth? Where was marketing to *demand* from the company the higher order of quality, reliability and durability that was being insisted on by the customer? Where was marketing to *insist* on the innovation that allows companies to build quality in, from the start? If marketing in the 1970's was at the helm, where it should be in business, it must have been asleep.

"Of course, I'm generalizing, and there were exceptions. In both decades, a leadership group of U.S. companies responded to the challenge of product and service innovation: from Merrill Lynch to McDonald's, from Federal Express to Disney, from Texas Instruments to Emerson Electric. And the same with selected products: from Miller Lite to Boeing's 747—products in tune with the times.

"But, let's face it, the 1970's really belonged to someone else. The news of the Seventies was the absolutely devastating way in which the Japanese had managed to decode the U.S. market: They undermined us on marketing fundamentals and innovation—while we were polishing technique. Their focus on ends, not means, led them, *forced* them, to do a better job of figuring out what society was valuing, how people were living, what customers really wanted.

"Where was *our* marketing? Twenty-five years after the United States came up with marketing as a comprehensive management concept, for most American companies it was still largely a theory in search of execution, an idea whose time had not yet come. We had mouthed the words, but the Japanese had heard the music.

"For the 1980's, we cannot predict much except the unpredictable. I have characterized innovation as the marriage of technology, whether product or service development, with the market insight—the market niche. Frankly, I'm more confident about technology's capability in this marriage than I am about marketing's. There is plenty of evidence to support my concern. Study after study shows the number one cause of new product failure is lack of a proper market focus.

"My concern is with the helm, with marketing. First, because it's crucial, second, because it's difficult. Marketing is synonymous with risk. Whatever the analysis and market research methodology, there's a lot of 'gut' to marketing. No amount of analysis will confirm an opportunity in advance. It's got to be the toughest perspective within business—far less tangible, far more deferrable than any other perspective a business can have. But the qualities that make it so difficult are precisely those that make it so important.

"Only the market vision, the outside cause, can rally people inside, can mobilize and animate a company. Only the market vision—with its focus on life, not things; on people, not products—can give meaning to what we do.

"When you think about it, we ought to be pretty good at this. It's in our roots, our tradition. Isn't that what we're supposed to be all about—listening, figuring out, and responding, to the paying fans?"

Source: Abridged excerpts from an address by John F. Welch, Jr., Chairman, General Electric Company, at The Conference Board's 1981 Marketing Conference. Reprinted by permission.

CASE 11
Langdale Lumber Company

Stan Sherman, vice-president for corporate planning of Clark Industries, Inc., leaned back in his plane seat as a late Friday afternoon flight carried him from Mississippi back to corporate headquarters in a major northern city. He had just spent two rather intense ten-hour days at the Langdale Lumber Company, a southern pine sawmill in a small town in Mississippi which had recently been acquired by Clark Industries, a large conglomerate. Although Clark Industries had been involved in the pulp and paper field for a number of years, along with a diverse array of other industrial and consumer goods businesses, this was the company's first venture into the lumber business. As corporate planning vice-president, it was Stan Sherman's job to oversee the planning activities of the company's various divisions. In the case of newly acquired firms such as the Langdale Lumber Company, which had never done any formal planning before, this could be quite a task, particularly when neither Mr. Sherman nor anyone else at corporate headquarters had had any working experience in the particular business involved, as in the case of lumber. Just prior to the Langdale acquisition, Sherman, whose background lay in marketing, had read up on the lumber industry, had collected reports and statistics from government and trade association sources, and had visited the Langdale mill several times. He had also recently talked with several large lumber wholesalers in the metropolitan area where Clark corporate headquarters were located. Right now, however, he was feeling frustrated in his efforts to get local management to use certain basic marketing concepts, such as market segmentation, to draw up a five-year marketing plan for Langdale.

While Stan Sherman was winging his way northward, Jim Benson, the new Langdale general manager, was sitting in his office at the mill in the late afternoon, after operations had closed down for the weekend, and was pondering over the many meetings he had had with Stan Sherman during the past two days. Mr. Benson's background lay chiefly in manufacturing, but he had also spent some time in log and pulpwood procurement. He had previously worked for a major pulp and paper company, not part of Clark Industries but located in the South. Unlike Stan Sherman, who had lived in the North all his life, Benson had grown up in Mississippi. Although less accustomed than Sherman to the analytical

---

This case is printed here with the permission of Professor Stuart U. Rich of the University of Oregon.

type of work required in business planning, Benson had a good feel for manufacturing operations, and had established a good relationship with the mill workforce. As one of his earlier supervisors at his previous company had remarked, "Jim can make the machines hum, and he has the ability to move among the workers in a mill in the right manner." Benson, who was given profit responsibility for the Langdale mill, currently reported to one of the regional vice-presidents of Clark Industries, who was mainly concerned with the company's pulp and paper operations in his region.

Reflecting on the planning job which lay ahead, Jim Benson said to himself, "Basically, the job isn't all that complex. Our marketing plan must answer three questions: Where are we now? Where do we want to go? And how can we get there?" What bothered him, however, was the extensive detail work that corporate headquarters seemed to call for, and the time demands this work would place on him and his small staff. He was thinking particularly of his sales staff, which consisted of Mathew Brady, who carried the title of sales manager, and Brady's assistant, Alice Perkins, who typed up the sales invoices, handled the sales correspondence, and did some telephone selling herself, chiefly during the infrequent occasions when Brady was away from the office.

Mathew Brady, unlike Sherman and Benson, had been part of Langdale Company's management prior to the acquisition. With the assistance of Alice Perkins, Brady had handled the company's sales activities for many years. He had lived in Mississippi all his life, his family was well known in the area, and the Brady family and the Langdale family (the company's previous owners) had been closely connected for several generations. Brady was about fifty, and Sherman and Benson were both about fifteen years younger. Mathew Brady prided himself on the close relationships he had built up with his customers over the years, although it had recently become Stan Sherman's opinion that Brady often seemed more concerned with protecting his long-time customers than aggressively expanding sales. Brady had attended several of the meetings held during the past two days, although he had spent most of the time listening to the discussions between Sherman and Benson, rather than playing an active role himself. When asked for his views about the need for expanding sales by entering new markets, Brady had replied that he did not want to go out and talk to new people until he was sure the mill could handle the extra production that might be required and still maintain its reputation for product quality and prompt service. Although the Langdale mill, like many others in the industry, was currently running at below one-shift capacity, Brady felt that when business conditions improved later in the year, the mill would be back up to its optimum level of operation, sustained largely by its regular customers and markets.

COMPANY BACKGROUND

The Langdale Lumber Company, located in Mississippi, had been founded in the early 1930s by Cyrus Langdale to manufacture boards and dimension lumber[1] from southern yellow pine. During its first 30 years of operation, the company had mainly sold direct to retail lumberyards in Mississippi and neighboring states and, to a lesser extent, to the export market through agents. Many of the sales were by letter and through personal visits, although by the 1960s the use of telephone WATS lines had largely replaced these earlier selling methods, and the company had expanded by selling to non-stocking (or "office") wholesalers, chiefly in the South, but also in the Midwest and a little in the Northeast.

In June of 1982, the Langdale Lumber Company, which had been purchased by Clark Industries from the Langdale family about a year earlier, was running one shift and producing at the rate of 100,000 board feet per day. Based on an industry average of 240 workdays per year, this translated into an annual rate of 24,000 MBF (MBF means thousand board feet). The company's theoretical one-shift capacity was 120 MBF per day, but the mill had seldom reached that level, even during boom times. The Langdale mill was considered to be in the small to medium-sized range among the 600 to 700 southern pine sawmills. Company sales volume in 1981 was $6,000,000, with a small loss reported, which was not unusual among lumber mills during current depressed industry conditions. Results so far in 1982 had been about the same, but improvement was expected in the second half-year, assuming the country started to pull out of the current housing slump.

Besides Jim Benson and Mathew Brady, other supervisory personnel at Langdale included a timber supply forester, a personnel coordinator, a maintenance foreman, sawmill foreman, dry kiln foreman, planing mill foreman, and shipping foreman. Total salaried personnel numbered 12, and total hourly workers numbered 120. Total personnel had been reduced about 10 percent since the acquisition by Clark Industries, as the plant had been considered overstaffed.

The company had two primary manufacturing lines. The band-saw line had the capability of producing either boards or dimension lumber, and the chipping-saw line produced primarily dimension lumber.[2] These

---

[1]A board is a piece of lumber less than two inches in nominal thickness and one inch or more in width. Dimension lumber is two inches up to, but not including, five inches thick, and is two inches or more in width. It is also referred to as framing lumber. (For definitions of these and other industry terms, the writer has drawn from "Terms of the Trade" by William Dean and David Evans of Random Lengths Publications, Eugene, Oregon.)

[2]A band saw consists of a continuous piece of flexible steel, with teeth on one or both sides, used to cut logs into cants, which are large timbers destined for further processing by other saws (e.g., cut into dimension lumber or boards).

A chipping saw or chipping heading (often called a "Chip-n-Saw" after a particular brand name) mills small logs simultaneously into lumber and chips. The machine chips away the entire outer part of the log and saws the inner part, usually into 2×4 dimension lumber.

two production lines gave the mill more flexibility than that available to many competitors who had only one type of production line, usually devoted to dimension lumber. The production costs of these more specialized mills were usually lower than those of a more versatile mill like Langdale.

Over the past year since the mill acquisition, Jim Benson, the general manager, had devoted nearly all of his time to improving the manufacturing efficiency of the mill and installing the many accounting and cost control reports which corporate headquarters now required. Sales and marketing had been left to Mathew Brady, who ran that end of the business much as he had done during his previous 15 years under the old family management. With a certain amount of urging by Stan Sherman, Benson was now starting to get involved in sales and marketing, although he felt that much remained to be done "to bring the manufacturing operation up to speed." For example, a bottleneck sometimes developed in the lumber drying process because of the lack of an adequate cooling ramp leading out of the dry kiln.[3] Similarly, the sorting chain on the planer mill needed to be extended so that the workers could more easily and quickly pull the finished lumber off the moving chain and stack it according to size, length, and grade.[4] The total cost of these two improvements was estimated at about $350,000.

Besides manufacturing, Jim Benson had also spent some of his time developing log supply sources. Although in earlier years Langdale had harvested a substantial portion of its logs from its own timberlands, very little productive timberland was included in the acquisition, and the company was now more dependent on outside raw material sources than many of its larger competitors. Log costs constituted approximately half of total lumber production costs. To get better product recovery from the logs, the company sold the chips which developed from its chipping-saw production line to a nearby pulp mill as raw materials for pulp manufacture.

INDUSTRY BACKGROUND

End Markets

The major markets for southern pine, and U.S. softwood lumber in general, were residential construction, nonresidential construction, re-

---

[3]A dry kiln is an oven-like chamber in which lumber is seasoned by applying heat and withdrawing moist air. Because of the tendency of green southern pine lumber to twist or crook, industry grading rules require that all grade-stamped southern pine dimension lumber be sold as kiln-dried down to a 15 percent moisture content. This is in contrast with Douglas fir and many other softwood species which are sold both as green and as kiln-dried lumber.

[4]A planer mill is where rough lumber is surfaced or dressed by a planing machine for the purpose of attaining smoothness of surface and uniformity of size on at least one side or edge.

pair and remodeling (or home improvement), and industrial uses. Lumber consumption by these markets since 1970 is shown in Exhibit 11-11, and a description of what constituted these markets is shown in Notes on Exhibit 11-11. This exhibit also gives figures on the regional sources of supply of the lumber consumed, and Notes on Exhibit 11-11 lists the states constituting the various regions. Exhibit 11-12 gives more detailed consumption figures for 1981 for the various market segments making up the four major market categories shown in Exhibit 11-11.

As these two exhibits show, the largest single market for softwood lumber was residential construction, particularly conventional, site-built, detached single-family homes. It was estimated that a site-built single-family house used on the average 10,500 board feet of lumber; a multifamily home used 4,200 board feet; and a mobile home, 2,000 board feet. About two-thirds of the lumber used in homes was framing lumber, and 90 percent of all single-family homes were built with wood frames. The relative importance of the residential construction market varied from year to year, reflecting the strength of the housing market, which is shown in Exhibit 11-13. In recent years, the repair and remodeling market had taken on increased importance, as shown in Exhibits 11-11 and 11-14. Finally, in terms of regional demand (not shown in the exhibits), the South's share of new housing starts rose from 38 percent of the U.S. total in 1975 to approximately 55 percent in 1981. In that year, the North Central region accounted for about 14 percent; the West, 22 percent; and the Northeast, 9 percent. The South's share continued to increase in 1982, and had reached 58 percent during the first five months. Within the South, certain metropolitan areas were currently experiencing strong housing demand even during the severe national housing slump. These areas included Houston and Dallas/Ft. Worth, Texas; Tampa and Orlando, Florida; Oklahoma City and Tulsa, Oklahoma; and Shreveport, Louisiana.

The export market, of less importance than any of the domestic markets noted above, is portrayed in Exhibit 11-15, which shows figures starting in 1970, as well as the relative importance of various species of lumber. Exhibit 11-16 gives a breakdown by both species and by country or region of destination for 1981, and a breakdown by country only for 1980 and the first quarter of 1982.

By late June, 1982, it was clear that earlier projections of housing demand and lumber demand for 1982 had been too optimistic, although longer-term projections still looked fairly good. Most of the forecasts which Stan Sherman had recently seen now predicted 1 million to 1.1 million starts in 1982, rising to 1.3 million in 1983. Some housing analysts were also challenging the conventional belief that a huge pent-up demand for single-family homes would be unleashed as soon as mortgage rates dropped to 13 or 14 percent from the current 17 percent. Revised 1980 Census Bureau data showed that the current housing stock of the nation was 92 million dwelling units, more than 2 million units greater than previously calculated. Many of these additional units had resulted from the conversion of schools, warehouses, and other nonresidential buildings, as well as

EXHIBIT 11-11　Estimated U.S. Softwood Lumber Consumption by Markets and Principal Sources, 1970–81 (in Million Board Feet)

	1970	1971	1972	1973	1974	1975	1976	1977	1978	1979	1980	1981
Markets (Demand):												
Residential Construction	12,380	17,654	20,025	17,945	11,952	11,065	14,497	18,580	18,573	15,827	11,639	9,825
Nonresidential Construction	6,785	6,563	6,424	6,302	6,449	5,748	5,704	5,699	6,134	6,318	5,668	5,790
Repair and Remodeling	6,164	6,336	6,450	6,502	6,639	6,922	7,357	7,477	7,940	8,041	7,788	7,720
Industrial	6,445	5,990	6,756	7,601	7,345	6,545	8,000	8,298	8,797	8,855	6,917	6,879
Total	31,774	36,493	39,655	38,350	32,385	30,280	35,558	40,054	41,444	39,041	32,012	30,214
Sources (Supply):												
Coast Region	7,017	8,064	8,785	8,102	7,010	6,579	7,594	8,237	8,320	7,622	5,898	5,589
Inland Region	9,092	10,144	10,374	10,204	8,762	8,307	9,478	10,017	9,815	9,397	7,463	7,043
Calif. Redwood Region	2,106	2,264	2,528	2,416	2,223	1,559	1,953	1,981	1,826	1,710	1,547	1,442
Southern Pine Region	6,957	7,832	8,008	7,681	6,684	7,074	7,360	8,147	8,134	7,737	6,401	5,918
Other U.S.	936	1,080	1,110	1,076	1,013	1,050	1,223	1,286	1,508	1,457	1,163	1,017
Total U.S.	26,108	29,384	30,805	29,479	25,692	24,569	27,608	29,668	29,603	27,923	22,472	21,009
Imports	5,666	7,109	8,850	8,871	6,693	5,711	7,950	10,386	11,841	11,118	9,540	9,205
Total	31,774	36,493	39,655	38,350	32,385	30,280	35,558	40,054	41,444	39,041	32,012	30,214

Source: Western Wood Products Association, "1980 Statistical Yearbook of the Western Lumber Industry."
Note: See Notes on Exhibit 11-11 for explanation of the above markets and sources.

Notes on Exhibit 11-11

Markets (Demand)

Residential Construction: Single-family; low-rise and high-rise multi-family; and mobile homes.

Nonresidential Construction: Commercial, industrial, public and other buildings; public utilities; sewer and water systems; highway construction; conservation and development projects; and nonresidential farm construction.

Repair and Remodeling: Residential and nonresidential.

Industrial: Products made for sale (e.g., furniture, shop lumber for uses such as window sashes and door frames, lumber for other remanufacturing uses); materials handling (e.g., crates, pallets, dunnage); mining timbers and railroad timbers.

Sources (Supply)

Coast Region: Washington and Oregon, west of the Cascades.

Inland Region: Washington and Oregon, east of the Cascades; California (except for central and northern coastal regions); Idaho, Nevada, Utah, Arizona, Montana, Wyoming, Colorado, New Mexico, southwestern South Dakota (Black Hills region).

California Redwood Region: Central and northern California coastal region.

Southern Pine Region: Tier of southern states of Oklahoma, Arkansas, Tennessee, and Virginia, plus all states directly south, viz., Texas, Louisiana, Mississippi, Alabama, Georgia, Florida, North Carolina, South Carolina.

Other U.S.: All other states not mentioned above (chiefly northeastern U.S. and Lake States).

---

the repartitioning of older houses, a trend which was expected to continue through the 1980s.

On the demand side, the 25- through 39-year-olds, a key buying group for housing, was increasing, and was expected to reach one-fourth of the total population by 1985, up from one-fifth 10 years earlier. However, federally subsidized housing, which accounted for an average of 240,000 housing starts per year throughout the 1970s, had been drastically curtailed and seemed unlikely to be a major factor during the 1980s. Finally, the purchase of homes (particularly single-family homes) as an investment had become less attractive because of the availability of new, high-yielding money market instruments, as well as the fact that home prices, which had been increasing at nearly twice the rate of inflation during the second half of the 1970s, had been falling in real terms since then.

Channels of Distribution

Channels of distribution for U.S. domestic markets and for overseas markets are shown in Exhibits 11-17 and 11-18, and brief descriptions

**EXHIBIT 11-12   1981 Estimated U.S. Softwood Lumber Consumption by
Market Segments (in Million Board Feet)**

I. Residential Construction		
Single-family		6,141
Multi-family		1,040
Condominium		
single-family	288	
multi-family	572	860
Factory-built (modular)		
single-family	682	
multi-family	111	793
Mobile homes		630
Second homes		416
Total		9,880
II. Nonresidential Construction		
Commercial (e.g., stores, offices, shopping centers, clinics)		1,550
Institutional (e.g., hospitals, churches, schools, government)		755
Industrial (e.g., factories, military buildings)		845
Agriculture		1,090
Other (e.g., highway construction, sewer and water systems)		1,460
Total		5,650
III. Repair and Remodeling		
Contractor		5,746
Do-It-Yourself		2,009
Total		7,755
IV. Industrial		
Products made for sale (e.g., furniture, shop lumber, lumber for other remanufacturing uses)		1,050
Other (chiefly materials handling, plus mining, railroads, etc.)		5,850
Total		6,900
Grand Total of Above Four Categories		30,185

Source: Western Wood Products Association.

of the various channel members are given in the Notes to these two exhibits. Of the various types of wholesalers in the domestic market, the
merchant wholesalers, both stocking and non-stocking, had traditionally
been the dominant channel for the distribution of lumber and other construction materials. However, by 1982, it was estimated that manufacturers' sales branches and sales offices, particularly those with large distri-

EXHIBIT 11-13 Private and Public Housing Starts and Mobile Home Shipments, 1970–81 (in Thousands of Units)

	1970	1971	1972	1973	1974	1975	1976	1977	1978	1979	1980	1981
Single-Family Starts	813	1,151	1,309	1,132	888	892	1,163	1,451	1,433	1,194	852	714
Multi-Family Starts	621	901	1,048	913	450	268	375	536	587	551	440	387
Total Private Housing Starts	1,434	2,052	2,357	2,045	1,338	1,160	1,538	1,987	2,020	1,745	1,292	1,101
Public Starts	35	32	22	13	15	11	10	15	16	15	20	16
Total Conventional Starts	1,469	2,084	2,379	2,058	1,353	1,171	1,548	2,002	2,036	1,760	1,312	1,117
Mobile Home Shipments	401	497	576	567	329	213	246	277	276	277	221	241
Total New Housing	1,870	2,581	2,955	2,625	1,682	1,384	1,794	2,279	2,312	2,037	1,533	1,358

Source: Western Wood Products Association, "1980 Statistical Yearbook of the Western Lumber Industry."

**EXHIBIT 11-14   Home Improvement Expenditures Versus New Housing
Expenditures, 1970–81 (in Billions of Dollars)**

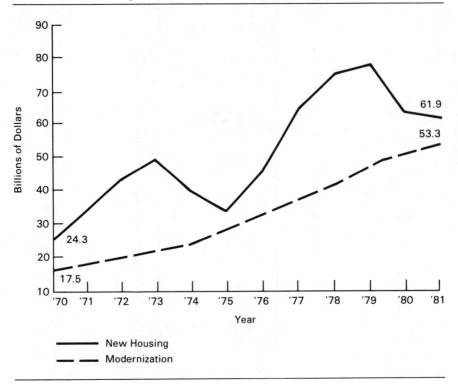

Source: *Building Supply News*, May, 1982.

bution yards, accounted for about 45 percent of the dollar sales of lumber
and other building materials, up from 32 percent ten years earlier. Independent merchant wholesalers accounted for 45 to 50 percent, with the
other channels, the remaining 5 to 10 percent.

Among the merchant wholesalers, those that carried inventory had
become the dominant channel in recent years, and many of the non-stocking (or "office") wholesalers had gone out of business. The major reason
for this trend was that the high cost of working capital had caused the
retail building materials dealers to push the inventory carrying function
back to the wholesale level. Retailers preferred to buy in smaller amounts
closer to their time of sale, making their purchases from nearby stocking
distributors, either independent merchant wholesalers or large manufac-
turer-owned distribution branches. Lumber mills selling to the large distribution yards of these two types of channel members shipped chiefly
straight carloads of lumber rather than mixed cars, which were sold to

EXHIBIT 11-15 U.S. Softwood Lumber Exports by Species, 1970–81 (in Million Board Feet)

	1970	1971	1972	1973	1974	1975	1976	1977	1978	1979	1980	1981
Douglas Fir	383	329	405	638	573	505	572	488	457	505	521	509
Other Fir	—	—	—	—	—	—	—	—	33	57	86	90
Southern Pine	78	65	64	94	76	68	140	158	131	196	261	211
Ponderosa and White Pines	118	127	161	178	157	177	214	211	162	200	239	302
Eastern Red and White Pines	—	—	—	—	—	—	—	—	42	46	53	62
Hem-Fir	142	119	191	395	343	317	294	264	272	464	511	390
Spruce	295	172	195	232	210	159	165	151	135	151	136	141
Redwood	30	33	50	72	39	37	61	48	34	30	27	38
Cedar	40	28	44	69	41	36	61	61	59	56	62	67
Other Softwoods	69	60	71	67	67	74	76	47	44	40	60	67
Softwood Rail and Mine Ties	—	—	6	4	30	28	16	9	5	36	20	16
Total	1,155	933	1,187	1,749	1,536	1,401	1,599	1,437	1,374	1,781	1,976	1,893

Source: Western Wood Products Association, "Statistical Yearbook of the Western Lumber Industry" (derived from U.S. Bureau of the Census, U.S. Exports—Schedule B—Commodity and Country, Report FT410).

EXHIBIT 11-16   U.S. Softwood Lumber Exports by Species and Destination, 1980, 1981, and 1st Quarter 1982 (in Million Board Feet)

	Spruce	Southern Pine	Douglas Fir	Hemlock	Western Red Cedar	Redwood	Other Species	1981 Total	1980 Total	1st Quarter 1982
Canada	19.1	6.9	121.3	21.0	31.3	25.3	269.2	494.1	359.8	70.4
Mexico	11.1	2.0	19.1	.1	.1	24.3	129.9	186.1	247.1	30.1
Caribbean	1.9	98.9	1.1	.3	.3	.6	13.9	116.6	88.5	26.5
United Kingdom	—	4.8	13.1	9.1	.5	—	3.1	31.2	53.5	6.4
Netherlands	.3	2.0	.7	.1	.1	.1	1.0	4.6	9.8	1.5
Belgium	.2	2.8	9.7	1.0	.3	.4	.2	14.9	26.2	5.0
France	—	1.2	3.8	.2	—	—	.9	6.0	14.8	.6
West Germany	.5	23.5	9.8	5.9	2.6	1.1	4.1	47.8	70.4	8.3
Spain	.1	9.8	4.8	—	.3	—	.7	15.7	46.4	5.8
Italy	.1	22.6	64.1	.6	—	.1	.8	88.3	186.0	16.9
Greece	—	.9	6.8	—	.1	.1	.4	8.2	10.6	3.4
Middle East	3.2	9.8	36.7	14.7	1.2	2.6	17.5	84.4	111.1	12.6
Japan	82.5	1.9	60.7	302.2	.2	.3	59.3	507.0	631.3	162.6
Australia	.1	—	110.1	5.0	2.5	2.0	2.5	122.8	90.6	28.4
Other Countries	22.3	24.1	47.2	30.0	1.8	15.1	14.8	155.0	16.7	30.4
Total	141.4	211.2	509.0	390.2	41.3	72.0	518.3	1,883.3	1,962.8	408.9

Sources: *Random Lengths Export*, March 17, 1982, and June 9, 1982 (derived from U.S. Bureau of the Census, U.S. Exports—Schedule B—Commodity and Country, Report FT 410).

Notes: Column and Row Totals may not always check out because of rounding. Species breakdown is slightly different from that in Exhibit 11-14. The Caribbean refers to the Caribbean rim countries as well as the islands.

the non-stocking or office wholesalers.[5] Another trend that was taking place (as portrayed in Exhibit 11-17) was a "lateral" channel of distribution from both stocking and non-stocking wholesalers to manufacturers' sales branches and sales offices and, to a lesser extent, to cooperative buying offices. Finally, there were increasing numbers of wholesalers who had become "remanufacturing wholesalers" who bought a product from the mill, altered it, and then resold it to retailers or industrial users. These products ranged from millwork items (door and window parts and decorative trim) to pressure-treated lumber.

A major trend at the retail level was the increasing importance of home improvement centers (or home centers) and the mass merchandisers who served the rapidly growing repair and remodeling market. They catered particularly to the homeowner or do-it-yourself (DIY) trade, but also sold to contractors and builders. They purchased their goods mainly from stocking merchant wholesalers, as well as from manufacturers' sales branches with distribution yards. Some of the major lumber items they handled were pressure-treated lumber for fencing and other outdoor use, such as 8-foot 4×4's, and shorter lengths and wider widths of pine boards for shelving and cabinets, such as 1×12's appearance (higher-quality) grades. A number of the major lumber and building materials manufacturers who had integrated forward into wholesaling had also gone a step further and established or acquired chains of national or regional retail outlets.[6]

In the overseas markets, the most common channel used followed this pattern: manufacturers to export merchant wholesalers to overseas sales agents to overseas merchant wholesalers to retailers to final overseas markets. (See Exhibit 11-18.) As in the case of domestic markets, although not nearly as strong a trend, a number of major manufacturers sold through their own captive wholesale distribution branches which sold to retailers and to end-use markets. Of the many channel members involved, the key role was generally played by the overseas sales agent who made daily price offers to importers on commodities based on telex-confirmed prices with the exporters (i.e., the manufacturers or their U.S.-based channel members). The agent arranged for shipments from the exporter, and followed up to make sure deliveries were made and payment received.

---

[5]A straight car is a loading of lumber and other wood products consisting entirely of one type of item and usually limited to one species, grade, and width. There may be a variation in length, such as in a random loading of dimension lumber. A mixed car consists of a variety of items, sizes, species, etc. Mixed-car items generally command a higher price than a comparable single item in a "straight" car.

[6]According to the most recent Bureau of Census figures (1977), there were in the United States 7,227 lumber, plywood, and millwork wholesalers, including manufacturers' sales branches. There were also 28,932 lumber and other building materials dealers (retailers). (Sources: U.S. Dept. Commerce, Bu. Census, 1977 Census of Wholesale Trade and Census of Retail Trade.)

EXHIBIT 11-17   Channels of Distribution for Lumber – Domestic Markets

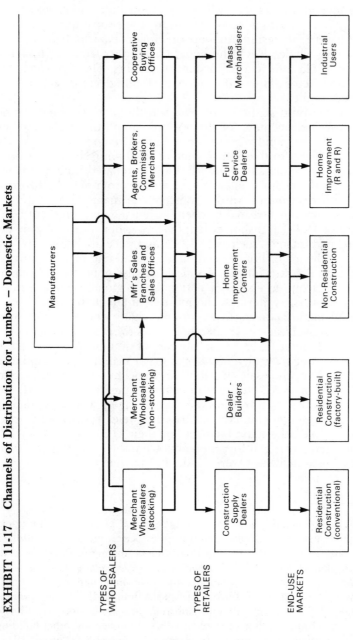

Note: The symbol ‿➤ indicates the bypassing of a layer of channel intermediaries. For example, manufacturers may sometimes bypass the wholesale level and sell direct to various types of retailers.

NOTES ON EXHIBIT 11-17

Types of Wholesalers

Merchant Wholesalers are independent firms which purchase products from manufacturers for the purpose of resale to dealers or retailers or industrial users. They take title to the goods they purchase and may or may not carry stock.

Agents, Brokers, and Commission Merchants are similar to merchant wholesalers, except that they do not take title to the products but only perform the sales function, and typically do not carry stock.

Manufacturers' Sales Branches and Sales Offices are establishments maintained by the manufacturers for marketing their products at the wholesale level. Captive wholesale distribution centers are also included in this category. If the sales branches or distribution centers sell primarily to household consumers or to local builders, however, they are not included in this category but in the appropriate retailer category. Finally, a mill salesforce, selling mainly the mill's output to establishments at the wholesale level, would not be considered as a sales branch or sales office, but rather as part of the mill operation.

Cooperative Buying Offices are maintained by a group of dealers or retailers who pool orders so that they can buy in quantity from mills and drop-ship partial carloads to the various yard locations of the dealer-members.

Types of Retailers

Construction Supply Dealers carry large inventories of bulky materials such as lumber, plywood, hardboard, and gypsum which they sell at near-wholesale prices to big-volume builders and contractors. These dealers may be involved in the manufacture of millwork items, such as cabinets and window frames, as well as roof trusses and wall panels.

Dealer-Builders sell building materials and also engage in either custom or speculative building of homes, farm buildings, major room additions, and general remodeling, using either their own or subcontracted crews.

Home Improvement Centers, also called Home Centers, are dealers or retailers who sell, chiefly to homeowners, a wide range of building materials and other products used for adding to, repairing, renovating, and maintaining the home.

Full-Service Dealers carry a complete line of building products, including appliances and kitchen cabinets, and serve both homeowners and builders. Service is emphasized, including design, cost estimating, and financing for small home builders.

Mass Merchandisers are retail institutions from outside the building materials field, including department stores, mail order/department stores, and discount stores. They may have home improvement or building supply departments in their regular stores, or may have chains of separate building supply centers.

EXHIBIT 11-18   Channels of Distribution for Lumber — Overseas Markets

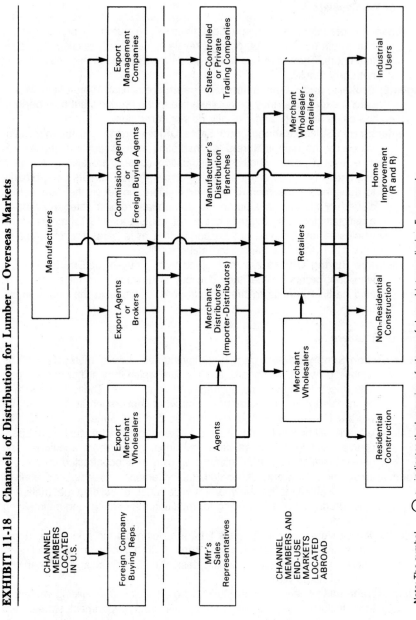

Note: The symbol ⟶ indicates the bypassing of a layer of channel intermediaries. For example, manufacturers may sometimes bypass the channel members located in the United States and sell direct to channel members located overseas.

NOTES ON EXHIBIT 11-18

Channel Members Located in U.S.

Export Merchant Wholesalers are the same as merchant wholesalers in the domestic market, but specialize in selling to channels and markets in the export trade.

Export Agents or Brokers are the same as agents and brokers in the domestic market, but specialize in selling to export channels and markets.

Commission Agents or Foreign Buying Agents are "finders" for foreign firms wanting to purchase U.S. products, and a commission is paid to them by their foreign clients.

Foreign Company Buying Reps are foreign company direct representatives, such as those sent here by Japanese trading companies.

Export Management Companies (also called EMCs) act as export departments for several manufacturers of noncompetitive products. They solicit and transact business in the name of the manufacturers they represent for a commission, salary, or retainer plus commission. Some may also take title and carry the financing for export sales.

Channel Members Located Abroad

Agents represent American exporters in the principal foreign lumber-buying ports. They develop sales with foreign importers, such as merchant wholesalers or industrial users. They do not take title to the goods, but are paid by commission.

Manufacturers' Sales Representatives take responsibility for a manufacturer's goods exported to a particular country or market area, and are paid by commission. They are more under the control of the manufacturer-exporter than are most categories of agents.

Merchant Distributors, unlike agents, take title to the goods they purchase from U.S. manufacturers or U.S.-located channel members. They resell the goods either direct or through wholesalers or retailers to end-user markets abroad. (Merchant Distributors are also called Importer-Distributors.)

Manufacturers' Distribution Branches have their own shipping terminals and storage facilities in foreign ports from which they sell their own mills' production as well as that of other U.S. mills. Their sales are to foreign wholesalers, retailers, or end-users.

State-Controlled Trading Companies are found in those countries which have state trading monopolies, where business is conducted by a few government-sanctioned and controlled trading entities. **Private Trading Companies** are privately owned merchant importers. In some countries, such as Japan, they may exercise considerable control over both the importation of goods and their distribution within the country.

Merchant Wholesalers take title to the goods purchased and may act as stocking wholesalers or drop shippers, and sell to retailers or direct to end markets.

Retailers typically buy from distributors or wholesalers and sell to building contractors, industrial users and home owners.

NOTES ON EXHIBIT 11-18   continued

Merchant Wholesaler-Retailers are firms involved in both wholesaling and retailing, and may own retail chains which sell to building contractors and
to the do-it-yourself market.

Note: For further detail on several of these channels, see U.S. Department of
Commerce, Industry and Trade Administration, "A Basic Guide to Ex-
porting," January, 1979.

Pricing

The process of price determination of most lumber items took place
in a nationwide (actually U.S.-Canadian) auction market. The lumber
wholesaler played a key role in matching what the mills were asking with
what the dealers or other purchasers were willing to pay, and in that way
determining the price at which a sale could take place. The mill's offering
price was influenced by its backlog of unfilled orders, by how much stock
it had on hand, and by the supply of raw material or logs which were
available. The price the dealer was willing to pay depended on his inventory and on the strength of market demand. This huge lumber auction
involved thousands of telephone transactions. The daily flood of buyer-
seller negotiations meant a highly volatile price structure, almost immediately responsive to supply and demand pressures. However, instead of
a single market price determining market equilibrium, as portrayed in
economic theory of price competition, there was more likely to be some
variation in the prices of the same items sold to the same general categories of purchasers. These price differentials stemmed from imperfect
knowledge of the market—for example, small, local wholesalers making
infrequent purchases versus large distributors plugged into a constant information stream of telephone inquiries and orders. The differing prices
were also caused by variations in the order mix shipped by different mills,
such as straight cars versus mixed cars, overgraded versus undergraded
lumber, and regular orders versus those requiring special handling or
packaging.

Position of the South

In the early 1980s the 12 southern lumber-producing states were
in a favorable position to capitalize on growing worldwide demand for
lumber and wood products. In contrast with the West, where over 60 percent of commercial forest land was in government ownership, in the South
10 percent was government-owned and 90 percent privately owned, either
by forest-products companies or by other forest land owners. Cuttings on
private holdings in the Northwest were being made at a rate faster than

timber growth, but at the same time there was a flat trend in federal timber sales. In the South, growth rate was greater than harvest rate because of the rapid growth and early maturity of southern pine, as well as more intensive forest management. It was estimated that the South grew timber at a rate one-fourth greater than the national average. Nearness to the major market areas of the Midwest and Northeast was another advantage of the southern mills, as compared with those on the West Coast, particularly with the rapid rise in freight rates. The faster increase in population in the Sunbelt states, with the South's increasing share of national housing starts noted earlier, also meant a stronger regional market for the southern lumber mills.

Most mills in the South were designed for the high-speed production of dimension or framing lumber, which constituted 85 percent of total southern pine lumber, with 13 percent consisting of boards, and the remaining 2 percent mostly timbers (i.e., lumber at least 5 inches in least dimension). Dimension lumber was used primarily for structural members and components such as floor and roof trusses, floor and ceiling joists, and roof rafters and studs in homebuilding. Boards were used in home construction for paneling, siding, and moldings or trim to finish off around window and door openings and walls. They were also used for shelving, cabinets, furniture parts, and ladders, and the lower grades were found in a wide variety of industrial uses such as crates and pallets. In earlier years, flooring had been a major market for boards, but with the popularity of wall-to-wall carpeting starting in the 1950s, plywood and particleboard had largely replaced lumber floorboards. Finally, the growing repair and remodeling market had caused an increase in the demand for boards. A major portion of the high-quality, "appearance" grades of boards were manufactured in the West, with ponderosa pine the leading species. Boards were also produced from other species in the West and Northeast, as well as from southern pine.

Besides boards, another type of lumber in current demand by the home improvement market was treated lumber, which was used particularly for fences and decks. Uses in other markets included wood foundation systems, bridges, and piers. Increasing amounts of treated lumber were also being exported to the Caribbean region. The wood-treating industry favored southern pine as it readily accepted preservative chemicals because of its high percentage of sapwood (the outer layers of growth between the bark and the heartwood). In 1981, 30 percent of all southern pine lumber produced was treated, up from 21 percent the year before. The most frequently treated items were #2 grade 2×4's and 2×6's in 16-foot and shorter lengths, as well as 4×4's in 8-, 10-, and 12-foot lengths.[7]

[7]The most commonly used species of framing lumber (except southern pine) are graded as follows: Standard and Better; #2 and Better; Utility; and #3. Major southern yellow pine grades are #1 Dense, #1, and #2, with "dense" referring to the number of annual rings per inch. The most frequently used board grades, including southern pine boards, are C and Better; D, #2 and Better; and #3.

Another reason for the increased popularity of treated lumber was the decreased availability of rot-resistant redwood and cedar, the traditional species for fences and decks and similar outdoor uses.

The dominant geographical market for the 6 to 7 billion board feet of annual production of southern pine in 1980 and 1981 was in the South, which got about 70 percent of its total softwood lumber needs from southern mills, a percentage which had remained fairly steady for the past 25 years. The second major source was Canada, which had recently surpassed the U.S. western states as a supplier. In fact, in the case of Georgia and Florida, over half of lumber consumption needs came from Canada, mainly in the form of dimension lumber. (Canadian mills had some advantages over U.S. mills, particularly those in the West, because of more favorable government timber sale policies, lower ocean shipping rates, lower rail transportation costs across Canada and into U.S. markets, and a favorable exchange rate for U.S. purchasers.)

In the case of Mississippi, which typically accounted for about 10 percent of total southern softwood lumber production, 84 percent of the state's softwood lumber consumption needs (slightly over 500 million board feet) came from southern mills, 11 percent from Canada, and 5 percent from the U.S. West. Mississippi mills, on the other hand, shipped about 18 percent of their output to points within the state. (Further detail on the distribution of southern pine lumber shipments from Mississippi is shown in Exhibit 11-19.) Although a major portion of their production was shipped out of the state, the Mississippi mills still supplied a large amount of the needs of the Mississippi market. The imports from Canada into that state were chiefly of Douglas fir and other western species.

In the overseas export market, southern pine lumber was expected to play an increasing role. World lumber consumption, excluding North America, was expected to increase by 30 percent between 1980 and 2000, according to FAO-UN projections. Currently, the world's leading exporters were Canada, Scandinavia, and Russia. However, U.S. softwood growth rates, particularly in the South, far exceeded those of Canada and Russia, and Scandinavia was already at the limit of sustainable yield production. Major export markets for southern pine were Western Europe and the Caribbean, that is, the Caribbean island nations and the countries around the rim of the Caribbean basin. (See Exhibit 11-16 for a further breakdown of southern pine and other lumber export destinations.) Southern pine lumber shipped to Europe was primarily clear (knot-free) material, used for paneling, furniture parts, and joinery.[8] A major portion of the pine shipped to the Caribbean was planed lumber used for structural purposes, particularly in roof structures.

---

[8]Joinery is a term used in Europe to denote the higher grades of lumber suitable for such uses as cabinetry, millwork, or interior trim.

EXHIBIT 11-19   Distribution of Southern Pine Lumber Shipments As Reported by 18 Mississippi Mills, 1981

Shipments to Southern Pine Producing States:	Thousand Board Feet	% Total	Rank
Alabama	90,392	16.6	2
Arkansas	11,046	2.0	15
Florida	12,452	2.3	14
Georgia	10,461	1.9	16
Louisiana	53,270	9.8	4
Mississippi	99,213	18.2	1
North Carolina	3,306	.6	20
Oklahoma	1,979	.4	22
South Carolina	3,325	.6	19
Tennessee	21,389	3.9	6
Texas	80,673	14.8	3
Virginia	7,326	1.3	17
Total	394,832	72.4	
Shipments to States Not Producing Southern Pine:			
Illinois	24,716	4.5	5
Indiana	16,307	3.0	9
Iowa	1,687	.3	23
Kansas	1,173	.2	25
Kentucky	15,223	2.8	11
Maryland	231	.0	29
Michigan	12,873	2.4	13
Missouri	15,994	2.9	10
Nebraska	13,071	2.4	12
New Jersey	684	.1	28
New York	873	.2	27
Ohio	17,563	3.2	8
Pennsylvania	1,052	.2	26
West Virginia	1,600	.3	24
Wisconsin	17,768	3.3	7
Other[a]	5,352	1.0	18
Total	146,167	26.8	
Export	3,021	.6	
Grand Total	544,020	99.8[b]	

[a]"Other" includes states not individually listed, principally the New England states.
[b]Does not add up to 100% because of rounding.
Source of figures: Southern Forest Products Association, *Distribution of Southern Pine Shipments*, March, 1982. (The sample of 18 mills accounts for approximately 70% of total Mississippi southern pine lumber production.)

PRODUCT LINE

Langdale's product line was broken down as follows: boards, 35 percent; dimension, 55 percent; flooring and siding, 6 percent; and SAPS and Prime, 4 percent.[9] The last two categories were the highest priced and most profitable items. As for the first two categories, boards were usually higher priced than dimension lumber of the closest similar size and grade. Board prices also fluctuated less widely than dimension prices. (See Exhibit 11-20). However, the sawing and planing process for boards took longer than for dimension. In addition, since boards were sawed to nominal one-inch thickness versus 2-inch thickness for dimension, there was greater raw material wastage in the form of sawdust when producing boards. Thus, manufacturing costs were high for boards, and the relative profitability of the two types of lumber varied according to their price relationship. Other factors determining the production emphasis on boards versus dimension were the types of logs available from local logging contractors and woodlot owners, competition from other mills, customer commitments, and overall market demand.

With a strong commitment to both boards and dimension lumber, the Langdale Company's product line was more complete than that of most of its competitors. Similarly, most of the company's shipments were in mixed carloads, rather than straight cars, enabling the company to charge higher prices to those customers who preferred mixed cars, such as office wholesalers and dealers. Product quality, in both boards and dimension, sometimes enabled Langdale to get slightly higher prices than many of its competitors in certain market uses, including boards used in finished work, such as cabinets, shelving, furniture, and window facings. In dimension lumber, wood truss manufacturers were a market which called for higher-quality lumber, with strength a major requirement.[10] Southern pine was good for trusses because of its strength, and the grades required were #1, and #2 Dense, the first of which was made by Langdale.

DISTRIBUTION, SALES, AND PRICING

Langdale's distribution channels were as follows: wholesalers, 65 percent; dealers or retailers, 15 percent; direct to industrial users, 10 percent; and export wholesalers or agents, 10 percent. Some 20 years earlier, the percentages through wholesalers versus retailers had been just re-

---

[9]Flooring and siding are higher-quality boards usually requiring more manufacturing steps than boards used for other purposes. For example, flooring is a tongue-and-groove piece of lumber, with the basic size 1″×4″.

SAPS and Prime are high-quality export grades of southern yellow pine boards, shipped mostly to Europe.

[10]A truss is an assemblage of wooden members which forms a rigid framework to support a roof or other part of a building.

EXHIBIT 11-20   Price Trends of Southern Pine Dimension Lumber Versus Southern Pine Boards, 1977–81

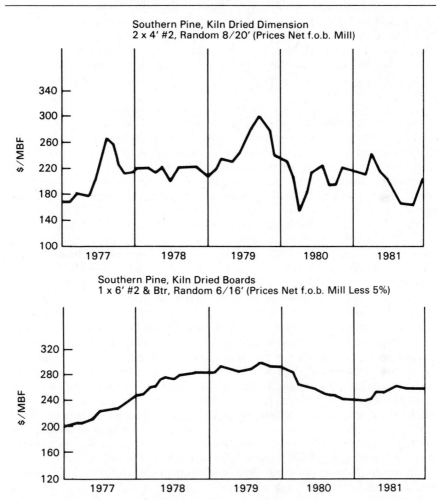

Source: Random Lengths Publications, *1981 Yearbook.*

versed. A major reason for the change was the increased importance of telephone selling and the use of WATS lines.[11] Other reasons for the in-

---

[11] A WATS (Wide Area Telephone Service) line enables a caller to phone anywhere in a designated area for a flat monthly fee. Many lumber wholesale firms use a WATS line in lieu of regular long-distance lines; some have toll-free incoming WATS lines that customers may use.

creasing importance of wholesalers for Langdale and for the industry generally were the shift of the inventory carrying function from retailer to wholesaler (described earlier), and the fact that the wholesaler could, in one telephone call, supply the retailer with all of his regular lumber needs in terms of species, sizes, types, and grades, thus saving much time that the retailer might have to spend dealing with many different mill salesmen. Wholesalers had also become more aggressive and were shaving the traditional 5 percent markup which they had taken on mill prices when they sold to retailers.

The majority of the company's sales to wholesalers were to office wholesalers (non-stocking merchant wholesalers). Those sales that went to stocking wholesalers were usually to the smaller, local ones, rather than to the big distribution yards which serviced retailers in larger areas. It was these large distribution yards, particularly those owned by large forest-products manufacturers, which had shown the fastest growth in recent years. Direct sales to industrial accounts included manufacturers of furniture, bleachers, toys, and laminated beams, as well as a little to a wood-treating firm. Other industrial users, such as truss manufacturers, were reached through wholesalers. The majority of the company's customers were in the home state of Mississippi, with some located in the adjoining states of Alabama, Tennessee, and Louisiana, and relatively few elsewhere.

Although during its early years Langdale had been very active in the export trade, this was no longer a market it was actively pursuing. It sold to this market through U.S. export wholesalers, and a few foreign-based agents. The most important of these had been an agent located in a major European lumber-importing country which had recently taken on the export business of a large U.S. forest-products firm and had apparently lost interest in selling Langdale products. If the company decided to expand its export sales, it would probably have to seek new export wholesalers and/or new overseas agents. It was generally accepted in the industry that success in selling to the export market required sorting out the higher-grade items in a mill's production, tight control over appearance and quality, rigid adherence to clearly drafted product specifications which often involved sizes and grades different from those in the domestic market, and first-hand knowledge of the trade customs, usage patterns, and government regulations of the various countries involved. It also helped if the U.S. exporter was willing to enter into long-term forward price commitments, since that was what foreign importers preferred. Since this represented a departure from the auction-market type of fluctuating price pattern to which U.S. firms had long been accustomed in the domestic market, few companies were willing to change. Most mills, including Langdale, tried to keep a 2- to 4-week order file, that is, not to give price quotes for any period more than 4 weeks ahead.

The company's pricing policy, following a long-established tradition of previous management, was to price somewhat higher than most competitors and not to engage in aggressive price cutting during a falling market, but rather to try to hold price and curtail production if inventory levels started rising too much. Mathew Brady, the Langdale sales manager, felt that such a policy was, in the long run, best for the company and for his established customers. However, Stan Sherman, planning vice-president from corporate headquarters, had questioned the desirability of this policy during the recent meetings at the Langdale mill. "We've got to make greater effort to maintain our sales volume," he said, "and if the market slides, there are two ways to do this: (1) lower price, or (2) expand our market through broadening our customer base, both geographically and through emphasizing new channels and new end-users." During a depressed market such as the company was currently experiencing, Sherman recommended lowering prices on a selective basis, in order to get new customers in new areas. Brady disagreed with this proposal. "If our inventory of particular items is getting too high, I would prefer to offer a one-time special sale to all our customers. To cut prices to new customers in other areas while at the same time charging higher prices to our long-established customers would raise a real moral issue with me. Furthermore," he continued, "these new customers would probably not stay with us for very long, but would go back to their established suppliers as soon as the market strengthened."

DEVELOPMENT OF A MARKETING PLAN

The five-year marketing plan which Langdale Company management was expected to draw up with the general assistance of Stan Sherman was to be part of the overall five-year long-range plan for Langdale. The main goal for the Langdale Company, which had been set by corporate headquarters, was to increase production capacity to 45,000 MBF over the next five years. To accomplish this, capital expenditures of between $500,000 and $750,000 had been tentatively planned. These expenditures included improvements in the dry kiln and planer mill noted earlier, as well as improvements in the log yard, and the chipping-saw and band-saw lines. The relative amount of expenditures on these two production lines depended on the future emphasis to be given to dimension lumber versus boards, as well as on the quality and sizes of the logs which could be procured.

How to sell the increased output of the mill over the coming five years was an issue which Stan Sherman felt had not really been addressed as yet. The purpose of his visit had been to get Langdale management moving ahead on drawing up a five-year marketing plan, which he believed should be a key component of the overall five-year long-range plan to be submitted to corporate headquarters for approval by the first of October. As Sherman had explained to Benson and Brady, the basic approach in marketing planning for Langdale, or for any company for that matter, should be to start out by identifying market segments in the industry that might be meaningful to the company, and to see to what extent the company was selling to these segments. In this way, a plan or program could be laid out detailing which segments should be emphasized, which ones deemphasized, and which ones, previously overlooked, should be cultivated. Both Benson and Brady agreed that this seemed like a good idea in principle; however, they did not appear to be convinced that a formalized approach such as this was necessary for a mill the size of Langdale. Furthermore, given the limited management personnel at Langdale, and current restrictions on additional hiring, there simply wasn't the time to do the analytical work and paperwork required for such a complete marketing plan.

There had been considerable discussion during the recent meetings of the sorts of data needed to draw up a complete marketing plan based on a market segmentation analysis. Some of the overall industry data had already been compiled by Stan Sherman. (These data consisted chiefly of the industry background exhibits and comments thereon already portrayed in the case.) Some of the industry trends were of particular significance to Langdale, and would have to be analyzed in more detail. More company sales information would also be needed in order to see where Langdale stood in relation to industry trends. Besides gathering the data, there was also the question of how to analyze it.

Prior to its acquisition by Clark Industries, the only data processing being used by the Langdale Company was a bank service to process its payroll. Now, using the data processing facilities of the parent corporation, the Langdale Company was planning to computerize other parts of its operations, including order entry, inventory, production, and sales analysis. An input terminal and printer had been ordered to provide the company with the devices necessary to control its data entry and report printing needs. As part of the current marketing planning efforts, Jim Benson, with the help of Sherman and Brady, was starting to determine how the company's sales invoices should be redesigned in order to secure the data necessary to do the sorts of sales analyses needed to improve the firm's customer service and marketing efforts. At that time, the invoices contained the following information: date of sale, name and address of customer, types of items purchased, number of units purchased, price charged per unit, and total dollar amount due. Stan Sherman pointed out that a lot could be learned about what market segments were being served simply by analyzing past company invoices. Jim Benson, however, preferred to wait a couple of months, when the new data processing system was supposed to be in place, before spending much time on such an analysis.

Another possible source of data which Stan Sherman felt would be useful in improving the company's marketing efforts was a telephone log. During his recent visits to several large lumber wholesalers, Sherman had noticed that some of the firms had required that their traders (those buying and selling lumber) keep such logs, or daily telephone call reports. These reports contained such information as the following: names of customer accounts (or supply sources) called, calls completed, price quotes made, orders bought (or sold), new accounts called, and new accounts sold.

Mathew Brady's reaction to such a phone log, however, was that he could keep all this information in his head, that he was too busy talking on the phone to write up such a log, and that even if such call reports were written out, they would be misleading to anyone trying to do sales analyses from them. The reason for this latter objection was that every customer was different. For example, some wanted to be called only at certain hours on certain days of the week, whereas others welcomed calls from him, or called him themselves, almost any time; some always liked to dicker on prices and items, whereas others quickly decided whether to accept or refuse an offer. Jim Benson had not yet decided how he felt about the telephone log idea.

CONCLUSION

As he neared the end of his flight, Stan Sherman decided to draft a memo over the weekend to be mailed to Jim Benson on Monday. This memo would first summarize what he perceived as the areas of common agreement reached during the recent meetings at the mill. The desirability of spending capital to increase the efficiency of the mill was one of these areas, and one which seemed to rank top priority with Benson in particular. The need to improve the Langdale Company's existing profit situation and to increase future sales were two other issues on which Sherman, Benson, and Brady agreed, although how best to go about doing this was an issue not yet resolved.

After describing these areas of general agreement, Sherman felt he should next reemphasize that some kind of market segmentation approach was the logical way to go, not only to improve profit performance, but also to reach the long-term sales goals that would be needed to sell out the mill's capacity during the coming years. He wondered if he should suggest several different ways to segment the lumber market and leave it up to Benson and Brady to choose the way, or ways, most applicable to Langdale. An alternative approach would be to lay out exactly what steps should be taken to analyze the market according to several different dimensions. This analysis would take the form of specific segmentation projects, a description of the benefits to be gained from each project, and timetables for their completion.

Finally, Sherman had not yet decided which other people, either within the Langdale mill or in other parts of Clark Industries, should receive copies of his memo to Jim Benson. He felt that both Benson and Brady were valuable men to the Langdale Company and to Clark Industries. However, something had to be done to "get Langdale on the march" toward developing a meaningful five-year marketing plan which was due at corporate headquarters on October first, just three months away.

PART SEVEN
Marketing Strategies

CHAPTER 12
Market Strategies

Three women and a goose make a marketplace.

Italian proverb

In the final analysis, all business strategies must be justified by the availability of a viable market. When a viable market is lacking, even the best strategy will flop. Additionally, the development of marketing strategies for each business should be realistically tied to the target market. Since market should be the focus for successful marketing, strategies aligned to market(s) point the way for each present business, serve as underpinnings for overall corporate-wide strategy, and provide direction for programming key activities and projects in all functional areas.

When corporate resources are scarce and corporate strengths are limited, it is fatal to spread them across too many markets. Rather, these critical resources should be concentrated on those key markets (key in terms of type of market, geographic location, time of entry, and commitment) that are decisive for a business's success. Merely allocating resources in the same way that other firms do will yield no competitive differential. If, however, it can be discovered which markets really hold potential, the business will be able to lever itself into a position of relative competitive superiority.

This chapter will identify different aspects of market strategies which companies commonly pursue and analyze their impact on performance vis-à-vis strategic business unit objectives. The use of these strategies will be illustrated with examples from the marketing literature.

The appendix at the end of this chapter summarizes each strategy in terms of definition, objectives, requirements, and expected results.

DIMENSIONS OF MARKET STRATEGIES

Market strategies deal with the perspectives of markets to be served. These perspectives can be determined in different ways. For example, a company may serve the entire market or dissect it into key segments on which to concentrate its major effort. Thus, market scope is one aspect of market strategy. The geographic dimensions of the market constitute another aspect: a company may focus on a local, regional, national, or international market. Another strategic variable is the time of entry into a market. A company may be the first, among the first few, or among the last to enter the market. Commitment to a market is still another aspect of market strategy. This commitment can be to achieve market dominance, to become a major factor in the market, or merely to play a minor role in it. Finally, a company may intentionally decide to dilute a part of its market as a matter of strategy.

Briefly, then, the following are the major market strategies that a company may pursue:

Market-scope strategy
Market-geography strategy
Market-entry strategy
Market-commitment strategy
Market-dilution strategy

MARKET-SCOPE STRATEGY

Market-scope strategy deals with the coverage of the market. A business unit may serve the entire market or concentrate on one or more parts of it. The three alternatives discussed in connection with this strategy are single-market strategy, multimarket strategy, and total-market strategy.

Single-Market Strategy

A variety of reasons may lead a company to concentrate its efforts on a single segment of the market. For example, a small company, in order to avoid confrontation with large competitors, may find a unique niche in the market and devote its energies to serving this market. Design and Manufacturing Corporation presents an illustration of a successful single-market strategy. In the late 1950s, Samuel Regenstrief studied the dishwasher market and found: (1) a high growth potential, (2) market domination by GE, and (3) absence of a manufacturer to supply large retailers like Sears with their own private brand. These conclusions led him to enter the dishwasher market, concentrating his efforts on the single segment of national retailers. Today the company is the largest producer of dishwashers in the world with over 25 percent of the U.S. market. A D&M executive states his company's strategy in the following words: "Sam knew precisely what segment of the market he was going after; he hit it at exactly the right time; and he has set up a tightly run organization to take full advantage of these opportunities."[1]

---

[1]"Design and Manufacturing Corporation," a case copyrighted in 1972 by the President and Fellows of Harvard College, p. 4.

The story of Tampax also illustrates the success of the single-market strategy. The product had a minimal share of the market dominated by Kimberly-Clark's Kotex and Personal Products' Modess sanitary pads. Tampax could not afford to compete head-on with these major brands to sell its different concept of sanitary protection. But the company found that newer, younger users are more open-minded in this matter and these customers are very loyal to a brand. Starting from a premise of greatest appeal to the young user—that internal protection offers greater freedom of action—Tampax concentrated on reaching young girls. The single-market strategy has proved to be highly beneficial to the company. Sales have grown to more than 35 percent of the total sanitary protection market. Even today the company's advertising is scarcely distinguishable from the firm's first efforts.[2]

In the competitive field of cosmetics Noxell Corporation, marketer of the popular Noxzema and Cover Girl brands of makeup and skin cream, has found success in a segment of the $11-billion cosmetics industry that its rivals disdain: the mass market. Its products are aimed primarily at teenagers and evoke the image of fresh-faced, natural beauty. Widely distributed and heavily advertised, Noxell's brands are easily recognizable by their low price. Content to sell its products in chains such as K-Mart and F. W. Woolworth, the company avoids more prestigious, but cutthroat, department and specialty store business. The determination to sell exclusively through mass merchandisers is based on Noxell's belief that distribution through department stores is unattractive because it requires leasing counter space, keeping large inventories on hand, and paying commissions to salespeople. Noxell's continued sales growth and healthy profit performance attest to the viability of concentrating on a single segment of the market.[3]

There is no magic formula in choosing a segment. A business should analyze the market carefully to find a segment that is currently being ignored or served inadequately. Then it should concentrate on the chosen segment wholeheartedly despite initial difficulties and in a manner that avoids competition from the established firms.

Often new segments emerge in the market as a result of changes in the environment. For example, the women's liberation movement motivated the General Broadcasting Corporation of New Haven, Connecticut, to orient its radio station strictly to working women. The station (rated among the "top 40 AM stations") features the Ladies Professional Golf Association before reporting on the Red Sox. It employs women on a two-to-one ratio and carefully screens advertising to avoid ads which may put down women in any way.[4]

---

[2]George W. Schiele, "How to Reach the Young Consumer," *Harvard Business Review*, March–April, 1974, p. 83.

[3]"Noxell Glows in the Mass Market," *Business Week*, February 14, 1983, p. 148.

[4]"A Radio Station with a Feminist Air," *Business Week*, October 2, 1978, p. 32.

The single-market strategy consists of seeking out a market segment which larger competitors may consider too small, too risky, or just plain unappealing. The strategy will not work in areas such as the extractive and process industries, where big-company market power becomes important in realizing economies of scale. Companies concentrating on a single market have the advantage of making a quick response to market opportunities and threats through appropriate changes in policies. For example, Rival Manufacturing Company strengthened its position in the sale of slow-cooking crockpots by gaining control over the sole source of earthenware liners, a backward-integration step that ensured its domination of this highly attractive, growing market segment.[5]

The single-market or niche strategy is often born of necessity. Lacking the resources to fight head-to-head battles across the board with larger, entrenched competitors, the winners typically seek out niches that are too small to interest the giants or can be captured and protected by sheer perseverance and by serving customers surpassingly well.

As far as the impact of the single-market strategy is concerned, it affects profitability in a positive manner. When effort is concentrated on a single market, and particularly when competition is minimal, it is feasible to keep costs down while prices are kept high, and thus earn substantially higher profits. Although the growth objective may not be achieved when this strategy is followed, a company may be able to increase its market share if the chosen segment is large enough vis-à-vis the overall market.

Multimarket Strategy

Instead of limiting business to one segment and thus putting all its eggs in one basket, a company may opt to serve several distinct segments. To successfully implement the multimarket strategy, it is necessary to choose those segments with which the company feels most comfortable and in which the company is able to avoid confronting companies that serve the entire market. The point can be illustrated with reference to Crown Cork & Seal Company. The company is a major producer of metal cans, crowns (bottle caps), closures (screw caps and bottle lids), and filling machinery for beer and soft-drink cans. The two dominant companies in this industry are American Can and Continental Group. The industry is characterized by a really dynamic environment: technological breakthroughs, new concepts of packaging, new materials, and the threat of self-manufacture by large users. Crown Cork & Seal, as a matter of strategy, decided to concentrate on two segments: (1) cans for such "hard-to-hold" products as beer and soft drinks, and (2) aerosol containers. The new strategy paid off. The company outperformed its two larger competitors both in sales

---

[5]Donald K. Clifford, Jr., "Thriving in Recession," *Harvard Business Review,* July–August, 1977, p. 63.

growth and in return on sales in the 1964–1975 period. As it should with any strategic choice, the company fully committed itself to its strategy despite the lure of serving other segments. For example, in spite of its 50 percent share in the motor-oil-can business, Crown Cork decided not to continue to compete aggressively in that market.[6]

The multimarket strategy can be executed in one of two ways: either by selling different products in different segments, or by distributing the same product in a number of segments. Texas Instruments, for example, introduced in 1978 the first all-electronic analog watch, showing the traditional hands on the face of a liquid-crystal display. The watch was directed toward that segment of people who like to stick to tradition whatever it costs. With Swiss-made stainless-steel and gold-plated cases, the four models of this watch ranged in price from $275 to $325. TI developed a new market by introducing a new product.[7] On the other hand, the Green Giant Company (now a division of Pillsbury) expanded itself into another segment by distributing an existing product more widely—i.e., supplying its frozen corn on the cob to all Church's Fried Chicken and some Kentucky Fried Chicken fast-food outlets.[8]

Total-Market Strategy

A company using the total-market strategy serves the entire spectrum of the market by selling different products directed toward different segments in the market. The strategy evolves over a great number of years of operation. Initially a company may start with a single product. As the market grows and different segments emerge, leading competitors may attempt to compete in all the segments. This may be done by employing different combinations of product, price, promotion, and distribution strategies. These dominant companies may also attempt to enter new segments as they emerge. As a matter of fact, the leading companies may themselves create new segments and try to control them at the outset.

A number of companies in different industries follow this strategy. General Motors, for one, has traditionally directed its effort to securing the entire market: "A car for every pocket and taste." With its five auto lines (Chevrolet, Pontiac, Oldsmobile, Buick, and Cadillac) and with a number of different models manufactured by each of these lines, the company attempts to compete in all conceivable segments.

IBM now also follows an across-the-board strategy. It has a system for meeting the requirements of all types of customers. In the middle

---

[6]E. Raymond Corey, "Key Options in Market Selection and Product Planning," *Harvard Business Review*, September–October, 1975, p. 119.

[7]"This Electronic Watch Has 'Hands,'" *Business Week*, July 31, 1978, p. 37.

[8]"Green Giant: The New Course That Makes It Attractive to Pillsbury," *Business Week*, October 2, 1978, p. 66.

1980s, as the personal computer segment emerged, IBM was somewhat slow in responding but finally developed a personal computer of its own. Similarly, in the consumer products area, Coca-Cola has the following soft drinks to satisfy different drinking tastes: Coca-Cola, Diet Coke, Tab, Sprite, Fresca, and Fanta. The company even has a brand of orange juice, Minute Maid, for the segment of consumers who drink juice rather than carbonated beverages.

The total-market strategy is highly risky. For this reason only a very small number of companies in an industry may follow this strategy. It requires a top-management commitment to embracing the entire market. Additionally, a company needs an ample amount of resources to implement this strategy. Finally, only companies in a strong financial position may find this strategy attractive. As a matter of fact, a deteriorating financial position may force a company to move backward from across-the-board market strategy. Chrysler Corporation's financial woes in the 1970s led it to reduce the scope of its markets overseas at a time when experts were looking to the emergence of a single global market. As a Chrysler official remarked: "The company has only a limited amount of management talent and money to go around. It can't go after every part of the U.S. market, let alone around the world."[9]

The total-market strategy can be highly rewarding in terms of achieving growth and market share. It may or may not lead to increased profitability.

Seeking Changes in Market Scope

There are only limited periods during which the "fit" between the key requirements of a market, and the particular competencies of a firm competing in that market, is at an optimum. Companies should not, therefore, get tied to a particular market strategy permanently. Environmental shifts may necessitate a new perspective from one time period to another. Consider the Household Finance Corporation (HFC). It gave such short shrift to its traditional business in the 1970s that the company appeared to be a prime candidate for a name change; in 1977 only 46 percent of its $139 million in net income came from consumer lending, compared with 78 percent in 1965. At the time, the big banks were beginning to promote their new national credit cards aggressively, mass merchandisers were touting their own credit cards more actively, and credit unions were capitalizing on their tax-exempt status to attract more borrowers with low-interest loans. In response to these trends the company had to take it easy in the household finance business as a defensive measure. Thus, HFC reduced the scope of its market. In 1978, as new opportunities emerged for

---

[9]"Chrysler Corp.: Bullish on the Future, BUT . . .," *Business Week*, November 20, 1978, p. 115.

expanding its financial services, the company decided to revitalize its position in the household finance market.[10] Similarly, Gerber Products had long dominated the U.S. baby food market, but a declining birth rate in the 1970s forced it to seek growth elsewhere. In the 1980s, as the birth rate began to turn up, the company began to concentrate again on its traditional business.[11]

The J. C. Penney Company, after 75 years of being identified as a retailer of private-label soft goods to price-conscious customers, decided around 1978 to change the scope of its market. The company transformed itself so that it occupied a position between a traditional department store and a discount store (something along the lines of a moderately priced department store chain with emphasis on higher-priced fashion) in hardgoods, housewares, and especially apparel.[12]

Disney's emphasis on the 5- to 13-year-old age market has been a phenomenon in itself. During the 1960s this segment continued to grow, providing the company with opportunity for growth and expansion. In the 1970s, however, this segment shrank; it was headed for a further decline in the 1980s. This led the company to change its strategic perspectives to begin serving the over-25 age group of customers by making changes in its current offerings and undertaking new projects. The result is the new Epcot Center attached to Disney World in Florida.[13]

Briefly, then, market is a moving target, and a company's strategic perspectives must undergo change accordingly.

MARKET-GEOGRAPHY STRATEGY

Geography has long been used as a strategic variable in shaping market strategy. Business history provides many examples of how businesses started locally and gradually expanded nationally or even internationally. Products like the automobile, telephone, television, and jet aircraft have brought all parts of the country together so that the distance factor ceases to be important. Thus, geographic expansion becomes an attractive choice when seeking growth.

Take the case of Ponderosa System, Inc., a fast-food chain of steak

---

[10]"Household Finance: Revitalizing the Business That Got It Started," *Business Week,* September 25, 1978, p. 129.

[11]"Gerber Concentrating on Babies Again for Slow, Steady Growth," *Business Week,* August 22, 1983, p. 80.

[12]"J. C. Penney's Fashion Gamble," *Business Week,* January 16, 1978, p. 66. See also Alan J. Resnick, Peter B. B. Turney, and J. Barry Mason, "Marketers Turn to 'Counter Segmentation,'" *Harvard Business Review,* September–October, 1979, pp. 100–106.

[13]"Can Disney Still Grow on Its Founder's Dreams?," *Business Week,* July 31, 1978, p. 59.

houses. The company started in 1969 with four restaurants in Indiana. By 1970 it had added ten more restaurants in Indiana and southern Ohio. At the end of 1975 there were almost 400 Ponderosa Steak Houses, from St. Louis to New York. The company continues to expand geographically; by the late 1980s, it is expected there will be Ponderosa Steak Houses coast to coast.

There are a variety of reasons for seeking geographic expansion: to achieve growth, reduce dependence on a small geographic base, use national advertising media, realize experience (i.e., economies of scale), utilize excess capacity, and guard against competitive inroads by moving into more distant regional markets.

This section examines various alternatives included in the market-geography strategy. The purpose here is to highlight strategic issues which may dictate the choice of a geographic dimension in the context of market strategy.

Local-Market Strategy

In modern days the relevance of the local-market strategy may be limited to (1) retailers and (2) service organizations such as airlines, banks, medical centers, etc. In many cases, geographic dimensions of doing business are decided by law. For example, until recently, an airline needed permission from the Civil Aeronautics Board (CAB) concerning the areas it could cover. By the same token, banks traditionally could only operate locally.

As far as retailers are concerned, of the 1.9 million retailers in the United States, about half had annual sales of less than $100,000 in 1980. Presumably, these are all local operations. Even manufacturers may initially limit the distribution of their new products to a local market.

The advantages of concentrating on local market is illustrated by Citytrust Bancorp, a Bridgeport, Connecticut, bank. Fifty *Fortune* 500 companies have their headquarters within an hour's drive of Citytrust Bancorp's offices. But this bank shuns them. As a matter of strategy, the bank has decided to serve the small, local businesses. As a bank officer says, "We want to treat the head of a $5 million, local firm the way Morgan Guaranty treats General Electric." By staying small and local the bank prospers despite its proximity to much bigger rivals in New York, Boston, and Hartford. It emphasizes services to companies with $1 million to $25 million in sales and located within 30 miles of its main office. The strategy has paid off. During the period 1977–83 the bank's earnings increased 25 percent a year.[14]

---

[14]Julie Salamon, "Bank in Connecticut Recovers by Ignoring the Big Companies and Small Consumers," *The Wall Street Journal*, August 16, 1983, p. 35.

Regional-Market Strategy

The regional scope of a business may vary from operations in two or three states to those spread over a section of the country such as New England, the Southwest, the Midwest, the West, etc. Regional expansion provides a good compromise between doing business locally and going national.

Regional expansion ensures that if business in one region is depressed, favorable conditions may operate in other regions so that overall business will be satisfactory. In the 1980s, Marshall Field, the Chicago-based department store, found itself pummeled by recent demographic and competitive trends in the city. Therefore, it decided to expand into new regions in the South and West. This way it could lessen its concentration in the Midwest and expand into areas where growth was expected.[15]

Further, it is culturally easier to handle a region than the entire country. The logistics of conducting a business are much simpler regionally than nationally. As a matter of fact, many companies prefer to limit their business to a region in order to avoid competition and keep control centralized.

Many businesses continue to operate successfully regionally. Large grocery chains such as the following, for example, are regional in character: Safeway in the West, Kroger's in the Midwest, and Stop & Shop in the East. Regional expansion of a business helps in achieving growth and, to an extent, in gaining market share. Simply expanding a business regionally, however, may or may not affect its profitability.

Geographic expansion of a business to a region may become necessary either to achieve growth, or to keep up with a competitor. For example, a small pizza chain with about 30 restaurants in a Ohio metropolitan area had to expand its territory to survive when Pizza Hut started to compete aggressively with it.

At times a regional strategy is much more desirable than going national. For example, a company operating nationally may do a major portion of its business in a region, with the remainder spread over the rest of the country. It may find it much more profitable to concentrate its effort on the region where it is most successful and divest itself of its business elsewhere. Although it is slowly expanding into other states, Coors Beer, for example, is distributed in only 24 percent of the U.S. market—a 20-state area where it has a 40 percent market share. If it expands its market nationally, it may lose some of the mystique attached to this brand.[16]

---

[15]"Marshall Field: Seeking New Markets in the South and West," *Business Week,* March 23, 1981, p. 125.

[16]"Coors Eats the Dust As the Giants Battle," *Business Week,* July 20, 1981, p. 54.

National-Market Strategy

Presumably, going from a regional to a national market further opens up opportunities for growth. This may be illustrated with reference to Acton Corporation. Traditionally a cable television and telephone interconnect business, it went into the consumer-product arena in 1977 by buying up a dozen regional snack-food companies. It became the nation's second largest potato- and corn-chip maker, doing business in 18 states including most of the Mid-Atlantic, Midwest, and Southwest. The company plans to go national in order to achieve further growth, thus providing stiffer competition for PepsiCo's Frito-Lay division.[17]

It was the prospect of growth that influenced the Radisson Hotel Corporation of Minneapolis to go national and become a major factor in the hotel business. The company operated 19 hotels in 1978. But to double its hotels to 37 by 1982, it decided to move into prime "gateway" markets such as New York, Los Angeles, Boston, Chicago, and San Francisco where it could compete against such giants as Marriott and Hyatt.[18]

In some cases the profit economics of the industry requires going national. For example, today success in the beer industry requires huge advertising outlays, new products such as light beer, production efficiencies, and wide distribution. Such characteristics of the industry forced Stroh Brewery Company to go national in 1979. The company bought F & M Schaefer Brewing Company to seek access to the Northeast market.[19]

Going national, however, is far from easy. Each year a number of brands enter the market, hoping eventually to become national brands. Ultimately, however, only a small percentage of them hit the national market, and a still smaller percentage succeed.

A national-market strategy requires a top-management commitment since a large investment is needed initially for promotion and distribution. This makes it easier for large companies to introduce new brands nationally, partly because they have the resources and are in a position to take the risk, and partly because a new brand can be sheltered under the umbrella of a successful brand. For example, a new product introduced under GE's name has a better chance of succeeding than if it is introduced by an unknown company.

To successfully implement the national-market strategy, a company needs to institute proper controls to make sure things are satisfactory in different regions. Where controls are lacking, competitors, especially regional ones, may find it easy to break in. If such a situation comes about,

---

[17]"Acton: A Switch to Snack Foods Has Turned It Profitable," *Business Week*, September 25, 1978, p. 126.

[18]"Radisson Hotel Corp.: A Budding Chain Challenges the Big Operators," *Business Week*, December 4, 1978, p. 113.

[19]"Another Regional Brewer Tries Going National," *Business Week*, December 3, 1979, p. 88.

the company may find itself losing business in one region after another. The national-market strategy, if implemented properly, can go a long way in providing growth, market share, and profitability.

International-Market Strategy

A number of corporations have adopted international-market posture. The Singer Company, for example, has for a long time been operating overseas. The international-market strategy became a popular method of growth for large corporations in the post–World War II period.

In attempts to reconstruct war-torn economies, the U.S. government provided financial assistance to European countries through the Marshall Plan. Since the postwar American economy emerged as the strongest in the world, its economic assistance programs in the absence of competition stimulated extensive corporate development of international strategies. As Sanford Rose remarked:

> . . . in those halcyon years, nothing seemed more seductive to U.S. business than a foreign climate. American manufacturing companies of all types trekked abroad in prodigious numbers, and wherever they migrated, their banks, advertising agencies, and accounting firms went with them. The book value of U.S. foreign direct investment swelled from about $12 billion in 1950 to more than $50 billion in 1966. It is now [1977] estimated at between $140 billion and $150 billion.[20]

At the end of 1982, according to a U.S. Department of Commerce report, the U.S. direct investment abroad stood at $241 billion, up from $164 billion in 1978.[21] About 75 percent of U.S. investments overseas have traditionally been in developed countries. However, as many less-developed countries (LDCs) gained political freedom after World War II, their governments also sought U.S. help to modernize their economies and improve their living standards. Thus, LDCs provided additional investment opportunities for U.S. corporations, especially in the more politically stable countries where U.S. foreign aid programs were in progress. It is interesting, though, that while for cultural, political, and economic reasons the more viable opportunities were found in Western Europe, Canada, and, to a lesser extent, Japan, the developing countries provided a better return on direct U.S. investments. For example, in 1981, LDCs accounted for about 40 percent of income but less than 30 percent of investments.[22]

In recent years, overseas business has become a matter of necessity from the viewpoint of both U.S. corporations and the U.S. government.

---

[20]Sanford Rose, "Why the Multinational Tide Is Ebbing," *Fortune*, August, 1977, p. 112.

[21]*Statistical Abstract of the U.S.*, 1984.

[22]*Ibid.*

The increased competition facing many industries, resulting from the saturation of markets and competitive threats from overseas corporations doing business domestically, has forced U.S. corporations to look to overseas markets. At the same time, the unfavorable balance of trade, partly due to increasing energy imports, has made the need to expand exports a matter of vital national interest. Thus, while in the 1950s and 1960s international business was considered to be a means of capitalizing on a new opportunity, in today's changing economic environment it has become a matter of survival.

Generally speaking, international markets provide additional opportunities over and above domestic business. In some cases, however, a company may find the international market segment as an alternative to the domestic market. Massey-Ferguson decided long ago to concentrate on sales outside of North America rather than compete with the powerful U.S. farm equipment producers. Massey's entire organization, including engineering, research, and production, is geared to market changes overseas. It has learned to live with the instability of foreign markets and to put millions of dollars into building its worldwide manufacturing and marketing networks. The payoff for the company from its emphasis on the international market has been encouraging. In 1975, with 70 percent of its sales abroad, Massey's return was more than the combined return for both Deere and International Harvester.[23]

With the world's biggest private inventory of commercial softwood timber, Weyerhaeuser has been able to build an enviable export business—a market its competitors have virtually ignored until recently. This has given Weyerhaeuser a unique advantage in a rapidly changing world market. Consumption of forest products overseas in the 1980s is projected to increase at double the domestic rate of 2 to 3 percent annually, with particularly dramatic growth in the Pacific Basin, which Weyerhaeuser is ideally located to serve. Moreover, dwindling timber supplies and high oil costs are putting European and Japanese producers at an increasing disadvantage even in their own markets, creating a vacuum that North American producers are now rushing to fill. With a product mix already heavily weighted toward export commodities and with unmatched access to deepwater ports, Weyerhaeuser is way ahead of its competitors in what is shaping up to be a U.S. forest-products export boom. Exports, which in 1981 accounted for 25 percent of Weyerhaeuser's sales and an even higher percentage of its profits, could account for fully half of the company's total revenues by the year 2000.[24]

---

[23]"Massey-Ferguson's Success Story," *Business Week*, February, 1976, p. 40.
[24]"Weyerhaeuser: An Early Lead in Exports Is About to Pay Off," *Business Week*, June 29, 1981, p. 116.

Other Dimensions of Market-Geography Strategy

A company may be regional or national in character, yet it may not be covering its entire trading area. These gaps in the market provide another opportunity for growth. For example, the Southland Corporation has traditionally avoided putting its 7-Eleven stores in downtown areas. About 6,500 of these stores in suburban areas provide it with over $2 billion in sales. In 1978 the company opened a store at 34th and Lexington in New York, signaling the beginning of a major drive into the last of the U.S. markets that 7-Eleven had not yet tapped.[25] Similarly, Hilton Hotels Corporation has hotels in all major cities, but not in medium-sized cities. This is a gap that the company may decide to fill. Bloom and Kotler label such strategic posture as "market fortification." The advantage of this strategy is to prevent the competition from moving in.[26]

Gaps in the market are left either because certain markets do not initially promise sufficient potential or because local competition appears too strong to confront. However, a corporation may find later on that these markets are easy to tap if it consolidates its position in other markets or if changes in the environment develop favorable conditions.

MARKET-ENTRY STRATEGY

The market-entry strategy refers to the timing of market entry. Basically, there are three options from which a company can choose: (1) be first in the market, (2) be among the early entrants, or (3) be a laggard. The importance of the time of entry may be shown with reference to computers. Experience has shown that if new product lines are acceptable to the user and if their impact is properly controlled through pricing and contractual arrangements, this can stimulate sales of an older line. Customers are more content to upgrade within the current product line if they know that a more advanced machine is available whenever they need it. A successful introduction, therefore, requires that the right product be announced at the right time. If it is announced too early, the manufacturer will make the product obsolete unnecessarily. If too late, the manufacturer will suffer a drop in revenues and a loss of customers to the competition.

---

[25]"Southland: Moving Downtown with Its 7-Eleven Food Stores," *Business Week*, October 30, 1978, p. 180.
[26]Paul N. Bloom and Philip Kotler, "Strategies for High Market-Share Companies," *Harvard Business Review*, November–December, 1975, p. 63.

First-In Strategy

To be the first in the market with a product provides definite advantages. The company can create a lead for itself which others will find difficult to match. Following the experience curve concept, if the first entrant gains a respectable share of the market, across-the-board costs should go down by a fixed percentage every time experience doubles. This cost advantage can be transferred to customers in the form of lower prices. Thus, competitors will find it difficult to challenge the first entrant in the market since in the absence of experience their costs, and hence prices, for a similar product will be higher. If the new introduction is protected by a patent, the first entrant has an additional advantage, of course, because a virtual monopoly will exist for the life of the patent.

The success story of Kinder-Care Learning Centers, Inc., illustrates the significance of being first in the market. In 1968, a real estate developer, Perry Mendel, had an idea that many people he talked to thought was outrageous, impractical, and probably immoral. He wanted to create a chain of child-care centers—and he wanted to use the same techniques of standardization he had seen work for motels and fast-food chains.

Convinced that the trend toward women working outside the home would continue, he took $200,000 in seed money and started Kinder-Care Learning Centers, Inc. In its brief history the company has become a dominant force in the commercial child-care industry. In 1981 there were 720 Kinder-Care centers in 36 states and two Canadian provinces. Revenues for fiscal 1981 were $87 million; they reached $161 million in 1983. Since 1976, in fact, Kinder-Care Learning Centers, Inc., has grown at a rate of 57 percent and has been considered one of the fastest-growing smaller public companies in the country.[27]

The strategy to be the first, however, is not without risks. The first entrant must stay ahead of technology in the field or risk being dethroned by competitors. Docutel Corporation provides an interesting case. This Dallas-based company was the first to introduce the automated teller machine (ATM) for banks in the late 1960s. These machines made it possible for customers to withdraw cash from and make deposits to their savings or checking accounts at any time by pushing a few buttons. It had virtually no competition until 1975, and as recently as 1976 the company had a 60 percent share of the market for ATMs. Then the downfall began. The market share fell to 20 percent in 1977 and 8 percent in 1978. Docutel's fortunes changed because the company failed to maintain its technological lead. Its second-generation ATM failed miserably and thus made way for the competitors. Diebold was the major beneficiary of Docutel's troubles: its share of the market jumped to 70 percent in 1978 from barely 15 percent in 1976. While Docutel's comeback effort in the 1980s shows promise,

---

[27]John Halbrooks, "Kinder-Care's Standard Formula for Success," *Inc.*, October, 1981, p. 84.

the company may never again occupy a dominant position in the ATM industry.[28]

A company whose strategy is to be the first in the market must stay ahead no matter what happens, since the costs of yielding the first position to someone else later can be very high. Through heavy investment in promotion, the first entrant must create a primary demand for the product where none exists. Competitors will find it convenient to piggyback since by the time they enter the market, the primary demand is already there. Thus, even if a company has been able to develop a new product for an entirely new need, it should carefully evaluate whether it has sufficient technological and marketing strength to command the market for a long time. Competitors will make every effort to break in, and if the first company is unsure of itself, it should wait. The strategy to be first, however, if properly implemented, can be highly rewarding in terms of growth, market share, and profitability.

Early-Entry Strategy

Several firms may be working on the same track to develop a new product. When one introduces the product first, the remaining firms are forced into early-entry strategy, whether they had planned to be first or had purposely waited for someone else to take the lead. If the early entry takes place on the heels of the first entry, there is usually a dogfight between the firms involved. By and large, the fight is between two firms, the leader and a strong follower (even though there may be several other followers). The reason for the fight is that both firms have worked hard on the new product and aspire to be the first in the market. Both of them have made a strong commitment to the product in terms of resources. In the final phases of their new-product development, if one of the firms introduces the product first, the other one must rush to the market right away to prevent the first one from creating a stronghold. Ultimately, the competitor with a superior marketing strategy in terms of positioning, product, price, promotion, and distribution comes out ahead.

After the two firms find their natural positions in the market and the market launches itself on the growth course, there may be other entrants. These firms exist on the growth wave of the market and exit as the market matures.

Back in the 1960s, the General Foods Corporation was working on the development of a new type of coffee produced by a freeze-drying process. The company already had a strong position in the regular and instant coffee markets. As General Foods was finalizing various aspects of the marketing strategy of its new coffee, later to be called Maxim, Nestlé introduced its own brand (Taster's Choice) of freeze-dried coffee. General

---

[28]"Docutel: Trying for a Comeback by Dovetailing the New with the Old," *Business Week*, October 30, 1978, p. 179.

Foods immediately followed suit, and the two firms aggressively fought for the market share. Nestlé carried the ball, however, since General Foods rushed to the market when it was not quite ready.[29]

Early entry on the heels of the leader is desirable if a company exhibits across-the-board superior marketing strategy and has the resources to fight the leader. As a matter of fact, the later entrant may get an additional advantage out of the groundwork (in the form of creation of primary demand) done by the leader. A weak early entrant, however, will be conveniently swallowed by the leader. The Docutel case discussed above illustrates the point. This company was the leader in the ATM market. However, being a weak leader, it paved the way for a later entrant, Diebold, to take over the market which Docutel had developed.

As the market reaches the growth phase, a number of other firms may enter it. Depending on the length of the growth phase and the point at which firms enter the market, some of them could be labeled as early entrants. Most of these early entrants prefer to operate in specific niches in the market rather than compete against the major firms. For example, a firm may concentrate on doing private branding for a major retailer. Many of these firms, particularly the marginal operations, may be forced out of the market as growth slows down.

Early entry, therefore, can be a rewarding experience if the entry is made with a really strong thrust directed against the leader's market or if it is carefully planned to serve an untapped market. The early entry can contribute significantly to profitability and growth. For the firm that takes on the leader, the early entry may also help in gaining market share.

Laggard-Market-Entry Strategy

The laggard-market-entry strategy refers to entering the market toward the tail end of the growth phase of the market or in the maturity phase of the market. There are two principal alternatives to choose from in making an entry in the market as a laggard: to enter as imitator or as initiator. An imitator will enter the market as a "me too" competitor, i.e., by developing a product which, for all intents and purposes, is similar to the one already on the market. An initiator, on the other hand, questions the status quo and, after doing some innovative thinking, enters the market with a new product. Between these two extremes there are companies which enter stagnant markets with modified products.

Entry into the market as an imitator is short-lived. Initially the company may be able to tap a portion of the market by capitalizing on the customer base of the major competitor(s). In the long run, however, as the leader discards the product in favor of a new or improved one, the imitator is left with nowhere to go. In the early 1970s Honeywell was faced

---

[29]John C. Maxwell, "Coffee Intake Rose in 1972, After Sliding for Five Years," *Advertising Age*, July 23, 1973, p. 68.

with the decision about which type of advanced computer system it should develop, an imitation of the IBM 360 or its own new version. As is evident from the following, the company favored the second alternative:

> But while the copy might make it easier to tap IBM's huge customer base, it was rejected on several counts. First, it relegated Honeywell to the status of a "me too" company. Secondly, even if a high performance/low cost system were developed, there was no assurance that customers would want an imitation. "After all, if you are looking for a Ford, you go to a Ford dealer." It was agreed that the Task Force would develop its own state-of-the-art system.[30]

This strategy worked well for Honeywell. The company developed a new series of computers especially suitable for manufacturing operations and made strong inroads into European markets.

Imitators have many inherent advantages which make it possible to run a profitable business. These advantages include: availability of latest technological improvements, feasibility of achieving greater economies of scale, ability to obtain better terms from suppliers, employees, or customers, and ability to offer lower prices. Thus, even without having superior skills and resources, an imitator may perform well.[31]

The initiator starts by seeking ways to dislodge the established competitor(s) in some way. Consider the following examples:

> The blankets produced by an electrical appliance manufacturer carried the warning: "Do not fold or lie on this blanket." One of the company's engineers wondered why no one had designed a blanket that was safe to sleep on while in operation. His questioning resulted in the production of an electric underblanket that was not only safe to sleep on while in operation, but was much more efficient: being insulated by the other bed clothes, it wasted far less energy than conventional electric blankets, which dissipate most of their heat directly into the air.
>
> A camera manufacturer wondered why a camera couldn't have a built-in flash that would spare users the trouble of finding and fixing an attachment. To ask the question was to answer it. The company proceeded to design a 35 mm camera with built-in flash, which has met with enormous success and swept the Japanese medium-priced single-lens market.[32]

The above two examples illustrate how through creativity and initiative a latecomer may be able to make a mark in the market. In other

---

[30]"Honeywell Inc.—EDP Division," a case copyrighted in 1975 by the President and Fellows of Harvard College, p. 10.

[31]George S. Yip, "Gateways to Entry," *Harvard Business Review*, September–October, 1982, pp. 85–92.

[32]Kenichi Ohmae, "Effective Strategies for Competitive Success," *The McKinsey Quarterly*, Winter, 1978, p. 55.

words, by exploiting technological change, avoiding direct competition, or changing the accepted business structure (e.g., a new form of distribution), the initiator has an opportunity to successfully establish itself in the market.[33]

The Wilmington Corporation adopted the middle course to enter the pressed glass-ceramic cookware market in 1977. Until that time, Corning Glass Works was the sole producer of this product, through a patent which expired in January, 1977. The Wilmington Corporation opted against entering the market with a me-too product to compete with Corning Glass. It sought entry into the market with a modified product line, i.e., round containers in solid colors, unlike Corning's product, which has a square shape, white color, and cornflower design. The company felt that these changes should enlarge the market by appealing to a broader range of consumer taste.[34]

Whatever course a company may pursue to enter the market, as a laggard it cannot expect much in terms of profitability, growth, or market share. At that stage the market is already saturated, and only established firms can operate profitably. As a matter of fact, their built-in experience affords an even greater advantage to the established competitors. The initiator, however, may be able to make a profitable entry, at least until the established firm adds the innovation to its own line.

MARKET-COMMITMENT STRATEGY

The market-commitment strategy refers to the degree of involvement that a company seeks in a particular market. It is widely held that not all customers are equally important to a company. Often, statements such as "17 percent of the customers account for 60 percent of the sales; 56 percent of the customers provide 11 percent of the sales, and so on," are made, which indicate that a company should make varying commitments to different customer segments. The commitment can be in the form of financial or managerial resources or both. Presumably, results from any venture will be commensurate with the commitment made, which explains the importance of the commitment strategy.

Commitment to a market may be categorized as strong, average, or light. Whatever the nature of the commitment, it must be honored; a company that fails to regard its commitment can get into trouble. Back in 1946 the Liggett & Myers Tobacco Company had a 22 percent share of the U.S. cigarette market. In 1978 its share of the market was down to less than 3.5 percent. A variety of reasons are ascribed to the company's declining fortunes, amounting to a lack of commitment to a market which at one time it commanded with an imposing market share. These reasons include

---

[33]George S. Yip, *op. cit.*
[34]"Wilmington Corporation," a case copyrighted in 1976 by the President and Fellows of Harvard College.

responding too slowly to changing market conditions, using poor judgment in positioning brands, and failing to attract new and younger customers. The company lagged behind when filters were introduced. It also missed industry moves to both king-size and extra-long cigarettes. It missed the market move toward low-tar cigarettes. Its major entry in the category, Decade, was not introduced until 1977, well after competitors had established similar brands.[35] The Liggett & Myers example illustrates that a company can lose a comfortable position in the market if it fails to adequately commit itself to its market.

Strong-Commitment Strategy

The strong-commitment strategy requires that the company plan to operate in the market optimally by realizing economies of scale in promotion, distribution, manufacturing, etc. If a competitor challenges the company's position in the market, the latter must fight back aggressively by employing different forms of product, price, promotion, and distribution strategies. In other words, since the company has a high stake in the market, it should do all it can to defend its position.

A company with a strong commitment to the market should refuse to be content with the way things are. It should foresee its own obsolescence by developing new products, improving product quality, and increasing expenditures for sales force, advertising, and sales promotion relative to the growth rate of the market.[36]

The point may be illustrated with reference to the Polaroid Corporation. The company continues to do research and development to stay ahead in the field. The original Land camera, introduced in 1948, produced brown-and-white pictures. Thereafter, the company developed film which took truly black-and-white pictures with different ASA speeds. Also, the time involved in the development of film was reduced from the original 60 seconds down to 10 seconds. In 1963, the company introduced a color-print film with a development time of 60 seconds; in the early 1970s, the company introduced the SX-70 camera, which made earlier Polaroid cameras obsolete. Since its introduction, a variety of changes and improvements have been made both in the SX-70 camera and in the film that goes into it. In brief, the Polaroid Corporation had a strong commitment to the instant-photography market, and it took all the necessary steps to maintain its position there. The end result has been Kodak's acceptance of second-place status in the instant market.[37]

---

[35]John Koten, "Liggett's Cigarette Unit Lags, and Some Believe It May Be Snuffed Out," *The Wall Street Journal*, November 27, 1978, p. 1.

[36]Robert D. Buzzell and Frederik D. Wiersema, "Successful Share-Building Strategies," *Harvard Business Review*, January–February, 1981, pp. 135–144.

[37]Linda Snyder Hayes, "What's Kodak Developing Now?," *Fortune*, March 23, 1981, p. 78.

The nature of a company's commitment to a market may, of course, change with time. Until 1971 Procter & Gamble had a light commitment in the coffee market, especially in the East. Its Folger's coffee was almost unknown east of the Mississippi. In the early 1970s the company made a strong commitment to the coffee market in the East, city by city. At that time a small company called Breakfast Cheer Coffee Company made $12 million a year in sales and had an 18 percent share of the coffee market in Pittsburgh. By 1974, because of P&G's strength, this company's sales had plummeted to $2.3 million and its market share had dwindled to under 1 percent. P&G became a major factor in coffee in the Pittsburgh market.[38]

Strong commitment to a market can be highly rewarding in terms of achieving growth, market share, and profitability. A warning is in order, however. The commitment made to a market should be based on the company's resources, strengths, and willingness to take risks to live up to this commitment. For example, P&G could afford to implement its commitment to the Pittsburgh market since it had a good rapport with distributors and dealers and the resources to launch an effective promotional campaign. A small company could not have afforded to do all that.

Average-Commitment Strategy

When a company has a stable interest in the market, it must stress the maintenance of the status quo. This leads it to make only an average commitment to the market. Adoption of the average-commitment strategy may be triggered by the fact that a strong-commitment strategy is not feasible. The company may lack the resources to make a strong commitment; strong commitment may be in conflict with top management's value orientation; or the market in question may not constitute a major thrust of the business in, for example, a diversified company.

In April, 1976, when the Eastman Kodak Company announced its entry into the instant-photography field, the company most worried was the Polaroid Corporation. This was because Polaroid had a strong commitment to the instant-photography market and did not like Kodak being there just for the sake of competition. As Polaroid's president commented: "This is our very soul that we are involved with. This is our whole life. For them it's just another field . . ."[39] Similarly, when Frito-Lay (a division of PepsiCo) entered the cookie business in 1982, the industry leader, Nabisco, had to adopt a new strategy to defend its title in the business. As an executive of the company noted: "We aren't going to sit on our haunches and let 82 years of business go down the drain."[40]

---

[38]Bill Henderickson, "Tiny Firms Are Losers in Coffee War Fought by Two Big Marketers," *The Wall Street Journal*, November 3, 1977, p. 1.

[39]*The New York Times*, April 28, 1976, p. 23.

[40]Ann M. Morrison, "Cookies Are Frito-Lay's New Bag," *Fortune*, August 9, 1982, p. 64.

A company with an average commitment to a market can afford to make occasional mistakes since it has other businesses to compensate. Essentially, this strategy requires keeping customers happy by providing them with what they are accustomed to. This can be done by making appropriate changes in the marketing program as desired by environmental shifts, thus making it difficult for competitors to lure the customers away. Where the commitment is average, however, the company becomes vulnerable to the lead company as well as the underdog. The leader may wipe out the average-commitment company by price cutting, which should be feasible because of the experience effect. The underdog may challenge the average-commitment company by introducing new products, focusing on new segments within the market, trying out new forms of distribution, or launching new types of promotional thrusts. The best defense for the company with an average commitment to the market is to keep the customers satisfied by being vigilant about the developments in the market.

Even an average commitment may be adequate, as far as profitability is concerned, if the market is growing. In a slow-growth market the average commitment is not conducive to achieving either growth or profitability.

Light-Commitment Strategy

A company may have only a passing interest in a market, by virtue of which it will make only a light commitment to it. The passing interest may be explained by the fact that the market is stagnant, its potential is limited, it is overcrowded with many large companies involved, etc. Additionally, a company may opt for light commitment to a market to avoid antitrust difficulties.

The General Electric Company maintains a light commitment in the color television market because the field is overcrowded, particularly by the Japanese companies. The Procter & Gamble Company, in the early 1970s, adopted the light-commitment strategy in the shampoo market presumably to avoid antitrust difficulties like those it had encountered with Clorox several years previously; P&G let its share of the shampoo market slip from around 50 percent to a little over 20 percent, delayed reformulating its established brands (Prell and Head and Shoulders), introduced only one new brand in many years, and substantially cut down on its promotional effort on shampoos.[41]

A company with a light commitment to a market operates passively without making any new moves. It is satisfied as long as the business continues to be in the black, and thus seeks very few changes in its marketing perspectives. Overall, this strategy is not of much significance for the company pursuing increasing profitability, greater market share, and/or growth.

---

[41]Nancy Giges, "Shampoo Rivals Wonder When P&G Will Seek Old Dominance," *Advertising Age,* September 23, 1974, p. 3.

MARKET-DILUTION STRATEGY

In many situations a company may find reducing a part of the business strategically more useful than expanding. The dilution strategy works out well when the overall benefit that a company derives from a market, either currently or potentially, is less than it could achieve elsewhere. Unsatisfactory profit performance, desire for concentration in fewer markets, lack of top-management knowledge of the market, negative synergy of the market vis-à-vis other markets that the company serves, and lack of resources to fully develop the market are other reasons for diluting market position.

There was a time when dilution of a market was considered to be an admission of failure on the part of management. In the 1970s dilution came to be accepted purely as a matter of strategy. Different ways of diluting the market include demarketing, pruning of marginal markets, key account strategy, and harvesting strategy.

Demarketing Strategy

Demarketing, in a nutshell, is the reverse of marketing. This term became popular in the early 1970s when, as a result of the Arab oil embargo, the supply of a variety of products became short. Demarketing may be defined as: ". . . attempts to discourage customers in general or a certain class of customers in particular on either a temporary or permanent basis."[42]

The demarketing strategy may be implemented in different ways. One way involves keeping close track of time requirements of different customers. Thus, if one customer needs the product in July and another in September, the former's order is filled first even though the latter confirmed the order first. A second way of demarketing is rationing supplies to different customers on an equitable basis. Shell Oil followed this route to institute demarketing strategy toward the end of 1978 when a gasoline shortage occurred. Each customer was sold up to ten gallons of gasoline at each filling. Third, recommending that customers use a substitute product temporarily is a form of demarketing. The fourth demarketing method is to divert a customer with an immediate need for the product to another customer to whom the company has supplied the product recently and who is not likely to use it until later. The company becomes an intermediary between the two customers, providing supplies of the product to the supplying customer whenever they are needed if present supplies are transferred to the customer in need.

The demarketing strategy is directed toward maintaining customer goodwill during times when customers' demands cannot be adequately met.

---

[42]Philip Kotler and Sidney J. Levy, "Demarketing, Yes Demarketing," *Harvard Business Review*, November–December, 1971, p. 74.

This is achieved by helping out customers in the different ways discussed above. The company does so hoping that the situation that requires de-marketing is temporary in nature and that when conditions are normal again, the customers will be favorably inclined toward the company. In the long run, the demarketing strategy should lead to increased profitability.

Pruning-of-Marginal-Markets Strategy

A company must undertake a conscious search for those markets which do not provide rates of return comparable to those that could be attained if it were to shift its resources to other markets. These markets potentially become candidates for pruning. The pruning of marginal markets may result in a much higher growth rate for the company as a whole. Consider two markets, one providing 10 percent and the other 20 percent on original investments of $1,000,000. After 15 years the first one will show an equity value of $4 million as opposed to $16 million for the second one. Pruning can improve the return on investment and growth rate by ridding the company of markets which are growing more slowly than the rest of the markets and by providing cash for investment in faster-growing, higher-return markets. Several years ago A&P closed over 100 stores in markets where its competitive position was weak. This pruning effort helped the company to fortify its position and concentrate on markets where it felt strong.[43]

Pruning also helps to restore balance in the business. A company may face an out-of-balance condition when the business has too many diverse and difficult markets to serve. By pruning, the company may limit its operations to growth markets only. Since growth markets require heavy doses of investment (in the form of price reductions, promotion, market development, etc.), and since the company may have limited resources, the pruning strategy can be very beneficial. Chrysler Corporation, for example, decided in 1978 to quit the European market to be able to use its limited resources to restore its position in the U.S. market. The pruning strategy is especially helpful in achieving market share and profitability.

Key-Markets Strategy

In most industries a few customers account for a major portion of the volume. This characteristic may be extended to markets. If the breakdown of markets is properly done, a company may find that a few markets account for a very large share of its revenues. Strategically, these key markets may call for extra emphasis in terms of selling effort, after-sales ser-

---

[43]"A&P Follows N.Y.C.'s Lead With 'Instant Money Game,'" *Advertising Age*, January 17, 1977, p. 50.

vice, product availability, etc. As a matter of fact, the company may decide to limit its business to these key markets alone.

The key-markets strategy may be illustrated with reference to Royal Crown Companies, Inc. (RC). For years this company, with a market share of 5.6 percent, pursued the mission to challenge head-on both Coca-Cola and PepsiCo, which had market shares of 35 percent and 21 percent, respectively. It tried to duplicate Coke and Pepsi in both product line and advertising. On his arrival in 1976 the new head of the company, Donald McMahon, decided to pursue the key-markets strategy. He put nearly all of RC's marketing efforts in markets where they were already successful, such as New York and Los Angeles. The key-markets strategy not only raised the company's market share in the soft-drink industry slightly, but led to a substantial increase in profitability as well. With growth in the industry settled down at 3.5 percent, the key-markets strategy worked out well for Royal Crown.[44]

The key-markets strategy requires:

(a) A strong focus tailored to environmental differences (i.e., don't try to do everything; rather compete in carefully selected ways with the competitive emphasis differing according to the market environment).
(b) A reputation for high quality (i.e., turn out high-quality products with superior performance potential and reliability).
(c) Medium to low relative prices complementing high quality.
(d) Low total cost to permit offering high-quality products at low prices and still show high profits.[45]

Harvesting Strategy

The harvesting strategy refers to a situation where a company may decide to deliberately let its market share slide down. The harvesting strategy may be pursued for a variety of reasons: to increase badly needed cash flow, to increase short-term earnings, or to avoid antitrust action. Usually only companies with high market share can expect to harvest successfully.

If a product reaches the stage where continued support can no longer be justified, it may be desirable to realize a short-term gain by raising the price or by lowering quality and cutting advertising to turn an active brand into a passive one. In any event, the momentum of the product may continue for years with sales declining but useful revenues still coming in.

A company may be prevented from implementing the harvesting strategy if there are exit barriers to reckon with, since they reduce the firm's strategic flexibility. Exit barriers refer to circumstances within an

---

[44]"Royal Crown Cola Gets a Lot More Fizz," *Business Week*, March 14, 1977, p. 84.
[45]Carolyn Y. Woo and Arnold C. Cooper, "The Surprising Case for Low Market Share," *Harvard Business Review*, November–December, 1982, pp. 106–113.

industry that discourage the exit of competitors whose performances in that particular business may be marginal. Three types of exit barriers are: (a) a thin resale market for the assets involved; (b) intangible strategic barriers (e.g., value of distribution networks, customer goodwill for the other products of the company, or strong corporate identification with the product) as deterrents to timely exit; and (c) management's reluctance to terminate a sick line.[46] When the exit barriers disappear, or their effect ceases to be of concern, the harvesting strategy may be pursued.

SUMMARY

This chapter illustrates various types of market strategies which a company may pursue. Market strategies rest on a company's perspective of the customer. This customer focus is a very important factor in market strategies. By diligently delineating the markets to be served, a company can effectively compete in an industry even with the established firms.

The five different types of market strategies and various alternatives under each strategy which were examined in this chapter are outlined below:

1. Market-scope strategy
   a. Single-market strategy
   b. Multimarket strategy
   c. Total-market strategy
2. Market-geography strategy
   a. Local-market strategy
   b. Regional-market strategy
   c. National-market strategy
   d. International-market strategy
3. Market-entry strategy
   a. First-in strategy
   b. Early-entry strategy
   c. Laggard-market-entry strategy
4. Market-commitment strategy
   a. Strong-commitment strategy
   b. Average-commitment strategy
   c. Light-commitment strategy
5. Market-dilution strategy
   a. Demarketing strategy
   b. Pruning-of-marginal-markets strategy
   c. Key-markets strategy
   d. Harvesting strategy

---

[46]Kathryn Rudie Harrigan and Michael E. Porter, "End-Game Strategies for Declining Industries," *Harvard Business Review*," July–August 1983, pp. 111–120.

Application of each strategy is illustrated by citing examples from marketing literature. The impact of each strategy is considered in terms of its effect on marketing objectives (i.e., profitability, growth, and market share).

DISCUSSION QUESTIONS

1. *What circumstances may lead a business unit to change the scope of its market?*
2. *Under what conditions may a company adopt across-the-board market strategy?*
3. *Can a company operating only locally go international? Discuss with examples.*
4. *Examine the pros and cons of being the first in the market.*
5. *What underlying conditions must be present before a company can make a strong commitment to a market?*
6. *Define the term demarketing. What circumstances dictate the choice of demarketing strategy?*
7. *List exit barriers which may prevent a company from implementing harvesting strategy.*

APPENDIX: PERSPECTIVES OF MARKET STRATEGIES

I. Market-Scope Strategy

A. Single-Market Strategy
Definition: Concentration of efforts in a single segment.
Objective: To find a segment which is currently being ignored or served inadequately and meet its needs.
Requirements: (1) Serve the market wholeheartedly despite initial difficulties. (2) Avoid competition with established firms.
Results: (1) Low costs. (2) Higher profits.

B. Multimarket Strategy
Definition: Serving several distinct markets.
Objective: To diversify the risk of serving only one market.
Requirements: (1) Careful selection of segments to serve. (2) Avoid confrontation with companies serving entire market.
Expected Results: (1) Higher sales. (2) Higher market share.

C. Total-Market Strategy
Definition: Serving the entire spectrum of the market by selling differentiated products to different segments in the market.
Objective: To compete across the board in the entire market.
Requirements: (1) Employ different combinations of price, product, promotion, and distribution strategies in different segments. (2) Top management commitment to embrace entire market. (3) Strong financial position.
Expected Results: (1) Increased growth. (2) Higher market share.

II. Market-Geography Strategy

A. Local-Market Strategy

Definition: Concentration of efforts in the immediate vicinity.

Objective: To maintain control of the business.

Requirements: (1) Good reputation in the geographic area. (2) Good hold on requirements of the market.

Expected Results: Short-term success; ultimately must expand to other areas.

B. Regional-Market Strategy

Definition: Operating in 2 or 3 states or over a region of the country (e.g., New England).

Objectives: (1) To diversify risk of dependence on one part of a region. (2) To keep control centralized.

Requirements: (1) Management commitment to expansion. (2) Adequate resources. (3) Logistical ability to serve regional area.

Expected Results: (1) Increased growth. (2) Higher market share. (3) Keep up with competitors.

C. National-Market Strategy

Definition: Operating nationally.

Objective: To seek growth.

Requirements: (1) Top management commitment. (2) Capital resources. (3) Willingness to take risks.

Expected Results: (1) Increased growth. (2) Increased market share. (3) Increased profitability.

D. International-Market Strategy

Definition: Operating outside national boundaries.

Objective: To seek opportunities beyond domestic business.

Requirements: (1) Top management commitment. (2) Capital resources. (3) Understanding of international markets.

Expected Results: (1) Increased growth. (2) Increased market share. (3) Increased profits.

III. Market-Entry Strategy

A. First-In Strategy

Definition: Entering the market before all others.

Objective: To create a lead over competition that will be difficult for them to match.

Requirements: (1) Willingness and ability to take risks. (2) Technological competence. (3) Strive to stay ahead. (4) Heavy promotion. (5) Create primary demand. (6) Carefully evaluate strengths.

Expected Results: (1) Reduced costs via experience. (2) Increased growth. (3) Increased market share. (4) Increased profits.

B. Early-Entry Strategy

Definition: Entering the market in quick succession to the leader.

Objective: To prevent the first entrant from creating a strong hold in the market.

Requirements: (1) Superior marketing strategy. (2) Ample resources. (3) Strong commitment to challenge market leader.

Expected Results: (1) Increased profits. (2) Increased growth. (3) Increased market share.

C. Laggard-Market-Entry Strategy

Definition: Entering the market toward tail-end of growth phase or during maturity phase. Two modes of entry are feasible: (1) *Imitator*—Entering market with "me-too" product. (2) *Initiator*—Entering market with unconventional marketing strategies.

Objectives: Imitator—To capture that part of the market which is not brand loyal. *Initiator*—To serve the needs of the market better than present firms.

Requirements: Imitator—(1) Market research ability. (2) Production capability. *Initiator*—(1) Market research ability. (2) Ability to generate creative marketing strategies.

Expected Results: Imitator—Increased short-term profits. *Initiator*—(1) Put market on a new growth path. (2) Increased profits. (3) Some growth opportunities.

IV. Market-Commitment Strategy

A. Strong-Commitment Strategy

Definition: Fighting off challenges aggressively by employing different forms of product, price, promotion, and distribution strategies.

Objective: To defend position at all costs.

Requirements: (1) Operate optimally by realizing economies of scale in promotion, distribution, manufacturing, etc. (2) Refuse to be content with present situation or position. (3) Ample resources. (4) Willingness and ability to take risks.

Expected Results: (1) Increased growth. (2) Increased profits. (3) Increased market share.

B. Average-Commitment Strategy

Definition: Maintaining stable interest in the market.

Objective: To maintain the status quo.

Requirements: Keep customers satisfied and happy.

Expected Results: Acceptable profitability.

C. Light-Commitment Strategy

Definition: Having only a passing interest in market.

Objective: To operate "in the black."

Requirements: Avoid investing for any long-run benefit.

Expected Results: Maintenance of status quo (no increase in growth, profits or market share).

V. Market-Dilution Strategy

A. Demarketing Strategy

Definition: Discouraging customers in general or a certain class of customers in particular, on either a temporary or a permanent basis, from seeking the product.

Objective: To maintain customer goodwill during periods of shortages.

Requirements: (1) Monitor customer time requirements. (2) Ration product supplies. (3) Divert customers with immediate needs to customers who have a supply of the product but no immediate need for it. (4) Find out and suggest alternative products for meeting customer needs.

Expected Results: (1) Increased profits. (2) Strong customer goodwill and loyalty.

B. Pruning-of-Marginal-Markets Strategy

Definition: Weeding out markets which do not provide acceptable rates of return.

Objective: To divert investments in growth markets.

Requirements: Willingness to disturb the status quo and drop traditional markets in favor of new growth markets.

Expected Results: (1) Long-term growth. (2) Improved return on investment. (3) Decrease in market share.

C. Key-Markets Strategy

Definition: Focusing efforts on selected markets.

Objective: To serve the selected markets extremely well.

Requirements: (1) Gain good knowledge of the chosen markets. (2) Concentrate all energies on these markets. (3) Develop unique strategies to serve the markets.

Expected Results: (1) Increased profits. (2) Increased market share in the selected markets.

D. Harvesting Strategy

Definition: Deliberate effort to let market share slide down.

Objectives: (1) To generate additional cash flow. (2) To increase short-term earnings. (3) To avoid antitrust action.

Requirements: High market share.

Expected Results: Sales decline but useful revenues still come in.

Nolte Freightlines, Inc.

"If Nolte Freightlines is going to serve its customers adequately it is going to have to break into the intermodal end of the business," said Chris Nolte, president of Nolte Freightlines, Inc. "With the introduction of these dedicated piggyback 'fast trains' by the Southern and R, F, and P [Richmond, Fredericksburg, and Potomac] Railroads, we can give customers what they want in freight rates as well as in time deliveries. We are losing business and will continue to lose business unless we respond to the needs of our customers by providing them with the type of pricing and service they want."

It was January 20, 1983, and Chris Nolte was addressing three of his siblings at a stockholders' meeting. Company profits had been on the decline for the past two years. However, the profit for 1982 was about half that of 1981, representing the largest drop since the company reorganized in 1975. The four stockholders, Hubble Nolte, Chuck Nolte, Kathleen Nolte Harrison, and Chris Nolte, had called the meeting to determine some course of action which might improve earnings in 1983.

COMPANY BACKGROUND

Nolte Freightlines, Inc., began in 1933 on a farm in Sharon, Connecticut. It was during the Great Depression when the dairy farms in the area needed a means of transporting milk to the larger city markets. Lynne Nolte, the mother of five sons and two daughters, won the contract from the Farmers' Cooperative to do the job. She purchased one truck, put one of her sons in the driver's seat, and Nolte Freightlines was born (although its name at that time was L. Nolte and Sons). A couple of years later, when the cooperative put the milk contract out for bids, L. Nolte lost the contract, forcing Mrs. Nolte and her sons to look for alternative sources of freight. They began hauling other farm products, such as fertilizer and produce, to New York and Boston, returning to the Sharon area with wool for the woolen mills.

The company experienced steady growth during the next forty years, expanding into a fleet of more than 500 tractor-trailer units and thirteen terminals on the Eastern Seaboard. The recession of 1973 and 1974, however, brought a crashing end to the growth which management had become accustomed to in those earlier years. Excessive Teamsters Union demands and poor management practices brought the company to the threshold of bankruptcy.

Alternatives to Chapter 11 bankruptcy are few, but in 1975, Chris Nolte brought about an ICC decision allowing Nolte Freightlines to sell to a competitor only its LTL (less-than-truckload) customers and goodwill, along with existing union contracts, selected equipment, and itemized properties. It was agreed that Nolte would be allowed to retain a small division with full operating authority to service TL (truckload) customers. All debts now reverted to this small division with any terminals and equipment not involved in the sale being liquidated.

The division, known as the Special Commodities Division, represents an entirely different niche in the transportation industry. Rather than the traditional corporate ownership of the tractor-trailer units with operations based in freight terminals, this operation recruits independent contractors who own their own tractors or tractor-trailer combinations and lease their equipment to Nolte. Nolte, in turn, provides the contractor with freight for a percentage of the gross revenue. No terminals are necessary, as only trailer-load freight is handled with the contractor going directly from pickup point to delivery point.

Since 1975, the company has paid past debts and again become profitable, allowing for expansion into three separate divisions: the Van Division, which handles all dry van traffic; the Flatbed Division, which handles lumber and other building materials; and the Refrigerated Division, which handles all refrigerated traffic. The corporation is now a $20-million operation leasing almost 200 independent contractors. The company has no employees other than office, management, and sales staff numbering about 130 people. Financial information on the company is contained in Exhibits 12-1 and 12-2.

Nolte's profits for the last two years have declined considerably as a result of the business environment; in two years the motor carrier industry has gone from a static environment to one of rapid change. The stimulus for this change was the Deregulation Act of 1980, which virtually eliminated all restrictions on competition. The Act widened authority for existing firms and admitted huge numbers of new motor carriers into an economy gripped by severe recession. Deregulation caused customer rates to plunge to their lowest levels since the early '70s, while the costs of operation, fuel, road taxes, equipment, and parts have greatly increased. Many well-established carriers have gone out of business, and many more are likely to follow. Exhibit 12-3 provides operating information on the competition.

MANAGEMENT HISTORY

The management of the family business over the years has followed a predictable path. The positions and titles have been distributed on the basis of age, although each of the four has 25 percent of the ownership and the same perquisites. Management has been highly centralized, especially since 1975, and decisions are in theory made by majority will.

While the oldest living Nolte, Hubble, is semiretired and involved

EXHIBIT 12-1   Nolte Freightlines, Inc.: Balance Sheet

	Year ended December 31,	
	1982	1981
Assets		
Current Assets:		
Cash	$ 484,355	$ 321,147
Accounts receivable	2,593,701	1,918,456
Prepaid taxes and expenses	1,052	10,572
Special deposits	1,164	1,164
Advances—contractors	196,570	181,009
Total current assets	3,276,842	2,432,348
Property and equipment:		
Real estate	1,293,907	1,491,907
Revenue and transportation equipment	594,772	343,871
Furniture and office equipment	343,837	137,630
Shop and garage equipment	1,389	1,389
	2,233,905	1,974,797
Less accumulated depreciation	530,988	352,219
	1,702,917	1,622,578
Other assets:		
Bond investment	7,765	7,143
Total assets	$4,987,524	$4,062,069
Liabilities and Stockholders' Equity		
Current liabilities—accounts payable and		
accrued liabilities	$1,747,863	$1,143,309
Loans payable	109,024	-0-
Other liabilities	123,299	80,669
Total liabilities	1,980,186	1,223,978
Stockholders' equity:		
Capital stock	383,107	383,107
Capital—land and buildings	1,004,351	1,142,401
Retained earnings	1,619,880	1,312,583
	3,007,338	2,838,091
Total liabilities and stockholders' equity	$4,987,524	$4,062,069

Source: Company records.

only on occasion, the other three family members divide the workload roughly by functional areas; sales, operations, and administration. In addition, each has taken special interest in certain divisions. The choice of work has been the result of personal preference and not of training, as none of the four had much formal education beyond high school.

All four except Hubble have progeny in the organization. Chris, the president and in charge of the operations area, has two children in

EXHIBIT 12-2   Nolte Freightlines, Inc.: Statement of Operations

(in thousands)	Year ended December 31, 1982	1981
Operating Revenues	$17,974	$19,920
Cost and Expenses:		
Salaries—officers and supervisory personnel	1,012	1,021
Salaries and wages	550	483
Fringes	221	217
Operating supplies and expenses	349	346
General supplies and expenses	824	939
Operating taxes and licenses	102	30
Insurance	199	194
Communication and utilities	432	282
Depreciation	187	93
Revenue equipment rental and purchased transportation	13,585	15,058
Gain or loss on disp. of operating assets (net)	(115)	-0-
Building and office equipment rentals	44	114
Total operating expenses	$17,390	$18,777
Net carrier operating income before taxes	584	1,143
Provision for income tax	-0-	-0-
Net income	$ 584	$ 1,143

Source: Company records.

the business: his daughter is the data processing manager, and his son is the director of safety and driver recruitment. Kathleen, the executive vice-president and in charge of the sales area, has a son who is coordinating research on a proposed new division. Chuck, the secretary-treasurer and in charge of the administrative area, has a daughter who is the vice-president of operations. All the third-generation Noltes have college degrees, and in some cases stepped into management above nonfamily members with longevity in the organization.

As more of the four Noltes near the age of retirement, concern about the future management of Nolte Freightlines becomes an ever-increasing issue. Differences in philosophies and management styles have created difficulties in setting corporate direction in the past and must be dealt with soon to set a course for the future.

EXPANDING OPERATING AUTHORITY AND THE REGULATORY ENVIRONMENT

When the industry was deregulated in 1980, the ability to apply for and obtain new authority from the ICC became a far simpler task than

EXHIBIT 12-3   Total Operating Income of Three Groups of U.S. Carriers (Excluding UPS and Household Goods), 1981–82

ITEM ($ amounts add 000)	1982		1981	
	AMOUNT	%	AMOUNT	%
Class I and Class II Carriers (497 carriers)				
Freight revenue—intercity common	$17,983,603	96.91	$19,167,889	97.18
Freight revenue—intercity contract	122,214	.66	80,016	.40
Freight revenue—local cartage	238,695	1.29	277,183	1.41
Intercity transportation for other carriers ...	79,428	.43	74,990	.38
Other operating revenue	132,433	.71	125,081	.63
Total operating revenue	$18,556,373	100.00	$19,725,159	100.00
Competitor Carriers Operating Within Nolte Freightlines Territory (122 carriers)				
Freight revenue—intercity common	$ 4,771,297	100.00	$ 4,951,455	100.00
Interstate Intermodal Carriers Operating Within Nolte Freightlines Territory (5 carriers)				
Freight revenue—intercity common	$ 47,094	100.00	$ 46,358	100.00

in the past. At that time, Nolte began applying for more authority in hopes of expanding their operating territory. In September, 1982, new operating rights were granted by the ICC to Nolte Freightlines for operations into the southeastern United States. (Nolte Freightlines operating territory and ICC authority before the expansion is shown in Exhibit 12-4.) Customers serviced by the company at the time were immediately informed of the new authority, and tariffs were published for expansion into the region.

The initial response of the customers was less than encouraging for Nolte's management. Only 1 percent of existing customers which had freight going into the Southeast used Nolte. The response from potential customers with freight coming out of the Southeast back into the Northeast was not much better. Customers in these areas had never heard of Nolte Freightlines, so special incentives were needed to encourage them to switch from carriers currently providing these services. This prompted management to publish extremely low rates out of the Southeast to stimulate interest and generate enough northbound traffic to balance what southbound traffic was available.

**EXHIBIT 12-4   Nolte Freightlines, Inc.: Operating Territory Before
Expansion**

This strategy, however, generated much more northbound traffic
than anticipated. Deadhead mileage (dispatching trucks with empty trailers) increased by 30 percent in order to service the new southeastern customers. Each empty mile cost Nolte out of pocket an average of sixty cents
(without taking into account the revenues lost by not running the truck
loaded). If opportunity costs were included in that figure, it would be
approximated at ninety-five cents a mile. Shown below are the empty-
mileage figures for October, November, and December, 1982.

MONTH	EMPTY MILES	LOADED MILES
October	200,550	1,050,020
November	260,700	1,140,000
December	261,200	1,145,010

In order to reduce the freight imbalance, reduce excess deadhead
miles, and increase profits in 1983, Chris Nolte believed there were three

strategic alternatives open to the company. Chris outlined these three options for his fellow stockholders to consider:

1. A "retrenchment" strategy
2. A "maintenance" strategy
3. A "growth" strategy

STRATEGIC ALTERNATIVES

The Retrenchment Strategy

The retrenchment strategy called for Nolte Freightlines to withdraw from the new southeastern market. The cost of doing business within the new market area was using up corporate profits at a time when the recession and new competition were dwindling Nolte's market share within established territories. Among the provisions of this strategy were the following:

1. Withdraw completely from new territories and revoke all published rates.
2. Analyze established territory to determine those areas which are unprofitable.
3. Provide services only in those areas which will produce the expected rate of return of 20 percent.
4. Reduce sales and office personnel by 15 percent.
5. Reduce administrative expenses by 10 percent.

The Maintenance Strategy

This strategy stressed maintenance of new and existing territories. A costly investment had already been made in the expansion territory, and the strategy sought a no-growth solution to the empty mileage problem. The key provisions of this approach were the following:

1. Raise rates by 5 percent on all northbound freight out of the Southeast to match competitor rates in the area.
2. Publish "point-to-point" rates as well as "continuous movement" rates for existing customers into and out of the Southeast. These special rates would pinpoint the customers Nolte wishes to service and bring about the establishment of traffic lanes to reduce empty mileage.
3. Keep the sales and office personnel at existing levels.
4. Keep administrative expenditures at current levels.
5. Concentrate efforts on preserving existing customers, not attracting new ones.

The Growth Strategy

The growth strategy called for the development of a new division, the Intermodal Division. For the past six months Kathleen's son had been researching the feasibility of starting such a division and had presented the material to the four owners. Basically, the idea behind the division is to use the railroads as a means of lowering deadhead mileage and capitalizing upon new train schedules to minimize the effects upon service time. Existing rates out of the Northeast could then be lowered as the cost savings were passed on to the customer, producing increased incentives for customers to use Nolte. The provisions for this strategy were outlined in the research material as follows:

1. Set up interchange agreements with the Southern and R, F, and P Railroads to allow Nolte to use railroad trailers. These agreements would set forth the daily charges that the railroads would bill Nolte for the use of their trailers as well as outline responsibility for damages.
2. Hire an operations person and a salesperson who have had experience with the railroads in a similar type of operation. Budget combined salaries at $65,000.
3. Develop a dispatching system capable of providing adequate controls for this type of operation.
4. Locate local carriers within the southeastern territory which would be willing to work with Nolte in providing service between the various major railheads (railroad piggyback terminals) and the customer.
5. Educate Nolte's present customers on this method of transportation and the cost savings from which the customer would benefit.
6. Begin a direct-mail advertising campaign within the southeastern and existing territories to manufacturers with selected SIC codes and financial characteristics. The mailing list would be purchased from Dunn & Bradstreet at a cost of fifty cents a name. Total expected price tag of the campaign would be $15,000.

THE INTERMODAL PROPOSAL

Management at Nolte Freightlines had considered the possibility of entering the intermodal market for the last fourteen months. However, only two of the owners had agreed on the need for such a division. Since a majority was needed to pursue start-up arrangements, the only course of action taken was to recently allow Kathleen's son Jonah to do some research into piggybacking.

Jonah Harrison had just graduated from a local college with a liberal arts degree and Kathleen wanted him to "get his feet wet" in the transportation field with this project. Short on experience but not on ideas, Jonah went about gathering as much information as was available on the subject of intermodal traffic. The trends were readily apparent in all the subject material, showing, as in Exhibit 12-5, that intermodal traffic was on the increase. The "plans" shown as column headings in the exhibit refer to the type of service provided. Jonah came to understand that the type of service that Nolte would provide if it entered the market would be Plan 2½, which involves using the railroads' trailers to haul the freight with Nolte providing pickup or delivery service to the customer. Motor carriers can use this plan if they are willing to pay the railroads' rates and have ICC authority to serve the points involved.

To gather more customer-related information, Jonah mailed a questionnaire to a random sampling of customers. This questionnaire was designed to get an idea of the support present for intermodal transit within Nolte's customer base (see Exhibit 12-6). Based upon the answers to the questionnaire, it was obvious to Jonah that there was a good-sized market for intermodal transit. He was surprised to find, however, that only 39 percent of the customers sampled knew of Nolte's recent expansion into the Southeast. This, he felt, helped to explain the poor response of customers providing freight shipments into this area. Realizing that this fact alone could scuttle the momentum building behind starting the Intermodal Division, Jonah neglected to highlight this fact in his report to the owners.

In his research, Jonah also found that the best transit times could be made by bypassing the Conrail System in the Northeast and going over the road to the connecting railroads at the Potomac Railroad yard in Al-

EXHIBIT 12-5   Trailers and Containers Loaded in Piggyback Service, 1976–82

YEAR	PLAN 1	PLAN 2	PLAN 2½	PLAN 3	PLAN 4	PLAN 5	TOTAL
1982	318,747	230,334	1,544,133	423,680	337,963	103,253	2,958,110
1981	281,022	216,855	1,431,568	363,814	273,143	84,348	2,650,750
1980	188,077	229,224	1,323,165	300,088	207,970	70,700	2,319,224
1979	119,453	255,339	1,215,283	199,625	163,101	71,687	2,024,488
1978	157,187	423,775	1,462,199	196,159	184,160	76,194	2,499,674
1977	183,278	488,585	1,425,746	147,061	196,534	67,823	2,509,027
1976	160,741	507,402	1,182,332	82,295	144,155	58,727	2,135,652
			Percent Change—1982 vs. 1976				
	+98.3%	−54.6%	+30.6%	+414.8%	+134.4%	+75.8%	+38.5%
			Each Plan as Percent of Total				
1982	10.8%	7.8%	52.2%	14.3%	11.4%	3.5%	100%

*Figures do not include empty trailers or containers originated that moved on revenue charges.

Source: Car Service Division, AAR.

EXHIBIT 12-6   Nolte Freightlines, Inc.: Selected Questions from Intermodal Sales Study of Existing Northeast Customers (500 selected, 342 responded)

QUESTIONS ASKED	YES	NO
1. As an existing Nolte Freightlines customer, are you aware that Nolte's territory has recently been expanded to include all points within the southeastern U.S.?	39%	61%
2. Are you presently using Nolte to service any of your southeastern customers?	2%	98%
3. Do you have branch plants within the Southeast with which interplant shipments are made?	28%	72%
4. Are you aware of Nolte Freightlines' low "continuous movement" rates designed for interplant shipments into and out of the Southeast?	1%	99%
5. Are you familiar with the terms "piggyback" or "intermodal"?	53%	47%
6. If Nolte Freightlines offered the same transit times that it has presently, and lowered rates (by approximately 7%) into the Southeast by using the railroad for a portion of the line haul, would you use Nolte Freightlines?	67%	33%
The next two questions were only asked of those that answered yes to Question #6.		
7. If the use of the railroad caused one additional day to be added to existing transit times, would Nolte Freightlines be used?	82%	18%
8. If the use of the railroad caused between two and three days to be added to existing transit times, would Nolte Freightlines be used?	31%	69%
9. If railroad trailers were used for freight pickup and delivery, would this pose a problem for your shipping dock?	3%	97%
10. Most railroad trailers are 40 feet in length and 13 feet 6 inches high, while Nolte's present fleet of trailers are 45 feet in length and 13 feet 6 inches high. Would the cubic footage requirements for present trailer loads be met if the smaller railroad trailer were used?	81%	19%

exandria, Virginia, where Southern and R, F, and P had new dedicated piggyback trains to southeastern points. By handling all northbound and southbound freight over the two piggyback loading/unloading ramps, two to three days could be eliminated from the traditional transit times into and out of the Northeast by existing intermodal carriers. This two- to three-day delay was virtually built into the Conrail System, as the tunnel used out of the Potomac yard was not high enough to accommodate a regular 13-foot, 6-inch-high trailer on a common railroad flatcar. Conrail had to use special low flatcars to transport these trailers into and out of the Northeast. Since low flatcars were always in short supply and trailers being interchanged from other railroads at Potomac yard had to be removed from existing flatcars and cross-loaded onto the lower flatcars, delays were inevitable.

Based on R, F, and P and Southern Railway schedules out of Alexandria, and on current Nolte transit times, a map showing transit times between representative points was prepared (see Exhibit 12-7). Since cus-

EXHIBIT 12-7   Nolte Freightlines, Inc.: Projected Operating Territory and Delivery Times for the New Intermodal Division

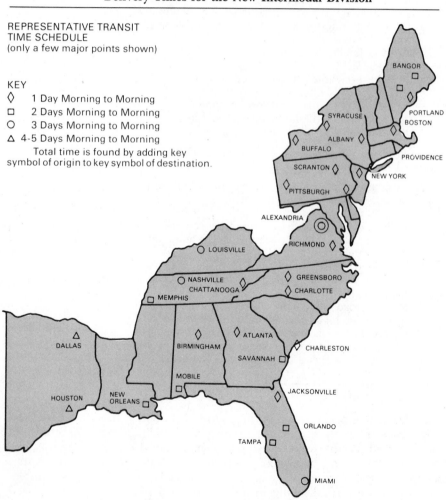

REPRESENTATIVE TRANSIT
TIME SCHEDULE
(only a few major points shown)

KEY
◊   1 Day Morning to Morning
□   2 Days Morning to Morning
○   3 Days Morning to Morning
△ 4-5 Days Morning to Morning
          Total time is found by adding key
symbol of origin to key symbol of destination.

tomer response in the questionnaire had revealed very little tolerance to
transit delays, it was necessary to present transit times under ideal conditions. Jonah recognized that these transit times were optimistic but that
they could be met if no unforeseen delays occurred.

When the transit schedule was composed, Jonah understood that
the vital element in making it work rested with the type of controls put
into practice at the dispatch level. Although Nolte Freightlines had had
fifty years' experience in the industry, the type of operation that the Intermodal Division represented would require a good deal of additional
expertise. Working closely with the railroads requires knowledge of the
railroad system and the paperwork necessary to expedite shipments. A
thorough understanding of the liabilities set forth in the railroad interchange agreements regarding trailer "per diem," or daily, rental charges,
tire repairs, interchanging trailers from one railroad to another, and trailer
damage could be the difference between a profitable operation and an
unprofitable one. In order to ensure the success of the operation, Jonah
saw it as a necessity to hire away from a competitor an operations person
with at least two years' experience in intermodal traffic. With the help of
the operations person, Jonah felt confident that an adequate dispatching
system could be developed that would overcome the many operational
hazards inherent in piggybacking.

Another vital element in the success of the new division was seen
by Jonah to be selling expertise. None of Nolte's present salespeople have
sold intermodal traffic, and since almost half of Nolte's present customer
base is unfamiliar with this type of transit, the need for an experienced
salesperson is self-evident. Training existing sales personnel, as well as
educating Nolte's customers, would be facilitated by an experienced salesperson. Duties would include the development of promotional materials
for the planned direct-mail campaign and all educational materials.

Management Views

Managerial reactions to Jonah's report have been almost as diverse
as the options open to pursue. Chris Nolte believes that the Intermodal
Division is vital to the improvement of Nolte's net profits. Chris understands that the immediate problem facing Nolte is the excess deadhead
miles generated from operations expanding into the Southeast. He also is
aware of a more fundamental problem in the present service mix which
Nolte offers its customers. The growing number of customers using intermodal services shows that more of them are giving up service time for
lower rates. Although Chris perceives the present surge in piggyback traffic
as being primarily due to the recession, he feels that customer needs are
changing and that growth in the intermodal market will continue over the
long term. He feels that starting the new division is a way not only of
eliminating the deadhead mileage problem but also of hedging Nolte's
profits against changes in customer preferences and needs.

Kathleen Harrison shares her brother Chris's views. She believes that the lost revenue will be too great if Nolte Freightlines does not enter the market. Kathleen is a firm believer in the old adage, "The best defense is a good offense."

Chuck Nolte's view on the present situation is basically middle-of-the-road. He does not see the need for an intermodal division and views the company's present problems as temporarily brought upon by the recession. He is in favor of pursuing a maintenance strategy and waiting out the recession.

Hubble Nolte finds himself again in the "swing vote" position. Over the years, he has positioned himself in this way to remain a powerful figure even though he is no longer involved in the day-to-day operations of the company. Hubble knows that if he sides with Chuck on the issue he will essentially vote-in the maintenance strategy, since the four owners would be at an impasse. He is not entirely convinced that the Intermodal Division will be the answer to Nolte's problems, but he does realize that the deadhead mileage problem has to be dealt with immediately if earnings are to improve. Hubble decides to look over the intermodal report again.

CHAPTER 13
Product Strategies

How many things there are here that I do not want.

Socrates

Product strategies specify the market needs which may be served by offering different products. It is the product strategies, duly related to market strategies, which eventually come to dominate both the overall strategy and the spirit of the company, and opportunities and threats are seen accordingly. Product strategies deal with such matters as number and diversity of products, product innovations, product scope, and product design. In this chapter different dimensions of product strategies are examined for their essence, their significance, their limitations, if any, and their contributions to objectives and goals. Each strategy will be exemplified with illustrations from marketing literature.

DIMENSIONS OF PRODUCT STRATEGIES

The implementation of product strategies requires cooperation among different groups, i.e., finance, R&D, corporate staff, and marketing. This makes product strategies difficult to develop and implement. The point may be illustrated with reference to what was said about the Chrysler Corporation in the 1970s—that the engineering department in the company had such dominance that all other considerations were subordinated. As a 1975 *Fortune* article noted:

> Engineering considerations . . . dictate what kinds of cars the company makes. In the late fifties, when the auto makers were developing their first compacts, Chrysler's management wanted to build a rear-engined compact to compete with GM's Corvair. "'Our engineers were not willing to go into the weight distribution that it would entail. There was no way this management could have even ordered that engineering department to do a rear-engined car." A decade later, as Ford and GM were preparing subcompacts, Chrysler's engineers concluded they could not design one that would both be competitive in styling and meet their standards for interior comfort.[1]

---

[1]Peter Vanderwicken, "What's Really Wrong at Chrysler," *Fortune*, May, 1975, p. 176.

According to the above author, too much engineering emphasis in arriving at strategic decisions was one of the major reasons for the Chrysler Corporation's poor showing in the turbulent 1970s.

As a matter of fact, in many companies, to achieve proper coordination among diverse business units, the product strategy decisions are made at the top-management level itself. At Gould Inc., for example, the top management decides what kind of a business it is and what type it wants to be. The company pursues products in the areas of electromechanics, electrochemistry, metallurgy, and electronics. The company works to dispose of products which do not fall strictly into its areas of interest.

In some companies, the overall scope of product strategy is laid out at the corporate level while actual design is left to business units. It is contended that this alternative is more desirable since in a diverse company it is difficult for the top management to deal with the details of product strategy. In this chapter the following dimensions of product strategies are recognized:

> Product-positioning strategy
> Product-repositioning strategy
> Product-overlap strategy
> Product-scope strategy
> Product-design strategy
> Product-elimination strategy
> New-product strategy
> Diversification strategy

Each strategy is examined from the point of view of a strategic business unit; the use of each strategy is discussed with reference to illustrations from marketing literature. The appendix at the end of this chapter summarizes each strategy, giving its definition, objectives, requirements, and expected results.

PRODUCT-POSITIONING STRATEGY

The term "positioning" refers to placing a brand in that part of the market where it will have a favorable reception compared to competing products. Since the market is heterogeneous, one brand cannot make an impact on the entire market. As a matter of strategy, therefore, the product should be matched with that segment of the market where it is most likely to succeed. The product should be so positioned that it stands apart from competing brands. Positioning tells what the product stands for, what it is, and how the customers should evaluate it.

Positioning helps in differentiating the product from competitive offerings. Positioning is achieved by using marketing-mix variables, especially through design and communication efforts. While differentiation through positioning is more visible in consumer goods, it is equally true of industrial goods. With some products positioning can be achieved on the basis of tangible differences (e.g., product features); with many others, intangibles are used to differentiate and position products. As has been said:

> Fabricators of consumer and industrial goods seek competitive distinction via product features—some visually or measurably identifiable, some cosmetically implied, and some rhetorically claimed by reference to real or suggested hidden attributes that promise results or values different from those of competitors' products.
>
> So too with consumer and industrial services—what I call, to be accurate, "intangibles." On the commodities exchanges, for example, dealers in metals, grains, and pork bellies trade in totally undifferentiated generic products. But what they "sell" is the claimed distinction of their execution—the efficiency of their transactions in their clients' behalf, their responsiveness to inquiries, the clarity and speed of their confirmations, and the like. In short, the *offered* product is differentiated, though the *generic* product is identical.[2]

The desired position for a product may be determined by use of the following procedure:

1. Analyze product attributes which are salient to consumers.
2. Examine the distribution of these attributes among different market segments.
3. Determine the optimal position for the product in regard to each attribute, taking into consideration the positions occupied by existing brands.
4. Choose an overall position for the product (based on the overall match between product attributes and their distribution in the population and the positions of existing brands).

For example, cosmetics for the career woman may be positioned as "natural" ones which supposedly make her appear as if she were wearing no makeup at all. An alternate position could be "fast" cosmetics: smoky mauve eye shadow and dark red lipstick to give the user a mysterious aura in the evenings. There can be still a third position: light cosmetics to be worn for tennis and other leisure activities.

Another example could be made in the positioning of beer. Two position decisions for beer are light vs. heavy and bitter vs. mild. The desired position for a new brand of beer can be determined by discovering its rating in the above attributes and the size of the beer market, which is divided into segments according to these attributes and the positions of other brands. It may be found that the heavy and mild beer market is

---

[2]Theodore Levitt, "Marketing Success Through Differentiation—of Anything," *Harvard Business Review,* January–February, 1980, p. 83. See also Theodore Levitt, "Marketing Intangible Products and Product Intangibles," *Harvard Business Review,* May–June, 1981, pp. 94–102, and William K. Hall, "Survival Strategies in a Hostile Environment," *Harvard Business Review,* September–October, 1980, pp. 78–85.

large and that Schlitz and Budweiser compete in it. In the light and mild beer market, another big segment, only Miller may be positioned. The management may decide to position the new brand in competition with Miller.

Six different approaches to positioning may be distinguished: (a) positioning by attribute (i.e., associating a product with an attribute, feature, or customer benefit); (b) positioning by price/quality (i.e., price/quality attribute is so pervasive that it can be considered as a separate approach to promotion); (c) positioning with respect to use or application (i.e., associating the product with a use or application); (d) positioning by the product user (i.e., associating a product with a user or a class of users); (e) positioning with respect to a product class (e.g., Lever Brothers' positioning of Caress soap as a bath oil product rather than a soap); and (f) positioning with respect to a competitor (i.e., making a reference to competition as in Avis's campaign: "We're number two, so we try harder."[3]

Two types of positioning strategy are discussed here: single-brand strategy and multiple-brand strategy. A company may have just one brand which it may place in one or more chosen segments in the market. Alternatively, it may have several brands positioned in different segments.

Positioning a Single Brand

To maximize its benefits with a single brand, a company must try to associate itself with a core segment in the market where it can play a dominant role. In addition, it may attract customers from other segments outside its core as a fringe benefit. Coors beer, for example, is mainly positioned in a limited geographic segment, the western states, and does very well there.

An alternative single-brand strategy would be to consider the market as undifferentiated and cover it with a single brand. Several years ago, for example, the Coca-Cola Company followed a strategy whereby Coke supposedly quenched the thirst of the total market. Such a policy, however, can only work in the short run. To seek entry into a market, competitors segment and challenge the dominance of the single brand by positioning themselves in small, viable niches. Even the Coca-Cola Company now has a number of brands to serve different segments: Coke, Diet Coke, Fanta, Sprite, Tab, Fresca, and even orange juice.

Take the case of beer. Traditionally brewers operated as if there were one homogeneous market for beer that could be served by one product in one package. Miller, in order to seek growth, took the initiative to segment the market and positioned its High Life brand to serve younger customers. Thereafter, it introduced a 7-ounce pony bottle which turned out to be a favorite of women and older people, who thought the standard

---

[3]David A. Aaker and J. Gary Shansby, "Positioning Your Product," *Business Horizons*, May–June, 1982, pp. 56–62.

12-ounce size was simply too much beer to drink. But Miller's big success came with the introduction of another brand in 1975, low-calorie Lite. Lite now stands to become the most successful new beer introduced in the United States in this century.[4]

To protect the position of a single brand, sometimes a company may be forced into introducing other brands. Kotler reports that Heublein's Smirnoff brand had a 23 percent share of the vodka market when its position was challenged by another brand, Wolfschmidt, priced at one dollar less a bottle. Instead of cutting the price of its Smirnoff brand to meet the competition, Heublein raised the price by one dollar and used increased revenues for advertising. At the same time it introduced a new brand, Relska, positioning it against Wolfschmidt, and also marketed Popov, a low-price vodka. This strategy effectively met Wolfschmidt's challenge and gave Smirnoff an even higher status. Thus, Heublein resorted to multiple brands to protect its single brand which was challenged by a competitor.[5]

Whether a single brand should be positioned in direct competition with the dominant brand already on the market or be placed in a secondary position is another strategic issue. The direct head-on route is usually risky, but some variation in this type of strategy is quite common. Avis seemingly accepted a number-two position in the market next to Hertz. Gillette, on the other hand, positioned Earth Born directly against Clairol's Herbal Essence, Johnson's Baby Shampoo, and P&G's Head and Shoulders.[6]

Generally a single-brand strategy is a desirable choice in the short run, particularly where the task of managing multiple brands will be beyond the managerial and financial capability of a company. Supposedly, this strategy is more conducive to achieving higher profitability since a single brand permits better control of operations than do multiple brands.

There are two requisites to successfully managing a single brand in the market: the brand must be so positioned in the market that it can stand competition from the toughest rival, and its unique position should be maintained by creating the aura of a different product. Take the case of Cover Girl in the cosmetics field, a crowded and highly competitive industry. The segment it has picked out—sales in supermarkets and discount stores—is one that large business companies such as Revlon, Avon, and Max Factor have not tapped. Cover Girl products are sold at a freestanding display without sales help or demonstration. As far as the second requisite is concerned, creating the aura of a different product, an example is VW's success in protecting its position in the small car market

[4]"Miller's Fast Growth Upsets the Beer Industry," *Business Week*, November 8, 1976, p. 58.
[5]Philip Kotler, *Marketing Management*, 5th Ed. (Englewood Cliffs, NJ: Prentice-Hall, 1984), p. 392.
[6]*Advertising Age*, June 17, 1974, p. 1.

until Japanese cars entered the market in the 1970s. Another example is Coors beer, which continues to protect its position through the mystique attached to its name. In other words, a single brand must have some advantage to save it from competitive inroads.

Positioning Multiple Brands

Business units introduce multiple brands to a market for two major reasons: (1) to seek growth by offering varied products in different segments of the market, and (2) to avoid competitive threats to a single brand. General Motors has a car to sell in all conceivable segments of the market. Coca-Cola has a soft drink to offer for each different taste. IBM sells computers for different customer needs. Procter & Gamble offers a laundry detergent for each laundering need. Offering multiple brands oriented toward different segments of the same market is an accepted route to growth.

To realize desired growth, multiple brands should be diligently positioned in the market so that they do not compete with each other and create cannibalism. For example, 20 to 25 percent of sales of Anheuser-Busch's Michelob Light brand are to customers who previously bought regular Michelob but switched because of the Light brand's low-calorie appeal.[7] General Foods' introduction of Maxim took sales away from its established Maxwell House brand. Ford's introduction of the Falcon as a "new-sized Ford" at a lower price led consumers to substitute Falcons for existing Ford models.[8] Thus, it is necessary to be careful in segmenting the market and to position the product through design and promotion as uniquely suited to a particular segment.

Of course, some sort of cannibalism is unavoidable. But the question is how much cannibalism is acceptable when introducing another brand. It has been said that 70 percent of Mustang sales in the car's introductory year were to buyers who would have purchased another Ford had the Mustang not been introduced; the remaining 30 percent of the sales came from new customers. Cadbury's experience with the introduction of a chocolate bar in England indicates that over 50 percent of its volume came from market expansion, with the remaining volume coming from the company's existing products. Both the Mustang and the chocolate bar were rated successful by the introducing companies. The apparent difference in cannibalism rates shows that cost structure, degree of market maturity,

---

[7]"Anheuser-Busch, Inc., Has Another Entry in 'Light Beer' Field," *The Wall Street Journal*, February 13, 1978, p. 4.

[8]William Copulsky, "Cannibalism in the Marketplace," *Journal of Marketing*, October, 1976, pp. 103–105.

and the competitive appeal of alternative offerings will affect cannibalism sales and their importance to the sales and profitability of a product line and individual items.[9]

An additional factor to consider in figuring out actual cannibalism is the vulnerability of an existing brand to a competitor's entry into the presumably open spot in the market. For example, suppose that a company's new brand derives 50 percent of its sales from customers who would have bought its existing brand. However, if 20 percent of the sales of this existing brand were susceptible to a competitor's entry (assuming a fairly high probability that the competitor would have indeed positioned its new brand in that open spot), the actual cannibalism should be considered as 30 percent. This is because 20 percent of the revenue from sales of the existing brand would have been lost to a competitive brand had there been no new brand.

Multiple brands can be positioned in the market either head-on with the leading brand or with an idea. The relative strengths of the new entry and the established brand will dictate which of the two positioning routes is more desirable. While head-on positioning usually appears risky, some companies have successfully carried it out. IBM's copier was positioned in head-on competition with Xerox. Bristol-Myers' Datril was introduced to compete directly with Tylenol. Positioning with an idea, however, may prove to be a better alternative, especially when the leading brand is well established. Positioning with an idea was attempted by Kraft Inc. to position three brands (Breyers and Sealtest ice cream and Light 'n' Lively ice milk) as complementary rather than competitive. Vick Chemical positioned Nyquil, a cold remedy, with the idea that Nyquil assured a good night's sleep. Seagram successfully introduced its line of cocktail mixes, Party Tyme, against heavy odds in favor of National Distillers' Holland House line by promoting it with the Snowbird winter drink.[10]

Positioning of multiple brands and their management in a dynamic environment calls for ample managerial and financial resources. When these resources are lacking, the company is better off with a single brand. Additionally, if a company already has a dominant position, its attempt to increase its share of the market by introducing an additional brand may invite antitrust action. Such an eventuality should be guarded against. On the other hand, there is also a defensive or share-maintenance issue to be considered here even if one has the dominant entry. A product with high market share may not remain in this position forever if competitors are permitted to chip away with unchallenged positions.

---

[9]Roger A. Kerin, Michael G. Harvey, and James T. Rothe, "Cannibalism and New Product Development," *Business Horizons*, October, 1978, p. 31.

[10]John P. Maggard, "Positioning Revisited," *Journal of Marketing*, January, 1976, pp. 63–66.

As a strategy, the positioning of multiple brands, if properly implemented, can lead to increases in growth, market share, and profitability.

PRODUCT-REPOSITIONING STRATEGY

Often a product may require repositioning. This can happen if (1) a competitive entry has been positioned next to the brand with an adverse effect on its share of the market, (2) consumer preferences have undergone a change, (3) new customer-preference clusters have been discovered with promising opportunities, or (4) a mistake has been made in the original positioning.

Citations from marketing literature will illustrate how repositioning becomes desirable under different circumstances. Simmons Company introduced its Hide-A-Bed (convertible sofa) in 1940. Soon after, hundreds of competitors followed suit and affected Simmons' business. At the same time consumer preferences shifted in favor of living room sofas, which plateaued the industry sales. Also, consumers were becoming more quality-conscious. These conditions led Simmons to reposition the product by reversing the emphasis—stressing that their product was not essentially a bed that converts to a sofa but a sofa that converts to a bed. The repositioning was implemented by making appropriate changes in product design (i.e., using high-quality upholstery and elegant style), and by advertising (i.e., stressing utilitarian demand for living room sofas, quality, and fashion consciousness). Following the repositioning in 1960, Simmons' sales increased rapidly.[11]

Over the years, Coca-Cola's position has been shifted to keep up with the changing mood of the market. In recent years, the theme of Coca-Cola's advertising has evolved from "Things go better with Coke" to "It's the real thing" to "Coke is it." The current perspective of Coca-Cola's positioning is to seek to reach a generation of young people and those young at heart. Recently Procter & Gamble changed the name of its brand of toothpaste, Gleem II, back to just Gleem to revitalize and reposition it primarily as a whitener with fresh taste, thereby reverting to Gleem's original position. In 1968 with the addition of fluoride to Gleem, P&G had emphasized Gleem's cavity-fighting properties and had changed its name to Gleem II. Continued poor performance of the brand, however, led to thorough research of the problem, which showed that Gleem was still perceived as a whitener despite its cavity-fighting emphasis. This is what led the company to seek again the original position for Gleem.[12]

The risks involved in positioning or repositioning a product or ser-

---

[11]Carl Spielvogel, "Brand Positioning and Repositioning," in Earl L. Bailey (ed.), *Marketing Strategies* (New York: The Conference Board, 1974), p. 10.

[12]Nancy Giges, "P&G Busy: Repositioned Gleem: Folger's Addition; Revamped Sure," *Advertising Age,* January 17, 1977, p. 1.

vice are high. The technique of perceptual mapping may be gainfully used to substantially reduce those risks. Perceptual mapping helps in examining the position of a product relative to competing products. It helps in:

—Understanding how competing products or services are perceived by various consumer groups in terms of strengths and weaknesses.
—Understanding the similarities and dissimilarities between competing products and services.
—Repositioning a current product in the perceptual space of consumer segments.
—Positioning a new product or service in an established marketplace.
—Tracking the progress of a promotional or marketing campaign on the perceptions of targeted consumer segments.[13]

The use of perceptual mapping may be illustrated with reference to the automobile industry. Exhibit 13-1 shows how different cars are positioned on the perceptual map. The map helps the marketing strategist in calculating whether the company's cars are on target. The concentration of dots representing competing models shows how much opposition there is likely to be in a specific territory on the map. Presumably, cars higher up on the graph should fetch a higher price than models ranked toward the bottom, where the stress is on economy and practicality. General Motors might find after looking at the map that its Chevrolet division, traditionally geared to entry-level buyers, ought to move down in practicality and more to the right in youthfulness. Another problem for GM on the map is the close proximity of its Buick and Oldsmobile divisions. That would suggest that the two divisions are waging a marketing war more against each other than against the competition.

Basically, there are three ways to reposition a product: among existing users, among new users, and for new uses. The discussion that follows will elaborate these repositioning alternatives.

Repositioning Among Existing Customers

Repositioning among existing customers is sought by the promotion of more varied uses of the product. DuPont adopted this strategy to revitalize its nylon business by promoting the "fashion smartness" of tinted hose.[14] The effort was directed toward expanding women's collections of hosiery by creating a new fashion image for hosiery: not simply a "*neutral* accessory to a central integration of fashion, but a *suitable* tint and pattern for each outer garment in the lady's wardrobe."

---

[13]William D. Neal, "Strategic Product Positioning: A Step-by-Step Guide," *Business,* May–June, 1980, p. 40.
[14]Examples of DuPont and General Foods discussed here and in the discussion that follows are from Theodore Levitt, "Exploit the Product Life Cycle," *Harvard Business Review,* November–December, 1965, pp. 81–94.

EXHIBIT 13-1   Perceptual Map of Brand Images

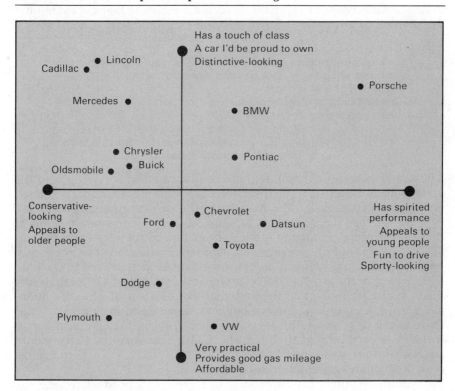

Source: Chrysler Corporation. Reprinted by permission.

General Foods Corporation repositioned Jell-O to boost its sales by promoting it as a base for salads. To encourage this usage, the company introduced a variety of vegetable-flavored Jell-Os. Similar strategy was adopted by 3M Company on behalf of Scotch tape, introducing a line of colored, patterned, waterproof, invisible, and write-on Scotch tapes for different types of gift wrapping.

The purpose of repositioning among current users is to revitalize the product's life by giving it new character as something which is needed not merely as a staple product, but also to keep up with new trends and new ideas. Repositioning among users should help the brand in its sales growth as well as its increasing profitability.

Repositioning Among New Users

Repositioning among new users requires that the product be presented with a different twist to the people who have not hitherto been favorably inclined toward it. In so doing, care must be taken to see that in the process of enticing new customers, the current customers of the product are not alienated. Miller's attempts to win over new customers for Miller High Life beer are noteworthy. Approximately 15 percent of the population consumes 85 percent of all the beer sold in the United States. Miller's slogan, "the champagne of bottled beer," tended to have more appeal for light users than heavy users. Also, the image projected too much elegance for a product like beer. Miller decided to reposition the product slightly to offer greater appeal to a wider range of beer drinkers without weakening the current franchise of the brand: "Put another way, the need was to take Miller High Life out of the champagne bucket, but not to put it in the bathtub." After conducting a variety of studies, Miller came up with a new promotional campaign built around this slogan: "If you've got the time, we've got the beer." The campaign proved to be highly successful. Through its new slogan the brand communicated three things: that it was a quality product worth taking time out for; that it was associated with a friendly, low-key informality; and that it offered relaxation and reward after the pressures of the workday.[15]

At DuPont new users of nylon were created by legitimizing among early teenagers and subteenagers the necessity of wearing hosiery. This was achieved by working out a new ad campaign with emphasis on the merchandising of youthful products and styles to tempt the young consumers. Jell-O attempted to develop new users among those who would not perceive Jell-O as a dessert or salad product. Thus, during the Metrecal boom, Jell-O was advertised with a new concept—a fashion-oriented, weight-control appeal.

The addition of new users to a product's customer base helps enlarge the overall market and thus puts the product on a growth route. Repositioning among new users also helps increase profitability, since very few new investments, except for promotional costs, have to be made to seek repositioning.

Repositioning for New Uses

Repositioning for new uses requires searching for latent uses of the product, if any. The case of Arm & Hammer's baking soda offers a classic example of an unexplored use of a product. Today this product is popular as a deodorizer, yet this was not the use originally conceived for the product. While new uses for a product can be discovered in a variety of ways, the best way to discover them is to gain insights into the customer's way of using the product. If it is found that a large number of customers are using the product for a purpose other than the one originally intended, this other use could be developed with whatever modifications are necessary.

---

[15]Carl Spielvogel, *op. cit,* pp. 13–16.

Repositioning for new uses may be illustrated with reference to a United States Borax & Chemical Corporation product. Initially it was positioned primarily as a laundry deodorant. The company stressed deodorizing and freshening as the benefits of the product. After nine years in the market, the company found that a large number of women who had a negative feeling about using a bleach considered a modified version of this company's product named Borateem (Borateem Plus) a good substitute for bleach. This led the United States Borax & Chemical Corporation to seek a new position for Borateem—that of a bleach substitute. The repositioning provided consecutive month-to-month sales gains for the product.[16]

At DuPont, new uses for nylon sprang up in the form of varied types of hosiery (such as stretch stockings and stretch socks), tires, bearings, etc. It is the new uses which kept nylon on the growth path: wrap knits in 1945, tire cord in 1948, textured yarns in 1955, carpet yarns in 1959, and so on. Without the new uses nylon would have hit the saturation level as far back as 1962.

As far as Jell-O is concerned, General Foods found that women used powdered gelatin dissolved in liquid as a means of strengthening their fingernails. Working on this clue, General Foods introduced a flavorless Jell-O as a nail-building agent.

The new-use strategy is directed toward revamping the sales of a product whose growth based on its original conceived use has slowed down. This strategy has the potential to increase sales growth, market share, and profitability.

PRODUCT-OVERLAP STRATEGY

The product-overlap strategy refers to a situation where a company decides to compete against its own brand. Many factors lead companies to adopt such a strategic posture. For example, the A&P stores themselves cannot keep the company's 42 manufacturing operations working at full capacity. Therefore, A&P decided to distribute many of its products through independent food retailers. A&P's Eight O'Clock coffee, for example, is sold through the 7-Eleven stores.[17] Procter & Gamble has different brands of detergents virtually competing in the same market. Each brand has its own organization for marketing research, product development, merchandising, and promotion. Although sharing the same sales force, each brand behaves aggressively to outdo the other in the marketplace. Sears, Roebuck's large appliances bearing its brand name are actually manufactured by the Whirlpool Corporation. Thus, Whirlpool's appliances compete against those it sells to Sears.

---

[16]*Ibid.*, pp. 11–12.
[17]Robert E. Weigand, "Fit Products and Channels to Your Markets," *Harvard Business Review*, January–February, 1977, p. 97.

There are alternative ways in which the product-overlap strategy may be operationalized. Principal among them are: having competing lines, doing private labeling, and dealing with original-equipment manufacturers. These are discussed in the ensuing pages.

Competing Brands

In order to gain a larger share of the total market, many companies introduce competing products to the market. When a market is not neatly delineated, a single brand of the product may not be able to make an adequate impact on the market. If the second brand is placed to compete with the first one, while there will be some cannibalism, overall sales of the two brands should increase substantially. In other words, the two competing brands provide a more aggressive front against the competitors.

Often the competing-brands strategy works out to be a short-term phenomenon. When a new version of the product is introduced, the previous version is allowed to continue until the new one has fully established itself. In this way competition is prevented from stealing sales during the time that the new product is coming into its own. In 1977 Gillette introduced the Atra razor, a revolutionary new product with a pivoting head mechanism that permits a closer shave. At the same time, its previous twin-blade razor, Trac II, introduced in 1971, continued to be promoted as before. It is claimed that the two brands put together have been very effective in the market. It is estimated that 46 percent of Atra users have converted from Trac II. If Trac II had not been promoted, this figure would have been 60 percent, and Atra would have become more vulnerable to the Schick Super II and other rigid Trac II lookalikes.[18]

To expand its overall coffee market, Procter & Gamble introduced in 1977 a more economical form of ground coffee under the Folger's label. A more efficient milling process which refines the coffee into flakes allows the hot water used in brewing to come into contact with more of each coffee particle, resulting in savings of up to 15 percent per cup. The new product is packaged in 13-, 26-, and 32-ounce cans yielding the same number of cups of coffee as standard 16-, 32-, and 48-ounce cans, respectively. Both the new and the old formulations were promoted aggressively, competing with each other and at the same time providing a strong front against brands belonging to other manufacturers.[19]

The competing-brands strategy is useful in the short run only. Ultimately each brand should find its special niche in the market. If that does not happen, they will create confusion among customers and sales will be hurt. Alternatively, in the long run, one of the brands may be

[18]"Gillette Renews Its Love for Television Sports," *Business Week*, October 23, 1978, p. 142.

[19]Nancy Giges, *op. cit.*, p. 1.

withdrawn, yielding its position to the other brand. This strategy is a useful device for achieving growth and increasing market share.

Private Labeling

Private labeling refers to manufacturing a product under another company's brand name. In the case of goods where middlemen have significant control of the distribution sector, private labeling or branding has become quite common. For large food chains, items produced with their label by an outside manufacturer contribute significantly to sales. Sears, J. C. Penney, and other such companies merchandise many different types of goods with their own brand names on them—textile goods, electronic goods, large appliances, sporting goods, and others.

The private-label strategy may be discussed from two viewpoints, that of the manufacturer and that of the middleman. A manufacturer offers a private brand if this will help increase total revenues. Of course, the manufacturer's first effort will be to push its own brand, but if the choice is between producing a private brand and having no business, it will seriously consider labeling for others. Many companies manufacture solely for others. For example, the Design & Manufacturing Corporation was begun exclusively for manufacturing privately branded dishwashers for large distributors. This can be a risky position, however, since the manufacturer is at the mercy of middlemen who will negotiate a hard bargain. They know the manufacturer is not known in the market and will be forced to come to terms. The situation becomes critical if the manufacturer deals mainly with one customer, such as Sears, for example. There have been many cases where a small manufacturer gave up and sold its business to a distributor with whom it did a major part of its dealings because it just could not operate profitably and still meet the distributor's demand for price reductions.

Many large manufacturers deal in private brands while simultaneously offering their own brands. In such a situation they are competing against themselves. They do so, however, hoping that overall revenues will be higher with the offering of the private brand than without it. Coca-Cola, for example, supplies to A&P stores both its own brand of orange juice, Minute Maid, and the brand it produces with the A&P label. At one time, many companies equated offering private brands with lowering their brands' images. But the business swings of the 1970s made them change their attitude on this issue. For example, Frigidaire appliances at one time were not offered under a private label. However, in 1975 Frigidaire started offering them under Montgomery Ward's name.

The middlemen's interest in selling goods under their own brand names is also motivated by economic considerations. They buy goods with their brand name on them at lower costs, then offer them to the customers at a price which is slightly lower than the price of a manufacturer's brand (also referred to as a national brand). The assumption is that the customer, motivated by the lower price, will buy a private brand, assuming that its quality is on a par with that of the national brand. This assumption is, of course, based on the premise that a reputable middleman will not offer something under its name if it is lacking in quality.

Dealing with Original-Equipment Manufacturers (OEMs)

Following the strategy of dealing with an OEM, a company may sell to competitors the components used in its own product. This enables the competitors to compete with the company in the market. For example, in the initial stages of color television, RCA was the only company that manufactured the picture tube. It sold these picture tubes to General Electric and other competitors, enabling them to compete with RCA color television sets in the market.

The relevance of this strategy may be discussed from the viewpoint of both the seller and the OEM. The motivation for the seller to engage in this strategy comes from two sources: desire to work at near-capacity level, and desire to have help in promoting primary demand. Working at full capacity becomes essential in the case of products where the experience effect (see Chapter 17) works. Thus, by selling a component to competitors, a company may reduce the across-the-board costs of the component for itself. This way it will have the price leverage to compete with those to whom it sold the component. Besides, the company will always have the option of refusing to do business with a competitor who becomes a problem.

The second type of motivation is based on the support which competitors can provide in stimulating primary demand for the new product. Many companies may be working on a new-product idea. One of them successfully introduces the product while others are unable to do so since they lack an essential component or technology which the former has. Since the product is new, the innovator may find it tedious to undertake the task of developing primary demand by itself. It may make a strategic decision to share the essential-component technology with other competitors, thus encouraging them to enter the market and share the burden of stimulating primary demand.

A number of companies follow the OEM strategy. Auto manufacturers sell parts to each other. Texas Instruments sold electronic chips to its competitors during the initial stages of the calculator's development. Back in the 1950s Polaroid bought certain essential ingredients from Kodak to manufacture film. IBM shared a variety of technological components with other computer producers. In many situations, however, the OEM strategy may be forced upon companies by the Justice Department in its efforts to promote competition in an industry. Both Kodak and IBM shared the products of their technology with competitors at the demand of the government. Thus, as a matter of strategy, when government interference may be expected, a company will gain more by sharing its components with others and assuming industry leadership. From the stand-point of results, this strategy is useful in seeking increased profitability, though it may not have much effect on market share or growth.

As far as the OEMs are concerned, the strategy of depending upon a competitor for an essential component will only work in the short run. This is because the supplier may at some point in time refuse entirely to sell or may make it difficult for the buyer by delaying deliveries or making enormous price increases.

PRODUCT-SCOPE STRATEGY

The product-scope strategy deals with the perspectives of the product mix of a company (i.e., the number of product lines and items in each line that the company may offer). The product-scope strategy is determined by making a reference to the business unit mission. Presumably, the mission defines what sort of business it is going to be, which helps in selecting the products and services which are to become a part of the product mix. Standard Brands Inc., for example, was traditionally in the business of food ingredients such as corn sweeteners; it also had such branded consumer products as Planter's nuts and Fleischmann's margarine. In 1977 the company wanted to add more branded food and beverage products to its business. It also wanted to branch out to nonfood products—for example, a product like Elmer's glue, which belonged to another food company, Borden, Inc. However, before arriving at any decision, the management felt that it should define the mission of its business: "A crucial choice is whether we define our mission as that of a consumer food company or, more broadly, as a consumer product company."[20]

The product-scope strategy must be finalized after a careful review of all facets of the business since it involves a long-term commitment. Additionally, the strategy must be reviewed from time to time to make any changes called for because of shifts in the environment. The point may be elaborated with reference to Eastman Kodak Company's decision to enter the instant-photography market in the early 1970s. Traditionally Polaroid bought the negatives, worth $50 million, for its films from Kodak. In 1969 Polaroid built its own negative plant. This meant Kodak would lose some $50 million worth of business and be left with idle machinery that had been dedicated to filling Polaroid's needs. Further, by producing its own film, Polaroid could lower its costs; if it then cut prices, instant photography might become more competitive with Kodak's business. Alternatively, if Polaroid held prices high, it would realize high margins and would soon be very rich indeed. Encouraged by such achievements, Polaroid could even develop a marketing organization rivaling Kodak's and threaten it in every sphere. In brief, Kodak was convinced that it would

---

[20]"Standard Brands: A Blueprint for a New Packaged Goods Drive," *Business Week*, February 6, 1978, p. 90.

be shut out of the instant-photography market forever if it delayed its entry any longer. Subsequently, however, a variety of reasons led Kodak to change its decision to go ahead with the instant-photography project. Its pocket instamatic cameras turned out to be highly successful, and some of the machinery and equipment allocated to instant photography had to be switched over to the pocket instamatics. Capital shortage also occurred, and Kodak, as a matter of financial policy, did not like to borrow to support the instant-photography project.[21] In 1976 Kodak again revised its position and did enter the field of instant photography. Determining the product-scope strategy to adopt required a thorough review of a large number of factors both inside and outside the organization.

The three variants of product-scope strategy which will be discussed in this section are single-product strategy, multiple-products strategy, and system-of-products strategy. It will be recalled that in the previous chapter three alternatives were discussed under market-scope strategy: single-market strategy, multimarket strategy, and total-market strategy. These market strategies may be related to the three variants of product-scope strategy, providing nine different product/market-scope alternatives.

Single Product

A business unit may have just one product in its line and try to live on the success of this one product. There are several advantages to this strategy. First, concentration on a single product leads to specialization, which helps in scale and productivity gains. Second, management of operations is much more efficient when a single product is the focus. Third, in today's environment where growth leads most companies to offer multiple products, a single-product company may become so specialized in its field that it can stand any competition. Lukens Steel Company ranks 19th in U.S. steel production. It specializes in plate steel, making more grades and sizes than anybody else in the industry. Even in its chosen field, Lukens has been a specialist in higher-margin lines, such as unusually heavy-gauge plates, low-sulfur grades, and special shapes such as dome-like caps. This sharp product focus differentiates Lukens from many larger competitors which have much broader product lines, and it has given the company much higher earnings than most. In 1977, a year when steel makers as a group barely broke even, its profits rose by 10.3 percent. In 1978, the industry enjoyed recovery although Lukens was far ahead of them all.[22]

---

[21]Bro Uttal, "Eastman Kodak's Orderly Two-Front War," *Fortune*, September, 1976, p. 123.

[22]"Lukens Steel: A Specialist Blankets a High-Margin Market," *Business Week*, December 11, 1976, p. 127. See also "Lukens: Broadening Its Product Mix Without Weakening Its Position in Steel," *Business Week*, September 6, 1982, p. 109.

A narrow product focus, i.e., cancer insurance, has given American Family Life Assurance Company of Columbus, Georgia, a fast track record. Cancer is probably more feared than any other disease in the United States today. Although it kills fewer people than heart ailments, its victims' suffering is often lingering and severe. Cashing in on this fear, American Family Life became the nation's first marketer of insurance policies that cover the expenses of treating cancer. Today 60 percent of all cancer policies in force have been written by American Family. The company ranked 69th in 1979 among North American life, accident, and health insurance companies as measured by premiums, while in 1969 its rank was 372. In just five years American Family's premium income increased 294 percent while earnings went up by 18 percent.[23]

Despite its obvious advantages, the single-product company has one drawback: if changes in the environment make the product obsolete, the single-product company can be in deep trouble. American history is full of instances where entire industries got wiped out. The disposable diaper, initially introduced by Procter & Gamble via its brand Pampers, pushed the cloth diaper business out of the market. The Baldwin Locomotive Company's steam locomotives were made obsolete by General Motors' diesel locomotives.

Currently another company, indeed the entire industry, is being challenged by technological inroads. DeLuxe Check Printers, Inc., has been a leader in the basic check-printing business for decades. But now the company must decide how to broaden its one-product revenue base because, as the more efficient electronic funds-transfer systems (EFTS) gain increasing acceptance in the 1980s and 1990s, growth in check printing is sure to decline. A recent study by IBM indicated that electronic funds transfer could displace as much as 20 percent of check transactions by 1990. Further slowdown is likely from a saturation of the check market. One reason for the recent high rates of check growth has been the wider use of checks. Two or more checking accounts in families with wives and teens working is not uncommon. But such growth prospects will decline by the end of the 1980s. In brief, DeLuxe needs to do something in the long run to offset the slowdown.[24]

The single-product strategy has an additional drawback. It is not conducive to seeking growth or market share. Its main advantage is profitability. If a company with a single-product focus is not able to earn higher margins, it is better to seek a new posture. Companies interested in growth and/or market share will find the single-product strategy to be of limited value.

---

[23]"American Family Life: Expanding Beyond Its Cancer Insurance Market," *Business Week,* January 15, 1979, p. 100.
[24]"DeLuxe Check Printers: Facing the Age of Electronic Banking," *Business Week,* August 28, 1978, p. 110.

Multiple Products

The multiple-products strategy amounts to offering two or more products. A variety of factors lead companies to choose this strategic posture. A company having a single product has nowhere to go if that product gets into trouble; with multiple products, however, poor performance by one product can be balanced out. In addition, it is essential for a company seeking growth to have multiple product offerings.

In 1970, when Philip Morris bought the Miller Brewing Company, it was a one-product business ranking seventh in beer sales. Growth prospects led the company to offer a number of other products. By May, 1978, the United States National Beer Competition showed Anheuser-Busch first with 23 percent of the market and Miller second with 15 percent of the market.[25] The Chicago-based Dean Foods Company is a $487 million (1983 sales) dairy concern. Over the years, diet-conscious and aging consumers have increasingly shunned high-fat dairy products in favor of low-calorie foods, and competition for the business that remains is increasingly fierce. To successfully operate in such an environment, the company in 1977 decided to add other refrigerated foods such as party dips and cranberry drink, which were faster-growing, higher-margin businesses than the company's traditional dairy business. Dean Foods' moves were so successful that while many milk processors were looking to sell out, it was concerned that it might be bought.[26]

Multiple products can be either related or unrelated. Unrelated products will be discussed later in the section on diversification. Related products consist of different product lines and items. For example, a food company may have a frozen vegetable line, a yogurt line, a cheese line, and a pizza line. In each line the company may have different items (such as strawberry, pineapple, apricot, peach, plain, and blueberry flavors in the yogurt line). Note that in this example there is a consistency in different lines of the food company on three counts: (1) they are sold through grocery stores, (2) they must be refrigerated, and (3) they are meant for the same target market. These underpinnings make them related products.

While not all products may be fast-moving items, they must complement each other in a portfolio of products. The subject of product portfolio was examined in Chapter 10. Suffice it to say here that the multiple-products strategy is directed toward achieving growth, market share, and profitability. Not all companies will get rich simply by having multiple products. This is because growth, market share, and profitability are the

---

[25]"Miller's Fast Growth Upsets the Beer Industry," *Business Week*, November 8, 1976, p. 58.
[26]"Dean Foods: Diversifying to Supplement a Low-Growth Business," *Business Week*, December 18, 1978, p. 74.

functions of a large number of variables, only one of which is having multiple products.

System of Products

The word "system" as applied to products is a post–World War II phenomenon. Two related forces have been responsible for the emergence of this phenomenon. These are the popularity of the marketing concept that businesses do not sell products but customer satisfaction, and the complexities of the product itself which call for the use of complementary products and after-sales services. For example, a cosmetics company does not sell lipstick but the hope of looking pretty; an airline should not be selling plane tickets but a pleasureful vacation. A person taking a vacation needs not only an airline ticket, but also hotel accommodations, ground transportation, and sightseeing arrangements. Following the systems concept, an airline may define itself as selling a vacation package which includes air transportation, hotel reservations, meals, sightseeing, etc.

IBM offers a single source for all of the customer's data processing requirements, including hardware, operating systems, packaged software, maintenance, emergency repairs, and consulting services to train customer personnel and assist them in using the system. Thus, IBM offers a system consisting of different products and services to solve data processing problems. Xerox sells a system for duplicating written documents consisting of the copying machine, repair service, and paper which is fed into the machine.

Offering a system of products rather than a single product is a viable strategy in a number of ways. It makes the customer fully dependent on the company, which in turn gains monopolistic control over the market. Additionally, the system-of-products strategy blocks the way for the competition to move in. With such benefits this strategy is extremely useful in seeking growth, profitability, and market share. If this strategy is stretched beyond its limits, however, a company can get into legal problems. IBM, for instance, was charged by the Justice Department with monopolizing the computer market. In the aftermath of this, IBM has had to make changes in its strategy.

The successful implementation of this strategy requires a thorough understanding of customer requirements, the processes and functions the consumer must perform when using the product. Effective implementation of this strategy broadens both the company's concept of its product and the market opportunities for it, which in turn help meet the product/market objectives of growth, profitability, and market share.

PRODUCT-DESIGN STRATEGY

A business unit may offer a standard or custom-designed product for each individual customer. The decision about whether to offer a standard or customized product can be simplified by asking these questions, among others: "What are our capabilities?" and "What business are we in?" With respect to the first question, there is a danger of overidentification of capabilities for a specific product. If capabilities are overidentified, the business unit may be in trouble when the need for the product declines, since it will have difficulty relating the capabilities to other products. It is, therefore, desirable for a business unit to have a clear perspective of its capabilities. The answer to the second question determines the limits within which customizing may be pursued.

Between the two extremes of standard and customized products, a business unit may also offer standard products with modifications. These three strategic alternatives which come under the product-design strategy are discussed below.

Standard Products

The offering of standard products leads to two benefits. First, standard products are more amenable to the experience effect than are customized products, giving the business unit a cost benefit. Second, standard products can be merchandised nationally much more efficiently. Ford's Model T is a classic example of a successful standard product. However, the standard product has one major problem. It orients management thinking toward realization of per-unit cost savings to such an extent that even the need for small changes in product design because of shifts in market requirements may be ignored.

There is considerable evidence to suggest that larger firms derive greater profits from standardization by taking advantage of economies of scale and long production runs to produce at a low price.[27] Small companies, on the other hand, must make use of the major advantage they have over the giants, i.e., flexibility. Hence the standard-product strategy is generally more suitable for large companies. Small companies are better off as job shops, doing customized individual work at a higher margin.

A standard product is usually offered in different grades and styles with varying prices. This way, even though it is a standard product, customers are offered broader choices. Likewise, distribution channels get the product in different price ranges. In terms of results, the standard-product strategy helps in achieving the product/market objectives of growth, market share, and profitability.

---

[27]See Sidney Schoeffler, Robert D. Buzzell, and Donald F. Heany, "Impact of Strategic Planning on Profit Performance," *Harvard Business Review*, March–April, 1974, p. 142. See also Lynn W. Phillips, Dae R. Chang, and Robert D. Buzzell, "Product Quality, Cost Position and Business Performance: A Test of Some Key Hypotheses," *Journal of Marketing*, Spring, 1983, pp. 26–43.

Customized Products

Customized products are sold on the basis of the quality of the finished product, i.e., the extent to which the product meets the customer's specifications. Usually, the producer works closely with the customer, reviewing the progress of the product until completion. Unlike standard products, for customized products price is not a factor to be reckoned with. A customer expects to pay a premium price for a customized product. As mentioned above, a customized product is more suitable for small companies to offer. This is a broad statement which should not be interpreted to mean that large companies cannot successfully offer customized products. This will actually depend on the nature of the product. A small men's clothing outlet is in a better position to offer custom suits than a large men's suit manufacturer. On the other hand, GE is better suited to manufacture a custom-designed airplane engine for a military craft than a smaller business.

Over and above the price flexibility, dealing in customized products provides the company with useful experience in developing new standard products. A number of companies have been able to develop mass market products out of their custom work experience on NASA projects. The microwave oven, for example, is an offshoot of experience that companies gained on government contracts. Customized products also provide opportunities for inventing new products to meet other specific needs. In terms of results, this strategy is directed more toward realizing higher profitability than are other product-design strategies.

Standard Product with Modifications

The standard-product-with-modifications strategy represents a compromise between the two strategies discussed above. In being offered a standard product, a customer may be given the option to specify a limited number of desired modifications. A familiar example of this strategy is provided by the auto industry. The buyer of a new car can choose from among a number of modifications: for example, type of shift (standard or automatic), air conditioning, power brakes, power steering, size of engine, type of tires, and color of the car. While some modifications may be free, for the most part the customer will be expected to pay extra.

This strategy is directed toward realizing the benefits of both a standard and a customized product. By manufacturing a standard product, the business unit seeks economies of scale; at the same time, by offering modifications, the product is individualized to meet the specific requirements of the customer. This is borne out by the experience of a small water pump manufacturer which sold its products through distributors nationally. The company manufactured the basic pump in its facilities in Ohio and then had it shipped to its four branches in different parts of the country. At each branch the pumps were finished according to specifications requested by the distributors. Following this strategy, the company saved money in transportation (since the standard pump could be shipped in quantity) even while it provided customized pumps to the distributors.

Among other benefits, this strategy permits the business unit to keep in close contact with market needs which may be satisfied through product improvements and modifications. It also enhances the organization's reputation for flexibility in meeting customer requirements. It may also encourage new uses of the product. Other things being equal, this strategy can be useful in seeking growth, market share, and profitability.

PRODUCT-ELIMINATION STRATEGY

Marketers have believed for a long time that sick products should be eliminated. It is only in recent years that this belief has become a matter of strategy. It is believed that a business unit's various products represent a portfolio and that each of these products has a unique role to play in making the portfolio viable. If a product's role diminishes or if it does not fit into the portfolio, it ceases to be important.

When a product reaches the stage where continued support can no longer be justified because its performance falls short of expectations, it is desirable to pull the product out. Poor performance of a product is easy to spot. It may be characterized by any of the following:

1. Low profitability
2. Stagnant or declining sales volume or market share which would be too costly to build up
3. Risk of technological obsolescence
4. Entry into a mature or declining phase of the product life cycle
5. Poor fit with the business unit's strengths or declared mission

Products which are not able to limp along must be eliminated. They are a drain on a business unit's financial and managerial resources, which can be used more profitably elsewhere.

The three alternatives in the product-elimination strategy are harvesting, line simplification, and total-line divestment.

Harvesting

Harvesting refers to getting the most from the product while it lasts. It may be considered as controlled divestment whereby the business unit seeks to get the most cash flow it can from the business. Usually, harvesting strategy is applied to a product or business whose sales volume and/or market share are slowly declining. An effort is made to cut the costs associated with such a business to help improve the cash flow. Alternatively, prices are increased without simultaneous increase in costs. Harvesting leads to a slow decline in sales. When the business ceases to provide positive cash flow, it is divested.

DuPont followed the harvesting strategy in the case of its rayon business. Similarly, BASF Wyandotte applied harvesting to soda ash.[28] As another example, a few years ago, General Electric Company harvested its artillery business. Even without making any investment or raising prices, the business continued to provide positive cash flow and substantial profits. Lever Brothers applied this strategy to its Lifebuoy soap. The company continued to distribute this product for a long time, since despite higher price and virtually no promotional support, it continued to be in popular demand.[29]

Implementation of harvesting strategy requires severely curtailing new investment, reducing maintenance of facilities, slicing advertising and research budgets, reducing the number of models produced, curtailing the number of distribution channels, eliminating small customers, and cutting service in terms of delivery time, speed of repair, or sales assistance.

Ideally, harvesting strategy should be pursued when the following conditions are present:

1. The business entity is in a stable or declining market.
2. The business entity has a small market share, and building it up would be too costly; or it has a respectable market share that is becoming increasingly costly to defend or maintain.
3. The business entity is not producing especially good profits or may even be producing losses.
4. Sales would not decline too rapidly as a result of reduced investment.
5. The company has better uses for the freed-up resources.
6. The business entity is not a major component of the company's business portfolio.
7. The business entity does not contribute other desired features to the business portfolio such as sales stability or prestige.[30]

Line Simplification

Line-simplification strategy refers to a situation where a product line is trimmed to a manageable size by pruning the number and variety of products or services being offered. This is a defensive strategy which is adopted to keep the falling line stable. It is hoped that the simplification effort will help to restore the health of the line. This strategy becomes especially relevant during times of rising costs and resource shortages.

The application of this strategy in practice may be illustrated with the example of General Electric Company's housewares business. In the early 1970s, the housewares industry faced soaring costs and stiff com-

---

[28]K. R. Harrigan and Michael E. Porter, "End-Game Strategies for Declining Industries," *Harvard Business Review*, July–August, 1983, p. 118.

[29]Philip Kotler, "Harvesting Strategies for Weak Products," *Business Horizons*, August, 1978, pp. 15–22.

[30]*Ibid.*, pp. 17–18.

petition from Japan. GE took a hard look at its housewares business and raised such questions as: "Is this product segment mature? Is it one we should be harvesting? Is it one we should be investing money in and expanding?" Analysis showed that there was a demand out there for housewares, but it was just not attractive enough for GE at that time. The company ended production of blenders, fans, heaters, and vacuum cleaners since they were found to be on the down side of the growth curve and did not fit in with GE's strategy for growth.[31]

The following excerpt indicates how and why a confectionery firm routinely simplifies its line:

> A maker of confectionery that offers more than one hundred brands, flavors and packagings prunes its lines—regularly or routinely—of those items having the lowest profit contribution, sales volume, and vitality for future growth.
>
> Since the early 1970's, each individual product has been ranked on these three factors, and an "index of gross profitability" has been prepared for each in conjunction with annual marketing plans. These plans take into account longer-term objectives for the business, trends in consumer wants and expectations, competitive factors in the marketplace and, lastly, a deliberately ordered "prioritization" of the company's resources. Sales and profit performance are then checked against projected targets at regular intervals through the year, and the indexes of gross profitability are adjusted when necessary.
>
> The firm's chief executive emphasized that even individual items whose indexes of profitability are ranked at the very bottom are nonetheless profitable and paying their way by any customary standard of return on sales and investment. But the very lowest ranking items are regularly reviewed; and, on a judgmental basis, some are marked for pruning at the next convenient opportunity. This opportunity is most likely to arrive when stocks of special ingredients and packaging labels for the items have been exhausted.
>
> In a recent year, the company dropped 16 items that were judged to be too low on its index of gross profitability. Calculated and selective pruning is regarded within the company as a healthy means of working toward the best possible mix of products at all times. It has the reported advantages of increasing efficiencies in manufacturing as a result of cutting the "down time" between small runs, reducing inventories, and freeing resources for the expansion of the most promising items—or the development of new ones—without having to expand productive capacity. Another important benefit is that the sales force concentrates on a smaller line containing only the most profitable products with the largest volumes. On the negative side, however, it is acknowledged that pruning, as the company practices it, may result in near-term loss of sales for a line until growth of the rest of the items can compensate.[32]

---

[31]"G.E.'s New Strategy for Faster Growth," *Business Week*, July 8, 1972, p. 54.
[32]David S. Hopkins, *Business Strategies for Problem Products* (New York: The Conference Board, Inc., 1977), p. 29.

The implementation of line-simplification strategy can lead to a variety of benefits: potential cost savings from longer production runs; reduced inventories; and a more forceful concentration of marketing, R&D, and other efforts behind a shorter list of products. According to one point of view, a business unit with an extensive line could trim costs and add to revenues by cutting 10 percent of the varieties being offered.[33]

Despite the obvious merits, simplification efforts may sometimes be sabotaged. Those who have been closely involved with a product may sincerely feel either that the line as it is will revive when appropriate changes are made in the marketing mix, or that the sales and profits will turn up once temporary conditions in the marketplace turn around. Thus, careful maneuvering is needed on the part of management to simplify the line unhindered by corporate rivalries and intergroup pressures. As has been said:

> . . . putting products to death—or letting them die—is a drab business, and often engenders much of the sadness of a final parting with old and tried friends. . . . Too often management thinks of this as something that should be done but can wait until tomorrow. . . . This is why a definite procedure for deletion of products should be set up, and why the authority and responsibility for the various activities involved should be clearly and definitely assigned.[34]

The decision to drop a product from the line is more difficult if it is one of those core products that served as a foundation for the company to start the business. Such a product achieves the status of motherhood, and a company may like to keep it for nostalgic reasons. For example, the decision by General Motors to drop the Cadillac convertible was probably a difficult one to make in light of the prestige attached to the vehicle. On the other hand, the BIC Pen Corporation probably had little difficulty in disposing of the nonprofitable Waterman pen and ink products because the company viewed the decision from purely a business perspective: "Marcel Bic [BIC Pen Corporation's founder] was not the founder of Waterman and supposedly did not have strong feelings about the product."[35] Despite the emotional aspects of a product-deletion decision, the need to be objective in this matter cannot be overemphasized.

Companies establish their own criteria to screen different products for elimination. An industrial company uses the following procedure to eliminate a product line:

[33]David S. Hopkins, "New Emphasis in Marketing Strategies," *The Conference Board Record,* August, 1976, p. 35.

[34]Ralph S. Alexander, "The Death and Burial of Sick Products," *Journal of Marketing,* April, 1964, pp. 1–7.

[35]"Bic Pen Corporation," a case copyrighted by the President and Fellows of Harvard College, 1974, p. 2.

Assuming that a product is beginning to show a decline in terms of profitability, we try to determine the causes. It may simply be volume; and, if so, this would be reflected by the fact that the product has a variable margin which is good but still inadequate to absorb fixed costs. In such cases, we try to determine why the sales are low and whether something can be done to change the situation.

If the variable margin is bad, we try to see if it cannot be changed by product design, better purchasing, or additional automation to reduce labor costs. In those cases where either the variable margin cannot be improved, or volume cannot be increased to absorb fixed costs, we have no alternative but to abandon the product.

All of these continuing efforts are examined annually when we update our three-year plan. All staff members participate in this effort; and it is not difficult to determine whether a problem product has a solution or whether it should be written off.

A specific example of this is our line of a component for electric motors. We began to get information back from the field that our prices were no longer competitive. On the other hand, an examination of costs indicated that if we lowered the price, the line would go from a marginally profitable position to one of significant loss.

We analyzed our manufacturing techniques and compared them with the reasonable knowledge that we had concerning our competition. It became apparent that without an expenditure of approximately $500,000 for new equipment, we would not be able to produce the product for a price that would approach that of our two major competitors.

At the time, we sold about $1 million worth of this product, and we projected that the increased investment in manufacturing would provide a profit of approximately $14,000 before taxes on this volume. We decided that a three-and-one-half-year payout was inadequate and, therefore, phased out the line.

We have benefitted from this decision. First, the capital was invested in other product lines, thus increasing their profitability. In addition, by focusing our strengths on fewer products, we were able to increase market penetration on those remaining products so significantly that our total sales today are probably much higher than they would have been had we continued to manufacture the special component.[36]

In finalizing the decision, due attention must be given to honoring prior commitments. For example, replacement parts must be provided even though an item is dropped. Alexander cautions: "The firm that leaves a trail of uncared-for 'orphan' products cannot expect to engender much goodwill from dealers or users. Provision for the care and maintenance of the orphan is a necessary cost of deletion."[37]

A well-implemented program of product simplification can lead to

---

[36]David S. Hopkins, *op. cit.*, p. 32.
[37]Ralph S. Alexander, *op. cit.*

both growth and profitability. It may, however, be done at the cost of market share.

Total-Line Divestment

Divestment is a situation of reverse acquisition. It may also be a dimension of market strategy. But to the extent that the decision is approached from the product's perspective (i.e., to get rid of the product which is not doing well even in a growing market), it is an aspect of product strategy. Traditionally companies resisted divestment for the following reasons, which are principally economic or psychological in nature:

1. Divestment means negative growth in sales and assets, which runs counter to the business ethic of expansion.
2. It suggests defeat.
3. It requires changes in personnel, which can be painful and can result in perceived or real changes in status or have an adverse effect on the entire organization.
4. It may have to be effected at a price below book and thus have an adverse effect on the year's earnings.
5. The candidate for divestment may be carrying overhead, buying from other business units of the company, or contributing earnings.

With the advent of strategic planning in the 1960s, divestment became an accepted option for seeking faster growth. More and more companies are now willing to sell a business if the company will be better off strategically. These companies feel that divestment should not be regarded solely as a means of ridding the company of an unprofitable division or plan; rather, there are some persuasive reasons supporting the divestment of even a profitable and growing business.

Divestment of businesses which no longer fit the corporate strategic plan can occur for a number of reasons. For example:

—There is no longer a strategic connection between the base business and the part to be divested.
—The business experiences a permanent downturn, resulting in excess capacity for which no profitable alternative use can be identified.
—There may be inadequate capital to support the natural growth and development of the business.
—It may be dictated in the estate planning of the owner that a business is not to remain in the family.
—Selling a part of the business may release assets for use in other parts of the business where opportunities are growing.
—Divestment can improve the return on investment and growth rate both by ridding the company of units which are growing more slowly than the basic business and by providing cash for investment in faster-growing, higher-return operations.

Whatever the reason, a business that may have fit well into the overall corporate plan in the past suddenly can find itself in an environment which causes it to become a drain on the corporation, either financially, managerially, or opportunistically. Such circumstances would suggest divestment of the business in question.

Divestment helps restore a balanced portfolio for a business. If the company has too many high-growth businesses, particularly those at an early stage of development, its resources may be inadequate to fund growth. On the other hand, if a company has too many low-growth businesses, it will often generate more cash than is required for investment and will build up redundant equity. For a business to grow evenly over time while showing regular earnings increments, a portfolio of fast- and slow-growth businesses is necessary. Divestment can help achieve this kind of balance. Finally, divestment helps restore a business to a size which will not raise the eyebrows of the Justice Department and lead it to an antitrust action against the company.

The use of this strategy is reflected in GE's decision to divest its computer business in the early 1970s. In order to realize a return which GE considered adequate, the company would have needed to make additional heavy investments in its computer business. It figured it could use the money to greater advantage in an area other than computers. Hence, it divested its computer business by selling it to Honeywell.[38]

Essentially following the same reasoning, Olin Corporation divested its aluminum business on the grounds that maintaining its small 4 percent share required big capital expenditures that could be more usefully employed elsewhere in the company. Westinghouse sold its major appliance line because it needed at least an additional 3 percent beyond the 5 percent share it held before it could compete effectively against the industry leaders, GE and Whirlpool, which divided about half the total market between them.

In 1978 Union Carbide Corporation sold eight small businesses and its European petrochemical interests, whose sales exceeded $300 million a year. The company considered these divestments necessary to transform itself into a manageable organization.[39]

It is difficult to prescribe generalized criteria to determine whether to divest a business. The Boston Consulting Group, however, suggests raising the following questions, the answers to which should provide a starting point for considering divestment:

1. What is the earnings pattern of the unit? A key question is whether the unit is acting as a drag on corporate growth. If so, then management must determine whether there are any offsetting values. For example, are earnings stable compared to the fluctuation in

---

[38]William E. Fruhan, Jr., "Pyrrhic Victories in Fights for Market Share," *Harvard Business Review*, September–October, 1972, pp. 100–107.

[39]Jeffrey A. Tannenbaum, "Sliding Earnings Spur Union Carbide Corp. to Big Reform Effort," *The Wall Street Journal*, January 3, 1979, p. 1.

other parts of the company; and if so, is the low growth unit a substantial contributor to the overall debt capacity of the business? Management should also ask a whole series of "what if" type of questions relating to earnings: the effect of additional funding? new management? a change in location? etc.

2. Does the business generate any cash? In many situations, a part of a company will be showing a profit but not generating any discretionary cash. That is, every dime of cash flow must be pumped right back into the operation just to keep it going at *existing levels*. Does this type of operation make any real contribution to the company? Will it eventually? What could the unit be sold for? What would be done with cash from this sale?

3. Is there any tie-in value—financial or operating—with the existing business? Are there any synergies in marketing, production, R&D? Is the business counter-cyclical? Does it represent a platform for growth—internally-based or through acquisitions?

4. Will selling the unit help or hurt the acquisitions effort? What will be the immediate impact on earnings (write-offs, operating expenses)? What effect, if any, will the sale have on the image in the stock market? Will the sale have any effect on potential acquisitions ("will I be sold down the river")? Will the divestment be functional in terms of the new size achieved? Will the smaller size facilitate acquisitions by broadening the "market" of acceptable candidates, or, by contrast, will the company become less credible because of the smaller size?[40]

In conclusion, a company should undertake a continuing in-depth analysis of the market share, growth prospects, profitability, and cash-generating power of each business. As a result of such a review, a business may have to be divested to maintain balance in the company's total business. This, however, is feasible only when the company develops enough self-discipline to avoid increasing sales volume beyond a desirable size and instead buys and sells businesses with the sole objective of enhancing overall corporate performance.

NEW-PRODUCT STRATEGY

New-product development is an essential activity for companies seeking growth. By adopting the new-product strategy as their posture, companies are better able to sustain competitive pressures on their existing products and make headway. The implementation of this strategy has become easier because of technological innovations and the willingness of customers to accept new ways of doing things.

In a recent survey of 700 companies, Booz, Allen & Hamilton reported that these companies were likely to derive 31 percent of their prof-

---

[40]"Divestment and Growth," an informal statement published by the Boston Consulting Group, 1969.

its over the next five years from new products.[41] This shows the importance that companies attach to new products. Despite their importance in strategy determination, implementation of new-product programs is far from easy. Too many products never make it in the market. The risks and penalties of product failure require that companies move judiciously in adopting the new-product strategy.

Interestingly, however, the mortality rate of new product ideas has declined considerably since the 1960s. In 1968, on average, 58 new product ideas were considered for every successful new product. In 1981, only seven ideas were required to generate one successful new product. However, there are variations by industry. Consumer nondurable companies consider more than twice as many new product ideas to generate one successful new product as industrial or consumer durable manufacturers.[42]

Top management can effect the implementation of new-product strategy: first, by establishing policies and broad strategic directions for the kinds of new products the company should seek; second, by providing the kind of leadership that will create the environmental climate needed to stimulate innovative drive in the organization; and third, by instituting review and monitoring procedures so that the manager is involved at the right decision points and can know whether or not work schedules are being met in ways that are consistent with the broad policy direction.[43]

The term "new product" is used in different senses. To avoid any confusion, new-product strategy for our purposes will be split into three alternatives: (1) product improvement/modification, (2) product imitation, and (3) new-product development.

Product improvement/modification is the introduction of a new version or improved model of the product, such as "new improved Crest." Usually the improvements and modifications are achieved by adding new features or style, changing processing requirements, and altering product ingredients. When a company introduces a product which is already on the market but new to the company, it is following product-imitation strategy. For example, Schick was imitating when it introduced a double-blade razor to compete with Gillette's Trac II. For our purposes, a new product will be defined as one which has a completely new approach in fulfilling customer desires (examples: Polaroid camera, television, typewriter, etc.) or one which replaces existing ways of satisfying customer desires (example: replacement of slide rules by pocket calculators).[44]

New-product development follows the experience curve concept—

---

[41]*New Products Management for the 1980s* (New York: Booz, Allen, & Hamilton Inc., 1982).

[42]*Ibid.*, p. 14.

[43]See Robert G. Cooper, "The Dimensions of Industrial Firms New Product Strategies," *Working Paper* (Montreal: Faculty of Management, McGill University, 1982).

[44]Ben M. Enis, Raymond La Garce, and Arthur E. Prell, "Extending the Product Life Cycle," *Business Horizons*, June, 1977, pp. 44–56.

that is, the more you do something, the more efficient you become at doing it (for additional details, see Chapter 17). Experience in introducing products enables companies to improve new-product performance. Specifically, with increased new-product experience, companies improve new-product profitability by reducing the cost per introduction. More precisely, with each doubling of the number of new-product introductions, the cost of each introduction declines at a predictable and constant rate. For example, for the 13,000 new-product introductions between 1976 and 1981 in the 700 companies surveyed by Booz, Allen & Hamilton, the experience effect yielded a 71 percent cost curve. At each doubling of the number of new products introduced, the cost of each introduction declined by 29 percent.[45]

Product Improvement/Modification

An existing product of a company may reach a stage which requires that something be done to keep it viable. The product may have reached the maturity stage of the product life cycle because of shifts in environment, thus ceasing to provide an adequate return. Or new-product, pricing, distribution, and promotion strategies employed by competitors may have reduced the status of the product to a "me-too" category. At that stage management has two options: either to eliminate the product or to revitalize it by making improvements and/or modifications. Improvements and/or modifications are achieved by redesigning, remodeling, or reformulating so that the product satisfies customer needs more fully. This strategy seeks not only to restore the health of the product, but also sometimes to help in distinguishing it from those of competitors. *Fortune*'s description of Kodak's strategy is relevant here:

> On the one hand, the longer a particular generation of cameras can be sold, the more profitable it will become. On the other hand, amateur photographers tend to use less film as their cameras age and lose their novelty; hence it is critical that Kodak keep the camera population eternally young by bringing on new generations from time to time. In each successive generation, Kodak tries to increase convenience and reliability in order to encourage even greater film consumption per camera—a high "burn rate," as the company calls it. In general, the idea is to introduce as few major new models as possible while ringing in frequent minor changes powerful enough to stimulate new purchases.
>
> Kodak has become a master of this marketing strategy. Amateur film sales took off with a rush after 1963. That year the company brought out the first cartridge-loading, easy-to-use instamatic, which converted many people to photography and doubled film usage per camera. A succession of new features and variously priced models fol-

---

[45]*New Products Management for the 1980s*, p. 18.

lowed to help stimulate film consumption for a decade. Then Kodak introduced the pocket instamatic, which once again boosted film use—both because of its novelty and because of its convenience. Seven models of that generation have since appeared.[46]

Kodak's strategy as described above points out that it is never enough just to introduce a new product. The real payoff comes if it is managed in such a way that it continues to flourish year after year in a changing and competitive marketplace.

It is said that Procter & Gamble has made 55 significant modifications in Tide since it was introduced in the 1950s.[47] GM's downsizing efforts in its different cars to meet the demands of the marketplace and the federal government for better gas mileage provide another illustration of the effectiveness and usefulness of the product-modification strategy. When the Arab oil embargo was imposed toward the end of 1973, GM had the worst average gas mileage, 12 miles per gallon, among U.S. automakers. Following the embargo in 1974, as buyers turned away from gas guzzlers in panic, GM's share of the U.S. new car market slid to 42 percent, its lowest share since 1952 (excluding the strike year of 1970). Just three years later, in the 1977-model year, the average mileage of GM cars, 17.8 miles per gallon, was the best among the three largest automakers. GM's big cars alone averaged 15 miles per gallon, or 3 miles per gallon better than the entire 1974 fleet. Largely as a result of the downsizing modifications, the company's market share in 1977 rebounded to about 46 percent.[48]

There is no magic formula for restoring the health of a product. Occasionally it is the ingenuity of the manager that may bring to light the desired cure for the product. Generally, however, a complete review of the product from marketing perspectives will be needed to analyze the underlying causes and come up with the modifications and improvements necessary to restore it to health.

To identify these options it may be necessary to tear down the competing product or products and make a detailed comparative analysis of quality and price. One framework for such an analysis is illustrated in Exhibit 13-2.

The basic premise of Exhibit 13-2 is that by comparing its product with that of its competitors, a company will be able to identify unique product strengths on the basis of which to pursue modifications and improvements. The use of the analysis suggested by Exhibit 13-2 may be illustrated with reference to a Japanese manufacturer. Back in 1978, Japan's amateur color film market was dominated by three companies, Kodak, Fuji, and Sakura, the last two being Japanese companies. For the past

---

[46]Bro Uttal, "Eastman Kodak's Orderly Two-Front War," *Fortune*, September, 1976, p. 123.

[47]Nancy Giges, *op. cit.*, p. 1.

[48]Charles G. Burck, "How G.M. Turned Itself Around," *Fortune*, January 16, 1978.

EXHIBIT 13-2   Product-Change Options After Competitive Tear-Down

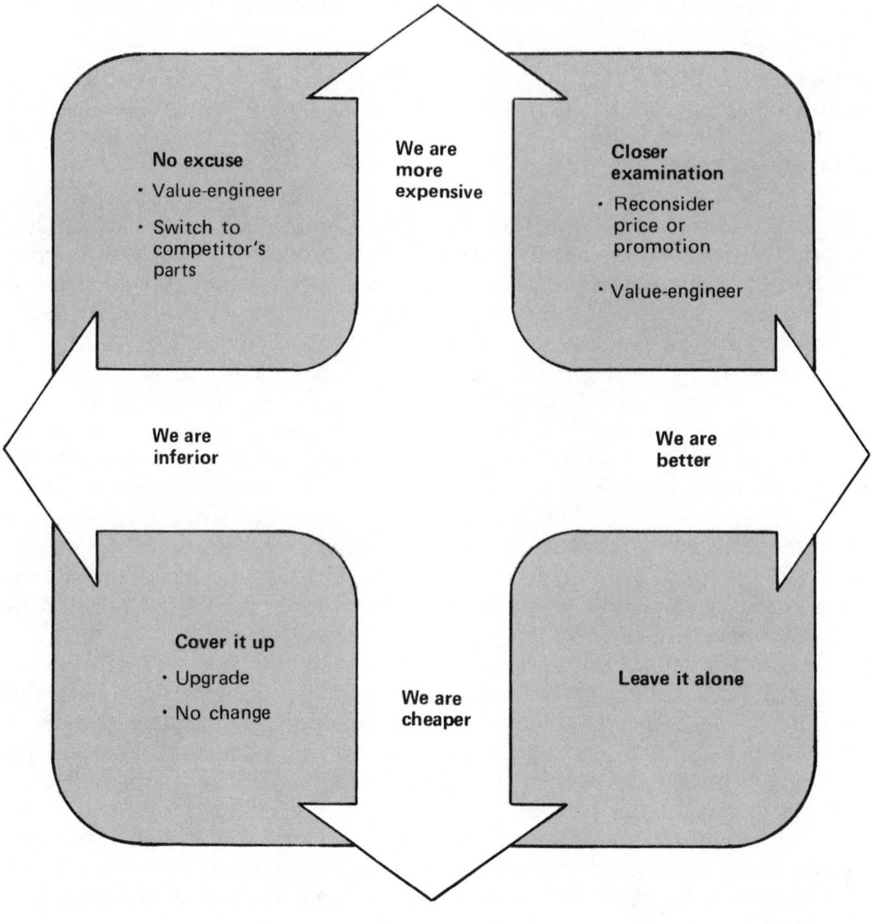

No excuse	We are more expensive	**Closer examination**
• Value-engineer		• Reconsider price or promotion
• Switch to competitor's parts		• Value-engineer

We are inferior   We are better

Cover it up		
• Upgrade		**Leave it alone**
• No change	We are cheaper	

Source: Kenichi Ohmae, "Effective Strategies for Competitive Success," *The McKinsey Quarterly,* Winter, 1978, p. 57. Reprinted by permission of the publisher.

15 years Fuji had been gaining market share, while Sakura, the market leader in the early 1950s with over half the market, was losing the market to both its competitors. By 1976 it held only about 16 percent of the market share. Marketing research showed that, more than anything else, Sakura was the victim of an unfortunate word association. Its name in Japanese means "cherry blossom," suggesting a soft, blurry, pinkish image. The name Fuji, however, was associated with the blue skies and white snow of Japan's sacred mountain. Being in no position to change perceptions,

the company decided to analyze the market from structural, economic, and customer points of view.

The company found a growing cost consciousness among film customers: Amateur photographers commonly left one or two frames unexposed in a 36-exposure roll, but they almost invariably tried to squeeze extra exposures onto the 20-exposure rolls. Here Sakura saw an opportunity. It decided to introduce a 24-exposure film. Its marginal costs would be trivial, but its big competitors would face significant penalties in following suit. Sakura was prepared to cut down its prices if the competition lowered the price of their 20-frame rolls. Its aim was twofold. First, it would exploit the growing cost-mindedness of users. Second, and more important, it would be drawing attention to the economic issue, where it had a relative advantage, and away from the image issue, where it could not win. Sakura's strategy paid off. Its market share increased from 16 percent to over 30 percent.[49] Overall, the product-improvement strategy is conducive to achieving growth, market share, and profitability alike.

Product Imitation

Not all companies like to be the first in the market with a new product. They let someone else take the initiative. If the innovation is successful, they ride the bandwagon of the successful innovation by imitating. In the case of innovations protected by patents, imitation must wait until the patent expires. In the absence of a patent, however, the imitating companies work diligently to design and produce a product not very different from the innovator's product to compete vigorously with the innovator.

The imitation strategy can be justified in that it transfers the risk of introducing the unproven idea/product to someone else. It also saves investments in research and development. This strategy particularly suits companies with limited resources. Many companies, as a matter of fact, develop such talent that they can imitate any product, no matter how complicated. With a limited investment in R&D, the imitator may sometimes have a lower cost, which gives it a pricing advantage in the market over the leader.

Another important reason for pursuing the imitation strategy may be to gainfully transfer the special talent a company may have for one product to other similar products. For example, the BIC Pen Corporation decided to enter the razor blade business since it thought it could successfully use its aggressive marketing posture there. In the early 1970s Hanes Corporation gained resounding success with L'eggs, an inexpensive pantyhose that sold on free-standing racks in food and drugstore outlets.

The imitation strategy may also be adopted on defensive grounds. Being sure of its existing product(s), a company may initially ignore new

---

[49]Kenichi Ohmae, "Effective Strategies for Competitive Success," *The McKinsey Quarterly,* Winter, 1978, pp. 56–57.

developments in the field. If the new developments become overbearing, however, they may cut into the ground held by the existing product. In such a situation, a company may be forced into imitating the new development as a matter of survival. Colorado's Adolph Coors Company conveniently ignored the introduction of light beer and dismissed Miller Lite as a fad. Many years later, however, the company was getting bludgeoned by Miller Lite. Also, Anheuser-Busch with its light beer began to challenge Coors' supremacy in the California market, where Coors' market share in 1977 went down from 41 percent to 23 percent. The matter became so serious that Coors decided to abandon its one-product tradition, and in the summer of 1978 it introduced a low-calorie light beer.[50]

Imitation also works well for companies that want to enter new markets without resorting to expensive acquisitions or special new-product development programs. For example, Owens-Illinois, Inc., is adapting heavy-duty laboratory glassware into novelty drinking glasses for home bars.

While imitation does prevent the risks involved in innovation, it is wrong to assume that every imitation of a successful product will succeed. The market program of an imitation should be as carefully chalked out and implemented as that of an innovation. This point may be illustrated with reference to R. J. Reynolds Tobacco Company's Real cigarette. Real, with 9 milligrams of tar, is suffering from the massive shakeout that is occurring in the low-tar segment (15 mg. or less) of the market. In less than three years, that segment came from almost nowhere to 25 percent of unit sales as millions found low-tar cigarettes to be an acceptable alternative which had a lower risk of damage to their health. Low-tar brands such as Reynolds' 11-mg. Vantage and Philip Morris's 9-mg. Merit are selling well because they were available before the low-tar craze took off. Kent Golden Lights did well because they capitalized on smokers' familiarity with parent brands. But the brands that were late entries, such as Real and Liggett & Myers' Decade, are hurting. Real's performance is disappointing because the company spent a huge amount of money in promoting it—almost $40 million in just six months. Among other reasons given, it is said that Real failed to perform well in the market because the company violated its own system by bypassing traditional test marketing.[51] Thus, even a proven imitation may fail unless all elements of the marketing mix are properly scrutinized and implemented.

Imitation strategy is most useful for seeking increases in market share and growth.

Product Innovation

Product-innovation strategy includes introducing a new product to replace an existing product in order to satisfy a need in an entirely dif-

---

[50]John Huey, "Men at Coors Beer Find the Old Ways Don't Work Anymore," *The Wall Street Journal*, January 19, 1979, p. 1.
[51]"Why Real Missed Its Target," *Business Week*, April 24, 1978, p. 27.

ferent way or to provide a new approach to satisfy an existing or latent need. This strategy connotes that the entrant is the first firm to develop and introduce the product. The ballpoint pen is an example of a new product which replaced the fountain pen. The electronic computer was a new approach for handling the information needs of people.

Product innovation is an important characteristic of U.S. industry. Year after year companies spend billions of dollars on research and development to innovate. In 1983, for example, American industry spent about $40 billion on R&D over and above the R&D supported by the federal government. R&D expenditures are expected to rise at an average of 3 percent annually throughout the 1980s.[52] This shows that industry takes a purposeful attitude toward new-product and new-process development.

Product innovation, however, does not come easily. Besides involving major commitment in terms of dollars, it requires heavy doses of managerial time spent in cutting across organizational lines. And still the innovation may fail to make a mark in the market. A number of companies have discovered the risks in this game. Among them is AM International Inc., which lost $245 million in 1981 as it faltered in an attempt to shift from its traditional electromechanical lines to electronic ones. AM is now in bankruptcy. A decade earlier, National Cash Register Company was forced to write off $139 million when it tried a similar game. RCA, General Electric and Sylvania—leaders in vacuum tube technology—lost out when transistor technology revolutionized the business.[53]

Most innovations are produced by large organizations. Initially an individual or a group of individuals may be behind it. But a stage is reached where individual efforts require corporate support to finally develop and launch the product in the market.

Typically the development of a product innovation passes through various stages such as idea, screening, business analysis, development of a prototype, test market, and commercialization. The idea may emerge from different sources such as customers, private researchers, university researchers, employees, research labs, and so on. An idea may be generated in recognizing a consumer need, or just in pursuing a scientific endeavor, hoping it may lead to a viable product. Companies follow different procedures to screen ideas and choose a few for further study. If an idea appears promising, it will be carried to the stage of business analysis, which may consist of investment requirements, revenue and expenditure projections, and financial analysis regarding return on investment, pay-back period, and cash flow. Thereafter, a few prototype products will be produced in order to examine engineering and manufacturing aspects of the product. A few sample products based on the prototype will be produced for market testing. After changes suggested in market testing

---

[52]Philip Kotler, *Marketing Management*, 5th Ed. (Englewood Cliffs, NJ: Prentice-Hall, 1984), p. 101.
[53]Richard N. Foster, "A Call for Vision in Managing Technology," *The McKinsey Quarterly*, Summer, 1982, p. 26.

have been incorporated, the innovation may be commercially launched.

Exhibit 13-3 shows a self-administered questionnaire for measuring the new-products management perspectives of a business unit. This questionnaire may be completed to determine what changes, if any, the business unit should make to revamp its new-products development effort.

Procter & Gamble's development of Pringle's is a classic case of recognizing a need in a consumer market and then painstakingly working away to meet it. To give the background of P&G's involvement in this product: Americans consume about $1 billion worth of potato chips annually. Manufacturers of potato chips face a variety of problems. Chips made in the traditional way are so fragile that they can rarely be shipped for more than 200 miles, and even then a quarter of the chips get broken. They also spoil quickly; their shelf life is hardly two months. These characteristics have kept potato-chip manufacture split into many small, regional operations, and nobody before P&G had applied much technology to the product since it was invented in 1853.

P&G knew these problems because it sold edible oils to the potato-chip industry, and it set out to solve them. Instead of slicing potatoes and frying them in the traditional way, P&G's engineers developed a process somewhat akin to papermaking. They dehydrated and mashed the potatoes and pressed them for frying into a precise shape, permitting the chips to be stacked neatly on top of each other in a hermetically sealed container that resembles a tennis ball can. Pringle's potato chips stay whole and have a shelf life of at least a year.[54]

After a new product is screened through the lab, the division that will manufacture it takes over and finances all further development and testing. In some companies division managers show little interest in taking on new products because the costs of introduction are heavy and hold down short-term profits. At P&G, executives ensure that a manager's short-term record is not marred by the cost of a new introduction.

Before a new P&G product is actually introduced in the market, it must prove that it has a demonstrable margin of superiority over its prospective competitors. A development team begins refining the product by trying variations of the basic formula, testing its performance under almost any conceivable condition, and altering its appearance. Eventually a few alternative versions of the product are produced and tested with a large number of P&G employees. If the product gets the approval of the employees, the company presents it to panels of consumers for further testing. P&G feels satisfied if a proposed product is chosen by fifty-five out of a hundred consumers tested. Though Pringle's potato chips passed all these tests, they have yet to show any profits for P&G.

There is hardly any doubt that if an innovation is successful, it pays off lavishly. However, it is a highly risky strategy requiring heavy commitment and having a low probability of achieving a breakthrough. Thus,

---

[54]Peter Vanderwicken, "P&G's Secret Ingredient," *Fortune*, July, 1974, p. 75.

EXHIBIT 13-3 New-Products Management Scorecard

To determine how well your business unit manages new products,
rate your business from 1 -10 points for each question:
10 = "Fully Meets"; 5 = "Partially Meets"; and 1 = "Does Not Meet"

	SCORE
1. Our corporate growth plan includes an explicit strategic description on the role of internally developed new products over the next five years.	_____
2. We have a well-defined new product strategy which identifies the financial gap and strategic roles which new products must satisfy.	_____
3. We establish different hurdle rates, based on associated risk.	_____
4. We have had a systematic, yet adaptive, new products process in place for at least five years.	_____
5. Idea generation for us begins **after** we have identified external market niches and assessed our internal competitive strengths.	_____
6. We have a formalized monitoring and tracking system in place to measure cost per introduction and new product performance against established objectives.	_____
7. We have compensation programs that encourage entrepreneurship, reward risk-takers, and reinforce innovative management.	_____
8. We have a clear understanding of who is responsible for new product development.	_____
9. Top management provides consistent commitment to new products in terms of funds and requisite managerial know-how.	_____
10. We adapt our new products organization to match the requirements of our new products portfolio.	_____
TOTAL	_____

SCORE

90-100	We are one of the best!
80-89	Improvement areas exist, but we're in good shape.
70-79	We should consider making changes to our new products program.
< 70	We better get some assistance in managing new products.

Source: *New Products Management for the 1980s* (New York: Booz, Allen & Hamilton, 1982). Reprinted by permission.

the choice of this strategy should be dictated by a company's financial and managerial strengths and willingness to take risks.

Suggested below is an approach which may be used to successfully manage innovations. As a company grows more complex and decentralized, its new-product development effort may fail to keep pace with change, weakening vital lines between marketing and technical people, leaving key decisions to be made by default, and resulting in ultimate loss of competitive edge. To solve the problem, as shown in Exhibit 13-4a, both technical and market opportunity may be plotted on a grid. From this grid, innovations may be grouped into three classes: *heavy emphasis* (deserving full support, including basic R&D); *selective opportunistic development* (i.e., may be good or may be bad; requires a careful approach and top management attention); and *limited defensive support* (i.e., merits only minimum support). Exhibit 13-4b lists the relevant kinds of programs for each area. The above approach helps in gearing research efforts to priority strategic projects.

DIVERSIFICATION STRATEGY

Diversification refers to seeking unfamiliar products or markets, or both, in pursuing growth. Every company is best at certain products; diversification requires substantially different knowledge, thinking, skills, and processes. Thus, diversification is at best a risky strategy, and a company should choose this path only when current product/market orientation does not seem to provide further opportunities for growth. A few examples will illustrate the point that diversification does not automatically promise success. CNA Financial Corporation faced catastrophe when it expanded the scope of its business from insurance to real estate and mutual funds and ended up being acquired by Loews Corporation. Schrafft's restaurants did little for Pet Incorporated. Pacific Southwest Airlines acquired rental cars and hotels, only to see its stock decline from $49^{1}/_{4}$ before diversification in 1969 to $4^{1}/_{4}$ in 1975.[55] The diversification decision is a major step which must be taken carefully. On the basis of a sample from 200 of the *Fortune* 500 firms and the PIMS database (see Chapter 17), Biggadike notes that it takes an average of 10 to 12 years before the ROI from diversification entries equals that of mature businesses.[56]

The term "diversification" must be distinguished from integration and merger. *Integration* refers to accumulation of additional business in a

---

[55]Paul I. Brown, "Diversifying Successfully," *Business Horizons*, August, 1976, p. 85. See also R. Timothy Breene and Stephen C. Coley, "Adding Value Through Diversification," *The McKinsey Quarterly*, Winter, 1984, pp. 64–73.

[56]E. Ralph Biggadike, "The Risky Business of Diversification," *Harvard Business Review*, May–June, 1979, pp. 103–111. See also E. Ralph Biggadike, *Corporate Diversification: Entry Strategy and Performance* (Boston, MA: Division of Research, Harvard Business School, 1979).

EXHIBIT 13-4   Managing Innovations

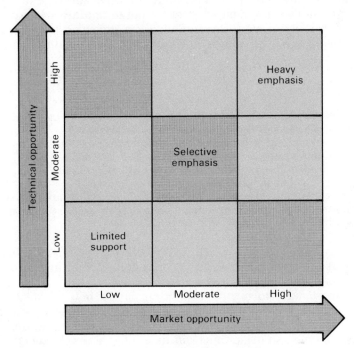

(a) The R&D Effort Portfolio

	R&D program elements					
R&D emphasis	Level of funding	Primary focus of work	Level of basic research	Technical risk	Acceptable time for payoff	Projects to exceed or maintain competitive parity
Heavy	High	Balance between new and existing products	High	High	Long	Many
Selective	Medium	Mainly existing products	Low	Medium	Medium	Few
Limited	Low	Existing processes	Very low	Low	Short	Very few

(b) Implied Nature of R&D Effort

Source: Richard N. Foster, "Linking R&D to Strategy," *Business Horizons*, December, 1980. Copyright, 1980, by the Foundation for the School of Business at Indiana University. Reprinted by permission.

field through participation in more of the stages between raw materials and the ultimate market, or through more intensive coverage of a single stage. *Merger* implies a combination of corporate entities which may or may not result in integration. Diversification is a strategic alternative which implies deriving revenues and profits from different products and markets.

Ansoff states the following factors which lead companies to seek diversification:

1. Firms diversify when their objectives can no longer be met within the product/market scope defined by expansion.
2. A firm may diversify because the retained cash exceeds the total expansion needs.
3. A firm may diversify when diversification opportunities promise greater profitability than expansion opportunities.
4. Firms may continue to explore diversification when the available information is not reliable enough to permit a conclusive comparison between expansion and diversification.[57]

Diversification can take place at either the corporate or the business unit level. At the corporate level, it typically entails entering a promising business outside the scope of existing business units. At the business unit level, it is most likely to involve expanding into a new segment of the industry in which the business now participates. The problems encountered at both levels are similar and may differ only in magnitude.[58]

Diversification strategies might include internal development of new products or markets (including development of international markets for current products); acquisition of an appropriate firm or firms; a joint venture with a complementary organization; licensing of new product technologies; and importing or distributing a line of products manufactured by another company. The final choice of an entry strategy in most cases involves a combination of the aforementioned alternatives. This combination is determined on the basis of available opportunities and of consistency with the company's objectives and available resources.

Caterpillar Tractor Company's entry into the field of diesel engines is a case of internal diversification. Since 1972 the company has poured over $1 billion into developing new diesel engines " . . . in what must rank as one of the largest internal diversifications by a U.S. corporation." By 1983 as much as 25 percent of Caterpillar's sales came from diesel engines. Caterpillar's decision was justified by soaring energy costs. Because a diesel is 45 percent more fuel-efficient than a gasoline engine,

---

[57]I. Igor Ansoff, *Corporate Strategy* (New York: McGraw-Hill Book Co., 1965), pp. 129–130.
[58]See Richard P. Rumelt, *Strategy Structure and Economic Performance* (Boston, MA: Division of Research, Harvard Business School, 1974).

Caterpillar has moved into a variety of smaller road and off-the-road vehicles.[59]

Hershey Foods' venture into the restaurant business was achieved by buying the Friendly Ice Cream Corporation. This illustrates diversification by acquisition. Hershey adopted the diversification strategy for growth since its traditional business, chocolate and candy, is stagnant because of the decline in candy consumption with the sharp increases in cocoa prices, and because of change in customer habits.

An empirical study on entry strategy shows that higher barriers are more likely to be associated with acquisition than with entry through internal development. Thus, in choosing between these two entry modes, business unit managers should take into account, among other factors, the entry barriers surrounding the market and the cost of breaching them. Despite high apparent barriers, the entrant's relatedness to the new entry may make direct entry financially more desirable.[60]

Essentially, there are three different forms of diversification which a company may pursue: concentric diversification, horizontal diversification, and conglomerate diversification.

Concentric Diversification

Concentric diversification bears a close synergistic relationship to either the company's marketing or its technology. Thus, new products that are introduced share a common thread with the firm's existing products either through marketing or production. Usually the new products are directed to a new group of customers. Texas Instruments' venture into digital watches illustrates this type of diversification. Using its expertise in integrated-circuits technology, the company developed a new product that appealed to a new set of customers. On the other hand, PepsiCo's venture into the fast-food business through the acquisition of Pizza Hut is a case of concentric diversification in which the new product bears a synergistic relationship to the company's existing experience in the area of marketing.

While a diversification move per se is risky, concentric diversification does not lead a company into an entirely new world, since in one of the two major fields (technology or marketing), the company will operate in familiar territory. The relationship of the new product to the firm's existing product(s), however, may or may not mean much. All that the

---

[59]"A Revved-up Market for Diesel Engine Makers," *Business Week,* February 5, 1979, p. 76.

[60]George S. Yip, "Diversification Entry: Internal Development Versus Acquisition," *Strategic Management Journal,* October–December, 1982, pp. 331–346. See also Malcolm S. Salter and Wolf A. Weinhold, "Choosing Compatible Acquisitions," *Harvard Business Review,* January–February, 1981, pp. 117–127.

realization of synergy does is make the task easier; it does not necessarily make it successful. For example, Gillette entered the market for pocket calculators in 1974 and digital watches in 1976, but abandoned both businesses later. Both pocket calculators and digital watches were sold to mass markets where Gillette had the expertise and experience. Despite the marketing synergy, it failed to successfully sell either calculators or digital watches. Gillette found that these lines of business called for strategies totally different from those it followed in selling its existing products.[61] Two lessons can be drawn from Gillette's experience. One, there may be other strategic reasons for successfully launching a new product in the market besides commonality of markets or technology. Two, the commonality should be analyzed in breadth and depth before drawing conclusions on the transferability of current strengths to the new product.

Philip Morris's acquisition of Miller Brewing Company illustrates how a company may achieve marketing synergies through concentric diversification. Cigarettes and beer are distributed through many of the same retail outlets, and Philip Morris had been dealing with them for years. In addition, both products serve hedonistic consumer markets. Small wonder, therefore, that the cigarette merchandising and marketing research techniques and emotional promotion appeals worked equally well for beer. Miller moved from seventh to second place in the beer industry in the short span of six years.

Horizontal Diversification

Horizontal diversification refers to new products which technologically are unrelated to a company's existing products, but can be sold to the same group of customers to whom existing products are sold. A classic case of this form of diversification is Procter & Gamble's entry into different businesses such as potato chips (Pringle's), toothpaste (Crest and Gleem), coffee (Folger's), etc. Traditionally a soap-products company, P&G diversified into the above products, which were aimed at the same customer who bought soap.

Note that in the case of concentric diversification, the new product may have certain common ties with the marketing of an existing product of the company, but it is sold to a new set of customers. In horizontal diversification the customers for the new product are drawn from the same ranks as those for the existing product.

Other things being equal, in a competitive environment the horizontal-diversification strategy is more desirable if the present customers are favorably disposed toward the company and if one can expect this loyalty to continue for the new product. Loyalty can help initially in successfully introducing the product; in the long run, however, the new prod-

---

[61]"Gillette: After Diversification That Failed," *Business Week*, February 28, 1977, pp. 58–62.

uct must stand on its own. Thus, for example, if product quality is lacking, or promotion is not effective, or the price is not right, the new product will flop despite customer loyalty to the company's other products. Thus, while Crest and Folger's made it for P&G, Pringle's has been disappointing, even though all these products are sold to the same "loyal" customers. In other words, horizontal diversification should not be regarded as a route to success in all cases. An important limitation of horizontal diversification is that the new product is introduced to be marketed in the same economic environment as the existing product, which leads to rigidity and instability. Stated differently, horizontal diversification tends to increase the company's dependence on a few market segments.

Conglomerate Diversification

In conglomerate diversification, the new product bears no relationship to either the marketing or the technology of the existing product(s). In other words, through conglomerate diversification a company launches itself into an entirely new product/market arena. International Telephone and Telegraph Corporation's ventures into bakery products (Continental Baking Company), insurance (Hartford Fire Insurance Company), car rentals (Avis Rent A Car System, Inc.), and the hotel business (Sheraton Corporation) illustrate the implementation of conglomerate diversification in practice. ITT divested some of these businesses a few years ago upon the demand of the Justice Department.

It is necessary to remember here that companies do not flirt with unknown products in unknown markets without having some hidden strengths to handle conglomerate diversification. For example, the managerial style required for a new product to prosper may be just the same as the one the company already has. Thus, managerial style becomes the basis of synergy between the new product and an existing product. By the same token, another single element may serve as a dominant factor in making a business attractive for diversification. As Conrad has said:

> Such could be the case for a cigarette manufacturer. Its general business acumen might not seem to suggest diversification opportunities, yet its extensive capabilities in advertising might hold an answer. Many companies would be afraid of the massive advertising techniques and budgets wielded in the cosmetics field, but this might be just what a cigarette company is basically suited to handle. Similarly, a cigarette manufacturer might do well in the razor blade business, and a razor blade manufacturer might succeed in the ballpoint pen business.[62]

Inasmuch as conglomerate diversification does not bear an obvious relationship to a company's existing business, there is some question as to

---

[62]Gordon R. Conrad, "Unexplored Assets for Diversification," *Harvard Business Review*, September–October, 1963, p. 71.

why companies adopt it. There are two major advantages of conglomerate diversification. One, it improves the profitability and flexibility of a firm by venturing into businesses which have better economic prospects than the firm's existing business. Two, a conglomerate firm, because of its size, gets a better reception in capital markets.

Overall, this type of diversification, if successful, has the potential of providing increased growth and profitability.

SUMMARY

Product strategies reflect the mission of the business unit and the business it is in. Following the marketing concept, the choice of product strategy should bear a close relationship to the market strategy of the company. The various product strategies and the alternatives under each strategy discussed in this chapter are:

1. Product-positioning strategy
   a. Positioning a single brand
   b. Positioning multiple brands
2. Product-repositioning strategy
   a. Repositioning among existing customers
   b. Repositioning among new users
   c. Repositioning for new uses
3. Product-overlap strategy
   a. Competing brands
   b. Private labeling
   c. Dealing with original-equipment manufacturers (OEMs)
4. Product-scope strategy
   a. Single product
   b. Multiple products
   c. System of products
5. Product-design strategy
   a. Standard products
   b. Customized products
   c. Standard product with modifications
6. Product-elimination strategy
   a. Harvesting
   b. Line simplification
   c. Total-line divestment
7. New-product strategy
   a. Product improvement/modification
   b. Product imitation
   c. Product innovation
8. Diversification strategy
   a. Concentric diversification
   b. Horizontal diversification
   c. Conglomerate diversification

The nature of different strategies was discussed, and their relevance for different types of companies was examined. Adaptations of different strategies in practice were illustrated with citations from published sources.

DISCUSSION QUESTIONS

1. *Discuss how a business unit may avoid problems of cannibalism among competing brands.*
2. *How may a church reposition itself among existing and new "customers" to increase its membership?*
3. *Conceptualize how a lagging brand (assume a grocery product) may be repositioned for new uses.*
4. *What criteria may be employed to determine the viable position for a brand in the market?*
5. *What conditions justify a company's dealing in multiple products?*
6. *Discuss the pros and cons of offering customized products.*
7. *Are there reasons other than profitability for eliminating a product? Discuss.*
8. *What factors must be weighed to determine the viability of divesting the entire product line?*
9. *Under what circumstances is it desirable to adopt product-imitation strategy?*
10. *Is conglomerate diversification a safe way to grow? Discuss why and why not.*

APPENDIX: PERSPECTIVES OF PRODUCT STRATEGIES

I. Product-Positioning Strategy

Definition: Placing a brand in that part of the market where it will have a favorable reception compared with competing brands.

Objectives: (1) To position the product in the market so that it stands apart from competing brands. (2) To position the product so that it tells customers what you stand for, what you are, and how you would like customers to evaluate you. In the case of positioning multiple brands: (1) To seek growth by offering varied products in differing segments of the market. (2) To avoid competitive threats to a single brand.

Requirements: Use of marketing-mix variables, especially design and communication efforts. (1) Successful management of a *single brand* requires (a) positioning brand in the market so that it can stand competition from the toughest rival; (b) maintaining its unique position by creating the aura of a different product. (2) Successful management of *multiple brands* requires careful positioning in the market so that they do not compete with each other and create cannibalism. Thus it is important to be careful in segmenting the market and to position an individual product through design and promotion as uniquely suited to a particular segment.

Expected Results: (1) Meet as much as possible the needs of specific segments of the market. (2) Limit sudden changes in sales. (3) Make customers faithful to the brands.

II. Product-Repositioning Strategy

Definition: Reviewing the current positioning of the product and its marketing mix and seeking a new position for it which seems more appropriate.

Objectives: (1) To increase the life of the product. (2) To correct an original positioning mistake.

Requirements: (1) If this strategy is directed toward existing customers, repositioning is sought through promotion of more varied uses of the product. (2) If the business unit wants to reach new users, this strategy requires that the product be presented with a different twist to the people who have not been favorably inclined toward it. In doing so, care should be taken to see that in the process of enticing new customers, the current ones are not alienated. (3) If this strategy aims at presenting new uses of the product, it requires searching for latent uses of the product, if any. While all products may not have latent uses, there are products which may be used for purposes not originally intended.

Expected Results: (1) Among existing customers: Increase in sales growth and profitability. (2) Among new users: Enlargement of the overall market, thus putting the product on a growth route, and increased profitability. (3) New product uses: Increased sales, market share, and profitability.

III. Product-Overlap Strategy

Definition: Competing against one's own brand through (a) introduction of competing products, (b) use of private labeling, and (c) selling to original equipment manufacturers.

Objectives: (1) To attract more customers to the product and thereby increase the overall market. (2) To work at full capacity and spread overheads. (3) To sell to competitors; to realize economies of scale and cost reduction.

Requirements: (1) Each competing product must have its own marketing organization to compete in the market. (2) Private brand should not become a profit drain. (3) Each brand should find its special niche in the market. If that doesn't happen, it will create confusion among customers and sales will be hurt. (4) In the long run, one of the brands may be withdrawn, yielding its position to the other brand.

Expected Results: (1) Increased share of the market. (2) Increased growth.

IV. Product-Scope Strategy

Definition: The product-scope strategy deals with the perspectives of the product mix of a company. The product-scope strategy is determined by taking into account the overall mission of the business unit. The company may adopt single-product strategy, multiple-product strategy, or system-of-products strategy.

Objectives: (1) Single product—To increase economies of scale by developing specialization. (2) Multiple products—To cover the risk of potential obsolescence of the single product by adding additional products. (3) System of products—To increase the dependence of the customer on the company's products as well as to prevent competitors from moving into the market.

Requirements: (1) Single product—Company must stay up to date on the product and even be the technology leader to avoid obsolescence. (2) Multiple products—Products must complement one another in a portfolio of products. (3) System of products—Company must have a close understanding of customers' needs and uses of the products.

Expected Results: Increased growth, market share, and profits with all three strategies. With system-of-products strategy, the company achieves monopolistic control over the market (which may lead to some problems with the Justice Department) and enlarges the concept of its product/market opportunities.

V. Product-Design Strategy

Definition: The product-design strategy deals with the degree of standardization of the product. The company has a choice among the following strategic options: standard product, customized product, and standard product with modifications.

Objectives: (1) Standard product—To increase economies of scale of the company. (2) Customized product—To compete against mass producers of standardized products through product-design flexibility. (3) Standard product with modifications—To combine the benefits of the two previous strategies.

Requirements: Close analysis of product/market perspectives and environmental changes, especially technological changes.

Expected Results: Increase in growth, market share, and profits. In addition, the third strategy allows the company to keep close contacts with the market and get experience in developing new standard products.

VI. Product-Elimination Strategy

Definition: Cuts in the composition of a company's business unit product portfolio by pruning the number of products within a line or by total divestment of a division or business.

Objectives: To eliminate undesirable products because their contribution to fixed cost and profit is too low, because their future performance looks grim, or because they do not fit in the business's overall strategy. The product-elimination strategy aims at shaping the best possible mix of products and balancing the total business.

Requirements: No special resources are required to eliminate a product or a division. However, since it will be impossible to reverse the decision once the elimination has been achieved, an in-depth analysis must be done to determine (a) the causes of the current problems; (b) the possible alternatives other than elimination that may solve the problems (e.g., are any improvements in the marketing mix possible?); and (c) the repercussions that elimination may have on the remaining products or units (e.g., is the product being considered for elimination complementary to another product in the portfolio? What are the side effects on the company's image? What are the social costs of an elimination?).

Expected Results: In the short run, cost savings from production runs, reduced inventories, and in some cases an improved return on investment can be expected. In the long run, the sales of the remaining products may increase since more efforts are now concentrated on them.

VII. New-Product Strategy

Definition: A set of operations that introduce (a) within the business, a product new to its previous line of products; (b) on the market, a product that provides a new type of satisfaction. Three alternatives emerge from the above: product improvement/modification, product imitation, and product innovation.

Objectives: To meet new needs and to sustain competitive pressures on existing products. In the first case the new-product strategy is an offensive one; in the second case, it is a defensive one.

Requirements: A new-product strategy will be difficult to implement if a "new product development system" does not exist within a company. Five components should be a part of this system:

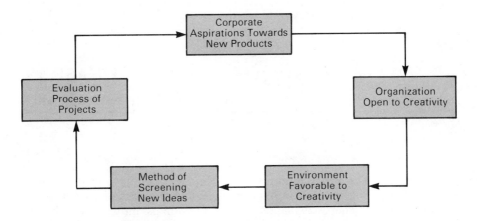

Expected Results: Increased market share and profitability.

VIII. Diversification Strategy

Definition: Developing unfamiliar products and markets through (a) concentric diversification (where the products introduced are related to the existing ones in terms of marketing or technology); (b) horizontal diversification (where the new products are unrelated to the existing ones but are sold to the same customers); (c) conglomerate diversification (where the products are entirely new).

Objectives: Diversification strategies respond to the desire for (a) growth when the current products/markets have reached maturity; (b) stability by spreading the risks of fluctuations in earnings; (c) security when the company may fear backward integration from one of its major customers; (d) credibility to have more weight in capital markets.

Requirements: In order to reduce the risks inherent in a diversification strategy a business unit should (a) diversify its activities only if the current product/market opportunities are limited; (b) have some good knowledge of the area in which it diversifies; (c) provide the products introduced with adequate support; (d) forecast the effects of diversification on the existing lines of products.

Expected Results: (1) Increase in sales. (2) Greater profitability and flexibility.

International Engineering, Inc.

In late 1970s much attention was focused on utility companies and the role they would play in supplying additional amounts of electricity to meet the growing energy demands created by business, industry, and home consumers. While geothermal, wind, and solar generating systems along with fusion and breeder reactors may be the energy sources of tomorrow, the electric utility companies rely on either fossil fuel or nuclear power plants to generate electricity today and will for the next few decades. Whereas nuclear power plants may in the future be the most economical and efficient means of producing electrical power, today they present many drawbacks, both economic and social, which have caused utilities to place more reliance on fossil fuel generating systems. Because of the relative scarcity of natural gas and the escalating cost of fuel oil, most of the fossil fuel plants that were in operation in 1980 or would be coming into operation in the next few years were of the coal-fired type.

One company that was heavily involved in serving the utility industry was International Engineering, Inc. (IEI), a Michigan-based firm that designed, manufactured, and sold fossil fuel and nuclear steam supply systems and components for use in generating electricity. Of the approximately 1,500 coal-fired power plants in operation in the United States in 1980, about 600 were designed, manufactured, and built by IEI. Exhibit 13-5 shows where most of these coal-fired plants were located and the areas where the growth of coal-fired plants was expected to occur over the next few years. Coupled with this growing market in coal-fired steam generating systems was a growing market in replacement sales, i.e., sales of those parts of a generating station that eventually wear out or break. The growth rate of this replacement market over the next few years had been estimated at about 5 percent per year. Replacement sales was a sizable amount of IEI's total sales picture, accounting for about 3 percent of total sales. Exhibits 13-6 and 13-7 show IEI's financial statements for the year 1979.

Realizing this growth potential of both coal-fired generating stations and the accompanying market for replacement parts, one could expect a steady growth of sales of each over the next few decades. Such was not the case, however, for one particular product in IEI's replacement line, coal pulverizer rings and rolls.

Prior to burning, coal to be used in the furnaces of generating plants

EXHIBIT 13-5   Present and Potential Areas for Coal-fired Power Generation Plants in the U.S.

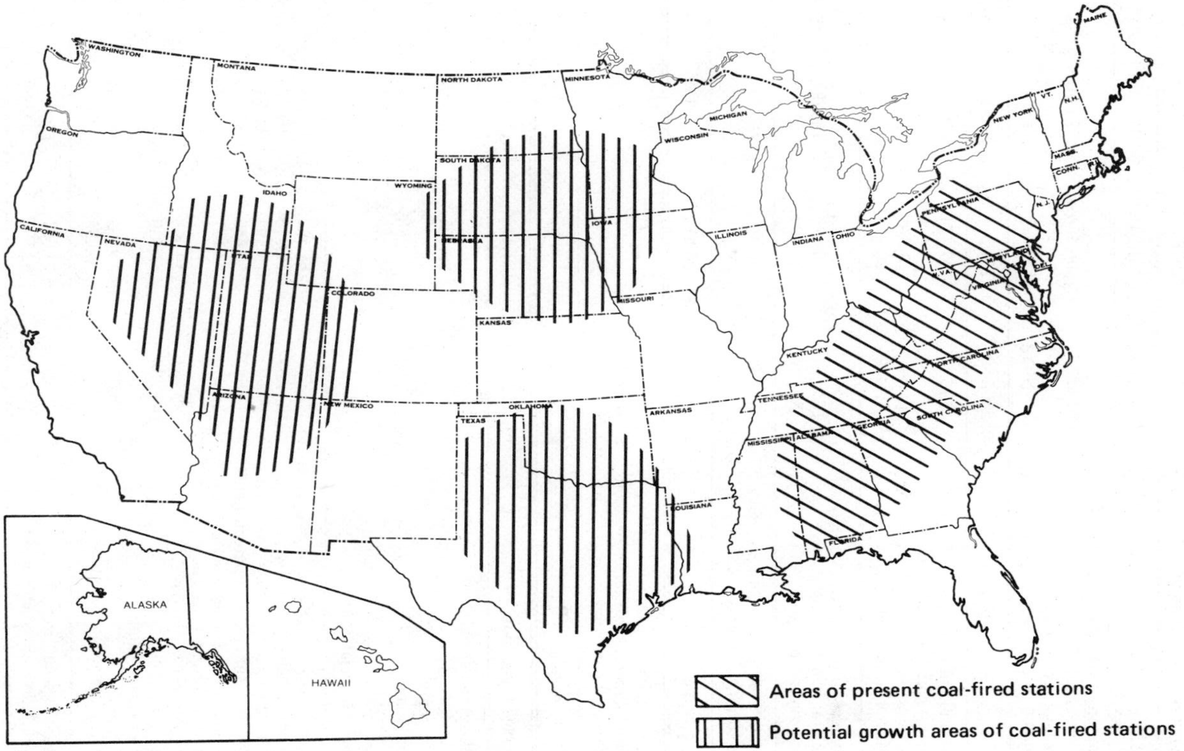

Areas of present coal-fired stations

Potential growth areas of coal-fired stations

Source: Company records.

EXHIBIT 13-6   International Engineering, Inc.: Comparative Financial Statistics, 1970–79

(in thousands, except per-share amounts) Summary of Operations	1979	1978	1977	1976
Net sales	$2,757,504	$2,331,751	$2,044,764	$1,830,925
Costs and expenses				
Cost of sales	$2,373,357	$2,006,266	$1,776,518	$1,601,773
Selling, general and administrative expenses	213,402	178,041	145,742	122,117
	$2,586,759	$2,184,307	$1,922,260	$1,723,890
Operating income	$ 170,745	$ 147,444	$ 122,504	$ 107,035
Other income and (deductions)				
Interest expense	(16,663)	(18,400)	(11,563)	(9,989)
Miscellaneous, net	32,499	29,972	22,068	8,147
Income before income taxes and extraordinary items	$ 186,581	$ 159,016	$ 133,009	$ 105,193
Taxes on income	88,940	78,700	65,820	50,990
Income before extraordinary items	$ 97,641	$ 80,316	$ 67,189	$ 54,203
Extraordinary items	—	—	—	—
Net income	$ 97,641	$ 80,316	$ 67,189	$ 54,203
Net income per share				
Income before extraordinary items	$ 5.96	$ 4.97	$ 4.17	$ 3.36
Extraordinary items	—	—	—	—
Net income	$ 5.96	$ 4.97	$ 4.17	$ 3.36
Average shares outstanding	16,371,638	16,171,116	16,117,125	16,121,660
Cash dividends declared				
Total	$ 35,892	$ 29,105	$ 24,098	$ 21,188
Per share				
Common	2.20	1.80	1.50	1.316
Preferred	—	.85	1.70	1.70
Other Financial Statistics				
Current assets	$1,428,639	$1,252,542	$1,086,841	$ 876,259
Current liabilities	1,144,337	978,948	894,123	663,412
Working capital	284,302	273,594	192,718	212,847
Property, plant and equipment, net	515,983	450,866	437,145	358,741
Investments and other assets	136,756	132,171	128,948	54,643
Deferred income taxes and investment tax credit	232,981	222,999	169,960	99,638
Long-term debt	144,386	139,639	147,270	128,176
Shareholders' equity				
Amount	559,674	493,993	441,581	398,417
Per share	34.26	30.58	27.30	24.31
Capital expenditures	$ 146,741	$ 74,904	$ 122,055	$ 81,446
Depreciation and amortization	66,138	52,567	39,630	33,030
Orders received	$2,897,763	$2,298,490	$2,111,246	$1,738,626
Unfilled orders	2,986,465	2,879,929	2,968,556	2,980,098
Employees	43,286	45,729	44,770	42,843
Shareholders of record	26,742	26,451	26,596	25,536

1975	1974	1973	1972	1971	1970
$1,711,151	$1,428,028	$1,168,578	$1,054,532	$ 960,910	$ 879,204
$1,513,297	$1,253,616	$ 998,987	$ 902,596	$ 819,794	$ 747,439
109,317	94,336	87,484	77,181	69,857	65,984
1,622,614	$1,347,952	$1,086,471	$ 979,777	$ 889,651	$ 813,423
$ 88,537	$ 80,076	$ 82,107	$ 74,755	$ 71,259	$ 65,781
(10,119)	(11,704)	(9,561)	(8,643)	(6,273)	(5,964)
5,024	5,472	6,885	6,387	3,845	3,135
$ 83,442	$ 73,844	$ 79,431	$ 72,499	$ 68,831	$ 62,952
38,850	33,660	36,340	32,980	32,100	30,630
$ 44,592	$ 40,184	$ 43,091	$ 39,519	$ 36,731	$ 32,322
—	(2,700)	—	(16,000)	—	—
$ 44,592	$ 37,484(1)	$ 43,091	$ 23,519	$ 36,731	$ 32,322
$ 2.77	$ 2.50	$ 2.70	$ 2.48	$ 2.34	$ 2.09
—	(.17)	—	(1.00)	—	—
$ 2.77	$ 2.33(1)	$ 2.70	$ 1.48	$ 2.34	$ 2.09
16,083,514	16,080,781	15,952,219	15,930,967	15,722,697	15,467,769
$ 20,137	$ 18,617	$ 16,320	$ 15,160	$ 14,195	$ 13,237
1.25	1.152	.997	.958	.917	.85
1.70	1.70	1.70	1.70	1.70	1.70
$ 717,029	$ 662,049	$ 523,588	$ 484,278	$ 458,427	$ 388,275
529,623	494,088	373,170	329,435	315,977	281,544
187,406	167,961	150,418	154,843	142,450	106,731
315,850	297,339	266,536	219,096	203,145	182,731
35,977	38,111	40,622	39,976	64,820	65,215
57,802	41,669	14,946	9,557	20,931	19,104
116,497	121,242	121,490	107,116	103,193	75,348
364,934	340,500	321,140	297,242	286,291	260,225
22.12	20.49	19.15	17.64	17.15	15.47
$ 50,621	$ 61,796	$ 57,330	$ 38,747	$ 42,336	$ 35,370
29,653	27,744	23,868	19,765	17,972	15,723
$1,527,288	$2,515,965	$1,999,142	$1,220,497	$ 979,133	$1,130,262
3,132,481	3,347,114	2,288,011	1,477,500	1,350,050	1,337,121
45,938	40,765	35,316	34,950	33,374	32,645
25,212	24,758	21,305	21,549	21,390	19,252

EXHIBIT 13-7   International Engineering, Inc.: Financial Reporting by Business Segments

The company's equipment, products and services are classified into the following business segments: (a) design, manufacture, installation and service of steam generating systems and equipment for the electric utility industry including nuclear steam supply systems; (b) design, engineering and construction services (principally through its subsidiary, The Lummus Company), primarily for the chemical, petrochemical and petroleum industries (or equipment supplied to industrial markets); and (d) products and services supplied to industrial markets. The following tables present financial data by business segment:

(in thousands)	1979	1978	1977
Sales			
Steam generating systems, equipment and services for the electric utility industry	$ 926,220	$ 815,767	$ 747,808
Design, engineering and construction services	351,719	308,438	300,698
Equipment for industrial markets	815,563	688,815	606,338
Products and services for industrial markets	664,002	518,731	389,920
Total	$2,757,504	$2,331,751	$2,044,764
Operating Profit			
Steam generating systems, equipment and services for the electric utility industry	$ 65,166	$ 56,985	$ 46,451
Design, engineering and construction services	27,979	27,663	24,664
Equipment for industrial markets	81,167	62,823	53,477
Products and services for industrial markets	25,948	20,819	13,147
Total	$ 200,260	$ 168,290	$ 137,739
Equity in net earnings of associated and other companies	4,340	1,397	1,775
Interest expense	(16,663)	(18,400)	(11,563)
Unallocated—			
Corporate expense	(16,356)	(14,443)	(12,141)
Miscellaneous, net	15,000	22,172	17,199
Consolidated income before income taxes	$ 186,581	$ 159,016	$ 133,009

EXHIBIT 13-7   continued

December 31,	1979	1978	1977
Identifiable assets			
Steam generating systems, equipment and services for the electric utility industry	$ 432,133	$ 385,962	$ 358,021
Design, engineering and construction services	151,989	135,746	135,230
Equipment for industrial markets	548,756	515,815	550,387
Products and services for industrial markets	451,069	349,927	334,883
Total	$1,583,947	$1,387,450	$1,378,521
Investments in associated and other companies (equity basis)	50,713	33,172	20,988
Corporate and unallocated assets, net	448,300	416,325	254,765
Consolidated	$2,082,960	$1,836,947	$1,654,274

is first fed into a coal pulverizer, where it is finely ground to the consistency of talcum powder to enable the coal to be burned much more efficiently. The ring and roll unit is responsible for crushing the coal. There are three ring and roll units per pulverizer and anywhere from five to ten pulverizers per power plant. The roll is capable of crushing anywhere from 250,000 to 500,000 tons of coal before having to be replaced, with the rings generally lasting up to three times as long as the rolls. IEI's replacement market for these rings and rolls was estimated to be in the neighborhood of $5 million to $6 million per year.

However, within the last two years IEI's market share of pulverizer replacement rings and rolls had been decreasing while the overall market for such items had been increasing. The reason for this decline in sales was that IEI had met stiff competition from two other manufacturers of rings and rolls, Helmick Corporation and Weatherly Company. They had succeeded in capturing a large percentage of the replacement market for rings and rolls by pricing their products lower than IEI's and by giving better delivery dates. Also, the quality of Helmick's rolls was believed to be superior to IEI's rolls; many customers were reporting longer life with Helmick's rolls than with IEI's rolls.

IEI's marketing department was faced with the problem of preventing future sales of rings and rolls from being lost to competitors and regaining the sales of those customers who had formerly purchased rings and rolls from IEI but were now purchasing from competitors.

BACKGROUND

International Engineering was originally formed in 1912 as a manufacturer of locomotive superheaters. Its growth was marked over a period of years by the acquisition of similar types of companies. Along the way it acquired much knowledge and experience in the field of fuel combustion which eventually enabled it to become one of the leading manufacturers of boilers and other steam-generating equipment.

With emphasis on growth and diversification, the company evolved as a diversified international company serving many markets with annual sales of about $1.7 billion. Through its design and manufacturing facilities it provided a variety of energy-related systems and engineering services worldwide to electric utility, petroleum, petrochemical, metallurgical, and other industrial markets. IEI produced nuclear and fossil fuel steam supply systems and oil and gas production processing equipment and also designed and constructed petrochemical, petroleum-refining chemical, and other related process plants. Other products included refractories and minerals, pulp-processing machinery, pollution-control equipment, and building products.

IEI was organized into four main groups to carry out the corporate functions as described above. These groups were the power systems group, the engineering group, the process equipment group, and the industrial products group. The largest of these was the power systems group, its principal market being the electric utility industry. This group was concerned primarily with the design and manufacture of fossil and nuclear-fueled steam supply systems and their related components. Within this group was power systems services, whose prime responsibility was serving the "after" market for energy-related projects. An organizational chart showing power systems services in the overall IEI structure is presented in Exhibit 13-8.

One "after" market was that of coal pulverizer replacement rings and rolls. Until 1974 IEI had experienced very little competition in the sale of replacement rings and rolls to electric utility companies. During the 1960s and early 1970s, the Griffin Wheel Company tried unsuccessfully to enter the market. Aggressive marketing programs on the part of IEI and the superiority of its product over that of Griffin Wheel forced the latter to withdraw from the market.

Concurrent with IEI's increasing sales of replacement rings and rolls during the early 1970s were increasing delays in delivery to customers. Being cast metal products, rings and rolls were manufactured at IEI's foundry in Middletown, Ohio. This foundry manufactured all of the cast metal parts in IEI's product line. Because of the large volume of work that was being done at the foundry in the early '70s and the resulting backlogs, delivery of rings and rolls could be promised for no sooner than 38 weeks. While plans were being made to expand the foundry in the near future, it would be some time before this increased capacity would enable the reduction of delivery time for rings and rolls. In the interim IEI found

EXHIBIT 13-8   International Engineering, Inc.: Power Systems Services Organizational Chart

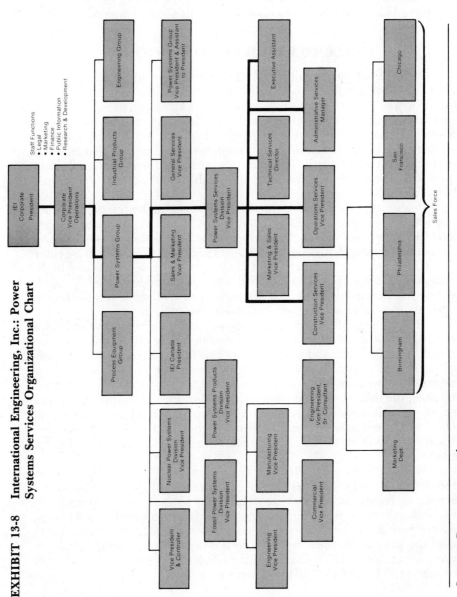

Source: Company records.

it necessary to acquire the services of an outside firm, Weatherly Foundry & Manufacturing Company, to help produce these rings and rolls. Even with Weatherly Company manufacturing all of the rings and the larger-sized rolls, IEI could only reduce its delivery time to 24 weeks.

ENTER HELMICK CORPORATION

In the final quarter of 1973, Helmick Corporation, a small company of about 87 employees with sales of approximately $3.5 million, purchased Griffin Wheel Company. Helmick Corporation was involved in the manufacture of gray iron and alloy castings. Helmick set up its own equipment and immediately entered the ring and roll market. It embarked on a strategic marketing program in an attempt to penetrate this market. This program consisted primarily of promising new customers delivery within 2 to 4 weeks and pricing their rings and rolls 30–40 percent lower than IEI's.

It also appeared that Helmick's rolls were of better quality than IEI's, with some utility companies claiming that Helmick's rolls lasted longer than IEI's rolls. This was probably due to the differences in construction and manufacturing techniques of the two rolls. The IEI roll had a center of gray cast iron with a 2-inch outer ring of Ni-hard, a nickel-base high-strength steel alloy. The Helmick roll was composed solely of Ni-hard. Because the Helmick rolls were made entirely of Ni-hard it was profitable for Helmick to buy back the old rolls from the utilities.

Helmick's initial marketing strategy of cutting delivery time and price evidently had worked, as an increasing number of utility companies were favoring Helmick rolls and rings over IEI. While price played an important part in the utilities' supplier selections, the promise of shorter delivery time and increased life influenced their decisions even more. With a shorter lead time, the utilities did not have to plan so much in advance. But more important, a shortened lead time coupled with a longer life meant that utilities would not have to stockpile as many rings and rolls for future use. This would result in savings on storage costs as well as on taxes for inventory.

From 1974 to 1976, Helmick enjoyed a steady growth in the sales of its rolls and rings. As sales increased, Helmick, like IEI, began to experience increases in delivery time. Though it was still able to promise 2- to 4-week delivery to new customers, established customers had a 24-week delivery period. Having successfully penetrated the market, Helmick also raised the price of its rolls and rings to the point where Helmick's prices were comparable to IEI's. During this period the prices of a typical roll manufactured by IEI and Helmick were as follows:

IEI price: $1,900   Helmick price: $2,100

$$\frac{-300}{\$1,800} \text{ (buy-back of used roll)}$$

WEATHERLY FIGHTS BACK

IEI had recently completed its expansion of the Middletown foundry at a cost of $7 million. With the availability of this additional foundry capacity, IEI no longer required the services of Weatherly Foundry & Manufacturing Company, which consequently faced a substantial drop in revenues from the loss of the ring and roll casting business it had been doing for IEI. Weatherly's total sales for 1979 had been $4.2 million, of which $2.2 million had been from rings and rolls. Unable to face such a large loss of sales, Weatherly made a major marketing effort to sell rings and rolls directly to the utilities. This did not prove to be difficult, because when they had been making rings and rolls for IEI they would often ship the finished product directly to the customer, rather than to IEI. Thus Weatherly not only acquired manufacturing expertise from IEI but became familiar with IEI's customers and dealt with them directly. With the elimination of IEI, Weatherly was now able to approach the utility companies and offer the same product that IEI had been selling but at a savings of about 60 percent over what IEI had been charging, and with a shorter delivery period.

IEI'S SALES PICTURE FOR RINGS AND ROLLS

The entrance of both Helmick and Weatherly into the coal pulverizer ring and roll replacement market had an adverse effect upon IEI's market position. Exhibit 13-9 shows IEI's market share of rings and rolls over the previous 10 years. In the years 1974–79, IEI's market share for rings went from a high of about 43 percent to a low of about 14 percent; and from a high market share for rolls of about 50 percent to a low of about 22 percent. Exhibit 13-10 gives a tabular breakdown of the purchase of rings by 55 utility companies for the period 1974 through 1979. Exhibit 13-11 shows 12 of IEI's customers who were either considering purchases of rings or had already purchased rings manufactured by IEI's competitors. It is evident from Exhibit 13-11 that the majority of IEI's sales of rings were being lost to Helmick, which in the past had been concentrating mainly on the roll market but was attempting to penetrate the ring market as well.

REFURBISHING OF ROLLS

A process whereby rings and rolls are refurbished by welding metal plates to their surfaces had been in existence since about the early 1950s, when the Cleveland Electric Illuminating Company began to hard-surface rings and rolls. The process did not catch on and until recently had insignificant effects upon the sales of new rolls. However, with the improvement of welding materials and depositing techniques, the process was starting to appeal to many of IEI's customers.

In this process the roll was cleaned by power brushing, mounted

EXHIBIT 13-9   IEI's Market Share of Rings and Rolls, 1970–79

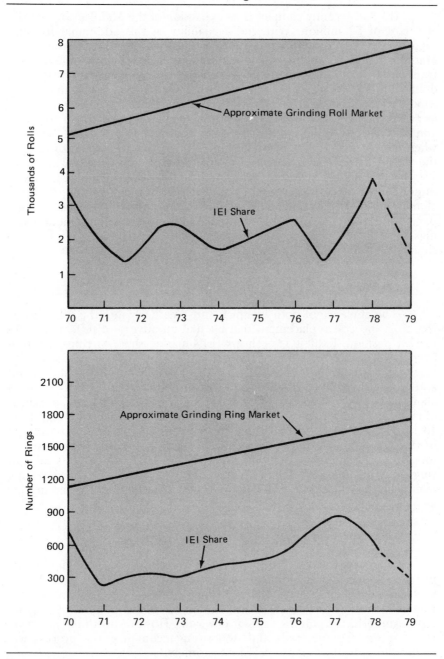

Source: Company records.

EXHIBIT 13-10   IEI Ring Sales Analysis by Customer

	1974	1975	1976	1977	1978	1979
Dairyland Power	0	3	3	6	6	0
Montana Power	2	0	0	4	0	0
Salt River Project	0	0	0	2	0	0
Southwestern Pub. Svc.	0	0	0	0	2	0
Alabama Power	1	11	48	16	7	0
Central Illinois Light	1	1	3	2	0	0
Central Illinois Pub. Svc.	5	2	3	0	5	0
Cincinnati Gas & Electric	23	6	8	14	14	0
Cleveland Electric	19	16	24	62	13	11
Columbus & Southern	12	7	5	9	13	0
Commonwealth Edison	0	20	22	13	11	0
Dayton Power & Light	4	3	5	5	2	0
Detroit Edison	11	15	15	13	12	0
Georgia Power	13	6	18	30	16	10
Gulf Power	10	11	13	9	0	10
Illinois Power	1		10	8	6	7
Indianapolis Power	13	7	5	30	15	1
Interstate Power	4	2	3	6	5	0
Iowa Power & Light	4	5	0	2	3	0
Kansas City Power	0	3	8	11	15	0
Kansas Power & Light	2	0	8	18	0	0
Louisville Gas & Electric	8	8	18	22	8	2
Metropolitan Edison	0	4	6	1	0	0
Minnesota Power & Light	3	3	9	6	8	2
N.Y. State Electric	1	7	15	21	18	1
Niagara Mohawk Power	0	2	11	28	7	6
Northern States Power	0	2	2	0	1	0
Ohio Edison	19	1	29	4	21	0
Pennsylvania Electric	11	35	33	45	0	4
Philadelphia Electric	0	0	7	30	0	0
Carolina Power & Light	7	6	10	22	3	12
Potomac Edison	0	0	1	0	3	2
Public Service of Indiana	0	4	13	8	6	0
Rochester Gas & Elec.	0	2	11	14	5	0
Upper Peninsula Gen.	3	4	5	1	5	0
Utah Power & Light	6	4	13	10	8	1
Virginia Electric Power Co.	0	0	0	0	0	19
Wisconsin Elec.	5	13	4	8	33	0
Pacific Power & Light	0	3	3	3	15	6
Consumers Power	19	15	3	16	32	5
Duke Power	8	35	24	47	14	0
Duquesne Light	0	5	8	6	8	6
Electric Energy	6	10	0	20	6	0

EXHIBIT 13-10   continued

	1974	1975	1976	1977	1978	1979
Northern Indiana Pub. Svc.	0	0	6	4	2	7
Otter Tail Power	0	0	0	0	0	2
Potomac Elec.	0	3	6	10	5	4
Union Electric	0	0	7	16	0	3
Wisconsin Pub. Svc.	3	0	1	4	0	0
Penn. Power & Light	8	12	22	22	12	0
So. Carolina Elec.	0	3	3	8	4	0
Tenn. Valley Authority	32	39	56	46	52	17
Arizona Public Svc.	1	1	2	1	2	0
Kentucky Utilities	3	1	7	3	0	0
New England Power	0	0	0	0	15	0
Florida Power	0	0	0	0	0	10

Source: Company records.

on a rotating surface, preheated, and welded. The process took up to eight hours for some of the larger rolls. Major equipment requirements were an automatic welder and positioner and rotating machinery. Initial capital costs were estimated at $75,000. Once a refurbishing facility was set up, it required only one or two workers for its complete operation, thus involving little additional capital outlay. The process was being aggressively marketed by two welding material suppliers.

EXHIBIT 13-11   Tabulation of Survey, Rings Investigation

Customer	Competitors Present
Cleveland Electric	Helmick
Consumers Power	Helmick
Central Illinois Pub. Svc.	Helmick
Duke Power	Helmick, Alabama Iron
Carolina Power & Light	Helmick
Detroit Edison	Helmick
Northern Indiana Pub. Svc.	Helmick
Pennsylvania Electric	Helmick, Weatherly
Penn. Power & Light	Helmick, Weatherly
Virginia Electric Power Co.	Helmick
Georgia Power	*Georgia Iron Works
Duquesne Light	Weatherly

*Minor purchase; emergency delivery required.

Source: Company records.

Several companies were already in the business of refurbishing and others were expected to enter the market shortly. Following is a list of the geographic areas that were being served by refurbishing companies:

West Coast—Rebuilders, Inc.
Southeast—Southern Tempering
Mid-Atlantic—Consolidated Metal Services, Inc.
Midwest—Kuhar Co. and A&R Industries

Rebuilders, Inc., had been quite successful in its operations, with the other four companies expected to gain an increasing amount of refurbishing business in the future. In addition, Detroit Edison, Consumers Power, and Dayton Power & Light were presently refurbishing rolls that had been purchased from IEI. The following utility companies were contemplating using the refurbishing process in the future:

Alabama Power	Louisville Gas & Electric
Cincinnati Gas & Electric	Montana Power
Columbus & Southern	Pacific Power & Light
Georgia Power	Salt River Project
Kansas Power & Light	Tennessee Valley Authority

Cost comparisons for new and refurbished rolls in 1980 are as follows:

Size	New	Refurbished
863	$1,620	$1,500
943	2,310	1,925
1003	5,270	2,500

It was evident that the cost of refurbishing was less than that of purchasing new rolls, especially larger rolls.

Once a roll had been refurbished its life appeared to be substantially improved over the life of a similar new roll. In particular, Detroit Edison and Pacific Power & Light reported longer life with refurbished rolls. To determine whether this was true, a test of a set of rolls that had been refurbished by Southern Tempering Company was undertaken at the Widows Creek Station of the Tennessee Valley Authority. At last report, the refurbished rolls had pulverized about 250,000 tons of coal and still showed no signs of failure. Based on current wear rates it was estimated that the rolls would probably be capable of crushing an additional 500,000 tons of coal before needing to be replaced or refurbished. In comparison, new rolls supplied by IEI for use at the Widows Creek Station had had an average life of about 250,000 tons.

A $75,000 refurbishing facility was capable of refurbishing 15 rolls a week, or 750 rolls per year. Ten of these facilities would therefore yield about 7,500 refurbished rolls per year, which represented approximately the total market available for IEI grinding rolls. Total replacement sales for IEI grinding rolls for the 1980 year would total about 2,000. In addition, a roll could be refurbished up to 15 times before having to be replaced. The recent trend among utility companies of refurbishing their old rolls instead of buying new ones posed a real threat to IEI's future in the highly profitable replacement coal-grinding roll business.

As an original equipment manufacturer, IEI had certain advantages over its lesser-known competitive suppliers in dealing with its utility customers. If it endorsed the refurbishing process, which was developed primarily by a welding metal supply company, IEI would jeopardize this advantage and lose the ability to differentiate its product. It would put its sales engineers at a disadvantage when, in the field, they were asked by the utility companies whether it was better to refurbish or to replace a grinding roll. IEI's acceptance and use of the process would encourage many utility companies to make the small investment necessary to set up their own refurbishing facilities, as several had already done. Lesser-known companies that were already involved in refurbishing would make use of IEI's acceptance of the process to increase their own business and compete on price.

Because refurbishing facilities could be small one- or two-worker operations requiring little capital investment, they would for the most part be regional or local businesses. If IEI were to enter the refurbishing market it would be necessary to establish several shops regionally located in order to compete favorably with local companies.

The refurbishing of old rolls would mean a definite loss of business for IEI's recently completed foundry expansion. Whether or not IEI decided to go into the refurbishing business, this loss of foundry business would continue. Since this loss was not acceptable, IEI would have to increase its sales of new grinding rolls to offset it.

IEI'S OPERATING PROCESS FOR RINGS AND ROLLS

IEI's sales department had the responsibility of getting new customers for coal pulverizer replacement rings and rolls. While there might be considerable contact between the sales engineers and the utility companies in the initial stages of acquiring them as customers, once the account had been established there was virtually no personal contact between IEI and the client utility companies when purchases of rings and rolls were made. For the most part the sales department was concerned with special or new orders, the ordering of replacement rings and rolls being a fairly routine matter on the part of both the utility companies and IEI.

Throughout the United States, IEI had several district offices to handle orders placed by utility companies for parts (see Exhibit 13-12). When a utility company wished to order a replacement ring or roll, it simply sent the order to the appropriate district office. The district office processed the order and sent it to the parts operations department in Plymouth, Michigan.

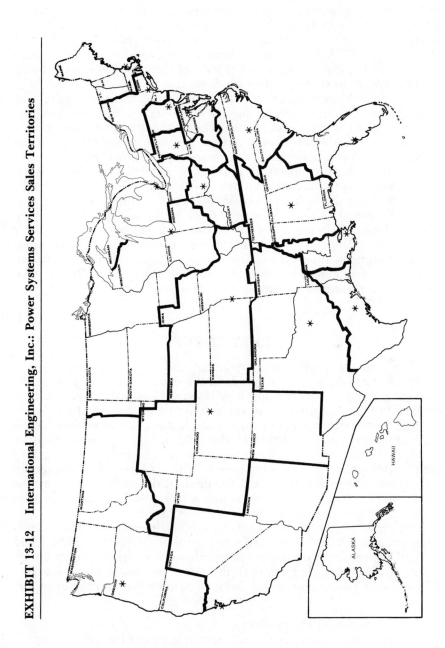

EXHIBIT 13-12   International Engineering, Inc.: Power Systems Services Sales Territories

The parts operations department had the responsibility of filling orders for all replacement and nonreplacement parts that IEI marketed for both nuclear and fossil fuel plants. The parts operations department handled orders for more than 50,000 parts. Total yearly sales for parts operations, in 1979, amounted to about $40 million for fossil fuel parts and $1 million for nuclear parts, the bulk of their work obviously being concerned with processing orders for fossil fuel parts.

The parts operations department checked each order against the original invoice to make certain that the customer was receiving the correct part. Once the order had been checked, the parts group then placed the order with the Middletown foundry. The foundry gave the parts operations department a shipping date based upon its current backlog of work. In turn, the parts operations department notified the customer when to expect shipment of the part. Shipment from the foundry was normally by truck, usually the fastest and cheapest means of transporting the part to the customer. Usually shipment by truck could be made to anywhere in the continental United States within two to three days.

To keep track of all orders that were placed with the parts operations department, IEI used a computerized tracking system. This system followed the order from its initial placement at the district office to final delivery to the customer, ensuring minimal delay in order processing and filling.

MARKET SURVEY

In order to provide the marketing and sales groups with information on current and future trends in the marketplace and to help the marketing group in determining how resources might be allocated over the next two years, a survey was conducted on a group of IEI customers in major metropolitan areas of the United States. The survey was developed, conducted, and tabulated by Health-width Inc., an independent survey company. In this survey 45 business executives of various IEI customer companies were personally interviewed. While the results of the entire survey cannot be presented herein, two areas of the survey were of prime interest to IEI in regard to its marketing problem with replacement sales of coal pulverizer rings and rolls.

One of these areas was concerned with determining what factors influence a purchaser to buy from a particular supplier. Exhibit 13-13 presents the results of this study. Respondents were asked to evaluate 20 factors on a 5-point scale ranging from "crucial" to "not at all considered." The following factors emerged as being very important in the buying decision:

(1) Quality of the product
(2) Ability to supply product within a reasonable time period
(3) Warranty or back-up service that accompanies product
(4) Responsiveness to customer needs
(5) Engineering and design capabilities

**EXHIBIT 13-13   Coal Pulverizer Rings and Rolls Market Survey Percentage
of Respondents Rating the Buying Factors as Crucial or
Very Important**

1. Dependability and quality of product or service	100.0%
2. Company reputation in this product or service category	87.8
3. Company's engineering capabilities	85.3
4. Company's reputation for meeting promised delivery date	82.9
5. Company's design capabilities	80.5
6. Responsiveness and flexibility of company to customer needs and requirements	78.1
7. Maintenance service and back-up capabilities offered by company	78.1
8. Promptness of reply to customer inquiries and requests	78.0
9. Length of company experience in this product or service category	75.6
10. Previous favorable experience with this company	73.9
11. Reputation of company for completion of projects on time and within budget	73.2
12. Company's field construction capabilities	63.3
13. Price of product or service	68.3
14. Amount of technical support information provided by company	63.4
15. Projected time of delivery	61.0
16. Quality of company's personnel	61.0
17. Commercial terms and conditions offered by company	51.2
18. Company's field labor relations	43.9
19. Recommendation by consulting engineer	24.4
20. Amount of sales support contact provided by company sales representatives	17.1

Source: Company records.

In another part of the survey the respondents were asked to evaluate how pricing affected their organization's decision-making process regarding the selection of supplier companies. The following is a list of the questionnaire statements and the percentage of respondents who agreed with them:

31.7% (A) In most cases, the lowest-priced quote for the product or service is the major determinant.

22.0% (B) In most cases, our firm will pay a small (up to 5%) price premium for a product or service if the supplier offers better quality, delivery, or service.

24.4% (C) In most cases, our firm will pay a meaningful premium (10% or more), assuming the quality, delivery, or service justifies such a premium.

14.6% (D) In most cases, the price of the product or service is one of the secondary considerations. Our firm bases its purchasing de-

cision on more primary factors such as performance, reputation of supplier, product quality, delivery, and service.
7.3% (E) No answer.

The information gained from this survey, while it pertained to sales
not just of rings and rolls but of the entire line of IEI's products and
services, gave the marketing department some insight concerning what
areas to concentrate on in their marketing strategy to regain their market
share of coal pulverizer ring and roll sales.

IEI'S MARKETING STRATEGY

It was evident that if IEI was to regain its former share of the replacement market for coal pulverizer rings and rolls, it would have to meet
or beat the competition in delivery time, quality, and price. The most crucial area, the one needing immediate improvement, was delivery. Longer
delivery times mean higher costs for utilities. IEI's delivery time of 24
weeks was clearly unacceptable. However, with the expansion of the Middletown foundry, IEI had the extra capacity it needed to manufacture,
within a reasonable time period, all the rings and rolls it could sell.

The $7-million foundry expansion was regarded as the most mod-
ern facility in the country, employing the latest casting techniques, including centrifugal casting. Both Weatherly and Helmick cast their rings
and rolls statistically, a more costly process because of the amount of labor
and time involved. Centrifugal casting was much more efficient and economical, requiring less labor and enabling parts to be cast at a faster rate.
It was unlikely that Helmick or Weatherly would be capable of making
similar major improvements in their foundries because of the large costs
involved. Neither company had the necessary cash for such an investment.
IEI's new facility, which would be devoted primarily to the manufacture
of rings and rolls, was capable of producing 21,000 rolls a year, with an
estimated market of 8,000 rolls a year. Thus, it was evident that IEI had
a definite edge on its competitors.

The entire foundry manufactured over 8,000 individual parts that
were sold by IEI. Because about 50 different types of rings and rolls were
manufactured by IEI, it was economically unfeasible to stock these items.
Instead, a system had been set up whereby all orders for rings and rolls
received by the foundry were to be guaranteed ready for shipment within
4 weeks, which essentially was the same as stocking an item. The district
sales offices and the parts operations group in Plymouth had been given
explicit instructions to expedite all orders for replacement rings and rolls.
Orders that had previously taken about 3 weeks to process would now be
processed within 2 weeks or less. Thus, the maximum lead time for rings
and rolls had been reduced from 24 weeks to 6 weeks.

The marketing department had the task of informing the utility
companies of the improved lead time. Two phases were planned. The first
phase, which had already started, would consist of personal contact by the

sales department with the utilities, while the second phase would consist of individual mailings to the utility companies. For these mailings a list would be drawn up of all past, present, and potential customers for IEI replacement rings and rolls. A letter would be sent to these firms telling of IEI's six-week delivery period. Enclosed with the letter would be a special four-page color brochure describing IEI's ring and roll line. This brochure would emphasize IEI's current position as a leader in the design, development, and construction of fossil fuel plants, a statement that could not be made by any of IEI's present competitors in the ring and roll replacement business.

The sales department, while not directly under the control of the marketing department (see Exhibit 13-8), relied heavily upon marketing and worked closely with this group. Thus, when the marketing people approached sales with the objective of and strategy for regaining IEI's market share of replacement rolls and rings, the sales group responded favorably. Immediately the sales department representatives were calling upon the utilities and informing them of the six-week delivery time for IEI's replacement rings and rolls.

Initial reports received by marketing from sales were not encouraging. Instead of taking advantage of the significantly shortened lead times, many of the utilities found it very difficult to believe that IEI could offer such lead times. The marketing people were now faced with the task of making believers out of these utility companies which had become disenchanted with IEI's service over the last few years. Perhaps the mailings, which would be going out very shortly, would have some impact on the utilities, but the marketing people felt that they would probably have to come up with some other means of enticing the utilities to purchase replacement rings and rolls from IEI. This enticement would probably have to be in the form of a price reduction or some type of allowance if IEI did not meet its promise of delivery within six weeks from the time the order was placed.

Improvement in the quality of IEI's rings and rolls was something that would take at least one to two years to materialize. Extensive support would be required from engineering in designing, analyzing, and testing various types of rings and rolls. To meet this challenge, $50,000 had been set aside to develop a better-quality roll. The objective of this program was to develop a roll that would last at least as long as that offered by the competition and at a price that was comparable to that of the competition. During the implementation of this program, the marketing group suggested that engineering look into the feasibility of developing a longer-wearing roll that would be incapable of being refurbished. It was unlikely that IEI's ring and roll competitors would be able to embark on such a development program because they lacked the engineering and technical resources that IEI possessed as an original equipment manufacturer.

Once the new foundry achieved full operation, IEI expected its price for replacement rings and rolls to drop by at least 10 percent. If this price reduction of rings and rolls was not enough to bring IEI's prices in line with its competitors', IEI was prepared to cut prices more. The marketing department was presently examining the profit margins, currently 36 to 40 percent of total cost, of the various rings and rolls sold by IEI to determine how much of a price cut could be withstood. It was realized that it might be necessary for IEI to take a loss on the sale of some of its rings and rolls in an effort to increase its market share.

CONCLUSION

Whether IEI's marketing tactics will succeed in reversing the trend of declining sales of replacement rings and rolls remains to be seen. IEI has clearly defined the reasons for this decline, i.e., price, quality, and delivery of their product vs. that of the competition. IEI is now taking the appropriate steps in improving their product to regain a larger share of the market. But one must question whether these problems could have been foreseen earlier and corrective action taken then to avoid the sudden decrease in sales of rings and rolls that apparently came about without much warning. The vice-president of marketing made the following comments on the whole problem and its solution:

It is obvious that IEI made a serious mistake in having Weatherly Company ship rings and rolls directly to IEI's utility customers. But even more serious may have been the lack of personal contact with the utilities in regard to sales of rings and rolls. Having successfully thwarted one would-be competitor, Griffin Wheel, from entering the ring and roll market, IEI may have felt, with their status as an OEM and being a leader in the field of fossil fuel plant development, that they occupied a position in the ring and roll market that was relatively safe from any outside competitive forces. It was this dominant position that possibly led IEI to believe that there was no need to have contact with the utility companies in supplying them with replacement rings and rolls. Had this contact been maintained through personal sales calls to the utilities, the utilities today might not have a despondent attitude toward IEI. It is no wonder that when smaller companies such as Helmick and Weatherly, which dealt more directly with the utilities and gave them what they wanted, i.e., better delivery, quality, and price of replacement rings and rolls, entered the scene the utilities favored doing business with them rather than with IEI.

If IEI should regain its market share of ring and roll sales, and hopefully it will, it must continue to remain in contact with the utilities for such routine orders as rings and rolls. IEI must let the utilities know that it cares about their wants and needs. If this contact is not maintained the situation that now exists may arise again in the years to come.

IEI must take a closer look at the refurbishing process as this poses a very serious threat to the ring and roll business in the future. It is obvious that for larger rolls refurbishing has definite cost advantages over buying new ones. And the fact that a refurbished roll will last up to three times as long as a new roll makes refurbishing look even more attractive. One way of overcoming this problem might be to sell new rolls to the utilities on a contractual basis. Under the terms of such a contract an agreement could be made between IEI and its customer utility companies whereby a purchased roll would be refurbished by IEI for a specified number of times at a specified price. The terms of the contract would be such that it would not be profitable for the utilities to refurbish the roll themselves or have some outside firm refurbish the roll. Or a contract might be set up whereby the utilities just purchase the use of the roll, thereby preventing them from having it refurbished by a competitor. While such arrangements probably would not be as profitable to IEI as selling a new roll every time one wears out, such alternatives would still allow IEI to acquire a sizable share of the market. Having the status of an OEM would make it easier for IEI to secure such contracts in comparison to their smaller competitors, provided the pricing of such contracts is competitive.

CHAPTER 14
Pricing Strategies

The real price of everything is the toil and trouble of acquiring it.

Adam Smith

Pricing has traditionally been considered a "me too" variable in developing marketing strategy. The stable conditions of the 1960s may be particularly responsible for the low status ascribed to the pricing variable. Strategically, the function of pricing was to provide adequate return on investment. Thus, the timeworn cost-plus method of pricing and its sophisticated version, return-on-investment pricing, have historically been the basis for arriving at a price.

In the 1970s, however, a variety of happenings gave a new twist to the task of making pricing decisions. Double-digit inflation, material shortages, the high cost of money, consumerism, and post–price-controls behavior all contributed to making pricing an important part of marketing strategy.

Despite the importance attached to it, effective pricing is not easy. Even under the most favorable conditions, a large number of internal and external variables must be systematically studied. For example, the reactions of a competitor often figure as an important consideration in developing pricing strategy. Simply knowing that a competitor has a lower price is insufficient; a price strategist must know how much flexibility the competitor has in further lowering the price. This presupposes a knowledge of the competitor's cost structure. In the dynamics of today's environment, however, where unexpected economic changes can render cost and revenue projections obsolete as soon as they are developed, pricing strategy becomes much more difficult to formulate.

This chapter provides a composite of pricing strategies. Each strategy is examined for its underlying assumptions and relevance in specific situations. The application of different strategies is illustrated with the help of examples from pricing literature. The appendix at the end of this chapter summarizes each strategy by giving its definition, objectives, requirements, and expected results.

REVIEW OF PRICING FACTORS

Basically, there are four factors a pricer needs to review to arrive at a price. These are pricing objectives, cost, competition, and demand.

EXHIBIT 14-1   Potential Pricing Objectives

1. Maximum long-run profits.
2. Maximum short-run profits.
3. Growth.
4. Stabilize market.
5. Desensitize customers to price.
6. Maintain price-leadership arrangement.
7. Discourage entrants.
8. Speed exit of marginal firms.
9. Avoid government investigation and control.
10. Maintain loyalty of middlemen and get their sales support.
11. Avoid demands for "more" from suppliers—labor in particular.
12. Enhance image of firm and its offerings.
13. Be regarded as "fair" by customers (ultimate).
14. Create interest and excitement about the item.
15. Be considered trustworthy and reliable by rivals.
16. Help in the sale of weak items in the line.
17. Discourage others from cutting prices.
18. Make a product "visible."
19. "Spoil market" to obtain high price for sale of business.
20. Build traffic.

Source: Alfred R. Oxenfeldt, "A Decision-Making Structure for Price Decisions," *Journal of Marketing*, January, 1973, p. 50. Reprinted by permission of the American Marketing Association.

This section briefly reviews these factors which underlie every pricing strategy alternative.

Pricing Objectives

Broadly speaking, pricing objectives can be either profit oriented or volume oriented. The profit objective may be defined either in terms of net profit percentage desired or as a target return on investment. Traditionally the latter objective has been more popular among large corporations. The volume objective may be stated as the percentage of market share that the firm would like to achieve. Alternatively, it may simply be stated as the desired sales growth rate. Many firms also consider the maintenance of a stable price as a goal. Particularly in cyclical industries, price stability helps to sustain the confidence of customers and thus keeps operations running smoothly through peaks and valleys.

For many firms, there can be pricing objectives other than those of profitability and volume, as shown in Exhibit 14-1. Each firm should evaluate the different objectives and choose its own priorities in the context of the pricing problems that the firm may be facing. The following are illustrations of pricing problems:

1. Decline in sales
2. Prices higher or lower than those of competitors
3. Excessive pressure on middlemen to generate sales
4. Imbalance in product-line prices
5. Distortion vis-à-vis the offering in the customers' perceptions of the firm's prices
6. Frequent changes in prices without any relationship to. environmental realities[1]

These problems suggest that a firm may have more than one pricing objective, even though these objectives may not be articulated as such. Essentially, pricing objectives will deal directly or indirectly with these three areas: profit (setting a high enough price to enable the company to earn an adequate margin for profit and reinvestment), competition (setting a low enough price to discourage competitors from adding capacity), and market share (setting a price below competition to gain market share).

Cost

Fixed and variable costs are the major concerns of a pricer. In addition, the pricer may sometimes have to consider other types of costs, such as out-of-pocket costs, incremental costs, opportunity costs, controllable costs, and replacement costs.

To study the impact of costs on pricing strategy, the following three relationships may be considered: (1) the ratio of fixed costs to variable costs, (2) the economies of scale available to a firm, and (3) the cost structure of a firm vis-à-vis competitors. If the fixed costs of a company in comparison with variable costs form a high proportion of its total costs, adding sales volume will be a great help in increasing earnings. Consider, for example, the case of the airlines, whose fixed costs are as high as 60 to 70 percent of total costs. Once fixed costs are recovered, any additional tickets sold add greatly to earnings. Such an industry would be called *volume sensitive*. There are some industries, such as the paper industry, where variable costs constitute a higher proportion of total costs. Such industries are *price sensitive* since even a small increase in price adds much to earnings.

If the economies of scale obtainable from a company's operations are substantial, one should plan to expand market share and, in considering long-term prices, take expected declines in costs into account. Alternatively, if the experience is expected to produce a decline in costs, then prices may be lowered in the long run to gain higher market share.

If a manufacturer is a low-cost producer relative to competitors, it will earn additional profits by maintaining prices at competitive levels. The additional profits can be used to promote the product aggressively and

---

[1]Alfred B. Oxenfeldt, "A Decision-Making Structure for Price Decisions," *Journal of Marketing*, January, 1973, pp. 48–53.

EXHIBIT 14-2   Effect of Costs on Pricing

COST PRICING		
COSTS	PRODUCT A	PRODUCT B
Labor (L)	$20	$30
Material (M)	40	20
Overhead (O)	10	20
Full Cost (L + M + O)	70	70
Incremental Cost (L + M)	60	50
Conversion Cost (L + O)	30	50
PRODUCT-LINE PRICES		
	MARKUP (M′)	PRODUCT A	PRODUCT B
Full-cost Pricing P = FC + (M′)FC	20%	$84	$84
Incremental-cost Pricing P = (L + M) + M′(L + M)	40%	84	70
Conversion-cost Pricing P = (L + O) + M′(L + O)	180%	84	140

Source: Philip Kotler, *Marketing Management: Analysis, Planning and Control,* 2d Ed., © 1972, p. 544. Reprinted by permission of Prentice-Hall, Inc., Englewood Cliffs, NJ.

increase the overall perspective of the business. If, however, the costs of a manufacturer are high compared to those of competitors, the manufacturer is in no position to reduce prices since this may lead to a price war which it is bound to lose.

Different elements of cost must be differently related in setting prices. Exhibit 14-2 shows, for example, how computations of full cost, incremental cost, and conversion cost may vary and how these costs affect product-line prices. Exhibit 14-3 shows the procedure followed for setting target-return pricing.

Competition

Exhibit 14-4 shows the competitive information needed for pricing strategy. The information may be analyzed with reference to the following competitive characteristics: number of firms in the industry, relative size of different members of the industry, product differentiation, and ease of entry.

In an industry where there is only one firm, competitive activity is absent and the firm is free to set any price, subject to constraints imposed

EXHIBIT 14-3   Computation of Target-Return Pricing

Manufacturing Capacity	200,000
Standard Volume (80%)	160,000
Standard Full Cost Before Profit	$100/unit
Target Profit	
Investment	$20,000,000
ROI Target	20%
ROI Target	$4,000,000
Profit Per Unit at Standard ($4,000,000 ÷ 160,000)	$25/unit
Price	$125/unit

by law. As an Illinois Bell executive said about pricing (before the AT&T split): "All we had to do was determine our costs, and then we would go to the commission—the Illinois Commerce Commission, and they would give us the allowable rate of return."[2] Conversely, in an industry comprising a large number of active firms there is fierce competition, which limits the discretion of a firm in setting its prices. Where there are a few firms manufacturing an undifferentiated product (such as in the steel industry), only the industry leader may have the discretion to change prices. Other industry members will tend to follow the leader in setting their prices.

The firm with a large market share in an industry will be in a position to initiate price changes without worrying about competitors' reactions. Presumably, a competitor with a large market share will have the lowest costs. The firm can, therefore, keep its prices low, thus discour-

EXHIBIT 14-4   Competitive Information Needed for Pricing Strategy

1. Published competitive price lists and advertising
2. Competitive reaction to price moves in the past
3. Timing of competitors' price changes and initiating factors
4. Information on competitors' special campaigns
5. Competitive product-line comparison
6. Assumptions on competitors' pricing/marketing objectives
7. Competitors' reported financial performance
8. Estimates of competitors' costs—fixed and variable
9. Expected pricing retaliation
10. Analysis of competitors' capacity to retaliate
11. Financial viability of engaging in price war
12. Strategic posture of competitors
13. Overall competitive aggressiveness

---

[2]Heywood Klein, "Illinois Bell Faces New Environment As Era of Competitive Pricing Nears," *The Wall Street Journal,* December 31, 1981, p. 9.

aging other members of the industry from adding capacity and further improving its cost advantage in a growing market.

If a firm operates in an industry where there are opportunities for product differentiation, it can have some control over pricing even if the size of the firm is small and there are many competitors in the industry. This may occur if customers consider one brand to be different from other competing brands; whether the difference is real or imaginary, they will not object to paying a higher price for their preferred brand. To establish product differentiation of their brand in the minds of consumers, companies spend heavily for promotion. Product differentiation, however, offers an opportunity to control prices only within a certain range.

In an industry which is easy to enter, the price setter has less discretion in establishing prices; if barriers to market entry exist, however, the firm already in the industry will have greater control over prices. Barriers to entry may take any of the following forms:

1. Capital investment
2. Technological requirements
3. Nonavailability of essential materials
4. Economies of scale which existing firms are enjoying and which would be difficult for a newcomer to achieve
5. Control over natural resources by existing firms
6. Marketing expertise

In an industry where barriers to entry are relatively easy to surmount, a firm will follow what can be called keep-away pricing. This is necessarily on the lower side of the pricing spectrum.

Demand

Exhibit 14-5 contains the information required for analyzing demand. Demand is based on a variety of considerations, of which price is just one. Some of these considerations are:

1. Ability of customers to buy
2. Willingness of customers to buy
3. Place of the product in the customer's lifestyle (whether a status symbol or a daily-use product)
4. Benefits that the product provides the customers
5. Prices of substitute products
6. Potential market for the product (if there is an unfulfilled demand in the market or if the market is saturated)
7. Nature of nonprice competition
8. Customer behavior in general
9. Segments in the market

EXHIBIT 14-5   Customer Information Needed for Pricing Strategy

1. The customers' value analysis of the product: performance, utility, profit-rendering potential, quality, etc.
2. Market acceptance level: the price level of acceptance in each major market, including the influence of substitutes
3. The price the market expects, differences in different markets
4. Price stability
5. The product's S-curve and its present position on it
6. Seasonal and cyclical characteristics of the industry
7. The economic conditions now and during the next few periods
8. The effect of depressions to anticipate; the effect of price change on demand in such a declining market (e.g., very little with luxury items)
9. Customer relations
10. Channel relations, and channel costs to figure in calculations
11. The mark-up at each channel level, company vs. intermediary goals
12. Advertising and promotion requirements and costs
13. Trade-in, replacement parts, service, delivery, installation, maintenance, preorder and post-order engineering; inventory, obsolescence, and spoilage problems and costs
14. The product differentiation that is necessary
15. Existing industry customs and reaction of the industry
16. Stockholder, government, labor, employee, and community reactions

Source: John M. Brion, *Corporate Marketing Planning*, p. 181. Copyright © 1967 by John Wiley & Sons. Reprinted by permission of John Wiley & Sons, Inc.

All these factors are interdependent, and it may not be easy to estimate their relationship to each other precisely.[3]

Demand analysis involves predicting the relationship between price level and demand while considering the effects of other variables on demand. The relationship between price and demand is called *elasticity of demand* or *sensitivity of price*. It refers to the number of units of a product that would be demanded at different prices. Price sensitivity should be considered at two different levels: total industry price sensitivity and price sensitivity for a particular firm.

Industry demand for a product is considered to be elastic if, by lowering prices, demand can be substantially increased. If lowering of price has little effect on demand, the demand is considered inelastic. The environmental factors previously mentioned will have a definite influence

[3]Benson P. Shapiro and Barbara B. Jackson, "Industrial Pricing to Meet Consumers' Needs," *Harvard Business Review*, November–December, 1978, pp. 119–127.

on demand elasticity. Let us illustrate with a few examples. In the 1970s during the energy crisis, the price of gasoline went up, which led consumers to reduce gasoline usage. By the same token, if by some miracle gasoline prices should go down, people would use gas more freely, driving large cars again and taking long-distance vacations by car. Thus, demand for gasoline can be considered somewhat elastic.

A case of inelastic demand is provided by salt. No matter how much the price fluctuates, people are not going to change the amount of salt they consume. Similarly, demand for luxury goods such as yachts is inelastic since yachts fit into the lifestyle of only a small proportion of the total population.

Sometimes the market for a product is segmented so that demand elasticity in each segment must be studied. Demand for certain types of beverages in the senior citizens' market might be inelastic, although it is especially elastic in the younger market. If the price of a product goes up, customers have the option of switching to another product. Thus, availability of substitute products is another factor that needs consideration.

When the total demand of an industry is highly elastic, the industry leader may take the initiative to lower prices. The loss in revenues due to decreased prices will be more than compensated for by the additional demand expected to be generated; therefore the total dollar market expands. Such a strategy is highly attractive in an industry where economies of scale are achievable. Where demand is inelastic and there are no conceivable substitutes, the prices may be increased, at least in the short run. In the long run, however, the government may impose controls, or substitutes may be developed.

The demand for the products of an individual firm will be derived from the total industry demand. An individual firm will be interested in finding out how much market share it can command by changing its own prices. In the case of undifferentiated standardized products, lower prices should help a firm to increase its market share as long as competitors do not retaliate by matching the firm's prices. Similarly, when business is sought through bidding prices, lower prices should be of help. In the case of differentiated products, however, market share can be improved even by maintaining higher prices (within a certain range). The products may be differentiated in various real and imaginary ways.

For example, by providing adequate guarantees and after-sale services, an appliance manufacturer may maintain higher prices and still increase market share. Brand name, an image of sophistication, and the perception of high quality are other factors which may help to differentiate the product and thus create for the firm an opportunity to increase prices and not lose market share. Of course, other elements of the marketing mix should reinforce the image suggested by the price. In brief, a firm's best opportunity lies in differentiating the product and then communicating this fact to the customer. A differentiated product offers more opportunity for increasing earnings through price increases.

The sensitivity of price can be measured by taking into account historical data, consumer surveys, and experimentation. Historical data can be either studied intuitively or analyzed through quantitative tools such as regression to see how demand goes up or down based on prices. A consumer survey to study sensitivity of prices is no different from any other market research study. Experiments can be conducted either in a laboratory situation or in the real world to judge what level of prices will generate what level of demand. For example, a company interested in studying the sensitivity of prices may introduce a newly developed grocery product in a few selected markets for a short period of time at different prices. Information obtained from this experiment should provide insights into elasticity of demand for the product. In one study, the prices of 17 food products were varied in 30 food stores. It was found that the product sales generally followed the "law of demand": When prices were raised 10 percent, sales decreased about 25 percent; an increase of 5 percent in prices led to a decrease in sales of about 13 percent; a lowering of prices by 5 percent increased sales by 12 percent; and a 10 percent decrease in price improved sales by 26 percent. In another study, a new deodorant priced at 63 cents and at 85 cents in different markets resulted in the same volume of sales. Thus, price elasticity was found to be absent, and the manufacturer set the product price at 85 cents.[4]

Laboratory experiments can be conducted in simulated environments to test the effects of various prices on demand. For example, consumers can be invited to an auditorium where they may be exposed to a number of products and asked to state their preferences. This information can then be analyzed to determine how demand behaved at various prices. Laboratory experiments can be performed in a variety of ways. In the studies that have been reported on laboratory experiments, students have generally been used as consumers. The consumers are asked to choose a brand from among several different ones without being shown the actual products, or they may be asked to go on a simulated shopping trip. In any event, if properly planned, the results obtained from laboratory experiments can be reliable.

To conclude the discussion on pricing factors, it would not be out of place to say that while everybody thinks businesses go about setting prices scientifically, very often the process is incredibly arbitrary. Although businesses of all types devote a great deal of time and study to determine what prices to put on their products, pricing often remains more art than science. In some cases, setting prices does involve use of a straightforward equation: material and labor costs, plus overhead and other expenses, plus profit, equals price. But in many other cases the equation includes psychological and other subjective factors so subtle that the decision may essentially rest on gut feeling.[5]

---

[4]Mark I. Alpert, *Pricing Decisions* (Glenview, IL: Scott, Foresman and Co., 1971), p. 96.
[5]See Jeffrey H. Birnbaum, "Pricing of Products Is Still an Art, Often Having Link to Costs," *The Wall Street Journal*, November 25, 1981, p. 29.

PRICING STRATEGIES FOR NEW PRODUCTS

Pricing strategy for a new product should be so developed as to make the desired impact on the market while at the same time discouraging the emergence of competition. There are two basic strategies that may be used in pricing a new product, skimming pricing and penetration pricing.

Skimming Pricing

Skimming pricing is the strategy of establishing a high initial price for a product with a view to "skimming the cream off the market" at the upper end of the demand curve. It is accompanied by heavy expenditure on promotion. A skimming strategy may be recommended when the nature of the demand is uncertain, when a company has expended large sums of money on research and development of a new product, when the competition is expected to develop and market a similar product in the near future, or when the product is so innovative that the market is expected to mature very slowly.

In these circumstances, a skimming strategy has several advantages. At the top of the demand curve, price elasticity is low. Besides, in the absence of any close substitute, cross elasticity is also low. These factors, along with heavy emphasis on promotion, tend to help the product make significant inroads into the market. The high price also helps in segmenting the market. Only non–price-conscious customers will buy the new product during the initial stage. Later on, the mass market can be tapped by lowering the price.

If there are doubts about the shape of the demand curve, and the initial price is found to be too high, the price may be slashed. But it is very difficult to start low and then raise the price later on. Raising a low price may annoy potential customers, and further anticipated drops in price may retard demand at a particular price. For a financially weak company, a skimming strategy may provide immediate relief. This model depends upon selling enough units at the higher price to cover promotion and development costs. If price elasticity is higher than anticipated, a lower price will be more profitable and "relief giving."

Modern patented drugs provide a good example of skimming pricing. At the time of its introduction in 1942, penicillin was priced as high as $20 for a 100,000-unit vial. By 1944 the price was down to $2, and it had decreased to a few cents in 1949. Many new products are priced following this policy. Color television, long-playing records, frozen foods, and instant coffee were all priced very high at the time of their initial appearance in the market. But different versions of these products are now available at prices ranging from very high to very low.

No conclusive research has yet been done to indicate how high the initial price should be in relation to the cost. The following suggestion provides a guideline:

A rule of thumb in the relationship between factory door cost and consumer's price is that the final price to the consumer should be at least three or four times the factory door cost. Such markup is frequently used to provide adequate margins for the promotional outlays needed for new-product flotation and for anticipated reductions in the retail price as distributor competition intensifies.[6]

The decision on how high a skimming price should be will depend on two factors: (1) chances of competitors entering the market and (2) price elasticity at the upper layer of the demand curve. If competitors are expected to bring out their own brands quickly, it may be safe to price rather high. On the other hand, if competitors are years behind in product development and a low rate of return to the firm would slow the pace of their research, a low skimming price would be useful. However, price skimming in the face of impending competition may not be wise if a larger market share might make entry more difficult. If limiting the sale of the new product to a few selected individuals will produce sufficient sales, a very high price may be desirable.

Determining the duration of time for keeping prices high will depend entirely upon the competition's activities. In the absence of patent protection, skimming prices may be forced down as soon as competitors join the race. However, in the case of products such as drugs, which are protected through patents, the first manufacturer slowly brings down the price as the patent period draws near an end, and then, a year or so before the expiration of the patent period, the first manufacturer saturates the market with a very low price. This is done to establish a foothold in the mass market before competitors enter it, thereby frustrating their expectations.

So far, skimming prices have been discussed as high prices in the initial stage. There are other forms of initial high prices, called *premium* and *umbrella* prices, which remain more or less high.[7] Some products carry premium prices (high prices) permanently and build an image of superiority for themselves. Where a mass market cannot be developed and the upper-end demand seems adequate, manufacturers will not take the risk of tarnishing the prestigious image by lowering prices and offering the product to everybody. Estee Lauder cosmetics, Olga intimate apparel, Brooks Brothers' clothes and Johnston & Murphy's shoes are products which fall into this category.

Sometimes higher prices are maintained in order to provide an umbrella for the small high-cost competitors. The umbrella pricing policy has been aided by limitation laws passed by state governments, which specify

---

[6]Joel Dean, *Managerial Economics* (Englewood Cliffs, NJ: Prentice-Hall, 1951), p. 419.
[7]Robert A. Lynn, *Price Policies and Marketing Management* (Homewood, IL: Richard D. Irwin, 1967), pp. 134–137.

minimum prices for a variety of products, such as milk.

DuPont provides an interesting example of a skimming-pricing strategy. The company tends to focus on higher-margin specialty products. Initially it prices them high, then it gradually lowers the prices as the market builds and competition grows.[8]

Penetration Pricing

Penetration pricing is the strategy of entering the market with a low initial price so that a greater share of the market can be captured. The penetration strategy is resorted to when an elite market does not exist and demand seems to be elastic over the entire demand curve, even during the early stages of product introduction. High price elasticity of demand is probably the most important reason for adopting the penetration strategy. The penetration strategy is also used to discourage competitors from entering the market. When competitors seem to be encroaching on the market, an attempt is made to lure them away by means of penetration pricing, which requires lower margins. A competitor's costs play a decisive role in this, since a cost advantage over the existing manufacturer might persuade a firm to enter the market, however low the margin of the former may be.

One may also turn to penetration strategy with a view to achieving economies of scale. Savings in production costs alone may not be an important factor in setting prices low, since in the absence of price elasticity it is difficult to generate sufficient sales. Finally, before adopting penetration pricing, one must make sure that the product will fit the lifestyles of the mass market. For example, while it might not be difficult for people to accept imitation milk, cereals made out of petroleum products would probably have difficulty in becoming popular.

How low the penetration price should be will differ from case to case. There are several different types of prices used in penetration strategy: *restrained prices, elimination prices, promotional prices,* and *keep-out prices.* Restraint is applied so as to maintain prices at a certain point during inflationary periods. In this case environmental circumstances serve as a guide to what the level of price should be. Elimination prices are fixed at a point where the survival of a competitor is threatened. A large, multiproduct company can lower prices to a level where a smaller competitor might be wiped out of the market. Pricing of suits at factory outlets illustrates promotional prices. Factory outlets constantly stress low prices for comparable quality. Keep-out prices are fixed at a level where the competitor is *just* prevented from entering the market. Here the objective is to keep the market to oneself at the highest chargeable price. A low price acts as the sole selling point under penetration strategy, but the market should be

---

[8]"Pricing Strategy in an Inflation Economy," *Business Week,* April 6, 1974, p. 43.

broad enough to justify low prices. Thus, price elasticity of demand is probably the most important factor in determining how low prices can go.

The point may be illustrated with an example.[9] Convinced that shoppers would willingly sacrifice convenience for price savings, an entrepreneur in 1981 introduced a concentrated cleaner called 4+1. Unlike such higher-priced cleaners as Windex, Fantastik, and Formula 409, this product did not come in a spray bottle and needed to be diluted with water. The entrepreneur hoped for 10 percent of the $160-million market. But the product did not sell well. The product was not price elastic as the entrepreneur had assumed: though the consumer tends to talk a lot about economy, the lure of convenience is apparently stronger than the wish to save a few cents. Ultimately, the product had to be withdrawn from most markets.

Unlike DuPont, Dow Chemical Company stresses a penetration-pricing strategy. It concentrates on lower-margin commodity products and low prices, builds a dominant market share, and holds on for the long pull.[10]

PRICING STRATEGIES FOR ESTABLISHED PRODUCTS

Changes in the marketing environment may require a review of prices of products already on the market. For example, an announcement by a large firm that it is going to lower its prices will make it necessary for other firms in the industry to examine their prices. In 1976 Texas Instruments announced that it would soon sell a digital watch for about $20. The TI announcement jolted the entire industry, since only 15 months earlier the lowest-priced digital was selling for $125. It forced a change in everyone's strategy and gave some producers real problems. Fairchild Camera & Instrument Corporation reacted with its own version of a $20 plastic-cased watch. So did National Semiconductor Corporation. American Microsystems, Inc., however, decided to get completely out of the finished watch business.[11]

A review of pricing strategy may also become necessary because of shifts in demand. In the late 1960s, for example, it seemed that with the popularity of miniskirts the pantyhose market would continue to boom. But the fashion emphasis on pants slowed down the growth. Pants hide runs or tears in pantyhose, making it unnecessary to buy as many pairs. The pants fashion has also led to a preference for knee-high hose over pantyhose. Knee-high hose cost less to the customer and mean lower prof-

---

[9] *The Wall Street Journal*, December 31, 1981, p. 9.
[10] "Pricing Strategy in an Inflation Economy," p. 43.
[11] "How T.I. Beat the Clock on Its $20 Digital Watch," *Business Week*, May 31, 1976, pp. 62–63. (For different reasons TI, a few years later, quit the digital watch business itself. But the point made here with reference to pricing is still relevant.)

its for the manufacturers. While the market was dwindling, two new entrants, Bic Pen Corporation and Playtex Corporation, were readying their brands for introduction. This made it necessary for the big three—Hanes, Burlington, and Kayser-Roth—to review their prices and protect market shares.[12]

An examination of existing prices may lead to one of three strategic alternatives: maintaining the price, reducing the price, or increasing the price.

Maintaining the Price

If the market segment from which the company derives a big portion of its sales is not affected by changes in the environment, the company may decide not to initiate any change in its pricing strategy. The gasoline shortage in the aftermath of the fall of the Shah of Iran did not affect the luxury-car market. Buyers of Cadillac, Mercedes-Benz, and Rolls-Royce were not concerned about higher gas prices. Thus, General Motors did not need to redesign the Cadillac to reduce gas consumption or lower its price to make it attractive to the average customer, despite its heavy gas usage.

This strategy will be appropriate in circumstances where a price change may be desirable, but the magnitude of change is indeterminable. This may be because the reaction of customers and competitors to a price change cannot be predicted. Alternatively, the price change may have an impact on the product image or sales of other products in the line, which it is not practical to assess. Back in the early 1970s, when Magnavox and Sylvania cut the prices of their color television sets, Zenith maintained prices at their current level. Since the industry appeared to be in good shape, Zenith could not determine why competitors were adopting such a strategic posture. Zenith continued to maintain prices for six years until 1977, when it sought multiple cuts in prices during a period of six months.[13] Thus, price may also be maintained when a company is not sure why a price change may be desirable.

Politics may be still another reason for maintaining prices. During 1978–79 President Carter urged voluntary control of wages and prices. Many companies restrained themselves from seeking price changes in order to align themselves behind government efforts to control inflation.

Concern for the welfare of society may be another reason for maintaining prices at current levels. Even when supply is temporarily short of demand, some businesspeople may continue to charge the current prices to adopt a socially responsible posture. For example, taxi drivers in a large

---

[12]"The New Sag in Pantyhose," *Business Week,* December 14, 1974, p. 98.
[13]"Troubled Zenith Battles Stiffer Competition," *Business Week,* October 10, 1977, p. 128.

city may choose not to hike fares when subway and bus service operators are on strike.

Reducing the Price

There are three main reasons for lowering prices. First, as a defensive strategy, prices may be cut in response to competition. For example, in October, 1978, Congress authorized deregulation of airlines. This gave airlines almost total freedom to set ticket prices. Thus, in 1981, in response to New York Air's $90 round-trip fare on its Cleveland–New York route, United Airlines had to meet the competitive fare; United's regular round-trip coach fare at the time was $296. Similarly, other carriers were forced to reduce their fares on different routes to match competitive prices.[14]

A second reason for lowering prices is offensive in nature. Following the experience curve concept (see Chapter 17), costs across the board go down by a fixed percentage every time experience doubles. This means that a company with greater experience will have lower costs than one whose experience is limited. Lower costs have a favorable impact on profits. Thus, as a matter of strategy in order to gain a cost and, hence, profit advantage, it behooves a company to shoot for higher market share and secure as much experience as possible.

Similarly, technological advances have made possible the low-cost production of high-quality electronics gear, and many companies have translated these advances into low retail prices to gain competitive leverage. For example, in 1978 a Sony clock radio, with no power backup and a face that showed nothing more than the current time, sold for $80. In 1981, a Sony clock radio priced at $39.95 had auxiliary power and showed the time at which the alarm was set as well as the current time.[15]

Texas Instruments has followed the experience curve concept in gaining cost reductions of integrated circuits for a long time. This has been duly reflected in its strategy to slowly lower prices of such products as electronic calculators. Even in other businesses such a strategy may work out. Take the case of Metpath Inc., a clinical laboratory. At about the time Metpath was formed in the late 1960s, the industry leader, Damon Corporation, was acquiring local labs all around the country; by the early 1970s, large corporations in the business, Revlon, Bristol-Myers, Diamond Shamrock, and W. R. Grace, began doing the same. Metpath, however, adopted a price-cutting strategy. In order to implement this strategy, it took a variety of measures to seek economies of scale, thus reducing costs. Figuring

---

[14]John Curley, "Decontrol of Airlines Shifts Pricing from a Cost to a Competition Basis," *The Wall Street Journal,* December 4, 1981, p. 37.

[15]Laura Landro, "Technology, Competition Cut Price of Electronics Gear As Quality Rises," *The Wall Street Journal,* December 1, 1981, p. 37.

that there were not many economies of scale involved in simply putting together a chain of local labs that continue to operate mostly as separate entities, Metpath focused on centralizing its testing at a super-lab that did have those economies and on creating a nationwide network to collect specimens and distribute test results. Metpath's strategy paid off well. In 1979 it was on the verge of becoming the industry leader with sales of $53.4 million in the $12-billion clinical-lab-testing field. Meanwhile, Damon, with revenues of $76 million in 1978, has been stumbling. Heavy price competition, much of it attributed to Metpath, led some of the big diversified companies, including W. R. Grace and Diamond Shamrock, to pull out of the business.[16]

The third and final reason for price cutting may be a response to customer need. If low prices are a prerequisite for inducing the market to grow, customer need may then become the pivot of marketing strategy, all other aspects of the marketing mix being developed accordingly. In the late 1970s continued inflation and higher prices made customers sensitive to shopping alternatives. Around this time, a new type of grocery store named Aldi opened its doors in the Chicago area. The biggest attraction of this store has been its rock-bottom prices. It carried only 450 food items (as against some 10,000 different food items in a large supermarket), most of them dry or canned foods; there was no fresh meat, eggs, milk, or anything refrigerated. Aldi provided no carry-out service, and there were no bags (customers brought their own bags), boxes, or check cashing. Needless to say, Aldi is doing well. As a matter of fact, it became a model for the establishment of similar stores throughout the country. Even some large chains moved in to adopt a strategic posture similar to Aldi's. The Jewel Companies initiated their generic product line with more than 100 products and introduced it in many of their Midwest supermarkets and in their Star Market Company subsidiary in New England. Generic products are those sold without brand names and marketed with labels reading "apple juice," "baking soda," and so on. It is expected that about 10 percent of the total industry sales of about $140 billion in the 1980s will go to stores like Aldi.[17]

In adopting a low-price strategy for an existing product, a variety of considerations must be taken into account. The long-term impact of a price cut against a major competitor is a factor to be reckoned with. For example, a regional pizza chain can cut prices to prevent Pizza Hut from gaining a foothold in the market only in the short run. Eventually Pizza Hut (a division of PepsiCo, Inc.) will prevail over the local chain through price competition. Pizza Hut may lower prices to such an extent that the

---

[16]"Metpath: Price Cutting with a Super-Lab Creates New Growth," *Business Week*, February 26, 1979, p. 128.

[17]David P. Garino and Paul Ingrassia, "No Frills Food Shops Attract Customers, Unsettle Supermarkets," *The Wall Street Journal*, April 27, 1978, p. 1.

local chain may find it difficult even to recover its costs. Thus, competitive strength should be duly evaluated in opting for low-price strategy.

In a highly competitive situation, a product may continue to command a higher price than other brands if it is marketed as a "different" product—for example, one of deluxe quality. If the price of this product is reduced, the likely impact on its position should be looked into. Sony television sets have traditionally been sold at a premium price since they were promoted as a quality product. Sony's strategy paid off: the Sony TV rose to prominence as a quality product capturing over 7 percent of the market between 1970 and 1975. Around that time, growing consumer-movement pressures led Sony dealers to reduce prices. This not only hurt Sony's overall prestige, but also made some retailers stop selling Sony since it had now become just one of the many brands they carried.[18] In other words, the price cut, though partly initiated by its dealers, lost Sony its distinction. Even if its sales might have increased in the short run, in the long run the price cut did not prove to be a viable strategy because it went against the perception consumers had of Sony's being a distinctive brand.[19] Ultimately, consumers may perceive Sony as just another brand, which will affect both sales and profits.

It is necessary to examine thoroughly the impact of a price cut of one product on other products in the line. Price is often considered to be an indication of product quality. Thus, the same product with a different price tag may be perceived differently. The impact of lowering prices can be illustrated with reference to the Bulova Watch Company. In 1972, the company was considering reducing the prices of its tuning-fork Accutron watches for men. Before finalizing the decision, the company had to consider the following effects of reducing the prices:

1. The pricing decision extended beyond Bulova's Accutron watches for men. In 1972 Bulova had, for the first time, started to market Accutron watches for women. This new line could more than double the market for Accutron watches. Also, in 1972 Bulova had started to market Accuquartz watches for men, Bulova's entry into the new market for quartz watches. If the prices for men's Accutron watches were reduced, the prices for the other two lines would have to be adjusted downwards as well.

2. A reduced-price Accutron line might affect Bulova's long-established conventional watch line. In 1972 the sale of "Bulova" brand watches—jeweled-lever watches retailing at prices across the entire mid-price segment of the market—continued a major piece of Bulova's business. In the past, a price gap separated most Bulova brand watches from those in the more expensive Accutron line. If the gap were closed, the company might find that it was trading sales of its

[18]Paul Ingrassia, "In a Color-TV Market Roiled by Price Wars, Sony Takes a Pounding," *The Wall Street Journal,* March 16, 1978, p. 1.

[19]See Zarrel V. Lambert, "Product Perception: An Important Variable in Price Strategy," *Journal of Marketing,* October, 1970, pp. 68–71.

most expensive Bulova brand watches for sales of its least expensive
Accutron watches.

3. The price reduction, if approved, could not be limited strictly to
   Bulova's domestic business. Bulova's watch prices overseas, though
   not identical with those in the United States, were related to its watch
   prices at home. Eventually, to maintain some sort of order on a
   worldwide basis, Bulova's foreign prices would have to ease down,
   too.

4. Related to point 3, Bulova's operations, particularly its manufacturing activities, were highly international in nature. Most of what
   the firm sold in the United States came from its overseas plants.
   But, with recurring monetary crises and currency realignments, the
   pricing decision had to be made against a backdrop of confused
   international economic conditions.

5. Finally, Bulova's financial performance in the preceding two years
   was nothing to cheer about. Declining defense orders since 1970
   had, by 1972, cut $26 million out of Bulova's sales, and even though
   increases in Bulova's consumer business had picked up some of the
   slack, profits had suffered badly. Bulova's net income for its fiscal
   year ending March 31, 1972, was $3.9 million, down 40% from its
   record 1970 net income of $6.8 million. While fiscal 1973 looked
   more promising, the company clearly had some distance to go to
   get back to its previous performance level.[20]

Finally, the impact of a price cut on a product's financial performance must be reviewed before the strategy is implemented. If a company
is financially so positioned that a price cut will weaken its profitability, it
may decide not to lower the price even if that may be in all other ways
the best posture to follow. It has been said that in the late 1960s, when
BankAmericard and Master Charge were made available to consumers free
of charge, the American Express Company was faced with a big dilemma.
To stop the growth of BankAmericard and Master Charge, it was considered strategically desirable to offer American Express at a nominal price,
i.e., $5 or even less as opposed to the former annual charge of $15. But
the American Express Company could ill afford loss of revenues. Since it
could not be sure that reducing the price of its card would generate enough
additional business to provide about the same amount of revenues, American Express decided to stick to its price.

Increasing the Price

An increase in price may be sought for various reasons. First, in an
inflationary economy, prices may have to be adjusted upward in order to
maintain profitability. During inflation all types of costs go up, and to

---

[20]"Bulova Watch Company, Inc. (A)," a business case copyrighted by the President
and Fellows of Harvard College, 1973, pp. 1–2.

maintain profits at an adequate level, increase in price becomes necessary. How much the price should be increased is a matter of strategy that varies from case to case. Conceptually, however, price should be increased to such a level that the profits before and after inflation are approximately equal. The increase in price should also take into account any decline in revenue caused by shift in demand due to the price increase. Strategically, the decision should be based on the long-term implication of short-run cost increases. Creative ways must be found to capture a competitive advantage by minimizing the effects of inflationary cost pressures on the company's strategy.[21]

Mention must be made that it is not always necessary for a company to increase prices to offset inflationary pressure. A company can take non-price measures as well to reduce inflationary effect. For example, many fast-food chains have increased their menus and seating capacity, thus partially offsetting the rise in costs. Similarly, a firm may substantially increase prices, much more than justified by inflation alone, and improve product quality and/or raise the level of accompanying services. High quality should help in keeping prices and profits up. Inflation-weary customers search for value in the marketplace. Improved product quality and additional services should provide such value.[22]

Prices may also be increased when a brand has a monopolistic control over the market segments that it serves. In other words, when a brand has a differential advantage over competing brands in the market, it may increase the price so as to maximize its benefits and take advantage of its unique position. The differential advantage may be real or may just exist in the mind of the consumer. In seeking a price increase in a monopolistic situation, the increase should be such that the customers will absorb it and still remain loyal to the brand. If the price increase is abnormal, the differential advantage may be lost, and the customer will choose a brand based on price. This may be illustrated with reference to coffee. Let us say there is a segment of customers who ardently drink Maxwell House coffee. In their minds Maxwell House has something special. If the price of Maxwell House coffee goes up (assuming prices of other brands of coffee remain unchanged), these coffee drinkers may continue with it because the brand has a virtual monopoly over their coffee-drinking behavior. There is a limit, however, to what these Maxwell House loyalists will

---

[21]See Joseph A. Pechman (ed.), *Economics for Policymaking, Selected Essays of Arthur M. Okun* (Cambridge, MA: The MIT Press, 1983), pp. 12–13. See also Arthur A. Thompson, Jr., "Strategies for Staying Cost Competitive," *Harvard Business Review*, January–February, 1984, pp. 110–117; and R. Dolan, "Pricing Strategies That Adjust to Inflation," *Industrial Marketing Management*, October, 1981, pp. 151–156.

[22]Mary Louise Hatten, "Don't Get Caught with Your Prices Down: Pricing in Inflationary Times," *Business Horizons*, March–April, 1982. pp. 23–28. See also Thaddeus H. Spratlen, "Industrial Marketers Need to Focus on Price in Relation to Other Marketing Mix Variables," *Marketing News*, May 1, 1981, p. 10.

pay for their favorite brand of coffee. Thus, if the price of Maxwell House coffee is increased too much, these customers may shift their preference.

This indicates that in monopolistic situations, strategically, the price of a brand may be set high to increase revenues. The extent of the increase will depend on many factors. Each competitor has a different optimum price level for a given end product for a given customer group. It is rare that such optimum prices will be the same for any two competitors. Each competitor has different options based on different cost components, capacity constraints, financial structure, product mix, customer mix, logistics, culture, and growth rate. The competitor with the lowest optimum price has the option of setting the common price; all others must follow or retreat. However, the continued existence of competitors depends upon each firm retreating from competition where it is disadvantaged until each competes primarily in a "competitive segment," a monopolistic situation, where it has an advantage compared to all others. That unique combination of characteristics, matched with differentials in the competitive environment, enables each firm to coexist and prosper in its chosen arena, where it has monopolistic control.

Sometimes prices must be increased to adhere to the industry situation. Of the few firms in an industry, one of them (usually the largest) emerges as a leader. If the leader firm raises its price, other members of the industry must do so too, if only to maintain balance of strength in the industry. If they refuse to do so, they are liable to be challenged by the leader. Usually no firm likes to fight the industry leader since it has more at stake than the leader.

In the U.S. auto industry there are four firms: General Motors, Ford, Chrysler, and American Motors. General Motors is the industry leader. If General Motors increases its prices, all other members of the industry follow suit. Thus, a firm may be compelled to seek a price increase in response to a similar increase by the industry leader. The leader also sets the limit to price increases, and followers frequently set their prices very close to those of the leader. While the increase is forced on a firm in this situation, it is a good strategic move to set a price which, without becoming obviously different, is higher than the leader's price.

Prices may also be increased to segment the market. For example, a soft-drink company may come out with a new brand and direct it toward busy executives/professionals. This brand may be differentiated as one that provides stamina and invigoration without adding calories. To substantiate the brand's worth and make it appear different, the price may be set at double the price of existing brands of soft drinks. Similarly, the market may be segmented by geography with varying prices in different segments. For example, in New York City, a 6.4-ounce tube of Crest toothpaste sold for $3.29 on Park Avenue, for $2.79 on the Upper East Side, and for $1.79 on the Lower East Side.[23]

---

[23]Jeffrey H. Birnbaum, "Location, Volume, Marketing Make Prices Vary Widely in New York City," *The Wall Street Journal*, December 3, 1981, p. 31.

Hewlett-Packard Company operates in the highly competitive pocket calculator industry, where the practice of price cutting is quite common. Nonetheless, Hewlett-Packard thrives by offering high-priced products for a select segment of the market. It seems to appeal to a market segment that is highly inelastic with respect to price, but highly elastic with respect to quality. The company equips its products with special features and then offers its calculators at a price that is much higher than the industry average. In other words, rather than running the business on the basis of overall volume, one can realize high price by becoming a specialist and serving a narrow segment. In cosmetics or automobiles, for example, there may be a tenfold cost difference between mass market products and those designed, produced, packaged, distributed, and promoted for small, high-quality niches. The up-market products are often produced by specialist companies like Daimler-Benz or BMW, which can compete successfully around the far larger producers of standard products.

Increase in price should be considered for its effect on long-term profitability, demand elasticity, and competitive moves. While in the short run a higher price may mean higher profits, the long-run effect of a price increase may be disastrous. The increase may encourage new entrants to the industry and competition from substitutes. Thus, before the price-increase strategy is implemented, its long-term effect should be thoroughly examined. Further, an increase in price may lead to shifts in demand which could be detrimental. Likewise, the increase may negatively affect market share if the competition decides not to seek similar increases in price. Thus, the competitive posture must be studied and predicted. Additionally, a company should review its own ability to live with higher prices. A price increase may mean decline in revenues, but increase in profits. Whether such a situation will create any problem needs to be looked into. Will laying off people or reassigning of sales territories be problematic? Is a limit to price increases called for as a matter of social responsibility? For example, in 1979 President Carter asked businesses to voluntarily adhere to 7 percent increases in prices and wages. In such a situation, should a company which otherwise finds a 10 percent increase in price strategically sound go ahead with it? Finally, the price increase should be duly reinforced by other factors of the marketing mix. A Chevy cannot be sold at a Cadillac price. A man's suit bearing a K-Mart label cannot be sold on a par with one manufactured by Brooks Brothers. An Estee Lauder cosmetic cannot be promoted by an ad in *TV Guide*. Thus, the increased price should be evaluated before being finalized to see whether the posture of other market-mix variables will substantiate such an increase.

PRICE-FLEXIBILITY STRATEGY

Price-flexibility strategy usually consists of two alternatives: a one-price policy and a flexible-pricing policy. Influenced by a variety of changes in the environment such as saturation of markets, slow growth, Japanese competition, and the consumer movement, more and more companies have been adhering in recent years to flexibility in pricing in different forms. The flexibility may consist of setting different prices in different markets based on geographic location, varying prices depending on the time of delivery, or customizing prices based on the complexity of the product desired.

One-Price Strategy

A one-price strategy means that the same price is set for all customers who purchase goods under essentially the same conditions and in the same quantities. The one-price strategy is fairly typical in situations where mass distribution and mass selling are employed. There are several advantages and disadvantages that may be attributed to a one-price strategy. Some advantages of this type of pricing strategy are that it allows for administrative convenience and that it serves to make the pricing process easier. Also, this strategy contributes to the maintenance of goodwill among customers because no one customer is receiving special pricing favors over another customer.

A general disadvantage of a one-price strategy is that the firm usually ends up broadcasting its prices to competitors, who may be capable of undercutting the price. Total inflexibility in pricing may have highly adverse effects on corporate growth and profits in certain situations. It is very important that the company remain responsive to general trends in the economic, social, technological, political/legal, and competitive environments. Realistically, then, a pricing strategy should be reviewed to incorporate environmental changes as they become pronounced. Any analysis of this type would have to include a close look at a company's position relative to the actions of other firms operating within the industry. As an example, it is generally believed that one reason for the success of discount houses is that conventional retailers rigidly hold to traditional prices and margins.

Flexible-Pricing Strategy

A flexible-pricing strategy refers to situations where the same products and/or quantities are offered to different customers at different prices. A flexible-pricing strategy is more common in industrial markets than in consumer markets. An advantage of a flexible-pricing strategy is the freedom allowed to sales representatives to make adjustments for competitive conditions rather than refuse an order. Also, a firm is able to charge a higher price to customers who are willing to pay it and a lower price to those who are unwilling. However, legal difficulties may be encountered if price discrimination becomes an issue. Besides, other customers may become upset upon learning that they have been charged more than their competitors. In addition, bargaining may tend to increase the cost of selling, and some sales representatives may let price cutting become a habit.

Recently many large U.S. companies have added new dimensions of flexibility to their pricing strategy. While companies have always shown some willingness to adjust prices or profit margins on specific products as and when market conditions varied, this kind of flexibility is now being carried to the state of a high art. The concept of price flexibility can be implemented in four different ways: by market, by product, by timing, and by technology.

Price flexibility with reference to the market can be achieved either from one geographic area to another or from one segment to another. Both Ford Motor Company and General Motors Corporation charged less for their 1984 compacts marketed on the West Coast than for those marketed anywhere else in the country. Different segments make different uses of a product. Many companies, therefore, consider customer usage in setting price. For example, a plastic sold to industry might command only 30¢ a pound, but sold to a dentist it might bring $25 a pound. Here again, the flexible-pricing strategy calls for different prices in the two segments.[24]

Price flexibility with reference to the product is implemented by considering the value that a product provides to the customer. Careful analysis may show that some products are underpriced and can stand an upgrading in the marketplace. But others, competitively priced to begin with, cannot stand any additional margin because the match-up between value and cost would be lost.

Costs of all transactions from raw materials to delivery at the customer's door may be analyzed, and if some costs are unnecessary in a particular case, due adjustments may be made in pricing a product to sell to a particular customer. Such cost optimization is very effective from the customer's point of view since the customer does not pay for those costs for which no value is received.

Price flexibility can also be practiced by adding to the price an escalation clause based on cost fluctuations. This is especially relevant in situations where there is a substantial time gap between confirmation of an order and delivery of the finished product. In the case of products susceptible to technological obsolescence, price is set to recover all sunken costs within a reasonable period of time.

There are two main characteristics of the flexible-pricing strategy: emphasis on profit or margins rather than simply volume, and willingness to change price with reference to the existing climate. Caution is in order here. In many instances building market share may be essential to cut costs and hence increase profits. Thus, where the experience curve concept makes sense, companies may find it advantageous to reduce prices

---

[24]"Flexible Pricing," *Business Week*, December 12, 1977, p. 81. See also Thomas Nagle, "Pricing as Creative Marketing," *Business Horizons*, July–August, 1983, pp. 14–19.

to hold or increase market shares. However, a reduction in price simply as a reactionary measure to win a contract is discounted. Implementation of this strategy requires that the pricing decision be instituted away from the salespeople in the field by someone high up in the organization. In some companies the pricing executive may report directly to the chief executive officer. Additionally, a systematic procedure for price review at quarterly or semiannual intervals must be established. Finally, an adequate information system is required to help the pricing executive examine different pricing factors.

PRODUCT-LINE-PRICING STRATEGY

A modern business enterprise manufactures and markets a number of product items in a line with differences in quality, design, size, and style. Products in a line may be complementary to or competitive with each other. This influences the cross elasticities of demand between competing products and the package-deal buying of products complementary to each other. For example, instant coffee prices must bear some relationship to the prices of the company's regular coffee since these items are substitutes for one another: therefore, this represents a case of cross elasticity. Similarly, the price of a pesticide must be related to that of a fertilizer if customers are to use both. In other words, a multiproduct company cannot afford to price one product without giving due consideration to the effect on other products in its line.

The pricing strategy of a multiproduct firm should be developed to maximize the profits of the entire organization rather than the profitability of a single product. For products already in the line, the pricing strategy may be formulated by classifying them according to their contribution as follows:

1. Products which contribute more than their pro rata share toward overhead after direct costs are covered
2. Products which just cover their pro rata share
3. Products which contribute more than incremental costs, but do not cover their pro rata share
4. Products which fail to cover the costs savable by their elimination

With such a classification in mind, management is then in a better position to study ways of strengthening the performance of its total product line. Pricing decisions on individual products in the four categories listed above are made in the light of demand and competitive conditions facing each product in the line. This means that some products (new products) may be priced to yield a very high margin of profit while others (highly competitive standard products) may have to show an actual loss. By retaining these marginal products to "keep the machines running" and to help absorb fixed overhead costs, management may be able to maximize the total profits from all of its lines. A few items which make no contribution may have to be kept to round out the line offered.

General Motors' pricing structure provides a good illustration of the above procedure. To offset the lower profit margins on lower-priced small cars, the company raises the prices of its large cars. Additionally, the prices of luxury cars are raised much more than those of standard cars. For example, in 1984 a Cadillac Seville sold for more than $24,000, four times the price of the lowest-priced car. Ten years ago the top of the line was three times as costly as the lowest-priced car. The gap is widening, however, since the growing market for small cars with low markups makes it necessary for the company to generate high profits on luxury cars to meet the profit goal. Thus, it is expected that by 1990 General Motors will be selling a Cadillac for $50,000.

For a new product being considered for addition to the line, strategy development will proceed with an evaluation of the role assigned to it. The following questions could be asked:

1. What would the effect be on the company's competing products at different prices?
2. What would be the best new-product price (or range), considering its impact on the total company offering as a whole? Should other prices be adjusted? What, therefore, would be the incremental gain or loss (volumes and profits of existing lines plus volumes and profits of the new line at different prices)?
3. Is the introductory product necessary for staying ahead of or catching up with competition anyhow?
4. Can it enhance the corporate image, and if so, how much is the enhancement worth?[25]

If the product/market strategy has been adequately worked out, it will be obvious whether the new product can profitably cater to a particular segment. If so, pricing will be considerably easier; costs, profit goals, marketing goals, experience, and external competition will be the factors around which price will be determined.

Where there is no specific product/market match, pricing strategy for a new product considered for the line will vary depending on whether the product is complementary or competitive vis-à-vis other products in the line. For the complementary product, examination of the industry price schedule, which will furnish the primary guides for the bottom price, top price, and conventional spread between items, may be necessary. There are three particularly significant factors in product-line-pricing strategy. The lowest price in the market is always the most remembered and unquestionably generates the most interest, if not the most traffic; having the top market price implies the ability to manufacture quality products;

---

[25]John M. Brion, *Corporate Marketing Planning* (New York: John Wiley & Sons, 1967), p. 183.

and a well-planned schedule structure (one that optimizes profit and at the same time is logical to the customers) is usually carefully studied and eventually followed by the competition regardless of who initiated it. In addition, however, there can be a product included in the line with the objective of pricing to obtain the principal profit from a product's supplies or supplementary components.

If the anticipated product is competitive, a start will have to be made with the following market analysis:

1. Knowledge of the industry's pricing history and characteristics regarding the line
2. Comparison of company vs. competitor items and volumes, showing gaps and areas of popularity
3. Volume and profit potentials of the company line as is
4. Volume and profit potentials with the new internally competitive product
5. Effect on company volume and profit if competition added the proposed product and the company did not
6. Impact of a possible introduction delay or speedup

With the above information on hand, the cost-plus-markup computations should be undertaken. Thereafter, the pricer has three alternatives to set the price: (1) to add a uniform or individual markup rate to the total cost of the product, (2) to add a markup rate that covers all the constant costs of the line, and (3) to add the rate necessary for achieving the goal. The three alternatives have different characteristics. The first one hides the contribution margin opportunities. The second alternative, while revealing the minimum feasible price, tends to spread the constant-cost coverage in such a manner that the product absorbing the most overhead is made the most price-attractive. The third alternative assigns the burden to the high-material-cost product, which may be competitively necessary. No matter which alternative is pursued, the final price should be arrived at only after it has been duly examined with reference to market and competitive factors.

LEASING STRATEGY

The major emphasis of a pricing strategy is on buying a product outright rather than leasing it. Except in housing, leasing is more common in the marketing of industrial goods than in that of consumer goods, though in recent years there has been a growing trend toward leasing of consumer goods. For example, some people lease cars. Usually by paying a specified sum of money every month, like a rental on an apartment, one can lease a new car. Again, as in the case of housing, a lease is binding for a minimum period, such as two years. Thus, the consumer can lease a new car every other year. Since repairs in the first two years of a car's life may not amount to much, one is saved the bother of such problems.

While there may be different alternatives for setting the lease price, the lessor usually likes to recover the investment within a few years. Thereafter, a very large portion of the lease price (or rent) will be profit. A lessor may set the monthly rental on a car so that within a few months, say 30, the entire cost can be recovered. For example, the monthly rental on a Chevette, based on the 1984 price (assuming no extras), may be about $150 a month. With the term set at 30 months, the dealer will get all his money back in about 27 months (it should be noted that a dealer gets a car at a wholesale price and not the sticker price, which is the suggested retail price). The important thing is to set the monthly lease rate and the minimum period for which the lease is binding in such proportions that the total amount which the lessee pays for the duration of the lease is less than what he or she would pay in monthly installments on a new car. As a matter of fact, the lease rate has to be substantially less than that in order for the buyer to opt to lease.[26]

Furniture renting may be attractive to young adults, people of high mobility (e.g., executives, stewardesses), and certain senior citizens whose children have left home and who need appropriate furnishings only temporarily when their children's families come to visit. In addition, apartment owners may rent furniture to provide furnished units to the tenants. The following excerpts from a case provide the pricing mechanics of furniture renting.

> Custom Furniture Rental Corporation (CFRC) leased home furnishings for one month or longer. On direct-to-tenant business the firm realized a nine-month payback (i.e., 11% per month of the purchase price) but 20 months, 5% on commercial.
>
> CFRC's customers had the option of buying part or all of the rented furniture. The purchase price amounted to 25 times the monthly rental fee. A selection of furniture carrying a monthly rental of $30 would bear, therefore, a total purchase price of $750. The purchase option offered provided that credit toward the total purchase price be given as follows:
>
> 100% of the first year's rent;
> 75% of the second year's rent;
> 50% of the third year's rent; or
> 80% of this credit could be applied to the purchase of a similar piece of new furniture
>
> Using the example of a $30-per-month rental and a $750 purchase price, the customer, having paid the first year's rental fees, would be given a credit of $360 and would pay the balance of $390 to complete the purchase. The customer who had completed making rental payments for two years would be given credit of $630 (100% of $360 plus 75% of $360) toward the $750 purchase price, leaving a balance of $120.

---

[26]Mark N. Dodosh, "Banks Are Offering Auto-Leasing Plans to Help Consumers Meet Soaring Prices," *The Wall Street Journal,* June 11, 1980, p. 44.

Persons opting to buy their rented furniture generally did so after the first year and certainly not beyond the second year. In 1971 there were 1,400 customers who decided to purchase one or more pieces of rented furniture. Gross receipts from those sales were $330,000. However, less than 8% of the total customer base exercised their buying option.

Used furniture was sent out for rental "like new," but the company openly invited all of its customers to return any piece that failed to meet the "like new" test.

A deposit of $35 was required for each account and was returned if the lease was in effect at least 12 months. This fee covered the cost of delivery and installation. Customers could make addition, deletions, or changes of items, but there was a $15 charge for each such order. The rate was in effect a delivery charge and applied to any and all pieces of furniture involved in the service call.

If the lessee moved, there was a $20 charge to shift the furniture. If a customer transferred to another geographical area serviced by CFRC, the lessee could return the furniture and ask for delivery at the new location.[27]

In industrial markets the leasing strategy is employed by essentially all capital goods and equipment manufacturers. Traditionally shoe machinery, postage meters, packaging machinery, textile machinery, and other heavy equipment have been leased. Recent applications of the strategy include the leasing of computers, copiers, cars, and trucks. As a matter of fact, just about any item of capital machinery and equipment can be leased. From the customer's point of view, the leasing strategy makes sense for a variety of reasons. First, it reduces the capital required to enter a business. Second, it protects the customer against technological obsolescence. Third, the entire lease price or rental may be written off as an expense for income tax purposes. This advantage, of course, may or may not be relevant depending on the source of funds the customer would have used for the outright purchase (i.e., his or her own money or borrowed funds). Finally, leasing gives the customer the freedom not to get stuck with a product which may prove later on not to be useful.

From the viewpoint of the manufacturer, the leasing strategy is advantageous in many ways. First, income is smoothed out over a period of years, which is very helpful in the case of equipment of high unit value in a cyclical business. Second, market growth can be boosted since more customers can afford to lease the product than can afford to buy. Third, revenues are usually higher when a product is leased than when it is sold.

The following quote from a book on the Xerox Corporation illustrates the manner in which a leasing strategy was adopted for a new product:

---

[27]"Custom Furniture Rental Corporation," a case in Harper W. Boyd, Jr., and Robert T. Davis, *Marketing Management Casebook* (Homewood, IL: Richard D. Irwin, 1976), pp. 11–12.

Immediately the plan had opponents. They argued vigorously. "When you sell a machine you instantly get your investment back, or a substantial part of it," they said. "That gives you the necessary capital to build more machines. But when you lease, at what has to be a small fee per month, your costs cannot be recouped for years. How can we afford to sink millions into this venture and get back only a small rental fee? How can we afford to wait a long time for our investment to be amortized before we can begin to show profits? We're too small to think of leasing. We simply haven't that much money to play with. We've got to sell copying equipment to regain our investment as quickly as possible. There's no other way to carry on."

Joe Wilson* listened attentively. Then he said, "If we try to sell a machine that costs upward of four thousand dollars to produce [as the first ones did], we'll have to charge more than eight thousand dollars, maybe more than ten thousand dollars to show any profit, allowing for maintenance, advertising, administration, and other costs. Will people make that big an investment in something so new and unproved? Won't it be easier to offer them the machine at a low rental price so that they don't have to gamble a big sum on reproducing papers?

"Another point to consider is this," Joe went on. "A rented machine will in time amortize its production costs. Thereafter all fees are profit, less an allowance for maintenance. So in the long run, with rental fees continuing, we're bound to show greater profits than an outright sale. IBM found the system works on other types of business equipment. Why shouldn't it work for us?"

"IBM has the financial resources for it. We haven't."

"We can borrow the resources," Joe said. "Or we can issue stock."

Then one of the men protested, "Suppose some other company comes out with a better copier that makes ours obsolete. The leased machines will quickly be returned to us. If this happens before rental fees have amortized our costs, we'll never recover our investment. And we'll never pay off our indebtedness. Haloid could be wiped out."

Joe granted, "There's no doubt that leasing means we have to produce a machine that's at all times the best on the market. This will be the responsibility of the research and development staff—always to stay ahead of competition. I'm confident they can do it."

In spite of his assurance, however, Joe Wilson had some grave doubts about one phase of leasing. It concerned the fee Haloid would have to charge if monthly payments were to amortize costs in a reasonable time, cover maintenance, yet yield a profit. They might amount to two hundred or even two hundred fifty dollars a month. Would potential users pay so much?

We all doubted it. A way had to be found, we all agreed, to reduce monthly rentals. Many of us sat at our desks with paper and pencil, trying to calculate the lowest fee we could profitably quote.

We could not ignore the fact that there was a subsidiary form of profit in leasing. This was pointed out by a tax-wise member of our

---

*President of the Haloid Company, which originally developed the xerographic process.

Board. Only the owner of a piece of equipment may claim a depreciation allowance on it. Therefore, if we sold a machine, its new owner would enjoy this tax deduction. But if we leased it, thereby retaining ownership, Haloid itself could claim the depreciation.

"Which," one director declared, "could amount to several million dollars a year if we ever get a hundred thousand or so machines on the market."[28]

BUNDLING-PRICING STRATEGY

Bundling, also called "iceberg" pricing, refers to the inclusion of an extra margin (for support services) in the price over and above the price of the product as such. This type of strategy has been popular with companies that lease rather than sell their products. Thus, the rental price when using a bundling strategy will include an extra charge to cover a variety of support functions and services needed to maintain the product throughout its useful life.

The bundling strategy is a very viable strategy for firms that lease their products. Since the unit profit increases sharply after the product completes the planned amortization life, it is desirable for the company to keep the product in good condition and hence enhance its working life for high resale or re-leasing value. The bundling strategy permits the company to do so since a charge for upkeep or "iceberg" services is included in the price.

IBM had traditionally followed the bundling strategy, whereby it supposedly charged rentals for hardware and provided service, software, and consultancy free to its customers. In 1969, however, the Justice Department charged IBM with monopolizing the computer market. Though the case proceedings were still in progress in 1984, the company unbundled its price in 1970. It started selling computers, software, service, and technical input separately.

Under the bundling strategy not only are costs of hardware and profits covered, but also included are the anticipated expenses for extra technical sales assistance, design and engineering of the system concept for a customer, software and applications to be used on the system, training of the customer's personnel, and maintenance. While the bundling strategy can be criticized for tending to discourage competition, one has to consider the complexities involved in delivering and maintaining a fault-free, sophisticated system. Without the manufacturer taking the lead in adequately keeping the system in working condition, customers would have to deal with a variety of people to make use of such products as computers. At least in the initial stages of a technologically oriented product, a bundling strategy is highly useful from the customer's point of view.

---

[28]John H. Dessauer, *My Years with Xerox* (New York: Doubleday and Co., 1971), pp. 68–70.

For the company, this strategy (1) covers the anticipated expenses of providing services and maintaining the product, (2) provides revenues for supporting after-sales service personnel, (3) provides contingency funds to meet unanticipated happenings, and (4) ensures the proper care and maintenance of the leased products.[29] The bundling strategy also permits an ongoing relationship with the customer. In this way the company gains firsthand knowledge of the customer's needs which may help to shift the customer to the new generation of the product. Needless to say, the very nature of the bundling strategy makes it most relevant to technologically sophisticated products, particularly those marked by rapid technological obsolescence.

On the negative side, the bundling strategy tends to inflate costs and distort prices and profitability. For this reason, in the inflationary years of the 1970s many businesses that had pursued this strategy began unbundling their services and charging separately for them. Grocery wholesalers, for instance, may pass through a straight invoice cost and then charge for delivery, packaging, etc., separately. A growing number of department stores now charge extra for home delivery, gift wrapping, and shopping bags. Thus, people who don't want a service need not pay for it.

PRICE-LEADERSHIP STRATEGY

The price-leadership strategy prevails in oligopolistic situations. One member of an industry, because of its size or command over the market, emerges as the leader of the entire industry. The leading firm then makes pricing moves which are duly acknowledged by other members of the industry. Thus, this strategy places the burden of making critical pricing decisions on the leading firm; others simply follow the leader. The leader is expected to be careful in making the decisions. A faulty decision could cost the firm its leadership since other members of the industry would then stop following in its footsteps. For example, if the leader, in increasing prices, is motivated only by self-interest, it will be left alone and will ultimately be forced to withdraw the increase in price.

The price-leadership strategy is a static concept. In an environment where growth opportunities are adequate, companies would rather maintain stability than fight each other by means of price wars. Thus, the leadership concept works out well in this case. In the auto industry, General Motors is the leader. The other three members of the industry have traditionally adjusted their prices to come very close to any price increase by General Motors.

Usually, the leader is the company with the largest market share, such as U.S. Steel Corporation or International Business Machines Cor-

---

[29]J. Thomas Cannon, *Business Strategy and Policy* (New York: Harcourt, Brace & World, 1968), p. 135.

poration. The leadership strategy is designed to stave off price wars and "predatory" competition which tend to force down prices and hurt all parties. Companies that deviate from this form are chastised through discounting or shaving by the leaders. Price deviation is quickly disciplined.

Successful price leaders are characterized by:

1. Large share of the industry's production capacity.
2. Large market share.
3. Commitment to a particular product class or grade.
4. New, cost-efficient plants.
5. Strong distribution system, perhaps including captive wholesale outlets.
6. Good customer relations such as technical assistance for industrial buyers, programs directed at end users, and special attention to important customers during shortage periods.
7. An effective market information system which provides analysis of the realities of supply and demand.
8. Sensitivity to the price and profit needs of the rest of the industry.
9. A sense of timing to know when price changes should be made.
10. Sound management organization for pricing.
11. Effective product-line financial controls, which are needed to make sound price leadership decisions.
12. Attention to legal issues.[30]

In an unfavorable business environment it may not be feasible to implement the leadership strategy. This is because firms may be differently placed to interact with the environment. Thus, the leader hesitates to make decisions on behalf of the entire industry since other firms may not always find its decisions to their advantage. For this reason, the price-leader–follower pattern may be violated.

In order to survive during unfavorable conditions, even smaller firms take the initiative to undercut the price leader. For example, during 1978, while the list prices of steel displayed similarity, companies freely discounted their prices. With increasing competition from overseas during the 1970s, the price-leadership strategy did not work in the chemical industry either. Thus, companies planned a variety of temporary allowances to generate business. The following quote from a 1977 article highlights the erosion of the leadership strategy in the glass container industry:

> Traditional patterns of price leadership also are breaking down in the glass container industry, with smaller companies moving to the fore in pricing. Last year, for example, Owens-Illinois, Inc.—which is larger than its next five competitors combined—increased its list prices by $4^1/_2\%$. Fearing that the increase would hurt sales to brewing companies that were just beginning to switch to glass bottles, the smaller companies broke ranks and offered huge discounts. The action not only

---

[30]Stuart U. Rich, "Price Leaders: Large, Strong, but Cautious About Conspiracy," *Marketing News,* June 25, 1982, p. 11.

negated O-I's increase but served notice that the smaller companies were after O-I's market share.[31]

An automatic response to a leader's price adjustment assumes that all firms are more or less similarly positioned vis-à-vis different price variables (i.e., cost, competition, and demand) and that different firms have common pricing objectives. Such an assumption, however, is far from being justified. The leadership strategy is an artificial way to force similar pricing response throughout the industry. It is a strategic mistake for a company to price in a manner identical to that of its competitors. It should price either above or below the competition to set itself apart.

PRICING STRATEGY TO BUILD MARKET SHARE

Recent work in the area of marketing strategy has delineated the importance of market share as a key variable in strategy formulation.[32] While market share has been discussed earlier with reference to other matters, this section examines the impact of market share on pricing strategy.

Time and again it has been noted that higher market share or experience leads to lower costs. Thus, the new product should be priced to gain experience and market share. This will give the company such a cost advantage that it cannot ever profitably be overcome by any competitor of normal performance. Competitors will be prevented from entering the market and will have to learn to live in a subordinate position.

Assuming the market is price sensitive, it is desirable to develop it as early as possible. One way of achieving this is to reduce the price. Unit costs are necessarily very high in the early stages of any product; if price is set to recover all costs, there may be no market for the product at its initial cost in competition with existing alternatives. Following the impact of the market share or experience on prices, it may be worthwhile to set prices at a level which will move the product. During the early stages operations may have to be conducted even at a loss. As volume is gained, costs go down, and even at the initial low price the company makes money. This implies that the competitive cost differential of the future should be of greater concern than current profitability. Of course, such a strategic posture makes sense only in a competitive situation. In the absence of competition there is every reason to set prices as high as possible, to be lowered only when total revenue would not be affected by such an action.

The lower the initial price set by the first producer, the more rap-

---

[31]"Flexible Pricing," *Business Week*, December 12, 1977, p. 81.

[32]Robert D. Buzzel, B. T. Gale, and R. G. M. Sultan. "Market Share—A Key to Profitability," *Harvard Business Review*, January–February, 1975, pp. 97–106. See also J. K. Newton, "Market Share—Key to Higher Profitability," *Long Range Planning*, February, 1983, pp. 37–41.

idly the producer builds up volume and a differential cost advantage over succeeding competitors and the faster the market develops. In a sense this is a purchase of time advantage. However, the lower the initial price, the greater the investment required before the progressive reduction of cost will result in a profit. This in turn means that the comparative investment resources of the competitors involved can become a significant, or even the critical, determinant of competitive survival.

Two limitations, however, make the implementation of this type of strategy difficult. First, the resources required to institute this strategy are more than those normally available to a firm. Second, the price, once set, will not be raised, but maintained until costs fall below price; therefore, the lower the price, the longer the time needed for any return and the larger the investment. When future return is discounted to present value, there is obviously a limit.[33]

It is these difficulties which lead many firms to set initial prices which cover all costs. This is particularly so when there is no clear competitive threat. As volume builds up and costs decline, this produces visible profitability which in turn induces new competitors to enter the field. As the competitors make their moves, the innovating firm has the problem of choosing between current profitability and market share. Strategically, however, pricing of a new product, following the relationship between market share and cost, should be dictated by a product's projected future growth.

SUMMARY

Pricing strategy is of interest to the very highest management levels of a company. Yet there are few management decisions that are more subject to intuition than pricing. There is a reason for this. Pricing decisions are primarily affected by factors which are difficult to articulate and analyze, such as pricing objectives, cost, competition, and demand. For example, assumptions must be made about what a competitor will do under certain hypothetical circumstances. There is no way to know that for certain; hence the characteristic reliance on intuition.

This chapter reviews the pricing factors mentioned above and examines important strategies which a pricer may pursue. The following strategies are discussed:

1. Pricing strategies for new products
2. Pricing strategies for established products
3. Price-flexibility strategy
4. Product-line-pricing strategy

---

[33]"New Product Pricing," an informal statement by the Boston Consulting Group, 1973.

5. Leasing strategy
6. Bundling-pricing strategy
7. Price-leadership strategy
8. Pricing strategy to build market share

There are two principal pricing strategies for new products, skimming and penetration. Skimming is a high-price strategy; the penetration strategy sets a low initial price to generate volume. Three strategies for established products are discussed: maintaining the price, reducing the price, and increasing the price. A flexible-pricing strategy provides leverage to the pricer in terms of duration of commitment both from market to market and from product to product. Product-line-pricing strategy is directed toward maintaining a balance between different products offered by a company. The leasing strategy constitutes an alternative to outright sale of the product. The bundling strategy is concerned with packaging products and associated services together for the purposes of pricing. Price-leadership strategy is a characteristic of an oligopoly where one firm in an industry emerges as a leader and sets the pricing tone for other members of the industry. Finally, the pricing strategy to build market share emphasizes the strategic significance of setting an initially low price to gain volume and market share and thereby achieve cost reductions.

DISCUSSION QUESTIONS

1. *Is the maintenance of a stable price a viable objective? Why?*
2. *Is there a conflict between profit and volume objectives? Doesn't one lead to the other? Discuss.*
3. *What are the advantages of using incremental costs instead of full costs for pricing? Are there any negative implications of using incremental costs which a pricing strategist needs to be aware of?*
4. *What assumptions need to be made about competitive behavior for formulating pricing strategy?*
5. *"Short-term price increases tend to depress industry profits in the long run by accelerating the introduction of new capacity and depressing market demand." Discuss.*
6. *Following the experience curve concept, the initial price of a new product should be set rather low; as a matter of fact, it may be below the cost. Taking into account the popularity of this thesis, discuss the relevance of the skimming strategy.*
7. *"Price policies are in fact a derived product of investment policies. Conversely, it appears that the true consequence of price changes is to affect the investment decisions of competitors." Discuss.*
8. *What factors are ascribed to the decline in popularity of the price-leadership strategy?*

APPENDIX: PERSPECTIVES OF PRICING STRATEGIES

I. Pricing Strategies for New Products

A. Skimming Pricing
Definition: Setting a relatively high price during the initial stage of a product's life.

Objectives: (1) To serve customers who are not price conscious while the market is at the upper end of the demand curve and competition has not yet entered. (2) To recover a significant portion of promotional and R&D costs through a high margin.

Requirements: (1) Heavy promotional expenditure to introduce product, educate consumers, and induce early buying. (2) Relatively inelastic demand at the upper end of the demand curve. (3) Lack of direct competition and substitutes.

Expected Results: (1) Market segmented by price-conscious and not-so-price-conscious customers. (2) High margin on sales which will cover promotion and R&D costs. (3) Opportunity for the firm to lower its price and sell to the mass market before competition enters.

B. Penetration Pricing
Definition: Setting a relatively low price during the initial stages of a product's life.

Objective: To discourage competition from entering the market by quickly taking a large market share and gaining a cost advantage by realizing economies of scale.

Requirements: (1) Product must appeal to a market large enough to support the cost advantage. (2) Demand must be highly elastic in order for the firm to guard its cost advantage.

Expected Results: (1) High sales volume and large market share. (2) Low margin on sales. (3) Lower unit costs relative to competition due to economies of scale.

II. Pricing Strategies for Established Products

A. Maintaining the Price
Objectives: (1) To maintain the position in the marketplace (i.e., market share, profitability, etc.). (2) To enhance the public image.

Requirements: (1) Firm's served market is not significantly affected by changes in the environment. (2) Uncertainty exists concerning the need for or result of a price change. (3) Firm's public image could be enhanced by responding to government requests or public opinion to maintain price.

Expected Results: (1) Status quo for the firm's market position. (2) Enhancement of the firm's public image.

B. Reducing the Price

Objectives: (1) To act defensively and cut price to meet the competition. (2) To act offensively and attempt to beat the competition. (3) To respond to a customer need created by a change in the environment.

Requirements: (1) Firm must be financially and competitively strong to fight in a price war if that becomes necessary. (2) Must have a good understanding of the demand function of its product.

Expected Results: Lower profit margins (assuming costs are held constant). Higher market share might be expected, but this will depend upon the price change relative to competitive prices and upon price elasticity.

C. Increasing the Price

Objectives: (1) To maintain profitability during an inflationary period. (2) To take advantage of product differences, real or perceived. (3) To segment the current served market.

Requirements: (1) Relatively low price elasticity, but relatively high elasticity with respect to some other factor such as quality, distribution, etc. (2) Reinforcement from other ingredients of the marketing mix; for example, if a firm decides to increase price and differentiate its product by quality, then promotion and distribution must address product quality.

Expected Results: (1) Higher sales margin. (2) Segmented market (price conscious, quality conscious, etc.). (3) Possibly higher unit sales, if differentiation is effective.

III. Price-Flexibility Strategy

A. One-Price Strategy

Definition: Charging the same price to all customers under similar conditions and for the same quantities.

Objectives: (1) To simplify pricing decisions. (2) To maintain goodwill among customers.

Requirements: (1) Detailed analysis of the firm's position and cost structure as compared with the rest of the industry. (2) Information concerning the cost variability of offering the same price to everyone. (3) Knowledge of the economies of scale available to the firm. (4) Information on competitive prices; information on the price that customers are ready to pay.

Expected Results: (1) Decreased administrative and selling costs. (2) Constant profit margins. (3) Favorable and fair image among customers. (4) Stable market.

B. Flexible-Pricing Strategy

Definition: Charging different prices to different customers for the same product and quantity.

Objective: To maximize short-term profits and build traffic by allowing upward and downward adjustments in price depending on the level of competitive conditions and how much the customer is willing to pay for the product.

Requirements: Have the information needed to implement the strategy. Usually, this strategy is implemented in one of four ways: (a) by market, (b) by product, (c) by timing, (d) by technology. Other requirements include (a) a customer-value analysis of the product, (b) an emphasis on profit margin rather than just volume, and (c) a record of competitive reaction to price moves in the past.

Expected Results: (1) Increased sales, leading to greater market share. (2) Increased short-term profits. (3) Increased selling and administrative costs. (4) Legal difficulties stemming from price discrimination.

IV. Product-Line-Pricing Strategy

Definition: Pricing a product line according to each product's effect on and relationship with other products in that line, whether competitive or complementary.

Objective: To maximize profits from the whole line rather than just certain members of it.

Requirements: (1) For a product already in the line, the strategy will be developed according to the product's contributions to its pro rata share of overhead and direct costs. (2) For a new product, a product/market analysis will determine whether this product will be profitable. Pricing will then be a function of costs, profit goals, experience, and external competition.

Expected Results: (1) Well-balanced and consistent pricing schedule across the product line. (2) Greater profits in the long term. (3) Better performance of the line as a whole.

V. Leasing Strategy

Definition: An agreement by which an owner (lessor) of an asset rents that asset to a second party (lessee). The lessee pays a specified sum of money, which includes principal and interest, each month as a rental payment.

Objectives: (1) To enhance market growth by attracting customers who cannot buy outright. (2) To realize greater long-term profits; once the production costs are fully amortized, the rental fee is mainly profit. (3) To increase cash flow. (4)

To have a stable flow of earnings. (5) To have protection against losing revenue because of technological obsolescence.

Requirements: (1) Necessary financial resources to continue production of subsequent products for future sale or lease. (2) Adequate computation of lease rate and minimum period for which lease is binding such that the total amount which the lessee pays for the duration of the lease is less than would be paid in monthly installments on an outright purchase. (3) Customers who are restrained by large capital requirements necessary for outright purchase and/or need write-off for income tax purposes. (4) The capability to match competitors' product improvements which may make the lessor's product obsolete.

Expected Results: (1) Increased market share because customers include those who would have forgone purchase of product. (2) Consistent earnings over a period of years. (3) Greater cash flow due to lower income tax expense from depreciation write-off. (4) Increased sales as customers exercise their purchase options.

VI. Bundling-Pricing Strategy

Definition: Inclusion of an extra margin in the price to cover a variety of support functions and services needed to sell and maintain the product throughout its useful life.

Objectives: (1) In a leasing arrangement, to have assurance that the asset will be properly maintained and kept in good working condition so that it could be resold or re-leased. (2) To generate extra revenues to cover the anticipated expenses of providing services and maintaining the product. (3) To generate revenues for supporting after-sales service personnel. (4) To establish a contingency fund for unanticipated happenings. (5) To develop an ongoing relationship with the customer. (6) To discourage competition with "free" after-sales support and service.

Requirements: This strategy is ideally suited for technologically sophisticated products which are susceptible to rapid technological obsolescence, since these products are generally sold in systems and usually require the following: (a) extra technical sales assistance, (b) custom design and engineering concept for the customer, (c) peripheral equipment and applications, (d) training of the customer's personnel, and (e) a strong service/maintenance department offering prompt responses and solutions to customer problems.

Expected Results: (1) Asset is kept in an acceptable condition for resale or re-lease. (2) Positive cash flow. (3) Instant information on changing customer needs. (4) Increased sales due to "total package" concept of selling, since customers feel they are getting their money's worth.

VII. Price-Leadership Strategy

Definition: This strategy is used by the leading firm in an industry in making major pricing moves, which are followed by the other firms in the industry.

Objective: To gain control of pricing decisions within an industry in order to support the leading firm's own marketing strategy (i.e., create barriers to entry, increase profit margin, etc.).

Requirements: (1) An oligopolistic situation. (2) An industry in which all firms are affected by the same price variables (i.e., cost, competition, demand). (3) An industry in which all firms have common pricing objectives. (4) Perfect knowledge of the industry conditions; an error in pricing means losing control.

Expected Results: (1) Prevention of price wars, which are liable to hurt all parties involved. (2) Stable pricing moves. (3) Stable market share.

VIII. Pricing Strategy to Build Market Share

Definition: Setting the lowest price possible for a new product.

Objective: To seek such a cost advantage that it cannot ever be profitably overcome by any competitor.

Requirements: (1) Enough resources to withstand initial operating losses which will be later recovered through economies of scale. (2) Price-sensitive market. (3) Large market. (4) High elasticity of demand.

Expected Results: (1) Start-up losses to build market share. (2) Creation of a barrier to entry to the industry. (3) Ultimately, cost leadership within the industry.

CASE 14
Dymond Electric and Gas Company

In the spring of 1983 a group of concerned managers gathered at the request of James T. Grover, senior vice-president of Dymond Electric and Gas Company and general manager of its gas business. All the attendees were cognizant of the meeting's purpose: declining sales (Exhibit 14-6) to its residential, commercial, and industrial customers had serious implications for the functions they represented and the customers the company served. Unless actions could be taken to reverse the trend or to mitigate its effects, the business would be entering a downward cycle which could seriously impair its ability to serve its customers.

INDUSTRY PERSPECTIVE

The natural gas industry has been federally regulated since the 1930s and has had wellhead price control since 1954. Traditionally, in this business, there has been a three-pronged partnership of producer, pipeline company, and distribution company with the pipeline company acting as middleman. The pipeline companies have constructed a massive system of transmission mains to bring natural gas from producers' wells in Texas and Louisiana to the distribution companies' franchise area; two major companies built facilities in New England in the early 1950s.

From the 1950s to the early 1970s, the Natural Gas Act created an artificially low price for gas transported out of producing states. Initially, lured by the low prices, the pipeline companies were able to provide sufficient gas to New England to accommodate the industry's growth. Annually, the pipelines would increase the contractual volumes deliverable to the New England gas distribution utilities on the basis of their projected growth. By the early 1970s, however, the artificially constrained pricing began to take its toll. Producer and pipeline company alike had no incentive to continue to sell their gas out of state when they could get higher prices intrastate. Some producers found it economically impossible to drill at the prices mandated. Distribution companies in nonproducing states experienced curtailment, a reduction in the pipeline company's contractual obligation. Shortages, economic in origin, came to a head in the 1977 winter; curtailed supplies of natural gas combined with severe weather forced hundreds of businesses, industries, and schools to close.

This situation led to public outcry and a congressional solution in the form of the Natural Gas Policy Act (NGPA). This extremely complex act created at least fifteen separate classifications of natural gas, depend-

EXHIBIT 14-6   Dymond Electric and Gas Company: Gas Sales, 1973–83

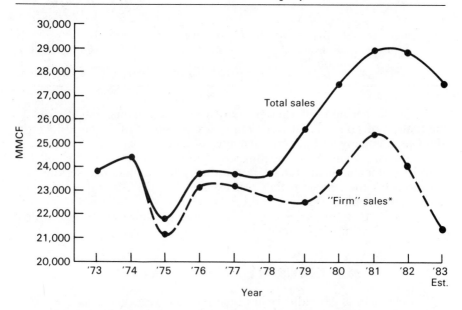

*Sales to customers to whom the company was contractually obligated to sell.

Source: Company records.

ing on the date the well was drilled, its depth, and its location. Each cat-egory had a price ceiling and an escalation formula designed to bring gas prices to parity with a fixed oil price in 1985. The result was increased production, exactly as desired; however, the balance of the supply mix produced began to alter as the "phased-in decontrol" schedule took effect. As might be expected, producers found it more profitable to drill for the higher-priced classifications of gas than to sell the "old" gas. Because of the lack of price competition in the tightly regulated market, pipeline companies began to outbid each other for reserve contracts by offering increasingly lucrative contract terms. Common contractual provisions were: "take or pay," which required a pipeline to purchase a specified percent-age of the contractual quantity or pay for it; "indefinite escalator clauses," which tied the decontrol price to some marker—120 percent of the No. 2 oil price was not unusual; and "most favored nations clauses," which allowed the price for that contract to match the highest price in that geo-graphic area for the same classification of gas. Many later contracts also contained "market out" clauses effective at the date of decontrol which would permit the pipeline to decline the purchase of gas which the pipe-line determined to be unmarketable at the price charged. The theory underlying the NGPA pricing structure and the phased deregulation was that a large volume of price-controlled "old" gas would remain to cushion the impact of including volumes of the higher-priced gas classifications in a weighted average price. As long as oil prices and economic conditions remained strong the market could support the higher prices. The declining economic situation in the mid-1970s had a substantial impact on the industrial sales market particularly in the Midwest, where some distribution companies lost as much as 25 percent of their load. The situation was exacerbated when oil prices dropped below the OPEC market price (Exhibit 14-7) and dual-fuel industrial customers began shifting from gas to oil. As local distribution companies lost large numbers of customers, the fixed costs of service had to be paid by the remaining customers, which led to higher rates and reduced sales even further.

The pipelines and producers had been relatively insulated from the results of their pricing policies while the distribution companies absorbed the initial impact of the sales decline; but by the time the pipelines' contract year had ended, it became apparent that reduced sales by distribution companies translated directly into reduced sales for the pipelines and producers as well. As was the case with the distribution companies, declining sales for pipelines meant higher unit costs. It was apparent that the industry would be trapped in a downward death spiral if actions were not taken immediately.

COMPANY PERSPECTIVE

Many New England gas distribution companies had resulted from the merging of small companies originally serving municipalities. Prior to the construction of major pipelines there was very little point in interconnecting towns; each had its own production facilities (usually making relatively low-Btu gas from coal or coke) and distribution mains to serve the customers within a reasonable distance from the plant. It had, however, become profitable for the local companies to merge, and by the early 1950s, when the major pipeline companies extended their transmission mains, New England was full of gas distribution companies serving towns physically removed from each other. In the case of Dymond Electric and Gas Company, the merging had been accomplished by electric companies, many of whom at one time or another had acquired gas properties as well. The final result was an electric company which covered a large but fairly integrated area and a gas business serving discrete areas within the electric system.

The introduction of the pipelines through the state alleviated the problems of the gas areas' physical separation to some extent by permitting flexibility in the amount of natural gas delivered to each town, but growth was limited by the relationship of the capacity available from the pipeline at each town's "gate station" and the peak shaving facilities (used to produce gas when customer requirements exceeded pipeline gas availability) in that town. Prior to 1970 the pipelines' reserves and the physical

EXHIBIT 14-7   Comparison of Gas and Oil Prices, 1976–82

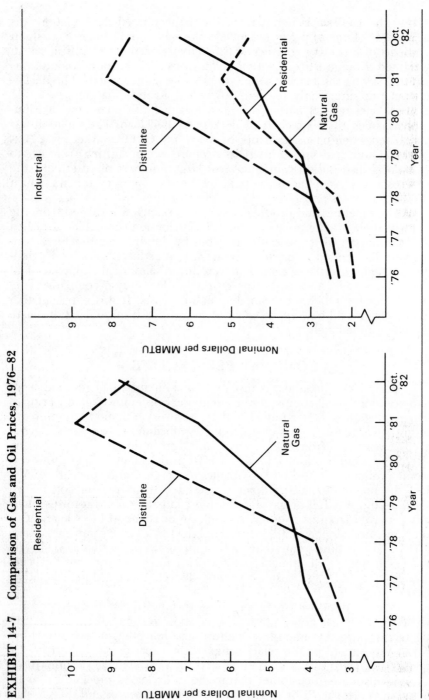

Source: Company records.

capacity of the line itself were sufficient to support their customers' growth. In actual practice, the pipelines delivered as much gas to their New England customers as their projected sales indicated necessary. During that period Dymond relied on commissioned sales personnel who had established very close relationships with the communities in which they worked.

The 1970s, however, were a period of substantial change for Dymond Electric and Gas Company. The OPEC oil embargoes brought conservation to the forefront, and the company's response was to reduce the size of its sales force, paying those remaining straight salaries, and to change its focus to conservation and energy management. During the same period, the pipelines, because of the national situation, not only did not allow their customers to increase their contract volumes each year as in the past but also imposed curtailment. The uncertainty of the pipeline supply caused Dymond Electric and Gas Company to seek supplies such as synthesized natural gas (produced locally from naphtha) and liquefied natural gas (imported from Algeria) to supplement the pipeline supply. These supplies, however, did not allow for any growth, and the company actually declared a moratorium on sales in the mid-'70s for this reason.

The picture changed dramatically beginning in 1978, when the National Gas Policy Act began to spur production and, as pipeline reserves increased, curtailments decreased and spot market purchases became available. This coincided with the second OPEC oil price spike and resulted in an unprecedented demand for natural gas by all customer classes. The company's energy management consultants (the former sales staff) became, in effect, order takers, coordinating service installations and contractor conversions. There had been no marketing strategy since the early '70s and none was formulated.

Coincident with the uncertainty about natural gas supplies and OPEC oil price spikes, the company had undergone the ordeal of attempting to divest itself of its gas business. The sale was undertaken in late 1972 but was officially terminated in 1979 because of the inability of the purchaser to raise the required financing. The intervening period, however, was one of great uncertainty, and many of the gas business's more promising employees accepted transfers to the electric side in order to ensure their futures with the company.

Additionally, the emphasis in the electric business had definitely shifted in the post-OPEC II period to conservation rather than growth. The company's energy management consultants conducted audits and advised customers on how to reduce energy consumption. Therefore, when the abrupt shift in gas supply from shortage to surplus occurred, the company was not prepared to take advantage of the opportunity to substantially increase sales because of limitations in organization and philosophy.

Current Situation

James Grover became senior vice-president and general manager of Dymond's gas business in 1981 and continued the organizational work

EXHIBIT 14-8   Dymond Electric and Gas Company: Corporate Organization

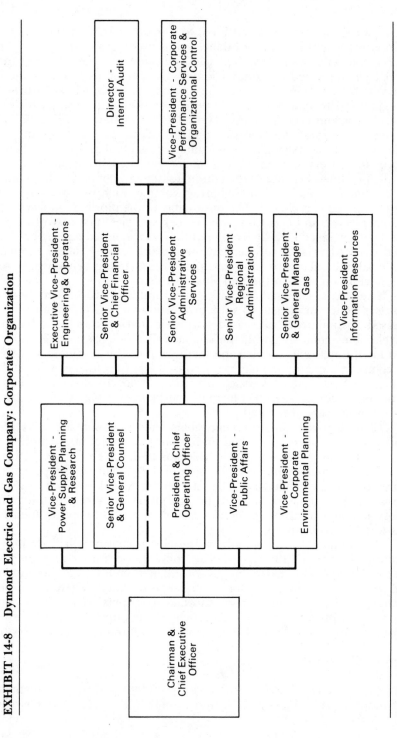

Source: Company records.

EXHIBIT 14-9   Dymond Electric and Gas Company: Gas Business Organization

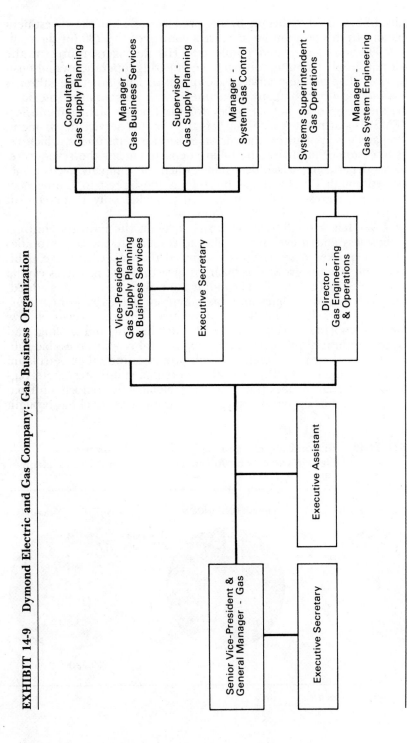

Source: Company records.

(Exhibits 14-8 and 14-9) begun by his predecessor after the divestment termination. In this position he has direct control of the 290 (of the company's 9,000-plus) gas-related employees. His managers represent the functions of supply planning, dispatch, engineering, operations, and business services. The business services group acts as liaison between the gas business and the other company departments with which it must interface. Grover, therefore, does not set policy for the Energy Management Services (EMS) Department, which markets the gas; the service department, which repairs gas appliances; the customer service department, which responds to customer inquiries; the billing department; or the revenue requirements department, which determines when the company needs a rate increase. Although Dymond's gas business is the largest in Connecticut and the fourth largest in New England, it provided only 13 percent of the company's revenues in 1982 (Exhibit 14-10).

Grover felt strongly that, with the focus of the industry shifting, the gas business must develop flexibility to respond to the opportunities which might quickly arise. He was convinced that in order to keep his business viable it must grow. Gas business growth is not nearly as capital intensive as electric (Exhibit 14-11) and, if the right type of load is added, the marginal costs of facilities and gas may even decrease. Most importantly, the gas markets are intensely competitive. There are relatively few uses for gas—cooking, drying, space and water heating and cooling, and some special industrial processes, all having several readily accessible substitutes (such as electricity, wood, coal, oil, propane, and other petroleum derivatives; see Exhibit 14-12) and other potential substitutes. State regulatory agencies grant utilities franchise areas, eliminating competition from similar regulated utilities, but deregulation on the federal level has brought

EXHIBIT 14-10 **Dymond Electric and Gas Company: Comparison of Electric and Gas by Revenues, Income, and Utility Plant, 1982**

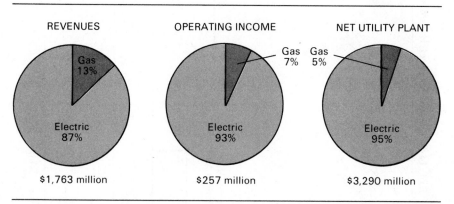

Source: Company records.

**EXHIBIT 14-11   Dymond Electric and Gas Company: Comparison of
Electric and Gas Capital Expenditures per Customer, 1982**

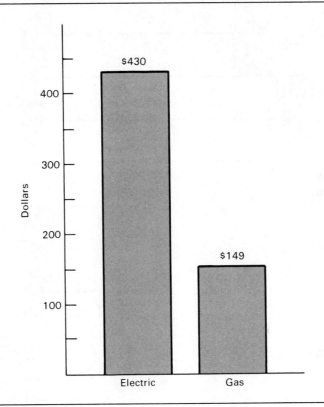

Source: Company records.

philosophical changes. It is now possible for a distribution company's own customer to purchase gas directly from a producer and merely use the pipeline and distribution companies as transporters. Potentially then, the threat of zero sales exists—if gas rate increases outpace the competition. In fact, as producer and pipeline prices to the distribution company (which must also add its margin for O&M and allowed return) escalated and the difference between oil prices and gas rates increased, it appeared from a comparison of gas rates and oil prices made in 1982 that the downward spiral had begun (Exhibit 14-13).

The Market

At the time of this study Dymond's gas business was serving approximately 153,000 customers with over 2,000 miles of distribution main

EXHIBIT 14-12   State Energy Consumption by Fuel Type in End-Use Markets

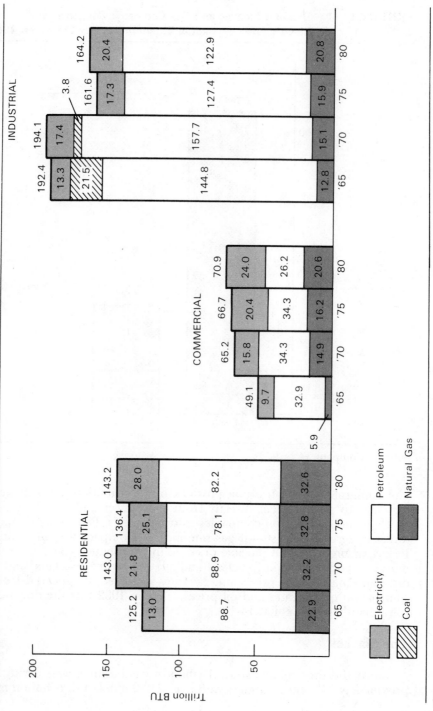

Source: Company records.

EXHIBIT 14-13   Dymond Electric and Gas Company: Comparison of Gas Rates and Oil Prices, Spring 1982

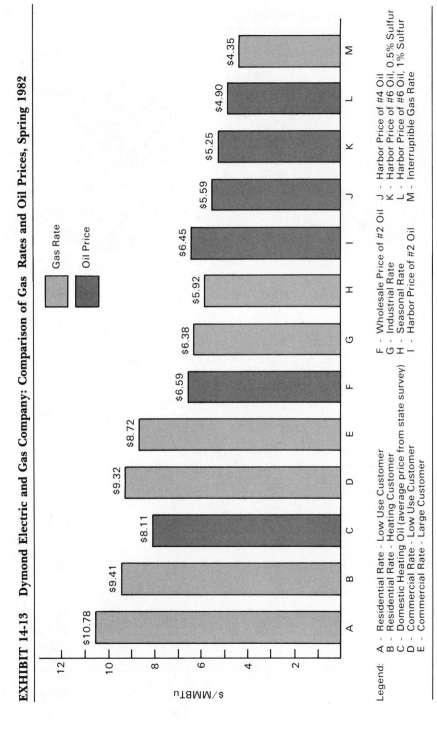

Legend: A - Residential Rate - Low Use Customer
          B - Residential Rate - Heating Customer
          C - Domestic Heating Oil (average price from state survey)
          D - Commercial Rate - Low Use Customer
          E - Commercial Rate - Large Customer

          F - Wholesale Price of #2 Oil
          G - Industrial Rate
          H - Seasonal Rate
          I - Harbor Price of #2 Oil

          J - Harbor Price of #4 Oil
          K - Harbor Price of #6 Oil, 0.5% Sulfur
          L - Harbor Price of #6 Oil, 1% Sulfur
          M - Interruptible Gas Rate

Source: Company records.

EXHIBIT 14-14   Dymond Electric and Gas Company: Sales Composition

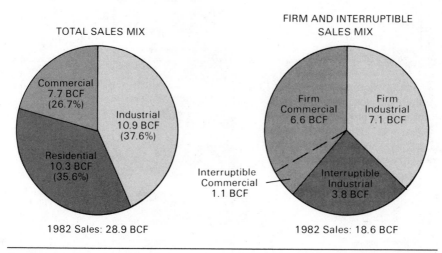

Source: Company records.

EXHIBIT 14-15   Dymond Electric and Gas Company: Analysis of Return by Rate, 1982

	RATES OF RETURN BY CURRENT RATES (%)
Residential Service Rate 2	
Regular Use	(0.862)
Space Heating	1.713
House Heating	10.174
Total Residential	6.374
Commercial & Industrial	
Rate 10 Small General Service	20.320
Rate 26 Large General Service – Firm	50.762
Rate 26 Interruptible	(18.129)
Rate 36 Seasonal	162.798
Sales for Resale	1.021
Total Commercial & Industrial	24.753
Rentals	(9.652)
Total Company	11.090

Source: Company records.

EXHIBIT 14-16 **State of Connecticut Market Share of Fuel Type by End Use, 1982**

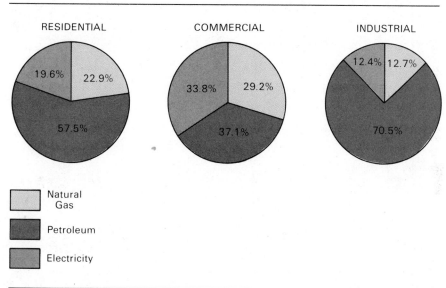

Source: Company records.

in 100 towns. The residential, commercial, and industrial customers to whom Dymond had a commitment to serve gas whenever the customer required it were termed "firm" customers, denoting the company's obligation to them. Since the bulk of the company's "firm" customers were heating customers, an unbalanced load profile resulted—i.e., winter heating requirements exceeded the summer gas demand. Such a profile usually involves the use of substantial amounts of supplemental (more expensive) gas during the winter. In order to purchase gas supplies on a more economic year-round basis, Dymond had designed sales rates to encourage customers whose gas requirements permitted turning off the gas or switching to an alternative fuel during periods of peak load. Customers of this type were termed "interruptible" because they contracted with the company to receive gas at a special rate with the understanding that the company might "interrupt" that gas at any time upon two hours' notice. The rate established for this customer class was based on the price of the alternative fuel (No. 6 oil, 1% sulfur) plus a margin for recovery of expenses. The company made no capital expenditures (i.e., extending gas mains) for interruptible customers other than metering expenses.

Dymond had experienced substantial rate switching from firm to interruptible in both its commercial and industrial customer categories (Exhibit 14-14) as larger firms had found it economic to install dual-fuel burner systems, which can burn either gas or oil with a minimum of

EXHIBIT 14-17 Dymond Electric and Gas Company: Forecasted Gas Supplies Assuming 3.5% Annual Sales Growth Rate (MMCF)

PIPELINE	83–84	84–85	85–86	86–87	87–88	88–89	89–90	90–91	91–92	92–93
Algonquin:										
F-1	13489	13466	13466	13466	13516	13466	13466	13466	13516	13466
WS-1	905	905	905	905	905	905	905	905	905	905
SNG-1	200	200	200	200						
STB withdrawn	546	546	546	546	546	546	546	546	546	546
STT withdrawn	357	363	363							
STC withdrawn					773	773	773	773	773	773
C-1				1683	2297	2297	2297	2297	2297	2297
Tennessee:										
CD-6	9980	9690	10466	10466	10508	10466	10466	10466	10508	10466
Other:										
Penn-York	465	390	698	631	518	704	743	863	49	94
Boundary	1065	1065	1582	3023	3171	3285	3285	3285	3188	3285
Sable Island									3216	3934
Consolidated										
To be purchased	179	181		292		441	1086	1681		
Supplemental Supplies:										
LNG-Everett	408	220								
LNG-Providence	255	363	378	385	385	385	401	405	392	390
LNG-Southern Connecticut	345	165	109	100	113	109	150	150	150	136
LNG-Satellites	336	518	777	779	766	772	713	710	724	739
Propane	345	222	488	436	297	397	560	788	116	123
Total gas required	27810	28294	29978	32912	33795	34546	35391	36335	36380	37154
Less: Required for injection	1455	1382	1349	1792	1953	2154	2195	2324	1452	1500
Total sendout	26355	26912	28629	31120	31842	32392	33196	34011	34833	35654

Source: Company records.

EXHIBIT 14-18   Dymond Electric and Gas Company: Forecasted Gas Supplies Assuming 10% Sales Increase in 83–84 (MMCF)

PIPELINE	83–84	84–85	85–86	86–87	87–88	88–89	89–90	90–91	91–92	92–93
Algonquin:										
F-1	13516	13466	13466	13466	13516	13466	13466	13466	13516	13466
WS-1	905	905	905	905	905	905	905	905	905	905
SNG-1		200	200	200						
STB withdrawn	546	546	546	546	546	546	546	546	546	546
STT withdrawn	363	363	363							
STC withdrawn					773	773	773	773	773	773
C-1				1913	2297	2297	2297	2297	2297	2297
Tennessee:										
CD-6	10508	10466	10466	10466	10508	10466	10466	10466	10508	10466
Other:										
Penn-York	973	909	1123	1107	1024	1085	1133	1196	358	477
Boundary		1429	1715	3023	3285	3285	3285	3285	3285	3285
Sable Island									5810	6445
Consolidated	181	181								
To be purchased	1338	794	1924	2113	1706	2067	2743	3241		
Supplemental Supplies:										
LNG-Everett	410	215								
LNG-Providence	255	363	398	385	386	386	428	437	410	390
LNG-Southern Connecticut	295	114	78	78	78	78	150	151	119	117
LNG-Satellites	374	573	789	802	801	801	687	677	736	759
Propane	1131	987	1498	1414	1290	1606	1776	2134	382	602
Total gas required	30995	31511	33471	36418	37115	37761	38655	39574	39645	40528
Less: Required for injection	2006	1937	2144	2564	2496	2561	2613	2679	1783	1910
Total sendout	28989	29574	31327	33854	34619	35200	36042	36895	37862	38618

Source: Company records.

EXHIBIT 14-19   Dymond Electric and Gas Company: Comparison of Commodity Gas Costs and Oil Prices

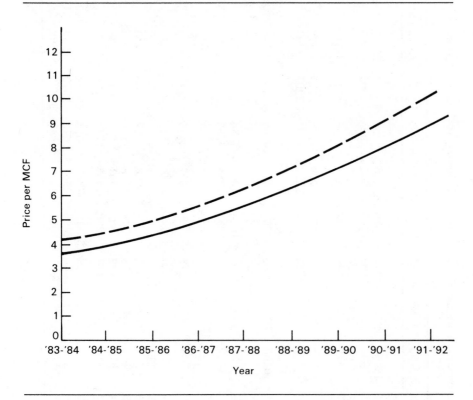

Source: Company records.

switchover. With this equipment customers can use gas when it is available and switch to oil either when gas is not available or when they can get oil at a lower price. The company believed that as total energy costs continued to increase in proportion to other production costs, this customer group would increase in number. Since their sensitivity to price differences between alternative fuels would result in great fluctuations in the company's sales, it would be extremely difficult to forecast and plan future supply acquisition.

The company's firm commercial and industrial rate classes had traditionally supplied the bulk of the return on the company's allowed rate base, as shown in Exhibit 14-15. Although it was a goal of both the company and the state regulatory agency to avoid cross-class subsidization, total equalization of rates would result in uncompetitively high residential rates.

(*Text continues on page 775.*)

EXHIBIT 14-20 Dymond Electric and Gas Company: Gas Business Potential Markets

	Rates Competitive With				Meets ROR*	Growth Potential	Favorable Operating Load
	Electric	No. 2 Oil	No. 6 Oil	Propane			
Residential Low-Use—New	X	—	—	—	—	Low	X
Residential Low-Use—Upgrade	X	X	—	X	—	Medium	X
Residential Heating—Upgrade	X	X	—	X	—	Medium	X
Residential—New	X	X	—	X	—	Low	—
Commercial	X	X	—	X	X	High	X
Industrial	X	X	—	X	X	Low	X
Interruptible—Existing	X	X	X	X	X	Low	X

*Rate of return.

Source: Company records.

EXHIBIT 14-21   Dymond Electric and Gas

AT DECEMBER 31,	1982	1981
	(Thousands of Dollars)	
Assets		
Utility Plant, at original cost:		
Electric	$3,037,882	$2,922,804
Gas	222,460	198,222
Other	33,926	35,959
	3,294,268	3,156,985
Less: Accumulated provision for depreciation	1,044,543	912,951
	2,249,725	2,244,034
Construction work in progress	1,223,578	894,078
Nuclear fuel, net of amortization	—	189,925
Total net utility plant	3,473,303	3,328,037
Other Property and Investments:		
Investments in regional nuclear generating companies, at equity	55,504	49,639
Other, at cost	15,996	21,296
	71,500	70,935
Current Assets:		
Cash and special deposits	4,177	24,000
Receivables, less accumulated provision for uncollectible accounts of $8,054,000 in 1982 and $4,920,000 in 1981	196,127	184,715
Accrued utility revenues	78,495	75,562
Fuel, materials and supplies, at average cost	130,021	126,060
Recoverable energy costs	—	35,768
Current portion of accumulated deferred income taxes	6,168	—
Prepayments and other	7,689	7,813
	422,677	453,918
Deferred Charges:		
Unamortized debt expense	5,317	3,864
Energy adjustment clauses, net	6,295	14,164
Canceled nuclear project	14,397	21,468
Deferred unusual operating expense	10,089	14,301
Other	25,061	18,894
	61,159	72,691
Total Assets	$4,028,639	$3,925,581

Source: Company records.

Company: Balance Sheet

AT DECEMBER 31,	1982	1981
	(Thousands of Dollars)	
Capitalization and Liabilities		
Capitalization:		
Common shareholders' equity	$1,159,698	$1,013,205
Preferred stock not subject to mandatory redemption	291,195	291,200
Preferred stock subject to mandatory redemption	103,893	65,401
Long-term debt	1,894,542	1,608,272
Total capitalization	3,449,328	2,978,078
Current Liabilities:		
Notes payable to banks	19,800	79,500
Commercial paper	37,725	146,135
Long-term debt due within one year	15,499	210,215
Preferred stock to be redeemed within one year	568	1,200
Nuclear fuel payable	—	26,900
Accounts payable	123,859	177,843
Accrued taxes	90,181	72,678
Refundable energy costs	10,783	—
Current portion of accumulated deferred income taxes	—	13,824
Accrued interest	40,790	44,962
Other	12,834	14,514
	352,039	787,771
Deferred Credits:		
Accumulated deferred income taxes	81,935	78,807
Accumulated deferred investment tax credits	128,845	66,798
Other	16,492	14,127
	227,272	159,732
Commitments and Contingencies		
Total Capitalization and Liabilities	$4,028,639	$3,925,581

EXHIBIT 14-22   Dymond Electric and Gas Company: Income Statement

FOR THE YEARS ENDED DECEMBER 31,	1982	1981	1980
	(Thousands of Dollars, except share information)		
Operating Revenues	$1,763,220	$1,655,057	$1,324,545
Operating Expenses:			
Operation—			
Fuel	464,654	511,776	420,138
Purchased and interchange power, net	46,022	97,915	18,385
Gas purchased for resale ..	147,637	111,651	89,366
Other	378,358	322,973	267,853
Maintenance	109,721	82,152	79,476
Depreciation	106,417	102,801	96,266
Federal and state income taxes	113,712	67,552	46,835
Taxes other than income taxes	140,031	131,458	113,959
Total operating expenses	1,506,552	1,428,278	1,132,278
Operating Income	256,668	226,779	192,267
Other Income:			
Allowance for equity funds used during construction ..	52,096	32,658	26,070
Equity in earnings of regional nuclear generating companies	8,570	6,148	3,692
Other, net	(1,994)	(2,999)	1,667
Income taxes applicable to other income—credit	37,898	37,705	22,433
Net other income	96,570	73,512	53,862
Income before interest charges	353,238	300,291	246,129
Interest Charges:			
Interest on long-term debt ...	175,866	158,883	120,588
Other interest	31,679	61,824	37,302
Allowance for borrowed funds used during construction, net of the income tax effect of $35,139,000 in 1982, $35,361,000 in 1981 and $22,144,000 in 1980	(37,081)	(42,146)	(25,960)
Total interest charges	170,464	178,561	131,930
Income after interest charges	182,774	121,730	114,199

EXHIBIT 14-22   continued

FOR THE YEARS ENDED DECEMBER 31,	1982	1981	1980
Preferred Dividends of Subsidiaries	31,532	26,612	25,447
Net Income	$ 151,242	$ 95,118	$ 88,752
Earnings Per Common Share	$ 1.76	$ 1.29	$ 1.31
Common Shares Outstanding (average)	85,777,230	73,783,201	67,555,006

Source: Company records.

EXHIBIT 14-23   Dymond Electric and Gas Company: Sources and Uses of Funds

FOR THE YEARS ENDED DECEMBER 31,	1982	1981	1980
	(Thousands of Dollars)		
Funds Generated From Operations:			
Net Income	$151,242	$ 95,118	$ 88,752
Principal noncash items:			
Depreciation and nuclear fuel amortization	154,722	142,191	126,988
Deferred income taxes, net	50,989	17,329	25,842
Amortization of deferred charges and other noncash items	8,995	1,327	4,441
Amortization of energy adjustment clauses	47,808	33,876	7,584
Allowance for equity funds used during construction	(52,096)	(32,658)	(26,070)
Total funds from operations ..	361,660	257,183	227,537
Less: Cash dividends paid on common shares	110,650	87,064	74,311
Net funds generated from operations	251,010	170,119	153,226
Funds Obtained From Financing:			
Proceeds from issuance of:			
Common shares	107,843	88,257	14,047
Preferred stock	38,054	14,453	24,680
Long-term debt	362,198	262,489	98,035
Proceeds from the sale of nuclear fuel to a third party trust (Note 6)	230,400	—	—
Increase (decrease) in short-term debt	(168,110)	(111,691)	169,436

EXHIBIT 14-23   continued

FOR THE YEARS ENDED DECEMBER 31,	1982	1981	1980
Increase (decrease) in nuclear fuel payable	(26,900)	4,600	175
Total	543,485	258,108	306,373
Less: Reacquisitions and retirements of long-term debt and preferred stock	274,641	7,778	30,147
Net funds from financing	268,844	250,330	276,226
Other Sources (Uses) of Funds:			
Decrease (increase) in net current assets (excluding short-term debt, long-term debt due within one year, preferred stock to be redeemed within one year and nuclear fuel payable):			
Cash and special deposits	19,823	(6,471)	(15,014)
Receivables and accrued utility revenues	(14,345)	3,890	(101,417)
Fuel, materials and supplies	(3,961)	(20,948)	(4,110)
Accounts payable	(53,984)	18,130	85,232
Accrued taxes	17,503	21,371	(26)
Other, net	(2,930)	7,745	1,949
Net change	(37,894)	23,717	(33,386)
Sale of utility plant	—	5,636	—
Deferred unusual operating expense	—	(10,949)	(4,034)
Energy adjustment clauses, net	2,886	(11,700)	(70,294)
Other, net	(3,040)	(1,602)	1,886
Net other sources (uses) of funds	(38,048)	5,102	(105,828)
Total Funds For Construction From Above Sources	481,806	425,551	323,624
Allowance for Equity Funds Used During Construction	52,096	32,658	26,070
GROSS PROPERTY ADDITIONS	$533,902	$458,209	$349,694
Composition of Gross Property Additions:			
Electric and other utility plant	$475,294	$360,118	$262,500
Gas utility plant	22,088	21,069	19,903
Nuclear fuel	36,520	77,022	67,291
Total	$533,902	$458,209	$349,694

Source: Company records.

EXHIBIT 14-24   Dymond Electric and Gas Company: Financial Data by Segments of Business

FOR THE YEARS ENDED DECEMBER 31,	1982	1981	1980
	(Thousands of Dollars)		
Operating information:			
Operating revenues—			
Electric	$1,538,773	$1,473,789	$1,179,161
Gas	224,447	181,268	145,384
Total	$1,763,220	$1,655,057	$1,324,545
Operating expenses excluding provisions for income taxes—			
Electric	$1,194,841	$1,204,896	$ 958,340
Gas	197,999	155,830	127,103
Total	$1,392,840	$1,360,726	$1,085,443
Pretax operating income—			
Electric	$ 343,932	$ 268,893	$ 220,821
Gas	26,448	25,438	18,281
Total	$ 370,380	$ 294,331	$ 239,102
Provision for income taxes—			
Electric	$ 106,290	$ 61,522	$ 43,477
Gas	7,422	6,030	3,358
Total	$ 113,712	$ 67,552	$ 46,835
Operating income—			
Electric	$ 237,642	$ 207,371	$ 177,344
Gas	19,026	19,408	14,923
Total	$ 256,668	$ 226,779	$ 192,267
Depreciation expense—			
Electric	$ 100,623	$ 97,401	$ 91,255
Gas	5,794	5,400	5,011
Total	$ 106,417	$ 102,801	$ 96,266
Capital expenditures:			
Electric	$ 511,814	$ 437,140	$ 329,791
Gas	22,088	21,069	19,903
Total	$ 533,902	$ 458,209	$ 349,694
Investment information at December 31:			
Identifiable assets (a)			
Electric	$3,325,950	$3,192,206	$2,899,412
Gas	186,483	169,792	154,057
Nonallocable assets	516,206	563,583	574,273
Total Assets	$4,028,639	$3,925,581	$3,627,742

Source: Company records.

EXHIBIT 14-25   Dymond Electric and Gas Company: Gas Business Operating Data

	1982	1981	1980	1979	1978
Source of Gas (Mcf-thousands)					
Purchased	29,263	29,158	28,342	26,048	24,809
Produced	464	573	410	454	358
Company use and unaccounted for	(810)	(702)	(1,206)	(936)	(1,468)
Net sold	28,917	29,029	27,546	25,566	23,699
Maximum Day Sendout (M-Therms)	2,068	2,036	1,854	1,772	1,467
Revenues: (thousands)					
Residential	$ 94,115	$ 75,500	$ 61,472	$ 48,221	$ 45,990
Commercial	58,189	44,143	31,772	21,472	19,383
Industrial	69,850	59,302	47,053	34,140	25,004
Miscellaneous	2,293	2,323	5,087	2,133	2,008
Total	$224,447	$181,268	$145,384	$105,966	$ 92,385
Sales: (Mcf-thousands)					
Residential	10,294	10,532	10,174	10,003	10,299
Commercial	7,722	7,103	6,075	5,175	4,973
Industrial	10,886	11,378	11,278	10,374	8,075
Other	15	16	19	14	352
Total	28,917	29,029	27,546	25,566	23,699
Customers: (average)					
Residential	137,204	135,992	134,075	131,634	131,036
Commercial	13,829	13,605	13,202	12,617	12,222
Industrial	1,296	1,304	1,297	1,274	1,273
Total	152,329	150,901	148,574	145,525	144,531
Average Annual Use Per Residential Customer (Mcf)	75.0	77.4	75.9	76.0	78.6
Average Annual Bill Per Residential Customer	$685.95	$555.18	$458.49	$366.33	$350.97
Average Revenue Per Mcf:					
Residential	$9.14	$7.17	$6.04	$4.82	$4.47
Commercial	7.54	6.21	5.23	4.15	3.90
Industrial	6.42	5.21	4.17	3.29	3.10

Source: Company records.

A recent survey conducted by Dymond's Energy Management Services Department revealed that in the home heating market Dymond had achieved only 38 percent saturation of homes located on its existing gas lines, leaving over 73,000 oil heating customers as potentials for conversions. Similar penetration studies had not been performed pertaining to commercial and industrial customers but, judging from statewide market share information generated by the U.S. Department of Energy (Exhibit 14-16), the results would probably not be too dissimilar.

Current estimates indicate that system gas supplies will be adequate to support substantial growth (Exhibits 14-17 and 14-18) and maintain the cost of gas to the company at less than the forecasted price of No. 6 oil to the area (Exhibit 14-19). The addition of a limited number of firm customers requiring gas at periods other than peak-load periods would actually result in a lower marginal cost of gas. A compilation of this information resulted in the matrix shown in Exhibit 14-20. Financial information on the company is given in Exhibits 14-21 to 14-25.

CONCLUSION

Grover has received assurances from the CEO and the president that they will support measures to ensure the viability of the gas business and the profitability of the company. He and his staff must formulate strategies for marketing gas which are consistent with the corporate mission of "providing safe, dependable, and reasonably priced energy and related services as an ethical and financial sound private enterprise committed to the efficient use of resources responsive to the needs of customers and their communities, sensitive to the well-being of employees, and yielding a fair return to the shareholders." The strategic marketing plan must also be responsive to the concerns of the state regulatory agency regarding the promotion of conservation.

Dymond Electric and Gas Company has no easy task if it is to reverse the trend of declining gas sales and gas rates escalating at rates higher than the alternative fuels. James Grover, with the help of his staff, must develop a viable marketing strategy suggesting innovative rate design which might help in reversing the declining sales trend.

The art of getting rich consists not in industry, much less in saving, but in a better order, in timeliness, in being at the right spot.

Ralph Waldo Emerson

Distribution strategies are concerned with the channels a manufacturer may employ to make its goods and services available to customers. The channels are organized structures of buyers and sellers which bridge the gap of time and space between the manufacturer and the customer.

Marketing is defined as an exchange process. In relation to distribution, exchange poses two problems. First, goods must be moved to a central location from the warehouses of producers who make heterogeneous goods and who are geographically widespread. Second, the goods that are accumulated from diversified sources should represent a desired assortment from the viewpoint of customers. These two problems can be solved by the process of sorting, which combines *concentration* (i.e., bringing the goods from different sources to a central location) and *dispersion* (i.e., picking an assortment of goods from different points of concentration). There are two basic strategic questions that need to be answered here. Who should perform the concentration and dispersion tasks—the manufacturer or intermediaries? Which intermediary should the manufacturer select to take the goods close to the customer? These questions are central to distribution strategies.

In addition to the above, there are other strategy-related matters which are discussed in this chapter. The focus of other strategic questions is on the scope of distribution (i.e., how widespread distribution may be), use of multiple channels to serve different segments, modification of channels to accommodate environmental shifts, resolution of conflict among channels, and use of vertical systems to institute control over channels.

Each strategic issue raised above is examined with reference to its relevance to different circumstances. The application of each strategy is illustrated with examples from marketing literature.

The appendix at the end of this chapter summarizes the definition, objectives, requirements, and expected results of each strategy.

CHANNEL-STRUCTURE STRATEGY

The channel-structure strategy refers to the number of intermediaries which may be employed in moving goods from manufacturers to customers. A company may undertake to distribute its goods to customers or retailers without involving any intermediary. This comprises the shortest channel and may be labeled a *direct* distribution strategy. Alternatively, goods may pass through one or more middlemen, such as wholesalers and/or agents. This is an *indirect* distribution strategy. Exhibit 15-1 shows alternative channel structures for consumer and industrial products.

The decision on channel-structure strategy is based on a variety of factors. To put the discussion in proper perspective, first a conceptual framework is presented. It is built around the principle of postponement-speculation theory. Then two different approaches for choosing channel structure are examined.

An underlying factor here is the use of middlemen in channel structure. The importance of using middlemen may be illustrated with reference to an example cited by Alderson.[1] In a primitive economy five producers produced one type of item each: hats, hoes, knives, baskets, and pots. Since all of them needed the others' products, a total of ten exchanges were required to accomplish trade. However, with a market (or middlemen), once the economy has reached equilibrium (that is, each producer-consumer has visited the market once), only five exchanges need take place to meet everyone's needs. Let n denote the number of producer-consumers. Then the total number of transactions (T) without a market is given by:

$$T_{\text{without}} = \frac{n(n-1)}{2}$$

and the total number of transactions with a market is given by:

$$T_{\text{with}} = n$$

The efficiency created in distribution by utilizing a middleman may be viewed as:

$$\text{Efficiency} = \frac{T_{\text{without}}}{T_{\text{with}}} = \frac{n(n-1)}{2} \times \frac{1}{n} = \frac{n-1}{2}$$

---

[1]Wroe Alderson, "Factors Governing the Development of Marketing Channels," in Richard M. Clewett (ed.), *Marketing Channels for Manufactured Products* (Homewood, IL: Richard D. Irwin, 1964), p. 7.

EXHIBIT 15-1   Typical Channel Structures

(a) Consumer Products

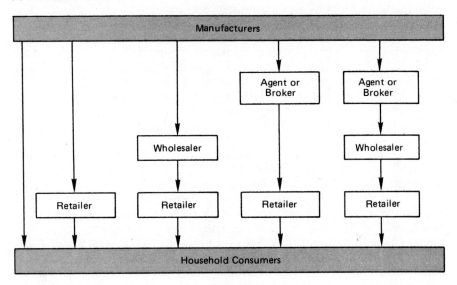

(b) Industrial Products

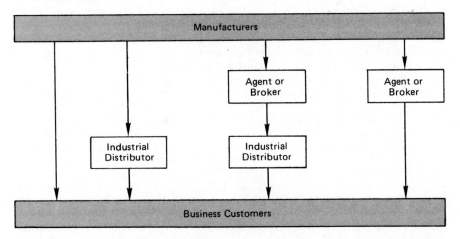

For the example with five producer-consumers, the efficiency of having a middleman is 2. The efficiency increases as n increases. Thus, in many cases middlemen may perform the task of distribution more efficiently than the manufacturers would.

Postponement-Speculation Theory

Conceptually, the selection of channel structure may be explained with reference to Bucklin's postponement-speculation framework.[2] The framework is based on risk, uncertainty, and costs involved in facilitating exchanges. Postponement seeks to eliminate risk by matching production/distribution with actual customer demand. Presumably, it should produce efficiency in marketing channels. For example, the manufacturer may produce and ship goods only on confirmed orders. Speculation, on the other hand, requires undertaking risk through changes in form and movement of goods within the channels. Speculation leads to economies of scale in manufacturing, reduces costs of frequent ordering, and eliminates opportunity cost.

Exhibit 15-2 shows the behavior of variables involved in the postponement-speculation framework. The vertical axis shows the average cost of undertaking a function for one unit of any given commodity; the horizontal axis shows the time involved in delivering a confirmed order. Together, the average cost and the delivery time measure the cost of marketing tasks performed in a channel with reference to delivery time. The nature of the following three curves in Exhibit 15-2 should be understood: C (costs to the buyer for holding an inventory), AD' (costs involved in supplying goods directly from manufacturer to buyer), and DB (costs involved in shipping and maintaining speculative inventories, i.e., in anticipation of demand).

Following Bucklin's framework, one determines the channel structure by examining the behavior of the C, AD', and DB curves:

1. The minimal cost of supplying the buyer for every possible delivery time is derived from curves AD' and DB. As may be seen in Exhibit 15-2, especially fast delivery service can be provided only by the indirect channel (i.e., by using a stocking intermediary). However, at some delivery time, I', the cost of serving the consumer directly from the producer will intersect and fall below the cost of indirect shipment. The minimal costs derived from both curves are designated DD'. From the perspective of channel cost, it will be cheaper to service the buyer from a speculative inventory if delivery times shorter than I' are demanded. If the consumer is willing to accept delivery times longer than I', then direct shipment will be the least expensive.

------

[2]Louis P. Bucklin, *A Theory of Distribution Channel Structure* (Berkeley, CA: IBER Special Publications, University of California, 1966); and "Postponement, Speculation and Structure of Distribution Channels," in Bruce E. Mallen (ed.), *The Marketing Channel: A Conceptual Viewpoint* (New York: John Wiley & Sons, 1967), pp. 67–74.

EXHIBIT 15-2   Using the Postponement-Speculation Concept to Determine Channel Structure

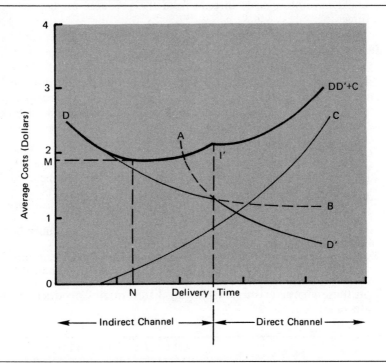

2. The minimal total cost curve for the channel with respect to delivery time is derived by summing the cost of moving goods to the buyer, DD', and the buyer's costs of holding inventory, C. The curve is represented in Exhibit 15-2 by DD' + C. Total channel costs initially fall as delivery time lengthens because increased buyer expenses are more than made up for by savings in other parts of the channel. Gradually, however, the savings from these sources diminish and buyer costs begin to rise more rapidly. A minimal cost point is reached, and expenses for the channel rise thereafter. Channel structure is controlled by the location of this minimum point. If, as in the present case, it falls to the left of I', then goods would be expected to flow through the speculative inventory (i.e., an intermediary). If, on the other hand, the savings of the buyer

from postponement had not been as great as those depicted, the minimum point would have fallen to the right of I' and shipments would have been made directly from the producer to the consumer.[3]

Goods Approach

The goods approach is advanced by Aspinwall. According to him, the marketing characteristics of a product determine the most appropriate and economical method for distributing it. The product characteristics considered here are:

1. *Replacement rate* (rate at which a product is bought and used by buyers in order to derive the satisfaction one expects from the product)
2. *Gross margin* (difference between sale price and direct costs incurred at different levels in bringing the goods closer to the buyer)
3. *Adjustment* (services that must be provided to ensure requisite satisfaction to the buyer from goods)
4. *Time of consumption* (time frame within which the product must be used to provide the required value)
5. *Searching time* (time that the buyer requires to travel to a retail store and the distance he or she must travel to purchase the product).[4]

Based on these characteristics, Aspinwall differentiates products in three color categories as follows:[5]

CHARACTERISTICS	COLOR CLASSIFICATION		
	RED GOODS	ORANGE GOODS	YELLOW GOODS
Replacement Rate	High	Medium	Low
Gross Margin	Low	Medium	High
Adjustment	Low	Medium	High
Time of Consumption	Low	Medium	High
Searching Time	Low	Medium	High

The above analysis may now be used to develop a schematic diagram showing how goods of different color classifications require differ-

---

[3]Louis P. Bucklin and Leslie Halpert, "Exploring Channels of Distribution for Cement with the Principle of Postponement-Speculation," in Peter D. Bennett (ed.), *Marketing and Economic Development* (Chicago: American Marketing Association, 1965), p. 699.

[4]Leo V. Aspinwall, "The Characteristics of Goods and Parallel Systems Theories," in *Four Marketing Theories* (Boulder, CO: Bureau of Business Research, University of Colorado, 1961).

[5]*Ibid.*

ent methods of distribution. Such a diagram is shown in Exhibit 15-3. A simple percentage scale of 0 to 100 is laid out on both coordinates, representing all possible gradations in goods from red through orange to yellow. For example, line AB represents a good with an ordinate value of 63, which indicates that it has 63 percent yellow characteristics and 37 percent red characteristics. Ladies' ready-to-wear is an example of such a good, sold through department stores and small specialty stores. Department stores are directly supplied by the factory, while small specialty stores

EXHIBIT 15-3   Schematic Array of a Few Selected Goods (Plotted in Terms of Yellow Goods)

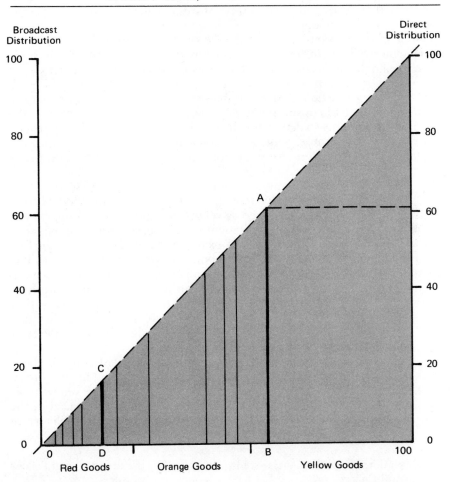

Source: Leo V. Aspinwall, *Four Marketing Theories* (Boulder, CO: Bureau of Business Research, University of Colorado, 1961). Reprinted by permission.

are served through specialty wholesalers. On the other hand, line CD represents a good which is characterized as 15 percent yellow and 85 percent red. A good of this type is soap, which is mainly sold through different types of intermediaries.

The 15 percent yellow characteristics might indicate specialty salespeople's activity involving factory drop shipments (direct distribution). A real-world example of this type of good is illustrated by the Bic pen. Back in 1979, Bic products were sold to retailers and commercial accounts by 120 company salespeople who called on approximately 10,000 accounts. These accounts represented large retailers (such as chains) as well as wholesale distributors. Through these 10,000 accounts Bic achieved distribution for its products in approximately two million retail outlets, of which 12,000 were commercial supply stores. In addition, the salespeople called on 20,000 independent retail accounts which were considered important in the marketplace. In the case of these accounts, the Bic salespeople merely filled orders for the distributors. Although Bic did do some direct selling (yellow characteristic), it was limited to chain retailers.[6]

The goods approach suggests that the color characteristic of a product, which is a function of five variables (replacement rate, gross margin, adjustment, time of consumption, and searching time), will determine the appropriate channel structure for the good. Thus, for yellow goods, direct distribution is desirable, while red goods should be channeled through middlemen. Distribution of orange goods may be partly direct and partly through middlemen.

Three reservations must be noted here, however. First, the color concept introduced here is dynamic in nature. Thus, many goods during introduction may be characterized as yellow. But as they reach the growth stage in their life cycles, the replacement rate increases and the goods shift toward the red end of the scale. For example, Texas Instruments at first distributed hand calculators directly. About five years later, as the product became popular, a large portion of the inventory moved through middlemen. When Hallmark Cards brought out a number of new products in the late 1970s—books, candles, jewelry, pewter, crystal items, etc.—they were considered to be yellow, since unquestionably the company's intention was to sell them exclusively through Hallmark dealers. Now, however, they may be characterized as red.[7]

Second, one or more of the five product characteristics noted above may be given higher importance for a particular good. This will mean that while four characteristics may qualify a product as the yellow type, one characteristic may be given such a high value that it is placed in the red category. For example, to provide customers with quick delivery of

[6]"Bic Pen Corporation (A)," a case study copyrighted by the President and Fellows of Harvard College, 1974.
[7]"Hallmark Now Stands for a Lot More Than Cards," *Business Week*, May 29, 1978, p. 57.

cassettes for use on videotape recorders, Paramount Pictures Corporation has collaborated with Fotomat stores for both the sale and the rental of its films. The customer can call a toll-free number to order a cassette, which can be picked up after twenty hours at a neighborhood Fotomat store.[8] Apparently, the searching time characteristic had a major influence in Paramount's decision to channel the films for household use through Fotomat.

The third reservation which must be noted here is that a company may always follow an innovative course to distribute its product. For example, Avon Products, Inc., distributes its products door to door, using about a quarter of a million saleswomen. This strategy not only suits the informal lifestyle of suburbia, but it also allows the customer to make a decision on an intimate product in the privacy of the home. In terms of the goods approach, beauty aids do not qualify for direct distribution, but this strategy helped to make Avon the world's largest cosmetics and toiletries company.[9] Similarly, Hanes Corporation decided to distribute L'eggs pantyhose directly to supermarkets and drugstores even though it was a "red" product. The company did so because their marketing research showed that the chief complaint of pantyhose customers was that they often could not find their size and type of pantyhose in stock. To overcome the out-of-stock problem that was hurting other hosiery manufacturers, L'eggs opted for direct store delivery and established a market information system which permitted regular replenishment of sold-out items.[10]

Financial Approach

With the financial approach, a manufacturer's choice of a channel should be determined by its financial resources and need to control the distribution of its product.[11] The term *control* refers to the desire of the manufacturer to determine retail price, distribution outlets, customer service, storage facilities, and advertising. Here the term will be used more broadly to include other factors involved in the selection of channel structure, such as the nature of the product, the nature of the market, and selectivity of distribution.

The relationship between these two determining factors for channel selection, i.e., financial resources and control, is an inverse one. The following are the four major channel alternatives:

1. Manufacturer to consumer
2. Manufacturer to retailer to consumer

---

[8]"Video Corp. of America: A Big Bet on Software for TV Recorders," *Business Week,* July 9, 1979, p. 76.

[9]"Troubled Avon Tries a Face-Lifting," *Business Week,* May 11, 1974.

[10]"Our L'eggs Fit Your Legs, " *Business Week,* March 25, 1972, pp. 96–100.

[11]Eugene W. Lambert, Jr., "Financial Considerations in Choosing a Marketing Channel," *MSU Business Topics,* Winter, 1966, pp. 17–26.

3. Manufacturer to wholesaler to retailer to consumer
4. Manufacturer to agent to wholesaler to retailer to consumer

Alternative 1 provides an organization with a good deal of control, but also requires an enormous amount of resources. Alternative 4, on the other hand, requires the least financial resources, but provides the firm with minimum control of distribution. Alternatives 2 and 3 stand between the two extremes. The above considerations provide a firm with four choices (A, B, C, and D) in selecting channel structure, as shown below:

Degree of Control Desired

		Maximum	Minimum
	Adequate	A	B
Financial Resources			
	Inadequate	C	D

In situations A and D, financial considerations do not play a major role because in the former case the firm has adequate resources, while in the latter the need for financial resources is minor. In situations B and C, however, financial considerations become a dominating factor. In the case of C, if the firm desires control, inadequacy of financial resources becomes a limiting factor. For example, the firm may want to use direct distribution to maintain control; however, lack of the financial resources needed to implement such a channel structure would prohibit such a choice. This may lead the firm to opt for indirect distribution through wholesaler (or wholesaler to agent) to retailer to consumer. In situation B the firm can choose among all four; since control is a determining factor here, the choice rests on financial resources alone. Commitment of the firm's financial resources, however, has to be made in the light of the opportunity cost of these resources in the firm elsewhere. In other words, in situation B, channel-structure strategy becomes a capital budgeting problem, and the investment in channels is evaluated vis-à-vis other investment opportunities available to the firm.

The importance of the control factor in choosing channel structure is demonstrated in a case study on petrochemicals. A characteristic of the petrochemical industry is that its base product can be finished in any of several different ways to produce several different end products. Therefore, in certain situations (such as sales in foreign countries a long way from a plant), it was found to be profitable to store the base product and finish it to an end product as and when the market dictated. This called for an effective control of channels to ensure that required inventories could be processed in time to provide timely delivery to the customer. Of extreme importance here were the logistics involved in setting up systems such as this. The distance between the end market and the main plant was so great that there was a high probability of stockouts and overstocks occurring because of fluctuating demands. The number of orders and amount of total sales were also major considerations in seeking control.[12] Another instance of the importance of control is provided by the Sherwin-Williams Company. Determining that its wholesalers and retailers were not expending the effort to do an effective job, the company instituted the necessary controls by establishing its own retail stores—as many as 2,000 outlets throughout the country.[13]

But even when control may necessitate opting for direct distribution, the financial resources of a company may not permit this. The point may be illustrated with reference to the J. B. Kunz Company, a leading supplier of savings passbooks to the U.S. banking industry. This small, family-run company sells to thousands of different banks spread over a wide region, relying on approximately 40 distributors to reach its bank customers. If the company wished to opt for direct distribution instead, it would have to acquire additional executives and hire more salespeople, a luxury it could neither afford nor justify.[14]

An intermediary for a financially weak company may provide a cushion even though this may not be realized when choosing a channel structure. In 1979, the Chrysler Corporation got into such trouble that it had to go to the federal government for a $1-billion advance against its taxes. At that time, while the government decision was still pending, its dealers offered aid in the form of a surcharge. The dealers' proposal called for imposing a special $50 surcharge on each vehicle delivered to them by the factory in the next three years. The extra $50 was proposed to be a direct investment in the company to help protect jobs and meet the cash-flow problem. The proposal was to generate $120 million in three years.[15] This illustrates how middlemen can come to the aid of a manufacturer in trouble.

Additional Considerations

The framework and the two approaches discussed above for determining channel structure are based primarily on economic considerations. Examined in this section are a variety of environmental influences

---

[12]"Tex-Fiber Industries: Petroloid Products Division (A)," a case study copyrighted by the President and Fellows of Harvard College, 1976.

[13]"A Paintmaker Puts a Fresh Coat on Its Marketing," *Business Week*, February 23, 1976, p. 95.

[14]"J. B. Kunz Company (A)," a case study copyrighted by the President and Fellows of Harvard College, 1977.

[15]"Chrysler Offered Aid by Its Own Dealers in the Form of Surcharge," *The Wall Street Journal*, August 10, 1979, p. 2.

on channel-structure strategy formulation. These influences may be categorized as technological, social and ethical, governmental, geographical,
and cultural. Many aspects of channel structure are affected by technological advances. For example, mass retailing in food has been feasible
because of the development of automobiles, highways, refrigerated cars,
cash registers, packaging improvements, and mass communications (television). In the coming years, television shopping with household computer
terminals should have a far-reaching impact on distribution structure.[16]
Technological advances permitted BSR Ltd., an English company, to become dominant in the U.S. market for low-priced phonograph record
changers. They developed a prepackaged, all-in-one changer which could
be sold through mass retailers so that even sales clerks without technical
know-how could handle customers.[17]

     How technology may be utilized to revamp the operations of a
wholesaler, making it worthwhile to adopt indirect channels, is illustrated
by the case of Foremost-McKesson, the nation's largest wholesale distributor. In the 1970s the company found itself in a precarious position. Distribution, although one of the company's most pervasive business functions, did not pay. It merely took manufacturers' goods and resold them
to small retailers through a routine process of warehousing, transportation, and simple marketing that offered thin profits. In 1975, the company earned a tiny 5.9 percent on equity, and its profit growth of 2 percent per year meant slow liquidation because of inflation. As a matter of
fact, the company came close to selling off drug wholesaling, its biggest
business. Instead, however, its new chief executive decided to add sophisticated technology to Foremost's operations, in order to make the
company so efficient at distribution that manufacturers could not possibly
do as well on their own. It virtually redefined the function of the middleman. Having used the computer to make its own operations efficient,
it devised ways to make its data processing useful to suppliers and customers in a way that made Foremost become, in essence, part of their
marketing teams. Since the company computerized its operations, Foremost has turned around dramatically. Profits that had grown at an average of 2 percent per year for five years until 1976 have since grown at
20 percent per year. Foremost earned $69.9 million on sales of $4.2 billion
in its fiscal year ending March 31, 1981. Here are the highlights of
Foremost's steps in reshaping its role:

- Acting as middleman between drugstores and insurance offices by
  processing medical insurance claims.
- Creating a massive "rack jobbing" service by providing crews to set
  up racks of goods inside retail stores, offering what amounts to a

[16]See John A. Quelch and Hirotaka Takeuchi, "Nonstore Marketing: Fast Track
or Slow," *Harvard Business Review,* July–August, 1981, p. 76.
[17]"Why BSR Dominates the Record-Changer Market," *Business Week,* June 7th, 1976,
pp. 84–85.

temporary labor force that brings both marketing knowhow and Foremost merchandise along with it.
* Taking waste products as well as finished goods from chemical manufacturers, and recycling the wastes through its own plants—its first entry into chemical waste management.
* Designing, as well as supplying, drugstores.
* Researching new uses for products it receives from manufacturers. Foremost found new customers, for example, for a Monsanto Co. food preservative, from among its contacts in the cosmetics industry.[18]

Social taboos and ethical standards may also affect the channel-structure decision. For example, Mallen reports that *Viva,* a woman's magazine, had achieved a high circulation in supermarkets and drugstores in Canada. When *Viva* responded to readers' insistence and to competition from *Playgirl* by introducing nude male photos, most supermarkets banned the magazine. Since supermarkets accounted for over half of *Viva*'s circulation, *Viva* dropped such photos so that it could continue to be sold through this channel.[19] The channel-structure strategy can also be influenced by local, state, and federal laws in a variety of ways. For example, door-to-door selling of certain goods may be prohibited by laws in some localities.[20] In many states (e.g., California and Ohio) wine can be sold through supermarkets, but other states (e.g., Connecticut) do not permit this.

Geographic size, population patterns, and typology also influence the channel-structure strategy. In urban areas direct distribution to large retailers may make sense. The rural areas, however, may be covered only by wholesalers.

Often it may appear that with the inception of large grocery chains, an accepted phenomenon, the independent grocery stores are dying. The truth is, however, that independent grocery stores as recently as 1975 accounted for 49 percent of all grocery sales in the country, i.e., over $70 billion. Thus, a manufacturer can ill afford not to deal with the independents, and to reach them it must go through wholesalers. Wetterau, Inc., for example, is a grocery wholesale firm in Hazelwood, Missouri, which did $832 million worth of business in 1978, serving only 700 IGA retail grocery stores and all of the Red & White grocery stores. It does not do any business with chain stores. But because of Wetterau's determination to offer its customers relatively low prices, a wide selection of brands, ser-

---

[18]"Foremost-McKesson: The Computer Moves Distribution to Center Stage," *Business Week,* December 7, 1981, p. 115. See also "Waldenbooks: Countering B. Dalton by Aping Its Computer Operations," *Business Week,* October 8, 1979, p. 116.
[19]Bruce Mallen, *Principles of Marketing Channel Management* (Lexington, MA: Lexington Books, 1977), p 179.
[20]See Marvin A. Jolson, "Direct Selling: Consumer vs. Salesman," *Business Horizons,* October, 1972, pp. 87–95.

vice programs carefully designed to make the brands more profitable, and a personal interest in their success, its customers are almost fanatically loyal. The company offers its customers—small, independent retail stores— a variety of services, such as lease arrangements, store design, financing packages, training, and computerized inventory systems. These services tend to enhance customers' competitiveness by reducing their operating costs and simplifying their bookkeeping, which in turn helps Wetterau to earn profits.[21] The Wetterau example shows that to reach smaller retailers, particularly in areas far removed from large metropolises, the indirect distribution strategy is appropriate. The wholesaler provides services to small retailers which a large manufacturer can never match on its own.

Finally, cultural traits may require the adoption of a certain channel structure in a setting which otherwise might seem an odd place for it. For example, in many parts of Switzerland, fruits and vegetables are sold in a central marketplace in the morning by small vendors even though there are modern supermarkets all over. This practice continues because it gives customers a chance to socialize with each other while shopping. Similarly, changing lifestyles among average American consumers and their desire to have more discretionary income for life-fulfillment activities appear to be making warehouse retailing more popular.[22] This is so because prices at warehouse outlets—grocery warehouses, for example—are substantially lower than at traditional stores.

DISTRIBUTION-SCOPE STRATEGY

For an efficient channel network, the manufacturer should clearly define the target customers it intends to reach. Implicit in the definition of target customers is a decision on the scope of distribution the manufacturer wants to pursue. The strategic alternatives here are exclusive distribution, selective distribution, and intensive distribution.

Exclusive Distribution

Exclusive distribution means that one particular retailer serving a given area is granted sole rights to carry the product. For example, Hart, Schaffner & Marx suits are distributed exclusively through one store in a town. There are several advantages to be gained by the use of exclusive distribution. It brings tremendous dealer loyalty, greater sales support, a

---

[21]"Wetterau: A Maverick Grocery Wholesaler," *Business Week*, February 14, 1977, p. 121.

[22]Jonathan N. Goodrich and Jo Ann Hoffman, "Warehouse Retailing: The Trend of the Future," *Business Horizons*, April, 1979, pp. 45–50. See also Frank E. James, "Big Warehouse Outlets Break Traditional Rules of Retailing," *The Wall Street Journal*, December 22, 1983, p. 27.

higher degree of control over the retail market, better forecasting, and better inventory and merchandising control. The impact of dealer loyalty can be helpful when the manufacturer has seasonal or other kinds of fluctuating sales. An exclusive dealership is more willing to finance inventories and thus bear a higher degree of risk than a more extensive dealership. Having a smaller number of dealers gives the manufacturer or wholesaler greater opportunity to provide each dealer with promotional support. And, with fewer outlets it is easier to control such aspects as margin, price, and inventory. Dealers are also more willing to provide data which may be used for marketing research and forecasts. Exclusive distribution is especially relevant for products that customers seek out. Examples of such products may include certain brands of appliances (such as GE dishwashers); clothing (such as Brooks Brothers suits); watches (such as Seiko); cameras (such as Minolta); and luggage (such as American Tourister briefcases).

On the other hand, there are several obvious disadvantages to exclusive distribution. First, sales volume may be lost. Second, the manufacturer places all its fortunes in a geographic area in the hands of one dealer. Exclusive distribution brings with it the characteristics of high price, high margin, and low volume. If the product is highly price elastic in nature, this combination of characteristics can mean significantly less than optimal performance. Having one sole retailer can mean that if sales are depressed for any reason, the retailer is then likely to be in a position to dictate terms to other channel members (i.e., the retailer becomes the channel captain).

For example, assume that a company manufacturing traditional toys deals exclusively with J. C. Penney. For a variety of reasons its line of toys may not do well. These reasons may be a continuing decline in the birthrate, an economic depression, the emerging popularity of electronic toys, higher prices of the company's toys compared to competitive brands, a poor promotional effort by Penney, etc. Penney, however, may put the blame on the manufacturer's higher prices since it is the exclusive distributor, and it may demand a reduction in prices from the manufacturer. Inasmuch as the manufacturer has no other reasons to give that could explain the poor performance, it must depend on Penney's analysis.

The last disadvantage of exclusive distribution is one that is easy to overlook. In certain circumstances exclusive distribution has been found to be in violation of antitrust laws because of its restraint on trade. The fine distinction between legal and illegal practices was shown in the *United States v. Sealy, Inc.* case, as described below:

> Another significant case was concerned with the arrangement under which bedding manufacturers were licensed to manufacture and sell in an exclusive territory under the Sealy brand name. The district court had held that the system of exclusive regional licensees used by Sealy was an effective way to achieve maximum market development and found no evidence that the system was developed for the purpose of protecting the markets of licensees or for eliminating competition among them. When the case reached the Supreme Court, however, the Court

decided that the arrangements among regional manufacturers and Sealy were essentially horizontal rather than vertical since Sealy was controlled by the regional franchise holders. Consequently, the effect was one of collusion and restraint of trade in which territorial restrictions were combined with unlawful price fixing and policing.[23]

As Sealy's case indicates, it is difficult to show that any given exclusive distribution channel is not set up to protect the markets of the retailers involved. Therefore, when one is dealing with exclusive distribution, the legal consideration should be one of the primary concerns.

The legality of an exclusive contract will vary from case to case. As long as an exclusive contract does not undermine competition and create a monopoly, it is acceptable. The courts appear to use the following criteria to determine if indeed an exclusive distribution lessens competition:

1. Whether the volume of the product in question is a substantial part of the total volume for the product type
2. Whether the exclusive dealership excludes competitive products from a substantial share of the market.[24]

Thus, a company considering an exclusive-distribution strategy should review its decision in the light of the above two ground rules. Based on past Supreme Court decisions, it would appear that exclusive distribution should be avoided unless it involves the reasonable use of a trademark or patent or is justified by unusual circumstances, such as the economic survival or maintenance of a company.

In recent years, the Justice Department has slightly mellowed its position. As has been said:

> Distributional practices may, under some circumstances, be used to adversely affect horizontal competition. But practices adopted independently by a firm (i.e., company) that restrict in some way the freedom of firms purchasing from it may be intended simply to increase the efficiency of the distribution process. For example, a manufacturer may attempt to limit competition among its retailers by restricting the territories that each may serve. Such vertical restrictions may be designed by the manufacturer to encourage retailers to provide services to consumers and to intensify their sales efforts in order to enhance the position of that manufacturer's product and allow it to compete more effectively in the market. Similarly, a firm's choices with respect to the granting of franchises or the grouping of goods and services for sale

---

[23]Edwin H. Lewis, *Marketing Channels: Structure and Strategy* (New York: McGraw-Hill Book Co., 1968), p. 77.

[24]Louis W. Stern and Adel I. El-Ansary, *Marketing Channels,* 2d Ed. (Englewood Cliffs, NJ: Prentice-Hall, 1982), p. 367.

may simply reflect the firm's judgment about the most efficient way to structure a marketing effort. Consumers may benefit substantially from resulting intensified interbrand competition among products and services.[25]

Yet careful review is needed when product-distribution issues take on antitrust significance.

Intensive Distribution

The inverse of exclusive distribution is intensive distribution. An intensive-distribution strategy makes a product available at all possible retail outlets. This may mean that the product is carried at a wide variety of different, and also competing, retail institutions in a given area. The distribution of convenience goods is most consistent with this strategy. If the nature of the product is such that a consumer will generally not bother to seek out the product, but will buy it on sight if available, then it is to the seller's advantage to have the product visible in as many places as possible. The Bic Pen Corporation is an example of a firm which uses this type of strategy. Bic makes its products available in a wide variety of retail establishments ranging from drugstores to "the corner grocery store" to large supermarkets. In all, Bic sells through 200,000 retail outlets representing competing as well as noncompeting stores. The advantages to be gained by this strategy are increased sales, wider customer recognition, and impulse buying. All of these qualities are desirable for convenience goods.

There are two main disadvantages associated with intensive distribution. First, the items are characteristically low-priced and low-margin products which require a fast turnover. Second, it is difficult to provide any degree of control over a large number of retailers. The uncontrolled distribution may not become a problem if the intensive distribution leads to increased sales. In the long run, however, it may have a variety of devastating effects. For example, if durable products such as Sony television sets were to be intensively distributed (i.e., through drugstores, discount stores, variety stores, etc.), Sony's sales would probably increase. But intensive distribution would lead to the problems of price discounting, provision of adequate customer service, and continued cooperation of traditional channels (e.g., department stores). Not only might these problems affect sales revenues in the long run, but the manufacturer might also

---

[25]Richard J. Favretto, "Antitrust Division Enforcement Priorities," Department of Justice News release (Washington, DC: September 18, 1981). See also Harry A. Garfield II, "Antitrust Risk Analysis for Marketers," *Harvard Business Review*, July–August, 1983, pp. 131–138.

lose some of its established channels. For example, a department store might decide to drop the Sony line for another brand of television sets. In addition, Sony's distinctive brand image could suffer. In other words, the advantages furnished by intensive distribution should be carefully related to the type of product to decide if this form of distribution is suitable. It is because of the problems outlined above that one finds intensive distribution limited to such products as candy, newspapers, cigarettes, aspirin, soft drinks, etc., where turnover is usually high and channel control is usually not as strategic as it would be, say, for television sets.

Selective Distribution

Between exclusive and intensive distribution, there is selective distribution. Selective distribution is the strategy in which several, but not all, retail outlets in a given area distribute the product. *Shopping goods* are frequently distributed through a selective-distribution strategy; these are goods which consumers seek on the basis of the most attractive price or quality characteristics. Because of this, competition among retailers is far greater for shopping goods than for convenience goods. Naturally they wish to reduce the competition as much as possible. This causes them to pressure the manufacturer to reduce the number of retail outlets in their area in order to reduce the competition.

The number of retailers should be limited by criteria which allow the manufacturer to choose only those retailers who will make a contribution to the firm's overall distribution objectives. For example, some firms may choose those retail outlets that can provide acceptable repair and maintenance service to consumers who have purchased their products. In the automotive industry selective criteria are used by the manufacturer in granting dealerships for given areas. These criteria consist of such considerations as showroom space, service facilities, and inventory levels.

The point may be illustrated with reference to Pennsylvania House, a furniture division of General Mills. In 1976 the company had 800 retail accounts, which by 1979 were cut to 500. This planned cut obviously limited the number of stores in which the company's product line was exposed. More limited distribution provided the company with much stronger support among the surviving dealers. Among the 500 dealers, there was a higher average amount of floor space devoted to Pennsylvania House merchandise, better customer service, better supplier relations, and most important for the company, an increase in sales per account from $35,000 annually to more than $100,000.[26]

Selective distribution is best applied under circumstances in which high sales volume can be generated by a relatively small number of retailers, or in other words, in which the manufacturer would not appre-

---

[26]Ronald L. Ernst, "Distribution Channel Detente Benefits Suppliers, Retailers and Consumers," *Marketing News,* March 7, 1980, p. 19.

ciably increase its coverage by adding additional dealers.

Selective distribution can also be used effectively in situations where a manufacturer requires a high-caliber firm to carry a full product line and provide necessary services. A dealer in this position is likely to require promotional and technical assistance. The technical assistance will be needed not only in conjunction with the sale, but also after the sale in conjunction with repair and maintenance service. Again, by limiting the number of retail outlets to a selected few which are capable of covering the market, the manufacturer can avoid unnecessary costs that may be associated with signing on additional dealers.

Obviously, the greatest danger associated with a strategy of selective distribution is the risk of not adequately covering the market for the product. The consequences of this error are greater than the consequences of initially having one or two extra dealers. Therefore, when in doubt, it is better to have too much coverage than not enough.

In selective distribution, it is extremely important for a manufacturer to choose those dealers (retailers) who most closely match the marketing goals and image intended for the product. There can be segments within retail segments; therefore, identifying the right retailers can be the key to penetrating a chosen market.

Thus, every department store cannot be considered the same. Among them there can be price, age, and image segmentation. One does not have to be very accurate in distinguishing between stores of the same type in the case of products that have no special image (i.e., those which lend themselves to unsegmented market strategies and mass distribution). But for products with any degree of fashion or style content or with highly segmented customer groups, a selective-distribution strategy requires a careful choice of outlets.[27]

To appraise what type of product would be suitable for what form of distribution, let us refer to Exhibit 15-4. This exhibit combines the traditional threefold classification of consumer goods (convenience, shopping, and specialty goods) with a threefold classification of retail stores (convenience, shopping and specialty stores) to determine the appropriate form of distribution. This initial selection may then be examined in the light of other considerations to make a final decision on the scope of distribution.

MULTIPLE-CHANNEL STRATEGY

The multiple-channel strategy refers to a situation in which two or more different channels are employed for distribution of goods and services. The market must be segmented so that each segment is provided the services it needs and pays for them, but is not charged for services it

---

[27]Arthur I. Cohen and Ana Loud Jones, "Brand Marketing in the New Retail Environments," *Harvard Business Review*, September–October, 1978, pp. 141–148.

EXHIBIT 15-4   Selection of Suitable Distribution Policies Based on the Relationship Between Type of Product and Type of Store

CLASSIFICATION	CONSUMER BEHAVIOR	MOST LIKELY FORM OF DISTRIBUTION
Convenience store/ convenience good	The consumer prefers to buy the most readily available brand of product at the most accessible store.	Intensive
Convenience store/ shopping good	The consumer selects his purchase from among the assortment carried by the most accessible store.	Intensive
Convenience store/ specialty good	The consumer purchases his favorite brand from the most accessible store carrying the item in stock.	Selective/ exclusive
Shopping store/ convenience good	The consumer is indifferent to the brand of product he buys but shops different stores to secure better retail service and/or retail price.	Intensive
Shopping store/ shopping good	The consumer makes comparisons among both retail-controlled factors and factors associated with the product (brand).	Intensive
Shopping store/ specialty good	The consumer has a strong preference as to product brand but shops a number of stores to secure the best retail service and/ or price for this brand.	Selective/ exclusive
Specialty store/ convenience good	The consumer prefers to trade at a specific store but is indifferent to the brand of product purchased.	Selective/ exclusive
Specialty store/ shopping good	The consumer prefers to trade at a certain store but is uncertain as to which product he wishes to buy and examines the store's assortment for the best purchase.	Selective/ exclusive
Specialty store/ specialty good	The consumer has both a preference for a particular store and for a specific brand.	Selective/ exclusive

Source: Louis P. Bucklin, "Retail Strategy and the Classification of Consumer Goods," *Journal of Marketing,* January, 1963, pp. 50–55; published by the American Marketing Association. The specific exhibit was developed in Burton Marcus, et al., *Modern Marketing,* copyright © 1975 by Random House, Inc. Reprinted by permission of Random House, Inc.

does not need. Usually, this cannot be done effectively by direct selling alone or by exclusive reliance upon distributors. The Robinson-Patman Act makes the use of price for segmentation almost impossible when selling to the same kind of customer through the same distribution method. Market segmentation, however, may be possible when selling to one class of customer directly and to another only through distributors, thus providing different services, prices, and support. Thus, a multiple-channel strategy permits optimal access to each individual segment.

Basically, there are two types of multiple channels of distribution, complementary and competitive.[28]

Complementary Channels

Complementary channels exist when each channel handles a different noncompeting product or noncompeting market segment. An important reason to promote a complementary channel is to reach market segments which cannot otherwise be served. For example, American Tourister sells to discount stores the same type of luggage it distributes through department stores, with some cosmetic changes in design. In this way the company is able to reach the middle- and low-income segments of consumers who may never shop for luggage in department stores. Similarly, magazines use newsstand distribution as a complementary channel to mailing subscriptions. Catalog business serves as a complementary channel for large retailers such as Sears and Penney.

The simplest way to create complementary channels is through private branding. This permits entry into markets which would otherwise be lost. The Coca-Cola Company sells its Minute Maid frozen orange juice to A&P to be sold under the A&P name. At the same time, the Minute Maid brand is available in A&P stores. Presumably, there are customers who perceive the private brand to be no different in quality from the manufacturer's brand. Inasmuch as the private brand is always a little less expensive than a manufacturer's brand, such customers prefer the former. Thus, private branding helps to broaden the market base.

There is another reason which may lead a manufacturer to choose this strategy. In instances where other firms in the industry have saturated the traditional distribution channels for a product, a new entry may be distributed through a different channel. This new channel may then in turn be different from the traditional channel used for the rest of the manufacturer's product line. Hanes, for example, decided to develop a new channel for L'eggs, supermarkets and drugstores, since the traditional channels were already crowded with competing brands. Likewise, R. Dakin developed nontraditional complementary channels to distribute its toys. While most toy manufacturers sell their wares through toy shops and department stores, Dakin distributes over 60 percent of its products

---

[28]Martin L. Bell, *Marketing* (Boston: Houghton Mifflin Co., 1972), pp. 711–712.

through a variety of previously ignored outlets such as airports, hospital gift shops, restaurants, amusement parks, stationery stores, and drugstores. This way it avoids direct competition. The success of Dakin's strategy is revealed by the fact that the company's sales went up from $11 million in 1975 to $457 million in 1979.[29] In recent years many companies have developed new channels in the form of mail ordering for such diverse products as men's suits, shoes, insurance, records, newly published books, and jewelry.

A company may also develop complementary channels to broaden the market when the traditional channel stops growing, particularly when the traditional channel happened to be a large account. For example, Easco Corporation, the nation's second-largest maker of mechanics' hand tools, had for years tied itself to Sears, Roebuck & Company, the world's largest retailer, supplying wrenches, sockets, and other tools for its Craftsman line. Sears accounted for about 47 percent of Easco's sales and about 62 percent of its pretax earnings as recently as 1976. But as Sears' growth slowed down, Easco had a critical strategic dilemma: What to do when one dominant customer stops growing and starts to slip? The company decided to lessen its dependence on Sears by adding some 500 new hardware and home-center stores for its hand tools.[30]

Complementary channels may also be necessitated on geographic grounds. Many industrial companies undertake direct distribution of their products in large metropolitan areas such as New York, Chicago, Detroit, and Cleveland. Since the market is dense, a salesperson can make over ten calls a day because of the proximity of customers to each other. The same company, however, uses manufacturer's representatives or some other type of middlemen in the hinterlands since the market there is too thin to support full-time salespeople.[31]

Another reason to promote complementary channels is to seek distribution of noncompeting items. For example, many food processors package fruits and vegetables for institutional customers in giant cans which have little market among household customers. These products, therefore, are distributed through different channels. Procter & Gamble manufactures toiletries for hotels, motels, hospitals, airplanes, etc., which need to be distributed through different channel arrangements. The volume of business may also require the use of different channels. Many appliance manufacturers sell directly to builders but use distributors and dealers for selling to household consumers.

The basis for use of complementary channels is to enlist customers

[29]"R. Dakin: Marketing Old-Style Toys Through Offbeat Outlets," *Business Week*, December 24, 1979, p. 94.

[30]"Easco: Turning to New Customers While Helping Sears Promote Tools," *Business Week*, October 6, 1980, p. 62.

[31]Robert E. Weigand, "Fit Products and Channels to Your Market," *Harvard Business Review*, January–February, 1977, pp. 95–105.

and segments which cannot be served when distribution is limited to a single channel. Thus, the addition of a complementary channel may be the result of a simple cost-benefit analysis. If by employing an additional channel the overall business can be increased without jeopardizing quality and/or service and without any negative impact on long-term profitability, it may be worthwhile to do so. Care is needed to ensure that the enhancement of the market through multiple channels does not lead the company to be charged by the Justice Department with monopolizing the market.

Competitive Channels

The second type of multiple-channel strategy is the use of competitive channels. Competitive distribution occurs when the same product is sold through two different and competing channels. This distribution posture may be illustrated with reference to a boat manufacturer, the Luhrs Company. It sells and ships boats directly to dealers, using one franchise to sell Ulrichsen wood boats and Alura fiberglass boats, and another franchise to sell Luhrs wood and fiberglass/wood boats. The two franchises could be issued to the same dealer, but they are normally issued to separate dealers. Competition between dealers holding separate franchises is both possible and encouraged.[32] The two dealers compete against each other to the extent that their products satisfy similar consumer needs in the same segment.

The reason for choosing this competitive strategy is the hope that it will provide increased sales. It is thought that if the dealers have to compete against themselves as well as against other manufacturers' dealers, the extra effort will serve to benefit the overall sales of the manufacturer. The effectiveness of this strategy does leave some room for debate. It could be argued that a program utilizing different incentives, such as special discounts for attaining certain given levels of sales, could be just as effective as this competition. It could be even more effective since the company would eliminate the costs associated with developing additional channels.

Sometimes a company may be forced into developing competing channels in response to a changing environment. For example, nonprescription drugs were traditionally sold through drugstores. But as supermarkets' merchandising perspectives underwent a change during the post–World War II period, grocery stores became a viable channel for such products since shoppers expected to find convenience drug products there. This made it necessary for drug companies to deal with grocery wholesalers and retail grocery stores along with drug wholesalers and drugstores.

The argument behind the competitive-channel strategy is that while

---

[32]"Bangor Punta Operations Inc.," a case study copyrighted by the President and Fellows of Harvard College, 1969, pp. 28–29.

two brands of the same manufacturer may be essentially the same, they appeal to different sets of customers. Thus, General Motors engages different dealers for its Buick, Cadillac, Chevrolet, Oldsmobile, and Pontiac cars. These dealers vigorously compete with each other. A more interesting example of competing multiple channels adopted by automobile manufacturers is provided by their dealings with car-rental companies, to whom they sell cars directly. Hertz, for example, buys from an assembly plant and regularly resells some of its slightly used cars in competition with new cars through its over 100 offices across the United States. Many of these offices are located in close proximity to manufacturers' new-car dealers.[33] Despite such competition, a manufacturer undertakes distribution through multiple channels to come off, on the whole, with increased business.

In adopting multiple competing channels, a company needs to make sure that it does not overextend itself; otherwise it may spread itself too thin and face competition to such an extent that the ultimate results are disastrous. McCammon cites the case of a wholesaler who adopted multiple channels and thus exposed itself to a grave situation:

> Consider, for example, the competitive milieu of Stratton & Terstegge, a large hardware wholesaler in Louisville. At the present time, the company sells to independent retailers, sponsors a voluntary group program, and operates its own stores. In these multiple capacities, it competes against conventional wholesalers (Belknap), cash and carry wholesalers (Atlas), specialty wholesalers (Garcia), corporate chains (Wiches), voluntary groups (Western Auto), cooperative groups (Colter), free-form corporations (Interco), and others. Given the complexity of its competitive environment, it is not surprising to observe that Stratton & Terstegge generates a relatively modest rate of return on net worth.[34]

One of the dangers involved in setting up multiple channels is dealer resentment. This is particularly true when competitive channels are established.[35] When this happens, it obviously means that an otherwise exclusive retailer will now suffer a loss in sales. Such a policy can result in the retailer electing to carry a different manufacturer's product line, if a comparable product line is available. For example, if a major department store like R. H. Macy is upset with a manufacturer like the Arrow Shirt Company for doing business with discounters (i.e., for adopting competing channels), it can very easily give its business to another shirt manufacturer.

---

[33]Weigand, *op. cit.*

[34]Bert C. McCammon, Jr., "Future Shock and the Practice of Management," a paper presented at the Fifth Annual Attitude Research Conference of the American Marketing Association, Madrid, Spain, 1973, p. 9.

[35]See John F. Cady, "Reasonable Rules and Rules of Reason: Vertical Restrictions on Distributors," *Journal of Marketing*, Summer, 1982, pp. 27–37.

Multiple channels also create control problems. National Distillers & Chemical Corporation had a wholly owned distributor, Peel Richards in New York, which strictly enforced manufacturer-stipulated retail prices and refused to do business with price cutters. Since R. H. Macy discounted National Distillers' products, Peel Richards stopped selling to them. R. H. Macy retaliated by placing an order with an upstate New York distributor of National Distillers.[36] National Distillers had no legal recourse against either R. H. Macy or the upstate New York distributor, who was an independent businessperson.

The above problems do not diminish the importance of multiple distribution. They only suggest the difficulties which may arise with the multiple-channel arrangement and which the management must live with. A manufacturer's failure to use multiple channels gives competitors an opportunity to segment the market by concentrating on one or the other end of the market spectrum. This is particularly disastrous to a leading manufacturer because the manufacturer must automatically forgo access to a large portion of the market potential if it cannot make use of the economies of multiple distribution.

CHANNEL-MODIFICATION STRATEGY

The channel-modification strategy is the introduction of a change into the existing distribution arrangements based on evaluation and critical review. Channel evaluation should be undertaken on an ongoing basis so that appropriate modification may be made as necessary. A shift in existing channels may become desirable for any of the following reasons:

1. Changes in consumer markets and buying habits
2. Development of new needs in relation to service, parts, or technical help
3. Changes in competitors' perspectives
4. Changes in relative importance of outlet types
5. Changes in manufacturer's financial strength
6. Changes in the sales volume level of existing products
7. Changes in product (addition of new products), price (substantial reduction in price to gain dominant position), or promotion (greater emphasis on advertising) strategies.

Channel Evaluation

Channels of distribution may be evaluated on such primary criteria as cost of distribution, coverage of market (penetration), customer service, communication with the market, and control of distribution networks. Occasionally such secondary factors as support of channels in the successful

---

[36]Weigand, *op. cit.*

introduction of a new product and cooperation with the company's promotional effort also become evaluative criteria. To arrive at a distribution channel which will satisfy all these criteria requires simultaneous optimization of every facet of distribution, something which is usually not operationally possible. Consequently, a piecemeal approach may be followed.

Cost of Distribution. A detailed cost analysis of distribution is the first step in evaluating various channel alternatives on a sales-cost basis. This requires classification of total distribution costs under various heads and subheads. Exhibit 15-5 gives an illustration of such a cost classification, based on general accounting practices; the information on each item should be conveniently available from the controller's office.

The question of evaluation comes up only when the company has been following a particular channel strategy for a number of years. Presumably, the company will have pertinent information to undertake distribution cost analysis by customer segment and product line. This sort of data allows the analyzer to find out how cost under each head varies with sales volume, e.g., how warehousing expenses vary with sales volume, how packaging and delivery expenses are related to sales, etc. In other words, the purpose here is to establish a relationship between annual sales and different types of cost. These relationships are useful in predicting the future cost behavior for the established dollar-sales objective, assuming present channel arrangements are continued.

To find out the cost of distribution for alternative channels, estimates should be made of all the relevant costs under various sales estimates. The cost information can be obtained from published sources and interviews with selected informants. For example, assume that a company has been selling through wholesalers for a number of years and is now considering distribution through its own branches. To follow the latter course, the company will need to rent a number of offices in important markets. Estimates of the cost of renting or purchasing an office can be furnished by real estate agents. Similarly, the cost of recruiting and hiring the additional help needed to staff the offices should be available through the personnel office. With the relevant information gathered, simple breakeven analysis can be used to compute the attractiveness of the alternative channel.

Assume that a company has 20,000 potential customers and, on an average, each of them must be contacted every two weeks. A salesperson making 10 calls a day and working 5 days a week can contact 100 customers every two weeks. Thus, the company will need $20,000 \div 100 = 200$ salespeople. If each salesperson receives $20,000 in salary and $10,000 in expenses, the cost of salespeople will be $6,000,000. Further, assume that 10 sales managers will be required for control and supervision, and each one will be paid, say, $35,000 a year. The cost of supervision would then be $350,000. Let $5,650,000 be the cost of other overheads, i.e., office and warehouse expenses, etc. The total cost of direct distribution will then be $6,000,000 + $350,000 + $5,650,000, or $12 million. Assume that

EXHIBIT 15-5   Representative List of Distribution Costs by Function

1. Direct Selling

   Salaries: Admin. & supervisory
   Clerical
   Salespeople
   Commission
   Travel and entertainment
   Training
   Insurance: Real & property
              Liability
              Workmen's comp.
   Taxes: Personal property
          Social security
          Unemployment ins.
   Returned-goods expense
     chargeable to salespeople
   Pension
   Rent
   Utilities
   Repair & Maintenance
   Depreciation
   Postage & office supplies
2. Advertising & Sales Promotion

   Salaries: Admin. & supervisory
             Clerical
             Advtg. production
   Publication space
     Trade journals
     Newspaper
   Product promotion
     Advtg. supplier
     Advtg. agency fees
     Direct mail expenses
     Contests
     Catalogs & price list
     Cooperative advtg.
       Dealers
       Retail stores
       Billboards
3. Product & Package Design

   Salaries: Admin. & supervisory
   Wages
   Materials
   Depreciation

4. Sales Discounts and Allowances

   Cash discounts on sales
   Quantity discounts
   Sales allowances

5. Credit Extension

   Salaries: Admin. & supervisory
             Credit representatives
             Clerical
   Bad-debt losses
   Forms and postage
   Credit-rating services
   Legal fees: Collection efforts
   Travel
   Financial cost of accounts
     receivable

6. Market Research

   Salaries: Admin.
             Clerical
   Surveys: Distributors
            Consumers
   Industry trade data
   Travel

7. Warehousing & Handling

   Salaries: Administration
   Wages: Warehouse services
   Depreciation: Furniture
                 Fixtures
   Insurance
   Taxes
   Repair & maintenance
   Unsalable merchandise
     Warehouse responsibility
   Supplies
   Utilities

8. Inventory Levels

   Obsolescence markdown
   Financial cost of carrying
     inventories

EXHIBIT 15-5   continued

9. Packing, Shipping, & Delivery	11. Customer Service
Salaries: Administration Clerical Wages: Truck drivers Truck maint. men Packers Shipping clerks Truck operators Truck repairs Depreciation: Furniture & fixtures Trucks Insurance Taxes Utilities Packing supplies Postage & forms Freight: Factory to warehouse Warehouse to customer Factory to customer Outside trucking service	Salaries: Administration Customer service representatives Clerical Stationery & supplies
10. Order Processing	**12. Printing and Recording of Accounts Receivable**
Order forms Salaries: Administration Wages Order-review clerks Order processing Equipment operators Depreciation: Order-processing equipment	Sales invoice forms Salaries: Clerical Administration Accounts receivable clerks Sales invoicing equipment operators Depreciation: Sales invoicing equipment
	13. Returned Merchandise
	Freight Salaries: Administration Clerical Returned-goods clerical Returned-goods processing: Material labor Forms & supplies

distribution through wholesalers (the arrangement currently being pursued) costs the company 25 percent of sales. Assuming sales to be x, we can set up the equation $.25x = \$12$ million and solve for x, which will be $48 million. This means that if the company decides to go to direct distribution, it must generate a sales volume of $48 million before it can break even on costs. Thus, if the sales potential is well above the $48-million mark, direct distribution is worth considering.

One problem with breakeven analysis is that the distribution alternatives which are considered equally effective may not always be so. It is a pervasive belief that the choice of a distribution channel affects the total sales revenue just as the selection of an advertising strategy does. For example, the retailer may receive the same number of calls under either of two channel alternatives: from the company's salesperson or from a wholesaler's salesperson. The question is, however, whether the effect of these calls is the same. The best way to handle this problem is to calculate the changes that would be necessary in order to make the channel alternatives equally effective. To an extent, this can be achieved either intuitively or by using one of the mathematical models reported in the marketing literature.[37]

Coverage of Market. An important aspect in predicting future sales response is the penetration which will eventually be achieved in the market. For example, in the case of a drug company, the customers can be divided into three groups: (1) drugstores, (2) doctors, and (3) hospitals.

One measure of the coverage of market (or penetration of market) will be the number of customers in a group contacted or sold, divided by the total number of customers in that group. Another measure may be the penetration in terms of geographical coverage of territory. But these measures are too general. Using just the ratio of customers contacted to the total number of customers does not give a proper indication of coverage, because not all types of customers are equally important. Therefore, customers may be further classified as follows:

CUSTOMER GROUP	CLASSIFICATION	BASIS OF CLASSIFICATION
Drugstores	Large, medium, and small	Annual turnover
Hospitals	Large, medium, and small	Number of beds
Doctors	Large, medium, and small	Number of patients attended

Then the desired level of penetration for each subgroup should be specified; e.g., 90 percent of the large, 75 percent of the medium, and 50 percent of the small drugstores may be penetrated. These percentages can be used for examining the effectiveness of an alternative channel.

An advanced analysis is possible, however, by building a penetration model. The basis of the model is that increments in penetration for equal time periods are proportional to the remaining distance to the aimed penetration. The increment in penetration in a time period t will be: $t = rp(1 - r)^{t-1}$, where p = targeted or aimed penetration, and r = penetration ratio. This ratio signifies how rapidly the cumulative penetration will approach aimed penetration. For example, if aimed penetration is 80 percent and if $r = 0.3$, then first-year penetration is $80 \times 0.3 = 24\%$. Next year, the increment in penetration will be $80 \times 0.3 \times 0.7 = 16.8\%$. Hence, cumulative penetration at the end of the second year will be $24 + 16.8 = 40.8$. The value of p for each subgroup is a matter of policy decision on

---

[37]Gary L. Lilien and Philip Kotler, *Marketing Decision Making* (New York: Harper & Row, 1983), Chapter 13.

the part of the company. The value of r depends on the time period during which aimed penetration is to be achieved and the sales efforts in terms of the number of medical representatives/salespeople and their call pattern for each subgroup.

For the existing channel (selling through the wholesalers), the value of r can be determined from past records. For the alternate channel (direct distribution), the approximate value of r can be computed in one of two ways:

1. The company executives should know how many salespeople would be kept on the rolls if the alternate channel is used. The executives can also estimate the average number of calls a day a salesperson would make and hence the average number of customers in a subgroup he or she could contact. With this information, the value of r can be determined as follows:

$$\frac{\text{Number of customers in a subgroup contacted under existing channel}}{\text{Number of customers in a subgroup that would be contacted in alternate channel}} = \frac{\text{Value of } r \text{ for existing channel}}{\text{Value of } r \text{ for alternate channel}}$$

2. A second approach may be to find out (or estimate) the penetration that would be possible after one year if the alternate channel is used, then substitute this in the penetration equation to find r when p and t are known.

The penetration model makes it easier to predict the exact coverage in each subgroup of customers over a planning period (say, five years hence). The marketing strategist should determine the ultimate desired penetration p and the time period in which it is to be achieved. Then the model would be able to predict which channel would take the penetration closer to the objective.

Customer Service. Level of customer service differs from customer to customer for each business. Generally speaking, the sales department, with feedback from the field force, should be able to designate the various services that the company should offer to different customer segments. If this is not feasible, a sample survey may be planned to find out which services the customers expect and which services are currently being offered by competitors. This information can be used to develop a viable service package. Then the capability and willingness of each channel alternative to provide these services may be matched to single out the most desirable channel. This can be done intuitively. A more scientific approach would be to list and assign weights to each type of service, then rate different channels according to their ability to handle these services. The cumulative scores can be used for the service ranking of channel alternatives. Conjoint measurement can be used to determine which services are most important to a particular segment of customers.[38]

Communication and Control. Control may be defined as the process of taking steps to bring actual results and desired results closer together. Communication refers to the information flow between the company and the customers. To evaluate alternate channels on these two criteria, the communication and control objectives should be defined. With reference to communication, for example, information may be desired on the activities of competitors, new products from competitors, the special promotional efforts of competitors, the attitudes of customers toward the company's and competitors' services, and the reasons for success of a particular product line of the company. Each channel alternative may then be evaluated in terms of its willingness, capabilities, and interest in providing the required information. In the case of wholesalers, the communication perspective may also depend on the terms of the contract. But the mere fact that they are legally bound by the contract may not motivate them to cooperate willingly. Finally, the information should be judged for accuracy, timeliness, and relevance.

Channel Modification

Environmental shifts, internal or external, may require a company to modify existing channel arrangements. A shift in trade practice, for instance, may render distribution through a manufacturer's representative obsolete. Similarly, technological changes in product design may require frequent service calls to customers which wholesalers may not be able to make, thus leading the company to opt for direct distribution.

To illustrate the point, consider jewelry distribution. For centuries jewelry was distributed through jewelry shops relying on uniqueness, craftsmanship, and mystique to reap fat margins on very small volumes. Traditionally, the big retailer had shunned jewelry as a highly specialized, slow-moving business that tied up too much money in inventory. But this has changed in the last few years. For example, between 1978 and 1982 jewelry stores' share of the jewelry market declined from 65 percent to less than 50 percent. On the other hand, relying on hefty advertising and deep discounting, mass merchandisers (i.e., Penney, Sears, Montgomery Ward, Target stores, and others) have been making fast inroads into the jewelry business. For example, in 1983 J. C. Penney became the fourth-largest retail jewelry merchant in the United States, behind Zale, Gordon Jewelry, and Best Products, the catalog showroom chain. Such a shift in

---

[38]Paul E. Green and Yoram Wind, "New Way to Measure Consumers' Judgments," *Harvard Business Review*, July–August, 1975, pp. 107–117.

trade practice requires that jewelry manufacturers modify their distribution arrangements.[39]

Similarly, as computer makers try to reach ever-broadening audiences with lower-priced machines, they need new distribution channels. Many of them, like IBM and Xerox, are turning to retail stores. Back in the 1970s people would have laughed at the idea of selling computers over the counter. But now it is a preferred way of doing business. The tantalizing opportunity to sell computers to consumers has also given birth to specialty chains such as Computerland, CompuShop, MicroAge, and Computer Store.[40]

Generally speaking, a new company in the market starts distribution through middlemen. This becomes necessary because during the initial period, the technical and manufacturing problems are big enough to keep the management busy. Besides, at this stage, the company has neither the insight nor the capabilities needed to successfully deal with the vagaries of the market. Therefore, middlemen are used. With their knowledge of the market they play an important role in establishing a demand for the company's product. But once the company establishes a foothold in the market, it may discover that it does not have the control of distribution it needs to make further headway. At this time, channel modification becomes essential.

Managerial astuteness requires that the company do a thorough study before deciding to change existing channel arrangements. Taking a few halfhearted measures could create insurmountable problems resulting in loose control and poor communications. Further, the middlemen affected should be duly taken into confidence about a company's plans and compensated for any breach of terms. Any modification of channels should match the perspectives of the total marketing strategy. This means that the effect of a modified plan on other ingredients of the marketing mix (such as product, price, and promotion) should be considered. The managers of different departments (as well as the customers) should be informed so that the change does not come as a surprise. In other words, care needs to be taken to ensure that a modification in channel arrangements does not cause any distortion in the overall distribution system.

CHANNEL-CONTROL STRATEGY

Traditionally channel arrangements consisted of loosely aligned manufacturers, wholesalers, and retailers, all of whom were trying to serve their own ends regardless of what went on elsewhere in the channel structure. In such arrangements, the channel control was generally missing.

---

[39]"Chain Stores Strike Gold in Jewelry Sales," *Business Week*, Feburary 6, 1984, p. 56.

[40]"The Retailing Boom in Small Computers," *Business Week*, September 6, 1982, p. 92.

Each member of the channel negotiated aggressively with others and performed a conventionally defined set of marketing functions.

Importance of Channel Control

For a variety of reasons, control is a necessary ingredient in running a successful system. Having control is likely to have a positive impact on profits since inefficiencies are caught and corrected in time. This is evidenced by the success of voluntary and cooperative chains, corporate chains, franchise alignments, manufacturer's dealer organizations, and sales branches and offices. Control also helps to realize cost effectiveness vis-à-vis experience curves. For example, centralized organization of warehousing, data processing, and other facilities will provide scale efficiencies. Through a planned perspective of the total system, effort is directed to achieving common goals in an integrated fashion.

Channel Controller

The focus of channel control may be any member of a channel system, such as the manufacturer, wholesaler, or retailer. Unfortunately there is no established theory to indicate whether any one of them makes a better channel controller than the others. When the literature was surveyed, it was found that one appliance retailer in Philadelphia with a 10 percent market share, Silo Incorporated, served as the channel controller. This firm had no special relationship with any manufacturer, but if a supplier's line did not do well, Silo immediately contacted the supplier to ask that something be done about it.[41] Sears (in addition to J. C. Penney, Montgomery Ward, and K-Mart) can be expected to be the channel controller for a variety of products. Among manufacturers, Kraft ought to be the channel controller for refrigerated goods in supermarkets. Likewise, Procter & Gamble is a channel controller for detergents and related items. Ethan Allen, Inc., decided to control the distribution channels for its line of Early American furniture by establishing a network of 200 dealer outlets.[42] As noted earlier, Sherwin-Williams decided to take over channel control to guide its own destiny since the traditional channels were not showing enough aggressiveness. The company established its own chain of 2,000 retail outlets.[43]

The above examples underscore the importance of someone taking over channel leadership in order to establish control. Conventionally, mar-

---

[41]"An Appliance Dealer with a Real Clout," *Business Week,* November 6, 1971, p. 76.

[42]"Ethan Allen Breaks with Tradition," *Business Week,* June 10, 1972, p. 22.

[43]"A Paintmaker Puts a Fresh Coat on Its Marketing," *Business Week,* February 23, 1976, p. 95.

ket leadership and the size of a firm determined its suitability for channel control. Strategically, a firm should attempt to control the channel for a product if it can make a commitment to fulfill its leadership obligations and if such a move is likely to be economically beneficial in the long run for the entire channel system.

Vertical Marketing Systems

Vertical marketing systems may be defined as:

> . . . professionally managed and centrally programmed networks [which] are pre-engineered to achieve operating economies and max-imum market impact. Stated alternatively, vertical marketing systems are rationalized and capital-intensive networks designed to achieve technological, managerial, and promotional economies through the in-tegration, coordination, and synchronization of marketing flows from points of production to points of ultimate use.[44]

The vertical marketing system is an emerging trend in the Amer-ican economy. It seems to be replacing all the conventional marketing channels as the mainstay of distribution. As a matter of fact, according to one estimate, the vertical marketing systems in the consumer-goods sector account for about 64 percent of the available market.[45] In brief, the ver-tical marketing system (sometimes also referred to as a centrally coordi-nated system) has emerged as the dominant ingredient in the competitive process and thus plays a strategic role in the formulation of distribution strategy.

Vertical marketing systems may be classified into three types: cor-porate, administered, and contractual. Under the corporate vertical mar-keting system, successive stages of production and distribution are owned by a single entity. This is achieved through forward and backward inte-gration. Sherwin-Williams owns and operates its 2,000 retail outlets in a corporate vertical marketing system (a case of forward integration). Other examples of such systems are Hart, Schaffner & Marx (operating over 275 stores); Singer; International Harvester; Goodyear; and Sohio.[46] Not only a manufacturer but also a corporate vertical system might be owned and operated by a retailer (a case of backward integration). Sears, like many other large retailers, has financial interests in many of its suppliers' busi-nesses. For example, about one third of DeSoto, Inc. (a furniture and

---

[44]Bert C. McCammon, Jr., "Perspectives for Distribution Programming," in Louis P. Bucklin (ed.), *Vertical Marketing Systems* (Glenview, IL: Scott, Foresman and Co., 1970), p. 43.

[45]Philip Kotler, *Marketing Management*, 5th Ed. (Englewood Cliffs, NJ: Prentice-Hall, 1984), p. 546.

[46]Louis W. Stern and Adel I. El-Ansary, *Marketing Channels*, 2d Ed. (Englewood Cliffs, NJ: Prentice-Hall, 1982), p. 343.

home furnishings manufacturer) stock is owned by Sears. Finally, W. W. Grainger, Inc., provides an example of a wholesaler-run vertical marketing system. This firm, an electrical distributor with 1983 sales of $498 million, has seven manufacturing facilities.[47]

In an administered vertical marketing system, a dominant firm within the channel system, such as the manufacturer, wholesaler, or retailer, co-ordinates the flow of goods by virtue of its market power. For example, the firm may exert influence to achieve economies in transportation, order processing, warehousing, advertising, merchandising, etc. As can be expected, it is the large organizations like Sears, Safeway, Penney, General Motors, Kraft, General Electric, Procter & Gamble, Lever Brothers, Nabisco, and General Foods which emerge as channel captains to guide their channel networks, while not actually owning them, to achieve economies and efficiencies.

In a contractual vertical marketing system, independent firms within the channel structure integrate their programs on a contractual basis to realize economies and market impact. Primarily, there are three types of contractual vertical marketing systems: wholesaler-sponsored voluntary groups, retailer-sponsored cooperative groups, and franchise systems. Independent Grocers Alliance (IGA) is an example of a wholesaler-sponsored voluntary group. At the initiative of the wholesaler, small grocery stores agree to form a chain to achieve economies with which to compete against corporate chains. The joining members agree to adhere to a variety of contractual terms, such as the use of a common name to help to realize economies on large orders. Except for these terms, each store continues to operate independently. A retailer-sponsored cooperative group is essentially the same. Retailers form their own association (cooperative) to compete against the corporate chains by undertaking wholesale functions (and possibly even a limited amount of production); i.e., they operate their own wholesale companies to serve the member retailers. This type of contractual vertical marketing system is operative primarily in the food line. Associated Grocers Co-op., Inc., and Certified Grocers are examples of retailer-sponsored cooperative groups.

A franchise system is an arrangement whereby a firm licenses others to market a product or service using its trade name in a defined geographic area under specified terms and conditions. In 1982, there were 1,700 franchisors in the United States offering for a fee the right to sell their products or services to about 466,000 franchised outlets, which sold a total of $437 billion in goods and services.[48] Four different types of franchise systems which can be distinguished are defined below:

1. The manufacturer-retailer franchise as exemplified by franchised automobile dealers and franchised service stations.
2. The manufacturer-wholesaler franchise as exemplified by Coca-Cola,

---

[47]*Ibid.*, p. 346.
[48]"A Franchise Investment in Every Pot," *Business Week*, April 12, 1982, p. 113.

Pepsi-Cola, Royal Crown Cola, and Seven-Up, which sell the soft drink syrups they manufacture to franchised wholesalers who, in turn, bottle and distribute soft drinks to retailers.

3. The wholesaler-retailer franchise as exemplified by Rexall Drug Stores and Sentry Drug Centers.

4. The service sponsor-retailer franchise as exemplified by Avis, Hertz, and National in the car rental business; McDonald's, Chicken Delight, Kentucky Fried Chicken, and Taco Tico in the prepared-foods industry; Howard Johnson's and Holiday Inn in the lodging and food industry; Midas and AAMCO in the auto repair business; and Kelly Girl and Manpower in the employment service business.[49]

Vertical marketing systems help in achieving economies that cannot be realized through the use of conventional marketing channels. In strategic terms, vertical marketing systems provide opportunities for building experience, thus allowing even small firms to derive the benefits of market power. If present trends are any indication, in the 1980s vertical marketing systems should account for over 85 percent of total retail sales. Considering their growing importance, conventional channels will need to adopt new distribution strategies to compete against vertical marketing systems. Stern and El-Ansary recommend that conventional channels take the following steps:

1. Develop programs to strengthen customers' competitive capabilities. This alternative would involve manufacturers and wholesalers in such activities as sponsoring centralized accounting and management reporting services, formulating cooperative promotional programs, and cosigning shopping center leases.

2. Enter new markets. For example, building supply distributors have initiated cash-and-carry outlets. Steel warehouses have added glass and plastic product lines to their traditional product lines. Industrial distributors have initiated stockless buying plans and blanket order contracts so that they may compete effectively for customers who buy on a direct basis.

3. Effect economies of operation by developing management information systems. For example, some middlemen in conventional channels have installed the IBM IMPACT program to improve their control over inventory.

4. Determine, through research, the focus of power in the channel and urge the channel member designated to undertake a reorganization of the marketing flows.[50]

Despite the growing trend toward vertical integration, it would be naive to consider it an unmixed blessing. Vertical integration has both pluses and minuses—more of the latter, according to one empirical study

---

[49]William P. Hall, "Franchising: New Scope for an Old Technique," *Harvard Business Review*, January–February, 1964, pp. 60–72.

[50]Stern and El-Ansary, *op. cit.*, p. 356.

on the subject.[51] For example, it requires a huge commitment of resources; in mid-1981, DuPont acquired Conoco Inc. in a $7.3-billion transaction. The strategy may not be worth it unless the company gains needed insurance as well as cost savings. As a matter of fact, some observers have blamed the U.S. automobile industry's woes, in part, on excessive vertical integration. As has been said: "In deciding to integrate backward because of apparent short-term rewards, managers often restrict their ability to strike out in innovative directions in the future."[52]

CHANNEL-CONFLICT-MANAGEMENT STRATEGY

It is quite conceivable that the independent firms which constitute a channel of distribution (i.e., manufacturer, wholesaler, retailer) may sometimes find themselves in conflict with each other. The underlying causes of conflict are the divergent goals that different firms may pursue. If the goals of one firm are being challenged because of the strategies followed by another channel member, conflict is the natural outcome. Thus, channel conflict may be defined as ". . . a situation in which one channel member perceives another channel member(s) to be engaged in behavior that is preventing or impeding him from achieving his goals."[53]

Disagreement between channel members may arise from incompatible desires and needs. Weigand and Wasson give four examples of the kinds of conflict that may arise:

> A manufacturer promises an exclusive territory to a retailer in return for the retailer's "majority effort" to generate business in the area. Sales increase nicely, but the manufacturer believes it is due more to population growth in the area than to the effort of the store owner, who is spending too much time on the golf course.
>
> A fast-food franchisor promises "expert promotional assistance" to his retailers as partial explanation for the franchise fee. One of the retailers believes that the help he is getting is anything but expert and that the benefits do not correspond with what he was promised.
>
> Another franchisor agrees to furnish accounting services and financial analysis as a regular part of his service. The franchisee believes that the accountant is nothing more than a "glorified bookkeeper" and that the financial analysis consists of several pages of ratios that are incomprehensible.
>
> A third franchisor insists that his franchisees should maintain a minimum stock of certain items that are regularly promoted through-

---

[51]Robert D. Buzzell, "Is Vertical Integration Profitable?" *Harvard Business Review*, January–February, 1983, pp. 92–102.

[52]Robert H. Hayes and William J. Abernathy, "Managing Our Way to Economic Decline," *Harvard Business Review*, July–August, 1980, p. 72.

[53]Stern and El-Ansary, *op. cit.*, p. 284.

out the area. Arguments arise as to whether the franchisor's recommendations constitute a threat, while the franchisee is particularly concerned about protecting his trade name.[54]

The four strategic alternatives available for resolving conflicts between channel members are: bargaining, boundary, interpenetration, and superorganizational strategies.[55] Under the *bargaining strategy*, one member of the channel takes the lead in activating the bargaining process by being willing to concede something, with the expectation that the other party will reciprocate. For example, a manufacturer may agree to provide interest-free loans for up to 90 days to a distributor if the distributor will carry twice the level of inventory that it previously did and will furnish warehousing for the purpose. Or a retailer may propose to continue to carry the television line of a manufacturer if the manufacturer will supply television sets under the retailer's own name (i.e., the retailer's private brand). The bargaining strategy will work out only if both parties are willing to adopt the attitude of give-and-take and if the bottom-line results for both are favorable enough to induce them to accept the terms of the bargain.

The *boundary strategy* handles the conflict through diplomacy; i.e., by nominating the employee most familiar with the perspectives of the other party to take up the matter with his or her counterpart there. For example, a manufacturer may nominate a veteran salesperson to communicate with the purchasing agent of the customer to see if some basis can be established to resolve the conflict. A department store manager may be upset with a manufacturer for the decision to start supplying the product to a mass retailer, such as Montgomery Ward. To resolve such a conflict, the manufacturer's salesperson may meet with the purchasing agent to talk over business in general, and in between the talks the salesperson may indicate in a subtle way that the company's decision to supply the product to Montgomery Ward for sale through catalogs is motivated by its desire to help the department store: in the long run, the department store will reap the benefits of the brand-name popularity triggered by the deal with Montgomery Ward. Besides, the salesperson may be authorized to propose that his or her company will agree not to sell the top of the line to Ward, thus ensuring that it will continue to be available only through major department stores. In order for this strategy to succeed, it is necessary that the diplomat (i.e., the salesperson in the above example) is fully briefed on the situation and is provided leverage with which to negotiate.

---

[54]Roert Weigand and Hilda C. Wasson, "Arbitration in the Marketing Channel," *Business Horizons*, October, 1974, p. 40.
[55]Discussion on resolving conflicts draws heavily on: Louis W. Stern and Adel I. El-Ansary, *Marketing Channels*, 2d Ed. (Englewood Cliffs, NJ: Prentice-Hall, 1982), pp. 292–302.

The *interpenetration strategy* is directed toward resolving conflict through frequent informal interactions with the other party to gain a proper appreciation of each other's perspectives. One of the easiest ways to develop interaction is for one party to invite the other to join its trade association. For example, several years ago television dealers were concerned because they felt that the manufacturers of television sets did not understand their problems. To help correct the situation, the dealers invited the manufacturers to become members of the National Appliance and Radio-TV Dealers Association (NARDA). Currently manufacturers take an active interest in NARDA conventions and seminars. According to industry sources, the channel relationships in the television industry have improved a great deal.[56]

Finally, the focus of *superorganizational strategy* is to employ conciliation, mediation, and arbitration to resolve the conflict. Essentially, a neutral third party is brought into the conflict to resolve the matter. *Conciliation* is an informal attempt by a third party to bring the two conflicting organizations together and make them come to an agreement amicably. For example, an independent wholesaler may serve as a conciliator between a manufacturer and its customers. Under *mediation,* the third party plays a more active role. If the parties in conflict fail to come to an agreement, they may be willing to consider the procedural or substantive recommendations of the mediator.

Arbitration may also be applied to resolve channel conflict. Arbitration may be compulsory or voluntary. Under *compulsory arbitration,* the dispute must by law be submitted to a third party, the decision being final and binding on both the conflicting parties. For example, the courts may arbitrate between two parties in dispute. Years ago, when automobile manufacturers and their dealers had problems relative to distribution policies, the court arbitrated. *Voluntary arbitration* is a process whereby the parties in conflict submit their disputes for resolution to a third party on their own. For example, in 1955 the Federal Trade Commission arbitrated between television set manufacturers, distributors, and dealers by setting up 32 industry rules to protect the consumer and to reduce conflicts over distribution. The conflict areas involved were: tie-in sales; price-fixing; mass shipments used to clog outlets and foreclose competitors; discriminatory billing; and special rebates, bribes, refunds, and discounts.[57]

Of all the methods of resolving conflict, arbitration is the fastest. Additionally, under arbitration, secrecy is preserved and less expense is incurred. Inasmuch as industry experts serve as arbitrators, one can expect a fairer decision. Thus, as a matter of strategy, arbitration may be more desirable than other methods for managing conflict.

---

[56]Henry Assall, "Constructive Role of Interorganizational Conflict," *Administrative Science Quarterly*, Vol. 14, 1969, p. 287.
[57]Stern and El-Ansary, *op. cit.*, p. 297.

SUMMARY

Distribution strategies are concerned with the flow of goods and services from manufacturers to customers. The discussion in this chapter is conducted from the manufacturer's viewpoint. Six major distribution strategies may be distinguished: channel-structure strategy, distribution-scope strategy, multiple-channel strategy, channel-modification strategy, channel-control strategy, and channel-conflict-management strategy.

The channel-structure strategy determines whether the goods should be distributed directly from manufacturer to customer or indirectly, through one or more intermediaries. Formulation of this strategy was discussed with reference to Bucklin's postponement-speculation theory, the goods approach advanced by Aspinwall, and the financial approach. The distribution-scope strategy specifies whether exclusive, selective, or intensive distribution should be pursued. The question of simultaneously employing more than one channel is discussed under multiple-channel strategy. The channel-modification strategy involves evaluating current channels and making necessary changes in distribution perspectives to accommodate environmental shifts. The channel-control strategy focuses on vertical marketing systems to institute control. Finally, resolution of conflict among channel members is examined under the channel-conflict-management strategy.

The merits and drawbacks of each strategy are discussed. Examples from marketing literature are given to illustrate the practical applications of different strategies.

DISCUSSION QUESTIONS

1. *What factors may a manufacturer consider to determine whether to distribute products directly to customers? Can automobiles be distributed directly to customers?*
2. *Is intensive distribution a prerequisite for gaining experience? Discuss.*
3. *What precautions are necessary to ensure that exclusive distribution is not liable to challenge as a restraint of trade?*
4. *What strategic factor makes the multiple-channel strategy a necessity for a multiproduct company?*
5. *What criteria may a food processor adopt to evaluate its channels of distribution?*
6. *What kinds of environmental shifts require a change in channel arrangements?*
7. *What reasons may be ascribed to the emergence of vertical marketing systems?*
8. *What strategies may conventional channels adopt to meet the threat of vertical marketing systems?*
9. *What are the underlying sources of conflict in distribution channel relations? Give examples.*
10. *What is the most appropriate strategy for resolving a channel conflict?*

APPENDIX: PERSPECTIVES OF DISTRIBUTION STRATEGIES

I. Channel-Structure Strategy

Definition: Using perspectives of intermediaries in the flow of goods from manufacturers to customers. Distribution may be either *direct* (from manufacturer to retailer, or from manufacturer to customer) or *indirect* (involving the use of one or middlemen, such as wholesalers and/or agents, to reach the customer).

Objective: To reach the optimal number of customers, in a timely manner, at the lowest possible cost, while maintaining the desired degree of control.

Requirements: Comparison of direct vs. indirect distribution on the basis of (a) cost; (b) product characteristics; (c) degree of control; (d) other factors.

Cost: (a) distribution costs; (b) opportunity costs incurred because product not available; (c) inventory holding and shipping costs.

Product characteristics: (a) replacement rate; (b) gross margin; (c) service requirements; (d) search time,

Degree of control: greater when direct distribution used.

Other factors: (a) adaptability; (b) technological changes (e.g., computer technology); (c) social/cultural values.

Expected Results: Direct distribution—high marketing costs; large degree of control; informed customers; strong image. Indirect distribution—lower marketing costs; less control; reduced channel management responsibilities.

II. Distribution-Scope Strategy

Definition: Establishing the scope of distribution—i.e., the target customers. Choices are *exclusive* distribution (one retailer is granted sole rights in serving a given area), *intensive* distribution (a product is made available at all possible retail outlets), and *selective* distribution (many, but not all, retail outlets in a given area distribute a product).

Objective: To serve the chosen markets at a minimal cost while maintaining desired product image.

Requirements: Assessment of (a) customer buying habits; (b) gross margin/turnover rate; (c) capability of dealer to provide service; (d) capability of dealer to carry full product line; (e) product styling.

Expected Results: (1) Exclusive distribution: (a) strong dealer loyalty; (b) high degree of control; (c) good forecasting capability; (d) sales promotion assistance from manufacturer; (e) possible loss in sales volume; (f) possible antitrust violation. (2) Selective distribution: (a) extreme competition in marketplace; (b) price discounting; (c) pressure from channel members to reduce number of outlets. (3) Intensive distribution: (a) low degree of control; (b) higher sales volume; (c) wide customer recognition; (d) high turnover; (e) price discounting.

III. Multiple-Channel Strategy

Definition: Employing two or more different channels for distribution of goods and services. Multiple-channel distribution is of two basic types: *complementary* (each channel handles a different, noncompeting product or market segment), and *competitive* (two different and competing channels sell the same product).

Objective: To achieve optimal access to each individual market segment to increase business. Complementary channels are used to reach market segments otherwise left unserved; competitive channels are used with the hope of increasing sales.

Requirements: (1) Market segmentation. (2) Cost/benefit analysis. Use of complementary channels prompted by (a) geographic considerations; (b) volume of business; (c) need to distribute noncompeting items; (d) saturation of traditional distribution channels. Use of competitive channels can be a response to environmental changes.

Expected Results: (1) Different services, prices, and support provided to different segments. (2) Broader market base. (3) Increased sales. (4) Possible dealer resentment. (5) Control problems. (6) Possible overextension: (a) decrease in quality/service; (b) negative effects on long-run profitability.

IV. Channel-Modification Strategy

Definition: Introducing a change in the existing distribution arrangements on the basis of evaluation and critical review.

Objective: To maintain an optimal distribution system given a changing environment.

Requirements: (1) Evaluation of internal/external environmental shifts: (a) changes in consumer markets and buying habits; (b) changes in the retail life cycle; (c) changes in manufacturer's financial strength; (d) changes in the product life cycle. (2) Continuous evaluation of existing channels. (3) Cost/benefit analysis. (4) Consideration of the effect of the modified channels on other aspects of the marketing mix. (4) Ability of management to adapt to modified plan.

Expected Results: (1) Maintenance of an optimal distribution system given environmental changes. (2) Disgruntled dealers and customers (in the short run).

V. Channel-Control Strategy

Definition: Takeover by a member of the channel structure in order to establish control of the channel and provide a centrally organized effort to achieve common goals.

Objectives: (1) To increase control. (2) To correct inefficiencies. (3) To realize cost effectiveness through experience curves. (4) To gain efficiencies of scale.

Requirements: Commitment and resources to fulfill leadership obligations. Typically, though not always, the channel controller is a large firm with market leadership/influence.

Expected Results (Vertical Marketing System): (1) Increased control. (2) Professional management. (3) Central programming. (4) Achievement of operating economies. (5) Maximum market impact. (6) Increased profitability. (7) Elimination of inefficiencies.

VI. Channel-Conflict-Management Strategy

Definition: Resolving conflict among channel members.

Objective: To devise a solution acceptable to the conflicting members so that they will cooperate to make it work.

Requirements: Choice of a strategy for solving the conflict.

(1) Bargaining: (a) Both parties adopt give-and-take attitude. (b) Bottom line is favorable enough to both parties to induce them to accept the terms of the bargain.

(2) Boundary: (a) Nomination of an employee to act as diplomat. (b) Diplomat is fully briefed on the situation and provided with leverages with which to negotiate. (c) Both parties are willing to negotiate.

(3) Interpenetration: (a) Frequent formal interactions with the other party to develop an appreciation of each other's perspectives. (b) Willingness to interact to solve problems.

(4) Superorganizational: A neutral third party is brought into the conflict to resolve the matter by means of (a) conciliation; (b) mediation; or (c) arbitration (compulsory or arbitrary).

Expected Results: (1) Elimination of snags in the channel. (2) Results that are mutually beneficial to the parties involved. (3) Need for management time and effort. (4) Increased costs. (5) Costs incurred by both parties in the form of concessions.

Oregon Pine Lumber Company

"I remember when this highway was lined with green and dry mills," remarked Jim Sutter, Oregon Pine Lumber's president and sales manager. "When this mill was built 36 years ago, about 1946, there wasn't much of anything else but mills around here. When we took over in 1973 there were several mills operating nearby. Now we're one of the few mills still running. For my partners and me this is the realization of a dream. We wanted to work for ourselves, and when the opportunity finally presented itself, we couldn't say no. We all left jobs with other forest-products companies and took over this operation. We didn't want anything big and fancy—just a small partnership, not a big corporation. Now the cost of timber, transportation, and credit are just about putting an end to all of it."

In the background the hum of the mill's saws, debarker, and finishing equipment was punctuated occasionally by the roar of a chain saw or lumber carrier. Several of the mill's 40 nonunion millworkers and one or two of its 10 woodland crew members darted back and forth, preparing to wind down another day on the job. The last semitrailer of the day pulled out for California with a load of green Douglas fir timbers lashed securely on board. A yellow Southern Pacific flatcar sat idle on a siding across the yard from Jim. Jim's two partners, Ross Gilbert and Charlie Olsen, joined him by the office. As they surveyed the small, neatly stacked piles of green Douglas fir dimension stock, they reminisced about their eight years in business together. They mused about how they swung the sale of the mill for $165,000 down and $1.1 million in debt. They were pleased that they had retired their original debt within six years even though economic conditions had forced them to shut down for 15 months in 1974 and 1975.

Ross Gilbert, the company's secretary-treasurer, was obviously concerned about the company's current financial condition as the end of 1981 approached. "We're overextended on federal timber sales which we bid when lumber prices were high and strong. Even with the federal set-aside programs for small mills, are paying a premium for our timber. We've got great relations with our bank and our bonding company, but we're likely to run into trouble if we can't sell our lumber at the prices we estimated when we committed ourselves to those timber sales."

This case is printed here with the permission of Professor Stuart U. Rich of the University of Oregon.

Charlie Olsen, log department manager, listened as Jim Sutter spoke of changes in the market for green Douglas fir timbers and dimension lumber. Jim said, "Even with our ability to cut special orders and special lengths, we're probably going to have to curtail our operations if the markets don't get stronger. The phone has been ringing a lot lately, but everybody is just fishing. The export business was taking up slack for our lost business in the Midwest and South, but lately things seem to be slowing down. There doesn't seem to be a lot of agreement about the strength of the export markets in the future."

As the hum of the mill machinery died down, Matt Kilkenney, the mill superintendent, joined the others to discuss the scheduling of orders for the next day. Collectively the group wondered what the future held for the mill.

RAW MATERIALS

Oregon Pine purchased all of its timber from U.S. Forest Service and Bureau of Land Management (BLM) timber sales. Currently, 90 million board feet of timber was under contract to be cut over the next three years. Since only Douglas fir logs were manufactured, other species in the timber sale such as hemlock, white fir, and cedar were separated at the logging site and sold direct to mills in the valley. Occasionally, mixed species were delivered to the mill. These logs were rebucked (sawed to length) and upgraded to add value, then sold on the open log market.

Because Oregon Pine employed fewer than 500 people, the company was allowed to bid on SBA set-aside sales.[1] Once a sale was put up for bid, Oregon Pine foresters cruised the timber to provide management with specific information on the quality and volume of timber being auctioned. Sometimes the U.S. Forest Service prospectus contained erroneous information that the unsuspecting purchaser based a bid on, thus resulting in financial distress to the firm.

Oregon Pine hired contract loggers to harvest and haul the timber from the woods to the mill. Charlie Olsen, the log department manager, was responsible for contract administration and coordination of logging activities to meet the daily production requirements of the mill. Because of the small log storage pond, Mr. Olsen and Mr. Kilkenney had to closely coordinate their logging and production schedules.

Douglas fir stumpage prices in the last decade had escalated rapidly (as shown in Exhibit 15-6). In search of less-expensive high-quality logs, Oregon Pine had expanded its procurement radius to 270 miles. At full mill capacity, delivered log costs (including transportation and stumpage costs) ran as high as $30,000 to $40,000 per day.

---

[1]Small Business Administration (SBA) set-aside sales are reserved by the U.S. Forest Service exclusively for small firms who can't bid competitively with large integrated and better-capitalized firms.

EXHIBIT 15-6   Average Stumpage Prices for Douglas Fir Sawtimber (West of the Cascades), 1970–81

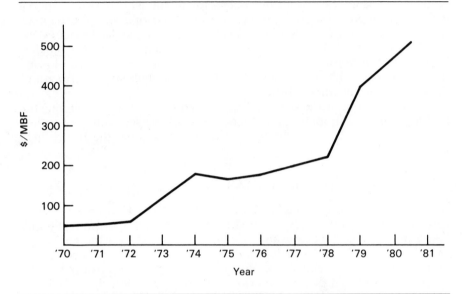

Source: U.S.D.A. Forest Service, "Production, Prices, Employment, and Trade in the Northwest Forest Industries" (Quarterly Report).

MANUFACTURING

The Oregon Pine sawmill was located on 13 acres of land leased from the Burlington Northern Railroad. In addition to a rail siding adjacent to the mill, Interstate 5, a major connecting link between Canada and Mexico, was four miles away by state highway. The mill ran one eight-hour shift per day, cutting approximately 100,000 board feet of green surfaced and rough-sawn Douglas fir lumber in this time period.

Logs were delivered by contract haulers to the mill and stored in a small log pond where they were sorted to provide Mr. Kilkenney with high-quality, properly sized logs. From the log pond, logs were moved to a debarker and converted into timbers, cants, and dimension lumber by a vertical bandsaw head rig.[2] Timbers, crossarms, and cants were trimmed and edged before they reached the sorting chain, where they were graded, stamped, and prepared for shipment. The falldown was resawn and trimmed into dimension lumber, then edged and planed to smooth the surfaces before it reached a green chain at the far end of the mill. Here it was sorted by length and width, graded, and placed in bins. As the bins

---

[2]For these and other technical terms, see Exhibit 15-7, "Glossary of Terms."

became full, a lumber carrier moved them to a small lumber storage area where their contents were strapped and loaded for shipment. High-quality green lumber was often stored in a covered shelter behind the main office to prevent checking or warping in hot weather.

Export clears and timbers were inspected for defects to insure that each product met or exceeded grading specification. Oregon Pine's reputation in the domestic and international markets was based on the high-quality Douglas fir used, and the finished product they manufactured. Their order file was filled with repeat customers who didn't mind paying a premium for excellent service and the assurance of a structurally superior product. Jim and Matt were proud of the fact they could cut any

EXHIBIT 15-7   Glossary of Terms

Band Saw. A saw consisting of a continuous piece of flexible steel, with teeth on one or both sides, used to cut logs into cants and also rip lumber.

Cant. A large timber cut from a log and destined for further processing by other saws.

Clears. Lumber free, or practically free, of all blemishes, characteristics, or defects.

Dimension. Lumber that is from two inches up to, but not including, five inches thick, and that is two or more inches in width; classified also as framing, joists, planks, rafters, etc.

Edger. A piece of sawmill machinery used to saw cants after they come off the head rig, squaring the edges and ripping the cants into lumber.

Export Clear. A high grade of lumber produced for shipment to overseas markets.

Falldown. Those lumber items of lesser grade or quality produced as an adjunct to the processing of higher-quality stock.

Green Chain. A moving chain or belt on which lumber is transported from saws in a mill. The lumber is pulled from the chain by workers and stacked according to size, length, species, and other criteria.

Green Lumber. Lumber whose moisture content has not been reduced by either air or kiln drying.

Head Rig. The primary saw in a sawmill operation, on which logs are first cut into cants before being sent on to other saws for further processing.

Hog (Hogged) Fuel. Fuel made by grinding waste wood in a hog (a machine for grinding wood into chips). Used to fire boilers or furnaces, often at the mill at which the fuel was processed.

Merchantable. An export grade that describes a piece of lumber suited for general construction use.

Planer. A machine with cutting knives mounted on cylindrical heads which revolve at high speeds to surface the faces and edges of rough lumber.

Timber. 1. Standing trees; stumpage. 2. A size classification of lumber that includes pieces that are at least five inches in least diameter.

Source: *Terms of the Trade: A Handbook for the Forest Products Industry*, Random Lengths, 1978.

size product up to 13″×13″ and 32′ long, and fill most orders the same day they were received.

Operating costs, net of residuals and stumpage, averaged $64 per thousand board feet ($64/MBF). Residuals sold in the form of planer shavings, sawdust, and hog fuel lowered this cost by $14/MBF.

PRODUCTS

Oregon Pine cut old-growth Douglas fir into clears, merchantable, and dimension lumber. Export clears were used primarily for cabinets, moldings, venetian blind slats, window trimmings, and other decorative wood product uses. Domestic clears had a variety of uses, including utility pole crossarms. Merchantable referred to export lumber that was good in appearance, strength, serviceability, and had no serious defects. Merchantable lumber was used in residential and commercial construction. Dimension lumber (2″ to 4″ thick) was used primarily for light framing and construction in the domestic market.

Jim Sutter indicated that they would essentially cut anything within the mill's capabilities that brought a premium price. This was reflected in Oregon Pine's product line. In search of a price premium, the company would cut 4″ clears for the export market. The company's ability to cut to a 32′ length also offered an opportunity for a premium price. Most of the company's competitors, within one hundred miles, cut instead 3″ clears and only up to 24′ lengths. About 15 percent of Oregon Pine's output was in dimension lumber. (A breakdown of the company's 1981 year-to-date product line for both domestic and export markets is presented in Exhibit 15-8.)

MARKETS

Oregon Pine sold to both the domestic and the overseas markets. Both Jim and Ross felt that, geographically, their domestic market had decreased in size as a result of high rail transportation rates and railroad shipping incentives aimed at accommodating large producers. (Exhibit 15-9 shows a similar decline for all Oregon lumber production.) Thus, the company's current domestic market consisted of the following areas: Oregon; Washington; western Idaho; California; Reno, Nevada; and Seward, Nebraska. Oregon Pine's export market included Western Europe (U.K., Switzerland, Greece, Italy) and Australia. Italy was an important market with primary interest in Douglas fir clears, while merchantable Douglas fir appealed more to the Australian market.

PRICES

Jim did not consult any price list when attempting to make a sale. He felt that a salesman needed to have the flexibility to change prices in

EXHIBIT 15-8   Oregon Pine Lumber Company: Lumber Sales, January–November, 1981

Clears	Board Feet	Percent of Total	Average Sales Price per MBF (thousand board feet)
1 × 2 & Wider	682,309	3.5%	$440.76
2 × 3 & Wider	954,717	5.0%	523.13
2-1/2 × 4 & Wider*	158,805	0.8%	810.35
3″ & Thicker*	1,576,217	7.9%	702.43
Dee &/or Reject*	1,111,791	5.5%	442.21
Misc. (Kiln Dried)	38,453	0.1%	570.00
	4,522,292	22.8%	563.78
Crossarms, Small Squares, Beams & Timbers			
Crossarms (Incl. Rej.)	3,070,610	15.5%	617.12
4 × 4 to 4 × 12 (#2&Btr)	4,231,552	21.4%	280.63
4 × 14 & Wider (#2&Btr)	11,022	—	584.17
6 × 6 & Wider (#2&Btr)*	2,564,729	12.9%	376.23
8 × 8 & Larger (#2&Btr)	151,862	0.7%	507.44
#3 (Util) S4S & Rgh	1,131,611	5.7%	127.28
#4 & Econ	203,325	1.0%	70.39
	11,364,711	57.2%	377.41
Dimension			
2 × 4 & Wider (#2&Btr)	2,168,771	10.9%	214.50
2 × 4 & Wider (#3)	642,125	3.3%	126.84
2 × 4 & Wider (Econ)	276,239	1.3%	72.93
	3,087,135	15.5%	183.60
Miscellaneous			
1 × 2 & Wider	642,894	3.2%	167.52
2 × 2 & Wider	264,950	1.3%	195.34
	907,844	4.5%	175.64
Totals:	19,881,982	100.0%	$/MBF 380.50

*Export sales
Notes: All products cut to ALS (American Lumber Standard) standards. The most commonly used species of framing lumber (except southern pine) are graded as follows: Standard and Better; #2 and Better; Utility; #3; and Economy. S4S means surfaced (planed) on four sides.

Source: Company records.

order to keep up with a fluctuating market. This flexibility was what Jim felt was one of Oregon Pine's distinctive competencies over the larger mills (where organizational structures often hampered rapid price adjustments to changes in the market). Oregon Pine's pricing policy was to price at

**EXHIBIT 15-9   Percentage of Total Lumber Production Shipped from
Oregon Sawmills to Various Markets**

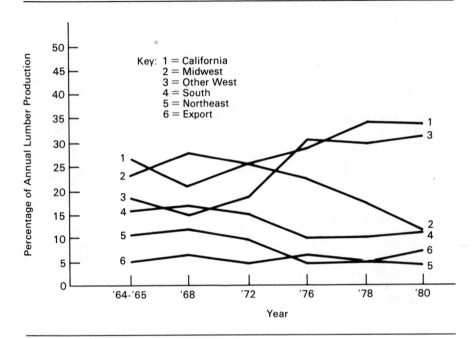

Key: 1 = California
     2 = Midwest
     3 = Other West
     4 = South
     5 = Northeast
     6 = Export

Source: *WWPA Statistical Yearbook* (for years listed).

what the market would bear. Jim's years of experience in lumber sales enabled him to quote a price that covered variable costs and that he felt was competitive with the rest of the industry. He admitted, however, that he received less than 2 percent of the orders on which he quoted. While the buyer might express interest in the quoted price, he was very likely to shop around for the lowest possible price offered.

Oregon Pine's year-to-date sales, through November, 1981, were $7.5 million. (Trends in monthly sales for the company are shown in Exhibit 15-10.)

CHANNELS OF DISTRIBUTION

To serve the domestic and export markets, Oregon Pine relied upon a network of wholesalers and stocking distributors.[3] The company did none of its business by consignment.

---

[3]Stocking distributors sell through their own salesforce or sales agents. Their product lines are generally quite broad. Their customers are retail building supply centers and retail lumber yards.

EXHIBIT 15-10   Oregon Pine Lumber Company: Average Monthly Sales Price (All Products)

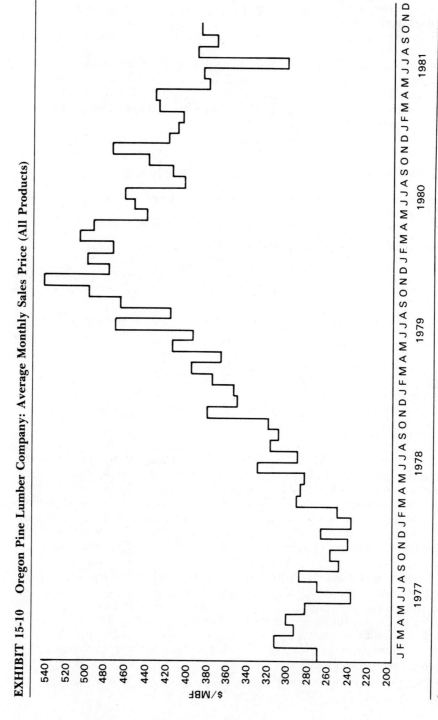

Source: Company records.

In the previous eleven months, Oregon Pine's sales in the export market had topped $1,878,000. Oregon Pine's sales manager estimated that between 25 and 30 percent of the company's annual production reached the export market through 22 channel intermediaries. Among these were the international distribution networks of several of the country's largest integrated forest-products companies. Two export wholesalers and one integrated forest-products company accounted for 45 percent of Oregon Pine's export business. (Exhibit 15-11 presents a generalized view of traditional export distribution channels.)

EXHIBIT 15-11   Traditional Export Distribution Channels

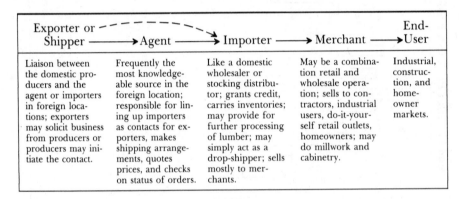

Source: Stuart U. Rich, "Distribution Channels in the Wood Products Export Market," *Forest Products Journal*, February, 1981, pp. 9–10.

Oregon Pine sold 70 to 75 percent of its annual production in the domestic market. Wholesalers and stocking distributors in the domestic market handled approximately 50 percent of the company's annual production for resale purposes. The remaining 20 percent was nearly evenly distributed direct to industrial end-users and remanufacturers. (Exhibit 15-12 presents distribution channels generally used by Northwest and Northern California Coast mills of between 20 and 30 million board feet annual production.)

Jim Sutter avoided direct retail sales channels and seldom sold direct to contractors. He felt that direct retail channels in particular involved unnecessary complications. He preferred to conduct business on wholesale terms (2/10 net 30) under an F.O.B. mill pricing policy. He believed that such conditions guaranteed prompt payment of receivables, and the channel intermediaries bore the costs of insuring and holding inventories. Off-loading these inventory carrying costs onto the distributors, he felt, was critical during periods of high interest rates and low product prices.

EXHIBIT 15-12   Distribution Channels Used by Coast Mills Between 20 and 30 Million Board Feet Annual Production

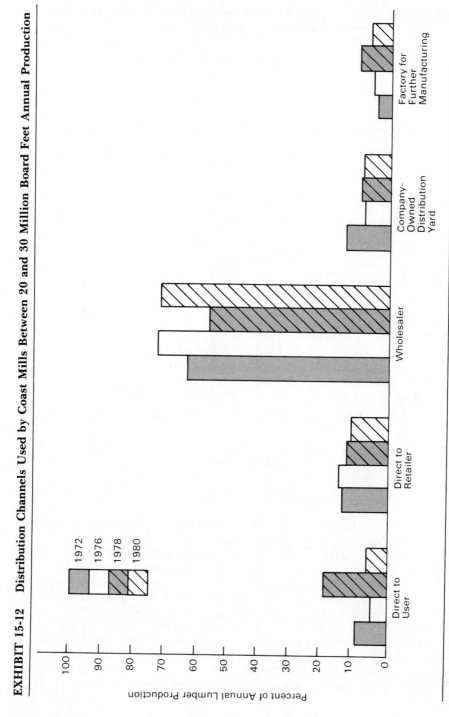

Source: *WWPA Statistical Yearbook* (for years listed).

EXHIBIT 15-13   Use of Shipping Modes by Coast Mills Between 20 and 30 Million Board Feet Annual Production

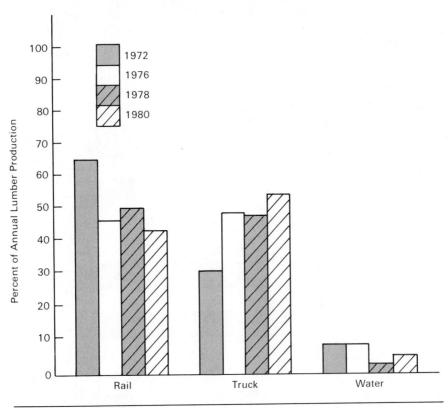

Source: *WWPA Statistical Yearbook* (for years listed).

TRANSPORTATION

A Southern Pacific rail spur and a state highway bounded the mill site on two sides, thus giving the company quick access to either rail or highway carriers. Under the F.O.B. mill pricing system, the distributor selected the appropriate transportation mode and the mill loaded the order.

Oregon Pine's modal mix, 20 percent rail and 80 percent truck, resulted from a large number of less-than-carload orders, its green lumber product line, the mill's quick-order-filling sales approach, and the lumber's destination. Oregon Pine's use of truck transportation was greater than that of most other coast mills in the same size class (as shown in Exhibit 15-13). However, it followed the trend toward increased reliance on truck transportation for all Oregon mills (as shown in Exhibit 15-14).

Rail transportation costs were in a state of flux because of recent federal legislation aimed at lessening the Interstate Commerce Commission's regulatory powers. Because the "deregulation" was still new, many carriers were experimenting with new rate structures. Shipments from Oregon Pine originated under the Southern Pacific's new carload point-to-point rates. Under the per-carload rates with weight ceilings, dry lumber producers enjoyed a cost advantage over green lumber producers such as Oregon Pine. The dry lumber producers could pack flatcars and boxcars with more board feet of lumber and remain within the weight limitations, thus achieving a lower transportation cost per thousand board feet than that for green lumber. Also, under the new system, the nearer an origin point was to a destination, the lower the per-carload rate. Therefore, the greatest cost advantages under this new rate system accrued to shipments of dry lumber from producers located closer to the destination point than their competitors producing either green or dry lumber.

EXHIBIT 15-14   Percentage of Total Lumber Production Shipped from Oregon Sawmills by Rail, Truck and Water

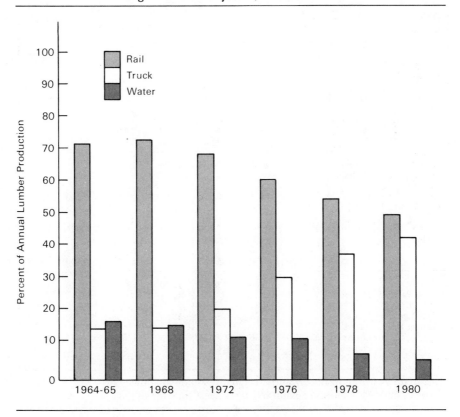

Source: *WWPA Statistical Yearbook* (for years listed).

EXHIBIT 15-15   Rail Rates for Lumber and Plywood, 1981

From	To	Per Carload Flatcars (Not Exc. 57')	Per MBF Green	Per MBF Dry	Per Carload Boxcars	Per MBF Green	Per MBF Dry
Portland, OR Oregon Branch Lines, i.e.,	S.F. Bay Area Modesto	1450	$24.25	$18.25	1100	$18.50	$13.75
Coos Bay Dallas Dawson	Fresno Bakersfield	1725	28.75	21.50	1350	22.50	17.00
Brownsville Toledo	Los Angeles Basin	2000	33.25	25.00	1600	26.75	20.00
Willamina Tillamook	Phoenix	2900	48.25	36.25	2400	40.00	30.00
Molalla Mill City West Stayton	Tucson	3000	50.00	37.50	2500	41.75	31.25
Salem Albany Eugene	S.F. Bay Area Modesto	1350	22.50	17.00	1050	17.50	13.25
Springfield Oakridge Drain	Fresno Bakersfield	1625	27.00	20.25	1275	21.25	16.00
	Los Angeles Basin	1900	31.75	23.75	1500	25.00	18.75
	Phoenix	2800	46.75	35.00	2300	38.50	28.75
	Tucson	2900	48.25	36.25	2400	40.00	30.00
Sutherlin Roseburg Dillard	S.F. Bay Area Modesto	1250	20.75	15.75	1000	16.75	12.50
Riddle Gilchrist Jct. Lakeview	Fresno Bakersfield	1475	24.50	18.50	1200	20.00	15.00
Alturas Canby	Los Angeles Basin	1700	28.50	21.25	1400	23.25	17.50
	Phoenix	2700	45.00	33.75	2200	36.75	27.50
	Tucson	2800	46.75	35.00	2300	38.50	28.75
Glendale Grants Pass Medford	S.F. Bay Area Modesto	1000	16.75	12.50	850	14.25	10.75
White City Klamath Falls	Fresno Bakersfield	1225	20.50	15.50	1075	18.00	13.50
	Los Angeles Basin	1450	24.25	18.25	1300	21.75	16.25
	Phoenix	2600	43.50	32.50	2100	35.00	26.25
	Tucson	2700	45.00	33.75	2200	36.75	27.50

Boards or Sheets: Both flatcar and boxcar rates same as shown above for flatcars.
Note: Per-MBF values are rounded to nearest quarter dollar.

Since the deregulation of rail rates in October, 1980, long-term contract arrangements between carriers and mills, or carriers and channel intermediaries, had assumed greater likelihood.[4] Such contracts usually involved a guarantee of a minimum monthly revenue to the rail carrier whether services were rendered or not. However, shippers might achieve large discounts on any traffic above the required minimums in the contract. (Exhibit 15-15 summarizes the flatcar and boxcar rates in use from Oregon towns and cities to specific Southern Pacific Railway points in California and the Southwest. Costs per thousand board feet on a carload basis of 60,000 board feet [green] and 80,000 board feet [dry] are also given.)

CONCLUSION

Toward the end of the conversation among the company managers, Jim turned to Ross and said, "None of our children seem interested in taking over the business, and we're all thinking about retiring in a few more years. I don't think we should be looking much further ahead than the next three or four years."

Ross agreed, but quickly added, "We would like to keep our sales volume up so that the business remains a going concern and continues its history of good service. I know the hassles of doing business, especially when all the regulations don't seem worth the returns, but we've got a really good operation here."

Matt Kilkenney spoke up: "The mill's in good shape. With a little regular maintenance we could run for another ten years, just so long as we don't try to make it a high-volume operation."

Jim said, "We don't have to do that, Matt. The big boys rely too much on us as a small specialty mill. We round out their product lines in ways that they can't. Without us they might lose some big accounts, especially some in foreign countries. I just wish I had a better idea about how we could sell more to customers who pay a premium for our products. I'd also like to figure out how we could stay flexible, but be better able to balance our domestic and foreign sales. We've been pretty good about switching to take advantage of premiums in either market, so far, and I hope we can continue. Sometimes, though, I feel like we may be missing something.

"Our total October sales were down $115,000 from the prior month, and prices continue to decline. Industry-wide production still exceeds demand and the pressure on prices is all downward. The market isn't or-

---

[4]No contracts had been entered into as yet, but negotiations between many shippers and producers were going on during 1981.

derly. Volume producers and dimension mills are pressing us in our best markets. We've been selling a larger volume of high grades, but I'm not sure this will continue. I'm concerned because the demand forecasts for the next six months don't indicate a turnaround. Why don't we review our basic business strategies and consider making some revisions to help us get through the next couple of years?"

CHAPTER 16
Promotion Strategies

Advertisements contain the only truths to be relied on in a news-paper.

Thomas Jefferson

Promotion strategies are concerned with the planning, implementation, and control of persuasive communication with customers. These strategies may be designed around advertising, personal selling, sales promotion, or any combination of these. The first strategic issue involved here is how much money may be spent on the promotion of a specific product/market. The distribution of the total promotional budget among advertising, personal selling, and sales promotion is another strategic matter. The formulation of strategies dealing with these two issues determines the role that each type of promotion may play in a particular situation.

Clear-cut objectives and a sharp focus on target customers are necessary for an effective promotional program. In other words, merely undertaking an advertising campaign or hiring a few salespeople to call on customers may not suffice. Rather, an integrated communication plan consisting of various promotion methods should be designed to ensure that customers in a product/market cluster get the right message and maintain a long-term cordial relationship with the company. Promotional perspectives must also be properly matched with the product, price, and distribution perspectives.

In addition to the strategic issues mentioned above, this chapter discusses strategies in the areas of advertising and personal selling. The advertising strategies examined here are media strategy and copy strategy. Strategic matters explored in the area of personal selling are those concerned with designing a selling program and supervising salespeople. The formulation of each strategy is illustrated with reference to examples from the literature. The definition, objectives, requirements, and expected results of each strategy are summarized in the appendix at the end of this chapter.

STRATEGIES FOR DEVELOPING PROMOTIONAL PERSPECTIVES

Promotion-Expenditure Strategy

The amount that a company may spend on its total promotional effort, which consists of advertising, personal selling, and sales promotion, is not easy to determine. There are no unvarying standards to indicate how much should be spent on promotion in a given product/market situation. This is so because the decision on promotion expenditure is influenced by a complex set of circumstances.

Promotion expenditure makes up part of the total marketing budget. Thus, the allocation of funds to one department, such as advertising, will affect the level of expenditure elsewhere within the marketing function. For example, it may be debated whether additional expenditures on advertising are more desirable than a new package design. In addition, the perspectives of promotion expenditure must be examined in the context of pricing strategy. A higher price obviously provides more funds for promotion than does a lower price. The amount set aside for promotion expenditure is also affected by the sales response of the product, which is very difficult to estimate accurately. A related matter here is the question of the cumulative effect of promotion. The major emphasis of research in this area, even where the issue is far from being resolved, has been on the duration of advertising effects. While it is generally accepted that advertising effects, and maybe that of other forms of promotion as well, may last over a long period, there is no certainty about the duration of these benefits. According to one source, the cumulative effect depends on the loyalty of customers, frequency of purchase, and competitive efforts, each of which may be influenced in turn by a different set of variables.[1]

Promotion expenditures will vary from one product/market situation to another. Consider the case of H. J. Heinz Company. In early 1977 the company decided to reverse its emphasis on overseas markets and concentrate on the United States. To successfully compete in the U.S. market, the company boosted its advertising budget from $34 million in 1976 to $63 million in 1977.[2] There is no way to be sure that the $63 million committed to advertising by Heinz was the optimum in light of a change in market strategy.

Promotion, however, is the key to success in many businesses. To illustrate the point, take the case of Isordil, a brand of nitrate drug prescribed to heart patients to prevent severe chest pains. Made by the Ives

---

[1]Nariman K. Dhalla, "Assessing the Long-Term Value of Advertising," *Harvard Business Review,* January–February, 1978, pp. 87–95.

[2]"Heinz Comes Home and Discovers Advertising," *Business Week,* November 14, 1977, p. 224.

Laboratories division of the American Home Products Corporation, it was introduced in 1959 and has since grown to claim 46 percent of the now $150-million-a-year market. Ives claims that Isordil is longer-acting and in certain ways more effective than other nitrate drugs on the market. No matter that the Food and Drug Administration has not yet approved all those claims, or that some doctors think that Isordil differs little from competing drugs, Ives has promoted its nitrate so aggressively for so long that many doctors think only of Isordil when they think of nitrates. The success of Isordil illustrates the key importance of promotion. As has been said, "Indeed, the very survival of a drug in today's highly competitive marketplace often depends as much on a company's promotion talents as it does on the quality of its medicine."[3]

Promotion induces competitors to react, and there is no way to accurately anticipate competitive response and thus decide on a budget. For example, from 1975 to 1977, Chesebrough-Pond's Inc. spent about $7.5 million annually to advertise its Ragu brand of spaghetti sauce. In 1977 Hunt-Wesson Foods, Inc., challenged Ragu with its Prima Salsa brand, and Ragu's market share went down from 63.5 percent in mid-1976 to 57.5 percent by early 1977. To regain its position, Chesebrough-Pond's, among other measures, increased its 1978 advertising budget to $11 million.[4] According to company sources, this proved helpful since in early 1979 Ragu's market share went up to 64 percent. Clearly the level of promotion must be adjusted as the competitive situation changes.

Despite the difficulties involved, practitioners have developed rules of thumb for determining promotion expenditures which are strategically sound. These rules of thumb may be distinguished as being of two types: breakdown methods and the buildup method.[5] Before discussing these methods, however, it will be worthwhile to briefly review the application of marginal analysis to the promotion expenditure decision.

Marginal Approach. The marginal approach was the earliest organized framework for developing a promotion budget. With this approach, the expenditure on each ingredient of promotion should be made so that marginal revenue is equal to marginal cost. For example, the outlay on advertising should be incurred to the point where it just equals the incremental profit earned on the additional business generated by advertising. Similarly, the expenditure on personal selling should be equal to the profit on sales generated by the sales force. For the communication mix as a whole, the optimum budget should be set so that the marginal

[3]Michael Waldholz, "Marketing Is the Key to Success of Prescription Drugs," *The Wall Street Journal,* January, 1982, p. 1.
[4]Stanley H. Slom, "Careful Planning, Aggressive Marketing Help Chesebrough-Pond's Stave Off Foes," *The Wall Street Journal,* March 23, 1979, p. 40.
[5]See G. David Hughes, *Marketing Management: A Planning Approach* (Reading, MA: Addison-Wesley Publishing Co., 1978), p. 368.

revenues per dollar of cost from advertising, personal selling, and sales promotion are equal. In other words, the appropriation for each of the three ingredients of promotion should be increased or decreased until marginal revenues are equal.

Theoretically the approach appears sound. However, measurement of marginal costs and revenues poses a difficult problem. Even if margins can be estimated, the marginal approach may not be feasible. For example, no firm may want to hire and fire salespeople in an attempt to reach the optimum point where marginal cost is equal to marginal revenue. Besides, what if the margin is reached at three-fourths of a salesperson? Likewise, in advertising, either one places an ad in a magazine or one does not advertise in a magazine at all. A half-page ad in *Time* costs approximately $80,000 (1984 estimate). Either one advertises in *Time* or one does not. Even though a firm may know that its margin is achieved at a level of expenditure which is much less than $80,000, it is not possible to haggle with *Time* over the cost of its advertising space. Measurement of the carryover effect of advertising or computation of profits may be still another problem.

The question of the carryover effect of advertising is a complex one, and there is no agreement on how long advertising affects sales. Traditionally it has been held that advertising's effect on sales lasts several years. Recent work in the area, however, suggests that the effect of advertising on sales is a short-term phenomenon, lasting between 3 and 15 months.[6] In brief, then, while the marginal approach for allocating promotional expenditures provides a good theoretical framework, its practical use is limited.

Breakdown Methods. There are a number of breakdown methods that can be helpful in determining promotion expenditures. Under the *percentage-of-sales approach*, promotion expenditure is a specified percentage of the previous year's or predicted future sales. Initially this percentage is arrived at by hunch. Later on, historical information is used to decide what percentage of sales should be allocated for promotion expenditure. The rationale behind the use of this approach is that expenditure on promotion must be justified by sales. This approach is followed by many companies since it is simple, it is easy to understand, and it gives managers the flexibility to cut corners during periods of economic slowdown. Among its flaws is the fact that basing promotion appropriation on sales puts the chicken before the egg. Further, the logic of this approach fails to consider the cumulative effect of promotion. In brief, this approach considers promotion a necessary expenditure that must be apportioned from sales revenue without considering the relationship of promotion to competitors' activities or its influence on sales revenues.

---

[6]Darral G. Clarke, "Econometric Measurement of the Duration of Advertising Effect on Sales," *Journal of Marketing Research*, November, 1976, pp. 345–347.

Another approach for allocating promotion expenditure is to *spend as much as can be afforded.* In this approach the availability of funds or liquid resources is the main consideration in making the decision on promotion expenditure. In other words, even if a company's sales expectations are high, the level of promotion will be kept low if its cash position is tight. This approach can be questioned on several grounds. It makes promotion expenditures dependent on the company's liquid resources, when in fact the best move for a cash-short company may be to spend more on promotion with the hope of improving sales. Further, this approach involves an element of risk. At a time when the market is tight and sales are slow, a company may spend more on promotion if it happens to have the resources available. This approach does, however, consider the fact that promotion outlays have long-term value, i.e., the cumulative effect of advertising. Also, under conditions of complete uncertainty, this approach is a cautious one.

Under the *return-on-investment approach,* promotion expenditures are considered as an investment whose benefits will be derived over the years. Thus, as in the case of any other investment, the appropriate level of promotion expenditure is determined by comparing the expected return with the desired return. The expected return on promotion may be computed by using present values of future returns. Inasmuch as some promotion is likely to produce immediate results, the total promotion expenditure may be partitioned between current expense and investment. Alternatively, the entire promotion expenditure can be considered as an investment, in which case the immediate effect of promotion can be conceived as a return in period zero. The basic validity and soundness of the return-on-investment approach cannot be disputed. But there are several problems in its application. First, determination over time of the outcomes of different forms of promotion may be difficult. Second, what is the appropriate return to be expected from an advertising investment? These limitations put severe constraints on the practical use of this approach.

The *competitive-parity approach* assumes that promotion expenditure is directly related to market share. The promotion expenditure of a firm should, therefore, be in proportion to those of competitors in order to maintain its position in the market. Thus, if the leader in the industry allocates 2 percent of its sales revenue on advertising, other members of the industry should spend about the same percentage of their sales on advertising. Considering the competitive nature of our economy, this seems a reasonable approach. There are, however, a number of limitations. First, the approach requires a knowledge of competitors' perspectives on promotion, and this information may not always be available. For example, the market leader may have decided to put its emphasis not on promotion per se but on reducing prices. Following this firm's lead in advertising expenditures without reference to its prices would be an unreliable guide. Second, one firm may get more for its promotion dollar through judicious selection of media, timing of advertising, skillful preparation of ads, a good sales-supervision program, etc. Thus it can realize the same results as another firm which has twice as much to spend. Since promotion is just one of the variables affecting market performance, simply maintaining a promotional parity with competitors may not be enough for a firm to preserve its market share.

Buildup Method. Many companies have advertising, sales, and sales promotion (merchandising) managers who report to the marketing manager. The marketing manager specifies the objectives of promotion separately for the advertising, personal selling, and sales promotion of each product line. Ideally the spadework for defining objectives should be done by a committee consisting of executives concerned with product development, pricing, distribution, and promotion. Committee work helps in bringing inputs from different areas; thus, the decision on promotion expenditure is made in the context of the total marketing mix. For example, it may be agreed that promotion should be undertaken to expose at least 100,000 household customers to the product; institutional customers may be sought through reductions in price.

In practice it may not always be easy to pinpoint the separate roles of advertising, personal selling, and sales promotion, since the three methods of promotion usually overlap to some degree. Each company must work out its own rules for a promotion mix. Once the tasks to be performed by each method of promotion have been designated, they may be defined formally as objectives and communicated to the respective managers. On the basis of these objectives, each promotion manager will probably redefine his or her own goals in more operational terms. These redefined objectives then become the modus operandi of each department.

Once departmental objectives have been defined, each area works out a detailed budget, costing each item required to accomplish the objectives of the program. As each department prepares its own budget, the marketing manager may also prepare a summary budget for each of them, simply listing the major expenditures in the light of overall marketing strategy. A marketing manager's budget is primarily a control device.

When the individual departments have arrived at their estimates of necessary allocation, the marketing manager meets with each of them to approve the budgets. At that time, the marketing manager's own estimates help in assessing the department budgets. Finally, an appropriation is made to each department. Needless to say, the emphasis on different tasks is revised and the total budget refigured several times before an acceptable program emerges. A committee, instead of just the marketing manager, may approve the final appropriation for each department.

The buildup method forces the managers to analyze scientifically the role they expect promotion to play and the contribution it can make toward achieving marketing objectives. It also helps maintain control over promotion expenditure and avoid the frustrations often faced by promotion managers as a result of cuts in promotion appropriations due to economic slowdown. On the other hand, this approach can become overly scientific. Sometimes profit opportunities which may require incurring additional promotion expenditure may appear unannounced. Involvement with the objective and task exercise to decide how much more should be spent on promotion will take time, perhaps leading to the loss of the unexpected opportunity.

The buildup method may be illustrated with the following example. International Products Company, Inc.,* a large grocery-products company, had successfully introduced its brand of freeze-dried coffee to the market back in the 1960s. In the mid-1970s, the company planned to introduce the freeze-dried coffee to the vending machine market. It followed the buildup method to budget promotional allocations for the purpose. As background on the subject, it was found that vending machines sold $10.2 billion of products in 1983 in the United States. There were approximately 8,000 operating companies directly concerned with the business of machine selling, and there were almost 11 million vending machines in over 1.4 million locations.

The following objectives were set up in each area of promotion:

Advertising
1. Make the entire population of vending machine operating companies aware of the International Products Company's freeze-dried coffee program within three years.
2. Make them knowledgeable about International's plan to help them by selling conversion kits for vending machines (i.e., kits to convert for use with freeze-dried coffee a machine designed for freshly brewed coffee).
3. Make the entire population of vending machine manufacturers aware of the desirability of converting their machines from freshly brewed to freeze-dried coffee within two years.

Personal Selling
1. Make calls on 2,000 selected vending machine operators to acquaint them with International's freeze-dried coffee program over a two-year period.
2. Follow up to finalize deals with at least 500 operators primarily in the East and Midwest.
3. Call upon five leading vending machine manufacturers to buy conversion kits from International.

Sales Promotion
1. Organize a one-day seminar at International's headquarters in Stamford, Connecticut, to be attended by top-management executives of selected vending machine operating firms. The attendees will be given an overview, in an elegant setting, of International's vending machines program.
2. Develop promotional material, which salespeople can leave with the vending machine operators, which is designed to restate the

---

*Disguised name.

sales pitch by characterizing different selling features (i.e., savings, profits, consumer acceptance, purchase or conversion assistance, and free products).

The above objectives were used to arrive at expenses for advertising, personal selling, and sales promotion. As far as possible, all direct items of cost were included. Due adjustments were made when intracompany transactions were involved. For example, International's sales force currently calling on vending machine operators was to be utilized to introduce freeze-dried coffee. It was agreed by top management that an amount equal to 5 percent of the sales force expenses should be charged to the new undertaking for the next three years.

An attempt was made to conceive each program in detail so that all expenses were included in the budget. For example, the one-day seminar program was detailed as follows:

Attending executives will receive "red carpet" treatment all the way: personal letters of invitation with round-trip first-class tickets enclosed; special limousines to meet arriving guests at airports; catered lunches, etc.

After a guided tour of the Stamford facilities, the visitors will be introduced to the freeze-dried coffee program by means of a two-step presentation:
1. A large flip chart outlining the advantages of freeze-dried coffee over fresh brew, the extra profits and other benefits for the operators, and the cooperation of the machine manufacturers in the program.
2. A preview of the audiovisual presentation which the International salespeople will make later in the fall to each operator's purchasing department

Following the presentation, the guests will be returned to the appropriate airports for their return flights.

Such a detailed outline of each aspect of promotion is helpful in making sure all items of expenditure have been included in the budget. The budgets are then submitted to marketing management for its approval.

Promotion-Mix Strategy

Another strategic decision in the area of promotion concerns the allocation of effort among the three different methods of promotion. *Advertising* refers to nonpersonal communication transmitted through the mass media (radio, TV, print, outdoors, and mail). The communication is identified with a sponsor who compensates the media for the transmission. *Personal selling* refers to face-to-face interaction with the customer. Unlike advertising, personal selling involves communication in both directions— from the source to the destination and back. All other forms of communication with the customer other than those included in advertising and personal selling constitute *sales promotion*. Thus, coupons, samples, demonstrations, exhibits, premiums, sweepstakes, trade allowances, sales and dealer incentives, cents-off packs, rebates, and point-of-purchase material are all sales promotion devices.

In recent years, a variety of new ways have been developed to communicate with the customer. These include telemarketing (i.e., telephone selling) and demonstration centers (i.e., specially designed showrooms to allow customers to observe and try out complex industrial equipment).[7] The discussion in this chapter will be limited to the three traditional methods of promotion. In some cases the three types of promotion may be largely interchangeable; however, they should be blended judiciously to complement each other for a balanced promotional perspective.[8] Illustrated below is the manner in which a chemical company mixed advertising with personal selling and sales promotion to achieve optimum promotional performance:

> An advertising campaign aimed at customer industries, employees, and plant communities carried the theme, "The little chemical giant." It appeared in *Adhesive Age, American Paint & Coating Journal, Chemical & Engineering News, Chemical Marketing Reporter, Chemical Purchasing, Chemical Week, Modern Plastics,* and *Plastics World.*
>
> Sales promotion and personal selling were supported by publicity. Editorial tours of the company's new plants, programs to develop employee understanding and involvement in the expansion, and briefings for local people in towns and cities where USIC [the company] had facilities provided a catalyst for publicity.
>
> Personal selling was aggressive and provided direct communication about the firm's continued service. USIC reassured producers of ethyl alcohol, vinyl acetate monomer, and polyethylene that "we will not lose personal touch with our customers."[9]

Development of an optimum promotion mix is by no means easy. Companies use haphazard, seat-of-the-pants procedures to determine the respective roles of advertising, personal selling, and sales promotion in a product/market situation. A Marketing Science Institute (MSI) study on the subject revealed the following:

1. Decisions on the promotional mix were often diffused among many decision makers. This inhibited the formation of unified promotion strategy, and indecision and conflict often occurred.

---

[7]See Benson P. Shapiro and John Wyman, "New Ways to Reach Your Customers," *Harvard Business Review,* July–August, 1981, pp. 103–110.

[8]See John A. Quelch, "It Is Time to Make Trade Promotion More Productive," *Harvard Business Review,* May–June, 1983, pp. 130–136.

[9]"USIC Chem. Ads Start to Support Effort to Double Sales in 5 Years," *Industrial Marketing,* June, 1976, pp. 1–4.

2. Personal selling plans were sometimes divorced from the planning of advertising and sales promotion.

3. Frequently the decision makers were not adequately aware of the objectives and broad strategies of the overall product program which the promotion plan was designed to implement.

4. Sales and market share goals tended to be constant, regardless of decreases or increases in promotional expenditures. Thus they became unrealistic as guides and directives for planning, or as criteria of promotional effectiveness, or even as a fair basis for application of the judgment of the decision makers.

5. The working planner was usually expected to prepare only one allocation plan for a product. . . . Alternate marketing or promotion strategies did not receive full consideration. . . . Decisions on the funds allocated among alternative promotional methods usually lacked objective measures of effectiveness or reliable sets of guidelines. Lacking alternative strategies, planners were unprepared to meet contingencies and to adapt the program readily to feedback of its effects or environmental changes.

6. Negative planning, to be implemented should expenditures be cut back, was missing. . . . Unforeseen cutbacks were perennial in most companies. . . . Promotion funds were often the first to be reduced when profits were threatened.

7. In most of the companies there seemed to be a minimum of emphasis on record keeping and a reluctance to worry about what actually happened in the past as opposed to what was intended.

8. Frequently, senior marketing . . . personnel were not clearly informed of assumptions and conditions underlying lower-echelon decisions. . . . the programs submitted for management review often lacked necessary details for upstream decision making.

9. Lower-echelon persons in some companies were not given the authority necessary to carry out their assignments. . . . yet they were responsible for results.

10. Top management seldom asked for support from knowledgeable line and staff groups in arriving at their final decisions. . . . these communications difficulties were a source of confusion and a demoralizing influence.

11. Expenditure levels for promotion were typically derived by working backward rather arbitrarily from sales revenue forecasts. . . . Quantifying the objective, and then referring all contributory factors to systematic and comprehensive promotional planning procedures, was rare. In those cases when this was found, it did not appear well documented or complete. . . .

12. The allocation of total budgets among the various tasks and tools of promotion was sometimes determined by: sheer intuition, comparing past patterns of decisions, mechanically working backward from the more fixed items to a residual for flexible items, relying on competent judgment of others, and arbitrary "rules of thumb."

13. In policy committee meetings, marketing management often presented well-rationalized, but not necessarily well-structured, arguments in favor of various promotional mixes. These presentations suffered in comparison with the more logical and rational financial and technical proposals presented by other line and staff

people. . . . Even less prevalent than systematic planning was the practice of looking at prior years' performances through postaudits or reviews intended to enhance the forward-planning process.

14. The present state of the art in marketing administration is such that cause and effect relationships, and other basic insights, are not sufficiently understood to permit knowledgeable forecasts of what to expect from alternate courses of action. Even identifying feasible alternatives can prove difficult.[10]

The MSI study clearly underlines the critical need for developing a conceptual framework to make promotion-mix decisions. A variety of factors need to be considered to determine the appropriate promotion mix in a particular product/market situation. These factors may be categorized as product factors, market factors, customer factors, budget factors, and marketing-mix factors,[11] as outlined in Exhibit 16-1. Discussed below is the significance of each of these categories in determining the promotion mix.

Product Factors. Factors in this category relate principally to the way in which the product is bought, consumed, and perceived by the customer. For industrial goods, especially technical products, personal selling is more significant than advertising since these goods usually need to be inspected and compared before being bought. Salespeople can explain the workings of a product and provide on-the-spot answers to customers' queries. For customer goods such as cosmetics and processed foods, advertising is of primary importance. In addition, advertising plays a dominant role for products which provide an opportunity for differentiation and for those being purchased with emotional motives.

The perceived risk of a purchase decision is another variable here. Generally speaking, the more risk a buyer perceives to be associated with buying a particular product, the higher will be the importance of personal selling over advertising. A buyer generally desires specific information on the product when the perceived risk is high, and this necessitates an emphasis on personal selling. Durable goods are bought less frequently than nondurables and usually require a heavy commitment of resources. These characteristics make personal selling of greater significance than advertising for durable goods. However, since many durable goods are sold through franchised dealerships, the influence of each type of promotion should be determined in light of the additional push it would provide in moving the product. Finally, products purchased in small quantities are presum-

[10]Patrick J. Robinson and David J. Luck, *Promotional Decision Making: Practice and Theory* (New York: McGraw-Hill Book Co., 1964), pp. 21–22. Reprinted by permission of the publisher.

[11]See Paul W. Farris, "Determinants of Advertising Intensity: A Review of the Marketing Literature," *Working Paper* (Cambridge, MA: Marketing Science Institute, 1977).

EXHIBIT 16-1   Criteria for Determining Promotion Mix

Product Factors
1. Nature of product
2. Perceived risk
3. Durable versus nondurable
4. Typical purchase amount

Market Factors
1. Position in its life cycle
2. Market share
3. Industry concentration
4. Intensity of competition
5. Demand perspectives

Customer Factors
1. Household versus business customers
2. Number of customers
3. Concentration of customers

Budget Factors
1. Financial resources of the organization
2. Traditional promotional perspectives

Marketing-Mix Factors
1. Relative price/relative quality
2. Distribution strategy
3. Brand life cycle
4. Geographic scope of market

---

ably purchased frequently and require routine decision making. For these products advertising should be preferable to personal selling. Often such products are of low value; therefore, a profitable business in these products can only be conducted on volume. This underlines the importance of advertising in this case.

Market Factors. The first market factor is the position of a product in its life cycle. The creation of primary demand, hitherto nonexistent, is the primary task during the introductory stage; therefore, a high level of promotion effort is needed to explain a new product to potential customers. For consumer goods in the introductory stage, the major thrust is on heavy advertising supported by missionary selling to help distributors move the product. Additionally, different devices of sales promotion (e.g., sampling, couponing, free demonstrations, etc.) are employed to entice the customer to try the product. In the case of industrial products, personal selling alone is useful during this period. During the growth phase there is increasing demand, which means enough business for all competitors. In the case of consumer goods, however, the promotional effort shifts to reliance on advertising. Industrial goods, on the other hand, begin to be advertised as the market broadens and continue to require a personal selling effort. In the maturity phase competition becomes intense, and advertising, along with sales promotion, is required to differentiate the product (a consumer good) from competitive brands and to provide an incentive to the customer to buy the product. Industrial goods during maturity call for intensive personal selling. During the decline phase, the promotional effort does not vary much initially from that during the maturity phase except that the intensity of promotion declines. Later on, as price competition becomes keen and demand continues to decline, overall promotional perspectives are reduced.

For a given product class, if market share is high, both advertising and personal selling are used. If the market share is low, the emphasis is placed on either personal selling or advertising. This is because high market share seems to indicate that the company does business in more than one segment and uses multiple channels of distribution. Thus, both personal selling and advertising are utilized to promote the product. Where market share is low, the perspectives of the business are limited, and either advertising or personal selling will suffice, depending on the nature of the product.

If the industry is concentrated among a few firms, advertising will achieve additional significance for two reasons. One, heavy advertising may help discourage other firms from entering the field. Two, it sustains a desired position for the product in the market. Heavy advertising constitutes an implied warranty of product performance and perhaps decreases the uncertainty consumers associate with new products. In this way new competition is discouraged and existing positions are reinforced.

Intensity of competition tends to affect promotional blending in the same way that market share does. When competition is keen, all three types of promotion are needed to sustain the product's position in the market. This is because promotion is needed to inform, remind, and persuade customers to buy the product. On the other hand, if competitive activity is limited, the major function of promotion is to inform and perhaps remind customers about the product. Thus, either advertising or personal selling is emphasized.

Hypothetically, advertising is more suited for products which have relatively latent demand. This is because advertising investment should open up new opportunities in the long run, and if the carryover effect is counted, expenditure per sales dollar would be more beneficial. If demand is limited and new demand is not expected to be created, advertising outlay would be uneconomical. Thus, future potential becomes a significant factor in determining the role of advertising.

Customer Factors. One of the major dimensions used to differentiate businesses is whether products are marketed for household consumption or for organizational use. There are several significant differences in the way products are marketed to these two customer groups, and these differences exert considerable influence on the type of promotion that should be used. In the case of household customers, it is relatively easy to identify the decision maker for a particular product; therefore, advertising is more desirable. Also, the self-service nature of many consumer-product sales makes personal selling less important. Finally, household customers do not ordinarily go through a formal buying process utilizing objective criteria as organizational customers do. This again makes advertising more useful for reaching household customers. Essentially the same reasons make personal selling more relevant in promoting the product among organizational customers.

The number of customers and their geographic concentration also influence promotional blending. For a small customer base, especially if it is geographically concentrated, advertising does not make as much sense as it does in cases where customers are widely scattered and represent a significant mass. Caution is needed here because some advertising may always be necessary for consumer goods, no matter what the market perspectives are. Thus, the above statements only provide a conceptual framework and should not be interpreted as exact yes/no criteria.

Budget Factors. Ideally the budget should be based on the promotional tasks to be performed. However, intuitively and traditionally, companies place an upper limit on the amount that they will spend on promotion. Such a limit may influence the type of promotion which may be undertaken. For example, a company with a promotional budget of $50,000 cannot afford insertions in a national magazine even though such coverage might provide the best results. Budget factors affect the promotional blend in two ways. First, a financially weak company will be constrained in undertaking certain types of promotion. For example, TV advertising necessitates a heavy commitment of resources. Second, in many companies the advertising budget has been traditionally linked to revenues as a percentage. This method of allocation continues to be used so that expected revenues will indicate how much might be spent on advertising in the future. The allocated funds, then, automatically determine the role of advertising.

Marketing-Mix Factors. The promotion decision should be made in the context of other aspects of the marketing mix. This section examines the relevance of other marketing decisions to the promotion mix. The price and quality of a product relative to competition impact the nature of its promotional perspectives. Higher prices must be justified to the consumer by actual or presumed product superiority. Thus, in the case of a product which is priced substantially higher, advertising achieves significance in communicating and establishing the product's superior quality in the minds of the customers.

The promotion mix is also influenced by the distribution structure employed for the product. If the product is distributed directly, the sales force will largely be counted on to promote the product. Indirect distribution, on the other hand, requires greater emphasis on advertising since the sales force push is limited. As a matter of fact, the further the manufacturer is removed from the ultimate user, the greater is the need for the advertising effort to stimulate and maintain demand. The influence of the distribution strategy may be illustrated with reference to two cosmetic companies, Revlon and Avon, which deal in similar products. Revlon distributes its products through different types of intermediaries and advertises them heavily. Avon, on the other hand, distributes directly to end users in their homes and spends relatively little on advertising.

Earlier, we examined the effect on the promotion mix of a product's position in its life cycle. The position of a brand in its life cycle also influences promotional perspectives. Positioning the new brand during the introduction phase in the desired slot in the market requires higher advertising. As it enters the growth phase, advertising will have to be blended with personal selling. In the growth phase the overall level of promotion will decline in scope. When an existing brand reaches the maturity phase in its life cycle, the marketer has three options: to employ life-extension strategies, to harvest the brand for profits, and/or to introduce a new brand which may be targeted at a more specific segment of the market. The first two options were discussed in Chapter 13. As far as the third option is concerned, the new brand will have to be treated like a new product as far as promotion is concerned.

Finally, the geographic scope of the market to be served is another consideration. Advertising, relatively speaking, is more significant for products marketed nationally than for those marketed locally or regionally. One study showed that even spot television advertising proved to be more expensive vis-à-vis the target-group exposures gained when the market was geographically limited.[12] Thus, since advertising works out to be an expensive proposition, regional marketers should rely less on advertising and more on other forms of promotion, or substitute for television advertising another element of the marketing mix. For example, a regional marketer may manufacture private-label brands.

Conclusion. While the above factors are helpful in establishing roles for different methods of promotion, actual appropriation among them should take into consideration the effect of any changes in the environment. For example, until 1977 soft-drink companies frequently used sales promotion (mainly cents off) to vie for customers. In 1978, however, the makers of soft drinks changed their promotion-mix strategy to concentrate more on advertising. This is evidenced by the fact that the five largest soft-drink makers spent about $200 million on advertising in 1979, 40 percent more than they spent in 1977. One reason for this change in promotional perspective has been the realization that price discounting hurt brand loyalties; since Coke and Pepsi had made colas into commodities by

---

[12]Michael E. Porter, "Interbrand Choice, Media Mix and Market Performance," *American Economic Review*, May 16, 1976, pp. 190–203.

means of cents-off promotion, the consumer now shopped for price.[13] Briefly, then, the promotion-mix strategy should be reviewed periodically to incorporate changes necessitated by environmental shifts both inside and outside the company.

In addition, the promotion mix may also be affected by a desire to be innovative. For example, Puritan Fashions Corporation, an apparel company, traditionally spent little on advertising. In the late 1970s, the company had been continually losing money. Then in 1977, the company introduced a new product, body-hugging jeans, and employed an unconventional promotion strategy. It placed the designer Calvin Klein's label on the jeans, sold them as a prestige trouser priced at $35 (double the price of nonlabeled styles), and advertised them heavily. This provided the company with instant success. Although Puritan had no previous experience in jeans, the company's production soared within one year to 125,000 pairs a week. This meant a 25 percent share of the $1-billion retail market.[14] While promotional innovation may not last long because competitors may soon copy it, it does provide the innovator with a head start.

Promotional blending requires consideration of a large number of variables, as outlined above. Unfortunately, it is difficult to assign quantitative values to the effect of these variables on promotion. Thus, the decision on promotion blending must necessarily be made subjectively. The above factors, however, provide a checklist for reviewing the soundness and viability of the subjective decision.

ADVERTISING STRATEGIES

Media-Selection Strategy

Media may be defined as those channels through which messages concerning a product or service are transmitted to the targets. The following media are available to advertisers: newspapers, magazines, television, radio, outdoor advertising, transit advertising, and direct mail. Selection of an advertising medium is influenced by such factors as the product or service itself, the target market, the extent and type of distribution, the type of message to be communicated, the budget, and the competitors' advertising strategy. Presumably, information on most of these factors is available inside the company, except for the advertising perspectives employed by the competition. To obtain this information, it may be necessary to undertake a marketing research project to find out what sort of ad-

---

[13]"Soft-Drink Companies Prime Their Weapons in Market-Share Battle," *The Wall Street Journal*, April 26, 1979, p. 1.
[14]"Puritan Fashions: Trying to Protect a Bonanza Built on Designer Jeans," *Business Week*, August 13, 1979, p. 56.

vertising strategy the competitors have used in the past and what might be expected of them in the future. In addition, selection of a medium also depends on the advertising objectives for the product/market concerned. These objectives form the basis for arriving at media objectives. With the above information in place, there are different methods which may be used to select a medium. Before finalizing the media strategy, however, it is desirable to evaluate it for viability against predetermined criteria.

Advertising Objectives. To build a good advertising program, it is necessary first to pinpoint the objectives of the ad campaign. It would be wrong to assume that all advertising leads directly to sales. A sale is a multiphase phenomenon, and advertising can be used to transfer the customer from one phase to the next: "Advertising attempts to move consumers from unawareness of a product or service—to awareness—to comprehension—to conviction—to action."[15] Thus, the advertiser must specify at what stage or stages he or she wants advertising to work. The objectives of advertising may be defined by any one of the following approaches.

Inventory Approach. A number of scholars have worked out an inventory of functions performed by advertising. The objectives of an ad campaign should be defined from an inventory based on a firm's overall marketing perspective. For example, the following inventory may be used to develop a firm's advertising objectives:

A. Increase sales by:
   1. Encouraging potential purchasers to visit the company or its dealers
   2. Obtaining leads for salesmen or dealers
   3. Inducing professional people (i.e., doctors, architects) to recommend the product
   4. Securing new distributors
   5. Prompting immediate purchases through announcements of special sales and contests
B. Create an awareness about a company's product or service by:
   1. Informing potential customers about product features
   2. Announcing new models
   3. Highlighting the unique features of the product
   4. Informing customers as to where the product may be bought
   5. Announcing price changes
   6. Demonstrating the product in use[16]

The inventory approach is helpful in highlighting the fact that there are different objectives which can be emphasized in advertising and that the selection of objectives cannot be made without reference to overall

---

[15]Russell H. Colley (ed.), *Defining Advertising Goals for Measured Advertising Results* (New York: Association of National Advertisers, 1961), pp. 49–60.
[16]Adapted from Harry D. Wolfe, et al., *Measuring Advertising Results,* Studies in Business Policy No. 102 (New York: The Conference Board, 1962), pp. 10–11.

marketing objectives. Thus, this approach helps the advertiser to avoid operating in a vacuum. However, inherent in this approach is the danger that the decision maker may choose nonfeasible and conflicting objectives if everything listed in the inventory seems worth pursuing.

Hierarchy Approach. According to Lucas and Britt, the objectives of advertising should be stated in an action-oriented psychological form. Thus, the objectives of advertising may be defined as: gaining customers' initial attention, perception, continued favorable attention, and interest; or affecting customers' comprehension, feeling, emotion, motivation, belief, intentions, decision, imagery, association, recall, and recognition. The thesis behind this approach is that customers move from one psychological state to another before actually buying the product. Thus, the purpose of advertising should be to move customers from state to state and ultimately towards purchasing the product. While it makes sense to define the purpose of an individual ad in hierarchical terms, it may become difficult to relate the purpose so defined to marketing goals. Besides, the measurement of psychological states which form the basis of this approach will be difficult and subjective compared to the measurement of goals such as market share.[17]

Attitudinal Approach. Boyd et al. consider advertising to be instrumental in producing changes in attitudes and therefore suggest defining advertising goals to influence attitudinal structures. According to them, advertising may be undertaken to accomplish any of the following goals:

1. Affect those forces which influence strongly the choice of criteria used for evaluating brands belonging to the product class.
2. Add characteristic(s) to those considered salient for the product class.
3. Increase/decrease the rating for a salient product class characteristic.
4. Change the perception of the company's brand with regard to some particular salient product characteristic.
5. Change the perception of competitive brands with regard to some particular salient product characteristic.[18]

The attitudinal approach is an improvement over the hierarchical approach since it attempts to relate advertising objectives to product/market objectives. This approach indicates not only the functions which advertising will perform, but also the specific results that it will achieve.

Advertising objectives should be defined by a person completely familiar with all the product/market perspectives. A good definition of objectives is an aid in writing appropriate ad copy and selecting the right

---

[17]Darrell B. Lucas and Stuart H. Britt, *Measuring Advertising Effectiveness* (New York: McGraw-Hill Book Co., 1962), p. 16.

[18]Harper W. Boyd, Jr., Michael L. Ray, and Edward C. Strong, "An Attitudinal Framework for Advertising Strategy," *Journal of Marketing*, April, 1972, pp. 29–30.

media. It should be recognized that different ad campaigns for the same product can have varied objectives. But all ad campaigns should be complementary to each other to maximize the total advertising impact.

Product/market advertising objectives may be used to derive media objectives. Media objectives should be defined so as to answer such questions as: Are we trying to reach everybody? Are we aiming to be selective? If housewives under 30 with children under 10 are really the target, what media objectives should be developed? Are we national or regional? Do we need to concentrate in selected counties? Do we need reach or frequency or both? Are there creative considerations which should control our thinking? Do we need color or permanence (which might mean magazines and supplements), or personalities and demonstration (which might mean TV), or the best reminder for the least money (which might mean radio or outdoor), or superselectivity (which might mean direct mail), or going all the way up and down in the market (which could mean newspapers)? The following is a sample of media objectives based on the questions raised above:

1. We need a national audience of women.
2. We want them between 18 and 34.
3. Because product is a considered purchase, we need room to explain it thoroughly.
4. We need color to show product to best advantage.
5. We have to keep after these women more than once, so we need frequency.
6. There's no way to demonstrate product except in store.[19]

Media-Selection Procedure. Media selection calls for two decisions: (1) which particular medium to use and (2) within a given medium, which specific vehicles to choose. For example, if magazines are to be used, which particular ones should ads be placed in? The following two approaches can be used in media selection: (1) cost-per-thousand-contacts comparison and (2) matching of audience and medium characteristics.

Cost-per-thousand-contacts Comparison. Traditionally the cost-per-thousand-contacts comparison has been the most popular method of media selection. Although simple to apply, the cost-per-thousand method leaves much to be desired. Basing media selection entirely on the number of contacts to be reached ignores the quality of contacts made. For example, an advertisement for a women's dress line appearing in *Vogue* would make more of an impact on those exposed to it than would the same ad appearing in *True Confessions*. Similarly, *Esquire* would perhaps be more appropriate than many less-specialized magazines for introducing men's fashions.

---

[19]The discussion on media objectives draws heavily on William J. Colihan, Jr., "How to Read and Judge a Marketing Plan," *Financial Executive*, March, 1975, pp. 26–30.

Further, the cost-per-thousand method can be highly misleading if one considers the way in which advertisers define the term *exposure*. According to the media definition, exposure occurs as soon as an ad is inserted in the magazine. Whether the exposure actually occurs is never considered. This method also fails to consider editorial images and the impact power of different channels of a medium.

Matching of Audience and Media Characteristics. An alternative approach to media selection is to specify the target audience and match their characteristics with those of the medium. The step-by-step procedure for using this method is described below:

1. Build a profile of customers detailing who they are, where they are located, when they can be reached, and what their demographic characteristics are. Media objectives defined earlier will be helpful in building the customer profile.
2. Study media profiles in terms of audience coverage. Implicit in this step is the study of the audience's media habits (i.e., an examination of who constitutes a particular medium's audience).
3. Match the customer profiles to media profiles. The customer characteristics for a product should be matched to the audience characteristics of different media. This should lead to the preliminary selection of a medium, based primarily on the grounds of coverage.
4. The preliminary selection should be examined further in regard to product and cost considerations. For some products, other things being equal, one medium will be superior to another. For example, in the case of beauty aids a demonstration should be helpful; hence, television would be a better choice than radio. Cost is another concern in media selection; information on cost is available from the media themselves. Cost should be balanced against the benefit expected from the campaign under consideration.
5. Finally, the total budget should be allocated to the different media and the various media vehicles. The final selection of a medium should maximize the achievement of the media objectives. For example, if the objective is to make people aware of a product, then the medium selected should be one that reaches a wide audience.

Basically, two types of information are required for medium selection: customer profile and audience characteristics. The advertiser should build a customer profile for this product/market.

Information on media is usually available from media owners. Practically all media have complete information available to them concerning their audiences (demographics and circulation figures). Each medium, however, presents the information in a way that makes the medium look best. It is desirable, therefore, to validate the audience information supplied by the media with reference to the audit bureaus of the various media, which authenticate this information. The Audit Bureau of Circulations, the Traffic Audit Bureau, and the Business Publications Audit of Circulation are examples of such bureaus.

There are many private sources which may also be tapped to collect media-related information. One prominent source is Standard Rate and Data Service, Inc., which supplies monthly directories of rates, mechanical requirements, circulation figures, and other information about the key media. In addition, various types of specific information may be sought from such sources as American Business Press (reports annual investment by business firms in business papers), Broadcast Advertisers Report (reports the costs of all network TV programs and monitors network and local television), Leading National Advertising, Inc. (gives monthly cumulative reports of schedules and expenditures in selected national magazines and supplements), and Media Records (provides monthly cumulative reports of schedules and expenditures in daily and Sunday newspapers). Most advertising agencies subscribe to information provided by the above sources and make it available to their clients. As a matter of fact, companies with large advertising departments may also purchase the information for in-house consumption. Additionally, the ad agencies may collect primary data as well on certain aspects for the benefit of their clients.

Evaluation Criteria. Before dollars are committed to a selected medium, it is desirable to review the medium's viability against a set of criteria. Colihan suggests using the following criteria to evaluate the medium decision: Is the decision maker being thorough, progressive (imaginative), measure-minded, practical, and optimistic?[20] Thoroughness requires that all aspects of media selection be given full consideration. For maximum impact, the chosen medium should be progressive: i.e., it should have a unique way of doing the job. An example of progressiveness is putting a sample envelope of Sanka coffee in millions of copies of *TV Guide.* Because of postal regulations, this could not be done in a magazine that is purchased primarily through subscriptions. But *TV Guide* is mainly a newsstand magazine. Measure-mindedness refers to more than just the number of exposures. It refers not only to frequency and timing in reaching the target audience, but also to the quality of the audience; i.e., the proportion of heavy to light TV viewers reached, proportion of men to women, working to nonworking women, etc. Practicality requires choosing a medium on factual, not emotional, grounds. For example, it is not desirable to substitute a weak newspaper for a strong one just because the top management of the company does not agree with the editorial policy of the latter. Finally, the overall media plan should be optimistic in that it takes advantage of the lessons to be learned from experience.

---

[20]*Ibid.*

Advertising-Copy Strategy

Copy refers to the content of an advertisement. In the advertising industry the term is sometimes used in a broad sense to include the words, pictures, symbols, colors, layout, and other ingredients of an ad. Copywriting is a creative job, and its quality depends to a large extent on the creative ability of the writers in the advertising agency or the company. However, creativity alone may not produce good ad copy. A marketing strategist needs to have his or her own perspectives incorporated in the copy (what to say, how to say it, and whom to say it to) and needs to furnish information on ad objectives, product, target customers, competitive activity, and ethical and legal considerations. The creative person will carry on from there. In brief, although copywriting may be the outcome of a flash of inspiration on the part of an advertising genius, it must rest on a systematic, logical, step-by-step presentation of ideas.

The point may be illustrated with reference to Perrier water, a brand of bottled water that comes from mineral springs in southern France. In Europe this product has been quite popular for some years; in the United States, however, it used to be a rare product available in gourmet shops only. In 1977, the company introduced the product to the U.S. market as a soft drink by tapping the adult-user market with heavy advertising. Perrier's major product distinction is that its water is naturally carbonated spring water. The product was aimed at the affluent adult population, particularly those concerned with diet and health, as a status symbol and a sign of maturity. Perrier faced competition from two sources: regular soft-drink makers and potential makers of a mineral water. The company took care of the soft-drink competition by segmenting the market on the basis of price (Perrier was priced 50 percent above the average soft drink) and thus avoiding direct confrontation. In regard to competition from new brands of mineral water, Perrier's association with France and the fact that it was constituted of naturally carbonated spring water were expected to continue as viable strengths. The above information was used to develop ad copy for placement in high-fashion women's magazines and in TV commercials narrated by Orson Welles. The results were astonishing. By the end of 1978, sales had soared to around $30 million from less than $1 million two years earlier.[21]

Essentially, ad copy constitutes an advertiser's message to the customer. To ensure that the proper message gets across, it is important that there is no distortion of the message because of what in communication theory is called *noise*. Noise may emerge from three sources: (1) dearth of facts (e.g., the company is unaware of the unique distinctions of its product); (2) competitors (e.g., competitors make changes in their marketing mix to counter the company's claims or position); and (3) behavior traits

---

[21]"Perrier: The Astonishing Success of an Appeal to Affluent Adults," *Business Week,* January, 1979, p. 64.

of the customers or audience. Often, failure to take into account the last source of noise is the missing link in developing ad copy. It is not safe to assume that one's own perspectives on what will appeal to the audience are accurate. It is desirable, therefore, to gain, through some sort of marketing research, insights into the behavior patterns of the audience and make this information available to the copywriter. For example, based on his research, Schiele provides the following clues for making an effective appeal to young customers:

1. *Never talk down to a teenager.* While "hip" phraseology and the generally flippant tone observed in the teenager's conversation may be coin of the realm from one youngster to another, it comes across as phony, foolish, and condescending when directed at him or her by an advertiser. Sincerity is infinitely more effective than cuteness. Entertainment and attention-getting approaches by themselves do little to attract a teenager to the merits of a product. In fact, they often dissuade the youngster from making a purchase decision.

2. *Be totally, absolutely, and unswervingly straightforward.* Teenagers may act cocky and confident in front of adults, but most of them are still rather unsure of themselves and are wary of being misled. They are not sure they know enough to avoid being taken advantage of, and they do not like to risk looking foolish by falling for a commercial gimmick. Moreover, teenagers as a group are far more suspicious of things commercial than adults are. Advertising must not only be noticed; it has to be believed.

3. *Give the teenager credit for being motivated by rational values.* When making a buying selection, adults like to think they are doing so on the basis of the benefits the product or service offers. Teenagers instinctively perceive what's "really there" in an offering. Advertising must clearly expose for their consideration the value a product or service claims to represent.

4. *Be as personal as possible.* Derived from the adult world of marketing, this rule has an exaggerated importance with teenagers. In this automated age, with so many complaining of being reduced en masse to anonymity, people are becoming progressively more aware of their own individuality. The desire to be personally known and recognized is particularly strong with young people, who are urgently searching for a clear sense of their own identity.[22]

The following findings from communications research are helpful in further refining the attributes of ad copy which an advertising strategist needs to spell out for the copywriter.

Source Credibility. An ad may show a celebrity recommending the use of a product. It is hoped that this will help give the ad additional credibility, which will be reflected in higher sales.

---

[22]George W. Schiele, "How to Reach the Young Consumer," *Harvard Business Review*, March–April, 1974, pp. 85–86.

Research on the subject has shown that an initially credible source, such as Miss America claiming to use a certain brand of hair spray, is more effective in changing the opinion of an audience than if a similar claim is made by a lesser-known source, such as a housewife. However, as time passes, the audience tends to forget the source or to dissociate the source from the message. Some consumers who might have been swayed in favor of a particular brand because it was recommended by Miss America may revert to their original choice, while those who did not initially accept the housewife's word may later become favorably inclined toward the product she is recommending. The decreasing importance of the source of the message over time has been called the *sleeper effect*.[23]

Several conclusions can be drawn from the sleeper effect. In some cases it may be helpful if the advertiser is dissociated as much as possible from the ad, particularly when the audience may perceive that a manufacturer is trying to push something. On the other hand, when source credibility is important, advertisements should be scheduled so that the source may reappear to reinforce the message.

Balance of Argument. When preparing copy, there is the question of whether only the good and distinctive features of a brand should be highlighted, or whether its demerits should be mentioned as well. Traditionally the slogan has been, "Put your best foot forward." In other words, the messages should be designed to emphasize only the favorable aspects of the product. Recent research in the field of communication has questioned the validity of indiscriminately detailing the favorable side. It has been noted that:

1. Presenting both sides of an issue was found to be more effective than giving only one side among individuals who were initially opposed to the point of view presented.
2. Better-educated people are more favorably affected by presentation of both sides; the poorly educated are more favorably affected by communication that gives only supporting arguments.
3. For those already convinced of the point of view presented, the presentation of both sides is less effective than a presentation featuring only those items favoring the general position being advanced.
4. Presentation of both sides is least effective among the poorly educated already convinced of the position advocated.
5. Leaving out a relevant argument is more noticeable and detracts more from effectiveness when both sides are presented than when only the side favorable to the proposition is being advanced.[24]

---

[23]See Carl I. Hoveland, Irving L. Janis, and Harold H. Kelley, *Communication and Persuasion* (New Haven, CT: Yale University Press, 1953), p. 225.

[24]Carl I. Hoveland, Arthur A. Lumsdaine, and Fred D. Sheffield, "The Effect of Presenting 'One Side' Versus 'Both Sides' in Changing Opinions on a Controversial Subject," in Wilbur Schramm (ed.), *The Process and Effects of Mass Communication* (Urbana, IL: University of Illinois Press, 1960), p. 274.

These findings have important implications for developing the copy. If one is trying to reach executive customers through an ad in the *Harvard Business Review,* it probably will be better to present both favorable and unfavorable qualities of a product. On the other hand, for status products and services such as Seiko diamond watches and Chanel No. 5 perfume, emphasis on both pros and cons can distort the image. Thus, when status is already established, a simple message is more desirable.

Message Repetition. Should the same message be repeated time and again? According to learning theory, reinforcement over time from different directions increases learning. It has been said that a good slogan never dies and that repetition is the surest way of getting the message across. However, some feel that while the central theme should be maintained, the message should be presented with variations.

Communication research questions the value of wholesale repetition. Repetition, it has been found, leads to increased learning up to a certain point. Thereafter learning levels off and may, in fact, change to boredom and loss of attention. Continuous repetition may even counteract the good effect created earlier.[25] Thus, advertisers must keep track of the shape of the learning curve and develop a new product theme when the curve appears to be flattening out. The Coca-Cola Company, for example, has regularly changed its message theme to maintain audience interest:

1886	Drink Coca-Cola
1905	Coca-Cola revives and sustains
1906	The Great National Temperance Beverage
1922	Thirst knows no season
1925	Six million a day
1927	Around the corner from everywhere
1929	The pause that refreshes
1938	The best friend thirst ever had
1948	Where there's Coke there's hospitality
1949	Along the highway to anywhere
1952	What you want is a Coke
1956	Makes good things taste better
1957	Sign of good taste
1958	The cold, crisp taste of Coke
1963	Things go better with Coke
1970	It's the real thing
1971	I'd like to buy the world a Coke
1975	Look up, America
1976	Coke adds life
1979	Have a Coke and a smile
1982	Coke is it[26]

---

[25] Donald F. Cox, "Clues For Advertising Strategists," *Harvard Business Review,* September–October, 1961, p. 170; and "Admen Suffer from Overskill," *Business Week,* October 17, 1970, p. 132.

[26] John Huey, "Lots of Hoopla About Three Little Words As Coca-Cola Kicks Off New Ad Campaign," *The Wall Street Journal,* February 5, 1982, p. 26.

Rational vs. Emotional Appeals. Results of studies on the effect of rational and emotional appeals presented in advertisements are not conclusive. Some studies show that emotional appeals have definite positive results.[27] However, Cox feels that arousing emotions may not be sufficient unless the ad can rationally convince the subject that the product in question will fulfill a need.[28] It appears that emphasis on one type of appeal—rational or emotional—will not be enough. The advertiser must strike a balance between emotional and rational appeals. For example, Procter & Gamble's Crest toothpaste ad, "Crest has been recommended by the American Dental Association," has a rational content; but its reference to "cavity prevention" also excites emotions. Similarly, Lever Brothers' Close-up toothpaste ad is primarily emotional in nature: "Put your money where your mouth is." However, it also has a economic aspect: "Use Close-up both as a toothpaste and mouthwash."

An interesting example of how emotional appeal complemented by service can get a market niche for an unknown company is provided by Singapore Airlines. Singapore is a Southeast Asian nation barely larger than Cleveland. Many airlines have tried to sell the notion that they have something unique to offer, but not many have succeeded. Singapore Airlines, however, thrives mainly on the charm of its exotic cabin hostesses, who serve the passengers with warm smiles and copious attention. A gently persuasive advertising campaign glamorizes the cabin hostess as "the Singapore girl." To convey the idea of in-flight pleasure of a lyrical quality, most of the airline's ads are essentially large, soft-focus color photographs of various hostesses. A commercial announces: "Singapore girl, you look so good I want to stay up here with you forever." Of course, its emotional ad appeals are duly supported by excellent service (rational appeals to complement emotional ones). It is claimed that the airline provides gifts, free cocktails, and free French wines and brandy even to economy-class passengers. The airline flies with an above-average load factor—higher than that of any other major scheduled international carrier.[29] In brief, emotional appeal can go a long way in the development of an effective ad campaign, but it must have rational underpinnings to support it.

Humor Appeals. Researchers have expressed divergent views on the role of humor in advertising. Some feel that appeals with a humorous touch are persuasive. Others find humor to be a regional, rather than universal, phenomenon which depreciates with repetition. A recent study

---

[27] Hoveland, Janis, and Kelley, *op. cit.,* p. 57.

[28] Cox, *op. cit.,* p. 166. See also Brian Sternthal and C. Samuel Craig, "Fear Appeals: Revisited and Revised," *Journal of Consumer Research,* December, 1974, pp. 22–34.

[29] Louis Kraar, "Flying High with the 'Singapore Girls,'" *Fortune,* June 18, 1979, pp. 132–139.

found humorous messages to be more effective when they did not interfere with comprehension. The study concluded that:

1. Humorous messages attract attention.
2. Humorous messages may detrimentally affect comprehension.
3. Humor may distract the audience, yielding a reduction in counter-argumentation and an increase in persuasion.
4. Humorous appeals appear to be persuasive, but the persuasive effect is, at best, no greater than that of serious appeals.
5. Humor tends to enhance source credibility.
6. Audience characteristics may confound the effect of humor.
7. A humorous context may increase liking for the source and create a positive mood. This may increase the persuasive effect of the message.
8. To the extent that a humorous context functions as a positive reinforcer, a persuasive communication placed in such a context may be more effective.[30]

Presentation of a Model's Eyes in Pictorial Ads. Traditionally it has been known that the size of the eye's pupil reflects mental attitude. The pupil tends to expand with excitement and contract when interest is lacking. One study tried to measure the effect of the size of the pupil and the direction of the model's eyes in an ad. The study found that:

> Enlarged pupil size is indicative of favorable attitude toward others and covertly influences consumers' interests and attitude toward the communicator. Message communication appears to be influenced by the direction of the eyes, and whether their angle is consistent with the appeal of the message and the receiver's attitude toward the message. When eye direction is to the right, rational and objective thoughts are reinforced; eyes directed toward the left reinforce emotional and subjective expressions.[31]

Apparently, if properly treated, eye size and direction in the picture can increase the effectiveness of an ad.

Comparison Advertising. Comparison advertising refers to the comparison of one brand with one or more competitive brands by explicitly naming them on a variety of specific product or service attributes. Such advertising became popular in the early 1970s; today one finds comparison ads for all forms of goods and services. While it is still debatable whether comparative ads are more or less effective than individual ads, limited

---

[30]Brian Sternthal and C. Samuel Craig, "Humor in Advertising," *Journal of Marketing,* October, 1973, p. 12.
[31]Albert S. King, "Pupil Size, Eye Direction and Message Appeal: Some Preliminary Findings," *Journal of Marketing,* July, 1972, p. 57.

research on the subject does indicate that in some cases such ads are more useful.[32]

Many companies have successfully used comparison advertising. One that stands out is Helene Curtis Industries, Inc. Starting in 1972, the company used comparison ads on TV for its Suave brand of shampoo. The ad said: "We do what theirs does for less than half the price." Competitors were either named or their labels were clearly shown. The message—that Suave was comparable to top-ranking shampoos—was designed to allay public suspicion that low-priced merchandise is somehow shoddy. In 1972 the brand had had less than 1 percent of the $850-million retail market for shampoo. The campaign was so successful, however, that Suave's sales and market share doubled in 1973, the campaign's first full year, and nearly doubled again in 1974. In 1976 Suave surpassed both Procter & Gamble's Head & Shoulders and Johnson & Johnson's Baby Shampoo in volume.[33] Clearly, comparison advertising provides an underdog with the chance to make a comeback.

PERSONAL SELLING STRATEGIES

Selling Strategy

There was a time when the problems of selling were simpler than they are today. In 1971, however, material shortages and spiraling costs produced a variety of changes in the selling strategies of businesses. The story is told of a drilling rig company in Texas which ordered a huge quantity of steel plate from the Los Angeles–based metal distributor Ducommun Inc. Ducommun could not possibly fill the order from its regular sources. To help the customer out, the Ducommun salesperson searched around and found a Rumanian factory which could supply steel plates to the drilling company. A Ducommun executive remarked, "Our salesmen have turned consultants on everything from scheduling a customer's future needs to drumming up substitute materials."[34] The complexities involved in selling in the 1970s required different perspectives from those in the 1960s. Future years may call for still different selling strategies. Discussed below are objectives and strategic matters pertaining to selling strategies.

---

[32]E. C. Hackleman and Subhash C. Jain, "An Experimental Analysis of Attitudes Toward Comparison and Non-Comparison Advertising," in William L. Wilkie (ed.), *Advances in Consumer Research,* Proceedings, Association for Consumer Research Conference, Miami, October 26–29, 1978, pp. 90–94.

[33]Gwen Kinkead, "A 'Me Too' Strategy That Paid Off," *Fortune,* August 27, 1979, pp. 86–89.

[34]"The Salesman's New Job: Drumming Up Suppliers," *Business Week,* October 26, 1974, p. 54.

Objectives. Selling objectives should be derived from overall marketing objectives and properly linked with promotional objectives. For example, if the marketing goal is to raise the current 35 percent market share in a product line to 40 percent, the sales manager may stipulate the objective to increase sales of specific product items by different percentage points in various sales regions under his or her control.

The sales management objectives may be broken down further into objectives for each region and even for each salesperson within a region. Using as a base the total sales management objectives, each sales office may work out its own objectives in terms of sales quotas for its territories and customers. The quotas may be further subdivided for each salesperson, who may set his or her own objectives (i.e., whom to call on and with what frequency, and which strategies to employ to sell to different customers).

Selling objectives are usually defined in terms of sales volume. The objectives, however, may also be defined for: (1) gross margin targets, (2) maximum expenditure levels, and (3) fulfillment of specific activities, such as converting a stated number of competitors' customers into company customers.

The sales strategist should also specify the role of selling in terms of personal-selling push (vis-à-vis advertising pull). This decision will depend on the consumer decision process, the influence of different communication alternatives, and the cost of these alternatives. Personal selling introduces flexibility and can offer sales presentations tailor-made for individual customers. Further, personal selling offers an opportunity to develop a tangible personal rapport with the customer which can go far toward building a long-term relationship. Finally, personal selling is the only method which can secure immediate feedback. This helps in taking timely corrective action and avoiding mistakes. The benefits of personal selling, however, must be considered in relation to its costs. For example, according to the research department of the McGraw-Hill Publications Company, per-call personal selling expenditures for all types of personal selling in 1980 came to $127, up by 31 percent from 1977.[35] Thus, the high impact of personal selling should be considered in light of its high cost.

Strategic Matters. As a part of selling strategy, several strategic matters should be resolved. The decision must be made on whether greater emphasis should be put on maintaining existing accounts or on converting customers. According to one study, the retention and conversion of cus-

---

[35] *Sales and Marketing Management*, February 23, 1981, p. 34. McGraw-Hill research also showed that the larger the sales force, the lower the cost. For instance, companies with fewer than 10 salespeople spent over $150 per call; companies with more than 50 spent less than $100. This underscores the significance of the experience effect (see Chapter 17).

tomers is related to the time salespeople spend with them.[36] Thus, before salespeople can make the best use of their efforts, they must know how much importance is to be attached to each of the two functions. The decision is influenced by such factors as the growth status of the industry, the company's strengths and weaknesses, the competitors' strengths, and marketing goals. For example, a manufacturer of laundry detergent will think twice before attempting to convert customers from Tide (Procter & Gamble's brand) to its own brand. On the other hand, there may be factors which make a company challenge the leader. For example, Bic Pen Corporation is aggressively promoting its disposable razor among Gillette's customers. The decision to maintain or convert customers cannot be made in isolation but must be considered in the context of the total marketing strategy.

An important strategic concern is how to make productive use of the sales force. In recent years, high expenses (i.e., cost of keeping a salesperson on the road), affordable technological advances (e.g., prices of technology used in telemarketing, teleconferencing, and computerized sales have gone down substantially), and innovative sales techniques (e.g., video presentations) have made it feasible for marketers to turn to electronic marketing to make the most productive use of sales force resources. For example, Gould Inc.'s medical products division in Oxnard, California, uses video support for a sales effort on a new product, a disposable transducer that translates blood pressure into readable electronic impulses. Gould produced two videotapes—a six-minute sales presentation and a nine-minute user-training film—costing $200,000. Salespeople were equipped with videorecorders—an additional $75,000 investment—to take on calls. According to Gould executives, video gives a concise, clear version of the intended communication and has added professionalism to their sales effort. Gould targeted its competitors' customers and maintains that it captured 45 percent of the $75-million transducer market in less than a year. By the end of nine months, the company achieved sales of more than 25,000 units per month, achieving significant penetration in markets they had not been able to get in before.[37]

Another aspect of selling strategy deals with the question of who should be contacted in the customer organization. The buying process may be divided into four phases: consideration, acceptance, selection, and evaluation. Different executives in the customer organization may exert influence on any of the four phases. The sales strategist may work out a plan specifying which salesperson should call upon whom in the customer organization and when. On occasion, a person other than the salesperson may be asked to call on the customer. Sometimes, as a matter of selling

---

[36]"Penstock Press," a case copyrighted by the President and Fellows of Harvard College, 1966.

[37]"Rebirth of a Salesman: Willy Loman Goes Electronic," *Business Week*, February 27, 1984, p. 103.

strategy a team of people may visit the customer. For example, Northrop Corporation, an aerospace contractor, assigns aircraft designers and technicians—not salesmen—to call on potential customers. When Singapore indicated interest in Northrop's F-5 fighter, Northrop dispatched a team to Singapore that included an engineer, a lawyer, a pricing expert, a test pilot, and a maintenance specialist.[38]

Van Leer cites this example from the literature: A manufacturer of vinyl acetate latex (used as a base for latex paint) built its sales volume by having its people call on the "right people" in the customer organization. The manufacturer recognized that its product was used by the customer to produce paint sold through its marketing department, not the purchasing agent or manager of research. So the manufacturer planned for its people to meet with the customer's sales and marketing personnel to find out what their problems were, what kept them from selling more latex paint, and what role the manufacturer could play to help the customer. It was only after the marketing personnel had been sold on the product that the purchasing department was contacted.[39] Thus, a good selling strategy requires a careful analysis of the situation to determine the key people to contact in the customer organization. A routine call on the purchasing agent may not suffice.

The selling strategy should also determine the size of the sales force needed to perform an effective job. This decision is usually made intuitively. A company starts with a few salespeople, adding more as it gains experience. Some companies may go a step beyond the intuitive approach to determine how many salespeople should be recruited. For instance, consideration may be given to factors such as the number of customers who must be visited, the amount of market potential in a territory, and so on. But all these factors are weighed subjectively. Discussed below are three different methods which may be employed in making an objective decision about the optimum size of the sales force.

Semlow recommends a step-by-step procedure for deciding how much should be spent on personal selling. He believes additional salespeople should be hired to the point where profit on sales generated by the additional staff is greater than or equal to the cost of these employees. Algebraically, this reads as follows:

$$S(p) - C > 0$$

S refers to the sales volume each additional salesperson is likely to produce, p is the expected profit margin on additional sales volume, and C denotes the total cost of maintaining the additional staff. In this equation

---

[38]Louis Kraar, "Everyone at Northrop Is in Marketing," *Fortune*, April 10, 1978, pp. 52–55.

[39]R. Karl van Leer, "Industrial Marketing with a Flair," *Harvard Business Review*, November–December, 1976, pp. 117–124.

the values of p and C are usually known. A company can devise its own methods for computing the value of S. Semlow has elaborated his procedure with an example. He discusses a simple case of 25 one-person territories. Semlow's method consists of:

1. Computing sales per one percent of potential for each territory by dividing its dollar sales by the percentage of the total potential for the same territory.
2. Smoothing out a trend line of sales volume per one percent of potential for territories of various sizes. This is achieved by plotting the percentage of potential of each territory and sales volume per one percent of potential on a graph.
3. Assigning a number of salespeople to territories based on different average percentage potentials, and computing sales per average salesperson in each case (assuming one salesperson for one percent of total potential). If territory size were taken to be 0.5 percent, 200 salesmen would be employed. Further, if sales per one percent of potential (with 0.5-percent-size territory) were $20,000, total sales would be $200,000. Dividing $200,000 by the number of salespeople, the sales per average salesperson comes to $1,000.

This process is repeated with different average territory sizes in percentages such as 2 percent, 3 percent, etc. Semlow's analysis shows that sales increased with the number of salespeople in territories rated high, but the increase in sales was less than proportionate to the increase in sales potential.

Semlow's method continues with the following procedures:

4. Estimating operating profit after deducting all costs from sales volume computed in point 3 above.
5. Determining total investment—plant investment and working capital—required at alternative sales volume.
6. Expressing operating profit as a ratio to sales volume and investment.

Semlow found that both these ratios were highest with 65 salespeople (in the case he was considering), which was then considered to be the optimum size of the sales force. With experience, one can derive a curve for various categories of products for ready reference as to the number of people needed for the selling job. Semlow's approach considers territorial sales potential to be the crucial factor in determining the size of the sales force.[40] While Semlow's method continues to be widely men-

---

[40]Walter J. Semlow, "How Many Salesmen Do You Need?," *Harvard Business Review*, May–June, 1959, pp. 126–132.

tioned in the literature, Lucas, Weinberg, and Clowes found his relationships to be spurious.[41]

The size of the sales force may also be determined based on the workload. For example, major customers may be grouped into different categories according to the desired frequency of calls. From this estimate, the total number of calls that must be made in a year is divided by the average number of calls a salesperson can make in a year. This gives the number of salespeople needed.

Suppose that a company has 10 customers to be called on 100 times a year, 80 customers to be called on 50 times a year, 140 customers to be called on 10 times a year, and 500 customers to be called on twice a year. Further, it is expected that a salesperson can make an average of 200 calls a year. Using this approach, this company needs 37 salespeople, as shown below:

$$N = \frac{10 \times 100 + 80 \times 50 + 140 \times 10 + 500 \times 2}{200}$$

$$= 7400/200 = 37$$

The size of the sales force can also be determined by comparing the expected monetary values of various sizes of sales forces in relationship to different market potentials. In other words, given the various levels of potential projections in a territory, different profits will accrue depending on the size of the sales force. Profit estimates for each market potential will give the expected values when multiplied by a probability of potential being realized. A summation of expected values for each decision rule (size of the sales force) can be prepared in order to pick the one which is highest. This specifies the desired number of salespeople.

Another model for determining the size of sales force that seeks to maximize company sales for a given sales force size has been developed by Glaze and Weinberg. Their model is a heuristic procedure that uses geographic information and account-specific sales response functions to locate salespersons in the territory, assign them to accounts, and allocate their time to these accounts. By running the model iteratively for different sizes of the sales force, a sales force response function may be developed.[42]

Examined above are the major strategic issues involved in developing selling strategy. In addition, matters of price concessions (within the

---

[41]H. C. Lucas, Jr., C. B. Weinburg, and K. W. Clowes, "Sales Response as a Function of Territorial Potential and Sales Representative Workload," *Journal of Marketing Research,* August, 1975, pp. 298–305.

[42]T. A. Glaze and C. B. Weinberg, "A Sales Territory Alignment Program and Accounting Planning System," in R. Bagozzi (ed.), *Sales Management: New Developments from Behavioral and Decision Model Research* (Cambridge, MA: Marketing Science Institute, 1979), pp. 325–343.

limits of law) to different customers and trial installations of the company's products on selected customers' premises may also occasionally require strategic inputs.

Sales-Motivation-and-Supervision Strategy

To ensure that salespersons perform to their utmost capacity, they must be adequately motivated and properly supervised. Often it has been found that salespeople fail to do well because the management has failed to carry out its part of the job, especially in the areas of motivation and supervision. While motivation and supervision may appear to be mundane day-to-day matters, they have far-reaching implications for marketing strategy. The purpose of this section is to provide insights into the strategic aspects of motivation and supervision.

Motivation. Salespeople may be motivated through both financial and nonfinancial means. Financial motivation is provided by monetary compensation. Nonfinancial motivation is usually tied in with evaluation programs.

Compensation. Most people work to earn a living; their motivation to work is deeply affected by the remuneration they receive. A well-designed compensation plan keeps turnover low and helps to increase an employee's productivity. A compensation plan should be simple, understandable, flexible (cognizant of the differences between individuals), and economically equitable. It should also provide incentive and build morale. It should not penalize salespeople for conditions beyond their control, and it should help in developing new business, provide stable income, and meet the objectives of the corporation. Above all, the compensation should be in line with the market price for salespeople.[43] Since some of these requisites may conflict with each other, there can be no one perfect plan. All that can be done is to try to balance each variable properly and design a custom-made plan for each sales force.

Different methods of compensating salespeople are: the salary plan, commission plan, and combination plan. Exhibit 16-2 shows the relative advantages and disadvantages of each plan.

The greatest virtue of the straight-salary method is the guaranteed income and security that it provides. However, it fails to provide any incentive to the ambitious salesperson and therefore may adversely affect productivity. Most companies work on a combination plan, which means that salespeople receive a percentage of sales as a commission for exceeding the periodic quotas set for them. Conceptually, the first step in designing a compensation plan is to define the objective, such as rewarding extraordinary performance, providing security, and so on. Every company

---

[43]*Marketing News,* February 5, 1982, p. 1.

EXHIBIT 16-2   Advantages and Disadvantages of Various Sales-Compensation Alternatives

SALARY PLAN

Advantages
1. Assures a regular income.
2. Develops a high degree of loyalty.
3. Makes it simple to switch territories or quotas or to reassign salesmen.
4. Ensures that nonselling activities will be performed.
5. Facilitates administration.
6. Provides relatively fixed sales costs.

Disadvantages
1. Fails to give balanced sales mix because salesmen would concentrate on products with greatest customer appeal.
2. Provides little, if any, financial incentive for the salesman.
3. Offers few reasons for putting forth extra effort.
4. Favors salesmen or saleswomen who are the least productive.
5. Tends to increase direct selling costs over other types of plans.
6. Creates the possibility of salary compression where new trainees may earn almost as much as experienced salesmen.

COMMISSION PLAN

Advantages
1. Pay relates directly to performance and results achieved.
2. System is easy to understand and compute.
3. Salesmen have the greatest possible incentive.
4. Unit sales costs are proportional to net sales.
5. Company's selling investment is reduced.

Disadvantages
1. Emphasis is more likely to be on volume than on profits.
2. Little or no loyalty to the company is generated.
3. Wide variances in income between salesmen may occur.
4. Salesmen are encouraged to neglect nonselling duties.
5. Some salesmen may be tempted to "skim" their territories.
6. Service aspect of selling may be slighted.
7. Problems arise in cutting territories or shifting men or accounts.
8. Pay is often excessive in boom times and very low in recession periods.
9. Salesmen may sell themselves rather than the company and stress short-term rather than long-term relationships.
10. Highly paid salesmen may be reluctant to move into supervisory or managerial positions.
11. Excessive turnover of sales personnel occurs when business turns bad.

COMBINATION PLAN

Advantages
1. Offers participants the advantage of both salary and commission.
2. Provides greater range of earnings possibilities.
3. Gives salesmen greater security because of steady base income.

EXHIBIT 16-2   continued

4. Makes possible a favorable ratio of selling expense to sales.
5. Compensates salesmen for all activities.
6. Allows a greater latitude of motivation possibilities so that goals and objectives can be achieved on schedule.

Disadvantages
1. Is often complex and difficult to understand.
2. Can, where low salary and high bonus or commission exist, develop a bonus that is too high a percentage of earnings; when sales fall, salary is too low to retain salesmen.
3. Is sometimes costly to administer.
4. Can, unless a decreasing commission rate for increasing sales volume exists, result in a "windfall" of new accounts and a runaway of earnings.
5. Has a tendency to offer too many objectives at one time so that really important ones can be neglected, forgotten, or overlooked.

Source: Reprinted by permission of the *Harvard Business Review*. Excerpt from "How to Pay Your Sales Force" by John P. Steinbrink, July–August, 1978, pp. 111–122. Copyright © 1978 by the President and Fellows of Harvard College; all rights reserved.

would probably prefer to grant some security to its people and, at the same time, distinguish the top employees through incentive schemes. In designing such a plan, the company may determine the going salary rate for the type of sales staff it is interested in hiring. The company should match the market rate to retain people of caliber. The total wage should be fixed somewhere near the market rate after making adjustments for the company's overall wage policy, environment, and fringe benefits.

A study of the spending habits of those in the salary range of salespeople should be made. Based on this study, the percentage of non-discretionary spending may be linked to an incentive income scheme whereby extra income could be paid as a commission on sales or as a bonus, or both. Care must be taken in constructing a compensation plan. In addition to being equitable, the plan should be simple enough to be comprehensible by the salespeople. Webster recommends the following procedure for constructing a compensation plan:

1. Establish clear and consistent compensation objectives, such as guaranteed income, stimulation, individual sales incentives, group incentives, and flexibility for local modification.
2. Determine the level of income for each salesperson.
3. Establish the proportions of fixed and incentive income.
4. Select measurement criteria for each component. For example, the size of the fixed component may be determined by the amount of servicing, follow-up work, and prospecting required. The incentive component may be determined by some measure of sales volume,

such as total sales in dollars, in units, or the gross formula.
5. Establish the compensation formula.
6. Pretest the formula.[44]

Once compensation has been established for an individual, it is difficult to reduce it. It is desirable, therefore, for management to consider all the pros and cons of fixed compensation for a salesperson before finalizing a salary agreement. While it is always possible to revise wages upwards, people are seldom penalized downwards. This raises an important ethical and managerial problem. Doesn't the equality concept demand periodic adjustments—both upward and downward—to the compensation? Some blue-collar workers are paid a piece rate and can be penalized for a bad showing. However, in a white-collar job such as that of a salesperson, no such penalties are planned. Thus, care in establishing the starting salary is important.

Evaluation. Evaluation is the measurement of a salesperson's contribution to corporate goals. For any evaluation, one needs standards. Establishment of standards, however, is a difficult task, particularly when salespeople are asked to perform different types of jobs. In pure selling jobs, quotas can be set for minimal performance, and salespeople achieving these quotas can be considered as doing satisfactory work. Achievement of quotas can be classified as follows: those exceeding quotas between 1 to 15 percent may be designated as average salespeople; those between 16 and 30 percent, well-performing; and, finally, those over 30 percent can be considered extraordinary salespeople. Sales contests and awards, both financial and nonfinancial, may be instituted to give recognition to salespeople in various categories. For example, NCR Corporation awards its well-performing salespeople with membership in its prestigious 100-points club (CPC). Nonfinancial awards are especially helpful in building morale and aspirations.

Subjective criteria may be used for measuring other work that a salesperson performs. Some companies use an evaluation form, such as the one shown in Exhibit 16-3 which is used by a paper manufacturer. The evaluation form reflects a salesperson's personality, attitude, and habits on the job as well as in interactions with associates in the company. In all, there are eleven criteria rated on a scale from 0 to 10. Salespeople who score in the outstanding range may be given awards in recognition of their performance. Awards may also be instituted for those in the excellent category.

---

[44]Fred E. Webster, Jr., "Rationalizing Salesmen's Compensation Plans," *Journal of Marketing*, January, 1966, pp. 55–58, as quoted in G. David Hughes, *Marketing Management* (Reading, MA: Addison-Wesley Publishing Co., 1978), p. 393. See also J. P. Steinbrink, "How to Pay Your Sales Force," *Harvard Business Review*, July–August, 1978, pp. 111–122.

EXHIBIT 16-3 Salesperson Evaluation Form

PERFORMANCE CRITERIA	POINT AWARD*				
	10 Outstanding	8 Excellent	5 Average	2 Poor	0 Unsatisfactory
1. Personal Habits (Appearance, absentee record, punctuality, etc.)					
2. Administrative Management (Timeliness, thoroughness, promptness of correspondence and other details involving customers and internal company. Does salesperson plan time wisely)					
3. Attitude (Overall, to company and to others—Is he or she the leader type)					
4. Continuing Education (Effort toward a better understanding of the business, its technology, the business environment, etc.—as evidenced by continuing education efforts—both within and outside the company)					
5. Outside Activities (Within the business such as graphic arts organizations, salespeople's associations, and/or community or other affairs that relate to his or her standing and importance within the industry or community and enhance both the salesperson's personal image and the company's)					
6. Customer Feedback (What do the customers say about the salesperson—has he or she impressed them sufficiently to warrant a compliment; while unsolicited, they are of most value, the regional manager will probably want to solicit feedback where it is not forthcoming)					

7. Care of Company Property & Finances
(What is the record in regard to company cars, the wiseness of expenditures on expense account; the settlement of R&A's, etc.)
8. Sales Training, Customer Education, etc.
(What is the track record in sales meeting-number and effectiveness; what other education or training has salesperson inaugurated for customers; how effective is he or she before these groups; manner and content of presentation)
9. Specifications Effort
(What is the extent and effectiveness of the salesperson's specifications efforts. Is he or she spending time conscientiously and aggressively in this area. If possible, measure results)
10. Market Development
(Addition of new merchants or customers; improvements in existing)
11. Merchandising Ability
(The extent and creativity with which salesperson uses advertising, promotional and public relations tools, and products developed within the company; or those that he or she has developed alone or in conjunction with a merchant or customer)

Source: Subhash C. Jain and Iqbal Mathur, *Cases in Marketing Management* (Columbus, OH: Grid Publishing, 1978), pp. 371–372. Reprinted by permission of the publisher.

*11 award categories were established with points that ranged from 0 to 10. That meant 110 points were possible to achieve. If $30 a point was awarded as bonus, an average performance warranted 55 points $\times$ $30 = $1,650 as bonus award, while an outstanding rated $3,300. In order to further award the top performers, there was an additional cash award to top 5 or 10 salespeople, i.e.,

#1—$3000   #2—$2000   #3—$1500   #4—$1000   #5—$ 500

What should be done about salespeople who repeatedly fail to perform according to standards? Miner suggests that, first, the underlying reasons for failure should be established. These may fall into the following categories: lack of intelligence and job knowledge, emotional problems, lack of motivation, physical disorders, family problems, problems with the groups at work, mistakes on the part of the company, and conflict with societal values and situational forces.[45]

After investigating the reasons for someone's poor performance, the sales strategist should take action to correct the situation, such as training, professional help, or transfer. If the company cannot do anything to improve the performance of a salesperson, dismissal may be the appropriate solution.

Supervision. Despite the best efforts in selecting, training, and compensating, salespeople may not perform as expected. Supervision is important to ensure that salespeople provide the services expected of them. Supervision is defined in a broader sense to include assignment of territory to a salesperson, control over his or her activities, and communication with the salesperson in the field.

Assignment. Salespeople are assigned to different geographic territories. An assignment requires solving two problems: (1) forming territories so that they are as much alike as possible in business potential, and (2) assigning territories so that each salesperson is able to realize his or her full potential. Territories may be formed by analyzing customers' locations and the potential business they represent. Customers can be categorized as having high, average, or low potential. Further, probabilities in terms of sales can be assigned to indicate how much potential is realizable. Thus, a territory with a large number of high-potential customers with a high probability of buying may be smaller in size (geographically speaking) than a territory with a large number of low-potential customers with a low probability of buying.[46]

Matching salespeople to the territories should not be difficult once the territories have been laid out. Regional preferences and the individual affiliations of the salespeople require that employees be placed where they will be happiest. It may be difficult to attract salespeople to some territories, while other places may be in great demand. Living in big metropolitan areas is expensive and not always comfortable. Similarly, people may avoid places with poor weather conditions. It may become necessary to provide extra compensation to salespeople assigned to unpopular places.

Control. Although salespeople are their own bosses in the field, the

---

[45]John B. Miner, *Management of Ineffective Performance* (New York: McGraw-Hill Book Co., 1972).

[46]Robert J. Zimmer and James W. Taylor, "Matching Profiles for Your Industrial Sales Force," *Business*, March–April, 1981, pp. 2–13.

manager must keep informed of their activities. To achieve that control, a system must be evolved for maintaining communication with employees in the field, for guiding their work, and for employing remedial methods if performance slackens. Firms use different types of control devices. Some companies require salespeople to fill in a call form giving all particulars about each visit to each customer. Some require their salespeople to submit weekly reports on the work performed during the previous week. Salespeople may be asked to complete several forms about sales generated, special problems they face, market information collected, and so on. Using a good reporting system to control the sales force should have a positive influence on performance. In recent years, more and more companies are using computer-assisted techniques to maintain control of sales force activities.[47]

Communication. Management communicates with salespeople through periodic mailings, regional and national conferences, and telephone calls. There are two areas of communication in which management needs to be extra careful to maintain the morale of good salespeople: (1) in representing the problems of the field force to people at the headquarters, and (2) in giving patient consideration to the salespeople's complaints. A sales manager serves as the link between the people in the field and the company and must try to bring their problems and difficulties to the attention of top management at the head office. Top management, not being fully aware of the operations in the field, may fail to appreciate the problems. It is, therefore, the duty of the sales manager to keep the top management fully posted about field activities and secure for the salespeople their favors. For example, a salesperson in a mountainous area may not be able to maintain the work tempo during the winter because of weather conditions. Management must consider this factor in reviewing the salesperson's work. There may also be occupational or personal problems bothering the salespeople, and it is the manager's duty to stand by and help.

Close rapport with the salespeople and patient listening can be very helpful in recognizing and solving the salespeople's problems. More often than not, a salesperson's problem is something the company can take care of with a little effort and expenditure if it is only willing to accept such responsibility. The primary thing, however, is to know the salesperson's mind. This is where the role of the supervisor comes in. It is said that the sales manager should be as much a therapist in solving salespeople's problems as the latter should be in handling customers' problems.

SUMMARY

Promotion strategies are directed toward establishing communication with customers. Three types of promotion strategies may be distin-

---

[47]Lad Kuzela, "Slicing Costs with Smarter Selling," *Industry Week*, February 22, 1982, pp. 59–61.

guished. Advertising strategies are concerned with communication transmitted through mass media. Personal selling strategies refer to face-to-face interaction with the customer. All other forms of communication, such as sampling, demonstration, cents off, contests, etc., are known as sales promotion strategies. Two main promotion strategies are examined in this chapter: promotion-expenditure strategy, which deals with the question of how much may be spent on the overall promotion, and promotion-mix strategy, which specifies the roles which the three ingredients of promotion (i.e., advertising, personal selling, and sales promotion) play in promoting a business.

Discussed also are two advertising strategies. The first is media-selection strategy, which focuses on the choice of different media to launch an ad campaign. The second is advertising-copy strategy, which deals with the development of appropriate ad copy to convey the intended message. The personal selling strategies examined here are selling strategy and sales-motivation-and-supervision strategy. The selling strategy emphasizes the approach that may be adopted to interact with the customer (i.e., who may call on the customer, whom to call on in the customer organization, when, and how frequently). The sales-motivation-and-supervision strategy is concerned with the management of the sales force and refers to such issues as sales compensation, nonfinancial incentives, territory formation and salespeople assignment, control, and communication.

Examples from marketing literature are cited to illustrate the practical application of each strategy.

DISCUSSION QUESTIONS

1. *Outline promotion objectives for a packaged food product, a small appliance, and a stereo system in assumed market segments.*
2. *Develop a promotion-expenditure strategy for a household computer to be marketed through a large retail chain.*
3. *Will promotion-expenditure strategy for a product in the growth stage of the product life cycle be different from that for a product in the maturity stage? Discuss.*
4. *How may a promotion budget be allocated among advertising, personal selling, and sales promotion? Can a simulation model be developed to figure out optimum promotion mix?*
5. *Is comparison advertising socially desirable? Comment.*
6. *Should the media decision be made before or after the copy is first developed? Discuss.*
7. *Which is more effective, an emotional appeal or a rational appeal? Are emotional appeals relevant for all consumer products?*

APPENDIX: PERSPECTIVES OF PROMOTION STRATEGIES

I. Promotion-Expenditure Strategy

Definition: Determination of the amount that a company may spend on its total promotional effort, which includes advertising, personal selling, and sales promotion.

Objective: To allocate enough funds to each promotional task, so that each is utilized to its fullest potential.

Requirements: (1) Adequate resources to finance the promotion expenditure. (2) Understanding of the products/services sales response. (3) Estimate of the duration of the advertising effect. (4) Understanding of each product/market situation relative to different forms of promotion. (5) Understanding of competitive response to promotion.

Expected Results: Allocation of sufficient funds to the promotional tasks to accomplish the overall marketing objectives.

II. Promotion-Mix Strategy

Definition: Determination of a judicious mix of different types of promotion.

Objective: To adequately blend the three types of promotion to complement each other for a balanced promotional perspective.

Requirements: (1) Product factors—(a) nature of product; (b) perceived risk; (c) durable vs. nondurable; (d) typical purchase amount. (2) Market factors—(a) position in the life cycle; (b) market share; (c) industry concentration; (d) intensity of competition; (e) demand perspectives. (3) Customer factors—(a) household vs. business customers; (b) number of customers; (c) concentration of customers. (4) Budget factors—(a) financial resources of the organization; (b) traditional promotional perspectives. (5) Marketing-mix factors—(a) relative price/relative quality; (b) distribution strategy; (c) brand life cycle; (d) geographic scope of the market. (6) Environmental factors.

Expected Results: The three types of promotion are assigned roles in a way that provides the best communication.

III. Media-Selection Strategy

Definition: Choosing the channels (newspapers, magazines, television, radio, outdoor advertising, transit advertising, and direct mail) through which messages concerning a product/service are transmitted to the targets.

Objective: To move customers from unawareness of a product/service – to awareness – to comprehension – to conviction – to the buying action.

Requirements: (1) Relate media-selection objectives to product/market objectives. (2) Media chosen should have a unique way of promoting the business. (3) Media should be measure-minded not only in frequency and timing in reaching the target audience, but also in evaluating the quality of the audience. (4) Base media selection on factual, not connotational, grounds. (5) Media plan should be optimistic in that it takes advantage of the lessons learned from experience. (6) Seek information on customer profiles and audience characteristics.

Expected Results: Customers are moved along the desired path of the purchase process.

IV. Advertising-Copy Strategy

Definition: Designing the content of an advertisement.

Objective: To transmit a particular product/service message to a particular target.

Requirements: (1) Eliminate "noise" for a clear transmission of message. (2) Consider importance of (a) source credibility; (b) balance of argument; (c) message repetition; (d) rational vs. emotional appeals; (e) humor appeals; (f) presentation of model's eyes in pictorial ads; (g) comparison advertising.

Expected Results: The intended message is adequately transmitted to the target audience.

V. Selling Strategy

Definition: Moving customers to the purchase phase of the decision-making process through the use of face-to-face contact.

Objective: Achievement of stated sales volume and gross margin targets, and the fulfillment of specific activities.

Requirements: (1) The selling strategy should be derived from overall marketing objectives and properly linked with promotional objectives. (2) Decision on maintenance of existing accounts vs. lining up new customers. (3) Decision on who should be contacted in customer's organization. (4) Determine optimal size of sales force.

Expected Results: (1) Sales and profit targets are met at minimum expense. (2) Overall marketing goals are achieved.

VI. Sales-Motivation-and-Supervision Strategy

Definition: Achieving superior sales force performance.

Objective: To ensure optimal performance of sales force.

Requirements: (1) Motivation—financial and nonfinancial. (2) Adequate compensation package. (3) Evaluation standards. (4) Appropriate territory assignment, activity control, and communication.

Expected Results: Business objectives are met adequately at minimum expense.

CASE 16
Eastern Insurance Company

Roger Knauth, project leader of Eastern Insurance Company's ActionShop Program, was concerned. The ActionShop concept had been developed by the Marketing Department in 1981 in response to the company's declining market share in Personal Lines insurance. Now, 30 months later, two shops had been implemented. A third was on the drawing board, but the senior vice-president had put this on hold until Knauth made his recommendations regarding the project. Specifically, the senior vice-president wanted to know whether the ActionShop concept was working; whether ActionShop III should be established; and if continued, whether the ActionShop concept should be franchised as recommended by the Marketing Department.

BACKGROUND

Early in the 1980s the insurance industry showed a marked trend: independent agents were losing a major share of the Personal Lines market (homeowners and auto) to direct writers such as Allstate. Independent agents represent a number of insurance companies through contractual arrangements, enabling their customers to choose among products, services, and prices. Direct writers are employed by one insurance company and represent only that company; the expense savings of this direct distribution channel are usually passed through to the customers.

Independent agents began to look to their insurance companies for help, but by early 1982, the *National Underwriter* echoed most agents' continuing sentiments:

> The long-heard "rumor" that agency companies are interested in Personal Lines is most certainly not confirmed in their advertising messages in the trade press . . . . It seems inconceivable that agency companies will continue to sit back and let the direct writers gain more of a market share in Personal Lines.

In response to declining market share and agencies' outcries, Eastern Insurance Company sought a plan whereby the company could (1) build consumer brand awareness of Eastern Insurance Company's Personal Lines products; (2) support its independent agency system to compete against the growing number of direct, "retail"-oriented insurance writers; and (3) increase market share in profitable lines of personal insurance products. The task of developing a strategy or strategies to meet these company objectives was assigned to the Marketing Department. The result was the ActionShop concept.

Previously, the company had served solely as a "wholesaler" of insurance products. Direct sales to consumers were made by independent agents, separate business entities representing multiple insurance companies. Eastern's venture into retail marketing—ultimately known as the ActionShop—was designed to take advantage of changing lifestyles and shopping behavior and to bring Eastern, as a company, into direct contact with the buying public. It involved establishing sales offices in enclosed shopping malls, utilizing retail promotional methods to build sales, and operating the offices in conjunction with selected independent agents representing Eastern. The company would provide the financing and technical knowledge to start the Shop, promote the product, and run the business; the independent agent would be responsible for the actual sales (so that the company would not have to have its employees licensed as insurance agents.) Ultimately, Eastern's strategy envisioned franchising ActionShops to independent agents.

A marketing consulting firm was commissioned to further develop the broad concept, and Eastern's Marketing Department presented it to the senior vice-president of Personal Lines for approval. As Project Leader Knauth explained:

> We knew it was a gamble. And presented it that way. The concept was different from anything we'd tried before. We knew the agents we chose would have to be specially trained and that the agencies themselves, while they could still represent other companies at other agency locations, would have to commit themselves to representing only Eastern in the ActionShop. The plan was for the company to develop a flexible modular store (to fit into irregularly shaped spaces rented in malls), an advertising campaign, and an intensive training program; the whole concept would be packaged and ultimately franchised to agents. While being tested, however, the Shops would be supervised by company marketing personnel.

In approving the concept, management set two additional objectives for the pilot:

1. Three ActionShops were to be established within 18 months to 2 years in diverse locations of the country. All were to be located in states specifically targeted for growth in Personal Lines business.
2. "All-Driver," a new Eastern product, was to be used as a drawing card for the ActionShops. As insurance is rarely an "impulse" item, this policy guaranteed anyone with a driver's license the opportunity to purchase auto insurance.

Roger Knauth, as project leader, was given total control of the concept. With an unlimited budget and direct management support, Knauth was able to cross divisional lines as well as access outside consultants to complete establishment of the first ActionShop (Exhibit 16-4).

EXHIBIT 16-4   Eastern Insurance Company: Organizational Chart (Overview)

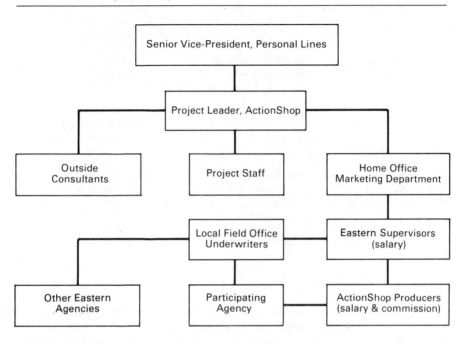

ActionShop I (February/March, 1982)

The first ActionShop was established in Hawthorn Center, a new residential community being built outside Chicago by a subsidiary of Eastern Insurance Company. The location was chosen because the subsidiary was having difficulty obtaining stores for its mall and would rent space to the ActionShop at a low cost. In addition, Illinois was targeted as a growth state for Personal Lines.

Eastern's Marketing Department provided a salaried supervisor to handle the actual operations of the ActionShop and monitor all production. Supervisors reported through the Marketing Department to the project leader. ActionShop agents were specially hired by the participating agency, were trained by Eastern, and were accountable to the Eastern supervisor and their respective agencies. Agents were compensated by their agencies—subsidized by Eastern via a salary and commission schedule based upon individual production goals set by Eastern and the agency. The local Eastern field office was responsible for handling all insurance policies, underwriting problems, and claims generated by the ActionShop. Barbara Sheridan, a field office underwriter responsible for maintaining ActionShop I's book of business, explained:

We really bent over backwards providing service to the ActionShop. The ActionShop supervisor was from the Home Office Marketing Department and so he was good at generating enthusiasm and sales, but he really didn't know too much about the technical side of the business. We know pricing and underwriting. He relied heavily on us. Some of the other agents felt slighted, I guess. They didn't want to make a commitment to become involved in the ActionShop, but they didn't want to lose out on service from our office, either. But we really didn't trouble the Home Office with our local problems; we wanted the ActionShop to succeed.

ActionShop I also marked the start-up of the ActionShop advertising campaign and, as Knauth explained, the Shop was a real learning experience from a promotional point of view:

We hired an outside firm to develop a promotional package for press, radio, and TV because our company didn't have the expertise in that area. We only knew insurance. But about six months into the campaign we realized we'd made a mistake. Promotional costs were sky-high and we weren't reaching our local audience because all media were based out of Chicago. In addition, the planned residential community was not generating the traffic we expected.

ActionShop II (January, 1983)

The Marketing Department sought to correct the promotional problems it saw in ActionShop I by choosing a more rural location for ActionShop II. In addition, an outside consulting firm, Opatow Associates, was hired to conduct a pre- and post-market audit to determine if Eastern's name was becoming better known.

Citadel Mall, Colorado Springs, was a well-established, well-visited shopping area when Eastern implemented its second ActionShop there in 1974. Opatow Associates noted in its benchmark study just prior to implementation that the ActionShop's target market, as determined by Eastern's Marketing Department, "differs from the current population as [the target market] is younger, more likely to be married, and in higher socioeconomic groups than the total population of Colorado Springs."

However, the viability of the mall (supported by an Eastern subsidiary) and the localized, low-cost media seemed to offer a perfect opportunity to test the promotional campaign developed in ActionShop I and to reintroduce All-Driver, which was beginning to experience underwriting losses in Illinois.

Mary Fragola, an agent hired by a participating agency to work in the ActionShop, discussed agent reactions to ActionShop sales:

Our training from Eastern was very good and stressed marketing of Personal Lines products using proven agency techniques—telephone solicitations, direct mail, cold calls. Other agents gave us some trouble because they felt they were "missing out" on some benefits. They didn't seem to understand that our activities and advertising also benefited them. All they could see was the short range: That Eastern was helping our agency write more Personal Lines business. They didn't seem to understand that the bulk of our sales didn't come from the existence of the ActionShop; they came from us soliciting business the same way we'd always developed business in the agency—phone calls, direct mail, and personal visits.

In fact, that led to the greatest problems we ever had with our ActionShop supervisor. He wanted us to stay on duty in the ActionShop; we wanted to be outside soliciting business. After all, that's where our commission dollars were.

The Marketing Department pointed out that Opatow's final market audit for ActionShop II showed that public awareness of Eastern had doubled in the nine months since the ActionShop had been established; however, the consulting firm could not determine whether establishment of the facility itself caused this change (Exhibit 16-5). Policy sales in ActionShop II as of the third quarter, 1983, were 35 percent greater than company objectives, and the Marketing Department felt that the Shop was meeting all expectations.

EXHIBIT 16-5   Eastern Insurance Company: Results of Pre- and Post-Market Audit of Name Awareness

Top-of-Mind Awareness, Regardless of Order of Mention	Projectable Sample	
	Benchmark	Follow-Up
(mentioned by 5% or more, either study)	(1,001 respondents)	(500 respondents)
Prudential	41%	36%
State Farm Mutual	31	38
Allstate	30	36
Farmers Insurance Group	25	28
Metropolitan	22	19
Mutual of Omaha	20	18
New York Life	18	15
Eastern	8	16
Hartford A&I	8	6
GEICO	8	7
Travelers Insurance Company	7	6
American Family Group	7	3
USAA	6	6
John Hancock	6	9
Blue Cross, Blue Shield	5	5

Source: Company records.

Year-End, 1983

By late 1983, Roger Knauth was considering implementation of a final experimental ActionShop and turning his staff's attention toward a possible franchise operation, as recommended by the Marketing Department. His staff's latest analysis, prior to Knauth's upcoming meeting with the senior vice-president, revealed the following information:

1. Rochester, New York, had been originally chosen as the site for ActionShop III. However, a recent internal market analysis recommended Syracuse as an alternative. A new mall was being built there, and Eastern would be assured first choice in shop

EXHIBIT 16-6   Eastern Insurance Company: ActionShop Expenditures, 1982–83

Expenditures by Eastern	
Outside professional design and communications consulting services	
ActionShop concept development	$ 25,000
Architectural professional services	35,000
Market research study	30,000
	$ 90,000
Sales module construction costs	
Hawthorn Center	$ 20,000
Citadel	23,000
	$ 43,000
Store interior construction costs	
Hawthorn Center	$ 36,000
Citadel	37,000
	$ 73,000
Advertising (developmental, production, media, direct mail)	$145,000
ActionShop supervisor and staff salaries	$153,000
Staff travel and entertainment	$ 20,000
Furniture and equipment	$ 8,500
Rent and utilities	$ 32,000
Agents' training	Unknown
Expenditures by Participating Agencies	
ActionShop I	$ 26,600
ActionShop II	19,500
	$ 46,100

Source: Company records.

EXHIBIT 16-7   Eastern Insurance Company: ActionShop Production Results (as of 12/83)

	Number of Policies YTD[a]	Loss Ratio[b]
ActionShop I	616	393%
Participating Agency	1,047	123%
Illinois Field Office	49,290	NA
ActionShop II	891	71.9%
Participating Agency	472	23.1%
Colorado Field Office	48,124	NA

[a]Can be interpreted as business generated during the year.
[b]Ratio of loss dollars expended to premium received (a loss ratio of 65 percent was considered breakeven by the company in Personal Lines).

Source: Company records.

location. In addition, because of the town's location, population characteristics, and localized media, Syracuse offered a "perfect" test market, often used by consumer-goods businesses. A strong Eastern agent in the area was eager to participate.

2. Third-quarter results revealed that ActionShop I had an underwriting profit of $13,424 but a net operating loss of $83,398, and that ActionShop II had a small underwriting loss of $3,991 and a net operating loss of $118,346. Net operating losses were largely attributed by the Marketing Department to high development costs, which could be offset by an expanded ActionShop network through franchising, and low start-up income flow (Exhibits 16-6 and 16-7).

3. The Marketing Department reported that the agent training program was a great success in teaching the basics of prospecting and selling by utilizing proven agency techniques—i.e., cold calls, direct mail, telephone solicitations. In addition, a highly flexible local advertising package would soon be ready for agents purchasing an ActionShop franchise. Agencies involved in the ActionShop pilot were pleased with the training and felt they had benefited from involvement in the pilot.

4. The Underwriting Department revealed that All-Driver was experiencing rapidly deteriorating underwriting results. These were severely impacting the production and profits of ActionShops I and II. However, retention of ActionShop business was running 10 percent and 25 percent higher than that sold through normal distribution channels in the same locations. This was considered a benefit, as the cost of retaining

business is lower than the cost of generating new business, all things being equal.

Knauth put the report on his desk and addressed his staff:

O.K., that's where we stand today. The question is, where do we go from here? What recommendations do I make to our senior vice-president?

PART EIGHT
Strategic Tools

CHAPTER 17 - Selected Techniques and Models

CHAPTER 17
Selected Techniques and Models

---

*The Red Queen said: "Now, here, it takes all the running you
can do to keep in the same place. If you want to get somewhere
else, you must run at least twice as fast as that."*

Lewis Carroll
Alice in Wonderland

Strategy development is by no means an easy job. Not only must
decision makers review a variety of inside factors, but they must also incorporate the impact of environmental changes in order to work out a
viable strategy. Strategists have become increasingly aware that the old
way of "muddling through" is not adequate to take care of the complexities involved in designing a future for the corporation. The 1970s were
especially difficult years, the uncertainties and dilemmas of the end of the
decade suggesting the shape of things to come in following years.

Economic uncertainty, shortages of energy and basic raw materials,
leveling off of productivity, international competition, tight money and
inflation, political upheavals, and environmental problems pose new challenges which corporations will have to cope with in the 1980s and 1990s
when planning their strategies. There is, therefore, a need for systematic
procedures for formulating strategy. This chapter discusses selected systems or models and techniques which serve as aids in strategy development.

A model or technique may be defined as an instrument which serves
as an aid in searching, screening, analyzing, selecting, and implementing
a course of action. Since marketing strategy interfaces with and/or affects
the perspectives of the entire corporation, the models and techniques of
the entire science of management can be considered relevant here. In this
chapter seven models or frameworks which have direct application to marketing strategies are dealt with. Discussed in this chapter are the experience curve concept, the PIMS model, the model for measuring sustainable
growth, the delphi technique, trend-impact analysis, cross-impact analysis,
and scenario building.

EXPERIENCE CURVE CONCEPT

Experience shows that practice makes perfect. It is common knowledge that beginners are slow and clumsy and that with practice they gen-

erally improve to the point where they can reach their own permanent levels of skill. As anyone with business experience knows, the initial period of a new venture or expansion into a new area will frequently not be profitable for some time. Many factors—such as making the name known to potential customers—are often cited as reasons for this. In brief, even the most unsophisticated businessperson acknowledges that experience or learning leads to improvement. Unfortunately the significance of experience is realized only in abstract terms, and its implications for strategy formulation are hardly ever considered. For example, managers in a new and unprofitable situation tend to think of experience in vague terms without ever analyzing it in terms of cost. This statement applies to all the functions of a business except production management, where cost improvements are commonly sought.

As growth continues, we anticipate greater efficiency and more productive output. But how much improvement can one reasonably expect? Generally management makes an arbitrary decision to ascertain what output reflects the optimum level. Obviously, in the great majority of situations, this decision is primarily based on pure conjecture. Ideally, however, one should be able to use historical data to predict the cost-volume relationship and learning patterns. Many companies have, in fact, developed their own learning curves, but only in the area of production or manufacturing, where tangible data are readily available and most variables can be quantified.

Several years ago the Boston Consulting Group observed that the concept of experience is not limited to production alone. The experience curve concept embraces almost all cost areas of a business:

> Unlike the well-known "learning curve" and "progress function," the experience curve effect is observed to encompass all costs—capital, administrative, research and marketing—and to have transferred impact from technological displacements and product evolution.[1]

In the rest of this section the application of the experience curve tool to marketing will be examined.

Historical Perspective

The experience effect was first observed in the aircraft industry. Since in this industry the expense incurred in building the first unit is exceptionally high, any reduction in the cost of succeeding units is readily apparent and becomes extremely pertinent in any management decision regarding future production. The phenomenon of an experience pattern in a manufacturing operation was first developed by the commander of Wright-Patterson Air Force Base in Dayton, Ohio, around 1925. It was observed that an "80 percent air frame curve" could be developed in the

---

[1]*Perspective on Experience* (Boston: The Boston Consulting Group, 1970), p. 1.

manufacture of airplanes. This curve depicts a 20 percent improvement every time production doubles (i.e., the fourth unit requires 80 percent as much time as the second unit, and so on).[2] Studies of the aircraft industry suggest that this rate of improvement seems to prevail consistently over the range of production under study; hence the label "experience" is applied to the curve. Even though this fact was fairly well established in the aircraft industry, it was not until eleven years later, in 1936, that T. D. Wright published the first account of this concept.[3]

Implications

Although the significance of the experience curve concept is corporate-wide, it bears most heavily on the setting of marketing objectives and the pricing decision. As already mentioned, according to the experience curve concept, all costs go down as experience increases. Thus, if a company acquired a higher market share, its costs would decline, enabling it to reduce prices. The lowering of prices would enable the company to acquire a still higher market share. The process is unending as long as the market continues to grow. But as a matter of strategy, the company may be wise, while aiming at a dominant position in the industry, to stop short of raising the eyebrows of the Antitrust Division of the U.S. Department of Justice.

During the growth phase, the company would keep making the desired profit. But in order to provide for this growth, the company would need to reinvest the profits. In fact, further resources might need to be diverted from elsewhere to support such growth. Once the growth comes to an end, the product would make available huge cash throw-offs which could be invested in a new product.

The Boston Consulting Group (BCG) claims that in the case of a second product, the accumulated experience of the first product should provide an extra advantage to the firm in reducing costs. However, experience is transferable only imperfectly. There is a transfer effect between identical products in different locations, but the transfer effect between different products occurs only if the products are somewhat the same (i.e., belong to the same family). This is true, for instance, in the case of the marketing-cost component of two products which are distributed through the same trade channel. Even in this case, however, the loss of buyer "franchise" can result in some lack of experience transferability.

---

[2]W. B. Hirschmann, "Profit from the Learning Curve," *Harvard Businiss Review,* January–February, 1964, pp. 125–139. See also John M. Dutton and Annie Thomas, "Treating Progress Functions as a Managerial Opportunity," *The Academy of Management Review,* April, 1984.

[3]T. D. Wright, "Factors Affecting the Cost of Airplanes," *Journal of Aeronautical Science,* February, 1936, pp. 122–128.

Exhibit 17-1 presents a diagram of the implications of the experience concept.

Some of the BCG's claims about the experience effect are hard to substantiate—in fact, may even be disputed—until enough empirical studies have been done on the subject.[4] But even in its simplest form the concept adds new importance to the market-share strategy.

Conceptual Framework for Marketing Application

The application of the experience curve principle requires sorting out various marketing costs and projecting their behavior for different sales volumes. It is hoped that the analyses will show a close relationship between the increase in cumulative sales volume and the decline in costs. The widening gap between volume and costs establishes the company's flexibility in cutting prices in order to gain higher market share.

The decline in costs is logical and occurs for reasons such as the following:

1. Economies of scale (e.g., lower advertising media cost)
2. Increase in efficiency across the board (e.g., ability of the salesperson to reduce time per call)
3. Technological advances

Conceivably, four different techniques could be used to project the cost at different levels of volume: regression, simulation, analogy, and intuition. Since historical information on growing products may be lacking, the regression technique may not go very far toward the projection of costs in future years. Simulation is a possibility, but it continues to be rare in practice since it is strenuous. Drawing an analogy between the subject product and the one that has matured perhaps provides the most feasible means of projecting various marketing costs as a function of cumulative sales. But analogy alone may not suffice. As with any other managerial decision, analogy may have to be combined with intuition.

The cost characteristics of experience curves can be observed in all types of costs, whether they are labor costs, advertising costs, overhead costs, marketing costs, development costs, or manufacturing costs. Thus, marketing costs, as well as those for production, R&D, accounting, service, etc., should be combined to see how the total cost varies with volume. Further, total costs over different ranges of volume should be projected while considering the company's ability to finance an increased volume of business, risk proneness, and relations with the Antitrust Division.

---

[4]George S. Day and David B. Montgomery, "Diagnosing the Experience Curve," *Journal of Marketing*, Spring, 1983, pp. 44–58. See also Walter Kiechel III, "The Decline of the Experience Curve," *Fortune*, October 5, 1981, p. 139.

EXHIBIT 17-1   Schematic Presentation of Implications of the Experience Concept

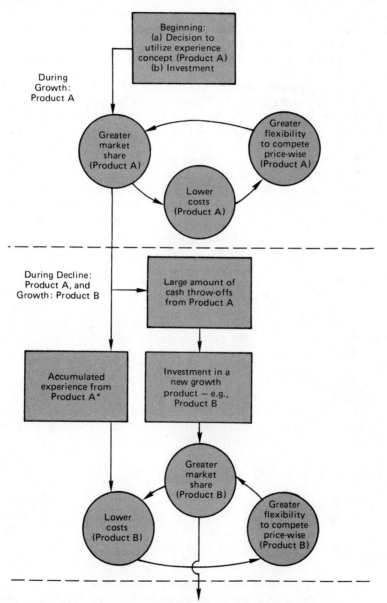

During
Growth:
Product A

During Decline:
Product A, and
Growth: Product B

Process continues through successive products

*An assumption is made here that Product B is closely related to Product A.

Source: Subhash C. Jain, "Translating Experience into Growth," *Managerial Planning*, March–April, 1975, p. 2. Reprinted by permission.

Each element of cost included in the total cost may have a different slope on a graph. The aggregation of these elements will not necessarily produce a straight line on logarithmic coordinates. Thus the cost-volume relationship curve is necessarily an approximation of a trend line. Also, the cost derivatives of the curve are not based on accounting costs, but on the accumulated cash input divided by the accumulated end-product output. The cost decline of the experience curve is the rate of change in that ratio.

The management should establish a market share objective which projects well into the future. Estimates should be made of the timing of price cuts in order to achieve designated market share. If at any time a competitor happens to challenge the firm's market share position, the firm should go all out to protect its market share and never surrender it without an awareness of its value. Needless to say, the perspective of the entire corporation will have to be changed if the gains expected from the market share strategy are to become a reality. Thus, proper coordination among different functions becomes essential for the timely implementation of related tasks.

Prerequisites for Application

While the experience effect is independent of the life cycle, of growth rate, and of initial market share, as a matter of strategy it is safer to base one's move on experience when the following conditions are operating: (1) the product is in the early stages of growth in its life cycle; (2) no one competitor holds a dominant position in the market; (3) the product is not amenable to nonprice competition—e.g., emotional appeals, packaging. Since the concept demands taking a big offensive in a battle that might last many years, a well-drawn long-range plan should be in existence. The top management should be capable of undertaking risks and going through the initial period of fast activity involved in sudden moves to enlarge the company's operations; the company should also have enough resources to support the enlargement of operations.

Barriers to Application to Marketing

The experience effect has been widely accepted as a basis for strategy in the aircraft industry, and some application can also be found in the petroleum industry and maintenance-related areas. The application of this concept to marketing has been minimal. The following reasons are given for this:

1. Skepticism that improvement can continue.
2. Difficulty with the exact quantification of different relationships in marketing.
3. Inability to recognize experience patterns even though they are already occurring.

4. Lack of awareness that the improvement pattern can be subjectively approximated and that the concept can apply to groups of employees, as well as to individual performance across the board in different functions of the business.
5. Inability to predict the effect of future technological advances, which can badly distort any historical data.
6. Accounting practices which may make it difficult to segregate costs adequately.

Despite these obstacles, however, the concept is too exciting for one to give up striving for its smooth application to marketing.

Conclusion

The acceptance of the experience concept leads naturally to recognizing the importance of gaining and sustaining market share. The linkage is direct. Increases in relative volume result in increases in relative experience; increases in relative experience result in cost advantages over less-experienced competitors.

Strategy is based upon competitive differences. If the experience curve permits a business to predict with confidence that one competitor can and should have a lower cost than another one, then the experience curve also permits prediction that the low-cost competitor can and should displace the higher-cost competitor if it provides identical products to identical customers with identical values at identical margins.

The long-term profitability of a product is related to the producer's ability to increase and hold the market share and to the amount that must be spent in doing so. There is, in fact, a conceptually best market share for each product. This "target" share is that which provides the greatest long-term value, measured in terms of the present worth of all future cash flows related to the product.[5]

Assume that a business unit has a cost-experience curve for one of its products and can make assumptions regarding the product's industry growth rate and the manner in which price will decline with industry experience. This information is sufficient to project the future cash flows of the product under the assumptions of maintaining current market share and increasing share to any specified level. From this, the incremental cash flows attributable to the share increase can be determined, and the present value of these incremental cash flows can be computed with the use of the discounted cash-flow technique. This present value can then be balanced against the estimated cost of obtaining the increase in market share. This cost typically takes the form of "expensed investments" for price reduction or such nonprice inducements as improved quality or ser-

---

[5]See Paul N. Bloom and Philip Kotler, "Strategies for High Market-Share Companies," *Harvard Business Review,* November–December, 1975, pp. 63–72.

vice. When the values of specific share increases are traded off against the costs of achieving them, the highest attainable market share which justifies the cost can be determined. Plans may then be developed for acquiring this target share. The type of analysis described above can be very useful in developing product/market strategy.[6]

Increasing market share is proportionately much easier, less costly, and more profitable with products having higher growth rates. Growth rates higher than that of the economy, however, cannot be sustained indefinitely. The industry growth rate for all products eventually must slow down. Because it is difficult to gain share in slow-growth markets, the objective of a producer in a rapidly growing market must be to achieve cost dominance. The competitor who has the lowest unit cost when growth subsides is in a nearly impenetrable position.

Achieving cost dominance requires a long-term perspective. Cash spending for capacity may exceed earnings until the growth rate declines. If it is a true growth product, however, the future cash inflows for the dominant producer will have a present worth far higher than the current cash outflows.

Once growth slows down, the strategy of the dominant producer may simply be to retain its dominance at the least cost. The producer can do so by continuing to achieve the full cost-reduction potential of the experience gains, thus prompting undesirable investments in increased share on the part of the competitors. If, instead, the high-market-share producer in a slow-growth market fails to maintain the industry norm of cost reduction (by failing to continue product development or process improvement), the producer will gradually relinquish its dominance.

Even if the high-share producer remains cost-effective, infringement on its dominance will be invited if the market is viewed by current or potential competitors as an attractive one for significant investment. This will occur if the producer holds a price umbrella which makes the product particularly profitable for less-experienced competitors despite their higher unit cost levels or if the producer gives the competitors reason to believe that it will not protect its dominant position.

One of the dominant producer's main weapons against such infringement is price or, equivalently, nonprice inducements. The objective of the pricing strategy must be to find the balance between getting the highest possible profit and maintaining market share and, hence, the cost advantage and the stability of the market. The concepts and techniques of experience curve analysis can be invaluable in helping the dominant producer find this balance.

A sound strategy for the dominant producer is to keep the constant dollar price, as plotted on its experience curve graph, parallel to the cost curve and at a height where the profitability of the strongest competitor

---

[6]"Experience Curves Applied to Product Strategy," an informal statement by the Boston Consulting Group, 1969.

is just tolerable. This strategy, however, should be tempered by an assessment of the competition. If, for example, a less-experienced competitor is viewed by the dominant producer as less competent in terms of seeing the strategic advantage of increased share, having a lower appraisal of the market's potential, or having inadequate resources to commit to buying an increased share, then the dominant producer may be able to maintain a higher price without risking market-share erosion. Similarly, if the dominant producer can convince the competitor that attempts to increase share will be aggressively countered, this is also reason to set a higher price than would otherwise be set.

The approach to price strategy vis-à-vis the experience curve concept is significantly different from traditional pricing theory. The traditional approach is to lower the price only if unit margin times volume (considering price sensitivity) will be increased. This approach emphasizes short-term profitability and ignores both the experience effect and competition. The dominant producer who follows it is susceptible to the competitor who is willing to sacrifice short-term profit by reducing price in return for increased market share and the resulting greater long-term profits.

It can be seen that once industry growth slows down, marginal producers are virtually at the mercy of the leader. If the leader is and has been cost-effective and follows a pricing strategy which makes investment in increased share undesirable for its competitors, there are only three alternatives open to the other producers: (1) to be satisfied with a marginal return, (2) to find a product/market segment for concentration in which there is a good chance for dominance, or (3) to get out of the market entirely.

The strategy-development activity of the smaller competitor in a slower-growth market must begin with an assessment of the dominant producer. The types of questions to be asked are: Is the dominant producer losing cost-effectiveness? Has it raised a price umbrella? How quickly, if at all, could it meet a price cut or nonprice inducements? In view of the total product mix, how important is the dominant producer's current profitability in regard to this product? The answers to such questions should form the basis for a decision on whether attempting to displace the leading producer on a broad scale is worthwhile.[7]

If the smaller producer concludes that the industry leader is not vulnerable in terms of the total product/market, the former should explore the possibility of concentrating all of its resources on those segments which maximize its strengths while minimizing those of the leader. The process of segmentation is one of making explicit choices from among the

---

[7]See Carolyn Y. Woo, "Evaluation of Strategies and Performance of Low ROI Market Share Leaders," *Strategic Management Journal*, April/June, 1983, pp. 123–125.

various product characteristics and customer requirements within the total market on which to focus the attempt for dominance.

The smaller competitor's decision on whether and where to concentrate should be based on an assessment of its functional skills (development, production, marketing, distribution, etc.) relative to the market leader and of the importance of these skills in serving specific market segments. An analysis to determine in which skill areas the producer is most experienced and, hence, most likely to have a cost advantage will facilitate the decision.

This same segmentation strategy may be desirable for the smaller producer in a high-growth market if it is determined that competing with larger producers on a broad scale is unlikely to result in dominance before the industry growth subsides. If successful segmentation is not possible, the best strategy for the smaller producer in the high-growth market is to withdraw.

To summarize, the experience curve concept leads to the conclusion that all producers must achieve and maintain the full cost-reduction potential of their experience gains if they hope to survive. Furthermore, the experience framework has implications for strategy development, as shown in Exhibit 17-2. The appendix at the end of this chapter describes the experience curve construction procedure, showing how the relationship between costs and accumulated experience can be empirically developed.

PROFIT IMPACT OF MARKETING STRATEGY (PIMS)

The PIMS program was initiated in 1972 at the Marketing Science Institute, a nonprofit organization associated with the Harvard Business School, to determine the profit impact of marketing strategies. As a matter of fact, the initiation of this program is ascribed to the General Electric

EXHIBIT 17-2   Experience Curves: Strategy Implications

		MARKET POWER	
		HIGH	LOW
INDUSTRY GROWTH RATE	HIGH	Continue to invest in increased market share up to "target" level.	Assess competition; then either invest heavily in increased share, segment market, or withdraw.
	LOW	Obtain highest possible earnings consistent with maintaining market share.	Assess competition; then either challenge, segment market, or withdraw.

Company. In 1960, the vice-president of marketing services at GE authorized a large-scale project (called PROM, for "profitability optimization model") to examine the above question. Several years of effort finally produced a computer-based model that identified the major factors responsible for a great deal of the variation in return on investment. Since the data used in the model came from diverse markets and industries, it is often referred to as a "cross-sectional" model. Even today cross-sectional models are popularly used at GE.

The scope of the PIMS program increased so much and its popularity gained such momentum that a few years ago its administration moved to the Strategic Planning Institute, a new organization established for PIMS.

The PIMS program is based on the experience of more than 200 companies in more than 1,700 "businesses." "Business" is synonymous with "strategic business unit" (SBU) and is defined as an operative unit which sells a distinct set of products to an identifiable group of customers in competition with a well-defined set of competitors. Essentially, PIMS is a cross-sectional study of the strategic experience of profit organizations. The information on experience has been gathered from the businesses in the form of about 200 pieces of data supplied by them in a standardized format. The gathered information deals with such items as:

1. Market served (in terms of growth, stability, etc.)
2. Competitive environment (number and size of competitors and customers)
3. Position of the business (market share, comparative product quality, comparative price, etc.)
4. Strategy employed (changes in position, discretionary budget allocations, product quality, etc.)
5. Operating results obtained (profit, cash flow, etc.)[8]

Overall Results

The PIMS project (Phases I and II) indicated that the profitability of a business is affected by 37 basic factors, explaining the more than 80 percent profitability variation among the businesses studied. Of the 37 basic factors, six proved to be of primary importance (Exhibit 17-3). Among these six factors, investment intensity ranked first and market share second in terms of their impact on profitability.

The PIMS program actually has two models, one for predicting ROI and another for predicting cash flow. The latter model shows that a large variance in cash flow among businesses is explained by 19 factors. Some of the variables in the cash-flow model were also found to be significant in the ROI model. The PIMS study is advocated on the grounds that it is necessary to learn about strategy from experience—something which

---

[8]See Sidney Schoeffler's speech delivered at the Strategic Planning Conference at Indiana University, November, 1975.

relationship of NCFO to ROI?

EXHIBIT 17-3   ROI and Key Profit Influences

Return on investment (ROI):
The ratio of net pretax operating income to average investment. Operating income is what is available after deduction of allocated corporate overhead expenses but before deduction of any financial charges on assets employed. "Investment" equals equity plus long-term debt or, equivalently, total assets employed minus current liabilities attributed to the business.

Market share:
The ratio of dollar sales by a business, in a given time period, to total sales by all competitors in the same market. The "market" includes all of the products or services, customer types, and geographic areas that are directly related to the activities of the business. For example, it includes all products and services that are competitive with those sold by the business.

Product (service) quality:
The quality of each participating company's offerings, appraised in the following terms: What was the percentage of sales of products or services from each business in each year which were superior to those of competitors? What was the percentage of equivalent products? Inferior products?

Marketing expenditures:
Total costs for sales force, advertising, sales promotion, marketing research, and marketing administration. The figures do not include costs of physical distribution.

R&D expenditures:
Total costs of product development and process improvement, including those costs incurred by corporate-level units which can be directly attributed to the individual business.

Investment intensity:
Ratio of total investment to sales.

Corporate diversity:
An index which reflects 1) the number of different 4-digit Standard Industrial Classification industries in which a corporation operates, 2) the percentage of total corporate employment in each industry, and 3) the degree of similarity or difference among the industries in which it participates.

Source: Reprinted by permission of the *Harvard Business Review*. Exhibit from "Impact of Strategic Planning on Profit Performance" by Sidney Schoeffler, Robert D. Buzzell, and Donald F. Heany, March–April, 1974, p. 140. Copyright © 1974 by the President and Fellows of Harvard College; all rights reserved.

---

requires diversity. From this diverse experience have been derived "principles" which are usually expressed in the form of a 3 × 3 matrix (three levels of each of three variables with ROI as the criterion). For example, Exhibit 17-4 shows that low market share combined with high investment intensity leads to a very poor return on investment, and vice versa.

EXHIBIT 17-4   Impact of Strategic Planning on Profit Performance: Investment Intensity and Market Share

INVESTMENT INTENSITY	MARKET SHARE		
	UNDER 12%	12%–26%	OVER 26%
Under 45%	21.2%	26.9%	34.6%
45%–71%	8.6	13.1	26.2
Over 71%	2.0	6.7	15.7

Source: Reprinted by permission of the *Harvard Business Review*. Exhibit from "Impact of Strategic Planning on Profit Performance" by Sidney Schoeffler, Robert D. Buzzell, and Donald F. Heany, March–April, 1974, p. 143. Copyright © 1974 by the President and Fellows of Harvard College; all rights reserved.

Relevance of the Program

Not only does the PIMS program provide interesting insights into relationships among crucial variables in a business setting, but it can also be used by a business seeking strategy guidance. In 1977 the PIMS program began providing four different sets of output reports to participating businesses: the par report, the cash flow par report, the strategy sensitivity report, and the optimum strategy report. The first two reports analyze the performance of a business in the last three years and evaluate the contribution of a number of factors to its return on investment and cash flow. The third report predicts the outcome of various strategic moves for both the long and the short run.

Exhibit 17-5 shows an example of a par report. The par ROI shown here is 26.3 percent, while the average ROI of all PIMS businesses is 16.7 percent. The former figure represents the return normally expected from an average management team with average luck. The net difference between the average ROI and the PIMS par ROI for the business under consideration is called the "impact of strategic factors on par ROI." Thus, for the business analyzed in Exhibit 17-5, the impact works out to be 9.6 percent (i.e., 26.3 − 16.7), based on rating of the seven categories listed. The 35 separate factors included in these categories are listed in Exhibit 17-6.

A sample of a cash flow par report is shown in Exhibit 17-7. The average cash flow for all PIMS businesses was 2.0 percent, while the cash flow par for the business studied here was 0.3 percent. The difference, −1.7 percent, is based on rating of the 19 factors listed in Exhibit 17-7.

A strategy sensitivity report is shown in Exhibit 17-8. This report is based on the strategy move of "no planned change." It was prepared

**EXHIBIT 17-5   Sample PIMS Report: Par Return on Investment (Pretax)
1972–1974**

Par return on investment is an estimate of the pretax return on investment (ROI)
that in 1972–74 was normal for businesses facing market and industry conditions
equivalent to those of your business and occupying a similar market position.

For Business No. 87041, Pretax
Par ROI 26.3%
Actual ROI 25.4
Impact on Par ROI of the Factors by Category

Par ROI equals the sum of the total impact and the average ROI of all businesses
in the PIMS data base.

CATEGORY	IMPACT ON PAR ROI (PRETAX)%
Attractiveness of business environment	3.1
Strength of your competitive position	0.1
Differentiation of competitive position	1.2
Effectiveness of use of investment	13.4
Discretionary budget allocation	−6.8
Company factors	−1.2
Change/action factors	−0.2
Total impact	9.6
Average ROI, all PIMS businesses	16.7
Par ROI, this business	26.3%

Source: From Derek Abell, "Tex-Fiber Industries—Petroloid Products Division
(D)," p. 3. Harvard Business School Case 9-577-040. Copyright © 1976
by the President and Fellows of Harvard College. Reprinted by permission.

assuming the "most likely" environment, as shown in Exhibit 17-9. For the
strategy sensitivity report, the model based the forecast of trends in the
market environment and in the cost structure on the firm's recent performance. This forecast was then used to predict future performance. Although the strategy sensitivity report shown in Exhibit 17-8 is based on
the strategy of "no planned change," the model could be used to spell out
the likely impact of various changes in the strategy; i.e., market share,
degree of vertical integration, and investment intensity could be varied
and the probable outcomes of such moves could be examined.

Finally, the optimum strategy report is concerned with isolating a
particular combination of strategic moves which optimize a particular criterion (e.g., profit, cash, or growth). This, again, is based on the past experience of others in similar situations.

PIMS operates from the premise that certain structural factors (e.g.,
market position, capital intensity, etc.) of a business influence, if not de-

EXHIBIT 17-6 Sample PIMS Report: The Impact on Par ROI of Each Factor in the Par Profit Equation (Points of ROI)

FACTORS	BASE PERIOD VALUES FOR:			IMPACT OF FACTOR	
	ALL PIMS BUSI-NESSES	THIS BUSINESS	THIS TYPE OF BUSINESS	ON ROI	PAR (%)
Attractiveness of Business Environment					
Industry (SIC) growth, long-run	8.0	21.3	8.2	3.2	
Market growth, short-run	5.9	21.4	5.9	1.4	
Industry exports (% totl shpts)	7.6	0.0	9.6	−1.1	
Sales direct to end user (%)	51.0	60.0	64.5	−0.4	0.1
Strength of Your Competitive Position					
Your market position	22.5	20.5	24.2	−0.1	
Share of 4 largest firms (SIC)	51.6	72.0	52.1	0.6	
Instability of your mkt share	2.9	0.9	3.3	1.1	
Buyer fragmentation index	13.6	15.0	13.8	−1.5	
Differentiation of Competitive Position					1.2
Price relative to competition	2.7	3.0	2.7	−1.2	
Relative pay scale	6.4	6.0	6.4	−0.4	
Product quality	23.2	0.0	24.7	1.1	
New product sales (% totl sales)	12.1	20.0	12.1	0.6	
Manufacturing costs/sales	30.7	22.0	33.6	1.1	
Effectiveness of Use of Investment					13.4
Investment intensity	63.8	61.9	71.3	−12.1	
Fixed capital intensity	57.5	78.2	61.2	−0.5	
Receivables/sales	14.4	12.9	14.9	0.2	
Vertical integration	58.8	81.4	60.1	17.5	
Capacity utilization	75.7	113.7	75.9	5.4	

EXHIBIT 17-6 continued

FACTORS	BASE PERIOD VALUES FOR:			IMPACT OF FACTOR	
	ALL PIMS BUSI-NESSES	THIS BUSINESS	THIS TYPE OF BUSINESS	ON ROI	PAR (%)
Raw & in proc. invent./purchase	33.2	35.2	39.3	0.2	
Sales/employees	47730.	50077.	42860.	2.7	−6.8
Discretionary Budget Allocation					
Mktg less sales forc exp/sales	4.1	14.6	3.0	−7.8	
R&D expenses/sales	2.9	4.8	3.4	1.1	−1.2
Company Factors					
Corporate payout (%)	62.0		63.2	−0.0	
Degree of corp diversification	2.1		2.3	−1.2	
Corporate size	1588.0		1431.0	0.0	
Growth rate of corporate sales	10.1		10.3	0.0	−0.2
Change/Action Factors					
Change in your market share	2.3	−3.4	3.1	−0.7	
Change in product quality	3.2	0.0	3.3	−0.0	
Change in price index	2.9	13.0	2.3	0.2	
Competitive market activity	0.1	−6.5	0.1	−0.0	
Change in capital intensity	−3.3	−22.7	−4.3	−0.7	
Change in vertical integr (%)	0.5	−9.2	0.3	0.6	
Point change adv & prom/sales	−0.1	−1.9	−0.1	−0.7	
Change in sales forc exp/sales	−0.3	−0.8	−0.3	−0.4	
Point change return on sales	1.1	0.2	1.3	1.4	

Notes

1. Components of "your market position" impact:

Your market share	22.5	20.5	24.2
Your market share/share big 3	54.3	37.0	58.8

2. Components of "investment intensity" impact:

Investment/sales	63.8	61.9	71.3
Investment/(value added −.5ni)	120.0	82.5	125.3

3. Only the combined net effect of "investment intensity," "vertical integration," and "sales/employees" should be given an interpretation, not the individual impacts:

$$-12.14 + 17.48 + 2.68 = 8.03$$

4. Interpretation of relative scales:

"Price relative to competition" "relative pay scale"

if "2" your price is higher   if "4" your pay scale is lower
"4"   lower   "8"   higher

Column 3, the means for this type of business (industrial), is for reference only and is not used to calculate the impacts except when used to replace missing data (noted with an *). Company factors are not shown for reasons of data security.

Source: From Derek Abell, "Tex-Fiber Industries—Petroloid Products Division (D)," pp. 4–5. Harvard Business School Case 9-577-040. Copyright © by the President and Fellows of Harvard College. Reprinted by permission.

EXHIBIT 17-7   PIMS Cash Flow Par Report

	PIMS MEAN	THIS BUSINESS	IMPACT	SENSITIVITY CHANGE OF	CHANGES IMPACT BY
Decision Use of Cash			-2.6		
1 Market share growth rate	3.2	-1.7	2.5	2.00	-1.02
2 Marketing expense growth rate	10.3	25.3	-1.6	2.00	-0.22
3 New product sales (% tot sales)	13.1	20.0	-1.0	5.00	-0.96
4 R&D expense/sales	2.4	4.8	-1.2	0.50	-0.34
5 Marketing expense/sales	10.3	18.1	-1.2	2.00	0.11
Change in Investment/Sales			3.6		
6 Point change investment/sales	-4.7	-7.3	3.6	2.00	-2.38
Forced Use of Cash			-7.0		
7 Real market growth, short run	8.2	21.7	-7.3	2.00	-1.07
8 Selling price growth rate	6.4	6.5	-0.1	1.00	-0.75
9 Industry (SIC) growth, long run	9.3	19.4	0.4	1.00	0.04

Strength of Competitive Position					
10 Market share	23.3	20.5	-0.8	5.00	1.23
Relative market share	60.6	37.0			
Differentiation from Competitors			-0.5		
11 Price relative to competition	1.030	1.000	0.0	0.01	-0.01
12 Relative product quality	23.5	0.0	-0.1	5.00	0.15
13 Price diff from competitors	0.040	0.000	-0.5	0.01	0.13
Capital and Production Structure			5.6		
14 Investment/sales	58.3	61.9	-2.3	5.00	-1.04
15 Vertical integration	59.8	82.5	5.8	2.00	0.62
16 Value added per employee	29.3	40.3	0.5	5.00	0.11
17 Capacity utilization	80.6	113.7U	1.7	5.00	0.00
18 Replacement value/GBV of P&E	185.4	180.0	-0.1	10.00	0.11
19 Employees unionized (%)	51.3	50.0	0.1	5.00	-0.08

(U) Capacity utilization compressed to upper limit of 110.0

EXHIBIT 17-8   PIMS Strategy Sensitivity Report: Version 002C (611010)-5 Details
STRATEGY MOVE: NO PLANNED CHANGE

	RECENT POSITION (1972–74)	DURING STRATEGY IMPLEMENTATION (1977)	NEW STEADY-STATE POSITION (1979)	NEW LONG-TERM POSITION (1984)
Net sales (current $)	476.4	643.0	803.3	1415.7
Net income	74.7	101.4	128.1	225.1
Average investment	294.8	345.3	472.6	862.4
Net cash flow	9.3	33.8	0.4	34.6
Return on investment	25.4%	29.4%	27.1%	26.1%
Return on sales	15.7%	15.8%	15.9%	15.9%
FACTORS:				
Competitive Position:				
Market share	20.5	20.8	21.1	21.1
Relative market share	37.0	37.7	38.3	38.3
Relative price index	3.0	3.1	3.0	3.0
Product quality	0.0	−12.5	−3.0	−3.0
Use of Investment:				
Investment/value added	82.5	73.0	78.6	81.3

Investment/sales	61.9	53.7	58.8	60.9
Fixed capital intensity	78.2	68.7	71.2	74.1
Net book/gross book value	52.9	49.6	54.0	54.7
Value added/sales	81.4	79.9	81.4	81.4
Working capital/sales	20.5	19.6	20.4	20.4
Capacity utilization	113.7	112.8	111.5	113.0
Sales/employees	50077.	50671.	53431.	61648.
Budget Allocations:				
Marketing expenses/sales	18.1	17.8	18.1	18.1
R&D expenses/sales	4.8	4.0	4.8	4.8
PERFORMANCE MEASURES:				
Discounted net income 10yr	816.2			
Discounted cash flow 10yr	99.7			
Average net income 3yr	92.5			
Discounted cash flow yield rate 10yr	15.1%			
Average return on investment 5yr	27.9%			

Source: From Derek Abell, "Tex-Fiber Industries—Petroloid Products Division (D)," p. 14. Harvard Business School Case 9-577-040. Copyright © 1976 by the President and Fellows of Harvard College. Reprinted by permission.

EXHIBIT 17-9   PIMS Strategy Sensitivity Report: Version 002C (611010)-5 Summary

	"Most Likely" Environment Key Assumptions 1975–78	1978–84
Industry sales growth rate	10.0%	12.0%
Annual change in selling price	5.0%	3.0%
Annual change in wage rates	8.0%	
Annual change in material cost	8.0%	
Annual change in plant cost	8.0%	6.0%
Time discount rate	10.0%	
Capital charge rate	0.0%	
Tax rate	50.0%	
Dividend payout rate	0.0%	
"Quantum" of additional capacity	2.0%	
Targeted capacity utilization	113.0%	
Annual depreciation rate	12.0%	

	Actual Historical	Assumed Future
Deviations from:		
Par ROI	−1.3	−1.3
Delta ROI	−3.0	0.0

Source: From Derek Abell, "Tex-Fiber Industries—Petroloid Products Division (D)," p. 12. Harvard Business School Case 9-577-040. Copyright © 1976 by the President and Fellows of Harvard College. Reprinted by permission.

termine, the return of that business. The PIMS approach is to gather data on as many actual business experiences as possible and to search for relationships that appear to have the most significant effect on the ROI. A model of these relationships is then developed so that an estimate of a business's ROI can be made from the structural factors describing the business. Obviously the PIMS conceptual framework must be modified on occasion in the real world. For example, repositioning the structural factors may be impossible and the costs of doing so may be prohibitive. Besides, actual performance may reflect some element of luck or some unusual event. Additionally, the results may be influenced by the transitional effect of a conscious change in strategic direction. Despite these reservations, the PIMS framework can be beneficial in the following ways:

1. It provides a realistic and consistent method for establishing potential return levels for individual businesses.
2. It stimulates managerial thinking on the reasons for deviations from par performance.

3. It provides insight into strategic moves which will improve the par ROI.

4. It encourages a more discerning appraisal of business unit performance.

GROWTH POTENTIAL

Growth is a common objective of business organizations. Growth requires resources; therefore, adequate management of corporate resources constitutes an important part of a strategic planning process. Zakon has said:

> Most importantly, in an environment where the perception of a corporation's worth—and hence the long-run interests of its shareholders—is largely in terms of growth, the chief financial officer possesses what for many firms are the most potent strategic weapons. The firm that grows the fastest is the one which generates enough money to add to its assets at the fastest rate. The firm that grows the fastest is the one which sustains the highest rate of return on its equity capital (and reinvests these funds). The firm that grows the fastest is the one that brings to bear the greatest force of resources in the face of its competitors.[9]

Resources for growth can be generated either internally or externally. Internally, resources are provided through retention of earnings. The amount of earnings that can be plowed back is a function of dividend payout. Among the two external sources, debt capital costs less than equity capital. But a corporation cannot use debt indiscriminately for a variety of reasons, an important one being the unwillingness of management to accept the risk attached to a high debt ratio. Interest on debt is a fixed expense which must be appropriated regardless of the company's profit position. Thus, when times are bad and profits low, debt further aggravates the situation by absorbing profits or by further increasing losses. Finally, there are limits to the amount of debt a corporation can raise. As far as equity is concerned, new issues of stock may dilute existing stockholders' equity, and there is a point beyond which the corporation cannot go if it will hurt the stockholders' interest. Besides, money market conditions may not be favorable enough for the corporation to raise money by issuing stock. In essence, then, in order to maximize its growth, a company needs to sustain the optimum mix of strategic resources. This, of course, varies according to place, time, and amounts involved.

The sustainable growth rate for a company can be determined to an extent by the rate at which it can generate funds for investment in growth businesses and by the return it can expect to earn on these funds.

---

[9]Alan Zakon, *Growth and Financial Strategies* (Boston: The Boston Consulting Group, 1968), p. 3.

Usually retained earnings, debt, and new equity constitute the sources of funds. The availability of funds depends upon dividend payout and capital turnover. Finally, rate of return and the risk characteristics of investment projects will determine the effectiveness of their use. Thus, a company's perspectives regarding debt, dividends, and rate of return underlie the growth rate the company can sustain.

The relationship between debt, dividends, and rate of return and their impacts on corporate growth can be studied with reference to the following formula:

$$g = \frac{D}{E}(r - i) + rp \qquad$$ where g = rate of growth in earnings
D = debt
E = equity
i = interest rate
r = return on assets
p = percent of earnings retained[10]

Hypothetical data can be used to find the growth rate for a hypothetical company, as follows:

$$D = 10.0 \text{ million} \qquad p = 50\%$$
$$E = 10.0 \text{ million} \qquad i = 6\%$$
$$r = .7/10 = .07$$

$$g = \frac{10}{10}(.07 - .03)(.5) + (.07)(.5) = 5.5\%$$

Thus, for the hypothetical company discussed here, the sustainable growth rate comes out to be 5.5 percent. To achieve the highest achievable growth, it is necessary to combine rate of return, debt, and dividends in an optimum fashion. While a firm should work out its own optimum mix of strategic resources, it is unwise to emphasize one factor at the expense of others since this can put a major burden on corporate performance. To elucidate the point, let us compute the effect of a 10 percent change in each variable at a time, holding the others constant. This is shown in Exhibit 17-10. The changes in each of these variables affect growth differently, earning power being the most effective. But a positive change in earning power cannot be achieved at the discretion of management. Next to earning power is the plowing back of earnings, which seems to have an impact on growth almost equal to that of earnings. As far as the debt-equity ratio is concerned, small increases in leverage do not make much difference. Thus, in order to have a noticeable effect on growth because of leverage, the increase in debt must be substantial. Changes in interest rate do not seem to be very influential. In practice, the position of these

---

[10]*Ibid.*, p. 10.

EXHIBIT 17-10   Impact of Different Variables on Growth

VARIABLE	GROWTH RATE	CHANGE IN GROWTH IN RESPONSE TO A 10% CHANGE IN VARIABLE
Earning Power		
6.3%	4.80%	
7.0%	5.50%	
7.7%	6.20%	12.7%
Interest Rate		
3.3%	5.35%	
3.0%	5.50%	
2.7%	5.65%	2.7%
Debt-Equity Ratio		
0.9:1.0	5.30%	
1.0:1.0	5.50%	
1.1:1.0	5.70%	3.6%
Earning Retention		
45.0%	4.95%	
50.0%	5.50%	
55.0%	6.05%	10.0%

variables must be set in combination with each other so that growth can be maximized at the discretion of management by adjusting the values of different variables. The technique of computer simulation can be used to figure out the optimum combination. Having discovered the maximum growth that is achievable with the given inputs, the management can specify the measurement objectives (i.e., return on investment, return on stockholders' equity, and the pretax profit desired).

DELPHI TECHNIQUE

The delphi technique, named after Apollo's oracle at Delphi, is a method of making forecasts based on expert opinion. Traditionally, expert opinions were pooled in a committee situation. The delphi technique was developed to overcome the weaknesses of the committee method. Wedgewood lists some of the problems that occur when issues are discussed in committees:

1. The influence of a dominant individual.
2. The introduction of a lot of redundant or irrelevant material into the committee workings.
3. Group pressure which places a premium on compromise.

4. It is a slow, expensive, and sometimes painful way to reach a decision.
5. The difficulty of holding members accountable for the actions of the group.[11]

All of the above factors provide certain psychological drawbacks to people in face-to-face communication situations. Often, because people may feel pressure to conform, the most popular solution, instead of the best one, prevails.

With the delphi technique, a staff coordinator questions selected individuals on various issues. The following is a sample of questions asked:

1. The probability of a future event occurring. Example: By what year do you think there will be widespread use of robot services for refuse collection, as household slaves, as sewer inspectors, etc.?
   a. 1980 b. 1990 c. 2000 d. 2010
   e. 2020 f. 2030 g. 2040 h. 2050
2. How desirable is the event in question 1?
   a. needed desperately b. desirable c. undesirable but possible
3. What is the feasibility of the event in question 1?
   a. highly feasible b. likely c. unlikely but possible
4. What is your familiarity with the material in question 1?
   a. fair b. good c. excellent

The coordinator compiles the responses, splitting them into three groups: lower, upper, and inner. The division into groups may vary from one investigation to another. Frequently, however, the lower and upper groups are 10 percent each, while the inner group takes the remaining 80 percent. When a person makes a response in either the upper or lower group, it is customary to ask him or her the reasons for the "extreme" opinion.

In the next round the respondents are given the same questionnaire along with a summary of the results of the first round. The data feedback includes the majority consensus and minority opinion. During the second round the respondents are asked to specify by what year the particular product or service will come to exist with 50 percent probability and 90 percent probability. Results are once again compiled and fed back. This process of repeating rounds can be continued indefinitely. However, rarely has any research to date been conducted past the sixth round. In recent years the delphi technique has been refined by the use of interactive computer programs to obtain inputs from experts, to present summary estimates, and to store revised judgments in data files, retrievable at user terminals.

---

[11]H. C. Wedgewood, "Fewer Camels, More Horses: Where Committees Go Wrong," *Personnel*, July–August, 1967, p. 64.

The delphi technique is gradually becoming important for long-range forecasting. The Rand Corporation has done extensive research on the technique.[12] The delphi technique has been used primarily to predict future events objectively. In 1970, according to *Business Week,* about 50 to 100 corporations were using this technique for forecasting purposes.[13] Since then, many more corporations must have begun to use the technique.

Some of the advantages of the delphi technique are listed below:

1. It is a rapid and efficient way to gain objective information from a group of experts.
2. It involves less effort for a respondent to answer a well-designed questionnaire than to participate in a conference or write a paper.
3. It can be highly motivating for a group of experts to see the responses of knowledgeable persons.
4. The use of systematic procedures applies an air of objectivity to the outcomes.
5. The results of the delphi exercises are subject to greater acceptance on the part of the group than are the consequences arrived at by more direct forms of interaction.[14]

Delphi Application

Change is an accepted phenomenon in the modern world. Change coupled with competition makes it necessary for a corporation to pick up the trends in the environment and determine their significance for company operations. Then, in the light of the changing environmental situation, the corporation must evaluate and define strategic posture in order to be able to face the future boldly. Two types of changes can be distinguished: cyclical and developmental. A cyclical change is repetitive in nature; managers usually develop routine procedures to meet these changes. A developmental change is innovative and irregular; having no use for the "good" old ways, it abandons them. The developmental change appears on the horizon so slowly that it may go unrecognized or ignored until it becomes an accomplished fact with drastic effects. It is this latter category of change which assumes importance in the context of strategy development. The delphi technique can be fruitfully used to analyze developmental changes. Functionally, a change may fall into one of the following categories: social, economic, political, regulatory, or technological. The delphi technique has been used by organizations to study emerging perspectives in all these areas.

---

[12]Norman C. Dalkey, *The Delphi Method: An Experimental Study of Group Opinion* (Santa Monica, CA: Rand Corp., 1969).

[13]"Forecasters Turn Group Guesswork: Delphi Technique," *Business Week,* March 14, 1970, p. 132.

[14]Dalkey, *op. cit.,* pp. 16–17.

An Illustration

The use of the delphi technique is illustrated in the following discussion of a study in which the author was involved as a consultant. The goal of the study was to assess the impact of emerging socioeconomic/political trends on the department store industry, using as a basis the set of 31 significant social trends identified by Yankelovich, Skelley and White, Inc. (see Exhibit 6-8). A list of areas of particular concern to department store executives (i.e., those areas having a direct bearing on the shopping behavior of department store customers) was prepared (see Exhibit 17-11).

The panel for the study consisted of 11 retailing executives in an Ohio metropolitan area. Before the panel was approached, however, a sample run was conducted using 28 students in the retailing class of a local university. Exhibit 17-12 shows the instructions for the questionnaire that was used. It should be noted that each prediction had to be rated on a scale ranging from 0 to 1 for its desirability, feasibility, and probability of occurrence. The panel responses on each round were sorted into lower, inner, and upper groups, as shown in Exhibit 17-12.

The percentage of respondents falling into each category on every

EXHIBIT 17-11   Aspects of the Department Store Industry That Are of Special Interest

A. Products
   1. Women's better dresses
   2. Housedresses and undergarments
   3. Children's clothing
   4. Men's socks and shirts
   5. Furniture
   6. Large appliances
   7. Towels, sheets, blankets, and spreads
   8. Kitchen utensils and small electrical appliances
B. Telephone shopping
C. Downtown vs. suburban (shopping center) shopping
D. Competition, such as from a discount store
E. Shopping motivations: convenience, fun, etc.
F. Nature and scope of services such as charge accounts, delivery, gift wrapping, sales clerks, etc.
G. Mail-order shopping
H. Fashion
I. Store decor
J. Advertisements and other aspects of promotion
K. Time preferences in shopping
L. Significance of comparison shopping, bargain hunting, impulse buying, browsing through the store, etc.

EXHIBIT 17-12 Delphi Study Questionnaire: Future Perspectives of Retailing

1. A well-known consulting organization has recognized 31 socioeconomic trends which it claims will have far-reaching impact on people's lifestyle. These trends are listed on the enclosed sheet. Our purpose here is to study the significance of these trends on the department store industry (especially the aspects listed on the enclosure, but not necessarily limited to them).
2. Please read and ponder over the trends and indicate below in column 1 all anticipated changes expected in the sphere of the department store industry. For each change, indicate the source—e.g., the particular trend(s) leading you to such an anticipation. Then evaluate each projected change with respect to the four factors at the right in view of the total environment as you see it.

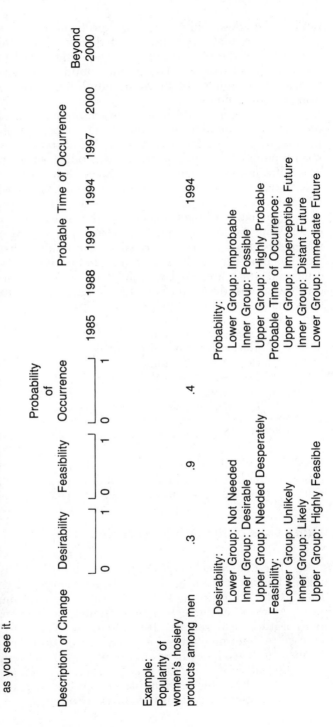

Description of Change	Desirability	Feasibility	Probability of Occurrence	Probable Time of Occurrence					
				1985	1988	1991	1994	1997	2000	Beyond 2000
	0 1	0 1	0 1							

Example:
Popularity of women's hosiery products among men   .3   .9   .4   1994

Desirability:
    Lower Group: Not Needed
    Inner Group: Desirable
    Upper Group: Needed Desperately
Feasibility:
    Lower Group: Unlikely
    Inner Group: Likely
    Upper Group: Highly Feasible
Probability:
    Lower Group: Improbable
    Inner Group: Possible
    Upper Group: Highly Probable
Probable Time of Occurrence:
    Upper Group: Imperceptible Future
    Inner Group: Distant Future
    Lower Group: Immediate Future

variable (i.e., desirability, feasibility, probability of occurrence, and time of occurrence) for a prediction was fed back to the panel members on the completion of the first round. The respondents were asked to complete the same questionnaire in the second round after they had had a chance to digest the findings of the first round. This process continued for as many as four rounds.

The process could have been continued further. But results of a comparison of round 3 with round 4 were statistically insignificant (results were significant between rounds 1 and 2 and rounds 2 and 3). Thus, there was no point in carrying on further. In other words, by conducting tests of significance (i.e., analysis of variances between two rounds), it can be determined whether it is worthwhile to undertake another round. Exhibit 17-13 shows a sample of the results obtained in the three rounds.

Tabulation of data obtained in the first round provided a long list of 37 changes in the area of concern in this study. After attrition and the screening out of irrelevant, trivial, and duplicate changes among those mentioned initially, in the final round 23 meaningful retailing predictions came out, which are listed in Exhibit 17-14. The most prominent trends (i.e., those most desirable, most highly feasible, and most likely to occur in the immediate future) that the panel predicted are the following:

1. Checkless shopping
2. Market for natural products
3. Door-to-door selling
4. Cooperative stores
5. Outfitting
6. International shopping
7. Store guarantee
8. Common products for men and women

Needless to say, these trends, if in fact they do occur, will have great significance for the department store industry. Their impact must be considered in designing corporate strategy.

Other Uses of the Delphi Technique

The delphi technique has great potential. It has so far been used mainly for predicting distant and abstract changes. Occasionally it has also been used for forecasting short-term sales and determining optimum bid price. As work on the technique continues, perhaps many more applications of it will be developed. It is safe to say that the delphi technique can be used to determine the value of any uncertain event. Even if the event happens to be completely unknown, at least initial insights into it can be gained (what statisticians call *prior distribution*). Then as more information becomes available, the original predictions can be revised with the use of statistical techniques such as the Bayes theorem.

EXHIBIT 17-13   Sample Results of the Delphi Technique (Three Rounds) — Percentage Responses

Prediction		Desirability			Feasibility			Probability of Occurrence			Probable Time of Occurrence		
		Not Needed	Desirable	Needed Desperately	Unlikely	Likely	Highly Feasible	Improbable	Possible	Highly Probable	Imperceptible Future	Distant Future	Immediate Future
1. Twenty-four-hour shopping	Round 1	75	20	5	38	40	22	57	28	15	55	30	15
	Round 2	58	35	7	49	38	13	44	47	9	62	27	11
	Round 3	43	46	11	54	35	11	29	62	9	69	21	10
2. New role of a salesclerk: "a doctor in waiting"	Round 1	27	45	28	40	33	27	32	56	12	38	44	18
	Round 2	31	58	11	45	39	16	28	62	10	26	52	22
	Round 3	28	63	9	48	42	10	21	70	9	3	68	29

EXHIBIT 17-14   Predictions: Retailing

1. Twenty-four-hour shopping
2. New role of salesclerk: "a doctor in waiting"
3. Shops for different moods
4. Declining market for "artificial" products
5. Checkless shopping
6. Growth through vertical integration
7. Increased emphasis on door-to-door selling
8. Computerized shopping
9. High-rise shopping centers
10. Recyclable clothes
11. Personal wear adjustable with physical growth
12. Universal merchandise standards
13. Rise of holding companies
14. Shopping across national boundaries
15. Frequent changes in store decor
16. Intellectual advertising
17. Customers' cooperative stores
18. Store's guarantee on merchandise
19. Trade-ins for unconventional merchandise
20. New forms of common products for men and women
21. Matching brands to moods and occasions
22. Temperature-proof clothes
23. Computerized service: what outfit to wear

Comments

The following are the points which become relevant in using the delphi technique:

1. Choice of panel members
2. Number of people on a panel
3. Number of rounds to be repeated
4. Impact of interactive variables

The choice of panel members should be related to the purpose for which the delphi technique is employed. If the purpose is to make broad predictions, an interdisciplinary team of experts would be most appropriate. On the other hand, if the forecast deals with a specific industry, persons knowledgeable about the industry would be preferred. But if the forecast is concerned with the company's perspective, in-house experts should make up the panel. Exhibit 17-15 suggests the appropriate qualification mix of experts for different types of forecasts.

As far as the size of the panel is concerned, experiments at Rand Corporation have shown a positive correlation between reliability of re-

EXHIBIT 17-15   Important Factors in the Selection of a Panel of Experts

SPECIFIC CORPORATE ORIENTATION TO THE FUTURE	EMPIRICAL DATA	JUDGMENT			DIVERSITY OF PARTICIPANTS		IMAGINATION	
		Specialized Expertise	Less Specialized Expertise	Informal Generalists	Close to Specialized Fields and Interests	Widely Diversified and Inter-Disciplinary	Extrapolative	Creative Conjecture
1. Broadened applications of existing technologies	high	high	high	low	high	low	high	medium
2. New alternatives evolving from existing knowledge	medium	medium to high	high	medium	medium	medium	medium	medium
3. New alternatives evolving from new knowledge derived from trends of research, analysis, and social developments	low	medium	high	high	medium to low	high	medium to low	high
4. New alternatives evolving from new knowledge derived from responsible, educated conjecture	low	medium to low	high	high	low	high	low	high
5. New alternatives from creative conjecture not discernable from any existing knowledge	low	low	high	high	low	high	low	high

Source: Robert M. Campbell and David Hitchin, "The Delphi Technique: Implementation in the Corporate Environment," in Subhash C. Jain and Surendra Singhvi, *Essentials of Corporate Planning* (Oxford, OH: Planning Executives Institute, 1973), p. 306. Reprinted by permission of the publisher.

sults and size of the panel. In other words, the error goes down with every increase in the size of the panel. For example, the error factor decreases from 1.2 in a one-man panel to .6 at panel size 9. In fact, the error continues to decline even at size 29. The Rand study does not pinpoint the exact desirable size for a panel. However, certain generalizations can be made. The minimum size should be somewhere between 9 to 11; it is helpful for the sake of reliability to go as high as 30. There are organizations, however, which have used panels of 140 people.[15]

The question of the number of rounds that should be tried in an experiment has already been discussed. Briefly, however, an additional round should be tried as long as the variances of the results of the previous two rounds are statistically significant. Once the improvement in results from the previous round is marginal (as proved by the analysis of variance), an additional round is unnecessary. The outcome of the last round need not be used as a final result, but would be of interest for proving that no further significant improvements in the results are possible.

One drawback of the delphi technique is that each trend is given unilateral consideration on its own merits. Thus, one may end up with conflicting forecasts, i.e., one trend may suggest that something will happen, while another may lead in the opposite direction. To resolve this problem, another forecasting technique called the *cross-impact matrix* (discussed later) has been used by some researchers. With this technique the effect of potential interactions among items in a forecast set of occurrences can be investigated. If the behavior of an individual item is predictable (i.e., if it varies positively or negatively with the occurrence or nonoccurrence of other items), the cross-impact effect is present. Thus, using the cross-impact matrix method, it can be determined whether the predicted event will have an enhancing or inhibiting influence upon each of the other events affected.

Recent research shows that the use of the delphi technique has undergone quite a change. The salient features of the revised delphi technique are: (a) to identify recognized experts in the field of interest; (b) to seek their cooperation and send them a summary paper on the topic being examined (based on a literature search); and (c) to conduct personal interviews with each expert based on a structured questionnaire, usually by two interviewers. Feedback and repeated rounds of questionnaire filling are no longer considered necessary.[16]

---

[15]Harper Q. North and Donald L. Pyke, "Probes of the Technological Future," *Harvard Business Review*, May–June, 1969, p. 68.
[16]Subhash C. Jain, "How to Scan the Environment," *Long Range Planning*, April, 1984.

TREND-IMPACT ANALYSIS

Trend-impact analysis is a technique developed by the Futures Group, Inc., a consulting firm, for projecting future trends from information gathered on past behavior. The uniqueness of this method lies in its combination of statistical methods and human judgment. If the future is predicted on quantitative data alone, it fails to take into account the impact of unprecedented future events. On the other hand, human judgment provides only subjective insights into the future. Therefore, since both human judgment and statistical extrapolation have their shortcomings, they should both be taken into consideration when predicting future trends.

In trend-impact analysis (TIA), past history is first extrapolated with the help of a computer. Then the judgment of experts is sought (usually by means of the delphi technique) to specify a set of unique future events which may have a bearing on the phenomenon under study and to indicate how the trend extrapolation would be affected by the occurrence of each of these events. The computer then uses these judgments to modify the trend extrapolation. Finally, the experts review the adjusted extrapolation and modify the inputs in those cases in which the input appears unreasonable.[17]

To illustrate the TIA method, let us consider the case of the average price of a new drug prescription in the 1980s and 1990s. As shown in Exhibit 17-16, the statistical extrapolation based on historical data shows that this cost will rise to $13 by 1990 and $14.23 by 1995. The events considered relevant here are shown in Exhibit 17-17. The first forecast, that generic dispensing will increase to 20 percent of all prescriptions filled, is shown to have a 75 percent chance of occurring by 1987. If this event does occur, it is expected that its first impact on the average price of a new prescription will begin right away. The maximum impact will occur after five years and will be a 3 percent reduction in the average price.

The combination of these events, probabilities, and impacts with the baseline extrapolation leads to a forecast markedly different from the baseline extrapolation (see Exhibit 17-16). The curve even begins to taper off in 1995. The uncertainty is indicated by quartiles above and below the mean forecast. (The quartiles indicate the middle 50 percent of future values of the curve, with 25 percent lying on each side of the forecast curve.) The uncertainty shown by these quartiles results from the fact that many of the events that have large impacts have relatively low probabilities.

At this juncture it is desirable to determine the sensitivity of these results to the individual estimates upon which they are based. For example, one might raise valid questions about the estimates of event prob-

---

[17]See "Trend Impact Analysis," a reference paper of The Futures Group, Glastonbury, CT, 1978.

EXHIBIT 17-16   Average Retail Price of a New Prescription

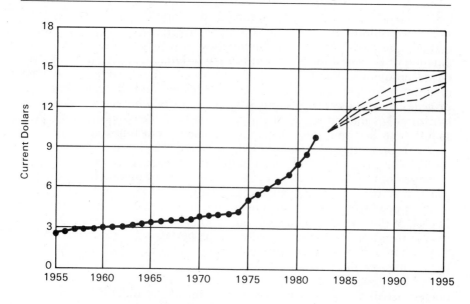

	Historical Data			Forecast		
				Lower Quartile	Mean	Upper Quartile
1952	2.17	1969	3.86	1983	10.65	10.70	10.74
1954	2.41	1970	4.02	1984	10.92	11.03	11.14
1956	2.78	1971	4.19	1985	11.21	11.40	11.61
1957	2.92	1972	4.32	1986	11.54	11.79	12.10
1958	2.99	1973	4.45	1987	11.83	12.15	12.54
1959	3.15	1974	4.70	1988	12.08	12.45	12.92
1960	3.22	1975	5.20	1989	12.30	12.74	13.25
1961	3.27	1976	5.60	1990	12.52	13.00	13.55
1962	3.26	1977	5.98	1991	12.74	13.25	13.83
1963	3.35	1978	6.44	1992	12.95	13.50	14.10
1964	3.42	1979	7.03	1993	13.17	13.75	14.38
1965	3.48	1980	7.66	1994	13.39	13.99	14.64
1966	3.56	1981	8.63	1995	13.60	14.23	14.90
1967	3.63	1982	10.37				
1968	3.70						

Source of historical data: *National Prescription Audit,* a service of IMS America, Ltd., Amber, PA (annual publication). Forecast source: Pharmaceutical PROSPECTS,® a service of Health-Care Forecasting Inc., Glastonbury, CT (annual publication). Reproduced by permission.

ability, the magnitude of the impacts used, and the delay time associated with these impacts. Having prepared these data in a disaggregated fashion, one can very easily vary such estimates and view the change in results. It may also be observed that intervention policies, whether they are institutional (such as lobbying, advertising, or new marketing approaches) or technological (such as increased R&D expenditures), can be viewed as a means of influencing the event probabilities or impacts.

TIA can be used not only to improve forecasts of time series variables, but also to study the sensitivity of these forecasts to policy. Of course, any policy considered should attempt to influence as many events as possible, rather than one as in this example. Realistically, corporate actions often have both beneficial and detrimental effects, since they may increase both desirable and undesirable possibilities. The use of TIA can make such uncertainties more clearly visible than is possible with traditional methods.

CROSS-IMPACT ANALYSIS

Cross-impact analysis is a technique used for examining the impacts of potential future events upon each other. It indicates the relative importance of specific events, identifies groups of reinforcing or inhibiting events, and unfolds relationships between events which appear unrelated. In brief, cross-impact analysis provides a future forecast, making due allowance for the effect of interacting forces on the shape of things to come.

Essentially, this technique consists of selecting a group of five to ten people to serve as project participants. They are asked to specify critical events having any relationship with the subject of the project. For example, in a marketing project the events may fall into any of the following categories:

1. Corporate objectives and goals
2. Corporate strategy
3. Markets or customers (potential volume, market share, possible strategies of key customers, etc.)
4. Competitors (product, price, promotion, and distribution strategies)
5. Overall competitive strategic posture, whether aggressive or defensive
6. Internally or externally developed strategies which might affect the project
7. Legal or regulatory activities having favorable or unfavorable effects
8. Other social, demographic, or economic events

The initial attempt presumably will generate a long list of alternatives which should be consolidated into a manageable size (e.g., 25–30

EXHIBIT 17-17   Events Used in Trend-Impact Analysis

EVENT NUMBER	FORECAST	ESTIMATED PROBABILITY BY YEAR SHOWN	YEARS TO FIRST IMPACT	YEARS TO MAXIMUM IMPACT	MAXIMUM IMPACT (PERCENT)	FORECAST SOURCE NUMBER(S)
496	Generic dispensing increases to 20 percent of all prescriptions filled. (1974 = 11 percent)	.75 1987	0	5	−3	6900
1346	Medicaid and Medicare prescription reimbursement is based on a fixed monthly fee per covered patient ("capitation plan").	.50 1984	0	2	−2.5	6226,6227,6228, 6229,7017
766	Private third-party insurance carriers institute cost containment programs for prescription drugs: MAC-type limits on generics, negotiated prices for single-source products, fixed fee per patient covered, etc.	.40 1990	0	5	−5	6900
207	Fifty percent decrease in the average rate of growth in prescription size.	.90 1983	0	5	−1	5557
492	Medicaid state funding replaced by block grants.	.50 1983	1	5	−1	5568,5569,5570, 5571,5572,5573, 5574,5575,5576
995	Prices of single-source or co-marketed drugs negotiated by state or federal government as major purchaser.	.35 1995	0	5	−3	6225,6230,7016, 7020

500	All outpatient drugs for persons over age 65 are covered by national health insurance or Medicare with some deductible or co-pay.	.40	1989	0	3	1	4479,5329,5330,5331,7021
483	Unit of use dispensing for at least one-fourth of all prescriptions: units prepared and packaged by manufacturer.	.35	1990	1	5	2	3908,4397,4496,6030,6031,6032
497	Nearly all drugs are covered under national health insurance with a maximum price schedule.	.30	1995	0	5	4	6900
478	Pharmacist dispensing fees and mark-ups for Medicaid and Medicare prescriptions increase at least 5 percent annually.	.40	1985	0	5	2	5559,5560,6231,7018,7019
499	Manufacturers increase prices of single-source drugs in response to government regulation of multi-source pharmaceuticals and the diminishing patent protection period.	.80	1985	0	2	2	6900
481	Drugs covered by expiring patents are displaced by new, single-source products at an accelerated rate.	.35	1985	0	5	5	6900
715	Government regulations increase manufacturers' cost of doing business for at least 5 percent above inflation for a three-year period.	.50	1985	1	3	4	6900

Source: Pharmaceutical PROSPECTS,® a service of HealthCare Forecasting Inc., Glastonbury, CT (annual publication). Reproduced by permission.

events) by means of group discussion, concentrated thinking, elimination of duplications, and refinement of the essence of the problem. It is desirable for each event to contain one and only one variable, thus avoiding the double counting of impacts. The selected events are represented in an "$n \times n$" matrix for developing the estimated impact of each event on every other event. This is done by assuming for each specific event that it has already occurred and will have an enhancing, an inhibiting, or no effect on other events. If desired the impacts may be weighted. The project coordinator seeks the impact estimates from each project participant individually and displays the estimates in the matrix in a consolidated form. The individual results, in summary form, are presented to the group. The project participants vote on the impact of each event. If the spread of the votes is too wide, the coordinator will ask those voting at the extremes to justify their positions. The participants are encouraged to discuss differences in the hope of clarifying the problem. Another round of voting takes place. During this second round the opinions usually converge, and the median value of the votes is entered in the appropriate cell in the matrix. This procedure is repeated until the entire matrix is complete.

In the process of matrix completion, the review of occurrences and interactions identifies those events which are strong actors and significant reactors and provides a subjective opinion on their relative strengths. This information then serves as an important input in formulating strategy.

The use of cross-impact analysis may be illustrated with reference to a study concerned with the future of U.S. automobile component suppliers. The following were the events set forth:*

> 1. Motor vehicle safety standards which come into effect between 1974 and 1978 will result in an additional 260 pounds of weight for the average-sized U.S. car.
> 2. The 1978 NO_x emissions regulations are relaxed by the EPA.
> 3. The retail price of gasoline (regular grade) is $1.00 per gallon.
> 4. U.S. automakers introduce passenger cars which will achieve at least 32 mpg under average summer driving conditions.

These events are arranged in matrix form as shown in Exhibit 17-18. The arrows show the direction of the analysis. For example, the occurrence of event A would be likely to bring more pressure to bear upon regulatory officials, so event B would be more likely to occur. Therefore, an enhancing arrow is placed in the cell where row A and column B intersect. Moving to column C, it is not expected that the occurrence of event A would have any effect on event C, so a horizontal line is placed in this cell. It is judged that the occurrence of event A would make event D less likely to occur, and an inhibiting arrow is placed in this cell. If event B were to occur, the consensus is that event A would be more likely, hence the enhancing arrow. Event B is not expected to affect event C, but would make event D more likely. The cells are completed in accordance with

---

*This illustration was developed before the 1979 gas price increases.

EXHIBIT 17-18   Basic Format for Cross-Impact Matrix

If This Event Were to Occur	Then the Impact upon This Event Would Be			
	A	B	C	D
A MVSS ('74 through '78) require 260# additional weight for "average" U.S. auto.	✕	←	—	→
B 1978 NOₓ emissions requirements are relaxed by EPA.	→	✕	—	←
C Retail price of gasoline is $1.00/gallon.	←	→	✕	←
D U.S. automakers introduce cars capable of 32 mpg in average summer driving.	←	→	→	✕

CODE: ← = enhancing
      — = no effect
      → = inhibiting

these judgments. Similar analyses for events C and D complete the matrix. The completed matrix shows the direction of impact of rows (actors) upon columns (reactors). An analysis of the matrix at this point reveals that reactor C has only one actor (event D) since there is only one reaction in column C. If the interest is primarily in event D, column D should be studied for actor events. Then each of those actor events should be examined to determine what degree of influence, if any, it is possible to have on these actors in order to bring about event D.

Next, the impacts should be quantified to show linkage strengths (i.e., to determine how strongly the occurrence or nonoccurrence of one event would influence the occurrence of each of the other events). To assist in quantifying the interactions, a subjective rating scale such as the one shown below may be used.

Voting Scale	Subjective Scale	
+8	Critical: essential for success	
+6	Major: major item for success	
+4	Significant: positive, helpful, but not essential	Enhancing
+2	Slight: noticeable enhancing effect	
0	No effect	
−2	Slight: noticeable inhibiting effect	
−4	Significant: retarding effect	Inhibiting
−6	Major: major obstacle to success	
−8	Critical: almost insurmountable hurdle	

Consider the impact of event A upon event B. It is felt that the occurrence of event A would significantly improve the likelihood of occurrence of event B. Both the direction and degree of enhancing impact are shown in Exhibit 17-19 by the +4 rating in the appropriate cell. Event A's occurrence would make event D less likely; therefore, the consensus rating is −4. This process is continued until all interactions have been evaluated and the matrix is complete. There are a number of variations in the quantification techniques. For example, the subjective scale could be 0 to 10, rather than −8 to +8 as shown in the above example.

Another technique involves the use of probabilities of occurrence. If the probability of occurrence of each event is assessed before the construction of the matrix, then the change in that probability can be assessed for each interaction. As shown in Exhibit 17-20, the probabilities of occurrence can be entered in an information column preceding the matrix. Next, the matrix is constructed in the conventional manner. Consider the impact of event A on the probable occurrence of event B. It is judged to be an enhancing effect, and the consensus is that the probability of oc-

EXHIBIT 17-19 Cross-Impact Matrix Showing Degrees of Impact

If This Event Were to Occur	Then the Impact upon This Event Would Be			
	A	B	C	D
A MVSS ('74 through '78) require 260# additional weight for "average" U.S. auto.	✕	+4	0	-4
B 1978 NO$_x$ emissions requirements are relaxed by EPA.	+2	✕	0	+4
C Retail price of gasoline is $1.00/gallon.	-4	+4	✕	+2
D U.S. automakers introduce cars capable of 32 mpg in average summer driving.	+2	-2	-2	✕

currence of event B will change from 0.8 to 0.9. The new probability is, therefore, entered in the appropriate cell. Event A is judged to have no effect upon event C; therefore, the original probability, 0.5, is unchanged. Event D is inhibited by the occurrence of event A, and the resulting probability of occurrence is lowered from 0.5 to 0.4. The occurrence of event B will increase the probability of occurrence of event A from 0.7 to 0.8. Event B has no impact upon event C (0.5, unchanged), and will increase the probability of event D to 0.7. This procedure is followed until all of the cells are completed.

An examination of the matrix at this stage reveals several important relationships. For example, if we wanted event D to occur, then the most likely actors would be events B and C. We would then examine columns B and C to determine what actors we might influence. Often, influences which bring about the desired results at the critical moment are secondary, tertiary, or beyond. In many instances the degree of impact is not the only important information to be gathered from a consideration of interactions. The time relationships are often very important and can be shown in a number of ways. For example, in Exhibit 17-20, time information has been added within parentheses. It shows that if event A were to occur, it would have an enhancing effect upon event B, raising B's probability of occurrence from 0.8 to 0.9; this enhancement would occur immediately. If event B were to occur, it would raise the probability of occurrence of event D from 0.5 to 0.7; it would take two years to reach the probable time of occurrence of event D.[18]

SCENARIO BUILDING

Traditionally plans for the future were developed on a single set of assumptions. This was all right during times of relative stability. But in the 1980s and 1990s, as the turbulent years of the 1970s have shown, it may not be desirable to commit the organization to the "most probable" future alone. It is equally important to make allowances for unexpected or less probable future trends which may seriously jeopardize the strategy. One way to focus on different futures within the planning process is to develop scenarios, then design the strategy so that it has enough flexibility to accommodate whatever future occurs. In other words, by developing multiple scenarios of the shape of things to come, a company can make a better strategic response to the future environment. A scenario in this sense is a synopsis depicting potential actions and events in a likely order of development, beginning with a set of conditions which describe a current situation or set of circumstances. In addition, scenarios depict a possible course of evolution in a given field. The two stages in scenario building can be labeled as "identification of changes" and "evolution of programs."

Changes are picked up in the environment and can be grouped into two classes: (1) scientific and technological and (2) socioeconomic-politi-

---

[18]*A Guide to Cross-Impact Analysis* (Cleveland, OH: Eaton Corp., no date).

EXHIBIT 17-20 Cross-Impact Matrix Showing Interactive Probabilities of Occurrence

If This Event Were to Occur	Having This Probability of Occurrence	Then the Impact upon This Event Would Be			
		A	B	C	D
A MVSS ('74 through '78) require 260# additional weight for "average" U.S. auto.	0.7	✕	0.9 (immed.)	0.5	0.4 (immed.)
B 1978 NO_x emissions requirements are relaxed by EPA.	0.8	0.8 (immed.)	✕	0.5	0.7 (+2 yrs.)
C Retail price of gasoline is $1.00/gallon.	0.5	0.6 (+1 yr.)	0.9 (+1 yr.)	✕	0.7 (+2 yrs.)
D U.S. automakers introduce cars capable of 32 mpg in average summer driving.	0.5	0.8 (immed.)	0.6 (immed.)	0.4 (+1 yr.)	✕

cal. Chapter 6 on environmental scanning dealt with the identification of these changes. This identification should be done by taking into consideration the total environment and its possibilities: What changes are taking place? What shape will they take in the future? How are other areas related to the changes? What effect will the changes have on other related fields? What opportunities and threats are likely?[19]

The scenario should be developed without any intention of predicting the future. It should be a time-ordered sequence of events bearing a logical cause-and-effect relationship to each other. The objective of a scenario exercise should be to clarify certain phenomena and/or study the key points in a series of developments in order to evolve new programs. One can follow an inductive or a deductive aproach in building a scenario. The deductive approach, which is predictive in nature, studies the broader changes and analyzes the impact of each change on the company's existing lines, at the same time generating ideas about new areas which seem feasible. Under the inductive approach, the future of each product line is simulated by exposing its current environment to various changes foreseen in the future. Through a process of elimination those changes which bear relevance to one's business can be studied more deeply for possible action. Both approaches have their merits and limitations. The deductive approach is much more demanding, however, since it calls for proceeding from unknowns to specifics. At different levels in the organization both approaches have some contribution to make. At the strategic level, the deductive approach to building a scenario is likely to be more useful. In operations planning, however, the inductive approach is likely to prove more useful.

Exhibit 17-21 describes how scenarios are constructed at the General Electric Company. Scenarios are not a set of random thoughts, but logical conclusions based on past behavior, future expectations, and the likely interactions of these two. As a matter of fact, a variety of analytical techniques (i.e., the delphi technique, trend-impact analysis, and cross-impact analysis) are used at GE to formulate scenarios.

Scenarios may be analyzed following Linneman and Kennell's ten-step approach, which is stated below:

1. Identify and make explicit your company's mission, basic objective, and policies.
2. Determine how far into the future you wish to plan.
3. Develop a good understanding of your company's points of leverage and vulnerability.
4. Determine factors that you think will definitely occur within your planning time frame.
5. Make a list of key variables that will have make-or-break consequences for your company.

---

[19]See Harold E. Klein and Robert E. Linneman, "The Use of Scenarios in Corporate Planning—Eight Case Histories," *Long Range Planning*, October, 1981, pp. 69–77.

EXHIBIT 17-21   Scenario-building Method at General Electric Company

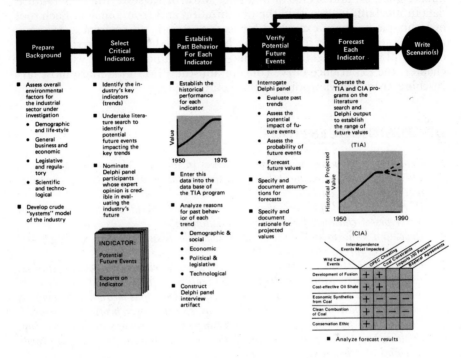

Note: TIA = Trend-impact analysis; CIA = Cross-impact analysis.

Source: General Electric Company. Reprinted by permission.

6. Assign reasonable values to each key variable.
7. Build scenarios in which your company may operate.
8. Develop a strategy for each scenario which will most likely achieve your company's objectives.
9. Check the flexibility of each strategy in each scenario by testing its effectiveness in the other scenarios.
10. Select—or develop—an "optimum response" strategy.[20]

SUMMARY

This chapter presents a variety of tools and techniques which are helpful in different aspects of strategy formulation and implementation. These include experience curves, the PIMS model, the model for mea-

[20]Robert E. Linneman and John D. Kennell, "Shirt-Sleeve Approach to Long-Range Plans," *Harvard Business Review*, March–April, 1977, pp. 141–151.

suring sustainable growth, the delphi technique, trend-impact analysis, cross-impact analysis, and scenario building. Most of these techniques require data inputs both from within the organization and from outside. Each tool or technique has been examined for its application and usefulness. In some cases procedural details for using a technique have been illustrated by means of examples from the field. Of the many techniques dealt with in this chapter, the experience curve concept and the PIMS model are most far-reaching from the viewpoint of marketing strategy.

DISCUSSION QUESTIONS

1. *Explain the relevance of experience curves in formulating pricing strategy.*
2. *The experience curve concept seems to suggest that antitrust laws are dysfunctional. Comment on this.*
3. *Discuss how the delphi technique may be used to generate innovative ideas for new types of channels for distributing automobiles.*
4. *Develop a scenario on the use of the automobile, assuming acute shortages and high prices for gasoline in the 1990s.*
5. *Explain how PIMS judgments can be useful in developing marketing strategy.*
6. *Experience curves and the PIMS model both seem to imply that market share is an essential ingredient of a winning strategy. Does that mean that a company with a low share of the market has no way of running a profitable business?*
7. *Describe how par reports may help a business in its strategic decision making.*
8. *Explain how the amount paid out in the form of dividends affects the growth potential of a business.*
9. *Explain the use of cross-impact analysis with reference to an emerging trend: the use of computers in households. Make appropriate assumptions.*

APPENDIX: EXPERIENCE CURVE CONSTRUCTION

The experience curve concept can be used as an aid in developing marketing strategy. The curve construction procedure discussed below describes how the relationship between costs and accumulated experience can be empirically developed.

The first step in the process of constructing the experience curve is to compute experience and accumulated cost information. *Experience* for a particular year is the accumulation of all volume up to and including that year. It is computed by adding the year's volume to the experience of the previous years. *Accumulated cost* (constant dollars) is the total of all constant costs incurred for the product up to and including that year. It is computed by adding the year's constant dollar cost to the accumulated costs of the previous years. A year's constant dollar cost is the real dollar cost for that year, corrected by inflation. It is computed by dividing the cost (actual dollars) by the appropriate deflator.

The second step is to plot the initial and annual experience/accumulated cost (constant dollars) data on log-log graph paper (see Exhibit 17-22). It is important that the experience axis of this graph be calibrated so that its point of intersection with the accumulated cost axis is at 1 unit of experience. The accumulated cost axis may be calibrated in any convenient manner.

EXHIBIT 17-22   Accumulated Cost Diagram

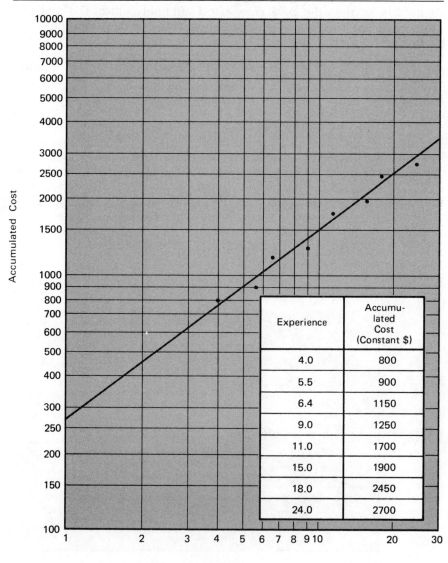

Experience	Accumulated Cost (Constant $)
4.0	800
5.5	900
6.4	1150
9.0	1250
11.0	1700
15.0	1900
18.0	2450
24.0	2700

The next step is to fit a straight line to the points on the graph, which may be accomplished by using the least-squares method (Exhibit 17-22). It is useful at this point to stop and analyze the accumulated cost diagram. In general, the closer the data points are to the accumulated cost curve, the stronger is the evidence that the experience effect is present. Deviations of the data points from the curve, however, do not necessarily disprove the presence of the experience effect. If the deviations can be attributed to heavy investments in plant, etc. (as is common to very capital-intensive industries), the experience effect still holds, but in the long run (since in the long run the fluctuations are averaged out). If, on the other hand, significant deviations from the line cannot be explained as necessary periodic changes in the rate of investment, then the presence of the experience effect, or at least its consistency, is open to question. In Exhibit 17-23 there is one deviation (see point X) that stands out as significant. If this can be ascribed to heavy investment (in plant, etc.), the experience effect is still viable here.

The next step in the process of constructing the experience curve is to calculate the intensity of the product's experience effect. *Intensity* is the unit-cost-reduction percentage achieved each time the product's experience is doubled. As such, it determines the slope of the experience curve. To compute the intensity from the accumulated cost curve, arbitrarily select an experience level on the experience axis (e.g., point E_1 in Exhibit 17-24). Draw a line vertically up from E_1 until it intersects the accumulated cost curve. From that point on the curve, draw a line horizontally left until it intersects the accumulated cost axis. Read the corre-

EXHIBIT 17-23   Interpretation of Deviations from Accumulated Cost Curve

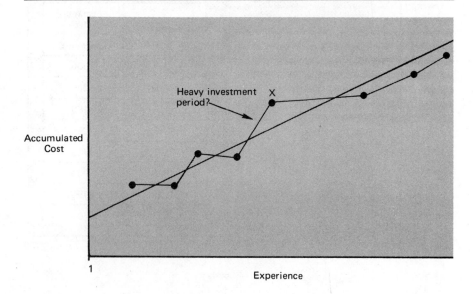

sponding accumulated cost (A_1) from the scale. Follow the same procedure for experience level E_2, where E_2 equals E_1 times 2, to obtain A_2. Divide A_2 by A_1, divide the result by 2, and subtract the second result from the number 1. The final answer is the product's intensity. With the information given in Exhibit 17-24, the intensity works out to be 16.7 percent:

$$1 - \left(\frac{2500}{1500} \times \frac{1}{2} \right) = .167 = 16.7\%$$

When the intensity has been computed, the slope of the experience curve is determined. However, as shown in Exhibit 17-25, this in itself is not sufficient for constructing the curve. This is because all of the lines in Exhibit 17-25, since they are parallel, have the same slope and represent the same intensity. To construct the experience curve, it is necessary to find a point (C_1) on the unit cost axis. This can be achieved in the following manner. Find the "intensity multiplier" corresponding to the product's intensity from the table specially prepared for the purpose (Exhibit 17-26). If the intensity falls between two values in Exhibit 17-26, the appropriate intensity multiplier should be determined by interpolating between the two closest intensity multipliers from the exhibit. Read the value on the accumulated cost axis where the curve intersects that axis. Multiply this value by the intensity multiplier. The result is C_1.

EXHIBIT 17-24   Product Intensity Computation

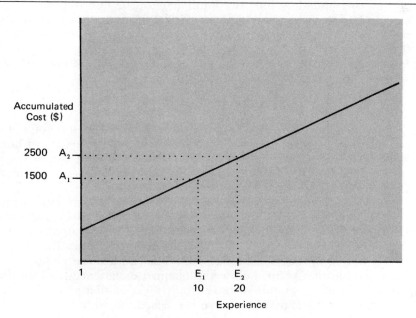

EXHIBIT 17-25   Slopes of Parallel Lines

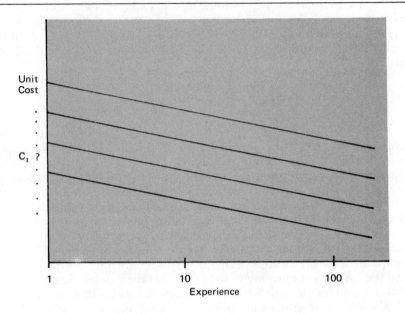

The intensity was calculated above as 16.7 percent. By using Exhibit 17-26, the corresponding intensity multiplier can be interpolated as approximately 0.736. As shown in Exhibit 17-22, the accumulated cost at the point of intersection can be read as approximately $260. Multiplying $260 by 0.736 yields a C_1 of $191. The experience curve can now be plotted on log-log graph paper. Position C_1 on the unit cost axis. Multiply C_1 by the quantity (1 − intensity) to obtain C_2:

$$\$191 \,(1 - 0.167) = \$159$$

Locate C_2 on the unit cost axis. Find the point of intersection (y) of a line drawn vertically up from 2 on the experience axis and a line drawn horizontally right from C_2 on the unit cost axis. Draw a straight line through the points C_1 and y. The result is the product's experience curve (Exhibit 17-27).

The application of the experience curve concept in marketing strategy requires the forecasting of costs. This can be achieved by using the curve above. To accomplish this, determine the current cumulative experience of the product. Add to this value the planned cumulative volume from the present to the future time point. The result is the planned experience level at that point. Locate the planned experience level on the experience axis of the graph. Move vertically up from that point until the line extension of the experience curve is reached. Move horizontally left

EXHIBIT 17-26 Intensity Multipliers

INTENSITY	INTENSITY MULTIPLIER	INTENSITY	INTENSITY MULTIPLIER
5.0%	.926	20.5%	.669
5.5	.918	21.0	.660
6.0	.911	21.5	.651
6.5	.903	22.0	.642
7.0	.895	22.5	.632
7.5	.888	23.0	.623
8.0	.880	23.5	.614
8.5	.872	24.0	.604
9.0	.864	24.5	.595
9.5	.856	25.0	.585
10.0	.848	25.5	.575
10.5	.840	26.0	.566
11.0	.832	26.5	.556
11.5	.824	27.0	.546
12.0	.816	27.5	.536
12.5	.807	28.0	.526
13.0	.799	28.5	.516
13.5	.791	29.0	.506
14.0	.782	29.5	.496
14.5	.774	30.0	.485
15.0	.766	30.5	.475
15.5	.757	31.0	.465
16.0	.748	31.5	.454
16.5	.740	32.0	.444
17.0	.731	32.5	.433
17.5	.722	33.0	.422
18.0	.714	33.5	.411
18.5	.705	34.0	.401
19.0	.696	34.5	.390
19.5	.687	35.0	.379
20.0	.678	35.5	.367

from the line to the unit cost axis. Read the estimated unit cost value from the scale. The unit cost obtained above is expressed in constant dollars, but can be converted to an actual dollar cost by multiplying it by the projected inflator for the future year.

Cost forecasts can also be used to determine the minimum rate of volume growth necessary to offset an assumed rate of inflation. For example, with an assumed inflation rate of 3.8 percent, a producer having an intensity of 20 percent must realize a volume growth of approximately 13 percent per year in order to just maintain the unit cost in real dollars. Should growth be slower, or should full cost-reduction potential not be realized, the producer's unit cost would rise.

EXHIBIT 17-27   Experience Curve Estimation

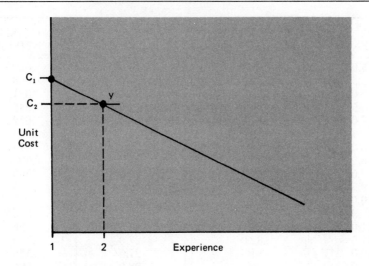

Competitor cost is one of the most fundamental, yet elusive, information needs of the producer attempting to develop marketing strategy. The experience curve concept provides a sound basis for estimating the cost positions of competitors as well. With certain assumptions, the competitors' curves can be estimated.

Sigtronics, Inc.

In such a diversified company, it is extremely difficult to properly allocate limited financial resources among what appear to be so many attractive investment opportunities. Unfortunately, there are no easy solutions, only difficult choices.

In the spring of 1978, Sandra Greenberg, special projects analyst in the corporate planning department of Sigtronics, Inc., a highly diversified manufacturing company based on the West Coast with 1977 sales of approximately $730 million and over 30 separate product divisions, was concerned with improving the methods by which "strategic expenditures" were allocated and spent within the company.

STRATEGIC EXPENDITURES

Strategic expenditures were considered to be those funds invested for the future position of the company. They were not those expenses necessary to manufacture and sell current products, but rather were "investments" made to improve the business(es) in the years ahead. Such "strategic expenditures" could be capital expenditures as well as expense items, but Greenberg's current interest was primarily in controlling strategic expenses. These were significant in that the company recently had been spending about $35 million a year in the strategic expense category, and in a typical year, such an amount was larger than either capital expenditures or after-tax profits.

Strategic expenses included a variety of improvements in capability which were considered crucial for the survival and success of a business. Illustrative of the types of projects which would qualify for categorization as strategic expenses were the following:

New product development
Improvement of existing products
New market development
Cost and operating expense reduction

This case was prepared by Professor Edwin A. Murray, Jr., of Boston University and is printed here with his permission.

Increase capital turnover
Advertise the company and its products
Marketing and distribution improvements

The effective management of strategic expenses was of major importance because they represented basically a reduction of current profits, and they could substantially affect the size, direction of growth, and future profitability of the company's various divisions. In general, management sought to control strategic expenditures so as to derive the maximum possible future benefit for the company. Whereas the capital investments were handled separately and consisted of after-tax dollars, the strategic *expense* items had in the past been mixed in with operating costs. However, if they were isolated for a typical division of Sigtronics, they would represent about 5 percent of the division's annual revenue. (In an "average" division, "product costs" would constitute about 60 percent of the division's sales, "operating costs" another 30 percent, and pre-tax profits would be approximately 5 percent.)

Division management traditionally had had wide discretion in trading off strategic expenses for current profits and vice versa. However, there were practical limits on the degree to which one could be forgone for the sake of the other—at least at the corporate level. Without adequate current profits, the company would incur the risk of adverse investor reaction and a concomitant unavailability (or at least increased cost) of capital with which to finance future growth. On the other hand, unless certain minimal strategic expenditures were made on an ongoing basis, the long-term competitive (and profit) position of the company would deteriorate. Nevertheless, within such limits, management had considerable discretion.

THE COMPANY

Both current and future profitability were of high priority to Sigtronics' corporate management. Said Robert Ferris, President:

> Like many major diversified corporations, we aspire to "Blue Chip" status in the eyes of the investment community. This has meant a steadfast commitment to rewarding our shareholders with a consistently and dependably high return on their investment. As a consequence, we cannot afford to forgo either short-range or long-range profitability, even for the cause of trading off one temporarily for the other. We need to preserve both at all times, at least insofar as it is within our ability to do so.

The company operated, as did many "diversified majors," with a sizable corporate staff and used six group vice-presidents to oversee the operations of the divisions which were grouped according to like markets and technologies. (See Exhibit 17-28 for an organization chart.) Each group vice-president had four to six divisions for which he was responsible, and this involved participation in their long-range planning and budgeting processes.

EXHIBIT 17-28   Sigtronics, Inc.: Partial Organization Chart

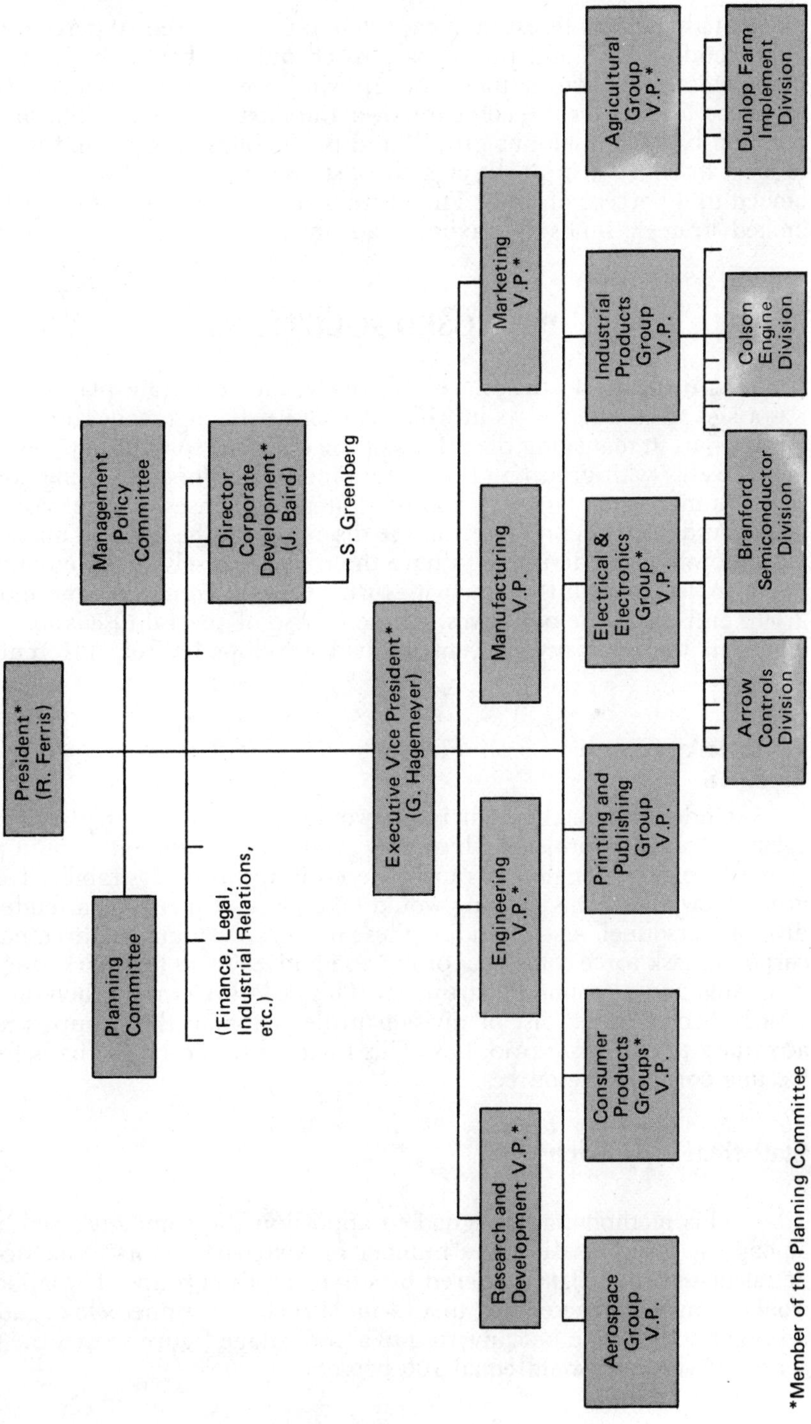

*Member of the Planning Committee

With prime interest rates expected to go above the 10 percent mark by the end of 1978 and profit margins chronically below those of many of its major competitors, there was growing concern that external funds would be limited for the company over the next few years. Still, the corporation had set ambitious growth and profitability targets, and in order to meet its short-term profit objectives, strategic expense funds would be limited to 4 percent of sales. Therefore, management sought to spend its limited strategic funds to maximum advantage.

PROPOSED SOLUTIONS

In order to do this more effectively, the corporate planning staff was asked to consider ways in which corporate management could take a greater part in managing the affairs of the divisions so that they coincided more readily with group and corporate interests. One area being considered for more attention was that of strategic expenses. In the past, they had been decided upon largely at the discretion of the division managers, but it now seemed desirable to have them more closely reviewed and adjusted to accord with those activities which would contribute the most to group and corporate objectives. In the course of several discussions with others in the company, Greenberg had developed three different approaches:

Project Approach

Under this method, divisions would submit to their group managements various projects which the group vice-presidents would then consolidate into a single list, rank-ordered in terms of desirability from a group viewpoint. This ranking would take place at meetings attended by division personnel. Also attending these meetings would be a three-person corporate task force consisting of representatives from the marketing, engineering, and planning departments. This task force would then develop a single, consolidated list of division projects for all the groups ranked according to corporate priorities. This final list would be the basis for allocating corporate resources.

Statistical Approach

This method was designed to apportion the company's resources among the groups based on a number of "external factors" which could be calculated from data gathered by surveying the groups. These factors would be averaged according to a formula such as the one below, and the resulting score would be converted to a percentage figure so that the total for all the groups would equal 100 percent.

$$\text{Overall Group Score} = \frac{\text{Factor 1} + \text{Factor 2} + \text{Factor 3}}{3}$$

Where Factor 1 = 1987 Market + 10-Year Growth + Technological Growth Potential[1]

Factor 2 = 1987 Market + Technological Growth Potential

Factor 3 = 1977 Sales + 1977 Market + 1987 Market + 10-Year Growth + Technological Growth Potential

Analytic Approach

The purpose of this method was to maximize the ratio:

$$\frac{\text{Corporate Profit Before Taxes}}{\text{Corporate Strategic Expenses}}$$

$$\text{Where} \quad \frac{\text{Corp. PBT}}{\text{Corp. SE}} = \frac{\Sigma (PBT_1 + PBT_2 + \ldots + PBT_n)}{\Sigma (SE_1 + SE_2 + \ldots + SE_n)}$$

and $1, 2, \ldots, n$ refer to divisions 1 to n.

In general, the idea was to allocate the individual amounts of SE on the basis of the estimated improvements of PBT which would result, always attempting to gain the largest increase in PBT for a given amount of SE. More specifically, the divisions were asked to estimate their 1983 PBT based upon their actual SE budgeted for 1978, 0.9 × actual, and 1.5 × actual. It was then possible to computerize a procedure whereby all divisions were cut back to 0.9 × their budgeted amounts and the resulting funds reallocated to those divisions projecting the greatest increase in PBT provided funds could be restored (to 1.0 × actual) or increased (to 1.5 × actual). In this way, the same absolute amount of strategic expenses was expected to yield a PBT for the corporation about 15 percent higher than if every division proceeded as planned with its budgeted strategic expenses. This approach would be applicable at the group level as well as to individual projects within a division.

---

[1]Technological Growth Potential was a ranking assigned to each of the company's six groups. It was arrived at by assigning arbitrary weights to each of four factors for each group's major product lines: breakthrough opportunity (the probability of major technological developments being introduced to the product line by 1982); new product potential (the relative number of new products conceivable for each group); importance of cost reduction (the degree to which cost reduction was important to the product line's success); and styling (the relative importance of styling on the success of the product line). A score for each major product line was thus calculated and these were combined to give a group score which was then used to develop a group ranking.

A TRIAL APPLICATION

While examining ways to more satisfactorily allocate strategic expense funds, Greenberg had come up with the idea of using the simplified situations of four representative divisions to test both the logic and the practicality of some of the methods proposed. She thought that by trying to cope with a specific problem involving the distribution of strategic expense funds, the planning committee[2] would be able to evaluate the methods described above or perhaps devise new and more effective approaches to the problem. In any event, they would be able to focus on the main issues from a new and more concrete perspective. Greenberg explained this approach to the planning committee:

> In many ways, these four divisions are representative of the diversity inherent in a firm like Sigtronics. What is not so clear is how we are to go about making intelligent investments for the future in such dissimilar units. Our task will be that of allocating limited strategic expense funds to these four divisions in a way that best serves the long-term interests of the corporation.
>
> We have past performance data and future projections for each division, along with a short summary of respective product lines and industries. Histories of strategic expenditures and forecasted needs for strategic funds have also been provided. For simplicity, let's assume that in each division depreciation funds are reinvested in new plant and equipment to remain competitive. Let us further assume that net worth is proportional to sales in each case.
>
> If strategic expense funds within the company are going to be constrained to about 4 percent of sales, one would expect to be able to predict the level of future strategic funds for these divisions. However, whereas past performance data show total strategic expenditures for the four divisions around 4 or 5 percent of aggregate sales, strategic fund requests for 1978 through 1982 far outstrip that percentage of sales. [At this point, Greenberg displayed Exhibit 17-29 shown on page 949.]
>
> The real challenge will be to resolve the discrepancies between what is available (presumably an amount approximating 4 percent of sales) and what has been requested by the divisions. To do this properly, we must not only keep within the limit of funds available, but we must allocate these funds to the four divisions in a manner which would most effectively improve the future position of Sigtronics.

Greenberg then distributed thumbnail sketches of the four sample divisions which were intended to provide some basis for distributing the strategic funds for 1978. These descriptions follow.

---

[2]Consisted of nine of the top officers of the company, including Ferris, President; Hagemeyer, Executive Vice-President; and Baird, Director of Corporate Development.

EXHIBIT 17-29   Strategic Expense Funds—Available and Requested
               (Dollar Amounts in Millions)

	Year	Available Strategic Funds for 4 Divisions (Based on 4% of Actual or Projected Sales)	Strategic Funds Invested or Requested by 4 Divisions (Based Upon Their Past and Projected Needs)
	1973	$4.3	$4.5
Actual	1974	4.7	5.0
Operating	1975	5.1	5.6
History	1976	5.4	6.0
	1977	5.8	6.7
	1978	6.3	8.5
	1979	6.9	11.2
Estimated	1980	7.6	15.0
	1981	8.3	20.5
	1982	9.0	29.0

ARROW CONTROLS DIVISION

The products of this division included a wide range of circuit breakers, automatic switches, bus ducts, and miscellaneous electrical controls and accessories. Most of the products were for industrial use and were sold nationally to original equipment manufacturers or to industrial supply houses. All of the manufacturing operations were concentrated in one location in facilities which had been built largely during World War II.

Past Performance

Sales growth in recent years had been rapid, growing at a 12 percent compound annual rate, and 1977's net sales were in excess of $42 million. This division enjoyed the largest market share in the industry, with the next two competitors having approximately 15 percent each and most of the remaining sales divided among a dozen smaller firms. Largely because of this industry leadership, the division had been able to command healthy margins. As a consequence, it had been one of the most profitable divisions in Sigtronics. (Operating results for the past five years are shown in Exhibit 17-30.)

Looking Ahead

The outlook for the industry largely influenced the Arrow Controls Division's projections for future operations. After an anticipated market

EXHIBIT 17-30   Arrow Controls Division
(Dollar Amounts in Millions)

Year Ended Dec. 31	Net Sales	Net Income*	Market Share	Strategic Funds Invested*
Past Operating Results				
1973	$27.1	$2.0 (7.4%)	30.4%	$1.3 (4.8%)
1974	30.3	2.1 (6.9%)	31.2	1.4 (4.6%)
1975	33.7	2.7 (8.0%)	31.7	1.7 (5.0%)
1976	37.6	3.2 (8.5%)	32.0	1.9 (5.0%)
1977	42.6	3.8 (8.9%)	32.8	2.1 (4.9%)

Year Ended Dec. 31	Net Sales	Net Income*	Market Share	Strategic Funds Requested*
Projected Results				
1978	$48.5	$4.4 (9.1%)	33.5%	$2.4 (4.9%)
1979	55.8	4.5 (8.1%)	34.7	2.8 (5.0%)
1980	63.2	5.1 (8.1%)	35.5	3.2 (5.1%)
1981	70.8	5.3 (7.5%)	36.0	3.8 (5.4%)
1982	78.0	5.5 (7.1%)	36.1	4.6 (5.9%)

*Figures in parentheses indicate percentage of sales.

growth of 11 percent in 1978, it was expected that primary demand for electrical controls would plateau or even decline to a more stable 5 percent growth per annum. Through heavy investments in aggressive marketing programs, however, the division forecast sales growth rates up to 15 percent per annum and an increased market share. (Projections are shown in Exhibit 17-30.)

BRANFORD SEMICONDUCTOR DIVISION

The division produced and marketed many electronic components including diodes and rectifiers, transistors, and a number of special devices and circuit elements. Most of the division's output went to industrial supply houses where it was further distributed to manufacturers of electronic components. Some of the division's products were sold to other divisions within Sigtronics.

Past Performance

Semiconductor devices had been in great demand since the mid-1950s, largely as a result of the great scientific and technological development effort precipitated by the launching of Sputnik. Growth in the industry had been rapid and sustained; 1977's total market sales had increased by as much as 20 percent from 1976's volume. In general, 15 percent per annum in sales had characterized the industry.

The Branford Semiconductor Division had matched industry sales growth, but had never managed to sustain superior growth. This was because many firms competed with the division, and consequently, product innovations within the industry were frequent and often short-lived. Great amounts of research and development funds were necessary just to remain competitive with the more than 200 firms in the industry. No one of these firms seemed capable of achieving more than a 15 percent share of the market. However, there were signs of the industry entering a consolidation phase, and the companies that emerged would be larger and more profitable than most present firms.

Division profits had been uneven and well below corporate averages due to start-up expenses in the mid-1950s and depressed semiconductor business in the early 1960s and 1970s. Even in 1974 and 1976 losses of $100,000 and $400,000, respectively, had been incurred. (Operating results for the past five years are shown in Exhibit 17-31.)

Looking Ahead

Profits were regarded as having excellent possibilities for growth as shown in the division's five-year projections. According to the division manager:

> For the immediate future we see no slowdown in the projected industry sales growth rate of 15 percent per year. By investing as we have in product development projects, we should be able to maintain our share of market at 5 percent or even increase it slightly.
>
> For example, we have plans to develop a wide range of new products which are either offered by others or are under development. These products include thermoelectric cooling and generating devices, solar cells, and micro-miniature circuits. Although they are much more complex and costly to develop than previous products, only by keeping up with other firms can we remain competitive.
>
> At the same time, we feel that additional strategic funds will be necessary to provide for improved production methods so that we can increase our yields. Only by making these investments now can we expect to become respectably profitable within the next few years. Our projections reflect these improved operations. Frankly, if we don't become more profitable soon, the company may have to rethink its decision to stay in the electronic component field.

(The projections for the division are shown in Exhibit 17-31.)

COLSON ENGINE DIVISION

This division was characterized by a stable, concentrated product line of gasoline engines under 3 horsepower which were used to power a

EXHIBIT 17-31   Branford Semiconductor Division
(Dollar Amounts in Millions)

Year Ended Dec. 31	Net Sales	Net Income*	Market Share	Strategic Funds Invested*
Past Operating Results				
1973	$16.4	$0.1 (0.6%)	4.8%	$0.7 (4.3%)
1974	19.8	−0.2 (–%)	4.9	0.9 (4.5%)
1975	23.0	0.1 (0.4%)	4.9	1.1 (4.8%)
1976	26.2	−0.4 (–%)	4.9	1.5 (5.7%)
1977	30.7	0.6 (2.0%)	5.0	2.2 (7.2%)

Year Ended Dec. 31	Net Sales	Net Income*	Market Share	Strategic Funds Requested*
Projected Results				
1978	$35.2	$0.7 (2.0%)	5.0%	$3.2 (9.1%)
1979	40.8	1.2 (2.9%)	5.0	4.9 (12.0%)
1980	47.8	1.9 (4.0%)	5.1	7.3 (15.3%)
1981	55.0	2.8 (5.1%)	5.1	11.0 (20.0%)
1982	64.0	4.5 (7.0%)	5.1	17.0 (26.6%)

*Figures in parentheses indicate percentage of sales.

variety of devices such as compressors, power lawn mowers, rototillers, irrigation pumps, etc. All of the division's production output was sold to original equipment manufacturers and industrial supply houses (for replacement use).

There had been very few technological changes in recent years. Consequently, one corporate executive expressed the opinion that development costs (such as a staff of 20 product development engineers) were a needless expense in such a division:

> This is a very mature field, and about all they [the development engineers] do is change the appearance now and then and occasionally rearrange the controls. From a corporate standpoint, we might do much better to invest elsewhere.

Past Performance

As shown in Exhibit 17-32, profitability had been well above the corporation average of 4 percent return on sales, with 1977's net income representing 9 percent of sales. The cash throw-off in 1977 was slightly more than $8 million, making the division a substantial generator of funds within the company.

EXHIBIT 17-32   Colson Engine Division
(Dollar Amounts in Millions)

Year Ended Dec. 31	Net Sales	Net Income*	Market Share	Strategic Funds Invested*
Past Operating Results				
1973	$46.0	$3.7 (8.0%)	57.0%	$1.6 (3.5%)
1974	47.4	4.0 (8.4%)	56.0	1.7 (3.6%)
1975	49.0	4.2 (8.6%)	55.3	1.7 (3.5%)
1976	50.3	4.5 (8.9%)	54.8	1.8 (3.6%)
1977	52.0	4.7 (9.0%)	55.0	1.8 (3.5%)

Year Ended Dec. 31	Net Sales	Net Income*	Market Share	Strategic Funds Requested*
Projected Results				
1978	$53.6	$4.8 (9.0%)	55.2%	$1.9 (3.5%)
1979	51.1	4.9 (9.6%)	55.0	2.0 (3.9%)
1980	57.0	5.1 (8.9%)	55.0	2.2 (3.9%)
1981	58.8	5.3 (9.0%)	55.1	2.3 (3.9%)
1982	60.6	5.5 (9.1%)	55.2	2.4 (4.0%)

*Figures in parentheses indicate percentage of sales.

Outlook

Although market share had dropped from 57 percent in 1973 to 55 percent in 1977, it was expected that the division could match industry sales growth in the future, thus retaining its share of the market. The annual growth rate for the industry was forecast as a steady 3 percent, down from 5 percent in 1973. Strategic funds would be needed in moderate amounts to support promotional programs aimed at maintaining market share. (Projections were as shown in Exhibit 17-32.)

DUNLOP FARM IMPLEMENT DIVISION

For many years this division had attempted to gain entry to the huge farm equipment market. It offered a limited line of high quality, multipurpose implements for use on small farms, where it was thought operators could not afford the substantial inventory of specialized equipment typically found on larger farms. Distribution of this division's product line was handled through a small group of independent farm equipment dealers.

Because the farm implement industry was dominated by a few large

EXHIBIT 17-33   Dunlop Farm Implement Division
(Dollar Amounts in Millions)

Year Ended Dec. 31	Net Sales	Net Income*	Market Share	Strategic Funds Invested*
		Past Operating Results		
1973	$18.3	$0.8 (4.4%)	2.1%	$0.9 (4.9%)
1974	19.8	1.1 (5.6%)	2.2	1.0 (5.1%)
1975	22.0	−0.5 (−%)	2.3	1.1 (5.0%)
1976	21.6	−3.2 (−%)	2.2	0.8 (3.7%)
1977	20.7	−1.7 (−%)	2.0	0.6 (2.9%)

Year Ended Dec. 31	Net Sales	Net Income*	Market Share	Strategic Funds Requested*
		Projected Results		
1978	$20.9	−2.0 (−%)	1.9%	1.0 (4.8%)
1979	21.2	−1.0 (−%)	1.9	1.5 (7.1%)
1980	21.5	0.0 (−%)	1.8	2.3 (10.7%)
1981	21.7	1.0 (4.6%)	1.7	3.4 (15.7%)
1982	22.0	1.0 (4.5%)	1.7	5.0 (22.7%)

*Figures in parentheses indicate percentage of sales.

manufacturers with extensive distribution channels, product acceptance was hampered by lack of a strong nationwide service organization.

Past Performance

Extensive product development costs had depressed the division's profitability in recent years, and the industry as a whole had suffered a sharp decline in the *rate* of sales growth in 1975. That same year, the Dunlop Division had introduced a new product line with disappointing sales results, leading to a loss in excess of $3 million. (Results for the past five years are shown in Exhibit 17-33.)

Outlook

With farm equipment sales growth projected at 5 percent per year, division management anticipated a decline in market share unless substantial increases in strategic funds could be obtained for expanding channels of distribution and service facilities. By aggressively marketing existing product lines, it was thought that stable profitability could be achieved by 1981.

INDEX